S0-BEB-784

HOUGHTON MIFFLIN HARCOURT

WRITE SOURCE

TEACHER'S EDITION

Grade 9

Authors

Dave Kemper, Patrick Sebranek, and Verne Meyer

Illustrator

Chris Krenzke

Education Resource Center
University of Delaware
Newark, DE 19716-2940

GREAT
SOURCE.

HOUGHTON MIFFLIN HARCOURT

Teacher Consultants

Patty Beckstead
St. George, Utah

Amy Goodman
Anchorage, Alaska

Debra McConnell
Williston, Vermont

Steve Mellen
Temple Hills, Maryland

Reviewers

Ilene R. Abrams
Cobb County School District
Marietta, Georgia

Doreen A. Caswell
Mary G. Montgomery
Semmes, Alabama

Marilyn Erbentraut
Randall Consolidated
Bassett, Wisconsin

Mary M. Fischer
Arlington Public Schools
Arlington, Massachusetts

Michelle Gallagher
Pinellas County Schools
Largo, Florida

Cullen Hemstreet
Jefferson Parish Schools
Metairie, Louisiana

Alberta Lantz
School District of Waukesha
Waukesha, Wisconsin

Rita Martin
Jenks Public Schools
Jenks, Oklahoma

Inge Noa
Unified School District 475
Junction City, Kansas

Mary Osborne
Pinellas County Schools
Largo, Florida

Tamara Jo Rhomberg
Rockwood School District
St. Louis, Missouri

Deborah Richmond
Ferry Pass Middle School
Pensacola, Florida

Robert Wright
Sebastian River Middle
  School, Indian River S.D.
Sebastian River, Florida

WRITE SOURCE Online
www.hmheducation.com/writesource

Photo credits: TE-8 ©Mike Kemp/Getty Images; TE-10–11 ©Andrzej Tokarski/Alamy; TE-12 (bl) ©Image Source/Getty Images; TE-12 (cm, bm) ©Bananastock/Jupiterimages/Getty Images; TE-16–17 (teacher) ©Blend Images/Alamy; TE-16–17 (students) ©SuperStock RF/SuperStock.

Text credits: TE-61–68 Common Core State Standards © Copyright 2010. National Governors Association Center for Best Practices and Council of Chief State School Officers. All rights reserved.

This product is not sponsored or endorsed by the Common Core State Standards Initiative of the National Governors Association Center for Best Practices and the Council of Chief State School Officers.

Copyright © 2012 by Houghton Mifflin Harcourt Publishing Company

All rights reserved. No part of this work may be reproduced or transmitted in any form or by any means, electronic or mechanical, including photocopying or recording, or by any information storage or retrieval system, without the prior written permission of the copyright owner unless such copying is expressly permitted by federal copyright law.

Permission is hereby granted to individuals using the corresponding student's textbook or kit as the major vehicle for regular classroom instruction to photocopy copying masters from this publication in classroom quantities for instructional use and not for resale. Requests for information on other matters regarding duplication of this work should be addressed to Houghton Mifflin Harcourt Publishing Company, Attn: Paralegal, 9400 South Park Center Loop, Orlando, Florida 32819.

Printed in the U.S.A.

ISBN 978-0-547-48462-4

4 5 6 7 8 9 10   0877   19 18 17 16 15

4500547626   B C D E F G

Program Overview

Professional Development for Writing

THE FORMS, THE PROCESS, AND THE TRAITS

WRITING WORKSHOP AND GRAMMAR

WRITING ACROSS THE CURRICULUM, ACADEMIC VOCABULARY, AND TEST PREPARATION

DIFFERENTIATION

RESEARCH

Teacher Resources

Contents

The Writing Process

The Forms of Writing

The Tools of Learning

Basic Grammar and Writing

A Writer's Resource

Proofreader's Guide

Credits

Copy Masters

Index

How does *Write Source* work?

*W**rite Source*** is a complete language arts curriculum focused on writing and grammar in print and digital formats.

With writing instruction at the core, grammar, usage, and mechanics are taught in an authentic writing context.

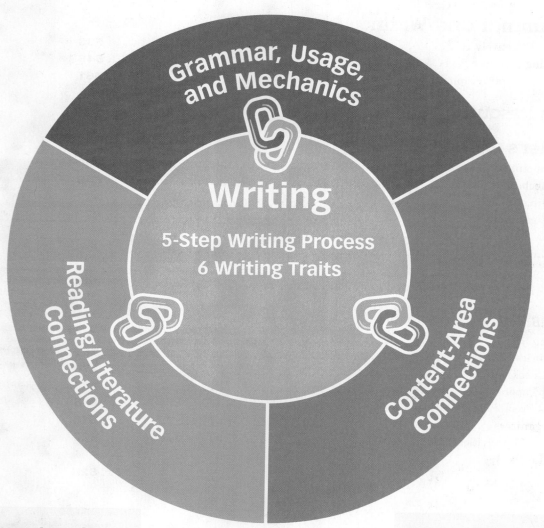

Grammar, Usage, and Mechanics

Writing
5-Step Writing Process
6 Writing Traits

Reading/Literature Connections

Content-Area Connections

The Six Traits of Effective Writing
- Ideas
- Organization
- Voice
- Word Choice
- Sentence Fluency
- Conventions

Steps of the Writing Process
- Prewriting
- Writing
- Revising
- Editing
- Publishing

Introduce the writing form:

- Preview the form by focusing on a key concept or skill.
- Analyze a model paragraph.
- Write a paragraph.

Each core forms of writing unit follows the same instructional path—a consistent writing curriculum across all grade levels.

Explore the writing form:

 Read authentic, real-world fiction or nonfiction that models the writing form.

- Analyze a model story or essay.
- Use the writing process to write a story or essay.

 Use the six traits to revise and to edit for conventions.

- Repeat these steps for on an additional writing assignment.

Write for the assessment:

- Write a piece in the same writing form for assessment.

 Read an essay or other response that models the form.

Write in other content areas:

 Write in a variety of forms across the major content areas in science, social studies, math, and the arts.

Write Source prepares students for success in the 21st century.

What are the main components of Write Source?

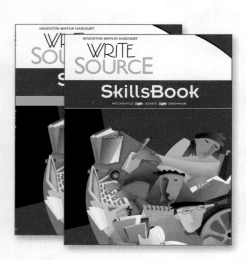

The **Assessment** book provides a pretest, progress tests, and a post-test.

The **Daily Language Workouts** build student grammar skills through quick, daily editing and proofreading activities.

The *Write Source* **Student Edition** reflects the latest research on writing instruction. The **Teacher's Edition** has all the support you need to help students become confident, proficient writers.

The **SkillsBook** helps students practice and improve grammar, usage, and mechanics skills.

Write Source Online
www.hmheducation.com/writesource

- Discover the power of writing instruction with **Net-text**, an interactive, collaborative online worktext.

- Engage students in grammar through **GrammarSnap**, the grammar practice Web application.

- Transform writing instruction through high-functioning **Interactive Whiteboard Presentations**.

- Support instruction with a searchable **File Cabinet** teacher resource.

- Score essays accurately and efficiently with online **Essay Scoring**.

How does the Teacher's Edition support instruction?

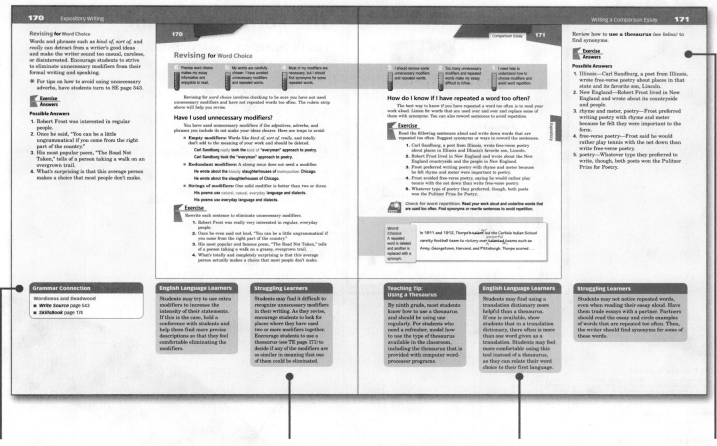

Grammar Connections support grammar, usage, and mechanics instruction.

Differentiated Instruction for struggling learners and advanced learners is provided throughout the core instructional units.

The Teacher's Edition provides consistent support for **English language learners.**

Teaching suggestions and activity answers provide the support you need to implement writing instruction.

Additional Resources

- Common Core State Standards Correlation
- Yearlong Timetable
- Professional Development
- Reading-Writing Connection
- Benchmark Papers
- Graphic Organizers

How is *Write Source* organized?

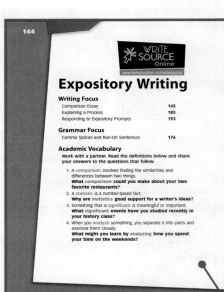

The Forms of Writing

Units focus on instruction in the following writing forms:

- Narrative Writing
- Expository Writing
- Persuasive Writing
- Response to Literature
- Creative Writing
- Research Writing

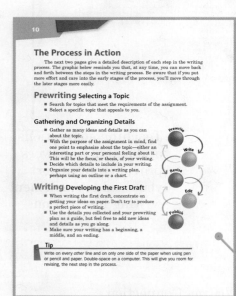

10

The Process in Action

The next two pages give a detailed description of each step in the writing process. The graphic below reminds you that, at any time, you can move back and forth between the steps in the writing process. Be aware that if you put more effort and care into the early stages of the process, you'll move through the later stages more easily.

Prewriting Selecting a Topic

- Search for topics that meet the requirements of the assignment.
- Select a specific topic that appeals to you.

Gathering and Organizing Details

- Gather as many ideas and details as you can about the topic.
- With the purpose of the assignment in mind, find one point to emphasize about the topic—either an interesting part or your personal feeling about it. This will be the focus, or thesis, of your writing.
- Decide which details to include in your writing.
- Organize your details into a writing plan, perhaps using an outline or a chart.

Writing Developing the First Draft

- When writing the first draft, concentrate on getting your ideas on paper. Don't try to produce a perfect piece of writing.
- Use the details you collected and your prewriting plan as a guide, but feel free to add new ideas and details as you go along.
- Make sure your writing has a beginning, a middle, and an ending.

Tip

Write on every *other* line and on only one side of the paper when using pen or pencil and paper. Double-space on a computer. This will give you room for revising, the next step in the process.

The Writing Process

This unit introduces students to the steps in the writing process and integrates instruction on the six traits of effective writing.

Writing Across the Curriculum

This section helps students prepare for writing assignments in other content areas.

The Tools of Learning

This section helps students improve important classroom skills: listening and speaking, note taking, critical reading, summarizing, and test taking.

Basic Grammar and Writing

This section covers the fundamental building blocks of writing: words, sentences, and paragraphs.

A Writer's Resource

This section is a writing guide with information about development and presentation of writing.

Proofreader's Guide

This section addresses the conventions of standard English: punctuation, mechanics, spelling, grammar, usage, and sentence structure.

How does *Write Source* support today's digital-age learners?

Write Source Online taps into the power of interactivity, collaboration, and motivation to deliver a coordinated, comprehensive technology program for writing and grammar.

With *Write Source Online*, teachers and students:

- personalize their writing experience through a **customizable dashboard, community network,** and **electronic portfolios**

- easily transition from reading to build a **solid foundation in writing and grammar**

- experience **interactive guided instruction** using Net-text, an online worktext with comprehensive writing support, tools for peer-to-peer collaboration, and point-of-use grammar practice

Write Source Online
www.hmheducation.com/writesource

Preparing students and teachers for success in the 21st century

What are the components of Write Source Online?

Set the stage for success with Interactive Whiteboard Lessons, high-functioning multimedia presentations that help you generate interest, promote engagement, and build background skills in each major form of writing.

Transform students into writers with Net-text, an innovative online worktext that features interactive instruction, online document creation, peer-to-peer commenting, and integrated grammar—all supported by tools that help you monitor progress and give feedback.

Engage students in grammar with GrammarSnap, a multimedia application that reinforces and extends understanding of key topics through videos, games, and quizzes that make learning about grammar fun.

Students are motivated to earn SkillSnap points to unlock a variety of accessories for their avatar character.

Tap into the power of publishing with the *Write Source Online* Portfolio, a customizable resource that gives students an authentic forum for sharing and reflecting on their writing.

Students and classrooms can connect in My Network to share and comment on each other's published portfolios.

Simplify the management of daily work with the Assignment Manager, a tool that delivers automatic student notifications about due dates and next steps while providing you with linked access to student work for commenting and grading.

Energize instruction with an innovative, integrated online writing program.

instructional videos   plays   literature connections   graphic organizers

satire

presentation   creative writing   online peer reviewing   compar

process   poetry   grammar   writing   writing in the arts

descriptive writing   voice   mechanics   word ch

collaboration

prewriting   expository writing   assessment

paragraph

stories   rubric   publishing

traits   **Write Source Online**
www.hmheducation.com/writesource   editing

ideas   interactive instrucion

writing across the curriculum

essay scoring   narrative writing   essay   organization

revising

sentence fluency   conventions   usag

informative   writing forms

benchmark papers   games

writing in math   persuasive writing   mpt

Additional Resources

- **Bookshelf** eBooks of *Write Source* print components
- **Essay Scoring** Prompts for additional writing practice with automatic scoring and evaluation

- **File Cabinet** Thousands of printable teacher resources, such as blackline masters and additional assessments, that help you minimize planning time and differentiate instruction.

Professional Development for Writing

This section of the *Write Source* Teacher's Edition provides information to help you make the most of *Write Source* in your classroom. The program's instructional design includes comprehensive support for the topics that matter most to teachers: grammar, writing workshops, academic vocabulary, test preparation, the use of technology, and so much more. Whether you are a new teacher or a veteran, the information in the following pages will show how *Write Source* can help you meet your classroom goals.

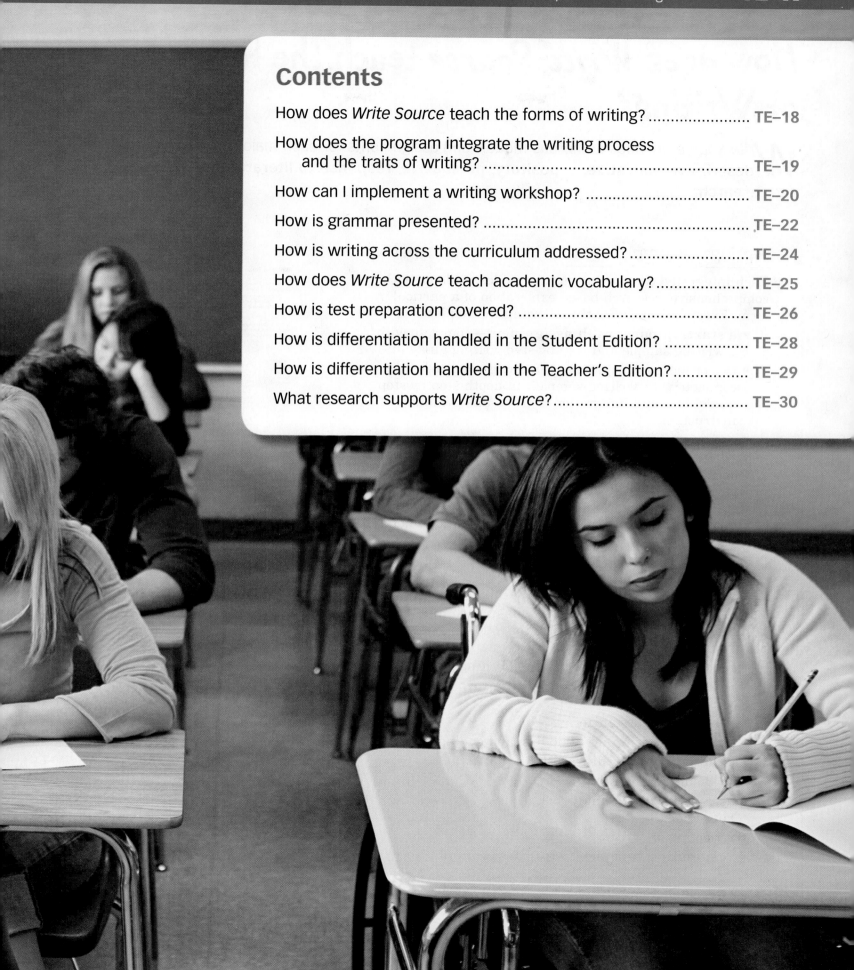

Contents

How does *Write Source* teach the forms of Writing?

Write *Source* provides numerous models and assignments for each major form of writing: **descriptive, narrative, expository, persuasive, response to literature, creative,** and **research**.

Writing Assignments

Each integrated core writing unit provides students with a comprehensive, research-based exploration of a particular form. Every unit includes the following writing lessons:

- a **start-up paragraph assignment**—complete with a writing sample and step-by-step writing guidelines
- two or more **multiparagraph assignments**—complete with writing samples, in-depth step-by-step guidelines, and integration of traits and grammar instruction
- one **assessment writing assignment**—complete with a sample response to a prompt plus writing tips

A separate section—**Writing Across the Curriculum**—provides students with authentic writing assignments from the major content areas and the world of work. Each assignment includes step-by-step instruction and annotated models.

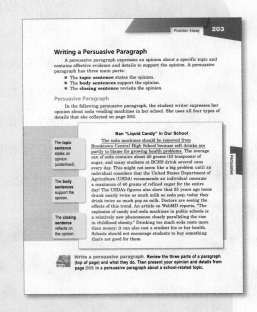

Writing Skills and Strategies

As students develop their compositions in each unit, they will gain valuable experience with the following skills and strategies:

- reading and responding to texts (writing models)
- **integrating the traits of writing into the writing process**
- using graphic organizers
- developing beginnings, middles, and endings
- **practicing grammar skills in context**
- publishing (presenting) writing
- assessing with an analytical, mode-specific scoring rubric
- reflecting on writing
- **responding to a prompt for assessment**

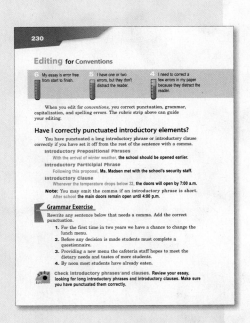

How does the program integrate the writing process and the traits of writing?

Throughout each core forms of writing unit, the six traits of effective writing are integrated into the steps of the writing process. As students develop their writing, they develop an understanding of and appreciation for each trait of writing. In addition, checklists, guidelines, and activities are used to ensure that each piece of writing is completely traits-based.

The Process and the Traits in the Core Units

Understanding Your Goal

The beginning of each main essay assignment helps students understand the goal of their writing. A chart listing the traits of writing as they relate to the form helps students meet that goal.

Focus on the Traits

As students develop each composition, they will find valuable discussions of the six traits at different steps in the writing process.

Revising and Editing for the Traits

When students are ready to revise and edit, they will find step-by-step instruction, traits-based guidelines, strategies, and checklists to help them improve their writing.

Rubrics for the Core Units

A traits-based rubric concludes each major assignment. This rubric ties directly to the goal chart at the beginning of the unit and the rubric strips presented on the revising and editing pages.

Special Note: For more information about the writing traits, we recommend *Creating Writers Through 6-Trait Writing Assessment and Instruction*, 4th ed., by Vicki Spandel (Addison Wesley Longman, 2005) and *Write Traits®* by Vicki Spandel and Jeff Hicks (Houghton Mifflin Harcourt, 2011).

How can I implement a writing workshop?

Write Source supports a writing workshop through both print and technology resources. The program includes minilessons for instruction, high-quality models to encourage writing, support for whole-class sharing, and much more.

Integrated Minilessons

As a starting point, **Interactive Whiteboard Lessons** provide short, focused teaching opportunities designed to lay a foundation in key concepts. Students build on this foundation as they move through the core forms of writing units, where each step in the writing process presents additional opportunities for minilessons targeting individual needs. Both the print book and the **Net-text** lessons teach students to:

- preview the trait-based goal of a writing assignment
- select a topic and use a graphic organizer to gather details
- create a focus (thesis) statement
- organize ideas
- create a strong beginning, a coherent middle, and an effective ending
- receive (and provide) peer responses
- revise for the traits
- edit and proofread for conventions
- publish a finished piece
- use an analytical, mode-specific rubric

Mon	Tues	Wed	Thurs	Fri
Writing Minilessons (10 minutes as needed)				
Status Checks (2 minutes) Find out what students will work on for the day.				
Individual Work (30 minutes) Writing, Revising, Editing, Conferencing, or Publishing				
Whole-Class Sharing Session (5 minutes)				

Graphic Organizers

Write Source contains a wealth of graphic organizers that can serve as the subjects of minilessons. The graphic organizers modeled in print and technology include the following:

Pie graph	Sensory chart	Process diagram	"Why" chart	Topic list
Web	Plot chart	Venn diagram	Basics-of-life list	Character chart
Cluster	Storyboard	Circle graph	5 W's chart	Picture diagram
T-chart	Bar graph	Cycle diagram	Cause-effect chart	Comparison-contrast chart
Outline	KWL chart	Gathering grid	Problem-solution chart	Time line

High-Quality Models

Each assignment begins with a high-interest model, complete with annotations pointing out key features. The **Net-text** provides additional tools for exploring each model, including online interaction with classroom peers to rate and comment on the model. Once students have read and analyzed each model, they will be ready—and excited—to begin their own writing. Other models and examples throughout each unit offer specific techniques that students can use in their writing.

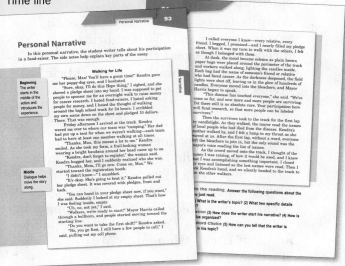

Individual Writing

Write Source makes it easy for writing-workshop students to work on their own. It also provides specific help whenever students have questions about their writing. Here are some of the areas that are addressed:

- catching the reader's interest
- providing background information
- developing strong paragraphs
- elaborating on ideas
- organizing ideas by time, location, importance, logic
- quoting, paraphrasing, and summarizing
- using transitions
- drawing conclusions
- calling the reader to act

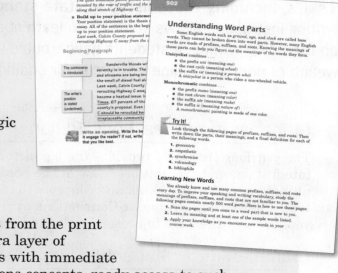

In addition to supporting these and other key concepts from the print components, the *Write Source* **Net-text** provides an extra layer of scaffolding for independent writing, including exercises with immediate feedback, at-a-click support for grammar and conventions concepts, ready access to such resources as a dictionary and thesaurus, and an application for creating and managing work online.

Peer and Teacher Response

Write Source teaches peer responding and provides a peer response sheet. Consistent integration of the traits into the writing process allows students and teachers to speak a common language as they conduct response sessions. Traits-based checklists help pinpoint just what is working—and what could work better—in each piece of writing. The *Write Source* **Net-text** provides additional support for teacher-to-student and student-to-student response, including a commenting tool and commenting notifications.

Whole-Class Sharing

Write Source helps students complete and prepare their work for whole-class sharing—whether in a traditional presentation or in the public section of the **Online Portfolio**. In addition, the program provides a wealth of suggestions for publishing work in a variety of forms and for a variety of audiences.

Most writing units include information on evaluating written compositions. Even the evaluation process is modeled with sample essays and assessments. A reflection sheet also helps students think about what they have learned and internalize the lessons to use in the future.

How is grammar presented?

If you follow the suggested yearlong timetable, you will cover all the key grammar skills, including those listed in state standards. Grammar instruction integrated into writing instruction allows students to learn about grammar in context when they are working on their own writing. If students have trouble with a particular concept, you can refer to a wealth of print and online resources for additional support.

Grammar in the Teacher's Edition

The yearlong timetable provides the big picture of grammar integration, and the unit overview at the beginning of each unit shows grammar skills and concepts to teach while teaching writing. Grammar Connections at point of use help you pinpoint the time to present skills and concepts.

Grammar in the Student Edition

Forms of Writing

Each core forms of writing unit includes grammar instruction integrated into the revising and editing steps in the main assignment. Instruction on grammar skills includes examples and practice and application activities, and it links to students' writing.

Basic Grammar and Writing

For more grammar in the context of writing, refer to "Using Words Effectively" and "Understanding Sentence Style." Use these minilessons to teach specific grammar and style skills that students can apply to their writing. These pages include instruction and examples as well as practice activities.

Proofreader's Guide

This section serves as a complete conventions guide, providing rules, examples, and activities for grammar, usage, punctuation, mechanics, and spelling.

⚡Write Source Online

The *Write Source* **Net-text** offers interactive instruction and practice for the conventions topics embedded in the core writing units. *Write Source* **GrammarSnap** provides additional instruction, practice, and basic skills reinforcement through videos, minilessons, games, and quizzes.

Grammar in Other Program Components

The *SkillsBook* provides more than 130 grammar, usage, punctuation, mechanics, sentence-construction, and spelling activities. The *Assessment* book contains a pretest, benchmark tests, and a post-test for basic writing and editing skills. *Daily Language Workouts* includes a year's worth of sentences (daily) and paragraphs (weekly) for editing practice.

Planning Grammar Instruction

Should I implement *all* of the suggested basic grammar activities?

In the course of the year, if you assigned every grammar exercise listed in the daily lesson schedules (located in the unit overviews of your TE), your students would complete **all** of the "Basic Grammar and Writing," "Proofreader's Guide," *SkillsBook*, and GrammarSnap activities.

Because the most effective teaching of grammar happens in context, grammar instruction appears at appropriate times during revising and editing in the core writing forms units. As the teacher, you must choose the type and number of activities that will best meet the needs of your students.

How are all the grammar resources related?

The *SkillsBook* grammar activities parallel and expand on the rules and exercises found in the "Proofreader's Guide." In "Basic Grammar and Writing," brief exercises function well as minilessons and may be assigned on an as-needed basis. GrammarSnap offers additional support for key grammar topics in an engaging, interactive format.

How do I use the daily lesson schedule charts?

The sample below from the "Persuasive Writing" unit is followed by an explanation of how to read and use the charts.

Suggested Persuasive Writing Unit (Five Weeks)

	Day	Writing and Skills Instruction	Student Edition		SkillsBook	Daily Language Workouts	Write Source Online
			Main Pages	Resource Units*			
WEEK 1	1–5	**Persuasive Warm-Up Paragraph**	201–203			32–33	*Interactive Whiteboard Lessons*
		Skills Activities:					
		• Direct Quotations		616 (+), 632 (+)			
		• Shifts in Verb Tense			183		*GrammarSnap*
	opt.	*Making Oral Presentations*	393–403				
WEEK 2	6	**Persuasive Writing: Position Essay** (Model) Literature Connections "I Have a Dream"	204–206			34–35	

* Th......... located in the back of the ...... Edition. Res......... elude "Basic Gram........ riting," "A Writer's Res......." ....d "Proofreader's Guide."

1. The Resource Units column indicates the Student Edition pages that cover rules, examples, and exercises for corresponding skills activities.
2. The *SkillsBook, Daily Language Workouts*, and **Write Source Online** columns indicate pages and information from those particular resources.

How do I use *Daily Language Workouts*?

Daily Language Workouts is a teacher resource that provides a high-interest sentence for each day of the year and weekly paragraphs for additional editing and proofreading practice. This regular practice helps students develop the objectivity they need to effectively edit their own writing.

How is writing across the curriculum addressed?

Write Source program provides a wide variety of cross-curriculum activities and assignments. It promotes *writing to show learning, writing to learn new concepts,* and *writing to reflect on learning.*

Writing to Show Learning

Writing to show learning is the most common type of writing that content-area teachers assign. The following forms of writing covered in the program are commonly used for this purpose.

- Narrative paragraph and essay
- Expository paragraph and essay
- Persuasive paragraph and essay
- Response paragraph and essay
- Summary
- Research report

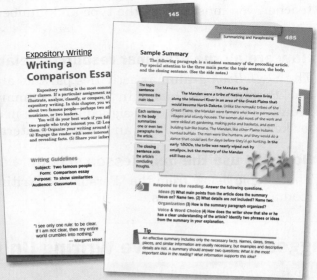

Sample Writing-Across-the-Curriculum Assignments

Specific content-area assignments let students show learning.

Writing in Science

Lab Report
Cause-Effect Essay
Science-Article Summary

Writing in Social Studies

Descriptive Report
Editorial-Cartoon
 Response
Document-Based Essay

Writing in Math

Article Summary
Problem Analysis
Creation of a Chart or
 Graph
Response to a Math
 Prompt

Writing in the Applied Sciences

Process Essay
Essay of Identification
Persuasive Poster

Writing in the Arts

Response to an Art Prompt
Research Report

How does *Write Source* teach academic vocabulary?

Write *Source* gives students the opportunity to learn and use academic vocabulary terms so essential for success in school.

Academic Vocabulary in *Write Source*

Academic vocabulary refers to the words students must know in order to understand the concepts they encounter in school. Academic vocabulary terms such as *element, analyze, substantial*, and *consistent* are not specific to any one subject but rather denote key ideas and skills relevant to many subject areas. In a sense, academic vocabulary is the language of school. To be successful in school, students must understand and be able to use academic vocabulary as they write about and discuss what they learn in class.

The *Write Source* Academic Vocabulary feature gives students the opportunity to learn and practice using new academic vocabulary in a collaborative activity. This feature, which appears at the beginning of each unit of the Student Edition, provides a brief explanation of each academic vocabulary word, followed by a prompt that motivates students to practice using the term.

- Academic vocabulary is taken from words appearing in the unit.
- Students work with a partner to read the explanations of academic vocabulary words used in the unit.
- Each explanation is accompanied by an activity or question that prompts students to demonstrate their understanding of the new word.

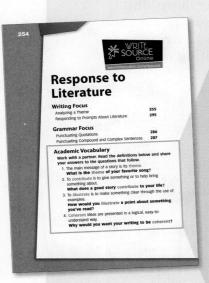

Academic Vocabulary

Work with a partner. Read the definitions below and share your answers to the questions that follow.

1. The main message of a story is its **theme**.
   What is the theme of your favorite song?

2. To **contribute** is to give something or to help bring something about.
   What does a good story contribute to your life?

3. To **illustrate** is to make something clear through the use of examples.
   How would you illustrate a point about something you've read?

4. **Coherent** ideas are presented in a logical, easy-to-understand way.
   Why would you want your writing to be coherent?

How is test preparation covered?

Each core forms of writing unit in the Student Edition prepares students for responding to testing prompts. **If students complete their work in each of the core units, they will have learned the skills necessary for success on any type of writing assessment.** Here are some of the main features in the Student Edition that address testing.

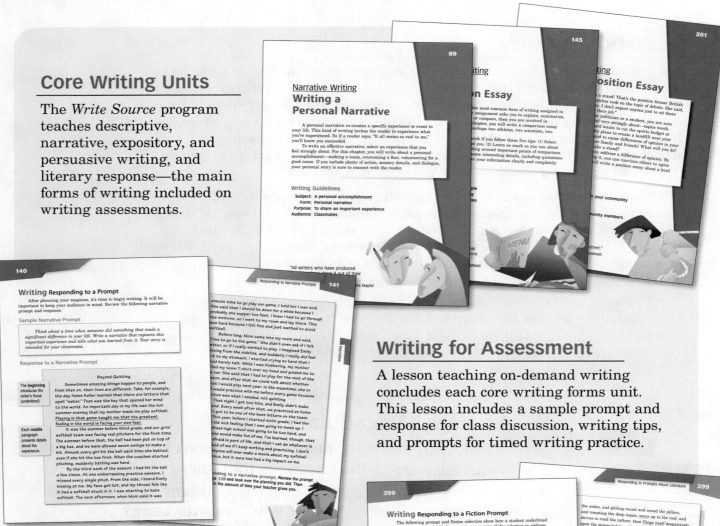

Core Writing Units

The *Write Source* program teaches descriptive, narrative, expository, and persuasive writing, and literary response—the main forms of writing included on writing assessments.

Writing for Assessment

A lesson teaching on-demand writing concludes each core writing forms unit. This lesson includes a sample prompt and response for class discussion, writing tips, and prompts for timed writing practice.

Responding to Literature

Special attention is given to assessing literary response. Included in the Response to Literature unit are samples, writing tips, and prompts for responding to short stories, nonfiction articles, and speeches.

Taking Classroom Tests

The chapter on test taking includes a section entitled "Taking Essay Tests" that helps students analyze the key words in writing prompts.

Writing Across the Curriculum

The writing-across-the-curriculum assignments help students prepare for on-demand writing on content-based tests.

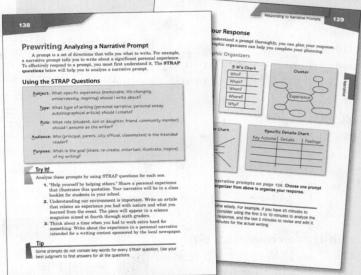

Test Prep for Grammar Skills

Tests at the end of each section in the "Proofreader's Guide" follow a standardized test format. Familiarity with this formatting will help students do their best on these important tests.

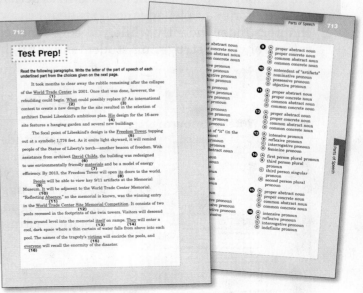

How is differentiation handled in the Student Edition?

Write Source texts, by design, **provide differentiation** in writing instruction—from struggling learners and English language learners to advanced, independent students.

Core Forms of Writing Units

Implementation Options: You can implement the forms of writing units, one assignment after another, as delineated in the yearlong timetable (pages TE-32–35), helping individuals or small groups of students as needed. Or you can differentiate instruction in any number of ways. Here are three of the many possibilities:

- Have **struggling learners** focus on the single-paragraph writing assignment in each unit while other students complete a multiparagraph assignment.
- Have **advanced learners** work individually or in small groups on a multiparagraph composition assignment, while you guide struggling learners step-by-step through the development of a composition.
- Conduct a **writing workshop** (pages TE-20–21), asking students to develop one or more assignments in a unit at their own pace.

Basic Grammar and Writing

"Basic Grammar and Writing" covers the basics in three chapters: "Using Words Effectively," "Understanding Sentence Style," and "Writing Effective Paragraphs." You can differentiate instruction with these chapters as needed. For example, advanced students can complete the work in these chapters independently while you cover the lessons more carefully and selectively with struggling students and English language learners.

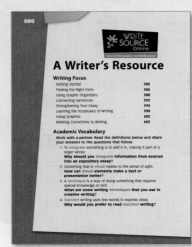

A Writer's Resource

Advanced students can find their own answers to writing questions in this section, while you can find minilesson ideas for struggling learners and English language learners with specific writing needs.

How is differentiation handled in the Teacher's Edition?

The Teacher's Edition provides point-of-use differentiation for struggling learners, English language learners, and advanced learners.

Struggling Learners

The Struggling Learners notes allow you to customize lessons to meet the needs of students who may have difficulty completing the work. These notes provide alternative approaches, extra practice, or additional insights.

English Language Learners

The English Language Learners notes help you to guide students with limited language skills through the lessons. These notes provide extra practice, alternative approaches, connections to first languages, glossaries of new terms, demonstration ideas, and more.

Advanced Learners

The Advanced Learners notes help you enhance the lessons for students who need to be challenged. Some of the notes extend the lessons.

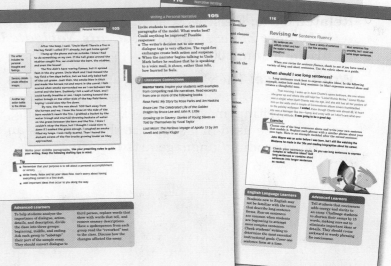

What research supports the *Write Source* program?

Write Source reflects the best thinking and research on writing instruction.

Applying the Process Approach to Writing

Research: The process approach, discussed by educators Donald M. Murray and Donald H. Graves, among others, breaks writing down into a series of steps—prewriting through publishing. Research has shown that students write more effectively and more thoughtfully, if they approach their work as a process rather than as an end product.

Graves, Donald. H. *Writing: Teachers and Children at Work*. Heinemann, 2003.

Murray, Donald. M.; Newkirk, Thomas; Miller, Lisa C. *The Essential Don Murray: Lessons from America's Greatest Writing Teacher*. Boynton/Cook Heinemann, 2009.

Write Source: All writing units and assignments are arranged according to the steps in the writing process. This arrangement helps students manage their work, especially in the case of longer essay or research report assignments.

Sequencing Assignments

Research: Writing instructor and researcher James Moffett developed a sequence of writing assignments—known as the "universe of discourse"—that has over the years, served countless English/language arts classrooms. Moffett sequences the modes of writing according to their connection or immediacy to the writer. Moffett suggests that students first develop descriptive and narrative pieces because the students have an immediate, personal connection to this type of writing. Next, they should develop informational pieces that require some investigation before moving on to more challenging, reflective writing, such as persuasive essays and position papers.

Moffett, James. *Teaching the Universe of Discourse*. Boynton/Cook, 1987.

Related Title: Fleischer, Cathy; Andrew-Vaughn, Sarah. *Writing Outside Your Comfort Zone: Helping Students Navigate Unfamiliar Genres*. Heinemann, 2009.

Write Source: The writing units and assignments in the *Write Source* texts are arranged according to the "Universe of Discourse," starting with descriptive and narrative writing, moving on to expository writing, and so on. These assignments are designed to be used in a sequence that supports an existing writing curriculum or integrated reading/language arts program.

Implementing a Writing Workshop

Research: Countless respected writing instructors and researchers have touted the importance of establishing a community of writers in the classroom. Teachers can establish such a community by implementing a writing workshop. In a writing workshop, students are immersed in all aspects of writing, including sharing their work with their peers.

Atwell, Nancie. *In the Middle: New Understandings About Writing, Reading, and Learning.* Heinemann, 1998.

Write Source: The units in *Write Source* are so clearly presented so that most students can work independently on their writing in a workshop. In addition, the core forms of writing units contain innumerable opportunities for workshop minilessons.

Producing Writing with Detail

Research: Rebekah Caplan learned through her teaching experience that students don't automatically know how to add details to their personal, informational, and persuasive writing. She discovered with her students that adding detail to writing is a skill that must be practiced regularly. To address this problem, Caplan came up with the "show-me" sentence strategy, in which students begin with a basic idea—"My locker is messy"—and create a brief paragraph that shows rather than tells the idea.

Caplan, Rebekah. *Writers in Training: A Guide to Developing a Composition Program.* Dale Seymour Publications, 1984.

Related Title: Bernabi, Gretchen S.; Hover, Jayne; Candler, Cynthia. *Crunchtime: Lessons to Help Students Blow the Roof Off Writing Tests—and Become Better Writers in the Process.* Heinemann, 2009.

Write Source: *Daily Language Workouts* contains a series of show-me sentences that teachers can implement as a regular classroom warm-up.

Meeting Students' Diverse Needs

Research: Many students in today's classrooms struggle with writing. For struggling students, following the writing process is not enough. According to the research done by James L. Collins, struggling students need specific strategies and aids to help them become better writers. Collins found that these students benefit from the following: *skills instruction integrated into the process of writing, color coding and signposts in the presentation of instructional material, the use of graphic organizers, instructions presented in discreet chunks of copy, and so on.*

Collins, James L. *Strategies for Struggling Writers.* Guilford Press, 1998.

Write Source: The core writing forms units contain all the key features from Collins' work. As a result, the units are well suited to struggling learners and English language learners.

Yearlong Timetable

This suggested yearlong timetable presents **one possible sequence** of writing and language skills units based on a five-days-per-week writing class. The sequence can support an existing writing curriculum or integrated reading/language arts program.

First Quarter

Week	Writing Lessons	*Write Source*	Grammar and Writing Skills
1	Getting Started (TE-80) **Why write?** **Understanding the Writing Process** **Narrative Paragraph**	1–5 7–12 89–91	**Skills Assessment:** Using the Right Word 698–699 — Marking Punctuation 646–647 Nouns, prepositions, commas, pronouns
2	**Taking Notes** **One Writer's Process**	467–472 13–32	**Skills Assessment:** Checking Mechanics Test Prep 670–671
3	**Understanding the Traits of Writing**	39–54	**Skills Assessment:** Understanding Sentences 758–759
	Using a Rubric **Publishing Your Writing** **Creating a Portfolio**	61–72 73–82 83–87	
4	**Writing a Personal Narrative: A Personal Accomplishment** (Model, Prewriting, Writing) **Listening and Speaking**	92–106 463–466	**Skills Assessment:** Spelling *SkillsBook* page 51
5	**Personal Narrative** *(cont'd)* (Revising, Editing, Publishing) **Peer Responding**	107–123 55–60	**Skills Assessment:** Parts of Speech 736–737
6	**Personal Narrative** *(cont'd)* (Assessing, Reflecting) **Writing Effective Paragraphs** Keeping a Learning Log	124–128 561–579 408–409	Word choice, capitalization, abbreviations, numbers, using the right word
7	**Critical Reading** **Taking Tests**	473–482 521–531	
8	**Understanding Writing Assignments** **Expository Paragraph**	491–500 145–147	Parallelism, using the right word, verbs
9	**Writing a Comparison Essay: Two Famous People:** (Prewriting)	148–156	Conjunctions, commas (compound sentences and introductory clauses and phrases), pronouns

Second Quarter

Week	Writing Lessons	*Write Source*	Grammar and Writing Skills
1	**Comparison Essay:** *(cont'd)* (Writing, Revising) **Peer Responding**	157–174 55–60	Parallelism, wordiness and deadwood, clauses, rambling sentences, compound and complex sentences
2	**Comparison Essay:** *(cont'd)* (Editing, Publishing, Assessing, Reflecting) **Responding to Expository Prompts**	175–184 193–194	Apostrophes, comma splices and run-on sentences, capitalization
3	**Response to Literature: Analyzing a Theme—Short Story Warm-Up Paragraph and Essay** (Model, Prewriting)	258–266	Punctuating titles
4	**Analyzing a Theme** *(cont'd)* (Writing, Revising) **Peer Responding**	267–284 55–60	Figures of speech, misplaced and dangling modifiers, pronouns (relative, indefinite, interrogative, demonstrative)
5	**Analyzing a Theme** *(cont'd)* (Editing, Publishing, Assessing, Reflecting)	285–294	Tense shifts, punctuating compound and complex sentences, punctuating quotations, end punctuation
6	**Persuasive Writing: Warm-Up Paragraph—Community Controversy**	200–203	Direct quotations
	Persuasive Writing: Position Essay—Community Controversy (Model, Prewriting)	204–210	
7	**Position Essay** *(cont'd)* (Writing)	211–216	
8	**Position Essay** *(cont'd)* (Revising) **Peer Responding**	217–228 55–60	Complete sentences (fragments), sentence types, adverbs, adjectives
9	**Position Essay** *(cont'd)* (Editing, Publishing, Assessing, Reflecting) **Responding to Persuasive Prompts** Portfolio Review *SkillsBook* Posttests	229–238 247–251	Spelling, hyphens and dashes, tenses (irregular verbs), commas with introductory phrases and clauses, pronoun-antecedent agreement

Third Quarter

Week	Writing Lessons	*Write Source*	Grammar and Writing Skills
1	**Biographical Narrative** (Model, Prewriting, Writing, Revising, Editing, Publishing)	129–136	Transitions, conjunctions, pronouns (review), end punctuation, using the right word, pronoun shifts, commas (appositives, in a series, to separate adjectives)
2	**Responding to Narrative Prompts**	137–143	
3	**Writing Stories** (Model, Prewriting, Writing, Revising, Editing, Publishing)	313–320	Punctuating dialogue, conjunctions and interjections, verbs, modeling sentences, sentence problems, subject-verb agreement
4	**Responding to Prompts About Literature**	295–311	
5	**Expository Writing: Explaining a Process** (Model, Prewriting, Writing, Revising, Editing)	188–192	Specific nouns, sentence variety, subject-verb agreement, sentence problems (comma splices, run-ons, fragments), commas
6	**Persuasive Writing: A Pet-Peeve Essay** (Model, Prewriting, Writing, Revising, Editing)	239–246	Sentence combining, adjectives, using the right word, nonstandard language, capitalization
7	**Writing Plays** (Model, Prewriting, Writing, Revising, Editing, Publishing)	323–332	Punctuating dialogue, interjections, pronouns, end punctuation (review)
8	**Making Oral Presentations** (Presenting plays)	393–403	
9	**Writing Across the Curriculum** (Teacher's Choice) *SkillsBook* Posttests	405–461	

Fourth Quarter

Week	Writing Lessons	*Write Source*	Grammar and Writing Skills
1	**Writing Poems: Free-Verse Poem** (Model, Prewriting, Writing, Revising, Editing)	353–357	Prepositions, prepositional phrases, parts of speech (review), adverbs, basic sentence patterns, phrases, spelling, commas (review)
	Blues Poem, Senyru	338	
2	**Research Writing Skills**	343–354	
	Taking Notes	467–472	
	Summarizing and Paraphrasing	483–490	
3	**Research Report: Important Development in History of Media in United States** (Model)	355–363	
4	**Research Report** *(cont'd)* (Prewriting)	364–372	
5	**Research Report** *(cont'd)* (Writing)	373–384	
6	**Research Report** *(cont'd.)* (Revising)	385–388	Active and passive verbs, mood of verbs, word choice, commas (in a series, to set off appositives, to separate adjectives), sentences (review), brackets, ellipses, colons, semicolons, parentheses, and other forms of punctuation
7	**Research Report** *(cont'd)* (Editing, Publishing)	389–392	Comma rules (review), sentence problems (review), pronoun-antecedent agreement, subject-verb agreement, using the right word, shifts in construction
8	**Making Oral Presentations**	393–403	Spelling (review), proofreading (review)
	Oral Presentations *(cont'd)*	393–403	
9	**Freestyle Writing Project** *(choice)* **Journal and Portfolio Review Final Reflection Essay** *SkillsBook* Posttests		

Reading-Writing Connection

The literary works listed on pages TE-36 through TE-43 provide high-interest **mentor texts** that you can use to inspire your students as you teach the different forms of writing. Use these texts to accentuate **writer's craft**:

- Read **strong beginnings** or **strong endings** to inspire students as they create their own beginnings and endings.
- Read paragraphs that **elaborate ideas** or demonstrate **strong organization**.
- Read from two different examples to **contrast voice** and **word choice**.
- Read from different authors to examine their **sentence fluency**.

Narrative Books for Grades 9–10

We Are All the Same: A Story of a Boy's Courage and a Mother's Love
Jim Wooten, 2004

Persepolis: The Story of a Childhood
Marjane Satrapi, 2004

The Catcher in the Rye
J. D. Salinger, 1951

The Burn Journals
Brent Runyon, 2004

Finding Their Stride: A Team of Young Runners and Their Season of Triumph
Sally Pont, 2001

Life of Pi: A Novel
Yann Martel, 2002

Crow Lake: A Novel
Mary Lawson, 2003

Truth and Bright Water: A Novel
Thomas King, 2000

The Secret Life of Bees
Sue Monk Kidd, 2003

Damage
A. M. Jenkins, 2001

A Painted House
John Grisham, 2001

Peace Like a River
Leif Enger, 2002

Grayson
Lynne Cox, 2006

My Losing Season
Pat Conroy, 2002

Hacker Cracker: A Journey from the Mean Streets of Brooklyn to the Frontiers of Cyberspace
David Chanoff, Ejovi Nuwere, 2002

March
Geraldine Brooks, 2005

The Road from Coorain
Jill Ker Conway, 1989

A Separate Peace
John Knowles, 1959

She Said Yes: The Unlikely Martyrdom of Cassie Bernall
Misty Bernall, 1999

A Killing in Plymouth Colony
Carol Otis Hurst, Rebecca Otis, 2003

Legend Days: Part 1 of the Ghost Horse Cycle
Jamake Highwater, 1984

No Promises in the Wind
Irene Hunt, 1970

Abraham Lincoln: Letters from a Slave Girl (Dear Mr. President)
Andrea Davis Pinkney, 2001

The Examination
Malcolm Bosse, 1994

Cleopatra VII: Daughter of the Nile, Egypt, 57 B.C. (The Royal Diaries)
Kristiana Gregory, 1999

The Shining Company
Rosemary Sutcliff, 1992

My Brother Sam Is Dead
James Lincoln Collier, 1984

Notes from the Midnight Driver
Jordan Sonnenblick, 2006

Over a Thousand Hills I Walk with You
Hanna Jansen, Elizabeth D. Crawford, 2006

Growing Up in Slavery: Stories of Young Slaves as Told by Themselves
Yuval Taylor, 2005

That Was Then, This Is Now
S. E. Hinton, 1971

Between a Rock and a Hard Place
Aron Ralston, 2004

Lost Moon: the Perilous Voyage of Apollo 13
Jim Lovell, 1994

Pilgrim at Tinker Creek
Annie Dillard, 1974

Shoeless Joe
W. P. Kinsella, 1982

Teen Angst? Naaah . . . A Quasi-autobiography
Ned Vizzini, 2000

Rosa Parks: My Story
Rosa Parks, Jim Haskins, 1992

Bruce Lee: The Celebrated Life of the Golden Dragon
Bruce Lee, John R. Little, 2000

Barrio Boy
Ernesto Galarza, 1971

Shabanu: Daughter of the Wind
Suzanne Fisher Staples, 1989

Expository Books for Grades 9–10

Police Lab: How Forensic Science Tracks Down and Convicts Criminals
David Owen, 2002

Vietnam: A War on Two Fronts
Sidney Lens, 1990

The Race to Save the Lord God Bird
Phillip Hoose, 2004

Getting Away with Murder
Chris Crowe, 2003

Photo by Brady: A Picture of the Civil War
Jennifer Armstrong, 2005

In the Land of White Death
Valerian Albanov, 2000

When I Was Puerto Rican
Esmeralda Santiago, 1993

Zarafa: A Giraffe's True Story, from Deep in Africa to the Heart of Paris
Michael Allin, 1998

The Endurance: Shackleton's Legendary Antarctic Expedition
Caroline Alexander, 1998

George Washington, Spymaster: How the Americans Outspied the British and Won the Revolutionary War
Thomas B. Allen, 2004

With Courage and Cloth: Winning the Fight for a Woman's Right to Vote
Ann Bausum, 2004

Wake Up Our Souls: A Celebration of African American Artists
Tonya Bolden, 2004

Flags of Our Fathers: Heroes of Iwo Jima (Young Reader's Abridged Edition)
James Bradley, Ron Powers, Michael French, 2003

Close to Shore: The Terrifying Shark Attacks of 1916
Michael Capuzzo, 2003

Counting Coup: A True Story of Basketball and Honor on the Little Big Horn
Larry Colton, 2000

Out of Harm's Way
Terry Crisp, 1997

The Day the World Came to Town: 9/11 in Gander, Newfoundland
Jim DeFede, 2002

Seeing in the Dark: How Backyard Stargazers Are Probing Deep Space and Guarding Earth from Interplanetary Peril
Timothy Ferris, 2002

Ben Franklin's Almanac: Being a True Account of the Good Gentleman's Life
Candace Fleming, 2003

In Defense of Liberty: The Story of America's Bill of Rights
Russell Freedman, 2003

Coal: A Human History
Barbara Freese, 2003

Hole in My Life
Jack Gantos, 2002

Meltdown: A Race Against Nuclear Disaster at Three Mile Island: A Reporter's Story
Wilborn Hampton, 2001

Fields of Fury: The American Civil War
James M. McPherson, 2002

Stiff: The Curious Lives of Human Cadavers
Mary Roach, 2003

Working Fire: The Making of an Accidental Fireman
Zac Unger, 2004

The Hot Zone
Richard Preston, 1994

Motorcycle: Evolution, Design, Passion
Mick Walker, 2006

Buzz: The Intimate Bond Between Humans and Insects
Josie Glausiusz, Volker Steger, 2004

Streetball: All the Ballers, Moves, Slams, & Shine
Chris Palmer, 2004

Dream Job Profiles
Donna Hayden Green, 2006

The Driving Book: Everything New Drivers Need to Know but Don't Know to Ask
Karen Gravelle, Helen Flook, 2005

Making the Most of High School: Success Secrets for Freshmen
Carol Carter, 2004

Yes Yes Y'All: The Experience Music Project Oral History of Hip-Hop's First Decade
Jim Fricke, Charlie Ahearn, 2002

Teens Cook: How to Cook What You Want to Eat
Megan Carle, Jill Carle, Judi Carle, Jessica Boone, 2004

Chess (From First Moves to Checkmate)
Daniel King, 2001

In a Different Light
Carolyn Meyer, 1996

We Just Want to Live Here: A Palestinian Teenager, an Israeli Teenager—An Unlikely Friendship
Amal Rifa'i, Odelia Ainbinde, Sylke Tempel, 2003

They Broke the Law—You Be the Judge: True Cases of Teen Crime
Thomas A. Jacobs, 2003

How Rude! The Teenagers' Guide to Good Manners, Proper Behavior, and Not Grossing People Out
Alex J. Packer, 1997

Persuasive Books for Grades 9–10

You Can Save the Animals: 251 Simple Ways to Stop Thoughtless Cruelty
Ingrid Newkirk, 1999

Save Our Land, Save Our Towns: A Plan for Pennsylvania
Thomas Hylton, Blair Seitz, 2000

Eating to Save the Earth: Food Choices for a Healthy Planet
Linda Riebel, Ken Jacobsen, 2002

Inside Dope: How Drugs Are the Biggest Threat to Sports, Why You Should Care, and What Can Be Done About Them
Richard W. Pound, 2006

Tons of Trash: Why You Should Recycle and What Happens When You Do
Joan Rattner Heilman, Nancy Schill, 1992

101 Reasons to Love the Red Sox: And 10 Reasons to Hate the Yankees
David Green, 2005

Let's Clear the Air: 10 Reasons Not to Start Smoking
Lobster Press, 2007

The Loch Ness Monster: The Evidence
Steuart Campbell, 2004

AIDS (Introducing Issues with Opposing Viewpoints)
Andrea C. Nakaya, 2005

Gangs (Introducing Issues with Opposing Viewpoints)
Scott Barbour, 2005

Gun Control (Introducing Issues With Opposing Viewpoints)
Beth Rosenthal, 2006

Stop Global Warming: The Solution Is You!
Laurie David, 2006

50 Ways to Save the Ocean
David Helvarg, Philippe Cousteau, Jim Toomey, 2006

Ultimate Weight Solution for Teens: The 7 Keys to Weight Freedom
Jay McGraw, Phil McGraw, 2003

Pollution: Problems & Solutions
National Wildlife Federation, 1998

Conflict Resolution: The Win-Win Solution
Carolyn Casey, 2001

Cosmetic Surgery for Teens: Choices and Consequences
Kathleen Winkler, 2003

Teens Can Make It Happen: Nine Steps for Success
Stedman Graham, 2000

Friends, Cliques, and Peer Pressure: Be True to Yourself
Christine Wickert Koubek, 2002

Teen Fads: Fun, Foolish, or Fatal?
Ray Spangenburg, Kit Moser, 2003

Propaganda: Understanding the Power of Persuasion
Ray Spangenburg, Kit Moser, Diane Moser, 2002

Tattooing and Body Piercing: Understanding the Risks
Kathleen Winkler, 2002

The Debate over Human Cloning: A Pro/Con Issue
David Goodnough, 2003

Books About Literary Response for Grades 9–10

American Indian Themes in Young Adult Literature
Paulette F. Molin, 2005

Theme-Sets for Secondary Students: How to Scaffold Core Literature
Jeannine D. Richison, Anita C. Hernandez, Marcia J. Carter, 2006

The Most Wonderful Books: Writers on Discovering the Pleasures of Reading
Michael Dorris, Emilie Buchwald, 1997

Books I Read When I Was Young: The Favorite Books of Famous People
M. Jerry Weiss, Bernice E. Cullinan, and National Council of Teachers of English Commission on Literature, 1980

Characters in Children's Literature
Raymond E. Jones, 1997

Characters in Young Adult Literature
John T. Gillespie, 1997

Traveling Literary America: A Complete Guide to Literary Landmarks
B. J. Welborn, 2005

Words About Pictures: The Narrative Art of Children's Picture Books
Perry Nodelman, 1989

The Young Actor's Book of Improvisation: Dramatic Situations Based on Literature, Plays, and Films: Ages 12–16
Sandra Caruso, Susan Kosoff, 1998

Romeo & Juliet: The Contemporary Film, The Classic Play
William Shakespeare, 1996

Guts: The True Stories Behind Hatchet and the Brian Books
Gary Paulsen, 2001

Brian's Song (Screenplay)
William Blinn, 1983

Drama for Reading and Performance: Collection 1
Aurand Harris, Horton Foote, Gary Soto, and Wendy Wasserstein, 2000

Classic Readers Theatre for Young Adults
Suzanne I. Barchers, Jennifer L. Kroll, 2002

Building Literature Circles
Jimmie Aydelott, 2003

Making Literature Circles Come Alive: A Time-Saving Resource
Amy Hamra, 2003

Discovering Florida Through Literature
Elizabeth Knowles, Martha Smith, 2002

Sketching Stories, Stretching Minds: Responding Visually to Literature
Phyllis Whitin, 1996

Ready-to-Tell Tales (American Storytelling)
David Holt, 1995

The Annotated Night Before Christmas: A Collection of Sequels, Parodies, and Imitations of Clement Moore's Immortal Ballad About Santa Claus
Martin Gardner, 2005

Fact, Fiction, and Folklore in Harry Potter's World: An Unofficial Guide
George W. Beahm, Tim Kirk, Britton McDaniel, 2005

Beauty: A Retelling of the Story of Beauty and the Beast
Robin McKinley, 1978

Dear Author: Students Write About the Books That Changed Their Lives
Weekly Reader's Read Magazine, 1995

Books About Creative Writing for Grades 9–10

Whatcha Mean, What's a Zine?
Esther Pearl Watson, Mark Todd, 2006

The DC Comics Guide to Writing Comics
Dennis O'Neil, 2001

Prepare to Board! Creating Story and Characters for Animation Features and Shorts
Nancy Beiman, 2007

A Teen's Guide to Getting Published: Publishing for Profit, Recognition, and Academic Success
Jessica Dunn, Danielle Dunn, 2006

Teen Ink: Love and Relationships (Teen Ink Series)
Stephanie Meyer, 2002

Twice Told: Original Stories Inspired by Original Artwork
Scott Hunt, 2006

Be a Writer: Your Guide to the Writing Life
Steve Peha, 2006

Be a Better Writer: Power Tools for Young Writers! Essential Tips, Exercises and Techniques for Aspiring Writers
Steve Peha, 2006

Beyond Roses Are Red Violets Are Blue: A Practical Guide for Helping Students Write Free Verse
Benjamin Green, Anita Punla, 1996

Image to Word: Art and Creative Writing
Kathleen Walsh-Piper, 2003

Like It Was: A Complete Guide to Writing Oral History
Cynthia Stokes Brown, 1988

Nonstandardized Quests: 500+ Writing Prompts That Matter
David E. LeCount, 2002

Web Design for Teens
Maneesh Sethi, 2004

A Fire in My Hands: Revised and Expanded Edition
Gary Soto, 2006

Out of The Dust
Karen Hesse, 1997

Names Will Never Hurt Me
Jaime Adoff, 2004

Fe-Vers: Feeling Verses for Teens
Cynthia Blomquist Gustavson, 2006

Red Hot Salsa: Bilingual Poems on Being Young and Latino in the United States
Lori Marie Carlson, 2005

I Am the Darker Brother: An Anthology of Modern Poems by African Americans
Arnold Adoff, Benny Andrews, 1997

Necessary Noise: Stories About Our Families as They Really Are
Michael Cart, 2006

An Island Like You: Stories of the Barrio
Melanie Kroupa, 1995

Big City Cool: Short Stories About Urban Youth
M. Jerry Weiss, Helen S. Weiss, 2002

No Easy Answers: Short Stories About Teenagers Making Tough Choices
Donald R. Gallo, 1999

America Street: A Multicultural Anthology of Stories
Anne Mazer, 1993

Reference Books for Grades 9–10

The American Heritage High School Dictionary: Fourth Edition
Houghton Mifflin, 2007

The American Heritage Essential Student Thesaurus
Houghton Mifflin, 2003

100 Research Topic Guides for Students
Barbara Wood Borne, 1996

100 More Research Topic Guides for Students
Dana McDougald, 1999

On Speaking Well
Peggy Noonan, 1999

Painless Speaking
Mary Elizabeth, 2003

The New York Public Library Student's Desk Reference
Frommer's, New York Public Library, Press Stonesong, 1995

An Encyclopedia of the History of Technology
Ian McNeil, 1996

Building the World, Volumes 1 and 2: An Encyclopedia of the Great Engineering Projects in History
Frank Davidson, Kathleen Lusk-Brooke, 2006

Mightier Than the Sword: How the News Media Have Shaped American History
Rodger Streitmatter, 1998

The New York Public Library Amazing African American History: A Book of Answers for Kids
The New York Public Library, Diane Patrick, 1997

American Heritage Science Dictionary
Houghton Mifflin, 2005

Technology in World History
Oxford, 2005

Encyclopedia of American Folklife
Ed. J. Simon Bronner, 2006

Unexplained: An Encyclopedia of Curious Phenomena, Strange Superstitions, and Ancient Mysteries
Judy Allen, 2006

National Geographic Atlas of the World
National Geographic, 2005

Atlas of the United States
Oxford, 2006

Opposing Viewpoints in American History: Volumes 1 and 2
William Dudley, 2007

The World Book Encyclopedia of People and Places
Ed. Thomas S. Richardson, 2007

Timelines of History
Grolier, 2005

Encyclopedia of Architectural and Engineering Feats
Donald Langmead, Christine Garnaut, 2001

You Are Here: High School Internet Guide
Eric Leebow, 2001

Find It Online, Fourth Edition: The Complete Guide to Online Research
Alan M. Schlein, 2004

The New York Times Almanac 2007
John W. Wright, 2006

Scope and Sequence

Skills taught and/or reviewed in the *Write Source* program, grades 8–10, are featured in the following scope and sequence chart.

FORMS OF WRITING	Grades 8	9	10
Narrative Writing			
biographical narrative essay	■	■	
historical narrative			■
narrative prompts	■	■	■
paragraph	■	■	■
personal experience essay		■	
phase autobiography essay	■		■
Expository Writing			
cause-effect essay			■
classification essay	■		
comparison essay		■	
comparison-contrast essay	■		
essay of definition			■
explaining a process essay	■	■	
expository prompts	■	■	■
paragraph	■	■	■
Persuasive Writing			
editorial essay			■
paragraph	■	■	■
personal commentary essay	■		
persuasive prompts	■	■	■
pet-peeve essay		■	
position essay	■	■	■
problem-solution essay			■
Response to Literature			
analyzing a theme essay	■	■	■
letter to an author	■		
paragraph	■	■	■
response prompts	■	■	■

	Grades 8	9	10
Creative Writing			
blues poem		■	
changing relationship play		■	
circle poem	■		
coming of age story	■		
conflict within character story			■
couplet	■		
found poem	■		
free-verse poem		■	■
getting to know someone story		■	
learning a lesson play			■
lune poem			■
photograph poem	■		
senryu poem		■	
skeltonic verse			■
Research Writing			
engineering report			■
important place report	■		
multimedia presentation	■		■
news media report		■	
oral presentation		■	■
summary paragraph	■		
The Tools of Learning			
business letters		■	■
critical reading		■	■
improving vocabulary		■	■
journal writing	■		
note taking	■	■	■
paraphrase paragraph		■	■
summary paragraph		■	■
taking tests	■	■	■
understanding writing assignments	■	■	■

THE WRITING PROCESS

Prewriting			
Selecting a Topic			
answer questions		■	
brainstorm	■		
charts	■	■	■
cluster	■	■	■

Selecting a Topic (Continued)	Grades 8	9	10
focus statement	■		■
freewriting	■	■	■
line diagram	■		
list	■	■	■
sentence starters	■	■	■
T-chart	■		
table diagram	■		
time line		■	
topic sentence	■	■	
Gathering Details			
anecdote		■	
answer questions	■	■	
avoid plagiarism	■	■	■
charts	■	■	■
counter an objection	■	■	■
five W's and H	■		
freewrite		■	■
gathering grid	■	■	■
gather objections	■	■	■
list	■	■	■
media grid	■		
note cards			■
quotations		■	■
sensory chart	■	■	
sentence starters	■	■	
T-chart	■	■	
table diagram	■		
time line	■	■	
tracking sources	■	■	
Organizing Details			
consonance		■	
developing viewpoint	■		
gathering grid		■	■
list	■	■	
logical order		■	
note cards	■	■	■
onomatopoeia	■		
order of importance	■	■	
order of location	■		

	Grades	8	9	10
outline ideas		■	■	■
repetition			■	
thesis statement		■	■	
time line		■	■	■
time order		■		
topic sentence		■	■	■
Venn diagram		■		

Sizing Up Your Topic

		8	9	10
list key details		■	■	
research			■	■
write questions		■		

Writing

Beginning Paragraph

		8	9	10
amusing anecdote			■	
ask a question		■	■	■
background information		■	■	■
connect with reader		■	■	
dialogue			■	■
exciting action			■	
focus statement		■		
interesting fact		■	■	■
introduce main character and conflict		■	■	■
introduce topic and thesis			■	■
middle of action		■	■	■
personal story				■
position statement		■	■	
quotation		■	■	■
statistic			■	
surprising statement			■	■
thesis statement			■	■
time and place		■		■
topic sentence		■		

Middle Paragraph

		8	9	10
action words		■		■
anecdote		■	■	
background information				■
build to high point		■	■	■
cite sources		■	■	■
comparisons		■		

Middle Paragraph (Continued)

Grades	8	9	10
counter an objection	■	■	■
dialogue	■	■	■
explain terms	■	■	■
facts	■	■	■
figures of speech		■	
key actions		■	■
main points	■	■	■
middle of action		■	
paraphrase information		■	■
personal feelings	■	■	■
quotations		■	■
repeating key words	■	■	
sensory details	■	■	■
show, don't *tell*		■	
specific details	■	■	■
statistics			■
supporting details	■	■	■
suspense		■	■
topic sentences	■	■	■
transitions	■	■	■

Ending Paragraph

	8	9	10
call to action			■
final scene	■	■	
final thought/insight	■	■	■
interesting fact	■	■	
key idea	■		■
new information		■	
quotation	■	■	■
refer back to beginning	■		■
reflect on experience	■	■	■
restate position	■	■	
restate thesis	■	■	■
revisit theme	■	■	
solution to problem		■	■
summarize	■	■	■

Grades 8 9 10

Revising

Ideas

	8	9	10
accurate facts			■
clear message	■	■	
comparisons	■		
compelling reasons			■
conflict	■	■	■
definitions	■		
dialogue	■	■	
errors in logic		■	
explanations	■	■	
focus statement	■		
fuzzy thinking	■		
interesting details	■		■
memory details	■		
opinion statement			■
paraphrasing		■	
quotations	■	■	
reflective details	■		
response to objection	■		
sensory details	■	■	■
show, don't *tell*	■	■	■
sources	■	■	■
specific reasons			■
support for opinion		■	■
surprising details	■	■	
thesis statement			■
unnecessary details		■	■

Organization

	8	9	10
beginning grabs reader's attention		■	■
build to high point	■	■	■
check overall organization	■	■	
chronological order	■		
clear beginning, middle, and ending	■	■	■
clearly connected details	■		■
connect beginning and ending		■	■

Organization (Continued)	Grades 8	9	10
evaluate unity		■	■
final thought		■	
key word or idea			■
line breaks and indents	■	■	■
logical order	■	■	■
order of importance	■	■	
order of location	■		
point-by-point details		■	
supporting details	■		■
thesis statement	■		
time order	■		
topic sentences	■		■
transition words	■	■	■
two-part focus statement	■		
Peer Response	■	■	■
Voice			
active/passive	■		
appropriate for topic	■	■	■
balance of facts and feelings	■		
confident	■		■
connects with reader	■	■	
consistent point of view	■		■
convincing		■	■
dialogue	■	■	■
engaging		■	■
enthusiastic	■		■
fits audience	■	■	
formal/informal	■		
interested	■	■	■
knowledgeable		■	■
natural	■	■	
original	■		
tone	■		

	Grades 8	9	10
Word Choice			
active voice		■	■
adjectives and adverbs	■		
connotation	■	■	■
descriptive words	■	■	
figures of speech		■	■
helping verbs			■
inflammatory words		■	
literary terms	■		■
modifiers	■	■	
poetic techniques	■		
precise terms	■	■	■
qualifiers	■	■	
quotations	■		
repeated words		■	■
sensory words			■
show, don't *tell*			■
specific action verbs	■	■	■
specific nouns	■	■	■
technical terms	■	■	■
unfair words	■		■
unnecessary modifiers	■	■	■
vivid verbs	■	■	■
Sentence Fluency			
balanced sentences	■		■
choppy sentences	■		
combining sentences	■		■
complete sentences	■		
complex sentences		■	
compound sentences		■	
conjunctions	■		
expanding sentences	■		■
long sentences		■	■
loose sentences	■		
rambling sentences	■		■
rhythm	■	■	■
short sentences	■	■	■
smooth flow	■	■	■
transitions		■	

Sentence Fluency (Continued)	Grades 8	9	10
variety of beginnings	■	■	■
variety of lengths	■	■	■
variety of types		■	■
verb tense shift		■	
wordy sentences	■		

Editing

Capitalization

	8	9	10
beginning of sentences	■	■	■
proper adjectives	■	■	■
proper nouns	■	■	■
speaker's first word in quoted dialogue		■	■

Grammar

	8	9	10
correct forms of adjectives		■	■
correct forms of verbs	■	■	■
double subjects	■		■
homophones	■		
pronoun-antecedent agreement	■	■	■
shifts in verb tense		■	
subject-verb agreement	■	■	■
using the right word	■	■	■

Punctuation

	8	9	10
apostrophes to show possession	■	■	■
commas after introductory phrases and clauses	■	■	■
commas after items in a series	■		
commas in compound sentences	■	■	■
commas with parenthetical expressions	■		
end punctuation	■	■	■
punctuating complex sentences	■	■	■
punctuating dependent clauses	■		
punctuating dialogue	■	■	■
punctuating titles	■	■	■
punctuating works-cited page	■	■	■
quotation marks around direct quotations	■	■	■

Spelling

	8	9	10
catching errors spell-checker missed	■	■	■
double-checking words	■	■	■

WRITING ACROSS THE CURRICULUM

	Grades 8	9	10
Writing in Science			
article summary	■	■	■
cause-effect essay		■	■
classification essay		■	■
classroom notes		■	■
definition essay		■	■
field trip report	■		
lab report		■	■
learning-log entry		■	■
natural formation	■		
observation report	■		
opposing-views essay		■	■
persuasive graph	■		
position essay		■	■
problem-solution essay		■	■
process essay		■	■
reading notes		■	
Writing in Social Studies			
classroom notes		■	■
descriptive report		■	■
document-based essay		■	■
editorial	■		
editorial-cartoon response		■	■
eyewitness report	■		
historical moment	■		
learning-log entry		■	■
news report	■		
response to a historical photo	■		
Writing in Math			
article summary		■	■
autobiography	■		
chart or graph		■	
classification paragraph or essay		■	■
classroom notes		■	■
definition paragraph or essay		■	■
describing an object	■		
descriptive paragraph or essay		■	■
explaining a mathematical operation	■		

Writing in Math (Continued)	Grades 8	9	10
learning-log entry		■	■
math-prompt response		■	■
narrative paragraph or essay		■	■
position essay		■	■
problem analysis		■	
process paragraph or essay		■	■
research report			■
statistical argument	■		■
written estimate			■

Writing in the Applied Arts/Practical Writing

	8	9	10
business letter	■		
classification essay			■
classroom notes		■	
comparison-contrast essay			■
descriptive essay			■
e-mail message	■	■	
essay of analysis			
essay of identification		■	
evaluation form	■		
lab report		■	
learning-log entry		■	■
letter of application			■
letter of complaint		■	
memo	■		
narrative essay			■
observation/accident report		■	
persuasive poster		■	
press release		■	
problem-solution essay			■
process essay		■	■
project proposal	■		■
résumé		■	
work order/estimate		■	

	Grades	8	9	10

Writing in the Arts

	8	9	10
classroom notes		■	■
creative writing		■	■
descriptive writing		■	■
expository writing		■	■
learning-log entry		■	■
narrative writing		■	■
persuasive writing		■	■
research report		■	■
response to a prompt		■	■

GRAMMAR

Understanding Sentences

	8	9	10
agreement of pronoun and antecedent		■	■
agreement of subject and verb		■	■
arrangements of sentences		■	■
clauses	■	■	■
diagramming sentences	■	■	■
direct objects	■	■	■
indirect objects	■		
kinds of sentences		■	■
modifiers	■		
phrases	■	■	■
subjects and predicates	■	■	■
types of sentence constructions		■	■

Using the Parts of Speech

Adjectives

	8	9	10
articles	■	■	■
common adjectives	■		
compound adjectives	■		
demonstrative adjectives	■		
forms of adjectives	■	■	■
indefinite adjectives	■		
irregular forms	■		
types of adjectives	■	■	■

Adverbs

	8	9	10
conjunctive adverbs	■		
forms of adverbs	■	■	■
irregular forms	■		
types of adverbs	■	■	■

	Grades 8	9	10
Conjunctions			
coordinating conjunctions	■	■	■
correlative conjunctions	■	■	■
subordinating conjunctions	■	■	■
Interjections	■	■	■
Nouns			
abstract nouns	■	■	■
case of nouns		■	■
collective nouns	■	■	■
common nouns	■	■	■
compound nouns	■		
concrete nouns	■	■	■
gender of nouns	■	■	■
object nouns	■		
possessive nouns	■		
predicate nouns	■		
proper nouns	■	■	■
singular and plural nouns	■	■	■
subject nouns	■		
Prepositions			
common prepositions	■	■	■
prepositional phrases	■	■	■
Pronouns			
antecedents	■	■	■
case of pronouns	■	■	■
classes of pronouns	■	■	■
gender of pronouns		■	■
person of pronouns	■	■	■
singular and plural pronouns	■	■	■
subject pronouns	■	■	■
Verbs			
action verbs	■	■	■
active and passive voice	■	■	■
auxiliary verbs	■	■	■
irregular verbs	■	■	■
linking verbs	■	■	■
mood of a verb		■	■
person of a verb		■	■

	Grades	8	9	10
singular and plural verbs		■	■	■
tenses of verbs		■	■	■
transitive and intransitive verbs		■	■	■
verbals		■	■	■

Mechanics

Abbreviations

	8	9	10
acronyms	■	■	■
common abbreviations	■	■	■
correspondence abbreviations	■	■	■
initialisms	■	■	■

Capitalization

	8	9	10
abbreviations	■	■	■
days, months, holidays	■	■	■
first words	■	■	■
geographic names	■	■	■
historical events	■	■	■
letters	■	■	■
names of people	■	■	■
official names	■	■	■
organizations	■	■	■
particular sections of the country	■	■	■
proper nouns and adjectives	■	■	■
races, languages, nationalities, religions, certain religious words	■	■	■
sentences following colons		■	■
sentences in parentheses		■	■
titles	■	■	■
titles of courses	■	■	■
titles used with names	■	■	■
words used as names	■	■	■

Numbers

	8	9	10
comparing numbers	■		
numbers in compound modifiers	■	■	■
numerals only	■	■	■
numerals or words	■	■	■
time and money	■	■	■
very large numbers	■	■	■
words only	■	■	■

	Grades 8	9	10
Plurals			
adding an *s*	■	■	■
collective nouns		■	■
compound nouns	■	■	■
irregular spelling	■	■	■
nouns ending in *ch, sh, s, x,* and *z*	■	■	■
nouns ending in *f* or *fe*	■	■	■
nouns ending in *ful*	■	■	■
nouns ending in *o*	■	■	■
nouns ending in *y*	■	■	■
plurals that do not change	■		
words discussed as words	■	■	■
Punctuation			
Apostrophes			
in contractions	■	■	■
in place of omitted letters or numbers	■		
to express time or amount	■	■	■
to form certain plurals	■	■	■
to form plural possessives	■	■	■
to form possessives with compound nouns	■	■	■
to form possessives with indefinite pronouns	■	■	■
to form singular possessives	■	■	■
to show shared possession	■	■	■
Brackets			
around an editorial correction		■	■
to set off added words		■	■
to set off clarifying information		■	■
Colons			
after salutations	■	■	■
between numbers in time	■	■	■
between titles and subtitles		■	■
for emphasis	■	■	■
to introduce lists	■	■	■
to introduce sentences or quotations	■	■	■
Commas			
between items in a series	■	■	■
for clarity or emphasis		■	■
in compound sentences	■	■	■
in dates and addresses	■	■	■
in direct address	■	■	■

	Grades 8	9	10
to enclose parenthetical elements	■	■	■
to keep numbers clear	■	■	■
to separate contrasted elements		■	■
to separate equal adjectives	■	■	■
to separate introductory clauses and phrases	■	■	■
to set off appositives	■	■	■
to set off dialogue	■	■	■
to set off interjections	■	■	■
to set off interruptions	■	■	■
to set off nonrestrictive phrases and clauses	■	■	■
to set off titles or initials	■	■	■
Dashes			
for emphasis	■	■	■
to indicate interrupted speech	■	■	■
to indicate a sudden break	■	■	■
to set off an introductory series		■	■
to set off parenthetical material		■	■
Diagonals			
to show a choice		■	■
when quoting poetry		■	■
Ellipses			
at the end of a sentence		■	■
to show omitted words	■	■	■
to show pauses	■	■	■
Exclamation Points			
to express strong feelings	■	■	■
Hyphens			
between numbers and fractions	■	■	■
in a special series		■	■
in compound words	■	■	■
to avoid confusion	■	■	■
to create new words	■	■	■
to divide words	■	■	■
to form adjectives	■	■	■
to join letters to words	■	■	■
to join numbers		■	■
Italics and Underlining			
for scientific and foreign words	■	■	■
for special uses	■	■	■
in handwritten material	■	■	■

Punctuation (Continued)	Grades 8	9	10
in printed material	■	■	■
in titles	■	■	■
Parentheses			
to set off explanatory or added information	■	■	■
with full sentences		■	■
Periods			
after abbreviations	■	■	■
after initials	■	■	■
as decimal points	■	■	■
at end of sentences	■	■	■
Question Marks			
at end of direct questions	■	■	■
at end of indirect questions	■	■	■
short question within a sentence		■	■
to show uncertainty	■	■	■
Quotation Marks			
for quotations within quotations	■	■	■
for special words	■	■	■
placement of punctuation	■	■	■
to punctuate titles	■	■	■
to set off long quoted material	■	■	■
to set off quoted material	■	■	■
to set off a speaker's exact words	■		
Semicolons			
to join two independent clauses	■	■	■
to separate groups that contain commas	■	■	■
with conjunctive adverbs	■	■	■
Usage			
Spelling			
consonant endings	■	■	■
i before *e*	■	■	■
silent *e*	■	■	■
words ending in *y*	■	■	■
Understanding Idioms		■	■
Using the Right Word	■	■	■

Meeting the Common Core State Standards

The following correlation clearly shows how the *Write Source* program helps you meet grade-specific **Common Core State Standards for English Language Arts,** along with their companion **College and Career Readiness (CCR)** standards. Students are expected to meet grade-specific standards by the end of the school year, thereby working steadily toward meeting the more general expectations described by the CCR standards.

Pages referenced below appear in the Teacher's Edition as well as the Student Edition.

Writing Standards

Text Types and Purposes

College and Career Readiness Standard 1. Write arguments to support claims in an analysis of substantive topics or texts, using valid reasoning and relevant and sufficient evidence.

Grade 9 Standard 1. Write arguments to support claims in an analysis of substantive topics or texts, using valid reasoning and relevant and sufficient evidence.

a. Introduce precise claim(s), distinguish the claim(s) from alternate or opposing claims, and create an organization that establishes clear relationships among claim(s), counterclaims, reasons, and evidence.	**Student Edition pages:** 203, 205–206, 207, 209–210, 212–216, 219, 220–221, 240–241, 243, 244, 248–249, 250–252, 253, 567, 594–595 **Net-text:** Persuasive Writing
b. Develop claim(s) and counterclaims fairly, supplying evidence for each while pointing out the strengths and limitations of both in a manner that anticipates the audience's knowledge level and concerns.	**Student Edition pages:** 202, 203, 205–206, 207, 209–210, 211, 212, 213–216, 218–219, 240–241, 242, 244, 249, 250–251, 450–451, 567, 569–570, 597 **Net-text:** Persuasive Writing
c. Use words, phrases, and clauses to link the major sections of the text, create cohesion, and clarify the relationships between claim(s) and reasons, between reasons and evidence, and between claim(s) and counterclaims.	**Student Edition pages:** 214–215, 220, 244, 577, 592–593 **Net-text:** Persuasive Writing

Text Types and Purposes (continued)

d. Establish and maintain a formal style and objective tone while attending to the norms and conventions of the discipline in which they are writing.	**Student Edition pages:** 222–223, 225 **Net-text:** Persuasive Writing
e. Provide a concluding statement or section that follows from and supports the argument presented.	**Student Edition pages:** 203, 206, 211, 212, 216, 241, 244, 251, 596 **Net-text:** Persuasive Writing

College and Career Readiness Standard 2. Write informative/explanatory texts to examine and convey complex ideas and information clearly and accurately through the effective selection, organization, and analysis of content.

Grade 9 Standard 2. Write informative/explanatory texts to examine and convey complex ideas, concepts, and information clearly and accurately through the effective selection, organization, and analysis of content.

a. Introduce a topic; organize complex ideas, concepts, and information to make important connections and distinctions; include formatting (e.g., headings), graphics (e.g., figures, tables), and multimedia when useful to aiding comprehension.	**Student Edition pages:** 17, 42–43, 44–45, 76–78, 149–150, 151, 156, 158, 159–162, 164, 167, 179, 186–187, 189, 190, 195, 196–197, 199, 259–260, 261, 266, 267, 268, 269–272, 297, 298–299, 300–301, 304–305, 306–307, 310, 311, 357–362, 371, 372, 373, 375–380, 410–411, 412–413, 414–415, 420–421, 422–423, 424, 430, 434–435, 436–437, 438–439, 440–441, 446–447, 448–449, 456–457, 458–460, 528–529, 566, 571–574, 594–595, 602–603 **Net-text:** Expository Writing, Response to Literature, Research Writing
b. Develop the topic with well-chosen, relevant, and sufficient facts, extended definitions, concrete details, quotations, or other information and examples appropriate to the audience's knowledge of the topic.	**Student Edition pages:** 16, 18–19, 20–21, 35, 43, 146, 149–150, 153–154, 155, 159–162, 164–165, 186–187, 189, 196–198, 199, 259–260, 264–265, 267, 270–271, 274–275, 357–362, 376–379, 420–421, 446–447, 448–449, 456–457, 458–460, 566, 569–570, 597 **Net-text:** Expository Writing, Response to Literature, Research Writing
c. Use appropriate and varied transitions to link the major sections of the text, create cohesion, and clarify the relationships among complex ideas and concepts.	**Student Edition pages:** 157, 190, 267, 271, 277, 446, 577, 592–593 **Net-text:** Expository Writing, Response to Literature
d. Use precise language and domain-specific vocabulary to manage the complexity of the topic.	**Student Edition pages:** 48–49, 170–171, 172–173, 280–281, 534, 538, 543, 548 **Net-text:** Expository Writing, Response to Literature

Text Types and Purposes (continued)

e. Establish and maintain a formal style and objective tone while attending to the norms and conventions of the discipline in which they are writing.	**Student Edition pages:** 46–47, 48–49, 52, 168 **Net-text:** Expository Writing
f. Provide a concluding statement or section that follows from and supports the information or explanation presented (e.g., articulating implications or the significance of the topic).	**Student Edition pages:** 147, 150, 158, 162, 166, 187, 190, 197, 257, 260, 268, 272, 276, 301, 307, 311, 362, 380, 410–411, 412–413, 448–449, 460, 596 **Net-text:** Expository Writing, Response to Literature, Research Writing

College and Career Readiness Standard 3. Write narratives to develop real or imagined experiences or events using effective technique, well-chosen details, and well-structured event sequences.

Grade 9 Standard 3. Write narratives to develop real or imagined experiences or events using effective technique, well-chosen details, and well-structured event sequences.

a. Engage and orient the reader by setting out a problem, situation, or observation, establishing one or multiple point(s) of view, and introducing a narrator and/ or characters; create a smooth progression of experiences or events.	**Student Edition pages:** 91, 93–94, 98, 100, 101, 102, 103–106, 110–111, 130–131, 133, 134, 140–141, 316–317, 318, 319, 564 **Net-text:** Narrative Writing, Creative Writing
b. Use narrative techniques, such as dialogue, pacing, description, reflection, and multiple plot lines, to develop experiences, events, and/or characters.	**Student Edition pages:** 93, 98, 99, 100, 101, 102, 104–105, 108, 112, 130–131, 134, 314–315, 316–317, 551, 564 **Net-text:** Narrative Writing, Creative Writing
c. Use a variety of techniques to sequence events so that they build on one another to create a coherent whole.	**Student Edition pages:** 98, 102–106, 110–111, 314–315 **Net-text:** Narrative Writing, Creative Writing

Text Types and Purposes (continued)

d. Use precise words and phrases, telling details, and sensory language to convey a vivid picture of the experiences, events, setting, and/or characters.	**Student Edition pages: 48**–49, 90, 95, 97, 102, 105, 109, 110, 114–115, 132–133, 319, 534, 538, 543, 548, 564 **Net-text:** Narrative Writing, Creative Writing
e. Provide a conclusion that follows from and reflects on what is experienced, observed, or resolved over the course of the narrative.	**Student Edition pages:** 91, 94, 102, 106, 111, 131, 134, 141, 317, 319, 596 **Net-text:** Narrative Writing, Creative Writing

Production and Distribution of Writing

College and Career Readiness Standard 4. Produce clear and coherent writing in which the development, organization, and style are appropriate to task, purpose, and audience.

Grade 9 Standard 4. Produce clear and coherent writing in which the development, organization, and style are appropriate to task, purpose, and audience. (Grade-specific expectations for writing types are defined in standards 1–3 above.)	**Student Edition pages:** 9, 10, 12, 17, 18–19, 20, 24–25, 40, 41, 44–45, 48–49, 50–51, 53, 54, 58–59, 65, 92, 98, 99, 100, 102, 108–109, 110–111, 114–115, 116–117, 118, 133, 139, 140–141, 143, 148, 154, 155–156, 158, 159–162, 166–167, 170–171, 172–173, 189, 195, 196–197, 199, 204, 209, 212, 220–221, 224–225, 226–227, 243, 249, 250–251, 252, 253, 258, 265, 266, 268, 276–277, 280–281, 282–283, 297, 311, 319, 337, 375, 376–381, 386–387, 388, 424, 436, 446, 448, 456, 458, 486, 538–539, 540–541, 546–547, 548, 549–560, 571–574, 577–579 **Interactive Whiteboard Lessons:** Narrative Writing, Expository Writing, Persuasive Writing, Response to Literature, Creative Writing, Research Writing **Net-text:** Narrative Writing, Expository Writing, Persuasive Writing, Response to Literature, Creative Writing, Research Writing

College and Career Readiness Standard 5. Develop and strengthen writing as needed by planning, revising, editing, rewriting, or trying a new approach.

Grade 9 Standard 5. Develop and strengthen writing as needed by planning, revising, editing, rewriting, or trying a new approach, focusing on addressing what is most significant for a specific purpose and audience.	**Student Edition pages:** 2, 10, 14, 20, 40, 46–47, 54, 138, 140, 142, 143, 188, 191, 194, 198, 222–223, 248, 252, 410, 424, 450, 456, 515, 586–587 **Interactive Whiteboard Lessons:** Narrative Writing, Expository Writing, Persuasive Writing, Response to Literature, Creative Writing, Research Writing **Net-text:** Expository Writing, Persuasive Writing

Production and Distribution of Writing (continued)

College and Career Readiness Standard 6. Use technology, including the Internet, to produce and publish writing and to interact and collaborate with others.

Grade 9 Standard 6. Use technology, including the Internet, to produce, publish, and update individual or shared writing products, taking advantage of technology's capacity to link to other information and to display information flexibly and dynamically.	**Student Edition pages:** 28, 34–38, 74, 75, 76–78, 79–81, 82, 123, 136, 179, 192, 233, 246, 289, 337, 346, 348, 392, 398, 402–403, 602–603 **Interactive Whiteboard Lessons:** Narrative Writing, Expository Writing, Persuasive Writing, Response to Literature, Creative Writing, Research Writing **Net-text:** Narrative Writing, Expository Writing, Persuasive Writing, Response to Literature, Creative Writing, Research Writing

Research to Build and Present Knowledge

College and Career Readiness Standard 7. Conduct short as well as more sustained research projects based on focused questions, demonstrating understanding of the subject under investigation.

Grade 9 Standard 7. Conduct short as well as more sustained research projects to answer a question (including a self-generated question) or solve a problem; narrow or broaden the inquiry when appropriate; synthesize multiple sources on the subject, demonstrating understanding of the subject under investigation.	**Student Edition pages:** 42–43, 132–133, 148–179, 204–233, 256–289, 356–363, 364–392, 424–430, 458–460, 493, 495–499 **Net-text:** Narrative Writing, Expository Writing, Persuasive Writing, Response to Literature, Research Writing

College and Career Readiness Standard 8. Gather relevant information from multiple print and digital sources, assess the credibility and accuracy of each source, and integrate the information while avoiding plagiarism.

Grade 9 Standard 8. Gather relevant information from multiple authoritative print and digital sources, using advanced searches effectively; assess the usefulness of each source in answering the research question; integrate information into the text selectively to maintain the flow of ideas, avoiding plagiarism and following a standard format for citation.	**Student Edition pages:** 16, 153–154, 177, 344–354, 356–353, 366–368, 369, 373–380, 381–384, 424–430, 434–435, 450, 458–460, 471, 473–478, 486–487, 488–490 **Net-text:** Expository Writing, Creative Writing, Research Writing

Research to Build and Present Knowledge (continued)

College and Career Readiness Standard 9. Draw evidence from literary or informational texts to support analysis, reflection, and research.

Grade 9 Standard 9. Draw evidence from literary or informational texts to support analysis, reflection, and research.

a. Apply grades *9–10 Reading standards* to literature (e.g., "Analyze how an author draws on and transforms source material in a specific work [e.g., how Shakespeare treats a theme or topic from Ovid or the Bible or how a later author draws on a play by Shakespeare]").

Student Edition pages: 98, 133–134, 256, 257, 262, 263–266, 268, 269–272, 274, 292–293, 314–315, 316–317, 318, 319–320, 321, 322, 327–328, 330, 340, 479–480, 481–482, 539, 544, 586–587, 600–601

Net-text: Narrative Writing, Response to Literature, Creative Writing,

b. Apply grades *9–10 Reading standards* to literary nonfiction (e.g., "Delineate and evaluate the argument and specific claims in a text, assessing whether the reasoning is valid and the evidence is relevant and sufficient; identify false statements and fallacious reasoning").

Student Edition pages: 90, 92, 93–94, 98, 99, 103–106, 108–109, 114–115, 126–127, 130–131, 135, 148, 149–150, 159, 164–165, 190, 208–209, 210, 214–216, 218–219, 224–225, 228, 237, 240–241, 242, 245, 263, 274, 278–279, 280–281, 286, 345, 366, 385–387, 456–457, 474–478, 495–499, 537, 538, 539, 541, 544, 545, 546, 551, 552 564, 565, 592–593, 600–601

Net-text: Narrative Writing, Expository Writing, Persuasive Writing, Response to Literature, Research Writing

Range of Writing

College and Career Readiness Standard 10. Write routinely over extended time frames (time for research, reflection, and revision) and shorter time frames (a single sitting or a day or two) for a range of tasks, purposes, and audiences.

Grade 9 Standard 10. Write routinely over extended time frames (time for research, reflection, and revision) and shorter time frames (a single sitting or a day or two) for a range of tasks, purposes, and audiences.

Student Edition pages: 2–3, 5, 8, 9, 11, 12, 14 15, 19, 31, 41, 42, 43, 44, 45, 47, 48, 49, 50, 53, 57, 58, 60, 65, 66, 67, 68, 71, 85, 86, 87, 90, 91, 94, 96, 98, 99, 103, 105, 106, 121, 131, 132, 134, 138, 141, 143, 146, 147, 150, 153, 155, 156, 159, 161, 162, 166, 168, 170, 183, 187, 189, 190, 197, 199, 202, 203, 206, 208, 209, 210, 213, 215, 216, 220, 224, 225, 237, 241, 244, 257, 260, 262, 263, 266, 269, 271, 272, 275, 276, 278, 279, 283, 287, 293, 301, 303, 307, 309, 319, 326, 330, 332, 334, 336, 338, 339, 341, 365, 371, 374, 375, 379, 380, 408, 411, 415, 419, 423, 433, 434, 440, 447, 449, 451, 457, 460, 485, 487, 490, 495, 496, 497, 498, 499, 515, 519, 526, 528, 535, 536, 537, 541, 542, 551, 562, 564, 565, 566, 567, 572, 573, 575, 576, 578

Interactive Whiteboard Lessons: Narrative Writing, Expository Writing, Persuasive Writing, Response to Literature, Creative Writing, Research Writing

Net-text: Narrative Writing, Expository Writing, Persuasive Writing, Response to Literature, Creative Writing, Research Writing

Language Standards

Conventions of Standard English

College and Career Readiness Standard 1. Demonstrate command of the conventions of standard English grammar and usage when writing or speaking.

Grade 9 Standard 1. Demonstrate command of the conventions of standard English grammar and usage when writing or speaking.

a. Use parallel structure.	**Student Edition pages:** 451, 550 **GrammarSnap:** Appositives and Appositive Phrases, Restrictive/Nonrestrictive Relative Clauses and Relative Pronouns
b. Use various types of phrases (noun, verb, adjectival, adverbial, participial, prepositional, absolute) and clauses (independent, dependent; noun, relative, adverbial) to convey specific meanings and add variety and interest to writing or presentations.	**Student Edition pages:** 287, 540–541, 542, 545, 554, 555, 556, 557, 608–609, 618–619, 726–727, 732–733, 742–743, 744–745 **Net-text:** Response to Literature

College and Career Readiness Standard 2. Demonstrate command of the conventions of standard English capitalization, punctuation, and spelling when writing.

Grade 9 Standard 2. Demonstrate command of the conventions of standard English capitalization, punctuation, and spelling when writing.

a. Use a semicolon (and perhaps a conjunctive adverb) to link two or more closely related independent clauses.	**Student Edition pages:** 176, 618, 619, 748 **Net-text:** Expository Writing **GrammarSnap:** Sentence Types
b. Use a colon to introduce a list or quotation.	**Student Edition pages:** 620, 621 **GrammarSnap:** Colons
c. Spell correctly.	**Student Edition pages:** 656, 664–671

Conventions of Standard English (continued)

College and Career Readiness Standard 3. Apply knowledge of language to understand how language functions in different contexts, to make effective choices for meaning or style, and to comprehend more fully when reading or listening.

Grade 9 Standard 3. Apply knowledge of language to understand how language functions in different contexts, to make effective choices for meaning or style, and to comprehend more fully when reading or listening.

a. Write and edit work so that it conforms to the guidelines in a style manual (e.g., *MLA Handbook, Turabian's Manual for Writers*) appropriate for the discipline and writing type.

Student Edition pages: 355–392
Net-text: Research Writing

Getting-Started Activities

The *Write Source* Student Edition is full of helpful resources that students can access throughout the year while they are developing their writing skills. Getting-started activities are provided as copy masters on TE pages 823–825. They will

- help students discover the kinds of information available in different sections of the book,
- teach students how to access that information,
- familiarize students with the layout of the book.

The more familiar students are with the text, the more proficient they will be in using its resources.

Scavenger Hunts

Students enjoy using scavenger hunts to become familiar with a book. The scavenger hunts we provide can be done in small groups or as a class. They are designed for oral answers, but you may want to photocopy the pages for students to write on. Also, you may want to vary the procedure, first having students take turns finding the items and then, on the next scavenger hunt, challenging students to "race" for the answers.

After your students have done each scavenger hunt, you can challenge them to create their own versions. For example, small groups can work together to create "Find It!" scavenger hunts and then exchange their "hunts" with other groups.

Special Challenge: Develop questions that teams of students try to answer using the book. Pattern this activity after a popular game show.

Other Activities

- Give students the following assignment: Across the top of a sheet of paper, write down three things you find difficult about school (e.g., taking notes, taking tests, writing essays, spelling, using commas). Then explore your book to find chapters, sections, examples, and so on, that might help you with your problem area. Under each problem, write the titles or headings and the page numbers where you can find help. Keep this sheet to use throughout the year.

- A variation on the above activity is to have students write down all the subject areas they study and list under each heading the parts of the book that might help them in that subject.

- Have students write a thought-trap poem: After reviewing the book, close it. The first line of your poem will be the title of the book. Then list thoughts and feelings about the book, line by line. When you have listed everything you want to say, "trap" your thoughts by repeating the title.

- Have pairs of students create poster-size advertisements for the book. Each ad should have a headline, list important features (what is in the book) and benefits (whom it can help and how), show an example of illustrations (made by tracing or copying), and urge readers of the ad to get their books now!

- Have students imagine they are going to send a copy of *Write Source* to a pen pal in another state. Have each student write a letter to send along with it to tell the pen pal about the book.

HOUGHTON MIFFLIN HARCOURT

WRITE SOURCE

Authors
Dave Kemper, Patrick Sebranek, and Verne Meyer

Illustrator
Chris Krenzke

GREAT
SOURCE.

HOUGHTON MIFFLIN HARCOURT

Welcome to the Teacher's Edition!

Strong writing brings success throughout high school—and beyond.

The student edition demystifies writing for your students. Using step-by-step instruction and concrete writing strategies, *Write Source* helps every student succeed at writing.

In the same way, the teacher's edition demystifies teaching writing. Simply have your class turn to any writing chapter—narrative, expository, persuasive, response to literature, creative, or research—and begin teaching. It's that simple. Of course, the teacher's edition also provides plenty of support to help you customize the instruction:

- Writing Traits Tips
- Teaching Tips
- Integrated Grammar, Literature, Writer's Craft, and Technology
- Assessment Options and Test Prep
- Notes for English Language Learners
- Accommodations and Modifications for Struggling Students
- Enrichments for Advanced Students

Thanks to the Teachers!

This program would not have been possible without the input of many teachers and administrators from across the nation. As we originally developed this K–12 series, we surveyed hundreds of teaching professionals, and as we revised this series, we implemented the feedback of even more. Our thanks goes out to each of you. We couldn't have done it without you!

Reviewers

Jonathan Benbow
Roxbury High School
Succasunna, NJ

Randolph C. Bernard
Lafayette Parish School System
Lafayette, LA

Edmund Desmond
Hofstra University
Hempstead, NY

Laura L. Doolan
Westminster High School
Carroll County Public Schools
Westminster, MD

Beth Gaby
Carl Schurz High School
Chicago, IL

Dr. Tim Hart
Cincinnati Public Schools
Cincinnati, OH

Shara W. Holt
St. Johns County School District
St. Augustine, FL

Guy M. Kinney
Orange County Public Schools
Orlando, FL

Raymond Klejmont
Desoto County
Arcadia, FL

Jenny R. May
Mason City Schools
Mason, Ohio

Christine Neuner
Iberia Parish School System
New Iberia, LA

Geraldine L. Ortego
Lafayette Parish District Office
Lafayette, LA

Marie T. Raduazzo
Artlington Public Schools
Arlington, MA

Marianne Raver
William R. Boone High School
Orlando, FL

Stephanie Saltikov-Izabal
Huntington Beach Union High
  School District
Huntington Beach, CA

Ann Marie Seely
Henrico County Public Schools
Richmond, VA

www.hmheducation.com/writesource

Copyright © 2012 by Houghton Mifflin Harcourt Publishing Company

All rights reserved. No part of this work may be reproduced or transmitted in any form or by any means, electronic or mechanical, including photocopying or recording, or by any information storage and retrieval system, without the prior written permission of the copyright owner unless such copying is expressly permitted by federal copyright law. Requests for permission to make copies of any part of the work should be addressed to Houghton Mifflin Harcourt Publishing Company, Attn: Paralegal, 9400 South Park Center Loop, Orlando, Florida 32819.

Printed in the U.S.A.

ISBN 978-0-547-48507-2

1 2 3 4 5 6 7 8 9 10 0914 19 18 17 16 15 14 13 12 11 10

4500000000   A B C D E F G

If you have received these materials as examination copies free of charge, Houghton Mifflin Harcourt Publishing Company retains title to the materials and they may not be resold. Resale of examination copies is strictly prohibited.

Possession of this publication in print format does not entitle users to convert this publication, or any portion of it, into electronic format.

Quick Guide

Contents iii

The *Write Source* Voice

For over 30 years, our student books have spoken directly to students. We see ourselves as writers speaking to other writers.

As a result, the *Write Source* voice is always encouraging, like a mentor who genuinely wants another student to succeed. We believe that every student can learn to write and that every writer can improve. Throughout this book, your students will hear a voice that says, "You can do it!"

In the same way, the material in the wraparound text speaks directly to you. After all, we are simply teachers speaking to other teachers, so we use the same encouraging voice.

Whether you're a seasoned writing teacher or a fresh new face, we are certain that these materials in your hands can make a big difference for your students. We hope you agree!

Getting to Know *Write Source*

Just as we helped you learn about *Write Source* in the TE pages entitled "Professional Development," you can use these pages to help orient your students.

Here are suggestions for pointing out the key features of the program:

- **Writing guidelines:** "How many of you get writer's block? *Write Source* is designed to be a writer's-block buster. This book breaks down the writing process into simple, concrete steps so you never get stuck."
- **Checklists:** "How many of you like to revise? *Write Source* makes the process much easier. Revising checklists help you decide what changes will improve your writing, and specific revising strategies don't leave you guessing as to what to do."
- **Rubrics:** "How many of you have an easy time judging writing? *Write Source* uses rubrics throughout the writing process to help you know what your goals are as you write and how to improve your work as you revise and edit. Rubrics also help you respond to the writing of your peers."

A Quick Tour of *Write Source*

Write Source contains many key features that will help you improve your writing and language skills. Once you become familiar with this book, you will begin to understand how helpful these features can be.

Contents v

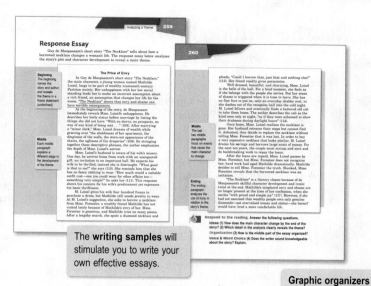

The **writing samples** will stimulate you to write your own effective essays.

Graphic organizers show you how to organize your ideas for writing.

Links to the traits help you appreciate the importance of different traits at different points in the writing process.

- **Writing samples:** "In basketball, you have a net to shoot for. In football, you have the goal line and the goalpost. In writing, you should also look at your goal before you begin. *Write Source* provides many models to help you know just what you are shooting for."

- **Graphic organizers:** "Have you ever heard that writing is thinking on paper? Well, graphic organizers are ways to draw out your thoughts. Graphic organizers help you think and sort out your ideas. They're just another way to make writing clear and easy."

- **Links to the traits:** "The traits of writing give us a common language for talking about what makes writing strong. As we go through the writing units in this book, we'll be talking a lot about ideas, organization, voice, word choice, sentence fluency, and conventions."

Understanding the Writing Process

The first section of the book provides an introduction to (or review of) the writing process.

The chapter "One Writer's Process" lets students see how another freshman writer works through the process of prewriting, writing, revising, editing, and publishing.

Integrating the Six Traits

Write Source fully integrates the six traits +1 of writing into the writing process. *Prewriting* focuses on **ideas** and **organization**. *Writing* adds a focus on **voice**. *Revising* focuses on the **first three traits** and also **word choice** and **sentence fluency.** *Editing* zeroes in on **conventions,** while *publishing* features the +1 trait of **presentation.**

Wraparound Feature

Focus on the Traits

Organization
Throughout the Teacher's Edition, trait boxes give you special tips for using the traits to help your students evaluate, discuss, and improve their writing.

---

contents

The Writing Process

The Forms of Writing

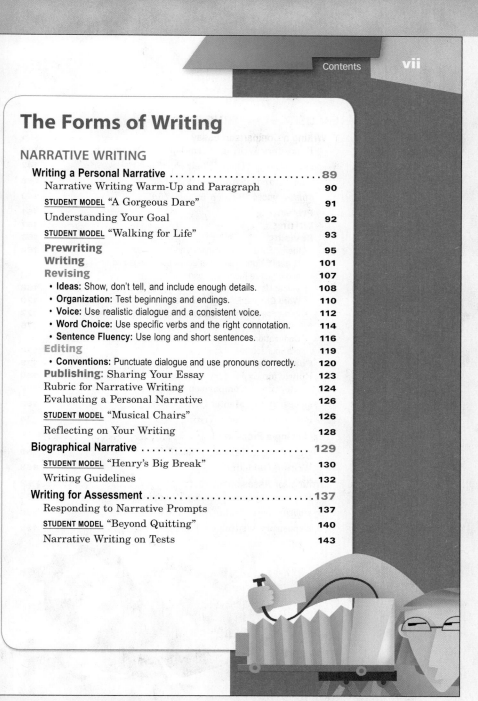

Creating the Forms of Writing

The writing units in *Write Source* focus on creating the fundamental forms of writing:

- Narrative
- Expository
- Persuasive
- Response to Literature
- Creative
- Research

Each writing assignment includes instruction, models, and activities that lead students through the writing process. The material works well for whole-class instruction, writing-workshop minilessons, and self-paced individual work time.

Wraparound Features

Copy Masters

These features tell you what copy masters are available to help you deliver the lesson.

Benchmark Papers

Check this feature to find out what benchmark papers you can use to show your students a range of performance.

Teaching the Core Units

The core writing units focus on the forms that are most often tested—narrative, expository, persuasive, and response to literature.

Each unit begins with an accessible model with response questions, helping students make the reading-writing connection.

Afterward, the text leads students step by step through the process of creating a similar piece of writing. Concrete activities help students do the following:

- select a topic
- gather details
- organize details
- create a focus statement
- write a strong beginning
- build a solid middle
- create an effective ending
- revise for ideas, organization, voice, word choice, and sentence fluency
- edit for conventions
- publish work with a polished presentation
- assess writing using traits-based rubrics

Each unit ends with an invitation for reflection, the point at which students internalize what they have learned.

Wraparound Features

Grammar Connection

Each unit overview suggests grammar activities to cover in the unit. Grammar Connection boxes then help you pinpoint the places to integrate instruction.

contents

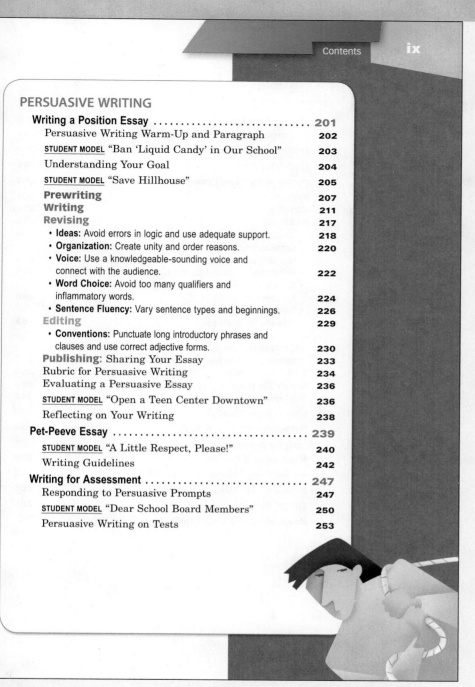

Using Rubrics Throughout the Process

You'll find that the traits-based rubrics in *Write Source* help guide your students throughout the process. Each core writing unit begins with a goal rubric that helps your students think about what they are trying to accomplish. Then, as your students revise and edit, rubric strips guide their work, helping them improve their writing in ways large and small.

Preparing for Assessment

Every core unit teaches students process-based strategies, which they internalize as "thinking moves" that will help them in on-demand writing situations. Each unit also ends with a sample on-demand writing prompt and response, as well as additional prompts for practice with high-stakes writing situations.

Efficacy studies from around the United States have demonstrated significant improvements from pretest to posttest scores for students using the *Write Source* series.

Wraparound Features

Teaching Tip

Throughout the wraparound, you'll find special strategies for making the lessons come alive for your students.

Test Prep!

These features give suggestions for preparing your students for high- and low-stakes writing and grammar tests.

Literature Connections

Each unit contains numerous student models. By reading them and responding to them, students tune their minds to a given genre before beginning to write in it.

Also, the response to literature unit focuses on age-appropriate novels, short stories, biographies, and articles that your students may have read—or may want to read. Here are the literature-based student models in the response to literature unit.

- **Response Paragraph:** "Gift Giving"
- **Response Essay Key Model:** "4 Little Girls"
- **Response Essay Working Model:** "Sweet Forgiveness"
- **Response Essay Assessment Model:** "Dying to Succeed"
- **Responding to a Fiction Prompt:** "Sleeping in Church?"
- **Responding to a Nonfiction Prompt:** "Instant Replay"

Writing Workshop

If you use the writing workshop approach, note how each activity in the core writing units can function as a minilesson. You can use these minilesson activities . . .

- to direct the whole class before individual writing time,
- to instruct a group of writers who are ready to learn a new skill, or
- to provide scaffolding for an individual writer who gets stuck.

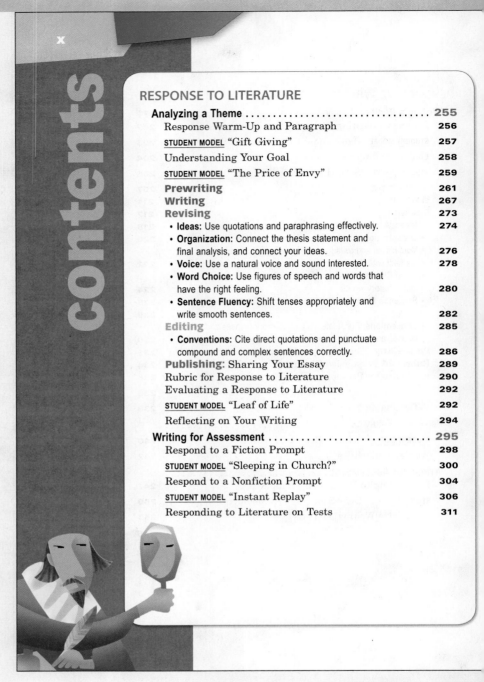

contents

x

RESPONSE TO LITERATURE

Wraparound Feature

 Literature Connections

These features help you use literary works to teach students special writing techniques. You'll find interesting insights into the works and lives of favorite writers as well as fresh ways to use literature to teach writing.

CREATIVE WRITING

Tapping Creativity

The *Write Source* series promotes creativity even in academic writing assignments. However, this section allows you and your students to develop forms that are especially inventive:

- Short Story
- Play
- Free-Verse Poem
- Blues Poem
- Senryu Poem

Research shows a direct connection between enjoyment and learning. Think how quickly a student masters a favorite video game or learns all the words to a favorite song. By letting students write for the joy of it, you can awaken in them a lifelong love of writing.

The Craft of Writing

Writing is an art. Art teachers teach techniques for creating perspective or formulas for the proportions of a human face, but then art students must internalize these techniques and use them to craft something new and wonderful.

Writing teachers need to do the same. In the wraparound, you'll find suggestions for helping students develop their writing style and voice, going beyond concrete skills to discover the craft of writing.

Wraparound Feature

 Writer's Craft

These features help you inspire students to write the way professional writers do. They feature techniques used by the masters as well as interesting anecdotes and quotations.

Training Researchers

In this Internet age, strong research skills are more important than ever. Students must be able to evaluate sources and avoid the lure of plagiarism. This section equips students to succeed using traditional and digital source materials.

The step-by-step instructions in the "Research Writing" section help students learn to do the following:

- use the library
- use the Internet
- evaluate sources
- summarize, paraphrase, and quote
- avoid plagiarism
- cite sources (according to MLA style)
- use a gathering grid and create note cards
- outline a research report
- create a works-cited page

The section also helps students present their material in a traditional report form—or as a multimedia presentation!

Wraparound Feature

 Technology Connections

In these features, you'll see connections to *Write Source Online* www.hmheducation.com/writesource. *Write Source* includes *Interactive Whiteboard Lessons, Net-text, Bookshelf, GrammarSnap, Portfolio, File Cabinet,* and *Essay Scoring.*

RESEARCH WRITING

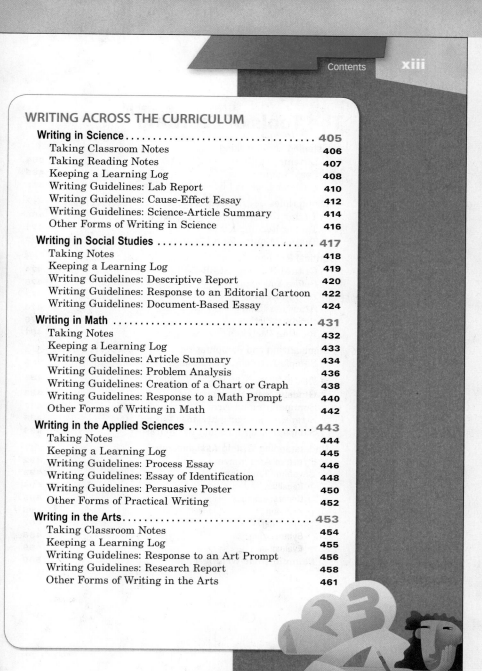

Writing Across the Curriculum

Special chapters help your students write in their content areas: science, social studies, math, the applied sciences, and the arts. These sections help you partner with content-area teachers to make sure that students can use writing to show knowledge, to think through difficult concepts, and to succeed throughout the school day.

Chapters feature note taking, learning logs, and a number of subject-specific assignments. The social studies chapter culminates in instruction for answering document-based questions—a type of on-demand writing that is often required on social studies tests.

Equipping Students to Learn

This section focuses on crucial skills for academic success: oral language use, note taking, critical reading, summarizing, paraphrasing, writing for different purposes, analyzing words, writing in the workplace, and taking tests.

Organized topically, these chapters can be taught as minilessons when your students most need them. Here are some suggested applications:

- **Use "Listening and Speaking"** when setting up a writing workshop so that students understand the ground rules for group discussion.
- **Present "Taking Notes"** at the beginning of the year to help students write to learn in all their classes.
- **Use "Critical Reading"** to equip students with the crucial study habits they need to succeed in all of their course work.
- **Present "Summarizing and Paraphrasing"** in tandem with the "Research Report" chapter.
- **Work through "Understanding Writing Assignments"** to deepen students' thinking through the use of Bloom's Taxonomy.

contents

The Tools of Learning

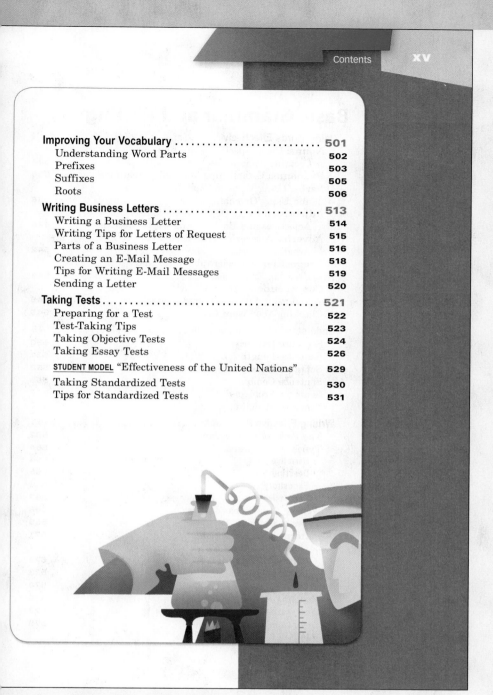

- **Present "Improving Your Vocabulary"** to help students analyze different word parts and derive meaning for unfamiliar terms.
- **Teach "Writing Business Letters"** in tandem with the persuasive writing unit, asking students to create persuasive letters in the correct format.
- **Use "Taking Tests"** to help students improve their performance on low- or high-stakes assessments.

Teaching Grammar and Writing

With clear rules, simple explanations, high-interest examples, and engaging activities, "Basic Grammar and Writing" provides short minilessons to help students understand and use the different parts of speech.

As you work through the writing units earlier in the book, you will find cross-references to these pages and those in the "Proofreader's Guide." The *Write Source* series fully integrates its grammar components within its writing units—including every activity in the student book and the *SkillsBook*. Integrated grammar instruction allows students to use the rules in context and understand not just the "what" of grammar, but also the "why."

You can use all the grammar that is suggested—or can target the grammar to your students' specific needs. The choice is yours.

Differentiating Instruction

Throughout the Teacher's Edition, you'll find useful hints for modifications and accommodations to help all students learn. Watch for the wraparound features shown below. Also, because the *Write Source* series follows a consistent format throughout its K–12 line, students who need further differentiation can work at a grade below (or above) their classmates.

Basic Grammar and Writing

Wraparound Features

English Language Learners

These boxes provide differentiation tips to help English language learners.

Struggling Learners

Consult this feature to adjust the lesson for those who are struggling.

Advanced Learners

These boxes feature tips for challenging students who excel.

A Writer's Resource

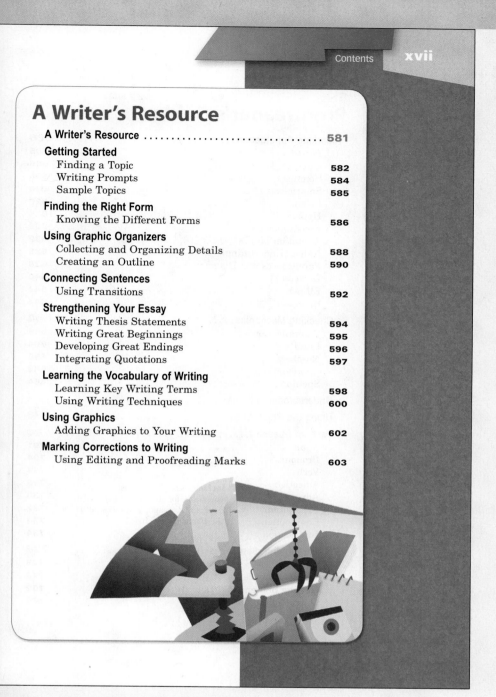

Contents   xvii

Creating Resourceful Writers

This section equips students with specific strategies that they will use over and over during the writing process. Students will find strategies for getting started, for gathering and organizing ideas, for connecting their thoughts, and for strengthening their essays.

Using the +1 Trait: Presentation

Sometimes the traits are referred to as the six traits +1 because presentation is so crucial to the success of any form of writing. Each of the core units includes a page that focuses on presentation and publishing. This section also provides support for effectively presenting ideas on the page.

Perfecting Conventions

The "Proofreader's Guide" includes the rules of punctuation, mechanics, idioms, usage, parts of speech, and sentence creation. The rules are accompanied by engaging example text and activities to test knowledge.

Also, as the "Test Prep!" box indicates, the major sections end with test-prep pages to help students study for grammar tests.

Cross-references in this TE connect to other resources—*SkillsBook* activities and *Write Source Online* GrammarSnap.

Proofreader's Guide

Test Prep!

The "Proofreader's Guide" includes test-prep pages to help you study for tests on punctuation, mechanics, usage, sentences, and the parts of speech.

Why Write?

Have you ever seen pictures of primitive cave drawings? These drawings suggest that since the earliest times, human beings have felt the need to record their experiences, to describe their lives, and to show what is important to them.

Perhaps you have felt the same need to record your thoughts, feelings, and experiences. Today, though, instead of crawling into a cave with a hunk of charcoal, you can stay right where you are. All you need is a pencil, a piece of paper, and the endless thoughts that tumble through your head.

This chapter addresses the question "Why write?" It also explores other basic questions you may have about writing and provides many answers. Maybe your own personal answer to the question "Why write?" will be like that of writer Anne Lamott: "The act of writing turns out to be its own reward."

- **Reasons to Write**
- **Getting Started**
- **Using a Writer's Notebook**

"Writing is not apart from living. Writing is a kind of double living."
—Catherine Drinker Bowen

Why Write?

Take this opportunity to explain why writers keep a journal or notebook. Tell students that writers answer the question "Why write?" each time they create an entry.

Have students copy the question "Why write?" at the top of the first page in their writer's notebook. Then tell them to record today's date and write a one-sentence response to the question. Don't give students any parameters to guide their response; simply tell them to answer the question honestly and from a personal point of view.

From time to time during the year, ask students to return to this question to revise or add to their original response, based on recent writing experiences and what they have learned about writing. At the end of the year, students should have a well-developed purpose statement for writing.

Quotations about writing, such as the one at the bottom of the page, appear on the introductory page of each chapter. Use these quotations to engage students in lively discussions about the philosophy, purpose, and act of writing.

English Language Learners

Some students may not have a strong tradition of writing in their first language. To motivate them to respond to "Why write?", have them brainstorm places in their communities where they have seen writing (books, menus, magazines, posters). Then ask them to write about how writing has been helpful to them.

Copy Masters

Sensory Chart (TE p. 2)

Reasons to Write

Books about writing can provide extensive insight into the writing process. If possible, make some of these books available in the classroom for students to explore at their leisure, or ask the school librarian to order copies for the school library.

- *Bird by Bird: Some Instructions on Writing and Life* by Anne Lamott
- *Writing Reminders: Tools, Tips, and Techniques* by Jim Burke
- *Writing Down the Bones: Freeing the Writer Within* by Natalie Goldberg
- *Breathing In, Breathing Out: Keeping a Writer's Notebook* by Ralph Fletcher

Provide photocopies of the reproducible Sensory Chart (TE page 820). Ask students to record their sensory observations of different places and situations for one week. At the end of the week, have them review their charts and ask themselves these questions:

- What new insights have I gained about myself and my surroundings as a result of this exercise?
- How can I use these observations in my writing?

Reasons to Write

In his book *Writing Reminders*, writing teacher Jim Burke says, "In the act of composing, writers learn about themselves and their world and communicate their insights to others." In one sentence, Mr. Burke has answered the question "Why write?" in many ways. The rest of this page helps analyze the ideas in that one sentence.

Writing helps you . . .

Learn more about yourself.

Writing lets you look deep within yourself, sometimes with surprising results. When you keep a writer's notebook of your thoughts and feelings, you may, as you read your entries later, see yourself in a whole new light.

Learn more about your world.

By recording observations of the world around you (what you hear and see and sense), you can learn from the events that shape you. Your observations also serve as a fascinating record of your time in history. Finally, writing about your classes helps you remember and make sense of what you are learning.

Share your ideas and insights.

Sometimes writing is the best way to share your thoughts with others. Unlike conversation, writing gives you time to decide exactly what you want to say before anyone else "hears" it.

Express what you know.

Writing actually helps you become a better thinker. It lets you review what you already know, reflect on it, and add new thoughts. Think of writing as exercise for your mind.

Tip

Remember, writing is a skill. As with all other skills, the more you practice, the better you will become.

Write to learn. Think of the most important piece of writing you have ever completed. Write freely for 5 minutes about this piece, exploring why it was important to you.

Getting Started

Think of writing as a skill. Just as you set aside time to improve your musical or athletic skills, do the same with writing. Exercise your mind as well as your body. Keep sharp as well as in shape. Improvement will come if you make an honest effort.

Where should I write?

Write in school. Here are ways you can write throughout your school day:
- Take classroom notes.
- Keep a learning log in each of your classes.
- Complete writing assignments and papers.

Write at home. Writing in your spare time can help you gain fluency—the ability to write quickly and easily. Here are ways to write at home:
- Write e-mail messages and letters.
- Keep a writer's notebook. (See pages **4–5**.)
- Create short stories and poems.

Write wherever you are. Write in a car, on the bus, or on the subway. In her book *Writing Down the Bones*, Natalie suggests that you write wherever you feel comfortable.

What should I write about?

You can write about anything and everything. The more you write, the more you learn. Here are just a few things you can write about:
- **Observations:** What is happening around you right now? What do you think about what is happening?
- **Memories:** What was the best moment of your day? Your week? Your year? What was the worst moment?
- **Hopes and dreams:** What do you want in life? What do you wish for your future?
- **People:** What person means the most to you? What person do you admire? What sort of person do you not understand?
- **Places:** Where are you right now? Where do you wish you were? Where do you never want to be again?
- **Things:** What is your favorite possession? Your least favorite? What one invention would you like to outlaw, and why?

 Write freely for 5 to 10 minutes using one of the ideas listed above as a starting point. Then read what you have written and circle at least two ideas that interest you or surprise you.

Getting Started

Point out to students that writing skills directly relate to success in school, and even in life. Have students brainstorm real-life everyday reasons for writing (for example, a letter requesting a refund for a product or service, an invitation, a contract, or a college or job application). Tell students that the more they write, the easier it will become for them.

Focus on the *Where should I write?* list. Ask students if, based on this list, they are writing as much as they could be. Have them make a personal checklist of ways they can add to the writing they do in school, at home, and wherever they are. Set a goal for students to check off a new item on their list every day for a week.

Repeat the freewriting activity every day for at least two weeks. Tell students to write once about each item listed under *What should I write about?* At the end of the two weeks, students will have identified several interesting ideas that they can refer to when they need topic ideas for future writing assignments.

Struggling Learners

Suggest that students ask themselves *who, what, when, where,* and *why* questions if they choose to freewrite about an observation or a memory.

When students complete their freewriting, instead of rereading it, have them exchange it with a partner. The partner can circle the most interesting and surprising ideas.

Using a Writer's Notebook

Take this opportunity to remind students of your requirements for keeping a writer's notebook.

- Make sure students know when you will be examining individual notebooks and how you will assess them.
- If students use their notebooks to explore personal issues, establish criteria for how you can evaluate the notebook without invading their privacy. For example, students can select pages for you to read, or you can just flip through the notebook without reading.
- Although students can use any kind of blank book for a notebook, point out that a three-ring binder allows pages to be inserted, moved around, and removed.

Explain that when Ralph Fletcher compares a writer's notebook to a compost heap, he is making a surprising comparison. Tell students that writers often use **similes and metaphors** *(see below)* to make these kinds of comparisons.

4

Using a Writer's Notebook

Your most powerful writing tool can be a notebook reserved exclusively for daily writing. A **writer's notebook** (also called a *journal*) is a place to record your thoughts on any topic. As you write regularly in your notebook, you will make countless discoveries about your world.

In his book *Breathing In, Breathing Out: Keeping a Writer's Notebook*, Ralph Fletcher compares a writer's notebook to a compost heap. Over time, all the cuttings and leftovers that a gardener composts turn into rich fertilizer. In the same way, all the thoughts and feelings that you record can turn into useful starting points for your future writing.

Ensuring Success

To make sure that your writer's notebook is a success, consider the quantity, quality, and variety of your entries. Also follow the rules at the bottom of the page.

- **Quantity:** Teachers often require a certain number of pages or entries per grading period. Know your teacher's expectations for your notebook.
- **Quality:** Approach each entry with a high level of enthusiasm and interest. Develop your ideas fully with sensory, memory, and reflective details.
- **Variety:** Write some of your entries from different points of view. For example, after an argument with a friend, write about it from your friend's point of view, or from the perspective of someone who overheard the argument.

Rules for a Writer's Notebook

- **Date each entry.** The date on an entry helps you find it later and puts it in perspective with other entries.
- **Write freely.** Don't worry about producing perfect copy. Just get your ideas on paper.
- **Write regularly.** Develop the habit of writing daily.
- **Reflect on your work.** Reread your entries to consider the discoveries you have made and to look for writing ideas.

English Language Learners

Students may think that similes and metaphors are used only in poetry. Encourage students to use these figures of speech to enrich all of their writing. Point out that, like Fletcher, they can use similes and metaphors to compare ideas in a way that readers will find interesting and memorable.

For practice, have students create their own similes or metaphors using this sentence starter: *A writer's notebook is (a, an,* or *like) . . .*

✱ For definitions and examples of simile, metaphor, and other figures of speech, see SE page 340.

English Language Learners

In their notebooks, students can ask you questions about English language concepts that they don't understand. Your responses can model good English writing. Check students' notebooks frequently to clear up any language misconceptions before they become ingrained.

Process

Taking It Personally

Here is a page, from a student writer's notebook, that focuses on both the writer's past and on a favorite pair of shoes. This entry does a lot of important things. It . . .

- captures a moment in time,
- describes something that is important to the writer,
- starts with a "seed idea" (a worn-out pair of shoes), and
- reflects on the writer's life.

Sample Notebook Entry

February 6, 2011

While cleaning out my closet, I came across my favorite pair of sneakers from seventh grade. They seemed out of place among my heels, cross-trainers, and boots. They look awful, old and cracked, and the laces are done for. But they bring back so many memories.

I remember opening the box they came in. I was so excited to have cool new shoes. I wanted to go to school so that I could show them off.

I remember wearing them as I ran to the bus, late as usual, thinking that my new shoes helped me run faster. I also remember wearing them when I waded through the icy water in a tunnel that ran under the road. I didn't think my feet would ever feel warm again! I put those shoes through a lot.

I'm sad to throw them away. It's like saying good-bye to an old friend. I'll never forget them or the person I was when I wore them. Hmm. I wonder what adventures I'll remember when my new cross-trainers look like these old friends.

Remember: Keeping a writer's notebook lets you look at ordinary things in new ways, describe your feelings, choose good descriptive words, and practice writing until you feel confident.

Write a quick reflection. Think about an object that was once very important to you. Write freely for 5 to 10 minutes about that object and what it meant—and still means—to you.

Use the sample entry to help students understand how much information they can store in a notebook entry. First, have students identify specific details that show how the entry accomplishes the following:

- The entry captures a moment in time (cleaning out a closet).
- It describes something that is important to the writer (old sneakers that are *awful, old and cracked,* but that are like an old friend).
- It starts with a "seed idea" (favorite pair of sneakers).
- It reflects on the writer's life (sneakers helped the writer run faster; worn while wading through icy water; now seem out of place next to heels, cross-trainers, and boots).

Then ask students what they learned about the writer that isn't stated directly but can be inferred from the details. Possible responses:

- The heels show that the writer is a girl.
- She wears cross-trainers, which suggests she's athletic.
- She probably doesn't clean out her closet often.

English Language Learners

Define the following words before reading the passage:

- came across (found)
- cross-trainers (special workout sneakers)
- awful (very bad)
- done for (ruined)
- waded (walked in)

Explain to students that in a writing notebook they do not need to use formal English; they can use slang and casual expressions as this author did *(done for)*. Their goal is to express their ideas, so they should not worry too much about grammar or formal voice.

Struggling Learners

Students may experience difficulty thinking of a suitable object to write about. Provide suggestions such as a book, a CD, a photograph, or an item of clothing. Then organize a brainstorming session to help students gather ideas about why the object has special significance.

The Writing Process Overview

Common Core Standards Focus

Writing 5: Develop and strengthen writing as needed by planning, revising, editing, rewriting, or trying a new approach, focusing on addressing what is most significant for a specific purpose and audience.

Writing 6: Use technology, including the Internet, to produce, publish, and update individual or shared writing products, taking advantage of technology's capacity to link to other information and to display information flexibly and dynamically.

Language 1: Demonstrate command of the conventions of standard English grammar and usage when writing or speaking.

Language 2: Demonstrate command of the conventions of standard English capitalization, punctuation, and spelling when writing.

Writing Process

- **Prewriting** Select a specific topic, and gather and organize details into a writing plan.
- **Writing** Complete a first draft, using the prewriting plan as a guide to getting everything down on paper.
- **Revising** Review the first draft for five key traits; then delete, move, add to, and rewrite parts of the text.
- **Editing** Check revised writing for conventions and proofread the final copy.
- **Publishing** Share the work with others.

Focus on the Traits

- **Ideas** Presenting a clear focus supported by specific ideas and details
- **Organization** Creating a meaningful whole with interesting beginning, middle, and ending parts
- **Voice** Reflecting the writer's personality in a way that is engaging and appropriate for the audience
- **Word Choice** Choosing precise words that deliver a clear message
- **Sentence Fluency** Using a variety of sentences that connect ideas smoothly
- **Conventions** Checking for errors in punctuation, capitalization, spelling, and grammar

Technology Connections

 Write Source Online
www.hmheducation.com/writesource

- *Net-text*
- *Bookshelf*
- *GrammarSnap*
- *Portfolio*
- *Essay Scoring*
- *Writing Network features*
- *File Cabinet*

 Interactive Whiteboard Lessons

Suggested Writing Process Unit (Three Weeks)

	Day	Writing and Skills Instruction	Student Edition		SkillsBook	Daily Language Workouts
			Main Pages	Resource Units*		
WEEK 1	1–2	**Getting Started** (activities, page TE-69) **Why Write?**	1–5	678–696 and Test Prep, 698–699	57	6–7
	3	**Understanding the Writing Process**	7–9			
	4–5	(continued)	10–12	605–644 and Test Prep, 622–623, 646–647	3–4	
WEEK 2	6–7	**Taking Notes**	467–472			8–9
		One Writer's Process (goals)	13–14			
		(Prewriting, Writing)	15–19			
	8–9	(Revising, Editing, Publishing)	20–30	648–668 and Test Prep, 670–671	41–42	
	10	(Assessing, Reflecting)	31–32			
WEEK 3	11–13	**Understanding the Traits of Writing**	39–54	738–756 and Test Prep, 758–759	127, 131, 136, 148, 153, 157–158, 163–164, 181	10–11
	14	**Using a Rubric**	61–72			
		Publishing Your Writing	73–82			
	15	**Creating a Portfolio**	83–87	700–734 and Skills assessment—Parts of Speech, Test Prep, 712–713, 736–737	69, 75, 89, 107, 117	

* These units are also located in the back of the *Teacher's Edition*. Resource Units include "Basic Grammar and Writing," "A Writer's Resource," and "Proofreader's Guide."

(+) This activity is located in a different section of the *Write Source Student Edition*. If students have already completed this activity, you may wish to review it at this time.

Using the Writing Process

Each chapter description below will help you decide which parts of the unit to teach.

Writing Focus

Understanding the Writing Process (pages 7–12)

Writing is approached as a process of exploration and discovery rather than as an end product. The text provides a concise explanation of each step in the writing process plus additional tips and insights into the craft of writing. The presentation on SE page 12 of how the traits of writing are connected to the writing process is a reference students may return to throughout the year.

One Writer's Process (pages 13–32)

Each step of one writer's process is modeled from prewriting to publishing. The complexity of the process is demonstrated, with ideas and words being cut or moved and new material added as the writer improves and refines his work. Direct students to this chapter whenever they need a refresher on any part of the writing process.

Writing with a Computer (pages 33–38)

Computers facilitate all aspects of the writing process. They do have drawbacks, however. Software does not always pick out mistakes (spelling, wrong word, and so on).

Understanding the Traits of Writing (pages 39–54)

Even the best writers can improve their writing by understanding and recognizing specific traits of effective writing. This chapter defines and models each trait.

Peer Responding (pages 55–60)

Peer responding is a critical component in the revising process. Using the language of the traits of writing helps students focus their feedback. Specific guidelines are provided for students in their roles as writer-reader and listener-responder.

Using a Rubric (pages 61–72)

A well-written paper is not just perfect grammar and spelling. Rubric strips are used throughout the book to present goals of writing based on the assignment, to revise for each of the six traits, and to evaluate a finished piece of writing.

Publishing Your Writing (pages 73–82)

Different purposes of publishing are presented: class assignments, school paper, writing contests, and so on. In each case, a refined, finished product favorably impacts the audience.

Creating a Portfolio (pages 83–87)

Students are encouraged to keep their best writing so that they can see how their writing has improved.

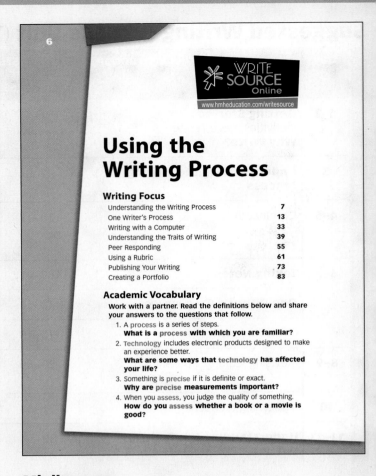

WRITE SOURCE Online
www.hmheducation.com/writesource

Using the Writing Process

Writing Focus

Academic Vocabulary

Work with a partner. Read the definitions below and share your answers to the questions that follow.

1. A process is a series of steps.
   What is a process with which you are familiar?
2. Technology includes electronic products designed to make an experience better.
   What are some ways that technology has affected your life?
3. Something is precise if it is definite or exact.
   Why are precise measurements important?
4. When you assess, you judge the quality of something.
   How do you assess whether a book or a movie is good?

Minilessons

Idea Chain   Understanding the Traits of Writing

■ As a class, **BEGIN** a topic chain with a general subject category (See "Basics of Life" on page 583). Each student **NAMES** a specific topic that could be part of that category. (For example, the category of health could have topics like aerobic exercise, jogging, fasting). **KEEP** an idea chain going as long as possible. **SWITCH** categories.

Mock Trial   Peer Responding

■ **READ** a sample essay from the textbook to a small group. Group members **RESPOND** using the peer-response format on page 60. Finally, **CRITIQUE** the responders. Were they too personal, negative, vague, or hesitant to give constructive criticism?

Measuring Success   Using a Rubric

■ **READ** the essay on pages 429–430. **USE** the rubric on pages 180–181 to evaluate the essay. **DISCUSS** your assessment with a classmate.

7

Understanding the Writing Process

Skilled athletes work very hard to perform at a high level. They train individually, practice with their teams, compete, assess their performances, and consult with their peers and coaches. To do their best, athletes must repeat this process again and again.

Skilled writers also follow a process. For specific projects, they gather and organize their thoughts (prewriting), connect their ideas on paper (writing), make changes as needed (revising and editing), and assess and share their finished copy (publishing). To do their best work, writers must address these steps for each piece they develop.

This chapter will help you learn the writing process and build some valuable writing habits at the same time.

- **Building Good Writing Habits**
- **Understanding the Writing Process**
- **The Process in Action**
- **Focusing on the Traits**

"What is written without effort is in general read without pleasure."
—Dr. Samuel Johnson

Understanding the Writing Process

Objectives
- build good writing habits
- demonstrate an understanding of the five steps in the writing process
- learn the six traits of effective writing

Engage students in a friendly debate by having them respond to these questions:
- Why do athletes accept that they have to practice to improve, yet some writers think that their first efforts are the best they can do?
- Is it harder to become a good athlete or a good writer?

Students can have fun debating the questions and, at the same time, can come to realize that becoming a good writer requires a fundamental willingness to improve.

Academic Vocabulary

Read aloud the academic terms, as well as the descriptions and questions. Model for students how to read one question and answer it. Have partners monitor their understanding and seek clarification of the terms by working through the meanings and questions together.

Copy Masters

Time Line, 5 W's Chart, T-Chart, Venn Diagram, Sensory Chart, Details Chart, Quick List (TE p. 10)

Building Good Writing Habits

For some students, the only writing they do is required writing for assignments. If you have not already set aside some class time for students to write and reflect regularly, set aside 10 to 15 minutes daily for students to explore topics that interest them. To ensure that students use this time to develop and practice their writing skills and not to catch up on homework, tell them to remove all other books and papers from their desks and have them write in their writer's notebook.

As an alternate idea for the freewriting activity at the bottom of the page, ask students to write a personal response to one of the quotations on the page. For example, if they choose to respond to the Willa Cather quotation, they can list three or four events from their lives that could be the foundation for a story idea.

8

Building Good Writing Habits

Writing success begins with good writing habits. Follow the tips below and you will see real improvement in your writing.

When to Write

Set aside time each day to write. Regular writing will help you develop fluency—the ability to write quickly and easily.

"When I am working on a book or a story, I write every morning as soon after the first light as possible."

—Ernest Hemingway

Where to Write

Write in school and at home. Write on the bus or in a coffee shop. Just keep writing wherever you can.

"I type in one place, but I write all over the house."

—Toni Morrison

What to Write

Write about anything and everything that interests you—personal experiences, current events, music, books, or sports.

"Most of the basic material a writer works with is acquired before the age of fifteen."

—Willa Cather

How to Write

Relax and let the words flow. Share your true feelings and, before long, your distinctive writing voice will develop.

"Any writer overwhelmingly honest about pleasing himself is almost sure to please others."

—Marianne Moore

 Write about your day. Think about something that has happened to you today. Write nonstop for 5 to 10 minutes about this experience. Let the words flow freely! Afterward, underline any thoughts or ideas that surprise you.

English Language Learners

Students may find it difficult to write continuously for 10 minutes in English. Allow them to write in their first languages for at least part of the freewriting time. This will allow students to concentrate on expressing their ideas without becoming stuck on grammar or vocabulary. The resulting improvement in students' overall writing skills will transfer into English. Ask them to translate some of their ideas after the initial 10-minute freewriting session.

Advanced Learners

Encourage students to create a personal collection of quotations that have special meaning or significance to them. Point out that these quotations can serve as a source of inspiration for their own writing. Remind students to record the name of the writer and the source of the quotation.

Understanding the Writing Process

Before a piece of writing is ready to share, it should have gone through a series of steps called the *writing process*. This page contains brief descriptions of these steps.

The Steps in the Writing Process

Prewriting

 The first step in the writing process involves selecting a specific topic, gathering details about it, and organizing those details into a writing plan.

Writing

 During this step, the writer completes the first draft using the prewriting plan as a guide. This draft is a writer's *first* chance to get everything on paper.

Revising

 During revising, the writer first reviews the draft for five key traits: *ideas, organization, voice, word choice,* and *sentence fluency.* After deciding what changes to make, the writer deletes, moves, adds to, and rewrites parts of the text.

Editing

 Then the writer edits the revised draft for the *conventions* of punctuation, capitalization, spelling, and grammar. A writer should also proofread the final copy before sharing it.

Publishing

 This is the final step in the writing process. Publishing is the writer's opportunity to share his or her work with others.

 Analyze your process. Which step in the writing process is easiest for you? Which step is hardest, and why? Explain one way to make that step easier for yourself.

Understanding the Writing Process

Review each step in the writing process with students. Some students may be seeing these steps for the first time. To reassure them, explain the following:

- They may already intuitively follow these steps when they write.
- They may have followed these steps in other classes, using different labels for the steps.
- They will be given detailed information about the steps and will have many opportunities to practice each step throughout the year.

Help students understand that all writers struggle at one time or another with different steps of the writing process. Talk about the step that you find most difficult and tell what you have done to make that step easier. Then invite volunteers to share ideas for making each step easier.

English Language Learners

To help students refer to the steps of the writing process as they work, display a poster that shows each step in a different color and in order. Include key words and phrases for each step. For example: *Prewriting—use strategies to select topic, gather details, organize details.*

Writing—get ideas down on paper.

The Process in Action

Prewriting **Selecting a Topic**

Ask students why they don't watch movies on topics that don't appeal to them. (Most students will say they would get bored and wouldn't enjoy the movie.) Explain that the same thing happens when writers **select topics** *(see below)* that don't appeal to them—they get bored and they don't enjoy writing.

Prewriting **Gathering and Organizing Details**

Display a variety of graphic organizers and discuss which ones work well for particular assignments and why. Copy masters for graphic organizers are available on TE pages 816–822.

Writing **Developing the First Draft**

Explain to students that when they start to write, they have to figure out how to present ideas so that readers will be interested in the topic. One way to spark a reader's interest is with a great beginning.

✱ For more about writing great beginnings, see SE page 595.

The Process in Action

The next two pages give a detailed description of each step in the writing process. The graphic below reminds you that, at any time, you can move back and forth between the steps in the writing process. Be aware that if you put more effort and care into the early stages of the process, you'll move through the later stages more easily.

Prewriting Selecting a Topic

- Search for topics that meet the requirements of the assignment.
- Select a specific topic that appeals to you.

Gathering and Organizing Details

- Gather as many ideas and details as you can about the topic.
- With the purpose of the assignment in mind, find one point to emphasize about the topic—either an interesting part or your personal feeling about it. This will be the focus, or thesis, of your writing.
- Decide which details to include in your writing.
- Organize your details into a writing plan, perhaps using an outline or a chart.

Writing Developing the First Draft

- When writing the first draft, concentrate on getting your ideas on paper. Don't try to produce a perfect piece of writing.
- Use the details you collected and your prewriting plan as a guide, but feel free to add new ideas and details as you go along.
- Make sure your writing has a beginning, a middle, and an ending.

 Tip

Write on every *other* line and on only *one* side of the paper when using pen or pencil and paper. Double-space on a computer. This will give you room for revising, the next step in the process.

Teaching Tip: Select Topics

Assure students that when it comes time to select a topic, there are many ways to generate ideas, such as freewriting, making lists, brainstorming, and looking through notebooks, personal journals, and family albums. Books and Web sites are also good sources for topics.

English Language Learners

Ask students to use their writer's notebooks to jot down questions they have about the steps on SE pages 10 and 11. Later, when they have studied each step in more detail and looked at the examples in the chapter, ask students to look back at these questions to see if they have been answered; if not, address the questions as needed.

Struggling Learners

Read the bulleted information for each step and pause to invite students' comments and questions based on their experience with the process.

Process

Revising Improving Your Writing

- Set aside your first draft for a while so you can return to it with a fresh perspective.
- Read your first draft slowly and critically.
- Use these questions as a revising guide:
  - Is my topic interesting for the reader?
  - Does the beginning catch the reader's attention?
  - Are the ideas in order and easy to understand?
  - Have I included enough details to support my central idea?
  - Does the ending leave the reader with something to think about?
  - Do I sound interested in, and knowledgeable about, the topic?
  - Are the nouns specific and the verbs active?
  - Are the modifiers (adjectives and adverbs) clear and descriptive?
  - Does the whole piece read smoothly?
- Ask at least one other person to review your writing and give suggestions.
- Make as many changes as necessary to improve your writing.

Editing Checking for Conventions

- Check for errors in punctuation, capitalization, spelling, and grammar.
- Have at least one other person check your writing for errors.
- Prepare a neat final copy.
- Proofread the final copy before publishing it.

Publishing Sharing Your Writing

- Share your writing with friends, classmates, and family.
- Consider submitting your writing to a newspaper or other publication.
- Also consider including the writing in your portfolio.

Tip

For assignments, save all your work. Refer to your original writing and to the teacher's comments on the graded piece for ideas and inspiration for future writing projects.

 Consider the process. Think about a recent writing assignment. Did you go through a process like the one explained on these two pages? Write about the differences between the process you followed and this one.

Revising Improving Your Writing

Ask students if they have ever been in a discussion and later wished that they had made one more point or had ended the discussion by saying something clever to leave a lasting impression. Point out that in the revising step of the writing process, writers have the chance to go back and insert that one last point, and to rewrite the ending to make a greater impression on their audience.

✱ For more about developing great endings, see SE page 596.

Editing Checking for Conventions

Students may not like the idea of having someone else check their work. Explain that a person who is seeing the piece for the first time and who is not concerned with style or content can more readily identify errors in punctuation, capitalization, spelling, and grammar.

Publishing Sharing Your Writing

Tell students they will have the opportunity to explore a variety of publishing formats and venues. For example, students who are not comfortable reading their work aloud can make their writing available on the class Web site or in printed form in the classroom or school library.

English Language Learners

If students are inexperienced with speaking and writing in English and are concerned about having someone check their grammatical errors, explain that they will only be responsible for conventions they have studied. If their work is edited by a peer, instruct the editing student to correct only for certain conventions.

Advanced Learners

Students who are comfortable with their writing will approach the writing process in a way that works best for them. They may skip or combine steps, devote more time to one step, or even change direction in the middle of the process. Assure these students that their work will be evaluated on rubrics, not on process.

Focusing on the Traits

Some students may have had limited exposure to the traits of writing. Later in the unit (SE pages 39–54), the traits are explained in depth. To introduce and explain the traits before students read SE page 12, have them read the descriptions of the traits in the Traits of Writing chart on SE page 40.

Assess your students' awareness and understanding of the traits before assigning the **Try It!** activity. Students may benefit from doing this activity later in the unit when they have developed a greater understanding of the traits and their application.

Focusing on the Traits

Writing is complicated, so you can't focus on everything at once. For example, you can't check punctuation and the effectiveness of your beginning and ending paragraphs at the same time. The writing process lets you focus on the different traits of good writing at different times. (See pages **39–54**.)

Connecting the Traits to the Writing Process

Prewrite

Ideas	What topic should I write about? What part of the topic should I focus on? What details should I include?
Organization	How should I organize my details? Which graphic organizer should I use for my planning?
Voice	What is my attitude about the topic?

Write

Ideas	What do I want to say?
Organization	How do I want to arrange my ideas?
Voice	How do I want to sound?

Revise

Ideas	Are my ideas clear and complete?
Organization	Do my beginning, middle, and ending work well?
Voice	Did I create an appropriate tone?
Word Choice	Have I chosen specific nouns and active verbs?
Sentence Fluency	Are my sentences varied? Do they read smoothly?

Edit

Conventions	Have I used correct punctuation, capitalization, spelling, and grammar?

Publish

Ideas, Organization, Voice, Word Choice, Sentence Fluency, Conventions What do you think of my work?

Try It!

Reflect on the traits. Answer the following questions:

1. Which trait is it easiest for you to work with? Explain.
2. Which trait is it hardest for you to work with? Explain.

One Writer's Process

Every writer approaches writing differently, but the best writers have this in common: They approach writing as a process. Step-by-step, they show that they care not only about their topic but also about the writing itself.

This chapter shows how student writer Dario Ramirez used the steps in the writing process to develop an expository essay about computer graphics (CG) used in films. As you follow his work, you'll see how he shaped his initial ideas into an effective piece of writing.

- **Previewing the Goals**
- **Prewriting**
- **Writing**
- **Revising**
- **Editing**
- **Publishing**
- **Assessing the Final Copy**
- **Reflecting on Your Writing**

"Easy writing makes hard reading, but hard writing makes easy reading."

—Florence King

One Writer's Process

Objectives
- examine the goals for expository writing
- evaluate one writer's work step by step through the writing process
- review one writer's final essay and self-assessment

Give students an opportunity to skim SE pages 13–38. Ask them to share their expectations about what they will learn on these pages. Possible responses:
- comparing their writing process to a model
- improving their writing
- assessing their writing
- writing with a computer

Previewing the Goals

As a class, preview the rubric for expository writing on SE pages 180–181. Assure students that they will learn more about using a rubric later in this unit (SE pages 61–72). Tell them that throughout the year, they will use assessment rubrics to guide their writing.

Call attention to the Traits of Expository Writing chart on this page and tell students that in each unit a list of goals like these will guide them through the writing process. Then have students compare the goals in the chart to the rubric on SE pages 180–181. Point out that the writer's goal for each trait is to aim for the highest rating.

Try It!
Answers

1. He should select a topic that interests him.
2. It should explore an important part of the topic.
3. He should use words and details that fit the audience and his purpose for writing.

Previewing the Goals

Before Dario Ramirez began writing his essay, he previewed the goals for expository writing, which are shown below. Dario also looked over the rubric for expository writing on pages **180–181**. Both of these activities helped him get started.

Traits of Expository Writing

- **Ideas**
  Select a specific topic that captures your interest. Create and support a thesis statement that explores an important part of the topic.

- **Organization**
  Organize your essay's ideas into three main parts—beginning, middle, and ending—and connect them smoothly.

- **Voice**
  Use words and details that fit the audience and the purpose of your writing.

- **Word Choice**
  Choose precise words that clearly explain your topic.

- **Sentence Fluency**
  Use a variety of sentences that connect your ideas smoothly.

- **Conventions**
  Use punctuation, mechanics, and grammar properly.

Try It!

Answer the following questions about the goals of Dario's assignment:

1. What must Dario remember when selecting a topic?
2. What should the thesis statement do?
3. What must Dario remember about voice?

English Language Learners

To help students gain a clearer idea of how voice is determined by audience and purpose, compare several passages, perhaps one from a textbook and one from a children's book on the same topic. Point out the words that convey the writers' voice. Discuss how audience and purpose determine the language and tone of each piece.

Prewriting Selecting a Topic

Dario's teacher wrote this expository writing prompt on the board.

> Explain how *technology affects...*
>
> Publishing   Movies   Live Drama   TV
> Periodicals   Music   Comic Books   Art

Dario wrote down several of the suggested subjects and listed ways that technology had affected each one. When he found the specific topic that interested him, he underlined it.

> Publishing (e-books, audio books)   Music (P2P file sharing, videos)
> TV (DVD collections, DVRs)   Movies (digital filming, CG)

Reflecting on the Topic

Dario did some freewriting in his journal to think about his topic.

> I want to write about movies. My cousin Luis is studying film and CG animation, and he takes me to the movies whenever he visits. When we see a movie on DVD, Luis tells me about moviemaking techniques while we watch it. Now I even watch for those special features on my own.
>
> With CG, movies have much better-looking aliens, ghosts, and special effects than they used to. Luis told me that Apollo 13 had a lot of CG to make the space scenes. He also said the last Spider-Man movie we saw had a huge amount of CG action. I loved the dinosaurs in the Jurassic Park movies—they were incredibly realistic.

Try It!

Freewrite for 10 minutes on one of the other topics above. Write about why the topic interests you and how you would write about it.

Prewriting Selecting a Topic

Ideally, students should select topics that interest them. You can provide students with interesting topics to consider by doing the following:

- Early in the year, have students fill out a card listing their hobbies, interests, and goals. These can be completed anonymously. Draw from the cards when you need to assign a specific topic.
- Set aside a portion of a classroom bulletin board for students to post news clippings, photographs, online articles, current events, headlines, or editorials. Encourage students to add items all year for a continuous source of topics.

Prewriting Reflecting on the Topic

Remind students that a reflection is not supposed to be a complete piece of writing. They should think of it more as an exploration. Tell students that as thoughts about a topic come into their heads, they should jot them down.

English Language Learners

Ask students to restate the **Try It!** instructions in their own words to make sure they use the time to explore a topic from the list. Preview and define any related vocabulary students will need for their freewriting. Give them some extra time if they are still writing after 10 minutes.

Struggling Learners

Some students may find that the connection to technology makes the **Try It!** activity too difficult. If so, invite students to write about their personal interest in one of the topics, for example, the kind of music they enjoy. Alternatively, have them freewrite about an invention that interests them.

Prewriting Gathering Details

Discuss how students can tell whether an Internet source is reliable. Point out that anyone with a moderate level of computer skills and Internet knowledge can create a Web site on any topic. The creator of a Web site is not necessarily an expert on the topic of the site, so Web sites may contain misinformation. Explain that the following guidelines will help students find reliable Web sites:

- Look for sites that end in *.edu* or *.gov.*
- Look for sites that are maintained by experts and specialists in the field, for example, a site maintained by a well-known, award-winning animator.
- Look for sites maintained by respected magazines and organizations, such as *National Geographic* or PBS.
- Check the date to see when the Web site was last updated to make sure the information is current.

Extend the **Try It!** activity by having students create note cards to record the source information they find.

Prewriting Gathering Details

Dario went to the library and looked for details about computer graphics (CG) in books, in magazines, and on the Internet. He used search engines and keywords like "CG," "CGI," and "special effects."

Sources of Information

To keep track of his research, Dario recorded complete source information on note cards.

> Rickitt, Richard. Special Effects: The History & Technique. New York: Watson-Guptill, 2000. Print.

> Thompson, Anne. "F/X Gods: The 10 Visual-Effects Wizards Who Rule Hollywood." Wired. Condé Nast Digital, Feb. 2005. Web. 10 Apr. 2011.

Quotations and Paraphrases

During his research, Dario recorded quotations and paraphrases. Dario's teacher asked students to use quotations or paraphrases from at least two sources.

Quotation

> "People didn't go to The Day After Tomorrow because of the acting, directing, and writing," says Scott Ross of Digital Domain. "They went to see New York flooded and L.A. ripped apart by a twister."
> Source: Thompson, "F/X Gods," p.10

Paraphrase

> Lucasfilm made the first CGI character—a knight made of stained glass—for Young Sherlock Holmes in 1985.
> Source: Carlson, "CGI Historical Time Line"

 Try It!

What keywords would you use to locate information about the topic that you explored on page 15? Find one book and one magazine that contain information on the topic.

English Language Learners

Help students choose effective keywords for their topic search.

If students are not familiar with certain periodicals, review their choices to make sure that the periodicals are reliable sources.

Forming a Thesis Statement

Once Dario had enough information, he was ready to write a *thesis statement* for his essay. (A thesis statement identifies the focus of the writing.) An effective thesis statement consists of two parts: a specific topic plus a particular feeling or opinion about it. Dario used the formula below to write his thesis.

A specific topic + a particular feeling = **an effective thesis statement.**

Dario's thesis statement

CG (specific topic) **allows filmmakers to show things in the movies that people could only imagine before** (particular feeling).

Organizing the Essay

Next, Dario wrote a topic outline for the body of his essay. This step organized the details that supported his thesis.

Dario's Outline

Thesis statement: CG allows filmmakers to show things in the movies that people could only imagine before.

I. Creates totally imaginary characters
  A. Stained-glass knight, Young Sherlock Holmes
  B. Dinosaurs in Jurassic Park
  C. Gollum (Andy Serkis), The Two Towers
  D. Aliens, Revenge of the Sith
II. Creates totally imaginary settings
  A. Temple in Indiana Jones and the Kingdom of the Crystal Skull
  B. Looking down at rocket in Apollo 13
  C. Seeing inside and around tornadoes in Twister
III. Creates dangerous effects
  A. Tidal waves—Deep Impact
  B. Fire & lava effects—Dante's Peak
  C. Entire armies using just a few people—Return of the King
IV. Can overwhelm a film
  A. Too much CG doesn't help story—Ross quote
  B. Spielberg quote about Jaws and CG shark

Prewriting Forming a Thesis Statement

It is important for students to be able to recognize an **effective thesis statement** *(see below)* and understand how it focuses and directs a piece of writing.

In the formula for an effective thesis statement, some students may associate the word *feeling* with emotions. Explain that *feeling* in this case means what you think about the topic. Have students focus their thoughts by considering these aspects of their topic:
- feature of the topic (its purpose, use, or function)
- idea about the topic (its impact or influence)
- opinion about the topic (how it might change)

Prewriting Organizing the Essay

Discuss the outline with students. Explain that each Roman numeral tells an important point that supports Dario's thesis statement. The lettered details help explain that point. Later, students will see how Dario transforms each section of the outline into the middle paragraphs of his essay. Point out that Dario used phrases in his outline, but he could have used full sentences.

✳ For examples of full-sentence outlines, have students turn to SE pages 156, 356, and 591.

Teaching Tip: Effective Thesis Statements

Explain that an effective thesis statement guides the writer because it dictates the kind of details the writer can include in the piece. The only details that should be included are those that support the main idea presented in the thesis statement.

Provide samples of short expository texts with effective thesis statements. Have students work in pairs or small groups to identify the thesis statement in each sample and to break it down into the two-part formula (specific topic + particular feeling). Then ask students to analyze how all the details relate to and support the main idea presented in the thesis statement.

Writing Developing Your First Draft

Encourage students to read Dario's draft once for meaning. Then ask them to read it again, paying attention to whether Dario achieved the goals of the Traits of Expository Writing on SE page 14.

As students read the draft, point out that Dario effectively uses a variety of pronouns to create a smooth flow and to establish a knowledgeable and confident voice. Tell students that they can use pronouns for the same purposes when they write. Remind them to make sure each personal pronoun they use has a clear noun referent. For example, in the first sentence, the pronoun *they* has no clear referent—*they* could be anyone. This is something that Dario will later revise for clarity.

✳ For more about using pronouns, see SE pages 536–537.

Writing Developing Your First Draft

Dario referred to his outline as he wrote his first draft. At this point, he needed to get all his ideas on paper and not worry about getting everything just right.

Dario's First Draft

The first paragraph introduces the topic and ends with the thesis statement.

Each middle paragraph covers one part of the topic.

Sources of information are given in parentheses.

The Sky's Not the Limit

I always laugh at the older stuff they used for special effects on film. They used model buildings. They used hand-drawn cartoons. They used stop-motion animation. Still, the effects never seem real enough. In the last twenty years, however CG has made it possible to create special effects in movies. CG allows filmmakers to show things in the movies that people could only imagine before.

CG can create totally imaginary characters that look real. An early example is a knight coming through a stained-glass window in Young Sherlock Holmes. Later on, CG showed us the amazing dinosaurs of Jurassic Park III. Motion-capture suits allow actors to help animate a CG character. The voice and acting of Andy Serkis combined with CG to create the incredible character of Gollum (The Two Towers). Today, CG often replaces older special effects. Yoda, a mere puppet in the original, is an example of this. Now, even the most fantastic creatures can seem real in the movies.

CG also allows film makers to tell the stories they want. CG animaters can imagine what ancient buildings might have looked like. They made an anceint temple for Indiana Jones and the Kingdom of the Crystal Skull. Computers even let film makers look at stuff in new ways, like watching a rocket blast off from overhead (Apollo 13). Film makers can change little things in a setting to add interest, like creating spider web rope.

English Language Learners

Define the following words and phrases before reading the sample first draft:

- stop-motion animation (a kind of special effect in older movies)
- CG (computer graphics)
- imaginary (not real)
- motion-capture suits (computer equipment that was worn by someone to capture motion and simulate it for animation.)
- animators (artists who make cartoons or computer graphics)
- blast off (take off, fly)
- tidal wave (huge, destructive ocean wave)
- awesome (fearful and amazing)
- overwhelm (be too much)
- indulging (overusing)

Advanced Learners

Ask students to read the sample first draft with a critical eye, looking for repeated, overused, or vague adjectives, nouns, or phrases (*stuff, amazing, tons of actors*). Have students suggest better word choices. Tell them to save their notes to compare their evaluation with the revision and the peer evaluation that follow.

Process

One Writer's Process **19**

In addition, CG lets film makers create dangerous effects such as an erupting volcano or a tidal wave. Nobody gets hurt and nothing gets damaged, since it's all in the computer. CG can even create an awesome army on the battlefield from only a few figures. They save millions of dollars by not hiring tons of actors. CG can show stuff too dangerous to shoot before.

CG makes movies better, usually. But it can easily overwhelm a film. Scott Ross of Digital Domain says they saw The Day After Tomorrow "to see New York flooded and L.A. ripped apart by a twister" (qtd. in Thompson 84). In fact, some of the best movies use your mind to complete what you don't see. In the movie Jaws, the excitement comes from not seeing the shark. Director Steven Spielberg admits "The shark would be fully CG" today and it wouldn't be a better movie" (qtd. in Westbrook 8). CG leaves nothing to the imagination, and that can ruin a movie. CG can't make a movie alone.

Computers let directors make movies with imaginary people, places, and effects. The only limits with CG now are the filmmakers' imaginations. Most directors balance CG effects with stories. Steven Spielberg states, "We must rescue ourselves from indulging in the technology we now have. . . . CG is just another tool—a means to an end. It shouldn't be an end itself" (qtd. in Westbrook 8). CG can't replace a story, but it can help make it great.

> Direct quotations are used.

> The ending paragraph sums up the topic and provides one last thought.

Try It!

Look through Dario's outline and first draft. Then answer these questions. Does Dario's first draft contain all the details from his outline (page **17**)? Does he add any new details? If so, what are they? What other movies could Dario have included in his discussion? Try to name at least one.

Try It! Answers

Dario's first draft uses most of the details from his outline but does not include details about
- the aliens in *Revenge of the Sith,*
- seeing inside and around tornadoes in *Twister,* and
- the names of specific movies in the paragraph about dangerous effects.

Dario adds new details to support main points and to explain other details. New details include
- motion-capture suits,
- replacing older special effects/Yoda, and
- saving millions of dollars by not hiring actors.

Dario could have included the movies in his outline that he didn't identify in his essay. These are *Revenge of the Sith, Twister, Deep Impact, Dante's Peak,* and *Return of the King.* He also could have named any of the more recent *Star Wars* movies.

Revising Improving the Writing

Students may wonder how Dario is able to recognize weak areas in his draft and know how to improve them. Explain that thoughtful writers revisit their goals and reflect on their writing before making changes. Writers must then take the time to rework the weak areas, even if it means rewriting entire sections of their work.

Reassure students that as they use the traits to inform their writing, they will become more skilled at recognizing weaknesses and knowing how to revise them. In addition, the more they write and share their writing, the more willing they will be to revise and polish their writing.

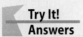

Try It! Answers

Possible Answers

- **Ideas:** Explain what made the dinosaurs in *Jurassic Park III* amazing.
- **Organization:** Add dates to show the development of CG over time.
- **Voice:** Use more specific nouns. For example, the word *things* in the first sentence sounds vague and does not convey the writer's knowledge about the topic.

Revising Improving the Writing

After Dario completed his first draft, he set aside his essay for a day. Then he rechecked the goals on page **14** before reviewing his first draft. Dario's thoughts below reveal the changes he planned to make.

Ideas

Select a specific topic that captures your interest. Create and support a thesis statement that explores an important part of the topic.

> "I've included my basic ideas, but some of them don't fit my thesis statement. I also need more details to support my main points."

Organization

Organize your essay's ideas into three main parts—beginning, middle, and ending—and connect them smoothly.

> "My middle is weak. I need more examples to illustrate my ideas. I also need more transitions."

Voice

Use words and details that fit the audience and the purpose of your writing.

> "I need to use third person (he/she/they) instead of first person (I/we) to sound more objective. I need a stronger opening statement to sound more confident about my topic."

Try It!

Choose a classmate to be your partner. Together, review the changes in Dario's first revision on page **21**. What other changes in ideas, organization, or voice would you make to Dario's essay? Try to name two.

English Language Learners

Students who are not proficient in English may have difficulty pinpointing how they would change Dario's voice for the **Try It!** activity. Have students limit their focus to changes they might make in ideas and organization (see the suggestions in the **Try It!** answers).

Dario's First Revision

Here are the revisions that Dario made in the first part of his essay.

The voice in the opening sentence is made more formal. A technical abbreviation is defined.

Unnecessary details that do not support the topic sentence are deleted.

Details that show the writer's knowledge of the subject are added.

> Ever since people began making movies, filmmakers
> ~~I always laugh at the older stuff they used for special~~
> have tried to put imaginary things
> ~~effects~~ on film. They used model buildings. They used hand-drawn cartoons. They used stop-motion animation. Still,
> the effects never seem real enough. In the last twenty
> computer graphics (CG)
> years, however, ~~CG~~ has made it possible to create special
> effects in movies. CG allows filmmakers to show things in
> the movies that people could only imagine before.
>
> CG can create totally imaginary characters that look
> real. An early example is a knight coming through a stained-glass window in <u>Young Sherlock Holmes</u>. Later on, CG showed
> us the amazing dinosaurs of <u>Jurassic Park III</u>. ~~Motion-capture~~
> ~~suits allow actors to help animate a CG character~~. The
> voice and acting of Andy Serkis combined with CG to create
> the incredible character of Gollum (<u>The Two Towers</u>). Today,
> CG often replaces older special effects. Yoda, a mere
> The Empire Strikes Back
> puppet in ~~the original~~, is an example of this. Now, even the
> most fantastic creatures can seem real in the movies.
>
> CG also allows film makers to tell the stories they want. CG
> animaters can imagine what ancient buildings might have
> and placed it in the Amazon rainforest
> looked like. They made an anceint temple for <u>Indiana Jones</u>
> <u>and the Kingdom of the Crystal Skull</u>. Computers even let film
> makers look at stuff in new ways, like watching a rocket blast
> or seeing inside a tornado (<u>Twister</u>)
> off from overhead (<u>Apollo 13</u>).

Revising Dario's First Revision

Ask students to examine Dario's revisions and identify the changes that they think are most effective. Have them explain their choices. Students may point out these changes:

- The original opening sentence used the first-person pronoun *I* and sounded too personal and informal. The revision gives the essay a more serious tone. Since the third-person point of view is used throughout the rest of the essay, this change also makes the voice consistent.
- The detail about motion-capture suits is confusing and interrupts the flow of ideas. Deleting this detail improves the sense and flow of the paragraph.
- Replacing vague words (*the original*) with a specific movie title makes the writer sound more knowledgeable.
- Adding details such as where the temple was placed shows the writer's knowledge of the subject.

Process

Revising Using a Peer Response Sheet

Give students time to study the Rubric for Expository Writing on SE pages 180–181 to see what Christine based her suggestions on. Then help students understand the goals of each part of the Peer Response Sheet.

"What I liked about your writing" highlights the writer's successes and helps to establish a spirit of trust between writer and responder.

"Changes I would suggest" provides specific ideas for improvement and notes questions the reader has about the topic.

Point out that the responder used "Could you," instead of the more demanding "You should," in making her suggestions. This invites the writer to consider the change and to be the person who makes the final decision.

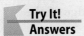
Try It!
Answers

Answers will vary, but suggestions should be specific, should be reasonable, and, ideally, should reflect the goals in the Rubric for Expository Writing.

Revising Using a Peer Response Sheet

Christine evaluated Dario's essay using a rubric like the one on pages 180–181. Her suggestions on the response sheet below showed Dario where he could make additional improvements.

Peer Response Sheet

Writer: <u>Dario Ramirez</u> Responder: <u>Christine Whitney</u>

Title: <u>The Sky's Not the Limit</u>

What I liked about your writing:

- <u>You chose an interesting topic.</u>
- <u>You show that you really know a lot about movies and CG.</u>
- <u>You cover your topic well, from characters to settings to</u>
  <u>story actions.</u>

Changes I would suggest:

- <u>I don't know all the movies you mentioned in the second</u>
  <u>paragraph. Could you add dates to show us when these movies</u>
  <u>were made?</u>
- <u>Could you come up with a more specific topic sentence in the</u>
  <u>third paragraph? What keeps filmmakers from telling their</u>
  <u>stories?</u>

Try It!

Review Christine's suggestions for improvement above. Which suggestion seems to be the most important? Explain why. Add at least one new suggestion to improve Dario's writing. Look at the explanations of ideas, organization, and voice on page **20** to help you make that suggestion.

English Language Learners

Students may find it difficult to comment effectively about the work. Pair them with English-proficient partners to complete the **Try It!** activity. Ask proficient students to explain their rationale to their partners to help them learn how to comment on future writing.

Struggling Learners

Have students work in pairs to review the explanations on SE page 20 before making their suggestion to improve Dario's essay. Remind them to use courteous language when they suggest changes.

Dario's Revision Using a Peer Response

Using Christine's comments, Dario revised his essay again. The changes that he made in three middle paragraphs are shown here.

Process

Dates of the movies are added for clarity.

The topic sentence is improved.

Ideas are made more specific and clear.

Specific details are added.

CG can create totally imaginary characters that look real. An early example is a knight coming through a stained-glass window in Young Sherlock Holmes. (1985) Later on, CG showed us the amazing dinosaurs of Jurassic Park III. (2001) The voice and acting of Andy Serkis combined with CG to create the incredible character of Gollum (The Two Towers). (2002) Today, CG often replaces older special effects. Yoda, a mere puppet in The in new movies of a series Empire Strikes Back, is an example of this. (1980) is CG in the new movies. Now, even the most fantastic creatures can seem real in the movies.

CG also allows film makers to tell the stories they wherever and however want. CG animaters can imagine what ancient buildings might have looked like. They made an anceint temple and placed it in the Amazon rainforest for Indiana Jones and the Kingdom of the Crystal Skull. (2008) Computers even let film use CG to makers look at stuff in new ways, like watching a rocket blast off from overhead (Apollo 13) or seeing inside a 1995 what it looks like tornado (Twister). Film makers can change little things in a 1996 setting to add interest, like creating spider web rope (Spider-Man 3). 2007

In addition, CG lets film makers create dangerous a rampaging forest fire, effects such as an erupting volcano or even a tidal wave swallowing New York City. (Deep Impact, 1998) Nobody gets hurt and nothing gets damaged. CG can even create an awesome army on the . . .

Dario's Revision Using a Peer Response

Have students point out the specific changes Dario made to the essay, based on Christine's response.

Point out that a peer response sheet can be helpful if the comments are accurate and the suggestions are reasonable and valid. Provide the following guidelines:

- If a writer does not understand a responder's comment or suggestion, the writer should ask for clarification.
- If a writer does not agree with a comment or suggestion, the writer should seek a second opinion or request a conference with you.
- The final decision to make a change is in the writers' hands, but they should strongly consider making any change that everyone agrees would improve their writing.

Struggling Learners

To make sure students look carefully at the changes Dario made to his essay, have them work in small groups. Assign each group one paragraph of the essay. Have the group make note of each revision and compare each change to the first draft.

Point out the side notes on SE pages 23 and 25 to identify

how Dario revised his draft. For example, he improved word choice by substituting *crashing* for *coming* and *believable* for *amazing*; he improved organization by adding the transitions *for instance* and *in addition*.

Revising Focusing on Style

Remind students that one of the most efficient ways for writers to identify problems with word choice and sentence fluency is to read their writing aloud. When they read aloud, they will often hear stylistic problems that aren't evident during silent reading. Some problems that can be highlighted by reading aloud include:

- words that are overused,
- too many sentences that begin the same way, and
- short, choppy sentences that could be combined.

Try It!
Answers

Possible Answers

- He could say *come alive on-screen* instead of *seem real on-screen*.
- He could replace the word *things* in the last sentence of the first paragraph with *characters and events*.
- He could add the transition *For example* in front of *Yoda*.

Revising Focusing on Style

Dario also reviewed his writing for its flow and style. His thoughts below tell you what changes he planned to make.

Word Choice

Choose precise words that clearly explain your topic.

> "I should use more technical terms to improve the level of language. I also want to add more exciting verbs and modifiers."

Sentence Fluency

Use a variety of sentences that connect your ideas smoothly.

> "I need to combine some of my choppy sentences in order to create a better flow in the text."

Try It!

Review Dario's improved essay on page **23**. What other changes in word choice could he make? Name one or two. What other changes could he make to improve the sentence fluency? Name one.

English Language Learners

Help students avoid repetitive language in their writing. Make sure students know how to find synonyms in a classroom thesaurus or word processing program. Have students practice with words from Dario's essay, and encourage them to use new words in their own writing by keeping a personal vocabulary list.

Dario's Improvements in Style

Dario next reviewed the style and sound of his writing. He focused on improving his word choice and sentence structure.

> **[Combining sentences improves sentence fluency.]**
>
> Ever since people began making movies, filmmakers have tried to put imaginary things on film. They used model buildings. ~~They used~~ hand-drawn cartoons, ~~They used~~ stop-motion animation. Still, the effects never seem real enough. In the last twenty years, however computer graphics (CG) has made it possible to create **realistic** special effects in movies. CG allows filmmakers to show things ~~in the movies~~ **on-screen** that people could only imagine before.
>
> **[Word choice is improved.]**
>
> CG can create totally imaginary characters that look real. An early example is a knight ~~coming~~ **crashing** through a stained-glass window in <u>Young Sherlock Holmes</u> (1985). Later on, CG showed us ~~the amazing~~ **believeable** dinosaurs ~~of~~ **in** <u>Jurassic Park III</u> (2001). **More recently,** The voice and acting of Andy Serkis combined with CG to create the incredible character of Gollum (<u>The Two Towers</u>, 2002). Today, CG ~~often~~ **even** replaces older special effects **technologies** in new movies of a series. Yoda, a mere puppet in <u>The Empire Strikes Back</u> (1980), is CG in ~~the new movies~~ **Revenge of the Sith (2005).** Now, even the most fantastic creatures **from folklore to science fiction** can seem real in the movies.
>
> **[Transitions make the sentences flow more smoothly.]**
>
> CG also allows film makers to tell stories wherever and however they want. **For instance,** CG animaters can imagine what ancient buildings might have looked like. They made an anceint temple and placed it in the Amazon rain forest . . .

Revising Dario's Improvements in Style

Help students understand how making simple changes in word choice can improve the overall impact of their writing. Ask students why Dario made the following word changes.

- *on-screen* for *in the movies* (*On-screen* is more specific and more technical. It makes Dario sound knowledgeable.)
- *crashing* for *coming* (*Crashing* is more precise and more vivid. It adds richness to the essay.)
- *believable* for *the amazing* (*Amazing* is an overused, vague adjective. *Believable* is more specific; it implies that the dinosaurs were lifelike.)

Also point out that the writer spells out the term *computer graphics* the first time it appears and then uses the abbreviation *CG* throughout the rest of the essay.

Editing Checking for Conventions

Tell students that when they edit their own work they should look for errors in punctuation, capitalization, spelling, and grammar that they tend to repeat. For example, if they frequently make mistakes with subject-verb agreement, then they should check their sentences to make sure that all singular subjects have singular verbs, and all plural subjects have plural verbs.

When students do the **Try It!** activity, some may argue that the term *computer graphics* is a plural noun that requires a plural verb. Explain that *computer graphics* appears plural in form but it is singular in meaning, so the term takes a singular verb.

✱ For more on subject-verb agreement, see SE page 752.

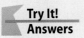
Try It!
Answers

Possible answers are shown in red on SE page 27.

26

Editing Checking for Conventions

Finally, Dario was ready to edit his essay. He checked his work for punctuation, capitalization, spelling, and grammar errors.

Editing Checklist

Conventions

Use punctuation, mechanics, and grammar properly.

> "I'll look carefully at my essay for punctuation, capitalization, spelling, and grammar errors."

For help with conventions, Dario used the "Proofreader's Guide" in the back of his *Write Source* textbook and the checklist below.

PUNCTUATION

_____ **1.** Do I use end punctuation correctly?
_____ **2.** Do I use commas correctly?
_____ **3.** Do I correctly italicize or use quotation marks for titles?
_____ **4.** Do I use apostrophes correctly?

MECHANICS (Capitalization and Spelling)

_____ **5.** Have I capitalized all the proper nouns and adjectives?
_____ **6.** Have I spelled words correctly?
_____ **7.** Have I used the spell-checker on my computer?
_____ **8.** Have I double-checked words my spell-checker may have missed?

GRAMMAR

_____ **9.** Do I use the proper tense and voice for my verbs?
_____ **10.** Do my subjects and verbs agree in number?
_____ **11.** Do my pronouns clearly agree with their antecedents?

DOCUMENTATION

_____ **12.** Are sources properly presented and documented?

Try It!

Find three or four errors in Dario's revised draft on page 25. Did you find the same errors as Dario found (on page 27)?

English Language Learners

Students will benefit from short lessons based on the editing checklist, such as verb tense, subject-verb agreement, and pronoun-antecedent agreement. Focus on the conventions with which students have recurring problems in their writing.

Dario's Editing

Here is Dario's editing for the first part of his essay. (See the inside back cover of this textbook for common editing and proofreading marks.)

> A verb-tense error, a number, and a punctuation error are corrected.

Ever since people began making movies, filmmakers have tried to put imaginary things on film. They used model buildings, hand-drawn cartoons, and stop-motion animation. Still, the effects never ~~seem~~ seemed real enough. In the last ~~twenty~~ 20 years, however‸ computer graphics (CG) has made it possible to create realistic special effects in movies. CG allows filmmakers to show things on-screen that people could only imagine before.

> A spelling error and a punctuation error are corrected.

CG can create totally imaginary characters that look real. An early example is a knight crashing through a stained-glass window in Young Sherlock Holmes (1985). Later on, CG showed us ~~believeable~~ believable dinosaurs in Jurassic Park III (2001). More recently, the voice and acting of Andy Serkis combined with CG to create the incredible character of Gollum (The Two Towers, 2002). Today, CG even replaces older special‸ effects technologies in new movies of a series. Yoda, a mere puppet in The Empire Strikes Back (1980), is CG in Revenge of the Sith (2005). Now, even the most fantastic creatures from folklore to science fiction can seem real on-screen.

> Additional spelling errors are corrected.

CG also allows film makers to tell stories wherever and however they want. For instance, CG ~~animatore~~ animators can imagine what ancient buildings might have looked like. They made an ~~anceint~~ ancient temple and placed it in the Amazon rainforest for . . .

Editing Dario's Editing

If students are not familiar with the editing and proofreading marks listed on the inside back cover of the book, have them look at the list now. Encourage students to refer to this list whenever they revise and edit their work or the work of their peers.

Suggest that students who are working on a computer should always print out their essay and mark the changes by hand. For their final copy, they can also use the computer's spell-checker to find any errors they may have introduced when they made the corrections.

If students are not sure why Dario changed the word *twenty* to the numeral 20, explain that numbers from one to nine are usually written as words, and numbers 10 and higher are written as numerals.

✱ For more on using numbers, see SE pages 658–659.

Publishing Sharing Your Writing

Compare Dario's revisions with his final copy. Discuss the obvious differences and point out that

- writers improve their writing with multiple revisions, and
- the final copy bears no evidence of revision so as not to distract the reader.

Also, make sure it's easy for students to follow your formatting requirements for final copy submissions. If possible, distribute a handout that lists your requirements, or display them prominently.

28

Publishing Sharing Your Writing

Dario used the information below to produce a clean and effective copy of his final essay.

Tips for Handwritten Copies

- Use blue or black ink and write clearly.
- Write your name according to your teacher's instructions.
- Skip a line and center your title on the first page; skip another line and begin your essay.
- Indent each paragraph and leave a one-inch margin on all four sides.

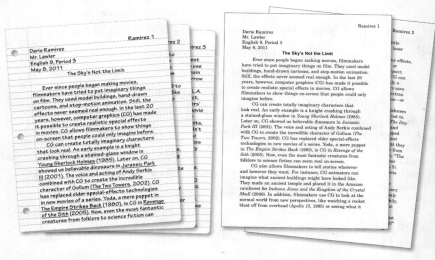

Tips for Computer Copies

- Use an easy-to-read font set at 12-point type size.
- Double-space the text and set your margins so that you have a one-inch space around the outside of each page.
- For more tips on using a computer, see pages **33–38**.

Dario's Final Copy

Dario proudly presented a printed copy of his essay to Mr. Lawler and volunteered to share his writing about movies with the class.

Ramirez 1

Dario Ramirez
Mr. Lawler
English 9, Period 3
May 8, 2011

The Sky's Not the Limit

Ever since people began making movies, filmmakers have tried to put imaginary things on film. They used model buildings, hand-drawn cartoons, and stop-motion animation. Still, the effects never seemed real enough. In the last 20 years, however, computer graphics (CG) has made it possible to create realistic special effects in movies. CG allows filmmakers to show things on-screen that people could only imagine before.

CG can create totally imaginary characters that look real. An early example is a knight crashing through a stained-glass window in *Young Sherlock Holmes* (1985). Later on, CG showed us believable dinosaurs in *Jurassic Park III* (2001). The voice and acting of Andy Serkis combined with CG to create the incredible character of Gollum (*The Two Towers*, 2002). CG has replaced older special-effects technologies in new movies of a series. Yoda, a mere puppet in *The Empire Strikes Back* (1980), is CG in *Revenge of the Sith* (2005). Now, even the most fantastic creatures from folklore to science fiction can seem real on-screen.

CG also allows filmmakers to tell stories wherever and however they want. For instance, CG animators can imagine what ancient buildings might have looked like. They made an ancient temple and placed it in the Amazon rainforest for *Indiana Jones and the Kingdom of the Crystal Skull* (2008). In addition, filmmakers use CG to look at the normal world from new perspectives, like watching a rocket

Publishing Dario's Final Copy

Discuss Dario's final essay with the class. Use the goals on SE page 14 and the rubric on SE pages 180–181 to evaluate the writing and help students recognize why it is a good example of an expository essay.

Ideas

- The writer has selected a topic that interests him.
- The writer uses specific details to explore a particular feature of the topic.

Organization

- The beginning captures the reader's interest.
- The middle paragraphs support the thesis statement and flow smoothly from one idea to the next, using transitions.

Voice

The writer uses technical terms, movie titles, and dates to create a knowledgeable voice.

English Language Learners

Students may rush through assignments if they lack confidence in their English skills. Help motivate such students by asking them to read Dario's final copy and then reread his first draft. Point out how much better the final copy is because Dario thoroughly worked through each step of the process. Tell students that by using the writing process and getting some assistance from peer readers, they will be able to express their ideas better, and they will also improve their English.

Ramirez 2

blast off from overhead (*Apollo 13*, 1995) or seeing what it looks like inside a tornado (*Twister*, 1996). Filmmakers can change little things in a setting to add interest, too, like creating spider web rope (*Spider-Man* 3, 2007).

In addition, CG lets filmmakers create dangerous effects, such as a rampaging forest fire, an erupting volcano, or even a tidal wave swallowing New York City (*Deep Impact*, 1998). Nobody gets hurt, and nothing gets damaged. CG can even create a realistic army on the battlefield from only a few figures. Filmmakers save millions of dollars by not having to hire thousands of extras. With CG, people can see stories that were too dangerous—or impossible—to shoot before.

CG definitely enhances many movies. The best producers and directors, though, know when to use it—and when not to. Scott Ross of Digital Domain says, "People didn't go to *The Day After Tomorrow* [2004] because of the acting, directing, and writing. They went to see New York flooded and L.A. ripped apart by a twister" (qtd. in Thompson 84). In fact, some of the best movies have relied on the viewers' minds to complete what they don't see. In the movie *Jaws* (1975), the excitement comes from rarely seeing the shark. Director Steven Spielberg admits, "The shark would be fully CG" today, and "it wouldn't be a better movie. I would have used the shark too much" (qtd. in Westbrook 8). Fortunately, most audiences realize that even cool CG effects can't tell a story or make a good movie by themselves.

Computers provide new tools for filmmakers to create movies they never could attempt before. CG creates imaginary people, places, and effects that seem totally realistic. The only limits with CG now are the filmmakers' imaginations. Luckily, most directors know they should balance CG effects with the stories. Steven Spielberg states, "We must rescue ourselves from indulging in the technology we now have. . . . CG is just another tool—a means to an end. It shouldn't be an end itself" (qtd. in Westbrook 8). CG can't replace a story, but it can help make it great.

Assessing the Final Copy

Dario's teacher used a rubric like the one found on pages 180–181 to assess his final copy. A **6** is the very best score that a writer can receive for each trait. The teacher also included comments under each trait.

One Writer's Process **31**

Process

6 Ideas
Your topic is interesting. I learned a lot about CG special effects. The quotations are very effective. Your essay convinced me to see some movies I've never wanted to watch.

5 Organization
Your writing is well organized and very clear. The beginning, middle, and ending paragraphs all work well together.

5 Voice
You obviously have a great deal of interest in your topic. Your voice conveys a sense of confidence about your topic.

4 Word Choice
You miss a few opportunities to teach new words to your readers. You also overuse these words: filmmakers, imaginary, real, realistic.

5 Sentence Fluency
You use a wide variety of sentences. Your sentences all read smoothly from one idea to another.

6 Conventions
Your writing is free of careless errors.

 Review the assessment. Do you agree with the scores and comments made by Dario's teacher? Why or why not? In a brief paragraph, discuss your own reaction to Dario's essay and how you would grade it.

Assessing the Final Copy

The benefit of using a written assessment is that it allows you to praise students' efforts while offering constructive criticism. A separate written assessment also eliminates the need for you to mark up a student's final copy with comments and corrections in red ink; even professional writers can find this discouraging. If possible, try to deliver assessments during individual **writing conferences** (see below).

Invite volunteers to share their analysis of the assessment with the class. Students can agree or disagree with Dario's teacher's comments and suggestions, but they should be prepared to support their opinions with specific reasons and make alternate suggestions, when appropriate.

Teaching Tip: Writing Conferences

Scheduling individual writing conferences can help students gain enough confidence to respond to your assessments.

Plan to begin the conference by returning the final copy, unmarked and ungraded, with your assessment sheet. After giving the student a few minutes to look it over, ask if the student agrees with the ratings. This approach will allow the student to feel in charge of the writing while affording you the opportunity to provide the guidance the student needs to achieve the goals of the assignment.

English Language Learners

Students may not want to disagree with your comments because in some cultures it is considered disrespectful to question a teacher. Explain that in a writing conference, the teacher and the writer exchange opinions. Assure students that questioning is an important tool for improving their writing.

Reflecting on Your Writing

If students will be expected to reflect on their writing throughout the year, discuss ways to make the reflecting process as effective as possible. When used regularly, reflections can help students become better writers. Tell students that honest, thoughtful reflections can help them

- identify stumbling blocks that prevent them from becoming better writers and
- see how their writing has progressed and improved over time, which will inspire them to try for even greater improvement.

Ask students if they think Dario has provided a thoughtful reflection on his writing experience, and have them discuss how this reflection can help him grow as a writer.

Reflecting on Your Writing

After the whole process was finished, Dario filled out a reflection sheet. This helped him think about the assignment and plan for future writing. (Complete a reflection sheet like this right after you finish your writing.)

Dario Ramirez
Mr. Lawler
English 9, Period 3
May 8, 20011

Expository Essay: The Sky's Not the Limit

1. **The best part of my essay is . . .**
   my conclusion. It covers the entire topic and uses quotations to show good points and bad points.

2. **The part that still needs work is . . .**
   my word choice. I need to make sure that I don't overuse certain words.

3. **The most important part of my prewriting and planning was . . .**
   exploring the history of CG special effects and the people who used them. That gave me the details I needed to explain my topic.

4. **During revising, I spent a lot of time dealing with . . .**
   adding more details from my notes to support my main points.

5. **What I've learned about this type of essay is . . .**
   that it's important to find a variety of details. Telling about the misuse of CG gives the end of my essay energy and surprises my readers.

6. **Here is one question I still have . . .**
   Are there other ways to note sources in a paper without using the parentheses?

English Language Learners

Add a seventh sentence to prompt reflection about students' English language growth so that they can monitor their progress throughout the year: *I improved my English writing by . . ..* When students complete a reflection, ask them to complete the sentence with examples of new concepts they learned.

Struggling Learners

To help students focus on Dario's reflection, ask the following questions:

- Do you agree with Dario that the conclusion is the best part of the essay? Why or why not? If not, what part do you think is the best part? Why?

- What part of the essay do you think still needs work? Why?
- What questions do you have about Dario's writing process?

Writing with a Computer

Writing with a Computer

A computer is more than just an alternative to writing with pen and paper. It's a valuable writing tool. Computers can aid writers at every step in the writing process, helping them produce effective essays, articles, and reports.

In this chapter, you will learn strategies for planning and writing with a computer. As you will see, there is no better tool for gathering and organizing information, creating a first draft, and improving a draft through revisions. The computer also takes a lot of the guesswork out of editing and proofreading. And once all the changes are made, a computer makes publishing the writing an easy process.

- ■ **Understanding the Basics**
- ■ **Prewriting**
- ■ **Writing**
- ■ **Revising**
- ■ **Editing**
- ■ **Publishing**

"I work on a word processor for the first draft, but for revisions I always print out a copy and do my corrections by hand."

—Betsy Byars

Objectives

- • demonstrate an understanding of how a computer works as a writing tool
- • learn to use a computer to plan, write, revise, edit, and publish a piece of writing

By ninth grade, most students will have more than a basic understanding of how computers work and how they can be used to write. Based on the proficiency of your students in this area, you can choose to present this section of the unit in class or assign it for at-home reading. If students will be reading this section on their own, set aside some class time for them to ask questions about any concepts in this section that are unfamiliar or that they don't understand.

Understanding the Basics

To heighten interest in the material presented here, invite volunteers to take part in a dramatic presentation. If there is no computer available, have students use a prop.

- Have a knowledgeable student play the role of an instructor of a class for people of all ages who are not familiar with computer basics.
- Other students can play the roles of pupils in the class. They should ask questions that elicit definitions of the terms used.
- Encourage students to incorporate their own knowledge of computers into the presentation and to make it as informative as they can.

Ask the computer technology person at your school to keep you informed about any changes to the school's computer system and **software** *(see below)*.

Understanding the Basics

Basically, a computer is a machine that receives information (*input*), *processes* it, and *outputs* the results. Here is a quick overview of how a computer works as a writing tool.

Input: You'll most often provide input by using a keyboard or mouse. Tablet and pocket computers may have a touch screen, on which a stylus is sometimes used.

- **Keyboard:** A keyboard contains letters, numbers, and other characters. It allows users to type faster than they can write longhand.
- **Mouse:** The mouse allows users to select items with an arrow, position the cursor, or highlight areas of text.
- **Stylus:** A stylus is like a pencil for writing on an electronic drawing pad or a touch-sensitive computer screen. It can also point and select like a mouse.

Process: Input is processed by a program loaded into the computer's memory from storage. Knowing the difference between memory and storage can save you a lot of trouble.

- **Memory:** Often called RAM, computer memory operates only when the power is on. If you shut down your computer before you save your work, that work is lost—so save often.
- **Storage:** Most computers have a built-in hard drive for permanent storage. Data saved on the hard drive is kept when the computer shuts down. Removable storage includes CD's, DVD's, and flash memory devices. (Pocket computers use internal flash memory instead of a hard drive.)
- **Program:** Often called software, programs are instructions a computer uses to recognize input, process it, store it, and output it.

Output: After information has been processed, the computer must output it to the user.

- **Monitor:** Often referred to as a computer screen, a monitor shows the user immediate results of her or his input.
- **Printer:** A printer allows a computer to output text and graphics on paper. This printout is commonly called hard copy.

Tip

Most computer programs have built-in help files. Look for "Help" in the program's menu. You can browse those files to learn more about the program.

Teaching Tip: Software

Review the features available in the software used on the school computers.

Software is constantly being upgraded, and some upgrades may affect the shortcut keys that students use automatically as they write. Have computer-literate students create a printout of shortcut keys, and display the list for easy reference. Revise the list whenever software is upgraded.

When new software is added to the computer system, invite the school's IT (information technology) person to demonstrate the new program for your class.

English Language Learners

Depending on their length of time in the United States and experiences in their home countries, students may not have logged many computer hours. Arrange time for a preliminary evaluation of students' computer skills, and provide skill development time if necessary.

Process

Prewriting

For some prewriting strategies, pencil and paper may work well. For others, a computer can speed up the process. This page discusses ways a computer can help during prewriting.

Selecting a Topic

- **Journaling:** Use a computer to keep a personal journal or learning log. Review your entries when you need ideas for essays or stories. Then copy and paste material into a new file, and start writing!
- **Freewriting:** Use a computer to write freely to discover possible writing ideas. Simply let your thoughts flow. It's helpful to begin with a focus in mind—one that is related to your assignment.

Gathering and Organizing Details

- **Creating Graphic Organizers:** Use the table function on your word processor to create T-charts, sensory charts, 5 W's charts, time lines, and gathering grids. The table automatically expands to include as much information as you add.

T-Chart

Cause	Effect

Sensory Chart

See	Hear	Smell	Taste	Touch

Time Line

First	
Next	
Then	
After	

- **Researching:** Use your computer and its Internet connection to conduct research. Search for relevant Web sites and print out pages that seem to be helpful. Be sure to keep track of useful Web sites as *favorites* or *bookmarks*.
- **Listing and Outlining:** Use the computer to list main points and details. Then rearrange the details in logical outline order. Activate the outline function of your computer so that it automatically labels each new line of your outline with the correct letter or number.

Try It!

Create graphic organizers. Use your word processor's table function to create a T-chart, a sensory chart, or a time line.

Prewriting

If students want to keep their writer's notebook on a school computer, make sure that there is a way for them to set a user's password for privacy.

Students often select the same topic for research reports. If you have a class Web site, use it to bookmark or create links to reliable Web sites and encourage students to explore these for topic ideas. If you prefer, assign trustworthy students to bookmark Web sites for the class.

Most students have had the experience of trying to squeeze information into small boxes on a paper copy of a graphic organizer. The **Try It!** activity will show them the advantages of creating a graphic organizer on the computer.

Writing

Encourage students to write with a computer even if they don't know how to type well. However, if students find they are focusing more on the keyboard than on their ideas, they should continue to handwrite their work until they can acquire basic typing skills.

Share the following computer tips with students.

- When they can't think of what to say next, they can use ellipses (. . .). Later, they can use the computer's "Find" function to quickly return to these places.
- If they are not satisfied with how they have worded some passages, they can use the computer's highlighting feature to highlight those chunks of text in a bright color. During revising, they can scroll through the document and easily find those sections.

If you require students to turn in their prewriting materials as well as their first drafts, remind them to print out or forward dated copies of these files.

Writing

Once you know how to type or keyboard, writing a first draft on a computer is much easier than writing a draft longhand. Here are some helpful writing tips.

Getting Started

- **Start a new document.** Always begin a new document for each project. In this way, you will keep your outline or organizer intact in the file.
- **Let your ideas flow.** Refer to your outline as you write, but feel free to include new ideas as they come to mind. For now, don't worry about getting every word or sentence just right.

Tip

If you can't resist the temptation to make a lot of changes during first drafts, turn down the resolution on your monitor. This should help you maintain a free flow of ideas, because you won't see what you're writing.

Keeping It Going

- **Stay with your writing.** Using a computer will help you to thoroughly develop a piece of writing. If you are having trouble with one part, fill it in with placeholder text, or just write a note to yourself.
- **Save often.** Learn the shortcut key to save your text (often pressing "Control" or "Command" and "S"). By saving often, you will avoid unexpectedly losing your work to a cranky computer or a power outage. Also consider setting your computer's "auto-save" feature to save your work every few minutes.
- **Share your work.** Writing on a computer makes it easier for you to share early drafts. You can simply print out a copy for others to read. By sharing your work, you become more aware of a real audience.

Try It!

Find out how often your computer is set up to save your work. Check the main toolbar for "Help" and click on it. In the help screen, type "save options" or "auto save." Then check your help file to find out how to retrieve "last save" versions of your file.

Process

Revising

On handwritten copy, making revisions can be messy. There will be crossed-out sentences, words written in the margins, and circled ideas. When writing on a computer, the text automatically reflows with every change, so there's no mess. The tips below can help you get the most out of revising on a computer.

Managing Your Document

- **Start with a printout.** Begin by reading a printed copy of your first draft. Then make changes on this copy before you make changes on the computer. (It's easier to make quick notes and experiment on a printed copy of your work.)
- **Save each round of revisions.** Save a printed copy of each set of revisions; also save each set separately on the computer (*revision 1, revision 2,* and so on). If you work in this way, you will have an accurate history of the changes you have made.
- **Save major deletions.** Dump large chunks of deleted text into a separate file so that you can easily review them if necessary.
- **Use the windows features.** For example, you can keep two files open when you need to move text from one file to another.

FYI

Using a computer during revising makes it easier to conduct group-advising sessions because everyone can have a clean printout to read and respond to.

Employing the Features

- **Use "Cut," "Copy," and "Paste."** Use these features to delete, add, or rearrange words, phrases, sentences, and paragraphs.
- **Learn to drag text.** This feature allows you to move text: You highlight the part you want to move; click on it again, holding down the button; and drag it to a new spot.
- **Try out "Track Changes."** Your computer may allow you to keep track of the changes you make. (See your help file.)
- **Learn about other revising features.** Look for features such as *search and replace, word count,* and *dictionary functions.*

Try It!

Take a toolbar tour. Click on each item on your main toolbar and check each drop-down menu. Explore some of these features.

Revising

To encourage students to make revision notes on printed copies of their first drafts, require them to turn in their notated drafts with their final copies.

Emphasize the importance of naming files clearly, especially if students are working on more than one writing project at a time. The file name should include a working title of the piece (may be abbreviated), the draft or revision number, the course title, and the student's last name. Tell students to join each piece of information with one stroke of the underline key instead of using commas, periods, or spaces, and to be sure the file name ends with *.doc.* For example:

CG_R1_English9_Ramirez.doc

To ensure that students don't write over a previous draft, show them how to use the "Save As" function and change the revision number each time they open it. Then if they want to review a section of text in a previous draft, they will be able to access that version.

Also demonstrate how to store work for assignments in separate, labeled folders. This way students can easily access concurrent projects without scrolling through numerous documents.

Editing

Demonstrate the importance of proofreading a final copy after using the computer's editing functions.

- Prepare a piece of writing that has several mistakes in punctuation, capitalization, spelling, and grammar. Be sure that some of the mistakes include misuse of homophones and words that are spelled correctly but are the wrong word (for example, *from* instead of *form*).
- Divide students into pairs. Have one partner edit a printout of the writing.
- Have the other partner use the computer's spelling- and grammar-check functions to edit the writing.
- Have the partners compare their edited copies to see that using both methods helps to find and correct mistakes.

Publishing

If students will be turning in a piece of writing soon, present the information on SE pages 76–78 now. Otherwise, have students skim these pages to get a general idea of how to use a computer to design their writing.

38

Editing

Most word-processing programs offer two main tools to help with editing and proofreading: the grammar checker and the spell-checker.

Understanding Your Grammar Checker

- **Watch for agreement errors.** Pay attention to underlined subject-predicate pairs. The underlining means that the grammar checker has identified an agreement problem. Select the best change suggested by the checker.
- **Watch for passive sentences.** Note when a whole sentence is underlined. Typically this means it is passive in construction. Consider reworking the sentence in the active voice. (See **722.2**.)
- **Keep a critical eye.** Be aware that grammar checkers can be wrong in what they flag as a problem. When in doubt, check the "Proofreader's Guide" in this book before following a suggestion.

Using Your Spell-Checker

- **Set the spell-check option to "Auto-Correct."** This feature corrects misspellings when they are first typed in.
- **Watch for underlined words as you type.** Correct errors yourself or let the checker suggest replacements.
- **Spell-check the final document.** When you finish editing, run the spell-checker on the whole document. The checker flags any word that isn't in its database. Carefully monitor the changes your checker makes. Always proofread a printout of the final copy. A spell-checker won't catch a homophone (*their, there, they're*) or a word that is spelled correctly that is not the word you want.

▶ Try It!

Explore the options available on your grammar and spell-checkers. Enable and disable different features by clicking on them. Decide which settings work best for you.

Publishing

Before you share your final copy, be sure that the document itself is well designed. See pages **76–78** for information about designing your writing with a computer.

Struggling Learners

Students might not understand why they should avoid using passive verbs. Present the following definitions and examples:

- When the subject of a sentence does the acting, the verb is in the active voice: *The guide took us to the exhibit.*

- When the subject of the sentence is acted upon, the verb is in the passive voice: *We were taken to the exhibit by the guide.*

Explain to students that using the active voice will make their writing clearer and more forceful.

Understanding the Traits of Writing

At times, jazz musicians stay with the beat, playing within a specific rhythm or pattern; at other times, they improvise, suddenly breaking out of the basic structure to create a whole new sound. Good writers often work in a similar way. They start with a basic plan, but as they go along, new ideas may come to mind, taking them in more interesting directions.

You will do your best writing if you keep an open mind, always expecting to take a few side trips that reveal new ways of thinking about your topic. Writing that isn't forced, that is formed "partly though accident," will likely display the **traits** found in all good writing— *stimulating ideas, engaging voice, original word choice,* and so on. This chapter will introduce you to all the traits of writing.

- Introducing the Traits
- Understanding the Traits
- Guide for Effective Writing

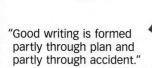

"Good writing is formed partly through plan and partly through accident."
—Ken Macrorie

Understanding the Traits of Writing

Objectives
- demonstrate an understanding of each of the six traits of effective writing
- apply the concepts of the traits to writing

Emphasize that good writing can't be forced and that writers must be open to improvising and experimenting. To demonstrate:

- Divide students into groups. Give each group a piece of paper with the same sentence at the top. Use the following sentence, or make up one of your own: *When the sun rose that morning, none of us were prepared for what the day would bring.*
- Tell students to pass the paper from student to student. Each student should add one or two sentences, based on the sentences that come before, to help tell a story.
- Set a time limit. Have groups share their stories to see how they differ and to see if they can identify some features of good writing.

Introducing the Traits

Call attention to Maya Angelou's quotation at the top of the page. Invite volunteers to describe something they have read that seemed to slide "through [their] brain and [go] straight to [their] heart." It might be a poem, a short story, a novel, an article, or any piece of writing. Ask students to use specific examples to explain how the writing affected them.

Ask students the following questions to heighten their awareness of the seamless way in which good writers apply the traits to their writing.

- When you are reading, which trait is the most obvious? (Possible response: ideas)
- Which trait or traits can be the least obvious, even though they are very important? (Possible responses: organization, conventions, voice)
- What would be the result if a writer did not apply the traits of word choice or sentence fluency? (Possible responses: The ideas would be confusing and difficult to follow.)

40

"The idea is to write so that people hear it, and it slides through the brain and goes straight to the heart."

—Maya Angelou

Introducing the Traits

The chart below identifies the main features of effective writing. If you write with these traits in mind, you will be pleased with the results.

Traits of Writing

- **Ideas**
  Strong writing presents a clear focus, or message. The writing contains specific ideas and details that support the focus.

- **Organization**
  Effective writing creates a meaningful whole—with interesting beginning, middle, and ending parts. The supporting details are arranged in the best order.

- **Voice**
  Writing that has voice reflects the writer's personality. It is engaging and appropriate for the audience.

- **Word Choice**
  Good writing contains strong words, including specific nouns, verbs, and modifiers. Word choice helps deliver a clear message.

- **Sentence Fluency**
  Effective writing flows smoothly from sentence to sentence. None of the sentences cause the reader to stumble or become confused.

- **Conventions**
  Strong writing follows the rules for punctuation, capitalization, spelling, and grammar. It is carefully edited to be error free.

FYI

Also consider the trait of presentation. An effective final copy looks neat and follows the guidelines for margins, indenting, spacing, and so on. The writing's appearance affects the reader's overall impression of it. (See pages **76–78**.)

Struggling Learners

For students who find the six traits overwhelming, plan to work on just one or two traits at a time. Provide a visual reminder by having students create and display a poster that lists the traits.

Advanced Learners

Have students create a bulletin board to display good examples of the six traits. They can create brief writing samples from their favorite books or pull them from newspapers or magazines.

The Traits in Action

The following excerpt from a personal narrative by Latrisha Jones displays the effective use of the traits of writing.

Ramadan Feast

The narrative starts with an interesting topic.

The sun was setting behind me as I walked into the Islamic Center. I'd never been in a mosque, but now I was going to a feast to celebrate the holiest month of the Islamic year: Ramadan.

The details are arranged chronologically.

I wondered what to expect. Would I see veils, pillows, and incense burners, like in the old movies? No. Instead, I saw linoleum floors, painted cinder blocks, and ceiling tiles. On the walls hung kids' drawings that celebrated Ramadan, posters with the words of the prophet Mohammed, and handwritten essays about being Muslim in America.

The writer's personal voice comes through.

"Latrisha!" called a voice. I turned to see my friend Helah hurrying toward me. She wore a hooded caftan, a silk robe that reached to her ankles, and she was beaming.

"Helah," I said as I took her hands. "I'm so nervous!" I touched the Kente hat I'd worn, knowing girls were supposed to cover their heads.

Specific nouns and verbs create clear images.

Helah smiled, "I like the hat, but you didn't have to cover your head. We know you're not Muslim. We just want you to celebrate with us." She led me into the gym, decked out like the Student Council banquet, with round tables and folding chairs and a buffet that steamed with Persian food. Helah took a deep breath. "I can't wait to taste the lamb."

Varied sentences engage the reader.

"Me, too," I said, my stomach rumbling. I'd fasted all day—no food or drink since sunup. "You do this every day for the whole month of Ramadan? I've never fasted before."

"You fasted today?" Helah asked, and she gave me a hug. "Muslims fast because it's one of the Five Pillars, or duties to honor Allah." She looked slyly at me. "But you fasted because you're my friend."

Correct punctuation makes the writing easy to read.

I nodded as we took our seats among the others. There were dates on a plate in the middle of the table. "So, friend, when do we eat?"

 Respond to the reading. Which two traits stand out in this narrative? Explain.

The Traits in Action

Point out that, like most narratives, Latrisha's writing is told in chronological order. Chronological order, or time order, is the order in which events happen in time.

❋ For more on using chronological order, see SE page 571.

Respond to the reading.

Possible Answers

- **Ideas:** The writer presents a clear picture of the Ramadan celebration, with specific, colorful details.
- **Organization:** Events are arranged in chronological order, which makes sense and is easy to follow.
- **Voice:** The writer's voice is natural and reflects her personality. She wonders what to expect. She covers her head out of respect for her friend.
- **Word Choice:** The writer uses specific nouns such as *mosque, incense burners, Ramadan, caftan,* and *Kente,* to present a vivid account of her experience.

English Language Learners

Define the following words before reading the excerpt:

- Ramadan (Islamic religious holiday)
- Islamic (from Islam, a religion)
- mosque (religious building)
- veils (thin cloths to cover faces or objects)
- linoleum (common material used for making floors)
- decked out (decorated)
- buffet (many foods set out together to be self-served)
- Persian (from Persia, now Iran)
- rumbling (making noise)
- Allah (name of god in Islam)

Advanced Learners

Have students use a debate format to defend one of the traits they chose for the **Respond to the reading** question. Students should work in pairs, each offering one trait from the essay and explaining why it stood out. After stating their choices, students should take turns discussing why their trait was the more effective one.

Understanding Ideas

Selecting Effective Ideas

To help students understand how a writer connects with the topic, write the following on the board:

Connecting with Ideas

Then ask students how they connect with ideas. Write their suggestions on the board. Possible responses include . . .

- through personal experiences
- because of genuine interest
- due to prior knowledge
- because of curiosity

 Respond to the reading.

Answers

- **Focus:** Leonardo DaVinci as an inventor
- **Supporting Details:** 6,000 sketchbook pages; sketches of military weapons and factory equipment; bizarre flying machines; description of the aerial screw, which may have inspired the design of early helicopters

---

Understanding Ideas

Quality ideas drive good writing, making it possible to develop strong essays, research papers, articles, and stories. No other trait is even remotely as important. As writer Joyce Carol Oates says, "As soon as you connect with your true subject [your ideas], you will write."

Selecting Effective Ideas

If you start out with effective ideas, there's a good chance that the rest of your writing will go smoothly. Follow these tips.

1. Begin with a specific topic. (Make sure that it genuinely interests you and meets the requirements of the assignment.)
2. Focus on an interesting or important part of the topic. (This will help you develop a more unified paper.)
3. Collect specific details that support the topic.

Sample Paragraph

Carefully read the following paragraph, paying close attention to the topic, the focus, and the specific details.

A Man with Imagination

People know Leonardo da Vinci (1452–1519) as a famous painter, but do they know that he was a famous inventor, too? The National Museum of Science and Technology in Milan, Italy, has more than 6,000 sketchbook pages of da Vinci's invention ideas. Included in the collection are sketches of military weapons and factory equipment. In addition, ideas for bizarre flying machines show da Vinci's incredible imagination. One of the most famous machines is called the aerial screw. It features a flattened spiral of fabric winding around a central pole. In theory, spinning the fabric "propeller" would lift the machine. Although such a machine couldn't actually work, the idea inspired other inventors. Some experts say that it may have inspired the early designs of the helicopter. Da Vinci will always be known for famous paintings like the *Mona Lisa*, but he has made significant contributions in other areas.

 Respond to the reading. What part of the topic does the paragraph focus on? What supporting details seem especially important? Name two.

English Language Learners

Define the following words before reading the paragraph:

- sketchbook (drawing journal)
- military weapons (tools for fighting wars)
- bizarre (strange, weird)
- aerial (of or in the air)
- propeller (spinning blades, like on a boat or plane)

Struggling Learners

Help students explore good topic ideas in small groups. Have each student write a topic idea on an index card and place it in a paper bag. Students take turns drawing a card from the bag and recording questions about the topic that group members generate. Have students rate the topic's interest level. Post topics for later use.

Process

Finding Important Details

Details are the information that supports the focus of your writing. When the details are clear and complete, the writing has impact. Consider using the four types of details listed below. (See pages **569–570** for other types of details.)

Types of Details

- **Facts** are details that can be proven.
- **Statistics** present numerical information.
- **Examples** illustrate a main point.
- **Quotations** are statements from other people.

Sample Paragraph

Read the following paragraph, paying close attention to the types of details that it includes.

Up in Smoke

Smoking continues to be a health problem in the United States, despite the accompanying risks. According to the American Heart Association, more than 20 percent of women and 25 percent of men in the United States are smokers. The American Lung Association states that in 2005, 2.5 percent of teens smoked. Smokers suffer from yellow stains on their teeth and hands, increased colds, insomnia, nervousness, and high blood pressure. They are more prone to arthritis, heart disease, and lung disease, among other ailments. A 2006 report reveals that the decline in teenage smoking has stopped. This troubling discovery may be linked to more advertising by the tobacco industry as well as the trend toward more frequent use of cigarettes in movies. These teen smokers are risking an early and painful death. Smoking is one habit that all people should avoid at all costs.

 Respond to the reading. Name one fact included in the paragraph. Name one example. Name one statistic.

 Try It!

Write a paragraph about a topic of your choice. Include three or four types of details listed above.

Understanding Ideas
Finding Important Details

Explain to students that they will use the types of details shown when they do expository writing, persuasive writing, and research reports.

✳ For more on using different types of details effectively, see SE pages 569–570.

Respond to the reading.

Possible Answers

- **Facts:** Smokers suffer from yellow stains on their teeth and hands, increased colds, insomnia, nervousness, and high blood pressure; they are prone to arthritis, heart disease, and lung disease.
- **Examples:** This troubling discovery may be linked to more advertising by the tobacco industry as well as the trend toward more frequent use of cigarettes in movies.
- **Statistics:** More than 20 percent of women and 25 percent of men in the United States are smokers; in 2005, 2.5 percent of teens smoked.

English Language Learners

Define the following words before reading the paragraph:

- despite (even though)
- accompanying (going with)
- stains (permanent spots)
- increased (more)
- insomnia (inability to sleep)
- prone (likely to have)
- ailments (disorders or sicknesses)

Understanding Organization

Working Deductively

Because deductive and inductive organization may be confusing for some students, **use a graphic** *(see below)* to explain these concepts.

 Respond to the reading.

Answers

The first sentence contains the topic (global warming) and the focus (it's changing the face of our world, and evidence suggests it will soon become an even bigger problem).

Supporting details

- The number of glaciers in Glacier National Park has shrunk from 150 in 1850 to 35 today.
- Experts suggest that by 2030 all the glaciers there will have melted.
- Glaciers of Antarctica are melting and crashing into the ocean.
- Sea levels are rising.
- Cities could flood, causing incalculable damage.

Understanding Organization

Writer Donald Murray states that strong writing stems from "the solid construction of thoughts." A clear plan of organization gives writing unity, which makes it easy to follow from one point to the next.

At a basic level, writing can be organized **deductively** or **inductively**. Most scientific and informative writing requires deductive organization, making complicated material easier to understand. Personal and some types of informational writing use inductive organization.

Working Deductively

You are working deductively when you start with a topic sentence or thesis statement and follow with supporting details. The informational paragraph below opens with a main point about global warming and follows with supporting details.

Sample Paragraph

A Critical Meltdown

Global warming is changing the face of the world, and evidence suggests it will soon become an even bigger problem. Its effects can be seen in this country in Montana's Glacier National Park, where the number of glaciers in the park has shrunk from 150 in 1850 to just 35 today. Some experts suggest that by the year 2030, all the remaining glaciers there will have melted. Elsewhere, the glaciers of Antarctica are melting and crashing into the ocean, causing an ecological nightmare for the animals living on that continent. The resulting rising sea levels will eventually impact many aspects of life. For example, if global warming continues at its current rate, it could affect the coastal areas of the earth's continents, flooding some cities and causing incalculable damage. Unfortunately, it may be too late to address this impending crisis.

 Respond to the reading. Which sentence contains both the topic and focus of this paragraph? Which supporting details seem the most critical?

 Try It!

Write an informational paragraph that follows the deductive pattern of organization. Use the sample paragraph above as a guide.

Teaching Tip: Use a Graphic

Students may benefit from a graphic explanation of deductive organization.

- Draw a large arrow, point down, along the side of the chalkboard. At the top of the arrow, write the label *Topic and Focus.* Along the length of the arrow shaft, write the words *Supporting details*.

- Then have students read the paragraph and do the **Respond to the reading** activity together as a class. Add answers to the graphic on the board as students supply them.
- Students can copy the graphic and use it as a guide to write a paragraph that follows the deductive pattern of organization for the **Try It!** activity.

- Repeat this process to help explain inductive organization on SE page 45, but invert the direction of the arrow and rearrange the labels accordingly.

Process

"Work hard to master these tools of writing. Simplify, prune, and strive for order."

—William Zinsser

Working Inductively

You are working inductively when you start with specific details and lead up to an important summary statement. In the sample personal paragraph below, the final sentence is a summary topic sentence. When you write inductively, you hold the reader's interest because he or she must read to the end to discover the specific topic. Details that are organized inductively build in suspense or lead to a logical conclusion.

Sample Paragraph

Read the following paragraph, paying close attention to the way specific details are used to lead up to a summary or key point.

Building in Force

The day had been muggy, the heat relentless as the hazy sun baked the ground. As the morning progressed, the haze turned to clouds, at first too thin to hide the sun, but growing thicker as they inched their way to the east. Then the sun was completely covered, and a low growl rumbled from the black western sky, accompanied by quick snake-tongues of lightning. The muggy air began to stir, and little dust clouds spun across the driveway. Thunder rolled across the darkening sky. A large drop of rain hit my cheek, followed by another and another. Then, with a crash, the sky parted, and the rain poured down in pulsing sheets. The predicted thunderstorm had arrived.

 Respond to the reading. What is the topic of this paragraph? Which sentence states the specific topic? What is the role of the other sentences?

 Try It!

Write a paragraph that follows the inductive pattern of organization. (Your topic can be informational or personal.) Use the sample paragraph above as a guide.

Understanding Organization

Working Inductively

Have students examine paragraphs and essays they have written for other classes to see how often they used deductive organization and how often they used inductive organization.

? Respond to the reading.

Answers

- The topic is the arrival of the predicted thunderstorm.
- The last sentence states the topic.
- The other sentences contain details describing the events leading up to the storm.

English Language Learners

Define the following words before reading the paragraph:

- muggy (humid, damp)
- relentless (without mercy)
- hazy (lightly cloudy)
- progressed (continued)
- inched (moved slowly)
- growl (low sound)
- rumbled (made noise)
- pulsing (beating like a heart)

To help students model their work after the example, tell them to write descriptively about a day they remember well. Make sure they have the English vocabulary for their sensory details.

Struggling Learners

Writing deductively or inductively will be difficult for some students. Encourage them to choose a topic they know well or can observe directly. Suggest that they describe concrete objects rather than abstract ideas. Help them gather details in a web or list before writing.

Understanding Voice

Knowing Your Audience

While students can quickly grasp the importance of having good ideas and solid organization, the importance of establishing one's own voice is often more difficult to understand and to achieve.

First, remind students that voice is the way their writing sounds to readers. Voice can be described using terms such as *excited, interested, enthusiastic, serious, humorous,* and so on. Explain that writers often are known by their voice. Tell students that when they truly connect with their ideas, their writing voice will sound enthusiastic and interested. Encourage students to read aloud their writing whenever possible so that they can listen for their voice and decide whether it sounds natural.

 Respond to the reading.

Answers

- Audience: the school principal
- The writer engages the reader's interest by mentioning the Student Council and by requesting the creation of a student lounge.
- Appropriate/appealing words include *request you consider, good grades and behavior, deserve . . . privilege, perfect place, easily be stored, hope you will consider, encourage students to work hard.*

Understanding Voice

Voice is the special quality that attracts a reader to your writing. Novelist Kurt Vonnegut says that a writer whose unique voice comes through in his or her work serves as a "good date" for the reader.

Knowing Your Audience

Writing with an appealing voice will help you connect with your reader. Your writing will always have voice if you . . .

- keep your purpose in mind,
- show respect for your reader,
- engage your reader's interest, and
- anticipate and address your reader's questions.

Sample Paragraph

Carefully read the following paragraph, paying attention to its voice.

> **To the Principal:**
>
> On behalf of the Student Council Spirit Committee, I would like to request that you consider creating a student lounge. Such a room would be designated for students who have shown through good grades and behavior that they deserve such a privilege. Students with a 2.5 average and no disciplinary problems for a full term would be issued a pass to use the lounge during their study halls. The student council could locate donated furniture for the room and decorate it. As for space, the large storage room off the cafeteria would be the perfect place. It is basically unused, and the few supplies kept there could easily be stored in the supply room by the kitchen. I hope you will consider this proposal. Offering a student lounge would encourage students to work hard.

 Respond to the reading. Who is the intended reader or audience? How does the writer engage the reader? Identify any two appropriate and/or appealing words, phrases, or ideas.

Try It!

Write a paragraph, either to your principal or to your classmates, addressing a school-related topic. Make sure to connect with your reader.

English Language Learners

Define the following words before reading the paragraph:

- on behalf of (representing)
- lounge (room for relaxing and visiting with others)
- designated (assigned)
- disciplinary (having to do with behavior)

- issued (given)
- donated (free, given as a gift)
- proposal (idea)
- encourage (support, motivate)

Voice may be difficult for students to understand if they are not proficient in English. If possible, share examples of voice.

Struggling Learners

Students may be tempted to adopt a stiff or formal voice for the topic in the **Try It!** activity. Remind them to avoid the temptation to sound too formal or too knowledgeable. On the other hand, they should not adopt a voice that is too informal. Tell students to use words and phrases that they use in polite conversation.

Process

> "By the time I reach the fifth version, [my writing] begins
> to have its own voice."
>
> —Ashley Bryan

Sounding Interested

Your writing voice will be heard loud and clear if you are enthusiastic and interested in your topic. Of course, to sound interested, you ought to know a lot about your topic. In the following sample, the writer's enthusiasm is evident.

Sample Paragraph

Programmed Pets

The pet world has just expanded, thanks to the world of robotics. An impressive range of robotic pets is available, including dogs, cats, parrots, and even frogs. Adorable robo-dogs are programmed to be affectionate and do a variety of tricks, while charming robo-cats purr when they are petted. Designed to look futuristic but friendly, the pets are made out of plastic that is either brightly colored or shimmering with a metallic finish. Robotic pets are a good option for people with allergies and for people with hectic schedules. While these toys won't replace golden retrievers or Siamese cats, they do appeal to techno fanatics. Instead of feeding the dog, the next generation of pet owners will simply recharge a battery.

 Respond to the reading. How does the writer's enthusiasm come through? What interesting information does the writer include? Name two details. How does the closing sentence add appeal?

 Try It!

Write freely for 5 to 10 minutes about a topic that truly interests you. When you finish, underline three or four phrases or ideas that show your enthusiasm.

Advanced Learners

For the **Try It!** activity have students write two paragraphs. In one paragraph they should use neutral language that does not reveal feelings or interest. In another paragraph they should use language that shows an attitude (affectionate, humorous, disdainful) toward the topic. Have students exchange paragraphs with a partner and identify the voice in each paragraph.

Understanding Voice

Sounding Interested

Discuss ways that students can develop interest and enthusiasm for a topic that is new to them. For example, they can watch a related documentary, or they can discuss the topic with an expert who can share both knowledge and enthusiasm for the topic.

 Respond to the reading.

Possible Answers

- Words such as *impressive, adorable, charming,* and *friendly* convey the writer's enthusiasm.
- Interesting details: robo-dogs that are affectionate and do tricks; robo-cats that purr when petted; materials used to make the robotic pets
- The closing sentence explains how easy it will be to care for robotic pets.

Understanding Word Choice

Choosing Words Carefully

Tell students that when they want to replace a vague, overused, or dull word with a clearer, more colorful one, they can use a thesaurus or a synonym finder. Remind students that synonyms have similar dictionary meanings, or denotations, but sometimes they have different **connotations** *(see below),* or shades of meaning. Using a word with the wrong connotation can change the tone of their writing.

 Respond to the reading.

Answers

- Topic: childhood experience of getting lost
- Action verbs: *played, examining, snuck, slipped, thrust, heard, crawled, formed, rolling, drip, sobbing, parted, peeked, shouted, pulled, enveloped*
- Modifiers: *circular, silky, smiling, strange*

Understanding Word Choice

Writer Dorothy Parker once said, "I can't find five words but that I change seven." Like all experienced writers, Parker appreciated the importance of word choice. She knew that her message would be delivered only with strong words.

Choosing Words Carefully

Since your words will communicate your message, you should choose them carefully. As you read the following sample, pay careful attention to the clear, colorful word choice.

Sample Paragraph

> **Peekaboo!**
>
> When I was little, Mom always played hide-and-seek with me at home, so I never thought that it would be a problem playing it at the store. While Mom was examining new bath mats, I snuck across the aisle to a circular dress rack. I slipped between the silky dresses where I waited, knowing at any moment Mom would thrust her smiling face inside the cave and yell, "Peekaboo!" But she didn't. Instead, I heard her ask someone to help her look for me. By this time, I realized I had done something wrong. For some reason, I held still as the seconds crawled by. What if Mom never found me? Tears formed and started rolling down my cheeks. My nose began to drip, and I started sobbing. Then the dresses parted and a strange lady peeked in at me. She shouted to my mother, who pulled me out and enveloped me in a hug. After that, I saved my games for home.

 Respond to the reading. What is the topic of this paragraph? Which verbs communicate specific actions? Name two or three. Which modifiers create clear or colorful images? Name two or three.

Try It!

Write freely for 5 to 10 minutes about a recent experience. Afterward, circle four words in your writing that seem especially colorful and clear, and underline three words that could be improved. Then substitute better choices for your underlined words.

Teaching Tip: Writer's Notebook

Remind students that a word's connotation is the general feeling that it evokes. Tell students that when selecting words from a group of synonyms, they should consider the positive or negative feelings associated with each word, as well as the subtle differences in their meanings.

- Point out the word *thin* in the sample paragraph on SE page 45.
- Ask students for several synonyms for *thin* and write them on the board. (Possible responses: *slim, skinny, slender, lean, bony, emaciated, lanky, skeletal*)

- Have students discuss the positive and negative feelings associated with these words, and the shades of difference in their meanings.
- Discuss why none of these synonyms should replace *thin* in the paragraph.

Process

Watching Out for Adjective Overload

Mark Twain once gave this piece of advice, "When you catch an adjective, kill it." He knew from experience that using too many adjectives can sound forced and unnatural. (See pages **540–541** for more information.)

Too Many Adjectives

A tall, shocking **column of** thick yellow **smoke marked the** exact **spot.**

Adjectives Used Selectively

A column of thick yellow **smoke marked the spot.**

Sample Paragraph

As you read the following paragraph, pay careful attention to the adjectives; they are used selectively.

Treasure Hunt

Whenever I feel down, I head straight to my tall dresser where I keep my memory bowl. It's just a plain red ceramic bowl with blue flowers painted around the outside, but it holds my most treasured possessions. There's the crystal geode my older brother and I found by the river. He split it open and gave me half when he left for college. He kept the other half, telling me that meant we would always be connected. Also in my bowl is my grandfather's prized fishing lure. The colorful feathers remind me of the fun we have fishing when he comes to visit. At the bottom of the bowl rests a scuffed baseball with fraying stitches. It is the game ball from last year when we won the conference championship. When I look at it, I remember the fun we had, and I look forward to next year's season. Looking at the things in my memory bowl always cheers me up.

 Respond to the reading. Which adjectives seem especially effective? Name two. Which verbs communicate specific actions? Name two.

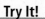 **Try It!**

In a brief paragraph, describe the inside of your locker. Then underline the adjectives that you have used.

Understanding Word Choice

Watching Out for Adjective Overload

When students are advised to use descriptive language, they tend to use too many adjectives. Explain that using too many adjectives can dilute, or weaken, their ideas and confuse readers. In fact, the use of too many or inappropriate adjectives is a sure signal to readers that the writer lacks the confidence to communicate ideas in simple language.

✳ For more about using adjectives effectively, see SE pages 540–541.

 Respond to the reading.

Possible Answers

- Effective adjectives: *plain red, blue, most treasured, crystal, prized, colorful, scuffed, fraying*
- Action verbs: *head, split, gave, rests, won, remember, looking, cheers*

Understanding Sentence Fluency

Checking for Variety

Ask students to identify transitions in the sample paragraph that help the sentences flow smoothly (*At first, soon, at last*). What are some other transitions that could be used in the paragraph? (Possible responses: *then, suddenly*)

From time to time, have students select a piece of writing from their reading assignments to check for sentence fluency. Have students check the passage for seamless style and sentence variety.

 Respond to the reading.

Answers

1. Column 1: *The, Multicolored, Bold, At, People, Blasts, Behind, At*
2. Column 2: 6, 8, 5, 15, 10, 9, 11, 5
3. Column 3: *dimmed; danced; grew; thundered, roared; stamped, clapped; drowned; appeared; began*

Understanding Sentence Fluency

Strong writing is seamless—meaning that the sentences are easy to follow from start to finish. To ensure this seamless style, William Zinsser says that he writes "entirely by ear, reading everything aloud before letting it go out into the world."

Checking for Variety

In effective writing, the sentences are not predictable. They vary in the way they begin, in length, and in verb choice. Use the following strategy to ensure sentence variety in your writing.

1. In one column on a piece of paper, list each sentence's opening word. (Decide if you need to vary some sentence beginnings.)
2. In another column, write the number of words in each sentence. (Decide if you need to change the length of some sentences.)
3. In a third column, list the verbs in each sentence. (Decide if you need to change any general verbs—*is, are, look,* and so on.)

Sample Paragraph

Read the following brief paragraph, paying careful attention to the flow of the sentences.

Bold Buildup

The lights dimmed in the amphitheater. Multicolored spotlights danced overhead, bouncing off the ceiling. Bold sounds grew in intensity. At first, the sounds thundered in the distance, but soon they roared in our heads. People all around stamped their feet and clapped their hands. Blasts from a bass guitar drowned out the fans. Behind a blinding flash of light, the band appeared on stage. At last, the concert began.

 Respond to the reading. On your own paper, use the three-step strategy above to test the sentences in the sample paragraph.

 Try It!

Write freely for 5 to 10 minutes about a concert or sporting event you have attended. Then test your sentence variety using the strategy above.

Advanced Learners

Ask students to identify the topic (concert) and focus (the moments leading up to the start of the concert) of the sample paragraph. Then ask whether the paragraph is organized inductively or deductively (inductively). Students should be prepared to share reasons for their answers.

Process

Adding Style to Your Sentences

You can learn about sentence style by examining the sentences in professional essays, articles, and stories. Experienced writers often use *loose* and *cumulative* sentences.

- A **loose sentence** expresses the main idea near the beginning (in blue below) and adds details as needed.

  The regimental flags led, **men trailing out behind each flag in a V-shaped mass, struggling over rocks and logs.**

  —"Missionary Ridge," Bruce Catton

- A **cumulative sentence** places the main idea in the middle (in blue below) with modifiers coming before and after it.

  Each afternoon during the wonderful spring, I had to stay in, **two hours a day for six weeks, working long division.**

  —*Good Old Boy,* Willie Morris

Try It!

Write sentences modeled after each example below. (You do not have to follow the examples exactly.) One sentence has been modeled for you.

Wil nodded to himself and slipped away, **softly as a mouse, toward the back of the house where the tourists were never taken.**

—"A Room Full of Leaves," Joan Aiken

Student Version: *Josie smiled to herself and jogged along,* **gracefully as a deer,** *toward the pond in the park where many ducks were always feeding.*

He was born around 1840, **by the Belle Fourche River, near Bear Butte, in what is now South Dakota.**

—*Crazy Horse,* Larry McMurtry

I spent hours in the bedroom playing with the set, **studying the directions, and working one experiment after another.**

—*Gifted Hands,* Ben Carson

Born in 1927, my mother, Johnny Florence Gooch, was her mother's right hand, **just as I am to her.**

—*An American Story,* Debra J. Dickerson

Creeping through her bones, the pain had become insistent, **nearly without letup.**

—*A Tidewater Morning,* William Styron

Understanding Sentence Fluency

Adding Style to Your Sentences

The terms *loose* and *cumulative* are used to describe different arrangements of words and ideas in sentences. Make sure students do not confuse loose or cumulative sentences with run-on sentences, which occur when two sentences are joined without punctuation or a conjunction.

✱ For more about sentence arrangements, see SE page 750.

When writing loose or cumulative sentences, students may encounter problems with misplaced or dangling modifiers. Before assigning the **Try It!** activity, display the following sentence on the board:

Josie smiled to herself and jogged along toward the pond in the park where many ducks were always feeding, gracefully as a deer.

Help students identify the misplaced modifier (gracefully as a deer). After students complete the **Try It!** activity, encourage them to check their sentences to make sure they have not included misplaced or dangling modifiers.

✱ For more about avoiding sentence problems, see SE pages 557–559.

English Language Learners

The **Try It!** activity may be difficult for students who have not yet mastered English, so pair them up with English-proficient partners to complete the activity. To ensure that both partners contribute, ask them to take turns writing every other phrase to complete each sentence.

Understanding Conventions

Knowing the Basic Rules

Checklists are helpful because they provide a quick and easy way to address common errors made by writers. Students will encounter similar checklists during the editing stage of all the core writing units (narrative, persuasive, expository, response to literature). Tell students that to make these checklists work better for them, they can add questions about specific punctuation, capitalization, spelling, or grammar errors that they tend to make when they write. The added questions will remind them to check for these errors.

52

Understanding Conventions

Effective writing is easy to read because, among other things, it follows the conventions for punctuation, capitalization, spelling, and grammar. Writer and editor Patricia T. O'Conner summarizes the importance of punctuation in this way: "When you write, punctuation marks are the road signs that guide the reader, and you wouldn't be understood without them."

Knowing the Basic Rules

The English language is always growing; it includes more words than any other "living" language. It stands to reason that there are a lot of rules for using English. The checklist below can guide you as you check your writing for conventions. Also see the "Proofreader's Guide" (pages **604–763**).

Conventions

PUNCTUATION

_____ **1.** Do I use end punctuation after all my sentences?

_____ **2.** Do I use commas and semicolons correctly?

_____ **3.** Do I use apostrophes to show possession (*that boy's keys* and *those boys' keys*)?

_____ **4.** Do I use quotation marks and italics correctly?

CAPITALIZATION

_____ **5.** Do I start each sentence with a capital letter?

_____ **6.** Do I capitalize the proper names of people and places?

SPELLING

_____ **7.** Have I checked my spelling using a spell-checker?

_____ **8.** Have I also checked the spelling with a dictionary?

GRAMMAR

_____ **9.** Do I use correct forms of verbs (*had eaten,* not *had ate*)?

_____ **10.** Do my subjects and verbs agree in number (*the dog barks* and *the dogs bark*)?

_____ **11.** Do I use the correct word (*their, there,* or *they're*)?

English Language Learners

Students may be overwhelmed by the number of conventions on the checklist. Assure them that they will be expected to look only for errors in conventions that they have been explicitly taught, and in many cases they will work with a partner who will help them check their work.

Process

"Cut out all those exclamation marks. An exclamation mark is like laughing at your own joke."

—F. Scott Fitzgerald

Creating a Smooth-Reading Rhythm

Carefully selected punctuation can help the reader follow the ideas in your writing. For example, if you use commas and semicolons especially well, they can give your writing an effective rhythm.

Sample Paragraph

Read the following paragraph to see how the punctuation controls the flow of ideas.

Flying Solo

Amelia Earhart never flew in an airplane until 1920, but by 1922, she had already set the women's altitude record at 14,000 feet. In 1932, Earhart became the second person to fly solo across the Atlantic, exactly five years after Charles Lindbergh's historic flight. Two years later, Earhart accepted her greatest challenge, flying around the world. She flew more than 22,000 miles—from California to Florida; across South America, Africa, and Asia; and then out across the Pacific. She departed from New Guinea on July 2. A few hours later, after a last cryptic radio message, Earhart and her airplane disappeared.

 Respond to the reading. How many of the sentences contain commas? How many contain semicolons? Which sentence seems especially rhythmic? Write it on your paper and explain your choice. Does any sentence contain punctuation that you don't normally use? Explain.

Try It!

Write a brief paragraph about someone you know and admire. Include a few sentences that require commas and one sentence that uses a semicolon.

Understanding Conventions

Creating a Smooth-Reading Rhythm

Students may associate the term *rhythm* with music or poetry. Explain that good writing also has rhythm. The rhythm of poetry often has a distinctive beat, creating its musical quality. Tell students that although prose can have a musical quality, the rhythm of prose depends primarily on the natural, smooth flow of ideas created by the arrangement of words and the punctuation.

Respond to the reading.

Answers

- Five sentences have commas.
- One sentence contains semicolons.
- *She flew more than 22,000 miles—from California to Florida; across South America, Africa, and Asia; and then out across the Pacific.*

  This sentence is rhythmic because the ideas flow naturally, taking the reader from one place to the next.
- Possible response: One sentence contains a dash and semicolons.

If students have recently completed a piece of writing, encourage them to use the Guide for Effective Writing to check their work. If they have not yet completed a writing assignment for this class or in any other curriculum area, have them apply this checklist to the sample expository essay "The Sky's Not the Limit" on SE pages 29–30 or the personal narrative "Ramadan Feast" on SE page 41. Analyzing how a piece of writing exhibits the traits of effective writing will help students better understand what to aim for when they write.

54

Guide for Effective Writing

If a piece of writing meets the following standards, it exhibits the traits of effective writing. Check your work using these standards.

- **Ideas**

  The writing . . .

  _____ maintains a clear, specific focus or purpose.

  _____ presents interesting details that support the focus.

  _____ holds the reader's attention (and answers her or his questions about the topic).

- **Organization**

  _____ includes a clear beginning, middle, and ending.

  _____ arranges the details in the best order.

  _____ contains transitions to connect ideas.

- **Voice**

  _____ speaks in a sincere, natural way.

  _____ shows that the writer is knowledgeable about and interested in the topic.

  _____ effectively addresses the reader (audience).

- **Word Choice**

  _____ contains specific, clear nouns and verbs.

  _____ presents an appropriate level of formality or informality.

- **Sentence Fluency**

  _____ flows smoothly from sentence to sentence.

  _____ includes sentences that vary in beginning, length, and style.

- **Conventions**

  _____ adheres to the rules of punctuation, spelling, and grammar.

  _____ follows established guidelines for presentation.

55

Peer Responding

If you're like most students, you're reluctant to make changes after working hard to write a first draft. But as you know, first drafts seldom, if ever, turn out clear and convincing. Unless you continue to work with it, your writing will never be as good as it could be.

Participating in peer-response sessions can help you stay with your writing. Classmates can point out what works well in your writing and what may need improving. At first, you may find it hard to share your writing. However, once you see how helpful peer responses can be, you'll come to appreciate them. Think of yourself and your responders as teammates who share the same goal: to make your writing the best it can be.

- ■ **Peer-Responding Guidelines**
- ■ **Using the Traits to Respond**

"Listen to good criticism, but pick your critics carefully."
—Paula Danziger

Peer Responding

> ### Objectives
> - demonstrate an understanding of the role of the author and the role of the responder in peer responding
> - learn how to give helpful responses
> - practice using a peer response sheet

Tell students that you sympathize with their reluctance to share their writing with their classmates. Then explain how you overcame your own unwillingness to share your writing with peers, and give specific examples of how it helped to improve your writing. Invite volunteers who have participated in peer-response sessions in other writing classes to share their experiences and to discuss the benefits they have derived from these experiences.

Peer-Responding Guidelines

The Author's Role

Before students read the guidelines on this page, ask them what they think is the hardest part of peer responding for the author. Possible responses:

- watching the expression on responders' faces
- worrying about the responders' reactions
- listening to criticism
- wondering how much rewriting will be necessary
- caring too much or not enough about what other people think of the writing

Explain to students that constructive criticism offers suggestions for improvements that will make the writing stronger and more enjoyable to read.

Peer-Responding Guidelines

The guidelines below will help you conduct effective response sessions. (If you're just starting out, work in small groups of two or three classmates.)

The Author's Role

Come prepared with a meaningful piece of writing. Make a copy for each responder. Also come to the session with an open mind. If you are defensive about your work, you may not "hear" all the comments. Follow these tips.

- **Introduce your writing.** Briefly explain what your writing is about, but don't go into too much detail.
- **Read your writing out loud.** You may, instead, ask the group members to read your writing silently.
- **Ask for comments.** Listen carefully. You don't have to make every change that is suggested, but keep an open mind.
- **Take notes.** Write comments on your copy as the session progresses, so you can remember exactly where changes need to be made.
- **Answer questions.** It's okay to say, "I don't know. I'll have to look into that," if you are unsure.
- **Ask for help.** If you are having trouble with something in your writing, ask for advice.

Asking for Constructive Criticism

To get constructive criticism, ask for it in the right way:

First ask . . .

"What do you think works best in my writing? Why?"

Then ask . . .

"What parts do you think could be improved? How?"

By asking for comments in this way, you create a cooperative relationship with responders. The answers to "Why?" and "How?" will help you to significantly improve your writing.

English Language Learners

Peer responding may be daunting for students who are not confident in their language skills. To ease the process, set some extra guidelines before beginning.

- Ask peers to comment only on certain aspects of the writing.
- Remind responders not to edit grammar and spelling mistakes unless an error affects comprehension.

The Responder's Role

Respond honestly but be sensitive to the author's feelings. Express your comments politely; be sure that they are constructive and helpful. Follow these tips.

- **Listen carefully.** You owe it to the author to pay close attention.
- **Take notes.** Mark places in the margins of your copy so that you can show the author exactly where revisions may be needed.
- **Start with what is good.** Find something positive to say about the author's writing. Be specific about what you liked.
- **Ask questions.** If you are not sure about something, ask for clarification.
- **Make suggestions.** Even when you are pointing out a problem, be positive and constructive. (See below.)

Process

Giving Constructive Criticism	
Don't give commands . . . "Change the beginning so that it grabs my attention."	**Do give suggestions . . .** "The beginning would be stronger if it grabbed my attention right away."
Don't focus on the writer . . . "You jumbled up the middle paragraphs."	**Do focus on the writing . . .** "The argument would be clearer if the details came in a different order."
Don't focus on the problem . . . "There aren't enough details to support your focus."	**Do focus on the solution . . .** "More details would make your essay even more informative."
Don't give general comments . . . "Your sentences are boring."	**Do give specific advice . . .** "You could try changing some of the passive verbs to active verbs."

Try It!

Rewrite the unhelpful comments below to make them more constructive.

1. You didn't use any transition words or phrases to connect your ideas.
2. The last paragraph doesn't leave me with any kind of final thought.
3. Cut out the sentence that compares highways to arteries.
4. You sound really unsure of yourself.

Peer-Responding Guidelines

The Responder's Role

After students read the guidelines for the responder, ask pairs of volunteers to role-play the parts of author and responder, as shown in "Asking for Constructive Criticism" on SE page 56, and "Giving Constructive Criticism" on SE page 57. Students can add appropriate comments of their own to the comments shown.

Try It!
Answers

Possible Answers

1. The flow would be smoother if you added transition words or phrases to connect your ideas.
2. The ending would be more effective if you left the reader with one final thought.
3. Your argument would be stronger if you left out the sentence that compares highways to arteries.
4. You could try adding more special terms to show your knowledge of the topic and to create a more confident voice.

Struggling Learners

Student responders might fail to notice weaknesses in an essay containing opinions that they agree with or a topic they think is interesting. Conversely, they might find fault in an essay with an opinion they disagree with or a topic they find uninteresting. Work with students to distinguish between emotional responses and objective criticism.

Advanced Learners

Remind students that in addition to being positive in their comments, they should remember to be serious, thorough, and considerate regardless of the level of the writing they are assessing. Remind them to look at content, organization, and style.

Using the Traits to Respond

Addressing Ideas, Organization, and Voice

When setting up peer-responding sessions, consider having each student in the group respond to only one trait for a particular piece of writing. One responder could address ideas, one could address organization, and one could address voice. The advantage of this is twofold. By focusing their attention on one trait, responders become more familiar with that trait and can offer the author more helpful comments. In addition, the author benefits by receiving more focused responses.

Using the Traits to Respond

As a responder, your goal is to help an author rethink, refocus, and revise her or his writing. You may find it helpful to base your responses on the traits of writing. Early in the process, focus on these three traits: *ideas, organization,* and *voice.*

Addressing Ideas, Organization, and Voice

Ideas: Help the author focus on the ideas.
- How would you state the main idea of your writing?
- It seems to me that you're trying to say . . . Is that right?
- Are these points the main ideas in your writing?
- The most convincing details include . . .
- A few more details like . . . may strengthen your work.
- Details like . . . may distract from your main idea.
- Your writing left me thinking . . . Is that what you intended?

Organization: Help the author focus on the organization.
- You got my attention in the beginning by . . .
- This sentence seems to state your focus. Is that correct?
- Are the middle paragraphs organized according to . . . ?
- Why did you place the information about . . . in the fourth paragraph?
- Is the purpose of your ending to . . . ?
- I wonder if a transition is needed between the second and third paragraphs.

Voice: Help the author focus on the voice.
- The sentences that most clearly show your personality are . . .
- I would describe your attitude about this topic as . . .
- What audience do you want to reach with your writing?
- In this paragraph, your writing sounds too formal/informal.
- The overall feeling I get from this writing is . . .
- Are you too subjective in the middle part of your essay?

Try It!

Why are these three traits important early in the revising process? Explain.

Process

Addressing Word Choice and Sentence Fluency

Later in the process, you may respond to the author's word choice and sentence fluency.

Word Choice: Help the author focus on the nouns, verbs, and modifiers.
- The strongest verbs in the writing are . . .
- I found these general nouns: . . . What specific nouns could you use instead?
- Do you think all the modifiers in the second paragraph are necessary?
- What does . . . mean? Could you define it in your writing?
- The words . . . seem to have the wrong feeling. Could you replace them with words that are more . . . ?
- Have you used . . . too often in the first part of your writing?

Sentence Fluency: Help the author focus on the sentences.
- I like the flow of the sentences in the beginning paragraph.
- Do too many sentences in the middle paragraphs begin the same way?
- How could you vary the sentences in the closing paragraph?
- Could some of the sentences in the second paragraph be combined?
- For the most part, your sentences have a nice rhythm.

Tip

Listen carefully to your peers' comments, but don't think that you have to act on all of them. Peer responders offer their opinions, but you should weigh the value of each comment and proceed accordingly. The following tips will help you get the most out of response sessions.

- Trust your own judgment about your writing.
- Determine which issues are the most important.
- Pay attention to comments made by more than one responder.
- Get another opinion if you are not sure about something.
- Be patient. Focus on one problem area at a time.

Try It!

Why are word choice and sentence fluency important in the revising process? Share your comments with your classmates.

Addressing Word Choice and Sentence Fluency

Tell students that when responding to word choice, responders should also help the author identify the following problems:
- commonly overused words, such as *very* and *thing*
- empty modifiers, such as *kind of, really, like,* and *sort of*
- slang or colloquial expressions that have become part of regional speech patterns, such as *you guys, you know, like,* and *awesome*

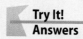
Try It!
Answers

Possible Answers

Word Choice You can make your description of the events even more vivid if you use action verbs.

Sentence Fluency Using a mix of simple, compound, and complex sentences can make the rhythm of your sentences even better.

Sample Peer Response Sheet

For another example of a peer response sheet, have students look back at the sample peer response sheet on SE page 22. Then invite volunteers to explain how the comments and suggestions on both peer response sheets can help the authors gain confidence and improve their writing. Use these questions:

- Which comments and suggestions are most helpful for the specific piece of writing?
- Which comments could the writer apply to future writing assignments?

Sample Peer Response Sheet

Use a response sheet like the one below to make comments about one of your classmate's essays. (Sample responses are included.)

Peer Response Sheet

Writer: <u>Riley Carruthers</u>   Responder: <u>Thea Karas</u>

Title: <u>Buckling Up Is Not Enough</u>

What I liked about your writing:

- You made a topic that I never thought about (Formula One racing) very interesting.
- You obviously know a lot about safety issues with racing.
- I like the little story in the beginning paragraph.
- You clearly explain complicated concepts like the Head-and-Neck Support system.

Changes I would suggest:

- Many of your sentences seem to be the same length. Could you make some long and some short?
- Would the thoughts and feelings of an actual driver make your paper even more interesting?
- You use a few terms—"external circuit breakers" and "faceplates"—that need more explanation.

Try It!

Exchange a recent piece of writing with a classmate.

1. Read the paper once to get an overall feel for it.
2. Read the paper again, paying careful attention to its strengths and weaknesses.
3. Fill out a response sheet like the one above.

61

Using a Rubric

How can you assess your writing? Most word-processing programs can count the number of words in an essay, and even find errors in grammar, but they can't begin to assess the ideas, organization, and voice in your writing. With a rubric in hand, though, you can evaluate your work and the work of others.

Rubrics aren't just for final assessment, either. They can help you get started on a project, guide your early writing, and provide specific suggestions for making improvements. In fact, by using a rubric throughout the process, you can expect to produce a final draft that you can be proud of. In this chapter, you will learn about all of these uses of a rubric—and more.

- **Understanding Rubrics**
- **Reading a Rubric**
- **Getting Started with a Rubric**
- **Revising and Editing with a Rubric**
- **Assessing with a Rubric**
- **Assessing in Action**
- **Assessing an Expository Essay**

"I have kind of an internal
monitor. . . . I'm trying to make
the story suitable for me."
—Christopher Paul Curtis

Copy Masters

Assessment Sheet (TE page 68)

Using a Rubric

Objectives
- demonstrate an understanding of the rating scale on a rubric
- learn how to read a rubric
- use a rubric to revise, edit, and assess writing

Rubric strips appear in the revising and editing sections of the core units in the student edition. Emphasize that the rubrics can be used throughout the writing process as well as for assessment.

Ask students to share any previous experiences they have had using rubrics.
- When and how did they use them?
- Did they find them useful? If so, in what way?

Understanding Rubrics

Give students a chance to study the sample rubric strip, which shows the numbers in the rating scale and the single-word ratings that the numbers represent. The more familiar students become with the rubrics, the more quickly they'll associate number ratings with their level of accomplishment and need for improvement.

Rating Guide

Emphasize that a rubric is a tool, not a grading system. The numerical ratings (accompanied by helpful comments) provide students with a gauge that shows them what they're doing well and what they need to do to improve.

Tell students they shouldn't be discouraged if, at first, their writing earns lower ratings than they expected. Reiterate that the more effort they put into the writing and the more they care about it, the more likely it is that their ratings will go up.

Understanding Rubrics

A **rubric** is simply a rating scale. Have you ever rated the popularity of something on a scale of 1 (terrible) to 10 (fantastic)? With rubrics, you can rate your writing—in this case on a scale of 6 (amazing) to 1 (incomplete).

| 6 Amazing | 5 Strong | 4 Good | 3 Okay | 2 Poor | 1 Incomplete |

The quality of any piece of writing can be rated on the basis of six traits: *ideas, organization, voice, word choice, sentence fluency,* and *conventions.* (For an introduction to these traits, see pages **39–54**.) A single essay might be well organized (score of 5) but have repetitive, general word choice (score of 3).

Rating Guide

Here's a brief description of the rating scale.

A **6** means that the writing is **amazing**.
It far exceeds expectations for a certain trait.

A **5** means that the writing is very **strong**.
It clearly meets the requirements for a trait.

A **4** means that the writing is **good**.
It meets most of the requirements for a trait.

A **3** means that the writing is **okay**.
It needs work to meet the main requirements for a trait.

A **2** means that the writing is **poor**.
It needs a lot of work to meet the requirements of a trait.

A **1** means that the writing is **incomplete**.
The writing is not yet ready to be assessed for a trait.

English Language Learners

To prevent students from feeling pressured by the rubric, set individual goals for students' assignments. For example, at the beginning of the school year, tell a student that his or her goal should be a score that would realistically reflect his or her language proficiency.

Explain that using a rubric throughout the year can help students monitor their progress both in writing and in English acquisition.

Reading a Rubric

Rubrics in this book are color coded according to the trait. *Ideas* appear in a green strip, *organization* in a pink strip, and so forth. There is a description for each rating to help you assess your writing for a particular trait.

Using a Rubric   63

Rubric for Expository Writing

6 Ideas	5	4
The topic, thesis, and details make the essay unforgettable.	The essay is informative with a clear thesis and specific details.	The essay is informative with a clear thesis. More specific details are needed.
Organization		
The organization and transitions make the essay crystal clear and compelling.	The beginning interests the reader. The middle supports the focus. The ending works well. Transitions are used.	The essay is divided into a beginning, a middle, and an ending. Some transitions are used.
Voice		
The writer's voice has the confident, knowledgeable sound of a professional writer.	The writer's voice sounds knowledgeable and confident. It fits the audience.	The writer's voice sounds knowledgeable most of the time and fits the audience.

Guiding Your Writing

A rubric helps you . . .

- **plan your work**—knowing what is expected,
- **create a strong first draft**—focusing on *ideas, organization,* and *voice,*
- **revise and edit your work**—considering each trait, and
- **assess your final draft**—rating the traits throughout the whole piece of writing.

 Think about the rubric. Read the level-5 descriptions above and consider what they have to say about ideas, organization, and voice. What should the essay include? What should each part of the writing do? How should a writer's voice sound?

Reading a Rubric

Encourage students to think of each color-coded strip on a rubric as a writing coach who provides them with hints and tips for improving a specific aspect of their writing. If they continue to "listen" to their coaches, they should eventually see a marked improvement in all parts of their writing.

Guiding Your Writing

Encourage students to use a rubric at every step in the writing process, not just during revising and editing.

Think about the rubric.

Answers

- The essay should include a clear thesis statement, supported by specific details.
- The beginning should be interesting and capture the reader's attention. The middle paragraphs should support the focus. The ending should be strong. Transitions should be used to connect ideas.
- The writer's voice should sound knowledgeable and confident and should fit the audience.

Getting Started with a Rubric

Ask students to study the Understanding Your Goal page and the Rubric for Expository Writing on SE pages 180–181. Then ask them to explain the different purposes of the two features. Students should recognize that

- the Understanding Your Goal page provides guidelines for planning and writing a specific form of expository writing—a comparison essay, and
- the rubric provides guidelines for evaluating the strengths and weaknesses of all forms of expository writing.

Remind students that they can use both the goals page and the rubric throughout the writing process to help them focus on individual traits.

64

Getting Started with a Rubric

Each of the writing units in this book includes a page like the one below. This page, which is arranged according to the traits of writing, explains the main requirements for developing the essay in the unit. Studying the "goals" page will help you get started with your planning.

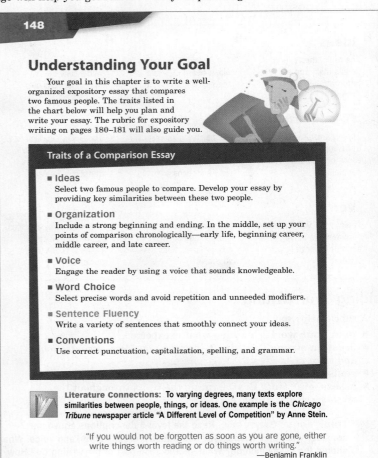

148

Understanding Your Goal

Your goal in this chapter is to write a well-organized expository essay that compares two famous people. The traits listed in the chart below will help you plan and write your essay. The rubric for expository writing on pages 180–181 will also guide you.

Traits of a Comparison Essay

- **Ideas**
  Select two famous people to compare. Develop your essay by providing key similarities between these two people.

- **Organization**
  Include a strong beginning and ending. In the middle, set up your points of comparison chronologically—early life, beginning career, middle career, and late career.

- **Voice**
  Engage the reader by using a voice that sounds knowledgeable.

- **Word Choice**
  Select precise words and avoid repetition and unneeded modifiers.

- **Sentence Fluency**
  Write a variety of sentences that smoothly connect your ideas.

- **Conventions**
  Use correct punctuation, capitalization, spelling, and grammar.

Literature Connections: To varying degrees, many texts explore similarities between people, things, or ideas. One example is the *Chicago Tribune* newspaper article "A Different Level of Competition" by Anne Stein.

"If you would not be forgotten as soon as you are gone, either write things worth reading or do things worth writing."
—Benjamin Franklin

A Closer Look at Understanding Your Goal

The following steps will help you get an overview of the assignment in each writing unit.

1. **Read through the traits chart** to familiarize yourself with the unit's goals.
2. **Focus on *ideas, organization,* and *voice*** at the start of the project, when you are prewriting and writing. These traits form the foundation of good writing.
3. **Identify specific requirements** for each trait (such as using "a point-by-point organizational pattern" and "a knowledgeable-sounding voice").
4. **Ask questions** if you aren't sure about any part of the assignment.

Process

A Special Note About the Traits

Different traits are important at different stages of the writing process. The following chart shows when the specific traits are important.

> During **prewriting** and **writing**, focus on the *ideas, organization,* and *voice* in your work.
>
> During **revising**, focus on *ideas, organization, voice, word choice,* and *sentence fluency.* (For some assignments, your teacher may ask you to pay particular attention to one or two of these traits.)
>
> During **editing** and proofreading, concentrate on *conventions*—spelling, punctuation, capitalization, and grammar.
>
> When you are **assessing** your final copy, consider all six traits. (For some assignments, your teacher may ask you to assess the writing for just a few of the traits.)

Exercise

Write a paragraph. Review the goals on page **64**. Then write an expository paragraph comparing two people, places, or things. Keep the traits in mind as you write.

A Closer Look at Understanding Your Goal

Have students take a few moments to locate and look at the Understanding Your Goal page and the rubric for each of the core units.

- Narrative writing: SE pages 92, 124–125
- Expository writing: SE pages 148, 180–181
- Persuasive writing: SE pages 204, 234–235
- Response to literature: SE pages 258, 290–291

Suggest that students bookmark these pages when they begin a writing assignment for a particular form of writing. If students lose their focus at any stage in the writing process, the bookmarks will help them easily find these pages. Students can then check their goals or read trait descriptions to get back on track.

A Special Note About the Traits

Before students write their paragraph for the **Exercise**, have them work together to generate a list of topics suitable for a brief comparison. Then review the basics of **writing a paragraph** *(see below)*. When students have finished writing their paragraph, invite them to share their work with the class. Have them explain when and how they used the traits to plan and write their paragraph.

Teaching Tip: Writing a Paragraph

Remind students that a paragraph has three main parts: a topic sentence, body sentences, and a closing sentence. In a comparison paragraph,

- the topic sentence introduces the two people, places, or things and identifies a point of comparison between them,

- the body sentences support the point of comparison, and
- the closing sentence completes the comparison.

✱ For more on planning and writing a comparison paragraph, see SE pages 146–147.

Revising and Editing with a Rubric

Invite volunteers to read aloud each of the steps for rating a piece of writing. Tell students that most of their writing will probably fall between the 5 and 3 ratings.

Although it will be obvious to most students, point out that the rubric applies to an essay, but for the **Try It!** activity, they are rating a brief paragraph. They should keep this in mind when determining their rating.

Try It!
Answers

Possible Answer

Students may give the paragraph a 4. It shows three similarities and one important difference. Adding more details that show differences could improve the rating to 5.

Revising and Editing with a Rubric

6 My essay shows strong similarities between the two people and is full of surprising contrasts.

5 My essay shows the similarities and differences between the two people.

4 My essay shows how the two people are similar, but it could use more details showing differences.

In this book, the pages that deal with revising and editing begin with a rubric strip. Each strip focuses on one trait of writing and will help you improve your first draft. The strip on these two pages focuses on the *ideas* for an expository comparison essay.

How can rubric strips help me assess my writing?

A rubric strip can help you look objectively at your writing. Follow these steps as you use the rubric strip to consider each trait:

1. Begin by reading over the number 5 description (a rating of strong).
2. Decide if your writing rates a 5 for that trait.
3. If not, check the 6 or 4 descriptions.
4. Continue until you find the rating that most closely matches your writing.
5. Notice how levels 4, 3, 2, and 1 offer suggestions on how you can improve your writing.

> *George H. W. Bush* and *George W. Bush* have a lot in common beyond family and presidential ties. Both men followed two-term presidents into office, and both confronted Saddam Hussein. Each president waged a war in the Middle East. The outcome of their work was quite different. While the first President Bush presided over a brief war, the second President Bush captured Hussein but had to deal with a much more extended fight afterward. That's one other great difference between the two men.

Try It!

Review the expository paragraph above. Then rate it for ideas using the strip at the top of these two pages as a guide. Give reasons for your rating.

3 I need more details that show the similarities and differences between the two people.

2 I need to address the similarities and differences between the two people.

1 I need to understand how to compare and contrast two people.

How can rubric strips help me revise and edit?

Once you have rated your writing for a given trait, you will see ways to improve your score. The writer of the paragraph on page **66** gave his ideas a score of 4, meaning that the writing meets *most* of the requirements for the trait. The score description told him just what he needed to do to improve his work: include "more details showing differences." (Scores of 4 or lower offer suggestions for improving your writing.)

In the main writing units, each rubric strip is followed by brief lessons that will help you revise or edit your writing to improve that trait. There are separate rubric strips and lessons for each trait—ideas, organization, voice, word choice, sentence fluency, and conventions.

Making Changes

The writer decided to add another detail and a surprising contrast to finish in a more dramatic way. He made the following changes.

Ideas
Added details help make the contrast clearer.

A new closing sentence strengthens the paragraph.

> . . . The outcome of their work ,though, was quite different. While the first President Bush presided over a brief war that failed to capture Hussein, the second President Bush captured Hussein but had to deal with a much more extended fight afterward. That's one other great difference between the two men. The legacy of H. W. is clear, but the legacy of W. is still being written.

 Revise your paragraph for ideas. Revise the paragraph you wrote on **page 65**, using the strip on these two pages as a guide.

Ask students to compare the rating they gave to the paragraph on SE page 66 to the rating the writer gave it. Have them also compare and discuss the reasons for each rating.

Give students a few minutes to skim SE pages 164–173 and 176–177 to help them focus on ways to address or improve the individual traits during revising and editing.

Before students revise the paragraphs that they wrote on SE page 65, suggest that they use the numbered steps on SE page 66 to rate their paragraphs. Then have them exchange paragraphs and ratings with a partner to see if the partner agrees with the rating. If partners disagree, they can provide their own ratings and give reasons for them.

Assessing with a Rubric

Students can make their own assessment sheet, or you can distribute photocopies of the reproducible Assessment Sheet on TE page 766.

Be sure students have a chance to examine the sample assessment sheet on SE page 71 before they attempt to complete one themselves. Encourage them to ask questions about anything they don't understand.

Assessing with a Rubric

Follow these four steps when you use a rubric (see pages **70–71**) to assess a piece of writing.

1. **Create an assessment sheet.** On your own paper, write each of the key traits from the rubric, preceded by a short line. Under each trait, leave two or three lines to allow for comments.

2. **Read the final copy.** First, get an overall feeling for the writing. Then read more carefully, paying attention to each trait.

3. **Assess the writing.** Use the rubric to rate each trait. First, check the level-5 rubric description and then go up or down the scale until you find the correct rating. Write the score next to the trait on your assessment sheet.

4. **Provide comments.** Under each trait, make whatever comments would be helpful for improving the writing.

Response Sheet   Title: _____

_____ Ideas

_____ Organization

_____ Voice

_____ Word Choice

_____ Sentence Fluency

_____ Conventions

Evaluator: _____

Exercise

Assess your expository paragraph. Make an assessment sheet like the one above. Evaluate your paragraph using the rubric on pages **180–181**. For each trait, write a comment about something you did well and something you'd like to improve. (See the sample on page **71**.)

Struggling Learners

Have students orally complete the self-assessment of their expository paragraph. They can work in pairs or in small groups, using the rubric. As students talk about their writing, they will discover strengths and weaknesses and find ideas for revision.

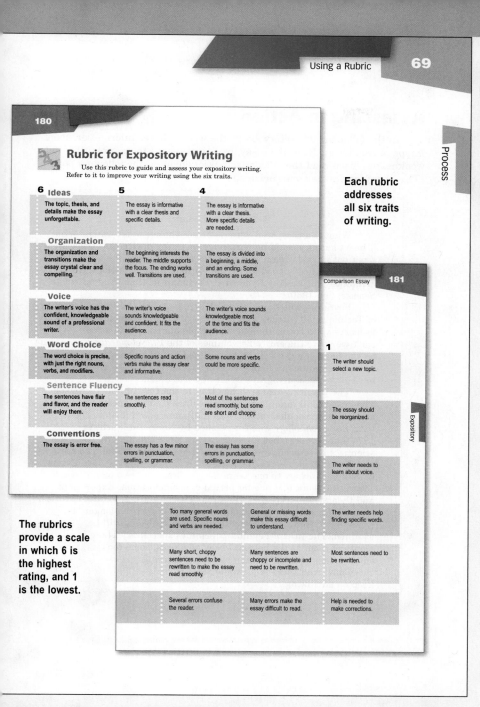

Each rubric addresses all six traits of writing.

The rubrics provide a scale in which 6 is the highest rating, and 1 is the lowest.

Ask if students have any questions about the arrangement, purpose, and practical application of the rubric. Depending on the level of questions students have, you can do a quick review or a more extensive review of the elements of a rubric.

✱ The complete six-point rubric for expository writing is found on SE pages 180–181. Reproducible six-, five-, and four-point rubrics for expository writing are available on TE pages 768, 772, and 776.

Assessing in Action

Have students work independently to read and assess the essay "A Shrinking Dream." Photocopy the reproducible Assessment Sheet on TE page 766 if you wish. Tell students not to look at the sample self-assessment on SE page 71 until after they have read the essay and jotted down their own ratings for each trait and their reasons for the ratings. Tell students to use the Rubric for Expository Writing on SE pages 180–181 to determine their ratings.

Assessing in Action

In the following expository essay, the writer shares information about a type of technology. Read the essay, paying attention to its strengths and weaknesses. Then read the student self-assessment on the following page. **(The essay contains some errors.)**

A Shrinking Dream

What if a computer were no bigger than a wrist-watch? What if heart surgery could be performed by a tiny device that travels a patient's bloodstream and operates from within? These are just two possibilities opened up by the world of nanotechnology, a world brilliantly initiated by Richard P. Feynman in 1959 (*Engineering & Science*, Feb 1960).

Feynman was speaking to physicists at the California Institute of Technology (Caltech), and he put forth a challenge of historical proportions to them. He had one simple question, and asked: "Why can't we write the entire 24 volumes of the *Encyclopaedia Britannica* on the head of a pin?" Then he outlined a world where wires might be only ten atoms in diameter, where a letter could be encoded on a metal cube measuring five by five by five atoms!

The resulting research has lead to the field of nanotechnology. The design and manufacture of machines that are measured in atoms and molecules rather than millimeters and inches. The term *nanotechnology* was first coined by Norio Taniguchi in 1974 (nanodot.org), but in all the years since the historic speech, scientists have been working to bring Feynman's dream into reality.

In 2006, the Foresight Institute awarded the Feynman Prizes in Nanotechnology to one team for the first time two prizes, one for theoretical work and one for actual experimentation. Experiment and theory are meeting in research. Theories are becoming realities.

Feynman's question about nanotechnology is no longer "Is it possible?" Now, we are wondering when his goals will be attained. The title of Feynman's seminal speech is: "There is plenty of room at the bottom." New advances, some too small to see with the human eye, are occurring every day! And there is plenty of room to keep on shrinking.

English Language Learners

Define the following words before reading the essay:

- device (object)
- initiated (started)
- proportions (size)
- outlined (described)
- manufacture (process of building)
- coined (said, used)
- theoretical (thought about)
- attained (reached)
- seminal (influential)

Process

Sample Self-Assessment

The student who wrote "A Shrinking Dream" created the following assessment sheet to evaluate her essay. She used the expository rubric on pages **180–181** as her assessment guide. Under each trait, she wrote comments about the strengths and weaknesses of her writing.

> **Response Sheet**   **Title:** _A Shrinking Dream_
>
> **4 Ideas**
>   The topic seems interesting.
>   A clearly stated thesis is needed.
>
> **3 Organization**
>   My essay follows my plan.
>   The middle part needs much more development.
>
> **4 Voice**
>   I sound interested.
>   I could have learned more about the topic.
>
> **4 Word Choice**
>   My words are accurate.
>   I could have used more specific verbs.
>
> **4 Sentence Fluency**
>   I used different sentence structures.
>   Some of my sentences are too long, and there is
>   one fragment.
>
> **5 Conventions**
>   I caught many errors.
>   I used "lead" instead of "led" in one sentence.
>
>   **Evaluator:** _Katrina_

Exercise

Review the assessment. On your own paper, explain why you agree with the responses above (or why you don't). Consider each trait carefully.

Sample Self-Assessment

As students write their review of the self-assessment, tell them to refer to the ratings and the reasons they jotted down when they read the essay.

Have students share their reviews with the class so that you can evaluate how well students understand the purpose of rubrics and self-assessments.

Assessing an Expository Essay

Note: In each core unit (narrative, expository, persuasive, and response to literature) there are two additional writing samples that teachers can use with students for further assessment practice (TE pages 783–814). A reproducible, blank assessment sheet, based on the traits of writing, and genre-specific rubric checklists allow you and students to rate the writing samples. Finally, a completed rubric checklist and comments sheet are provided to guide you through the assessment.

Assessing an Expository Essay

Read the essay below, focusing on its strengths and weaknesses. Then follow the directions at the bottom of the page. **(The essay contains errors.)**

H. G. Wells: A Science Fiction Original

Herbert George Wells was born in 1866. His books are still read today. Although he wrote many books between 1895 and 1946, he is best remembered for four science fiction novels he wrote during the late 1890s. (*Britannica*, v12, 574).

The Time Machine was published in 1895. The novel was an imaginative story about a man who wished to travel to the past, but instead went nearly a million years into the future! He found a peaceful society but learned that there was still evil and suffering. Like all of Wells works, the book makes a statement about his world, as well as his imaginary world.

The Island of Dr. Moreau in 1896 was also popular. Wells wrote about a mad scientist trying to make creatures better than humans. It is a classic story of a man trying to play God and failing.

Next, in 1897, came *The Invisible Man*. It is Wells' "scientific romance" about a scientist who discovers a potion that makes him disappear. He uses it to terrify the people of Sussex, England.

Wells' preceding books were overshadowed in 1898 with *The War of the Worlds*. It was the first popular story about an alien invasion of Earth. The book is full of action and horror, though it ends with hope. It has left a storytelling legacy that continues up to the modern day, as well as a genre of "little green men" alien invasion stories (*War*, xii).

After witnessing two world wars and many personal difficulties, Herbert George Wells became pessimistic about the future of humankind. But these four books are still popular, and his stories are still being retold. It is a legacy that any author would be proud to enjoy.

Exercise

Use an expository rubric. Assess this expository essay, using the rubric on pages **180–181** as your guide. To get started, create an assessment sheet like the one on page **68**. *Remember:* After each trait, try to write one comment about a strength and one about a weakness.

73

Publishing Your Writing

When you first learn to play an instrument, you're not ready for an audience. You're unsure of yourself and make too many mistakes. However, once you become more skilled, you'll be ready to share your talent with others.

The same is true of writing. Some of it is not ready for an audience, especially your personal writing. However, the essays and stories that you develop are meant to be shared. Publishing makes all that hard work worth the effort.

Publishing your writing can be as simple as reading it to a friend or classmate or as complex as submitting it to a literary magazine. In any form, publishing is a very important step in the writing process. It helps you see how well you are doing. The purpose of this chapter is to help you with all of your publishing needs—from preparing a piece for publication to launching your own Web site.

- ■ **Preparing to Publish**
- ■ **Publishing Ideas**
- ■ **Designing Your Writing**
- ■ **Publishing Online**
- ■ **Creating Your Own Web Site**
- ■ **Finding Places to Publish**

"You learn ways to improve your writing by seeing its effect on others."

—Tom Liner

Publishing Your Writing

Objectives
- explore a variety of publishing options
- learn how to format and design writing for publication
- demonstrate an understanding of how to publish online
- plan a Web site

Reassure students that they are not expected to have their writing published in a professional publication. Of course, students always have the option of submitting a piece of writing to a magazine, newspaper, or book publisher. However, throughout this text, the term *publishing* simply means "sharing the final copy of a piece of writing with an audience."

Tell students that their audience will usually be their teacher and their classmates. In some cases, they may choose to share their writing with a wider audience, including family members, the general school population, and the community.

Materials

A variety of current magazines
(TE page 76)

Preparing to Publish

If more than one editor reviews students' writing for content and conventions, have each editor use a different color for marking revisions, errors, and making comments. Then, if students have a question about any of the marks or comments, the color coding will identify the editor.

Most students are eager to get to the publishing stage in the writing process. Others, however, may be reluctant to give up a piece of writing because they want to keep trying to make it better. This won't be a common problem because assignment deadlines usually are not arbitrary. However, if the problem does arise, encourage students to follow all the tips to prepare their writing for publication. Then have them choose a reasonable date on which their writing will be finished and ready to be shared.

Preparing to Publish

Your writing is not ready to share until you have taken it through all the steps in the writing process. The tips below will help you prepare your writing for publication.

Publishing Tips

- **Take advantage of peer-response sessions.**
  Make sure that you have addressed the important concerns identified by your classmates.
- **Check for the traits of writing.** (See pages **39–54**.)
  The ideas, organization, voice, word choice, sentence fluency, and conventions in your writing are all important.
- **Put forth your best effort.**
  Continue working until you feel good about your writing from start to finish.
- **Save all drafts for each writing project.**
  Then you will be able to double-check the changes you have made.
- **Seek editing help.**
  Ask at least one trusted editor to check your work for conventions. Another person may spot errors that you miss.
- **Prepare a neat final copy.**
  Use a pen (blue or black ink) and one side of the paper if you are writing by hand. Select a typestyle that is easy to read if you are using a computer. (Always use a computer when you submit your writing to outside publishers.)
- **Consider different publishing options.**
  There are many ways to publish writing. (See page **75**.)
- **Follow all publishing guidelines.**
  Each publisher has certain requirements for publishing. Be sure to follow their directions exactly.

Try It!

Prepare to publish. Select a piece of writing that you would like to publish. Review the tips listed above. Is there anything more to do before the writing is truly ready to publish?

"I tend to do as much revising as editors will let me do."
—Tom Wolfe

English Language Learners

If possible, allow students to publish pieces for class even if they do not correct all spelling and grammar. Some students may be motivated by being able to show their work to others, but others might resist if they have to edit for language concepts that they haven't yet mastered. A more appealing option for these students may be to read their work aloud.

Publishing Ideas

The simplest way to publish your writing is to share it with a friend or classmate. Other publishing ideas, such as entering a writing contest, take more time and effort. Try a number of these publishing ideas during the school year. All of them will help you grow as a writer.

Self-Publishing
- Newsletter
- Greeting Cards
- Personal Book
- Web Site
- Blog (Web Log)

Performing
- Sharing with Classmates
- Reading to Other Audiences
- Multimedia Presentation
- Open-Mic Night

Sending It Out
- Local Newspaper
- Magazines
- Web Sites or E-zines
- Writing Contests
- Young Writers' Conferences

Sharing in School
- Literary Magazine
- Writing Portfolio
- Classroom Collection
- School Newspaper/Yearbook

Posting
- Bulletin Boards
- Display Cases
- Business Windows
- Literary/Art Fairs

 Plan your publishing. What types of publishing have you tried in the past? In what way would you like to publish the piece of writing that you identified on page 74? Why? How else would you like to publish? Explain.

Publishing Ideas

Early in the year, work with students to establish a regularly scheduled forum for students to share their writing. For example, they may decide that every first Wednesday of the month they will decorate a space in the school to resemble a coffeehouse, where students can read their own stories, articles, and poems, accompanied, if they like, by music of their choosing. Students can open the forum to just their classmates or to the entire school.

Designing Your Writing

To prevent students from choosing inappropriate fonts, prepare and distribute a list of acceptable fonts that they can use in their final designs.

At first, limit the number of graphic elements, and remind students to use only those that help explain their ideas.

✱ For more about adding graphics to writing, see SE pages 602–603.

Have a variety of current magazines on hand for students to use to complete the **Try It!** activity.

Designing Your Writing

Always focus first on the content of your writing. Then consider its design, or appearance. For most types of publishing, you'll want to use a computer for your final copy. These guidelines will help you to design your writing.

Selecting an Appropriate Font

- **Choose an easy-to-read font.** In most cases, a serif typestyle is best for the text, and a sans serif style works for any headings.
  > The letters of **serif** fonts have "tails"—as in this sentence.
  > The letters of **sans serif** fonts are plain, without tails—as in this sentence.
- **Include a title and headings.** Use the title to introduce your paper and use headings to guide the reader through the text. Headings break a long report into readable parts.

Using Consistent Spacing and Margins

- **Set clear margins.** Use a one-inch margin (top, bottom, left, and right).
- **Indent paragraphs.** Use a half-inch indent.
- **Use one space after every period.** This will improve the readability of your paper.
- **Avoid awkward breaks.** Don't leave a heading or the first line of a paragraph at the bottom of a page or a column. Never split a hyphenated word between pages or columns.

Including Graphic Elements

- **Use lists if appropriate.** Use numbered lists if your points have a clear number order. Otherwise, use bulleted lists (like the ones on this page).
- **Include graphics.** Use tables, charts, or illustrations to help make a point. Keep graphics small within the text. If a graphic needs to be large, display it on its own page.

Try It!

Working with a partner, compare the design features of articles from two different magazines. How are the design features the same? How are they different? Decide which design is the most effective, based on the magazine's audience and purpose.

Effective Design in Action

The following two pages show a well-designed student essay. The side notes explain the design features.

Process

Ilse Haraldson
Ms. Serapio
General Science
January 28, 2011

Secrets of the Moon Illusion

Why is it that the moon looks larger on the horizon than overhead? People have pondered this question for thousands of years. Scholars from Greece and China posed the question as early as the 7th century B.C.E. Aristotle wrote about it in 350 B.C.E, and the Arab scientist Ibn Alhazan studied the problem around 1000 C.E. Many explanations have been offered for this "moon illusion," but none have yet proved true.

Refraction Hypothesis

The earth's atmosphere distorts light and makes the day sky look blue and the night stars seem to twinkle. When the moon is low on the horizon, its color is darkened and it seems flattened. Does the atmosphere swell the moon's image? No. Measuring the moon's image with a bent paperclip held at arm's length proves this. This measurement can be taken when the moon is low and high, and its image remains the same size.

Context Cues Hypothesis

Another explanation for the moon illusion involves context. When the moon is overhead, there is nothing for comparison; but when it is on the horizon, buildings and trees make it seem larger. However, pilots in flight, with no context cues, see the moon illusion. If a person bends over and looks with his or her head upside down, the moon on the horizon no longer looks bigger. So context cues don't explain this.

Flattened-Sky-Dome Hypothesis

Some scholars think that the moon illusion happens because people view the sky as a flattened dome. (See diagram.) They say this makes the moon seem closer overhead, so the brain adjusts to make it look smaller. This seems logical in a diagram,

> The title is 18-point sans serif type, centered.

> Centered subheadings (14-point sans serif type) identify main sections.

> The body text is 12-point serif type, double-spaced.

Effective Design in Action

Have students read the essay through once to understand the content. Suggest that they ignore the side notes in their first reading. When students have finished reading the essay, ask the following questions to help them evaluate the effectiveness of the design.

- What is the topic of the essay? (the moon illusion, which makes the moon look larger on the horizon than overhead)
- How does the design of the essay help you predict what the essay will be about and what it will explain? (The title identifies the topic. The subheadings indicate specific points related to the topic. The graphic illustrates one of those points.)
- In your opinion, does the design make the essay easy to read? Why or why not? (Most students will agree that breaking the text into chunks with separate subheadings makes the ideas in the essay easy to follow. The use of the graphic also clarifies an idea explained in the text and makes the essay visually appealing.)

Give students time to look through past writing assignments to find an essay or report suitable for the **Try It!** activity at the bottom of the page. Encourage students to select an essay or report that they are proud of and that they enjoyed writing. Their pride and enthusiasm should carry over and inspire them to create an effective design for it.

Explain that students should create a design that complements the tone and topic of the essay or report. For example, a report on the history of roller coasters might have a less formal design than an essay on the causes of the Civil War.

78

Haraldson 2

but it doesn't make sense. If the moon seems closer overhead, it should look bigger—not smaller.

Complex Human Vision

Experts who study vision say many things could contribute to the moon illusion:

A graphic helps to clarify an idea and adds visual appeal.

A bulleted list helps the reader digest related information.

- **Focal distance:** Depth of focus changes the apparent size of objects. When the moon is on the horizon, people focus at maximum stereoscopic distance (50–100 feet); when it is overhead, they focus at resting distance (3–6 feet).
- **Linear and angular size:** Seen through a window, a mountain looks both bigger (linear size) and smaller (angular size) than the window. The eyes and brain together decipher these two perspectives and judge size and distance of that mountain—and of the moon.

Moon Sky Dome

Apparent Sky Dome

Horizon Observer

Sky Dome

- **Visual orientation:** People see things better up close and on the same level than far away and high or low. People's sense of balance affects their vision, which is why the moon illusion disappears when looking upside down.
- **Age:** The moon illusion decreases with age, as the brain acquires more experience in judging size and distance.

Obviously, the reasons for the moon illusion are not simple. This subject continues to fascinate scholars and probably will for years to come.

Try It!

Design a page. Create an effective design for an essay or a report you've written. Then share that design with a classmate. Does the design appeal to the reader's eye? Is it clear and easy to follow? Does it distract the reader in any way?

Publishing Your Writing 79

Process

Publishing Online

The Internet offers many publishing opportunities, including online magazines and writing contests. The information below will help you submit your writing for publication on the Net. (At home, always get a parent's approval first. In school, follow all guidelines established by the administration.)

Checking Local Sites

Ask your teacher whether your school has a Web site where students can post work. Also check with local student organizations to see if any of them have Web sites that accept submissions.

Finding Other Sites

Use a search engine to find sites that publish student work. Pay special attention to online magazines for young adults. If you don't have any luck with getting published, consider creating your own Web site. (See pages 80–81.)

Submitting Your Work

Once you find online sites where you would like to submit your work, carefully follow these tips.

- **Understand the publishing guidelines for each site.** Be sure to share this information with your teacher and your parents.
- **Send your writing in the correct form.** Some sites have online forms. Others will ask you to send your writing by mail or e-mail. Always explain why you are sending your writing.
- **Provide contact information.** Don't give your home address or any other personal information unless your parents approve.
- **Be patient.** Within a week or so of your submission, you should receive a note from the publisher verifying that your work has been received. However, it may take many weeks for the publisher to make a decision about publishing it.

Try It!

Surf the Net. Look for Web sites that accept student submissions for publication. List two or three possibilities. Print out the submissions guidelines for each one.

Publishing Online

Make sure students are aware of school policy regarding Internet use. If the school has a printed copy of the policy, make it required reading for all students early in the year.

Encourage interested students to work together to generate a list of Web site addresses of online magazines that publish young adult writers. This can complement the list of print sources provided on SE page 82. Take time to review the students' list for appropriateness before displaying the addresses in the classroom or distributing it to students.

Make it a habit, when reviewing student writing, to write a note to the student when you think a piece of writing is worthy of submission for a writing contest or to an online publication.

Creating Your Own Web Site

Consider working together as a class to create a class Web site. If the class already has a Web site, design pages to link to the home page.

If you do not feel that you have the expertise to guide students in all the stages of Web site design, ask for assistance from the computer technology person on the school staff or from an older student or parent with Web design knowledge and experience.

Creating Your Own Web Site

To create a Web site on your home computer, check with your Internet service provider to find out how to get started. If you are using a school computer, ask your teacher for help. Then follow these steps.

Planning Your Site

Begin by answering the following questions:
- What will be the purpose of this Web site?
- How are my favorite sites set up?
- How many pages will I include?
- How will my pages be linked together?

Creating the Pages

First plan your pages by sketching them out. Then create each page as a text file. Most word-processing programs let you save a file as a Web page. If yours doesn't, you will have to add hypertext markup language (HTML) codes to format the text and make links to graphics and other pages. You can find instructions about HTML on the Net or check out an HTML book from the library to help you master the basics.

Testing Your Pages

Use your browser to open your first page. Then follow any links to make sure they work correctly. Finally, be sure that all the pages look the way that you want them to look.

Uploading the Site

Ask your Internet provider how to upload your finished pages. (If you're working at home, make sure to get your parents' approval first. If you're using school equipment, work with a teacher.) When you complete this step, visit your site to make sure it still works.

Publicizing the Site

Once your site is up, e-mail your friends and tell them to visit it. Ask visitors to your site to spread the word to other people they know.

 Try It!

If you're interested in creating a personal Web site, plan your site. Then sketch out your pages.

Designing a Home Page

This home page includes links to the student's art, his blog site, and his best writing. It also gives information about one of his favorite hobbies—skateboarding.

Sample Home Page

Process

DJ's Skateboarding Site

DJ's Home Page
* * * * * * * * * * * * * * * * * * *

My Original Art   My Blog   My Best Writing

Skateboarding is one of my favorite activities. I am always working on some new tricks!

A little background on skateboarding . . .

With the evolution of skateboard parks (or skateparks) and ramp riding, the skateboard began to change. Originally, skateboarders did two-dimensional tricks like these:

- Riding on only the front wheels (nose manual)
- Spinning like an ice-skater on the back wheels (a 360)
- High-jumping over a bar
- Long-jumping from one board to another

Around 1978 or so, street riding became transformed by the invention of the "ollie," the first modern skateboarding trick.

Useful skateboarding links
* * * * * * * * * * * * * * * *

The Board Room
Skateboards and Skate Gear
The Science of Skateboarding
KDT

Links to other sites I like
* * * * * * * * * * * * * * * *

ArtByU.com
CompGaming
Fab Fotos
Krintzbel's Home Page

Sample Home Page

Ask students to study the sample home page, and have them tell what they like about it and what they would change.

If necessary, explain that the word *blog* is a shortened form of *Weblog*. A Weblog is similar to a personal journal. It is written by the person who is the author of the Web site, is updated regularly, and is posted online for anyone who visits the Web site to read.

Finding Places to Publish

Consider establishing a regular Submissions Day every month, when students can plan to submit a piece of writing for publication. Having a specific date to work toward and knowing that other students are willing to take the risk might encourage reluctant students to submit their work. Students can also do the following:

- help each other create letters to submit to the publisher, along with the piece of writing
- review each other's work to make sure it is ready for submission
- support each other through the process

Finding Places to Publish

The suggestions below will help you research places you can publish your writing. Before you submit writing anywhere, however, be sure you understand the conditions of the publication and share this information with your parents.

School Days

If you have written about a topic that interests or affects others in your age group, school publications provide some good publishing options. Your school's newspaper is a good choice for expository or persuasive writing about school-related topics. A student literary magazine or journal offers publishing opportunities for a variety of writing forms, but especially for narrative writing, literary criticism, and poetry. There may even be a page for student writing on your school's Web site. If there isn't, perhaps you should be the one to start it!

Your Own Backyard

The people in a community generally share some interests or background— that's what brought them together as a community in the first place. As a result, ideas that draw your attention may also appeal to your community as a whole. You may find that local publications, such as a local newspaper or neighborhood newsletter, are interested in publishing your writing.

Explore the Possibilities

If you have a favorite national or regional magazine, it may accept writing from outside writers on certain topics. There are also writing contests that accept submissions; many of these contests are even geared toward young writers. A librarian can help you research the possibilities. You can also look in *Writer's Market*—available in most libraries—for more places to publish.

Thanks to modern technology, there are publishing options such as blogs that were not available in the past. By posting comments, readers can interact with other writers on a blog. Additionally, authors—including best-selling authors—have self-published their work for many years, but advances in technology have opened up many new possibilities. Enter "self publishing" into a search engine to investigate whether it has potential for you as a writer.

Tip

Before submitting your work to a publication, check the submission guidelines to be sure your writing is in an acceptable form and style. Include a self-addressed stamped envelope when submitting your work to help ensure that you receive a response, as well as your returned work if it is not published.

Creating a Portfolio

A **writing portfolio** is a collection of your work that shows your skill as a writer. In most cases, you will be asked to compile a *showcase portfolio*—a collection of your best writing for a school term. Compiling a portfolio gets you involved in the assessment process. You decide which writing to include; you decide how to present your work; and you reflect on your writing progress. In short, compiling a portfolio puts you in control.

A writing portfolio is like a photo album. Instead of showing just one picture of you as a writer, a portfolio shows a series of pictures at different points in your development as a writer. An album of your writing gives a very clear picture of your writing abilities.

- ■ **Understanding Portfolios**
- ■ **Parts of a Portfolio**
- ■ **Creating a Cover Sheet**
- ■ **Completing an Evaluation Checklist**

"It's not what a piece of writing is about, but how it's written, that makes good writing good."
—Katie Wood Ray

Creating a Portfolio

Objectives
- demonstrate an understanding of the types of portfolios
- demonstrate an understanding of the parts of portfolios

If you plan to use portfolios, be sure to tell students
- ■ what they are expected to have in their portfolios for each review and
- ■ the dates and times that individual reviews will take place.

Plan to stagger the review dates so that you are not overwhelmed with too many portfolios.

Understanding Portfolios

Ask students to reflect on their progress regularly using a form of the reflection sheet on SE page 32. In the beginning of the year, you can help students evaluate their progress based on your comments and feedback from their reviewers.

Consider placing a file cabinet in the classroom specifically for student portfolios. This will give students a safe place to store their work.

Understanding Portfolios

There are four basic types of writing portfolios: a *showcase portfolio,* a *growth portfolio,* a *personal portfolio,* and an *electronic portfolio.*

A **growth portfolio** shows your progress as a writer. It contains writing assignments that show how your skills are developing.

A **showcase portfolio** presents the best writing you have done during a term. This type of portfolio is used for evaluation.

An **electronic portfolio** is any type of portfolio available online or on digital media. It often includes writing, graphics, video, and sound.

A **personal portfolio** contains writing you want to keep and share with others. Many writers and artists keep personal portfolios arranged according to themes, styles of writing, and so on.

Creating a Portfolio

Use these tips as a guide when you develop a writing portfolio. Also make sure to follow your teacher's instructions.

Tip

- **Know what is expected of you.** Make sure that you understand all of the requirements for your portfolio.

- **Keep track of all your work.** Save all your prewriting notes, rough drafts, and revisions for each writing project. Then you will have everything you need when compiling your portfolio.

- **Store your papers in a safe place.** Reserve a special folder to keep all of your work.

- **Set a reasonable schedule for creating your portfolio.** You can't put together an effective portfolio by waiting until the last minute.

- **Take pride in your work.** Make sure that your portfolio shows you at your best.

English Language Learners

If students are required to keep a growth portfolio, add a special writing skills checklist to it. The checklist should be developed for each student individually, based on his or her level. When students check off a skill they have mastered, ask them to refer to an example of the skill used correctly in one or more pieces of their writing. In addition to showcasing their successes, this checklist can be shown to parents during conferences.

Process

Parts of a Portfolio

Most showcase portfolios contain the following parts. (Before creating your portfolio, though, make sure to check with your teacher for specific requirements.)

- A **table of contents** lists the material included in your portfolio.
- A **brief essay or letter** introduces your portfolio, telling how you put it together, how you feel about it, and what it means to you.
- A **collection of writing samples** presents your best work. (Your teacher may require that you include all of your planning, drafting, and revising for one or more of your writings.)
- A **cover sheet** for each sample explains why you selected it.
- **Evaluations, reflections, or checklists** identify the skills you have mastered, as well as the skills that you still need to work on.

Writing Your Opening Pages

The first two pages of a showcase portfolio are shown here.

Table of Contents

Opening Letter

Dear Ms. Keller,

    I was surprised at how much I wrote this semester. My goal for this class was to keep up with my assignments, and I met that goal. I enjoyed choosing my own topics. It was easier to get to work on my writing and not put it off like I did before. I'm glad I took this class, and I've chosen my best work for my showcase portfolio.

    My first piece is my personal narrative about sledding when I was little. I usually don't like to write personal narratives, but I honestly liked this one. All the prewriting helped for that assignment. (I included my life map and list of memories from early childhood with my rough draft.) Comparing my rough draft to my final copy, I can see that I added a lot of sensory details about the snow and how my breath came out in little crystal puffs. I think I finally understand what "show, don't tell" means.

    I also included my persuasive essay because I have a definite opinion about whether or not only athletes should earn letters. I could tell that it was a good topic because it sparked so much discussion in our writing workshop.

    My favorite piece in this portfolio is the expository essay I wrote comparing and contrasting Sylvia Plath and Virginia Woolf. When I started writing, I didn't know much about these writers except that they were women. As I found out more about them, though, I got excited about being a writer myself. I found out I wasn't just comparing them to each other, but comparing them to me.

    In the future, I'd like to focus on my word choice and vocabulary. I'll be reading my favorite authors this summer to inspire me.

    Have a great summer, and I'll see you next year.

Sincerely,
Justine Grady

Try It!

Imagine that you are putting together a showcase portfolio. Think of two pieces of writing that you would include in it. In a brief paragraph, explain the reasons for your choices.

Parts of a Portfolio

If you have already established criteria for student portfolios, review that criteria now and make sure students understand exactly what is expected of them.

Provide additional samples of portfolio introductory letters for students to use as examples when preparing their introductory letters. Remind students to apply the traits of writing (ideas, organization, voice, word choice, sentence fluency, and conventions) to their portfolio opening letter and to their cover sheet.

Creating a Cover Sheet

Before students write a sample cover sheet for the **Try It!** activity, encourage them to review the items listed below for their piece of writing. Reviewing these materials can help them recall the writing experience and give them greater insight into why they feel the way they do about the piece of writing.

- all prewriting materials, including notes, gathering grids, outlines, and other graphic organizers
- first draft and revisions
- reflection sheets
- peer-responding sheets
- self-assessment sheets
- teacher assessments

86

Creating a Cover Sheet

For a showcase portfolio, it's common to attach a cover sheet to each writing project in your portfolio. (See the cover sheet below written for a student essay comparing Sylvia Plath and Virginia Woolf.) Your cover sheet should do one or more of the following things:

- Explain why you chose the piece for your portfolio.
- Tell about the process of writing you used, including any problems that you faced.
- Describe the strong points and the weak points in the writing.
- Reflect on the writing's importance to you.

Sample Cover Sheet

Our assignment was to compare two writers. I read short biographies of several writers, and was surprised by the similarities between Sylvia Plath and Virginia Woolf. They were interesting, and I thought it would be fun to see just how much they were alike.

When I began, I thought it would be easy to compare the two. But I found it was a lot tougher to come up with important ways they were different. I also had some trouble setting up the paper. I actually wrote two first drafts, setting up the information in two different ways, before I could decide what the final format should be.

I think my strongest point in this paper is my voice. As I did my research, I found that both writers were really brilliant but sad people, and I felt really sorry for them. I think my feelings showed in my writing, and that helped make the subjects seem more real, both to me and to the reader. My weakest point was probably my organization. Sometimes my details seemed out of place, even after I rearranged them.

I always thought that a writer was a writer, and gender didn't matter, so I was really surprised to learn how hard it used to be for a woman to be a writer. I also learned how hard it was just to be a writer, period.

Try It!

Write a sample cover sheet for a piece of writing that you would like to include in a portfolio.

Completing an Evaluation Checklist

In a portfolio, it's also common to include a final evaluation checklist in which you review your strengths, weaknesses, and progress as a writer.

Sample Evaluation

The evaluation checklist below covers one student's progress as a writer.

Process

Evaluation

Writer: _Justine Grady_   Class & Term: _English/2_

Skills Mastered:
1. I finally figured out how to use a cluster to find a topic.
2. I now write a first draft without making it perfect right away. My writing sounds more like me from the start!
3. I learned to read my writing backward, one sentence at a time, to edit for spelling and punctuation.

Skills to Work On:
1. I have to be careful when I'm collecting my details. I still tend to put too much information in my writing.
2. My introductions and conclusions are still too short. I have to work more on making them interesting.
3. I still have some trouble with transitions. I don't always use the best words to connect my ideas.
4. I don't always use proofreading marks. I should learn them.

Goals:
1. I would like to make my thoughts flow more smoothly.
2. I also want to learn to build longer, more interesting sentences.

Final Thoughts:
1. I think my writing has really improved. I organize my thoughts more effectively.
2. I'm a more careful editor with punctuation.

Try It!

Create a checklist like the one above on your own paper. Then fill it out to evaluate your own progress as a writer.

Completing an Evaluation Checklist

Like the reflection sheet that students learned about on SE page 32, students can also use an evaluation checklist to monitor their progress as a writer. When assigning the **Try It!** activity, suggest that students take the time to look over any past reflection sheets they may have, as well as teacher assessment sheets. Students can use the comments on these sheets to generate ideas for their evaluation checklist.

Narrative Writing Overview

Common Core Standards Focus

Writing 3: Write narratives to develop real or imagined experiences or events using effective technique, well-chosen details, and well-structured event sequences.

Language 2: Demonstrate command of the conventions of standard English capitalization, punctuation, and spelling when writing.

Writing Forms

- narrative paragraph
- personal narrative essay
- biographical narrative essay
- writing for assessment

Focus on the Traits

- **Ideas** Re-creating an experience by using action, sensory details, and dialogue to *show* rather than *tell*
- **Organization** Including a strong beginning that grabs the reader's attention, a middle that is organized chronologically, and an ending that reveals why the event is important to the writer
- **Voice** Creating a consistent narrative voice that sounds natural and that uses dialogue to reveal the speaker's personality
- **Word Choice** Choosing specific words with the appropriate connotation
- **Sentence Fluency** Using long and short sentences that flow smoothly from one idea to the next
- **Conventions** Checking for errors in punctuation, capitalization, spelling, and grammar

WAC: Learning Logs for Earth Science, Geography, Math, Sewing, Art (watercolor)

 Literature Connections

- **"The Rights to the Streets of Memphis"** from *Black Boy* by Richard Wright
- **Chapter 8 of** *Seabiscuit: An American Legend* by Laura Hillenbrand

 Technology Connections

 Write Source Online
www.hmheducation.com/writesource

- *Net-text*
- *Bookshelf*
- *GrammarSnap*
- *Portfolio*
- *Essay Scoring*
- *Writing Network features*
- *File Cabinet*

 Interactive Whiteboard Lessons

Suggested Narrative Writing Unit (Five Weeks)

Day	Writing and Skills Instruction	Student Edition		SkillsBook	Daily Language Workouts	Write Source Online
		Main Pages	Resource Units*			
1–5 (WEEK 1)	**Narrative Warm-Up Paragraph** (Model)	89–91			12–13	*Interactive Whiteboard Lessons*
	Skills Activities: • Nouns		701–703	71, 74		*GrammarSnap*
	• Prepositions		544–545, 732			*GrammarSnap*
	• Commas (in compound sentences and after introductory clauses and phrases)		552, 608–609, 610, 744 (+)	8, 11		*GrammarSnap*
	• Pronouns (classes)		536 (+), 537 (+), 706–707, 708–709	77		*GrammarSnap*

* These units are also located in the back of the *Teacher's Edition*. Resource Units include "Basic Grammar and Writing," "A Writer's Resource," and "Proofreader's Guide."
(+) This activity is located in a different section of the *Write Source Student Edition*. If students have already completed this activity, you may wish to review it at this time.

Day	Writing and Skills Instruction	Student Edition		SkillsBook	Daily Language Workouts	Write Source Online
		Main Pages	Resource Units*			
WEEK 2 6–10	**Narrative Essay** (Model, Prewriting, Writing) Literature Connections "The Rights to the Streets of Memphis" from *Black Boy*	92–106			14–15	*Net-text*
WEEK 3 11–13	(Revising)	107–118			16–17	*Net-text*
	Skills Activities: • Tone (transitive and intransitive verbs)		538, 716–717	98, 99		*GrammarSnap*
	• Verbals (participles, infinitives)		554, 726–727, 742–743	100, 132		*GrammarSnap*
	• Pronouns		536 (+), 537 (+), 704–705, 706 (+), 708 (+), 710 (+)	76, 78, 79, 81, 82		*GrammarSnap*
	• Active vs. Passive Voice		722–723	95		
	• Sentences		552 (+), 553, 750–751			
	Peer Responding	55–60				
14–15	(Editing and Publishing)	119–123				*Net-text, Portfolio*
	Skills Activities: • Punctuating Dialogue		616–617, 632–633	34		
	• Pronoun-Antecedent Agreement		756–757	154		*GrammarSnap*
	• Spelling and Plurals		654–657	51, 52, 53		
WEEK 4 16–17	(Assessing, Reflecting)	124–128			18–19	
18	**Keeping a Learning Log**	408–409				
opt.	*Making Oral Presentations*	393–401				
19–20	**Responding to Narrative Prompts**	137–143				
SECOND FORM WEEK 1 1–5	**Biographical Narrative** (Model, Prewriting, Writing, Revising) Transitions Literature Connections Chapter 8 of *Seabiscuit: An American Legend*	129–135	592–593		20–21	*Net-text*
	Skills Activities: • Conjunctions		546, 547 (+), 734	118		
	• Pronouns Review		536 (+), 537 (+), 704 (+), 706 (+), 708 (+), 710 (+)	83		*GrammarSnap*
	(Editing and Publishing)	136				*Net-text, Portfolio*
	Skills Activities: • End Punctuation		605–607	5		
	• Using the Right Word		678–679, 680–681	58		
	• Pronoun Shifts		708 (+), 710 (+), 756 (+)	181		
	• Commas (appositives, in a series, to separate adjectives)		535 (+), 540 (+), 610–611	9		*GrammarSnap*

* These units are also located in the back of the *Teacher's Edition*. Resource Units include "Basic Grammar and Writing," "A Writer's Resource," and "Proofreader's Guide."
(+) This activity is located in a different section of the *Write Source Student Edition*. If students have already completed this activity, you may wish to review it at this time.

Narrative Writing

This overview for narrative writing includes some specific teaching suggestions for the unit. The description of each chapter will help you decide which parts of the unit to teach.

Writing Focus

Personal Narrative (pages 89–128)

In a personal narrative, students share one specific incident from their past. Good narrative writing has a sense of immediacy to it. The paragraph model in this chapter deals with a challenging personal accomplishment, climbing a steep mountain. The narrative doesn't talk about the experience; it takes the reader on the hike. Other models will lead the students through the process of narrative writing.

Biographical Narrative (pages 129–136)

In this unit, students will focus on an important experience in the life of another person. To do this well, they will need to know their subject, so writers are advised to write about a family member or a friend. Students will use the same pattern they used for writing a personal narrative.

Responding to Narrative Prompts (pages 137–143)

Assessment writing often involves a narrative prompt. Students' responses demonstrate their ability to convincingly plan, organize, write, and convey a life event. A sample response is shown and STRAP questions are introduced to facilitate student responses.

Grammar Focus

For support with this unit's grammar topics, consult the resource units (Basic Grammar and Writing, A Writer's Resource, and Proofreader's Guide).

Academic Vocabulary

Read aloud the academic terms, as well as the descriptions and questions. Model for students how to read one question and answer it. Have partners monitor their understanding and seek clarification of the terms by working through the meanings and questions together.

88

WRITE SOURCE Online
www.hmheducation.com/writesource

Narrative Writing

Writing Focus

Personal Narrative	89
Biographical Narrative	129
Responding to Narrative Prompts	137

Grammar Focus

Punctuating Dialogue	120
Pronoun-Antecedent Agreement	121

Academic Vocabulary

Work with a partner. Read the definitions below and share your answers to the questions that follow.

1. Something that is specific is definite or particular, not general.
   How do specific details help a story seem real?
2. Maintain means to keep something as it is.
   Why is it important to maintain a consistent voice throughout a piece of writing?
3. Something is complex if it is made up of many parts, details, or ideas and may be hard to understand.
   What activities would you describe as complex?
4. Conventions are accepted practices, such as the widely accepted patterns of English grammar, capitalization, punctuation, and spelling.
   What is one punctuation convention that helps a reader understand what you have written?

Minilessons

First I Was Born — Writing a Personal Narrative

■ **CUT** or **TEAR** a sheet of paper into 15–20 thin strips. On each of three or four strips, **WRITE** a sentence about a major accomplishment in your life. On the remaining strips, **WRITE** complete sentences expressing important points about those accomplishments. **ORGANIZE** the strips into outline form on the desk in front of you. **IMAGINE** how you would use the outline to compose your narrative.

Dramatic Scenario — Biographical Narrative

■ **CHOOSE** a famous person from the field of art, music, science, or history (for example, Picasso, Mozart, Einstein, Napoleon). **READ** about that person online or in an encyclopedia or other book. **CHOOSE** an important moment in that person's life. **WRITE** your imagining of that person's thoughts at the crucial moment of a crucial day.

Narrative Writing
Writing a Personal Narrative

A personal narrative re-creates a specific experience or event in your life. This kind of writing invites the reader to experience what you've experienced. So if a reader says, "It all seems so real to me," you'll know you succeeded.

To write an effective narrative, select an experience that you feel strongly about. For this chapter, you will write about a personal accomplishment—making a team, overcoming a fear, volunteering for a good cause. If you include plenty of action, sensory details, and dialogue, your personal story is sure to connect with the reader.

Writing Guidelines

Subject: **A personal accomplishment**
Form: **Personal narrative**
Purpose: **To share an important experience**
Audience: **Classmates**

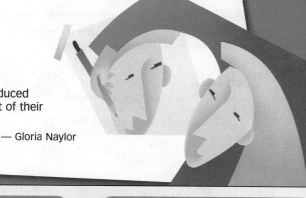

"All writers who have produced anything have done it out of their specific experience."

— Gloria Naylor

Writing a Personal Narrative

Objectives

- understand the purpose, content, and form of a personal narrative
- choose a topic (a personal accomplishment) to write about
- plan, draft, revise, and edit a personal narrative essay

A **personal narrative** tells the story of something that happened to the writer. Discuss the Gloria Naylor quotation at the bottom of the page. Point out that Naylor doesn't mean good writers write *only* about their own experiences. Ask what genres of writing are not based on writers' experiences (science fiction, fantasy, biography).

Ask students how writers' experiences can influence their work.
- Experiences help to determine writers' topics.
- They help writers understand other people's experiences.
- Experiences help writers create vivid descriptions.

Tell students that in this section they will write about their own experiences, in a narrative paragraph and also in an extended personal narrative.

 Technology Connections

Use this unit's Interactive Whiteboard Lesson to introduce narrative writing.

 Interactive Whiteboard Lessons

Copy Masters

Time Line (TE p. 91)

Details Chart (TE pp. 97, 100)

5 W's Chart (TE p. 109)

Assessment Sheet (TE p. 127)

Benchmark Papers

It's a Boy! (good)
⬤ TE pp. 783–787

My Cousin's Wedding (poor)
⬤ TE pp. 788–791

Narrative Writing Warm-Up: Being Selective

Discuss ways of thinking about using details. For example, suggest that choosing details is like using spices in cooking. A cook adds spices to create an interesting taste, but too many spices will overpower the dish. Similarly, a writer who uses too many details will overwhelm the reader. Also, point out that just as different cuisines call for different seasonings, different types of writing call for different levels of detail.

Explain that a writer must achieve a balance, choosing the details that add the following characteristics:

- interest
- clarity
- authenticity

Suggest that students use an assortment of different kinds of details. Using a mixture of descriptions and examples, with an occasional fact or definition, adds interest and variety.

✳ For more about types of details, see SE pages 569–570.

90

Narrative Writing Warm-Up: Being Selective

When you write a personal narrative, it's important to include specific details. However, a reader doesn't need to know every little thing—like the color of the shoes you wore to a band concert. You need to be selective, choosing those details that are key to appreciating the experience.

A writer compiled the list of details below for a narrative paragraph. After reading through his ideas, he crossed out those that weren't important enough to include.

Sample Details List

> **Climbing Mount Chocorua**
> - climbed the mountain last summer
> - in New Hampshire
> - ~~not the highest peak in White Mountains~~
> - ~~drove up Mount Washington first~~
> - did it on a dare by my brother
> - ~~he also dared me to do other things~~
> - took a few energy bars and bottled water
> - trail started easy
> - saw waterfalls, rivers, and jutting rocks
> - path steeper above tree line
> - ~~no trees above a certain point~~
> - had to climb a rocky wall
> - brother determined to continue
> - ~~no rest stations~~
> - saw a dog and other people at top
> - missed the easier path at one point
> - gorgeous view

Note: This final list of details guided the writer as he wrote a paragraph about his experience. (See the next page.)

 Try It!

Think of an exciting experience in your life. List key details related to this experience. Afterward, review your list and cross out any details that are really not that important.

English Language Learners

Students may have difficulty listing details related to an experience and determining the importance of each detail. Have students discuss their lists with cooperative partners. This will help them learn which details are important for the listener to understand the experience. It will also help them add details that answer the listener's questions.

Advanced Learners

Note that as people recount stories and anecdotes, they may be tempted to embellish the story. Ask students to suggest common ways stories are embellished (making something seem more dangerous than it was, claiming to have a more central role than is true).

Point out that when sharing personal experiences, being truthful can create a more believable and compelling story. For example, the story of watching someone else save a cat and helping in just one small way can be just as interesting as claiming to have been the hero.

Writing a Narrative Paragraph

A personal narrative paragraph shares a specific experience. The paragraph has three parts:

- The **topic sentence** introduces the experience.
- The **body sentences** share details that re-create the experience.
- The **closing sentence** reflects on the experience.

Sample Narrative Paragraph

In the following narrative paragraph, the writer shares a challenging personal experience—climbing a mountain.

Narrative

The topic sentence introduces the experience.

The body sentences share the important details in chronological order.

The closing sentence reflects on the experience.

A Gorgeous Dare

Last summer, I climbed a huge mountain, Mount Chocorua in New Hampshire. I wasn't sure that I could make it, but my brother Travis dared me to join him. At first, the rocky trail seemed easy enough. Crystal clear rivers ran along the path, and we stopped in different places to admire a waterfall and fantastic rock formations. After a while, the trail got steeper, and we found ourselves hiking up sharply angled rock faces. After a few hours, we were above the tree line. It was hotter now without any shade and harder to climb, harder to breathe, and the path seemed to disappear. We picked out what we thought was the path, but it led us to a steep rocky wall. Determined not to turn back, my brother began climbing the wall hand over hand, holding on to rocky ledges and cracks. I followed behind, trying to make the same moves that Travis made. Finally, we reached the top, and to our surprise, we were greeted by a dog! A little farther along, there were a lot of people, admiring the view. We discovered that the path that had "disappeared" came up around the other side, and made a much easier, safer climb. We laughed at ourselves as we ate our energy bars. Looking around at the gorgeous scenery, we were glad that we had kept going. **Rough or not, our climb had been worth it.**

Write your narrative paragraph. Review the three parts of a paragraph (top of page) and what they do. Then use your details list from page **90** to write a narrative paragraph about *your* experience.

Writing a Narrative Paragraph

Discuss how the writer achieves a smooth flow of sentences in the model paragraph.

- Introductory phrases such as *last summer* and *at first* provide transitions and clarify time order.
- The structure of most of the sentences avoids repetition.

Point out the kinds of details the writer uses in each part of the paragraph. For example, the topic sentence focuses on setting details; the body sentences include more setting details and details that describe the sequence of events; and the closing sentence includes details about the writer's feelings.

✷ For more information about writing effective paragraphs, see SE pages 561–579.

Struggling Learners

To reinforce the chronological organizational pattern in the model paragraph, distribute copies of the reproducible Time Line (TE page 816) to students. Then do a Think Aloud to complete the time line of the events recounted in the model paragraph.

Grammar Connection

Nouns
- **Proofreader's Guide** pages 701–703
- **GrammarSnap** Nouns
- **SkillsBook** pages 71, 74

Prepositions
- **Proofreader's Guide** page 732
- **GrammarSnap** Prepositions
- **Write Source** pages 544–545

Commas
- **Proofreader's Guide** pages 608–609, 610, 744 (+)

- **Write Source** page 552
- **GrammarSnap** Commas after Introductory Words, Phrases, and Clauses
- **SkillsBook** pages 8, 11

Pronouns
- **Proofreader's Guide** pages 706–707, 708–709
- **Write Source** pages 536 (+) 537 (+)
- **GrammarSnap** Pronoun-Antecedent Agreement
- **SkillsBook** page 77

Understanding Your Goal

Three traits relate to the development of the content and the form. They provide a focus during prewriting, drafting, and revising.
- Ideas
- Organization
- Voice

The other three traits relate more to form. They are more important during the revising and editing processes.
- Word Choice
- Sentence Fluency
- Conventions

✳ The six-point rubric on SE pages 124–125 is based on these traits. Reproducible six-, five-, and four-point rubrics for narrative writing can be found on TE pages 767, 771, and 775.

Note that the chart on SE page 92 lists the goal for each trait. The rubric on SE pages 124–125 helps the writer evaluate whether these goals are achieved. After reading each goal, ask students to read the complete rubric strip for that trait. The lower scores show the possible pitfalls a writer might encounter (for example, in organization, allowing the beginning, middle, and ending to run together).

Literature Connections

In the personal narrative "The Rights to the Streets of Memphis," an excerpt from *Black Boy,* author Richard Wright describes a time in his life when he was forced to stand up for himself.

Discuss with students how the author uses dialogue to bring a sense of reality to his narrative. For additional models of narrative writing, see the Reading-Writing Connections beginning on page TE-36.

Understanding Your Goal

Your goal in this chapter is to write a narrative essay about a personal accomplishment or victory in your life. The traits in the following chart can help you do your planning and writing. The rubric for narrative writing on pages **124–125** will also guide you.

Traits of Narrative Writing

- **Ideas**
  Choose an important accomplishment in your life. Re-create the experience with plenty of specific details.

- **Organization**
  Present the experience in chronological order. Include a strong beginning, middle, and ending.

- **Voice**
  Sound natural, believable, and interested. Use dialogue to make the experience seem real and to reveal the people in your essay.

- **Word Choice**
  Choose specific words with the appropriate connotation, or feeling.

- **Sentence Fluency**
  Use sentences that flow smoothly from one idea to the next.

- **Conventions**
  Be sure that your punctuation, capitalization, spelling, and grammar are correct.

 Literature Connections: "The Rights to the Streets of Memphis," an excerpt form Richard Wright's autobiography *Black Boy,* is a personal narrative about facing difficult circumstances and fighting to earn respect.

"No tears in the writer, no tears in the reader. No surprise for the writer, no surprise for the reader."
—Robert Frost

English Language Learners

Students may need help understanding that *content* refers to the topic or subject of the story and *form* refers to the way the author organizes ideas and uses language to tell the story.

If students are overwhelmed by the rubric on SE pages 124–125, reassure them that you will help them work on one or two traits at a time to help them improve their written English.

Personal Narrative

In this personal narrative, the student writer tells about his participation in a fund-raiser. The side notes help explain key parts of the essay.

Narrative

Walking for Life

"Please, Max! You'll have a great time!" Kendra gave me her puppy-dog eyes, and I hesitated.

"Sure, okay, I'll do this Hope thing," I sighed, and she shoved a pledge sheet into my hand. I was supposed to get people to sponsor me for an overnight walk to raise money for cancer research. I hated fund-raisers, I hated asking people for money, and I hated the thought of walking around the high school track for 24 hours. I scribbled my own name down on the sheet and pledged 10 dollars. There. That was enough.

Friday afternoon I arrived at the track. Kendra waved me over to where our team was "camping." Her dad had put up a tent for when we weren't walking—each team had to have at least one member walking at all times.

"Thanks, Max, this means a lot to me." Kendra smiled. As she took my form, a frail-looking woman wearing a bright bandana around her head came up to us.

"Kendra, don't forget to register," the woman said. Kendra hugged her, and I suddenly realized who she was.

"Thanks, Mom, I'll go now. Come on, Max." We started toward the registration booth.

"I didn't know—" I mumbled.

"It's okay. She's going to beat it." Kendra pulled out her pledge sheet. It was covered with pledges, front and back.

"You can hand in your pledge sheet now, if you want," she said. Suddenly I looked at my empty sheet. That's how I was feeling inside, empty.

"Uh, no, not yet," I said.

"Walkers, we're ready to start!" Mayor Harris called through a bullhorn, and people started moving toward the starting line.

"Do you want to take the first shift?" Kendra asked.

"No, you go first. I still have a few people to call," I said, pulling out my cell phone.

Beginning
The writer starts in the middle of the action and introduces the experience.

Middle
Dialogue helps move the story along.

Personal Narrative

Work through this model essay with the class, pointing out the elements that make it a good personal narrative.

Ideas

- The experience is carefully recreated.
- The essay includes dialogue and many specific details.
- The writer shows how an important experience caused him to change his attitude.

Organization

- The opening begins in the middle of the action (*in medias res*) and makes the reader curious about the topic.
- The details are presented in chronological order.

Voice & Word Choice

- The writer uses a lot of dialogue to make the story realistic and to give an idea of each speaker's personality.
- The voice in the descriptions sounds natural and authentic.
- The writer chooses vivid, precise words to describe the scene, express feelings, and recreate the experience.

English Language Learners

As students read the essay, work with them so that you can identify those individuals who have difficulty with embedded dialogue in text. Then work with these students as a group to introduce the concept and conventions of embedded dialogue.

- Ask students how they would respond to being told they would have to walk around a track for 24 hours.
- Use a two-column chart to record each response on the board.
- Model using appropriate punctuation and capitalization as you rewrite students' responses. Use a variety of dialogue tags.

Point out the moment when the narrator's attitude about the fund-raiser changes. Is it effective? (Most should agree that it is.) Why? Possible responses include the following:

- The narrator does not say explicitly what happened.
- The narrator uses visual information (the sudden appearance of the frail woman) to convey his shock.
- He uses voice (*I mumbled* instead of *I said*) to show that he was shaken.

 Respond to the reading.

Answers

Ideas 1. his part in a 24-hour fund-raising walk for cancer research

2. Possible choices include:

- The writer didn't want to do the fund-raiser at first.
- The issue became personal for him when he learned Kendra's mother had cancer.

Organization 3. with dialogue, in the middle of the action

4. chronological order

Voice & Word Choice 5. Answers will vary but should include examples such as *I called everyone I knew, I felt a lump in my throat, I knew I was accomplishing something important.*

94

I called everyone I knew—every relative, every friend. I begged, I promised—and I nearly filled my pledge sheet. When it was my turn to walk with the others, I felt as though I belonged with them.

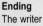 **Middle** Specific details help the reader "see" the experience.

At dusk, the mood became solemn as plain brown paper bags were placed around the perimeter of the track and workers walked along, lighting the candles inside. Each bag had the name of someone's friend or relative who had faced cancer. As the darkness deepened, the field lights were shut off, leaving us in the glow of hundreds of candles. Everyone moved into the bleachers, and Mayor Harris began to speak.

"This disease has touched everyone," she said. "We've come so far, and now more and more people are surviving. Yet there still is no absolute cure. Your participation here will fund research, so that more people can be labeled survivors."

Then the survivors took to the track for the first lap by candlelight. As they walked, the mayor read the names of local people who had died from the disease. Kendra's mother walked by, and I felt a lump in my throat as she waved at us. After the first lap, without a word, everyone left the bleachers to join in, but the only sound was the mayor's voice reading the list of names.

 Ending The writer shares the importance of the experience.

As the crowd moved onto the track, I thought of the money I was raising, of how it would be used, and I knew that I was accomplishing something important. I closed my eyes and listened as the last names were read. Then I took Kendra's hand, and we silently headed to the track to join the other walkers.

Respond to the reading. Answer the following questions about the narrative you just read.

Ideas (1) What is the writer's topic? (2) What two specific details stand out?

Organization (3) How does the writer start his narrative? (4) How is the narrative organized?

Voice & Word Choice (5) How can you tell that the writer is interested in his topic?

Personal Narrative **95**

Prewrite → Write → Revise → Edit → Publish

Prewriting

Your personal narrative will be about an accomplishment in your life. In your prewriting, you will choose a specific topic, gather your details, and organize your thoughts.

Narrative

Keys to Effective Prewriting

1. **Think about personal successes and accomplishments you could share.**

2. **Choose one special accomplishment to be your topic.**

3. **Gather specific details about the experience.**

4. **Identify the key sensory details related to this time.**

5. **Organize your ideas chronologically.**

6. **Use dialogue to add personality to your writing.**

Prewriting
Keys to Effective Prewriting

Remind students that the prewriting stage in the writing process is when the writer selects a topic, gathers details, and decides how to organize those details.

Keys to Effective Prewriting list the process students will be guided through on SE pages 96–100.

To help students think about topics, discuss the sorts of topics that interest them. Talk about different kinds of personal successes—and assure students that they do not have to write about life-and-death topics. Smaller-scale stories, such as the first time they ever beat an older sibling at chess, can be told in interesting ways.

Writing Workshop

The activities in the prewriting, writing, revising, and editing sections of this chapter can serve as minilessons for whole-group instruction, small-group work, or independent work time.

Technology Connections

Students can use the added features of the Net-text as they explore this stage of the writing process.

⚡ Write Source Online *Net-text*

English Language Learners

To prepare students for sharing their finished essays in class, use the following strategies:

- During the writing process, have students work with English-proficient partners.
- Ask students to restate their partners' suggestions to make sure they understand what revisions to make.
- Have partners respond to the revisions.

Prewriting Selecting a Topic

Invite students to devise a different sentence starter. Some students may find it helpful to use visual prompts. If possible, assign topic selection as homework; encourage students to look through a personal photo collection to generate ideas. Students can list ideas in their **writer's notebook** (*see below*).

✴ For more about choosing topics, see SE pages 582–585.

Prewriting Reflecting on Your Topic

After freewriting and underlining key details, have students

- choose partners and take turns telling each other the story they plan to write,
- jot down three to five details that stood out as they listened to their partner's story, and
- tell their partner these details and discuss any additional issues that arise.

Ask students to compare the details that impressed their listener to the ones they underlined in the freewriting. Were they the same? Students may wish to revise their plans based on the feedback they receive.

Prewriting Selecting a Topic

Andy completed the sentence starter "I am very proud that I . . ." in four different ways. The activity helped him think of personal accomplishments for his narrative. He put an asterisk next to the one that he wanted to write about.

Sentence Starter

> I am very proud that I . . .
>   completed a 20-mile bike race.
>   learned CPR and first aid.
>   helped my grandfather tend his garden.
>   *prevented a brush fire from getting out of control.

 Complete the sentence starter. Try to come up with at least three things you are proud of. Put an asterisk (*) next to the one you would like to write about.

Reflecting on Your Topic

To gather his initial thoughts, Andy wrote freely about his chosen topic. Then he underlined key details that he could use in his narrative.

> I remember the day the hay field caught fire. I had to <u>run from the outer fence to the house to get to the phone</u>. Man that was a long way to run! Then I had to <u>run around the corral by the barn to get to the water trough.</u>
> There was a lot of dry grass that wasn't baled yet. The fire chief told Uncle Mark that somebody probably tossed a cigarette out of the window of a passing car, and the grass caught fire. That made me mad!
> The smell of the smoke—that weird odor of burning orchard clover. And there was the <u>incredible heat</u> too—when the wind shifted, <u>it hit like a wall and made it really really hard to breathe.</u>
> The smoke stung! <u>I had to stop the fire before it got to the barn.</u> My arms were sore from swinging that bucket of water! A firefighter asked me if I was going to be one of them. . . .

 Collect your first thoughts. Write freely for 5 to 10 minutes about your accomplishment. Underline key details that you could use in your narrative.

English Language Learners

Students may need additional help with vocabulary to share their story in English. Allow these students to record their ideas as lists of words or phrases instead of writing complete sentences during the freewriting activity. Encourage them to develop their ideas with cooperative partners.

Teaching Tip: Keeping a Writer's Notebook

Keeping a writer's notebook can provide additional writing practice and can be a great place to record possible topics. Have students use a writer's notebook to

- make personal connections to required reading,
- respond to interesting books, articles, or films, and
- reflect on responses to writing projects in progress.

Explain that you will collect and review the notebooks occasionally to see if you can provide additional suggestions for how to use the notebook.

✴ For more about writer's notebooks, see SE pages 4–5.

Narrative

Gathering Different Types of Details

An effective personal narrative contains three types of details: *actions,* *sensory details,* and *personal thoughts.* Andy completed a chart to gather details for his narrative.

- **Actions** relate what you (and others) did in a situation.
- **Sensory details** show what you saw, smelled, heard, tasted, or touched.
- **Personal thoughts** reveal what you thought during your experience.

Details Chart

Actions	Sensory details	Thoughts
Checking fences	Smelled smoke; saw flames	Get help!
Spotted fire; ran to house to call 911	Tired legs	The fire could spread to the barn!
Called Uncle Mark	Listened to voice mail	I'm all alone!
Ran to corral/barn	Hard breathing; couldn't see in smoke	That hose won't reach far enough.
Grabbed water bucket; threw water on grass	Horses snorting; felt wall of heat from fire	This is scary!
Firefighters arrived	Sirens, flashing lights, aching arms	Relieved

Prewrite **Create a details chart.** Refer to your freewriting on page 96 for the main details of your experience. Then fill in a chart like the one above with specific details about what you did, sensed, and thought.

Focus on the Traits

Ideas Action is the skeleton of a narrative, but sensory details and thoughts are the muscles that keep it moving. Include all three types of details in your writing.

Prewriting Gathering Different Types of Details

Provide photocopies of the reproducible Details Chart (TE page 821) for students to fill in. To help students collect details for composing dialogue later on, have them add a column to the chart with the heading *What was said.* They can use this column to record specific things they remember hearing or saying at the time.

Focus on the Traits

Ideas

Review sensory details, and encourage students to add a variety of these to their chart. Identify the sensory details listed in the sample chart:

- Sight—saw flames, couldn't see in smoke, flashing lights
- Sound—listened to voice mail, hard breathing, horses snorting, sirens
- Smell—smoke
- Feeling—tired legs, wall of heat from fire, aching arms

English Language Learners

Students may not understand the skeleton and muscles analogy presented in the **Focus on the traits** activity. Use pictures to contrast the static, immoveable skeleton (actions), with a dynamic, muscled body (actions plus details and thoughts).

Struggling Learners

Have students interview each other to gather details. The interviewers will take notes, which they will give to their partners. Students can use the notes to help fill in the details chart.

Possible interview questions:

  What happened?

  What did you do?

How did you feel?

What happened next?

Was anyone else there?

What did they do?

How did you feel when it was over?

Prewriting Building Narrative Suspense

Ask students to suggest elements that can contribute to creating suspense. Responses may include the following:

- a problem that does not have an immediately obvious solution
- a time limit or other constraint that adds to the sense of urgency
- actions that may temporarily make the problem seem worse

Focus on the Traits

Organization

Point out that keeping in mind the plot line while **plotting the narrative** *(see below)* helps prevent the writer from giving away too much too quickly, which would spoil the suspense. If the writer develops the rising action in multiple steps that increase in intensity, the story will sustain the reader's interest.

✱ For more about plot lines, see SE pages 314–315.

Prewriting Building Narrative Suspense

Memorable narratives are suspenseful; they make the reader want to know what happens next. Here's how to build suspense into your narrative:

Start with a problem (conflict)—some type of physical or mental obstacle in your way. The problem in Andy's narrative is a brush fire that he has to deal with.

Work in actions that respond to the problem. Andy does a series of things—calls the fire department and his uncle, throws water on the fire, and so on. Each of these actions builds suspense into the story.

Build toward the climax or high point. This is the most exciting part of the narrative, in which the writer does or does not overcome the challenge. Andy's narrative builds to the point when the firefighters finally arrive and control the fire. This part should happen near the end of the narrative.

Focus on the Traits

Organization Narratives follow the classic shape of a plot line. The beginning grabs the reader's attention by identifying the problem. Then rising action builds suspense. (Include at least two or three key actions.) The climax brings the writer face-to-face with the problem. The falling action quickly leads to the resolution. The resolution tells how the person is changed.

Plot Line

Climax
The firefighters finally arrive.

Rising Action
I do a series of things in response to the fire.

Falling Action
Uncle Mark arrives.

Beginning
I discover a fire on my uncle's property.

Resolution
I learn that I can act calmly under pressure.

Create a story line. Plot out the main actions of your narrative in a story line like the one above. Be sure that you include details that build suspense into your writing. Use your details chart from page 97.

Prewrite

Teaching Tip: Plotting the Narrative

As an alternative to the graph-like depiction of the events in the narrative, some students may want to plan their story pictorially, as a cartoon, or in story-board format. They may find that this strategy helps them to focus and organize their ideas.

Struggling Learners

To help students use a plot line as an organizing strategy, work as a class to graph a story line for a familiar short story. Then ask students to create their own story line, using a chapter from a favorite book, a scene from a film, or a television episode.

Adding Dialogue

Dialogue makes a personal narrative come alive with added information about the experience. It reveals the speakers' personalities and keeps the action moving. The chart below shows how a writer can express the same idea with or without dialogue. (The dialogue examples are taken from the model on pages **93–94**.)

	Without Dialogue	**With Dialogue**
Show a speaker's personality	I reluctantly got involved with a fund-raiser.	"Sure, okay, I'll do this Hope thing," I sighed, . . .
Keep the action moving	Kendra said that I could turn in my pledge sheet, which was totally empty of pledges.	"You can hand in your pledge sheet now, if you want," she said. Suddenly I looked at my empty sheet. That's how I was feeling inside, empty.
Add information	I discovered that Kendra's mom was battling cancer.	"I didn't know—" I mumbled. "It's okay. She's going to beat it." Kendra pulled out her pledge sheet.

Consider dialogue for your narrative. For practice, write some dialogue that would be appropriate near the beginning of your narrative. (See page **120** for information about punctuating dialogue.)

Prewrite

Narrative

Prewriting Adding Dialogue

As they write dialogue, have students refer to the planning notes they've made so far.

- If students added a dialogue column to the details chart they made for SE page 97, have them refer to it for ideas.
- Have students examine the plot line they drew. Can the story begin in the middle of the action with dialogue (as on SE page 93)? Can any of the rising action be developed with dialogue?

Suggest additional ideas that might help students create realistic-sounding dialogue. For example:

- Ask students to write a few lines of dialogue for each person who appears in the story, if possible. The dialogue should be expressive of the character who says it.
- Have students read their dialogue aloud to make sure it **sounds realistic** *(see below)*, like real conversation.

Writer's Craft

Voice: Everyone has a distinctive voice, so novelists use dialogue to reveal the personalities of characters. John R. King, author of *The Shadow of Reichenbach Falls*, wrote: "Once I can hear a character speaking, I know who the person is. Outward descriptions don't do it. Actions don't do it. I need to hear the person speak."

Teaching Tip: Writing Dialogue That Sounds Realistic

To give writers tools for creating realistic dialogue, review the use of dashes and ellipses. Explain that both represent a pause in speech.

- Dashes indicate an abrupt break because the speaker has suddenly stopped or someone has interrupted:
  "You mean—"
  "That's right!" he cried.

- Ellipsis points indicate speech that has trailed off because the speaker is hesitant to say something or is having a slow realization:
  "Wait . . . is it . . . "

* For more about dashes and ellipses, see SE pages 640–643.

Prewriting Reviewing Features of a Narrative

Ask students how suspense is created in the model essay even though there is little physical action. Possible answers:

- Suspense is created by the obstacle (the narrator's fear of public speaking) and the time constraint (the audience was waiting).
- The narrator's physical manifestations of his fear create a sense of suspense.

 On your own paper

Possible Answers

Action: *I breathed deeply; the words started to flow; I lost it in a couple of spots, until I checked my note cards; I eased into my seat and sighed*

Sensory details: *eyes watering; knees shaking; stomach flip-flopping; pale wood; sun warming my face*

Dialogue: Any words in quotation marks, except "Golf is life."

Personal thoughts: *I felt like I was drowning; I figured I'd never have to make a speech once I was out of school; What was I going to do; my mind was frozen; Maybe someday I'll win the Masters'*

Prewriting Reviewing Features of a Narrative

Remember, memorable personal narratives include action, sensory details, dialogue, and personal thoughts. Look for these features as you read "Fore!"

> ### "Fore!"
> I looked at the sea of faces and felt like I was drowning. Why did we have to take a public speaking class anyway? I figured I'd never have to make a speech once I was out of school! Yet there I stood, my eyes watering, my knees shaking, and my stomach flip-flopping.
>
> "Brendan, you may begin whenever you're ready," Ms. Dailey said from the back of the room. What was I going to do? I had to begin, but my mind was frozen.
>
> "Take a deep breath," Ms. Dailey said. "Focus on what you want to say." I didn't want to say anything, but I breathed deeply. It seemed to help. I grasped the pale wood of the podium. Glancing at my first note card, I saw the words "Golf is life." I tried to imagine being on a golf course, the sun warming my face.
>
> "Golf is life. At least that is the way that I look at it," I said. As I continued talking, the words started to flow. "When I make a perfect swing, I know that life is good." I felt good as long as I talked about my game. I lost it in a couple of spots, until I checked my note cards.
>
> "So, anytime you want a little fresh air and exercise, as well as a mental challenge, I suggest you head for the nearest golf course."
>
> I was done! Chelsea gave me a thumbs-up, and Ms. Daily said, "Thank you, Brendan."
>
> I eased into my seat and sighed. One speech down, six more to go. And who knows? Maybe someday I'll win the Masters, and then I will have to give a speech! Now I'll be ready.

 On your own paper, identify at least one example of each narrative feature—*action, sensory details, dialogue,* and *personal thoughts*—in the sample above. Then make sure to include these elements in your own personal narrative.

"You want the reader to feel swept along, as if on a kind of trip, from sentence to sentence."

—Russell Freedman

English Language Learners

Some students may have difficulty identifying examples of action, sensory details, and personal thoughts in the model essay. Allow them to read and discuss the essay with English-proficient partners. Have them work together to fill in a photocopy of the reproducible Details Chart (TE page 821) to help identify details used in the model essay.

Advanced Learners

Help students analyze the effect of using dialogue in a personal narrative. Have them read the dialogue in "Fore!" Ask them to find examples that communicate action, sensory details, and personal thoughts.

Then have students analyze the dialogue they wrote for practice on SE page 99 for examples of the same features.

Writing

Now that you have planned your narrative, you're ready to write your first draft.

Narrative

Keys to Effective Writing

1. Tell the complete story—the beginning, the middle, and the ending.

2. Grab the reader's interest in the beginning, build suspense in the middle part, and, in the ending, tell how you were changed by your experience.

3. Use the details you gathered and organized as a general guide. Feel free to add new ideas as they come to mind.

4. Include dialogue whenever it makes sense to do so.

5. Write on every other line, leaving space for additions and changes later on.

English Language Learners

Some students may be so concerned about neatness, perfection, and the rules of written English that they are not able to focus on developing their ideas. Call special attention to item 5: *Write on every other line, leaving space for additions and changes later on.* Assure them that they will be able to revise and edit later.

Writing

Keys to Effective Writing

Remind students that the writing stage is when they get to write, or draft, their ideas on paper.

Keys to Effective Writing lists the process students will be guided through on SE pages 102–106.

Draw students' attention to the second sentence of item 3, *Feel free to add new ideas as they come to mind.* Tell students that new ideas and approaches will come up during the writing process. Remind students that they have done a lot of planning, but explain that although they should consult their planning notes regularly, they should not feel tied to the notes.

If students will be using a computer to create their drafts, remind them to set their word processing programs to double-space the printouts.

✻ For more about working with computers, see SE pages 33–38.

Writing Workshop

One key concept of the writing workshop is to write with your students. On an overhead or on the board, draft a few opening sentences as you speak about opening sentences. Write a few sentences of description. By writing, you embolden your students to write as well—and you create a writing community in your class.

Technology Connections

Students can use the added features of the Net-text as they explore this stage of the writing process.

✻ *Write Source Online* **Net-text**

Writing Getting the Big Picture

Draw students' attention to the tip at the bottom of the page and note that how they shape the narrative will also depend on the subject matter they've chosen. For example, if the topic is the unexpected death of a pet, the narrative will most likely be shaped in a way that expresses the writer's sudden feelings of sadness and loss.

Ask students to suggest adjectives that could be used to describe the impact of a story. In addition to *suspenseful* or *sad,* these might include the following:
- humorous
- dramatic
- frightening
- uplifting

For each adjective suggested, ask students to think of at least one story they've read that creates that effect. Then encourage students to analyze those stories to see how the authors achieved these effects.

Suggest that students pay extra attention whenever they find themselves enjoying what they are reading. What effect is the author creating? How? Encourage students to analyze how they can use some of the same techniques in their own writing.

Writing Getting the Big Picture

The chart below shows how the parts of a personal narrative fit together. (The examples shown are from the essay on pages **103–106**.) As you begin your first draft, be sure you have

- collected plenty of details about your personal accomplishment,
- decided how you will build narrative suspense, and
- considered using dialogue.

Beginning	Opening Sentences
The **beginning** identifies the problem and grabs the reader's attention.	Late last summer, I was checking fences on my uncle's property when I smelled smoke. I looked up to see the hay field was on fire!

Middle	
The **middle** paragraphs use a variety of details to show what happened. Dialogue keeps the narrative moving.	"There's a brush fire just east of where Highway 9 crosses the White River!" I hung up the phone and ran outside. I knew I had to do something on my own. I coughed as smoke filled my lungs.

Ending	Closing Sentences
The **ending** explains how the experience changed the writer.	I had been scared, but I learned that I could handle emergencies and not panic when things got tough. Learning that about myself was just a bonus on top of helping to save the barn that day.

Tip

How you shape your narrative depends on what you want your story to do. If you want to keep readers in suspense, leave out anything that blows the ending. If you want to make the readers laugh, you'll have to surprise them. Make them expect one outcome but show them another.

Personal Narrative **103**

Beginning
Middle
Ending

Narrative

Starting Your Personal Narrative

Once you've planned the main parts of your narrative, you're ready to write your first draft. An effective opening paragraph will

- **grab your reader's attention,**
- **start in the middle of the action,**
- **introduce the main problem, and**
- **include important background information about the experience.**

Beginning Paragraph

The writer introduces the problem and gains the reader's attention.

Late last summer, I was checking fences on my uncle's property when I smelled smoke. I looked up to see the hay field was on fire! Since I was the only one there, I had to do something. First, I hopped the split-rail fence and ran to the house. When I got there, I grabbed the phone in the kitchen and dialed 911.

Using Transitions

Transitions move the reader smoothly through your writing by signaling time shifts. Choose natural-sounding transitions from the chart below to express the passage of time. For additional choices, see pages **592–593**.

Transition Words and Phrases					
about	besides	later	second	today	when
after	but	meanwhile	so far	tomorrow	whenever
as soon as	during	next	soon	until	while
at	finally	now	then	until now	yesterday
before	first	recently	this time	usually	

Write your beginning. On your own paper, write the first paragraph of your personal narrative. Use transitions to connect your ideas. Afterward, circle any transitions that you have used.

Write

Writing Starting Your Personal Narrative

Talk about different styles of opening paragraphs. Look back at the beginnings of the models in the unit (the SE page 93 essay starts with dialogue, the SE page 100 essay starts with student's thoughts).

Read several opening paragraphs of published short stories or essays. Discuss why each opening is effective. Tell students that **studying literary models** *(see below)* can help them improve their own writing.

✱ For more about great beginnings, see SE page 595.

Writing Using Transitions

Point out that although time-order transitions are needed for narratives, students may want to use other kinds of transitions to add variety.

After students have reviewed the information on SE pages 592–593, try this group exercise:
- Make up a sentence.
- Have a volunteer use a transition to create a second sentence following the first.
- Continue adding sentences.

Teaching Tip: Studying Literary Models

One of the best ways for students to internalize the qualities of good writing is to imitate it.

- Have students choose an opener from a story they admire.
- Ask them to write an opening for their own narrative (either the one they are working on

now or one for the future), trying to imitate the structure of their model.

- Have students read both the model and their own opening aloud to the group.
- Ask students to explain the model author's strategy and to tell why it appeals to them for their own work.

Struggling Learners

To help students determine if their opening paragraph is effective, have them read aloud the paragraph to a small group. Ask group members to answer the following questions:

- What is interesting in the paragraph?
- Does it make you want to know more?
- Does it tell too much?

Writing Developing the Middle Part

Share any writing tips you have with the class and invite students to do the same. These might include the following:

- While working on the draft, if an idea comes up that doesn't quite fit in the part you are working on at the moment, quickly add it to your planning notes so you won't forget about it.
- It can be helpful to take breaks if your flow of ideas starts to dry up, or you become distracted or unsure of what to do next. Before putting your writing away for the day, make some notes about why you stopped.
- Even when a computer is available, some people prefer to create their drafts on paper. Experiment with both keyboarding and writing on paper to see what works best for you.

Writing Developing the Middle Part

The middle part of your narrative shares the important information related to your experience. *Remember:* Your goal is to tell a good story and hold the reader's interest. Use the tips below as a guide when you develop this part of your writing.

- **Include the key actions,** showing how you reacted to your problem. (See page **97** for help.)
- **Add sensory details** to create effective images (word pictures).
- **Work in your personal thoughts** and feelings whenever they add interest to your narrative.
- **Maintain suspense!** (See page **98**.)

Middle Paragraphs

> The writer shows his personality through the dialogue.

"911. What's the nature of your emergency?"

"There's a brush fire just east of where Highway 9 crosses the White River!"

"Your name and address, sir?"

"I'm Andy Summers at 47113 Hammer Lane. This is Greenwood Stables. When will you guys get here?"

"It'll take at least 10 minutes to get out to you. What I need you to do now—"

"Oh man! The barn could be on fire by then!"

"Stay calm, sir. I need you to—"

> Each new action builds the suspense.

I hung up and called my uncle's cell phone. The phone rang four times before he picked up. "This is Mark—"

"Uncle Mark! There's a fire—" I yelled, but his voice kept going.

"—Greenwood Stables. Please leave me a voice-mail message after the beep and let me know where and when to call you back. Thanks."

Narrative

The writer includes his personal thoughts and feelings.

Sensory details create effective images.

Another key action builds to the climax.

After the beep, I said, "Uncle Mark! There's a fire in the hay field! I called 911 already, but get home quick!"

I hung up the phone and ran outside. I knew I had to do something on my own. If the tall grass around the stables caught fire, we could lose the barn, the stables, and even the house!

The fire didn't have roaring flames, but it spread fast in the dry grass. Uncle Mark and I had mowed the hay field a few days before, but we had only baled half of the cut grass. Just then, the smoke blew in thick and made the horses run and snort in the corral. I felt scared when smoke surrounded me as I ran between the corral and the barn. Suddenly I hit a wall of heat, and I could hardly breathe or see. I kept running toward the water trough on the other side of the hay field fence, hoping I could slow the fire down.

By now, the fire was about 100 feet away from the horses and me. I knew the hose on the side of the barn wouldn't reach the fire. I grabbed a bucket by the water trough and started throwing buckets of water on the grass between the barn and the fire. I knew I couldn't stop the blaze, but I thought I could slow it down if I soaked the grass enough. I coughed as smoke filled my lungs. I was really scared. Then I heard the distant sirens of the fire trucks growing louder as they approached.

 Write your middle paragraphs. Use your prewriting notes to guide your writing. Keep the following drafting tips in mind.

Tip

- Remember that your purpose is to tell about a personal accomplishment or victory.
- Write freely. Relax and let your ideas flow. Don't worry about having everything correct in a first draft.
- Add important ideas that occur to you along the way.

Invite students to comment on the middle paragraphs of the model. What works best? Could anything be improved? Possible responses:

- The writer's decision not to use many dialogue tags is very effective. The rapid-fire exchanges create both action and suspense.
- When the narrator begins talking to Uncle Mark before he realizes that he is speaking to a voice mail, it *shows*, rather than *tells*, how hurried he feels.

 Literature Connections

Mentor texts: Inspire your students with examples from compelling real-life narratives. Read excerpts from one or more of the following books:

Rosa Parks: My Story by Rosa Parks and Jim Haskins

Bruce Lee: The Celebrated Life of the Golden Dragon by Bruce Lee and John R. Little

Growing Up in Slavery: Stories of Young Slaves as Told by Themselves by Yuval Taylor

Lost Moon: The Perilous Voyage of Apollo 13 by Jim Lovell and Jeffrey Kluger

---

Advanced Learners

To help students analyze the importance of dialogue, action, details, and description, divide the class into three groups: beginning, middle, and ending. Ask each group to "sabotage" their part of the sample essay. They should convert dialogue to third person, replace words that show with words that tell, and remove sensory descriptions. Have a spokesperson from each group read the "reworked" text to the class. Discuss how the changes affected the essay.

Writing Ending Your Personal Narrative

Note that the ending consists of multiple paragraphs, not just one. Point out that this allows the writer to wind down after the climax, before providing the final thought.

Encourage students to experiment with the pacing of their ending paragraphs. Is their topic better suited to a sudden, dramatic ending or a more gradual one? If they aren't sure, suggest that they write two different endings, share them with a partner, and choose the one that works the best.

106

Writing Ending Your Personal Narrative

The ending of your personal narrative shows how you overcame your problem and accomplished something. It is your chance to reflect on the experience and tell what you learned about yourself.

Beginning

Middle

► Ending

Ending Paragraphs

The writer builds suspense up to this point.

Through the smoke, I saw the flashing lights of the fire engines. A tanker truck on the highway began to spray water on the eastern side of the fire. Another tanker truck pulled into the driveway behind me. Firefighters started to spray around the barn. I was relieved when Uncle Mark's truck skidded to a stop at the barn.

Uncle Mark yelled, "Andy? You okay?"

The conclusion tells what the writer learned.

I smiled at him and said, "I guess so." I had been scared, but I learned that I could handle emergencies and not panic when things got tough. Learning that about myself was just a bonus on top of helping to save the barn that day.

Write

Write your ending and form a complete first draft. Complete your essay by sharing the climax of your personal accomplishment and telling what you learned from the experience. Then write a final copy of your narrative, double-spacing so you have room to revise your writing.

Tip

■ If you are having difficulty with the ending, put your writing aside for a while. Stepping away from your work for a time will make it easier to reflect on the importance of the experience.

■ Consider these suggestions if you're finding it hard to write your ending:

• Think in terms of *before* and *after*. What were you like before the experience, and how were you different after it?

• What one word describes how you felt after the experience (*proud, mature, happy*)? Why did you feel that way?

• Consider the *good* and the *bad*. What did you do well during this experience, and what could you have done better?

Revising

Your first draft is your first look at a developing narrative. During the revising step, you improve your first draft by adding to, rewriting, or reorganizing different parts. Focus on these traits when you revise: *ideas, organization, voice, word choice,* and *sentence fluency.*

Narrative

Keys to Effective Revising

1. Set aside your first draft for a day or two, if possible, before you review your writing.

2. Be sure each main part—the beginning, the middle, and the ending—works well.

3. Revise any parts that seem confusing or incomplete.

4. Pay special attention to your writing voice. Do you sound truly interested in the experience?

5. Use specific words that reflect your feelings about the experience.

6. Be sure your sentences read smoothly.

Revising

Keys to Effective Revising

Remind students that the revising stage is when writers have an opportunity to make improvements to their first drafts. At this stage they can think about refinements they might not have considered when they were drafting.

Keys to Effective Revising lists the process students will be guided through on SE pages 108–118.

In preparation for the following pages, review the proofreader's marks on the inside back cover of the pupil edition. Explain that these marks are used by writers and editors to indicate changes and corrections. Point out that students can also find these marks in many dictionaries.

Peer Responding

Prior to revision, have students read and respond to each other's drafts. A constructive peer response helps students pinpoint the traits that need revision. On the following pages, students can find the specific strategies they need to improve their writing.

Technology Connections

Have students use the Writing Network features of the Net-text to comment on each other's drafts.

Write Source Online **Net-text**

English Language Learners

Depending on their stage of English language acquisition, students may not be able to recognize errors in word order and word choice. Limited vocabularies make it difficult to substitute appropriate synonyms independently. Throughout the revising step, allow these students to work with proficient English-speaking partners who can help them revise their writing.

Revising for Ideas

The rubric strips that run across all of the revising pages (SE pages 108–117) are provided to help students focus their revising on specific traits and are related to the full rubric on SE pages 124–125.

The essay on SE pages 93–94 provides good examples of *showing* details. Have students identify the examples.

■ Max's sigh at the beginning shows that he doesn't want to do the fund-raiser.

■ His reaction to Kendra's mother shows that he is changing his attitude.

■ His refusal to turn in his pledge sheet at first shows that he's going to take action.

■ The candle-lighting and the reading of names show that many have been affected by cancer.

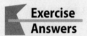

Exercise
Answers

1. tells
2. tells
3. shows (he ran very hard)
4. shows (winter is coming)
5. tells
6. shows (people live under the boardwalk)
7. Students may say it *tells* that the ride is going to be bumpy or *shows* that the writer is resigned to a bumpy ride.

108

Revising for Ideas

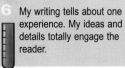

6 My writing tells about one experience. My ideas and details totally engage the reader.

5 My narrative "shows" my ideas with details that hold my reader's interest.

4 I have enough details, but my narrative should "show" more ideas, not "tell" them.

When you revise for *ideas*, be sure your narrative "shows" your experience and doesn't just "tell" it. Be sure you have included enough details to make the narrative clear. The rubric above will help guide you as you revise and improve your ideas.

Do I *show* rather than *tell* in my narrative?

Your narrative *shows* if sentences contain action, sensory details, dialogue, and your personal thoughts and feelings. Writing that shows makes a personal narrative come alive for the reader. Review the sentences that follow to see the difference between showing and telling in writing.

Telling: It looked like rain.

Showing: Dark gray clouds loomed overhead and thunder rumbled in the distance.
(Sensory details create a strong image.)

Exercise

Decide whether each of the following sentences *shows* or *tells*.

1. Grace had never seen the aurora borealis.
2. We saw many neat things in the desert.
3. Marcus staggered across the finish line, nearly doubled over in pain.
4. The sky was black with birds, all racing to the south.
5. Jeff told me that the sound system wasn't working.
6. Under the boardwalk, a few homeless people hang up sheets, lay out old clothes, and stack up full plastic bags.
7. I knew I was in for a bumpy ride when Dad said, "Let's use the old pickup."

Review your sentences. Be sure that your narrative contains enough action, details, and dialogue to show rather than tell.

Revise

English Language Learners

Students may have insufficient vocabulary to determine whether the sentences in the exercise *show* or *tell*. To demonstrate how the use of sensory details helps readers "see" the picture the writer is creating, have students sketch pictures for contrasting sentence pairs such as the following:

There were birds in the sky. The sky was black and alive with birds.

Compare students' sketches and discuss how the details in the second sentence help create a more vivid picture that shows what the writer intended.

3 I should focus on one experience and use more sensory details.

2 I should focus on one experience and use more details.

1 I should include more details about my topic or choose a different experience.

Have I included enough details?

You have included enough details if the reader has a complete picture of your experience. Use the 5 W's and H—*who? what? when? where? why?* and *how?*—to learn whether you have covered the experience thoroughly enough.

Exercise

Read the following paragraph about a personal experience. Then, on your own paper, list the 5 W's and H for the experience.

> To complete pull-ups in Mr. Brown's gym class is a major accomplishment. I found that out last week when we had fitness tests in the gym. We had to start a pull-up by hanging from the bar with our arms straight. Our palms had to face toward the bar. As we raised ourselves, our bodies had to remain straight. Mr. Brown tapped our stomachs with a yardstick if we started to bend or wiggle. Our chins had to rest on the bar. I wasn't sure how I would do because I hadn't worked out too much. . . .

Revise

Check your details. Review the first draft of your personal narrative to be sure that it answers the 5 W's and H. If it does not answer one or more of these questions, add the necessary details.

Ideas
A variety of details are added to help show the experience.

Just then, the smoke blew in thick and made the horses
~I felt scared when smoke surrounded me as~
run and snort in the corral. I ran between the corral and the
and I could hardly breathe or see.
barn. Suddenly I hit a wall of heat, but I kept running toward
the water trough on the other side of the hay field fence.
hoping
~I just hoped~ I could slow the fire down.

Provide copies of the reproducible 5 W's Chart (TE page 817) for students to fill out for the exercise and for their own essays. Note that for future essays (especially if students discover that they skipped more than one or two of these details), students may wish to fill out a 5 W's and H chart during prewriting instead of during revisions.

Exercise Answers

Who—the writer and fellow students, the gym teacher Mr. Brown
What—pull-ups
When—last week
Where—in the gym
Why—to fulfill fitness test requirements
How—hanging from the bar with arms straight, pulling up while keeping the body straight, and resting the chin on the bar

 Writer's Craft

Narrative components: Note that by answering the 5 W's and H, writers are gathering the main components of a narrative:

Question	Answer
Who?	Character
What?	Conflict
Where?	Setting (place)
When?	Setting (time)
Why?	Theme
How?	Plot

Revising **for** Organization

Students may be reluctant to revisit their drafts and revise them in a substantial way. To help them get over this hurdle, have students pick one of the strategies on the page (or another strategy of their choice) and write alternative beginnings for their narratives, even if they're satisfied with their original start. Then ask them to read both beginnings to a partner.

- Which beginning does the partner prefer?
- Which does the writer prefer now?
- Are there elements of both beginnings that could be combined into an ideal opening paragraph?

Encourage students to approach the exercise with an open mind. Acknowledge that it can be very difficult to cut or change what they have written, but usually it improves the writing.

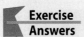

Exercise Answers

1. personal thought
2. creates image (could also be considered middle of the action)
3. middle of the action

Revising **for** Organization

6 The organization makes my narrative very enjoyable to read.

5 My narrative has a clear beginning, middle, and ending. My transitions are effective.

4 My narrative is clearly organized. My beginning or ending could be stronger. I use transitions.

When you revise for *organization*, be sure all parts of your narrative work smoothly together. Use the rubric above to guide you.

Does my beginning grab the reader's attention?

Your beginning grabs the reader's attention if it does one of these things: (1) starts in the middle of the action, (2) creates a clear image with sensory details, or (3) opens with a personal thought.

- Start in the middle of the action.
  Number 44 kicked the ball. It soared high above our heads as the teams charged down the field.

- Create an image with sensory details.
  The rain hit my helmet, like a soft tapping on a door. I pulled my chin strap tighter and snapped it on the other side.

- Give a personal thought.
  Fourth down in overtime . . . this is the stuff dreams are made of.

Exercise

Decide whether each opening starts in the middle of the action, creates an image, or gives a personal thought.

1. I guess all kids go through a pretending stage. Why dressing up was so important to me, though, I don't know.
2. The train screeched to a halt, just far enough up the hill for me to see a waterfall cascading into a deep ravine.
3. "Jermaine, get into the game for Eddie," Coach Lee said. "On defense, switch with Terrell. I want you to guard Adams, and don't let him get to the basket."

Reread your beginning. If your beginning seems a little flat, improve it by trying one of the strategies above.

Revise

Personal Narrative **111**

Narrative

3 My beginning or ending is weak. Some details are out of order. I need more transitions.

2 I need clearer beginning, middle, and ending parts. I should use transitions.

1 My narrative is very confusing. I should organize my writing chronologically.

Does my ending work well?

You know you have created an effective ending if you can answer *yes* to these four questions.

1. Does my essay build to my personal victory or accomplishment?
2. Does my personal narrative end soon after the most intense or most important moment?
3. Will my reader know why this event is important to me?
4. Are all my reader's questions answered?

If any of these questions leads to a *no* answer, revise your ending to make it solid and satisfying.

Revise

Check your ending. Answer the questions above in order to improve your essay's ending.

Organization
The writer adds details about what he learned.

> Uncle Mark yelled, "Andy? You okay?"
>
> I smiled at him and said, "I guess so." I had been
> and not panic when things got tough
> scared, but I learned that I could handle emergencies.
> Learning that
> ~~What I learned~~ about myself was just a bonus. ~~What really~~
> on top of helping to save the barn that day.
> ~~mattered was that the fire didn't wreck anything.~~

Tip

To conclude a speech, speakers often say, "In closing, I would like to leave you with this . . . " To end your narrative, make sure to leave the reader with a thought that truly puts your experience in perspective.

Divide students into small **writers' groups** *(see below)* of three or four and have them read each other's narratives. Then have the groups talk about each essay, focusing on key questions *(Why is this event important to the writer? Were all your questions answered? and so on).*

- Ask writers to take detailed notes as they receive feedback about their work.
- Remind students that the readers' answers don't need to match the writer's intentions exactly, but if they're very far off, it might indicate that something could be clarified.
- If readers have a lot of unanswered questions, the writer should look at how the essay is organized to see where key information has been misplaced or omitted.

Teaching Tip:
Writers' Groups

Encourage students to work in groups. Explain that the benefits of group work become more apparent over time. Invite interested students to form a regular writers group, either with your participation or on their own.

Revising for Voice

To practice natural voice in dialogue, do a group exercise:

■ Write a flat piece of dialogue on the board.

■ Have students rewrite the dialogue in a voice to match an adjective in the box on the page or another adjective they like.

■ Have students read their rewritten dialogue aloud, without revealing the adjective they chose.

■ Challenge the class to guess the adjective for each piece of dialogue.

■ For additional practice, have each student pass the rewritten dialogue (without revealing the adjective they chose) to another student, who reads it aloud.

■ Did the reader capture the voice that the writer intended? Can the class guess the adjective?

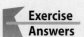
Exercise Answers

Possible Answers

1. awkward, shy, worried
2. confident, bold
3. knowledgeable, practical, hopeful
4. suspicious, worried

Revising for Voice

6 My writer's voice captures the experience perfectly.

5 My dialogue sounds realistic, and my narrative voice is consistent.

4 My dialogue sounds realistic, but I need to make my narrative voice more consistent.

When you revise for *voice*, be sure your dialogue sounds realistic and your narrative voice is consistent. The rubric above can guide your revision.

Does my dialogue sound realistic?

Your dialogue sounds realistic if it reveals the speaker's personality. Here are some adjectives that can describe both the words and personality of a speaker.

eager	bubbly	suspicious	hopeful	bold	elegant
angry	cautious	awkward	bored	confused	worried

Flat Dialogue
"I just heard that I was chosen for the debate team." (flat voice)

Dialogue That Shows Personality
"This rocks! I made the debate team!" (eager)
"How did this happen? I never tried out for the debate team . . . " (suspicious)

Exercise

Read the dialogue below and write an adjective that best describes each speaker's personality.

1. "I'm no good at talking in public."
2. "Nobody can beat me in an argument."
3. "The key to winning any debate is to conduct careful research."
4. "I think the other debate team is up to something."

Revise

Check your dialogue. Think of an adjective to describe the personality of each speaker in your narrative. Does that adjective also describe the words of that person? Rework your dialogue until it sounds realistic.

English Language Learners

Students' spoken and written language reflects their internalized sense of how English works. The dialogue they write may sound awkward. Help students hear and correct one or two constructions in their spoken English before helping them revise for more realistic dialogue in their writing.

Narrative

3 My dialogue needs to sound more natural, and my narrative voice needs to be more consistent.

2 My dialogue sounds unnatural, and I don't have a narrative voice.

1 My writer's voice needs work. It is inconsistent, sounds unnatural, and lacks dialogue.

Have I created a consistent narrative voice?

You have created a consistent narrative voice if your writing sounds like you throughout the piece. Any parts of your writing that sound unnatural will distract the reader.

Exercise

Read the following paragraph. Identify two sentences that sound unnatural. Rewrite them to fit the predominant narrative voice.

When I was little, my dad decided that I should learn about farm animals. So he took me to the petting zoo in the city park. His initial action was to deposit me in the goat containment. The wobbly little goats just quietly stared at me—until the keeper set a milk bottle in my hand. Suddenly, the spindly mob charged me, bleating and fighting for food. I held the bottle higher, which made the animals start to climb me! My father quickly rescued me after I started sobbing. I did not hold these animals in high regard, but over time, I learned to enjoy them. I just always left the feeding to the caretaker.

Revise

Check your narrative voice. Read your narrative aloud and listen for sentences that introduce an unnatural voice. Rework them.

Voice
The dialogue is made more realistic, and the voice is made consistent.

"911. What's the nature of your emergency?"
"~~I have~~ a brush fire ~~at the junction~~ of Highway 9 ~~and the~~ White River!"
There's ... *just east* ... *where crosses*
"Your name and address, sir?"
"~~Where you at, kid?~~"

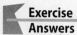

His initial action was . . .
I did not hold these animals . . .

Possible rewrites:
- The first thing he did was put me in the goat pen.
- That was terrifying, but eventually I started to like the little guys.

After making revisions to their own narratives, suggest that students ask a friend or family member to read their narrative aloud to them. This can help students focus on how the words work together to create the writer's voice. The writer should ask the reader to mark the page wherever
- dialogue doesn't sound natural and realistic,
- the reader has to reread any part more than once, or
- the narrative voice interrupts the flow of ideas.

Advanced Learners

Remind students that the goal of creating natural-sounding dialogue should be to attempt to recall what was actually said—not to fabricate conversations. Discuss how memories of events and verbal exchanges vary. For example, two friends who recount the same argument will often give conflicting accounts.

Also encourage students to try not to filter another person's voice through their own speech patterns, but instead to recall and find that person's natural voice. Ask students how an adult, a teenager, and a toddler each might ask for a glass of water. Then discuss how replacing the teen's wording with the toddler's would change a story.

Revising for Word Choice

Be sure to note that, as with adding details, the key is to strike the right balance between specific and general verbs. A narrative with only specific verbs would sound unnatural and forced. For example, using the general verb *said* in a **dialogue tag** *(see below)* helps a writer identify the speaker without drawing attention away from the words being spoken.

Although vivid or specific verbs are effective in moderation, too many can sound overwrought:

> "Ouch!" George yelped.
> "What's the matter?" I called.
> "Mind your own business," he snapped.
> "I thought you might need help," I cried.
> "Well, I don't," he snarled.

✱ For more about specific verbs, see SE page 538.

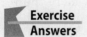
Exercise Answers

Possible Answers

1. scampers, bounces
2. shout, squeak
3. back, run; races, skitters
4. calls, sings out
5. wagging, wiggling

114

Revising for Word Choice

6 My word choice captures the experience and relates it vividly.

5 My word choice is specific and conveys the right feeling.

4 Most of my words have the right feeling, but they aren't always specific enough.

When you revise for *word choice*, be sure to use specific verbs and words with the right connotation, or feeling. Use the rubric strip above as a guide.

Have I used specific verbs?

You know you have used specific verbs when your sentences share clear actions. General verbs do not create a clear picture.

General Verbs	Specific Verbs	
move	shift	amble
	wobble	dawdle
	dart	sneak
look	gaze	study
	stare	peek
	gawk	view

Exercise

In the following sentences, replace the underlined words with specific verbs. Use a thesaurus if you need help.

1. The yapping dachshund <u>moves</u> across the sidewalk.
2. I <u>say</u>, "Watch out! It sounds mean!"
3. Jill and I <u>walk</u> away, but the dachshund <u>comes</u> after us.
4. Suddenly a boy <u>says</u> the dog's name and whistles.
5. The dachshund turns and starts <u>moving</u> its tail.

Check for specific verbs. Make sure that your verbs give a clear idea of what is happening in your narrative. If you need to replace a general verb, check a thesaurus.

Teaching Tip: Dialogue Tags

Ask students to look at sample dialogue in a novel the class is reading (or provide examples for students to look at).

- Have students note the different verbs used in the dialogue tags.
- Point out that the tags are often omitted when it's clear who is speaking. This avoids the necessity of repeating *say* and *said* and it also speeds up the action and makes the conversation more realistic.
- Encourage students to continue to check the books they're reading for pointers about writing dialogue.

English Language Learners

Not all thesauruses provide enough context to be helpful resources for these students. Encourage students to discuss suggested synonyms with English-proficient classmates and/or use bilingual dictionaries to determine which synonyms best capture the intended meanings.

Personal Narrative **115**

Narrative

3 I need to use more specific words and words with the appropriate feeling.

2 My words are very general. I need to find words with the right feeling.

1 I need help finding the right words. My words do not express my feelings.

Do my verbs have the right connotation?

Your verbs have the right connotation when they create the feeling you want. *Connotation* is the suggested meaning or feeling of a word. Notice the different feeling in each set of verbs below.

yell	call	bellow
laugh	giggle	jeer
smile	grin	sneer
discuss	debate	argue

Exercise

For each verb below, write one synonym that has a different connotation. Use a thesaurus if you need help.

1. watch   **4.** repeat   **7.** laugh

2. change   **5.** say   **8.** go

3. walk   **6.** look   **9.** take

Revise

Check connotations. Read through your narrative and watch for verbs with the wrong feeling. Replace them to create the tone or the feeling that fits your story.

Word Choice
Specific words with the right feeling create a stronger tone.

                  roaring
The fire didn't have ~~big~~ flames, but it spread fast in the

dry grass. Uncle Mark and I had mowed the hay field a few

                          baled up
days before, but we had only ~~gathered~~ half the cut grass.

Remind students to consult the dictionary to double-check the meaning of any words they aren't certain about. To demonstrate the subtle (and not so subtle) differences between words, have students find a group of synonymous verbs in an **indexed thesaurus** *(see below)*. As a class, discuss the similarities and differences between the words. For example, the following are all ways of moving quickly:

- *run, race* (*race* implies the idea of a competition)
- *sprint, dash* (both suggest fairly short distances)
- *scamper, scramble* (both imply playfulness; *scramble* is often used for climbing)
- *jog, trot* (both are slower than running)

Exercise Answers

Possible Answers

1. see, observe, spy
2. modify, switch, swap
3. stride, march, amble
4. echo, mimic, redo, restate
5. shout, command, speak
6. stare, peer, glare
7. chuckle, guffaw, snort
8. depart, exit, attend
9. steal, pick up, buy

Teaching Tip: The Indexed Thesaurus

The indexed thesaurus is ideally suited for browsing and for exposing readers to words.

- Provide indexed thesauruses for students to use.
- Demonstrate how to use the index, with its numbered categorization system.

- Show students how each category is divided into groups of synonyms belonging to the various parts of speech.
- Encourage students to browse freely in the category for their word. This may give them other ideas.

Struggling Learners

Modify the **Exercise** so it applies directly to the words students have used in their narrative. Have students look for and discuss synonyms for words they have used often in their writing or words they're not sure of. Throughout the year, have students record synonyms in personal vocabulary notebooks to use as a reference.

Revising for Sentence Fluency

Review compound and complex sentences, longer sentence forms that should be familiar to students:

- Compound—two or more independent clauses joined by a coordinating conjunction.
- Complex—a complete sentence with one or more dependent clauses.

Talk about other types of long sentences, such as those that

- start with a series of details and end with the main idea (periodic sentences),
- start with the main idea and end with a series of details (loose sentences), and
- give details both before and after the main idea (cumulative sentences).

✳ For more about periodic, loose, and cumulative sentences, see SE page 552.

Remind students to avoid the run-on sentence. If necessary, review how to correct run-ons.

✳ For more about run-on sentences, see SE page 557.

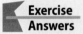

Exercise Answers

Answers will vary.

116

Revising for Sentence Fluency

6 My sentences are skillfully written and hold the reader's interest throughout.

5 I have a variety of sentences that flow smoothly.

4 Most sentences flow smoothly, but I could use some longer sentences.

When you revise for *sentence fluency*, check to see if you have used a variety of long and short sentences. Use the rubric above as a guide.

When should I use long sentences?

Long sentences work best to express complex ideas. In the following example, notice how each long sentence (in blue) expresses several ideas and creates a thoughtful tone.

That morning, I woke up in Aunt Chante's spare bedroom, the one where she grew up and where she still kept her "Lionel Richie Shrine." Lionel Richie was a singer when Aunt Chante was my age, and she still had all her posters of him on the walls and a couple of Commodores album covers thumbtacked to the paisley wallpaper. **I smiled.** Even though Chante was almost 40, at heart she was a teenager like me—funny and crazy with an I-don't-care-what-you-think-of-me attitude. **It was going to be a good day.**

Exercise

Choose one of the long sentences above and write your own sentence that models it. Replace each phrase with a similar phrase about your own topic. Here is an example modeled after the second sentence:

John Wayne was an actor before I was born, but I still like watching the Westerns he made in the '50s and reading biographies about his career.

Check your sentence style. Do you use long sentences to express complex or reflective ideas? Add long sentences or combine short sentences into longer sentences as needed.

Revise

English Language Learners

Students new to English may not be familiar with the terms that describe long sentence forms. Run-on sentences are common when students are beginning to attempt more complex sentences. Check students' writing to determine the most essential instructional goals. Cover one sentence form at a time.

Advanced Learners

Tell students that conciseness adds energy and clarity to an essay. Challenge students to shorten their essays by 15 words, making sure not to eliminate important ideas or details. They should revise awkward or wordy phrasing for conciseness.

Narrative

3 Too many sentences are the same. I should use some long and some short sentences.

2 My sentences are choppy or incomplete, making them hard to read and understand.

1 Most of my sentences should be rewritten.

When should I use short sentences?

Short sentences work well to deliver especially important ideas. Use them like an exclamation point to give a powerful punch. The short sentence in the following example (in blue) makes the reader sit up and take notice.

> **Chante took me to Trinity Church where she sang in a choir with more than 300 people, all of them in Kente cloth and all of them swaying as they belted out Gospel music.** Chante sang a solo.

A series of short sentences can quicken the pace, like a heart beating faster and faster.

> She sang *Amazing Grace*, low and smooth. Then the key changed. Chante took the song up a few steps. The choir sang faster and louder. Chante overtopped them all. They all reached the final chord. What a chord it was! **I suddenly wished that Lionel Richie could see Chante now, wished that I were up there singing with her, too.**

Check your sentence style. Watch for places in your narrative where a single short sentence could deliver an important idea to the reader. Watch for places where a series of short sentences could speed up the pace. **Consider adding or changing sentences.**

Sentence Fluency

Combine short sentences to convey complex ideas.

> I grabbed a bucket by the water trough. ^and^ I started throwing buckets of water on the grass between the barn and the fire. I knew I couldn't stop the blaze, ^, but^ I thought I could slow it down if I soaked the grass enough. . . .

Suggest that students underline the short sentences in their drafts so they stand out for evaluation.

Ask students to consider how and why short sentences help to quicken the pace. Responses may include the following:

- Readers understand short sentences more quickly because there are no extra words to complicate the meaning.
- Short sentences tend to center around active verbs.
- If you read a series of short sentences aloud, you actually have to breathe more quickly.
- Short sentences can work the way quick camera cuts work in films, switching the focus rapidly from one image to another and creating a feeling of speed.

✱ For more about writing short sentences, see SE page 551.

 Writer's Craft

Rhythm: Rhythm isn't just for poets. Prose writers also carefully craft their sentences to create a pleasing flow of thought. Encourage advanced learners to experiment with the pacing of their sentences and even with the rhythm of stressed and unstressed syllables.

Revising Improving Your Writing

Encourage students to browse through "Basic Grammar and Writing" at the back of the student edition (SE pages 532–579). Tell students they will find additional information about the items on the checklist and they will also encounter other topics that can help them as they refine and improve their writing.

Suggest that students approach the checklist after taking a break from their essay. This will give them a fresher outlook and make it more likely that they'll appraise their work realistically.

118

Revising Improving Your Writing

 Check your revising. On your own paper, write the numbers 1 to 12. Put a check by the number if you can answer "yes" to that question. If not, continue revising that part of your personal narrative.

Revising Checklist

Ideas

_____ **1.** Do I focus on one personal accomplishment?
_____ **2.** Do I include action, sensory details, and personal thoughts?
_____ **3.** Do I *show* more than *tell*?

Organization

_____ **4.** Are my beginning, middle, and ending parts effective?
_____ **5.** Do the actions in the middle part create suspense?
_____ **6.** Are the actions and details organized chronologically?

Voice

_____ **7.** Does my dialogue sound realistic?
_____ **8.** Do I have a consistent narrative voice?

Word Choice

_____ **9.** Do I use specific nouns and verbs and explain technical terms?
_____ **10.** Do I use verbs with the right connotation?

Sentence Fluency

_____ **11.** Do I use some long sentences to express complex thoughts?
_____ **12.** Do I use short sentences to pick up the pace or deliver an important idea?

 Make a clean copy. When you've finished revising your essay, make a clean copy to edit.

Grammar Connection

Tone
- **Proofreader's Guide** pages 716–717
- **Write Source** page 538
- **GrammarSnap** Transitive and Intransitive Verbs
- **SkillsBook** pages 98–99

Verbals
- **Proofreader's Guide** pages 726–727, 742–743
- **Write Source** page 554

- **GrammarSnap** Verbals: Gerund, Participle, and Infinitive
- **SkillsBook** pages 100, 132

Pronouns
- **Proofreader's Guide** pages 704–705, 706 (+), 708 (+), 710 (+)
- **Write Source** pages 536 (+), 537 (+)
- **GrammarSnap** Pronoun-Antecedent Agreement
- **SkillsBook** pages 76, 78, 79, 81, 82

Active vs. Passive Voice
- **Proofreader's Guide** pages 722–723
- **SkillsBook** page 95

Sentences
- **Proofreader's Guide** pages 750–751
- **Write Source** pages 552 (+), 553

Editing

Once you've made your revisions, you can edit your writing for conventions: punctuation, capitalization, spelling, and grammar.

Keys to Effective Editing

1. Use a dictionary, a thesaurus, and the "Proofreader's Guide" on pages 604–763 in this book to guide your corrections.

2. Check for any words or phrases that may be confusing to the reader.

3. Check your narrative for correct use of punctuation, capitalization, spelling, and grammar.

4. Edit on a printed computer copy and then enter your changes on the computer.

5. Use the editing and proofreading marks on the inside back cover of this book to note your changes.

Narrative

Editing

Keys to Effective Editing

Remind students that during the editing stage they have a chance to find and correct errors in

- punctuation,
- capitalization,
- spelling, and
- grammar.

Keys to Effective Editing lists the process students will be guided through on SE pages 120–122.

Point out that while input from **outside readers** *(see below)* is helpful at any stage, it is extremely important during editing. Writers can be so sure of what the words are *supposed* to say that certain mistakes become invisible to them. Errors may stand out more for someone who is unfamiliar with the piece. Suggest that students have someone else read the essay after they have edited it themselves. That way, the reader can help catch any errors that may have been overlooked.

Suggest that students always mark editing changes using colored ink or pencil that will stand out on the page. This makes the corrections easier to see when students make a clean copy.

 Technology Connections

Students can use the added features of the Net-text as they explore this stage of the writing process.

Write Source Online *Net-text*

Teaching Tip: Outside Readers

Remind students that although outside readers bring a fresh eye to the piece, they may not know what to look for when they proofread. Encourage students to ask a classmate to be an outside reader and suggest that they give a copy of the editing checklist to their reader.

Grammar Exercise
Answers

1. Angie said, "Do you believe that guy?"
2. Was Marta joking when she said, "Talk about attitude!"?
3. Crystal screamed, "Don't you know who he was?"
4. "Yeah!" Ora shrieked. "That guy was Phil Axis, the record producer!"
5. That guy asked Angie, "Do you want to be on my record?"

Editing **for** Conventions

6 My grammar and punctuation are correct, and the copy is free of spelling errors.

5 I have a few minor errors in grammar, spelling, or punctuation, but they won't confuse the reader.

4 I must correct a number of errors in punctuation, spelling, or grammar that may distract the reader.

When you edit for *conventions*, you check punctuation, capitalization, spelling, and grammar. Use the rubric strip above to help you edit your writing for conventions.

Have I punctuated dialogue correctly?

You have punctuated dialogue correctly if you have followed the three rules shown below.

- Use a comma to set off a speaker's exact words from the rest of the sentence.
  "Bob Taylor, it's a pleasure to meet you," said Melissa Moore.

- Place periods and commas inside quotation marks.
  "Hello," Bob said. "It's a pleasure to meet you."

- Place an exclamation point or a question mark outside quotation marks when it punctuates the main sentence, and inside when it punctuates the quotation.
  What if someone said to you, "You've won a million dollars!"?
  I would say, "Are you kidding me?"

Grammar Exercise

On your own paper, punctuate these sentences correctly.

1. Angie said Do you believe that guy?
2. Was Marta joking when she said Talk about attitude!?
3. Crystal screamed Don't you know who he was?
4. Yeah! Ora shrieked That guy was Phil Axis, the record producer!
5. That guy asked Angie Do you want to be on my record?

Edit

Edit your dialogue. Use the rules and examples in the middle of this page to be sure you've punctuated the dialogue correctly. Also see **616.1** and **632.1–632.2**.

Grammar Connection

Punctuating Dialogue
- **Proofreader's Guide** pages 616–617, 632–633
- *SkillsBook* page 34

English Language Learners

Students' errors in punctuation, spelling, and capitalization may be related more to the effort it takes to write in a new language than to carelessness. Effective proofreading requires native-like language proficiency.

After students attempt to edit the piece themselves, allow them to work with cooperative partners to correct the one or two errors that most interfere with a reader's ability to comprehend the piece.

Personal Narrative **121**

Narrative

3 I need to correct some errors that will confuse my reader.

2 I need to fix many errors that make my writing hard to read and understand.

1 I need help finding errors and making corrections.

Have I used pronouns correctly?

You have used pronouns correctly if they agree with their antecedents. (An *antecedent* is a noun or pronoun that a pronoun replaces or refers to.) A pronoun must agree with its antecedent in number, person, and gender.

A pronoun must agree with its antecedent in number (singular or plural), person (first, second, or third person), and gender (masculine, feminine, neuter, or indefinite). (See pages **708–711**.)

Mr. Lucas **owns 10 horses, and** he **trains** them.

(*Mr. Lucas* is the antecedent for *he*. Both words are singular, third person, and masculine. *Horses* is the antecedent for *them*. Both words are plural, third person, and indefinite.)

Grammar Exercise

Write sentences following the directions below.

1. Use a singular first-person pronoun and antecedent.
2. Use a plural third-person pronoun and antecedent.
3. Use a singular third-person masculine pronoun and antecedent.

 Check your pronouns. Review your personal narrative to make sure that you have used pronouns correctly. Use the information above as a guide.

Conventions
Punctuation is added and a pronoun-antecedent agreement problem is corrected.

> After the beep, I said, "Uncle Mark! There's a fire in the
> hay field! I called 911 already, but get home quick!"
> I hung up the phone and ran outside. I knew we had
> to do something on ~~our~~ my own. If the tall grass around the . . .

Focus on ambiguous pronouns, a common error for writers. Explain that an ambiguous pronoun occurs when there is more than one possible antecedent for a pronoun. Sometimes the effect is confusing, and sometimes it is comical. Write examples of ambiguous pronoun usage on the board and challenge students to suggest ways to correct the problem.

■ *Anil told Josh that he couldn't make plans for the weekend.* (Does *he = Anil* or *Josh*?)
■ *Puppies will chew on your shoes if you're not careful, so always keep them locked in the closet.* (Does *them = puppies* or *shoes*?)

✱ For more about the agreement of pronouns and their antecedents, see SE page 756.

Grammar Exercise Answers

Students' sentences will vary but should include the following pronouns:
1. *I, me, my,* or *mine*
2. *they, them, their,* or *theirs*
3. *he, him,* or *his*

English Language Learners

Number and gender of nouns and pronouns are not universal concepts. Have students tab the appropriate pages in the Parts of Speech reference section (SE pages 700–737) that address their specific errors. Encourage students to refer to these pages every time they edit their writing.

Grammar Connection

Pronoun-Antecedent Agreement
■ **Proofreader's Guide** pages 756–757
■ *GrammarSnap* Pronoun-Antecedent Agreement
■ *SkillsBook* page 154

Editing Checking Your Writing

Give students a few moments to look over the Proofreader's Guide (SE pages 604–763). Tell them that throughout the year they can refer to the guidelines, rules, and examples to clarify any checklist items or to resolve questions about their own writing.

Remind students that the editing checklist includes selected items only, and that there are many other important conventions.

Creating a Title

Talk about conventions for capitalization in titles. Draw students' attention to each of the three model titles in turn.

■ Models 1 and 2: Why is *Against* capitalized, while *with* is lowercase? (Some publishers choose to capitalize longer prepositions and lowercase only short prepositions such as *with*. Other publishers lowercase all prepositions.)
■ Model 3: Why is *Up* capitalized? Isn't it a short preposition? (No. In this sentence, it is an adverb.)

Note that sometimes writers lowercase *is* in titles, perhaps because it's so short. This is an error. Example: *A Star Is Born*.

✱ For more about capitalizing in titles, see SE page 650.

122

Editing Checking Your Writing

Check your editing. On a piece of paper, write the numbers 1 to 12. Put a check by the number if you can answer "yes" to that question. If not, continue to edit your narrative for that convention.

Editing Checklist

Conventions

PUNCTUATION

_____ 1. Do I use end punctuation after all my sentences?
_____ 2. Do I use commas after longer introductory word groups?
_____ 3. Do I use commas correctly in compound and complex sentences?
_____ 4. Do I punctuate my dialogue correctly?
_____ 5. Do I use apostrophes to show possession (a girl's book)?

CAPITALIZATION

_____ 6. Do I start all my sentences with capital letters?
_____ 7. Do I capitalize all proper nouns?

SPELLING

_____ 8. Have I spelled all my words correctly?
_____ 9. Have I double-checked the words my spell-checker may have missed?

GRAMMAR

_____ 10. Do I use correct forms of verbs (had gone, not had went)?
_____ 11. Do my pronouns agree with their antecedents?
_____ 12. Do I use the right words (to, too, two; their, there, they're)?

Creating a Title

■ Focus on the tone or the overall feeling created by the words in your essay: **Racing Against a Fire**
■ Use alliteration, the repetition of a consonant sound: **Face-to-Face with Fire**
■ Play with words: **Almost Up in Smoke!**

Grammar Connection

Spelling and Plurals
■ **Proofreader's Guide** pages 654–657
■ *SkillsBook* pages 51, 52, 53

Advanced Learners

To help students analyze the tone or feeling of titles, ask them to bring to class the Living, Arts, or Style section of the newspaper. Have students scan the section for clever headlines. Discuss why each headline works. Ask students to identify any creative devices that are used.

Publishing Sharing Your Essay

After you have completed revising and editing, you can make a neat final copy of your story to share. Other publishing ideas include recording your narrative, presenting it in a class blog, or simply sharing it with a group of your peers. (See the suggestions below.)

Make a final copy. When you write your final copy, follow your teacher's instructions or use the guidelines below. (If you use a computer, see pages **76–78** for formatting tips.) Create a clean copy of your personal narrative and carefully proofread it.

Focus on Presentation

- Use blue or black ink and write neatly.
- Write your name in the upper left-hand corner of page 1.
- Skip a line and center your title; skip another line and begin your essay.
- Double-space your narrative.
- Indent every paragraph and leave a one-inch margin on all four sides.
- Write your last name and the page number in the upper right-hand corner of every page after the first one.

Record Your Narrative

Produce a recording of your narrative. Use an expressive voice that matches the tone of your work. Give the recording and a printed copy of the narrative to friends and family as a gift.

Create a Class Blog

Encourage all of your classmates to submit their stories to a class blog or Web site. Use graphics to illustrate each narrative.

Perform Your Narrative

Turn your narrative into a script. Assign roles and perform the story for the class or for other audiences. (See pages **323–332** for help.)

Publishing
Sharing Your Essay

Encourage students to consider submitting their essays for publication, either online or in print.

Remind students to be careful to choose organizations with good reputations—they should never have to pay anyone to publish their work. Tell students they should read the submission guidelines carefully and they should also take time to read the Web site or magazine to make sure their work will fit in.

✱ For more on publishing online, see SE page 79.

Technology Connections

Remind students that they can use the Writing Network features of the Portfolio to share their work with peers.

✴ **Write Source Online** *Portfolio*

✴ **Write Source Online** *Net-text*

English Language Learners

Students may become discouraged because they do not realize it takes many years to become fully proficient in a new language. Reviewing students' written work and having them listen to recordings of themselves collected throughout the year gives them a sense of the progress they have made.

Rubric for Narrative Writing

Remind students that a rubric is a chart that helps them evaluate their writing.

- The rubrics in this book are based on a six-point scale in which a score of 6 indicates an amazing piece of writing, and a score of 1 means the writing is incomplete and not ready to be assessed.
- Explain that the purpose of the rubric is to help students break down the assessment process by evaluating each of the six traits individually—ideas, organization, voice, word choice, sentence fluency, and conventions.
- Point out that rubrics are also helpful during the writing process. They can guide the writer whenever he or she writes because they tell what elements to include in the writing and how to present them.
- Explain to students that they will most likely have different ratings for the traits. For example, they may give themselves a 5 for ideas but a 4 for organization.

✱ Reproducible six-, five-, and four-point rubrics for narrative writing can be found on TE pages 767, 771, and 775.

Rubric for Narrative Writing

Use the following rubric as a guide for assessing your narrative writing. Refer to it whenever you want to improve your writing.

6 Ideas	**5**	**4**
The narrative shares a memorable event. Details bring the essay to life.	The writer shares an interesting experience. Specific details help maintain interest.	The writer tells about an interesting experience. Details need to show, not tell.

Organization		
The structure of the narrative makes it enjoyable and easy to read.	The narrative has a clear beginning, middle, and ending. Transitions are helpful.	For the most part, the narrative is organized. Most of the transitions are helpful.

Voice		
The writer's voice captures the experience for the reader.	The writer's voice sounds natural. Dialogue helps hold the reader's interest.	The writer's voice creates interest in the essay, but dialogue needs to sound more natural.

Word Choice		
The writer's excellent word choice creates a vivid picture of the event.	Specific nouns, verbs, and modifiers create clear images and feelings.	Some stronger nouns, verbs, and/or modifiers would create a clearer picture.

Sentence Fluency		
The sentences are skillfully written to hold the reader's interest.	The sentences show variety and are easy to understand.	The sentences are varied, but some should flow more smoothly.

Conventions		
The narrative has no errors in spelling, grammar, or punctuation.	The narrative has a few minor errors in punctuation, grammar, or spelling.	The narrative has some errors that may distract the reader.

Narrative

3	2	1
The writer should focus on one event. Some details do not relate to the essay.	The writer should focus on one experience. More details are needed.	The writer should select an experience and provide details.
The order of events must be corrected. More transitions are needed.	The beginning, middle, and ending all run together. The order is unclear.	The narrative must be organized.
The writer's voice can usually be heard. More dialogue is needed.	The voice is weak. Dialogue is needed.	The writer sounds uninvolved or disinterested in the essay.
More specific nouns, verbs, and modifiers would paint a clearer picture of the event.	Better words are needed. Words are overused or too general to paint a clear picture.	The writer has not considered word choice or has used words incorrectly.
A better variety of sentences is needed. Sentences do not flow smoothly.	Many incomplete or short sentences make the writing choppy.	Few sentences are written well. Help is needed.
The narrative has several errors.	Numerous errors make the narrative hard to read and confusing.	Help is needed to find errors and make corrections.

Test Prep!

The six traits of writing were first identified in the 1960s by Paul Diederich and a group of 50 professionals who reviewed student papers and brainstormed the qualities that made writing strong. In 1983, a group of educators in Beaverton, Oregon, learned of Diederich's work and replicated it, settling on a similar set of six traits. A separate team in Missoula, Montana, simultaneously ran a study that identified the same basic group of traits.

Put simply, the six traits provide a universal set of criteria for strong writing. They correlate very well to the rubrics used in most state testing. Using the traits throughout the writing process, therefore, prepares students for any writing test they will face.

Evaluating a Personal Narrative

Ask students if they agree with the sample self-assessment on SE page 127. If they agree with the overall comments, ask them to suggest improvements based on the comments. If they disagree with any comment, ask them to explain why.

Challenge students to identify the conventions errors in the model. Possible responses:

- In paragraph 2, *flutter* should be *fluttered*.
- In paragraphs 5, 14, and 16, correct the punctuation in the dialogue—there should be commas after *Jan, time,* and *job,* not periods.
- At the end of paragraph 5, put the question mark inside the quotation marks.
- At the beginning of paragraph 8, add a period after *Ms.*
- Later in paragraph 8, replace the period after *once* and lowercase *But* to make a compound sentence.
- In paragraph 11, add a hyphen to create the adjective *brand-new.*
- In paragraph 17, place a comma after *know.*

Evaluating a Personal Narrative

As you read the narrative below, focus on the writer's strengths and weaknesses. (**The essay contains a few errors.**) Then read the student's self-assessment on page **127**.

Musical Chairs

Ever since I began playing trumpet in fifth grade, being first chair in the high school band has been my dream. I had worked up to second chair in freshman band, just behind Luis. Now I was challenging him for first chair.

Luis and I sat in the band room after school, waiting for our director, Ms. Reilly. Luis nervously twirled his trumpet, while I fingered the keys on mine. Had I oiled them enough? I flutter the tabs up and down, making quick little "thumpa-thumpa" sounds in the valve casings.

I had worked for this moment, practicing every night. I had changed my embouchure and breathing to get more volume and a fuller sound. I looked at Luis. He was a good guy, and I felt guilty challenging him.

"I'm sorry about this, Luis," I mumbled.

"Hey, it's okay, Jan." he said. "Ya gotta do what ya gotta do." Then he kind of smirked a little. "Besides, who said you're gonna win"?

I laughed. "Well, I'll give it my best shot."

"Me, too."

Ms Reilly arrived and said, "Okay, let's start. Luis, you can go first." He played the trumpet solo from one of our band pieces. He sounded pretty good. Then I played the same piece. I cracked once. But it wasn't too bad. Before that we had run through some short exercises, playing high notes and low notes. Trills and turns. It was cool—like a "dueling trumpets."

"Very nice! Try this one."

She gave us each another piece of music, and this time I went first. It had some tricky fingering, but I got through it. When Luis played, his staccato notes weren't as clean as mine. I started to relax.

Then Ms. Reilly said, "Let's try a brand new piece." I felt my nerves return. Luis looked worried, too.

"To be fair, I want you to play it together first," Ms. Reilly said. "Ready? Start at the andante. One-two, one-two—"

Struggling Learners

To help students assess the essay, break up the evaluation into several readings. In their first reading, they should pay attention to the ideas. Then they should reread to evaluate more closely for organization and voice. In their final scan, they should search solely for errors in word choice, sentence fluency, and conventions.

Narrative

> As I got into the piece, I concentrated on the notes. Luis and I both messed up in a few places.
>
> "Now one at a time." Ms. Reilly said. "Jan, you go first."
>
> I was surprised how much easier it seemed the second time. At his turn, Luis made more mistakes than I did. Finally we were finished.
>
> "You both did a great job." Ms. Reilly said. "I'm sorry, Luis, but it looks like Jan gets to be first chair."
>
> Luis gave a half grin and said, "Pretty good, Jan. But you know I'll just have to challenge you next."
>
> "I'll be ready," I said.

Student Self-Assessment

Narrative Rubric Checklist

Title: Musical Chairs
Writer: Jan Maggin

6 Ideas
- Is the essay about an important accomplishment?
- Does it have enough specific details about the event?
- Does it *show* the event rather than *tell* about it?

5 Organization
- Does the beginning grab the reader?
- Does the middle part follow chronological order and increase the narrative tension?
- Does the ending work well?

5 Voice
- Is the dialogue realistic?
- Is the narrative voice natural and consistent?

4 Word Choice
- Do the words have the right connotation?
- Are the nouns and verbs specific?

5 Sentence Fluency
- Is there a good variety of sentences?
- Do the sentences flow smoothly?

4 Conventions
- Does the essay avoid errors in punctuation, spelling, and grammar?
- Is the dialogue punctuated correctly?

OVERALL COMMENTS:
The details of my narrative are complete and clear.

The events are in the right order, except for the part about the exercises before the challenge.

My voice and dialogue sound interesting and natural.

I should have explained technical terms like "embouchure," "trills and turns," and "staccato."

My sentences flow well.

I need to review how to punctuate dialogue.

Review your narrative. Rate your narrative and write comments about why you gave yourself the scores you did.

Student Self-Assessment

To give students additional practice with evaluating a narrative essay, use a reproducible Assessment Sheet (TE page 766), the Narrative Rubric Checklist (TE page 779), and one or both of the **benchmark papers** listed in the Benchmark Papers box below. For your benefit, a completed checklist and comments are provided for each benchmark paper.

Consider scheduling one-on-one writing conferences with students to discuss their self-evaluations. This will help you assess their understanding of the narrative rubric. It will also give you a sense of how to help them look at their own work critically.

In the conference, encourage students to explain why they scored their essays as they did. Tell them what you agree with and, as needed, discuss points they might have missed.

English Language Learners

Not all of the items on the Self-Assessment checklist will be meaningful to students. To modify the Student Self-Assessment activity, have students evaluate their progress only on the specific errors they addressed throughout the unit. Have them focus on correcting these errors in all writing until new goals are established.

Benchmark Papers

It's a Boy! (good)
TE pp. 783–787

My Cousin's Wedding (poor)
TE pp. 788–791

Reflecting on Your Writing

Tell students they may freewrite any additional thoughts they have about their essays on the back of the reflections page.

Have students put the essay title and the date at the top of the page and file the reflection, along with the corresponding essay, in their portfolio. Remind them that it is helpful to go back through their reflections from time to time, especially as they begin a new project. This will

- show students how much they've improved,
- pinpoint areas that still need improvement,
- remind them of important discoveries they've made about the writing process, and
- refresh their memory of ideas they wanted to pursue further.

Reflecting on Your Writing

You've worked hard to write a personal narrative that your classmates will enjoy. Now take some time to think about your writing. Finish each of the sentence starters below on your own paper. Thinking about your writing will help you see how you are growing as a writer.

My Narrative

1. The strongest part of my personal narrative is . . .

2. The part that still needs work is . . .

3. The main thing I learned about writing a personal narrative is . . .

4. In my next personal narrative, I would like to . . .

5. One question I still have about writing personal narratives is . . .

Narrative Writing
Biographical Narrative

Writing a personal narrative gives you a chance to revisit an experience that affected or changed you. In the same way, writing a biographical narrative offers you an opportunity to re-create a significant event in the life of someone you know. An effective biographical narrative makes the experience come alive for the reader by including dialogue, action, and specific details.

In this chapter, you will read a biographical narrative about the writer's great-grandfather, who became famous in the newspaper industry. Then you will write a biographical narrative of your own.

Writing Guidelines

Subject: An important experience in another person's life
Form: Biographical narrative
Purpose: To share a life-changing event
Audience: Classmates

"To write about people you have to know people, to write about bloodhounds you have to know bloodhounds, to write about the Loch Ness monster you have to find out about it."

—James Thurber

Biographical Narrative

Objectives
- choose a topic for a biographical narrative (an important experience in the life of someone the student knows)
- gather details for the essay and organize them chronologically
- write, revise, and edit a biographical narrative

A **biographical narrative** is about the experiences of a person other than the writer. In this section, students will work on biographical narratives about friends or family members.

Alternatively, you may wish to give students the option to coordinate the exercise with a topic they are studying for social studies or history and write about historical figures. If so, follow all steps as described in the section, but allow additional time for students to research their chosen subjects during the prewriting stage.

✱ For information about research writing, see SE pages 342–392.

Struggling Learners

To help students connect with the concept of biographical narratives, remind them that the stories family members recount about their lives or the lives of their other relatives and ancestors are oral versions of such narratives. Ask a few students to share a favorite family story about a grandparent or other relative.

Discuss why these stories are captivating: Do they contain an element of surprise? Did the relative overcome an obstacle? Are the stories funny? Do they engender pride? Are the details vivid?

Copy Masters

Time Line (TE p. 133)

Sample Biographical Narrative

Draw students' attention to the dialogue in the essay and use this as a starting point for a discussion about the purpose of and audience for a biographical narrative. Discuss the following ideas:

- Julie can't know exactly what was said during this conversation, unless her great-grandfather told her.
- A professional biographer's audience would expect the book to be as factual and accurate as possible.

Note, however, that students' biographical narratives have a different purpose. Their goal is to practice telling a compelling story—and dialogue is one of the best ways to do that. Suggest that students think of their narratives as biographies that contain elements of historical fiction.

 Literature Connections

Biographical writing: For an inspiring glimpse into another person's life, see the graphic novel *Persepolis: The Story of a Childhood* by Marjane Satrapi. Through words and images, the author reveals what it was like to live through the Iranian cultural revolution of 1979. This book may be especially illuminating to struggling students and English Language Learners (for whom the visuals will aid comprehension), as well as students from other cultures.

130

Sample Biographical Narrative

A biographical narrative shares a specific experience from someone else's life. Julie wrote about the day her great-grandfather became a news reporter.

Beginning
The first paragraph sets the scene.

Middle
The middle part starts right in the middle of the action.

Explanations are added as needed.

Details capture specific actions.

Henry's Big Break

My great-grandfather, Henry A. Benson, is the most famous person in our family. He rose from delivering newspapers in his small hometown of Cross Plains, Texas, to becoming the editor in chief of one of the biggest papers in the state. He tells many stories about his days as a reporter, but his favorite one takes place on a late spring afternoon in 1941. That's the day Great-granddad got his big break.

Inside the offices of the *Center State Chronicle*, 15-year-old Henry took a deep breath. The warm air of the print room filled his lungs, and the smell of hot ink lingered in his nose. He stuffed his hands into the pockets of his worn-out jeans so the paper's editor, Mr. Walsh, wouldn't see how nervous he felt.

"Mr. Walsh," Henry said, "I've delivered your paper for three years now. I've never missed one day. If you make me a reporter, I won't let you down."

"Henry," Mr. Walsh replied, "there's a big difference between being a delivery boy and being a reporter. Maybe after you've finished school."

Trying not to let his disappointment show, Henry left the newspaper office. What was he going to do? The paper route just didn't earn him enough money to help his mom. He got his battered bicycle and pedaled across town toward home.

Near an old bridge, Henry saw skid marks on the pavement. Tire tracks showed where a car had recently left the road. Henry spotted a sedan lying at the bottom of the ravine.

Henry flagged down a passing car to fetch an ambulance. Then he scrambled down the ravine. The car's right front tire was shredded, which must have been why the car ran off the road. The driver lay slumped over the steering wheel. He was a middle-aged man wearing a

English Language Learners

Read the first paragraph with students and ask if they understand the idiom *big break*. Explain that it means a sudden or unexpected chance to do something.

Narrative

rumpled brown suit. A dark bruise marked the driver's forehead.

Dialogue adds realism.

"Are you all right?" Henry asked the man.

". . . Can't move my right arm," the driver mumbled.

Henry opened the car door and took a look. He tried not to let the man see how scared he felt. "It looks broken," Henry said. "I'll do what I can to help until the ambulance gets here."

Henry tried to talk to the injured man to keep him awake, but the man passed out anyway. Henry understood the seriousness of the situation and stayed with the man until an ambulance came. Only when the man was safely on his way to the hospital did it occur to Henry that the accident was newsworthy. Maybe this was the story that could make him a real reporter!

He raced home and typed up an account of the accident. Then he pedaled as fast as he could back to the *Chronicle* offices. Editor Walsh ran the story and began to realize that Henry had the right stuff to become a reporter.

Ending
The final paragraph explains the importance of the experience.

In the years that followed, my great-grandfather learned to be a great reporter. Later, he became one of the most respected newspaper editors in Texas. No matter how famous he became, though, he always loved to tell about the day he got his big break. His story still inspires me whenever I think about what kind of job I might love.

 Respond to the reading. Answer the following questions about the sample biographical narrative.

Ideas (1) What specific event does the writer share? (2) What is the most exciting part of the narrative?

Organization (3) How are the beginning and ending parts different from the middle part?

Voice & Word Choice (4) Which words or phrases help create specific images? Name three or four.

Literature Connections: In Chapter 8 of *Seabiscuit: An American Legend* by Laura Hillenbrand, you can find a biographical narrative about the jockey Red Pollard and one of his rides on the famous racehorse Seabiscuit.

As a group, discuss students' responses to the reading, focusing especially on questions 2 (what is most exciting) and 4 (most evocative words and phrases). Students will likely have different answers. Encourage them to explain why they feel as they do.

 Respond to the reading.

Answers

Ideas 1. how her great-grandfather broke into newspaper reporting **2.** Answers may vary. Possible answers: Some students may identify the discovery of the accident, while others may point to Henry's realization that he could write about his experience.

Organization 3. The middle part uses dialogue and action to create a fast-paced story. The beginning and ending are more descriptive; they frame the story by setting the scene and telling the outcome of the events, respectively.

Voice & Word Choice 4. Possible answers: *The warm air of the print room; the smell of hot ink; worn-out jeans; battered bicycle; the car's right front tire was shredded; middle-aged man wearing a rumpled brown suit*

 Literature Connections

"What Makes a Winner?" (an excerpt from *Seabiscuit: An American Legend*), by Laura Hillenbrand, is an example of a biographical narrative. Though the author must research and report facts accurately, she engages the reader by setting up feelings of tension and concern about the events of the story.

Discuss with students some techniques that a biographer can use, such as foreshadowing, to build suspense in the same way that a fiction writer does. For additional models of narrative writing, see the Reading-Writing Connections beginning on page TE-36.

Prewriting **Selecting a Topic**

After reviewing cluster diagrams with students, suggest that they use a different color of ink for each person they include in their clusters. This will make it easy to see at a glance which person on the diagram is associated with which ideas.

✳ For more about cluster diagrams, see SE page 582.

Prewriting **Gathering Details**

Talk about the fact that, since she was writing a story that had been passed down in her family, Julie already knew many of the details she would include in her narrative. This would not necessarily be true if she had decided to write about someone outside of her family, or if she hadn't been able to remember much of the story.

Tell students not to be discouraged if they have trouble remembering details about their topic.

Emphasize that freewriting is the perfect time to note questions they have about details they'd like to include.

✳ For more about freewriting, see SE page 582.

 Technology Connections

Students can use the added features of the Net-text as they explore this stage of the writing process.

➤ *Write Source Online* **Net-text**

Prewriting **Selecting a Topic**

Julie used a cluster to identify possible topics for her biographical narrative. Next to each name, she listed one or two possible story ideas.

Cluster Diagram

first newspaper job · meets Great-grandma · performs in musical · Great-grandfather · Jill · people I know · Uncle Liam · moves to Ireland · works on ship to Hong Kong

 Choose your topic. Create a cluster, naming different people you know and their stories. Put an asterisk (✳) next to the story that you would like to write about.

Gathering Details

Next you need to gather details for the narrative. Julie wrote freely about her story idea to determine what she remembered about the experience. Here is part of her freewriting.

Freewriting

> My great-grandpa, Henry A. Benson, was a famous news reporter, but he really had to work for everything that he got. He started by delivering papers in a small town. But he wanted to do more, so my great-grandpa asked if he could be a reporter. The editor said that he was too young, but soon Great-grandpa got to prove his ability. . . .

 Freewrite to gather details. Write for 10 to 15 minutes about your story idea. Let your ideas flow, writing down everything that comes to mind about the topic.

Struggling Learners

To help students choose a topic, work as a class to create a list of people students know. Encourage them to think about the people connected to the different places where they spend time. They can then review the list to get ideas for a topic.

- School—friends, classmates, teachers, other staff
- Home—family of every generation, neighbors
- Activities—club members, team members, coaches

Advanced Learners

Suggest that students repeat the freewriting exercise from the perspective of another person involved in the event. By reviewing this second freewrite, students may discover new details and dialogue to use in their writing. If the event does not involve another person, they may use an imaginary participant.

Asking Questions

After reviewing her freewriting, Julie realized that she needed to ask her grandpa a few questions about his dad. Here are some of her questions:

1. Where did Henry live?
2. How old was he when this experience happened?
3. What was the name of the paper and the editor?

Gather more details. Review your freewriting and write down all the questions you have. Talk to someone who knows about the event to find your answers.

Organizing Your Details

A biographical narrative is a type of story, and stories are almost always told chronologically. Julie used a time line to organize the details she had gathered about her great-grandfather's story. Above the line, she listed key events or actions related to the story, and below the line, she listed details.

Time Line

asks to be reporter	sees car wreck	helps driver	writes first story
-needs money	-near old bridge	-flags down car	-rushes home
-talks to Mr. Walsh	-sees tire tracks	-goes in ravine	-writes first story
-turned down	-car in ravine	-helps driver	-gets job

Create a time line. Organize the details of your story. List key events above the line and details below it.

Focus on the Traits

Organization The beginning paragraph in the narrative on pages 130–131 introduces the person and his story. The ending paragraph tells what happened because of the experience. In this way, the beginning and ending paragraphs frame the story, which is told in the middle.

Prewriting Asking Questions

Remind students that this is a good time to confirm and clarify details from their freewriting.

If time permits, encourage students to do additional research. This could mean talking to other people, reading family papers, or, in some cases, conducting library or Internet research.

Note that because Henry's account of the event was published, it's possible that Julie could have gotten a copy of the article to read by contacting the newspaper or by going to her local library. Her great-grandfather became well known, so she might also have been able to find published information about him.

Prewriting Organizing Your Details

Distribute a copy of the reproducible Time Line (TE page 816) for students to fill out. Note that although the reproducible Time Line is vertical, it can be used the same way as the sample horizontal time line. The vertical time line also allows more space for **note taking** (see below).

✱ For more about chronological order, see SE page 571.

Teaching Tip: Note Taking

Point out that the chart format of the graphic does not always allow space for detailed notes. Suggest that students can expand the organizers by using index cards. When they fill the space on the chart, have them continue writing on a numbered index card.

Writing Creating Your First Draft

Explain to students that it isn't necessary for them to write the beginning, middle, and ending parts of their narratives in order, unless they want to. It may be easier for them to tell the story first, and then add the "framing" paragraphs—the beginning and ending. Or, if they have a great idea for an ending, they can capture that on paper first; then they can fill the rest in.

Remind students to check their planning notes regularly as they write, so they don't accidentally leave out an important detail. They may find it helpful to cross details off their planning notes after they mention them in the draft.

✱ For more about writing narrative paragraphs, see SE page 564.

 Technology Connections

Students can use the added features of the Net-text as they explore this stage of the writing process.

🔆 *Write Source Online* **Net-text**

Writing Creating Your First Draft

To write your biographical narrative, use your time line of events and details as a guide. Also read through the tips listed on this page. They will help you develop the three main parts of your writing—the beginning, the middle, and the ending.

| Beginning |
| Middle |
| Ending |

Writing Your Beginning Paragraph

Set the stage for your story. Introduce the character and his or her story. Give just enough information to grab the reader's interest.

> . . . That's the day Great-granddad got his big break.

Creating Your Middle Paragraphs

Let the reader share your experience. Here are four ways to do that.

- Start right in the middle of the action.
  Inside the offices of the Center State Chronicle, 15-year-old Henry took a deep breath. The warm air of the print room filled his lungs, and the smell of hot ink lingered in his nose.
- Provide specific details. Show, don't tell.
  He stuffed his hands into the pockets of his worn-out jeans so the paper's editor, Mr. Walsh, wouldn't see how nervous he felt.
- Add dialogue. Reveal the person's character.
  "Mr. Walsh," Henry said, "I've delivered your paper for three years now. . . ."
- Include explanations and thoughts as needed.
  Trying not to let his disappointment show, Henry left the newspaper office. What was he going to do?

Finishing with a Strong Ending Paragraph

Bring your narrative to a close. Tell what happened because of the experience or why it was important.

> **In the years that followed, my great-grandfather learned to be a great reporter. . . . His story still inspires me whenever I think about what kind of job I might love.**

Write

Write your first draft. Use your time line (page 133) and the tips above to guide your writing. Your aim is to get all your ideas on paper.

Struggling Learners

To help students complete their ending paragraphs, ask them to read the beginning and middle parts to a partner and then explain why they chose this story to write about. Encourage the partner to ask questions about why the story matters to the author. By talking it over casually, the importance and meaning of the story may come more easily to mind. Using these fresh insights, students may then return to writing their final paragraphs.

Revising Improving Your Writing

Use the following checklist to decide how to improve your writing.

Revising Checklist

Ideas

_____ **1.** Is my subject's story an interesting one?
_____ **2.** Do I include enough specific details?

Organization

_____ **3.** Does my beginning paragraph introduce the person and story?
_____ **4.** Do the middle paragraphs re-create the experience?
_____ **5.** Does the ending tell why the experience was important?

Voice

_____ **6.** Does my interest in the story come through?
_____ **7.** Does the dialogue sound natural?

Word Choice

_____ **8.** Have I used specific nouns?
_____ **9.** Do I capture the experience with vivid verbs and modifiers?

Sentence Fluency

_____ **10.** Do my sentences read smoothly?
_____ **11.** Have I used a variety of long and short sentences?

Creating a Title

- Be clever: **Accidental Reporter**
- Use an expression: **A Reporter Is Born**
- Use a line from the narrative: **Skid Marks on the Pavement**

Check your first draft and add a title. Use the checklist above to review your first draft. Then use one of the strategies above or an idea of your own to add a title to your narrative.

Revising Improving Your Writing

Focus briefly on checklist item 8, about specific nouns. Review the different types of nouns (common, proper, concrete, and abstract). Challenge students to call out examples of specific nouns that exemplify each type.

✱ For information about specific nouns, see SE page 534.

Creating a Title

Tell students they should remain open to the possibility that the perfect title idea could come to them at any stage in the writing process. Whenever they think of titles, students should immediately jot them down on their planning notes, so they won't forget about them.

Challenge students to come up with two or more possible titles, using a different strategy for each. Which one works best?

 Writer's Craft

Titles: Different writers approach titles differently. Here are two quotations to share with your students:

"Sometimes people give titles to me, and sometimes I see them on a billboard."

—Robert Penn Warren

"A good title should be like a good metaphor; it should intrigue without being too baffling or too obvious."

—Walker Percy

 Technology Connections

Have students use the Writing Network features of the Net-text to comment on each other's drafts.

 Write Source Online **Net-text**

Grammar Connection

Conjunctions
- **Proofreader's Guide** page 734
- *Write Source* pages 546, 547 (+)
- *SkillsBook* page 122

Pronouns Review
- **Proofreader's Guide** pages 704 (+), 706 (+), 708 (+), 710 (+)
- *Write Source* pages 536(+), 537 (+)
- *GrammarSnap* Relative Pronouns, Reflexive and Reciprocal Pronouns
- *SkillsBook* page 83

Editing Checking for Conventions

Tell students who would like more editing guidance to refer back to the process described earlier in the unit (SE pages 119–122). Encourage them also to consult the Proofreader's Guide (SE pages 604–763) as often as they need.

Note that nearly everyone has a grammatical weak point that takes extra work to master, such as remembering the difference between *its* and *it's* *(see below)*. Encourage students to

- use their writer's notebook to keep a running list of the errors they make repeatedly,
- watch extra carefully for those errors in their work, and
- study the correct approaches in the Proofreader's Guide section.

Publishing Sharing Your Writing

To prepare for reading their work to the class, have students work in pairs. Taking turns, each student can practice reading his or her essay aloud, while the other "directs" (provides helpful feedback to improve the performance).

Technology Connections

Remind students that they can use the Writing Network features of the Portfolio to share their work with peers.

Write Source Online **Portfolio**

Write Source Online **Net-text**

Teaching Tip: *Its* versus *It's*

Review the difference between *its* and *it's*:

- Possessive pronouns never have an apostrophe *(his, hers, its)*.
- Contractions always have an apostrophe—and *it's* is the contraction made by combining *it* and *is*.

Editing Checking for Conventions

Once you have revised your narrative, you're ready to edit your writing for conventions. Use the following checklist to guide your editing.

Editing Checklist

Conventions

PUNCTUATION

_____ 1. Do I use end punctuation correctly?

_____ 2. Do I use apostrophes to show possession *(Henry's Big Break)*?

_____ 3. Do I use commas correctly?

CAPITALIZATION

_____ 4. Do I capitalize all proper nouns?

_____ 5. Do I capitalize each speaker's first word in quoted dialogue?

SPELLING

_____ 6. Have I checked my spelling?

GRAMMAR

_____ 7. Do I use the correct forms of verbs *(didn't earn,* not *didn't earned)*?

_____ 8. Do my subjects and verbs agree in number *(We were going,* not *We was going)*?

_____ 9. Do I use the right words *(your, you're)*?

Correct your narrative. Use the checklist above to find and correct any errors. Also ask someone else to check your work. Then create a neat final copy and proofread it.

Publishing Sharing Your Writing

Sharing your narrative with the subject of your writing (if possible) and with family and classmates is an important part of the writing process.

Share your biographical narrative. If you plan on reading your narrative out loud, be sure to practice first.

Grammar Connection

End Punctuation

- **Proofreader's Guide** pages 605–607
- *SkillsBook* page 5

Using the Right Word

- **Proofreader's Guide** pages 678–679, 680–681
- *SkillsBook* page 58

Pronoun Shifts

- **Proofreader's Guide** pages 708 (+), 710 (+), 756 (+)
- *SkillsBook* page 185

Commas

- **Proofreader's Guide** pages 610–611
- *Write Source* pages 535 (+), 540 (+)
- *GrammarSnap* Commas after Introductory Words, Phrases, and Clauses
- *SkillsBook* page 9

Writing for Assessment
Responding to Narrative Prompts

137

An important part of life is sharing personal experiences. ("Guess what happened to me.") When you were younger, you may have shared just a few details about each experience. But now that you are older, your personal stories are probably richer and more detailed.

An effective personal story does more than simply tell what happened. It often tells what the writer learned from the experience, and why it is important to her or him. In this chapter, you will learn how to share a personal experience in response to a narrative writing prompt. And besides the story's details, you'll tell why the experience is important to you.

Writing Guidelines

Subject: Narrative prompt
Form: Response to a prompt
Purpose: To demonstrate competence
Audience: Instructor

"Experience is a hard teacher because she gives you the test first, the lesson after."

—Vernon Saunders Law

Responding to Narrative Prompts

Objectives
- use the STRAP questions to help formulate a response to a narrative prompt
- adapt the stages of writing to test-taking situations
- practice writing for assessment

If your students must take school, district, or state assessments this year, focus on the writing form on which they will be tested.

Explain to students that in the next section they'll learn how to approach narrative writing for tests. Most specifically, they will learn how to move efficiently from one stage of the writing process to another.

Tell students that as they become more confident about the test-taking process, they'll also waste less time worrying. This allows them to concentrate more on what they've been asked to write about, and this, in turn, will improve what they write.

Copy Masters

Time Line (TE p. 139)

5 W's Chart (TE p. 139)

Details Chart (TE p. 139)

Prewriting Analyzing a Narrative Prompt

Acknowledge that students may be nervous when they encounter writing prompts. This makes it important to learn techniques for approaching them. Tell students that by rigorously and systematically using the five STRAP questions, they will eliminate any chance of misunderstanding prompts or overlooking important parts of them.

Prewriting Using the STRAP Questions

Work through one or more of the **Try It!** prompts as a group. For example, you might use the first prompt in the following way:
- Subject—a personal experience illustrating "help yourself by helping others"
- Type—a personal narrative for a class booklet
- Role—Note that the role depends on the subject. For example, if the story features the writer's family, the role will be son/ daughter or brother/sister.
- Audience—fellow students
- Purpose—share and inspire

138

Prewriting Analyzing a Narrative Prompt

A prompt is a set of directions that tells you what to write. For example, a narrative prompt tells you to write about a significant personal experience. To effectively respond to a prompt, you must first understand it. The **STRAP questions** below will help you to analyze a narrative prompt.

Using the STRAP Questions

> **Subject:** What specific experience (memorable, life-changing, embarrassing, inspiring) should I write about?
>
> **Type:** What type of writing (personal narrative, personal essay, autobiographical article) should I create?
>
> **Role:** What role (student, son or daughter, friend, community member) should I assume as the writer?
>
> **Audience:** Who (principal, parent, city official, classmates) is the intended reader?
>
> **Purpose:** What is the goal (share, re-create, entertain, illustrate, inspire) of my writing?

Try It!

Analyze these prompts by using STRAP questions for each one.

1. "Help yourself by helping others." Share a personal experience that illustrates this quotation. Your narrative will be in a class booklet for students in your school.
2. Understanding our environment is important. Write an article that relates an experience you had with nature and what you learned from the event. The piece will appear in a science magazine aimed at fourth through sixth graders.
3. Think about a time when you had to work extra hard for something. Write about the experience in a personal narrative intended for a writing contest sponsored by the local newspaper.

Tip

Some prompts do not contain key words for every STRAP question. Use your best judgment to find answers for all the questions.

English Language Learners

Comprehending prompts can be especially problematic. Have students create STRAP organizers on which they can write the subject, type, role, audience, and purpose for each of the **Try It!** prompts. Encourage them to create STRAP organizers for all narrative assessments.

Advanced Learners

Ask students to write prompts, using the STRAP questions as a guide. Encourage students to be creative. Unusual prompts are allowed as long as the prompts answer the five STRAP questions. As a class, share and analyze the student prompts.

Planning Your Response

Once you understand a prompt thoroughly, you can plan your response. The following graphic organizers can help you complete your planning.

Narrative Graphic Organizers

Narrative

Reread the narrative prompts on page 138. Choose one prompt and a graphic organizer from above to organize your response.

Tip

Be sure to use your time wisely. For example, if you have 45 minutes to respond to a prompt, consider using the first 5 to 10 minutes to analyze the prompt and plan your response, and the last 5 minutes to revise and edit it. That leaves 30 to 35 minutes for the actual writing.

Prewriting **Planning Your Response**

Provide photocopies of the reproducible Time Line, 5 W's Chart, and Details Chart (TE pages 816, 817, and 821) for students to use for organizing their responses.

Point out to students that in test-taking situations they won't have these blank graphic organizers. They should take the time to become so familiar with the organizers that they can reproduce them as needed. Suggest that students devise simplified forms of the charts.

■ A time line chart can be reduced to a vertical line at the left of the page with a tick mark beside each item. It isn't necessary to write in *first, next, then,* etc.

■ The 5 W's can become five clusters of notes, each labeled with one of the questions.

■ The details chart can be three columns labeled *Actions, Details, Feelings.*

Writing Responding to a Prompt

Before students begin writing, refer them to the information about taking essay tests on SE pages 526–529.

Test Prep!

Point out how similar this narrative is to the narratives that students have written using the writing process. By working carefully through the process of creating a narrative, students have internalized the skills they need to generate a narrative in an on-demand writing situation.

Students need to quickly select a topic (based on the prompt), gather and organize details, write a first draft, and review their writing to make adjustments and corrections.

Writing Responding to a Prompt

After planning your response, it's time to begin writing. It will be important to keep your audience in mind. Review the following narrative prompt and response.

Sample Narrative Prompt

Think about a time when someone did something that made a significant difference in your life. Write a narrative that captures this important experience and tells what you learned from it. Your story is intended for your classmates.

Response to a Narrative Prompt

Beyond Quitting

The **beginning** introduces the writer's focus. (underlined)

Sometimes amazing things happen to people, and from then on, their lives are different. Take, for example, the day Helen Keller learned that there are letters that spell "water." That was the key that opened her mind to the world. An important day in my life was the hot summer evening that my mother made me play softball. <u>Playing in that game taught me that the greatest feeling in the world is facing your own fear.</u>

Each **middle** paragraph presents details about the experience.

It was the summer before third grade, and our girls' softball team was facing real pitchers for the first time. The summer before that, the ball had been put on top of a big tee, and we were allowed seven swings to make a hit. Almost every girl hit the ball each time she batted, even if she hit the tee first. When the coaches started pitching, suddenly batting was hard.

By the third week of the season, I had hit the ball a few times. At one embarrassing practice session, I missed every single pitch. From the side, I heard Emily hissing at me. My face got hot, and my throat felt like it had a softball stuck in it. I was starting to hate softball. The next afternoon, when Mom said it was

English Language Learners

Depending on how long students have been in the United States, some of them may be exempt from high-stakes district or state assessments. Find out which students will be tested and what accommodations are allowed. If bilingual dictionaries are permitted, help students identify how and when to use them during timed tests. Encourage students to use their dictionaries to clarify the prompts but suggest that they use the dictionaries sparingly or not at all during the actual writing.

Narrative

almost time to go play our game, I told her I was sick. She said that I should lie down for a while because I probably ate supper too fast. I knew I had to go through the motions, so I went to my room and lay there. This was hard because I felt fine and just wanted to avoid softball.

Before long, Mom came into my room and said, "Time to go to the game." She didn't even ask if I felt better, or if I really wanted to play. I imagined Emily hissing from the sideline, and suddenly I really did feel sick to my stomach. I started crying so hard that I could barely talk. While I was blubbering, my mother pulled my team T-shirt over my head and guided me to the car. She said that I had to play for the rest of the season, and after that we could talk about whether or not I would play next year. In the meantime, she or Dad would practice with me before every game because practice was what I needed, not quitting.

That night I got two hits, and Emily didn't make a sound. Every week after that, we practiced at home until I got to be one of the best hitters on the team.

This year, before I started ninth grade, I had the same old sick feeling that I was going to mess up. I was afraid high school was going to be too hard, and someone would make fun of me. I've learned, though, that being afraid is part of life, and that I can do whatever is expected of me if I keep working and practicing. I don't think anyone will ever make a movie about my softball experience, but it sure has had a big impact on me.

The **ending** tells what the writer learned from the experience.

Practice responding to a narrative prompt. Review the prompt you chose on page **139** and look over the planning you did. Then write a response in the amount of time your teacher gives you.

Write

Encourage students to talk about the model essay. What might they change? Possible responses:
- The focus sentence does not express its idea completely. The good feeling comes not from just facing fear, but from succeeding despite fear.
- More dialogue could have been used for showing details.
- The prompt asks about *a time when someone did something that made a significant difference.* It would be good to mention the mother (that *someone*) in the last paragraph to emphasize her role and demonstrate the student's thorough reading of the prompt.

What are the strong points of the essay? Possible answers:
- Many readers (the audience) will relate to the subject.
- The writer did a good job of describing what happened in chronological order.
- Using the example of Helen Keller's breakthrough really describes the feeling the writer is talking about.

Revising Improving Your Response

Remind students that because it may be practical to allot only four or five minutes to the revision stage, they must take care to keep their changes simple. Discuss the kinds of small changes that can be most effective when revision time is short. For example, students can make sure that . . .

- their ideas and details support the topic,
- the organization is clear, and
- their writer's voice is consistent.

Editing Checking for Conventions

Encourage students to familiarize themselves with this short editing checklist. With practice, they can learn to watch for the answers to all five questions while reading the essay once—which may be all they have time for during a test.

Suggest that students practice quickly using the checklist in other situations, such as when they read over e-mail messages just before sending them.

142

Revising Improving Your Response

Most writing tests allow you to make neat changes to your response, but be sure you know the number and kinds of changes that are allowed.

Using the STRAP Questions

The following STRAP questions can serve as a revising guide.

Subject:	Does my response focus on a specific personal experience related to the prompt?
Type:	Have I written the appropriate type of response (narrative, essay, article)?
Role:	Have I assumed the role indicated in the prompt (student, friend, community member)?
Audience:	Have I kept my intended audience in mind (principal, parents, city official, classmates)?
Purpose:	Does my writing accomplish the goal set by the prompt (share, re-create, entertain, illustrate, inspire)?

Improve your work. As you reread your response, ask yourself the STRAP questions. Make changes neatly in the time allotted by your teacher.

Editing Checking for Conventions

Finally, it is a good idea to read through your draft again to check for punctuation, capitalization, spelling, and grammar errors.

Conventions

_____ **1.** Have I used commas and end punctuation correctly?
_____ **2.** Have I capitalized proper nouns and first words of sentences?
_____ **3.** Have I checked my spelling?
_____ **4.** Do my subjects and verbs agree (*she was*, not *she were*)?
_____ **5.** Have I used the right words (*there*, *they're*, or *their*)?

Check for conventions. Use the checklist above to check your response for punctuation, capitalization, spelling, and grammar errors. Make corrections neatly in the time allotted by your teacher.

Struggling Learners

Finding the time to check their test papers for all five items during a testing situation may not be feasible for students. Have them focus their conventions check on punctuation, capitalization, and spelling.

Narrative Writing on Tests

The following tips will guide you whenever you are asked to write a response to a narrative prompt.

Before you write . . .

- **Understand the prompt.**
  Use the STRAP questions and remember that a narrative prompt asks you to share or re-create an experience.
- **Plan your response.**
  Spend several minutes planning your response. Use an appropriate graphic organizer to help you. (See page **139**.)

As you write . . .

- **State the focus of your writing in the beginning.**
  Keep your purpose *(to share, to illustrate)* in mind as you write.
- **Be selective.**
  Include specific details that effectively re-create your experience.
- **End in a meaningful way.**
  Tell why the experience has been important to you.

After you write your first draft . . .

- **Check for completeness and correctness.**
  Use the STRAP questions to revise your work. Then check for errors in punctuation, capitalization, spelling, and grammar.

 Plan and write a response. Analyze one of the prompts below using the STRAP questions. Then plan and write your response. Complete your work within the time allotted by your teacher.

Narrative Prompts

> - "Experience is the best teacher." In a personal narrative, share a specific time in your life that illustrates this quotation. Make sure to tell what you learned from your experience. Your intended audience is middle school students.
> - In an article for your school newspaper, share your most meaningful school-related experience from the past year. Make the experience come alive with vivid details and dialogue.

Narrative (side tab)

Narrative Writing on Tests

Point out that students must approach writing-on-demand assignments differently from open-ended writing assignments.

Narrative Prompts

To give students practice with timed assessments, give them the same amount of time to write their response essay as they will be allotted for school, district, or state assessments. Break down each part of the process into clear chunks of time. For example, give students

- 15 minutes for note taking and planning,
- 20 minutes for writing, and
- 10 minutes for editing and proofreading.

Start the assignment at the top of the hour or at the half-hour to make it easier for students to keep track of the time. Tell students when time is up for each section.

Advanced Learners

Give students more practice with timed tests. After students complete a practice test in the time allowed, speed things up. Have students write a response to the second prompt with less time (5 or 10 minutes less). Knowing they can beat the clock will keep students calm during an actual exam.

Expository Writing Overview

Common Core Standards Focus

Writing 2: Write informative/explanatory texts to examine and convey complex ideas, concepts, and information clearly and accurately through the effective selection, organization, and analysis of content.

Language 1b: Use various types of phrases (noun, adjectival, adverbial, participial, prepositional, absolute) and clauses (independent, dependent, noun, relative, adverbial) to convey specific meanings and add variety and interest to writing or presentations.

Language 2a: Use a semicolon (and perhaps a conjunctive adverb) to link two or more closely related independent clauses.

Writing Forms

- comparison paragraph
- comparison essay
- how-to essay
- writing for assessment

Focus on the Traits

- **Ideas** Focusing on a significant similarity and including details to support the thesis
- **Organization** Including a strong beginning and ending, and arranging points of comparison chronologically in the middle paragraphs
- **Voice** Engaging the reader by sounding knowledgeable
- **Word Choice** Selecting precise nouns, active verbs, and no unnecessary modifiers
- **Sentence Fluency** Constructing simple, compound, and complex sentences that read smoothly
- **Conventions** Checking for errors in punctuation, capitalization, spelling, and grammar

WAC: **Science**—Lab Report, Cause-Effect Essay, Science Article Summary
Social Studies—Descriptive Report, Document-Based Essay
Math—Math Article Summary, Analysis of a Problem, Graphic Response
Applied Science—Recipe, Essay of Identification
Arts–Research Report

Literature Connections

- **"A Different Level of Competition"** by Anne Stein

Technology Connections

 Write Source Online
www.hmheducation.com/writesource

- **Net-text**
- **Bookshelf**
- **GrammarSnap**
- **Portfolio**
- **Essay Scoring**
- **Writing Network features**
- **File Cabinet**

 Interactive Whiteboard Lessons

Suggested Expository Writing Unit (Five Weeks)

Day	Writing and Skills Instruction	Student Edition		SkillsBook	Daily Language Workouts	Write Source Online
		Main Pages	Resource Units*			
1–5	**Understanding Writing Assignments**	491–500			22–23	
WEEK 1	**Expository Warm-Up Paragraph: Comparison of Two People** (Model)	145–147				*Interactive Whiteboard Lessons*
	Skills Activities:					
	• Parallelism		550	176		
	• Using the Right Word		682–683, 684–685	59		

* These units are also located in the back of the *Teacher's Edition*. Resource Units include "Basic Grammar and Writing," "A Writer's Resource," and "Proofreader's Guide."
(+) This activity is located in a different section of the *Write Source Student Edition*. If students have already completed this activity, you may wish to review it at this time.

Day	Writing and Skills Instruction	Student Edition		SkillsBook	Daily Language Workouts	Write Source Online
		Main Pages	Resource Units*			
WEEK 1						
1–5 cont.	• Verbs (review)		714 (+), 716 (+), 718 (+), 722 (+), 724 (+)	105–106	22–23	*GrammarSnap*
WEEK 2						
6	**Expository Essay: Comparison of Two Famous People** (Model) Ⓛ Literature Connections "A Different Level of Competition"	148–150			24–25	
7–10	(Prewriting, Writing)	151–162				*Net-text*
WEEK 3						
11–13	(Revising)	163–174			26–27	*Net-text*
	Skills Activities:					
	• Parallelism		550 (+)	177–178		
	• Wordiness and Deadwood		543	174		
	• Rambling Sentences		558	170		
	• Compound and Complex Sentences		748–749	141		*GrammarSnap*
	• Clauses		612–613, 744 (+)	16–17, 138, 139, 140		*GrammarSnap*
14–15	(Editing and Publishing)	175–179				*Net-text, Portfolio*
	Skills Activities:					
	• Apostrophes		628–629, 630–631	29, 30, 31, 32		
	• Comma splices and Run-On Sentences		557	165, 166		*GrammarSnap*
	• Capitalization		648–649	43, 46		*GrammarSnap*
WEEK 4						
16–18	(Assessing, Reflecting)	180–184			28–29	
opt.	*Making Oral Presentations*	393–401				
19–20	**Responding to Expository Prompts**	193–199				
SECOND FORM WEEK 1						
1–5	**Explaining a Process** (Model)	185–187			30–31	
	(Prewriting, Writing)	188–190				*Net-text*
	(Revising)	191				*Net-text*
	Skills Activities:					
	• Specific Nouns		534, 701–703 (+)	70, 72, 73		*GrammarSnap*
	• Sentence Variety		553 (+), 746–747	129, 162		*GrammarSnap*
	(Editing)	192				*Net-text, Portfolio*
	Skills Activities:					
	• Subject-Verb Agreement		738–739, 740–741, 752–753, 754–755	128, 130, 149, 151		*GrammarSnap*
	• Sentence Problems (comma splices, run-ons, fragments)		557–558 (+)	167, 169		
	• Commas		614–615	19		

* These units are also located in the back of the *Teacher's Edition*. Resource Units include "Basic Grammar and Writing," "A Writer's Resource," and "Proofreader's Guide."
(+) This activity is located in a different section of the *Write Source Student Edition*. If students have already completed this activity, you may wish to review it at this time.

Expository Writing

This overview for expository writing includes some specific teaching suggestions for this unit. The description of each chapter will help you decide which parts of the unit to teach.

Writing Focus

Comparison Essay (pages 145–184)

In a comparison essay, a writer compares two subjects to better understand the similarities and differences between them. An effective comparison essay will either help readers become better acquainted with new, unfamiliar subjects or share fresh insights about familiar subjects. In this unit, the paragraphs and essay focus on comparing two people. The first sample in this chapter compares two people related to the writer, while other essays compare two famous people.

Explaining a Process (pages 185–192)

In a process essay, students explain how to do something or how something works. Their challenge is to write clearly, carefully, and completely so that their readers can easily follow the directions or explanations. When developing their essays, students should assume that their readers are unfamiliar with most, or all, of the steps in the process.

Responding to Expository Prompts (pages 193–199)

Because of time constraints, responding to an expository prompt on an assessment test is a challenge for most students. This chapter provides useful tips to help students determine what they need to say and how to say it, using STRAP questions and graphic organizers.

Grammar Focus

For support with this unit's grammar topics, consult the resource units (Basic Grammar and Writing, A Writer's Resource, and Proofreader's Guide).

Academic Vocabulary

Read aloud the academic terms, as well as the descriptions and questions. Model for students how to read one question and answer it. Have partners monitor their understanding and seek clarification of the terms by working through the meanings and questions together.

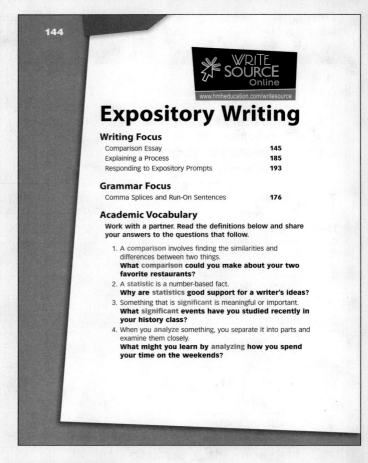

144

Expository Writing

Writing Focus

Grammar Focus

Academic Vocabulary

Work with a partner. Read the definitions below and share your answers to the questions that follow.

1. A **comparison** involves finding the similarities and differences between two things.
   What comparison could you make about your two favorite restaurants?
2. A **statistic** is a number-based fact.
   Why are statistics good support for a writer's ideas?
3. Something that is **significant** is meaningful or important.
   What significant events have you studied recently in your history class?
4. When you **analyze** something, you separate it into parts and examine them closely.
   What might you learn by analyzing how you spend your time on the weekends?

Minilessons

Just Like That — Comparison Essay

- **READ** page 146. In a T-chart, **LIST** two athletes, two politicians, two movie stars, and two fairy-tale characters. **WRITE** a specific point of comparison for each group of two. Then **WRITE** a possible specific point of comparison for one of the actors and one of the politicians or one of the athletes and one of the movie stars or fairy-tale characters. **SHARE** your results with the class.

Butter Up! — Explaining a Process

- **READ** "Making Jiaozi" on pages 186–187. **NOTE** the steps used in the process. **LIST** five steps necessary to butter a piece of toast. **COMPARE** your list with the lists of several classmates in a small group. **DISCUSS** which list best explains the process.

Following the Leader — Explaining a Process

- **CHOOSE** a how-to topic that you could pantomime. First, **PANTOMIME** the process for a partner. Then, **WRITE** the directions in a brief paragraph.

145

Expository Writing
Writing a Comparison Essay

Expository writing is the most common form of writing assigned in your classes. If a particular assignment asks you to explain, summarize, illustrate, analyze, classify, or compare, then you are involved in expository writing. In this chapter, you will write a comparison essay about two famous people—perhaps two athletes, two scientists, two musicians, or two leaders.

You will do your best work if you follow these five tips: (1) Select two people who truly interest you. (2) Learn as much as you can about them. (3) Organize your writing around important points of comparison. (4) Engage the reader with some interesting details, including quotations and revealing facts. (5) Share your information clearly and completely.

Writing Guidelines

Subject: Two famous people
Form: Comparison essay
Purpose: To show similarities
Audience: Classmates

"I see only one rule: to be clear. If I am not clear, then my entire world crumbles into nothing."

— Margaret Mead

Writing a Comparison Essay

Objectives
- understand the form and content of a comparison essay
- identify and develop the main point of comparison between two subjects
- plan, draft, revise, edit, and publish a comparison essay

A **comparison essay** is a piece of writing that
- compares two people, places, or things;
- explains how the two subjects are alike; and
- is organized by points of comparison.

Focus students' attention on the five tips that provide a mini-guide for writing an effective comparison essay. Point out that like any tips, they work only if they're applied.

Students can bookmark this page or copy the tips on a note card or in their writer's notebook.
- Tell students that they can copy the tips exactly or they can paraphrase them.
- Encourage students to keep the tips handy throughout the writing process to use as a writing guide.

Technology Connections

Use this unit's Interactive Whiteboard Lesson to introduce expository writing.

Interactive Whiteboard Lessons

Copy Masters

T-Chart (TE pp. 146, 155)

Details Chart (TE p. 152)

Assessment Sheet (TE p. 183)

Benchmark Papers

Pull the Plug and Play Corks (good)
- TE pp. 792–795

Changing Students (poor)
- TE pp. 796–799

Expository Writing Warm-Up: Key Points of Comparison

Before asking students to do the **Try It** activity, make sure they understand that they are selecting a topic for a comparison paragraph, not for an essay.

Students may not have thought of two people they know as having things in common. To stimulate ideas, brainstorm a list of experiences, activities, professions, and interests/hobbies people may share—growing up during the 1960s, coaching a sport, working as a health-care provider, gardening, and so on.

Provide photocopies of the reproducible T-Chart on TE page 818 for students to use to list details for their comparison paragraph.

As students compose their **topic sentence** *(see below)*, stress that they should not introduce any new ideas about either of the two people here. They should simply identify the people and tell what that they have in common.

146

Expository Writing Warm-Up: Key Points of Comparison

When you write a comparison essay, be sure that you focus on key points of comparison between your two topics. Tim Williams was planning a comparison of his two grandfathers. He knew that one important point of comparison was their involvement in World War II. During his planning, he made a T-chart and listed wartime details about each grandfather.

T-Chart

Point of Comparison: Involvement in WWII	
Grandfather Capewell	**Grandfather Williams**
– wanted to join the British army	– wanted to join the U.S. Navy
– denied because of heart murmur	– denied because of poor eyesight
– worked for aviation industry	– accepted in the army
– inspected crashed airplanes	– fought in Europe

 Try It!

Think of two people you know well who have things in common—perhaps two aunts, two friends, or two neighbors. Also think of an important or interesting point of comparison between the two people (growing up, involvement in a sport, education, and so on). On a piece of paper, write the point of comparison. Then make a T-chart to list details related to this idea for each person. (See the example above.)

Writing Your Topic Sentence

A specific point of comparison can usually be covered in one paragraph. To plan for his paragraph, Tim wrote this topic sentence, which identified the point of comparison to be covered.

My grandfathers (subjects) **proudly served their countries during World War II** (point of comparison).

 Try It!

Using your list of comparison details, write a topic sentence that identifies your subjects and point of comparison. Use the sample sentence above as a guide.

Teaching Tip: Writing an Effective Topic Sentence

Students will benefit from having your guidance and in-class time to write strong, effective topic sentences. Emphasize the following:

- The purpose of a topic sentence is to introduce the two people and the point of comparison.
- Students will use their topic sentences to guide their writing, so they need to develop ones that reflect their purposes and capture the readers' interest.
- Details that do not support the comparison stated in the topic sentence do not belong in the paragraph.

Provide help as needed. Point out that writing effective topic sentences now for their paragraphs will help them write thesis statements later for their essays.

Writing a Comparison Paragraph

A paragraph in a comparison essay should cover one main point of comparison between the two subjects. Tim wrote the following comparison paragraph about his two grandfathers. Remember that a paragraph has three main parts:

- The **topic sentence** introduces the two people and the point of comparison.
- The **body sentences** support the point of comparison.
- The **closing sentence** completes the comparison.

Expository

Doing Their Part

Topic Sentence

My grandfathers proudly served their countries during World War II. As soon as the war started, Thomas Capewell, my grandfather in England, wanted to join the British army. As soon as he graduated from high school, John Williams, my grandfather in the United States, wanted to join the navy. Things didn't work out well for either of them. The draft board wouldn't take

Body

Thomas because he had a heart murmur as a kid, and the navy wouldn't take John because his eyesight wasn't good enough. That didn't stop either of the men. Because Thomas was trained as an engineer, he helped design airplanes for his country. He was also part of a group that inspected enemy warplanes that were shot down. John passed the physical for the United States Army and served in the infantry for three years. John was in Germany when the German army surrendered. He said that he and his war buddies really celebrated that night. Both of my

Closing Sentence

grandfathers say that the war taught them more than any other experience in their lives.

 Write your own comparison paragraph. Use your planning from page **146** and the paragraph above as a guide for your writing.

Writing a Comparison Paragraph

Review the three main parts of a paragraph and the purpose of each in a comparison paragraph.

✴ For information about the parts of a paragraph, see SE pages 562–563.

Then have students explain how each of these parts fulfills its purpose in the model comparison paragraph. Encourage students to use specific details from the paragraph in their explanations.

Have students note the parallel construction that the writer uses in the sample paragraph to highlight the comparison. For example, point out the repetition of the introductory phrase _as soon as_ in sentences two and three, and the repetition of the words _wouldn't take_ in sentence five. Students may want to use a similar technique when they write their paragraph, to ensure that the comparison between the two people is clear.

✴ For more about writing effective paragraphs, see SE pages 561–579.

English Language Learners

Before students read the model paragraph, define the following words:

- draft board (group that judges whether people can join the military service)
- heart murmur (problem in heart functioning)
- engineer (person who uses science and math concepts to design things)
- infantry (foot soldiers)

Struggling Learners

Have students look in the model paragraph for words that signal comparisons _(either, and, both)_. Remind them that these words and others, such as _like_ and _similarly,_ can help a writer clearly state points of comparison. Encourage students to use words of comparison in their draft.

✴ For a list of transition words that signal comparison, refer students to SE page 592.

Grammar Connection

Parallelism
- **Write Source** page 550
- _SkillsBook_ page 176

Using the Right Word
- **Proofreader's Guide** pages 682–683, 684–685
- _SkillsBook_ page 59

Verbs (Review)
- **Proofreader's Guide** pages 714 (+), 716 (+), 718 (+), 722 (+), 724 (+)
- _GrammarSnap_ Specific Verbs, Transitive and Intransitive Verbs
- _SkillsBook_ pages 105–106

Understanding Your Goal

Three traits relate to the development of the content and the form. They provide a focus during prewriting, drafting, and revising.

- **Ideas**
- **Organization**
- **Voice**

The other three traits relate more to form. They are more important during the revising and editing processes.

- **Word Choice**
- **Sentence Fluency**
- **Conventions**

✳ The six-point rubric on SE pages 180–181 is based on these traits. Reproducible six-, five-, and four-point rubrics for expository writing can be found on pages 768, 772, and 776.

Encourage students to apply these traits of writing to all their comparison writing assignments across the curriculum. Point out that if they apply the traits consistently and conscientiously, they should notice continued improvement in their writing.

Refer students to the comparison traits list as you work through the model essay on SE pages 149–150, so that students have concrete examples of how to apply the traits.

Literature Connections

"A Different Level of Competition," a newspaper article by Anne Stein, explores the world of competitive sports for people with disabilities.

Discuss with students how the author's use of anecdotes and direct statements helps to reinforce her main idea. For additional models of expository writing, see the Reading-Writing Connections beginning on page TE-36.

Understanding Your Goal

Your goal in this chapter is to write a well-organized expository essay that compares two famous people. The traits listed in the chart below will help you plan and write your essay. The rubric for expository writing on pages **180–181** will also guide you.

Traits of a Comparison Essay

- **Ideas**
  Select two famous people to compare. Develop your essay by providing key similarities between these two people.

- **Organization**
  Include a strong beginning and ending. In the middle, set up your points of comparison chronologically—early life, beginning career, middle career, and late career.

- **Voice**
  Engage the reader by using a voice that sounds knowledgeable.

- **Word Choice**
  Select precise words and avoid repetition and unneeded modifiers.

- **Sentence Fluency**
  Write a variety of sentences that smoothly connect your ideas.

- **Conventions**
  Use correct punctuation, capitalization, spelling, and grammar.

Literature Connections: To varying degrees, many texts explore similarities between people, things, or ideas. One example is the *Chicago Tribune* newspaper article "A Different Level of Competition" by Anne Stein.

"If you would not be forgotten as soon as you are gone, either write things worth reading or do things worth writing."
—Benjamin Franklin

English Language Learners

If students are only beginning to learn English, ask them to focus on just a few traits for this assignment. Voice and word choice may be difficult for students to express if they have limited English vocabularies. If possible, teach students how to use a thesaurus, and have thesauruses available during all steps of the writing process.

Comparison Essay

In the following expository essay, a professional writer compares two wild-life conservationists who changed the way the world thought about great apes. The notes in the left margin explain the key parts of the essay.

Expository

Beginning
The first paragraph introduces the two people and gives the thesis statement (underlined).

Middle
The topic sentence in each middle paragraph focuses on one main point of comparison.

Women in the Wild

In the first half of the twentieth century, most people thought that great apes were ferocious beasts like King Kong. By the middle of the century, though, a young Englishwoman named Jane Goodall and a young American named Dian Fossey began to change people's minds. By going to live with great apes, Goodall and Fossey taught the world about these gentle giants.

Goodall and Fossey began their careers by following their childhood dreams of working with animals in Africa. In her late twenties, Goodall finally saved up enough money to travel to Cape Town, South Africa, where she met the famous paleontologist Louis Leakey. He hired her as his secretary and by 1960 convinced her to study chimpanzees in the wild. Leakey funded Goodall's expedition to Tanzania, and she took her mother with her. In a speech that Goodall gave in 2002, she said, "I had a wonderful, supportive mother. She encouraged me to follow my ridiculous dream to go to Africa and live with animals (qtd. in "Jane"). In 1963, Fossey first met Leakey, but she had a harder time impressing him. After paying 14 shillings to look around his dig site, she slipped down a rock slope, landed on his fossil find, sprained her ankle, and because of the pain, threw up on the specimen ("Dian"). Still, by 1966, Leakey had funded an expedition for Fossey to study mountain gorillas in the Congo and Rwanda.

Over the next two decades, Goodall and Fossey became world-renowned primatologists, or ape researchers. Since neither woman was a trained scientist, they shared a unique approach to their research. Instead of numbering the apes like test subjects, the women named them and developed close relationships with them. Goodall discovered that chimpanzees live in extended tribal groups and have individual personalities, emotions, and awareness. Perhaps her most startling discovery, though, was that chimpanzees

Comparison Essay

Work through this model essay with the class, pointing out the elements that make it a good comparison essay.

Ideas

- The thesis statement identifies the focus of the essay.
- The beginning introduces the two people and summarizes the main similarity between them.
- The writer supports the comparison with details, paraphrases, and anecdotes.

Organization

- Each middle paragraph focuses on one point of comparison.
- The writer presents ideas point by point in chronological order, using dates and time-order words to make the order clear.
- The ending reinforces the comparison by emphasizing the similar goals and accomplishments of the two people.

Voice & Word Choice

- The writer's use of facts and statistics shows knowledge of the topic.
- Anecdotes and quotations help to engage the reader's interest.
- Precise nouns and verbs make the writer's ideas vivid.

English Language Learners

If possible, before reading, show students pictures of Jane Goodall and Dian Fossey working in their fields to promote further understanding. Also, define the following words:

- ferocious (savage, angry)
- paleontologist (someone who studies early humans and related animals)

- expedition (research trip)
- shillings (British money)
- specimen (sample)
- crouched (sat on heels)
- dwindling (becoming smaller in number, less)
- poaching (illegal hunting)
- habitat (the area where something lives)

- foundations (organizations)
- bounty (reward paid to catch someone)

Check student comprehension of the essay before asking them to answer the questions at the bottom of SE page 150.

Point out the use of the plural forms throughout the essay. Some examples are *apes, beasts, people, giants, gorillas, chimpanzees,* and *personalities.* Remind students of the following:

- Most plurals are formed by adding *-s* or *-es* to the singular form of the noun.
- Some nouns change their spellings to form the plural.
- Some nouns have irregular plural forms.
- When using plurals, students should pay special attention to subject-verb agreement and the use of the possessive form.

✱ For more information about forming plurals, see SE page 656.

 Respond to the reading.

Answers

Ideas 1. That both women named and developed close personal relationships with the apes seems most important. Because of this, they both fought to save the apes, which led to Fossey's murder.

Organization 2. time

Voice & Word Choice 3. Yes. The writer provides background details about each woman, as well as specific examples of how each woman followed her dream and made discoveries about the apes.

150

The writer uses paraphrases, facts, statistics, quotations, and anecdotes to make the comparison clear.

make tools, stripping leaves off twigs and using the twigs to "fish" termites from their mounds (Shadow). For her part, Fossey learned that gorillas live in small family groups and show compassion even to non-gorillas. Once, when Fossey crouched alone and depressed in the woods, a gorilla named Digit put his arm around her and comforted her ("Gorillas"). Over the years, both women discovered that great-ape populations are dwindling because of poaching and habitat loss. At Leakey's suggestion, Goodall and Fossey each went to Cambridge to earn PhD's, which helped them fight for the survival of great apes.

Later in their careers, the two women worked hard to save the great apes. Goodall wrote papers and books, traveled and lectured, and created foundations to save chimpanzees and other animals. As a result, the United Nations named her a "Messenger of Peace," and she was the only non-Tanzanian to receive the Medal of Tanzania ("Biography"). Fossey also did these things, but when the gorilla populations she studied were attacked, she declared a public war on poachers. She put a bounty on any poachers and organized patrols to protect gorillas. In 1985, her war ended when she was murdered in her cabin, most likely by a poacher ("Dian").

Ending
The final paragraph reflects on the subjects' importance.

Though Goodall and Fossey were born ten thousand miles apart, each woman followed her dream of going to Africa. They worked with Louis Leakey, wrote and lectured, and set up foundations to save the creatures they loved. Most of all, these two conservationists shared a message that Fossey expressed in her final journal entry: "When you realize the value of all life, you dwell less on what is past and concentrate on the preservation of the future" (qtd. in "Dian").

 Respond to the reading. Answer the following questions.

Ideas (1) Which point of comparison seems the most important? Explain.

Organization (2) How is the comparison of the two women organized—by time, location, or order of importance?

Voice & Word Choice (3) Does the writer sound knowledgeable about the two subjects? Explain.

Advanced Learners

To extend the analysis of a comparison essay (**Respond to the reading**), encourage students to bring in examples of comparative writing they have come across in their individual reading, such as magazine articles or informational Web sites that compare people, animals, scientific phenomena, and so on.

Have students use the **Respond to the reading** questions to analyze the presentation of ideas, organization, voice, and word choice in their selected articles.

Comparison Essay **151**

Prewriting

Your comparison essay will be about two people who share several important similarities. In your prewriting, you will choose two people, gather your details, and organize your thoughts.

Keys to Effective Prewriting

1. Select a topic (two famous people) that interests you and will interest your readers.

2. Research the two people to learn as much as you can about them.

3. Write a thesis statement that focuses your thoughts about the key points of comparison between the two people.

4. Use a point-by-point chronological organization pattern.

5. Organize your details in an outline (or another graphic organizer).

Expository

Prewriting

Keys to Effective Prewriting

Remind students of the purpose of the prewriting stage in the writing process: It is when the writer selects a topic, gathers details, and decides how to organize those details.

Keys to Effective Prewriting lists the process students will be guided through on SE pages 152–156.

- As students consider people for their topic (item 1), suggest that they keep in mind the distinction between the terms *famous* (popular for positive contributions to society) and *infamous* (popular as a result of negative behavior), and focus on people who meet the first criteria.
- Encourage students to think about their own special fields of interest and careers they are considering, and to select people in these fields and careers. Then they are more likely to select people who interest them and about whom they already have some knowledge.

Writing Workshop

Use the activities in this section (and in writing, revising, and editing) as minilessons in your writing workshop. Each activity introduces and models a key skill and helps students apply the skill to their own writing.

Technology Connections

Students can use the added features of the Net-text as they explore this stage of the writing process.

Write Source Online **Net-text**

English Language Learners

Encourage students to consider famous people from their own cultures. It will make the assignment easier if students have some familiarity with the two people.

If students do choose people from their cultures, allow them to gather information from sources written in their first languages. Ask students to show you their sources, even if you cannot read them, to make sure that they seem to have enough information before they begin writing.

Prewriting Selecting a Topic

Many students will not be aware of what things famous people have in common with other famous people. Offer these tips:

- Look through texts in a variety of curriculum areas. For example, art texts usually group artists according to their techniques and the periods in which they worked.
- Ask parents and older siblings which two people from history, science, sports, or the arts they admire most. People tend to admire people with similar qualities and traits.

Provide photocopies of the reproducible Details Chart (TE page 821) for students to use to create their famous-people chart.

Focus on the Traits

Ideas

Be sure students read **Focus on the Traits** before they mark a topic. Suggest that they do some preliminary research on the people to see if they have enough in common. There should be a minimum of three points of comparison between the pair.

Prewriting Selecting a Topic

The first step in writing a comparison essay is to choose two people who interest you. To do this, Rafael Hernandez first listed categories of people and chose three categories that interested him. He wrote them across the top of a piece of paper. Next, he listed pairs of athletes, scientists, and leaders/rulers that could be compared. Finally, he selected the two people he wanted to write about.

actors	athletes	leaders/rulers
activists	business people	musicians
artists	explorers	scientists
astronauts	inventors	writers

Famous-People Chart

Athletes	Scientists	Leaders / Rulers
Phil Mickelson Anthony Kim	Roy C. Andrews Jack Horner	Queen Elizabeth I Queen Victoria
Venus Williams Steffi Graf	Marie Curie Gertrude B. Elion	Robert E. Lee Ulysses S. Grant
Jim Thorpe * Jesse Owens		Winston Churchill Franklin Roosevelt

Create a famous-people chart. Choose three categories of people from the list at the top of the page. Write the categories at the tops of three columns. Then under each heading, list pairs of famous people who interest you. Put an asterisk (*) next to the pair you would like to write about.

Focus on the Traits

Ideas When you choose two people to compare, focus on two people who you know are similar in a number of ways. Though Ronald Reagan and Henry VIII were both powerful politicians, they may not have had enough in common to prompt a solid comparison essay.

English Language Learners

If students choose people from their own culture with whom you are not familiar, ask them to tell you what their three points of comparison will be. Ask to see materials in English, if they are available, so that you can familiarize yourself with the individuals. Students may be able to use Internet sites that you can translate online so that you can help them focus their ideas.

Struggling Learners

Two people famous for the same thing aren't necessarily good subjects for a comparison essay. As students research two people, have them jot down the answers to these questions:

- Why is each person famous?
- What is each person's most important contribution or accomplishment, and why is it noteworthy?

- What motivates each person's actions? Is it his or her philosophy? Life experiences? Dreams or ideals?

Students can then review the answers to these questions to help them assess whether the two people have enough significant similarities for comparison.

Gathering Details

Check books, Web sites, and magazines to learn as much as possible about the two people you chose. Rafael used a gathering grid to keep track of the details he found. In parentheses, he listed the source in which he found each piece of information. For additional information, he used note cards. (See the next page.)

Gathering Grid

Questions	Jim Thorpe	Jesse Owens
When and where was he born?	Born in 1888 in a one-room cabin, Prague, Oklahoma (nativeamericans.com)	Born in 1913 in Alabama (jesseowens.com)
What was his family like?	Poor, Native American name "Wa-tho-huck" meant "Bright Path" (All-American)	Poor, moved to Cleveland for better life (Jesse: The Man Who Outran Hitler)
When did his talent first appear?	At the Carlisle Indian School in PA (nativeamericans.com)	At Cleveland East Technical High on track team ("Jesse")
What was his first big success?	Scored 25 touchdowns and 198 points in last season at Carlisle, All-American two years (wmgww.com)	Tied one world record and set three more—all with an injured back! (jesseowens.com)
What was his biggest success?	Pentathlon and decathlon winner at 1912 Olympics, decathlon score stood for 20 years (All-American)	Went to Berlin Olympics in 1936, won four gold medals in front of Hitler (World Book Encyclopedia)
What happened after his biggest success?	Medals stripped for "professionalism," played pro baseball/football, movie extra, Chicago Park Dist. staff (nativeamericans.com)	No endorsement deals, raced against motorcycles and racehorses, became public speaker ("Jesse")

Prewrite

Create a gathering grid. Write questions about the two people you are researching. Then fill in the rest of your grid.

Expository

Prewriting Gathering Details

Suggest that students review the information on SE pages 153–154 at the same time to help them understand how note cards can be used to extend the usefulness of the gathering grid.

Point out the Web addresses noted on the grid and discuss the importance of **using reliable Web sites as resources** *(see below)*.

Writer's Craft

Organization: Comparison-contrast essays—like any two-part essays—are challenging to organize. Writers have to decide how to handle each subject as well as the similarities and differences between them. This chapter helps students create a point-by-point comparison, dealing with one point for each subject before moving on to the next point. Other organizational patterns include the following:

- **subject-by-subject:** first treat one subject fully; then treat the other subject fully.
- **similarities and differences:** first tell how the two subjects are alike; then tell how they are different.

Teaching Tip: Using Reliable Web Sites as Resources

Explain to students that not all Web sites on a topic provide reliable and accurate information for that topic.

- The ease of creating and uploading a Web site onto the World Wide Web has led to the proliferation of sites created by people who are not necessarily experts on topics.

- This does not mean that all the facts and details on a given Web site are incorrect, but they may not be entirely accurate or unbiased.

Encourage students to take time to evaluate the Web sites they use as resources.

- Sites that end in *.edu* or *.gov* are usually reliable.
- Sites that are created and maintained by the subject of the site (for example, an author's official Web site) also provide reliable information.

Prewriting Creating Note Cards

Emphasize the importance of copying quotations exactly to avoid plagiarism. Remind students that plagiarism is illegal and unethical. When people plagiarize, they steal the words and ideas of others, and use them as their own.

Remind students to record all sources accurately as they do research. This will save time and avoid confusion later when they have to create a works-cited page or when they want to check a fact or other detail.

 Writer's Craft

Elaboration: Make sure that students gather a variety of details, including paraphrases, quotations, explanations, statistics, anecdotes, and so forth. By gathering a rich set of details, writers can move beyond a simple listlike structure to create paragraphs that deeply elaborate the comparisons and contrasts.

Prewriting Creating Note Cards

A gathering grid is an effective way to collect and organize details for an essay. However, sometimes you need more space, especially to record a quotation, to paraphrase important information, or to explain or define something. In these cases, you should use note cards.

Number each new card, and write the question at the top. Then answer the question with a paraphrase, a quotation, or an explanation. If necessary, identify the source of the information at the bottom of the note card.

Sample Note Cards

> ① **Paraphrase**
> What was Jim Thorpe's family like?
>   Thorpe's twin brother, Charlie, died when Jim was nine, and his mother died shortly afterward. Thorpe attended one Indian school after another in Oklahoma, Kansas, and Pennsylvania before his athletic talent was recognized.
>   —"Thorpe"

> ② **Quotation**
> What was Jesse Owen's biggest success?
>   Owens befriended the top German long jumper, Luz Long. Owens later said, "You can melt down all the medals and cups I have, and they wouldn't be a plating on the 24-karat friendship I felt for Luz Long."

> ③ **Explanation**
> What happened to Jim Thorpe after his biggest success?
>   Explanation of "professionalism"— Professional athletes were not allowed to compete in the Olympics, and Thorpe had earned $15 a week playing minor-league baseball.

 Prewrite **Create note cards.** Make note cards like the examples above whenever your answers are too long to fit on your gathering grid.

Struggling Learners

Remind students that *paraphrasing* means writing information from a source *in one's own words*. When taking notes, students should paraphrase or jot down information as phrases. This will help ensure that students will use their own words when writing their essay.

Advanced Learners

Some students may not feel the need to take many notes. They may want to begin writing as soon as they find a couple of sources. Explain that organized note taking will save them time by helping them sort and organize information *before* they begin to write. Emphasize that good note taking will help students conduct research and write effectively in all classes.

Focusing on Points of Comparison

After gathering details about your subjects, it's time to decide on the key points of comparison that you will make in your essay. (See pages 146–147 for more information.) After reviewing the assignment goals and his gathering grid, Rafael decided to focus on four points of comparison.

Points of Comparison

- Childhood
- Beginning career
- Middle career
- Late career

Select the points of comparison. Review your gathering grid and decide on three to five important points of comparison that you would like to use. (You can use those shown above if they work with your subjects.)

Listing Details

Next, you should list the details that relate to each subject for each point of comparison. Here is how Rafael listed the details for his first two points of comparison: childhood and beginning career.

Childhood

Jim Thorpe
- born in 1888 in Prague, OK
- very poor
- Native American
  name "Wa-tho-huck" means
  "Bright Path"

Jesse Owens
- born in 1913 in Alabama
- very poor
- African American
- moved to Cleveland
- worked odd jobs, couldn't
  make all track practices

Beginning Career

- led Carlisle Indian football team
  to huge upsets
- named All-American

- track star of East Tech High
- at Ohio State, tied one world
  record and broke three

Arrange your details. List each point of comparison on a piece of paper, leaving seven or eight lines between each one. Then list the appropriate details for your subjects under each point of comparison.

Prewriting Focusing on Points of Comparison

Many students will choose to use the four points of comparison shown here (Childhood, Beginning career, Middle career, Late career), which are generic enough to fit almost any topic. Encourage the class to brainstorm other points of comparison (for example, College Years, Family Life), and list their ideas on the board for reference.

Prewriting Listing Details

Students might like to use photocopies of the reproducible T-Chart on TE page 818 for listing details (see SE page 146). Emphasize that students should list details for each point of comparison they plan to use and that there should be approximately the same number of details for each person for each point of comparison.

As students list details, they may discover that there is only one detail to compare for a point of comparison. If that's the case, they can broaden that point of comparison to include other ideas (for example, Childhood and Young Adulthood), or, if possible, they can combine it with one of their other points (for example, Beginning/Middle Career).

Struggling Learners

If students have difficulty listing details, suggest that they answer the following questions:

- What kind of background or family history does each person have?
- What are each person's main personality traits (creative, hard working, athletic)? At what point in his or her life did each one demonstrate these traits?
- What goals did each person have? At what point in his or her career did each one achieve those goals?

Prewriting **Writing a Thesis Statement**

Give students sufficient time to write their thesis statements. Set a time limit, however. If students have not developed the perfect wording for their thesis statements by the end of that time, suggest that they go with statements that establish the main similarity between the two people and that will help guide their writing. Later, during the revising stage, they can rework their thesis statements to their satisfaction.

Prewriting **Outlining Your Essay**

The last line of directions for preparing a sentence outline tells students that they do not need to include every detail in their outline.

- Make sure students understand that this means that they do not have to include every detail from their gathering grid, note cards, and list of details.
- As an example, point out item E in the sample outline. Then have students flip back to the details list on SE page 155. Have them note that the detail about Jesse Owens not making all track practices is not included in the outline. The writer may still include the detail in the essay, however.

156

Prewriting Writing a Thesis Statement

The thesis statement of your essay should name the two people and summarize the main similarity between them. Here is Rafael's thesis statement.

Write your thesis statement. Use the model above to create a thesis statement for your essay. Try different versions until you are satisfied.

Outlining Your Essay

Before you write your first draft, you should outline the main information that you will include in the middle part of the essay to support your thesis statement. Below is the first part of Rafael's sentence outline. (See page 372 for more about outlining.)

Prepare a sentence outline. Begin with your thesis statement. Then include each point of comparison (I., II., III.) and supporting details (A., B., C.). You need not include every detail in your outline.

Struggling Learners

Students who feel overwhelmed by the amount of prewriting required for the essay might rush to write a thesis statement and end up with one that does not capture the *main* similarity between the two people. Emphasize the importance of a thesis statement and remind students that it should tell the reader the main idea of the essay. Explain that a well-written thesis statement also guides the writer during the writing process.

To help students write their thesis statements, have them answer the following questions:

- What is the point of this essay?
- What do I want the reader to understand about the two people I chose?

* For more information on thesis statements, refer students to SE page 594.

Comparison Essay **157**

Prewrite · **Write** · Revise · **Edit** · Publish

Writing

Now that you have finished prewriting, you're ready to write your first draft. As you write, refer to your outline and your research notes.

Expository

Keys to Effective Writing

1. Include a thesis statement in the first paragraph and a topic sentence about a point of comparison in each middle paragraph.

2. Put all your ideas down on paper in your first draft.

3. Use your outline as a guide.

4. Add specific details to explain each point of comparison.

5. Use transition words and phrases to connect your ideas.

6. Write on every other line to leave room for later changes, or double-space if you're working on a computer.

Writing

Keys to Effective Writing

Remind students that the writing stage is when they get to write, or draft, their ideas on paper.

Keys to Effective Writing lists the process students will be guided through on SE pages 158–162.

- Have students check that their thesis statements identify the two people along with the main similarity between them.
- Stress that the other points of comparison that they plan to explain (item 4) should all lead to or be a result of this main similarity.

Writing Workshop

Make sure to model your own writing in front of your students. After all, you aren't just an instructor: You're also a writer. Use an overhead or the board to create your own beginning sentences or comparison sentences— and you'll simultaneously be helping to create a writing community.

Technology Connections

Students can use the added features of the Net-text as they explore this stage of the writing process.

✳ *Write Source Online* **Net-text**

Writing Getting the Big Picture

Encourage students to scan SE pages 159–162 to see how the items in this graphic actually reflect the bigger picture of the student essay. Suggest that when students have finished their first drafts they return to this page and fill in a similar graphic for their own essays.

- If students have used their prewriting notes and followed the steps presented on SE pages 159–162, they should see their own "big picture" clearly emerge.
- This will also highlight any gaps in their drafts that they can fill in when they revise.

Explain that the topic sentences for the **Middle** section of the graphic come from the student writer's prewriting outline. Have students turn back to the sample outline on SE page 156 to see that the sentence for section I is the first topic sentence in the graphic here.

- Provide time for students to review their own outlines now to make sure that they have written complete topic sentences for each point of comparison they plan to make.
- Stress that these outline sentences will become topic sentences for each middle paragraph of their essays.

158

Writing Getting the Big Picture

Now that you have finished prewriting, you are ready to write a first draft of your essay. The graphic that follows shows how the parts of your essay should fit together. (The example came from the student essay on pages **159–162**.)

Beginning

The **beginning** captures the reader's interest, introduces the two famous people, and states the thesis.

Thesis Statement
Jim Thorpe and Jesse Owens were great athletes who overcame poverty and prejudice.

Middle

The **middle** contains a paragraph for each point of comparison and includes supporting details, paraphrases, and quotations.

Topic Sentences
Both of these great athletes started life poor. **(Childhood)**

As young adults, Thorpe and Owens used their natural talents to achieve greatness. **(Beginning career)**

These great American athletes then went on to succeed against the world's best athletes. **(Middle career)**

Following their days of Olympic glory, however, Thorpe and Owens both returned to harsh realities. **(Late career)**

Ending

The **ending** revisits the thesis and reflects on the importance of the two famous people.

Closing Sentences
Jim Thorpe and Jesse Owens overcame poverty and prejudice to become two of the greatest athletes of all time. Their accomplishments live on in the sports they helped to integrate and in the world they helped to change.

Comparison Essay **159**

Starting Your Essay

The beginning of your essay should capture the reader's interest, introduce your two subjects, and state your thesis. Here are some ways to get the reader's attention:

Beginning	
Middle	
Ending	

- **Ask a question.**
  Who is the greatest American athlete of all time?
- **Start with a quotation.**
  "Sir," the King of Sweden said to Jim Thorpe, "you are the greatest athlete in the world."
- **Use a surprising statistic.**
  During one Big Ten meet, Jesse Owens tied one world record and set three more—all with an injured back!
- **Connect with the reader.**
  Imagine being a high school athlete who could beat world records.

Beginning Paragraph

Rafael starts his essay by asking a question. He then includes details leading to his thesis statement, which introduces the focus of his writing.

The writer captures the reader's interest and leads up to his thesis statement (underlined).

> Who is the greatest American athlete of all time? Most people think of people like Muhammad Ali, Jackie Joyner-Kersey, or Babe Ruth. However, there are two other great American athletes that some people may have forgotten about. These two people caught the world's attention many years ago, and they still inspire us today. Jim Thorpe and Jesse Owens were great athletes who overcame poverty and prejudice.

Write your beginning. Use one of the suggestions above to get the reader's interest. Then build to your thesis statement.

Focus on the Traits

Organization These transitions may help you make comparisons.

also	by contrast	likewise	similarly
both	each	on the one hand	though
but	however	on the other hand	yet

Expository

Writing Starting Your Essay

To help students start their essay, suggest that they read over the sample beginnings shown here and decide which they find most interesting and engaging. Tell them to use that same strategy to write their beginnings.

Focus on the Traits

Organization

Remind students that transitions will make their ideas flow more smoothly and make those ideas easier for readers to follow and understand.

To help students recognize how transitions can be used to make comparisons, have students locate and discuss the use of transitions in the model paragraph on SE page 147 and the model essay on SE pages 149–150. Have students add the comparison transitions in the list and any new comparison transitions they find to their **Writer's Notebook** (see below).

Teaching Tip: Writer's Notebook

Discuss the benefits of keeping a Writer's Notebook.

- Point out that students can record their thoughts and feelings on different topics. Then when they need an idea for a writing assignment, they can refer to their notebooks.
- Students can use their notebook to improve and increase their writing

vocabularies. Suggest that they designate a certain section of their notebooks (the back of the book may work best) for vocabulary. Encourage students to jot down interesting words and phrases that they hear or read; new words and their definitions; and groups of words such as the transitions on SE page 159.

If students aren't keeping notebooks yet, suggest that they begin. They can use any kind of blank book, but many writers like to use loose leaf binders with ruled pages so that they can insert additional pages anywhere in the notebooks.

✴ For more information about using a writer's notebook, see SE pages 4–5.

Writing Developing the Middle Part

Remind students that the topic sentence in each middle paragraph on SE pages 160–161 was part of the "big picture" on SE page 158 and came from the writer's outline. If they haven't already identified these topic sentences, have them do so now. Reinforcing this framework will help students understand how to use their own outlines to create their drafts.

Ask students to point out specific facts and statistics in the essay. Then consider the following questions for discussion:
- What level of interest do these facts and statistics add to the comparison?
- How do these facts and statistics make the writer sound more knowledgeable?
- Have I gathered enough facts and statistics to make my comparison as interesting and as informative?

If students determine that they need to do more research, have them come to you to discuss revising the due date for submitting their draft.

Beginning

Middle

Ending

Writing Developing the Middle Part

Follow your outline to write the middle part of your essay. Be sure to expand on the key ideas with additional information from your note cards.

Middle Paragraphs

> Topic sentences identify each main point of comparison.
>
> A paraphrase puts information in the writer's own words.
>
> Facts and statistics produce a knowledgeable voice.

Both of these great athletes started life poor. In 1888, Jim Thorpe was born on a farm near Prague, Oklahoma. His parents named him Wa-tho-huck, a Native American name that means "Bright Path" ("Jim"). Still, he didn't have a bright early life. Thorpe's twin brother, Charlie, died when Jim was nine, and his mother died shortly afterward. Thorpe attended one Indian school after another in Oklahoma, Kansas, and Pennsylvania before his athletic talent was recognized. Jesse Owens also had a tough childhood. He was born in 1913 into a poor Alabama family. They moved north to Cleveland, hoping for a better life, but couldn't find one. During high school, Owens worked so many odd jobs that he couldn't make afternoon practices for the track team. However, track coach Charlie Riley recognized Owens' talent and offered to train him in the morning ("Jesse").

As young adults, Thorpe and Owens used their natural talents to achieve greatness. In 1911 and 1912, Thorpe led the Carlisle Indian School varsity football team to victory over powerful teams such as Army, Georgetown, Harvard, and Pittsburgh. Thorpe scored 25 touchdowns and 198 points in his last season, and he was named All-American for two years running ("Jim"). In the same way, Owens became a track star in high school and college. At Cleveland East High School, he tied the world-record time for the 100-yard dash. At Ohio State University, he tied one world record and set three more, all in less than an hour and with an injured back! Owens broke the broad-jump record by placing a handkerchief at the old mark—26 feet 2 1/2 inches—and jumping nearly 6 inches beyond it ("Jesse").

Struggling Learners

Caution students about two mistakes that are sometimes made when writing topic sentences for middle paragraphs:
- being too specific
- using first-person point of view

Write these examples on the board, and have students identify why each would not work as a topic sentence:

- Thorpe led his high school team to victory, and Owens was a high school track star.
- I'm now going to talk about Thorpe's and Owens's athletic accomplishments as young adults.

Work with students to rewrite these sentences as good topic sentences.

For example: *Even as young adults, Thorpe and Owens performed tremendous athletic feats.* Make sure students see the difference between this sentence (more general) and the example it replaces (too specific).

Expository

These great American athletes then went on to succeed against the world's best athletes. Jim Thorpe was chosen to represent the United States in the Stockholm Olympics of 1912. There he easily won the pentathlon and set a decathlon score (8,413 points) that wouldn't be topped for 20 years ("Jim"). The king of Sweden even declared Thorpe "the greatest athlete in the world," to which Jim replied, "Thanks, King" (qtd. in "Thorpe"). Twenty-four years later, in 1936, Jesse Owens represented this country in the so-called "Hitler Olympics." Adolf Hitler believed the Aryan race was superior, but as he watched, Owens won four gold medals, breaking an Olympic record and a world record. But Owens' greatest accomplishment was winning the hearts of the German people. Even Luz Long, the top German long jumper, befriended Jim in front of Hitler. Owens later said, "You can melt down all the medals and cups I have, and they wouldn't be a plating on the 24-karat friendship I felt for Luz Long" (qtd. in "Track").

Following their days of Olympic glory, however, Thorpe and Owens both returned to harsh realities. The Olympic committee removed Thorpe's medals because of complaints about his "professionalism." (Professional athletes were not allowed to compete, and Thorpe had earned $15 a week playing minor-league baseball.) Thorpe returned to playing baseball and football, became a Hollywood extra, and finally ended up on the recreation staff of the Chicago Park District ("Jim"). Owens became a "runner-for-hire," racing against ballplayers, motorcycles, or even racehorses ("Biography"). "It was bad enough to have toppled from the Olympic heights to make my living competing with animals," Owens once said, "but the competition wasn't even fair. No man could beat a racehorse, not even for 100 yards" (qtd. in "Quotes"). Unlike Thorpe, though, Owens kept an optimistic spirit, which launched him into a new career: motivational speaking.

> **Quotations** add insight into Owens' personality.

> **An explanation** makes the meaning clear.

Write your middle paragraphs. Follow your outline and use transitions to connect your ideas.

Have students identify the quotation by Owens in the third middle paragraph and discuss how it helps readers understand the athlete. Then discuss the difference between **using direct quotations and paraphrasing** (see below).

Remind students to refer to their prewriting notes—specifically their outline and details list—as they write their middle paragraphs.

It would benefit all students to point out that in the essay parentheses are used in three ways:
- to provide additional information (8,413 points)
- to cite sources ("Jim") ("Thorpe")
- to explain (Professional athletes were not allowed . . .)

Sometimes students may have to use an indirect source. An indirect source is a source cited within another source. For such indirect quotations, instruct students to use "qtd. in" to indicate the sources they actually consulted. Also inform students it is better to attempt to find the original source, rather than citing an indirect source.

Teaching Tip: Using Direct Quotations and Paraphrasing

Explain to students that when using information from another source, they can quote directly from the source or they can paraphrase it.

- To paraphrase, students should put information from a source in their own words.

- To use a direct quotation, students must copy the information exactly from the source and enclose it in quotation marks. In a brief essay, it is advisable to limit the use of direct quotations and to keep them short.

　✳ For more about punctuating direct quotations, see SE pages 632–634.

Whether they use a direct quotation or paraphrasing, students must give credit to the source in the essay and cite the source on the works-cited page.

Writing Ending Your Essay

After reviewing the options for writing an effective ending and the sample ending, focus attention on Donald Murray's quotation at the end of the page.

- Ask students if they agree or disagree with the quotation.
- Have them provide examples from their own reading experience to support their opinions.

Writing Ending Your Essay

Your ending should be strong since it contains the last thoughts for your reader. Here are some ways to create a strong ending.

Beginning
Middle
Ending

- **Reflect on the importance of your subjects.**
  Athletes such as Jim Thorpe and Jesse Owens paved the way for other athletes like Mia Hamm and Tiger Woods.

- **Provide an effective quotation.**
  Jesse Owens summed up his winning spirit this way: "Friendships are born on the field of athletic strife and are the real gold of competition. Awards become corroded; friends gather no dust."

- **Include additional information of interest.**
  In 1982, 30 years after his death, the Olympic committee returned Thorpe's medals to his family.

Ending Paragraphs

The writer revisits the thesis and reflects on the importance of the subjects.

> Eventually, these two athletes got the recognition they deserved. In 1976, President Ford gave Owens the Medal of Freedom, the highest honor a civilian can receive ("Biography"). In 1982, thirty years after his death, the Olympic committee returned Thorpe's medals to his family ("Jim"). Jim Thorpe and Jesse Owens overcame poverty and prejudice to become two of the greatest athletes of all time. Their accomplishments live on in the sports they helped to integrate and in the world they helped to change.

Write your ending. Write the final paragraph of your essay, using one or more of the strategies above.

> "We need important information at the beginning to attract the reader, but what the reader remembers is usually at the end of the paragraph."
>
> —Donald Murray

English Language Learners

For their ending paragraphs, students may have the tendency to summarize what they have already written, as it is easier and uses less new language. To avoid this, encourage students to do the following:

- Refer back to their outline for details that they haven't used.

- Include some of these details as new ideas in their conclusion.

Provide help as needed with word choice so that the final paragraph does not sound like a simple summary.

Prewrite · Write · **Revise** · Edit · Publish

Revising

Go Online!

When you revise, you improve your writing. You add important new information, delete unnecessary details, change the order of ideas, and rework parts that do not sound right.

Expository

Keys to Effective Revising

1. Read your essay aloud to get a feeling for how well it works.

2. Be sure your thesis statement and topic sentences are clear.

3. Check your supporting details. Do they work and are there enough of them?

4. Consider your voice. It should sound knowledgeable and engaging.

5. Check your words and sentences for clarity and variety.

6. Use the editing and proofreading marks inside the back cover of this book.

Revising

Go Online!

Keys to Effective Revising

Remind students that the revising stage is when writers have an opportunity to make improvements to their first drafts. At this stage they can think about refinements they might not have considered when they were drafting.

Keys to Effective Revising lists the process students will be guided through on SE pages 164–174.

Emphasize that reading their essays aloud (item 1) is one of the best ways for students to identify problems. Mistakes in the misuse of words, organization, or gaps in information seem to jump out much more quickly when they are heard than when they are viewed. Alternately, students might ask someone else to read their essay aloud to them. Then the writer can listen and take notes.

Peer Response

Ask students to read and review each other's first drafts. Peer response is a crucial yardstick with which students can measure their work. Constructive peer responses can help students determine which of the following revision strategies can make the largest difference for their writing.

Technology Connections

Have students use the Writing Network features of the Net-text to comment on each other's drafts.

Write Source Online Net-text

Revising for Ideas

The rubric strips that run across all of the revising pages (SE pages 164–173) are provided to help students focus their revising and are related to the full rubric on SE pages 180–181.

Have students discuss why the first sample thesis statement is weak and the second is strong.

- Ask students to name singers from several different genres, including rock, jazz, classical, pop, theater, and so on.
- Guide students to see that all of these people can be identified as singers. However, not every one of them helped introduce Latin music to the United States. This fact is what makes a comparison between Gloria Estefan and Selena interesting.

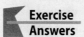

Exercise Answers

1. Queen Elizabeth and Queen Victoria ruled during England's most powerful and profitable periods.
2. The voyages of Christopher Columbus and Ferdinand Magellan changed the course of European history.
3. Elizabeth Cady Stanton and Susan B. Anthony shared a vision of equality for all women everywhere.

Revising for Ideas

6 My essay shows the strong similarity between two people, and it is full of supporting details.

5 My essay shows interesting similarities between the two people and one good contrast.

4 My essay shows how the two people are similar, but it could use more details and a better contrast.

When you revise for *ideas*, you ensure that the central similarity between the two people is clear. You also decide whether you should include a surprising contrast. The rubric strip above will help you revise.

Have I focused on a significant similarity?

You have focused on a significant similarity if you show an *important* way that the two people are alike. Start by checking your thesis statement.

A weak thesis statement: Gloria Estefan is a singer, as was Selena.

A strong thesis statement: Singers Gloria Estefan and Selena helped introduce Latin music to the United States.

Exercise

Read the pairs of thesis statements below. Which one shows a more important similarity between the two people?

1. Queen Elizabeth I and Queen Victoria came to the throne because male heirs could not be found.
   Queen Elizabeth I and Queen Victoria ruled during England's most powerful and profitable periods.
2. Christopher Columbus and Ferdinand Magellan believed they could sail around the world.
   The voyages of Christopher Columbus and Ferdinand Magellan changed the course of European history.
3. Elizabeth Cady Stanton and Susan B. Anthony shared a vision of equality for all women everywhere.
   Elizabeth Cady Stanton and Susan B. Anthony lived in the East but traveled across many states.

Review your thesis statement. Does it show a significant similarity? If not, rewrite it. Then be sure your main points of comparison fit the thesis.

English Language Learners

Students may have difficulty determining whether their thesis statements show a significant similarity. If they are comfortable doing so, encourage students to share their work with a partner who is more proficient in English. Have the partner do the following:

- Read the thesis statement.
- Help decide if it shows an important way the subjects are alike.
- If it doesn't, offer suggestions on how to revise it.

3 I need more details that show the similarities between the two people and a contrast.

2 I need to address the similarities between the two people.

1 I need to understand how to compare two people.

Comparison Essay **165**

How can a surprising contrast improve my essay?

A surprising contrast will add interest to your essay. The contrast should point out a significant difference between your chosen subjects.

Exercise

Decide which of each pair of contrasts is more surprising.

1. Madeleine Albright and Condoleeza Rice come from different parts of the country.
   Many of Condoleeza Rice's foreign-policy decisions completely overturned those made by Madeleine Albright.

2. Bruce Lee was the most famous martial-arts star, but Jackie Chan may have overtaken him.
   Bruce Lee's fighting style was derived from karate and kung fu, while Jackie Chan's style also draws from comedians like Buster Keaton and Charlie Chaplin.

3. Hemingway enjoyed traveling the world, while Faulkner preferred staying in Oxford, Mississippi.
   Hemingway was more popular at first, but Faulkner has become very popular.

Revise

Search for surprising contrasts. Find a few important ways in which your subjects are/were different. Include some contrasts in your essay.

Ideas
A surprising contrast gives insight into both men.

. . . *Owens once said, "but the competition wasn't even fair. No man could beat a racehorse, not even for 100 yards"* (qtd. in "Quotes").

Unlike Thorpe, though, Owens kept an optimistic spirit, which launched him into a new career: motivational speaking.

Expository

Point out to students that no matter how similar two people appear to be, there are bound to be contrasts in their lives. Usually, the most significant differences have to do with their basic beliefs or their singular approach to a particular aspect of their life.

Exercise Answers

1. The second statement is more surprising because the difference between the decisions of these women emphasizes the differences between the two administrations they served.

2. The second statement is more surprising because most people would probably not guess that Jackie Chan's style draws from two old-time, slapstick comedians.

3. The first statement is more surprising because readers may expect all famous authors to enjoy traveling all over the country and the world.

✱ For a list of transition words that show contrasts, see SE page 593. Encourage students to use these words to help them introduce contrasts in their essay.

Struggling Learners

Students may be confused as to why contrasts are introduced into a comparison essay. A brief class discussion can help illustrate the interest that a surprising contrast can add to their essays.

- First, ask students to think of a friend, cousin, or sibling who is similar to themselves.

- Call on a volunteer to name the similarities he or she identified. List the similarities on the board.
- Then ask the volunteer to name two differences between them. (We have different hobbies; we come from different cultures, and so on.)
- Invite the class to decide which difference is more surprising.

Explain that no two people share everything in common, and adding a contrast into a comparison essay will add an element of interest and will make the comparison seem more real or honest to the reader.

Revising for Organization

Peer responders *(see below)* may feel more comfortable and give more thoughtful responses if they have time to read the essays, think about them, and write responses on their own.

- Have writers copy the questions in the sample "Beginning-Ending Review Sheet" onto paper, leaving several lines of space between questions.
- Tell writers to give the peer reviewers the sheet of questions along with their drafts.
- Provide time for peer reviewers to read the beginnings and endings and write responses.
- Writers and peer reviewers can then meet and discuss the reviewing process.

166

Revising for Organization

 6 The key points of comparison and transitions make the essay engaging.

5 The beginning, middle, and ending paragraphs provide a clear comparison.

4 The essay is complete, but the organization in some of the middle paragraphs seems unclear.

When you revise for *organization*, be sure that your beginning and ending work well and that each middle paragraph covers a key point of comparison. The rubric strip above can guide your revision.

Do my beginning and ending sentences work well?

You know your beginning and ending sentences work well if your writing creates a strong first impression and an even stronger final impression. The best way to find out is to ask a classmate to review these sentences.

 Exercise

Ask for a peer response. Have your partner read your beginning and ending and then answer the questions below. (Use the sample responses as a guide.)

> **Beginning-Ending Review Sheet**
>
> 1. **Do the first few sentences capture your interest? Why or why not?** Mostly. I like sports, so I like knowing about the greatest athletes.
>
> 2. **How could I create a stronger beginning?** You could include the names of some famous athletes from the last century.
>
> 3. **Do the last few sentences leave you with a final thought? Explain.** They make me think that even if people aren't fair to you during your life, you should just hang on. You'll probably get recognized eventually.
>
> 4. **How could I create a stronger ending?** You could use the words "greatest athletes of all time" to refer back to the beginning.

 Reread your beginning and ending. Use your partner's responses to help you improve the beginning and ending of your essay.

Revise

Teaching Tip: Peer Responders

Provide these basic rules for peer responders to follow to help them provide useful responses.

- Be specific. Simple "yes" or "no" answers do not tell the writer enough.
- Be honest and offer constructive criticism. The writer is asking for your opinion to help improve the piece of writing.

- Be considerate and polite. Evaluate and criticize the writing, not the writer.

✳ For examples of constructive criticism, see SE page 57.

3 The beginning or ending is weak. The middle should have a paragraph for each key point of comparison.	2 The beginning, middle, and ending all run together. Point-by-point organization should be used.	1 The essay should be reorganized.

How can I check the organization of the middle part?

Check the organization of the middle to be sure that your comparisons balance. Create a scale diagram for each main point of comparison and weigh the details in it. Here is a sample diagram for a comparison of the early careers of Fred Astaire and Gene Kelly.

Scale Diagram

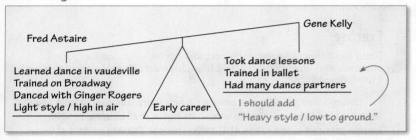

Fred Astaire

Learned dance in vaudeville
Trained on Broadway
Danced with Ginger Rogers
Light style / high in air

Early career

Gene Kelly

Took dance lessons
Trained in ballet
Had many dance partners

I should add
"Heavy style / low to ground."

Revise

Check your point-by-point details. Review your paragraphs. If one seems out of balance, create a scale diagram to compare the weight of details.

Organization
Suggestions from a classmate improve the beginning paragraph.

Who is the greatest American athlete of all time?
other
There are two great American athletes that some people
may have forgotten about. . . .

Most people think of people like Muhammad Ali,
Jackie Joyner-Kersey, or Babe Ruth. However,

Expository

Model how to use the scale diagram.
- Draw a fulcrum on the board or on chart paper.
- Ask a volunteer to read aloud a paragraph from his or her draft.
- Then have the writer read the paragraph one sentence at a time, pausing at the end of each sentence.
- Ask students to identify details in each sentence, and as they do, list the details on either side of the fulcrum.
- After the writer finishes reading the paragraph, have the class examine the filled-in scale diagram to determine if the comparison for that paragraph is balanced.

Revising for Voice

Using facts, statistics, and quotations will make a writer's voice sound knowledgeable. Remind students to double-check their notes and their sources to make sure that their essays are accurate.

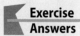

Exercise Answers

Possible Answers

- **Facts:** presidencies came a century apart; 1860; Lincoln granted freedom to most of those slaves in the Emancipation Proclamation; June 11, 1963
- **Statistics:** 31 million people; thirteen percent of those, or nearly four million, were slaves
- **Quotation:** "One hundred years of delay . . . until all its citizens are free."

These specific facts, statistics, and quotations show that the writer has done extensive research to learn as much as possible about the subject. They show a clear and in-depth understanding of the topic, thereby creating a knowledgeable voice.

168

Revising for Voice

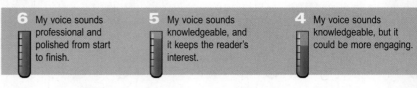

| **6** My voice sounds professional and polished from start to finish. | **5** My voice sounds knowledgeable, and it keeps the reader's interest. | **4** My voice sounds knowledgeable, but it could be more engaging. |

When you revise for *voice*, you add details that make your writing sound knowledgeable and engaging. The rubric strip above can help you revise.

Does my writing voice sound knowledgeable?

Your writing voice sounds knowledgeable if you effectively use facts, statistics, and quotations. **Facts** are details that can be proven to be true. **Statistics** are facts that include precise numbers, and **quotations** are someone's exact words.

Exercise

Read the following paragraph and identify at least one fact, one statistic, and one quotation. Tell how these details make the voice sound knowledgeable.

Though their presidencies came a century apart, Abraham Lincoln and John F. Kennedy both worked to ensure the rights of all citizens. In 1860, Lincoln presided over a nation of 31 million people. Thirteen percent of those, or nearly four million, were slaves ("Census"). Lincoln granted freedom to most of those slaves in the Emancipation Proclamation, but freedom did not translate into equality. "One hundred years of delay have passed since President Lincoln freed the slaves," announced Kennedy on June 11, 1963, "yet their heirs, their grandsons, are not fully free. . . . And this nation, for all its hopes and all its boasts, will not be fully free until all its citizens are free" (qtd. in "Civil"). Kennedy saw himself as a partner working to complete the job Lincoln had begun.

Revise

Revise for voice. Use facts, statistics, or quotations to make your writing voice sound more knowledgeable.

English Language Learners

It may be necessary to give some background before assigning the **Exercise**. Explain the conditions for African Americans at the time of the US Civil War and the civil rights movement to promote understanding of the passage and the activity.

| 3 | More details and personal connections would improve my voice. | 2 | My voice sounds uncertain and uninteresting. I should add facts, statistics, quotations, and anecdotes. | 1 | I need help understanding how to create a strong expository voice. |

Does my writing voice sound engaging?

Your voice sounds engaging if it creates a personal connection between your topic and your reader. One way to do this is to use an **anecdote**. An **anecdote** is a little story that reveals something about the person. The following paragraph includes an anecdote about Lincoln:

> Lincoln and Kennedy faced terrible challenges near the end of their presidencies, but they kept their feelings of compassion. For example, during Grant's final advance in the Civil War, Lincoln found three orphaned kittens in the telegraph hut at City Point, Virginia. Lincoln listened to reports of battle while he held the kittens in his lap. "Kitties, thank God you are cats," he said, "and can't understand this terrible strife that is going on" (qtd. in Sandburg 679). Lincoln even asked someone on Grant's staff to take care of the kittens.

 Revise

Check for anecdotes. Review your research, looking for little stories that reveal something significant about the person you are describing. Consider adding an anecdote to your essay.

Voice

A statistic and an anecdote create a more knowledgeable and engaging voice.

> There he easily won the pentathlon and set a decathlon
> (8,413 points)
> score that wouldn't be topped for 20 years ("Jim"). Twenty-
> four years later, in 1936, Jesse Owens represented this
> country in the so-called "Hitler Olympics." . . .
>
> The king of Sweden even declared Thorpe "the greatest athlete in the world," to which Jim replied, "Thanks, King."

Expository

Most well-written biographies include interesting and entertaining anecdotes about the subject. These anecdotes are what make the person "real" for readers. If students do not have anecdotes in their research notes that they can use in their essays, suggest that they look in the following sources:

- published biographies and autobiographies of the people they are comparing (these should be available at most libraries)
- recent articles in newspapers and magazines
- official Web sites of high-profile people and celebrities

Remind students to choose appropriate anecdotes that will enhance their ideas and engage the reader. Caution them to avoid the following:

- offensive and inappropriate anecdotes
- anecdotes that may be interesting but are completely unrelated to the ideas in the essay

Revising for Word Choice

Words and phrases such as *kind of, sort of,* and *really* can detract from a writer's good ideas and make the writer sound too casual, careless, or disinterested. Encourage students to strive to eliminate unnecessary modifiers from their formal writing and speaking.

✳ For tips on how to avoid using unnecessary adverbs, have students turn to SE page 543.

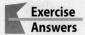
Exercise
Answers

Possible Answers

1. Robert Frost was interested in regular people.
2. Once he said, "You can be a little ungrammatical if you come from the right part of the country."
3. His most popular poem, "The Road Not Taken," tells of a person taking a walk on an overgrown trail.
4. What's surprising is that this average person makes a choice that most people don't make.

170

Revising for Word Choice

6 Precise word choice makes my essay informative and enjoyable to read.

5 My words are carefully chosen. I have avoided unnecessary modifiers and repeated words.

4 Most of my modifiers are necessary, but I should find synonyms for some repeated words.

Revising for *word choice* involves checking to be sure you have not used unnecessary modifiers and have not repeated words too often. The rubric strip above will help you revise.

Have I used unnecessary modifiers?

You have used unnecessary modifiers if the adjectives, adverbs, and phrases you include do not make your ideas clearer. Here are traps to avoid:

■ **Empty modifiers:** Words like *kind of, sort of, really,* and *totally* don't add to the meaning of your work and should be deleted.

> Carl Sandburg really took the kind of "everyman" approach to poetry.
>
> Carl Sandburg took the "everyman" approach to poetry.

■ **Redundant modifiers:** A strong noun does not need a modifier.

> He wrote about the bloody slaughterhouses of metropolitan Chicago.
>
> He wrote about the slaughterhouses of Chicago.

■ **Strings of modifiers:** One solid modifier is better than two or three.

> His poems use natural, casual, everyday language and dialects.
>
> His poems use everyday language and dialects.

Exercise

Rewrite each sentence to eliminate unnecessary modifiers.

1. Robert Frost was really very interested in regular, everyday people.
2. Once he even said out loud, "You can be a little ungrammatical if you come from the right part of the country."
3. His most popular and famous poem, "The Road Not Taken," tells of a person taking a walk on a grassy, overgrown trail.
4. What's totally and completely surprising is that this average person actually makes a choice that most people don't make.

Grammar Connection

Wordiness and Deadwood
■ *Write Source* page 543
■ *SkillsBook* page 174

English Language Learners

Students may try to use extra modifiers to increase the intensity of their statements. If this is the case, hold a conference with students and help them find more precise descriptions so that they feel comfortable eliminating the modifiers.

Struggling Learners

Students may find it difficult to recognize unnecessary modifiers in their writing. As they revise, encourage students to look for places where they have used two or more modifiers together. Encourage students to use a thesaurus (see TE page 171) to decide if any of the modifiers are so similar in meaning that one of them could be eliminated.

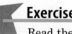

3 I should remove some unnecessary modifiers and repeated words.

2 Too many unnecessary modifiers and repeated words make my essay difficult to follow.

1 I need help to understand how to choose modifiers and avoid word repetition.

How do I know if I have repeated a word too often?

The best way to know if you have repeated a word too often is to read your work aloud. Listen for words that are used over and over and replace some of them with synonyms. You can also reword sentences to avoid repetition.

Exercise

Read the following sentences aloud and write down words that are repeated too often. Suggest synonyms or ways to reword the sentences.

1. Carl Sandburg, a poet from Illinois, wrote free-verse poetry about places in Illinois and Illinois's favorite son, Lincoln.
2. Robert Frost lived in New England and wrote about the New England countryside and the people in New England.
3. Frost preferred writing poetry with rhyme and meter because he felt rhyme and meter were important to poetry.
4. Frost avoided free-verse poetry, saying he would rather play tennis with the net down than write free-verse poetry.
5. Whatever type of poetry they preferred, though, both poets won the Pulitzer Prize for Poetry.

Revise

Check for word repetition. Read your work aloud and underline words that are used too often. Find synonyms or rewrite sentences to avoid repetition.

Word Choice
A repeated word is deleted and another is replaced with a synonym.

In 1911 and 1912, Thorpe's ~~talent~~ led the Carlisle Indian School
powerful
varsity football team to victory over ~~talented~~ teams such as
Army, Georgetown, Harvard, and Pittsburgh. Thorpe scored . . .

Expository

Review how to **use a thesaurus** *(see below)* to find synonyms.

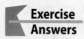

Exercise Answers

Possible Answers

1. Illinois—Carl Sandburg, a poet from Illinois, wrote free-verse poetry about places in that state and its favorite son, Lincoln.
2. New England—Robert Frost lived in New England and wrote about its countryside and people.
3. rhyme and meter, poetry—Frost preferred writing poetry with rhyme and meter because he felt they were important to the form.
4. free-verse poetry—Frost said he would rather play tennis with the net down than write free-verse poetry.
5. poetry—Whatever type they preferred, though, both poets won the Pulitzer Prize for Poetry.

Teaching Tip: Using a Thesaurus

By ninth grade, most students know how to use a thesaurus and should be using one regularly. For students who need a refresher, model how to use the type of thesaurus available in the classroom, including the thesaurus that is provided with computer word-processor programs.

English Language Learners

Students may find using a translation dictionary more helpful than a thesaurus. If one is available, show students that in a translation dictionary, there often is more than one word given as a translation. Students may feel more comfortable using this tool instead of a thesaurus, as they can relate their word choice to their first language.

Struggling Learners

Students may not notice repeated words, even when reading their essay aloud. Have them trade essays with a partner. Partners should read the essay and circle examples of words that are repeated too often. Then, the writer should find synonyms for some of these words.

Revising for Sentence Fluency

Advise students to aim for a variety of sentence types in their essays. Point out that too many of one pattern can create an awkward sound and flow. On the other hand, a balanced mix of sentence patterns will add interest and create a smoother flow.

✱ For more information on using commas and coordinating conjunctions in compound sentences, see SE pages 608 and 734.

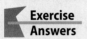
Exercise Answers

Possible Answers

1. Pocahontas's brother captured John Smith, and her father decided that Smith had to be put to death.
2. Smith was tied up and helpless, yet Pocahontas embraced him and cradled him in her arms.
3. Tribes were suspicious of the expedition of Lewis and Clark, but the presence of Sacagawea reduced their suspicions.
4. Sacagawea knew the plants and animals along the route, for she had lived there many years before.

172

Revising for Sentence Fluency

6 My sentences are skillfully written and easy to follow.

5 My sentences flow well because I have used a variety of sentence types.

4 Most of my sentences flow well, but I could use a few more compound or complex sentences.

To revise for *sentence fluency,* be sure you have used a combination of simple, compound, and complex sentences in your writing. The rubric strip above can guide your revision.

When should I use compound sentences?

You should use compound sentences to show that two ideas are closely related. You create a compound sentence by joining two simple sentences using a comma and a coordinating conjunction (*and, but, or, nor, for, so,* or *yet*).

Two Simple Sentences
Pocahontas helped the settlers at Jamestown survive.
Sacagawea did the same for the Lewis and Clark expedition.

One Compound Sentence
Pocahontas helped the settlers at Jamestown survive, and **Sacagawea did the same for the Lewis and Clark expedition.**

Exercise

Use a comma and a coordinating conjunction to join each pair of simple sentences into a compound sentence.

1. Pocahontas's brother captured John Smith.
   Her father decided that Smith had to be put to death.
2. Smith was tied up and helpless.
   Pocahontas embraced him and cradled him in her arms.
3. Tribes were suspicious of the expedition of Lewis and Clark.
   The presence of Sacagawea reduced their suspicions.
4. Sacagawea knew the plants and animals along the route.
   She had lived there many years before.

Create compound sentences. Read your work and look for simple sentences with related ideas. Consider joining some with a comma and a coordinating conjunction.

Grammar Connection

Compound and Complex Sentences

- **Proofreader's Guide** pages 748–749
- *GrammarSnap* Sentence Types: Simple, Compound, Complex, and Compound-Complex, Compound Sentences, Complex Sentences
- *SkillsBook* page 141

Comparison Essay **173**

3 More compound and complex sentences would create a better flow.

2 My sentences do not flow. I could create variety with compound and complex sentences.

1 I need help to learn how to create different types of sentences.

When should I use complex sentences?

You should use complex sentences to show a relationship between ideas. The ideas may be related by time or place (*when, where*), by cause and effect (*because, in order that*), by comparison (*as if, as though*), or by contrast (*although, whereas*). A subordinating conjunction shows the relationship. (Relative pronouns such as *which* or *that* can also be used to form complex sentences.)

Subordinating Conjunctions

after	because	since	when
although	before	that	where
as if	in order that	though	whereas
as though	provided	unless	while

Two Simple Sentences
Pocahontas traveled to England. She was reunited with John Smith.

Two Complex Sentences
Pocahontas traveled to England where she was reunited with John Smith.
When Pocahontas traveled to England, she was reunited with John Smith.

 Revise

Create complex sentences. Review your essay and watch for simple sentences that have a special relationship. Consider joining some of these.

Sentence Fluency
Two simple sentences are joined to form a complex sentence.

which
Unlike Thorpe, though, Owens kept an optimistic spirit. ~~This spirit~~ launched him into a new career: motivational speaking.

Expository

Invite volunteers to explain the differences between simple, compound, and complex sentences.

- A simple sentence has one independent clause.
- A compound sentence has two independent clauses connected by a comma and a coordinating conjunction.
- A complex sentence has one independent clause and at least one dependent clause, joined to the independent clause by a subordinating conjunction.

✳ For more information about using subordinating conjunctions, see SE pages 547 and 734.

 Writer's Craft

Signaling relationships: Point out to students that the conjunctions used on these pages do more than simply connect ideas. They signal relationships between ideas. A word such as "because," or "though" binds two ideas together into a larger idea. By creating such relationships, writers make words on a page come to life.

English Language Learners

Help students identify places in their essays where a complex sentence would work better than two short sentences. Have students refer to the list of subordinating conjunctions, and guide them in choosing which one would work best to tie two sentences together.

✳ For more subordinating conjunctions, direct students to the list on SE page 734.

Revising Improving Your Writing

Encourage thoughtful consideration of each question on the checklist.

- Ask students to jot down at least one example from their essay that justifies each of their "yes" answers.
- Then have students exchange papers with a partner who can review the revisions and the writer's responses to the checklist questions. If the partner disagrees with any of the writer's responses, the two of them should meet for a discussion.

Schedule **writing conferences** (*see below*) to discuss any areas that students determine need more revision.

Revising Improving Your Writing

 Check your revising. On a piece of paper, write the numbers 1 to 14. If you can answer "yes" to a question, put a check mark after that number. If not, continue to revise that part of your essay.

Revising Checklist

Ideas
_____ **1.** Have I chosen interesting people to compare?
_____ **2.** Does my thesis statement focus on a significant similarity?
_____ **3.** Do I include details that support my thesis?

Organization
_____ **4.** Does my beginning capture the reader's interest?
_____ **5.** Do I have a middle paragraph for each point of comparison?
_____ **6.** Are the details in each paragraph arranged point by point?
_____ **7.** Does the ending leave the reader with a strong final thought?

Voice
_____ **8.** Does my voice sound knowledgeable?
_____ **9.** Does my voice sound engaging?

Word Choice
_____ **10.** Have I avoided unnecessary modifiers?
_____ **11.** Have I avoided repeating words?
_____ **12.** Have I chosen specific nouns and active verbs?

Sentence Fluency
_____ **13.** Have I used simple, compound, and complex sentences?
_____ **14.** Do my sentences read smoothly?

 Make a clean copy. When you've finished revising, make a clean copy of your essay. This makes editing easier.

Grammar Connection

Parallelism
- **Proofreader's Guide** page 550 (+)
- *SkillsBook* pages 177–178

Rambling Sentences
- *Write Source* page 558
- *SkillsBook* page 170

Clauses
- **Proofreader's Guide** pages 612–613, 744 (+)
- *GrammarSnap* Restrictive/Nonrestrictive Relative Clauses and Relative Pronouns in Complex Sentences
- *SkillsBook* pages 15, 16, 17–18, 138–139, 140

Teaching Tip: Writing Conferences

In individual conferences with students, discuss how they can revise specific parts of their essays to improve them.

- Using the Revising Checklist, address each area of concern (items that are not checked) in order.
- Ask students what they think the problem is (for example, the beginning is dull) and if they have suggestions in mind for fixing the problem. If not, provide good examples that will give students options for revising that part of their essays.
- Read over the problem areas together. It's possible that there is an easy fix that will quickly become apparent upon rereading.
- Do not tell the student how to fix the problem, but do offer constructive advice that will help him or her arrive at a solution.

Prewrite → Write → Revise → Edit → Publish

Editing

Once you have finished your revisions, you're ready to edit your work for punctuation, capitalization, spelling, and grammar. These rules of English are called *conventions*.

Expository

Keys to Effective Editing

1. Edit your work with the help of a dictionary, a thesaurus, and the "Proofreader's Guide." (See pages 604–763.)

2. Check your writing for punctuation, capitalization, spelling, and grammar errors.

3. If you're using a computer, edit on a printed copy. Then enter your changes on the computer.

4. Use the editing and proofreading marks located inside the back cover of this book.

Editing

Keys to Effective Editing

Remind students that during the editing stage, they have a chance to find and correct errors in

- punctuation,
- capitalization,
- spelling, and
- grammar.

Keys to Effective Editing lists the process students will be guided through on SE pages 176–178.

Encourage students to read carefully for errors and to not rely solely on a word processor's spell-checking function to catch all spelling mistakes.

- Remind students that a spell checker will not catch misused words that are spelled correctly (*their* for *there*) or typographical errors that result in existing words (*rose* for *rise*).
- To encourage students to make it a habit to edit on a printed copy, have them submit their marked revised-and-edited copy with their final clean copy. Students who prefer to edit using the computer can submit a copy that shows tracked changes.

Technology Connections

Students can use the added features of the Net-text as they explore this stage of the writing process.

Write Source Online Net-text

English Language Learners

Throughout the editing process, encourage students to use the Proofreader's Guide (SE pages 604–763) to edit independently. Then schedule a conference with students to make any additional changes necessary before they write their final copies.

Have students focus on only a few English grammar concepts at first, gradually adding additional conventions as students become more skilled.

Editing for Conventions

Point out that comma splices and run-on sentences often occur when writers attempt to combine ideas during revising to add sentence variety. Advise students to check their writing carefully for these problems.

✱ For more about how to avoid these kinds of sentence problems, see SE page 557.

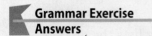

Grammar Exercise Answers

Possible answers. Errors may be corrected with a comma and coordinating conjunction, a semicolon, or by creating two separate sentences.

1. comma splice—Katharine Hepburn was born in 1907 in Connecticut, and Audrey Hepburn was born in 1929 in Belgium.

2. run-on—Katharine won her first Oscar for *Morning Glory*. She starred in the film the year after Audrey was born.

3. run-on—In 1939, Katharine starred in *The Philadelphia Story* on Broadway; Howard Hughes bought her the film rights.

Editing for Conventions

| **6** My writing is error free, and I have credited my sources correctly. | **5** I have a few minor errors, but I have credited my sources correctly. | **4** I have errors in conventions and in crediting my sources that must be corrected. |

Editing for *conventions* involves checking the punctuation, capitalization, spelling, and grammar of your writing. These two pages will help you correct any comma splices and run-ons you may have. They will also show you how to give credit to sources. The rubric strip above can guide you.

Have I fixed any comma splices or run-on sentences?

You can fix comma splices or run-ons by correctly connecting two simple sentences. (A compound sentence needs both a comma and a coordinating conjunction.) You can also correct these errors with a semicolon or by creating two sentences. (See page **557** for more information.)

Comma Splice (coordinating conjunction missing)
Katharine and Audrey Hepburn had the same last name, they weren't sisters.

Corrected Sentence (coordinating conjunction added)
Katharine and Audrey Hepburn had the same last name, but they weren't sisters.

Run-On (comma and coordinating conjunction missing)
Katharine and Audrey Hepburn had the same last name they weren't sisters.

Two Sentences (separated with a period and a capital letter)
Katharine and Audrey Hepburn had the same last name. They weren't sisters.

Grammar Exercise

Identify each error as a comma splice or a run-on and correct it.

1. Katharine Hepburn was born in 1907 in Connecticut, Audrey Hepburn was born in 1929 in Belgium.

2. Katharine won her first Oscar for *Morning Glory* she starred in the film the year after Audrey was born.

3. In 1939, Katharine starred in *The Philadelphia Story* on Broadway Howard Hughes bought her the film rights.

 Check for comma splices and run-ons in your essay. Correct any you find.

Grammar Connection

Comma Splices and Run-On Sentences
- *Write Source* page 557
- *GrammarSnap* Comma Splices and Run-On Sentences
- *SkillsBook* pages 165, 166

Advanced Learners

To extend this activity, invite students to compose two run-on sentences and two sentences with comma splices. Then have them do the following:

- Exchange papers.
- Identify the type of error in each sentence.
- Correct the error.

Encourage students to work together to create a poster using several examples each of these run-on sentences and comma splices, along with their corrected versions. Display the poster in the classroom as a reference.

3 I have errors in conventions and errors in crediting sources that may confuse the reader.

2 I must correct many errors that make my essay confusing and hard to read.

1 I need help finding errors and making corrections.

Expository

Have I credited my sources correctly?

You have credited your sources correctly if you have cited them in the text of your paper, using parenthetical citations, and creating a works-cited page. Use the guidelines below and pages 381–384 to cite sources.

- **Cite the author and title** in your text when possible.
  In her autobiography, *Me: Stories of My Life,* Katharine Hepburn shares her struggles and victories.

- **Use the author's last name** or, if the author is unknown, the first significant word from the title in the parenthetical reference.
  Audrey was strongly shaped by her experiences in Nazi-occupied Belgium ("Audrey").

- **Give the page number** if you are citing only part of a work.
  Katharine, likewise, was deeply shaken by the loss of her beloved older brother (Ormand 54).

- **Place the period after** a parenthetical reference.
  Audrey Hepburn's life story appears in a book by her son (Ferrer).

Edit

Credit sources. Review your essay to be sure you have correctly credited your sources. Create a works-cited page (see pages 381–384).

Conventions
A parenthetical citation credits the source of information.

Thorpe returned to playing baseball and football, became a Hollywood extra, and finally ended up on the recreation staff of the Chicago Park District. Owens became a . . .
("Jim")

If this is the first time students are being asked to submit a works-cited page, set aside some time to review the guidelines on SE pages 381–384 together. If possible, have students create their works-cited page in class. Then if students have any problems understanding the guidelines or applying them to their sources, you can work together to clarify these problems.

Remind students that each of their sources needs to be documented. Some students may need to revisit their sources to get the correct and complete information before they can create a works-cited page.

Editing Checking Your Writing

Give students a few moments to look over the Proofreader's Guide (SE pages 604–763). Throughout the year, they can refer to the instruction, rules, and examples to clarify any checklist items or to resolve questions about their own writing.

Creating a Title

Students will probably enjoy brainstorming clever, entertaining titles for their essays.
- Divide students into pairs or small groups.
- Suggest that students summarize their essays for their partners or groups.
- Then have them spend a few minutes suggesting titles for each other.

Editing Checking Your Writing

 Check your editing. On a piece of paper, write the numbers 1 to 10. If you can answer "yes" to a question, put a check mark after that number. Continue editing until you can answer "yes" to all the questions.

<u>Editing Checklist</u>

Conventions

PUNCTUATION

_____ **1.** Do I correctly punctuate compound and complex sentences?

_____ **2.** Have I cited sources correctly in my essay?

_____ **3.** Have I correctly formatted a works-cited page?

CAPITALIZATION

_____ **4.** Have I capitalized proper nouns and adjectives?

_____ **5.** Do I begin each sentence with a capital letter?

SPELLING

_____ **6.** Have I spelled all my words correctly?

_____ **7.** Have I double-checked the words my spell-checker may have missed?

GRAMMAR

_____ **8.** Do I use correct forms of verbs (*he saw*, not *he seen*)?

_____ **9.** Do my subjects and verbs agree in number?

_____ **10.** Have I used the right words (*there, their, they're*)?

Creating a Title

Even when you write informational essays and reports, it's important to engage your reader with an attention-getting title. Here are some ideas:

- Sum up the comparison:
  Natural Talents Bring National Fame
- Be clever:
  Breaking Records and Making History
- Use an idea from your essay:
  Overcoming Poverty and Prejudice

Grammar Connection

Apostrophes
- **Proofreader's Guide** pages 628–629, 630–631
- *SkillsBook* pages 29, 30, 31, 32

Capitalization
- **Proofreader's Guide** pages 648–649
- *GrammarSnap* Common uses of Capitalization
- *SkillsBook* pages 43, 46

English Language Learners

Before students address items 8, 9, and 10 on the checklist, review each concept that you anticipate students will find difficult. For example, if you have seen errors in subject-verb agreement when working with students, remind them that for regular verbs they should add an *s* to the third person singular form, as in *he walks,* and so on.

Advanced Learners

Divide students into groups of three or four and have them do a round-robin edit of one another's essays. Each group member should use a different-colored pen, and each should begin by editing his or her own essay. Later, if a student has a question about a particular notation or comment, he or she can consult the peer editor who used that color pen.

Publishing Sharing Your Essay

After editing your essay, make a neat final copy, proofread it, and share it. You may post your essay on a Web site, role-play your subjects with a classmate, or turn your writing into a multimedia presentation. (See the suggestions below.)

 Make a final copy. Follow your teacher's instructions or use the guidelines below to format your essay. (If you are using a computer, see pages 76–78.) Create a clean final copy of your essay and carefully proofread it.

Focus on Presentation

- Use blue or black ink and write neatly.
- Write your name in the upper left-hand corner of page 1.
- Skip a line and center your title; skip another line and start your writing.
- Indent every paragraph and leave a one-inch margin on all four sides.
- Write your last name and the page number in the upper right corner of every page after page 1.

Post on a Web Site

Upload your paper to a school or personal Web site. Add photos and graphic elements to enhance your comparison.

Role-Play Your Essay

Find a partner and read your comparison essay with that person. Then choose the person each of you will role-play. Finally, improvise a conversation that reveals your similarities (and differences).

Create a Multimedia Presentation

Rework your essay into an effective speech script (see pages 393–403). Create visual aids such as posters or computer slides to complement and strengthen your speech. Give your presentation to the class.

Publishing
Sharing Your Essay

If your school or class has a Web site and students plan to publish their essays on it, make sure they have the current Web site addresses for uploading, and that they adhere to school policy and procedures when doing so.

By ninth grade, many students will be proficient enough using the computer to create slide-show presentations. However, not all students will have the equipment at home to create such presentations. Discuss what equipment is available at school with students and then work out a schedule for students who would like to use this equipment to share their essays.

 Technology Connections

Remind students that they can use the Writing Network features of the Portfolio to share their work with peers.

 Write Source Online **Portfolio**

Write Source Online **Net-text**

Expository

Rubric for Expository Writing

Remind students that a rubric is a chart that helps them evaluate their writing.

- The rubrics in this book are based on a six-point scale, in which a score of 6 indicates an amazing piece of writing, and a score of 1 means the writing is incomplete and not ready to be assessed.
- Explain that the purpose of the rubric is to help students break down the assessment process by evaluating each of the six traits individually—ideas, organization, voice, word choice, sentence fluency, and conventions.
- Point out that rubrics are also helpful during the writing process. A rubric can guide students whenever they write because it tells them what elements to include in their writing and how to present them.
- Explain to students that they will most likely have different ratings for the traits. For example, they may give themselves a 5 for ideas but a 4 for organization.

* Reproducible six-, five-, and four-point rubrics for expository writing can be found on pages 768, 772, and 776.

180

Rubric for Expository Writing

Use this rubric to guide and assess your expository writing. Refer to it to improve your writing using the six traits.

6 Ideas	**5**	**4**
The topic, thesis, and details make the essay unforgettable.	The essay is informative with a clear thesis and specific details.	The essay is informative with a clear thesis. More specific details are needed.
Organization		
The organization and transitions make the essay crystal clear and compelling.	The beginning interests the reader. The middle supports the focus. The ending works well. Transitions are used.	The essay is divided into a beginning, a middle, and an ending. Some transitions are used.
Voice		
The writer's voice has the confident, knowledgeable sound of a professional writer.	The writer's voice sounds knowledgeable and confident. It fits the audience.	The writer's voice sounds knowledgeable most of the time and fits the audience.
Word Choice		
The word choice is precise, with just the right nouns, verbs, and modifiers.	Specific nouns and action verbs make the essay clear and informative.	Some nouns and verbs could be more specific.
Sentence Fluency		
The sentences have flair and flavor, and the reader will enjoy them.	The sentences read smoothly.	Most of the sentences read smoothly, but some are short and choppy.
Conventions		
The essay is error free.	The essay has a few minor errors in punctuation, spelling, or grammar.	The essay has some errors in punctuation, spelling, or grammar.

Expository

3	2	1
The thesis of the essay should be clearer, and more specific details are needed.	The topic should be narrowed or expanded. Many more specific details are needed.	The writer should select a new topic.
The beginning or ending is weak. The middle needs a paragraph for each main point. More transitions are needed.	The beginning, middle, and ending all run together. Paragraph breaks and transitions are needed.	The essay should be reorganized.
The writer sometimes sounds unsure, and the voice needs to better fit the audience.	The writer sounds unsure. The voice needs to fit the audience.	The writer needs to learn about voice.
Too many general words are used. Specific nouns and verbs are needed.	General or missing words make this essay difficult to understand.	The writer needs help finding specific words.
Many short, choppy sentences need to be rewritten to make the essay read smoothly.	Many sentences are choppy or incomplete and need to be rewritten.	Most sentences need to be rewritten.
Several errors confuse the reader.	Many errors make the essay difficult to read.	Help is needed to make corrections.

Test Prep!

Throughout *Write Source,* students use formative, traits-based rubrics. These rubrics break the traits apart so that students can learn discrete strategies for improving their writing.

Many state writing tests use summative rubrics—sometimes combining all the traits holistically and at other times rating each trait on a 4- or 5-point scale.

The difference is simple. Formative rubrics are created to help students. Summative rubrics are created to help *graders*.

There's no need to worry, though. The formative rubrics in Write Source correlate very well to the summative rubrics used on most writing tests.

Evaluating a Comparison Essay

Ask students if they agree with the sample self-assessment on SE page 183. If they agree with the overall comments, ask them to suggest improvements based on the comments in the self-assessment. If they disagree with any comment, ask them to explain why.

Possible comments and suggestions:

Ideas—All the specific facts and details, including names of people and places, and dates, make the essay informative. Introducing contrast (for example, the different language preferences of the writers) also adds interest.

Organization—The beginning is especially engaging to readers who are familiar with Frodo Baggins and Aslan.

Voice—An anecdote would have brought the authors to life, but the writer does sound knowledgeable.

Word Choice—The use of the phrase *tough childhood* does not sound serious enough. The writer should replace *tough* with *difficult,* and delete the words *as well* the first time they appear in the last paragraph.

Sentence Fluency—The flow of the sentences is smooth. The sentence patterns do not sound repetitive.

Conventions—Add sources.

182

Evaluating a Comparison Essay

Read the comparison essay that follows and focus on its strengths and weaknesses. Then read the student self-assessment on the next page. (**This student essay contains some errors.**)

Men of Letters

In a small pub in Oxford, England, a group of men got together to read the books they were writing. One man read a chapter he had just written about Frodo Baggins. Another read a chapter about the giant lion Aslan. These men were known as the Inklings, led by J.R.R. Tolkien and C.S. Lewis, who were the first authors of fantasy.

In their early lives, both Tolkien and Lewis were raised by kind, friendly strangers. Tolkien was born in 1892 in South Africa, but after his father's death four years later, his family returned to England. They moved several more times before Tolkien's mother also died. Tolkien was only 12 when he and his brother Hilary became orphans. They were raised by a local priest, and they attended boarding schools as teenagers ("Who"). Lewis also was born to an English family, although they lived in Northern Ireland. After his family returned to England, his mother died. Lewis was only 10 when he and his brother Warnie entered one boarding school after another ("Chronology"). During their boarding-school years, both Lewis and Tolkien fell in love with language and mythology. Lewis enjoyed Greek and Roman mythology while Tolkien focused the Anglo-Saxon myths.

When World War I began, both men joined the British army. Tolkien signed up along with his three closest friends from school. Lewis signed up on his own but met up later with one of his best buddies, Paddy Moore. All of these men fought in the Battle of the Somme, but only Tolkien and Lewis survived. Still, Lewis was seriously injured, and Tolkien came down with "trench fever." They each returned to England where they eventually recovered. These war experiences made a lasting impression on them. Both men later wrote about young people going to war.

Back in England, the two young men found jobs at universities. Lewis went to Oxford and Tolkien went to the University of Leeds. When Tolkien later moved to Oxford, the two professors met each other and became friends. Lewis later wrote, "Friendship is born at that moment when one person says to another, 'What! You too? I thought I was the only one!'" (qtd. in "Quotes"). Shortly afterward, Tolkien and Lewis created a group called the "Inklings." The group talked about writing, philosophy, and theology. At their meetings, Tolkien read parts of his new novel *The Lord of the Rings,* and C.S.

English Language Learners

Before students read the sample essay, define the following words:

- pub (public house that serves alcoholic drinks)
- fantasy (fictional stories that could not happen, usually including magic)
- boarding school (school where students live and study)
- mythology (cultural stories and beliefs that often explain how or why things came to be in the world)

Expository

Lewis read parts of his series the Chronicles of Narnia. Both works have become classics of fantasy and have been made into major motion pictures.

Lewis and Tolkien both had a tough childhood. Their parents died when they were young, and they were sent away to boarding schools. Then, both men fought in the War to End All Wars and lost friends and almost died as well. Still, when Lewis and Tolkien finally met each other, they had discovered a real friendship. Lewis described Tolkien and the other Inklings as "those who speak one's own language" (qtd. in Carpenter 126). Their friendship helped Lewis and Tolkien create new worlds in their fantasy novels. Millions of other people have gotten to explore these worlds as well.

Student Self-Assessment

Expository Rubric Checklist

Title: _Men of Letters_

Writer: _Bryce Johnson_

5 **Ideas**
• Is the essay informative?
• Does it have a clear thesis?
• Are the details specific?

5 **Organization**
• Is the beginning interesting?
• Does the middle support the focus?
• Does the ending work well?

4 **Voice**
• Is the voice knowledgeable?
• Does it sound confident?
• Does the voice fit the audience?

5 **Word Choice**
• Are the verbs active?

4 **Sentence Fluency**
• Are the sentences varied?
• Do the sentences read smoothly?

4 **Conventions**
• Does the essay avoid most errors in punctuation, spelling, or grammar?
• Are sources correctly cited?

OVERALL COMMENTS:

I enjoyed writing my comparison because I like the two authors. Other students were interested because they had seen the movies.

I graded myself down for voice because I forgot to put in any anecdotes.

Many of my sentences start with the subject. I should try to vary them a little more.

I forgot to cite my sources in the third paragraph.

 Review your essay.
Rate your essay and write comments that explain why you gave yourself the scores you did.

Student Self-Assessment

To give students additional practice with evaluating an expository essay, use a reproducible Assessment Sheet (TE page 766), the Expository Rubric Checklist (TE page 780), and one or both of the **benchmark papers** listed in the Benchmark Papers box below. For your benefit, a completed checklist and comments sheet are provided for each benchmark paper.

Benchmark Papers

Pull the Plug and Play Corks (good)
○ TE pp. 792–795

Changing Students (poor)
○ TE pp. 796–799

Reflecting on Your Writing

Students are often reluctant or unable to identify either the strongest or the weakest parts of their writing.

Suggest that students consider comments you and peers have provided during various stages of the writing process, including your comments on students' final essays, to identify weak and strong points in their writing.

Have students refer to earlier reflections to see how they assessed their strengths. At the same time, they can evaluate how much progress they have made in areas where they identified weaknesses.

Reflecting on Your Writing

With your comparison essay finished, take a few moments to reflect on this writing experience. On your own paper, finish each sentence starter below. Reflecting helps you to learn more about writing and to apply what you've learned to future assignments.

My Comparison Essay

1. The strongest part of my essay is . . .

2. The part that still needs work is . . .

3. The prewriting activity that worked best for me was . . .

4. The main thing I learned about writing a comparison essay is . . .

5. In my next comparison essay, I would like to . . .

6. One question I still have about writing a comparison essay is . . .

185

Expository Writing
Explaining a Process

How does a florist arrange a bouquet? What's the best way to find hidden clues in a video game? What are the steps to building a bat house? How do you set up a blog? When you explain how to do something in an essay, you are doing expository writing.

In this chapter, you'll read a sample expository essay about making jiaozi—Chinese dumplings. Then you will write your own essay based on personal experience and expertise. Your how-to essay should tell the reader what materials are needed and what steps to take to finish the project. Choose a process you know well and care about in order to do your best writing.

Writing Guidelines

Subject: **Something you know how to do or how to make**
Form: **How-to essay**
Purpose: **To explain a process**
Audience: **Classmates**

"Good writing is clear thinking
 made visible."

—Bill Wheeler

Copy Masters

Time Line (TE p. 189)

Explaining a Process

Objectives

- understand the form and content of a how-to essay
- use effective strategies to explain a process
- plan, draft, revise, edit, and share a how-to essay

A **how-to essay** explains how a process works, or how to do or make something. It includes the steps in a process and any materials needed.

- Explain to students that the terms *how-to essay* and *process essay* are often used interchangeably.
- Students may worry that they will have to explain a complicated process. Assure them that the goal is to explain a process clearly and accurately, and that they can choose a relatively simple process.

How-To Essay

Before students read the model how-to essay, ask them to preview the formatting used in the essay. What elements stand out? In particular students should notice the following:

- subheadings
- numbered items
- bulleted items

Point out that as well as adding visual interest, the format

- helps the writer present information clearly and efficiently, and
- helps readers follow the explanation and find information more quickly.

186

How-To Essay

In the following expository essay, Chen Wei Wu explains how to prepare a traditional Chinese food.

Beginning
The title and opening part identify the topic.

Making Jiaozi

The Chinese dumpling, or jiaozi, is the most popular food in China. There is a common saying in China: "There is nothing more delicious than jiaozi." So you can see that Chinese people have great love for this food. To make your own jiaozi with a basic meat filling, follow these directions:

Making the Dumpling Skins

To make the dumpling skins, you will need three basic ingredients: a small package of white flour, very cold water, and salt. Combine the ingredients in this way:

Middle
The steps are carefully explained.

1. Stir a teaspoon of salt into two cups of very cold water.
2. Then add the water to the flour, a little at a time. Use only as much water as necessary to make workable dough.
3. Knead the dough very well before refrigerating it. (Kneading means to work and press the dough with your hands.)

When you are ready to use the dough, break off a piece about the size of a walnut. Form the piece of dough into a ball and, with a rolling pin, flatten it into a thin, three-inch circle. Continue this process until you have made enough dumpling skins.

Subheadings and lists (numbered and bulleted) help the reader follow the explanation.

Making the Meat Filling

A basic meat filling contains the following ingredients mixed together:

- Ground pork (one pound)
- Finely chopped cabbage (one cup)
- Finely chopped onion (a few tablespoons)
- Grated ginger
- Soy sauce (two tablespoons)
- Minced garlic (one or two cloves)
- Salt and pepper (to taste)

Struggling Learners

Emphasize that proper sequencing is crucial in how-to writing. Numbered steps, as well as transition words *(first, next, then*, and *finally)*, help the writer present information that is clear to the reader.

To reinforce the importance of correct sequencing, do the following:

- Have volunteers take turns telling how to get from your classroom to another place in the building (library, lunch room, office, and so on).
- As each volunteer gives directions, have listeners raise their hand whenever a direction seems out of sequence.
- Have the volunteer revise the sequence until listeners agree.

Expository

Special attention is given to design in the essay.

Completing the Dumplings

Form the dumplings in this way:

1. Place one tablespoon of filling in the middle of each skin. Then fold the skin over and seal the dumpling by pressing together both sides. Continue until you have made all of your dumplings.

2. Next, bring a large pot of water to a boil. Add enough dumplings to cover the bottom of the pot. Cover the pot.

3. When it returns to a boil, add a cup of cold water. Cover until the dumplings again come to a boil. Repeat this process one more time, and then the jiaozi are ready. Serve with rice vinegar or soy sauce.

Chinese people put more than 3,000 kinds of stuffing into their dumplings. The ones made in the United States usually are stuffed with a meat filling or with vegetables. By trying this recipe, you will get to enjoy one of the most popular tastes of China.

Ending Additional information brings the essay to an interesting close.

 Respond to the reading. Answer the following questions.

Ideas (1) Will readers be interested in this topic? Explain.

Organization (2) How are the middle paragraphs organized?

Voice & Word Choice (3) What words or phrases show the writer's attention to providing an accurate how-to essay? List three.

 Literature Connections: You can find instructional documents in many types of books and magazines—cookbooks, popular science magazines, computer magazines—but you will also encounter them in your everyday life. The next time you follow directions to use a new computer application, for example, you will have relied on a common form of "how-to" writing.

Call attention to the use of prepositions in the model essay. Point out that prepositions such as *into, to, before, with, by,* and *of* are important for explaining exactly what to do and when.

✻ For more about prepositions, see SE page 732.

 Respond to the reading.

Answers

Ideas 1. Readers who are familiar with this Chinese food would be interested in learning how to make it. Readers who have never heard of jiaozi will still be interested because most people like learning about new foods and how to make them.

Organization 2. The middle paragraphs (or sections) are organized logically, in the order they should be done.

Voice & Word Choice 3. Possible choices: *teaspoon of salt; two cups of very cold water; add water to flour a little at a time; Kneading means; piece the size of a walnut; thin, three-inch circle; specific amounts of ingredients for the filling; one tablespoon of filling; bring water to a boil; cover bottom of the pot; cup of cold water; again come to a boil.*

Literature Connections

Have students read the procedural document addressing how to scan, edit, and save an image for use on a Web page.

Challenge students to revise this selection to make it either more or less complex, and discuss how clear, accurate directions can make a complicated task easier to perform. For additional models of writing to describe a process, see the Reading-Writing Connections beginning on page TE-36.

Advanced Learners

To illustrate the idea in the Tip, invite pairs of students to present skits to the class that show how confusing unclear details can be.

- Encourage students to choose a familiar process with at least five steps, such as making a book cover.
- Give partners time to write an explanation of the process that contains unclear details (for example, *cut out paper and fold it*) and to gather necessary props.
- Have one partner read the explanation while the other acts out each step.

While entertaining for the class, this activity will help all students understand the importance of using transitions and precise language when describing a process.

Prewriting Selecting a Topic

Suggest that students use ideas in the sample Topics List as a springboard for their own topics lists. For example, they may not ride a mountain bike, but they may skateboard. They may not make an origami swan, but they may make a dream catcher.

Prewriting Focusing Your Topic

After students mark the two or three topics they like best, have students briefly explore each topic on paper to determine if they

- know enough about the topic to explain the process logically,
- know where to find details they are not sure about,
- can fit all the steps and ingredients or materials in three or four middle paragraphs.

Tell students to circle the topic that meets these requirements.

Technology Connections

Students can use the added features of the Net-text as they explore this stage of the writing process.

 Write Source Online **Net-text**

Focus on the Traits

Ideas
Have students identify interesting and informative details in the model how-to essay on SE pages 186–187. Ask students to explain how these details show that Chen enjoyed the topic and understood it well.

English Language Learners

Students may know a skill or recipe in their first language but lack the ability to express their ideas in English. Have students describe and/or draw the steps of the process for a partner. The partner can help number the steps and choose the correct English vocabulary.

Prewriting Selecting a Topic

The purpose of your essay is to explain how to do or how to make something. To find a topic for his essay, Chen made a list of things he knew how to do or make. He then put an asterisk next to three topics that he liked the best.

Topics List

> **Things I know how to do or make:**
>
> ride a mountain bike   play shortstop in softball*
>
> make jiaozi*   water-ski
>
> build a bat house   draw Pegasus*
>
> create a blog   make an origami swan

Focusing Your Topic

You should pick a how-to topic that is the "right size" for an essay. A topic that is too narrow won't provide enough information for an essay. One that is too broad may lack focus or run too long. Chen decided that playing shortstop was too broad and drawing Pegasus was too narrow. He selected making jiaozi for his topic because it seemed to be the right size for an essay.

 Select a topic and find a focus. Write the heading "Things I know how to do or make." List at least five ideas and put an asterisk (*) next to the two or three topics you like best. Then focus your topic so that it is the right size for your essay.

Focus on the Traits

Ideas A good how-to essay is more than just a list of directions. It should include details that will interest and inform the reader. In order to do this, choose a topic that you enjoy and understand well.

Struggling Learners

Give students practice identifying whether a topic is the right size for an essay. Present the following topics and ask students to tell whether each is too broad, too narrow, or just right for a how-to essay.

- planting a garden in the yard (too broad)
- planting a container garden (just right)
- formatting a process essay on a computer (just right)
- turning on a computer (too narrow)
- playing winter sports (too broad)
- sharpening ice skates (just right)
- sewing a shirt (just right)
- threading a needle (too narrow)

Gathering and Organizing Details

Ease your reader into the steps of your how-to essay with some background information. Chen used interesting details and a quote about the food to encourage the reader to read on. Other ideas are listed here:

- How you got interested in the topic (*I learned that there are more than 3,000 stuffings for jiaozi.*)
- How you learned to make or do it (*My mother taught me.*)
- Why you enjoy it (*Jiaozi is part of my culture.*)

Once you have your background information, you'll need a list of the materials necessary to complete the process.

Materials List

Dough	Filling	
White flour	Ground pork (one pound)	Grated ginger
Cold water	Finely chopped cabbage	Soy sauce (two tablespoons)
Salt	(one cup)	Minced garlic (one or two cloves)
	Finely chopped onion (a few	Salt and pepper (to taste)
	tablespoons)	

Next, you must organize the process logically, as in a time line.

Time Line

Make the dumpling skins —
— Stir salt into cold water
— Add salt water to flour
— Knead dough and refrigerate
— Roll the skins

Make the filling —
— Mix ground pork,
chopped cabbage and onion,
grated ginger, soy sauce, and
minced garlic

Complete the dumplings —
— Place filling on skin and seal
— Boil, adding cold water, repeat

Gather and organize details. Decide how to introduce your topic with background information. List the materials needed. Then write the steps for your how-to topic in proper order, using a time line.

Prewrite

Prewriting Gathering and Organizing Details

Allow time for students to confirm the steps and any materials or ingredients needed to complete the process. This may involve speaking to a family member or doing *minimal* research at the library or online. Students should have chosen topics that they know well, not ones they have to research. If they have to spend an extensive amount of time (more than an hour) to find the missing details they need, then they probably have not chosen an appropriate topic. Have them return to their topics list to choose a more suitable topic.

Point out that the items on the left side of the sample time line correspond to the subheadings in the model essay on SE pages 186–187. Suggest that students take a few moments to develop subheadings for their essay. (Students can revise and improve them later.) Then provide photocopies of the reproducible Time Line on TE page 816. Tell students to write their subheadings on the left side of the time line and to list steps and materials on the right side, in proper order.

Writing Creating Your First Draft

Before students start to write their drafts, have them review their time lines to make sure that they have included all the steps and materials needed for the successful completion of the processes.

- If a step is out of order, they should circle the step and draw an arrow to show where it belongs in the process.
- If a step or an ingredient is missing, they should write it in the margin and draw an arrow to show where to insert the information.

Taking time to review and edit their time line now can help students avoid extensive revising later.

Remind students that the main purpose of each middle paragraph of their how-to essays is to explain what steps to follow or what materials are needed to complete the process. Like all good expository writing, these paragraphs should be well-organized and include specific details.

 For more about constructing effective expository paragraphs, see SE page 566.

Technology Connections

Students can use the added features of the Net-text as they explore this stage of the writing process.

 Write Source Online **Net-text**

Writing Creating Your First Draft

The tips below describe how to write each part of the essay. Use these tips as a guide for writing your first draft.

Writing Your Beginning Paragraph

The **beginning** grabs the reader's attention, gives some background, and includes the thesis statement. Here are strategies for capturing your reader's interest.

- Give an important detail about the topic.
  Chinese dumplings, or jiaozi, are the most popular food in China.
- Tell what makes the topic fun.
  Chinese dumplings are as much fun to make as they are to eat.
- Open with an intriguing question.
  Do you know what food all Chinese people love?

Creating Your Middle Paragraphs

The **middle** paragraphs should tell what materials are needed and share the steps in the process.

- Develop a paragraph (or two) for each step or main point.
- Include details to fully explain each step.
- Use transition words and phrases to connect your ideas.

Finishing with a Strong Ending Paragraph

The **ending** must conclude the explanation in a satisfying way. Use one or more of the following strategies.

- Give the reader new information to think about.
  Chinese people put more than 3,000 kinds of stuffing into their dumplings.
- Summarize the process.
  In just a few simple steps, the dumplings are done, steaming hot, and ready to eat.
- Suggest that the reader try the process.
  By trying this recipe, you will get to enjoy one of the most popular tastes of China.

 Write your first draft. Use your prewriting work (pages 188–189) and the tips above as a guide for your writing.

Struggling Learners

Before they begin to write their drafts, students will benefit from viewing good models of how-to essays. Consult the school librarian to find articles that explain processes at appropriate reading levels. Together, find good examples of introductory paragraphs, clear and well-sequenced instructions, and motivating conclusions. Discuss words and phrases the author uses to engage the reader.

Advanced Learners

Remind students that if they have chosen topics that are unfamiliar to many readers, they need to define specialized or technical language. For example, if a student is writing about rock climbing, he or she should not assume that readers know what a *carabiner* is (a metal clasp used to attach rope and gear together), or what *rappelling* means (descending by sliding down a rope). Students should always keep their audience in mind when writing.

Revising Improving Your Writing

After you write your first draft, set it aside for a while. When you come back to your writing, use the checklist below as your revising guide.

Revising Checklist

Ideas

_____ **1.** Have I focused on an interesting process?

_____ **2.** Have I clearly explained the process in easy steps?

_____ **3.** Do I provide enough detail for each step?

Organization

_____ **4.** Does my essay have a strong beginning, an interesting middle, and a thoughtful ending?

_____ **5.** Have I put the how-to steps in a sequential order?

_____ **6.** Does each paragraph cover a key step or a main point?

_____ **7.** Have I used transitions to connect my ideas?

Voice

_____ **8.** Does my voice fit the topic and the audience?

_____ **9.** Does my voice show my interest in the topic?

Word Choice

_____ **10.** Have I used specific nouns, verbs, and modifiers?

_____ **11.** Have I explained any technical or unfamiliar terms?

Sentence Fluency

_____ **12.** When I read the essay out loud, do my sentences flow smoothly?

_____ **13.** Have I used a variety of sentence types?

Improve your first draft. Use the checklist as you review your first draft and make changes. (Consider asking a partner to review your writing, too.)

Expository

Revising Improving Your Writing

Students may discover that in an attempt to make their directions clear and easy to follow—which is important—they have neglected to write interesting sentences that flow smoothly and that vary in pattern and style. Instead, they may have used a preponderance of short, simple sentences that create a choppy and boring sound.

■ Suggest that students revisit the model essay on SE pages 186–187, paying special attention this time to how the writer creates interest with varied sentence patterns, while still keeping the ideas and directions clear.

■ Encourage students to review their own drafts, looking for short, choppy sentences that they can combine to add interest and variety to their essays.

✱ For information about combining short, choppy sentences, see SE page 555.

 Technology Connections

Have students use the Writing Network features of the Net-text to comment on each other's drafts.

 Write Source Online *Net-text*

Grammar Connection

Specific Nouns

■ **Proofreader's Guide** pages 701–703 (+)

■ *Write Source* page 534

■ *GrammarSnap* Nouns

■ *SkillsBook* page 70, 72, 73

■ **Sentence Variety**

■ **Proofreader's Guide** page 746–747

■ *Write Source* page 553 (+)

■ *GrammarSnap* Compound Sentences

■ *SkillsBook* pages 129, 162

Editing Checking for Conventions

Suggest that students use a red pen to edit their own drafts, and that partners use a different-colored pen to mark corrections. Then, writers can easily see both their own corrections and their partner's corrections when preparing their final drafts.

Publishing Sharing Your Writing

Students may enjoy compiling their how-to essays into class resource books. They can organize essays according to categories, such as recipes, games, sports, crafts, and construction projects. Students can display their books in the school library or make photocopies to distribute to family members and friends.

If time allows, consider scheduling several days for students to present their essays as demonstration speeches. This is a good opportunity for students to practice listening skills as well as speaking skills.

✳ For information about turning an essay into an oral presentation, see SE pages 393–403. For information about listening and speaking skills, see SE pages 463–466.

Technology Connections

Remind students that they can use the Writing Network features of the Portfolio to share their work with peers.

✳ *Write Source Online* **Portfolio**

✳ *Write Source Online* **Net-text**

Advanced Learners

Some students may wish to publish their writing by creating a video presentation. Using a cooking- or home improvement-type television show as a model, students can show how to do each step as they explain it.

192

Editing Checking for Conventions

When you have finished revising, it's time to edit your how-to essay for punctuation, capitalization, spelling, and grammar.

Editing Checklist

Conventions

PUNCTUATION

_____ 1. Have I used end punctuation correctly?

_____ 2. Have I used commas correctly in compound and complex sentences?

CAPITALIZATION

_____ 3. Did I capitalize all proper nouns and proper adjectives?

_____ 4. Did I capitalize the first word in each sentence?

SPELLING

_____ 5. Have I caught any errors my spell-checker may have missed?

_____ 6. Have I double-checked the spelling of any special terms?

GRAMMAR

_____ 7. Have I used the correct forms of verbs *(I did, not I done)*?

_____ 8. Do my verbs and subjects agree in number?

_____ 9. Have I used the right word *(to, too, two)*?

Edit your how-to essay. Use the checklist above to edit your work. Ask a partner to check your work, too. Then write a correct final copy and proofread it.

Publishing Sharing Your Essay

After working so hard on your essay, be sure to share it with friends or family. You can also present your essay as a demonstration speech, a poster, or a Web page.

Publish your essay. Give your writing to classmates or family members to read. Also consider the speech, poster, or Web-page ideas.

Grammar Connection

Subject-Verb Agreement

- *Proofreader's Guide* pages 738–739, 740–741, 752–753, 754–755
- *GrammarSnap* Subject-Verb Agreement
- *SkillsBook* pages 128, 130, 149, 151

Sentence Problems

- *Write Source* pages 557–558 (+)
- *SkillsBook* pages 163, 165

Commas

- *Proofreader's Guide* pages 614–615
- *SkillsBook* page 19

Writing for Assessment
Responding to Expository Prompts

Explanations can be tricky. Giving directions or sharing information requires that you thoroughly understand the topic and present your ideas in a clear and concise way. Beyond that, the reader must feel drawn to your explanation because it is interesting. The best explanations begin and end with good information, so the key is to work with solid ideas right from the start.

On a test, you may be asked to write explanations in response to expository prompts. You can create the best responses by following the steps in the writing process. This chapter will show you how to adapt the writing process to response writing, when you have limited time to complete your work.

Writing Guidelines

Subject: Expository prompt
Form: Response essay
Purpose: To demonstrate competence
Audience: Instructor

"Never underestimate your reader's intelligence or overestimate his or her information."
—Anonymous

Copy Masters

Time Line (TE p. 195)

T-Chart (TE p. 195)

Venn Diagram (TE p. 195)

Quick List (TE p. 195)

Responding to Expository Prompts

Objectives
- apply what has been learned about expository writing
- practice writing for assessment

If your students must take school, district, or state assessments this year, focus on the writing form on which they will be tested.

Call attention to the quotation at the bottom of the page. Discuss how both assumptions could result in an ineffective explanation.
- Underestimating the reader's intelligence leads a writer to include too many unnecessary and minute details that muddle the explanation and confuse the reader.
- Overestimating the amount and quality of the reader's information leads a writer to omit important details that will make the explanation clear and useful.

Both problems emphasize the importance of understanding the audience.

Prewriting Analyzing an Expository Prompt

Make sure that students understand that the ideas given in parentheses for each of the STRAP questions are provided as examples of possible responses to that question. Each response, of course, depends on the specific prompt.

Try It!
Answers

Some answers may vary where specific information is not given in the prompt.

1. **Subject:** adjusting to ninth grade **Type:** article **Role:** experienced classmate **Audience:** new ninth graders **Purpose:** compare and contrast

2. **Subject:** my hero or heroine **Type:** article **Role:** student **Audience:** students and school staff **Purpose:** explain

3. **Subject:** friends/friendship **Type:** essay **Role:** friend **Audience:** teacher, other students **Purpose:** define the word *friend*

Prewriting Analyzing an Expository Prompt

Most writing tests ask you to respond to a prompt. A prompt is a set of directions that tells you what to write. It's crucial for you to analyze the prompt carefully so that you write a response that fits the requirements of the test. When you analyze a prompt, answer the following **STRAP questions:**

> **Subject:** What topic (school schedule, homework policy, healthy living, friendships) should I write about?
>
> **Type:** What form (essay, letter, announcement, report, article) of writing should I create?
>
> **Role:** What position (student, community member, son or daughter, friend) should I assume as writer?
>
> **Audience:** Who (classmates, teacher, principal, parents, city council) is the intended reader?
>
> **Purpose:** What is the goal (inform, explain, evaluate) of my writing?

The following key words are often found in **expository** prompts: *inform, explain, analyze, compare and contrast, outline,* and *define.*

Try It!

Analyze these prompts by using the STRAP questions.

1. The principal has asked for student essays for next year's "Freshman Survival Guide." Write an article that compares and contrasts eighth grade with ninth grade. Focus on providing information to help new freshmen adjust to ninth grade.

2. Your school newspaper is printing a series of articles about heroes and heroines. Write about someone who is a hero or heroine to you. That person may be someone you know or someone you have read about. Explain why you believe this person is heroic.

3. "That's what friends are for." Most people know the word "friend," but everyone has a different idea of what makes a friend. Define the word "friend" and include clear examples.

Tip

Some prompts do not contain key words for every STRAP question. You will have to use your best judgment to answer these questions.

Struggling Learners

Give students practice answering STRAP questions for prompts that do not contain key words that signal expository writing. For example:

- What does *freedom* mean to you? Do you think freedom can have limits? Provide examples that support your opinion. (**Subject:** the meaning of *freedom* **Type:** essay **Role:** a citizen in a free country **Audience:** teacher, other students **Purpose:** define *freedom*)

- Education comes from many sources, not just books or formal education. What person or experience has taught you a valuable lesson about life? Make sure to provide details about that lesson. (**Subject:** an important lesson in life **Type:** essay **Role:** student **Audience:** teacher, other students **Purpose:** describe and explain)

Guide students to see that these prompts both ask the student to write an expository essay.

Planning Your Response

Once you have answered the STRAP questions, you should quickly plan your response. The following graphic organizers can help.

Graphic Organizers

Quick List (Any Essay)
1. First Point
   —Detail 1
   —Detail 2
2. Second Point
   —Detail 1
   —Detail 2
3. Third Point
   —Detail 1
   —Detail 2

Time Line (How-To/Process)
First
Next
Then
After
Last

T-Chart (Two-Part Essay)
Topic:
Part A | Part B

Venn Diagram (Compare-Contrast)
Topic A   Topic B
Similarities
Differences

Cluster (Definition/Classification)
Topic

Reread the expository prompts on page 194. Choose one prompt and use one of the graphic organizers above to quickly organize a response to the prompt.

Prewrite

Tip

Always allow time for prewriting and for revising and editing. For example, with 45 minutes to respond to a prompt, use 5 to 10 minutes to analyze the prompt and plan your response, 30 to 35 minutes for your writing, and the last 5 minutes for revising and editing.

Expository

English Language Learners

Before students begin to use one of the graphic organizers, ask them individually to tell you what the prompt is asking them to do. Clear up any misinterpretations of the objective, and remind students to use the STRAP questions to help them respond to the prompt.

Prewriting Planning Your Response

Students should be familiar with all of the graphic organizers shown and understand how and when to use each one. However, to be sure, ask students which organizer they would use to prepare a response for *each* of the prompts on SE page 194 and to explain why it is the best choice for them for that particular prompt. (Possible responses: 1. T-chart or Venn diagram; 2. cluster diagram or quick list; 3. cluster or quick list)

Test Prep!

For most on-demand writing tests, the ability to quickly plan a response is crucial. Graphic organizers are key. By becoming familiar with many different graphic organizers during classroom writing, students can be better equipped to use graphic organizers in a testing situation. Some writing assessments actually require students to hand in any graphic organizers they used in planning. Other tests go so far as to have students analyze graphic organizers and answer multiple-choice questions about them. Familiarity with these organizers can help students succeed.

Writing Responding to a Prompt

Work as a class to answer the STRAP questions for the sample expository prompt. If necessary, have students turn back to SE page 194 to recall what each letter stands for in the acronym. Point out that even though their audience for a test response is usually a teacher, they can suggest other possible audiences as well.

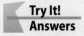

Try It!
Answers

Subject: community improvement **Type:** essay **Role:** community member **Audience:** teacher, community members **Purpose:** explain, persuade

Before students practice responding to an expository prompt (SE page 197), review the main traits of expository writing. Ask students to look for these traits as they read the sample response:

- an interesting beginning that engages the reader
- a clearly-stated thesis statement
- middle paragraphs that support the thesis and help explain the topic
- specific, interesting details that create a knowledgeable voice
- a strong ending that leaves readers with a final thought about the topic

---

Writing Responding to a Prompt

After answering the STRAP questions and using a graphic organizer to plan your response, it's time to begin writing. Make sure to use a tone and level of language appropriate to your topic and to your audience. Review the sample prompt and response that follow.

Sample Expository Prompt

> *What could be done to make your community better? Could something be done to make it safer? Could there be more opportunities for young people? In an essay, explain one idea that you have to improve your community.*

Try It!

Answer the STRAP questions for this prompt. Remember that answering these questions will help you understand the prompt and form your response. (See page **194**.)

Response

Beginning
The beginning paragraph states the thesis (underlined).

Make Way for Walking and Biking

To drive from one end of New London to the other takes 15 minutes. On the north end of town, there is a small shopping mall, plus a new grocery store. The downtown, in the middle of New London, contains a few shops, restaurants, and the Crown Movie Theater. A medical clinic, another grocery store, and a hardware store anchor the south end of town. What makes New London inconvenient is getting from one shopping area to another—when not driving a car. <u>New London would be a better community if it were more accessible for pedestrians and cyclists.</u>

Walking is difficult because there are very few continuous sidewalks. Some sidewalks end halfway down

Responding to Expository Prompts **197**

a block. In order to continue, pedestrians have to walk across front lawns until they come across more sidewalk. If it's wet or muddy, they have to walk in the street. As silly as it sounds, there are parts of town with only one or two small sections of sidewalk on some blocks. If all homeowners were required to have sidewalks, New London would be a safer place to walk.

Middle
Each middle paragraph covers one main point.

Riding a bike is not any safer than walking. The streets in New London are very narrow, and many people park their cars on the street. Riding a bike through this obstacle course can be dangerous. Even experienced cyclists have been known to clip a parked car and crash. It would be impractical to include a bike lane because the streets are so narrow. But many cities have made old railroad paths into bike trails. This could work in New London because of the unused railroad tracks running through town.

Ending
The ending explains the importance of the topic.

A lot has been said about the value of cutting back on driving to save energy. That would certainly be possible if people didn't have to drive everywhere in New London. Walking or biking would also give some New Londoners more opportunity to get some exercise. Continuous sidewalks and a bike path would give them different ways to get around town and clearly make the community a better place to live.

Expository

Practice responding to an expository prompt. Review the prompt you chose from page **194**, reminding yourself of the STRAP questions and the graphic organizer you have created. Then write a response to the prompt in the amount of time your teacher gives you.

Students may lack confidence as they begin their response to an expository prompt. Encourage students to draw on the experience they gained writing their comparison essay. To help students realize that they know how to write an expository essay, and to ease their anxiety, point out the similarities between the comparison essay they wrote and the sample prompt response on SE pages 196–197.

- When students wrote their comparison essay, their goal was to compare two people. They identified the two people and stated the most important similarity between them in the thesis statement. They reinforced the similarity point-by-point in the middle paragraphs. They used specific details and examples to explain each point of comparison.

- In the sample response, the writer's goal is to explain an idea that will improve his or her community. In the thesis statement, the writer identifies an idea for improvement and explains its importance. The writer reinforces the need for this improvement point-by-point in the middle paragraphs. The writer uses specific details and examples to explain each point.

Revising **Improving Your Response**

Provide time for students to practice revising with the STRAP questions so that they can see where they need to focus when planning a prompt response.

Editing **Checking Your Response**

Students are likely to make careless mistakes on a timed test when they feel pressured, especially with commonly misused words such as *there, they're,* and *their.* Tell students to pay particular attention when they're editing to find and correct these kinds of mistakes.

✱ Refer students to "Using the Right Word," SE pages 678–696.

Revising **Improving Your Response**

Most writing tests allow you to make corrections to improve your work, though you should find out ahead of time how many changes are allowed. Always make changes and corrections as neatly as possible. If the test allows revising and editing, use the STRAP questions to guide your changes.

> **Subject:** Does my response focus on the topic in the prompt? Do the main points in my response support the thesis?
>
> **Type:** Have I followed the correct form (essay, letter, article)?
>
> **Role:** Have I assumed the position indicated in the prompt?
>
> **Audience:** Have I used the right level of language for my audience?
>
> **Purpose:** Does my writing accomplish the goal set forth in the prompt?

Improve your work. Reread your response, asking yourself the STRAP questions above. Make neat changes in the time your teacher allows.

Editing **Checking Your Response**

Check your response for punctuation, capitalization, spelling, and grammar. You don't want any careless errors that confuse the reader.

Conventions

_____ **1.** Have I used end punctuation for every sentence?
_____ **2.** Have I capitalized all proper nouns and first words of sentences?
_____ **3.** Have I checked my spelling?
_____ **4.** Have I made sure my subjects and verbs agree?
_____ **5.** Have I used the right word (*there, they're, their*)?

Check your conventions. Review your response for punctuation, capitalization, spelling, and grammar. Make neat corrections in the time your teacher allows.

> "Grammar is an ever-evolving set of rules for using words in ways that we can all agree on."
>
> —Patricia T. O'Conner

Expository Writing on Tests

Use the following tips as a guide whenever you respond to an expository writing prompt.

Before you write . . .

- **Understand the prompt.**
  Use the STRAP questions listed on page 194.
  Remember that an expository prompt asks you to *explain.*
- **Plan your time wisely.**
  Spend several minutes making notes and planning before starting to write. Use the last few minutes to read over what you have written.

As you write . . .

- **Decide on a focus or thesis for your essay.**
  Keep your main idea or purpose in mind as you write.
- **Be selective.**
  Use examples and explanations that directly support your focus.
- **End in a meaningful way.**
  Remind the reader about the importance of the topic.

After you've written a first draft . . .

- **Check for completeness.**
  Use the STRAP questions on page 198 to revise your work.
- **Check for correctness.**
  Check for errors in punctuation, capitalization, spelling, and grammar.

 Plan and write a response. Analyze one of the prompts below using the STRAP questions. Then plan and write a response. Complete your work within the time your teacher gives you.

Expository Prompts

- Explain why it is good for a person to play a competitive sport, participate in musical performances, or belong to a school organization.
- Explain how to build something or how to do something. Give your reader enough information to actually do what you are explaining.

Expository

Expository Writing on Tests

Point out that students must approach writing-on-demand assignments differently from open-ended writing assignments and that timed writing creates pressures for everyone.

Expository Prompts

Allow students the same amount of time to write their response essay as they will be allotted for school, district, or state assessments. Break down each part of the process into clear chunks of time. For example, you might give students

- 15 minutes for note taking and planning,
- 20 minutes for writing, and
- 10 minutes for editing and proofreading.

Tell students when time is up for each section. Start the assignment at the top of the hour or at the half-hour to make it easier for students to keep track of the time.

Advanced Learners

After students have responded to a prompt, have them meet in a small group with others who responded to the same prompt. Using the STRAP questions (SE page 194), students should share their responses and analyze the strengths and weaknesses of each one.

Persuasive Writing Overview

Common Core Standards Focus

Writing 1: Write arguments to support claims in an analysis of substantive topics or texts, using valid reasoning and relevant and sufficient evidence.

Writing 7: Conduct short as well as more sustained research projects to answer a question (including a self-generated question) or solve a problem; narrow or broaden the inquiry when appropriate; synthesize multiple sources on the subject, demonstrating understanding of the subject under investigation.

Language 1b: Use various types of phrases (noun, adjectival, adverbial, participial, prepositional, absolute) and clauses (independent, dependent, noun, relative, adverbial) to convey specific meanings and add variety and interest to writing or presentations.

Writing Forms

- persuasive paragraph
- position essay
- pet-peeve essay
- writing for assessment

Focus on the Traits

- **Ideas** Including solid reasons that defend a position, and avoiding errors in logic
- **Organization** Creating a beginning that states a position, a middle that provides support and answers an objection, and an ending that restates the position
- **Voice** Connecting with the reader by sounding knowledgeable
- **Word Choice** Choosing fair and precise words, and avoiding inflammatory words
- **Sentence Fluency** Writing clear, complete sentences with varied beginnings
- **Conventions** Checking for errors in punctuation, capitalization, spelling, and grammar

WAC: Social Studies—Editorial Cartoons
Applied Science—Safety Posters

 Literature Connections

- **"I Have a Dream"** by Martin Luther King, Jr.
- **"Primal Screen"** by Ellen Goodman

 Technology Connections

 Write Source Online
www.hmheducation.com/writesource

- **Net-text**
- **Bookshelf**
- **GrammarSnap**
- **Portfolio**
- **Essay Scoring**
- **Writing Network features**
- **File Cabinet**

 Interactive Whiteboard Lessons

Suggested Persuasive Writing Unit (Five Weeks)

Day	Writing and Skills Instruction	Student Edition		SkillsBook	Daily Language Workouts	Write Source Online
		Main Pages	Resource Units*			
WEEK 1 1–5	**Persuasive Warm-Up Paragraph**	201–203			32–33	Interactive Whiteboard Lessons
	Skills Activities:					
	• Direct Quotations		616 (+), 632 (+)			
	• Shifts in Verb Tense			183		GrammarSnap
opt.	*Making Oral Presentations*	393–403				
WEEK 2 6	**Persuasive Writing: Position Essay** (Model) Ⓥ Literature Connections "I Have a Dream"	204–206			34–35	

* These units are also located in the back of the Teacher's Edition. Resource Units include "Basic Grammar and Writing," "A Writer's Resource," and "Proofreader's Guide."
(+) This activity is located in a different section of the Write Source Student Edition. If students have already completed this activity, you may wish to review it at this time.

Day	Writing and Skills Instruction	Student Edition		SkillsBook	Daily Language Workouts	Write Source Online
		Main Pages	Resource Units*			
WEEK 2 (CONT.)						
7–8	(Prewriting)	207–210			34–35	*Net-text*
9–10	(Writing)	211–216				*Net-text*
WEEK 3						
11–13	(Revising)	217–228			36–37	*Net-text*
	Skills Activities:					
	• Complete Sentences		558 (+) (fragments), 738 (+), 740 (+)	168		
	• Sentence Types		746 (+)	143		*GrammarSnap*
	• Adverbs		542, 730–731	112, 113, 114, 115		*GrammarSnap*
	• Adjectives		540 (+), 541 (+), 608 (+), 728–729	109, 110, 111		*GrammarSnap*
14–15	(Editing, Publishing)	229–233				*Net-text, Portfolio*
	Skills Activities:					
	• Spelling		664–669	54		
	• Hyphens and Dashes		624–625, 626–627, 640–641	25–28		
	• Tenses (irregular verbs)		720–721	101–104		*GrammarSnap*
	• Commas with Introductory Phrases and Clauses		553 (+), 610 (+)	12, 129		*GrammarSnap*
	• Pronoun-Antecedent Agreement		756 (+)	155		*GrammarSnap*
WEEK 4						
16–17	(Assessing, Reflecting)	234–238			38–39	
opt.	*Making Oral Presentations*	393–401				
18–20	**Responding to Persuasive Prompts**	247–253				
SECOND FORM WEEK 1						
1–5	**Pet-Peeve Essay** (Model) Literature Connections "Primal Screen"	239–241			40–41	
	(Prewriting, Writing)	242–244				*Net-text*
	(Revising) order of importance	245				
	Skills Activities: • Sentence Combining		555, 556, 742 (+), 744 (+), 748 (+)	159–160		*GrammarSnap*
	• Adjectives		540–541, 728 (+)	108		*GrammarSnap*
	(Editing, Publishing)	246				*Net-text, Portfolio*
	Skills Activities: • Using the Right Word		686–687, 688–689	60		
	• Nonstandard Language		559 (+)	175		
	• Capitalization (titles)		648 (+), 652–653	44		*GrammarSnap*

* These units are also located in the back of the *Teacher's Edition*. Resource Units include "Basic Grammar and Writing," "A Writer's Resource," and "Proofreader's Guide."
(+) This activity is located in a different section of the *Write Source Student Edition*. If students have already completed this activity, you may wish to review it at this time.

Persuasive Writing

This overview for persuasive writing includes some specific teaching suggestions for the unit. The description of each chapter will help you decide which parts of the unit to teach.

Writing Focus

Position Essay (pages 201–238)

In a position essay, a writer takes an assertive and authoritative stand on a significant issue. A position essay is a form of argumentative writing offering reasons for the writer's position, entertaining alternative points of view, and, in closing, reaffirming the initial position. When writing a position paragraph or essay, students' primary purpose is to convince the reader to think the way that they do about a timely issue. To accomplish this goal, students need to establish a well-reasoned, thoughtful argument that they feel strongly about.

Pet-Peeve Essay (pages 239–246)

When writing about pet peeves, students react humorously or sensibly to a common, everyday annoyance. When developing these reactions, students should go beyond a simple statement of what bothers them and analyze their pet peeve—describing the cause of the annoyance, identifying possible remedies, and so on. Essentially, they should do some basic cause-and-effect reasoning. Although such an essay may be very convincing, the main point is that the writer can express his or her annoyance about something without using insulting or degrading language. For a selecting activity, have students complete "Don't you hate it when . . . " statements. Students may work with partners. Each pair should generate as many ideas as possible.

Responding to Persuasive Prompts (pages 247–253)

Taking assessment tests, timed or not, that call for a response to a persuasive prompt can be intimidating for students. However, if they use the guidelines included in this chapter, they will be able to concentrate on what they are writing. A sample prompt and response are included.

Grammar Focus

For support with this unit's grammar topics, consult the resource units (Basic Grammar and Writing, A Writer's Resource, and Proofreader's Guide).

Academic Vocabulary

Read aloud the academic terms, as well as the descriptions and questions. Model for students how to read one question and answer it. Have partners monitor their understanding and seek clarification of the terms by working through the meanings and questions together.

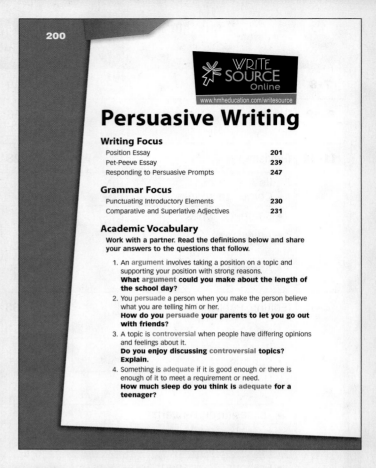

Minilessons

Seeing It My Way — Position Essay

- **THINK** about concerns you have for your school or community. **CHOOSE** three controversial issues that interest you, and **WRITE** a topic sentence for and a topic sentence against each one.

Choosing a Pet-Peeve — Pet-Peeve Essay

- **CHECK** in a local or a large city newspaper for a pet-peeve essay. You many find one on the opinion page or in a particular writer's column. **LIST** those points that convince you the article is a pet peeve rather than a position essay. How would you have written about the issue? **BRING** the article and your written answers to class for discussion.

Tug-of-War — Responding to Persuasive Prompts

- **CREATE** a T-chart of pro/con points about the merits or lack thereof of having an after-school job.

Persuasive Writing
Writing a Position Essay

Don't just sit there; take a stand! That's the position former British Prime Minister Margaret Thatcher took on the topic of debate. She said, "I love argument; I love debate. I don't expect anyone just to sit there and agree with me; that's not their job."

Whether you are a famous politician or a student, you are sure to encounter topics that you feel very strongly about—topics worth debating. Maybe the school board wants to cut the sports budget at your school, or perhaps your city plans to create a landfill near your home. Issues like these are bound to cause differences of opinion in your community and even among your family and friends! What will you do? Will you sit there, or will you take a stand?

Persuasive writing helps you address a difference of opinion. By stating an opinion and defending it, you can convince others to agree with you. In this chapter, you will write a position essay about a local controversy in your community.

Writing Guidelines

    Subject: **A local controversy in your community**
       Form: **Position essay**
  Purpose: **To defend a position**
Audience: **Classmates and community members**

"Understanding is a two-way street."
—Eleanor Roosevelt

Writing a Position Essay

Objectives

- take a position on a controversial issue
- use specific reasons to defend the position
- write a beginning that states a position, a middle that provides support and answers an objection, and an ending that restates the position effectively
- assess and reflect on a persuasive essay

A **position essay** establishes a writer's stance on a controversial issue and includes specific reasons to defend that stance.

Help students recognize all sides of issues by providing time for them to examine the pros and cons, and to express their opinions on those that directly affect them, their school, and their community.

Technology Connections

Use this unit's Interactive Whiteboard Lesson to introduce Persuasive writing.

Interactive Whiteboard Lessons

Copy Masters

Assessment Sheet (TE p. 237)
Persuasive Rubric
  Checklist (TE p. 237)

Benchmark Papers

Athlete of the Century (good)
⬤ TE pp. 800–803

ATVs vs. Snowmobiles (poor)
⬤ TE pp. 804–807

Persuasive Writing Warm-Up: Using Support

Discuss the kinds of details that students generally find most convincing in any argument.

■ Have students read the sample list of details for a persuasive paragraph.

■ Ask students which details have the greatest impact on them and why.

■ Point out to students that **achieving objectivity** *(see below)* should always be the goal when writing persuasively.

Persuasive Writing Warm-Up: Using Support

When you write a persuasive paragraph or essay, it's important to include plenty of effective supporting details. You can include, among other things, facts, statistics, quotations from experts, and personal experiences. (See pages **569–570** for additional types of details.)

The notebook page below shows supporting details that one student collected to support her opinion about soft-drink machines in schools.

Details for Persuasive Paragraph

Ban "Liquid Candy" in School

personal experience	Some of my friends drink three or four sodas per day in school.
statistics	According to the USDA, teens 25 years ago drank almost twice as much milk as soda pop. Today they drink twice as much soda pop as milk.
facts	The USDA recommends only 40 grams of refined sugar for the entire day.
quotation	"The explosion of candy and soda machines in public schools is a relatively new phenomenon closely paralleling the rise in childhood obesity." —WebMD

 Try It!

On your own paper, express an opinion about an important topic in your school. Then find at least three different types of details to support your opinion. Use the information above as a guide.

Grammar Connection

Direct Quotations

■ **Proofreader's Guide** pages 616 (+), 632 (+)

Teaching Tip: Achieving Objectivity

Students may not understand the difference between objectivity and subjectivity or how to achieve objectivity in persuasive writing. To help students understand the concept of objectivity, explain the following:

● Objectivity in persuasive writing is the ability to present information without personal bias.

● To achieve objectivity in persuasive writing, students should present reliable and accurate facts, statistics, and examples in support of their positions.

Writing a Persuasive Paragraph

A persuasive paragraph expresses an opinion about a specific topic and contains effective evidence and details to support the opinion. A persuasive paragraph has three main parts:

- The **topic sentence** states the opinion.
- The **body sentences** support the opinion.
- The **closing sentence** revisits the opinion.

Persuasive Paragraph

In the following persuasive paragraph, the student writer expresses her opinion about soda vending machines in her school. She uses all four types of details that she collected on page **202**.

The **topic sentence** states an opinion (underlined).

The **body sentences** support the opinion.

The **closing sentence** reflects on the opinion.

Ban "Liquid Candy" in Our School

The soda machines should be removed from Brooktown Central High School because soft drinks are partly to blame for growing health problems. The average can of soda contains about 40 grams (10 teaspoons) of sugar, and many students at BCHS drink several cans every day. This might not seem like a big problem until an individual considers that the United States Department of Agriculture (USDA) recommends an individual consume a maximum of 40 grams of refined sugar for the entire day! The USDA's figures also show that 25 years ago teens drank nearly twice as much milk as soda pop; today they drink twice as much pop as milk. Doctors are seeing the effects of this trend. An article on WebMD reports, "The explosion of candy and soda machines in public schools is a relatively new phenomenon closely paralleling the rise in childhood obesity." Drinking too much soda costs more than money; it can also cost a student his or her health. Schools should not encourage students to buy something that's not good for them.

Write a persuasive paragraph. Review the three parts of a paragraph (top of page) and what they do. Then present your opinion and details from page **202** in a persuasive paragraph about a school-related topic.

Struggling Learners

Review the difference between *facts* and *opinions*. Facts are statements that can be proved, and opinions are statements that describe what someone feels or believes. Emphasize that opinions should be supported with facts. Ask which of these two sentences is more effective and why:

- The menu in the school cafeteria needs to be changed because the meals are gross.

- The menu in the school cafeteria needs to be changed because the meals are repeated too often.

(The second one backs up the writer's opinion with a fact that can be proved, rather than with another opinion.)

* Refer students to SE page 569 for examples of details that can be used to support an opinion.

Writing a Persuasive Paragraph

Review the three main parts of a paragraph and their purposes in a persuasive paragraph.

* For more about Writing Effective Paragraphs, see SE pages 561–579.

Focus particular attention on the topic sentence in the sample paragraph and discuss why it is effective. Students should notice that it has a dual purpose.

- It states the opinion. (Soda machines should be removed.)
- It provides a strong reason that makes the opinion valid. (Soft drinks are partly to blame for growing health problems.)

Explain that if the topic sentence does not also provide a reason for the opinion, readers could be inclined to dismiss it. Here, readers are probably more inclined to ask, "What kind of health problems?" and then read on to find out. Tell students to write topic sentences that state their opinions and provide reasons for the opinions.

Grammar Connection

Shifts in Verb Tense

- *SkillsBook* pages 92–93
- *GrammarSnap* Past Perfect and Past Continuous Verb Tenses

Understanding Your Goal

Three traits relate to the development of content and form. They provide a focus during prewriting, drafting, and revising.

- Ideas
- Organization
- Voice

The other three traits relate more to form. They should be carefully addressed during the revising and editing processes.

- Word Choice
- Sentence Fluency
- Conventions

✳ The six-point rubric on SE pages 234–235 is based on these traits. Reproducible six-, five-, and four-point rubrics for persuasive writing are available on TE pages 769, 773, and 777.

Make sure students understand the distinction between defending a position with valid and reasonable details and examples, and being defensive, which is usually an emotional response based on incomplete information.

 Literature Connections

Watch a TV commercial with students. Explain how the ad tries to persuade the audience. Then show several other commercials and have students analyze them. Can the students identify the main focus of the ad? The facts and statistics used? The ads' voices?

For additional models of how to write a position essay, see the Reading-Writing Connections beginning on page TE-36.

204

Understanding Your Goal

Your goal in this chapter is to write a well-organized persuasive essay that defends a position. The traits listed in the chart below will help you plan and write your essay. The rubric for persuasive writing on pages 234–235 will also guide you.

Traits of Persuasive Writing

- **Ideas**
  Use specific reasons to defend a clear position on a controversial issue in your community.

- **Organization**
  Create a beginning that states your position, a middle that provides support and answers an objection, and an ending that restates your position.

- **Voice**
  Use a persuasive voice that is appropriate for your topic and audience.

- **Word Choice**
  Choose fair and precise words to state and defend your position.

- **Sentence Fluency**
  Write clear, complete sentences with varied beginnings.

- **Conventions**
  Check your writing for errors in punctuation, capitalization, spelling, and grammar.

 Literature Connections: You will encounter persuasion in all types of media—from TV commercials advertising the latest clothing fad to works of literature with lasting appeal. For example, Dr. Martin Luther King Jr.'s famous "I Have a Dream Speech," which persuaded people to support civil rights legislation in the 1960s, continues to inspire people today.

English Language Learners

When you introduce the rubric on SE pages 234–235, also point out the single-trait rubric strips that run across the revising pages (SE pages 218–227).

- Students may have an easier time using the rubric strips because they are written in the first person.
- Have students use the rubric strips to set personal goals for their writing.
- Encourage students to refer to the rubric strips to guide their writing.

Position Essay

A position essay clearly states where you stand on an issue. By stating and defending your position, you may be able to convince others to agree with you. In this sample essay, the student writer defends his position on keeping open a local home for mentally challenged adults.

Beginning
The beginning introduces the topic and states the position (underlined).

Middle
The first middle paragraph supports the writer's position with statistics and a personal experience.

The second middle paragraph provides interesting facts.

Persuasive

Save Hillhouse

Hillhouse is the big, old house on the hilltop near Beecher and Main Streets. It is a home for mentally challenged adults. Yesterday the Journal Express printed an article about closing Hillhouse. It said that Hillhouse needs more than $100,000 worth of repairs, and there isn't enough money available to get them done. The city wants to close Hillhouse and tear the building down. Is closing it the best way to solve the problem? No. <u>The best solution is to pull together as a community and keep Hillhouse open.</u>

First, keeping Hillhouse open is very important to the people who live and work there. If Hillhouse shuts down, twenty-six residents will need to find new homes, and seven staff members will lose their jobs. Half of the adults at Hillhouse have lived there for five years or more. For some, it's the only place they have lived since leaving their parents' homes. One resident is named John. He is 34 and has been at Hillhouse since he was 18. John has no family, and he thinks of himself as the official caretaker. He is always the first one to welcome a new resident and to make sure that he or she feels like a part of the Hillhouse family. John says that he would make the repairs by himself, if he knew how. Moving from Hillhouse would mean that people like John would have to adjust not only to a new home but to new friends, new caretakers, a new neighborhood, and maybe even a new city!

A second reason to keep Hillhouse open is the house itself. Hillhouse was built in 1870, just five years after the Civil War ended. It has had many well-known local owners, and some people in the community want it declared a historical landmark. If the building was made a landmark, then the city could not close it down. As a landmark, it might even be eligible to get some government money to fix it up. The local historical society is willing to work with

---

Position Essay

Work through this model essay with the class, pointing out the elements that make it a good persuasive essay.

Ideas

- The focus statement states the position that the community should work together to keep Hillhouse open.
- The writer supports this position with details that strengthen the argument.
- The writer counters an objection to the position.

Organization

- The middle paragraphs build the argument with strong reasons.
- The reasons are presented in order of importance.
- The ending restates the position and recaps possible solutions.

Voice & Word Choice

- The use of specific facts creates a knowledgeable voice.
- The writer deals with an opposing point of view respectfully and reasonably.

English Language Learners

Focus on the language in the introduction that defines a position essay. Make sure students understand that

- *where you stand on an issue* means "stating your opinion" and
- *defending your position* means "giving good reasons for your opinion."

Advanced Learners

Analyzing published opinion pieces can help students see the practical importance of persuasive writing and can provide style and organizational ideas for students' own writing. Have students look in local newspapers to locate op-ed or editorial pieces about topics that interest them. Ask students to bring in examples to share in small groups.

Call attention to the words *twentieth century* at the top of the page. Remind students that numbers such as *twentieth* are always written as words, not numerals. Then have students find examples of other numbers written as numerals and numbers written as words elsewhere in this essay.

✱ For more about writing numbers, see SE page 658.

 Respond to the reading.

Answers

Ideas 1. Hillhouse is important to the people who live and work there. Hillhouse could be declared a historical landmark. Keeping Hillhouse open shows the community cares for its people.

Organization 2. order of importance **3.** The fifth paragraph answers the objection that Hillhouse residents should be moved to Hawthorn Manor.

Voice & Word Choice 4. Yes. The use of specific details (for example, twenty-six residents, 1870 building date, President Taft's stepbrother Charles), and the anecdote based on personal experience make the writer sound knowledgeable. The writer's appeal for people to work together to help fix the house and raise money is persuasive.

206

the Heritage Museum to try to get the Hillhouse building on the National Register of Historical Places. President William Howard Taft's stepbrother, Charles Phelps Taft, lived in the house at the turn of the twentieth century. Also, several early mayors have lived there.

 The third middle paragraph appeals to a sense of community.

Lastly, the best reason for keeping Hillhouse open is to show that the community cares for its people. If everyone gets together and conducts fund-raisers, organizes volunteer efforts, and donates time and money, it will show that this city is a great place to live and that the citizens look out for each other. Businesses can step up and donate materials, and individuals can donate time to help fix things up. Certainly, the people of Hillhouse would want to help if needed. The city needs to get busy and help them with what they need.

The last middle paragraph defends the position against an important objection.

Some people think that the residents of Hillhouse should move to Hawthorn Manor, which is more like a nursing home. These people don't understand that the residents don't need daily nursing care. They can do a lot by themselves. They are somewhat independent and want keep their "family" together. Tearing down the house and breaking apart that special family can't be a good thing.

Ending
The ending restates the writer's position.

Everyone needs to pull together as a community and keep Hillhouse open. Community members can all find ways to help with the repairs so that the residents won't need to move, and the staff won't lose their jobs. Maybe Hillhouse can stay open if it is declared a historical landmark. Someday soon it would be nice to read an article in the *Journal Express* about the amazing way the community solved the Hillhouse problem.

 Respond to the reading. Answer the following questions about the sample essay.

Ideas (1) What three reasons support the writer's position?

Organization (2) What method of organization does the writer use (time order, order of importance, order of location)? **(3)** Which paragraph answers an objection?

Voice & Word Choice (4) Does the writer sound knowledgeable and persuasive? Explain.

English Language Learners

Help students understand that an objection in a position essay is an opinion that does not agree with the writer's position. Point out the position statement (SE page 205) that expresses the writer's opinion. Then work with students to identify the sentence in the last middle paragraph that expresses the objection.

Struggling Learners

Make sure students can identify valid supporting reasons. Write the following sentences on the board:

1. Hillhouse should be saved because it is important.
2. Hillhouse should be saved because it provides a home and "family" for twenty-six people in our community.
3. Hillhouse should be saved because everyone thinks it is a great place.

Ask students which sentence provides a valid reason to save Hillhouse (the second statement). Have them consider why the other reasons are not good support for the writer's opinion. (The first statement is an opinion that is unsupported; the third statement is a generalization.) Guide students to see that effective opinion statements are supported with *specific, objective* reasons.

Prewriting

Prewriting for a position essay involves selecting a controversial issue in your community, gathering reasons and details to support a position on that issue, and organizing your ideas. Careful prewriting makes persuasive writing easier and more effective.

Keys to Effective Prewriting

1. Choose a controversial local issue in your community. Decide what your position is.

2. Write a clear position statement to guide your writing.

3. Gather the best reasons and details to support your position. Rank the reasons —1, 2, 3—from least important to most important.

4. Select an important objection that you can address.

Persuasive

Prewriting

Keys to Effective Prewriting

Remind students of the purpose of the prewriting stage in the writing process: It is when the writer selects a topic, gathers details, and decides how to organize those details.

Keys to Effective Prewriting lists the process students will be guided through on SE pages 208–210.

Young adults are greatly influenced by the opinions of their peers and may not take the time to evaluate how they truly feel about various issues. When it's time for students to decide on their positions (item 1) and generate reasons to support them (item 3), have students ask themselves:
- Is this really my position or is it someone else's?
- Can I defend this position with three carefully formed reasons?

If students realize that their positions and/or reasons do not represent their personal beliefs and feelings, they should consider choosing other issues.

Writing Workshop

The activities in prewriting can function as minilessons in your writing workshop. Use them to introduce, model, and teach specific strategies to the whole class, to small groups, or to individual students.

Technology Connections

Students can use the added features of the Net-text as they explore this stage of the writing process.

Write Source Online **Net-text**

Prewriting Selecting a Controversy

Students who belong to a debate club can suggest issues that they have debated that would work as topics for position essays.

Some local controversies could affect students on a personal level. Depending on the nature of these issues, discussing these controversies in class may cause discomfort and, perhaps, unnecessary conflict among students. While students should be encouraged to write about real issues, to avoid creating an uncomfortable situation, have students submit topic ideas ahead of time for your approval.

Focus on the Traits

Ideas

Have current regional, local, and school newspapers on hand for students to use to identify community controversies and some reasons for taking a stand one way or the other on these issues.

Tell students to keep these questions in mind as they proceed:

■ Where can I find factual information to support my position?

■ Can I address an opposing view with objectivity?

Prewriting Selecting a Controversy

A controversy happens when there is a disagreement about an important issue. To find a writing topic, student writer Keefe Collum answered two key questions about local controversies in his community. He put an asterisk next to the controversy that he wanted to write about.

List of Local Controversies

> In the past two weeks, what local controversies have been covered most often on the front page of our local newspaper?
> * the upcoming school referendum
> * rerouting Highway C away from Sanderville Woods *
> * building a fire station on the far north side of town
> * the need for more security at local sports events
>
> What local controversies have we discussed in class recently?
> * the upcoming school referendum
> * the city council's decision to make recycling mandatory
> * the accuracy of bacteria testing at New Eastland Beach

List controversies. On your own paper, answer the two key questions above. Try to come up with at least three topics for each question. Then choose one controversy that you feel strongly about. Write a sentence that states your position and explain the reason for your choice.

> Highway C should be moved away from Sanderville Woods. I picked this issue because I've started to become really interested in wildlife and their habitats. Many birds and animals live in that area, but the highway puts them in great danger. I would like to see our community consider the wildlife for a change when it decides to do something.

Focus on the Traits

Ideas Choose an issue that you can defend with several clear, convincing reasons. The more knowledge you have about your topic, the easier it will be for you to defend your position.

English Language Learners

Students may not have enough knowledge of community controversies to have formed opinions about them. Encourage students to read bilingual newspapers, if available, to ask family members for their opinions on local issues, and to meet in small groups (see **Struggling Learners**). Hearing others express differing opinions can help them form their own.

Struggling Learners

Some students may need assistance selecting a controversial issue that is a matter of public debate. Provide local newspapers and highlight several articles that discuss community issues.

● As a class, develop a list of interesting local controversies.

● Have students work in small groups to discuss the issues involved in some of these controversies, and see if they feel strongly about any of the positions.

Once students establish an issue and a position, provide reading material (or suggest specific resources) to give them more information about the controversy.

Gathering Reasons to Support Your Position

After you have stated your position, you need to gather reasons to support it. Making a "why" chart helped Keefe gather reasons that supported his position.

"Why" Chart

Why should Highway C be moved away from Sanderville Woods?		
because ②	Deer are getting hit by cars.	• increase in deer population • dead deer on highway • accidents injure people
because ③	Birds and animals are being driven away by traffic noise.	• sandhill cranes making a comeback in our state • cranes nesting near the woods • noise and exhaust fumes drive cranes away
because ①	People who live near the woods oppose commercial development and noise in the area.	• built homes near the woods to get away from noise of the city

*(left margin: Why?)* *(right margin: Details)*

(right edge tab: Persuasive)

Prewrite

Create a "why" chart. Create your own chart. At the top of the chart, write your position in the form of a "why" question. In the boxes below it, write three reasons that answer the question. Then add details about each reason.

Focus on the Traits

Organization Persuasive essays are often organized by order of importance. After you have finished your chart, rank your reasons—1, 2, 3—from least important to most important.

Gathering Reasons to Support Your Position

If, after researching the issue, a student can come up with only one good reason to support his or her position, he or she should find a new issue to write about. Students may be able to build a solid argument with two very good reasons.

Point out to students that each of the "because" sections in the chart will become a separate paragraph in their essays.

Focus on the Traits

Organization
Some reasons may appear to have equal weight. If students can't decide how to rank their reasons, they can seek advice from two or three classmates who are familiar with the issues. Tell students to
■ write the reasons on separate slips of paper and
■ have each classmate arrange the reasons in order from least to most important.

Students can then use these rankings to make a final decision.

Struggling Learners

Give students practice ranking the order of importance of reasons that support a position. Write on the board the following reasons why a new shopping center should be built on an abandoned lot:

A. It will help the town's economy.

B. It will raise the value of properties near the shopping center.

C. The closest shopping center is 20 miles away.

Have pairs of students work together to rank these reasons according to order of importance.

Prewriting Gathering Objections

Encourage students to identify objections to an issue by looking at editorials and letters to the editor on the op-ed page of newspapers and the letters pages of journals. Point out that students may also find new or stronger supporting reasons for their positions there. If time permits, provide students with some tips for **evaluating editorials and letters to the editor** *(see below)*.

Money often fuels the strongest objections in any community argument. However, it may not be the most important objection to the student writer. As an example, have students turn back to the essay on SE pages 205–206. The writer points out but does not *specifically* counter the objection that money ($100,000 worth of repairs) is needed to keep Hillhouse open. However, in the middle paragraphs, the writer shows ways that the money issue can be addressed (government money if Hillhouse is declared a historical landmark; fund-raisers, volunteer efforts, local business donations as part of a community effort), and in the ending the writer explicitly states that citizens can *find ways to help with the repairs.*

Prewriting Gathering Objections

Once you have a solid list of reasons that support your position, you should anticipate any arguments that the reader might have. If your position is that something *should* be done, come up with reasons someone might argue that it *should not* be done. By planning how to answer objections, you can make your position even stronger.

Identifying Objections

Here are several ways to identify objections.

- Read newspaper articles and listen to local news reports to see how these sources present different sides of an issue.
- Think about debates you've had about the issue. Try to recall opposing positions and reasons.
- Ask the opinions of your friends and family. Try to debate positions that differ from yours.

Keefe listed the following objections to his argument.

> *County Highway C is a scenic drive.*
> *County Highway C has become a popular alternate route to Taborville.*
> *Moving the highway will cost a lot of money.*✱

 Gather objections. Use the strategies above to identify and list three objections to your position. Put an asterisk next to the strongest objection.

Countering an Objection

Countering an objection is simply arguing against it. Keefe counters the strongest objection in three ways.

> *Moving the highway will cost a lot of money.*
> 1. The woods represents years of history and a vital ecosystem.
> 2. No one can put a price tag on natural resources.
> 3. As the city expands, this peaceful place should be saved for future generations.

 Counter an important objection. Write down the strongest objection to your argument. Try to counter it in two or three ways.

Teaching Tip: Evaluating Editorials and Letters to the Editor

Students will be shown how to recognize illogical reasoning and disrespectful and inflammatory language on SE pages 218, 223, and 225. However, they can benefit now from seeing how these flaws negatively impact the persuasiveness of an opinion piece.

Provide examples of newspaper editorials and letters to the editor about community issues. Try to provide a balance of well-written pieces with those that contain flaws in reasoning.

Divide students into groups and have them evaluate each piece of writing for the following points.

- Does the writer state the position clearly?
- Does the writer provide logical reasons to support the position?
- Does the writer's language show respect for readers and other people in the community?
- Is the writer convincing?

Writing

Now that you have planned your essay, you are ready to get your ideas on paper.

Keys to Effective Writing

1. Get all your ideas on paper in your first draft.

2. Write on every other line to allow room for changes.

3. Introduce the controversy and state your position in the first paragraph.

4. In the middle paragraphs, use specific reasons and details to support your position. Also address an important objection.

5. In the ending, restate your position and summarize your support.

Persuasive

Writing

Keys to Effective Writing

Remind students that the writing stage is when they get to write, or draft, their ideas on paper.

Keys to Effective Writing lists the process students will be guided through on SE pages 212–216.

If students will be working on a computer, remind them to double- or triple-space to allow for changes during revising.

Provide an opportunity for students to review their prewriting materials to make sure they are complete.

- Do they have three reasons to defend their position?
- Have they gathered enough facts, statistics, quotations from experts, and personal anecdotes to support their reasons?
- Do they know how they will respond to an important objection?
- Have they ranked their reasons in order of importance?

Writing Workshop

Use an overhead or the board to compose sample sentences of your own so that your students can see you writing. It's crucial that they see you not just as an instructor, but as a writer as well. This is one key strategy for creating a writing community in your classroom.

 Technology Connections

Students can use the added features of the Net-text as they explore this stage of the writing process.

 Write Source Online **Net-text**

Writing Getting the Big Picture

Encourage students to skim SE pages 213–216 to see how this graphic reflects the organization of ideas in the sample essay.

Explain that the first three topic sentences for the middle section of the graphic come from the student writer's "why" chart. Have students look back at this chart on SE page 209 to see how Keefe created topic sentences from the reasons in the second column of the chart, and how he put them in order.

Have students create "big picture" charts before they begin writing. Tell them to return to their "why" charts to create topic sentences for each of their reasons, as well as for their objection for their middle paragraphs. Explain that they can use their "big picture" chart to guide their writing.

212

Writing Getting the Big Picture

As you prepare to write your first draft, study the following graphic to see how the parts of your essay should fit together. (The examples are from the student essay on pages **213–216**.)

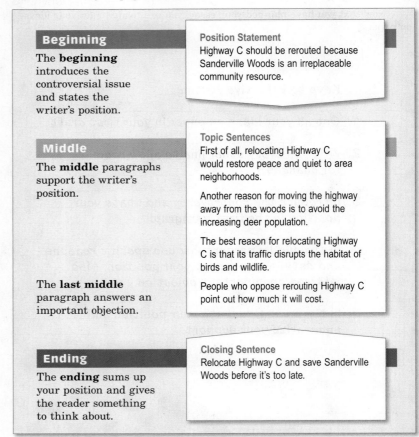

Beginning

The **beginning** introduces the controversial issue and states the writer's position.

Position Statement
Highway C should be rerouted because Sanderville Woods is an irreplaceable community resource.

Middle

The **middle** paragraphs support the writer's position.

Topic Sentences
First of all, relocating Highway C would restore peace and quiet to area neighborhoods.

Another reason for moving the highway away from the woods is to avoid the increasing deer population.

The best reason for relocating Highway C is that its traffic disrupts the habitat of birds and wildlife.

The **last middle** paragraph answers an important objection.

People who oppose rerouting Highway C point out how much it will cost.

Ending

The **ending** sums up your position and gives the reader something to think about.

Closing Sentence
Relocate Highway C and save Sanderville Woods before it's too late.

English Language Learners

Some students may come from cultures that do not organize information using the linear outline structure commonly used in the United States.

- Before students create "big picture" charts, make sure they understand that the topic sentences are listed in order of importance.

- Guide students as they return to their "why" charts to create topic sentences and make sure that their ranking of reasons is accurate.

Starting Your Essay

The beginning paragraph of your essay should get the reader's attention, introduce the topic, and state your position.

- **Begin with a powerful lead sentence.**
  Get the reader's attention in the first sentence with a strong opening idea.
  Don't let Sanderville Woods lose its natural beauty and serenity.

- **Provide important background information.**
  Be honest, creative, and even dramatic as you introduce the controversy.
  The quiet woodland paths, ponds, and streams are being invaded by the roar of traffic and the smell of diesel fuel along that stretch of Highway C.

- **Build up to your position statement.**
  Your position statement is the thesis statement for your entire essay. All of the sentences in the beginning paragraph should lead up to your position statement.
  Last week, Calvin County proposed solving the problem by rerouting Highway C away from the woods. . . .

Beginning Paragraph

The controversy is introduced.

The writer's position is stated (underlined).

> Sanderville Woods with its natural beauty and serenity is in trouble. The quiet woodland paths, ponds, and streams are being invaded by the roar of traffic and the smell of diesel fuel along that stretch of Highway C. Last week, Calvin County proposed solving the problem by rerouting Highway C away from the woods. This idea has become a heated issue. In a poll taken by the Pine Valley Times, 67 percent of those responding agreed with the county's proposal. Even more support is needed. Highway C should be rerouted because Sanderville Woods is an irreplaceable community resource.

Write an opening. Write the beginning paragraph of your essay. Does it engage the reader? If not, write another version or two. Choose the one that you like best.

Persuasive

English Language Learners

Some students may find it difficult to write multiple versions of their beginnings. Help them write engaging openings by having them rehearse ideas for lead sentences orally with you before they write.

Writing Starting Your Essay

Discuss why the lead sentence in the sample beginning paragraph works. Explain that it is an example of one extremely effective persuasive technique used in writing and speaking—making every single member of the audience believe that he or she has the power to make something happen.

- By beginning the paragraph with the sentence, "Sanderville Woods with its natural beauty and serenity is in trouble," the writer is saying to each individual reader, "You can stop this consequence. This situation is in your hands. You are responsible."
- Many readers will embrace this sense of empowerment.

Suggest that students may want to at least try this approach to write their opening.

Writing Developing the Middle Part

Point out that while many times it is perfectly acceptable to put the topic sentence in the middle or at the end of a paragraph, in this case, in order to build a solid argument, students should

- begin each of their first three middle paragraphs with a topic sentence that contains a specific reason in support of their position, and
- begin each of these topic sentences with transitions that help show the order of importance of their reasons.

✱ For more about using transitions, see SE pages 592–593.

Remind students to use the "big picture" chart they created (TE page 212) to guide their writing.

214

Writing Developing the Middle Part

Begin each middle paragraph in your essay with a topic sentence and add details that support it. Refer to your "why" chart (page **209**) for ideas for this part of your essay. Remember to address a significant objection in your last middle paragraph.

Beginning
Middle
Ending

Using Transitions

Transitions will help you show order of importance in your paragraphs. The following chart includes transitions that could connect your first three middle paragraphs.

Paragraph 1	Paragraph 2	Paragraph 3
First of all, ⟶	Another reason . . . ⟶	The best reason . . .
To begin, ⟶	Also ⟶	Finally,
To start with, ⟶	In addition, ⟶	Most importantly,

Middle Paragraphs

A topic sentence (underlined) introduces each middle paragraph.

The middle paragraphs build to the most important reason.

First of all, relocating Highway C would restore peace and quiet to area neighborhoods. Before Highway C became a busy road, many people built homes near Sanderville Woods. They wanted a quiet woodland setting where they could relax and enjoy nature. They didn't bargain for a noisy highway.

Another reason for moving the highway away from the woods is to avoid the increasing deer population. Why is that important? The number of deer being hit on the highway has increased 30 percent since last year. Hitting a deer can cause a serious accident. Protecting the lives of people as well as animals is an important reason for relocating the highway.

The best reason for relocating Highway C is that its traffic disrupts the habitat of birds and wildlife. For example, the marsh at the edge of Sanderville Woods has become a habitat for sandhill cranes. Until recently,

English Language Learners

The transitions shown in the chart may be unfamiliar to students. Introduce and reinforce how these transitions *sound* by having volunteers substitute the alternate transitions as they read aloud the underlined sentences. Point out that when replacing *Another reason* and *The best reason*, the word *for* should be dropped.

Struggling Learners

Remind students that transition words should also be used to connect ideas within the body of each paragraph. As students refer to the lists on SE pages 592–593, have them analyze the sample middle paragraphs for transition words that add or clarify information (*for example, in addition, also*), and that show a comparison or contrast (*however*).

sandhill cranes had nearly disappeared in our state. Now they are making a comeback. They nest near Sanderville Woods. The noise and traffic on Highway C may drive them away. Other wild animals, like raccoons and foxes, may be forced to leave the area, too.

The last middle paragraph counters an objection.

<u>People who oppose rerouting Highway C point out how much it will cost.</u> However, no one can put a price tag on natural resources. Sanderville Woods is a gold mine of local history and ecology. In addition, it is a popular place for quiet sports like hiking, snowshoeing, bird-watching, and so on. Many school children enjoy science field trips to Sanderville Woods. It also provides a peaceful habitat for wildlife. This valuable resource should be preserved for future generations.

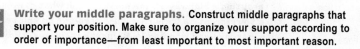

Persuasive

Write your middle paragraphs. Construct middle paragraphs that support your position. Make sure to organize your support according to order of importance—from least important to most important reason.

Tip

- **Use transitions** between paragraphs to show order of importance.
- **Include clear reasons** and avoid sounding too emotional.
- **Support your reasons** with facts, statistics, quotations from experts, and personal anecdotes.
- **Respond to a significant objection** by countering it in a thoughtful, reasonable way.

Call attention to the last bulleted tip at the bottom of the page. During revising on SE pages 222–225, students will learn how to avoid overly emotional (inflated bias) and disrespectful language (dismissing an objection with a label or put-down). However, discussing these issues now will put students on the right track.

Make sure that students recognize the difference between strong, moving persuasive language and language that is too emotional or disrespectful.

- Persuasive language is convincing when it appeals to a reader's sense of reason while sticking to facts. Have students point out words and details in the last sample middle paragraph that help counter the objection in a respectful, convincing way.
- Emotionally charged language reveals too much of the writer's own feelings and does not convey careful thought on the topic. Critical readers seldom connect with these feelings. Provide this example: *I just love the wildlife in the woods, and it will kill me if the highway drives it away.*
- Disrespectful language attacks people's beliefs and intelligence. It places readers on the defensive. Provide this example: *You have to be crazy to agree with this plan.*

Writing Ending Your Essay

Point out to students that their readers want to do the right thing. As students write their endings, they want to communicate to readers, "Okay, you know my position, and I've provided some good reasons why it makes sense. Now, readers, do the right thing and support my position." Have students reread their ending to make sure that it gets this message across.

During revising, students will use an extensive checklist to evaluate how well they have applied the traits of writing to their essay. For now, students can use the bulleted items in the Tip section as a mini checklist. Suggest that students turn each item into a question and use these questions to check their essays for major flaws.

For example, the first question they would ask is *Have I introduced the topic and stated my opinion?* If the answer to any question is "no," students can focus on this problem during revising.

216

Writing Ending Your Essay

At this point, you have stated your position, supported it with solid reasons, and responded to an objection. Now you are ready to write your ending paragraph. Follow these guidelines.

- Revisit your position and add a final insight.
- Sum up the main reasons that support your position.
- Sum up your response to the objection.
- Leave the reader with a final thought.

Ending Paragraphs

The position is restated.	<u>Clearly, Highway C should be moved away from Sanderville Woods.</u> Relocating the highway would restore peace and quiet to area neighborhoods, decrease the number of deer being hit by cars, and, most importantly, help preserve vital wildlife habitat. If current development continues along Highway C, it will become an extended strip mall. From the perspective of long-term value, the cost of rerouting a highway seems smaller than what it would take to re-create a thriving nature preserve complete with marshes and woodlands. Relocate Highway C and save Sanderville Woods before it's too late.
The paragraph sums up support points and revisits the response to the objection.	
The reader is left with a final thought.	

Write your ending and form a complete first draft. Write the final paragraph of your essay. Restate your position and summarize your reasons. Leave the reader with something new to think about. Then prepare a copy of your entire essay. Write on every other line if you write by hand, or double-space if you use a computer. This will give you room for revising.

Tip

If you have followed the traditional persuasive essay structure, your first draft should have turned out quite well. That structure follows:

- Introduce the topic and state your opinion.
- Support your opinion.
- Answer an objection.
- Wrap up your argument.

English Language Learners

Some students will not be used to working with the linear outline structure (checklists, bulleted lists, outlines) used so often in the United States. To provide practice understanding the relationship between such a list and a written essay, have students review the essay on SE pages 205–206 and identify those parts of the essay that address each of the checklist items in the Tip Section.

Revising

When you revise, you may add or delete details, rearrange parts of your writing, and work on improving your voice. You should also check your word choice and refine your sentences.

Keys to Effective Revising

1. Read your essay aloud and decide if it sounds convincing.

2. Make sure you have clearly stated your position.

3. Check your paragraphs to make sure that they contain convincing support.

4. Work on your writer's voice so it sounds informed and confident.

5. Check your writing for strong words and varied sentences.

6. Use the editing and proofreading marks found inside the back cover of this book.

Persuasive

Revising

Keys to Effective Revising

Remind students that the revising stage is when writers have an opportunity to make improvements to their first drafts. At this stage they can think about refinements they might not have considered when they were drafting.

Keys to Effective Revising lists the process students will be guided through on SE pages 218–228.

Point out that after using sound reasoning, the most important element of a persuasive position essay is probably word choice (item 5). Emphasize that

- overly emotional or disrespectful language can anger readers and turn them off; but
- strong, convincing language appeals to readers' intelligence and sense of responsibility. When readers feel comfortable, confident, and empowered, they are much more likely to agree with an idea than to dismiss it.

Peer Responding

Have students read and review each other's writing and provide constructive feedback. A thoughtful peer response can show students the traits they need to improve, and can help them select the best revision strategies from the many that appear on the following pages.

Technology Connections

Have students use the Writing Network features of the Net-text to comment on each other's drafts.

Write Source Online *Net-text*

Revising for Ideas

The rubric strips that run across all of the revising pages (SE pages 218–227) are provided to help students focus their revising and are related to the full rubric on SE pages 234–235.

Provide students with these additional tips for checking for illogical conclusions and exaggerations in their essay.

- Illogical conclusions: Look for the *if . . . then* construction (if this happens, then this will happen) in their sentences.
- Exaggerations: Look for absolute words such as *never, always, no one,* and *everyone.*

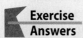
Exercise
Answers

1. *With cell phones, people never have to worry about anything* jumps to a conclusion. Cell phones can help in emergency situations, but they don't eliminate every danger.
2. *They can get anything they need* is an exaggeration. People can't use a cell phone to get good health or happiness.

218

Revising for Ideas

6 My position is very well defended and compels the reader to act.

5 My position is supported with logical reasons, and I respond to an important objection.

4 Most of my reasons support my position. I respond to an objection.

When you revise for *ideas,* make sure the reasons you use are accurate and logical. Also make sure that you have adequately supported your opinion. The rubric strip above can guide you.

How can I avoid errors in logic?

You can avoid errors in logic by eliminating statements that are hard to support. Here are some types of logic errors you should remove from your writing.

- **Statements that jump to a conclusion**
  If County Highway C isn't rerouted, Sanderville Woods will be replaced by a strip mall.

This statement is hard to support because you cannot prove that the woods will become a strip mall.

- **Exaggerations**
  No one will visit Sanderville Woods if Highway C stays where it is.

To support this statement you must prove that *no one* will visit Sanderville Woods.

Exercise

Identify at least two logic errors in the paragraph below. Explain why they are errors.

1   All kids should have cell phones. A cell phone is handy for calling a
2   family member for a ride or just making plans with a friend. Cell phones
3   can also be safety devices in an emergency. With cell phones, people never
4   have to worry about anything. They can get anything they need.

Check for logic errors. Read the body of your essay. Look for exaggerations and statements that jump to a conclusion. Revise any errors that you find.

English Language Learners

Explain that statements that jump to a conclusion are those that state an idea even though the writer has no supporting details (facts, statistics). As students read their essays looking for logic errors, have them answer the question, "What facts in my essay support this statement?"

Struggling Learners

For more practice identifying errors in logic, write this ad on the board, and have students analyze its logic flaws:

If you wear Coolest jeans, you'll be the envy of your friends. Everyone looks great in Coolest jeans! Once you wear Coolest, you'll never wear anything else!

(Sentence 1: illogical if-then conclusion; sentences 2 and 3: exaggerations)

3 I need more supporting reasons and a more convincing response to an objection.

2 I need to rethink my position from start to finish.

1 I need to learn how to defend a position.

Have I included adequate support for my opinion?

You have effectively supported your opinion if you include clear, provable details. The following checklist can help you decide how well you have supported your opinion.

_____ **1.** Do you strongly believe in the opinion that you are developing?

_____ **2.** Do you include convincing supporting details? Name the different types of details that you used.

_____ **3.** Do you address an important objection? What other objections are there? How important are they?

Check your essay. Answer the questions in the checklist above. Continue to work with those parts that you were not able to answer with a "yes."

Revise

Persuasive

Ideas
A new detail adds support to the topic sentence.

Sanderville Woods with its natural beauty and serenity is in trouble. The quiet woodland paths, ponds, and streams _and the smell of diesel fuel_ are being invaded by the roar of traffic along that stretch of Highway C. Last week, Calvin County proposed solving the problem by rerouting Highway C away from the woods. This idea has become a heated issue. In a poll taken by the _67 percent_ Pine Valley Times, ~~almost all~~ of those responding agreed with . . .

An exaggeration is replaced by a statistic.

A new perspective and a fresh eye can help students identify problems that they don't see in their own writing. Help students identify problems in their writing by using these strategies:

■ List what you will be looking for in their essays.

■ Model the revising process, using your own writing or a sample paper (see TE pages 236–237).

■ Schedule a **writing conference** _(see below)_ to help students finalize their revisions.

 Writer's Craft

Elaboration: In conversation, when we understand a general idea but want more details, we ask, "Can you elaborate?" Providing a depth of varied support is called _elaboration_.

If a student needs to elaborate support in a specific middle paragraph, have him or her write down the main idea of the paragraph. Then have the student answer the question "Can you elaborate?" three times for the main idea. Encourage the writer to answer the question using different types of support. Then suggest that the student incorporate some or all of the details into the middle paragraph.

Teaching Tip: Writing Conference

Students who are reluctant to identify their own writing problems often benefit from a writing conference during the revising process.

To foster a casual, comfortable atmosphere in which a student is more likely to open up, consider conducting conferences in a non-classroom setting. For example, if weather permits, meet outdoors. The library,

school lounge, and cafeteria are other possibilities.

If you have been writing along with the class, share your draft during the conference and suggest revisions to your work. Then have students review their own essays, using the checklists on SE pages 219 and 221. Agree on where revisions should be made before ending the conference.

Revising **for** Organization

As students check their essays for unity, tell them to underline each topic sentence in red.

- Next, students should determine if each topic sentence gives a key reason in support of their positions.
- Then, although it may seem laborious, they should read each detail sentence in each paragraph and ask themselves, "How does this detail support the topic sentence?" If they cannot find an obvious relationship between the detail and the topic sentence, they should rewrite the detail sentence to make sure it does relate, or delete it if they find it does not support the position.

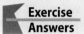

Exercise
Answers

Possible Answer

A poll shows that 80 percent of students support building a skate park next to North Beach, but some area residents have safety concerns. Although the park will have a boundary fence, some residents think skaters might skate outside the fence and get hurt. In addition, residents think the skate park will bring gangs to the beach.

Revising **for** Organization

| **6** All of the parts of my essay work together to build a thoughtful, convincing position. | **5** My overall organization is clear, and my reasons are arranged effectively. | **4** Most parts of my essay are organized well except for one part. |

When you revise for *organization*, you check the structure of your essay. Be sure that your paragraphs are connected in a logical way and your reasons are arranged by order of importance. The rubric strip above can be used as a guide.

Is my essay unified?

Your essay is unified if all of the parts work together. If your essay doesn't have unity, the reader won't be able to follow your argument. The following checklist will help you evaluate the unity in your essay.

_____ **1.** Does my first paragraph include my position statement?
_____ **2.** Does the topic sentence of each middle paragraph give a key reason in support of the position statement?
_____ **3.** Do all of the sentences in each paragraph support the topic sentence?
_____ **4.** Does my final paragraph sum up my position?

How can I improve unity with transitions?

You can improve unity in your essay by using transitions to tie ideas together between sentences and between paragraphs.

Exercise

Improve the paragraph below by using transitions between sentences or combining some sentences. For a list of transitions, see pages **592–593**.

A poll shows that 80 percent of students support building a skate park next to North Beach. Some area residents have safety concerns. The park will have a boundary fence. Some residents think skaters might skate outside the fence and get hurt. Residents think the skate park will bring gangs to the beach.

Check for unity. Revise your essay using the checklist above as a guide. Also check your essay for effective use of transitions.

Position Essay **221**

3 I need to reorganize the middle part of my essay from least important reason to most important.

2 I need to include a beginning, a middle, and an ending in my essay.

1 I need to learn how to organize a persuasive essay.

Do I present my reasons in the best order?

The reasons in your essay are in the best order if they are presented according to order of importance. Check for order of importance by using the checklist below.

_____ **1.** Does the topic sentence of my first middle paragraph address my least important supporting reason?

_____ **2.** Does the topic sentence of my second middle paragraph address the next important reason?

_____ **3.** Does the topic sentence of my third middle paragraph address the most important reason?

| Position statement |
| Least Important Reason |
| Next Important Reason |
| Most Important Reason |
| Position Summary |

Revise

Check the organization of your essay. Make sure you have built your argument from the least important to the most important supporting reason. Rearrange any paragraphs that are out of place.

Persuasive

Organization
A transition is changed to improve unity.

A sentence that does not support the topic sentence is removed.

The best
~~Another~~ reason for relocating Highway C is that its traffic disrupts the habitat of birds and wildlife. For example, the marsh at the edge of Sanderville Woods has become a habitat for sandhill cranes. ~~Each year there is a crane count.~~ Until recently, sandhill cranes had nearly disappeared in our state. Now they are slowly making a comeback. They nest near Sanderville Woods. The noise and traffic on Highway C may drive them away. . . .

Although students have had multiple opportunities to check the order of importance of their reasons, encourage them to check one more time. Point out that the most important reason is usually the one that affects the most people. To determine which reason is least important and which is most important suggest that students ask themselves the following questions:

- Which reason has the least impact on people in general? (least important)
- Which reason has the greatest impact on the largest number of people? (most important)

Revising for Voice

Students may wonder how they can write about issues that they care about without making emotional appeals. Help students understand that by eliminating overly emotional words from their essays, they are not eliminating their concerns about the topics. Emphasize the following:

■ Their goal is to help readers understand their positions and to convince them to promote these positions in the community.

■ Overly emotional language is ineffective because readers cannot or may not want to identify with such personal feelings.

■ Readers are much more receptive to feelings and opinions supported by reasonable facts. Then they have more of a tendency to think, "Yes, I feel that way, too, and for that very reason."

222

Revising for Voice

6 My knowledgeable voice creates total confidence in my position.

5 My voice is persuasive and respects my audience. I balance facts and feelings.

4 My voice respects my audience, but I need to sound more persuasive and knowledgeable.

When you check for *voice,* make sure that you have focused primarily on facts rather than personal feelings in your essay. A knowledgeable-sounding voice will connect with your reader. The rubric strip above will guide your revising.

Have I used a knowledgeable-sounding voice?

You have used a knowledgeable-sounding voice if you focus primarily on factual information in your essay. (Persuasive writing succeeds when it contains reliable facts and details that support the main position.) On the other hand, if you focus too heavily on your personal feelings, your voice will sound overly emotional, impulsive, and unconvincing.

Notice the difference between the two passages below. In the first one, the writer sounds too emotional. There is nothing thoughtful or convincing about his voice. In the second passage, the writer effectively balances facts with personal feelings. As a result, he sounds much more convincing.

Overly Emotional Voice

The new rules at the video arcade are the worst. The manager hates kids. He hired a security guard to stand at the door. That makes kids feel like they are being watched all the time. The arcade used to be fun, but now it feels like a prison.

Knowledgeable-Sounding Voice

The video arcade has upgraded its security. The manager became concerned about fights in the arcade, so he hired a security guard. Now, going to the arcade isn't as much fun as it used to be. According to Mike Kuhn, an arcade user, "The security guard creates . . ."

Revise

Check your dialogue. As you review your essay, make sure that you sound knowledgeable and thoughtful rather than too emotional. Revise accordingly for voice.

Advanced Learners

Voice may seem elusive because it reveals so much about the writer and the writing situation. Voice reveals the following:

● The writer's **personality**: *authoritative, thoughtful, witty, meticulous*
● The writer's opinion of the **topic**: *hopeful, knowledgeable, sarcastic, annoyed*
● The writer's relationship to the **reader**: *conversational, friendly, respectful, nagging*

● The writer's relationship to **language**: *direct, flowery, spare, rich, fluent*
● The writer's **purpose** for writing: *compelling, entertaining, informative, helpful*

Use a style matrix to diagram the parts of a writing situation. Then encourage advanced learners to brainstorm adjectives that describe different types of voice based on each part.

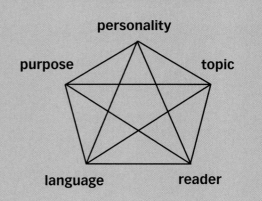

Position Essay **223**

3 My voice has a few problems sounding respectful and knowledgeable.

2 My voice may not respect my audience, and I sound too emotional and unconvincing.

1 I need to learn how to create a respectful, knowledgeable voice.

Do I connect with my audience?

You connect with your audience if, among other things, you address any objections in a respectful way. Your audience may include people who have not made up their minds about the issue, as well as people who feel differently about it. Dealing with an objection in a respectful way will make you sound more convincing. In the following paragraph, the writer addresses an objection in a disrespectful way.

> **Extending the landfill to Harrison Road is a really dumb idea. It would mean chopping down lots of trees. People in nice homes on Harrison Road don't want to look at a big, ugly landfill. Everyone knows that a landfill stinks.**

Exercise

Rewrite the paragraph above so that it addresses the objection in a respectful way. Trade papers with a classmate. Decide if your partner's voice connects more respectfully with the reader.

Revise

Review for voice. Read the paragraph that counters an objection to your position. Does it sound respectful? If not, revise it until it does.

Persuasive

Voice
One sentence is deleted and another is revised to create a more respectful voice.

People who oppose rerouting Highway C point to how much it will cost. ~~They are being very unreasonable. It is~~ However, no one can ~~stupid to~~ put a price tag on natural resources. Sanderville Woods is a gold mine of local history and ecology. In addition, . . .

Ask students how they feel when someone says to them, "That's a stupid idea" or "How can you go along with such a dumb plan?" Explain to them that readers will have the same negative reaction if writers address objections in a similar way.

Before asking students to rewrite the paragraph for the **Exercise** activity, read aloud the paragraph, emphasizing the language that is not respectful to the reader. This can help students recognize the effect of such language on their audience.

Exercise Answers

Possible Answer

Extending the landfill to Harrison Road is not a good idea because it would mean chopping down acres of trees. Besides destroying the beautiful landscape, it would destroy a natural barrier between the landfill and homes in the surrounding area.

Revising for Word Choice

Many students (adults, too) practice careless speech, which is characterized by the overuse of qualifiers and **unnecessary modifiers** (*see below*). Remind students that the conversational voice they use when talking to friends wouldn't translate into a confident, knowledgeable voice in their academic writing.

Exercise Answers

Possible Answer

The mayor will meet with us to discuss our plan. He has indicated that he is pleased with our proposal. The mayor has set aside money for such a project. As a result, we may soon have a stoplight at the corner by our school.

224

Revising for Word Choice

6 My words make a powerful case for my position.

5 Carefully chosen words make my writing persuasive and effective.

4 I have avoided inflammatory (unfair) words, but I need to remove a few qualifiers.

Checking for *word choice* means making sure that you have used the best words to build your argument. It also means making sure that you have not overused qualifying words or used inflammatory words. The rubric strip above can guide you.

Did I overuse qualifiers in my essay?

You have overused qualifiers in your essay if too many of your sentences contain words like these: *seems, appears, maybe, somewhat, rather, quite,* or *might*. Such words make a writer sound unsure.

> **Sentence with Qualifiers**
>
> It seems that the mayor is somewhat willing to meet with us.

> **Sentence with Qualifiers**
>
> The mayor is willing to meet with us.

Exercise

Read the paragraph below. Rewrite it in a straightforward, convincing way.

1 Apparently the mayor will meet with us to discuss our plan. He
2 indicated that he was quite pleased with the proposal we sent him. If he
3 agrees with our position, then maybe we can eventually get a stoplight at
4 the corner by our school. It seems the mayor has already set aside money
5 for a project somewhat like this.

Revise

Check your word choice for balance. Change any sentences that may contain too many qualifying words.

Teaching Tip: Unnecessary Modifiers

Explain that words such as *kind of, sort of, really,* and *totally* are unnecessary modifiers that can weaken students' arguments by making them sound less knowledgeable and less sure of their positions. Encourage them to look for and eliminate unnecessary modifiers from their essays.

＊ For more about unnecessary modifiers, see SE pages 170 and 543.

English Language Learners

Students may find it easier to identify unnecessary modifiers if they can hear how they make a writer sound unsure.

- Find sentences in their essays that contain qualifiers.
- Read aloud each sentence.
- Read the sentence again, omitting the qualifiers and using a more convincing tone of voice to emphasize the difference.

3 I need to change some inflammatory words and remove some qualifiers.

2 I need to change my unfair language to make a believable position.

1 I need to learn what words are inflammatory and how to use qualifiers.

How can I avoid inflammatory words?

You can avoid inflammatory words by expressing your opinion without blame. Strong language aimed at someone or something only weakens your argument. Here are some examples of inflammatory words.

greedy	foolish	stupid	dumb	so-called
phony	unfit	mean	disgusting	

Note: Being sarcastic can also be inflammatory. Don't call something a great idea when you clearly mean that it is *not* a good idea.

Exercise

Identify inflammatory statements in the paragraph below. Then rewrite the paragraph so that it convinces without blame or sarcasm.

> HGR Inc. is being unreasonable and mean. Their so-called East Side Improvement Plan includes tearing down the recreation center. How ridiculous! That center is where kids go for fun after school. What a brilliant plan—send kids to the streets. HGR should remodel the center and offer more activities.

Review for inflammatory words. Read your essay carefully. Rewrite any parts that blame or use sarcasm.

Word Choice
The argument is strengthened by removing two qualifying words.

> Clearly, Highway C should be moved away from Sanderville Woods. ~~Perhaps,~~ relocating the highway would restore peace and quiet to area neighborhoods, ~~maybe~~ decrease the number of deer being hit by cars, and, most importantly, help . . .

Persuasive

Before asking students to rewrite the **Exercise** paragraph, have them identify the inflammatory words (*unreasonable, mean, ridiculous*) and the sarcasm (*so-called East Side Improvement Plan, What a brilliant plan*).

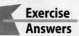

Exercise Answers

Possible Answer

The East Side Improvement Plan by HGR Inc. involves tearing down the recreation center. That center provides a safe place for students to go after school to meet with friends and participate in fun activities. HGR should remodel the center and offer more activities.

English Language Learners

Hearing examples will help students understand that using sarcasm can be saying something nice about someone or something when you mean the opposite. Ask volunteers to express examples of sarcastic comments such as, "I just love surprise math quizzes."

Struggling Learners

Use this whole-class activity to help students recognize and avoid inflammatory words. Read aloud the following examples, placing emphasis on the underlined words. Then have students suggest more appropriate wordings.

- Anyone who disagrees with this position is <u>foolish</u>. (not fully aware of the issue; uninformed; coming to a premature conclusion)

- The new building is <u>hideous</u>. (doesn't fit with the city's architecture; blocks the view of the harbor; should have been one-story tall)
- The project hasn't been approved because the mayor is <u>cheap</u>. (concerned about the budget; worried about voter support; submitting bids to contractors)

Revising for Sentence Fluency

Remind students that sentence variety adds interest and creates a smooth flow of ideas within and between paragraphs.

✱ To learn more about using sentence variety, have students turn to SE page 746.

Point out the words *call to action* in the explanation of imperative sentences. Explain that a call to action asks readers to do or believe in something, and that persuasive writing often ends with one. Have students check their ending for a call to action. Invite volunteers to read aloud their calls to action as examples for those who haven't written them.

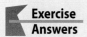

Exercise Answers

Declarative-5, Interrogative-2, Imperative-2

- Interrogative appear in the beginning and in the middle of the paragraph. By placing questions here, the writer helps readers recognize their own personal connection to the issue.
- Imperatives appear in the last two sentences. They leave readers with a sense of urgency to respond to the writer's call to action.

226

Revising for Sentence Fluency

| **6** My sentences spark the reader's interest in my position. | **5** My sentences are skillfully written with varied beginnings. | **4** I use different sentence types, and most of the beginnings are varied. |

To revise for *sentence fluency,* check to see that you have used different kinds of sentences and that your sentences have varied beginnings. The rubric strip above will help you.

Have I used a variety of sentence types effectively?

You have used different kinds of sentences effectively if they help you develop your argument. Here are the three types of sentences that you can use.

Declarative sentences make statements.
(Most of your sentences should be declarative.)

Interrogative sentences ask questions.
(Asking a question or two in your essay may help you connect with the reader.)

Imperative sentences make commands or requests.
(Use imperative sentences when you want to make a call to action.)

Exercise

Read the following paragraph. How many declarative, interrogative, and imperative sentences does it contain? Where do the interrogative sentences appear? Why? Where do the imperative sentences appear? Why?

1 Signs that old Southport lighthouse is crumbling include chipped
2 mortar and loose bricks. Isn't it time to restore this historic landmark? Even
3 though the lighthouse hasn't been used for years, it has been an important
4 symbol in our community. For many years, it was open to the public. Did
5 you ever climb all those spiraling stairs to the top and look out at the ocean
6 far below? The lighthouse should be fixed so that it can be reopened. Next
7 week, the city council will vote to repair it or tear it down. Call your council
8 person today. Ask for a yes vote.

Review your sentences. Read your essay. Have you used different kinds of sentences effectively?

Grammar Connection

Sentence Types

- **Proofreader's Guide** page 746 (+)
- *GrammarSnap* Sentence Types: Simple, Compound, Complex, and Compound-Complex
- *SkillsBook* page 143 (+)

English Language Learners

Revising their entire essays for all sentence types may be overwhelming for some students. Because a persuasive essay should compel a reader to act, focus instruction on creating shorter imperative sentences. Have students practice giving oral commands and writing them before asking students to revise their endings.

Struggling Learners

To ensure that students have included a variety of sentence types, have them underline imperative sentences and circle interrogative sentences. If students find none or very few imperatives and interrogatives, have them revise their essays to include these different sentence types. If necessary, review the purposes of the different sentence types.

Position Essay   **227**

Invite a volunteer to read aloud the Similar Beginnings and the Varied Beginnings paragraphs. Students should hear the liveliness of the second paragraph, created by the varied sentence beginnings.

✳ For more on varying sentence beginnings, see SE page 553.

3 I use different types of sentences, but I need to vary my sentence beginnings.	**2** Most of my sentences are the same type and begin the same way.	**1** I need to learn about different types of sentences and how to vary the beginnings.

Have I varied my sentence beginnings?

You have varied your sentence beginnings if all of your sentences do not begin with the main subject. Compare the following paragraphs.

Similar Beginnings

A bike trail near Lang Road will attract people to other recreation areas in our community. The trail will pass the recreation center, the city playground, and Wentworth Beach. Families can combine a bike ride with other activities along the way. Older kids can use the trail as a safe way to get to places to meet their friends.

Varied Beginnings

A bike trail near Lang Road will attract people to other recreation areas in our community. In addition to the recreation center, the trail will pass the city playground and Wentworth Beach. When families go bike riding, they can enjoy other activities along the way. For older kids, the trail will provide a safe way to get to places to meet their friends.

Revise

Check your sentence beginnings. Read your essay looking at sentence beginnings, especially the subject-followed-by-a-verb pattern. Revise by adding words, phrases, or clauses to the beginnings of some sentences.

Sentence Fluency
An interrogative sentence is added.

Another reason for moving the highway away from the woods is to avoid the increasing deer population. Why is that important? The number of deer being hit on the highway has increased 30 percent since . . .

Persuasive

English Language Learners

If students are not using a variety of sentences, introduce one specific sentence pattern, such as beginning sentences with simple adverbial phrases that describe when or where.

- Describe a picture or class event, using the target sentence pattern, and write the model sentences on the board.
- Have students refer to the sentence frame to practice using the pattern orally before they attempt to incorporate the pattern into their writing.

Struggling Learners

Have students attempt to circle each sentence where the subject appears at the beginning. Encourage students to revise at least half of the sentences that begin with a subject. Then have them read aloud their essay to hear how the revised sentences flow.

Revising **Improving Your Writing**

You may want to focus special attention on specific items in the checklist. For example, you may want students to underline their position statements, put an asterisk next to each supporting reason, circle any transitions, and so on.

Revising **Improving Your Writing**

 Check your revising. On a piece of paper, write the numbers 1 to 12. If you can answer "yes" to a question, put a check mark after that number. If not, continue to work with that part of your essay.

Revising Checklist

Ideas

_____ **1.** Do I state my position clearly?

_____ **2.** Have I included solid reasons that support my position?

_____ **3.** Do I effectively respond to an important objection?

Organization

_____ **4.** Does the overall structure of my essay work well?

_____ **5.** Are my reasons arranged by order of importance?

_____ **6.** Have I used transitions to create unity in my writing?

Voice

_____ **7.** Is my voice appropriate for my topic?

_____ **8.** Have I shown my audience the proper respect?

Word Choice

_____ **9.** Have I avoided overusing qualifiers?

_____ **10.** Have I removed inflammatory language and sarcasm?

Sentence Fluency

_____ **11.** Have I used different kinds of sentences?

_____ **12.** Do I vary my sentence beginnings?

 Make a clean copy. When you have finished revising, make a clean copy of your essay before you edit. This makes checking for conventions easier.

Grammar Connection

Complete Sentences
- **Proofreader's Guide** pages 738 (+), 740 (+)
- **SkillsBook** page 168

Sentence Types
- **SkillsBook** page 143
- **GrammarSnap** Sentence Types: Simple, Compound, Complex, and Compound-Complex

Adverbs
- **Proofreader's Guide** pages 730–731
- **Write Source** page 542
- **GrammarSnap** Adverbs
- **SkillsBook** pages 112, 113, 114, 115

Adjectives
- **Proofreader's Guide** pages 608 (+) 728–729
- **Write Source** pages 540 (+), 541 (+)

- **GrammarSnap** Comparative and Superlative Adjectives
- **SkillsBook** page 109, 110, 111

Fragments
- **Write Source** page 558 (+)

Editing

After you finish revising your essay, you are ready to edit for *conventions:* punctuation, capitalization, spelling, and grammar.

Persuasive

> **Keys to Effective Editing**
>
> 1. Use a dictionary, a thesaurus, and the "Proofreader's Guide" in the back of this book (pages 604–763) to check your writing.
>
> 2. Use the editing and proofreading marks inside the back cover of the book to mark your writing.
>
> 3. If you are using a computer, edit on a printed computer copy. Then enter your changes on the computer.
>
> 4. Check for any words or phrases that may be confusing to the reader.
>
> 5. Check your writing for punctuation, capitalization, spelling, and grammar errors.

English Language Learners

Errors in conventions may be related to the effort it takes to write in the second language, not to carelessness. Allow students to work with an English-proficient partner after editing independently.

Editing

Keys to Effective Editing

Remind students that during the editing stage, they have a chance to find and correct errors in punctuation, capitalization, spelling, and grammar.

Keys to Effective Editing lists the process students will be guided through on SE pages 230–232.

Call attention to item 3. Point out that new mistakes can occur when entering revision and editing changes on the computer.

- After students have made these changes, tell them to print out their essay one more time.
- Then tell them to do one last proofread, paying particular attention to changes.

Technology Connections

Students can use the added features of the Net-text as they explore this stage of the writing process.

Write Source Online *Net-text*

> **Test Prep!**
> According to research, grammar instruction is most effective when it is integrated into regular writing. Teaching grammar in isolation does not allow students to apply what they are learning, and so the rules remain only in short-term memory and are forgotten once the grammar test is done. Use grammar errors in student writing as the basis of grammar instruction so that students learn concepts in context.

Editing **for Conventions**

Ask students if they have any questions about using a comma after introductory elements. Make sure students can distinguish between a participial phrase and a **gerund phrase** (see below) used as a subject.

✱ For more about using a comma after introductory phrases and clauses, see SE page 610.

> **Grammar Exercise**
> **Answers**

1. For the first time in two years, we have a chance to change the lunch menu.
2. Before any decision is made, students must complete a questionnaire.
3. Providing a new menu, the cafeteria staff hopes to meet the dietary needs and tastes of more students.
4. This sentence does not need a comma although students should not be marked wrong if they add one. (By noon, most students have already eaten.)

Editing **for Conventions**

6 My essay is error free from start to finish.

5 I have one or two errors, but they don't distract the reader.

4 I need to correct a few errors in my paper because they distract the reader.

When you edit for *conventions,* you correct punctuation, grammar, capitalization, and spelling errors. The rubric strip above can guide your editing.

Have I correctly punctuated introductory elements?

You have punctuated a long introductory phrase or introductory clause correctly if you have set it off from the rest of the sentence with a comma.

Introductory Prepositional Phrases
With the arrival of winter weather, **the school should be opened earlier.**

Introductory Participial Phrase
Following this proposal, **Ms. Madsen met with the school's security staff.**

Introductory Clause
Whenever the temperature drops below 32, **the doors will open by 7:00 a.m.**

Note: You may omit the comma if an introductory phrase is short. After school **the main doors remain open until 4:00 p.m.**

> **Grammar Exercise**

Rewrite any sentence below that needs a comma. Add the correct punctuation.

1. For the first time in two years we have a chance to change the lunch menu.
2. Before any decision is made students must complete a questionnaire.
3. Providing a new menu the cafeteria staff hopes to meet the dietary needs and tastes of more students.
4. By noon most students have already eaten.

Edit

Check introductory phrases and clauses. Review your essay, looking for long introductory phrases and introductory clauses. Make sure you have punctuated them correctly.

Grammar Connection

Commas with Introductory Phrases and Clauses

- **Proofreader's Guide** page 610 (+)
- *Write Source* page 553 (+)
- *GrammarSnap* Commas after Introductory Phrases and Clauses
- *SkillsBook* page 11

Teaching Tip: Gerunds and Gerund Phrases

Help students to distinguish between gerund phrases and participial phrases at the beginning of sentences.

- A gerund is a verb form that ends in *-ing* and functions as a noun. A gerund phrase contains a gerund and all of its modifiers. When a gerund phrase functions as a subject, the phrase is not followed by a comma. (*Walking in my bare feet gave me blisters.*)

- A participle is a verbal that ends in *-ing* or *-ed* and functions as an adjective.
- A participial phrase includes a participle and its modifiers. When a participial phrase appears at the beginning of a sentence, it is followed by a comma. (*Carrying a set of blueprints, the builder approached the construction site.*)

3 I need to correct several errors in my paper because they confuse the reader.

2 I need to correct the many errors because they make my essay difficult to read.

1 I need help finding errors and making corrections.

Have I used the correct forms of adjectives?

You have used the correct forms of adjectives if they make the proper comparisons. The *comparative* form compares two people or things; the *superlative* form compares three or more people or things.

- **Comparative adjectives** (*-er, more,* or *less*) compare two things.

    bigger   more profitable   less economical

- **Superlative adjectives** (*-est, most,* or *least*) compare three or more things.

    biggest   more profitable   less economical

Grammar Exercise

Correct each underlined adjective below by making it either comparative or superlative.

1. The fall festival will be the <u>challenging</u> project our service club has done.
2. Extra volunteers will make this festival <u>enjoyable</u> than last year's.
3. We believe this will be the <u>great</u> festival in the history of our school!

Check for forms of adjectives. Add more punch to your essay by including some comparative and superlative adjectives.

Conventions
A comma is added.

The form of an adjective is corrected.

From the perspective of long-term value, the cost of
rerouting a highway seems ~~small~~ *smaller* than what it would take to
re-create a thriving nature preserve complete with marshes
and woodlands. Relocate Highway C and save Sanderville . . .

Persuasive

Explain to students that the overuse of superlatives can lead to illogical reasoning, which can weaken their positions.

✱ For more about the forms of adjectives, see item 728.2 on SE page 728.

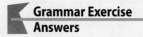

Grammar Exercise Answers

Possible Answers

1. most challenging
2. more enjoyable
3. greatest

Editing Checking for Conventions

Give students a few moments to look over the Proofreader's Guide (SE pages 604–763). Throughout the year, they can refer to the instruction, rules, and examples to clarify any checklist items or to resolve questions about their own writing.

As students edit their essays, encourage them to pay particular attention to the spelling and capitalization of people's names. Explain that when writers are trying to persuade the community at large to agree with their positions, they should be careful not to offend anyone in the community. Point out that people are often offended when their names are spelled wrong.

Creating a Title

Encourage students to experiment with all three types of title ideas. Suggest that they look at the sentence that states their position at the beginning of their essay to get an idea for a way to sum up the controversy.

Advanced Learners

Encourage students to be creative with their titles. Have students write three possible titles for their essays, using rhyme, alliteration, puns, or other catchy language. Have small groups review one another's possible titles and give feedback on their favorites.

232

"Fortunately both my wife and my mother-in-law seem to love digging up mistakes in spelling and punctuation. I can hear them in the next room laughing at me."

—Sherwood Anderson

Editing Checking Your Writing

 Check your editing. On a piece of paper, write the numbers 1 to 9. If you can answer "yes" to a question, put a check mark after that number. If not, continue to edit for that convention.

Editing Checklist

Conventions

PUNCTUATION
_____ 1. Do I use end punctuation after all my sentences?
_____ 2. Do I use commas after long introductory phrases and introductory clauses?

CAPITALIZATION
_____ 3. Do I start all my sentences with capital letters?
_____ 4. Do I capitalize all proper nouns and adjectives?

SPELLING
_____ 5. Have I spelled all words correctly?
_____ 6. Have I checked the words my spell-checker may have missed?

GRAMMAR
_____ 7. Do my subjects and verbs agree in number (*She and I are going*, not *She and I is going*)?
_____ 8. Do my pronouns agree with their antecedents?
_____ 9. Have I used the correct forms of adjectives?

Creating a Title

- Sum up the controversy: **Save Sanderville Woods**
- Write a slogan: **Cast a Vote for Peace and Quiet**
- Be creative: **Don't Make Nature Take a Backseat**

Grammar Connection

Spelling
- **Proofreader's Guide** pages 664–669
- *SkillsBook* page 54

Hyphens and Dashes
- **Proofreader's Guide** pages 624–625, 626–627, 640–641
- *SkillsBook* pages 25–28

Tenses
- **Proofreader's Guide** pages 720–721
- *GrammarSnap* Past Perfect and Past Continuous Verb Tenses
- *SkillsBook* pages 101–104

Pronoun-Antecedent Agreement
- **Proofreader's Guide** page 756 (+)
- *GrammarSnap* Pronoun-Antecedent Agreement
- *SkillsBook* page 155

Publishing Sharing Your Essay

After writing, revising, and editing your persuasive essay, make a neat final copy to share. You may also present your essay in a debate, publish it in a newspaper, or send it to an official in your community.

 Make a final copy. Follow your teacher's instructions or use the guidelines below to format your essay. (If you are using a computer, see pages 76–78.) Create a clean final copy of your essay and carefully proofread it.

Focus on Presentation

- Use blue or black ink and write neatly.
- Write your name in the upper left corner of page 1.
- Skip a line and center your title; skip another line and start your writing.
- Indent every paragraph and leave a one-inch margin on all four sides.
- Write your last name and the page number in the upper right corner of every page after page 1.

Contact an Official

Think of a community or state official who has the authority to take action on your issue. Send your essay to that person along with a letter briefly stating your position and asking for help. In the letter, explain that your essay includes important reasons to support your opinion.

Publish a Letter

Reformat your essay as a letter to the editor of your community newspaper. Check submission guidelines. Then submit your letter.

Stage a Debate

Gather a group of family members or friends who hold opposing opinions on your issue. Try to include one neutral person who has not formed an opinion. Stage a debate. Present and defend your position; allow others to present and defend theirs. Then ask the neutral person to form an opinion based on the debate.

Publishing
Sharing Your Essay

People tend to respond negatively when they are misquoted. Students who plan to publish their essays in any public forum can avoid problems if they take the time to contact the people they have quoted (by phone or e-mail) to get final approval for the quotations before they publish their essays.

Technology Connections

Remind students that they can use the Writing Network features of the Portfolio to share their work with peers.

Write Source Online **Portfolio**

Write Source Online **Net-text**

Rubric for Persuasive Writing

Remind students that a rubric is a chart that helps you evaluate your writing.

- The rubrics in this book are based on a six-point scale, in which a score of 6 indicates an amazing piece of writing, and a score of 1 means the writing is incomplete and not ready to be assessed.
- Explain that the purpose of the rubric is to help students break down the assessment process by evaluating each of the six traits individually—ideas, organization, voice, word choice, sentence fluency, and conventions.
- Point out that rubrics are also helpful during the writing process. They can guide students whenever they write because rubrics tell them what traits to include in writing and how to present those traits.
- Explain to students that they will most likely have different ratings for the traits. For example, they may give themselves a 5 for ideas but a 4 for organization.

✱ Reproducible six-, five-, and four-point rubrics for persuasive writing can be found on TE pages 769, 773, and 777.

234

Rubric for Persuasive Writing

Refer to the following rubric for guiding and assessing your persuasive writing. Use it to improve your writing using the six traits.

6 Ideas	**5**	**4**
The position is convincingly supported and defended; it compels the reader to act.	The position is supported with logical reasons; an important objection is countered.	Most of the reasons support the writer's position. An objection is addressed.
Organization		
All of the parts of the essay work together to build a very thoughtful, convincing position.	The opening states the position, the middle provides clear support, and the ending reinforces the position.	Most parts of the essay are organized adequately except for one part.
Voice		
The writer's voice is extremely confident, knowledgeable, and convincing.	The writer's voice is persuasive, knowledgeable, and respectful.	The writer respects the audience but needs to sound more persuasive or knowledgeable.
Word Choice		
The writer's choice of words makes a powerful case.	The writer's word choice helps persuade the reader.	The writer avoids inflammatory (unfair) words but needs to remove some qualifiers.
Sentence Fluency		
The sentences spark the reader's interest in the essay.	Variety is seen in both the types of sentences and their beginnings.	Variety is seen in most of the sentences.
Conventions		
The writing is error free.	Grammar and punctuation errors are few. The reader is not distracted by the errors.	Distracting grammar and punctuation errors are seen in a few sentences.

English Language Learners

If students found it easy to use the rubric strips for each trait on PE pages 218–231 (English Language Learners, TE page 204), allow them to use those (instead of the master rubric) to rate their essays.

3	**2**	**1**
More supporting reasons and a more convincing response to an objection are needed.	A clearer position statement is needed. Better support for the position must be provided.	A new position statement and reasons are needed.
Some parts of the essay need to be reorganized.	The beginning, middle, and ending run together.	The organization is unclear and incomplete.
The writer's voice needs to be more persuasive and respectful.	The writer's voice sounds too emotional and unconvincing.	The writer needs to learn about voice in persuasive writing.
The writer needs to change some inflammatory words and remove some qualifiers.	The words do not create a clear message. Some inflammatory words are used.	Word choice for persuasive writing has not been considered.
More variety is needed in the beginnings or kinds of sentences used.	Too many sentences are worded in the same way.	Sentence fluency has not been considered.
There are a number of errors that may confuse the reader.	Frequent errors make the essay difficult to read.	Nearly every sentence contains errors.

Persuasive

Test Prep!

The six traits of writing were first identified in the 1960s by Paul Diederich and a group of 50 professionals who reviewed student papers and brainstormed the qualities that made writing strong. In 1983, a group of educators in Beaverton, Oregon, learned of Diederich's work and replicated it, settling on a similar set of six traits. A separate team in Missoula, Montana, simultaneously ran a study that identified the same basic group of traits.

Put simply, the six traits provide a universal set of criteria for strong writing. They correlate very well to the rubrics used in most state testing. Using the traits throughout the writing process, therefore, prepares students for any writing test they will face.

Evaluating a Persuasive Essay

Ask students if they agree with the sample self-assessment on SE page 237. Ask them to suggest improvements based on the comments. When they disagree with the assessment, ask them to explain why.

Ideas—It's illogical to say a teen center would help the relationship between all teens and all store owners or to base the argument on one letter.

Organization—A transition, such as *another reason, also,* or *in addition,* is needed to move the reader into the second middle paragraph.

Voice—The addition of statistics about teen centers in other communities would create a more knowledgeable voice.

Word Choice—The repetition of *stuck* in the first paragraph sounds informal, and in the fifth paragraph, *this person couldn't be more wrong* sounds disrespectful.

Sentence Fluency—The majority of the sentences are worded in the same way. Add a few questions and commands.

Conventions—Reduce the number of contractions. Correct the spelling of *bored (board)* in the fourth paragraph.

236

Evaluating a Persuasive Essay

Read the position essay below and focus on its strengths and its weaknesses. Then read the student self-assessment on the next page. **(The student essay that follows contains some errors.)**

Open a Teen Center Downtown

Ninth graders get stuck in the middle. They're not kids, but they're still too young to drive. After school, juniors and seniors drive places to meet friends and have fun. Ninth graders are stuck finding places within walking distance from the high school, or places they can get to on public transportation. Last week, Mayor Steve Ricchio recommended to the common council that it should "seriously consider an after-school program for students at Pine Ridge High." He's right! It's time for a teen center downtown where kids can go after school.

First of all, a downtown teen center would be most convenient, especially for nondrivers. About a third of Pine Ridge students head downtown after school because it's so close to the high school. A teen center downtown would be easy for students to get to. It would also be near the public library, so if they wanted to study with their friends at the teen center, they could get study materials from the library first. Best of all, all city buses stop downtown at the Transit Center, so students would have a way to get home without calling their folks to come and get them.

A downtown teen center would help the relationship between all teens and downtown store owners. Many times, it's cold or rainy outside, so kids hang out in the stores. Store owners don't like this. They either don't let students in at all, or they can only come in two at a time. A teen center would get kids out of the stores and into a place that's better for meeting with friends. That would make both the store owners and the kids happy.

The most important reason for a downtown teen center is to have a definite place to go after school. Right now, kids hang out on street corners, in coffee shops, and at the park. There isn't much to do in those places, so it's easy to get board. A teen center would provide a safe place where kids could listen to music, dance, play games, and have fun with their friends.

The adults in town believe that teens are troublemakers. In a recent letter to the local newspaper, one adult wrote, "If we provide a place for teens to congregate downtown, there will be nothing but

English Language Learners

Read the essay aloud one paragraph at a time. Have students discuss each paragraph to clarify ideas and new words.

Struggling Learners

The more practice students have reviewing the writing of others, the better they will be at revising their own work.

- Before students read the Student Self-Assessment, have them work in small groups to evaluate the essay.
- Then have them compare their comments with the self-assessment on SE page 237.

trouble. Downtown will become a dangerous place, and more people will go to the suburbs to shop." This person couldn't be more wrong! A few kids cause trouble, but most kids just want a safe place to study with friends, learn new things, and just have fun.

A downtown teen center is a great idea! It would be easy for students to get to, and it's near places they need to go, like the library. It would get kids out of stores and create a place where they can get together and have fun. Best of all, it would help the adults in town see that young people are good, law-abiding citizens.

Student Self-Assessment

Persuasive Rubric Checklist

Title: Open a Teen Center Downtown
Writer: Janelle Jones

__4__ **Ideas**
- Does my essay have a clear position statement?
- Is my position backed with solid reasons?
- Does my essay have any logic errors?

__5__ **Organization**
- Does the beginning introduce the issue and state my opinion?
- Are my reasons arranged by order of importance?
- Does my ending sum up my reasons and opinion and leave the reader with something to think about?

__4__ **Voice**
- Is the tone of my writing appropriate?
- Did I connect with my audience?

__3__ **Word Choice**
- Did I use too many qualifying words?
- Does my essay have any inflammatory words?

__5__ **Sentence Fluency**
- Did I use different kinds of sentences?
- Did I vary my sentence beginnings?

__5__ **Conventions**
- Does my essay avoid most errors in punctuation, spelling, and grammar?

OVERALL COMMENTS:

My position essay shows that I feel strongly about having a teen center downtown. I backed up my opinion with good reasons because my friends and I have talked about it a lot.

I graded down for ideas because I had some logic errors, like including everyone when I just meant some people.

I graded down for voice because I think I sounded too emotional in some places. My word choice could have been better. I found some blaming words in my essay.

I think I did an excellent job of organizing my essay, and I didn't have many mistakes in conventions, either.

Review your essay.
Rate your essay and write comments that explain why you gave yourself the scores you did.

Persuasive

Benchmark Papers

Athlete of the Century (good)

● TE pp. 800–803

ATVs vs. Snowmobiles (poor)

● TE pp. 804–807

Student Self-Assessment

To give students additional practice with evaluating persuasive essays, use the reproducible Assessment Sheet (TE page 766), the Persuasive Rubric Checklist (TE page 781), and one or both of the **benchmark papers** listed in the Benchmark Papers box below. You can use an overhead transparency while students refer to their own copies made from the copy masters. For your benefit, a completed checklist and comments sheet are provided for each benchmark paper.

Reflecting on Your Writing

It is important to set aside time for everyone to have an opportunity between writing assignments to celebrate successes and explore challenges in order to grow and improve as writers.

Reflecting on Your Writing

After you finish your position essay, take time to reflect on your writing experience. On your own paper, complete each of the sentences below. This exercise will reinforce what you learned from the writing experience and help you apply that knowledge to future assignments.

My Position Essay

1. The strongest part of my essay is . . .

2. The part that still needs work is . . .

3. The prewriting activity that worked best for me was . . .

4. The main thing I learned about writing a position essay is . . .

5. In my next persuasive essay, I would like to . . .

6. One question I still have about writing a position essay is . . .

239

Persuasive Writing
Pet-Peeve Essay

If someone is "peevish," it means that they like to complain. A pet peeve is something annoying that someone likes to complain about. Nearly everybody has a pet peeve. You probably have a few of your own. Maybe it bothers you when the neighborhood dog barks every morning, starting around five o'clock. Maybe people talking on cell phones while they drive really burns your toast. Maybe you are annoyed by classmates who tap their pencils on their desks during algebra tests.

Writing about a pet peeve is a form of persuasive writing. In this form, the writer complains about something annoying, without really expecting to change it. A pet-peeve essay gives the writer a chance to vent some frustration, often in an entertaining way.

In this chapter, you'll read a sample pet-peeve essay. Then you'll write your own essay about something that irritates you.

Writing Guidelines

Subject: **Something that annoys you**
Form: **A pet-peeve essay**
Purpose: **To complain**
Audience: **Classmates**

"A man has to live with himself, and he should see to it that he always has good company."
—Charles Evans Hughes

Pet-Peeve Essay

Objectives
- recognize a pet-peeve essay as a form of persuasive writing
- use what was learned about persuasive writing to create a pet-peeve essay
- plan, draft, revise, edit, and share a pet-peeve essay

A **pet-peeve essay** is a brief piece of writing in which the writer complains about an annoying problem that he or she finds particularly irritating.

- A pet-peeve essay incorporates elements of persuasive writing but usually has a less formal tone than other forms of persuasive writing.
- A pet-peeve essay does not usually end with a call to action, because the writer's purpose is to air a complaint; the writer does not really expect to trigger any kind of change.

Pet-Peeve Essay

After students read the pet-peeve essay on SE pages 240–241, ask what they notice about a pet-peeve that makes it similar to and yet different from the position essay they wrote earlier. Students may notice the following characteristics:

Similar:
- The essay clearly states a position—that cell phones can be distracting, annoying, and dangerous.
- It builds the argument with supporting reasons that are organized according to order of importance.
- It counters the objections that cell phones help keep people safe and connected, and that some people, such as doctors, need to receive and answer calls at all times.

Different:
- The essay has an informal, conversational tone.
- It uses language that is highly personal and clearly emotional, especially when expressing frustration.

240

Pet-Peeve Essay

In the following pet-peeve essay, Devon complains about people who use—or misuse—cell phones in public.

Beginning
The beginning grabs the reader's attention and introduces the pet peeve.

Middle
The writer devotes one paragraph to each way this topic is annoying.

The writer relates an anecdote to illustrate his pet peeve.

A Little Respect, Please!

What is it about cell phone users that makes them think they are the only people in the world? Cell phones are great inventions and help keep people safe and connected when necessary. I keep my cell phone with me at all times to check in with my parents or to talk with my friends. But when used improperly, cell phones can be distracting, annoying, and even downright dangerous!

Just look at people who take or make calls in a theater. There are usually announcements in movies, asking viewers to turn off all cell phones or pagers. True, some people, such as doctors, need to have their phones turned on in case of emergency calls. However, most cell phones can be set to a silent vibrating mode. Then a person can check an incoming call to see if it's important and, if it is, leave the theater to answer it. Yet some people insist on keeping their phones—and ringers—turned on. Is the news so vital that the person can't go two hours without getting—or worse, making—a phone call? Why are these people in the theater to begin with if they want to talk?

Then there are the people who think they have to talk extra loud—in public—to be heard on their cell phones. Maybe they have a poor connection and have to shout to be heard, but most cell phones are pretty sensitive and can pick up a whisper. In any case, it seems odd that a person would want to discuss personal issues where others can hear them. Sometimes, listening to calls is downright embarrassing! One time, I couldn't help overhearing a conversation about someone I knew. I heard things I wished I hadn't, and it was really hard to talk to my friend after that! How hard is it for someone to simply say, "Can I call you back later?"

English Language Learners

Before students read the model essay, build background by asking them to describe their feelings about hearing other people answering their cell phones in public places, such as restaurants, theaters, or buses.

Key facts illustrate the pet peeve.

Probably the worst cell phone misusers are the many people who talk on their handheld phones while driving. Studies have shown that talking on handhelds while driving may cause accidents, because drivers are either distracted or unable to react quickly. Many cities and some states have either introduced or accepted laws against handheld cell phone use by drivers. Some countries, such as Brazil, Japan, and England, have already enacted restrictions. Still, on any street or highway, there will be many people yakking away with only one hand on the wheel. Those drivers are accidents waiting to happen.

Ending
The writer repeats his complaint from a new angle.

So what can be done? I have been tempted to tap an offender on the shoulder and ask him or her to please make the call some other time or place, but I've never done that. I'm too polite. I am also too polite to share my phone conversations in public or disrupt or endanger another person's life with thoughtless or reckless use of a cell phone.

Persuasive

Respond to the reading. Answer the following questions.

Ideas (1) Has the writer chosen a timely topic? Explain. (2) How does the writer relate the problem to the reader?

Organization (3) How did the writer organize the middle paragraphs?

Voice & Word Choice (4) List three words or phrases that show the writer's annoyance.

Literature Connections: In the essay "Primal Screen," newspaper columnist Ellen Goodman complains that Americans watch too much television. Goodman's essay is both persuasive and entertaining.

Respond to the reading.

Answers

Ideas 1. Yes. Almost everyone has a cell phone today. Indiscriminate use of cell phones is a growing problem for people just about everywhere.
2. The writer provides familiar examples that just about everyone who goes out in public has experienced to some extent. The writer also connects to readers by asking questions that make readers feel like the writer is talking directly to them.

Organization 3. In order of importance, from least important (disruptive), to more important (rude and embarrassing), to most important (dangerous).

Voice & Word Choice 4. Possible choices: *What is it about; downright dangerous; some people insist; is the news so vital; why are these people in the theater to begin with; talk extra loud; downright embarrassing; how hard is it; yakking away; tempted to tap an offender; thoughtless or reckless use of a cell phone.*

 Literature Connections

In "Primal Screen," author Ellen Goodman argues that watching TV night after night is an addictive behavior that can cause problems between family members.

Discuss with students their TV watching habits, and how that behavior might be affecting their relationships at home. For additional models of pet-peeve essay writing, see the Reading-Writing Connections beginning on page TE-36.

English Language Learners

Students may be confused by the more personal and casual tone of the model pet-peeve essay. Explain that although a pet-peeve essay is persuasive writing, it

- uses a less serious tone;
- includes personal feelings; and

- sounds informal, as though the writer were talking to a friend, as opposed to formal, like a letter of complaint would be.

When discussing Voice & Word Choice, ask volunteers to identify words and phrases that make the essay sound like the writer is talking to a friend.

Prewriting Selecting a Topic

Remind students that this is a chance for them to address an issue that has annoyed them for a long time. If they can't think of anything right away, suggest that they look through past entries in their journals to see if they have written about some particularly annoying problems there. It's possible that they will have explored these topics to an extent that gives them a place to start writing their essays. Emphasize the point that students should select topics that are appropriate to share and that can be addressed in a light way, perhaps with some degree of **humor** *(see below)*.

Technology Connections

Students can use the added features of the Net-text as they explore this stage of the writing process.

 Write Source Online **Net-text**

Focus on the Traits

Ideas

Explain to students that the anecdote from the pet-peeve essay on SE pages 240–241 recounts a serious incident. Point out that students can add humor to their essays by choosing amusing anecdotes.

✱ For more about using an anecdote to emphasize a point about a topic, see SE page 569.

242

Prewriting Selecting a Topic

We all suffer annoyances. Your brother uses all the hot water just before you get into the bathroom. Your neighbor lets his dog, well, use your lawn. Your friend chews gum with an open mouth. Even a small problem can really get to you, and it can make a good topic for a pet-peeve essay. To find a topic for his pet-peeve essay, Devon started freewriting about things that annoyed him.

Freewriting

> What little things bother me the most? There is always something distracting going on. Yesterday at a movie, someone's cell phone went off. I missed a whole chunk of dialogue because this person answered the call. Maybe I should write about people who aren't considerate about using cell phones in public. They talk so loud. Don't they realize everyone's listening to them? People who use them while driving really bug me. They weave around and are dangerous. How dumb!

Choose your topic. Focus on an average day and freewrite about things that annoy you. Keep writing until you discover something you can complain about in a pet-peeve essay. Pick a topic that is appropriate to share and can be addressed with some humor.

Focus on the Traits

Ideas Adding details will make your pet-peeve essay interesting to your audience. Here are two ways to add interesting details.

- **Use an anecdote.** An anecdote is a brief story that illustrates a main point.

  One time, I couldn't help overhearing a conversation about someone I knew. I heard things I wished I hadn't, and . . .

- **Use irony.** Irony is saying one thing and meaning something else.

  And I'm always lucky enough to sit next to them.

Create details. Write one anecdote and one ironic statement about your topic. If you like how they turn out, try to work them into your essay.

Teaching Tip: Humor

Students may benefit from a review of literary techniques writers use to create humor:

- **sarcasm** a form of ridicule that says one thing while conveying the exact opposite sentiment of what the words mean
- **exaggeration** (hyperbole) outrageous magnification of the true facts
- **puns** creative play on words that have more than one meaning
- **irony** words that say one thing but mean something else

✱ For examples of literary techniques, see SE pages 600–601.

Struggling Learners

When choosing topics for a pet-peeve essay, make sure students choose general problems that affect many of their readers. Point out that writing about one particular annoying person or personal problem would not be appropriate. Have the class brainstorm pet peeves and list them on the board to provide appropriate topics.

Organizing Details

You can organize a pet-peeve essay by logical order or by order of importance. With **logical order**, all of your reasons are of equal importance. They can be placed in any order, but you must move from one idea to the next in a way that flows well and makes sense.

With **order of importance**, you explain the most important reason either first or last. Placing the most important reason first allows you to reinforce the idea throughout the essay. Placing it last allows you to build up to the best reason. This is the order Devon used in his essay.

Devon's Main Reasons

- Cell phones are disruptive in theaters.
- Loud private conversations are rude and embarrassing.
- Using cell phones while driving is dangerous.

Least important
↓
Most important

Organize your details. List the main reasons you will use in your essay. Organize them by *logical order or by order of importance*.

Prewrite

Focus on the Traits

Sentence Fluency Vary your sentences to make your pet-peeve essay read smoothly; remember to vary your sentence beginnings and lengths. Notice how the sentences in the first passage below follow the same basic pattern.

I've had to listen to calls that are downright embarrassing. I couldn't help one time overhearing a conversation about someone I knew. I heard things I wished I hadn't. It was really hard to talk to my friend after that!

Now read the same passage with sentences that are varied. (Some new words have been added.) This writing flows better and is more enjoyable to read.

Sometimes, when waiting in line somewhere, I have had to listen to calls that are downright embarrassing. One time, I couldn't help overhearing a conversation about someone I knew. I heard things I wished I hadn't, and it was really hard to talk to my friend after that!

Persuasive

Prewriting Organizing Details

Suggest that students turn back to SE page 214 to review organizing reasons by order of importance. If students choose to organize reasons logically, but are not sure if they have listed their reasons in the most logical order, have them discuss their ideas with a partner who can provide helpful feedback.

Focus on the Traits

Sentence Fluency
Read aloud each passage so that students can hear how the same basic sentence pattern in the first passage creates a choppy, monotone sound while the sentences in the second passage have a smooth flow and interesting sound.

Before students move on to the writing stage, remind them to avoid writing **short, choppy sentences** *(see below)* and to vary their sentence patterns to create a smooth flow of ideas.

Teaching Tip: Short, Choppy Sentences

Remind students that the repeated use of short sentences will make a piece of writing sound choppy. To avoid this problem, students should combine short sentences that have related ideas into longer, more interesting sentences.

For practice, have students revisit an earlier piece of writing to find short, choppy sentences that could be combined.

✱ For more information about short, choppy sentences, see SE page 555.

English Language Learners

Students who express ideas in short, simple sentences may not be ready to combine sentences. If you have already introduced one sentence pattern as a model (English Language Learners, TE page 227), introduce a different sentence pattern to help students expand their sentence repertoire.

Writing Creating Your First Draft

Remind students that each middle paragraph of their pet-peeve essays should present points that help explain why the pet peeves are so bothersome to the writer. Like all good persuasive writing, these paragraphs should include supporting details that help build the arguments. Paragraphs should also be well organized and contain transitions that help connect ideas.

✳ For more about constructing effective persuasive paragraphs, see SE page 567.

Because students are writing about annoying problems, there may be a tendency for them to overuse the word *annoy* (and other forms of it) in their essays. Before students start to write, suggest that they brainstorm a variety of words and phrases to use in place of *annoy*. Post a list of synonyms that they think of; as they write and find new words and phrases, they can add them to the list for easy reference. Some ideas are *irritate, get on my nerves, bug me, infuriate, exasperate, bother, upset, aggravate, drive me crazy,* and so on.

Technology Connections

Students can use the added features of the Net-text as they explore this stage of the writing process.

⚡ *Write Source Online* **Net-text**

Writing Creating Your First Draft

Though a pet-peeve essay is a lighter form of persuasive writing, it still should follow a definite pattern. Use the guidelines below.

Writing Your Beginning Paragraph

Start by getting the reader's attention and sharing your thesis or focus statement. Here are several strategies.

- Introduce your pet peeve and tell why it bothers you.
- Ask questions about the topic.
- Use an amusing anecdote about an annoying experience you've had.
- Open with a startling fact or statistic related to your pet peeve.

Writing Your Middle Paragraphs

Discuss your pet peeve. Show the reader why the topic annoys you. Use examples, statistics, and anecdotes to illustrate your pet peeve. Organize your middle paragraphs logically or by order of importance.

- Start each paragraph with a well-crafted topic sentence.
- Develop a paragraph for each main point.
- Support each topic sentence with effective details.
- Use transition words and phrases to connect your ideas.

Finishing with a Strong Ending Paragraph

Wrap up your essay in a satisfying way. Your ending can be serious and reasonable or entertaining and light. Just make sure that it makes sense within the context of the entire essay. Try one of the following strategies to create a strong ending for your pet-peeve essay.

- Offer a humorous or serious suggestion for solving the problem.
- Summarize your feelings about your pet peeve.
- Suggest ways to handle or adjust to the pet peeve.

 Write the first draft. Use your list of reasons and any details you've gathered to write the first draft of your pet-peeve essay. Get all your ideas on paper, including new ones that come to mind as you write.

Struggling Learners

To help students organize their thoughts, have them create a list of grievances for their pet-peeve essays before starting their first drafts.

Revising Improving Your Essay

Take a break after finishing your first draft. Let it sit for a while. The following questions can help you decide what to change in your pet-peeve essay.

Revising Checklist

Ideas

_____ **1.** Have I chosen a timely topic and stated my complaint clearly?

_____ **2.** Have I included effective ideas and details to prove my point?

_____ **3.** Do I need to cut any details that are off the topic or unclear?

Organization

_____ **4.** Are my details and paragraphs arranged logically or by order of importance?

_____ **5.** Are my sentences and paragraphs easy to follow?

Voice

_____ **6.** Do the anecdotes I use sound genuine and personal?

_____ **7.** Am I convincing throughout my essay?

Word Choice

_____ **8.** Have I used effective descriptive words?

_____ **9.** Have I avoided name-calling and overly negative words?

Sentence Fluency

_____ **10.** Have I used a variety of sentences?

_____ **11.** Have I used transitions to connect my ideas and my paragraphs?

Revise your essay. Use the tips above as you review your essay and make changes.

Revise

Persuasive

Revising Improving Your Essay

If possible, give students a one- or two-day break between writing and revising their pet-peeve essays. During this time, encourage students to talk about their pet-peeve essays with others. Point out that it is always a good idea to take a break after finishing the first draft of a piece of writing. Explain that professional writers do this all the time because during such a break

■ they may think of new details that will improve a piece of writing, or

■ they may be inspired to say something in a better way.

 Technology Connections

Have students use the Writing Network features of the Net-text to comment on each other's drafts.

Write Source Online **Net-text**

Struggling Learners

Emphasize that in a pet-peeve essay, the voice should convey the writer's irritation with the topic. To check that the voice is convincing, have writing partners exchange essays and read each other's draft aloud, using tone and expression to show annoyance and humor. The writer should be able to hear whether the writer's voice conveys appropriate irritation.

Grammar Connection

Sentence Combining
■ **Proofreader's Guide** pages 742 (+), 744 (+), 748 (+)
■ *Write Source* pages 555, 556
■ *GrammarSnap* Compound Sentences
■ *SkillsBook* pages 159–160

Adjectives
■ **Proofreader's Guide** page 728 (+)
■ *Write Source* page 540–541
■ *GrammarSnap* Comparative and Superlative Adjectives
■ *SkillsBook* page 108

Editing Checking for Conventions

Have students read through their essays once, using the checklist to look for mistakes in punctuation and grammar. Then have them read through their essays again, this time starting at the end and reading one sentence at a time, to catch spelling errors. This process often helps writers spot misspellings.

Publishing Sharing Your Writing

Make sure students who plan to post their essay on a school or class Web site use the correct address and the proper instructions for uploading files.

Technology Connections

Remind students that they can use the Writing Network features of the Portfolio to share their work with peers.

✳ *Write Source Online* **Portfolio**

✳ *Write Source Online* **Net-text**

Advanced Learners

Point out that many stand-up comedians use pet peeves as the basis of their routines. Invite students to create comedy routines based on their pet-peeve essays. Set aside class time for volunteers to present their routines.

246

Editing Checking for Conventions

After you've revised your pet-peeve essay, it's time to edit it. The following checklist can help you spot any errors in punctuation, mechanics (spelling and capitalization), or grammar.

Editing Checklist

Conventions

PUNCTUATION

_____ **1.** Did I end sentences with the proper punctuation?

_____ **2.** Have I used commas correctly?

_____ **3.** Did I use quotation marks correctly?

MECHANICS

_____ **4.** Did I properly capitalize proper nouns?

_____ **5.** Did I capitalize the beginnings of sentences and direct quotations?

_____ **6.** Did I use a dictionary and/or the computer's spell-checker to check spelling?

GRAMMAR

_____ **7.** Do all my subjects and verbs agree in number?

_____ **8.** Did I use the "Proofreader's Guide" in the back of this book to check grammar?

Edit your essay using the tips above. Mark your changes on the printout. After fixing any errors, create a final copy and proofread it one last time.

Publishing Sharing Your Writing

Your pet-peeve essay may amuse your friends, family, or even the whole world. After you've finished the writing, find a way to share it with others.

Share your pet-peeve essay. Publish your essay in one of the following ways.

- Share copies of your essay with your class.
- Read your essay aloud to friends or family.
- Post your essay on the Web. (Get permission from your teacher and parents first.)

Grammar Connection

Using the Right Word
- **Proofreader's Guide** pages 686–687, 688–689
- *SkillsBook* page 60

Nonstandard Language
- *Write Source* page 559 (+)
- *SkillsBook* page 175

Capitalization (Titles)
- **Proofreader's Guide** pages 648 (+), 652–653
- *GrammarSnap* Common Uses of Capitalization
- *SkillsBook* page 44

247

Writing for Assessment
Responding to Persuasive Prompts

Throughout your lifetime, you will have many opportunities to persuade others to agree with you. Perhaps you'll try to convince a friend to see a certain movie, ask a teacher to let you take a makeup exam, or persuade your parents to give you certain privileges. The art of persuasion can be learned. The best arguments are carefully thought out and well structured. They are designed to make your audience think like you do on an issue.

You may be asked to respond to a persuasive prompt on a writing test. Within time limits, you must structure your argument and arrange it in a logical way. This chapter will show you how to use the writing process to create a clear, persuasive response.

Writing Guidelines

Subject: **Persuasive prompt**
Form: **Response essay**
Purpose: **To demonstrate competence**
Audience: **Instructor**

"There is no point asserting what the heart cannot believe."
—Aleksander Solzhenitsyn

Copy Masters

T-Chart (TE p. 249)

Quick List (TE p. 249)

Responding to Persuasive Prompts

Objectives
- apply what has been learned about persuasive writing
- practice writing for assessment

Call attention to the quotation at the bottom of the page and discuss its meaning. Remind students that if they don't truly care about a topic, they will have a difficult time persuading readers to care about it, or even more importantly, to follow a call to action.

Prewriting Analyzing a Persuasive Prompt

Make sure students understand that the ideas given in parentheses for each of the STRAP questions are examples of possible responses to that question. Each response, of course, depends on the specific prompt.

Try It!
Answers

1. **Subject:** eliminating the school art program **Type:** letter **Role:** member of student body **Audience:** school board **Purpose:** argue for or against keeping the art program

2. **Subject:** the decision to reduce the number of school assemblies **Type:** editorial **Role:** member of student body **Audience:** school staff and students **Purpose:** defend the decision or persuade the principal to reconsider the decision

3. **Subject:** city library's new reading partners program **Type:** newspaper article **Role:** reporter/student **Audience:** teens **Purpose:** persuade teens to volunteer for the reading program

Prewriting Improving Your Response

Before you respond to a prompt, you must analyze it to be sure that your response will fit the requirements of the test. One way to analyze a prompt is to answer the following **STRAP questions** about it:

<u>S</u>ubject:	What topic (lockers, policy, decision, program) should I write about?
<u>T</u>ype:	What form (essay, letter, editorial, article, report) of writing should I create?
<u>R</u>ole:	What position (student, son or daughter, friend, employee) should I assume as the writer?
<u>A</u>udience:	Who (teacher, principal, parents, classmates, employer) is the intended reader?
<u>P</u>urpose:	What is the goal (persuade, respond, evaluate, explain, tell, describe) of my writing?

The following key words are often found in **persuasive** prompts: *convince, argue, defend, persuade.*

Try It!

Analyze these prompts by using STRAP questions.

1. The school board has decided to eliminate the school art program because of budget constraints. Write a letter arguing for or against the board's decision.

2. Your principal has reduced the number of school assemblies for the year. The school newspaper editor wants you to write about the decision. Write an editorial either defending the decision or urging the principal to reconsider.

3. To promote literacy, the city library is starting a new reading program pairing teens with younger children. Write a newspaper article calling for teens to volunteer for the program.

Tip

Some prompts may not contain key words for every STRAP question. Use your best judgment to answer those questions.

Planning Your Response

Once you have answered the STRAP questions, you should quickly plan your persuasive response. The following graphic organizers can help you.

Countering an Opposing Point of View

Each persuasive graphic organizer includes space for both pro and con arguments. You must consider points from both sides of an issue to see where your strongest argument lies. Facts usually make the strongest arguments; however, your strong feelings about the issue can be important, too.

When planning your persuasive writing, make sure to counter or address at least one opposing point of view. Presenting another opinion tells your reader that you have carefully examined the issue. And effectively countering the point can actually strengthen your overall argument.

Reread the persuasive prompts on page 248. Choose one prompt and use a graphic organizer to plan your response.

Tip

In a timed writing test, plan carefully. Allow yourself time for planning before you write and for revising and editing after you write. For example, if you have 45 minutes to respond to a prompt, use the first 5 to 10 minutes to analyze the prompt and plan your response, the last 5 minutes to revise and edit it, and the 30 to 35 minutes in between for writing.

Planning Your Response

Discuss the benefits of using each type of graphic organizer to gather and organize ideas for a persuasive prompt response.

Encourage students to draw their own graphic organizers to practice for responding to test prompts.

Countering an Opposing Point of View

Review the definitions of fact and opinion.
- A fact is a statement that can be proved by checking a reliable source.
- An opinion is a statement that expresses the beliefs of the writer (or speaker). An opinion cannot be proved or checked.

Caution students against stating an opinion as a fact. Consider the following statement: *The after-school teen center prevents teens from committing crimes.* The writer believes that the after-school teen center will keep teens off the street and prevent them from committing petty crimes. This is the writer's opinion, stated as a fact. Ask students to rewrite the statement as an opinion. (I believe that the center prevents teens from committing crimes.)

Struggling Learners

Students may find that the pressure of writing under a time constraint interferes with their thinking process.
- Focus attention on the Tip and emphasize the importance of planning and organizing when answering a test prompt. Point out, however, that students should not spend too much time planning.
- Give students many opportunities to practice planning responses within 10 minutes.
- Encourage students to use graphic organizers whenever they are planning responses.

Advanced Learners

To dramatize for the class the different points of view that one might take in prompts 1 and 2 (SE page 248), invite students to role-play a conversation between two people who take different stands on each issue.

Writing Responding to a Prompt

Work as a class to answer the STRAP questions for the sample persuasive prompt.

Try It!
Answers

Subject: funding after-school student center **Type:** letter **Role:** student **Audience:** school board **Purpose:** argue for or against funding the center; explain benefits, or problems, the center could create; answer a counter-argument.

Review the main traits of persuasive writing. Ask students to look for these traits as they read the sample response:

- an interesting beginning with a clearly stated opinion statement
- middle paragraphs that support the position and help build the argument
- a final middle paragraph that counters an objection
- a strong ending that summarizes the argument and presents a call to action

---

250

Writing Responding to a Prompt

Once you have answered the STRAP questions and planned your response with a graphic organizer, you can begin writing.

Persuasive Prompt

Your school board is considering funding an after-school student center, but some board members feel it is a waste of funds. Write a letter to the board arguing for or against the center, explaining the benefits it will provide or the problems it could create for students, parents, and the community.

Try It!

Analyze the above prompt using the STRAP questions. Be sure to write your answers out before proceeding.

Response

Beginning
The beginning paragraph states the opinion (underlined).

Dear School Board Members:

If students are not involved in after-school activities or do not have a job, they may face long afternoons after the final bell rings. Many parents work until 5:00 or later in the evening. Students with time on their hands often look for something to do. Without guidance, they often get into trouble. At the very least, they might just go home and flop in front of the TV. An after-school teen center could create a positive environment for teens.

Middle
Each middle paragraph presents a main supporting point.

A teen center provides a supervised place for students. In a teen center, adults are always available to make sure nothing inappropriate happens. Students can be with friends in a safe, supervised atmosphere.

A properly equipped teen center offers a positive place for students, many activities, and healthy snacks. Students are encouraged to engage in physical activity. Sports are usually part of a center as well. With a few simple pieces of equipment, students can engage in activities such as table tennis, weight training, or aerobics. If the center has space outside, a basketball hoop or volleyball court encourages physical activity in good weather. An indoor gym could give students a place to be active even in bad weather.

The teen center could offer homework help. Volunteers could provide assistance. A computer lab supervised by an adult would help students do research, check e-mail, and have some fun. This environment could encourage students to do their homework.

Concession
The writer addresses a possible objection.

Some people might argue that the district can't afford such a facility, but there are ways to make an expensive dream an affordable reality. For one thing, the center could sell snacks and juices to help with expenses. The upper-class students could volunteer to help younger students with class work, earning volunteer service hours for their efforts. Local businesspeople might be willing to mentor students in different areas, working with them at the center. Another resource might be parents. Service organizations could donate materials to help support such a worthy community project. Of course, fund-raisers could be held to support the center.

Ending
The ending offers a final plea and summarizes the argument.

All the school board members must consider the importance of a teen center. The youth of today are the parents and citizens of tomorrow. A teen center that offers safe, supervised activities and homework tutoring could show how a community can work together for the betterment of all.

Sincerely,
Alia Santos

Practice responding to a persuasive prompt. Review the prompt you chose on page 249, your answers to the STRAP questions, and your graphic organizer. Then write a response to the prompt in the amount of time your teacher gives you.

Encourage students to draw on the confidence and experience they gained writing their position essay (SE pages 204–238) as they practice responding.

- In their position essays, the goal was to defend their positions on controversial community issues. They stated their position in the beginning paragraph. In the middle paragraphs they built their argument with strong reasons, organized in order of importance, and they countered an objection. At the end of their essays, they issued a call to action to members of the community.

- In the sample response, the writer's goal is to defend a position on an after-school center. The writer states an opinion in the beginning paragraph and builds a strong defense in the middle paragraphs, presenting reasons in order of importance. The writer counters an objection in the last middle paragraph and concludes the essay with a call to action to the community.

Struggling Learners

For all students, but especially for those who are struggling, the best way to prepare for a test is to practice under similar conditions. If your state assessment is administered in the library, for example, try to arrange a test prep experience in that setting. If students write on lined paper in an exam book, try to provide a similar looking workspace for them to practice.

Revising Improving Your Response

Make sure students know how much time they will have for revising. Emphasize once again the importance of answering the STRAP questions before students even plan their response. If they discover that their responses need major revisions after they write, there is a strong possibility that they will run out of time to make major revisions.

Editing Checking Your Response

As students edit their responses, remind them that a singular subject takes a singular verb, and that a plural subject takes a plural verb. Point out that mistakes in subject-verb agreement usually occur when descriptive words and phrases separate, or come between, the subject and verb.

✱ For more about subject-verb agreement, see SE page 752.

Revising Improving Your Response

Before you begin a writing test, find out whether you will be allowed to make changes in your writing. If this is allowed, always make your changes and corrections as neatly as possible. The STRAP questions below can help.

Subject:	Does my response focus on the topic of the prompt? Do my main points support the opinion stated in the beginning of my response?
Type:	Have I used the form requested in the prompt (essay, letter, article)?
Role:	Have I assumed the position called for in the prompt?
Audience:	Do I use appropriate language for my audience?
Purpose:	Does my writing accomplish the goal set forth in the prompt?

Improve your work. Reread your response, asking yourself the STRAP questions above. Make whatever changes are necessary to your response.

Editing Checking for Conventions

A final read-through of your essay gives you the chance to check for punctuation, capitalization, spelling, and grammar errors.

Editing Checklist

Conventions

_____ **1.** Have I used end punctuation for every sentence?
_____ **2.** Have I capitalized all proper nouns and the first words of sentences?
_____ **3.** Have I checked my spelling?
_____ **4.** Have I made sure my subjects and verbs agree?
_____ **5.** Have I used the right words (*effect, affect*)?

Check for conventions. Read through your response one final time, checking your punctuation, capitalization, spelling, and grammar. Make all of your corrections neatly in the time allowed.

Persuasive Writing on Tests

Use this guide when preparing to respond to a persuasive writing prompt.

Before you write . . .

- **Understand the prompt.**
  Use the STRAP questions, and remember that a persuasive prompt asks you to use facts and logical reasons to persuade or convince.
- **Plan your time wisely.**
  Spend 5 to 10 minutes planning before starting to write.

As you write . . .

- **Decide on a focus for your essay.**
  Keep your main idea or purpose in mind as you write. Be sure all your points clearly support your argument.
- **Be selective.**
  Use examples that directly support your opinion.
- **End in a meaningful way.**
  Remind the reader about the topic and your point of view.

After you write your first draft . . .

- **Check for completeness and correctness.**
  Use the STRAP questions to revise your work. Then check for errors in punctuation, capitalization, spelling, and grammar.

Try It!

Plan and write a response. Choose one of the prompts below. Analyze it using the STRAP questions; use a graphic organizer to gather details and plan; then write, revise, and edit your response.

- Your school budget will allow for an additional class to be offered in the coming school year, and your principal has asked students to make suggestions. Write a letter to the principal explaining what class you think should be offered and why.
- As a class project, your English teacher wants to view and analyze a current movie. In preparation for this unit, she would like students to recommend a movie to study. In a memo or an e-mail, convince your teacher to use the movie of your choice.

Persuasive

Persuasive Writing on Tests

Point out that students must approach writing-on-demand assignments differently from open-ended writing assignments and that timed writing creates pressures for everyone.

Try It! Answers

Break down each part of the process into a clear chunk of time. For example, you might give students

- 15 minutes for note taking and planning,
- 20 minutes for writing, and
- 10 minutes for editing and proofreading.

Tell students when time is up for each section. Start the assignment at the top of the hour or at the half-hour to make it easier for students to keep track of the time.

Response to Literature Overview

Common Core Standards Focus

Writing 9: Draw evidence from literary or informational texts to support analysis, reflection, and research.

Language 1b: Use various types of phrases (noun, adjectival, adverbial, participial, prepositional, absolute) and clauses (independent, dependent, noun, relative, adverbial) to convey specific meanings and add variety and interest to writing or presentations.

Language 2a: Use a semicolon (and perhaps a conjunctive adverb) to link two or more closely related independent clauses.

Writing Forms

- analysis paragraph
- response essay
- writing for assessment

Focus on the Traits

- **Ideas** Developing a thesis statement that explains the interpretation of the theme and selecting details to support that statement
- **Organization** Creating clear beginning, middle, and ending paragraphs, connected by transitions
- **Voice** Using a natural, engaging voice that sounds interested in the analysis
- **Word Choice** Quoting words and phrases from the story and using the author's figures of speech to prove a point
- **Sentence Fluency** Using a variety of sentence types and lengths and using correct verb tenses
- **Conventions** Checking for errors in punctuation, capitalization, spelling, and grammar

 Literature Connections

- **Review of "4 Little Girls"** by Roger Ebert

 Technology Connections

 Write Source Online
www.hmheducation.com/writesource

- *Net-text*
- *Bookshelf*
- *GrammarSnap*
- *Portfolio*
- *Essay Scoring*
- *Writing Network features*
- *File Cabinet*

 Interactive Whiteboard Lessons

Suggested Response to Literature Unit (Three Weeks)

Day	Writing and Skills Instruction	Student Edition		SkillsBook	Write Source Online
		Main Pages	Resource Units*		
1–3	**Response to Literature Warm-Up Paragraph: Analyze Theme of a Short Story** (Model)	255–257			*Interactive Whiteboard Lessons*
	Critical Reading	473–482			
	Skills Activities: • Punctuating Titles		634–635, 636–637	33, 36, 45	*GrammarSnap*
4–5	**Response to Literature: Analyze a Theme of a Short Story** (Model) ⓘ Literature Connections Review of "4 Little Girls"	258–260			
	Summarizing and Paraphrasing	483–490			
	(Prewriting)	261–266			*Net-text*
6–7	(Writing)	267–272			*Net-text*
8–10	(Revising)	273–284			*Net-text*
	Skills Activities: • Figures of Speech		598–599, 600–601, 672–677 (+)		
	• Misplaced and Dangling Modifiers		559	172–173	
	• Pronouns (relative, indefinite, interrogative, demonstrative)		537 (+), 704 (+), 706 (+)	86–88	*GrammarSnap*
11–12	(Editing)	285–288			*Net-text*
	Skills Activities: • Tense Shifts		718–719, 722 (+)	184	*GrammarSnap*
	• Punctuating Compound and Complex Sentences		744–745, 748 (+)	21–22, 144, 161	*GrammarSnap*
	• Punctuating Quotations		616 (+), 632(+)	35	
	• End Punctuation		605 (+), 606 (+)	6	
13	(Publishing, Assessing, Reflecting)	289–294			*Net-text, Portfolio*
opt.	*Making Oral Presentations*	393–401			
14–15	**Responding to Prompts About Literature**	295–311			

* These units are also located in the back of the *Teacher's Edition*. Resource Units include "Basic Grammar and Writing," "A Writer's Resource," and "Proofreader's Guide."
(+) This activity is located in a different section of the *Write Source Student Edition*. If students have already completed this activity, you may wish to review it at this time.

Response to Literature

This overview for response to literature includes some specific teaching suggestions for this unit. The description of each chapter will help you decide which parts of the unit to teach.

Writing Focus

Analyzing a Theme (pages 255–294)

Analysis is one of the most challenging forms of writing in any content area. As students analyze a piece of literature to identify and discuss a theme of the work, they develop valuable thinking, learning, and writing skills. They learn to develop interpretations of what they read and become aware of stylistic devices. Another key skill students will need in all disciplines is the ability to support important ideas through accurate and detailed references to the text. They can also learn to identify and assess the impact of perceived ambiguities, nuances, and complexities within the text.

Responding to Prompts About Literature
(pages 295–311)

Because students often face literature prompts in assessment tests, they need to know how to respond in a timely manner. This chapter provides direction and several examples for responding to fiction and to nonfiction.

Grammar Focus

For support with this unit's grammar topics, consult the resource units (Basic Grammar and Writing, A Writer's Resource, and Proofreader's Guide).

Academic Vocabulary

Read aloud the academic terms, as well as the descriptions and questions. Model for students how to read one question and answer it. Have partners monitor their understanding and seek clarification of the terms by working through the meanings and questions together.

Minilessons

A Theme in Metaphor
Analyzing a Theme

■ **READ** the definition of the word "theme" on SE page 599 and the definition of "metaphor" on SE page 601. Then **CHOOSE** one of your favorite short stories and **WRITE** a theme for the story in one sentence. Finally, **CREATE** a one-sentence metaphor that captures the story's theme. **CONSIDER** how the metaphor could inspire your writing about the theme of the story. **DISCUSS** your answers with a classmate.

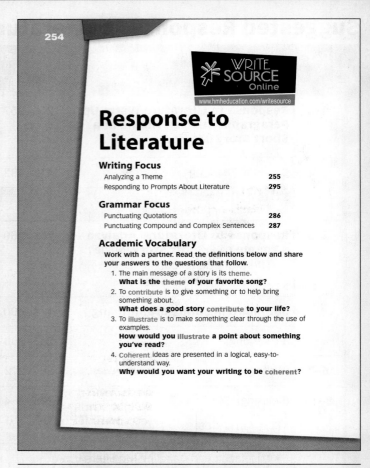

254

Response to Literature

Writing Focus

Grammar Focus

Academic Vocabulary

Work with a partner. Read the definitions below and share your answers to the questions that follow.

1. The main message of a story is its theme.
   What is the theme of your favorite song?

2. To contribute is to give something or to help bring something about.
   What does a good story contribute to your life?

3. To illustrate is to make something clear through the use of examples.
   How would you illustrate a point about something you've read?

4. Coherent ideas are presented in a logical, easy-to-understand way.
   Why would you want your writing to be coherent?

A Pair of Phrases   Responding to Prompts About Literature

■ Sometimes an analysis asks for a paraphrase of what's being said in a work of literature. Other times, the writer must quote exact phrases. In the following excerpt, **QUOTE** two phrases in a simple sentence to **DEMONSTRATE** the theme that real fear generates real courage.

When the bear had wandered into camp, Rick's quick thinking lured the bear away, letting his friends escape. He expected the bear would soon stop following him. However, the grizzly's unrelenting pace soon wore him out. Out of breath and unaccustomed to the altitude, Rick desperately looked over his shoulder and felt the ground shake as the grizzly suddenly charged straight for him. With certain death pounding his way, Rick considered the chasm between the cliff he was on and the nearby cliff that might mean safety. Feeling trapped, Rick ignored the terrifying drop and leaped. He slammed into the rocky surface on the other side completely exhausted. As he watched, the huge bear rumbled to a stop on the edge of the cliff, snorted, and then walked away. Rick's fear dissolved into laughter that echoed up the rock walls above him.

255

Response to Literature
Analyzing a Theme

To analyze means to break down a topic into smaller parts and determine how the parts relate to one another. Sportswriters are often asked to analyze sporting events. For example, a baseball writer may break down a particular game according to three main parts—fielding, pitching, and hitting—and then determine how each part contributed to a team's overall performance.

In this chapter, you will analyze the theme or main point of a short story. You will base your essay on a close examination of two key elements—the **plot** *(key events)* and **characterization** *(the thoughts and actions of the main character)*.

Writing Guidelines

Subject: A short story
Form: Essay
Purpose: To analyze a theme
Audience: Classmates

"What all good story writers certainly have in common is the ability to make the best choices before the story is finished."

—William Boone

Analyzing a Theme

Objectives

- understand the content and form of an essay that analyzes a theme
- plan, draft, revise, edit, and publish an analysis of a theme in a short story

Point out that breaking something down into its component parts is a good way to master any complicated process. For example, it is a strategy that helps sportswriters understand a sport, and it is also a strategy that athletes use. Athletes perfect their techniques by focusing on specific tasks such as improving muscle tone, improving stamina, and doing offensive and defensive drills.

Explain that in the following pages, students will learn how to analyze short stories by breaking them down into manageable parts. Looking at the different parts in a systematic fashion will help them consider what the stories mean as a whole.

Technology Connections

Use this unit's Interactive Whiteboard Lesson to introduce response writing.

Interactive Whiteboard Lessons

Copy Masters

Time Line (TE p. 264)

Assessment Sheet (TE p. 293)

Response-to-Literature Rubric Checklist (TE p. 293)

Benchmark Papers

The Color Purple (good)
 TE pp. 808–811

The Call of the Wild (poor)
 TE pp. 812–814

Writing Warm-Up: Finding Themes

To aid students as they complete the **Try It!** activity, provide dictionaries of proverbs to browse through. Good examples include the following:

- *Cassell's Dictionary of Proverbs*
- *The Concise Oxford Dictionary of Proverbs*
- *The Prentice-Hall Encyclopedia of World Proverbs*

Information is available online as well. Students can try the following:

- www.bartelby.com for the searchable version of *The New Dictionary of Cultural Literacy* (devotes a chapter to proverbs) or
- The Phrase Finder (www.phrases.org.uk).

Be sure that students understand they are not obligated to use proverbs or other common sayings to express their ideas about themes. They should feel free to describe the ideas in their own words.

256

Writing Warm-Up: Finding Themes

In literature, the **theme** is usually a lesson learned or a statement about life. Sometimes the theme is openly stated in the story but more often it is not. In some long pieces of literature, there may be more than one significant theme. One way to think about literary themes is to consider lessons that are often learned from experience. For example, in *To Kill a Mockingbird*, Scout Finch learns not to prejudge people. Study the cluster of life lessons below. (Some of these lessons are familiar proverbs.)

Cluster

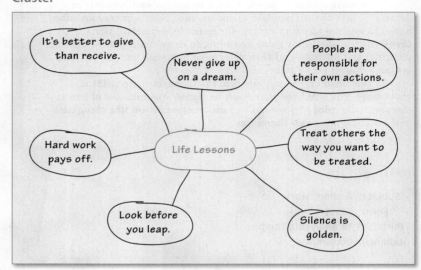

▶ Try It!

Work with a classmate to create a cluster diagram. See how many life lessons you can list. If you get stuck, think of familiar proverbs. Then identify a story you've read that uses one of these life lessons as its theme.

> "Reading is actually plunging into one's own identity and, one hopes, emerging stronger than before."
>
> —Amalia Kahana-Carmon

Struggling Learners

Theme can be difficult to recognize. Ask the following questions to help them identify the themes of familiar stories.

- What is the main lesson of the story?
- What does the story say about that idea?

Writing an Analysis Paragraph

Analyzing a Theme **257**

You can analyze the theme of a short story in one paragraph. Here is one way to develop the analysis:

- In the **topic sentence,** name the title, author, and theme of the story.
- In the **body sentences,** focus on the actions of the main characters.
- In the **closing sentence,** explain how these actions reveal the theme.

Sample Paragraph Analysis

In the following paragraph, a student writer does a brief thematic analysis.

> The **topic sentence** introduces the author, the story, and the theme (underlined).

> The sentences in the **body** focus on the main characters' actions.

> The **closing sentence** analyzes the theme.

Gift Giving

The theme of "The Gift of the Magi" by O. Henry is <u>love means making sacrifices.</u> A husband and wife named Jim and Della want to give each other a special holiday gift, even though they are poor. Della wants to give Jim a gold chain for his gold watch, and Jim wants to give Della a set of expensive combs for her beautiful, long hair. Jim and Della both sacrifice something they treasure. Della's prized possession is her hair, but she has it cut and sells it to a wig maker so she can afford to buy a gold chain for Jim's watch. Jim's prized possession is his gold watch, but he sells it to buy Della special combs for her hair. When they open their gifts, each of them realizes the sacrifice that the other has made. In the end, their best gift is knowing that they love each other so much that they would sacrifice their prized possessions for one another.

Literature

Write an analysis paragraph. Using the story you identified on the previous page, write a paragraph in which you briefly analyze the story's theme. Be sure to include the three parts explained above.

Writing an Analysis Paragraph

Before asking students to comment on the model paragraph, have them read the brief short story "The Gift of the Magi" (available online at the Project Gutenberg Web site, www.gutenberg.org). Do they agree with the student writer's analysis? Ask students to explain their answers.

Have students point out strengths of the model paragraph and ask them to give suggestions for improvement.

Remind students that although their chosen stories may have more than one theme, the brief paragraph format allows for discussion of only one theme. Students should focus on the theme they consider the most interesting or important.

✳ For more about writing effective paragraphs, see SE pages 561–579.

English Language Learners

Before reading "Gift Giving," define the following words to help students understand the analysis:

- sacrifices (things that are given up)
- expensive (worth a lot of money)
- possession (something someone owns)
- afford (have enough money to buy)

Advanced Learners

Have students use the analysis in the SE, or their own reading of "The Gift of the Magi," to explore alternate themes (for example, "Love is more important than possessions" or "The true gift is love"). Remind students that theme reveals a truth about human behavior and makes us think about why the story affects us.

Grammar Connection

Punctuating Titles

- **Proofreader's Guide** pages 634–635, 636–637
- *SkillsBook* pages 33, 36, 45
- *GrammarSnap* Common Uses of Capitalization

Understanding Your Goal

Three traits relate to the development of the content and the form. They provide a focus during prewriting, drafting, and revising.

- **Ideas**
- **Organization**
- **Voice**

The other three traits relate more to form. Make them a part of your focus during the revising and editing processes.

- **Word Choice**
- **Sentence Fluency**
- **Conventions**

＊ The six-point rubric on SE pages 290–291 is based on these traits. Reproducible six-, five-, and four-point rubrics for responses to literature are available on TE pages 770, 774, and 778.

Under Word Choice, draw students' attention to the reference to literary terms. Tell students they will use literary terms such as *simile* and *metaphor* to describe **figures of speech** *(see below)* the author uses. To review these and other literary terms, encourage students to consult two glossaries—"Learning Key Writing Terms" and "Using Writing Techniques"—in "A Writer's Resource."

＊ The glossaries are on SE pages 598–601.

 Literature Connections

In his review of the movie *4 Little Girls*, Roger Ebert uses quotes, historical facts, and personal reflection to discuss how well the film portrays a particularly tragic example of racism in the 1960s that resulted in the deaths of 4 young girls.

Have students write a review of a film they have seen recently. Discuss how the inclusion of details not presented in the film can help make the review more effective. For additional models of analyzing a theme, see the Reading-Writing Connections beginning on page TE-36.

258

Understanding Your Goal

Your goal in the rest of the chapter is to write an essay that analyzes a short story in order to reveal its main theme. The chart below lists the key traits of such an essay. Consult this chart and the rubric on pages **290–291** for guidance as you write.

Traits of a Response to Literature

- **Ideas**
  Write a thesis statement that explains your interpretation of the theme of the story. Then select specific details to support the statement.

- **Organization**
  Write clear beginning, middle, and ending paragraphs. Use transitions to effectively connect sentences and paragraphs.

- **Voice**
  Sound interested in, and knowledgeable about, the story you are analyzing.

- **Word Choice**
  Quote words and phrases from the story that support the theme. Use literary terms that reveal your understanding of the story.

- **Sentence Fluency**
  Write sentences that read well and flow smoothly.

- **Conventions**
  Correct all punctuation, capitalization, spelling, and grammar errors.

 Literature Connections: Professional critics respond to, or review, literature, but you may be more familiar with movie reviews. The famous movie critic Roger Ebert, for instance, has reviewed thousands of films. One example is his review of Spike Lee's 1997 documentary *4 Little Girls*.

Teaching Tip: Learning Figures of Speech

To help students study the figures of speech, have them make flash cards with the name of a particular type on one side of an index card and its definition on the other. They can challenge a partner to give examples of the figures of speech.

English Language Learners

Students may have difficulty understanding figures of speech in English. To aid understanding, make a chart that defines the literary terms they will be asked to use in their writing. Include examples, along with explanations of the examples. Display the chart for reference.

Response Essay

Guy de Maupassant's short story "The Necklace" tells about how a borrowed necklace changes a woman's life. The response essay below analyzes the story's plot and character development to reveal a main theme.

Beginning
The beginning names the story and author and reveals the theme in a thesis statement (underlined).

The Price of Envy

In Guy de Maupassant's short story "The Necklace," the main character, a young woman named Mathilde Loisel, longs to be part of wealthy nineteenth-century Parisian society. Her unhappiness with her low social standing leads her to make an incorrect assumption about a rich friend, an assumption that changes her life for the worse. <u>"The Necklace" shows that envy and shame can have terrible consequences.</u>

At the beginning of the story, de Maupassant immediately reveals Mme. Loisel's unhappiness. He describes her lowly status before marriage by listing the things she did not have: "With no dowry, no prospects, no way of any kind of being met . . ." (108). After marrying a "minor clerk," Mme. Loisel dreams of wealth while grieving over "the shabbiness of her apartment, the dinginess of the walls, the worn-out appearance of the chairs, the ugliness of the draperies" (108). By stringing together these descriptive phrases, the author emphasizes the depth of Mme. Loisel's sorrow.

Middle
Each middle paragraph explains a different stage in the development of the theme.

Mme. Loisel's husband is aware of his wife's misery. One day, he arrives home from work with an unexpected gift: an invitation to an important ball. He expects his wife to be thrilled; instead she is distraught. "What good is that to me?" she says (110). She reminds him that she has no fancy clothing to wear. "How much would a suitable outfit cost—one you could wear for other affairs too—something very simple?" he asks her (111). This response shows his concern for his wife's predicament yet expresses his basic thriftiness.

M. Loisel gives his wife four hundred francs to purchase a dress, but Mathilde still needs jewelry to wear. At M. Loisel's suggestion, she asks to borrow a necklace from Mme. Forestier, a wealthy friend Mathilde has not visited lately because of Mathilde's envy of her. Mme. Forestier is generous, and Mathilde tries on many pieces. After a lengthy search, she spots a diamond necklace and

Literature

Response Essay

Work through this model essay with the class, pointing out the elements that make it a good response to literature. If possible, have students read the short story as homework to prepare for reading the model essay.

Ideas

- The focus statement identifies the theme.
- The writer describes events that show how the main character got into difficulty and then struggled to do the right thing.

Organization

- The opening includes the story's title and the author.
- The middle describes the events in chronological order.
- The ending tells how the character is changed.

Voice & Word Choice

- The writer uses a natural but serious voice that is appropriate for the subject matter.
- The writer uses quotations from the story to illustrate examples.
- The vocabulary used is appropriate to the audience.

English Language Learners

To aid students' understanding, define the following words and phrases before reading the essay:

- dowry (money or property that a woman brings to her husband in marriage)
- prospects (expectations of finding a husband)
- shabbiness (in an ill-kept state; poorly cared for)
- dinginess (in a dirty state)

- draperies (heavy curtains)
- distraught (agitated with doubt or mental conflict)
- thriftiness (very concerned about spending money)
- belle of the ball (most popular or beautiful woman)
- drabness (in a dull, faded condition; without cheer)
- scrimp (to be stingy or frugal)
- imitation (not real)

Ask for students' comments about the essay. How does the writer reveal Mathilde's desperate desire to fit in with the wealthy Parisian society? Possible responses:

- The writer describes how Mathilde feels that a new dress is not enough for her to appear wealthy (see fourth paragraph).
- The writer describes how Mathilde "dashes out of the reception hall" so that she isn't seen wearing her "everyday shabby coat".

 Respond to the reading.

Answers

Ideas 1. She is no longer envious of Mme. Forestier by the time she confesses to replacing the necklace. **2.** The theme is revealed in the last paragraph, when the writer explains that Mathilde "would have lived a more comfortable life" if she had not placed such a high value on money and status.

Organization 3. chronologically

Voice & Word Choice 4. Yes. The detailed explanation of the story shows the writer's knowledge.

---

pleads, "Could I borrow that, just that and nothing else?" (112). Her friend readily gives permission.

Well dressed, beautiful, and charming, Mme. Loisel is the belle of the ball. For a brief moment, she feels as if she belongs with the people she envies. But her sense of shame is triggered when it is time to leave. She has no fine furs to put on, only an everyday shabby coat, so she dashes out of the reception hall into the cold night. M. Loisel follows and eventually finds a battered old cab to take them home. The author describes the cab as the kind seen only at night, "as if they were ashamed to show their drabness during daylight hours" (114).

Once home, Mme. Loisel realizes the necklace is gone. Her husband retraces their steps but cannot find it. Ashamed, they decide to replace the necklace without telling Mme. Forestier that it was lost. In order to buy a very expensive necklace that looks similar, M. Loisel drains his savings and borrows large sums of money. For the next ten years, the couple must scrimp and save and do backbreaking work to repay the loans.

After the loans are repaid, Mme. Loisel passes by Mme. Forestier, but Mme. Forestier does not recognize her; hard work had aged Mathilde dramatically. Mathilde decides to tell Mme. Forestier the truth. Shocked, Mme. Forestier reveals that the borrowed necklace was an imitation.

"The Necklace" is a literary classic because of de Maupassant's skillful character development and ironic twist at the end. Mathilde's misplaced envy and shame are no longer present at the time of her confession, when she smiles "with proud and simple joy" (117). However, if she had not assumed that wealthy people own only genuine diamonds—not overvalued money and status—she herself would have lived a more comfortable life.

Middle
The last two middle paragraphs focus on events that cause the main character to change.

Ending
The ending paragraph analyzes the use of irony in relation to the story's theme.

 Respond to the reading. Answer the following questions.

Ideas (1) How does the main character change by the end of the story? **(2)** Which detail in the analysis clearly reveals the theme?

Organization (3) How is the middle part of the essay organized?

Voice & Word Choice (4) Does the writer sound knowledgeable about the story? Explain.

Analyzing a Theme 261

Prewriting

The writing process begins with prewriting. The first step in writing your essay is to choose a story you have read recently and would like to analyze.

Keys to Effective Prewriting

1. Select an interesting story, one that you have recently read and enjoyed.

2. Identify a main theme in the story.

3. Looking at the beginning, middle, and ending of the story, find the key plot events and the characters' actions that reveal the main theme.

4. Write a clear thesis statement about the theme.

5. Decide how to organize the information in your middle paragraphs.

6. Write a topic sentence for each middle paragraph.

Literature

Prewriting
Keys to Effective Prewriting

Remind students of the purpose of the prewriting stage in the writing process: It is when the writer selects a topic, gathers details, and decides how to organize those details.

Keys to Effective Prewriting lists the process students will be guided through on SE pages 262–266.

Encourage students to make specific **story recommendations** *(see below)* if they think they know of a story that classmates would like.

Point out that item 2 on the list specifies that students should focus on a single theme in this essay. Encourage them to keep this in mind as they decide on a story to write about. As with the warm-up paragraph, they should choose a story with a strong central theme.

Technology Connections

Students can use the added features of the Net-text as they explore this stage of the writing process.

Write Source Online **Net-text**

Teaching Tip: Story Recommendations

Provide display space where students can post story recommendations and brief reviews. Encourage students to read recommended short stories for entertainment and also to get ideas for topics for the future.

English Language Learners

If recommended stories are too difficult for students to read on their own, allow students to view films of short stories for their analyses. Or suggest simpler chapter books to analyze. It may also be possible for students to find translations of stories they have read in their first language.

Prewriting Finding Topic Ideas

Note that this section focuses on analyzing the story in terms of the main character's actions. Briefly meet with students to review their choices, guiding them to choose stories with strong main characters.

Prewriting Choosing a Topic

Explain that a good way for a writer to focus his or her thoughts is to write a single sentence describing what a story is about. If a student has trouble describing a story in one sentence, he or she may not have developed a clear enough understanding of the story—or perhaps the story is too complicated to use for an essay.

Prewriting Finding Topic Ideas

A graphic organizer like the ideas chart below can help you think of possible stories to write about. This chart lists favorite stories, a statement about the basic plot in each story, and a comment about the main character.

Ideas Chart

Story and author	What the story is about	What the main character is like
"The Birds" by Daphne du Maurier	Swarms of birds attack a family living on the coast of England.	Nat is a brave father who tries to protect his family.
"Helen on Eighty-sixth Street" by Wendi Kaufman	A girl tries to understand why her dad went away.	Vita is very smart.
*"Thank You, Ma'm" by Langston Hughes	A teenage boy tries to rob an old lady, and she drags him home with her.	Roger is a tough kid who is not so tough when he gets caught.

 Consider possible topics. Make an ideas chart like the one above. List short stories that you have read and liked. For each title, write one sentence that tells what the story is about and one sentence that tells about the main character.

Choosing a Topic

It will be easier to write your essay if you choose a story that you know and enjoy. Be sure that you have a clear understanding of the story's plot and the actions of the main character. In your analysis, you will be expected to trace the development of the theme through the main character's thoughts, feelings, and actions.

 Choose your topic. Review the stories in your chart. Put an asterisk next to the title you choose. Then write a few sentences that explain the reason for your choice. (Perhaps you identify with the main character, enjoy the author's writing style, or so on.)

Struggling Learners

Tell students to use the following suggestions to help them list possible topics:

- Find a story that you enjoyed.
- Look for a story that gives a lesson or message to think about.
- Choose a story with a memorable main character.

Finding a Theme

Sometimes a theme is clearly stated, but often it is found deep within a story. Here are three ways to uncover a theme.

- **Look for clues in the title.**
  "Irraweka, Mischief-Maker"

- **Look for the author's statements about life.**
  "The very best thing in all this world that can befall a man is to be born lucky."

  —Mark Twain, "Luck"

- **Identify a life lesson that the main character learns.**
  In the short story "To Build a Fire," the main character learns that he must accept his unfortunate fate.

▸ Try It!

Find a theme. Answer the following questions to find the theme of your story. Ask your teacher for help if you still can't identify the theme after answering these questions.

1. Does the title say anything about the main character? If so, what?

2. Does the title say anything about a life lesson? If so, what?

3. Does the author make any statements about life? List them.

4. How does the main character change in the story?

5. What does the main character learn?

Finish this sentence. After answering the "Try It!" questions, complete the sentence below to identify a main theme in your story.

A main theme in my story is _____.

Focus on the Traits

Ideas Authors sometimes use figures of speech to convey ideas to the reader. Figures of speech include *idioms, similes, metaphors,* the *oxymoron* and *hyperbole* (see pages **598–601**). Look for these as you analyze your short story. They often hold clues to theme and character development.

Literature

English Language Learners

Because figures of speech are difficult for students who are still learning English, have them focus on only one or two. Similes may be the easiest for students to recognize, because they often use *as* or *like* in the comparison. Ask students to look for similes in their story.

Prewriting Finding a Theme

Ask students to reread their stories, looking for clues to find the themes. Explain that it's important to be very familiar with a story before writing about it, and point out that it's often possible to find something new in a story when rereading it.

Focus on the Traits

Ideas
To help students become familiar with figures of speech, provide definitions and invite students to find examples in their stories.

- idiom—a phrase that means something different from what the words actually say
- simile—a comparison of two things using *like* or *as*
- metaphor—a comparison of two things without using *like* or *as*
- oxymoron—a connection of two words with opposite meanings
- hyperbole—exaggeration used to emphasize a point

Prewriting Gathering Details

Point out that students can think of this chart as a kind of time line because it addresses the story events in chronological order. Distribute photocopies of the reproducible Time Line (TE page 816) for students to use as a character chart, if desired.

Tell students that a common error for beginning writers is to summarize (just tell what happened) instead of doing an analysis (use what happened to explain the theme).

 Literature Connections

Author info: Encourage students to discover facts about the author's life and experiences. Inspire your students by reading from *Guts: The True Stories Behind* Hatchet *and the Brian Books* by Gary Paulsen. In this book, the famed young adult writer tells about the experiences he had that led to writing his stories of adventure and hardship. He tells of being an early responder in Colorado who, because of the great distances, witnessed more than one heart attack. He drew on these experiences when he wrote about the pilot's death by heart attack in *Hatchet*.

Read the first few pages to your students to inspire them to find similar background information about the stories or books that they are analyzing.

264

"My books deal with characters who feel rejected and have to painfully learn how to deal with other people."
—Alice Childress

Prewriting Gathering Details

One way to gather details for a story analysis is to make a chart of the main character's thoughts, feelings, and actions. The sample chart below is for the essay on pages **269–272**.

Character Chart

> **Story Title:** "Thank You, Ma'm"
>
> **Theme:** Forgiveness is sweet.
>
> **First Stage:** The main character's thoughts, feelings, and actions in the **beginning** of the story
> — tries stealing a woman's purse
> — falls down
> — grabbed by the woman and dragged to her apartment
>
> **Middle Stage:** The main character's thoughts, feelings, and actions in the **middle** part of the story
> — fears Mrs. Jones
> — wants to run away from her
> — admits stealing the purse because he needed money for shoes
> — discovers Mrs. Jones understands what it's like to be poor
> — wants to be trusted
>
> **Final Stage:** The main character's thoughts, feelings, and actions in the **last** part of the story
> — accepts money from Mrs. Jones for a pair of shoes
> — is too proud to say more than thank you

 Chart your main character. Make a chart like the one above. List your main character's thoughts, feelings, and actions during the beginning, middle, and ending parts of the story.

Prewrite

Advanced Learners

Challenge students to think about other clues that tell the reader what a character is like. For example:

- What does the character look like?
- What do other characters say about the character?

- What does the author say directly about the character?
- Why might these clues reveal more (or less) than the thoughts, feelings, and actions of the character?

Encourage students to share their ideas in a group discussion.

Using Direct Quotations

You can use quotations from the story to show how a character talks, acts, thinks, and feels. The student writer of the essay about "Thank You, Ma'm" gathered the following revealing quotations. Consider what each quotation reveals about the main character.

Sample Quotations

"He did not trust the woman not to trust him. And he did not want to be mistrusted now."
— not used to being trusted
— suddenly wants to be trusted

"He looked as if he were fourteen or fifteen, frail and willow-wild."
— thin, lonely, and scared
— looks weak, but proves to be strong

"He barely managed to say 'thank you' before she shut the door."
— got Mrs. Jones's message
— can't put what he's experienced into words

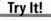

Try It!

Read the quotations above. Explain what each quotation reveals about the story and the main character.

Prewrite **Gather quotations.** Review your character chart (page 264). Make a list of direct quotations that reveal something about the main character.

Focus on the Traits

Organization You can't talk about the theme of a short story without also discussing the plot and the main character. (*Theme, plot,* and *characterization* are the three main elements of literature.) As you discuss the plot and characterization, your analysis will naturally be organized chronologically, or by time. However, an analysis can also be organized by order of importance.

Literature

Prewriting **Using Direct Quotations**

Encourage students to list quotations that express the story's theme or reveal things about the characters. For example, the quotation by Mark Twain on SE page 263 expresses a theme.

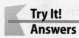 For more about using quotations, see SE pages 570 and 597.

Try It! Answers

If possible, have students read the short story "Thank you, Ma'm" before evaluating the quotations.

Possible answers:
1. The circular wording echoes the character's confused state of mind and expresses his desire for trust.
2. This describes the boy's appearance the way a casual observer would. It shows that the observer and the boy were strangers.
3. The boy can't express his gratitude, but he feels it.

Focus on the Traits

Organization
Ask students to tell why details in their essays will naturally be in chronological order. (Because analyzing the plot line means thinking about events in the order they happened.)

English Language Learners

Give students a mini lesson on how to use quotation marks correctly in English, as their usage may be different in their first languages. Point out the third example of the sample quotations on SE page 265, which shows the correct use of quotation marks within a quotation.

Prewriting Writing a Thesis Statement

Have students read and discuss the quotation by John Rowe Townsend. Encourage them to think of their stories as questions posed by the authors. The themes they choose to write about are possible answers to the questions.

Organizing the Middle Paragraphs of Your Essay

Acknowledge that it can be difficult to predict exactly how many middle paragraphs will be needed for the analysis. Have students use their character charts as a guide to write four topic sentences. Assure students that when they write their drafts they may rephrase or add to the sentences as needed.

266

"I'd like to explore moral problems, but I don't like to lay down the law about them! Books are for asking questions, not for answering them."
—John Rowe Townsend

Prewriting Writing a Thesis Statement

Now that you have gathered details, you are ready to write your **thesis statement**—the main point that your paper will illustrate and explain. The thesis statement connects the main character to the theme.

main character A teenager named Roger	+	**theme** Forgiveness is sweet.	=	**thesis statement** Roger learns that forgiveness is sweet.

Form a focus. Write a thesis statement for your response essay using the formula above.

Organizing the Middle Paragraphs of Your Essay

Each middle paragraph should address a different stage in the development of the theme. The writer of the sample essay on pages **269–272** planned his middle paragraphs by writing a topic sentence for each one.

Topic Sentence 1 (First Stage)

The story begins when Roger grabs a woman's purse.

Topic Sentence 2 (Middle Stage)

Mrs. Jones understands Roger better than he knows.

Topic Sentence 3 (Middle Stage)

Roger, however, still isn't sure about Mrs. Jones.

Topic Sentence 4 (Final Stage)

After supper, Mrs. Jones gives Roger ten dollars to buy some blue suede shoes.

Plan your middle paragraphs. Review your character chart from page **264**. Add any important details you may have left out. Write a topic sentence for each middle paragraph of your essay, covering the first, middle, and final stages of your story's theme.

Analyzing a Theme **267**

Writing

Once you have finished your prewriting, you can begin writing your essay. Your thesis statement, character chart, quotations, and topic sentences will guide your writing.

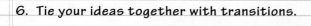

Keys to Effective Writing

1. Write on every other line so that you have room to make changes later.

2. Use your thesis statement and topic sentences to organize your paragraphs.

3. Support your topic sentences with specific details from the story.

4. Refer to your character chart and quotations for details, adding more if needed.

5. Get all of your thoughts on paper.

6. Tie your ideas together with transitions.

Literature

Writing

Keys to Effective Writing

Remind students that the writing stage is when they get to write, or draft, their ideas on paper.

Keys to Effective Writing lists the process students will be guided through on SE pages 268–272.

Students may benefit from creating an outline. This will help them organize the details they plan to use in each paragraph of their essays. Using the outline format, have students list the thesis statements and topic sentences as main points and then have them add their ideas for supporting details underneath each main point.

✳ For more about outlines, see SE pages 590–591.

Writing Workshop

On the next five pages, you'll find minilessons that help writers develop a strong beginning, middle, and ending during individual work time. These minilessons can also provide small-group or whole-class instruction.

Technology Connections

Students can use the added features of the Net-text as they explore this stage of the writing process.

 Write Source Online **Net-text**

Teaching Tip

Once students have created their outlines, remind them that they can still change their minds about the organization of their essays. Encourage students to reread their stories and look for new information and ideas. They can alter their outlines by adding, deleting, moving, or combining ideas.

Writing Getting the Big Picture

Tell students that they should now be ready to begin writing. Suggest that they complete these final preparatory steps during their first writing session:

- Review their planning notes, making sure they know how the information will be organized into the beginning, middle, and ending of their essays.
- **Reread** *(see below),* or at least skim through, the story one more time, looking for important details they might have missed.
- Add any new ideas to their planning notes.
- Refer to the notes as they begin to write. It may be helpful to cross off details as they are mentioned in the drafts.

268

Writing Getting the Big Picture

Remember that an essay includes three main parts—the beginning, the middle, and the ending. You are ready to begin writing your response if you have . . .

- discovered the theme,
- written a clear thesis statement that ties the theme to the main character, and
- planned and organized your middle paragraphs.

The chart below shows how the three parts of a response essay fit together. The examples are from the essay on pages **269–272**.

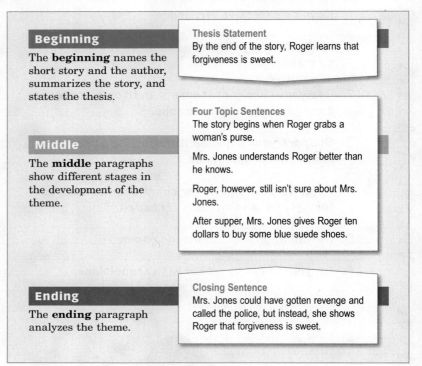

Beginning

The **beginning** names the short story and the author, summarizes the story, and states the thesis.

Thesis Statement
By the end of the story, Roger learns that forgiveness is sweet.

Middle

The **middle** paragraphs show different stages in the development of the theme.

Four Topic Sentences
The story begins when Roger grabs a woman's purse.

Mrs. Jones understands Roger better than he knows.

Roger, however, still isn't sure about Mrs. Jones.

After supper, Mrs. Jones gives Roger ten dollars to buy some blue suede shoes.

Ending

The **ending** paragraph analyzes the theme.

Closing Sentence
Mrs. Jones could have gotten revenge and called the police, but instead, she shows Roger that forgiveness is sweet.

Teaching Tip: Rereading

Encourage students to look back at their story as often as is necessary for them to become familiar with it. Suggest tips such as the following to help them do this more effectively:

- Use spare time—such as when they are riding on the bus or waiting for an appointment— for rereading.
- Try reading the story aloud at least once during the process.
- Use sticky notes to remember ideas that come to them as they read. They can use the notes to mark telling quotations.

Starting Your Essay

The opening of your analysis should include . . .

- **the title and author of the short story,**
- **background information about the plot and characters, and**
- **your thesis statement.**

Beginning Paragraph

The sample paragraph below names the title and the author of the short story. It also includes background information about the main character and the plot, and ends with a thesis statement identifying a main theme. (Also see the sample beginning on page **259**.)

> The first part introduces the story and gives the thesis statement (underlined).

"Thank You, Ma'm" by Langston Hughes is a short story about forgiveness. In the story, a boy named Roger tries to steal a woman's purse. The woman surprisingly grabs him and drags him home with her. While at this woman's house, Roger is forced to confront his actions but in a way that seems very positive and helpful. <u>By the end of the story, Roger learns that forgiveness is sweet.</u>

Write

Write your beginning. Write the beginning paragraph of your essay. Include the name of the story and its author, a brief plot summary, and your thesis statement. You may have to write more than one version of this paragraph before it says what you want it to say.

Tip

If you have trouble getting started, review these tips. One or more of them may trigger your thinking.

- **Talk about your story with a classmate** before you begin to write.
- **Write freely** without worrying about producing the perfect analysis right away. First drafts are often called *rough drafts* for a reason.
- **Include enough details** to support your thesis statement.
- **Show your personal interest** in the story and in your analysis by using precise, careful language.
- **Focus on these key traits of writing:** ideas, organization, and voice.

Writing Starting Your Essay

If students need additional help getting started, suggest that they take the following steps:

- Use the model paragraph as a template, copying the form but filling in the details specific to their own topics.
- Once students have filled in all the details, they should go back over their paragraphs, adjusting them as needed to express their own voices.

Struggling Learners

Some students may be unable to express their personal interest in their stories. Encourage them to make connections to the stories by thinking about the following:

- how the stories relate to them,
- how the stories make them feel, or
- how the characters in the stories feel.

Advanced Learners

Challenge students to write three openers on separate slips of paper. Have them mark their first, second, and third choices on the back of each slip. Then have them ask writing partners to rate them. See if they agree.

Writing Developing the Middle Part

Ask students to respond to the model paragraphs. Do the paragraphs focus on the feelings, thoughts, and actions of the characters? (Have students explain their answers.) Challenge students to tell how each paragraph supports the theme that "forgiveness is sweet." Possible responses:

- Paragraph 1: Describes Roger's crime and the woman's strong reaction. It isn't yet clear how she feels, so the boy is afraid.
- Paragraph 2: Describes the point in their relationship when Roger realizes that Mrs. Jones understands him. But she hasn't forgiven him, so he's still nervous.
- Paragraph 3: Roger remains worried, but Mrs. Jones's actions make it clear that she likes him. He wants to stay to hear her out.
- Paragraph 4: Mrs. Jones expresses her forgiveness by giving Roger good advice, giving him the money he needs, and letting him go. Roger experiences the sweetness of being forgiven.

270

Writing Developing the Middle Part

Each middle paragraph should explore a stage in the development of the story and how it relates to the theme. Your writing should focus on the thoughts, feelings, and actions of the characters during each stage.

Middle Paragraphs

These paragraphs show the development of the theme throughout the story.

> The first middle paragraph focuses on the first stage of the story.

The story begins when Roger grabs a woman's purse. Its heaviness makes Roger fall. This hyperbole makes clear the weight of the purse: "It had everything in it but hammer and nails" (211). The woman grabs Roger and shakes him until his teeth rattle. She says, "When I get through with you, sir, you are going to remember Mrs. Luella Bates Washington Jones" (211). Roger struggles to get free, but Mrs. Jones is strong. Hughes writes, "She dragged the boy inside, down a hall, and into a large kitchenette-furnished room at the rear of the house" (212). Finally, she turns Roger loose. In fear, "Roger looked at the door—looked at the woman—looked at the door" (212). However, he doesn't run. Instead, he obeys her order to wash his face. From his "frail and willow-wild" (212) appearance, she guesses he is hungry. But if he is hungry, Roger is too proud to say so. He tells Mrs. Jones that he stole the purse because he wanted money to buy some blue suede shoes.

> Each new paragraph begins with a topic sentence (underlined) that introduces a new stage in the story.

Mrs. Jones understands Roger better than he knows. She says that when she was young she wanted things that she couldn't get. She says that she did bad things, things that she won't tell Roger. This is when the two characters connect. They share an understanding of what it means to be poor.

Roger, however, still isn't sure about Mrs. Jones. He wants to run away, but something also makes him want to stay: "He did not trust the woman not to trust him. And he did not want to be mistrusted now" (213). As Mrs. Jones makes supper, Roger sits on the far side of the room where she can see him. Surprisingly, she isn't watching him. Even more surprising is the fact that she leaves her purse near him. It would be easy

English Language Learners

To help students understand the text, define the following words before reading the passage:

- rattle (shake together)
- struggles (fights)
- loose (free)
- obeys (follows)
- frail (weak)
- embarrass (to cause to feel self-conscious)

Struggling Learners

Have students write out and number their topic sentences. Then have them read the topic sentences in order. Does the order make sense? Are there clear transitions from one paragraph to the next?

Analyzing a Theme   **271**

The last stage shows how the main character deals with his surprising life lesson.

for Roger to take it and run, but he doesn't. They eat supper, and it's clear that she cares about him because she doesn't ask about his folks, where he lives, or anything else that will embarrass him.

After supper, Mrs. Jones gives Roger ten dollars to buy some blue suede shoes. She tells him not to make the mistake of stealing someone else's purse. She says, "Shoes come by devilish like that will burn your feet" (214). Then Mrs. Jones leads Roger to the door and reminds him to behave himself. Pride keeps Roger from saying more than "Thank you, ma'm" (214). He wants to say more, but he doesn't. Luella Bates Washington Jones shuts the door, and Roger walks away. They never see each other again.

Write

Write your middle paragraphs. Use your topic sentences, character chart, and direct-quotation list to guide your writing. Try to include one or two figures of speech from the story to enhance the theme for the reader. (For a list of figures of speech, see pages **600–601** in this book.)

Creating Coherence

When the details of an essay are tied together in a way that produces clear ideas, the essay has **coherence**. Repeating key words is one way to give your writing coherence. In the three examples below, the colored key word creates a transition between two sentences.

> From his "frail and willow-wild" (212) appearance, she guesses he is hungry. But if he is hungry, Roger is too proud to say so.

> Pride keeps Roger from saying more than "Thank you, ma'm" (214). He wants to say more, but he doesn't.

> Surprisingly, she isn't watching him. Even more surprising is the fact that she leaves her purse near him.

Literature

Ask students to point out the most effective details the student writer uses. Possible responses:

■ The quotation that begins "When I get through with you. . . . " sounds very threatening, but the reality turns out quite differently—and Mrs. Jones is correct that he will never forget her.

■ The dialogue that is paraphrased in the second middle paragraph describes the turning point in the relationship.

Writing **Creating Coherence**

Explain that **coherence** *(see below)* comes from the Latin verb meaning "to stick"; the ideas should "stick" together.

Point out that one way to create coherence is to use smooth transitions. Challenge students to suggest other ways to make writing *coherent*. Responses may include the following:

■ Use effective introductory phrases.

■ Make sure all pronouns have a clear antecedent.

■ Fully develop one idea at a time.

Teaching Tip: Coherence

To provide students with a good example of coherent writing, have them turn ahead to SE pages 304–305 and read the Booker T. Washington excerpt. Ask students to give examples of how Washington creates coherence. Possible responses:

● Repeating key words: *I was asked not long ago . . . Until*

that question was asked; would fall off the horse, and often I would fall with it; I would have to wait, sometimes for many hours . . . the hours while waiting

● Effective introductory transitions: *From the time that I can remember anything; Besides, when I was late getting home*

English Language Learners

Tell students that if they choose to repeat words, they should use each one only two or three times in some paragraphs. Ask students to use a thesaurus to vary their word choice in other paragraphs.

Writing Ending Your Essay

Explain that an effective ending paragraph often mentions something new related to the theme. Ask students to identify the new elements introduced by the student writer in the model ending. Possible responses:

- the idea that strength is not just physical force—it is also moral force
- the mention of the old saying "revenge is sweet" to emphasize the difference between Mrs. Jones's response and what Roger had expected

272

Writing Ending Your Essay

Beginning
Middle
Ending

Your essay starts with a thesis statement that connects the theme to a main character in the story. In the middle paragraphs, you show how the theme develops through the plot and the actions of the main character. The ending is your final chance to comment on and explore the theme. Here are some suggestions for this final part of your essay.

- Show how a character has changed.
- Use a quotation from the story.
- Predict how the theme might affect the character in the future.
- State the theme as a basic truth or saying about life.

Ending Paragraphs

The ending paragraph below shows what Roger learns and states the theme of the short story as a basic truth of life.

> The ending explores the main character's actions and restates the theme.

In the beginning of the story, Roger thinks that he can overpower Mrs. Jones and steal her purse. Then, as the story goes on, he learns that she is much stronger than he is, in more ways than one. She is both physically and morally strong. Even though Roger appears "frail and willow-wild," he proves that he, too, is strong and can handle a very humbling experience. There is an old saying that "Revenge is sweet." <u>Mrs. Jones could have gotten revenge and called the police, but instead, she shows Roger that forgiveness is sweet.</u>

Write

Write your ending and form a complete first draft. Using one or more of the suggestions at the top of the page, write the last paragraph of your essay. Then make a clean copy of your essay. Double-space or write on every other line so that you have room for revising.

"Good writing is about making good choices when it comes to picking the tools you plan to write with."
—Stephen King

English Language Learners

To help students understand the text, define the following words before reading the paragraph:

- overpower (beat down)
- morally (following "good" rules of conduct)
- humbling (humiliating)
- revenge (getting even)

Advanced Learners

Have each student use the suggestions at the top of the page to write a new ending paragraph for the sample essay. Then have students meet to compare and evaluate their new endings.

Revising

Now that your first draft is complete, you are ready to begin the revision process. Focus on ideas, organization, and other key traits to make changes that will improve your writing.

Keys to Effective Revising

1. Read your essay aloud to see whether it holds together from start to finish.

2. Check your thesis statement to be sure it includes the theme of the story.

3. Be sure that each middle paragraph analyzes the thesis statement.

4. Check your voice to see if it sounds knowledgeable.

5. Review your word choice and sentence fluency to be sure that your analysis reads smoothly.

6. Use the editing and proofreading marks inside the back cover of this book.

Literature

Revising

Keys to Effective Revising

Remind students that the revising stage is when writers have an opportunity to make improvements to their first drafts. At this stage they can think about refinements they might not have considered when they were drafting.

Keys to Effective Revising lists the process students will be guided through on SE pages 274–284.

Note that in addition to the six items on the revising list, the following pages will guide students through more detailed aspects of the revising process.

Suggest that as students work through the section, they can create their own "keys to revising list" by adding information they find helpful. They can clip their customized revising lists to this page of their books for future use.

Peer Responding

Have students read and respond to one another's writing. For more on promoting constructive peer responses, see TE pages 55–60.

Writing Workshop

Instead of assigning all of the revising activities, let peer responses or self-assessments direct students to the activities they need. As an alternative, use the activities as minilessons.

Technology Connections

Have students use the Writing Network features of the Net-text to comment on each other's drafts.

 Write Source Online **Net-text**

Struggling Learners

Students may feel that their first drafts are the best they can do. Remind them that most writers write and rewrite their first drafts many times. Suggest that students read their first drafts aloud to a parent or to a peer partner. Tell them to listen for places where word choice or fluency could be improved or to look for more effective ways to end or start their essays.

Revising for Ideas

The rubric strips that run across all of the revising pages (SE pages 274–283) are provided to help students focus their revising and are related to the full rubric on SE pages 290–291.

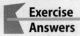
Exercise
Answers

1. description to show setting
2. specific phrase to clarify the idea
3. dialogue to help the reader understand the character
4. figure of speech to reinforce an idea related to the theme

---

274

Revising for Ideas

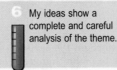

6 My ideas show a complete and careful analysis of the theme.

5 My essay has a clear thesis statement and uses quotations and paraphrasing.

4 My essay has a thesis statement but needs more supporting quotations.

When you revise for *ideas,* be sure that you have effectively used quotations from the story and that you have clearly paraphrased key ideas. Use the rubric strip above to help you revise.

Have I effectively used quotations?

You have effectively used quotations from the text if they clearly and effortlessly support the main points in your analysis. An author's exact words can add a great deal of meaning to your analysis. Here are some effective ways to use quotations from a text.

1. Use story dialogue to help the reader understand a character.
2. Use an author's figure of speech to reinforce an important idea related to the theme.
3. Include a description from the story to show its setting or mood.
4. Cite a specific word or phrase from the text to make an idea clearer.

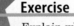
Exercise

Explain which of the ideas above is illustrated by each sentence below.

1. "She dragged the boy inside, down a hall, and into a large kitchenette-furnished room at the rear of the house" (212).
2. Mathilde . . . smiles "with proud and simple joy" (117).
3. She says, "When I get through with you, sir, you are going to remember Mrs. Luella Bates Washington Jones" (211).
4. The author describes the cab as the kind seen only at night, "as if they were ashamed to show their drabness during daylight hours" (114).

Tip

Remember that you cannot use an author's exact words as your own. This is called **plagiarism**. Always give the author credit when using a quotation. (See pages **369–370**.)

English Language Learners

If students have difficulty answering the **Exercise** questions independently, have them work with English-proficient partners. The partners can help clarify the meanings of the sentences and match them to the four uses of quotations.

3 I need to improve my thesis statement, and I need more supporting details.

2 I need a thesis statement and supporting details from the text.

1 I need to learn more about how to analyze a theme.

Have I paraphrased effectively?

You have paraphrased effectively if you clearly express an author's thoughts and ideas using your own words. (Paraphrasing means using your own words to restate someone else's ideas.)

Author's words: "She was a tiny woman who lit up the room when she entered. Everyone loved Ramona."

Paraphrase: Ramona was small, but her lively personality made everyone notice when she entered the room.

Exercise

Read the paragraph below. Then rewrite it as a paraphrase.

> Luke looked out at the empty field. He imagined himself kicking a field goal and winning the game for his team. A voice behind him said, "Hey, Mahoney." It was Hector Rodrigez, the team running back. "Whoa, dude, what's with the leg cast? Does Coach Karls know you're out for the season?"

Revise

Review your first draft for ideas. Be sure that you have used effective quotations from the story and that you have paraphrased important ideas using your own words.

Literature

Ideas
The writer adds a quotation from the story to support the idea of trust.

Roger, however, still isn't sure about Mrs. Jones. He wants to run away, but something makes him want to stay. As Mrs. Jones makes supper, Roger sits on the far side of the room . . .

"He did not trust the woman not to trust him. And he did not want to be mistrusted now" (213).

English Language Learners

If students are analyzing stories from their first languages, remind them to treat a direct translation like a quotation, not a paraphrase. Have students provide English definitions for key words and underline the original words, if handwritten, or use italics on a computer.

✳ See Foreign Words, SE page 636.

Struggling Learners

Tell students that before they begin paraphrasing, they should read the selection carefully at least twice, or until they know the story well enough to feel comfortable about retelling it.

Encourage students to look up any unfamiliar words.

Point out that paraphrasing is the most efficient way to explain important points that would otherwise require the use of long quotations. Paraphrasing is also useful if the students have already used quite a few quotations in their essays.

Encourage students to try to express the author's ideas in their own words (in writing or by retelling) whenever they want to check or reinforce their understanding.

Exercise Answers

Possible Paraphrase

Luke looks at the field and daydreams about kicking a winning field goal. Then he's brought back to reality by his teammate, Hector Rodrigez, who sees the cast on Luke's leg and asks if the coach knows yet that Luke is sidelined for the season.

Revising for Organization

276

Exercise Answers

Possible Answers

1. The word *beauty* is echoed in both sentences to help create coherence.
2. The right observer ("beholder") can find beauty even in unlikely places.
3. a rainbow

Revising for Organization

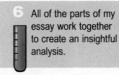

6 All of the parts of my essay work together to create an insightful analysis.

5 The beginning, middle, and ending of my essay work well together.

4 All my ideas flow smoothly. My thesis statement and my ending need a stronger connection.

Organization is the way ideas are arranged in an essay. The beginning, middle, and ending parts should all work well together. The rubric strip above will help you.

How can I connect my thesis statement and my final analysis?

You can connect your thesis statement and final analysis by sharing an insight about the story and the theme in your closing sentences.

Exercise

Read the following paragraph analysis. Then explain how the topic sentence (underlined) connects with the closing statement. What does the final statement say about the theme (topic sentence)? What are the flowers compared to?

> <u>In the story "The Window Box," Gretchen Bates discovers that beauty lies in the eye of the beholder.</u> Gretchen, a 20-something woman, lives alone in a rundown apartment building. When she looks out her third-story window, she sees only a dark alley below. One cool, autumn day, she sees an old woman in the alley planting something in a window box. She forgets about it until springtime when she sits at her window complaining about the cold draft. Suddenly, she sees a rainbow. Orange, yellow, and purplish-red tulips are spilling out of the window box, bringing life to the dismal alley. Just like a rainbow brightens a stormy sky, colorful flowers helped Gretchen to change her attitude. Gretchen learns that there can be beauty, even in a dark alley, if she looks for it.

Reread your first draft for connection. Decide if your thesis statement and your final analysis connect.

English Language Learners

When doing the **Exercise** activity, first discuss the closing statement in the paragraph. Then relate that statement to the topic sentence so that students can easily see the relationship between the parts.

Analyzing a Theme 277

3 I need more transitions to improve sentence flow, and I also need to rewrite the ending.

2 I need clearer topic sentences that relate to the theme.

1 I need to learn how to organize a response to literature.

How can I make my ideas flow smoothly?

Your ideas will flow smoothly if you use transitions to connect them. The bold words in the paragraph below are transitions that connect ideas.

> **By nightfall** he was fatigued, footsore, famishing. The thought of his wife and children urged him on. **At last** he found a road which led him in what he knew to be the right direction. It was as wide and straight as a city street. **Yet** it seemed untraveled. No fields bordered it, no dwelling anywhere.
>
> —Ambrose Bierce, "An Occurrence at Owl Creek Bridge"

► Exercise

Carefully read the following passage. Then identify the transitional words or phrases that were used to connect ideas.

1   At the beginning of the novel, Alfred Brooks, a high school dropout, has
2 few prospects. He is terrorized by a local gang and worries about losing his
3 best friend to a world of drugs and crime. Then, surprisingly, Brooks decides
4 to try boxing. While getting started, he meets Vito Donatelli, who becomes one
5 of the important influences in his life.

 Review your first draft for idea flow. Make sure that you have used transitions to make your ideas flow smoothly from beginning to end.

Revise

Organization
Two transitions are added.

> *Finally,*
> She turns Roger loose. In fear, "Roger looked at the
>
> door—looked at the woman—looked at the door" (212).
> *However,*
> He doesn't run. . . .

Literature

Invite a volunteer to read aloud the sample paragraph by Ambrose Bierce. Point out how transitions help the ideas in the sentences flow, one to the next, allowing the reader to move through them smoothly.

Challenge students to try other transitions in the sample, replacing *By nightfall, At last,* and *Yet.* Can students find other transitions that work as well to connect ideas? Why or why not?

✱ For more transition words, see SE pages 592–593.

Ask students to find a passage in the story they're writing about that shows effective use of transitions. Have several students read their passage to the class. Allow time for listeners to identify the transitions.

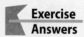 **Exercise Answers**

At the beginning of the novel; Then; While getting started

Revising for Voice

Note that the two sample passages are about the short story "To Build a Fire" by Jack London. Explain that the events describe the character's desperate attempts to survive extreme cold. Ask students to examine the passages. Have them suggest reasons the second (interested) example works better than the first (not interested). Responses may include the following:

- The first example simply tells what the man did, while the second gives details about how he did it (*he gripped a dry match between his teeth; ever so gently;* and so on).
- The first example uses long sentences with similar structure, while the second example uses sentences of varying lengths and structures.
- Use of the comment *Surprisingly* brings in the interested voice of the writer.

Revising for Voice

6 My writer's voice sounds distinctive and engaging right from the start.

5 My voice sounds interesting and natural throughout the analysis.

4 My voice sounds interesting, but it needs to be more natural.

Voice is the way your writing sounds. The rubric strip above and the information below will help you revise your analysis so that it sounds interesting, thoughtful, and natural.

Does my voice sound as if I am interested in my analysis?

Your writing voice will sound interesting if you do two things:

1. Show that you truly care about the story.
2. Demonstrate a clear understanding of one of the story's main themes.

Not Interested

In the passage below, the writer's ideas are too general.

> The man was unable to move his fingers, but he still got a fire started. If the fire threw off enough heat, he might survive. But then snow from a branch above him fell on the fire and put it out.

Interested

The voice in this passage clearly shows that the writer cares about, and understands, the story he is analyzing.

> The man's fingers were frozen stiff. So he gripped a dry match between his teeth and struck it against his jacket zipper. Surprisingly, the match lit. Then the man carefully set the match on a clump of dry moss, which also caught flame. Ever so gently, he started to build the fire. . . .

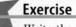

Exercise

Write the first five things that come to mind about a story you have read. Then rewrite your thoughts, making them sound more interesting.

Revise

Check for an interested voice. Read your analysis out loud to see whether you sound interested in the story. Revise any passages that display an uninterested voice.

Analyzing a Theme 279

3 My voice needs to sound more interesting and natural.

2 I need to create more voice in my analysis.

1 I need to learn more about voice.

Does my voice sound natural and engaging?

Your voice sounds natural and engaging if it reflects your personality and connects with the reader. Keep these tips in mind.

- Your writing should sound the way you do when you talk with a classmate in a "relaxed" classroom setting.
- Imagine yourself reading your essay aloud to the class. Your classmates should enjoy what you have to say. You should use words that they will understand.

Keeping It Natural

Avoid writing that sounds too formal or too informal.

Formal

The man was extremely shaken by his extraordinary experience, and he was exhilarated to return to his residence.

Informal

The guy got freaked out by what happened, and then he headed for home.

Natural and Engaging

After his strange experience, the man was happy to go home.

 Check for a natural voice. Reread your essay, marking any sections that sound too formal or too informal. Rewrite them so that they sound natural.

Revise

> **Voice**
> Overly formal language is rewritten.

> After supper, Mrs. Jones gives Roger ten dollars to
>   tells   not to
> buy some blue suede shoes. She ~~advises~~ him ~~to never again~~
>   mistake   else's
> make the ~~transgression~~ of stealing someone's purse.

Literature

As students read their work aloud, they should note

- whether the sentences are easy to read and follow, and
- whether the writing sounds natural, not hesitating or forced.

Tell students that if they stumble over sentences or must pause to get their bearings, they should revise those sentences for greater clarity.

Point out that the tone of a piece of writing depends on its purpose and audience. Note that although students have been instructed to aim for a relaxed, natural tone for this essay, there are times when their writing should be more or less formal. Talk about the kinds of writing that might be more formal and less formal.

- formal—a science report, a wedding invitation, a business letter
- informal—a letter or an e-mail message to friends or family, a journal entry, dialogue between characters in a story

English Language Learners

If students have difficulty monitoring the voice that they use in their writing, tell them to concentrate on making their writing clear so that it is easily understood by others.

Confer with students individually to make sure that their writing is not too informal.

Students learning English often grasp conversational language before academic language. For each informal word that you find, ask students to list the standard word in their journal or notebook so that they know which words to use in future assignments.

Revising **for Word Choice**

Note that some idioms are regional (from a particular part of the country); others just appeal to the people who use them or are handed down in families. Invite students to suggest idioms that they use or hear often. Where did they first hear them? What do they mean?

✳ For more about understanding idioms, see SE pages 672–677.

Ask students to look through their stories for examples of figures of speech.

Ask students to look for patterns that might relate to the theme:
- Does the author use one kind of figure of speech more than others? Why?
- Does the author use certain figures of speech to talk about one character and different figures of speech to talk about another? What might this indicate?

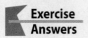

Exercise
Answers

1. simile; **2.** idiom; **3.** hyperbole or idiom; **4.** metaphor

---

280

Revising **for Word Choice**

6 My word choice demonstrates my careful thinking about the literature.

5 My word choice is appropriate, and I include figures of speech from the story.

4 My word choice is appropriate, but I need a few of the author's figures of speech in my analysis.

When you revise for *word choice*, make sure to include one or two figures of speech from the story in your analysis. Also make sure that your words effectively reflect the intent of your analysis. Use the rubric above and the information below to help you revise for word choice.

Do I use the author's figures of speech to prove a point?

You use figures of speech effectively if they help you prove or support a point in your analysis. Here are some common figures of speech that may appear in a short story.

- A **simile** compares two things using *like* or *as*. (*The dog danced around like loose litter in the wind.*)
- A **metaphor** compares two things without using *like* or *as*. (*At McKinley High School, football is king.*)
- A **hyperbole** is a highly exaggerated statement. (*Her heart melted when she saw the gift.*)
- An **idiom** is an expression that means something different from what the words actually say. (*Mr. Jung has an axe to grind with his landlord.*)

Exercise

Identify the figure of speech used in each literary passage below. Some sentences may have more than one.

1. "[The snapping turtle] struck like springsteel and the branch snapped like a stick of macaroni." ("The Turtle" by George Vukelich)
2. "This intelligence has driven a wedge between me and all the people I once knew." ("Flowers for Algernon" by Daniel Keyes)
3. "Dad hit the ceiling when I brought home my report card." ("Denton's Daughter" by Ellen Lowenberg)
4. "The guns and the dog were an armor against fear." ("The Old Chief Mishlanga" by Doris Lessing)

Grammar Connection

Figures of Speech
- **Proofreader's Guide** pages 672–677 (+)
- **Write Source** pages 598–599, 600–601

English Language Learners

Students may want to use idioms from their first language, especially if they are writing about a story from that culture. Have students explain the idioms they use so readers will understand them.

Advanced Learners

Challenge students to find figures of speech in poetry. Start by providing examples of your favorites. Have students read the poems aloud and discuss the imagery created by the figures of speech. Focus the discussion on what the figures of speech add to the meaning of the poem and how they help paint a picture with words.

Analyzing a Theme   **281**

3 I need to use more appropriate words and include one or two of the author's figures of speech.

2 I need to pay more attention to my word choice.

1 I need to learn more about word choice.

Do the words in my analysis have the right feeling?

The words in your analysis have the right feeling, or connotation, if, among other things, they accurately reflect the thoughts and actions of the main character. Read the paragraph below, paying close attention to the underlined words and phrases. These ideas clearly suggest the confused feelings of the main character.

> Robert looks <u>dazed</u> as an official tells him that he has been put under hypnosis as part of his driver's test. Robert <u>slowly nods</u>, as some scary images race through his mind. He was just about to collide with an oncoming vehicle, or <u>so he thought</u>. Now he is in a reclining chair, <u>trying to gather his wits</u>, trying to figure out what he has just experienced. Robert <u>has no idea how to react</u> as he slowly stands up.

Revise

Revise for word choice. Review the way that you use words in your analysis. Do they reflect the thoughts and actions of the main character? Replace words as needed.

Word Choice
New words and phrases are included to create the right feeling.

> The story begins when Roger ~~takes~~ *grabs* a woman's purse. Its heaviness makes Roger fall. This hyperbole makes clear the weight of the purse: "It had everything in it but hammer and nails" (211). The woman grabs Roger and shakes him ~~hard~~ *until his teeth rattle.* She says, "When I get through with you, sir, you are going to remember Mrs. Luella Bates Washington Jones" (211). Roger ~~moves~~ *struggles* to get free, but Mrs. Jones is strong.

Literature

Write on the board a word that describes a feeling and have students call out other words, verb phrases, or idioms that relate to it or that capture the same feeling. Write students' suggestions on the board as a list or a cluster diagram. For example, for the word *overjoyed*, students might suggest the following:

- *elated*
- *ecstatic*
- *blissful*
- *on cloud nine*
- *walking on air*
- *grinning from ear to ear*
- *more than happy*

Encourage each student to focus on the **author's choice of words** *(see below)* in the story he or she reviews.

Teaching Tip: The Author's Choice of Words

Have students find five examples of effective words in their chosen stories. Ask them to share one or more of these words (along with the sentences they're used in) with the class and explain why the words are effective.

Provide time for students to jot down interesting words in their journals or notebooks while reading. Encourage them to incorporate these new words into their own writing whenever appropriate.

Advanced Learners

Some students may feel that their work does not need revision. Suggest that they put aside their work for a short time. When they pick it up again, they will be able to see it with new eyes. Alternatively, writers can get a different perspective by reading their work aloud to a partner or by hearing it read aloud to them.

Revising for Sentence Fluency

Exercise Answers

The writer of the essay uses the present tense *(begins, pulls)*. Yet in the chosen quotation, the author of the story uses the past tense to talk about what happened *(looked, were, struck)* but uses the present tense to address the reader *(wait till I tell you).*

Writer's Craft

Tenses: The "literary present tense" gives a certain immortal quality to a work of literature. Just as the *Mona Lisa* still smiles mysteriously, so too the characters in great literature are forever living their lives. Even movie reviewers use the literary present tense to describe the actions of heroes and villains on the silver screen.

Interestingly, when fiction writers create proposals for their novels, they also cast the action in the literary present tense. By doing so, they create the sense that the characters are living right now and that the book already exists. Usually when they write their stories, though, authors use past-tense verbs.

282

Revising for Sentence Fluency

6 The sentences in my analysis make my ideas really stand out.	**5** My sentences read smoothly, and I have used the appropriate verb tense.	**4** Most of my sentences read smoothly, but I need to fix some tense shifts.

To revise for *sentence fluency*, check that you have used the correct verb tenses and that your sentences flow smoothly. The rubric strip above will help you.

When should I shift tenses in my analysis?

You should not shift tenses in your analysis unless there is good reason to do so. A response to literature (such as an analysis) is usually written in the present tense. Because the plot unfolds in the same way each time you read a story, it makes sense to discuss the story in the present tense.

Present tense: The girl trains diligently for the city races.

However, you may need to shift tenses when you include a quotation from the story. Authors often tell their stories using the past tense. *(She smiled. He blushed.)* So when you include a quotation in your analysis, you may shift from the present tense to the past tense. Notice the shift in the example below.

> In "The Cask of Amontillado," Poe **writes**, "He **had** a weak point—this Fortunato—although in other regards he **was** a man to be respected and even feared."

Exercise

Read the example below. Explain how the tenses shift.

1   "The Ransom of Red Chief" begins, "It looked like a good thing: but wait
2 till I tell you. We were down South, in Alabama—Bill Driscoll and myself—when
3 this kidnapping idea struck us." With these words, O. Henry pulls the reader
4 into the action.

Revise

Review your first draft. Read your essay and be sure that you have not shifted tenses without good reason.

English Language Learners

Assist students in using the correct verbs in their analysis. Have them pay close attention to the third person singular (–s in the present tense and –ed in the past tense for most regular verbs). Have them check all irregular verbs such as *to be* and *to have.*

✱ For irregular verbs, see SE page 720.

Analyzing a Theme 283

3 I need a variety of sentences and a consistent verb tense to improve the flow of my writing.

2 I need to pay more attention to verb tenses and my sentences.

1 I need to learn more about sentences.

Do all of my sentences read smoothly?

Your sentences will read smoothly if you use a variety of sentences. When too many sentences in a paragraph are the same length or follow the same pattern, your writing may sound choppy. Here are three basic types of sentences that you can use.

- **Simple Sentence**
  Eugenia Collier wrote the short story "Marigolds."

- **Compound Sentence**
  Lizabeth's friends view her as a leader, and they follow her example.

- **Complex Sentence**
  After she destroys Ms. Lottie's marigolds, Lizabeth learns about compassion.

Exercise

Think of a story you have recently read. Write one simple sentence, one compound sentence, and one complex sentence about the main character.

Revise for sentence fluency. Be sure that you have used a variety of sentence lengths and patterns in your essay.

Literature

Sentence Fluency
Simple sentences are combined for smooth reading.

Then Mrs. Jones leads Roger to the door. She reminds him
                                        ^and
to behave himself. Pride keeps Roger from saying more than
                                    ,but
"Thank you, m'am." He wants to say more. He doesn't.

Challenge students to define simple, complex, and compound sentences:

- **simple**—consists of one independent clause
- **compound**—two (or more) independent clauses joined by a coordinating conjunction or semicolon
- **complex**—an independent clause and one (or more) dependent clauses

Emphasize that a simple sentence does not have to be short—or uncomplicated. A simple sentence consists of a single independent clause, but it can

- include many modifying words and phrases (*By standing on tiptoe, he was just barely able to reach the top shelf of the old oak armoire*);
- have a compound subject (*Janice, Maria, and Stephanie live on the same street*);
- have a compound predicate (*Tonya looked out the window and decided to wear a hat*).

✳ For more information about types of sentence constructions, see SE page 748.

Revising Improving Your Writing

After working hard on a draft, students often find it difficult to commit to revising it in a substantive way. To help them with this task, suggest that they

- put the draft away for as long as is practical before beginning to revise it, so they can approach it with fresh eyes;
- look back over their self-assessments and reflections to remind themselves of ideas for improvements and to note progress made; or
- enlist the help of an informed outside reader to go over their essay with them, making sure that the reader has a copy of the revising checklist for reference.

284

Revising Improving Your Writing

Check your revising. On a piece of paper, write the numbers 1 to 12. If you can answer "yes" to a question, put a check mark after that number. If not, continue to work with that part of your essay.

Revising Checklist

Ideas

_____ 1. Have I written a clear thesis statement about the theme?
_____ 2. Have I used quotations from the story to support my analysis?
_____ 3. Have I effectively paraphrased the author's thoughts and ideas?

Organization

_____ 4. Have I written a clear beginning, middle, and ending?
_____ 5. Have I used transitions to connect ideas?
_____ 6. Do my thesis statement and final analysis connect?

Voice

_____ 7. Have I used a natural, engaging voice that fits the story?
_____ 8. Do I sound interested in the story and in my analysis?

Word Choice

_____ 9. Have I included at least one significant figure of speech used by the author?
_____ 10. Do I use words with the right connotation?

Sentence Fluency

_____ 11. Have I used a variety of sentence lengths and patterns?
_____ 12. Have I used the correct verb tenses in my sentences?

Make a clean copy. When you finish revising your essay, make a clean, double-spaced copy before you begin to edit.

Grammar Connection

Modifiers
- *Write Source* page 559
- *SkillsBook* pages 172–173

Pronouns
- **Proofreader's Guide** pages 704 (+), 706 (+)
- *Write Source* page 537 (+)
- *SkillsBook* pages 86–88
- *GrammarSnap* Relative Pronouns, Reflexive and Reciprocal Pronouns

Editing

After you've finished revising your essay, it's time to edit for the following conventions: punctuation, capitalization, spelling, and grammar.

Keys to Effective Editing

1. Use a dictionary, a thesaurus, and the "Proofreader's Guide" in the back of this book (pages 604–763).

2. Check quotations for correct punctuation.

3. Check your writing for correctness of punctuation, capitalization, spelling, and grammar.

4. If you use a computer, edit on a printed copy and enter your changes on the computer.

5. Use the editing and proofreading marks inside the back cover of this book.

Literature

Editing

Keys to Effective Editing

Remind students that during the editing stage, they have a chance to find and correct errors in

- punctuation,
- capitalization,
- spelling, and
- grammar.

Keys to Effective Editing lists the process students will be guided through on SE pages 286–288.

Point out that some errors will really stand out, but others won't be as obvious (for example, easily confused words such as *affect* and *effect*). Explain that students can improve their ability to catch errors if they

- continue to study the conventions,
- take note of errors they make frequently (perhaps keep a running list as a reminder of what to watch for), and
- use the Proofreader's Guide to look up anything they feel even a slight doubt about.

Technology Connections

Students can use the added features of the Net-text as they explore this stage of the writing process.

Write Source Online **Net-text**

Editing for Conventions

Point out that when citing direct quotations that end with a question mark or exclamation mark, students should place the punctuation inside the quotation marks. The citation will still be followed by a period:

> *The pupil edition poses the question, "How should I cite direct quotations?" (286).*

Remind students that one important task they should complete during the editing stage is to double-check each quotation they have used. Is the wording correct? Is the correct page number given?

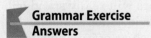

Grammar Exercise Answers

Possible Answer

Jack London wrote, "The man flung a look back . . ." (48).

286

Editing for Conventions

6	5	4
My grammar and punctuation are correct, and the copy is free of spelling errors.	I have one or two errors in grammar, spelling, or punctuation, but they won't distract the reader.	I need to correct a few errors in punctuation, spelling, or grammar that may distract the reader.

Conventions are the rules you follow for punctuation, capitalization, spelling, and grammar. To edit for conventions, use the rubric strip above and the information below.

How should I cite direct quotations?

You should cite direct quotations using the following method.

1. In most cases, start by giving credit to the author:
   O. Henry **writes . . .**

2. Put the direct quotation inside quotation marks.
   O. Henry writes, "There was clearly nothing to do but flop down on the shabby little couch and howl. So Della did it."

3. Write the page number from the text you are quoting. Place the number inside parentheses following the quotation. The period for the sentence follows the parentheses.
   O. Henry writes, "There was clearly nothing to do but flop down on the shabby little couch and howl. So Della did it" (34).

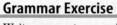

Grammar Exercise

Write one sentence using the information below to show how to cite a direct quotation.

Author: Jack London

Direct quotation: The man flung a look back along the way he had come. The Yukon lay a mile wide and hidden under three feet of ice. On top of this ice were as many feet of snow.

Page number: 48

Edit for punctuation of quotations. Be sure that you correctly cite any direct quotations that you use.

Grammar Connection

Punctuating Quotations

- **Proofreader's Guide** pages 616 (+), 632 (+)
- *SkillsBook* page 35

Advanced Learners

Encourage students to create a class resource book of rules for punctuating quotations to share with other students:

- Have them include quotations from their reading that demonstrate different rules (for example, exact words, dialogue, quotations within quotations).

- Have them show the correct punctuation of each quotation in another color or by highlighting.

- Each quotation should be followed by a statement of the relevant rule for punctuation.

* Refer students to SE pages 632–635 to confirm the appropriate punctuation of quotations.

3 I need to correct a number of errors.

2 I need to fix many errors that make my writing hard to read and understand.

1 I need help making corrections.

How should I punctuate compound and complex sentences?

Punctuate compound and complex sentences using these rules.

■ A **compound sentence** is made up of two independent clauses. The clauses must be joined by a semicolon, or by a comma and a coordinating conjunction.

> The story focuses on Celie's family; they face innumerable problems.
> Celie's life is extremely difficult, **but** slowly she discovers her true self.

■ A **complex sentence** contains one independent clause (in blue) and one or more dependent clauses (in black). Place a comma after the dependent clause when it comes first in a sentence.

> **As the hardships pile up,** the family discovers an inner strength.

Grammar Exercise

Rewrite the two sentences below using correct punctuation.

> Although she invited me to the party I did not want to go.
> It rained hard in the afternoon we played soccer anyway.

 Edit for conventions. Check your essay for the correct citations of quotations and the correct punctuation of your compound and complex sentences.

> **Conventions**
> A comma is added to a compound sentence.
>
> A page number is added.

Roger, however, still isn't sure about Mrs. Jones. He wants to run away, but something also makes him want to stay: "He did not trust the woman not to trust him. And he did not want to be mistrusted now." (213).

Note that confusion between compound sentences and sentences with a compound predicate can make it difficult to place commas correctly. Review the difference:

■ A sentence with a compound predicate has a single subject that governs two verbs. It does not require a comma before the conjunction: *We eat supper around seven o'clock and then spend an hour or so doing homework.* (subject = *We*, verbs = *eat, spend*)

■ A compound sentence contains a subject for each verb. There is a comma before the conjunction: *We eat supper around seven o'clock, and then we spend an hour or so doing homework.* (*We + eat, we + spend*)

Grammar Exercise
Answers

1. *Although she invited me to the party, I did not want to go.*
2. *It rained hard in the afternoon; we played soccer anyway. Or, It rained hard; in the afternoon we played soccer anyway.*

Struggling Learners

To review how to use commas between clauses, write the following sentences on the board, leaving out the commas:

We went to the library yesterday but we did not find the books we wanted.

If you want to go on the field trip you must sign up today.

Read the sentences aloud with no pauses. Help students place commas correctly and reread the sentences with correct pauses.

✷ For more on commas, see SE pages 608–612.

Grammar Connection

Punctuating Compound and Complex Sentences

■ **Proofreader's Guide** pages 744–745, 748 (+)
■ *SkillsBook* pages 21–22, 144–161
■ *GrammarSnap* Punctuating Compound and Complex Sentences

Editing **Checking for Conventions**

Give students a few moments to look over the Proofreader's Guide (SE pages 604–763). Throughout the year, students can rely on this section to resolve questions about conventions in their own writing.

Draw attention to item 9 on the list. Ask students why they can't trust the spell-checker to find all their spelling errors. (The computer can't reliably evaluate context. It only compares each word to a preprogrammed list.) Ask students to think of the kinds of errors spell-checkers can miss. Possible responses:

- similar-sounding words used incorrectly (*write / right*)
- words with letters left out or added (*manger / manager*)
- verb forms that differ by one letter (*named / names*)
- words with the same letters in a different order (*united / untied*)

Creating a Title

Remind students that one good way to create titles is to choose phrases from their essays.

288

Editing **Checking for Conventions**

 Check your editing. On a piece of paper, write the numbers 1 to 12. Put a check by the number if you can answer "yes" to that question. If not, continue to edit your essay for that convention.

__Editing Checklist__

Conventions

PUNCTUATION

_____ 1. Does each sentence have correct end punctuation?

_____ 2. Have I used quotation marks and correctly cited direct quotations?

_____ 3. Do I correctly punctuate compound and complex sentences?

_____ 4. Have I used parentheses to set off page numbers?

_____ 5. Do I use apostrophes to show possession (*in Poe's story*)?

CAPITALIZATION

_____ 6. Do I start all my sentences with capital letters?

_____ 7. Have I capitalized all proper nouns?

SPELLING

_____ 8. Have I spelled all my words correctly?

_____ 9. Have I double-checked the words my spell-checker may have missed?

GRAMMAR

_____ 10. Have I used correct verb tenses throughout?

_____ 11. Do my subjects and verbs agree in number (*Marigolds are,* not *Marigolds is*)?

_____ 12. Have I used the right words (*its, it's*)?

Creating a Title

- Focus on the theme: **Sweet Forgiveness**
- Refer to the character: **A Not-So-Tough Guy**
- Be creative: **Forget Revenge—Forgive**

Grammar Connection

Tense Shifts
- **Proofreader's Guide** pages 718–719, 722
- *SkillsBook* page 184
- *GrammarSnap* Past Perfect and Past Continuous Verb Tenses

End Punctuation
- **Proofreader's Guide** pages 605 (+), 606 (+)
- *SkillsBook* page 6

Struggling Learners

Tell students that they can think of their essay titles as an invitation to readers to start reading. Suggest that in addition to looking for a phrase in their essays, they might also consider turning exciting plot events into attention-grabbing titles.

Have students brainstorm a few titles. They can try them out on friends or family members before selecting one.

Publishing Sharing Your Essay

Now that you've finished writing, revising, and editing your essay, you can think about publishing it! See the suggestions in the boxes below for a variety of ways to present your essay.

 Make a final copy. Follow your teacher's instructions or use the guidelines below to format your paper. (If you are using a computer, see pages **76–78**.) Write a final copy of your essay and proofread it for errors.

Focus on Presentation

- Use blue or black ink and write neatly.
- Write your name in the upper left corner of page 1.
- Skip a line and center your title; skip another line and start your writing.
- Indent every paragraph and leave a one-inch margin on all four sides.
- Write your last name and the page number in the upper right-hand corner of every page after page 1.

Submit your Essay to a Literary Magazine

Ask your school or public librarian about young adult magazines that accept literary analyses. Submit your essay for publication. (See page 82.)

Give an Oral Presentation

Give a brief summary of the short story and then read your essay to the class. Ask if any of your classmates have read the story. Do they agree with your analysis?

Publish Your Essay Online

If your school has a Web page, submit your essay for publication. You may also explore other online sites that share reviews and analyses by teens.

Literature

Publishing
Sharing Your Essay

Instruct students to double-space their final versions. This will leave room for students to make last-minute corrections if they find proofreading errors. It will also provide space for you to write comments when you read their essays.

Tell students to include information about the source of their stories at the end of their essays *(see below)*.

Technology Connections

Remind students that they can use the Writing Network features of the Portfolio to share their work with peers.

- *Write Source Online* **Portfolio**
- *Write Source Online* **Net-text**

Teaching Tip: Citing Sources

Explain that short stories can appear in more than one collection, so it is important to provide the reader with correct source information so that he or she can easily find the quotations mentioned in the essay.

Review the correct format for citing a short story:

Author name. "Story Title." *Anthology Title*. Ed. Name of Editor. City: Publisher name, year of anthology's publication.

* For more about the format of works cited, see SE page 381.

Rubric for a Response to Literature

Remind students that a rubric is a chart that helps you evaluate your writing.

- The rubrics in this book are based on a six-point scale, in which a score of 6 indicates an amazing piece of writing, and a score of 1 means the writing is incomplete and not ready to be assessed.
- Explain that the purpose of the rubric is to help students break down the assessment process by evaluating each of the six traits individually—ideas, organization, voice, word choice, sentence fluency, and conventions.
- Point out that rubrics are also helpful during the writing process. They can guide you whenever you write because they tell you what elements to include in your writing and how to present them.
- Explain to students that they will most likely have different ratings for the traits. For example, they may give themselves a 5 for ideas but a 4 for organization.

✱ Reproducible six-, five-, and four-point rubrics for response writing are available on TE pages 770, 774, and 778.

290

Rubric for a Response to Literature

Use this rubric for guiding and assessing your writing. Refer to it whenever you want to improve your writing using the six traits.

6 Ideas	**5**	**4**
The ideas show a complete understanding of the reading.	The essay has a clear focus statement and necessary supporting details.	The essay has a clear focus statement. Unnecessary details need to be cut.
Organization		
All the parts work together to create an insightful essay.	The organization pattern fits the topic and purpose. All parts of the essay are well developed.	The organization pattern fits the topic and purpose. A part of the essay needs better development.
Voice		
The voice expresses interest and complete understanding. It engages the reader.	The voice expresses interest in and understanding of the topic.	The voice expresses interest but needs to show more understanding.
Word Choice		
The word choice reflects careful thinking about the reading.	The word choice, including the use of figures of speech, creates a clear message.	The word choice is clear, but more figures of speech would improve the essay.
Sentence Fluency		
The sentences in the essay make the ideas really stand out.	The sentences are skillfully written and keep the reader's interest.	No sentence problems exist. More sentence variety is needed.
Conventions		
Grammar and punctuation are correct, and the copy is free of all errors.	The essay has one or two errors that do not interfere with the reader's understanding.	The essay has a few careless errors in punctuation and grammar.

3	2	1
The focus statement is too broad. A variety of details are needed.	The focus statement is unclear. More details are needed.	The essay needs a focus statement and details.
The organization fits the essay's purpose. Some parts need more development.	The organization doesn't fit the purpose.	A plan needs to be followed.
The voice needs to be more interesting and express more understanding.	The voice does not show interest in or an understanding of the topic.	The writer needs to understand how to create voice.
The word choice is too general, and more figures of speech are needed.	Little attention was given to word choice.	The writer needs help with word choice.
A few sentence problems need to be corrected.	The essay has many sentence problems.	The writer needs to learn how to construct sentences.
The errors in the essay confuse the reader.	The number of errors makes the essay hard to read.	Help is needed to make corrections.

Literature

Test Prep!

Throughout *Write Source*, students use formative, traits-based rubrics. These rubrics break the traits apart so that students can learn discrete strategies for improving their writing.

Many state writing tests use summative rubrics—sometimes combining all the traits holistically and at other times rating each trait on a 4- or 5-point scale.

The difference is simple. Formative rubrics are created to help students. Summative rubrics are created to help *graders*.

There's no need to worry, though. The formative rubrics in *Write Source* correlate very well to the summative rubrics used on most writing tests.

Evaluating a Response to Literature

Ask students if they agree with the sample self-assessment on SE page 293. If they agree with the overall comments, ask them to suggest improvements based on the comments in the self-assessment. If they disagree with any comment, ask them to explain why.

Possible responses:

A direct quotation in the ending paragraph would help further illustrate Johnsy's change of heart and her decision to live.

The conventions score is generous. There should be a period after the parenthetical citation in each instance, and there are grammatical errors in several places:

- Paragraph 2, line 3: change comma to semicolon
- Paragraph 3, line 2: put a comma after *old*
- Paragraph 3, line 4: delete word *page* from citation
- Paragraph 4, line 7: put a comma after *mind*

✳ For more on nonrestrictive phrases, see SE page 612.

Evaluating a Response to Literature

Read the following analysis of a short-story theme. Then read the student's self-evaluation on the next page. **(There are errors in the essay below.)**

Leaf of Life

"The Last Leaf" by O. Henry is the story of two friends and a reluctant fight for life. Young artists Sue and Johnsy, who share a studio apartment, face the possibility of Johnsy's death when she comes down with pneumonia. Though at first Johnsy is not hopeful, her outlook changes and she ultimately survives. O. Henry uses irony and symbolism to cleverly convey his theme: Love and optimism can triumph over death.

Early in the story, the doctor tells Sue that Johnsy will probably die from her illness because she thinks she will. Sue finds that the doctor is right, that Johnsy does not expect to live. Johnsy has decided that her life will end when the last leaf falls from the vine outside her window. Unwilling to fight, she tells Sue, "I want to turn loose my hold on everything, and go sailing down, down, just like one of those poor, tired leaves." (93) Sue, acting brave, tries to convince her that she mustn't think that way, but Johnsy just keeps counting down as the leaves fall off the vine.

At this point, O. Henry introduces a new character, Behrman. Behrman is an old failed artist. O. Henry explains, "He had been always about to paint a masterpiece, but had never yet begun it." (page 93) His affection for the young women, though, is obvious when his eyes start "plainly streaming" after Sue tells him about Johnsy's plans to die.

There are only a few leaves left on the vine when Sue goes out to see Behrman, but O. Henry draws out the tension by having Sue pull down the shade in Johnsy's room. This way Johnsy can't see the vine, though she hears the wind from a cold storm. In the morning, when Johnsy asks Sue to pull up the shade, the reader is as worried as Sue is—and as relieved to see the last leaf still on the vine. That does not change Johnsy's mind however. She is sure the wind will knock off the leaf, and when it does, she is sure she will die.

Eventually, Sue grows a bit desperate and no longer pretends to be brave. "Dear, dear!" she cries, "think of me, if you won't think of yourself. What would I do?" (95) Johnsy doesn't answer. Sue also expects that the leaf will certainly fall soon. The day passes, followed by another windy rainy night. When Sue opens the shade the next morning, the leaf is still there.

English Language Learners

To help students understand the text, define the following words before reading the essay:

- reluctant (showing hesitation or unwillingness)
- pneumonia (a lung disease)
- optimism (hopefulness)
- masterpiece (a work done with extraordinary skill)
- tension (emotional unrest)
- desperate (having lost hope)
- relieved (free from anxiety)
- symbol (sign or token)
- sacrifice (something given up)

Seeing the last leaf still clinging suddenly changes Johnsy. It becomes a symbol of life. Johnsy decides that its wicked to want to die and she finds a reason to live—she wants to paint the Bay of Naples. In an ironic twist, O. Henry reveals that while Johnsy is recovering, Behrman has gotten pneumonia and died. He became sick when, out in the cold, he painted the leaf that Johnsy thought was real. Behrman's actions show love and selflessness. The leaf now represents his sacrifice and is his true masterpiece.

Student Self-Assessment

Response Rubric Checklist

Title: "Leaf of Life"

Writer: David Jenkins

5 **Ideas**
- Does my analysis focus on an interesting short story?
- Do I have a clear thesis statement?
- Do I include effective supporting details?

4 **Organization**
- Does the beginning identify the story and the thesis statement?
- Does the middle show how the theme develops?
- Does the ending share a meaningful analysis?

4 **Voice**
- Does my voice sound natural?
- Do I sound engaging?

4 **Word Choice**
- Do I use specific nouns and active verbs?
- Have I included one of the author's significant figures of speech?

5 **Sentence Fluency**
- Do I use tense shifts correctly?
- Do my sentences read smoothly?

4 **Conventions**
- Do I correctly cite sources?
- Are my punctuation, capitalization, spelling, and grammar correct?

OVERALL COMMENTS:

My first paragraph introduces the story and states the theme, though maybe I should have used a direct quotation somewhere in the paragraph.

I have a strong beginning, middle, and ending, but I could sound more interested in the story.

I included an important figure of speech from the story, but I didn't discuss it much.

I think my paper is mostly free of careless errors, but I'm not sure how to add page numbers to citations.

Use the rubric. Rate your essay using the rubric on pages **290–291.** Write comments about why you gave yourself the scores you did.

Literature

Student Self-Assessment

To give students additional practice with evaluating a response to literature, use a reproducible Assessment Sheet (TE page 766), the Response to Literature Rubric Checklist (TE page 782), and one or both of the **benchmark papers** listed in the Benchmark Papers box below. You can use an overhead transparency while students refer to their own copies made from the copy masters. For your benefit, a completed checklist and comments sheet are provided for each benchmark paper.

Before assessing the model essay, discuss *figures of speech.* The model uses a metaphor about leaves falling from a tree to illustrate Johnsy's fight for life.

Advanced Learners

After they have completed their evaluations, have students exchange them with a partner. Ask partners to give their opinion of the evaluations and offer any suggestions they have for further improvements.

Benchmark Papers

The Color Purple (good)
- TE pp. 808–811

The Call of the Wild (poor)
- TE pp. 812–814

Reflecting on Your Writing

Remind students to write the title of the essay and the date on their reflection page and to keep it with the finished analysis for future reference.

After students have finished their reflections, have them discuss their thoughts with the group.

- Invite students to share the main thing they learned during the writing process (item 3). Do they have any helpful guidance for how others could achieve the same results? Do classmates have any questions about how they did it?
- Ask students to read the question they still have about writing an analysis (item 5). Does anyone in the group have an answer or a helpful suggestion?
- Have students jot down notes from the class discussion on the back of their reflection page so this information will be available to them in future.

294

Reflecting on Your Writing

Reflect on your finished analysis of a short-story theme by completing each starter sentence below. These comments will help you check your progress as a writer.

My Literature Analysis

1. The strongest part of my essay is . . .

2. The part that most needs change is . . .

3. The main thing I learned about writing an analysis of a theme is . . .

4. In my next response to literature, I would like to . . .

5. Here is one question I still have about writing an analysis of a theme:

6. Right now I would describe my writing ability as . . . (excellent, good, fair, poor)

Writing for Assessment
Responding to Prompts About Literature

You may be asked to respond to a literature prompt on an assessment test. The prompt may be based on a piece of literature that you have previously read or on a story, a poem, or an article provided on the test itself. Your response will show how well you understand the main features of literature. To prepare for this type of writing, pay careful attention to discussions of *plot, character, theme, setting,* and *style* in your English classes.

This chapter will help you respond effectively to literature prompts. You will learn to analyze various types of prompts, to use the writing process in a test situation, and to respond to fiction and nonfiction.

Writing Guidelines

  Subject: **Literature prompt**
     Form: **Response to a prompt**
  Purpose: **To demonstrate competence**
 Audience: **Instructor**

"Great literature is simply language charged with meaning to the utmost possible degree."

—George Orwell

Copy Masters

T-Chart (TE pp. 297, 301)

Responding to Prompts About Literature

Objectives

- apply what has been learned about responding to various kinds of literature, including fiction, nonfiction, and poetry
- analyze literature prompts
- practice writing for assessment

If your students must take school, district, or state assessments this year, focus on the writing form on which they will be tested.

Tell students that knowing how to respond to a literature prompt is one of the most useful skills a student can develop. This assessment technique is used all the way through high school and college.

Explain that aside from helping students take tests, practice with analyzing literature helps students become better readers in everyday life. Not only will they understand what they read better, but they are likely to enjoy it more.

Prewriting Analyzing a Literature Prompt

Tell students to always read prompts twice before beginning to write. This reduces the chance that they'll miss an important part of the questions.

Try It!
Answers

Answers will vary. Possible answers:
1. *Inventor . . . was* <u>*remarkably successful*</u> *. . .* <u>*explain what characteristics contributed to her achievements*</u> *. . .* <u>*specific examples*</u>

Information needed: list personal qualities that helped Knight succeed; give examples of actions that show she had those qualities.
2. *. . . poem about* <u>*a boy's relationship with his parents*</u> *. . .* <u>*discuss the stanza that reveals the most*</u> *about the relationship.* <u>*How does this stanza clarify*</u> *. . .* <u>*the details*</u> *in the poem?*

Information needed: identify most revealing stanza; give specific details that stanza clarifies.

"The books that help you the most are those which make you think the most."
—Theodore Parker

Prewriting Analyzing a Literature Prompt

A prompt about literature asks you to respond to specific characteristics of a story, a poem, a novel, or a nonfiction selection. As you read a prompt, look for key words that tell you exactly what the prompt requires. In the sample prompt below, key words and phrases are underlined. The word describe gives the main direction or focus for the response.

Sample Prompt

> In the story "The Amigo Brothers," the <u>friendship</u> of two boys is <u>severely tested</u>. Write an essay in which you <u>describe</u> how the <u>crisis between them demonstrates</u> the ideal of <u>true friendship</u>. How do their <u>personal characteristics</u> lead to the crisis and the way it is resolved? <u>How does the author reveal</u> their similarities and differences? Support your thesis with <u>evidence from the story</u>.

Try It!

Copy the following sample prompts on a sheet of paper. Underline key words and phrases for each prompt and make notes about the kinds of supporting information that you would need for your response.

1. Inventor Margaret E. Knight, the subject of Susan Bivin Aller's article "A Lady in a Machine Shop," was remarkably successful. In an essay, explain what characteristics contributed to her achievements. Include specific examples to support your ideas.
2. "Our Son Swears He Has 102 Gallons of Water in His Body," by Naomi Shihab Nye, is a poem about a boy's relationship with his parents. In an essay, discuss the stanza that reveals the most about the relationship. How does this stanza clarify some of the details in the poem?

Planning Your Response

Once you analyze and understand a prompt, you are ready to plan your response. If a reading selection is provided, read it with the prompt in mind, picking out the information you need for your response. Then form your topic sentence and organize the details.

Sample Prompt and Selection

This excerpt from Charles Dickens's "A Christmas Carol" describes Scrooge. In a paragraph, discuss the feeling created by this description. What details create this feeling?

The cold within him froze his old features, nipped his pointed nose, shriveled his cheek, stiffened his gait; made his eyes red, his thin lips blue; and spoke out shrewdly in his grating voice. A frosty rime was on his head, and on his eyebrows, and his wiry chin. He carried his own low temperature always about with him; he iced his office in the dog-days, and didn't thaw it one degree at Christmas.

The underlined words refer to Scrooge's coldness.

Writing a Topic Sentence

After reading the prompt and selection above, one student wrote the following topic sentence.

Dickens's description of Scrooge (specific topic) shows a man who is cold to the core (particular focus related to the prompt).

Creating a Graphic Organizer

The writer used a T-chart to sort details for her response paragraph.

Scrooge	
cold from within him	cold affected his surroundings
"froze his old features"	"carried his own low temperature"
"nipped his pointed nose"	"iced his office in the dog-days"
"shriveled his cheek"	"didn't thaw it one degree at Christmas"
"stiffened his gait"	
"eyes red," "lips blue," "frosty rime"	

Literature

Planning Your Response

Remind students that if they are **writing from memory** *(see below)* and they don't have a photocopy of the story, they should write their notes on a separate piece of paper.

Writing a Topic Sentence

Note that the student writer created the topic sentence by

- paring the prompt down to its basics (*discuss Dickens's description of Scrooge*) and
- using the result to create a sentence starter (*Dickens's description of Scrooge . . .*).

Suggest that students try this strategy as well.

Creating a Graphic Organizer

Provide photocopies of the reproducible T-Chart (TE page 818). Explain that this chart fits the writer's needs because it helps identify two aspects of the feeling created by Scrooge's coldness. Other prompts might require different organizers. Suggest that students become familiar with different types of organizers so they can choose the one that works best.

Teaching Tip: Writing from Memory

Explain that in some tests students may be asked to write an essay about a story they have read, but they might not have a copy of the story to refer to as they write. Assure them that

- if they are expected to study a particular story for a test, they will be warned well in advance (students should then read the story several times, noting important details); and

- they will not be expected to provide exact quotations from a story that they write about from memory. Instead, they should try to provide accurate paraphrases in support of their theses.

Writing Responding to a Fiction Prompt

Ask students to read the prompt and identify the key words and phrases that should guide the writer. These include the following:

■ *Explain* how Dickens makes the wind seem more than it really is.
■ *What details* create this effect?

Test Prep!

Response-to-literature prompts are popular on many on-demand writing tests because of the following factors:

- They provide all students with the same starting point.
- They allow graders to assess students' use of source material.
- They test both reading and writing.

Use the various sample prompts in this text to help your students prepare to respond to literature in on-demand testing situations. For help preparing students to respond to document-based questions (DBQs), see TE pages 424–430.

Writing Responding to a Fiction Prompt

The following prompt and fiction selection show how a student underlined words and phrases and added some notes on a copy of the selection to address the focus of the prompt (red).

Sample Prompt and Selection

Most people are aware that Charles Dickens wrote the famous story "A Christmas Carol." They are less familiar with his other stories, including "The Chimes," celebrating that season of the year. Read the excerpt that follows from "The Chimes," which opens with a description of the winter wind. In an essay, explain how Dickens makes the wind seem more than it really is. What details create this effect?

From "The Chimes" by Charles Dickens

There are not, I say, many people who would care to sleep in a church. I don't mean at sermon-time in warm weather (when the thing has actually been done, once or twice), but in the night, and alone. A great multitude of persons will be violently astonished, I know, by this position, in the broad bold day. But it applies to night. It must be argued by night, and I will undertake to maintain it successfully on any gusty winter's night appointed for the purpose, with any one opponent chosen from the rest, who will meet me singly in an old churchyard, before an old church-door; and will previously empower me to lock him in, if needful to his satisfaction, until morning.

For the night-wind has a dismal trick of wandering round and round a building of that sort, and moaning as it goes; and of trying, with its unseenhand, the windows and the doors; and seeking out some crevices by which to enter. And when it has got in; as one not finding what it seeks, whatever that may be, it wails and howls to issue forth again: and not content with stalking through

The wind is "gusty."

Wind seems human as it plays a "trick," wanders, moans, and uses an "unseen hand."

Soaring and flinging itself down, the wind seems superhuman.

the aisles, and gliding round and round the pillars, and tempting the deep organ, <u>soars</u> up to the roof, and strives to rend the rafters: then <u>flings itself despairingly upon the stones below</u>, and passes, <u>muttering</u>, into the vaults. Anon, it comes up stealthily, and <u>creeps along the walls</u>, seeming to read, in whispers, the inscriptions sacred to the dead. At some of these, <u>it breaks out shrilly</u>, as with <u>laughter</u>; and at others, <u>moans and cries</u> as if it were <u>lamenting</u>.

Shrill laughter tied to "lamenting" creates an eerie, scary feeling.

Writing a Thesis Statement

After reading the excerpt and making notes, the student wrote the following thesis statement for his response essay.

> **The narrator presents the wind** (specific topic) **as an intruder that becomes more and more terrifying** (particular focus related to the prompt).

Creating a Graphic Organizer

The writer used a line diagram to organize specific details from the excerpt.

Literature

Writing a Thesis Statement

Tell students the wording of the prompt suggests that students might use a figure of speech in their responses. Challenge students to identify the figure of speech in the student's thesis statement (. . . *an intruder that becomes* . . .) and the words of the prompt that seem to suggest using it (metaphor—suggested by *makes the wind seem more than it really is*).

Creating a Graphic Organizer

Ask students to tell how the writer has organized the diagram:

- The main topic, "Wind," is at the top.
- The writer forms two categories, one for each place the wind goes.
- In each category, the writer lists descriptive words organized roughly in the order in which they're mentioned in the excerpt.

Have students choose the graphic organizer they think best suits this topic and take notes as if they were going to write the essay. Have students share their diagrams with the class.

✳ For descriptions of the line diagram and other graphic organizers, see SE pages 588–589.

Writing Student Response

Acknowledge that in a timed situation writers can't address the traits as thoroughly as they would otherwise. Note, however, that using figures of speech is a good way for students to show that they're knowledgeable about analyzing the elements in literature.

✳ For more about literary terms, see SE page 600.

Student Response

In this student response to the excerpt from "The Chimes," note how the writer used details from the story to support the thesis statement.

Sleeping in Church?

Beginning
The first paragraph leads up to the thesis statement (underlined).

The excerpt from "The Chimes" by Charles Dickens begins with the idea that isolated, old churches are much different places at night than they are during the daytime. The narrator challenges anyone who doubts this to be locked alone in an old church overnight. <u>The narrator presents the wind as an intruder that becomes more and more terrifying.</u>

Middle
One paragraph focuses on the wind outside the church.

Although the wind is first described as simply "gusty," it soon takes on human qualities, "wandering round . . . moaning as it goes." In addition to the mournful sounds, the wind begins "trying, with its unseen hand, the windows and the doors." The would-be sleeper seems trapped and surrounded by this persistent intruder seeking to get in.

The next paragraph focuses on the wind inside the church.

As if this stalker image were not enough, the wind changes into something superhuman and even more frightening as it enters the building. It starts out "stalking through the aisles" and "gliding round and round the pillars" almost as if in search of some prey. Then something truly alarming happens; the wind "soars up to the roof . . . then flings itself despairingly upon the stones below, and passes, muttering, into the vaults." Clearly the wind is beyond the reach of death itself even as it seems cursed to wander among the graves mournfully "lamenting." The narrator imagines the "moans and cries" are the wind's reactions to the inscriptions on the tombs.

Ending
The closing summarizes the main point.

   In an isolated country church at night, the wind is described as a mysterious and frightening intruder. What begins as natural gusts of wind on a winter night takes on a far more terrifying form. The narrator first personifies the wind as a sinister stalker and then as a haunted spirit moaning among the graves below. Throughout the excerpt, the narrator does his best to describe to anyone brave enough to take the dare what he or she might encounter.

Literature

 Respond to the reading. Answer the following questions about the student response.

Ideas (1) What part of the topic does the student focus on in the thesis statement? (2) What types of details does the student use to support his thesis?

Organization (3) How does the writer organize the middle part of the response?

Voice & Word Choice (4) Which words or phrases quoted from the story are the most effective? Name two.

Respond to the reading.

Answers

Ideas 1. the author's description of the wind as an increasingly terrifying intruder **2.** quotations from the story in chronological order that describe human emotions and actions and show the wind as ever more active and threatening

Organization 3. first middle paragraph—describes the wind's behavior outside the church; second middle paragraph—describes the even more terrifying things the wind does when it gets inside

Voice & Word Choice 4. Possible responses:
■ *wandering round . . . moaning as it goes*
■ *stalking through the aisles*

Advanced Learners

Point out that the student response makes use of well-chosen words and descriptive details to help readers hear, see, and feel the scene. Provide photocopies of the reproducible T-Chart (TE page 818). In the first column, have students record the two words or phrases they identified in **Respond to the reading (4)**. Then have them use the second column to tell how the words or phrases create a word picture for readers.

Practice Literature Prompt

Work through the process of responding to the prompt step-by-step, stopping to discuss students' thoughts and decisions along the way:

- Give students a few minutes to read and analyze the prompt. Then have them share their ideas with the group. What are the key words? What is the prompt asking them to do?
- Give students about 10 to 12 minutes to plan their essays. Then have them share their progress. Which graphic organizer did they choose?
- Allow students 20 minutes to write, and then immediately have them spend 10 minutes editing and proofreading.
- Finally, divide the class into small groups and have students read their essays to one another and discuss them. What can students learn from the different approaches their classmates took?

Practice Literature Prompt

Whenever you respond to a writing prompt, especially in a timed situation, begin by studying the prompt. Find the key word that indicates what you are to do in the response: *compare, explain, describe,* and so on. Be sure that you understand the prompt and any specific points you need to address in your response before you read the selection. Of course, it is important to quote examples and specific details from the selection to support your thesis. However, it is equally important to share your own insights about the selection.

Prompt and Selection

"An Experiment in Misery" by Stephen Crane is about two friends who are watching a homeless man, and they wonder what it would be like to be in his situation. One of the friends decides to put on some old clothes and pretend to be homeless in order to find out. The following excerpt follows the young man in his new role. Discuss how you think this experience will change his understanding of the homeless. Support your ideas with specific examples from the excerpt.

From "An Experiment in Misery" by Stephen Crane

It was late at night, and a fine rain was swirling softly down causing the pavements to glisten with hue of steel and blue and yellow in the rays of the innumerable lights. A youth was trudging slowly, without enthusiasm, with his hands buried deep in his trousers' pockets, toward the downtown places where beds can be hired for coppers. He was clothed in an aged and tattered suit, and his derby was a marvel of dust-covered crown and torn rim. He was going forth to eat as the wanderer may eat, and sleep as the homeless sleep. By the time he had reached City Hall Park he was so completely plastered with yells of "bum" and "hobo," and with various unholy epithets that small boys had applied to him at intervals, that he was in a state of the most profound dejection. The sifting rain saturated the old velvet collar of his overcoat, and as the wet cloth pressed against his neck, he felt that there no longer could be pleasure in life. He looked about him searching for an outcast of highest degree that they two might share miseries, but the lights threw a quivering glare over rows and circles of deserted benches that glistened damply, showing patches of wet sod behind them. It seemed that their usual freights had fled on this night to better things. There were only squads of well-dressed Brooklyn people who swarmed toward the bridge.

The young man loitered about for a time and then went shuffling off down Park Row. In the sudden descent in style of the dress of the crowd he felt relief, and as if he were at last in his own country. He began to see tatters that matched his tatters. In Chatham Square there were aimless men strewn in front of saloons and lodging-houses, standing sadly, patiently, reminding one vaguely of the attitudes of chickens in a storm. He aligned himself with these men, and turned slowly to occupy himself with the flowing life of the great street.

Through the mists of the cold and storming night, the cable cars went in silent procession, great affairs shining with red and brass, moving with formidable power, calm and irresistible, dangerful and gloomy, breaking silence only by the loud fierce cry of the gong. Two rivers of people swarmed along the sidewalks, spattered with black mud which made each shoe leave a scar-like impression. Overhead, elevated trains with a shrill grinding of the wheels stopped at the station, which upon its leg-like pillars seemed to resemble some monstrous kind of crab squatting over the street. The quick fat puffings of the engines could be heard. Down an alley there were somber curtains of purple and black, on which street lamps dully glittered like embroidered flowers.

Respond to a literature prompt. Read the practice prompt again to make sure that you understand its focus. Then carefully reread the fiction selection by Stephen Crane. Next, form a thesis statement, quickly arrange your main supporting details in a graphic organizer, and write your essay. After you finish, check your work for conventions.

Literature

After students discuss their essays with the small groups, return to the larger group. Encourage them to share what they have learned. For example:

- What is the basic question posed by the prompt? (Possible response: *How could pretending to be homeless change the young man's view of homelessness?*)
- Point out that since the excerpt doesn't say how the man originally felt about homeless people, students must address how he "will change" by focusing on how he might feel *after* the episode. They cannot speculate about before—unless they've read the story (if so, they should use their knowledge, but they must remain focused on the topic).
- Were students happy with the graphic organizer they chose, or do they think another would have worked better? If so, which one?
- Did the time allocated for each writing stage work well for them? Would they have preferred to divide it up differently? How?

English Language Learners

For students who find the prompt and the passage too difficult, provide vocabulary support as necessary. You might also paraphrase the prompt and text for them. Reassure students that if the passage were assigned prior to the test, they would be able to read it carefully several times before responding. Check students' understanding of the story before they begin to write.

Writing Responding to a Nonfiction Prompt

Note that the prompt asks two questions. The answers to these questions must also be included in the essay (and the writer did so, as students will see on SE pages 306–307). However, it might have been a good idea to mark the questions on the prompt to create visual reminders. Suggest that students circle any question marks in prompts so the questions will stand out.

Responding to a Nonfiction Prompt

The following prompt and nonfiction selection show how a student underlined words and phrases related to the prompt's focus. The writer also jotted notes in the margin of the selection in order to put together a brief outline before writing his response essay.

Sample Prompt and Selection

The following excerpt from Booker T. Washington's autobiography is about part of his childhood. What caused Washington to remember what his life had been like when he was young? As Washington recalls these experiences, what does he realize about his childhood? Using examples from your own childhood or from the experiences of people you know, explain whether or not you think that your generation will look back with some of the same feelings that Washington had.

From *Up from Slavery: An Autobiography*
by Booker T. Washington

Why Washington recalls his youth

I was asked not long ago to tell something about the sports and pastimes that I engaged in during my youth. Until that question was asked it had never occurred to me that there was no period of my life that was devoted to play. From the time that I can remember anything, almost every day of my life has been occupied in some kind of labour;

Realizations about his childhood

though I think I would now be a more useful man if I had had time for sports. During the period that I spent in slavery I was not large enough to be of much service, still I was occupied most of the time in cleaning the yards, carrying water to the men in the fields, or going to the mill, to which I used to take the corn, once a week, to be ground. The mill was about three miles from the plantation.

Feelings about his childhood

This work I always dreaded. The heavy bag of corn would be thrown across the back of the horse, and the corn divided about evenly on each side; but in some way, almost without exception, on these trips, the corn would so shift as to become unbalanced and would fall off the horse, and often I would fall with it.

Responding to Prompts About Literature   305

> As I was not strong enough to reload the corn upon the horse, I would have to wait, sometimes for many hours, till a chance passer-by came along who would help me out of my trouble. The hours while waiting for someone were usually spent in <u>crying</u>. The time consumed in this way made me late in reaching the mill, and by the time I got my corn ground and reached home it would be far into the night. The road was a lonely one, and often led through dense forests. I was always frightened. The woods were said to be full of soldiers who had deserted from the army, and <u>I had been told that the first thing a deserter did to a Negro boy when he found him alone was to cut off his ears. Besides, when I was late in getting home I knew I would always get a severe scolding or a flogging.</u>

His fears & experiences

Writing a Thesis Statement

After reading the excerpt, the student writer developed the following thesis statement for his response essay.

> **Young people today, like Washington in his childhood** (specific topic), **are not being given enough chances to play** (particular focus related to the prompt).

Creating a Graphic Organizer

The student used a simple outline to plan his response.

I.   Parents today forget kids need to play.
II. Some kids are locked into too much organized activity.
III. I got to play as a kid.
IV. Today's kids may grow up like Booker T., regretting their lack of true play time.

Literature

Writing a Thesis Statement

Note that this prompt is unlike the examples students have seen previously in the section; it asks writers not only to analyze literature but also to express an opinion based on their own experiences. The essay should therefore share the qualities of both a response to literature and a personal essay.

✱ For information about persuasive writing, see SE pages 200–253.

Creating a Graphic Organizer

Point out that the student's outline simply lists the basic idea he plans to address in each paragraph, without noting specific details. This is perfectly fine, and with practice, many students may choose to do this. However, at first they may benefit from jotting a few supporting details under each section of their outline.

Suggest that the T-chart might have been another possibility for a graphic organizer. The student could have used the two columns to compare his own and his friends' experiences to Washington's experiences.

Writing Student Response

Before students work on the **Respond to the reading** activity, explain the structure of the response.

- The writer states the thesis in the beginning paragraph.
- Next, he devotes one paragraph to telling what is similar about the lives of kids today and the childhood experience of Booker T. Washington.
- The third paragraph talks about the differences between the writer's own experience and that of people who never had free play time.
- Finally, the writer draws a unified conclusion about the thesis.

✱ For more about comparing and contrasting, see SE page 574.

Student Response

The following essay is a student response to the prompt and excerpt from Booker T. Washington's autobiography.

Instant Replay

Beginning
The first paragraph identifies the author of the selection, uses a quotation, and builds up to the thesis statement (underlined).

Booker T. Washington really didn't have a childhood. In a description of his early life, Washington says, "There was no period of my life that was devoted to play." Washington had never really thought about this until someone asked him "to tell something about the sports and pastimes" of his youth. He described having to spend his time doing dangerous and difficult chores, sometimes followed by "a severe scolding or a flogging." Of course, today's children are free from the terrible abuses of slavery. However, it is possible that young people today, like Washington in his childhood, are not being given enough chances to play.

Middle
The first middle paragraph gives examples of why kids today may relate to Washington's lack of free time.

Booker T. Washington "always dreaded" some of the things he had to do, but it wasn't the hardship that seemed to haunt him. Later in life, when he thought back on his childhood, he regretted not having had a chance to play sports—to do something just for the fun of it. It's possible that some kids today may look back on their early years in the same way. Many of my friends spent almost all their grade-school years being hauled around by their parents to music lessons, scout meetings, church retreats, and organized baseball or soccer games. This frantic pace continued all summer, when some of them also had to attend summer school.

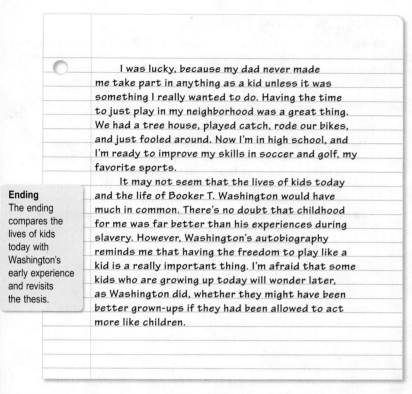

Responding to Prompts About Literature **307**

I was lucky, because my dad never made me take part in anything as a kid unless it was something I really wanted to do. Having the time to just play in my neighborhood was a great thing. We had a tree house, played catch, rode our bikes, and just fooled around. Now I'm in high school, and I'm ready to improve my skills in soccer and golf, my favorite sports.

It may not seem that the lives of kids today and the life of Booker T. Washington would have much in common. There's no doubt that childhood for me was far better than his experiences during slavery. However, Washington's autobiography reminds me that having the freedom to play like a kid is a really important thing. I'm afraid that some kids who are growing up today will wonder later, as Washington did, whether they might have been better grown-ups if they had been allowed to act more like children.

Ending
The ending compares the lives of kids today with Washington's early experience and revisits the thesis.

Literature

 Respond to the reading. Answer the following questions about the student response.

Ideas (1) What is the thesis of the student response? (2) What details does the student use to support the thesis? Name two or three.

Organization (3) How is this response organized—chronologically, spatially (by location), or logically?

Voice & Word Choice (4) Which words and phrases indicate the student's attitude toward the topic? Name two.

 Respond to the reading.

Answers

Ideas **1.** Kids today, like Booker T. Washington, might not get enough opportunity to play.
2. Possible responses:
- Washington talks about having to work instead of being allowed to play.
- The writer has friends who spent a lot of time as young children doing organized activities arranged by their parents.
- The writer was given time to himself; he feels that he was able to make the most of his childhood.

Organization **3.** logically

Voice & Word Choice **4.** Possible responses:
- *being hauled around*
- *this frantic pace*
- *I was lucky*
- *Having the time to just play . . . was a great thing.*
- *I'm afraid that*

Practice Writing Prompt

Before students begin to write the practice response essay, have them preview SE page 310 as a reminder of their goals. Then have them read the prompt; plan their answer; and write, revise, and edit the response. Depending on your students' needs, you might either keep track of the time for them or encourage them to decide how to allot the time themselves.

After students have finished, instruct them to choose a partner, read each other's essay, and discuss their work process. Make sure they talk about the three main items required by the prompt:

- Tell why Henry's speech was effective, using examples from the text.
- Tell his reasons for rebelling.
- Tell why he thought fighting was better than peace.

Have students share their planning notes and discuss the organizational methods they used.

Practice Writing Prompt

Whether you are reading and responding to fiction or nonfiction, remember that the author of the selection carefully chose the words to create a character, establish a setting, share information, arouse an emotion, and so on. You also need to carefully choose your words when you respond to a literature prompt.

Sample Prompt and Selection

The excerpt that follows is from a speech that Patrick Henry delivered on March 23, 1775. The final words of the speech became an inspiration to those who wanted to go to war against the British. In an essay, explain why Patrick Henry's speech was so effective. What reasons did Henry give his fellow colonists for rebelling? Why did he think that fighting was a better alternative than peace? What words, phrases, or sentence structures of Henry's seem especially convincing? Support your ideas with examples from the speech.

From Patrick Henry's
"Give Me Liberty or Give Me Death" speech

There is no longer any room for hope. If we wish to be free—if we mean to preserve inviolate those inestimable privileges for which we have been so long contending—if we mean not basely to abandon the noble struggle in which we have been so long engaged, and which we have pledged ourselves never to abandon until the glorious object of our contest shall be obtained—we must fight! I repeat it, sir, we must fight! An appeal to arms and to the God of hosts is all that is left us! They tell us, sir, that we are weak; unable to cope with so formidable an adversary. But when shall we be stronger? Will it be the next week, or the next year? Will it be when we are totally disarmed, and when a British guard shall be stationed in every house? Shall we gather strength by irresolution and inaction? Shall we acquire the means of effectual resistance by lying supinely on our backs and hugging the delusive phantom of hope, until our enemies shall have bound us hand and foot? Sir, we are not weak if we make a proper use of those means which the God of nature hath placed in our power. The millions of people, armed in the holy cause of liberty, and in such a country as that which we possess, are invincible by any force which our enemy can send against us. Besides, sir, we shall not fight our battles alone. There is a just God who presides over the destinies of nations, and who will raise up friends to fight our battles for us. The battle, sir, is not to the strong alone; it is to the vigilant, the active, the brave. Besides, sir, we have no election. If we were base enough to desire it, it is now too late to retire from the contest. There is no retreat but in submission and slavery! Our chains are forged! Their clanking may be heard on the plains of Boston! The war is inevitable—and let it come! I repeat it, sir, let it come.

It is in vain, sir, to extenuate the matter. Gentlemen may cry, Peace, Peace—but there is no peace. The war is actually begun! The next gale that sweeps from the north will bring to our ears the clash of resounding arms! Our brethren are already in the field! Why stand we here idle? What is it that gentlemen wish? What would they have? Is life so dear, or peace so sweet, as to be purchased at the price of chains and slavery? Forbid it, Almighty God! I know not what course others may take; but as for me, give me liberty or give me death!

Literature

? **Respond to a writing prompt.** Read the practice prompt on the previous page again to be sure that you understand its focus. Then reread the selection. Next, form a thesis statement, briefly list your main ideas in a graphic organizer, and write your response essay. Use the revising and editing tips on the next page to check your response before turning it in.

After students have turned in their essays, have them discuss the reading selection as a group:

Ask students to explain in their own words the reasons Patrick Henry gives for supporting rebellion. Possible responses:

- It is the only way to win freedom.
- The idea of liberty will inspire people to fight bravely.
- God is on the colonists' side.
- It is too late to withdraw with honor from the battle.
- Life in slavery is not worth living.

What words, phrases, and sentence structures are most convincing?

- repetition of words and phrases *(. . . we must fight! I repeat it, sir, we must fight!)*
- asking a series of questions *(But when shall we be stronger? Will it be the next week, or the next year? Will it be . . . ?)*
- use of strong words *(The battle, sir, is not to the strong alone; it is to the vigilant, the active, the brave.)*
- use of strong metaphors *(Our chains are forged! Their clanking may be heard . . .)*

Revising Improving Your Response

Acknowledge that students might normally spend as much time revising their first drafts as they spend writing them, but in timed tests, students will need to write first drafts that are close to the final version. They should think of the revision stage as a time to make limited changes.

Suggest that students study the revising questions until they are completely familiar with them. Tell students they should take extra care to address ideas and organization during the prewriting and writing phases. This way, during revision they can focus primarily on changes needed to perfect voice, word choice, and sentence fluency.

Editing Checking Your Response

Point out that there are items on the editing checklist that students have internalized by now (using end punctuation for sentences, capitalizing the first words). Suggest that when checking an essay during a test, students should focus their attention on the conventions that they know, from past experience, might cause them trouble.

Revising Improving Your Response

Always review your response at the end of a writing test. Make any changes and corrections as neatly as possible. Use the following questions to help you revise your response.

- **Ideas:** Does my thesis statement address the focus of the prompt? Do the details support the thesis?
- **Organization:** Have I included a beginning, a middle, and an ending? Does each paragraph have a focus? Did I conclude with an insight about the literature selection?
- **Voice:** Do I sound clear in my thinking?
- **Word Choice:** Do the words that I use reflect my clear understanding of the literature selection? Have I avoided any unnecessary repetition?
- **Sentence Fluency:** Are all of my sentences complete? Do my sentences flow smoothly from one to the next?

Improve your work. Reread your practice response, asking yourself the questions above. Make any changes neatly.

Editing Checking Your Response

In your final read-through, check your punctuation, capitalization, spelling, and grammar.

Conventions

_____	**1.**	Have I used end punctuation for every sentence?
_____	**2.**	Have I capitalized all proper nouns and first words of sentences?
_____	**3.**	Have I checked the spelling in my work?
_____	**4.**	Have I made sure my subjects and verbs agree?
_____	**5.**	Have I put quotation marks around the exact words that I quoted from the selection?

Check your response. Read over your work, looking for errors in punctuation, capitalization, spelling, and grammar. Make corrections neatly.

Responding to Literature on Tests

Use the following tips as a guide whenever you respond to a prompt about literature. These tips will help you respond to both fiction and nonfiction selections.

Before you write . . .

- **Be clear about the time limit.**
  Plan enough time for prewriting, writing, and revising.
- **Understand the prompt.**
  Be sure that you know what the prompt requires. Pay special attention to the key word that tells you what you need to do.
- **Read the selection with the focus of the prompt in mind.**
  Take notes that will help you form your thesis. If you're working on a copy of the selection, underline important details.
- **Form your thesis statement.**
  The thesis statement should identify the specific topic plus the focus of the prompt.
- **Make a graphic organizer.**
  Jot down main points and possible quotations for your essay.

As you write . . .

- **Maintain the focus of your essay.**
  Keep your thesis in mind as you write.
- **Be selective.**
  Use examples from your graphic organizer and the selection to support your thesis.
- **End in a meaningful way.**
  Start by revisiting the thesis. Then try to share a final insight about the topic with the reader.

After you write a first draft . . .

- **Check for completeness and correctness.**
  Use the questions on page **310** to revise your essay. Then check for errors in punctuation, capitalization, spelling, and grammar.

Try It!

Plan and write a response. Read a prompt your teacher supplies. Analyze it, read the selection, form a thesis statement, list ideas in a graphic organizer, and write your essay. Then revise and edit your response. Try to complete your work within the time your teacher gives you.

Literature

Responding to Literature on Tests

Point out that students must approach timed writing assignments differently from open-ended writing assignments.

**Try It!
Answers**

To give students practice with timed assessments, allow them the same amount of time to write their response essay as they will be allotted on school, district, or state assessments. Break down each part of the process into clear chunks of time. For example, you might give students

- 15 minutes for note taking and planning,
- 20 minutes for writing, and
- 10 minutes for editing and proofreading.

Tell students when time is up for each section. Start the assignment at the top of the hour or at the half-hour to make it easier for students to keep track of the time.

Creative Writing Overview

Common Core Standards Focus

Writing 3: Write narratives to develop real or imagined experiences or events using effective technique, well-chosen details, and well-structured event sequences.

Language 2: Demonstrate command of the conventions of standard English capitalization, punctuation, and spelling when writing.

Writing Forms

- short story
- play
- poems

Focus on the Traits

- **Ideas** Creating characters the reader will care about, developing a believable conflict, and establishing a setting
- **Organization** Building suspense that leads up to the climax
- **Voice** Using dialogue that sounds natural and reflects the characters' thoughts and feelings
- **Word Choice** Describing action to show rather than tell
- **Sentence Fluency** Writing a variety of sentences that flow smoothly
- **Conventions** Checking for errors in punctuation, capitalization, spelling, and grammar

Literature Connections

- **"The Most Dangerous Game"** by Richard Connell
- **The Frog Prince** by David Mamet
- **"Spring is like a perhaps hand"** and **"in Just-"** by E.E. Cummings
- **"Mother to Son"** and **"Theme for English B"** by Langston Hughes
- The haiku of Matsuo Bashō

Technology Connections

 Write Source Online
www.hmheducation.com/writesource

- **Net-text**
- **Bookshelf**
- **GrammarSnap**
- **Portfolio**
- **Essay Scoring**
- **Writing Network features**
- **File Cabinet**

 Interactive Whiteboard Lessons

Suggested Creative Writing Unit (5 Weeks)

Day	Writing and Skills Instruction	Student Edition		SkillsBook	Daily Language Workouts	Write Source Online
		Main Pages	Resource Units*			
WEEK 1 1	**Writing Stories** (Model) Literature Connections	313–317			42–43	Interactive Whiteboard Lessons
2–5	(Prewriting, Writing)	318–319				Net-text
WEEK 2 6–7	(Revising)	320			44–45	Net-text
	Skills Activities:					
	• Punctuating Dialogue		616 (+), 632 (+)	37		GrammarSnap
	• Conjunctions and Interjections		546 (+), 547, 734–735	119–121		
	• Verbs		538, 714–715, 716 (+), 718 (+), 720 (+), 721 (+)	90, 91, 92, 93, 94		GrammarSnap
	• Modeling Sentences		560	145		

* These units are also located in the back of the *Teacher's Edition*. Resource Units include "Basic Grammar and Writing," "A Writer's Resource," and "Proofreader's Guide."
(+) This activity is located in a different section of the *Write Source Student Edition*. If students have already completed this activity, you may wish to review it at this time.

Day	Writing and Skills Instruction	Student Edition		SkillsBook	Daily Language Workouts	Write Source Online
		Main Pages	Resource Units*			
8–9	(Editing)	320			44–45	*Net-text*
	Skills Activities: • Sentence Problems (review)		557 (+), 558 (+), 559 (+)	179–180, 187–188		
	• Subject-Verb Agreement			150		*GrammarSnap*
10 *opt.*	Other Story Patterns	321	752 (+), 754 (+)			
11	**Writing Plays** (Model) ◍ Literature Connections	323–326			46–47	
12–15	(Prewriting, Writing)	327–330				*Net-text*
16–17	(Revising)	331			48–49	*Net-text*
	Skills Activities: • Punctuating Dialogue		616 (+), 632 (+)			*GrammarSnap*
	• Interjections		734 (+)	118		
	• Pronouns		536–537, 704 (+), 710–711	80		
18–19	(Editing)	331				*Net-text*
	Skills Activities: • End Punctuation (review)		605–606 (+)	7		
20 *opt.*	*Advertising Script*	332				
21–22	**Writing Poems: Free-Verse Poem** (Model) ◍ Literature Connections	333–334			50–51	
	(Prewriting)	335–336				
	(Writing) Prepositions and Prepositional Phrases	336	544 (+), 545 (+), 732–733			*GrammarSnap*
23–24	(Revising)	337				
	Skills Activities: • Parts of Speech Review		534–547 (+), 700 (+), 701–734 (+)	123–124		
	• Adverbs		730 (+)	116		*GrammarSnap*
	• Basic Sentence Patterns		760–761, 762–763	142		
	• Phrases		742 (+), 744 (+)	135		
25	(Editing, Presenting)	337				*Net-text, Portfolio*
	Skills Activities: • Spelling		644 (+), 666–668 (+)	55		
	• Commas (review)		608–616 (+)	13		*GrammarSnap*
opt.	*Blues Poem* ◍ Literature Connections	338				
opt.	*Senryu Poems* ◍ Literature Connections	339				

* These units are also located in the back of the *Teacher's Edition*. Resource Units include "Basic Grammar and Writing," "A Writer's Resource," and "Proofreader's Guide."
(+) This activity is located in a different section of the *Write Source Student Edition*. If students have already completed this activity, you may wish to review it at this time.

Creative Writing

This overview for creative writing includes some specific teaching suggestions for the unit. The description of each chapter will help you decide which parts of the unit to teach.

Writing Focus

Writing Stories (pages 313–322)

The basic parts of every story (characters, a setting, a plot, and a theme) are presented in this chapter with examples. Although story writing is inventive, its roots are found in the experiences and memories of the writer. This chapter will help students blend fiction and fact into effective creative compositions.

Writing Plays (pages 323–332)

A play is a story brought to life on stage or in film. Once students understand that, they will generally find watching a play an interesting experience. At the same time, students will discover that, with a bit of imagination and effort, they can write simple plays. This chapter leads students through the various parts of playwriting, including character formation, conflict development and resolution, and stage direction. The advertising script presents a possible extension activity.

Writing Poetry (pages 333–341)

Put simply, reading and understanding poetry is challenging work. Explicating (analyzing) a poem is an excellent exercise in bringing personal insight and basic understanding of a text into focus in such a way as to reveal depth and meaning that would not be likely in a casual reading. Here intuition, along with sensitivity to sight, sound, and other sensual images, can be refined as skills to use in all analytical writing.

Writing good poetry is even more challenging. Nevertheless, students can learn to appreciate the deep human expression often found in poetry. Their attempts at creating poetry may help them better appreciate a finely crafted poem as well as open up a new area of self-expression rich in symbolism and insight. This chapter samples free verse, blues, and senryu poems. The techniques of poetry are shown with examples.

Academic Vocabulary

Read aloud the academic terms, as well as the descriptions and questions. Model for students how to read one question and answer it. Have partners monitor their understanding and seek clarification of the terms by working through the meanings and questions together.

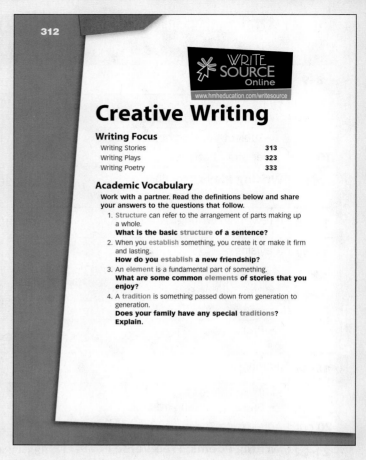

Minilessons

Story Circles   Writing Stories

- **FORM** story circles (small groups). **TAKE** turns as each student shares a personal true story or another person's story (anonymously). Afterward, **DISCUSS** your ideas for future creative-writing projects.

From Screen to Stage   Writing Plays

- **WORK** in small groups, based on a movie that you have all seen. On a sheet of paper, **WRITE** the basic plot line, **DESCRIBE** the main setting, and **LIST** the main characters. Could this movie be performed on a stage? **DISCUSS** your observations.

Poetry Sampler   Writing Poetry

- **WRITE** an example of each of the figures of speech shown on SE page 340. **WRITE** two examples using onomatopoeia and two examples using rhyme. (**SEE** SE page 341.)

Writing Stories

Writing about your own experiences is fairly easy, and so is writing about people that you know well. You simply tap into your memory and write. However, writing made-up stories is another matter. While the starting point for a story may be a real experience, the end result should be something new and imaginative.

To write effective stories, you must understand how stories develop. Usually, there is a main character doing some activity, and a problem, or conflict, occurs. The story then unfolds around the main character's attempts to solve the problem. You will begin to understand basic story structure if you read a variety of short stories and novels. The information in this chapter will get you started on your own story writing.

Writing Guidelines

Subject: **Getting to know someone**
Form: **Short story**
Purpose: **To engage and entertain**
Audience: **Classmates**

"I try to give the readers a slice out of life."
—Stephen Crane

Writing Stories

Objectives

- demonstrate an understanding of the content and structure of a short story
- choose a topic (getting to know someone) to write about
- plan, draft, revise, and edit a short story

Remind students that a **short story** usually has one main character with a problem or conflict.

- The *exposition* introduces the character, setting, and conflict.
- The *rising action* consists of a series of events or actions that lead to the climax or high point.
- The *climax* is the turning point—usually the most exciting moment—in the story. This is when the main character makes a life-changing decision or comes to a life-changing realization.
- The *falling action* shows how the main character deals with the change.
- The *resolution* brings the story to an end in a satisfactory way.

 Technology Connections

Use this unit's Interactive Whiteboard Lesson to introduce creative writing.

 Interactive Whiteboard Lessons

The Shape of Stories

To familiarize students with the short-story format, share several short stories throughout the unit.

Share your favorite short stories and authors with students. Then invite students to share their favorites. They can flip through their literature texts to recall stories they have read and enjoyed recently.

List suggested story titles on the board. Ask students to explain why they enjoyed reading these stories and how the stories fit the description for an effective short story (main character, problem or conflict, attempts to solve the problem, resolution).

Point out that recognizing what they enjoy reading will help students decide what they want to write. Remind students that writers do their best writing when they write about what they know best.

Suggest that students visit the library to look for good short-story collections. Or request that the librarian pull collections in advance of the unit and display them prominently in the library.

314

The Shape of Stories

Think of a special experience in your life: a concert, family trip, school play, championship game, or some other event. The best experiences gradually build in excitement to a high point—a big payoff—that really makes the event memorable. The best fictional stories do the same thing; they follow a classic plot line that builds to a climax.

Beginning with the Plot

The plot refers to the events or actions that move a story along from start to finish. A plot has five parts: *exposition, rising action, climax, falling action,* and *resolution*. The plot line below shows how these parts work together.

Exposition

The *exposition* is the beginning part of a story in which the main character, conflict, and setting are introduced. The conflict is the problem that the main character faces. The setting is where and when the action takes place.

Juan Lopez is about to leave school and head to the park. In one hand, he carries a copy of Conrad Richter's *The Light in the Forest,* and in the other hand, a suspension slip. He's been skipping classes, and now the principal has made his skipping official. "What do you want to do with your life?" the principal yells after him, the same thing Juan's father yelled that morning.

English Language Learners

Use a favorite picture book to show an example of plot development and to help students easily identify each part of a story without having to focus on the text. For example, *The Very Hungry Caterpillar* by Eric Carle shows all five parts of the plot.

Rising Action

In a short story, the *rising action* usually includes at least two or three important actions involving the main character and his or her problem. This builds suspense into the story.

First Action: Juan finishes *The Light in the Forest*, the story of a young man in Colonial America who is torn between two cultures. Juan, who recently moved to the United States from Puerto Rico, understands that feeling.

Second Action: Juan remembers hearing about a vision quest, in which a young Native American leaves his family and travels into the wilderness to discover his guardian spirit. (*Guardian* means "one who protects.")

Third Action: Juan looks for a guardian spirit. He sees a squirrel looking for food, and wishes he weren't stuck here, cold and hungry, on the park bench. He sees geese flying south and wishes he could fly to Puerto Rico.

Climax

The *climax* is the moment of truth or the most exciting action, when the character confronts her or his problem head-on. All the action leads up to the climax. In the best stories, the main character is changed by the climax.

A crow lands in front of Juan. The big, strong bird stares at him with calm confidence. The crow nods at Juan and then flies off, leaving a black feather. Juan has just found his guardian.

Falling Action

The *falling action* involves the main character as he or she learns how to deal with life after the moment of truth.

Juan walks home through the cold, dark streets and knows that he, like the crow, will overcome this harsh northern place. He'll show his principal, his father, and himself that he can succeed.

Resolution

The *resolution* brings the story to a natural, thought-provoking, or surprising conclusion. (In some stories, it's hard to tell the difference between the falling action and resolution because they are so closely related.)

Juan arrives home, and his father meets him at the door. "Where have you been?" Juan holds up the suspension slip and says, "I've been in a bad place, but I'm not there anymore. And it's more important where I'm going."

Creative Writing

Have students choose a story from one of the titles that you listed on the board, preferably one that all or most students know well. Have students identify the five parts of the story *(exposition, rising action, climax, falling action, and resolution)* to see how it fits the classic plot line. If the story is in the students' literature text, they can refer to the text to identify the parts.

Point out that writers can **use a plot line to plan a story** *(see below)*. Have students use a plot line to plan their stories.

Teaching Tip: Use a Plot Line to Plan a Story

To demonstrate how a writer can use a plot line, draw a plot line on the board. Then have students fill it in with details from the story outlined on SE pages 314 and 315.

Exposition: Juan Lopez has been suspended. He's going to the park. He's reading *The Light in the Forest*. He had an argument with his father.

Rising Action: 1. Juan finishes his book and identifies with the main character of the book, who is also torn between two cultures. 2. He recalls a Native American's vision quest in search of a guardian spirit. 3. He looks for his guardian spirit.

Climax: A crow leaves Juan a feather. Juan has found his guardian spirit.

Falling Action: Juan decides he will succeed in his new home.

Resolution: Juan tells his father he has learned what is important in life.

Sample Story

Read through this sample story with the class, pointing out the elements that make it a good short story.

Ideas

- The main character gets to know someone she didn't think she wanted to know.
- Actions and dialogue reveal the personalities of the characters.
- The main character learns an important lesson about life: *Appearances can be deceiving.*

Organization

The beginning puts two characters in conflict. The series of events that make up the rising action build suspense and naturally lead to the climax. An ending quickly follows the high point.

Voice & Word Choice

- The characters use language that sounds natural and contemporary.
- Sensory details such as *dingy green military coat, stale smoke and body odor, tapping a rhythm, shriek from a few seats back,* and *toy flying through the air* **show** instead of *tell* (see below) readers what is happening.

Sample Story

Read and enjoy the sample story by Gabe Roberts. The side notes indicate how the story develops from the exposition to the resolution.

> **Exposition**
> The writer identifies the characters, setting, and conflict.

> **Rising Action**
> Dialogue and details add to the suspense of the story.

Jack and Jill

"This creative writing?"

Jill looked up from the poem she had been laboring over. Looming in the classroom doorway was a tall, unkempt boy swathed in a dingy green military coat. A set of earphones embraced his neck, which showed hints of shaving stubble and grime.

"Yes, it is," replied Mrs. Hawkins, reading the crumpled slip he thrust at her. "John Powers."

"Jack," the boy mumbled, his eyes lowered beneath a shock of black hair.

"Jack," repeated Mrs. Hawkins with a smile. "Why don't you take that empty seat next to Jill there?"

The boy flopped into the seat, sending an unpleasant mix of stale smoke and body odor wafting across the aisle. Jill wrinkled her nose in distaste, then forced a weak smile. She was about to speak when the boy flipped up his coat collar and sank down, his long legs stretching to hook under the desk in front of him. *Fine,* thought Jill, shrugging slightly. *You don't want to be friendly, it's okay with me.* She turned her attention to wrestling with the poem once more.

A few days later, Jill got to class early and noticed Jack hunched over behind Mrs. Hawkins's desk, reading one of the teacher's poetry books. He looked different—his face seemed softer somehow, and his lips moved as he read. He chuckled softly, and she heard him murmur the word "quoth" once out loud, then again. "Quoth." Like he was tasting a new flavor. He looked up quickly and saw her.

"Whatcha starin' at?"

"N-nothing!" His face had fallen back to the old menacing hardness, and Jill backed out of the room, deciding to wait until the others got there.

After class, she talked to Mrs. Hawkins about Jack.

"He doesn't belong in creative writing," Jill complained. "He never writes anything, never talks in class, and in workshops he's absolutely useless. He never even smiles!"

"But he never disrupts class, either," the teacher smiled. "And he is listening. Does anyone ever talk to him? Jill, you're a writer. The most important thing a writer can learn is how

Teaching Tip: Show Instead of Tell

Remind students that a narrative *shows* rather than *tells* when the sentences contain action, sensory details, and dialogue that create vivid images in the reader's mind. Read aloud these examples:

- *(tells)* The boy sat down. He smelled bad.
- *(shows)* The boy flopped into the seat, sending an unpleasant mix of stale smoke and body odor wafting across the aisle.

English Language Learners

Define the following words before reading the story:

- unkempt (messy)
- dingy (dirty)
- stubble (whiskers)
- grime (dirt)
- menacing (scary)
- snagged (caught)
- siddown (variant pronunciation of *sit down*)
- cowered (moved fearfully)
- Kay (slang for *okay*)

to see beneath the surface. Jack didn't just appear on this earth sullen and alone. Don't you wonder what's behind that mask?"

Jill thought of Jack, shuffling down the hallway, his headphones firmly in place as though to drown out the world. She wondered if there could be more to him than she realized.

She watched Jack on the bus after school, his ever-present headphones plugged into his MP3 player. His hands made tiny flickers against the books on his lap, tapping a rhythm that Jill couldn't hear. His eyes, half closed, seemed focused on something only he could see.

Suddenly, she heard a shriek from a few seats back. A couple of bullies had grabbed a smaller child's stuffed animal and were tossing it around in a game of keep-away.

The toy was flying through the air, when a long arm in a green sleeve shot out and snagged it. Holding the toy, Jack swung himself up, his head nearly touching the top of the bus as he headed toward the back.

"Siddown!" yelled the bus driver, and Jack slid into the seat behind Jill, turning to face the kids in the back.

"Knock it off, you jerks," Jack growled, and at his dark look the bullies cowered into the back of their seats. "This yours?" he softy asked the crying child, who nodded. "Nice," Jack said, stroking the soft golden lion. "He got a name?"

"Simba," the child said softly, wiping his eyes.

"Good name. I had a tiger called Kiko." He handed the stuffed animal back to the child. "You hold onto Simba real tight, okay?" Jack whispered.

"Kay."

Jack smiled then, and with a jolt, Jill saw that he had a big gap where a tooth was missing. Jack turned and saw her looking at him, and his smile quickly closed.

"I'm Jill," she said. "From creative writing class?"

"I know," he said, starting to pull his earphones up into place. Jill's hand flashed out to stop him.

"Hey, do you like poetry? Maybe you could help me figure out what to do with this poem I'm trying to write for class." Jill reached for her backpack and shifted back to sit next to Jack. When she looked up again, she smiled at him.

After the smallest hesitation, he smiled back.

Rising Action
Additional action builds excitement and keeps the reader engaged.

Climax
Jill finally discovers the truth about Jack.

Falling Action & Resolution
The story comes to a satisfying end.

Creative Writing

Literature Connections: "The Most Dangerous Game" by Richard Connell is a story with a suspenseful plot and lots of dramatic action.

Point out that "Jack and Jill" is a successful short story because the writer clearly understands the two main characters. When writers know their characters, they write about them as if they are real people. Use the following questions to discuss believable characters.

■ Why is it important to readers that characters be believable? (They'll care about the characters and want to know what happens to them. They'll connect with them. They'll keep reading. They'll enjoy the story more.)

■ How do writers make characters believable? (by describing how they look and dress; by giving them habits and behaviors that readers can understand and identify with; by giving them natural-sounding dialogue)

Brainstorm with students some methods writers can use to get to know their characters. (Possible responses: Writers can create fictional biographies for their characters; they can talk about the characters with a partner; they can have a partner interview them as they take on the role of the characters; or they can draw pictures of them.)

 Literature Connections

In Richard Connell's short story "The Most Dangerous Game," a wealthy hunter plays a deadly game with the main character, trapping him on a jungle-covered island where people, rather than animals, are hunted for sport.

Discuss with students how the author builds suspense by introducing the main character to new conflicts throughout the story. For additional models of creative writing, see the Reading-Writing Connections beginning on page TE-36.

Prewriting Planning Your Writing

Point out that in a novel, writers have the luxury of developing a character and conflict over several pages or chapters. Short-story writers have only a few paragraphs to accomplish this same task, so every word and detail must help tell the story.

Encourage students to limit themselves to two or three important story characters and two to four important story events (rising action).

Have students use a plot line or a **story map** *(see below)* as they plan their story.

Technology Connections

Students can use the added features of the Net-text as they explore this stage of the writing process.

 Write Source Online **Net-text**

Prewriting Planning Your Writing

Professor John Tolkien was grading exams when he scribbled a now-famous line: "In a hole in the ground there lived a Hobbit." Tolkien didn't know what a Hobbit was or why it lived in the ground. Even so, a single character in a setting inspired him to write *The Hobbit* and a series of other fantastic stories.

Remember that most short stories start with a main character doing some activity, and a conflict occurs. As you start planning your story, identify at least the main character and her or his problem.

Creating Characters

Your story should be about getting to know someone. So think of two characters: a main character plus someone he or she learns about. Remember, though, not to embarrass anyone by making any of your characters too much like actual people.

The best stories have characters that you enjoy reading about and grow to care about. Don't, however, include so many characters that the reader becomes confused.

Developing a Conflict

Your main character can be in conflict with another person, with him- or herself, with nature, with society, or with fate. The main character in the sample story on pages **316–317** is primarily in conflict with herself: Jill is having a hard time dealing with a new student in her creative writing class.

Establishing a Setting

The *Hobbit* was set in "a hole in the ground" long ago. Your setting can be any place that allows your main character to deal with the conflict. Limit yourself, though, to one main location and a brief span of time.

Considering the Action

The conflict requires the main character to act, so list two or three actions that could move your story along. Also consider the climax, or moment of truth.

Plan your story. Think of at least two characters for your story, a conflict, and a setting. You could also list one or two actions that result from the conflict.

Teaching Tip: Story Map

Remind students that a story map, like a plot line, can be used as a planning tool to develop the basic elements of a story. A story map usually contains the following headings.

- Story Title
- Setting

- Main Characters
- Problem or Conflict
- Event 1
- Event 2
- Event 3
- Climax or Turning Point
- Ending

English Language Learners

If students find it difficult to get started due to limited English skills, suggest that they write versions of stories they know from their first languages. They can adapt them into English and add some original parts, such as new characters or different settings.

Writing Stories 319

Writing Creating Your First Draft

Build your story with a few interesting characters, realistic dialogue, and believable action. Also consider the following points about story writing.

Starting Your Story

To get the reader's attention, try starting your story in one of the following ways: (The sample story begins with dialogue.)

- **Start with an exciting action.**
  The dog lunged at Ming, and she climbed higher in the tree.
- **Begin with dialogue.**
  "I need to see some I.D.," said the security guard.
- **Make a surprising statement.**
  David wasn't worried about the trees along the ski trail; it was the bear that concerned him.

As you develop the beginning of your story, you should name the setting, introduce the main character, and identify the conflict.

Developing the Action

Place your characters in the first challenging action. Then build suspense with each new action or struggle, leading up to the climax.

- Create dialogue that sounds real and natural. Let the words reflect what the characters think and feel.
- Include sensory details. What do the characters see, hear, smell, taste, or feel?
- *Show* instead of *tell* what is happening. For example, instead of writing "Joe was happy," write "Joe's face split into a grin." Instead of writing "The boat was in trouble," write "A wave crashed over the side and swamped the boat."

Bringing the Story to a Close

After the climax, work quickly through the rest of the story. Show how the climax has changed your main character, and tell how she or he will act or live from now on. The ending of your story will fall into place if the other parts of your story work well together.

Write your first draft. Use your planning from page **318** plus the information above as a general guide for your writing.

Creative Writing

Writing Creating Your First Draft

Before students begin to write, have them return to the sample story on SE pages 316–317 to see how that story illustrates the points listed here.

- To start the story, the writer begins with a short piece of dialogue that immediately captures the reader's interest. Then the writer quickly introduces the main characters, the setting, and the conflict.
- To develop the action, the writer places the two characters in conflict right away. Jill is offended by Jack's unpleasant smell and unfriendly attitude when he sits beside her for the first time. The writer uses sensory details, dialogue, Jill's thoughts and feelings, and dynamic verbs that show, instead of tell, what is happening.

* For information about using verbs to *show* instead of *tell,* see SE page 538.

- To bring the story to a close quickly, the writer shows how Jill's attitude toward Jack changes after he comes to the aid of a small child.

Technology Connections

Students can use the added features of the Net-text as they explore this stage of the writing process.

☀️ *Write Source Online* ***Net-text***

English Language Learners

If students set their stories in their home cultures, suggest that they start their stories with a word or phrase from their first language to grab their readers' attention. Tell students to use words that are easily understood or to provide English translations for readers.

Struggling Learners

To spark students' sensory imaginations before they start writing, ask them to suggest random locations such as a park, a grocery store, or a mall.

Choose two locations and have the class brainstorm sensory details for the sites. Help students focus their thinking by asking for detailed descriptions of things they might see at the locations. For example, a park bench might be scratched or weathered. Then go through the remaining senses in a similar way. Encourage students to consider significant sensory details for their stories rather than just adding them for interest.

Revising Improving Your Story

Students may benefit from two rounds of revisions. First, have them review and revise their stories on their own, using the story checklist as a guide.

Then, divide students into groups for peer-responding sessions. The writers can read their stories aloud or provide printed copies for other students in the groups. To help the writers improve their stories, peer responders should point out

- dialogue that sounds forced or unnatural, or that doesn't fit a character's personality,
- actions that do not help to advance the plot, and
- details that *tell* instead of *show* what is going on.

✻ For more about peer responding, see SE pages 55–60.

Editing Checking for Style and Accuracy

Show students that it is sometimes easier to find spelling mistakes when they read from the end of the story to the beginning. Then they can concentrate on each word, instead of being distracted by the story ideas.

✻ For spelling rules and a list of commonly misspelled words, see SE pages 664–669.

 Technology Connections

Have students use the Writing Network features of the Net-text to comment on each other's drafts.

⟋ *Write Source Online* **Net-text**

320

Revising Improving Your Story

Ask yourself the following questions when you review and revise your first draft. (Also see page **322**.)

Story Checklist

_____	Do my characters talk and act like real people?
_____	Does the conflict really test my main character?
_____	Do all the actions build toward the climax?
_____	Does the main character learn about another person?

Revising in Action
An unneeded idea is deleted, and a new idea is added.

"N-nothing!" His face had fallen back to the old menacing hardness ~~when he saw her~~, and Jill backed out of
deciding to wait until the others got there
the room.

Editing Checking for Style and Accuracy

When you edit your revised story, check for capitalization, punctuation, grammar, and spelling errors.

Editing in Action
A spelling error is fixed.

Punctuation is corrected.

A set of earphones embraced his neck, which showed hints of shav~~e~~ing stubble and grime.

"Yes, it is," replied Mrs. Hawkins, reading the crumpled slip he thrust at her. "John Powers."

 Revise and edit your story. Use the information above to help you revise and edit the first draft of your story.

Grammar Connection

Punctuating Dialogue
- **Proofreader's Guide** pages 616 (+), 632 (+)
- *GrammarSnap* Punctuating Dialogue
- *SkillsBook* page 37

Conjunctions and Interjections
- **Proofreader's Guide** pages 734–735
- *Write Source* pages 546 (+), 547 (+)
- *SkillsBook* pages 119–121

Verbs
- **Proofreader's Guide** pages 714–715, 716 (+) 718 (+), 720 (+), 721 (+)
- *Write Source* page 538
- *GrammarSnap* Past Perfect and Past Continuous Verb Tenses
- *SkillsBook* pages 90, 91, 92, 93, 94

Modeling Sentences
- *Write Source* page 560
- *SkillsBook* page 145

Sentence Problems
- *Write Source* pages 557 (+), 558 (+), 559 (+)
- *SkillsBook* pages 179–180, 187–188

Subject-Verb Agreement
- **Proofreader's Guide** pages 752 (+), 754 (+)
- *GrammarSnap* Compound Sentences
- *SkillsBook* page 150

Story Patterns

Many short stories follow a basic pattern. Here are brief descriptions of some popular short-story patterns.

The Quest

The main character goes on a journey into the unknown, overcomes a number of obstacles, and returns either victorious or wiser. Heroic myths follow this pattern, but so do many modern stories.

A young woman fights for the right to join an all-male sports team.

The Discovery

The main character follows a trail of clues to discover an amazing secret. Mystery and suspense novels use this pattern.

A curious young man discovers that the bully at school is . . .

The Rite of Passage

A difficult experience changes the main character in a significant and lasting way. These stories are also called *Coming of Age* stories.

A young soldier learns about responsibility while on the battlefield.

The Choice

The focus in this type of story is a decision the main character must make. Tension builds as the decision approaches.

A young adult must decide to follow the crowd or follow her own conscience.

The Union

Two people fall in love, but they are held apart by a number of obstacles. Their struggle to come together only causes their love to grow stronger. Sometimes they succeed, and sometimes they fail.

A young deaf man falls in love with a gifted violinist and then struggles to understand the music he can't hear.

The Reversal

In this pattern, the main character follows one course of action until something causes him or her to think or act in a different way.

A young woman quits school, but then discovers her true love is painting and enrolls in an art school.

Creative Writing

Story Patterns

Review the list of story patterns and discuss their specific features.

■ Ask students to identify the pattern of the sample story on SE pages 316–317 (reversal) and the pattern of the story they just finished writing.

■ Then have students identify stories on the list they made at the beginning of this unit that fit the different story patterns. Ask them to explain how the stories fit the specific patterns. Students may notice that sometimes a story has elements of different patterns. Explain that in such cases one pattern is usually predominant.

English Language Learners

Explain each story pattern, pointing out that a *quest* is someone's deliberate search or mission to find the truth, and that a *rite of passage* is an important event in a person's life that marks a transition from one life stage to another, such as from adolescence to adulthood; it may be marked by a ritual or ceremony.

Struggling Learners

To practice recognizing the story patterns, have students divide into groups of three. Each should read his or her story aloud. All three should then determine which pattern or patterns each story follows.

Elements of Fiction

Review the elements of fiction with students. Ask students to offer examples of each element from novels or short stories they have read. As you discuss the terms, tell students to jot down any element that they don't completely understand. When you have reviewed the entire list, encourage students to ask for additional clarification for the terms they noted.

Suggest that students bookmark SE page 322 and return to it whenever they are discussing or writing about literary elements in short stories, novels, poetry, essays, and other literary works.

Elements of Fiction

The following terms describe elements of literature. This information will help you discuss and write about novels, poetry, essays, and other literary works.

Antagonist	The person or force that works against the hero of the story (See *protagonist*.)
Character	A person or an animal in a story
Conflict	A problem or clash between two forces in a story
	■ **Person vs. person** A problem between characters
	■ **Person vs. himself or herself** A problem within a character's own mind
	■ **Person vs. society** A problem between a character and society, the law, or some tradition
	■ **Person vs. nature** A problem with an element of nature, such as a blizzard or a hurricane
	■ **Person vs. destiny** A problem or struggle that appears to be beyond a character's control
Mood	The feeling a piece of literature creates in a reader
Narrator	The person or character who tells the story, gives background information, and fills in details between dialogue
Plot, Plot Line	See pages 314–315.
Point of View	The angle from which a story is told
	■ In **first-person point of view,** one character is telling the story.
	■ In **third-person point of view,** someone outside the story is telling it.
	■ In **omniscient point of view,** the narrator tells the thoughts and feelings of all the characters.
	■ In **limited omniscient point of view,** the narrator tells the thoughts of one character at a time.
	■ In **camera view** (objective), the narrator records the action from her or his own point of view without any other characters' thoughts.
Protagonist	The main character or hero in a story (See *antagonist*.)
Setting	The place and time period in which a story takes place
Theme	The author's message about life or human nature
Tone	The writer's attitude toward his or her subject (*angry, humorous,* and so on)

Struggling Learners

To help students remember the meanings of *antagonist* and *protagonist*, point out that the *ant* in antagonist stands for *anti*, which means "opposed to," and that the *pro* in protagonist means "for."

Have students note that the *ant*agonist is working *against* the hero and the *pro*tagonist is working *for* a positive goal.

323

Writing Plays

Playwriting has been a powerful means of communication for thousands of years, dating back to ancient Greece. Plays have changed in style through the years, but they still follow the same basic structure. A play tells a story with a beginning, a middle, and an ending. The main character is challenged and somehow changed by the events as they unfold.

Playwriting is a special form of creative writing. While plays are meant to be performed, they are often read as well. The story is "told" by the characters—their **dialogue** and their **actions**. Additional information in the form of **stage directions** helps the reader visualize what is happening.

In this chapter, you will read a play about the high school dating scene. Then you will develop a play of your own about a changing relationship.

Writing Guidelines

Subject:	**Changing relationships**
Form:	**Play**
Purpose:	**To entertain**
Audience:	**Classmates**

"Everything that I have written is closely related to something that I have lived through."
—Henrik Ibsen

Writing Plays

Objectives
- demonstrate an understanding of the content and structure of a play, including stage directions and stage terminology
- choose a topic (a changing relationship) for a play
- plan, draft, revise, and edit a play
- write an ad script for a commercial

A **play** is a story written to be performed on a stage. A play has the same fictional elements as a story—a setting, a plot, and memorable characters, who face a conflict.

To introduce the subject of plays and playwriting,
- encourage students to share their play-going experiences (professional and amateur), and
- have students offer their opinions about live theater. (Do they like it? Why or why not? What makes it unique? Do they prefer plays or movies? Why?) Encourage students to give reasons for their responses.

Sample Play

By ninth grade, most students will have been in a play or at least have read a play, and they are probably familiar with a script format. Use the sample play to review the following features that are unique to a play format and script.

■ **Cast of characters**—lists all the characters in the play, usually in the order that they appear on stage, with a brief description of who they are and how they are related to one another

■ **Speaker tag and dialogue**—tells the actor when to speak and exactly what to say. The tag usually appears in bold or capital letters and is followed by a colon. The dialogue is *not* enclosed in quotation marks.

■ **Stage directions**—tell the actors what to do onstage. They may also tell stage assistants and technicians what to do; for example, when to raise and lower the curtain or the lights. Stage directions usually appear in italics within parentheses or brackets.

324

Sample Play

In the following play by Brandi Lee, the main character discovers that she may be dating the wrong boy. The side notes identify key points in the development of the play.

Friends and More

Characters: **Gina**, a high school student
Jared, Gina's boyfriend
Beth, Gina's friend
Pete, Gina's best friend

(Gina and Jared are on a platform in a pool of light. Beth and Pete sit in chairs, one on each side of the stage.)

GINA: You're breaking our date?

JARED: Look, Gina, you want to go to that concert. I don't. My dad said he'll take me fishing, and I'd rather do that.

BETH: *(A light comes up on her.)* Jerk!

JARED: You could come with us. It would be fun!

PETE: *(A light comes up on him.)* Not for the fish!

GINA: No, that's all right. You should spend some time with your dad. *(The lights go down on Beth and Pete.)*

JARED: Great. I'll call you tomorrow, okay?

GINA: Sure.

(Beth rises and approaches Gina. Gina is practicing her ballet, doing deep and graceful dips.)

BETH: He dumped you? Oh, Gina, you poor thing!

JARED: *(His light comes up.)* Jeez, it's just a date! *(Light goes down.)*

GINA: *(Laughing and continuing her practicing.)* He broke a date, Beth, not my heart! Besides, he didn't dump me. We're still together.

BETH: Then why are you going to this concert alone? *(Gina stops dancing.)*

GINA: You want to come?

BETH: You have got to be kidding! Ask Pete! He loves that stuff.

Beginning
The characters and the problem are introduced.

English Language Learners

Define the following words before reading the play:

● platform (raised floor, for a play or a speech)
● jerk (insensitive person)
● approaches (moves closer)
● jeez (expression of annoyance or impatience)
● wimp out (back down)
● realization (understanding)

Struggling Learners

Even students with the best sense of humor sometimes forget that their creative writing can be funny. Point out that Pete's "Not for the fish," line is the kind of joke friends often make with one another. Remind students that their characters can be witty, too, if it fits the mood of the play or scene.

Middle
The interplay between the characters builds suspense.

(Pete rises and approaches Gina.)

PETE: A concert? Sure. Did Jared wimp out on you again?

GINA: What do you mean?

PETE: I mean, you always come to me whenever he doesn't want to do something.

GINA: I do?

JARED: *(Light comes up)* She does?

BETH: Um-hmm. *(Beth and Pete lean forward to listen.)*

GINA: I'm sor—I didn't mean to make you feel—

PETE: It's okay, Gina. I don't mind. I like doing stuff with you.

GINA: Well, that's why we're friends.

JARED: *(To Beth)* See, they're just friends.

PETE: *(Sighs)* Right. Friends.

BETH: Oh, yes. *(All characters' lights go down.)*

Middle
Stage directions set the scene.

(Gina and Jared move chairs together on the platform and sit facing the audience as though taking notes in school. Pete sits on a chair off to the side. Lights come up on platform.)

JARED: *(Whispering as though in class)* So how was your concert?

GINA: Shhh. Fine.

JARED: Sorry you had to go alone.

GINA: *(Whispering)* I didn't go alone. I went with Pete.

JARED: Oh, good. I'm glad you had fun.

GINA: You're not jealous that I went with Pete?

JARED: No. Should I be?

PETE: *(A light comes up on him.)* Gee, thanks. *(His light goes down. Beth's light comes up.)*

BETH: Well, maybe just a little. *(Her light goes down.)*

GINA: No.

JARED: You know, this works out great. You like to do things I don't, and Pete likes the same stuff you do.

GINA: Yes, he does.

JARED: It's great that you have so much fun with him.

Creative Writing

Read through the sample play with the class, pointing out the elements that make it a good play.

Ideas

- The main character has a believable problem: she and her boyfriend don't seem to have much in common.
- The dialogue reveals the personality of the characters and builds tension in the play.

Organization

- The beginning introduces the characters and sets the scene.
- The discussion between the four characters moves logically toward the conflict and leads to the final outcome of the play.
- The stage directions are clearly set off from the dialogue and are easy to understand.

Voice & Word Choice

The characters use language that sounds natural and appropriate for people their age.

English Language Learners

Plays are written to be acted, so ask several English-proficient students to dramatically read and act out the play for the class. Students who are not as English-proficient will benefit from watching the action and will gain better comprehension of the play and its elements.

Respond to the reading.

Answers

Ideas 1. Gina and her boyfriend Jared don't seem to want to do the same things, even though they're supposed to be a couple.

Organization 2. The stage directions tell the characters where they should be and what emotions they should show. They also tell the lighting technician where to direct the stage lighting.

Voice & Word Choice 3. The writer uses natural language that you would expect young people to use. Examples are:

- (Beth) *He dumped you?*
- (Jared) *Jeez, it's just a date!*
- (Pete) *Did Jared wimp out on you again?*
- (Gina) *I'm sor—I didn't mean to make you feel—.*

 Literature Connections

The Frog Prince, a play by David Mamet, is a new interpretation of an old fairy tale in which a peasant woman places a curse on a prince, condemning him to live as a frog unless a woman will willingly kiss him on the lips.

Ask students to observe how the dialogue between characters in the play allows the audience to make inferences about the characters. Discuss with students how a comedy can incorporate more serious elements while maintaining its sense of humor throughout. For additional models of creative writing, see the Reading-Writing Connections beginning on page TE-36.

326

Middle
The characters work out the problem.

GINA: *(Realization)* Yeah, we do have fun.
PETE: *(Light comes up on Pete and Beth and they look at each other.)* And there it is.
BETH: Surprise! *(Her light goes down.)*
JARED: *(Realization)* You have a lot more fun with him than with me, don't you? *(Pete turns and observes.)*
BETH: *(Her light comes up.)* Aha! *(Her light goes down.)*
GINA: *(Looks at Jared)* Yes, I do. *(They both nod.)* I'm sorry, Jared.
JARED: *(Shrugs)* Yeah. Still friends, right?

Ending
The main character sets a new course of action.

GINA: *(Smiles)* Sure. Maybe we can go fishing sometime.
(Jared laughs as Pete rises and approaches Gina. Jared moves to Pete's chair.)
GINA: Hey, Pete! Would you like to go to a movie?
PETE: What, doesn't Jared like movies now?
BETH: *(Her light comes up.)* Ouch!
GINA: It doesn't matter. I want to go with you. What do you say?
PETE: I say, that's what friends are for.
GINA: Friends. Yeah, well, we can work on that.
(They exit between the chairs. Jared and Beth watch them go out, then look at each other and smile. The lights go out.)

 Respond to the reading. Answer the following questions about the play.

Ideas (1) What is the conflict or problem in the play?

Organization (2) How do the stage directions help organize the play?

Voice & Word Choice (3) How does the writer make the dialogue sound realistic? Give three examples.

 Literature Connections: In *The Frog Prince* by David Mamet, the main character's transformation into a frog is not his only extraordinary change. He also learns humility through two special friendships.

Prewriting Selecting a Conflict

A play explores a conflict in the life of the main character. In the play you will write in this chapter, your main character should deal with a changing relationship.

When Brandi planned her play, she made a list of conflicts or problems that she could write about. Then she placed an asterisk beside the one that interested her the most.

List of Conflicts

> Becoming a friend with an elderly neighbor
> Dealing with a new coach
> * Breaking up with a boy- or girlfriend
> Working for a demanding employer
> Making a new friend

Make a list of possible conflicts. Your list may include one or two of the ideas in Brandi's list. Then put an asterisk next to the conflict that interests you the most.

Choosing a Main Character

After choosing a conflict, Brandi thought about a main character for her play. She felt this person should be a teenager. Not surprisingly, she decided on a teenage girl as her main character.

What would this main character be like? Brandi wrote freely about her to find out. Read part of Brandi's freewriting below:

Freewriting

> I'll call the main character Gina. She's 16 and cute, with long hair. She's really into the arts—especially classical music and ballet. She plays the oboe in the school orchestra. She's not into team sports right now, but would like to be. Gina is very easygoing and has a boyfriend named Jared. . . .

Select a main character. After you decide upon the main character, form your first thoughts about this person by writing freely about him or her.

Creative Writing

Selecting a Conflict

Young adults generally have no trouble at all finding the drama in their lives. Remind students that if they plan to select conflicts based on real-life experiences, they need to be careful not to embarrass anyone. They should avoid making their characters and events too closely reflect the lives of people they know, especially family members, teachers, and classmates.

To prevent students from choosing inappropriate conflicts, have them submit their prewriting materials before they write their first drafts. Review the materials and suggest modifications when necessary.

Choosing a Main Character

Remind students that writers do their best writing when they write about what they know best. It's not surprising that Brandi decided to make a teenage girl her main character, because Brandi is a teenage girl herself. Tell students that they don't have to choose a teenage girl or boy as their main character. They do, however, have to choose a character that they know well enough to portray realistically through dialogue and actions.

 Technology Connections

Students can use the added features of the Net-text as they explore this stage of the writing process.

Write Source Online **Net-text**

English Language Learners

Students who are immersed in another language and culture may feel that people do not understand the difficulty of interacting in a new language. Suggest that students use their personal experiences in a new country as the basis for their play.

Struggling Learners

To get student's ideas flowing, brainstorm situations that can cause conflicts in relationships. Begin with these ideas: friends try out for the same team and only one makes the cut; strangers are thrown together when the teacher makes them lab partners. As students suggest more situations, list them on the board.

Advanced Learners

To help students get the most out of their freewriting, suggest that they explore these characteristics of their character:

- attitude or personality
- background and history
- interests, hobbies, dislikes

Explain that developing these details will help them create realistic characters.

Prewriting Identifying Other Characters

Advise them to limit their important characters to a maximum of three or four. Depending on where and when their play takes place, they may have to add an extra character who has only a line or two and who is not important to the plot. For example, if a play is set in a store, the writer may need to have a salesperson as a minor character.

Prewriting Planning the Starting Point

If you think it will help students, suggest that they create story maps or plot lines before they write. But tell them not to let their planning get in the way of new ideas. If, as they write, students find that their plays naturally want to go in new directions, then they should let their imaginations go there.

Prewriting Identifying Other Characters

Brandi considered additional characters to include in her play. She listed three of them and described each one in a sentence.

Character List

> Jared—He is Gina's current boyfriend.
> Beth—She is Gina's friend who understands relationships.
> Pete—He is another friend with interests similar to Gina's.

 List additional characters for your play. Depending on the conflict, you may need only one or two more characters. Describe each one in a sentence or two.

Planning the Starting Point

Writing a play is a process of discovery. The story line will take shape *during* the process of writing. All you really need is a starting point. Brandi clustered possible starting points that would lead into the conflict of breaking up. Then she starred the one she wanted to use.

Cluster Diagram

 Cluster possible starting points. Think of actions that will naturally lead into the conflict of your play. Star the starting point that you will use.

 Try It!

Consider listing other actions or discussions that might take place in your play. But don't try to do too much planning at this point.

English Language Learners

Students may find it difficult to express all of their ideas in stage dialogue. Suggest that they make one of their characters a narrator who can give the audience necessary details from the third-person point of view (see SE page 322). Explain that the narrator can also describe the setting of the play for the audience.

Struggling Learners

To help students get started, suggest that they begin their plays with a question, a musing that alludes to the conflict, or a call to another character offstage. Read the opening lines from favorite plays. Use students' questions about what happens next to make a point about writing a beginning that grabs the interest of the audience from the first line. Encourage students to write several beginnings for their plays and try them out with partners to see which one would begin their plays effectively.

Writing Plays **329**

Thinking about Stage Directions

Part of developing a play is deciding where and how the action will take place on stage. For the most part, you give this information in **stage directions**. These directions appear at the beginning and also within the play, whenever it is important to say what a character is doing on stage.

Brandi decided to have all four characters on stage at all times. A light shines on them when they talk or do something. Here are the simple stage directions at the beginning of Brandi's play.

Stage Directions

(Gina and Jared are on the platform in a pool of light. Beth and Pete sit in chairs, one on each side of the stage.)

 Plan your initial stage directions. Describe where and how the opening action of your play takes place. Try to keep things simple.

Prewrite

Learning Stage Terminology

Below is a diagram of the basic acting areas on a typical stage and the shorthand used to refer to each area. All stage directions are given from the point of view of an actor facing the audience. So moving to the actor's left and toward the audience would be called *down left* or *DL*.

Stage Diagram

Thinking About Stage Directions

Emphasize the importance of keeping stage directions simple.

- Words and short phrases are usually sufficient to tell characters what emotions to show and how to act.
- Two or three sentences are usually enough to describe the setting.

Students can look back at the sample play on SE pages 324–326 to see more examples of stage directions. Students may also find plays with stage directions in their literature texts.

Learning Stage Terminology

Although stage terminology is important to know for play production, students may have difficulty trying to incorporate these terms into their play script. For now, suggest that they read over this information, but tell them not to include these terms in their play until they prepare the script for performance.

English Language Learners

Students may be confused by the convention of using only words or phrases for stage directions. To give students practice with this convention, have them find examples of stage directions from SE pages 324–326. On the board, write the following headings: *How the Actors Speak; How the Actors Move; Lighting Effects; Sound Effects.* Challenge students to list examples of stage directions for each heading. Suggest that they keep these examples in mind as they write stage directions for their plays.

Writing Creating Your First Draft

Tell students that before they start to write, they should create a chart that lists details describing the characters' personalities and the role each character will play.

Writing Developing the Three Parts

Point out that if there is any background information that the audience needs to know, student writers should incorporate the information into the narrator's or characters' dialogue.

The sample play on SE pages 324–326 has several lighting changes, used for dramatic effect. Suggest that students concentrate on telling the story through strong dialogue and try to avoid using any complicated staging techniques.

Technology Connections

Students can use the added features of the Net-text as they explore this stage of the writing process.

Write Source Online **Net-text**

Writing Creating Your First Draft

In your play, remember to let your characters tell the story through what they say and do in response to the play's conflict. As you develop your play, have the characters reveal their personalities. The main character in the sample play is developed in the following ways.

From what she says, the reader learns that Gina is understanding:

GINA: No, that's all right. You should spend some time with your dad.

From what she does, the reader learns (in the stage directions) that she is easygoing:

GINA: *(Laughing and continuing her practicing.)* He broke a date, Beth, not my heart!

From what others say, the reader realizes Gina takes Pete for granted:

PETE: I mean, you always come to me whenever he [Jared] doesn't want to do something.

Developing the Three Parts

Keep in mind the interplay of action and dialogue in a play. Use the following guide to help you write your play.

Beginning

- **Introduce the characters and the conflict.** Refer to your starting point on page **328** for help.
- **Share background information** that your audience needs to understand the conflict.

Middle

- **Add complications.** Introduce small problems that the character must overcome on the way to solving the main conflict. This will heighten the dramatic tension.
- **Create a clear climax.** The climax is the point at which the main character makes a decision about the problem.

Ending

- **Show the effects of the climax.** The main character should show or discuss any personal changes caused by her or his decision.
- **Bring your play to a close.** Wrap up the action with a clear, definite ending.

Write your first draft. Use the information above as a guide as you develop your play.

Revising Improving Your Writing

Read your play out loud or have someone else read it to you. Change any lines that sound forced or unnatural. Ask these questions as you revise.

Revising Checklist

Ideas

_____ **1.** Is the conflict believable?
_____ **2.** Have I built suspense into the play?
_____ **3.** Does each character's personality come through in the play?

Organization

_____ **4.** Does my play build to a climax?
_____ **5.** Have I included enough stage directions?

Voice

_____ **6.** Does the dialogue sound natural?

Sentence Fluency

_____ **7.** Are all of the ideas easy to follow?

Editing Checking for Conventions

Use the following checklist as a guide when you check your play for proper formatting and for conventions.

Editing Checklist

Conventions

_____ **1.** Does the play follow basic script form?
_____ **2.** Have I checked for punctuation and capitalization?
_____ **3.** Have I checked for spelling errors?

Revise and edit your writing. Use the checklist above as a guide when you revise and edit the first draft of your play.

Revise

Creative Writing

Revising Improving Your Writing

Have students work with partners to revise their plays. After partners have a chance to read the plays, writers can ask them to respond to the questions in the Revising Checklist. If the answer to any question is "no," partners should be prepared to point out specific problems in the plays and suggest possible solutions.

Editing Checking for Conventions

Tell students to make sure that they have used a colon after each speaker tag and to check that they have not used quotation marks to enclose the character's dialogue. Within dialogue, students should use the same punctuation conventions that they would use for writing prose.

✱ For rules on marking punctuation, have students refer to SE pages 605–647.

Technology Connections

Have students use the Writing Network features of the Net-text to comment on each other's drafts.

※ *Write Source Online* **Net-text**

Grammar Connection

Punctuating Dialogue
- **Proofreader's Guide** pages 616 (+), 632 (+)
- *GrammarSnap* Punctuating Dialogue

Interjections
- **Proofreader's Guide** page 734 (+)
- *SkillsBook* page 114

Pronouns
- **Proofreader's Guide** pages 704 (+) 710–711
- *Write Source* pages 536–537
- *SkillsBook* page 80

End Punctuation
- **Proofreader's Guide** pages 605–606 (+)

English Language Learners

Allow students to revise their work by having several peers read/perform the plays. Students will be able to hear how their English writing sounds when it is spoken by other people, and they can check whether the dialogue sounds natural. This is a good way for students to practice conversational English.

Sample Advertising Script

Explain that pyramid schemes have been in existence for many years, and that they're illegal. They get their name from the shape of a pyramid—there are many people at the bottom who contribute money, and a few people at the top who get the money.

Sample Advertising Script

You can create a commercial by writing an ad script. The following script satirizes (attacks with humor and sarcasm) get-rich-quick schemes.

The **beginning** establishes the setting and provides the first images.

PYRAMIDZ R US
Desert Exterior—Day

The Giza plateau sizzles beneath the sun, with two completed pyramids and the Great Pyramid half-built. While overseers bark, work gangs in loincloths haul gigantic stones across rolling logs. One beleaguered worker wears a sticker that says "Hello, I'm Jason." He staggers up in front of the camera and wipes his forehead.

JASON
Pyramid building is such a grind. Blazing sunlight, ten-ton stones—there's got to be a better way. . . .

ANNOUNCER (Voice–Over)
Now there is!

The **middle** uses a voice–over to convey a message.

FADE TO: INTERIOR BASEMENT—NIGHT
Jason sits on an old recliner. He flips through a telephone directory and dials a phone on an old TV tray.

JASON
Hello? I'm calling from Jason Industries. How would you like to make a million dollars this year? . . . Yes? Have I got a pyramid scheme for you!

The ad pokes fun at telemarketing.

ANNOUNCER (Voice–Over)
That's right—Pyramidz R Us can help you set up your own pyramid scheme. Like a pharaoh, you'll rise to the top by keeping everybody else on the bottom.

The **ending** includes a slogan and a strong final image.

A pyramid of cash erupts from the floor under Jason's chair, carrying him up out of the house until he is high in the sky. He laughs joyously.

JASON
Don't just make a pile of cash. Make a pyramid of it!

Try It!

Write an ad script. Think of a product or service to promote—or satirize. Create a commercial using images and words to convey your point.

English Language Learners

Define the following words before reading the script:

- pyramidz R (creative spelling of *pyramids are*)
- sizzles (burns)
- overseers (bosses)
- bark (yell out orders)
- loincloths (strips of cloth)
- haul (drag, carry)
- beleaguered (harassed)
- a grind (hard work)

Struggling Learners

Remind students that satire pokes fun at someone or something. Explain that exaggeration and absurdity are important elements of satire. Tell students that to satirize the ads for a product, they should ask: *What do these ads usually claim or show?* and *How can I exaggerate these claims or make them seem absurd?*

Writing Poetry

What is a poem? Robert Frost says, "Poetry is when an emotion has found its thought and the thought has found words."

That captures the process you use to create a poem. First, you recall a powerful feeling. Then, when the feeling is stirred up within you, your thoughts pour out in words. Finally, you polish your poem so that it best conveys your feeling to the reader.

In this chapter, you will learn to write a free-verse poem that shows a special feeling. You will also learn about two special forms of poetry: a blues poem and a senryu poem.

Writing Guidelines

Subject: **Sharing a special feeling**
Form: **Free-verse poem**
Purpose: **To entertain**
Audience: **Friends, family, and classmates**

"You will not find poetry anywhere unless you bring some of it with you."
—Joseph Joubert

Copy Masters

T-Chart, Sensory Chart (TE p. 335)

Writing Poetry

Objectives
- demonstrate an understanding of the content and structure of a free-verse poem and other forms of poetry
- choose a topic (a special feeling associated with a time or event) to inspire a poem
- use poetry techniques, including figures of speech and special sounds, in a poem
- plan, draft, revise, edit, and share a free-verse poem, a blues poem, and a senryu poem

Help students develop an appreciation of poetry and learn to observe poetry in the world around them. Dedicate one or two days a month to poetry. On those days, students can share a favorite poem or the words to a song.

Sample Free-Verse Poem

Work as a class to answer the **Respond to the reading** questions. Keep in mind that students' interpretation of the poem may differ widely. Accept and discuss all reasonable responses.

 Respond to the reading.

Answers

Ideas 1. It gives a feeling of nostalgia, a mix of happiness and longing for the past. The title of the poem and the photo of the statue, with its bright eyes and grin, set a cheerful mood. However, the poem reveals that the restaurant is closed permanently and the parking lot is empty, a turn of events that seems a little sad.

Organization 2. The first stanza and the last three stanzas focus on the closed restaurant. The second and third stanzas describe the statue. The imagery evokes the past as a happy, cheerful time. That is in direct contrast to the imagery in the other stanzas, which suggests that the present is lacking some of the life and flavor of the past.

Voice & Word Choice 3. bright-eyed with a mustached grin, rosy cheeks, perfect red bow tie, thumb raised

 Literature Connections

"Spring is like a perhaps hand" and "in Just-" are two free-verse poems by E.E. Cummings that describe different elements of springtime. Both poems experiment with grammar, syntax, and punctuation to convey mood and add meaning. Have students take note of the unique structure of each poem as they read.

Discuss how the length of each line and the spacing between words affects the way they read the poems. Ask students why the author might have written *eddieandbill* and *bettyandisbel,* rather than using simple names. For additional models of creative writing, see the Reading-Writing Connections beginning on page TE-36.

334

Sample Free-Verse Poem

Free-verse poems have a structure of their own and rarely rhyme. However, poets craft the sound and structure of each free-verse poem to make sure it conveys the right feeling. Deangelo Piccioni's free-verse poem expresses his feelings about a statue at a closed drive-in restaurant in his neighborhood.

The Smiling Chef

The restaurant is closed
   permanently

Still he stands
   bright-eyed with
   a mustached grin lifting
   rosy cheeks
   above a perfect red
   bow tie

And that thumb raised to say,
   "The food here is great!"

But the parking lot is empty
   permanently

All that remains
   is the vague scent of burgers
   and this cheery statue

Maybe his raised thumb is saying,
   "Can you give me a lift
   outta here?"

—Deangelo Piccioni

 Respond to the reading. On your own paper, reflect on the ideas, organization, and voice of the free-verse poem above.

Ideas (1) What feeling does this poem give you? Explain why.

Organization (2) The poem is divided into six stanzas. How does their arrangement share the focus of the poem?

Voice & Word Choice (3) What words or phrases give this poem an upbeat tone? List at least three.

 Literature Connections: E. E. Cummings wrote especially innovative free verse, experimenting with grammar, syntax, and punctuation. "Spring is like a perhaps hand" and "in Just-" are two examples.

English Language Learners

Define the following words before reading the poem:

- permanently (forever)
- grin (smile)
- rosy (red)
- vague (slight, weak)
- cheery (happy)
- lift (ride)
- outta (variant pronunciation of *out of*)

Advanced Learners

Students sometimes think that poetry is supposed to be written in scholarly, formal language. To help them understand that simple, informal language can have great poetic effect, have students reread the sample and note the difficulty level of the words. Point out that the poem uses simple, casual words, such as *grin, red,* and *burgers.*

Prewriting Choosing a Topic

Think about a time or an event that gave you a special feeling. If you keep a diary or journal, look there for "mood memories," or page through a photo album for ideas. Then again, you could just look at the world around you. Deangelo listed the following topic ideas. He then put an asterisk next to the topic he wanted to share in a poem.

List

Topic Ideas	Feelings
playing basketball—excitement	
biking down a steep hill—thrilling	
listening to Green Day—awestruck	
*statue at the old drive-in—cheerfulness	
talking to my older sister on the phone—closeness	

Gather possible topics. Make a list of topics, ideas, and feelings for your poem. Then put an asterisk next to the one that you want to write about in a poem.

Gathering Details

Like a painting, a poem creates a picture. As you think about your topic idea, consider different sights, sounds, smells, and so on. Deangelo created the following chart about a statue at a closed restaurant.

Sensory Chart

See	Hear	Smell	Taste	Feel
big raised thumb	silent parking lot	old asphalt		coarse statue material
mustached grin		faint smoke scent		flecks of paint
smiling eyes		old burger grease		cheerfulness and optimism
flushed cheeks				sad/funny
red bow tie				

Gather details. Make a chart like the one above to gather sensory details about your topic idea.

Creative Writing

Prewriting Choosing a Topic

Provide photocopies of the reproducible T-Chart (TE page 818) for students to use to generate their list of topic ideas and feelings.

Gathering Details

Have students compare the sensory details in the chart to the sensory images in the poem and determine which ones Deangelo used in "The Smiling Chef."

Provide photocopies of the reproducible Sensory Chart (TE page 820) for students to use to gather sensory details about their topic. Be sure students understand that they do not have to struggle here for the exact language they will use in their poems. Instead, they should concentrate on listing as many details as they can think of about their topics.

 Technology Connections

Students can use the added features of the Net-text as they explore this stage of the writing process.

※ *Write Source Online* **Net-text**

English Language Learners

Expressing emotion in writing may be a difficult skill to master. Allow students to gather ideas by brainstorming topics and emotions in their first languages. Then they can translate their lists into English. Check the translations to make sure their details express the emotions that they are trying to convey.

Struggling Learners

To help students understand that their poems need not be limited to one emotion, such as happiness or sadness, draw their attention to the "Feel" category in the sample Sensory Chart. Note that the writer listed the emotions *cheerfulness, optimism, sad,* and *funny,* which all came through effectively in his poem. Explain that sometimes conflicting feelings make for very interesting poetry by creating a conflict or tension that the writer seeks to understand.

Prewriting Using Poetic Techniques

Discuss the poetry techniques here, as well as the ones on SE pages 340–341.

Invite volunteers to offer their own examples of each technique, based on ideas in their sensory details chart. This will provide the class with additional examples and will also give the volunteers a head start on their poems.

Writing Developing Your First Draft

Remind students that the purpose of the drafting step in the writing process is to get their ideas on paper. They will have time to make changes when they revise.

Technology Connections

Students can use the added features of the Net-text as they explore this stage of the writing process.

Write Source Online **Net-text**

336

Prewriting Using Poetic Techniques

Poets often use figures of speech and special sound techniques in their writing. (See pages **340–341**.) For example, Deangelo uses *personification*, *repetition*, and *rhythm* in his poem.

Using Personification

Personification gives personality to an animal, object, or idea.

> And that thumb raised to say,
> "The food here is great!"

Adding Repetition

Repetition emphasizes a word or phrase and can unify a poem.

> The restaurant is closed
> permanently

> But the parking lot is empty
> permanently

Consonance is the repetition of consonant sounds anywhere in words. (Also see *alliteration* on page **340**.) The repetition of the *r* sound in the following words adds a pleasing rhythm to the poem.

> . . . lifting rosy cheeks above a perfect red bow tie.

Explore poetic techniques. In your sensory chart, underline any ideas that suggest one of the techniques above.

Writing Developing Your First Draft

The first draft of a poem should spill onto the page. These guidelines will help you write freely.

- **Think** about the idea and feeling you have chosen. Scan your sensory chart for details.
- **Let** the mood or feeling generated by the topic guide your writing.
- **Write** whatever comes to mind.

Write your first draft. Use the guidelines above as you write your poem. Also experiment with personification, repetition, and consonance.

Grammar Connection

Prepositions and Prepositional Phrases
- **Proofreader's Guide** pages 732–733
- **Write Source** pages 544 (+), 545 (+)
- **GrammarSnap** Prepositions

English Language Learners

Review repetition in poetry as a technique to make a strong point. Tell students that if they repeat a word or phrase, the repetition should improve the poem. Have them experiment with different key words or phrases to produce the desired effect.

Revising Focusing on the Traits

During the revising process, you improve your poem until it conveys the feeling you intend. In particular, look at the following traits.

- **Ideas** Do I use effective sensory details? Have I shared personal feelings or insights?
- **Organization** Do I use line breaks and indents to control the flow of my poem?
- **Voice** Do I sound interested in the poem's message?
- **Word Choice** Are my words precise? Have I used poetic techniques?
- **Sentence Fluency** Do the lines of the poem have an appealing rhythm?

 Revise your poem. Using the questions above as a guide, revise your poem until it is the best that it can be.

Editing Checking for Errors

Because poems are more concise than other types of writing, every word and punctuation mark is important. Careful editing is necessary.

- **Conventions** Is my poem free of errors that could distract the reader?

 Edit your poem. Poems sometimes break the rules, but never by accident. Edit your poem for careless errors and make a neat final copy.

Presenting Sharing Your Poem

Poetry is meant to be shared. Here are some ways to do that.

- **Post it.** Put it on a bulletin board, a Web site, or your refrigerator.
- **Submit it.** Send your poem to a contest or magazine.
- **Perform it.** Read your poem aloud to friends and family.
- **Send it.** Create an e-mail attachment with photos, animation, or other special effects.

 Present your poem. Allow other people to read or hear what you have created. Ask your teacher for other publishing ideas.

Creative Writing

Revising Focusing on the Traits

Remind students that a poem's sound is the result of the precise arrangement of words and syllables in each line and in each stanza or verse. Encourage students to read aloud their poems several times during the revising process to make sure that they have the sound and cadence they intend.

Editing Checking for Errors

Encourage students to examine several free-verse poems, including "The Smiling Chef" on SE page 334, to get a better idea of how poems sometimes break the conventional rules of punctuation.

If students still aren't sure where to break the lines in their poems, encourage them to read them aloud, adding slash marks where they pause or stop naturally.

Presenting Sharing Your Poem

Provide time for students to share their poems. Students whose poems are based on the same subjects, themes, or moods may enjoy presenting their poems during the same session.

 Technology Connections

Remind students that they can use the Writing Network features of the Portfolio to share their work with peers.

Write Source Online **Portfolio**

Write Source Online **Net-text**

Grammar Connection

Parts of Speech Review
- **Proofreader's Guide** pages 700 (+), 701–734 (+)
- *Write Source* pages 534–547 (+)
- *SkillsBook* pages 123–124

Adverbs
- **Proofreader's Guide** page 730 (+)
- *SkillsBook* page 116
- *GrammarSnap* Adverbs

Basic Sentence Patterns
- **Proofreader's Guide** pages 760–761, 762–763
- *SkillsBook* page 142

Phrases
- **Proofreader's Guide** page 742 (+), 744 (+)
- *SkillsBook* page 135

Spelling
- **Proofreader's Guide** pages 664 (+), 666–668 (+)
- *SkillsBook* page 55

Commas (Review)
- **Proofreader's Guide** pages 608–616 (+)
- *SkillsBook* page 13
- *GrammarSnap* Commas after Introductory Words, Phrases and Clauses

Blues Poem

If possible, play some blues music to get students into the mood for reading and writing blues poems.

Have students examine the rhyming pattern of the sample poem, "The Saturday Morning Blues." Students should notice that the second, fourth, and last line of each verse all have the same vowel sound as the word *blues*. Students can adopt this same internal rhyming pattern in their poems.

Tell students to select only rhyming words that fit the feeling and sense of their poem. Suggest that they consult a rhyming dictionary for ideas.

Invite students to read their poems with the blues music playing softly in the background. Encourage them to use good oral expression that reflects the "bluesy" quality of their poems.

Literature Connections

The rhythm of blues and jazz music was often reflected in the works of Harlem Renaissance poets such as Langston Hughes. The poems "Mother to Son" and "Theme for English B" are examples of how Hughes's writing is often rhythmically similar to blues music. Hughes's poetry provides insightful views into the lives of working-class African Americans in the 1920s, and the rhythmic style lends itself to being read aloud.

Discuss with students how the musical nature of Hughes's writing adds meaning to his poems. Does the writing style convey a particular mood or setting? For additional models of poetry writing, see the Reading-Writing Connections beginning on page TE-36.

338

Blues Poem

A **blues poem** follows the tradition of blues music. You express yourself about something that gets you down—and end up feeling good! Some blues poems use rhyme and repeated lines like a song; others are more like free verse. Leida Sulzman wrote a rhyming poem about being bored.

The Saturday Morning Blues

Well, it's Saturday morning,
And I've got nothing to do.
I said it's Saturday morning,
But I've got nothing to do.
I'm just sitting here on the couch,
With the boring old Saturday morning blues.

All I have is a rhyming dictionary
To keep myself amused.
Just a rhyming dictionary
For me to peruse.
Guess I could try writing a poem,
But I can't seem to get enthused.

Maybe I should go outside and exercise,
So I don't just sit here and stew.
I guess I could go outside and skate awhile
Up and down the avenue.
I could skate across a parking lot,
Along the hypotenuse.

I'll need my helmet, knee and elbow pads,
So that I don't get a bruise.
You have to use that safety gear,
If you don't want to be transfused.
Now I'm going to go get my skate stuff,
And bid this boring room adieu.

—Leida Sulzman

Tip

- **Choose a topic.** Think about something that gives you the blues.
- **Gather details.** Make a chart of details about the topic.
- **Write your poem.** Convey your feelings to the reader in a fun way.

Write your first draft. Use the tips above to guide your writing. Experiment with repetition, rhyme, and rhythm, but don't worry about getting things perfect.

Literature Connections: Poets of the Harlem Renaissance, such as Langston Hughes, captured the rhythm of jazz and blues. Examples of Hughes's poetry include "Mother to Son" and "Theme for English B."

English Language Learners

Students may benefit from several prewriting lessons in phonics in order to make their poems rhyme. Focus on the sounds of short and long vowels. Also show students vowel combinations that have similar sounds, such as in the words *blue, too,* and *shoe.* Allow them to write with partners to create more rhymes.

Struggling Learners

To help students better understand the format, dissect the sample poem as a class, focusing on these elements:

- Problem: the speaker is bored; there's nothing to do
- Details: it's Saturday and all she has for entertainment is a rhyming dictionary
- Feelings shown: boredom, lack of enthusiasm
- Solution: she decides to go out and skate

Writing Poetry **339**

Senryu Poems

A **senryu** (pronounced *sĕń-rē-ü*) is similar to a haiku. Both types of poems have three unrhymed lines, with five syllables in the first line, seven in the second line, and five in the last line. However, instead of focusing on an image from nature, as the haiku does, the senryu deals with human nature, and always with a touch of humor or irony.

**Laughing so hard we
forget what we are saying—
which brings more laughter**

**A heart in sand could
last forever, if not for
the nearby ocean**

**Like a helpful book
with an attractive cover—
the smiling teacher**

Write your own senryu. Think of something that amuses you about human nature and compose a senryu about it.

Literature Connections: Reading traditional haiku can help you better understand senryu. Consider reading the haiku of Mastuo Bashō.

Creative Writing

Senryu Poems

Have students explain how the sample poems explore human nature.

- *Laughing so hard . . . :* People get so carried away by laughter that they forget what made them start laughing in the first place, and their laughter makes them laugh more.
- *A heart in sand . . . :* A heart drawn in sand, signifying love, can't last, because once the tide comes in, the heart is washed away. Love is fleeting.
- *Like a helpful book . . . :* Friendly teachers are like the books they want us to learn from, resources filled with helpful information.

Brainstorm a list of topics about human nature and then narrow the list to five topics. Have students choose one of the five topics for their senryu poems. Invite volunteers to read their completed poems aloud so the class can hear different approaches to the same subjects.

 Literature Connections

The haiku of Matsuo Bashō established the tradition of focusing on nature and transformed haiku from a playful poetry style into a major genre of classical Japanese literature.

Discuss with students how Bashō's haiku effectively capture a scene in nature using only a few simple elements. For additional models of poetry writing, see the Reading-Writing Connections beginning on page TE-36.

English Language Learners

Counting the syllables in words may be difficult if students are unsure of the correct pronunciation. Check students' work to make sure that they are counting the syllables of each word correctly and offer suggestions if they have difficulty making the lines flow correctly.

Advanced Learners

To help students grasp the nature of senryu and find ideas for their poems, point out that in addition to dealing with the gentle ironies of human nature, senryu can also poke fun at and satirize behavior.

Suggest that as they seek ideas, students might focus on things they believe need improvement (such as cafeteria food) or that are silly (such as a popular fashion) or irritating (such as people in public places who talk loudly on their cell phones). Tell students that senryu can, in effect, be a creative way to vent.

Special Poetry Techniques

Have on hand several anthologies of poetry, or have students turn to the poetry section of their literature texts. After reviewing the poetry techniques described here and on SE page 341, give students time to find and read aloud poems that use one or more of these techniques. Ask listeners to identify the different techniques they hear.

Before moving on, ask students to find and share more poems that include these techniques. Encourage interested students to form groups where they can read, discuss, and share original poetry regularly.

Special Poetry Techniques

Poets use a variety of special techniques, and these two pages define the most important ones.

Figures of Speech

- A **simile** *(sĭm´ə-lē)* compares two unlike things with the word *like* or *as*.

  The water in the cooler burbled like a happy baby.

- A **metaphor** *(mĕt´ə-fôr)* compares two unlike things without using *like* or *as*.

  His fingers were acrobats tumbling down the row of keys.

- **Personification** *(pər-sŏn´ə-fĭ-kā´shən)* is a technique that gives human traits to something that is nonhuman.

  Distant mountains call, "Come closer."

- **Hyperbole** *(hī-pûr´bə-lē)* is an exaggerated statement, often humorous.

  She sliced a piece of cake so thin it fluttered to the plate.

Sounds of Poetry

- **Alliteration** *(ə-lĭt´ə-rā´shən)* is the repetition of consonant sounds at the beginning of words.

  A jester's job is to joust with jibes.

- **Assonance** *(as´ə-nəns)* is the repetition of vowel sounds anywhere in words.

  Still he stands bright-eyed

- **Consonance** *(kon´sə-nəns)* is the repetition of consonant sounds anywhere in words.

  A jester's job is to joust with jibes.

English Language Learners

Consonants often present challenges to students learning English. For example, the English /j/ sounds like /h/ in Spanish. Provide practice using consonant sounds they are mastering by having students create tongue twisters similar to the sample for alliteration in Sounds of Poetry.

Advanced Learners

Point out that letter sounds can help create specific moods or effects, and challenge students to use alliteration and consonance to this end. Explain that repeated sounds should match the subject. For example, a hard sound, such as /k/ (*crunch, cut, cold*) is suitable for a poem about cutting a fishing hole in ice. A soft /s/ sound (*sleepy, silken, silent*) is suitable for a poem about a boy rocking his baby sister to sleep.

Also point out that word choice can create more than one effect. For example, in a poem about making breakfast the soft /s/ sound could also evoke the sizzle of eggs and bacon frying in a pan.

Writing Poetry **341**

■ **Line breaks** help control the rhythm of a poem. The reader naturally pauses at the end of a line. There's also added emphasis on the last word in a line.

> a mustached grin lifting
> rosy cheeks
> above a perfect red
> bow tie

■ **Onomatopoeia** *(onˊə-matˊə-pēˊə)* is the use of words that sound like what they name.

> **The campfire** hissed **and** popped **for attention.**

■ **Repetition** *(rĕpˊĭ-tĭshˊən)* uses the same word or phrase more than once, for emphasis or for rhythm.

> Inching across the **walk,**
> inching across the **driveway,**
> inching across the **lawn,**
> and oh-so-slowly up the fence.

■ **Rhyme** means using words whose endings sound alike.

End rhyme happens at the end of lines.

> **What** wonder
> in thunder!

Internal rhyme happens within lines.

> Ask**ing** for crack**ers, and other** snack**s**

■ **Rhythm** *(rĭthˊəm)* is the pattern of accented and unaccented syllables in a poem. The rhythm of free-verse poetry tends to flow naturally, like speaking. Traditional poetry follows a more regular pattern, as in the following example.

> **What** wonder
> in thunder!

Try It!

Write your own example for one or more of the techniques explained on these two pages. Then expand one of your examples into a complete poem.

Creative Writing

Call attention to the definition for *onomatopoeia*. Point out that prose writers as well as poets use onomatopoeia because it allows them to *show* rather than *tell* readers what is happening. Invite students to look through their own poems to see if there are places where they have used or could use onomatopoeia.

✳ For more information about onomatopoeia, see SE page 539.

As an additional challenge, some students may enjoy working with a partner or in small groups to write pattern poems that use as many of the special poetry techniques as possible.

English Language Learners

Words for sounds vary greatly in different languages. To familiarize students with sound words in English, present short poems containing onomatopoeia, and ask students to find the sound words in the poems. Invite students to compare them to sound words in their first languages.

Research Writing Overview

Common Core Standards Focus

Writing 7: Conduct short as well as more sustained research projects to answer a question (including a self-generated question) or solve a problem; narrow or broaden the inquiry when appropriate; synthesize multiple sources on the subject, demonstrating understanding of the subject under investigation.

Writing 8: Gather relevant information from multiple authoritative print and digital sources, using advanced searches effectively; assess the usefulness of each source in answering the research question; integrate information into the text selectively to maintain the flow of ideas, avoiding plagiarism and following a standard format for citation.

Language 2: Demonstrate command of the conventions of standard English capitalization, punctuation, and spelling when writing.

Language 3a: Write and edit work so that it conforms to the guidelines in a style manual (e.g., *MLA Handbook*, Turabian's *Manual for Writers*) appropriate for the discipline and writing type.

Writing Forms

- research report
- oral presentation
- multimedia report

Focus on the Traits

- **Ideas** Stating the main idea clearly in a thesis statement and supporting it with enough details
- **Organization** Creating a sentence outline to organize topic sentences and details that support each topic sentence
- **Voice** Engaging the reader with a knowledgeable voice
- **Word Choice** Choosing specific nouns and active verbs, and avoiding unnecessary modifiers
- **Sentence Fluency** Varying sentence lengths and beginnings
- **Conventions** Checking for errors in punctuation, capitalization, spelling, and grammar

Technology Connections

 Write Source Online
www.hmheducation.com/writesource

- *Net-text*
- *Bookshelf*
- *GrammarSnap*
- *Portfolio*
- *Essay Scoring*
- *Writing Network features*
- *File Cabinet*

 Interactive Whiteboard Lessons

Suggested Research Writing Unit (Five Weeks)

Day	Writing and Skills Instruction	Student Edition		SkillsBook	Daily Language Workouts	Write Source Online
		Main Pages	Resource Units*			
1–4 WEEK 1	**Research Writing Skills**	343–354			52–53	
5	**MLA Research Report** (Model)	355–363				*Interactive Whiteboard Lessons*
6 WEEK 2	**Summarizing and Paraphrasing**	483–490			54–55	
	Taking Notes	467–472				
7–10	(Prewriting) Outlines	364–372	590–591			*Net-text*
	Beginnings, Endings		595–596			
11–15 WEEK 3	(Writing)	373–384			56–57	*Net-text*
	Thesis Statements		594			
	Integrating Quotations		597			
16–20 WEEK 4	(Revising) Transitions	385–388	577		58–59	*Net-text*
	Skills Activities: • Active and Passive Verbs and Mood of Verbs		722 (+), 724–725			*GrammarSnap*
	• Word Choice		548 (+)	142		
	• Commas (in a series, to set off appositives, to separate adjectives)		535, 610 (+)	10, 14, 134		*GrammarSnap*
	• Sentences Review		738–757 (+)	147		
	• Brackets, Ellipses, Colons, Semicolons, Parentheses, and Other Forms of Punctuation		618–619, 620–621, 638–639, 642–643, 644–645	23–24, 39–40		
21–22 WEEK 5	(Editing)	389–392			60–61	*Net-text, Portfolio*
	Skills Activities: • Comma Rules Review		608–616 (+)	20		
	• Sentence Problems Review		557–559 (+)	171		
	• Pronoun-Antecedent and Subject-Verb Agreement Review		752–753 (+), 754–755 (+), 756–757 (+)	152, 156		
	• Using the Right Word and Review		694–695, 696–697	62, 63–64		
	• Shifts in Construction			182, 186		
23	(Publishing)	392				*Net-text, Portfolio*
24–25 opt.	Multimedia Presentations	402–403				
	Skills Activities: • Spelling Review			56		
	• Proofreading Review			65–66		

* These units are also located in the back of the *Teacher's Edition*. Resource Units include "Basic Grammar and Writing," "A Writer's Resource," and "Proofreader's Guide."
(+) This activity is located in a different section of the *Write Source Student Edition*. If students have already completed this activity, you may wish to review it at this time.

Research Writing

Each chapter description below will help you decide which parts of the unit to teach.

Writing Focus

Research Skills (pages 343–354)

In an age filled with information, many sources are simply not trustworthy. This is true not only of the Internet but of books as well. However, the Internet is particularly vulnerable to misrepresentation and deceptive information. To be good researchers, students need to sort out the good from the bad. Using primary sources is one way to deal with possible misinformation. One of the best approaches is to examine several sources, which together represent all sides of an issue. In addition, students should not rely on only one type of information, for example, electronic media.

MLA Research Report (pages 355–392)

When students develop a research report, they gain experience with three important aspects of extended informational writing: (1) researching to learn about a relevant, interesting subject, (2) organizing their findings into a focused written report, and (3) crediting specific ideas and quotations from original sources. This chapter reviews the last two aspects of research writing (organizing writing, crediting sources). Students will see how to properly complete an MLA research paper by looking at the model, which is about the development of the news media in the United States.

Making Oral Presentations (pages 393–403)

Most students will eventually find themselves in a situation where they must make a presentation in front of an audience. This chapter will help them with initial planning, creating note cards, devising visual aids, practicing delivery, doing follow-up evaluation, and using other forms of multimedia.

Academic Vocabulary

Read aloud the academic terms, as well as the descriptions and questions. Model for students how to read one question and answer it. Have partners monitor their understanding and seek clarification of the terms by working through the meanings and questions together.

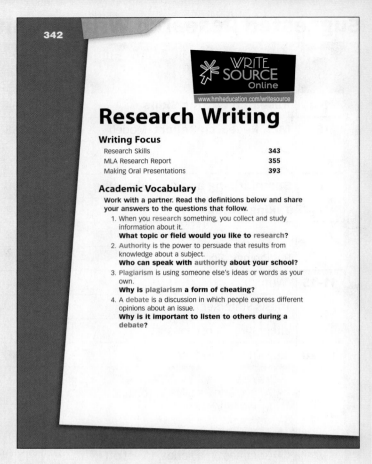

Minilessons

Dueling Detectives   Research Skills

- With a partner. **ASK** a question for which neither of you knows the answer. (For example: In what city was the Declaration of Independence signed? When was the printing press invented? Who drew the first map of the Americas?). Once you have decided on the question, work separately to see who can **FIND** the answer first in the library (not on the Internet or in a class textbook). Afterward, **COMPARE** notes about what you found and where and how you found it.

In the News   MLA Research Report

- With several classmates, **DEFINE** what "news" means. **LIST** the different types of news media. **DISCUSS** what connection the news has to you.

Show and Tell   MakingPresentations

- **RECALL** basic show-and-tell experiences you may have had in grade school. **SELECT** one item for a one-minute show-and-tell. **PLAN** your "speech" in a brief outline, Everything should **FOCUS** on your shared object. **PRESENT** your show-and-tell in a small group or for the whole class. **DISCUSS** the presentations. (See the checklist on SE page 399.)

343

Research Skills

Report Writing
Research Skills

How would you describe intelligence? Most people are impressed when someone has in-depth knowledge about a certain topic. However, intelligence means more than knowing facts. It also means knowing where to find information when you need it. To be an effective researcher, you need to know how to find reliable information. With the increased reliance on sources of information on the Internet, it is essential to know which sources you can trust, and which ones you can't trust.

In this chapter, you will learn how to use the Internet and the library, and you will also learn how to weigh the merits of the sources you find. These skills will prove valuable in the classroom and in the world of work.

- **Primary vs. Secondary Sources**
- **Evaluating Sources of Information**
- **Using the Internet**
- **Using the Library**
- **Using Reference Books**

"Knowledge is of two kinds. We know the subject ourselves, or we know where we can find information upon it."
—Samuel Johnson

Objectives
- distinguish between primary and secondary sources
- learn how to evaluate information sources
- demonstrate an understanding of how to use the Internet to do research
- demonstrate an understanding of how to access and use library reference materials
- know the elements of a dictionary page

Tell students that having good research skills can be helpful in many aspects of daily life. Encourage students to think of examples of when a person might want to research something in daily life. Responses may include the following:

- investigating a product before a purchase—for example, an MP3 player or a car;
- searching for information about a family's history; and
- learning about a disease or physical condition because someone close to you deals with it.

Copy Masters

T-Chart (TE p. 345)

Primary vs. Secondary Sources

Remind students that useful and reliable secondary sources include

- books, articles, and **blogs** (*see below*) by experts;
- reference books, such as encyclopedias; and
- television or radio interviews with experts.

Try It!
Answers

Possible answers:

1. interview with the governor; interview with someone who knows the governor; the governor's autobiography or articles written by the governor
2. a Web site, articles, books, or documentaries about deep-sea exploration

Primary vs. Secondary Sources

Primary sources are original sources. These sources (*diaries, people, events, surveys*) inform you directly, not through another person's explanation or interpretation. Ideally, when you research a topic, you should find as much primary information as possible. (See below.)

Primary sources include . . .

- **Diaries, Journals, and Letters** You can often find these in museums, in libraries, or at historic sites.
- **Presentations** A speaker at a museum or a historic site can give you firsthand information, but be aware of the presenter's own interpretation of events.
- **Interviews** Talk to an expert on your research topic. You can do this by phone, e-mail, or letter.
- **Surveys and Questionnaires** These tools help you gather a great deal of data from many people.
- **Observation and Participation** Your own observations of a person, a place, or an event provide excellent firsthand information. Participating in an event can give you insights that cannot be discovered through the reports of others.

Secondary sources are third-person accounts found in research done by other people. Much of the news (*television, radio, Internet, books, magazines*) can be considered a secondary source of information. Keep in mind that, by their very nature, secondary sources represent filtered information that may contain biases or misunderstandings.

Primary Sources	Secondary Sources
1. Reading the journal of a mountain climber	1. Exploring a Web site about mountain climbing
2. Listening to a presentation by a mountain climber	2. Reading a magazine article about mountain climbing
3. Interviewing a mountain climber	3. Watching a TV documentary about a mountain climber

Try It!

List primary sources you might use to learn about the governor of your state. Also list secondary sources you might use to write about deep-sea exploration.

Teaching Tip: Blogs

A *blog* (short for *Weblog*) is a Web site with ongoing discussion of a chosen topic. Journalism blogs are increasingly influential sources of news. Note the following:

- Students must choose blogs very carefully. Many "bloggers" are professional journalists or professors, but just as many are amateurs.

- Bloggers often include their opinions, so the information may be biased.
- Suggest that students explore journalism blogs, such as the columns on the Poynter Institute Web site (www.poynter.org) and the headline links on www.memeorandum.com.

English Language Learners

To help students understand that print sources can contain firsthand information, have them write a few sentences about a personal experience. Point out that the accounts contain firsthand information because the writer participated in the event.

Research Skills **345**

Evaluating Sources of Information

You may find a lot of information about your research topic. But before you use any of it, decide whether or not the information is dependable. Use the following questions to help you decide about the reliability of your sources.

Is the source a primary source or a secondary source?

You can usually trust the information you've collected yourself, but be careful with secondary sources. Although many of them are reliable, they can contain outdated or incorrect information.

Is the source an expert?

An expert knows more about a subject than other people. Using an expert's thoughts and opinions can make your paper more believable. If you aren't sure about a source's authority, ask a teacher or librarian what he or she thinks.

Is the information accurate?

Sources that people respect are usually very accurate. Big-city newspapers *(New York Times* or *Chicago Tribune)* and well-known Web sites (CNN or ESPN) are reliable sources of information. Little-known sources that do not support their facts or that contain errors may not be reliable.

Tip

Be especially cautious about the accuracy of information on the Internet. While there is an incredible amount of information available on the Net, there is also a lot of misinformation.

Is the information fair and complete?

A reliable source should provide information fairly, covering all sides of a subject. If a source presents only one side of a subject, its information may not be accurate. To make themselves sound better, politicians and advertisers often present just their side of a subject. Avoid sources that are one-sided, and look for those that are balanced.

Is the information current?

Usually, you want to have the most up-to-date information about a subject. Sometimes information changes, and sources can become outdated quickly. Check the copyright page in a book, the issue date of a magazine, and the posting date of online information.

Research

Evaluating Sources of Information

Discuss each question on the page, commenting on the information as appropriate. For example:

- Question 1: Remind students that collecting trustworthy information means understanding and **accurately recording** *(see below)* what they hear and see.
- Question 2: To confirm experts' credentials, students can find out what the individuals have published and where they work (for example, university professors are generally reliable).
- Question 3: Encourage students to become informed about well-known sources by learning the names of reliable networks, publishers, and newspapers.
- Question 4: Instead of simply avoiding a one-sided source, students can balance it with a source that expresses another side of an issue *(in addition to* using balanced information).
- Question 5: Students should not be concerned solely with locating the most current information. For example, the best biography of a historical figure may not be the latest biography.

Teaching Tip: Accurately Recording Information

Discuss ways students can record information.

- E-mail interviews will automatically be recorded in writing.
- In-person or telephone interviews can be recorded by writing notes or using an audio-recording device. Some telephone answering systems provide a recording feature. Explain that interviewers should always ask for permission before recording.
- Some students may have MP3 players with voice recording capabilities. Students should check their players if they're not sure.

English Language Learners

Students may need explicit instruction to understand that *outdated* means "no longer used," and *up-to-date* means "the newest." Use a copy of the reproducible T-Chart (TE page 818) and list some outdated items or sources in the first column. Have students provide the up-to-date versions in the second column (typewriter/computer; 1950 atlas/2010 atlas)

Using the Internet

Discuss ways to do **more effective Internet searches** *(see below)*.

- Many browsers allow you to search for a specific phrase by putting it in quotation marks. This is useful because, for example, a search for *white elephants* will find pages with both words, while a search for *"white elephants"* will find only pages with that phrase.

- Putting a minus sign before a word or phrase excludes it from the search. For example, if a search about the novel *Wuthering Heights* brings up too many pages about the movie, you can type *novel "wuthering heights" –movie* to eliminate the movie references.

- Search engines don't register capital letters, and punctuation is read as blank space. Type in *"margaret bourke white"* to search for information about the photographer Margaret Bourke-White.

- Many searches have an *Advanced* link. This leads to a detailed search form, with fields to help narrow results.

Using the Internet

Because you can access many resources by surfing the Web, the Internet is a valuable research aid. You can find government publications, encyclopedia entries, business reports, and firsthand observations on the Internet. The increasing speed of modern computers makes the Internet even more inviting. When researching on the Internet, keep in mind the following points.

Points to Remember

- **Use the Web wisely.** Sites that include *.edu, .org,* and *.gov* in the Web address are often reliable. Most of these sites are from educational, nonprofit, or government agencies. If you have questions about the reliability of a site, talk to your teacher. (See also page **345.**)

- **Try several search engines.** Because there is an enormous amount of information on the Web, no one search engine can handle it all. So employ at least two search engines when you surf the Web. Enter keywords to start your research or enter specific questions to zero in on your topic.

  When you type a term into a search engine's input box, the search engine scans its database for matching sites. Then the engine returns recommendations for you to explore.

- **Take advantage of links.** When you read a page, watch for links to other sites. These may offer different perspectives on your topic.

- **Experiment with keywords.** Sometimes you must ask a number of different questions or use different keywords to find the information you need. Remember to check the date of the Web site. Abandoned Web sites may contain outdated information.

- **Ignore Web sites that advertise research papers for sale.** Using these sites is dishonest. Teachers and librarians can recognize and verify when a paper is someone else's work.

- **Learn your school's Internet policy.** Using the computer at school is a privilege. To maintain that privilege, follow your school's Internet policy and any guidelines your parents may have set.

Try It!

Choose a topic to research. Enter the topic or related keywords into two search engines. What differences between search engines did you notice?

Teaching Tip: More Effective Internet Searches

One way to gauge the reliability of an unfamiliar site is to evaluate its appearance.

- Is the site well designed? Artwork, fonts, and colors should work well together.
- Do the links work? If not, the information may be either out-of-date or carelessly compiled.

- What sorts of ads are on the site? Good sites have reputable advertisers and few or no "pop-up" ads (ads that open by themselves).
- Are there many spelling errors? This is a sign that the creator of the site hasn't carefully evaluated the information.

English Language Learners

Some students may have limited experience with computers or may be unfamiliar with English-language Web sites. To reinforce Internet-related vocabulary, have students practice using the Internet while discussing this page. Alternatively, illustrate the points on an overhead.

Using the Library

The Internet may be a good place to initiate your research, but a library is often a more valuable place to continue your research. A library offers materials that are more in-depth and reliable than what you find on the Internet. Most libraries contain the following resources.

Books

- **Reference** books include encyclopedias, almanacs, dictionaries, atlases, and directories, plus resources such as consumer information guides and car-repair manuals. Reference books provide a quick review or overview of research topics.
- **Nonfiction** texts are a good source of facts that can serve as a foundation for your research. Check the copyright dates to be sure you are reading reasonably up-to-date information. (Some libraries organize nonfiction using the Library of Congress system, but most libraries use the Dewey decimal system as shown on page **349**.)
- **Fiction** can sometimes aid or enhance your research. For example, a historical novel can reveal people's feelings about a particular time in history. (Fiction books are grouped together in alphabetical order by the authors' last names.)

Periodicals

Periodicals (*newspapers* and *magazines*) are grouped together in a library. Use the *Readers' Guide to Periodical Literature* to find articles in periodicals. (See page **354**.) You will have to ask the librarian for older issues.

The Media Section

The media section of your library includes DVD's, CD-ROM's, CD's, and other audio-visual media. These resources can immerse you in an event. Keep in mind, however, that directors and screenwriters may present events in a way that accommodates their personal views.

Computers

Computers are available in most libraries, and many are connected to the Internet, although there may be restrictions on their use.

Try It!

Visit your school or public library. Familiarize yourself with the floor plan so that you will know exactly where to look for resources.

Research

Using the Library

Strongly encourage students to apply for a public library card and familiarize themselves with the library's resources.

Public libraries are rapidly responding to the growing popularity of the Internet. Many services, such as the following, are available to remote users:

- access to the library's computer catalog (see SE page 348)
- the option to request **interlibrary loans** and place **holds** (*see below*)
- access to the same electronic resources available in the library (such as the references listed on SE pages 350–351)

Find out what online services are available from your public library and show students how to access them. Gaining access usually involves entering the bar code from the library card, along with a personal password, into a log-in page on the library's site.

Teaching Tip: Interlibrary Loans and Holds

Explain these helpful library services to students:

- Interlibrary loans greatly increase the number of books available to users. If a local library doesn't have a book, it can be requested through an interlibrary loan. The book will then be sent to the local branch.

- A hold (putting a book on reserve) allows students to put their name on a waiting list for a book that's currently checked out. They'll be notified when the book is available.

English Language Learners

Some students may not have explored the public library. Advise students on the hours of operation and how to use public transportation to get to the library. Encourage students to learn if the library carries books, videos, or magazines in their first language, and give them a short assignment to complete at the library.

Using the Computer Catalog

Show students a sample screen from your local library's computer catalog, using the same title as in the sample. (Or have students look up the title themselves.) Ask them to compare the two screens and familiarize themselves with their library's format.

Note that, like online booksellers, many library catalogs now show a picture of the book's front cover and provide published reviews. Students who want access to more supplemental information can start their search for a book on the Web site of an online bookseller such as Amazon or Barnes & Noble. On these sites, they are likely to find the following:

- pictures of the book's back cover and jacket flaps,
- brief excerpts from the book,
- readers' comments (to be taken with a grain of salt), and
- information about when the latest edition was published (the library may have more than one edition available, and students may want the most recent).

After gathering information from the commercial site, students can look for the book in the library catalog.

348

Using the Computer Catalog

Some libraries still use a card catalog located in a cabinet with drawers. Most libraries, however, have put their entire catalog on computer. Each system varies a bit, so ask for help if you're not sure how the system in your library works. A **computer catalog** lists the books held in your library and affiliated systems. It lets you know if a book is available or if you must wait for it.

Using a Variety of Search Methods

When you are using a computer catalog, you can find information about a book with any of the following methods:

1. If you know it, enter the **title** of the book.
2. If you know the **author** of the book, enter the first and last names.
3. A general search of your **subject** will also help you find books on your topic. Enter either the subject or a related keyword.

Sample Computer Catalog Screen

The key to the right identifies the types of information provided for a particular resource, in this case, a book. Once you locate the book you need, make note of the call number. You will use this to find the book on the shelf.

Try It!

Use a computer catalog to find a book about a topic that interests you. Read all of the information on the catalog screen and then locate the book.

English Language Learners

Students who have limited experience with school and public libraries in the United States may need more explicit instruction about using the catalog system. Arrange for school media-center personnel or cooperative partners to work directly with these students to show them how to use the catalog system to locate books.

Advanced Learners

To extend the **Try It!** activity, encourage students to find more information about their topics by using a computer catalog. Have them locate different types of library materials, including books, periodicals, encyclopedias, and other reference works. Remind students to consult the librarian if they need help.

Understanding Call Numbers

All nonfiction books in the library have **call numbers**. The books are arranged on the shelves according to these numbers. Call numbers are usually based on the **Dewey decimal classification** system, which divides nonfiction books into 10 subject categories.

000–099	**General Works**	500–599	**Sciences**
100–199	**Philosophy**	600–699	**Technology**
200–299	**Religion**	700–799	**Arts and Recreation**
300–399	**Social Sciences**	800–899	**Literature**
400–499	**Languages**	900–999	**History and Geography**

A call number often has a decimal in it, followed by the first letter of an author's name. Note how the following call numbers are ordered.

973 M | 973.19 D | 973.2 De | 973.2 Do | 974 F | 974 H | 974.3 B | 974.3 R | 975 R | 975.5 Ry

Identifying the Parts of a Book

Each part of a book provides valuable information. The **title page** includes the title of the book, the author's name, and the publisher's name and city. The **copyright page** follows with the year the book was published. The **preface, foreword,** or **introduction** comes before the table of contents and tells why the book was written. The **table of contents** lists the names and page numbers of sections and chapters in the book. At the end of the book, you may find at least one **appendix,** containing various maps, tables, and lists. Finally, the **index** is an alphabetical list of important topics and their page numbers in the book.

Try It!

For a book from your library, write down its title and call number, its publisher's name and city, the year it was published, and the heading and page numbers for one section in the table of contents.

Research

Understanding Call Numbers

Libraries do not use Dewey decimal numbers for fiction in English (or English translations of foreign works). These are shelved alphabetically according to authors' names.

Assure students that finding reference materials, nonfiction books, foreign works, and biographies is not complicated. Signs and floor plans are posted in libraries to guide users to what they need. Students who use their library will soon become familiar with its layout. Remind students that they can consult a librarian whenever they need help.

Using Reference Books

Point out that some reference books are available in both the reference and the circulating sections of the library. If students find a reference book they want to take home, it's worth consulting the catalog to see if a circulating copy is available.

Referring to Encyclopedias

Encourage students to explore the print versions of encyclopedias, which are more likely than the electronic versions to inspire browsing through related articles.

To expand students' knowledge of online references, tell students the following:

- Many standard library reference books are available online at Bartleby.com and similar Web sites.
- The online encyclopedia *Wikipedia,* which contains vast amounts of information, should be used with extreme caution. The entries are written by volunteers and may contain bias and errors.

Using Reference Books

A reference book is a special kind of nonfiction book that contains specific facts or background information. The reference section includes encyclopedias, dictionaries, almanacs, and so on. Usually, reference books cannot be checked out, so you must use them in the library.

Referring to Encyclopedias

An encyclopedia is a set of books (or files or Web pages) that contains basic information on topics from A to Z. Topics are arranged alphabetically. Here are some tips for using encyclopedias.

Tips for Using Encyclopedias

- **At the end of an article, there is often a list of related articles.** You can read these other articles to learn more about your topic.

- **The index can help you find out more about your topic.** The index is usually in a separate volume or at the end of the last volume. It lists every article that contains information about a topic. For example, if you look up "newspapers" in the index, you would find a list of articles—"United States Media," "Freedom of the Press," and so on—that include information on that topic. (See below.)

- **Libraries usually have several sets of encyclopedias.** Review each set and decide which one best serves your needs. (Always check with your teacher first to see if you can use an encyclopedia as a source for your research.)

Sample Encyclopedia Index

Encyclopedia volume → **United States News Media U:** 383 with pictures
Associated Press **A: 340**
Free Press **F: 213**
Page numbers → Yellow Journalism **Y: 135–137**
See also the list of related articles in the United States News Media article.
Related topics → United States Magazines **U: 393**
United States Penny Press **U: 394**
Day, Benjamin **D: 85**
Political Factors **U: 395**

Consulting Other Reference Books

Most libraries contain several types of reference books in addition to encyclopedias.

Almanacs

Almanacs are books filled with facts and statistics about many different subjects. *The World Almanac and Book of Facts* contains celebrity profiles; statistics about politics, business, and sports; plus consumer information.

Atlases

Atlases contain detailed maps of the world, continents, countries, and so on. They also contain statistics and related information. Specialized atlases cover topics like outer space and the oceans.

Dictionaries

Dictionaries contain definitions of words and their origins. Biographical dictionaries focus on famous people. Specialized dictionaries deal with science, history, medicine, and other subjects.

Directories

Directories list information about groups of people, businesses, and organizations. The most widely used directories are telephone books.

Periodical Indexes

Periodical indexes list articles in magazines and newspapers. These indexes are arranged alphabetically by subject.

- The *Readers' Guide to Periodical Literature* lists articles from many publications. (See page **354**.)
- The *New York Times Index* lists articles from the *New York Times* newspaper.

Other Reference Books

Some reference books do not fit into any one category but are recognized by their names:

- *Facts on File* includes thousands of short but informative facts about events, discoveries, people, and places.
- *Facts About the Presidents* presents information about all of the presidents of the United States.
- *Bartlett's Familiar Quotations* lists thousands of quotations from famous people.

Research

Consulting Other Reference Books

To give students practice using references, have them choose a general topic (for example, owls) and look it up in different references listed here. Encourage students to use a mixture of books and electronic sources. As they work, students should jot down where they found each piece of information, as well as some notes on the topic.

When students have finished compiling their research, have them discuss what they discovered.

- Which reference was most helpful? Least helpful?
- Which reference was easiest to use? Why?
- Which do they prefer, books or electronic media? Why?
- Which references inspired students to browse for information on related topics?

English Language Learners

Have students work with cooperative partners to look up the general topic (owls) in different references. Before they begin the assignment, provide copies of the suggested discussion questions so that students can consider the value of the different references while using them.

Checking a Dictionary

Encourage students to explore different dictionaries. By looking up a word in several sources, they can learn more than if they use just one source. Suggest specific dictionaries, and discuss their characteristics.

■ *Oxford English Dictionary* (OED): contains perhaps the best and most detailed definitions, etymologies, and usage examples available; written primarily for British readers

■ *Webster's Third International Dictionary:* the largest American dictionary, but much smaller than the OED, so a library is more likely to have the latest edition; contains more American slang than the OED

■ *The American Heritage Dictionary of the English Language:* family dictionary that includes pictures, word histories, usage, and pronunciation keys on every two-page spread

Point out that additional features are available in the electronic versions of these dictionaries.

Checking a Dictionary

A dictionary gives many types of information:

■ **Guide words:** These are the first and last words on the page. Guide words show whether the word you are looking for will be found alphabetically on that page.

■ **Entry words:** Each word defined in a dictionary is called an entry word. Entry words are listed alphabetically.

■ **Etymology:** Many dictionaries give etymologies (word histories) for certain words. An etymology tells what language an English word came from, how the word entered our language, and when it was first used.

■ **Syllable divisions:** A dictionary tells you where you may divide a word.

■ **Pronunciation and accent marks:** A dictionary tells you how to pronounce a word and also provides a key to pronunciation symbols, usually at the bottom of each page.

■ **Illustrations:** For some entries, an illustration, a photograph, or a drawing is provided.

■ **Parts of speech:** A dictionary tells you what part(s) of speech a word is, using these abbreviations:

n.	**noun**	*tr. v.*	**transitive verb**	*adj.*	**adjective**
pron.	**pronoun**	*interj.*	**interjection**	*adv.*	**adverb**
intr. v.	**intransitive verb**	*conj.*	**conjunction**	*prep.*	**preposition**

■ **Spelling and capitalization:** The dictionary shows the acceptable spelling, as well as capitalization, for words. (For some words, more than one spelling is given.)

■ **Definitions:** Some dictionaries are large enough to list all of the meanings for a word. Most standard-size dictionaries, however, will list only three or four of the most commonly accepted meanings. Take time to read all of the meanings to be sure that you are using the word correctly.

Try It!

Ask your teacher for three words you can look up in the dictionary.

1. Identify the part(s) of speech for each word.
2. Provide the first one or two meanings for each word.
3. Identify the etymology (if given) for each word.

English Language Learners

Include bilingual dictionaries in your classroom. Clarifying meanings in bilingual dictionaries may be more helpful to students than reading through multiple meanings in English. Have students compare the information in their bilingual dictionaries with information in the classroom dictionaries.

Sample Dictionary Page

Guide words — Circle | Circularize   261

Entry word — **cir·cle** (sûr′kəl) n. **1.** A plane curve everywhere equidistant from a given fixed point, the center. **2.** A planar region bounded by a circle. **3.** Something, such as a ring, shaped like such a plane curve. **4.** A circular course, circuit, or orbit. **5.** A traffic circle. **6.** A curved section or tier of seats in a theater. **7.** A series or process that finishes at its starting point or repeats itself; a cycle. **8.** A group of people sharing an interest, activity, or achievement. **9.** A territorial or administrative division, esp. of a province, in some European countries. **10.** A sphere of influence or interest; domain. **11.** *Logic* A vicious circle. ❖ *v.* **-cled, -cling, -cles** —*tr.* **1.** To make or form a circle around; enclose. **2.** To move in a circle around. —*intr.* To move in a circle. —*idiom:* **circle the wagons** To take a defensive position. [ME *cercle* < OFr. < Lat. *circulus*, dim. of *circus*, circle < Gk. *kirkos, krikos*.] —**cir′cler** (-klər) *n.*

Etymology —
Syllable divisions — **circle graph** *n.* See **pie chart**.
                    cir·clet (sûr′klit) *n.* A small circle, esp. a circular ornament. [ME *cerclet* < OFr., dim. of *cercle*, circle. See CIRCLE.]
Pronunciation — **cir·cuit** (sûr′kit) *n.* **1a.** A closed, usu. circular line that goes and accent marks   around an object or area. **b.** The region enclosed by such a line. **2a.** A path or route that returns to its starting point. **b.** The act of following such a path or route. **c.** A journey made on such a path or route. **3.** *Electronics* **a.** A closed path followed by an electric current. **b.** A configuration of electrically or electromagnetically connected components or devices. **4a.** A regular or accustomed course from place to place; a round: *the lecture circuit.* **b.** The area or district thus covered, esp. a territory under the jurisdiction of a judge in which periodic court sessions are held. **5a.** An association of theaters among which plays, acts, or films move for presentation. **b.** A group of nightclubs, show halls, or resorts at which entertainers appear in turn. **c.** An association of teams or clubs. **d.** A series of competitions held in different places. ❖ *intr. & tr.v.* **-cuit·ed, -cuit·ing, -cuits** To make a circuit or circuit of. [ME, circumference < OFr. < Lat. *circuitus*, a going around < p. part. of *circuire*, to go around : *circum-*, circum- + *ire*, to go; see **ei-** in App.]

Illustration —

switch
💡
— battery

circuit
simple electrical circuit
system

Parts of speech — **circuit board** *n. Computer Science* An insulated board on which interconnected circuits and components such as microchips are mounted or etched.
                    circuit breaker *n.* An automatic switch that stops the flow of electric current in an overloaded electric circuit.
Spelling — **circuit court** *n.* A state court that holds sessions at several different places within a judicial district.
                    cir·cu·i·tous (sər-kyōō′ĭ-təs) *adj.* Being or taking a roundabout, lengthy course. [< Med.Lat. *circuitōsus* < Lat. *circuitus*, a going around. See CIRCUIT.] —**cir·cu′i·tous·ly** *adv.* —**cir·cu′i·ty, cir·cu′i·tous·ness** *n.*
                    circuit rider *n.* A cleric who travels from church to church.
                    cir·cuit·ry (sûr′kĭ-trē) *n., pl.* **-ries 1.** The design of or a detailed plan for an electric circuit. **2.** Electric circuits considered as a group.
                    cir·cu·lar (sûr′kyə-lər) *adj.* **1.** Of or relating to a circle. **2a.** Shaped like or nearly like a circle; round. **b.** Moving in or forming a circle. **3.** Circuitous; roundabout. **4.** Using a premise to prove a conclusion that in turn is used to prove the premise: *a circular argument.* **5.** Addressed or distributed to a large number of persons. ❖ *n.* A circular printed advertisement, directive, or notice. [ME *circuler* < AN < Lat. *circulāris* < *circulus*, circle. See CIRCLE.] —**cir′cu·lar′i·ty** (-lăr′ĭ-tē) *n.* —**cir′cu·lar·ly** *adv.*
                    circular function *n.* See **trigonometric function**.
Definitions — **cir·cu·lar·ize** (sûr′kyə-lə-rīz′) *tr.v.* **-ized, -iz·ing, -iz·es 1.** To publicize with circulars. **2.** To canvass or poll using a questionnaire. —**cir′cu·lar·i·za′tion** (-lər-ĭ-zā′shən) *n.*

ă	pat	oi	boy
ā	pay	ou	out
âr	care	ōō	took
ä	father	ōō	boot
ĕ	pet	ŭ	cut
ē	be	ûr	urge
ĭ	pit	th	thin
ī	pie	th	this
îr	pier	hw	which
ŏ	pot	zh	vision
ō	toe	ə	about,
ô	paw		item

Stress marks:
′ (primary);
′ (secondary), as in
lexicon (lĕk′sĭ-kŏn′)

Research

To expand students' knowledge of online dictionaries, suggest that they explore the following reliable Web sites:

- Merriam-Webster's online dictionary (www.m-w.com)
- *The American Heritage Dictionary* (http://education.yahoo.com/reference/dictionary)

Review the pronunciation symbols in the lower left corner of the sample dictionary page. Note that although these symbols aren't very difficult to master, this is one area in which electronic dictionaries can provide more than the paper versions. Nearly all electronic dictionaries offer audio files, which give the word's pronunciation (and sometimes an alternative pronunciation).

If an electronic dictionary is available, invite students to look up the three words they investigated for the **Try It!** activity on SE page 352 to hear the pronunciations.

Advanced Learners

Have students use a search engine (see SE page 346) to look up the word *media* in several different dictionaries. Ask students how the information provided varies from dictionary to dictionary.

Using Periodical Guides

Consider providing additional information about the *Readers' Guide to Periodical Literature.*

- The guide covers articles in more than 200 magazines as far back as the 1890s.
- The electronic guide often provides links to full text versions of recent articles, eliminating the step of **finding the article** *(see below)*.
- Printed volumes of the index are released as soft cover updates 10 times a year. These are then released in a hardcover volume at the year's end. Each volume lists articles published during the time indicated.
- For current articles, the online version of the guide is kept more up-to-date than the books (though not all libraries subscribe to this database).

Using Periodical Guides

Periodical guides are located in the reference or periodical section of the library. These guides alphabetically list topics and articles found in magazines, newspapers, and journals. Some guides are printed volumes, some are CD-ROM's, and some are on library Web sites. Ask your librarian for help.

Readers' Guide to Periodical Literature

The *Readers' Guide to Periodical Literature* is a well-known periodical reference source and is found in most libraries. The following tips will help you look up your topic in this resource:

- Articles are always listed alphabetically by author and topic.
- Some topics are subdivided, with each article listed under the appropriate subtopic.
- Cross-references refer to related topic entries where you may find more articles pertinent to your topic.

Sample *Readers' Guide* Format

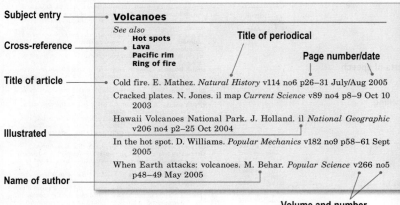

Subject entry	**Volcanoes**
	See also
Cross-reference	Hot spots / Lava / Pacific rim / Ring of fire — Title of periodical
Title of article	Cold fire. E. Mathez. *Natural History* v114 no6 p26–31 July/Aug 2005 — Page number/date
	Cracked plates. N. Jones. il map *Current Science* v89 no4 p8–9 Oct 10 2003
Illustrated	Hawaii Volcanoes National Park. J. Holland. il *National Geographic* v206 no4 p2–25 Oct 2004
	In the hot spot. D. Williams. *Popular Mechanics* v182 no9 p58–61 Sept 2005
Name of author	When Earth attacks: volcanoes. M. Behar. *Popular Science* v266 no5 p48–49 May 2005 — Volume and number of periodical

Tip

When you find a listing for your topic, write down the name and issue date of the magazine and the title and page numbers of the article. Your librarian may get the periodical for you, or you may need to find it yourself.

Teaching Tip: Finding the Article

Explain to students that if an electronic version of an article isn't available, they can submit a call slip to the reference librarian to request the following:

- the actual magazine or newspaper (probably possible only for newer articles), or
- a copy of the magazine on microfilm or microfiche.

Note that special magnifying readers are used to view microfilm and microfiche materials. If possible, arrange for a librarian to show students how to request periodicals and use the microfilm and microfiche readers.

Research Writing
MLA Research Report

Morning news, noon news, nightly news, special news reports, newspapers, news channels, news stations, newsmagazines, the Internet—the news media bombards us on all sides with late-breaking stories. Obviously, this hasn't always been the case. Ancient kings waited weeks or months for runners bearing news from the frontier, and the common people seldom knew about events outside their own communities. How then has our modern news media come into existence?

This chapter will help you to write an MLA research paper about an important aspect in the development of the news media in the United States. In the process, you may gain a better understanding of how and why the media operates as it does.

Writing Guidelines

Subject: **An important development in the history of the news media in the United States**

Form: **MLA research report**

Purpose: **To research and present historical information**

Audience: **Classmates**

"There's no use getting into a writing schedule until you've done the [research] and you have the material."

—Tom Wolfe

Copy Masters

Details Chart (TE p. 361)

Time Line (TE p. 365)

MLA Research Report

Objectives
- demonstrate an understanding of the form and purpose of a research report
- choose a topic (an interesting event in the development of the U.S. news media) for a research report
- plan, draft, revise, edit, and publish a research report

The information provided in this unit can be applied to subjects other than the news media. Since students will be working intensively to create an in-depth report—perhaps their first long paper—you may wish to have them focus on a topic they're studying in another subject area.

Consult with other teachers to determine suitable general subjects from which students could develop topics. Alternatively, collaborate with the teachers to compile a list of specific topic choices.

To ensure that students make the best use of the section, make sure that their topics center around interesting or influential historical events or the actions of interesting or influential historical figures.

 Technology Connections

Use this unit's Interactive Whiteboard Lesson to introduce research writing.

 Interactive Whiteboard Lessons

Title Page and Outline

Point out the specific elements of the cover page and outline:

- Cover—report title, student's name, teacher's name, class, date (no page number)
- Sentence Outline—page number in lowercase Roman numeral, report title, main headings (consisting of topic sentences), supporting details for each main heading or topic sentence

If you decide to have students do an outline (see SE and TE pages 372), ask them to submit an outline for your review before they begin their first draft. At that stage, you can

- comment on the draft outline, highlighting strong ideas and suggesting improvements as needed;
- invite students to schedule a conference to discuss your comments and ask further questions; and
- encourage students to take time to revise their outlines based on your comments before starting to write.

Have students resubmit their original draft outlines, and any revision to it, along with the final reports so you can assess their success at responding to feedback.

Title Page and Outline

Gabriella Neuhoff chose to write her research report about the start of the penny press in the United States in the 1830s. You can read her report starting on the next page. Below are the title page and outline of her paper. Some teachers require a title page and an outline. If your teacher does, follow any special instructions he or she may give you.

A Penny for Your Paper

Gabriella Neuhoff
Mr. Delnoce
English
7 May 2011

Title Page
Center the title one-third of the way down the page. Center and double-space the writer information two-thirds of the way down the page.

Outline
Center the title one inch from the top of the page. Double-space throughout.

A Penny for Your Paper   i

Introduction: The creation of the penny press paved the way for the modern daily newspaper.

I. Colonial newspapers in America were different from those today.
  A. They needed government authorization.
  B. John Peter Zenger was tried for libel for criticizing the governor.
  C. Freedom of the press became the focus of Zenger's trial.

II. Early newspapers were different from ours in other ways, too.
  A. Commercial papers had advertisements, ship schedules, product prices, money conversion tables.
  B. Political papers contained stuffy political statements.
  C. News in both types was out of date.
  D. These papers were mainly for the wealthy.

III. In the early 1800s, more people began to read newspapers.
  A. They liked interesting items like the police court reports.
  B. The nation was changing and growing.
  C. The masses were ready for a new type of paper.

English Language Learners

Some students may have limited experience with the linear pattern of organization represented by the sample outline. Explain that writers use an outline as a strategy to help them organize the ideas and details they want to include in their reports. Emphasize that the student writer developed the sample outline after researching the topic. Tell students they will create an outline on SE page 372.

Struggling Learners

Have students read the sample outline carefully. Tell them that as they read the report on SE pages 357–363, they should refer to the outline to see how the writer used it to organize her thoughts.

✳ If students want to see other sample outlines, refer them to SE pages 590–591.

Sample Research Report

The entire report is double-spaced.

1"

1/2"

Neuhoff 1 ← 1" →

Gabriella Neuhoff

Mr. Delnoce

English

7 May 2011

A Penny for Your Paper

Beginning
The writer introduces her topic and states her thesis (underlined).

Why did newsboys in old movies shout "Extra! Extra! Read all about it!"? Why do newspapers include an entertainment section and an opinion page? Who was the first Washington news correspondent? Studying the start of the "penny press" in the 1830s provides answers to these questions. <u>The creation of the penny press paved the way for the modern daily newspaper.</u>

← 1" →

Before the Penny Press

Middle
The first middle paragraphs tell about the topic's history.

Colonial newspapers in America were different from those today. For one thing, they could not be published without the approval of the government. In 1690, the publisher of the first newspaper in the colonies found this out the hard way. The government arrested him and destroyed all copies of his paper because he didn't get proper approval. In another case, John Peter Zenger published articles in the *New York Weekly Journal* that criticized the governor. Authorities arrested Zenger and tried him for libel ("Milestones").

1"

Research

English Language Learners

Some students may be distracted by trying to figure out unfamiliar vocabulary instead of paying attention to the structure of the report.

Have students work with cooperative English-proficient partners to read and discuss the content and features highlighted in the side notes on SE pages 357–362.

Point out the student writer's definition of the word *staid* on this page and of *impertinent* (bottom of SE page 360). Tell students that the decision about whether to add such explanations will depend on the audience. For a student audience, such as the one for this report, explaining unusual words can add another layer of information. But students should use such explanations sparingly—readers can always consult a dictionary if needed.

✱ Another use of brackets is demonstrated on SE page 362. You can choose to consult SE page 644 to discuss the use of brackets now or when you reach TE page 362.

Neuhoff 2

Freedom of the press became the focus of his famous trial in 1735. He was eventually set free.

The early newspapers were different from today's papers in many other ways, too. Colonial papers were usually "4-page weeklies containing local ads, . . . local hearsay, and large, unedited chunks of . . . news from the London press" ("Milestones"). Even after the American Revolution, newspapers lacked interesting and timely news. Commercial papers "were filled with advertisements, ship schedules, . . . product prices, money conversion tables, and stale news," and political papers "contained staid [stuffy] political discourses in addition to yesterday's or last week's or last month's news" (Thompson 2). These newspapers were expensive and read mostly by wealthy citizens.

Because of increased literacy in the early 1800s, more people began to read newspapers. Common people paid special attention to the more interesting sections, especially the coverage of the police court (Thompson 2). This was also a time of great change for the nation. The country elected Andrew Jackson, the first unaristocratic president. More immigrants were entering the country, and cities were growing rapidly (Younes 14). The stage was set for the penny press, a new type of newspaper that would appeal to the masses.

Ellipses show that words have been left out of a quotation.

Brackets show that a word has been added to explain something.

A source and page number are identified in parentheses.

Advanced Learners

One of the best ways to learn about writing mechanics and style is to study the work of published authors. As students do their research, have them notice the way authors of secondary sources use brackets within quotations. Have students bring in examples of quotations with bracketed text to share in small groups.

MLA Research Report **359**

Neuhoff 3

The Rise of the *Sun*

In 1833, Benjamin Day, the owner of a printing
company in New York, started the *Sun*, the first successful
penny paper. Walking to work each day, he passed
Chatham Street, where street vendors sold items for
a penny (Thompson 8). Day thought he could make a
penny newspaper to sell on the street. On September 3,
1833, he sold the first edition of the *Sun*. It was only a
single sheet of paper, folded in the middle. On the front
page, Day printed advertisements copied from other
papers. The other three pages contained a mix of ads
and news from other papers, two humorous tall tales,
and the police report copied from the *Courier & Enquirer*
(10–11). His paper was an instant success. Soon Day had
enough new ads to make the paper profitable even with
its penny price.

Day quickly realized that he needed help. While he
managed the business, someone would have to attend
the courts each day and write the police report. A man
named George Wisner became Day's court reporter and
partner (Thompson 13). Day and Wisner didn't always
agree, and the paper reflected their different opinions
(15–17). This debate of ideas set the *Sun* apart from the
older, more conservative political newspapers.

Day also needed help selling the paper. He decided
to use a system known as the "London plan." Under this

> The next part of the report focuses on the penny press.

> Each paragraph begins with a topic sentence, followed by supporting details.

Research

Ask students to focus on the section headings
used in the paper. What strategies would they
say the writer used in devising the headings?
Possible responses:

- creative word associations (*The Rise of the
  Sun, The Trumpeting of the Herald, The
  Conscience of the Tribune*)
- descriptions of how the information applies to
  the thesis (*Before the Penny Press, After the
  Penny Press*)

Note that strategies for devising section titles
are similar to those for coming up with titles
for papers. Remind students that a good title
for a section might occur to them as they write.
They should always make a note of such ideas
right away, so they don't forget them.

Encourage students to start paying extra
attention to the titles of newspaper articles.
Newspaper editors often use creative strategies
to come up with titles.

Struggling Learners

To help spark creative ideas for
titles and subheadings, have
students go through newspapers
and news magazines and cut out
headlines that seem particularly
creative or attention-grabbing.
Have students share their
headlines in small groups and
explain why they chose each
one. If students have trouble
articulating the reasons a
headline caught their attention,
guide them to pay attention to
interesting word choices, puns,
or similar letter sounds.

Point out that the writer refers to her sources by their full names on the first mention, but then uses only their last names. On this page, for example, she introduces James Gordon Bennett, and then she begins calling him Bennett. This is a common practice in nonfiction writing.

Explain that if the writer were to mention Bennett again later in the paper, she might choose to use his full name again, as a reminder to readers.

Neuhoff 4

plan, he offered newspapers at a reduced rate to people who then sold their copies and pocketed the profit. The first person to join him was a 10-year-old boy. Before long, "newsboys" were selling the papers all over New York (Thompson 12–13), and the *Sun* became the most popular paper in the city.

The Trumpeting of the *Herald*

In 1835, James Gordon Bennett started another successful penny paper in New York called the *Herald*. Bennett had lived in many places, from Canada to South Carolina, and had gained valuable experience as a writer and an editor. Historians say that he was America's first Washington news correspondent, for the *New York Enquirer*. These experiences helped prepare Bennett to start his own paper (Douglas 27–29). Bennett started out alone, in a dark cellar room, using a plank and two boxes as a desk. However, before long, the *Herald* would outsell the *Sun*. In fact, at its best, the *Herald* sold more copies worldwide than even the most respected European papers (Younes 16).

Bennett knew how to get the attention of readers. They liked the *Herald* because Bennett wrote opinion pieces that were "saucy, impertinent [disrespectful], and funny" (Thompson 34). Bennett also filled his paper with sensational news stories that made the *Sun* seem

Headings help the reader understand the report's organization.

Information from a key source is paraphrased.

MLA Research Report **361**

Neuhoff 5

> The writer's last name and page number appear on every page.

tame by comparison, and he placed these stories on the front page to gain more attention. Many historians give Bennett the credit for the first "crisis news reporting," based on his eyewitness news about New York City's Great Fire of 1835 and his writing about the Jewett murder trial (Douglas 30). The *Herald* also quickly became the best source of Wall Street news (Thompson 59). Along with these stories, Bennett included entertainment news. All of these things helped make the *Herald* a great success.

The Conscience of the *Tribune*

In 1841, Horace Greeley started another penny newspaper in New York. It was called the *Tribune*. Like the *Sun* and the *Herald*, the *Tribune* relied on advertising for its main income, and it included sensational stories to attract readers. However, Greeley believed that a newspaper should do more than just make money. He thought it should keep people informed about important events and educate them about important ideas.

> Quotations from experts add authority to the report.

The *Tribune* gave readers crime stories and stories about local events, but it "downplayed sensational stories by placing them on inside pages" (Thompson 97). This paper also included poetry and literature by respected authors. Under Greeley's direction, the *Tribune* showed

Research

Point out the student's name and the page number in the upper right corner of the page. Tell students that if they create their papers on a computer, there is a special "header" function that will allow them to add this information without having to type it on every page. The word-processing program will automatically keep track of the proper page number.

If necessary, demonstrate how to set up the header function so that it includes the student's last name and numbers the report from page 1 onward.

English Language Learners

Students may need explicit instruction about quotations. Have students work with partners to provide examples that clearly show they understand that quotations are the exact words used in a book or spoken by a person. Provide examples as necessary.

Advanced Learners

Distribute copies of the reproducible Details Chart (TE page 821) and have students compare and contrast the early newspapers described in this report. Then, in small groups, have them explain which of the newspapers they would have preferred to read and why.

Draw students' attention to the bracketed word *and* in the first paragraph on this page. Note that this use of brackets is different from the student writer's earlier addition of word definitions. In this case, the bracketed word is used to help the quotation fit grammatically into the sentence.

✳ For more about using brackets, see SE page 644.

Neuhoff 6

"a social conscience in its news columns and reform-minded editorials" (98).

The *Tribune* soon rivaled the *Herald* as the most popular paper of the time, and through the *Tribune*, Greeley became a well-known national figure. He influenced the opinion of Americans everywhere on topics like "labor, education, [and] temperance" (Thompson 112). Greeley showed that a newspaper could help shape a nation.

After the Penny Press

Modern newspapers and online news sites continue to focus on disaster and crime news, along with editorials and stories about business and entertainment. Also, topics in the public interest continue to appear in the news, just as they did in the *Tribune*. The obligation to the public that today's newspaper reporters and editors feel originated with the penny press. Further, modern newspapers still "rely heavily on advertising as a main source of income and that is also a main reason they are still being offered at relatively low prices today" (Vance). All these things show that "the age of modern-day journalism began with the penny press" (Thompson 3). The free press that grew from those early papers has helped to shape the nation, just as the Founding Fathers had hoped.

Ending
The conclusion discusses the topic in relation to the present.

The final sentence leaves the reader with something to think about.

Neuhoff 7

Works Cited

A separate page alphabetically lists sources cited in the paper.

Douglas, George H. *The Golden Age of the Newspaper.*
    Westport: Greenwood, 1999. Print.

"Milestones in the History of Media and Politics." *Now.*
    Public Affairs Television, Aug. 2005. Web. 27 Apr.
    2011.

Thompson, Susan. *The Penny Press.* Northport: Vision,
    2004. Print.

Second and third lines are indented half an inch.

Vance, Jennifer. "The Penny Press." *A Brief History
    of Newspapers in America.* University of Florida
    Interactive Media Lab, n.d. Web. 29 Apr. 2011.

Younes, Robert. "In for a Penny." *American Publisher*
    1 Oct. 2005: 14+. Print.

 Respond to the reading. After you have finished reading the sample research report, answer the following questions.

Ideas (1) What is the focus or main idea of this paper? (2) List at least three facts that support this main idea.

Organization (3) How do the headings help organize the report?

Voice & Word Choice (5) Does the writer sound knowledgeable about her topic? Explain.

Research

 Respond to the reading.

Answers

Ideas 1. The penny press paved the way for today's newspapers.

2. Possible choices:

- Zenger's libel trial introduced the idea of freedom of the press.
- From the beginning, penny papers used advertising to raise funds.
- Day and Wisner introduced the debate of ideas in the *Sun.*
- Bennett *(Herald)* wrote spirited opinion pieces and filled his paper with sensational stories.
- Greeley *(Tribune)* introduced the idea of informing and educating people about important events.

Organization 3. The headings

- help the writer organize and group related facts,
- break the text into manageable sections for the reader, and
- emphasize the chronological presentation of the information.

Voice & Word Choice 4. Yes.

- The details explain the sequence of events and support the thesis.
- Source references and quotations are used well.
- The voice is natural and knowledgeable.

English Language Learners

Students may be unfamiliar with the works-cited page included in a report. Have students turn to SE pages 381–384 to learn how to interpret the information on the works-cited page.

Struggling Learners

When considering voice, explain that not only does a writer need to show strong interest in the subject, but the writer also needs to engage the curiosity of the audience. Discuss with students whether Gabriella was successful in engaging their curiosity. Ask the following questions:

- How did you react to the title? Did you expect the report to be interesting?
- Was the report interesting? Why or why not?
- How did Gabriella engage your curiosity?
- How did your expectation about the topic compare to what you actually learned?

Prewriting

Keys to Effective Prewriting

Remind students that the purpose of the prewriting stage in the writing process is to select a topic, gather details, and decide how to organize those details.

Keys to Prewriting lists the process students will be guided through on SE pages 365–372.

Plan to tell students a few days ahead of time about the subject area or possible topics for their reports. Encourage them to give some thought to what they might like to write about and to investigate the possibilities in a general way before the class begins working through the step-by-step prewriting instructions. This will give students a little more information to work with as they consider what questions they want to explore about possible topics.

 Technology Connections

Students can use the added features of the Net-text as they explore this stage of the writing process.

 Write Source Online **Net-text**

Prewriting

To get to the top of a mountain, you must take one step at a time. The same is true of a research project. First, you need to choose an interesting topic. Next, you must carefully research the topic, establish a thesis, and plan your writing. Then you'll be ready to write.

Keys to Effective Prewriting

1. For your topic, choose an interesting event in the history of the news media in the United States.

2. List questions you want to have answered about the topic.

3. Be sure that there is enough information available about your topic.

4. Use a gathering grid to organize your research questions and answers. Use note cards to keep track of longer answers. (See pages 367–368.)

5. Be careful to cite the sources of any information you paraphrase or quote.

6. Write down the publication details of all your sources as you do your research. (See page 370.)

English Language Learners

Some students may find the task of thinking of appropriate research topics overwhelming. Meet with students to brainstorm ideas. Model step 2 to reinforce the idea that the best topics are those they want to investigate in order to answer questions they have.

Struggling Learners

Give students guidelines for doing light research to help them choose an appropriate topic for a research report. Remind them that it's important to avoid choosing a topic that is too broad. Have students evaluate the following report topics to determine whether or not each topic is too broad for a research report.

- the history of radio news (too broad)
- a specific era in radio news (appropriate)
- different newscasters (too broad)
- a comparison of two newscasters on national television (appropriate)

MLA Research Report 365

Selecting a Topic

When you are assigned a research report, your teacher will suggest a general subject area. Your job is to identify an interesting specific topic within that subject area. To consider possible topics about the news media, Gabriella decided to make a time line of developments that she had learned about in her history textbook. She then circled the topic she wanted to research.

Time Line

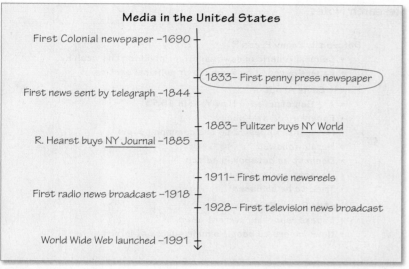

Media in the United States

First Colonial newspaper –1690

1833– First penny press newspaper

First news sent by telegraph –1844

1883– Pulitzer buys NY World

R. Hearst buys NY Journal –1885

1911– First movie newsreels

First radio news broadcast –1918

1928– First television news broadcast

World Wide Web launched –1991

Prewrite

Review possible topics. For a research report on news media in the United States, you may choose one of the topics in the sample time line above. Or you can consider other possible topics, including those listed below.

- How the "New Journalism" has shaped reporting
- The significance of the Hearst/Pulitzer conflict
- The *Progressive* magazine and the H-bomb
- The effect of advertising dollars on news coverage

Prewrite

Select a topic. Choose one specific topic for your research report. Then, on your own paper, explain the reason for your choice in a brief freewriting.

Research

Prewriting Selecting a Topic

If students are writing about a topic other than the news media, distribute photocopies of the reproducible Time Line (TE page 816) and have them use the appropriate textbook or other source to compile a time line related to the designated subject area.

Remind students that it's important to choose a topic that genuinely interests them because they will be immersing themselves in the topic for many hours. Encourage them to **use freewriting** *(see below)* to help them focus their thoughts about the topic.

Teaching Tip: Use Freewriting

To help students get the most out of the freewriting exercise, review questions they should keep in mind as they write:

- How much do I know about the topic? Would I like to know more?
- Will I have fun learning and thinking about the topic?

- Do I have a lot of interesting questions about it?
- Is it an important topic?

Give students a few minutes to think about the questions before writing. Remind them to keep their pencil moving—their goal is to capture all their thoughts on the paper.

English Language Learners

Modify the freewriting exercise for students who have difficulty expressing their ideas in complete English sentences. Instead of requiring sentences, allow students to communicate their ideas using sketches, words and phrases, and words from their first languages.

Prewriting Sizing Up Your Topic

If students are writing about historical figures rather than events, have them compile research notes for these basic areas:

(1) the circumstances before the person entered the scene,

(2) how the person acted to influence the situation, and

(3) how things changed as a result of the person's work.

Discuss using encyclopedias. Why is this a good way to start research?

■ They give a solid overview of topics in a compact, easy-to-access format.

■ They often tell where to find specific information.

Tell students that encyclopedias shouldn't be used as key references in a report because they are "general" sources. The basic information they provide is all available in primary and specialized secondary sources. Explain that specialized encyclopedias—for example, *History of the Mass Media in the United States: An Encyclopedia*—are acceptable references.

Prewriting Sizing Up Your Topic

An effective research report about a historical event related to the media in the United States should cover three basic areas: (1) the circumstances before the event, (2) how the event came about, and (3) how the event affected the development of the media.

Gabriella checked an encyclopedia and did a quick Internet search for basic facts about her topic. She took notes on her findings.

Research Notes

> **Before the Penny Press**
> • Colonial American newspapers printed for the wealthy
> • Papers devoted to business or political parties
>
> **How It Came About**
> • The <u>Sun</u> started in New York in 1833
> • Paper priced at a penny
> • News that appealed to the common people
> • <u>Herald</u> followed
> • Bennett an outspoken editor
> • Horace Greeley <u>Tribune</u>
> • Tried to be unbiased
>
> **After the Penny Press**
> • Papers reporting current news
> • Newspapers as people's main source of information

With these basic facts in hand, Gabriella knew that she could find enough information to write a research report about the penny press. She decided to focus on the first three penny newspapers: the *Sun*, the *Herald*, and the *Tribune*. She was confident that she could find more facts and details about these papers.

Size up your topic. Do some initial research about your topic using an encyclopedia and the Internet. List the key details you find. Will you be able to find enough information to write a research report? If not, consider another topic. (In most cases, your teacher will not want you to use an encyclopedia as an actual resource for your research report.)

Prewrite

English Language Learners

Students may have difficulty deciding which information in their sources to include in their notes. Be prepared to hold conferences with students frequently during the prewriting step to help them match the information they find with their research questions so that they know what to add to their notes.

MLA Research Report **367**

Using a Gathering Grid

A gathering grid can help you organize your research. Gabriella used a grid to guide her research about the first penny papers. Down the left-hand side, she listed questions she needed to answer about her topic. Across the top, she listed sources she found to answer those questions. For answers too long to fit in the grid, Gabriella used note cards. (See page **368**.)

Gathering Grid

PENNY PRESS	"Milestones in the History of Media and Politics" (Web)	The Penny Press (book)	The Golden Age of the Newspaper (book)	"In for a Penny" (magazine article)
1. What was the media like before the penny press?	Newspapers were "mouthpieces for political parties."	See note card #1.	Most colonial papers were published weekly. page 2	
2. How did the penny press come about?	Day's Sun and Bennett's Herald appealed to the masses with sensational stories and a low price.	Growing literacy, prosperity, and public education provided a new audience. page 2	See note card #2.	
3. What effect has the penny press had on modern media?			"In many ways, the age of modern day journalism began with the penny press." page 3	See note card #3.

 Create a gathering grid. Make a list of questions about your topic in the left-hand column. Across the top, list sources you will use. Fill in the grid with answers you find. Use note cards for longer, more detailed answers.

Prewrite

Research

Prewriting Using a Gathering Grid

Suggest that, if they prefer, students can write each question at the top of a sheet of notebook paper. Then they'll have plenty of room for notes (remind them to carefully identify the source for each answer).

Point out that in the sample gathering grid, the student writer doesn't list any primary sources. Challenge students to think of possible primary sources the writer could have found. Possible responses:

- excerpts from actual penny press papers
- letters, journals, or articles by one of the people mentioned
- contemporary accounts of the Zenger trial

Point out that the student writer started with these four sources and eventually used five (see SE page 363). This is a good number for a paper of this length. Students should try to use at least four sources and are welcome to use more.

English Language Learners

Draw attention to the use of quotations in the grid on this page and the note cards on SE page 368. Remind students that they should not copy all the answers from sources. Point out that the student writer used her own words to answer many of the questions. See TE page 368 for more on paraphrasing.

Prewriting Creating Note Cards

Provide additional note-taking hints. For example:

- Note cards (also called index cards) are available in assorted colors, as well as in plain white. Students could use a different color card for each question on their grids.
- Instead of copying the full questions onto the cards, students can number each question on the grids and then write the appropriate numbers on the cards.
- Suggest that students make a "works-cited" set of note cards, writing the reference information for each source on a card according to the formats shown on SE pages 381–384. Later, when they create their works-cited list for the report, they can copy this information onto it.
- Tell students that after copying a quotation onto a note card, students should double-check the wording to make sure they've copied it correctly. Emphasize the importance of making sure all quotations are accurate

368

Prewriting Creating Note Cards

While a gathering grid allows you to see all your research at a glance, sometimes an answer needs more space. Use note cards when that is the case. Number each new card and write the question at the top. Then answer the question with a paraphrase (see page **369**), a quotation, or a list. At the bottom of each card, identify the source of the information (including a page number if appropriate).

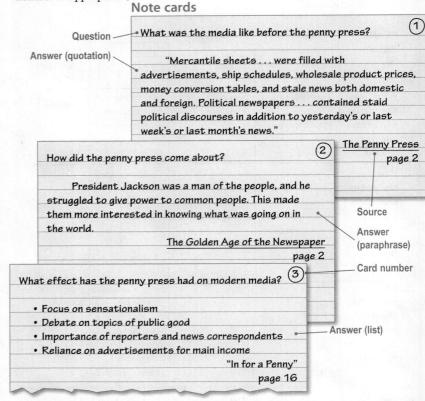

Note cards

Question → What was the media like before the penny press? ①

Answer (quotation) → "Mercantile sheets . . . were filled with advertisements, ship schedules, wholesale product prices, money conversion tables, and stale news both domestic and foreign. Political newspapers . . . contained staid political discourses in addition to yesterday's or last week's or last month's news."

The Penny Press
page 2

How did the penny press come about? ②

President Jackson was a man of the people, and he struggled to give power to common people. This made them more interested in knowing what was going on in the world.

The Golden Age of the Newspaper
page 2

Source

Answer (paraphrase)

Card number

What effect has the penny press had on modern media? ③

- Focus on sensationalism
- Debate on topics of public good
- Importance of reporters and news correspondents
- Reliance on advertisements for main income

"In for a Penny"
page 16

Answer (list)

Create note cards. Make note cards like the examples above whenever your answers are too long to fit on your gathering grid.

Prewrite

English Language Learners

Many students copy too much information verbatim because of the time it takes for them to think of the words they need to restate the ideas. Have students practice paraphrasing a few paragraphs of the model report on SE pages 357–362.

When students do their research, have them use white note cards to record paraphrased information and colored note cards to record quotations. This will help them see how often they copy directly from their sources.

Struggling Learners

Remind students that if they cite complete sentences from a source—even in their notes—they need to use quotation marks and provide a reference.

* Refer students to SE page 632 for ways to use quotation marks correctly.

MLA Research Report **369**

Avoiding Plagiarism

When you develop an essay or a report, you must give credit for information that is not your own or not common knowledge. Using other people's words and ideas without giving them credit is called **plagiarism**, and it is a form of intellectual stealing. Here are two ways to avoid plagiarism.

- **Paraphrase:** It's usually best to put ideas you find into your own words, so that your paper sounds like you. This is called *paraphrasing*. Still, you must give credit to the source of the idea.
- **Quote:** Sometimes it's best to use the exact words of a source to add authority to your report. Be sure you enclose those words in quotation marks and give credit to the source.

Paraphrase

> What effect has the penny press had on modern media?
> Newspapers today are cheap to buy because they get most of their money from advertising, just like the penny papers.
>
> Vance Web site

Quote

> What effect has the penny press had on modern media? ④
> "Newspapers rely heavily on advertising as a main source of income and that is also why they are still being offered at relatively low prices today."
>
> Vance Web site

Try It!

Read this excerpt from "In for a Penny." Then label two note cards with the question "What was the media like before the penny press?" On one card, *quote* a sentence from the excerpt. On the other, *paraphrase* the selection.

> In the earliest days of American newspapers, publishers could be arrested and tried for criticizing the government. In fact, the more accurate the criticism, the more damaging it was considered, and the greater the publisher's guilt. That changed when John Zenger was arrested in 1734 for publishing articles that criticized the governor of the New York colony. Andrew Hamilton argued to the jury that a law intended to protect the king in England should not be used to forbid complaint against a corrupt governor. The jury returned a verdict of "not guilty," setting a precedent for freedom of the American press.

Research

Prewriting Avoiding Plagiarism

Deciding whether or not a detail is common knowledge can be tricky. To help students better understand **plagiarism** *(see below),* discuss the difference between facts and ideas.

- Factual information is available from several sources and doesn't have to be credited.
- An idea or theory tells *how* or *why;* an interpretation suggests *what* something means. An idea, theory, or interpretation by someone other than the report writer should be credited.

Try It! Answers

Possible Answers

Quotation: *In the earliest days of American newspapers, publishers could be arrested and tried for criticizing the government.*

Paraphrase: *Before the penny papers and the trial of John Zenger, it was illegal for American newspapers to criticize the government.*

Teaching Tip: Plagiarism

To help students understand that plagiarism is stealing, explain that plagiarizing is like going into a person's home and stealing his or her belongings. Discuss the ethical and practical implications of using someone's ideas without giving proper credit.

Prewriting Keeping Track of Your Sources

Caution students not to assume that they'll be able to remember where they found a piece of information without making notes about it. Share the following with students:

- After doing a lot of research, they're likely to lose track of where they found details and to forget details they didn't write down.
- They may get confused and think they came up with an idea, when in fact they read it.
- It will be much easier for them to write down all the source details when they have the book (or information) in front of them.

Suggest that students mark this page with a sticky note so that it will be easy to find whenever they want to check what details are needed for citing different sources.

Prewriting Keeping Track of Your Sources

As you conduct your research, keep track of the sources you use so that you can correctly cite them in your final report. You'll need the following information to properly format your source citations later:

- **Book:** Author's name. Title. City of publication. Publisher. Copyright year. Medium of publication (such as print or Web).
- **Magazine:** Author's name. Article title. Magazine title. Date published (day, month, and year). Page numbers. Medium of publication.
- **Newspaper:** Author's name. Article title. Newspaper title. Date published (day, month, and year). Edition (if listed). Page numbers. Medium of publication.
- **Internet:** Author's name (if listed). Document or page title. Site title. Name of sponsoring organization. Date of publication (or last update). Medium of publication. Date accessed (day, month, year).
- **Video:** Title. Director's name. Distributor. Year released. Medium of reception (DVD, for example).

Source Notes

Source Notes

Book
Susan Thompson. The Penny Press. Northport. Vision. 2004. Print.

Magazine
Robert Younes. "In for a Penny." American Publisher. 1 Oct. 2005. Pages 14–17 and 21. Print.

Newspaper
Jerry Large. "Steady Trickle Alters the Flow of the Mainstream." Seattle Times. 17 Feb. 2010. C3. Print.

Internet
No author. "Newspapers in the Boston Public Library (Background)." BPL: Boston Public Library. Boston Public Library. Aug. 2001. Web. 9 May 2011.

Video
American Experience: Emma Goldman. Mel Bucklin. PBS. 2004. DVD.

Prewrite

List sources. Keep a list of each of your sources with the information shown above. Whenever you find a new source, add it to the list.

Struggling Learners

Students may be overwhelmed by the number of style guidelines for citing different types of sources. This may discourage them from using a variety of source materials. Tell students that in their notes they should jot down the key information for each source, not worrying about what should be underlined or where each period or comma should go. Explain that later, when they create their works-cited page, they can work with a partner to edit the sources for style, using the examples on SE pages 381–384.

Writing Your Thesis Statement

Once your research is completed, you should write a thesis statement. The thesis statement identifies the main idea of your paper, serving as the focus of your report. The following formula will help you write your thesis statement.

an interesting subject		a focus		a thesis statement
The creation of the penny press	+	paved the way for the modern daily newspaper	=	The creation of the penny press paved the way for the modern daily newspaper.

Sample Thesis Statements

The invention of the electric telegraph (an interesting subject) had a profound effect on people in this country (a focus).

The science of weather forecasting (an interesting subject) has saved millions of lives by predicting dangerous storms (a focus).

The global spread of radio and television (an interesting subject) helped to bring down the Berlin Wall and end the Cold War (a focus).

Prewrite

Form your thesis statement. Review your research notes and choose the main point you want to make about your topic. Using the formula above, write a thesis statement for your report. You may have to write more than one version of the thesis statement before it says exactly what you want it to say.

Research

Writing Your Thesis Statement

Point out to students that ideas for thesis statements may come to them at any time during the research process. Encourage students to make note of any thesis ideas that occur to them. They might try writing a thesis statement when they finish taking notes from an especially good source. Getting an early start on formulating a thesis statement will help them

■ focus their research,

■ begin refining the language they want to use in their thesis statement, and

■ think of additional questions about the topic.

✳ For more about writing thesis statements, see SE page 594.

Prewriting Outlining Your Ideas

If you will require students to turn in their outlines for approval before they write their first draft (see SE page 356), specify whether they should create a topic outline or a sentence outline.

Have students compare the outline excerpt shown (either this one, or the longer excerpt on SE page 356) to the text of the report (SE pages 357–358) to see how they relate to each other.

Point out that the student writer's first-level (Roman numeral) headings correspond very closely to the topic sentences for those paragraphs. Remind students that they don't have to write finished versions of their topic statements at this point—they can revise them as needed later.

✱ For more about creating outlines, see SE pages 590–591.

Prewriting Outlining Your Ideas

One way to organize and plan your report is to make an outline. An outline maps the ideas you plan to include in your paper. You can use either a topic outline or a sentence outline. A topic outline lists ideas as words or phrases; a sentence outline lists them as full sentences. (For an example of a topic outline, see page **590**.)

Below is the first part of a sentence outline for the report on pages **356–363**. Notice that the writer begins with the thesis statement. Next, after the Roman numerals (I., II., III., . . .), she lists the major points that she plans to cover in the middle part of her report. After the capital letters (A., B., C., . . .), she includes the details that support the major points. (Each major point serves as the topic sentence for a middle paragraph in the report.)

Sentence Outline

Remember, in an outline, if you have a I, you must have at least a II. If you have an A, you must have at least a B.

Thesis Statement	THESIS STATEMENT: *The creation of the penny press paved the way for the modern daily newspaper.*

Major Point (I., II.)	I. *Colonial newspapers in America were different from those today.*
	  A. *They needed government authorization.*
	  B. *John Peter Zenger was tried for libel for criticizing the governor.*

Supporting Details (A., B., C.)	C. *Freedom of the press became the focus of Zenger's trial.*
	II. *The early newspapers were different from ours in many other ways, too.*
	  A. . . .
	  B. . . .

Prewrite

Create your outline. Write a sentence outline for your report, using the details from your research. Be sure that each topic sentence (I., II., III., . . .) supports the thesis statement and that each detail (A., B., C., . . .) supports its topic sentence. Use your outline as a guide for writing the first draft of your report.

Writing

With your research and planning completed, you are ready to write the first draft of your research report. Don't worry about getting everything perfect in this first draft. For now, just get your ideas on paper in a way that makes sense to you. The following key points will help.

Keys to Effective Writing

1. Use your first paragraph to get your reader's attention, introduce your topic, and present your thesis statement.

2. In the next paragraph or two, explain how things were before your important event took place.

3. In the next several paragraphs, tell how the event came about.

4. In the final part of your report, discuss how the event influenced or affected the news media in this country.

5. Remember to cite, within your report, the sources of any ideas you paraphrase or quote; also list those sources alphabetically on a works-cited page.

Research

Writing

Keys to Effective Writing

Remind students that the writing stage is when they get to write, or draft, their ideas on paper.

Keys to Effective Writing lists the process students will be guided through on SE pages 374–384.

Tell students not to try to write the draft for a long report all at one sitting. Ask them to plan to spend time on it over two or three days (or more, if possible). Spending this amount of time has the following advantages:

- Students won't rush through the ending because they are getting tired.
- Students will be able to use spare moments when they're not writing to think about what they've written so far and plan what comes next.
- Students will have time to look at more sources if questions come up during the writing process.

Technology Connections

Students can use the added features of the Net-text as they explore this stage of the writing process.

Write Source Online **Net-text**

Citing Sources in Your Report

Emphasize the importance of including citations even at the rough-draft stage. Review the following points:

- Punctuate abbreviated titles in citations as usual. For an article (as in the example), the abbreviated title is in quotation marks; for a book, it is italicized.
- Citations can't be ambiguous. If two books on the citation list have authors with the same last names, students should include first initials in the citations. If two sources have titles that start the same way, the shortened titles must clearly distinguish between them.

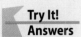

Try It!
Answers

Possible Answers

Having an independent news media is important to Americans. People need access to reliable information so they can participate fully in the democratic process (Bezanson 20).

Bezanson notes that having an independent news media is important to Americans. People need access to reliable information so they can participate fully in the democratic process (20).

374

Citing Sources in Your Report

Credit the sources of ideas and facts you use in your report.

When You Have All the Information

- The most common type of credit (citation) lists the author's last name and page number.

  In 1829, young Benjamin Day moved to New York to seek his fortune (Thompson 5).

- If you name the author in your report, just include the page number in parentheses.

  What made the *Herald* a success, George Douglas says, was the personality of its owner and editor (27).

When Some Information Is Missing

- If a source does not list an author, use the title and page number. (If the title is long, use only the first word or two.)

  "The press played an important role in the American Colonies' fight against British authorities and eventually for independence from Britain" ("Background" 302).

- If neither the author nor a page number is available, use the title (or a shortened version of it) alone.

  When John Peter Zenger published articles criticizing the governor in the *New York Weekly Journal* in 1735, he was jailed and tried for libel ("Milestones").

- Some sources (especially Internet sites) do not use page numbers. In those cases, include just the author (or, if the author is not listed, the title).

  "The changes made to the newspaper during the penny press era set a precedent for the way newspapers operate today" (Vance).

Try It!

Rewrite the following sentence, citing Randall P. Bezanson's article "Profits and Press Freedom" from *Human Rights*, page 20.

As a free and self-governing people, Americans depend upon the news media for information, and they expect that media to be independent in its own judgment.

Writing Starting Your Research Report

The opening paragraph of your research report should grab the reader's attention, introduce your topic, and present your thesis statement. Consider using one of the following effective ways to begin your opening paragraph.

- **Ask an interesting question.**

  Why did newsboys in old movies shout "Extra! Extra! Read all about it!"?

- **Start with a quotation.**

  "Before the coming of the penny press, newspapers weren't really news," says writer Robert Younes in an article called "In for a Penny."

- **Start with an interesting fact.**

  When George Day started publishing the *Sun* in 1833, he was mainly looking for a way to save his new printing business.

Beginning Paragraph

> Why did newsboys in old movies shout "Extra! Extra! Read all about it!"? Why do newspapers include an entertainment section and an opinion page? Who was the first Washington news correspondent was? Studying the start of the "penny press" in the 1830s provides answers to these questions. <u>The creation of the penny press paved the way for the modern daily newspaper.</u>

This beginning paragraph starts with an interesting question and ends with the thesis statement (underlined).

Write your opening paragraph. Make sure to grab the reader's interest in the beginning, then introduce your topic, and end with a clear thesis statement. You may have to write more than one version of this paragraph before it says exactly what you want it to say.

Research

Writing Starting Your Research Report

Suggest that students consider what caught their interest about their topics in the first place. How can they recreate that feeling for their readers?

Encourage students to try to write several versions of their opening paragraphs. Remind them, however, that they shouldn't let this paragraph sidetrack them. After a few tries, they should move on to the middle paragraphs. They can always try out other versions of the opener later, either while they're still writing their first drafts or during the revision stage. In fact, ideas for an opening can sometimes become clearer once the writer knows what will follow.

English Language Learners

Because of the time it takes for students to think about and write a single paragraph in English, asking them to write more than one version of their opening paragraph is not recommended. Encourage them to rehearse their opening paragraphs orally with you or with cooperative partners, who can record their ideas.

Writing Developing the Middle Part

Point out that if students have put careful thought into their outlines during prewriting, they have already done most of the planning work for their middle paragraphs.

Acknowledge that students' ideas may change as they begin writing. Encourage students to follow their outline closely only if it is working for them. They should feel free to make adjustments whenever it seems appropriate.

Remind students not to forget to consult their other research notes, such as the gathering grid, as they work. Suggest that they cross off each item on their outline and grid as they incorporate it into their writing.

376

Writing Developing the Middle Part

The middle part of your report should support or explain your thesis statement. Start by explaining what things were like before the event. Then discuss the development of the event in detail.

Each middle paragraph should cover one major point. This major point is presented in the topic sentence and followed by supporting details. Use your sentence outline as a guide for your writing.

Middle Paragraphs

The first middle paragraphs tell what the media was like before the event.

<u>Colonial newspapers in America were different from those today.</u> For one thing, they could not be published without the approval of the government. In 1690, the publisher of the first newspaper in the colonies found this out the hard way. The government arrested him and destroyed all copies of his paper because he didn't get proper approval. In another case, John Peter Zenger published articles in the <u>New York Weekly</u> Journal that criticized the governor. Authorities arrested Zenger and tried him for libel ("Milestones"). Freedom of the press became the focus of his famous trial in 1735. He was eventually set free.

All the details in each paragraph support the topic sentence (underlined).

<u>The early newspapers were different from today's papers in many other ways, too.</u> Colonial papers were usually "4-page weeklies containing local ads, . . . local hearsay, and large, unedited chunks of . . . news from the London press" ("Milestones"). Even after the American Revolution, newspapers lacked interesting and timely news. Commercial papers "were filled with advertisements, ship schedules, . . . product prices, money conversion tables, and stale news," and political papers "contained staid [stuffy] political discourses in addition to yesterday's or last week's or last month's news" (Thompson 2). These newspapers were expensive and read mostly by wealthy citizens.

Sources are cited in parentheses.

English Language Learners

Students who have difficulty putting their thoughts into writing will benefit from rehearsing orally before they begin writing. Have students tape record their ideas for each paragraph. Encourage them to begin writing as soon as they have recorded their ideas. Listen to the recordings to evaluate their progress.

Information from the source is paraphrased.

Because of increased literacy in the early 1800s, more people began to read newspapers. Common people paid special attention to the more interesting sections, especially the coverage of the police court (Thompson 2). This was also a time of great change for the nation. The country elected Andrew Jackson, the first unaristocratic president. More immigrants were entering the country, and cities were growing rapidly (Younes 14). The stage was set for the penny press, a new type of newspaper that would appeal to the masses.

The next middle paragraphs explain how the event came about.

In 1833, Benjamin Day, the owner of a printing company in New York, started the Sun, the first successful penny paper. Walking to work each day, he passed Chatham Street, where street vendors sold items for a penny (Thompson 8). Day thought he could make a penny newspaper to sell on the street. On September 3, 1833, he sold the first edition of the Sun. It was only a single sheet of paper, folded in the middle. On the front page, Day printed advertisements copied from other papers. The other three pages contained a mix of ads and news from other papers, two humorous tall tales, and the police report copied from the Courier & Enquirer (10–11). His paper was an instant success. Soon Day had enough new ads to make the paper profitable even with its penny price.

Sentences are arranged so that the reader can easily follow the ideas.

Day quickly realized that he needed help. While he managed the business, someone would have to attend the courts each day and write the police report. A man named George Wisner became Day's court reporter and partner (Thompson 13). Day and Wisner didn't always agree, and the paper reflected their different opinions (15–17). This debate of ideas set the Sun apart from the older, more conservative political newspapers.

Day also needed help selling the paper. He decided to use a

Research

Tell students that they may sometimes find it difficult to decide how best to present the information in the middle paragraphs. If they get stuck, encourage them to take a break from writing. As with many puzzles (such as math problems), they might find that the answer comes to them in an "ah ha!" moment—a sudden realization.

Encourage students to think about their drafts in progress occasionally when they aren't writing. Note that they'll be surprised at how much they can accomplish by spending just a minute or two thinking about how they want to proceed.

Struggling Learners

To help students follow the discussion in this report, point out words indicating sequence of events (such as *in the early 1800s, soon, while*). Guide students to use similar transitions to connect ideas in their reports.

✳ For more on transitions, see SE pages 592–593.

Make sure students understand how to use the "cut and paste" functions for their word-processing programs. This allows them to move large sections of text from one place to another without having to retype it.

✳ For more about writing using a computer, see SE pages 33–38.

A new term, the "London plan," is explained.

system known as the "London plan." Under this plan, he offered newspapers at a reduced rate to people who then sold their copies and pocketed the profit. The first person to join him was a 10-year-old boy. Before long, "newsboys" were selling the papers all over New York (Thompson 12–13), and the Sun became the most popular paper in the city.

In 1835, James Gordon Bennett started another successful penny paper in New York called the Herald. Bennett had lived in many places, from Canada to South Carolina, and had gained valuable experience as a writer and an editor. Historians say that he was America's first Washington news correspondent, for the New York Enquirer. These experiences helped prepare Bennett to start his own paper (Douglas 27–29). Bennett started out alone, in a dark cellar room, using a plank and two boxes as a desk. However, before long, the Herald would outsell the Sun. In fact, at its best, the Herald sold more copies worldwide than even the most respected European papers (Younes 16).

The author's interest in the subject is evident in the voice and word choice.

Bennett knew how to get the attention of readers. They liked the Herald because Bennett wrote opinion pieces that were "saucy, impertinent [disrespectful], and funny" (Thompson 34). Bennett also filled his paper with sensational news stories that made the Sun seem tame by comparison, and he placed these stories on the front page to gain more attention. Many historians give Bennett the credit for the first "crisis news reporting," based on his eyewitness news about New York City's Great Fire of 1835 and his writing about the Jewett murder trial (Douglas 30). The Herald also quickly became the best source of Wall Street news (Thompson 59). Along with these stories,

English Language Learners

To help students understand the side note about voice and word choice, have pairs of students scan the second and third paragraphs on the student page for specific examples of words and phrases that communicate the author's interest. Ask volunteers to share their ideas about why specific words are so effective.

Possible words and phrases:
- valuable experience
- first . . . news correspondent
- alone, in a dark cellar room, using a plank and two boxes as a desk
- outsell
- more copies . . . than even the most respected

- "saucy, impertinent [disrespectful], and funny"
- sensational
- tame by comparison
- "crisis news reporting"
- best source
- great success

Bennett included entertainment news. All of these things helped make the <u>Herald</u> a great success.

In 1841, Horace Greeley started another penny newspaper in New York. It was called the <u>Tribune</u>. Like the <u>Sun</u> and the <u>Herald</u>, the <u>Tribune</u> relied on advertising for its main income, and it included sensational stories to attract readers. However, Greeley believed that a newspaper should do more than just make money. He thought it should keep people informed about important events and educate them about important ideas.

The <u>Tribune</u> gave readers crime stories and stories about local events, but it "downplayed sensational stories by placing them on inside pages" (Thompson 97). This paper also included poetry and literature by respected authors. Under Greeley's direction, the <u>Tribune</u> showed "a social conscience in its news columns and reform-minded editorials" (98).

The <u>Tribune</u> soon rivaled the <u>Herald</u> as the most popular paper of the time, and through the <u>Tribune</u>, Greeley became a well-known national figure. He influenced the opinion of Americans everywhere on topics like "labor, education, [and] temperance" (Thompson 112). Greeley showed that a newspaper could help shape a nation.

> The transition "however" introduces an important point.

> Quotations are worked smoothly into the writing.

Write your middle paragraphs. Keep these tips in mind as you write.
- Write a topic sentence for each paragraph and support it with details.
- Refer to your outline for direction. (See page 372.)
- Give credit to all your sources. (See page 374.)

Research

Have students review the side notes for the sample middle paragraphs on SE pages 357–362, as well as in this section. Respond to students' questions about the side notes and give additional hints, if appropriate. For example:
- When deciding whether to define a term (see "London plan" example on SE page 378), students should consider whether they were familiar with it before they began researching the topic. If not, it may be best to define it.
- Terms specifically associated with the topic should also be defined.
- At the same time, too many definitions will interfere with the point the writer is trying to make. Students must strike a balance, choosing which specific terms are most important to mention and which ones are not needed.

Writing **Ending Your Research Report**

While reviewing the information on the page, remind students that when they reach this point it should be easy for them to restate the thesis. However, they may not know what final idea they'd like to leave their readers with.

To help students think of a final idea, have them work in groups of three or four.

- Have each student read the other group members' beginning and middle paragraphs.
- Ask each reader to write down the most important thing they learned about the topic and pass this feedback on to the writer.
- Encourage students to keep this feedback in mind as they contemplate their final paragraphs.

Writing **Ending Your Research Report**

Your ending paragraph should summarize your research report and bring it to a thoughtful close. To accomplish that, use the following guidelines.

- Tell how the event influenced or affected modern media.
- Restate the thesis.
- Leave the reader with something to add to his or her understanding of the topic.

Ending Paragraph

The report's conclusion discusses the topic's effect on modern media.	<u>Modern newspapers continue to focus on disaster and crime news, along with editorials and stories about business and entertainment.</u> Also, topics in the public interest continue to appear in the news, just as they did in the *Tribune*. The obligation to the public that today's newspaper reporters and editors feel, originated with the penny press. Further, modern newspapers
The writer restates the thesis (underlined).	still "rely heavily on advertising as a main source of income and that is also a main reason they are still being offered at relatively low prices today" (Vance). <u>All these things show that</u>
The reader is left with a final idea to think about.	<u>"the age of modern-day journalism began with the penny press" (Thompson 3).</u> The free press that grew from those early papers has helped to shape the nation, just as the Founding Fathers had hoped.

 Write your ending paragraph and review your first draft. Draft your ending paragraph using the guidelines above. Then read your draft to make sure it is complete. Check your research notes and outline to make sure you haven't forgotten any important details. In the margins and between the lines, make notes about anything you should change.

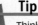 **Tip**

Think of your research report as one-half of a conversation with a reader you invent. Talk to your silent partner in a sincere and honest voice. Research reports should be informative and engaging.

Creating Your MLA Works-Cited Page

The purpose of a works-cited page at the end of a research report is to allow the reader to locate the sources you used. Pages **381–384** show the standard MLA format for common types of sources. Some sources will not match these formats exactly, so simply give as much detail as possible. When you are writing by hand, you may use underlining to represent italics.

Books

The standard works-cited entry for a book uses the following format.

Author or editor (if available, last name first). **Title** (in italics). **City of publication:**
Publisher, year published. Medium of publication (print, Web, etc.).

> Douglas, George H. *The Golden Age of the Newspaper.* Westport:
> Greenwood, 1999. Print.

If a book has two or three authors, list them in the order they appear on the title page. Reverse only the name of the first author. (Example: Brentano, Margaret, and Nicholson Baker.) For a book with four or more authors, list only the first author, followed by "et al."

A Single Work from an Anthology

To list an essay or a short story from an anthology, include the title of that work in quotation marks, followed by the title of the anthology and the editor.

> Ashabranner, Brent. "Helping Hands." *Read All About It: Great Read-Aloud
> Stories, Poems, and Newspaper Pieces for Preteens and Teens.* Ed. Jim
> Trelease. New York: Penguin, 1993. 42–47. Print.

An Article in a Familiar Reference Work

It is not necessary to list full publication details for dictionaries, encyclopedias, or other familiar reference works. If the article is initialed, check the index of authors for the author's full name.

Author (if available). **Article title** (in quotation marks). **Reference book title** (in
italics). **Edition** (if available). **Year published. Medium of publication.**

> "Day, Benjamin Henry." *Columbia Encyclopedia.* 6th ed. 2000. Print.

Research

Creating Your MLA Works-Cited Page

Point out that if students kept careful track of their resources during the research process, all they need to do now is format the sources correctly and arrange the information in alphabetical order.

Focus on the specialized abbreviations used in works-cited entries:

- The abbreviation *et al.* is Latin for "and others." There is a period after *al.* because it's an abbreviation of *alii,* which means "others."
- The word *editor* is abbreviated as *Ed.*—with a capital *E*—in references. The abbreviation *ed.*—with a lowercase *e*—stands for *edition.*

The information on citing sources (SE page 374) and creating a works-cited page (SE pages 381–384) is based on the documentation style developed by the Modern Language Association (MLA). This style is commonly used with literary and humanities papers. For more advanced research and papers in the sciences and social studies, the documentation style of the American Psychological Association (APA) is often used.

Periodicals

Bring in examples of each kind of periodical mentioned for students to examine. Point out items that they may not have paid much attention to in their casual reading of magazines and newspapers:

- Authors are not listed for all articles. Some periodicals don't give credit for short articles written by people on their editorial staffs. No authors are listed for newspaper articles created using information from "newswire services" such as the Associated Press (AP).
- Articles often don't run on consecutive pages of popular magazines or newspapers (scholarly journals tend to keep the pages together). They are arranged this way so the important articles begin in the front section of the periodical, which readers tend to look at first.

Point out the format used for dates in reference citations. They are listed with no commas in this order: day, abbreviated month, year.

Periodicals

Periodicals are publications issued on a regular, scheduled basis. This includes magazines, scholarly journals, and newspapers.

A Magazine

If a magazine is published weekly or biweekly, include the full date (day, month, year). If it is published monthly, bimonthly, or less often, include only the month and year. For an article not running on continuous pages, list the first page followed by a "+" sign.

> **Author** (if available, last name first). **Article title** (in quotation marks). **Title of the magazine** (in italics) **Date** (day, month, year): **Page numbers of the article. Medium of publication.**

> Younes, Robert. "In for a Penny." *American Publisher* 1 Oct. 2005: 14+. Print.

A Scholarly Journal

Scholarly journals are identified by volume number rather than by full date of publication.

> **Author** (if available, last name first). **Article title** (in quotation marks). **Title of the journal** (in italics) **Volume number. Issue number Year published** (in parentheses): **Page numbers of the article. Medium of publication.**

> Postman, Neil. "The Information Age: A Blessing or a Curse?" *Harvard International Journal of Press/Politics* 9.2 (2004): 3–10. Print.

A Newspaper

> **Author** (if available, last name first). **Article title** (in quotation marks). **Title of the newspaper** (in italics) **Date** (day, month, year), **edition** (if listed): **Section letter and page numbers of the article. Medium of publication.**

> Large, Jerry. "Steady Trickle Alters the Flow of the Mainstream." *Seattle Times* 17 Feb. 2003: C3. Print.

MLA Research Report **383**

Online Sources

Online sources include Web pages, documents in Internet databases, and e-mail messages.

A Web Page

> **Author** (if available, last name first). **Document title** (if available, in quotation marks). **Site title** (in italics). **Name of sponsor** (if available), **date posted or published** (or last updated) (if available). **Medium of publication** (Web). **Date accessed** (day, month, year).

> "Newspapers in the Boston Public Library (Background)." *BPL: Boston Public Library.* Boston Public Lib., Aug. 2001. Web. 9 May 2011.

An Article in an Online Database

Libraries often subscribe to online databases where articles are kept. To cite such an article, first give any details about the original print version. (See "Periodicals" on page 382.) Then list the database if known (in italics), followed by the medium of publication (Web). Then give your date of access.

> Weston, Beth Turn. "Papers for a Penny." *Cobblestone* Mar. 2005: 47. *MasterFILE Premier.* Web. 22 Mar. 2011.

E-Mail Message

> **Writer** (last name first). **Title from subject line** (in quotation marks). **Description of message, including recipient** ("Message to William Grady"). **Date received. Medium of delivery.**

> Faraday, Ralph. "Press No More." Message to William Grady. 31 Jan. 2011. E-mail.

Research

English Language Learners

If an online source cannot be easily found via a Web search, a URL should be included between angle brackets (< >) at the end of the source citation. Students who have limited knowledge of Web-related vocabulary may need examples of the proper way to include a line break in a URL.

- Have volunteers write a long URL as one line on the board or overhead.

- Then ask students to rewrite the URL, showing how the line can break after a slash.
- Point out and label the slash.

Make sure students understand they should not add a slash to the URL; they should simply break the line after a slash that already exists in the URL.

Other Sources

Suggest that students use a sticky note to bookmark SE pages 381–384 for easy reference when they need to check citation formats. Alternatively, to help students internalize the formats, have them make a compact reference sheet for themselves by copying all the different citation formats from SE pages 381–384 onto one sheet of paper. That way, all the information will be available at a glance.

Expand on the instruction that students need only to list resources they actually used (that is, resources they cited) in their final report. Explain that this is what is meant by "works cited." However, students may sometimes be required to list all the books they consulted while researching the paper, whether or not they specifically refer to those works in the paper. In that case, the list of resources is called a bibliography. Challenge students to find an example of a bibliography in one of their reference books.

Other Sources

Your research may include other sources, such as television programs, video documentaries, and personal interviews.

A Television or Radio Program

Episode title, if given (in quotation marks). **Program title** (in italics). **Series title** (if any). **Name of the network. Call letters, city of the local station** (if any). **Broadcast date** (day, month, year). **Medium of reception.**

> "NOVA scienceNOW." *Nova*. PBS. WMVS, Milwaukee. 19 Oct. 2005. Television.

Video, Etc.

Title (in italics). **Director's name** (if known, first and last). **Distributor, year released. Medium of reception** (DVD, VHS, slide program, etc.).

> *American Experience: Emma Goldman*. Dir. Mel Bucklin. PBS, 2004. DVD.

An Interview by the Author (Yourself)

Person interviewed (last name first). **Description** (Personal interview, Telephone interview, etc.). **Date of interview** (day, month, year).

> Faraday, Ralph. Personal interview. 19 Feb. 2011.

Format your sources. Check your report and your list of sources (page 370) to see which sources you actually used. Then follow these directions.

1. Write out the information for each of your sources using the guidelines above and on the previous three pages. Use a sheet of paper or note cards.

2. Arrange your sources in alphabetical order.

3. Create your works-cited page. (See the example on page 363.)

Struggling Learners

Students may have difficulty organizing their sources on their works-cited page. Remind them of these points:

- Sources are alphabetized according to the first word in the citation.
- When citing more than one work by the same author, the articles should be listed chronologically.

MLA Research Report **385**

Revising

Your focus during drafting is to get your thoughts on paper in a logical order. During the revising step, you make changes to ensure that your thoughts are clear and interesting, that your organization is easy to follow, that your voice sounds knowledgeable, and so on.

Keys to Effective Revising

1. Read your entire draft to get an overall sense of your research report.

2. Review your thesis statement to be sure that it clearly states your main point about the topic.

3. Make sure your beginning engages the reader. Then check that your ending leaves the reader with something to think about.

4. Be sure that the middle part clearly and completely supports the thesis statement.

5. Make sure that you sound knowledgeable and interested in the topic.

6. Check for effective word choice and sentence fluency.

Research

English Language Learners

Students may not have sufficient English skills to be helpful partners, but they can benefit from the ideas and suggestions of proficient English speakers. Modify the task, assigning these students to groups of three or four so they can listen to others' reactions to their writing.

Revising

Keys to Effective Revising

Remind students that the revising stage is when writers have an opportunity to make improvements to their first drafts. At this stage, they can think about refinements they might not have considered when they were drafting.

Keys to Revising lists the process students will be guided through on SE pages 386–388.

Acknowledge that it can be difficult to go back to a paper after putting a lot of energy into the draft. Remind students, though, that thoughtful revision is an absolute necessity in an extensive paper. To help them look at their work with fresher eyes, have them work with a partner:

- Ask partners to trade papers and read them with the keys to revision in mind, writing a response to each paragraph on a sticky note.
- Allow students time to discuss their responses. Ask them to first point out two or more strong points and then to suggest improvements that might be made in their partner's report.
- Encourage partners to continue to communicate as they revise.

Technology Connections

Have students use the Writing Network features of the Net-text to comment on each other's drafts.

Write Source Online **Net-text**

Revising Improving Your Writing

Draw students' attention to the revision that replaces a sentence in the passive voice with one in the active voice. Review voices of verbs by having students define the terms in their own words:

- Active voice: A verb form that expresses action the subject takes.
- Passive voice: A verb form that indicates the subject is acted upon.

Note that good writing may include sentences in both voices, but with the balance in favor of active sentences. Too many passive sentences can make writing sound flat. Also, passive sentences tend to be longer, because the passive voice always requires the auxiliary verb *to be*.

Challenge students to scan the excerpt on SE pages 386–387 for other sentences in the passive voice:

- *They could not be published . . .*
- *He was eventually set free.*
- *These newspapers were . . . read mostly by . . .*

✱ For more about the voice of a verb, see SE page 722.

386

Revising Improving Your Writing

A first draft is never a finished paper. There is always room for improvement. In the following sample paragraphs, Gabriella makes several important revisions. Each improves the *ideas, organization, voice, word choice,* or *sentence fluency* in the writing.

> Have you ever seen newsboys in a movie shouting "Extra! Extra! Read all about it!"? Have you ever wondered why newspapers include an entertainment section and an opinion page? Would you like to know who the first Washington news ~~reporter~~ *correspondent* was? You can find answers to these questions by studying the start of the "penny press" in the 1830s. The creation of the penny press ~~made~~ *paved the* way for the modern daily newspaper.
>
> *Before the Penny Press*
> Colonial newspapers in America were different from those today. *For one thing,* They could not be published without the approval of the government. In 1690, the publisher of the first newspaper in the colonies found this out the hard way. *The government arrested him and destroyed all copies of his paper* ~~He was arrested and all copies of his paper were destroyed~~ because he didn't get proper approval. In another case, John Peter Zenger published articles in the New York Weekly Journal that criticized the governor. Authorities arrested Zenger and tried him for libel ("Milestones"). Freedom of the press became the focus of his famous trial in 1735. He was eventually set free.

More precise words improve word choice.

A subheading is added.

A transition is added for better fluency.

Wording is changed to create the active voice.

Grammar Connection

Active and Passive Verbs and Moods of Verbs

- **Proofreader's Guide** pages 722 (+), 724–725
- *GrammarSnap* Subjunctive Mood

Word Choice

- *Write Source* page 548 (+)
- *SkillsBook* page 146

English Language Learners

Students who use only the active voice in their writing may be confused by the challenge to locate passive sentences in the model report. Work with students to look for passive sentences in other writing. Model how to rewrite these sentences to create active sentences.

✱ See SE pages 722–723.

> A sentence is moved to improve organization.

The early newspapers were different from ours in many other ways, too. Colonial papers were usually "4-page weeklies containing local ads, . . . local hearsay, and large, unedited chunks of . . . news from the London press" ("Milestones"). Even after the American Revolution, newspapers lacked interesting and timely news. These newspapers were expensive and read mostly by wealthy citizens. Commercial papers "were filled with advertisements, ship schedules, . . . product prices, money conversion tables, and stale news," and political papers "contained staid [stuffy] political discourses in addition to yesterday's or last week's or last month's news" (Thompson 2).

> An idea is added for clarity.

Because of increased literacy in the early 1800s, more people began to read newspapers. Common people paid special attention to the more interesting sections, especially *This was also a time of great change for the nation.* the coverage of the police court (Thompson 2). The country elected Andrew Jackson, the first unaristocratic president. More immigrants were entering the country, and cities were growing rapidly (Younes 14). The stage was set for the penny press, a new type of newspaper that would appeal to the masses.

Revise

Revise your research report and add subheadings. Check your first draft for problems with ideas, organization, voice, word choice, and sentence fluency. Make any needed changes. Also look for logical breaks in your report and add appropriate subheadings.

Research

Ask students to examine the circled sentence that begins *These newspapers*. How does moving it improve the organization of the paragraph? Possible responses:

- It allows the writer to explain first what newspapers were like after the Revolution and then tell who used to buy them.
- The phrase *these newspapers* works better when it refers to the more specific phrase *commercial papers* than when it must refer to the idea of all newspapers published after the American Revolution.
- Moving the sentence creates a better transition to the next paragraph, which begins with the idea that more people—not just the wealthy—began to buy papers in the early 1800s.

Revising Using a Traits Checklist

Review unnecessary modifiers (mentioned in item 11). Explain that well-chosen modifiers make the voice of a piece more lively and engaging.

388

Revising Using a Traits Checklist

On a piece of paper, write the numbers 1 to 13. If you can answer "yes" to a question, put a check mark after that number. Continue to revise until you can answer all of the questions with a "yes."

Revising Checklist

Ideas

_____ 1. Have I chosen an interesting event to write about?
_____ 2. Does my thesis statement clearly state the main idea of my paper?
_____ 3. Do I include enough details to support my thesis?
_____ 4. Do I give credit for ideas that I have paraphrased or quoted from other sources?

Organization

_____ 5. Does my beginning paragraph capture the reader's interest and introduce my topic?
_____ 6. Do my first middle paragraphs explain what things were like before this event?
_____ 7. Do my next middle paragraphs detail how the event developed?
_____ 8. Does my ending relate the event to present-day media?

Voice

_____ 9. Does my voice sound knowledgeable and engaging?

Word Choice

_____ 10. Have I used specific nouns and active verbs?
_____ 11. Do I avoid unnecessary modifiers?

Sentence Fluency

_____ 12. Do my sentences read smoothly?
_____ 13. Have I used a variety of sentence beginnings and lengths?

English Language Learners

For students who are working on putting ideas into their own words, add the following question to the ideas checklist: *Do I paraphrase (use my own words) when I write about ideas I find in resources?*

Grammar Connection

Commas
- **Proofreader's Guide** page 610 (+)
- **Write Source** page 535
- **GrammarSnap** Appositives and Appositive Phrases
- **SkillsBook** pages 10, 14, 134

Sentence Review
- **Proofreader's Guide** pages 738–757 (+)
- **SkillsBook** page 147

Brackets, Ellipses, Colons, and other Forms of Punctuation
- **Proofreader's Guide** pages 618–619, 620–621, 638–639, 642–643, 644–645
- **SkillsBook** pages 23–24, 39–40

Editing

When you have finished revising your research paper, all that remains is checking for conventions: spelling, punctuation, capitalization, and grammar.

Keys to Effective Editing

1. Read your research report out loud and listen for words or phrases that may be incorrect.

2. Use a dictionary, a thesaurus, your computer's spell-checker, and the "Proofreader's Guide" in the back of this book.

3. Look for errors in punctuation, capitalization, spelling, and grammar.

4. Check your report for proper formatting. (See pages 356–363.)

5. If you use a computer, edit on a printed copy. Then enter your changes on the computer.

5. Use the editing and proofreading marks inside the back cover of this book. Check all citations for accuracy.

Research

Editing

Keys to Effective Editing

Tell students that during the editing stage they have a chance to find and correct errors in
- punctuation,
- capitalization,
- spelling, and
- grammar.

Remind students to always plan to proofread their finished copies one last time before turning them in.
- If students used a computer, it's possible that they incorrectly typed some of the changes they entered during editing.
- Computer spell-checkers won't catch all misspellings (for example, spelling *right* for *write*).
- If students handwrote their reports, they might have introduced errors as they made the final copies of their drafts.

This final read-through is a good time to enlist the aid of an outside reader—preferably one who is a skilled proofreader.

Technology Connections

Students can use the added features of the Net-text as they explore this stage of the writing process.

 Write Source Online **Net-text**

Editing Checking for Conventions

If students are writing on computers, discuss the use of the grammar checker. Emphasize that current technology is not able to accurately evaluate complex sentence structures. Students should be aware that

- the suggestions that the grammar checker offers are often—perhaps even usually—wrong, and
- the checker can completely miss some kinds of errors.

Therefore, students should

- look very critically at each item flagged by the grammar checker and refer to the proofreader's guide whenever they have questions,
- use the checker only as a backup method—to help them spot-check their work, and
- always examine the whole report for errors that the grammar checker might have missed.

Checking for Conventions

After revising the first draft of her report, Gabriella checked the new version carefully for punctuation, spelling, and usage errors. She also asked a classmate to look it over. The passage below shows some of Gabriella's editing changes.

The Rise of the Sun

A spelling error is corrected.

In 1833, Benjamin Day, the owner of a printing company in New York, started the Sun, the first ~~succesful~~ *successful* penny paper.

An error in verb tense is corrected.

Walking to work each day, he passes Chatham Street, where street vendors sold items for a penny (Thompson 8). Day thought he could make a penny newspaper to sell on the street. On September 3, 1833, he sold the first edition of the Sun. It was only a single sheet of paper, folded in the

A capitalization error is marked.

middle. On the front page, day printed advertisements copied from other papers. The other three pages contained a mix of ads and news from other papers, two humorous

A missing citation is added.

tall tales, and the police report copied from the Courier & Enquirer. (10–11) His paper was an instant success. Soon Day had enough new ads to make the paper profitable even with its penny price.

Check your work for conventions. Use your computer spell-checker and grammar checker to correct your work. Then print a copy of your report and read it carefully for errors the computer cannot catch. Use the editing and proofreading marks on the inside back cover of this book.

MLA Research Report **391**

Editing Using a Checklist

On a piece of paper, write the numbers 1 to 12. If you can answer "yes" to a question, put a check mark after that number. Continue editing until you can answer all of the questions with a "yes."

Editing Checklist

Conventions

PUNCTUATION

_____ **1.** Do I correctly punctuate all my sentences?

_____ **2.** Have I correctly punctuated citations in my research paper?

_____ **3.** Do I use quotation marks around all quoted words from my sources?

_____ **4.** Do I use italics (or underlining, if handwriting) and quotation marks correctly for titles of works?

_____ **5.** Have I correctly formatted the works-cited page?

CAPITALIZATION

_____ **6.** Have I capitalized proper nouns and adjectives?

_____ **7.** Do I begin each sentence with a capital letter?

SPELLING

_____ **8.** Have I spelled all my words correctly?

_____ **9.** Have I double-checked the words my spell-checker may have missed?

GRAMMAR

_____ **10.** Do I use the correct forms of verbs (*he saw*, not *he seen*)?

_____ **11.** Do my subjects and verbs agree in number?

_____ **12.** Have I used the right words (*there, their,* or *they're*)?

Research

Editing Using a Checklist

Draw students' attention to item 12. To help students discover words that might cause them trouble, challenge them to use confusing words correctly.

- Write a potentially troublesome word (such as *affect*) on the board and have students use the word in a sentence.
- Invite students to read their sentences. If students used the word incorrectly, have them make note of the word and its correct usage.
- Repeat the process for several different confusing words.
- Alternatively, you could begin each writing instruction session by challenging students to use one confusing word correctly in a sentence.

✱ For information on using the right word, see SE pages 678–699.

Editing **Creating a Title**

Invite students who still need to decide on a title to seek their classmates' input. Writers should have at least two potential titles to share. Ask students to raise their hands to show their preference for one of the titles. Call on students to explain what they like about titles they vote for.

Publishing **Sharing Your Report**

Before students turn their papers in, have them write short descriptions of their reports on index cards. Circulate the cards and ask students to sign up for the reports they want to read. Make the reports available and allow time for students to choose one or two to read.

Suggest that students might choose a paper because
- they helped the writer with it at some stage in the writing process and want to see how it turned out,
- it's about an unfamiliar topic that interests them, or
- it's about a topic similar to their own and they want to read someone else's approach to the subject.

Encourage students to seek out the writers of the reports and give them positive feedback.

Technology Connections

Remind students that they can use the Writing Network features of the Portfolio to share their work with peers.

✳ *Write Source Online* **Portfolio**

✳ *Write Source Online* **Net-text**

392

Editing **Creating a Title**

Make sure that you have considered a title before you share your research report. Writer Randall VanderMey says that a title, like a good fish bait, should entice the reader. Each of the following approaches will help you write an effective title:

- Provide a creative hook:
  From Penny Press to Free Press
- Identify the topic of your report with special attention given to the sound and the rhythm of the words:
  A Penny for Your Paper
- Directly state the key point of your report:
  The Birth of the Modern Newspaper
- Focus on a theme that runs though your paper:
  Common News for Common People

Publishing **Sharing Your Report**

When you have finished your editing and proofreading, make a neat final copy to share. Consider making extra copies for family and friends.

 Make your final copy. Use the following guidelines to format your report. (Also see pages 76–78 for instructions about designing on a computer.) Create a clean final copy and share it with your classmates and family.

Focusing on Presentation

- Use blue or black ink and double-space the entire paper.
- Write your name, your teacher's name, the class, and the date in the upper left corner of page 1.
- Skip a line and center your title; skip another line and start your writing.
- Indent every paragraph and leave a one-inch margin on all four sides.
- For a research paper, you should write your last name and the page number in the upper right corner of every page of your report.
- If possible, type rather than handwrite your research paper.
- If your teacher requires a title page and outline, follow your teacher's instructions. (See page **356**.)

English Language Learners

Before asking students to state briefly what their reports are about, explain that a brief description does not contain all the details in the report. Model how to state information briefly. Use the thesis statement and topic sentences from the model outline to introduce the report, "A Penny for Your Paper."

Making Oral Presentations

393

Speaking in front of a group can be exciting, but it can also be scary. If the thought of any formal speaking situation makes you nervous, you are not alone. Speaking in front of a group is a common fear, but one that you can overcome.

Just think of speaking as a type of performance. You may already perform quite well on a basketball court, in a band, in a play, or at a dance. With planning and practice, you will also be able to give effective oral presentations.

In this chapter, you will learn how to prepare and present an oral presentation based on a research report you have written. You will also learn how to turn your presentation into a multimedia report.

- **Planning Your Presentation**
- **Creating Note Cards**
- **Considering Visual Aids**
- **Practicing Your Speech**
- **Delivering Your Presentation**
- **Evaluating a Presentation**
- **Preparing a Multimedia Report**

"Lend thy serious hearing to what I shall unfold."
—Shakespeare

Making Oral Presentations

Objectives
- select a previously written report to adapt as an oral presentation
- plan, practice, and deliver an oral presentation
- plan a multimedia report

Invite students to talk about any experiences they have had speaking or performing in front of an audience. How did they like it? How did they prepare?

Explain to students that in working through this section they will learn special techniques for planning oral presentations. The instructions will guide them step-by-step through the process, to prepare them for giving their presentation.

When students do perform, it will be in front of a familiar, friendly audience composed of their classmates. This will help them get a sense of what it might be like later on, when they speak in front of larger audiences, perhaps made up of strangers.

Planning Your Presentation

If students will make their presentations based on their research reports, note that the purpose of their presentation will be to inform.

If students have other research reports to choose from, encourage them to think about what they might enjoy most—informing, persuading, or demonstrating. Point out that each of these will require the speaker to take a slightly different approach.

Before students review their chosen reports, briefly discuss the fact that, unlike readers, listeners can't go back to review something that wasn't clear the first time (or stop to ponder meaning). This is a very helpful point to keep in mind when adapting a written report to an oral report. Encourage students to look over their reports carefully with this idea in mind.

- Are there long or complicated sentences that won't be so easy to follow when spoken aloud?
- Can the writer's voice be made more conversational (without becoming too casual)?
- Can visual aids be used, instead of words, to convey some of the information?

Planning Your Presentation

To transform a research report into an oral presentation, you need to consider your purpose, your audience, and the content of your report.

Determining Your Purpose

Your purpose is your reason for giving a presentation.

- **Informative** speeches educate by providing valuable information.
- **Persuasive** speeches argue for or against something.
- **Demonstration** speeches show how to do or make something.

Considering Your Audience

As you think about your audience, keep the following points in mind.

- **Be clear** so that listeners understand your main points immediately.
- **Anticipate questions** the audience might have and answer them. This helps keep the audience connected.
- **Engage the listeners** through thought-provoking questions, revealing anecdotes, interesting details, and effective visuals.

Reviewing Your Report

During an oral report, your audience obviously cannot go back and listen again to anything you have said, so you must be sure to share your ideas clearly from beginning to end. Review your report to see how the different parts will work in an oral presentation. Use the following questions as a review guide.

- Will my opening grab the listeners' attention?
- What are the main supporting points that listeners need to know?
- How many supporting details should I include for each main point?
- What visual aids can I use to create interest in my topic? (See page **398**.)
- Will the ending part have the proper impact on the listener?

Try It!

Adapt your research report. Rework any parts of your report that need to be adjusted to work well in an oral presentation. Pay special attention to the beginning and ending parts, which should be written out word for word. (See the next page for example adaptations.)

Advanced Learners

Some students may be proficient with presentation software. Encourage these students to create slides to accompany each major idea presented in their oral presentation. Slides can show a main idea statement, a quotation, a graph or chart, or an illustration. If possible, encourage proficient students to hold a training session for other students in the school computer lab.

Reworking Your Report

To create a more effective oral presentation, you may need to rewrite certain parts of your report. The new beginning below grabs the listeners' attention by using short, punchy phrases and asking questions. The new ending makes a more immediate connection with the beginning.

Written Report (page 357)

> Why did newsboys in old movies shout "Extra! Extra! Read all about it!"? Why do newspapers include an entertainment section and an opinion page? Who was the first Washington news correspondent? Studying the start of the "penny press" in the 1830s provides answers to these questions.

Oral Introduction

> "Extra! Extra! Read all about it! Latest news! Shocking stories! Political scandals! Just a penny a paper!" These are the things newsboys shouted to sell penny newspapers in the early 1800s. Creators of the penny press in the United States paved the way for modern daily newspapers.

Written Report (page 362)

> Modern newspapers continue to focus on disaster and crime news, along with editorials and stories about business and entertainment. Also, topics in the public interest continue to appear in the news, just as they did in the Tribune. The obligation . . .

Oral Conclusion

> So when you hear the cry "Extra! Extra!" in a movie, remember those enterprising men who advanced the idea of a people's press. Although the penny press was sensational, it developed and influenced a national readership and established the foundation for the media of today.

Reworking Your Report

Invite volunteers to read the sample selections aloud for the class. (Have them read both the written and oral versions for both the introduction and conclusion.) Which version holds listeners' attention better? (Students should agree that the oral presentation versions do.)

Have students talk about the differences between the two versions presented.
- The oral version is shorter than the written version.
- The written version gives more specific facts (for example, saying that the penny press started *in the 1830s,* instead of the oral version's *in the early 1800s*).
- The emphasis of the oral presentation has been shifted a bit to emphasize the sensationalism of the penny papers.

Struggling Learners

If students have difficulty determining which parts of their written reports need to be reworked for an oral presentation, have them work with a partner. Each partner should read his or her paper aloud, while the other partner provides a constructive critique. The listener should raise a hand for any section that presents too much information, and the writer should mark that section to rewrite it or to consider using a visual.

Creating Note Cards

Explain the advantages of using notes for the middle section of oral presentations, rather than using the full texts of the reports. For example:

■ Using brief reminders of what topics to cover helps the speaker sound less "scripted" and more conversational.

■ A speaker who isn't reading steadily from a page can make eye contact with the audience.

Discuss why students are asked to write out their beginnings and endings word-for-word. Possible responses:

■ The beginning must grab the listeners' attention, and the ending must be tied in with the beginning. It's important to carefully craft the wording of both.

■ Reading the beginning gives the speaker a little time to get used to being in front of an audience without worrying about how to begin.

396

Creating Note Cards

If you are giving a prepared speech rather than an oral reading of your report, you should use note cards to help you remember your ideas. The guidelines below will help you make effective cards.

Following Note-Card Guidelines

Write out your entire introduction and conclusion on separate note cards. In the body of your speech, write one point per card, along with specific details. Clearly number your cards.

■ Place each main point on a separate note card, using key words and phrases to help you remember your details.

■ Number each card.

■ Note the main idea at the top of each card.

■ Write supporting ideas on the lines below the main idea.

■ Highlight any ideas you especially want to emphasize.

■ Mark cards that call for visual aids.

Considering the Three Main Parts

As you prepare your note cards, keep the following points in mind about the three parts of your oral presentation: the introduction, the body, and the conclusion.

■ **The introduction** should grab the listeners' attention, identify the topic and the focus of your presentation, and provide any essential background information about the topic. (See pages **394–395**.)

■ **The body** should contain the main points from your report that you want to cover. Present these points in such a way that they have the most impact on the listener. Also jot down the visual aids that you plan to use. (See the bold notes on the sample cards on page **397**.)

■ **The conclusion** should restate your focus and leave the listener with a final thought about your topic. (See pages **394–395**.)

Try It!

Create your note cards. Review the note cards on the following page. Then create cards for your introduction, main points, and conclusion. Make notes on the cards where you want to use visual aids.

English Language Learners

Students who are sharing with a small group may find it difficult to speak from note cards, but they should follow the guidelines to create note cards for the body of their written report. Tell them they can limit their speech so that it is based on just one or two note cards of their choosing.

Sample Note Cards

Below are the note cards Gabriella used for her oral presentation. Note how she arranged and marked her details on each card.

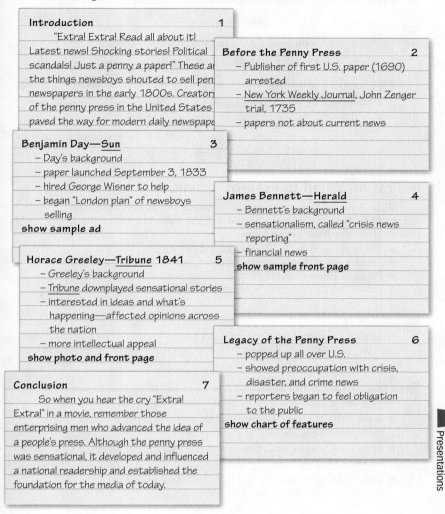

Sample Note Cards

Have students compare the sample note cards with the written research report on SE pages 357–362. What do students notice? Responses may include the following:

- The oral report focuses on the people who founded the first examples of the penny press papers. Many general details about newspapers—such as the paragraphs on SE page 358— are omitted.
- The information on card 6, that penny papers *popped up all over U.S.,* doesn't appear in the written version. It's an example of good word choice.
- The brief notes on the cards are just prompts. It's important to master the material in order to be able to talk about it. For example, the second note on card 2 about the John Zenger trial is a reminder to the speaker about what Zenger did and what the trial was about.

Considering Visual Aids

Students can draw posters and charts themselves, but finding other visual aids requires research. Have students review their sources, and familiarize students with good online sources of visual aids, such as the following:

- Web sites with good art and photography resources,
- the Library of Congress Web site (www.loc. gov), especially the American Memory section and the Prints and Photographs division,
- the New York Public Library Digital Gallery (http://digitalgallery.nypl.org), and
- the sites of state and local historical societies.

Note also that Google Web search has an image search option that can provide promising research leads (click the *images* link at www. google.com).

Considering Visual Aids

Consider using visual aids during your speech. They can make your presentation clearer and more meaningful. Here are some examples.

Posters	include words, pictures, or both.
Photographs	help people see what you are talking about.
Charts	explain points, compare facts, or show statistics.
Maps	identify or locate specific places being discussed.
Objects	show the audience important items related to your topic.
Computer slides	project your photographs, charts, and maps onto a screen and turn your speech into a multimedia presentation. (See pages 402–403.)

Indicating When to Present Visuals

Write notes in the margins of your note cards to indicate where a visual aid would be helpful. Gabriella considered the following visuals for her presentation about the penny press.

- A sample ad from Benjamin Day's newspaper
- Front page of James Bennett's newspaper
- Photo of Horace Greeley and the front page of his newspaper
- Chart listing the main features of penny press newspapers

Try It!

List possible visual aids. Identify two or three visual aids you could use in your presentation. Explain how and when you would use each one.

Tip

When creating visual aids, keep these points in mind.

- **Make them big.** Your visuals should be large enough for everyone in the audience to see.
- **Keep them simple.** Use labels and short phrases rather than full sentences.
- **Make them eye-catching.** Use color, bold lines, and simple shapes to attract the audience.

Advanced Learners

Some students may be experienced in using software to create charts and graphs. Encourage proficient students to demonstrate for other interested students how to create professional-looking charts and graphs that can be used as visual aids for their speeches.

Practicing Your Speech

Practice is the key to giving an effective oral presentation. Knowing what to say and how to say it will help eliminate those "butterflies" speakers often feel. Here are some hints for an effective practice session.

- **Arrange your note cards in the proper order.** This will eliminate any confusion as you practice.
- **Practice in front of a mirror.** That way you can check your posture and eye contact and determine if your visuals are easy to see.
- **Practice in front of others.** Friends and family can help you identify parts that need work.
- **Record a practice presentation.** A tape recording will let you know if you sound interested and if your voice and message are clear. (A videotape of your presentation would be even better.)
- **Time yourself.** If your teacher has set a time limit, practice staying within it.
- **Speak clearly.** Do not rush your words, especially later when you are in front of your audience.
- **Work on eye contact.** Look down only to glance at a card.
- **Speak up.** Your voice will sound louder to you than it will to the audience. Rule of thumb: if you sound *too* loud to yourself, you are probably sounding just right to your audience.
- **Look interested and confident.** This will help you engage the listeners.

Practice Checklist

To review each practice session, ask yourself the following questions.

- _____ **1.** Did I appear at ease?
- _____ **2.** Could my voice be heard and my words understood?
- _____ **3.** Did I sound like I enjoyed and understood my topic?
- _____ **4.** Were my visual aids interesting and used effectively?
- _____ **5.** Did I feel like I was rushing through my speech?
- _____ **6.** Did I miss anything I wanted to say?

Try It!

Practice your presentation. Practice your speech before your family or friends. Also consider videotaping your speech.

Presentations

Practicing Your Speech

Tell students that, with practice, they may memorize their opening and closing paragraphs. Caution them against memorizing the middle section. Instead, encourage them to think of ways to familiarize themselves with the information that will help them **speak clearly and audibly** *(see below)* and sound prepared and natural when they speak to their audience.

Provide additional suggestions for becoming comfortable with the material. For example:

- Practice telling parents and friends what the presentation is about in casual conversation.
- Encourage people to ask questions about the topic to see how well they can give spontaneous answers.

Teaching Tip: Speak Clearly and Audibly

To help students gauge the right pace and volume for public speaking, have them read aloud.

- Have students take turns reading their beginning and ending.
- If classmates cannot hear or understand the reader, have them raise their hand.

- Ask students to continue reading until they have a sense of the right pace and volume.
- As they read, remind students to speak loudly, clearly, and consistently.
- Have a volunteer sit farthest from the speaker and raise a hand when the volume and pace are just right.

Delivering Your Presentation

A day or two before students deliver their presentations, play a selection of famous speeches (both audio and video, if possible) for students. (The Web site HistoryChannel.com has a selection of speeches available online.)

After listening to each speech, discuss it as a group.

- What was most effective about it?
- What could use improvement?
- Describe the speaker's tone and the pacing of the speech.
- For video, did the speaker maintain eye contact with the audience? Did he or she follow all the tips listed on the page?

Delivering Your Presentation

When you deliver a speech, concentrate on your voice and body language. Voice quality and body language communicate as much as your words do.

Controlling Your Voice

Volume, tone, and *pace* are three aspects of your formal speaking voice. If you can control these three aspects of voice, your listeners will clearly follow your ideas.

- **Volume** is the loudness of your voice. Imagine you are speaking to someone in the back of the room and adjust your volume accordingly.
- **Tone** expresses your feelings. Be enthusiastic about your topic and let your voice show that.
- **Pace** is the speed at which you speak. For the most part, speak at a relaxed pace.

 Tip

You can make an important point by slowing down, by pausing, by increasing your volume, or by emphasizing individual words.

Considering Your Body Language

Your body language (*posture, gestures,* and *facial expressions*) plays an important role during a speech. Follow the suggestions given below to communicate effectively.

- **Assume a straight but relaxed posture.** This tells the audience that you are confident and prepared. If you are using a podium, let your hands rest lightly on the surface.
- **Pause before you begin.** Take a deep breath and relax.
- **Look at your audience.** Try to look toward every section of the room at least once during your speech.
- **Think about what you are saying** and let your facial expressions reflect your true feelings.
- **Point to your visual aids** or use natural gestures to make a point.

 Try It!

Deliver your presentation. As you deliver your speech, make sure to control your voice and exhibit the proper body language.

Evaluating a Presentation

Evaluate a presentation using the following evaluation sheet. Circle the description that best fits each assessed area. Then offer two comments: one positive comment and one helpful suggestion.

Peer Evaluation Sheet

Speaker _____ Evaluator _____

1. Vocal Presentation

Volume:
Clear and loud   Loud enough   A little soft   Mumbled

Pace:
Relaxed   A little rushed or slow   Rushed or slow   Hard to follow

Comments:
a. _____
b. _____

2. Physical Presentation

Posture:
Relaxed, straight   A bit stiff   Fidgeted a lot   Slumped

Eye contact:
Excellent contact   Made some contact   Quick glances   None

Comments:
a. _____
b. _____

3. Information

Thought provoking   Interesting   A few good points   No ideas

Comments:
a. _____
b. _____

4. Visual Aids

Well used   Easy to follow   Not clear   None used

Comments:
a. _____
b. _____

Evaluating a Presentation

Before students write their **responses to presentations** *(see below),* review the role of a peer responder.

- Remind responders that their comments should be polite, positive, and constructive.
- Note that one way to make a comment constructive is to phrase it as a question that requires an explanation as an answer (not a simple "yes" or "no"). It helps to use one of the 5 W's or H in phrasing a question. For example, *Could you explain a little more about why this event was influential?*
- To keep comments positive, focus on suggesting how to solve problems rather than just pointing them out.

✳ For more about the responder's role, see SE page 57.

Presentations

Teaching Tip: Responses to Presentations

Students will benefit from receiving feedback from more than one peer responder.

- Assign four or five student responders for each speaker (rotate responders, making sure that all students fill out an equal number of evaluations).

- Ask responders to take careful notes during or after each presentation they've been assigned to.
- Provide time after the presentations for responders to complete their evaluations.

Preparing a Multimedia Report

Demonstrate how to use any multimedia computer software available to students. Explain that they'll become more familiar with the software as they use it to prepare their reports.

Note that it can be helpful for the presenter of a multimedia report to have some help with the technical aspects. That way, he or she can concentrate on speaking effectively, while someone else controls the video and sound.

- After students have planned their multimedia reports, have them explain their plans to partners.
- Have partners help each other program the computer to present the audio and video.
- Give students time to rehearse their reports before making the final presentations.
- During the presentation, one student will speak while the other acts as a technical assistant, operating the computer.

Preparing a Multimedia Report

You can enhance an oral report using electronic aids such as slides and sound. In order to use these effectively, you must plan exactly where each slide or sound bite will fit into your speech.

Here is a planning script for a multimedia report on the penny press. What will be *seen* appears in the "Video" column, and what will be *heard* appears in the "Audio" column.

Planning Script

Video	Audio
1. Title Screen: "The Penny Press"	1. SPEAKER: Introduction SOUND: Music begins.
2. Slide 2: "Before the Penny Press" and picture of newsboys on city streets, early 1800s	2. SPEAKER: Read background of penny press. SOUND: Newspaper presses, boys' voices calling "Extra! Extra!"
3. Slide 3: Photo of Benjamin Day next to a picture of the NY Sun front page	3. SPEAKER: Give background of Benjamin Day and the Sun. SOUND: Ragtime music VOICE: Quotation about Day
4. Slide 4: Photo of Bennett and Herald	4. SPEAKER: Give background of James Bennett and the Herald. SOUND: Ragtime music VOICE: Quotation about Bennett
5. Slide 5: Photo of Greeley and Tribune	5. SPEAKER: Give background on Horace Greeley and the Tribune. SOUND: Ragtime music VOICE: Quotation about Greeley
6. Slide 6: Map of U.S. with New York pinpointed with large flag	6. SPEAKER: Explain impact of papers. SOUND: Music becomes Western.
7. Slide 7: Same map, with flags wherever other papers appeared	7. SPEAKER: Tell of spread of papers. SOUND: Music continues.
8. Slide 8: Pictures of printing presses then and now, side by side	8. SPEAKER: Conclusion SOUND: Printing presses running

English Language Learners

Some cultures view music differently than mainstream U.S. culture does. Some students may not be familiar with or have access to musical selections to include in their presentations. Encourage students who want to include music in future multimedia reports to work with partners at this time to learn how to do so.

Multimedia Report Traits Checklist

Use the following checklist to help you improve your multimedia report. When you can answer all of the questions with a "yes," your report is ready.

Revising Checklist

Ideas

_____ 1. Have I included the main ideas from my written report in my multimedia report?

_____ 2. Have I effectively supported my main ideas?

_____ 3. Does each slide or sound bite suit the audience and the purpose of the report?

Organization

_____ 4. Do I state the topic in my introduction?

_____ 5. Do I include the important main points in the body?

_____ 6. Do I restate my focus in the conclusion?

Voice

_____ 7. Do I sound interested and enthusiastic?

_____ 8. Is my voice clear, relaxed, and expressive?

Word and Multimedia Choices

_____ 9. Are the words and pictures on each slide easy to read and see?

_____ 10. Have I chosen the best audio and video clips?

Presentation Fluency

_____ 11. Does my report flow smoothly from point to point?

Conventions

_____ 12. Is each slide free of grammar, spelling, capitalization, and punctuation errors?

Presentations

Grammar Connection

Spelling Review
- **Proofreader's Guide** page 664 (+)
- *SkillsBook* page 56

Proofreading Review
- *SkillsBook* pages 65–66

Multimedia Report Traits Checklist

Point out that because students began working on the content of the reports and the visual aids earlier in the section, those elements should already be fairly solid. Students should evaluate items that apply to those aspects first—they should be able to check them off quickly. Then they can focus on the newest addition to their reports—the sound.

Ask students to talk about ideas to keep in mind while choosing sound bites. Possible responses:
- Find music that matches the historical period and geographic focus of the report.
- Find a song from any time period with lyrics that apply to the subject of the report.
- Think about the way sound effects are used in movies, and determine if sound effects would enhance their reports or detract from the content.

Writing Across the Curriculum Overview

Common Core Standards Focus

Writing 4: Produce clear and coherent writing in which the development, organization, and style are appropriate to task, purpose, and audience.

Writing 10: Write routinely over extended time frames (time for research, reflection, and revision) and shorter time frames (a single sitting or a day or two) for a range of tasks, purposes, and audiences.

Language 2: Demonstrate command of the conventions of standard English capitalization, punctuation, and spelling when writing.

Writing Forms

- learning log
- lab report
- cause-effect essay
- article summary
- descriptive report
- editorial-cartoon response
- document-based essay
- problem analysis
- chart or graph
- response to a prompt
- process essay
- essay of identification
- persuasive poster
- research report

Focus on the Traits

- **Ideas** Including the most important details that describe, explain, identify, and clarify the subject for the reader
- **Organization** Presenting information in the best order so that it is clear and easy to follow
- **Voice** Developing an appropriate voice that sounds interested and knowledgeable
- **Word Choice** Using specific nouns, active verbs, and correct terminology with definitions
- **Sentence Fluency** Writing smooth-flowing sentences
- **Conventions** Checking for errors in punctuation, capitalization, spelling, and grammar

 Technology Connections

 Write Source Online
www.hmheducation.com/writesource

- *Net-text*
- *Bookshelf*
- *GrammarSnap*
- *Portfolio*
- *Essay Scoring*
- *Writing Network features*
- *File Cabinet*

 Interactive Whiteboard Lessons

Teacher's Notes
for Writing Across the Curriculum

Each chapter description below will help you decide which parts of the unit to teach.

Writing in Science (pages 405–416)

Since observation and experimentation are key elements in science, much of science writing will have to do with facts, tests, and results. In this chapter, students will deal with taking notes, keeping learning logs, writing lab reports, developing cause-effect essays, and summarizing science articles.

Writing in Social Studies (pages 417–430)

Students will be asked to take notes and keep learning logs in social studies classes. This chapter also focuses on a descriptive report, a student's response to an editorial cartoon, and a document-based essay.

Writing in Math (pages 431–442)

Although math focuses on numbers, equations, and so on, there are times when math students are called upon to read and write as well. Therefore, this section will show students how to write a math article summary, how to analyze a word problem, how to graph the payments on a loan, and how to respond to a math prompt.

Writing in the Applied Sciences (pages 443–452)

In applied sciences, students take class notes and keep learning logs. They may also write an essay to explain a process, write an essay of identification, and write and design safety posters.

Writing in the Arts (pages 453–461)

Most students will find it impossible to remember everything they hear in class about music or artwork. Their class notes will help them remember, and their learning logs will reinforce specific learning points. Responses to a painting and a report on a musician's influence in the United States are presented to help students understand what is involved in such writing for the arts. Students often encounter writing in the arts in the form of book and movie reviews. Here the critique of works of art is modeled.

Academic Vocabulary

Read aloud the academic terms, as well as the descriptions and questions. Model for students how to read one question and answer it. Have partners monitor their understanding and seek clarification of the terms by working through the meanings and questions together.

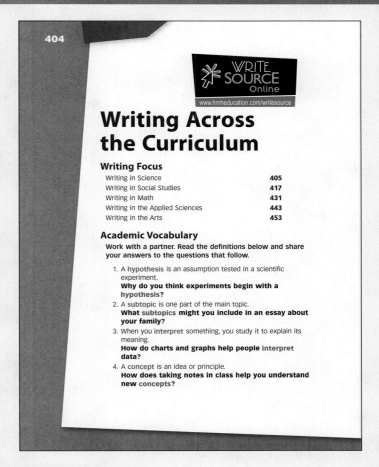

Minilessons

Why? Writing in Science

- **CHOOSE** a topic under "cause/effect" on SE page 585 or a topic of your own choice. **PRETEND** you are a kindergartner and **WRITE** a kindergartner's explanation of the cause.

My Space Writing in Social Studies

- **WRITE** a detailed description of a very small space. **SHARE** your description with a partner or the class. **ASK** the reader to identify the place.

Class Survey Writing in Math

- **CONDUCT** a brief survey of your class. **ASK** for each student's response to a question that poses three choices. **PLOT** your results on a simple graph. **SHARE** your graph with the class. **STATE** the summary of your graph as a mathematical ratio (for example, 2 out of 3 students . . .).

Recipe for Disaster Writing in the Applied Sciences

- **WRITE** a brief recipe that is sure to create a disaster. **INCLUDE** all the ingredients and directions for combining them. Then, **CHANGE** or **ADD** one final ingredient that could turn your recipe into a recipe for success.

404

www.hmheducation.com/writesource

Writing Across the Curriculum

Writing Focus

Academic Vocabulary

Work with a partner. Read the definitions below and share your answers to the questions that follow.

1. A hypothesis is an assumption tested in a scientific experiment.
   Why do you think experiments begin with a hypothesis?

2. A subtopic is one part of the main topic.
   What subtopics might you include in an essay about your family?

3. When you interpret something, you study it to explain its meaning.
   How do charts and graphs help people interpret data?

4. A concept is an idea or principle.
   How does taking notes in class help you understand new concepts?

Writing in Science

Simply put, science is a system of knowledge obtained by applying the scientific method—a method of testing hypotheses and drawing conclusions about the natural world. Throughout time, applying the scientific method has been one of the most powerful ways for human beings to learn about their world. In science classes—biology, life science, astronomy, or geology—you can learn how to explore the world for yourself and make many fascinating discoveries.

This chapter covers the types of science writing that will help you deepen your understanding of the world around you. It will also allow you to share that understanding with others.

- Taking Classroom Notes
- Taking Reading Notes
- Keeping a Learning Log
- Writing Guidelines: Lab Report
- Writing Guidelines: Cause-Effect Essay
- Writing Guidelines: Science-Article Summary
- Other Forms of Writing in Science

"Nothing in life is to be feared. It is only to be understood."

—Marie Curie

Writing in Science

Objectives
- practice taking notes for science
- keep a learning log for science
- apply the writing process and traits of writing to a lab report, cause-effect essay, and science-article summary

The lessons on the following pages provide samples of writing students might do in a science class. Assigning these forms of writing will depend on
- the skill level of your students,
- the subject matter they are studying, and
- the writing goals of your school, district, or state.

Taking Classroom Notes

Have students compare notes they took during a recent science class to the sample notes at the bottom of the page. Then have students use the following questions to evaluate their own note-taking habits. Since they probably practice these habits in all content areas, students can apply what they learn here to improve their note taking for all their studies.

- Did I date each entry?
- Did I note the topic?
- Are main points underlined or highlighted in some way?
- Do the notes contain clear and sufficient details?
- Have I written questions or made some other kind of notation about information I need clarified? Have I taken time to clarify this information?
- Are my notes legible?
- What changes should I make to take better notes?

Taking Classroom Notes

Note taking helps you focus on the information in a lecture, understand new material, and remember what's important. Here are tips on taking notes.

Before you take notes . . .

- **Set up your notes.** Use a three-ring binder so that you can add handouts to your notes, or use a notebook with a folder in the back.
- **Date each entry** and write down the topic.
- **Organize each page.** Consider using a two-column format, with lecture information on the left and questions on the right.

As you take notes . . .

- **Listen for key words.** Pay attention to information that comes after words like *for instance, as a result,* or *most importantly*.
- **Write down information the teacher puts on the board** or on an overhead. This is often the most important material.
- **Use your own words** as much as possible.
- **Write down any questions you may have** in the second column.
- **Draw pictures.** Use quick sketches to capture complex ideas.

After you've taken notes . . .

- **Reread your notes** after class. Add information to clarify your notes as necessary.
- **Research answers** to any questions that you wrote.
- **Review notes before the next class** to be ready for discussions.
- **Study your notes** to prepare for tests and exams.

The date and topic are noted.

Main points are underlined.

Dashes set off details.

March 16, 2011—Cell Structure

Two Types of Cells:
—prokaryotic = bacteria, basic life-forms
—eukaryotic = all other life

Eukaryotic Cell Structure
—cell membrane: skin around cell
—nucleus: home of DNA
—cytoplasm: part outside nucleus
—mitochondria: powerhouses
—lysosome: cell police
—endoplasmic reticulum (ER): roadway system of cell
—golgi: cell packing plant

Q: What structures are missing from prokaryotic cells?

A: They don't have a nucleus. Their DNA is just loose. It's in a shape called a plasmid. Also, these cells are tiny, like mitochondria in another cell.

English Language Learners

Students who are learning English may have difficulty separating new pieces of information when taking notes. To help them avoid confusion, tell students that when they reread their notes, they should highlight each new idea in a different color.

- Provide support by having students meet in small groups or with you to highlight their notes.
- Additionally, when giving students notes on the board or overhead, use different colors for each new concept.

Science

Taking Reading Notes

Taking notes while you read can increase your understanding and recall of a text. Here are some tips on taking reading notes.

Before you take notes . . .

- **Write the date, chapter, book, and topic** at the top of each entry.
- **Organize each page.** Try using a two-column format with wide margins. Put notes on the left and thoughts or questions on the right.
- **Quickly skim the assignment.** Read the title, introduction, headings, and chapter summaries. Look at graphics and charts.

As you take notes . . .

- **Write down headings or subtopics.** Note the most important details under each.
- **Put ideas in your own words** to be sure you understand the material.
- **Summarize graphics.** Write down or sketch the main ideas.
- **List vocabulary words.** Look up definitions later.

After you've taken notes . . .

- **Review your notes.** Write down any thoughts or questions you may have. Find answers and add them to your notes.

	March 16, 2011 Chapt. 10 <u>BioWorld</u> Cell structure and function

Reflections and questions are listed in the second column.

* Plant/animal cells both have membranes. Only plants have cell walls (rigid).
    1. Cell walls are made of cellulose.
    2. They protect a cell from damage.
    3. They give a plant its shape.
* Plant/animal cells have cytoplasm. Only plant cells have chloroplasts.
    1. Oval, green-colored structures
    2. Absorb sunlight, convert water and CO_2 into food (photosynthesis)

Flexible plant parts (leaves) have thinner cell walls.

Q: What is cytoplasm?

A: The liquid environment, mostly water, where cell activity happens.

Try It!

Take notes on the next chapter you read for a class assignment.

Taking Reading Notes

In addition to titles, headings, and subheadings, students can look for other print clues to recognize key ideas. Tell students to look for the following:

- words and terms in boldfaced type
- callouts from the text (These may appear in italics, a larger font size, or in a different color.)
- questions at the end of a section, chapter, or unit
- bulleted items

Many students try to write too much when they take reading notes. Their biggest challenge, after recognizing key ideas, may be the ability to condense these ideas into manageable notes. Using itemized or bulleted lists and knowing how to **summarize** *(see below)* will help.

Teaching Tip: Summarizing

Students may benefit from a refresher on summarizing. Remind them that a summary presents in shorter form the most important ideas from a longer piece of writing. To summarize, students should follow these steps:

- Identify the most important ideas in a passage or section of text.
- Think of how two or more of these ideas can be combined and condensed.
- Retell the ideas using their own words.

Select several passages from students' science textbook or from a science-magazine article and have students practice summarizing the ideas and putting them into note form.

English Language Learners

Students may have difficulty understanding texts if there are many vocabulary words they don't know. Tell students to read through texts once to identify unknown terms and look up the definitions. Then they should go back and reread passages, using the tips on this page to aid comprehension.

Keeping a Learning Log

Make sure students understand the distinction between class notes and learning log entries.

- Notes summarize and paraphrase facts and details presented in a classroom lecture or in a reading assignment. Notes are taken while listening to the lecturer or while reading.
- Learnings-log entries reflect one's thoughts about the facts and details from a lecture or reading assignment. Usually the entries are made after taking notes during a lecture or reading. A learning log is a tool students can use to think through concepts and to address questions they have.

Before students begin the **Try It!** activity, work together to analyze the sample learning-log entries on SE page 409, using the bulleted items under "As you make an entry" on SE page 408 and the call-outs on SE page 409 to guide the discussion.

Keeping a Learning Log

A **learning log** is a specialized journal in which you reflect on ideas and facts you are learning in class. In a learning log, you write about new concepts by connecting them to previous knowledge or experience. Here are some tips for keeping a learning log.

Before you make an entry . . .

- **Set up your learning log** in a three-ring binder or notebook.
- **Write the date and topic of each entry.**
- **Leave wide margins** so that you have room for reflections and questions.

As you make an entry . . .

- **Summarize key concepts** and compare them to familiar ideas.
- **Apply new ideas** to what you know and have experienced.
- **Write down questions** that you have about the topic.
- **Predict how the new ideas** may prove helpful in the future.
- **Make a connection** by explaining what the new ideas mean to you.

After you've made an entry . . .

- **Review your entries** to see how well you understand the class material.
- **Research any questions** you have and write down answers.
- **Continue your reflections** by writing new observations in the margins.

Tip

One way to approach your learning log is to stop and write. Stop in the middle of your reading or just after a lecture and freewrite immediate thoughts about what you've just learned. This can reveal how well you understand the material. Knowing which concepts are most difficult for you can help you better prepare for exams.

Try It!

Follow the guidelines above to set up your own learning log. Then, after a lecture or while reading an assignment, stop and write, reflecting on what you are learning. Explain what the ideas mean to you personally.

Learning-Log Entries

Here are sample learning-log entries from a student in an earth science class. The student reflects on the ideas raised in class, analyzing them and applying them to her own life.

Sample Learning Log

The date and topic are given, and ideas from the class are reviewed.

The student reflects on the topic and writes a question.

Another entry shows the student's growing understanding.

Answers to questions are also recorded.

October 19—Global Warming

Today we talked about global warming, which was confusing. Mr. Gull said that most scientists agree it is happening, and they have many ways to show it, like glaciers and ice caps melting and trees growing on the tundra where they never grew before.

Partly, I wonder why it matters if things get warmer. People say there was an ice age for tens of thousands of years, and then things got warmer. Maybe the earth just changes. That's the way it goes.

If global warming is real, how come it's been so cold around here lately?

October 23—Greenhouse Gases

Mr. Gull showed us an experiment with two clear-plastic zip-type bags. He filled one with air and zipped it. The other one he breathed into over and over before zipping it. Then he shined a hot light through each bag. The one with the regular air let the heat come right through—I could feel it on my hand. But the heat didn't come through the bag full of old breath (carbon dioxide). The CO_2 caught and held the heat. It's a greenhouse gas. The earth's CO_2 holds the sun's heat.

Why can't plants keep up? They take CO_2 and turn it into oxygen. Won't more CO_2 just mean bigger plants and more oxygen? Mr. Gull said that deforestation and destruction of plants in the oceans means the plants can't keep up with all the CO_2 people produce.

So, where does all the carbon dioxide come from? It's from breathing and from burning things. Ever since people discovered fire, they've been burning things—wood, coal, gasoline, natural gas. Unless people begin to get energy from cleaner sources, the planet will just keep heating up.

English Language Learners

Students may find it easier to write learning-log entries in their first languages so that their thoughts and reflections are not restricted by lack of vocabulary. When students are beginning new lessons, recommend that they write down new vocabulary and have translations or definitions handy for easy reference when they write in their logs.

Learning-Log Entries

Have students identify details in the sample learning log that show the writer's personal reflections. Students may suggest the following details:

- *Today we talked about global warming, which was confusing.*
- *I wonder why it matters . . .*
- *Maybe the earth just changes. That's the way it goes.*
- *If global warming is real, how come it's been so cold around here lately?*
- *I could feel it on my hand.*

Have students experiment with keeping a learning log for a semester. Teachers in every subject area can include them as part of in-class work. Once or twice a week, provide time for students to write learning-log entries. From time to time, ask students if and how these entries are helping them make connections in their learning.

Writing Guidelines

Lab Report

As you read each bulleted item in the Writing section, have students identify the corresponding element in the sample lab report on SE page 411. This will help students see how these guidelines can be implemented in a lab report.

Point out that a lab report is a combination of descriptive and expository writing. If necessary, remind students that

- descriptive writing creates a vivid mental picture, using sensory details; and
- expository writing explains an idea or a process, using specific facts and examples.

✱ For more about writing descriptive and expository paragraphs, see SE pages 565–566.

Writing Guidelines Lab Report

A **lab report** follows the scientific method. The report states a hypothesis, provides a method for testing it, records observations, and offers conclusions. Here are guidelines for creating a lab report.

Prewriting

- **Select a topic.** Follow your science teacher's assignment or (if given a choice) select a topic that interests you.
- **Plan the experiment.** Follow the planning your teacher provides. If you have selected the experiment, study it, gather materials, and make sure you understand each step.
- **Follow the proper format.** Use the lab-report format provided by your teacher or follow the lab-report model on page **411**, which is divided into seven separate parts.

Writing

- **Lay the groundwork.** State the purpose of your experiment— what it is designed to prove—and list materials needed. Also note the variables you will use in your test. Then write your hypothesis, explaining what you expect your experiment to prove.
- **Describe the procedure.** Use specific language to make each step clear.
- **Record your observations.** Describe exactly what happens during the experiment in chronological order.
- **Write a conclusion.** Tell whether your hypothesis was correct or not. Explain why.

Revising

- **Improve your writing.** Review your first draft for *ideas, organization,* and *voice.* Ask these questions: *Have I clearly stated my purpose, hypothesis, and conclusion? Have I described the experiment in chronological order and included enough details?*
- **Improve your style.** Check your *word choice* and *sentence fluency* by asking these questions: *Have I correctly used and explained scientific terms? Do my sentences read smoothly?*

Editing

- **Check for conventions.** Proofread your report for errors in punctuation, capitalization, spelling, and grammar. Fix any errors.
- **Prepare a final copy.** Make a neat final copy of your lab report.

Lab Report

The lab report below describes an in-class experiment dealing with acid-base reactions. The acid used is vinegar and the base is baking soda.

Sample Lab Report

The **beginning** states the purpose, the materials, the variables, and the hypothesis.

The **middle** outlines the procedure and records observations.

The **ending** tells whether the hypothesis was correct or not and why.

Acid-Base Reactions

PURPOSE: Show how an acid-base reaction is affected by foreign materials.

MATERIALS: Two 2-liter beakers, 3 cups water, 2 cups vinegar, 2 tsp. baking soda, 6 raisins

VARIABLES: Time and ingredients

HYPOTHESIS: The raisins will not change the acid-base reaction at all; the vinegar-baking soda reaction will still produce CO_2 bubbles.

PROCEDURE: I labeled the beakers A (test) and B (control). I poured 1.5 cups of water into each beaker and added 1 tsp. of baking soda to each beaker. I stirred each mixture until the powder dissolved in the water. Then I dropped the 6 raisins into beaker A. Afterward, I slowly poured 1 cup of vinegar into each beaker.

OBSERVATIONS: After a minute or so, the solution in each beaker began to bubble. Both solutions bubbled like carbonated soda, with bubbles clinging to the side of the beaker. The raisins in beaker A rose to the top of the liquid and then sank again. They continued to move up and down for the entire period.

CONCLUSION: My hypothesis was correct. The raisins did not affect the reaction. That's because the skin of the raisins isn't acidic or basic. (I wonder what would happen if the raisins were cut open.) However, the reaction <u>did</u> affect the raisins. The CO_2 bubbles formed by the acid-base reaction stuck to the raisins, causing them to rise to the top of the solution. The gas bubbles were released at the surface, causing the raisins to sink again. I was surprised that the acid-base reaction continued as long as it did.

Try It!

Perform a science experiment assigned by your teacher or devise one that interests you. Describe it completely in a lab report.

Lab Report

After reading and discussing the sample lab report, provide additional examples of lab reports. Have students
- point out what makes each report successful or less successful and
- suggest ways that the less successful reports could be improved.

Discuss the use of the first-person point of view in the lab report. Explain that if students are working on an experiment by themselves, they should use the singular personal pronoun *I*. If they are working with a partner or in a group, they should use the plural personal pronoun *we*. They should also clearly indicate who did what during the experiment. For example, *I labeled the beakers. My partner poured water into each beaker.*

English Language Learners

Define the steps of the lab report to ensure students know what each means:

- purpose (the goal of the experiment)
- materials (tools and ingredients)
- variables (things that could/will change the results)
- hypothesis (educated guess)
- procedure (steps followed)
- observations (results you notice)
- conclusion (summary of the results)

Advanced Learners

To enhance observation skills, point out that the sample lab report includes an observation not directly related to the hypothesis. Ask students to identify it (how the reaction affected the raisins). Emphasize that careful observation can reveal unexpected results. Encourage students to record any unexpected results in their own lab experiments.

Writing Guidelines

Cause-Effect Essay

Define the terms *cause* and *effect*.

- A *cause* is something that makes something happen.
- An *effect* is what happens as a result of a cause.

To make sure students can recognize cause-effect relationships when they do their research, have them identify cause-effect relationships in a current science article.

- Divide students into small groups and have them read their assigned article.
- Then have them work together to fill in a cause-effect graphic organizer similar to the one shown on SE page 588.

Writing Guidelines Cause-Effect Essay

Nature is full of causes and effects, and a science essay that explains them is called a cause-effect essay. It is common in a cause-effect essay to focus on one cause (the topic) and show its many effects. Follow these guidelines when you create a cause-effect essay.

Prewriting

- **Select a topic.** If your teacher does not assign a topic, review your class notes, learning log, or textbook for ideas. Choose a topic that shows a clear cause-effect relationship.
- **Gather details.** Research your topic so that you understand it thoroughly. Write down the cause and its effects. (Consider using a graphic organizer like the one on page 588.)
- **Outline your essay.** Write a thesis statement that names your topic (the cause) and the part you will focus on (the effects). Then write down the important details that explain the cause and the effects.

Writing

- **Connect your ideas.** Use your planning as a guide when you write your essay. Create a beginning that introduces the topic and leads to your thesis statement. Write a middle that explains the effects. Each middle paragraph should refer to a separate effect. Write an ending that reflects on the cause and its effects. (Refer to the model on the next page for ideas.)

Revising

- **Improve your writing.** Review your first draft for *ideas, organization,* and *voice.* Ask these questions: *Does my essay clearly illustrate a cause and its effects? Does my essay include enough details? Does my voice sound knowledgeable and appropriate?*
- **Improve your style.** Check your *word choice* and *sentence fluency,* asking these questions: *Have I correctly used and defined any scientific terms? Do my ideas flow smoothly from one to another?*

Editing

- **Check for conventions.** Proofread your essay for errors in punctuation, capitalization, spelling, and grammar.
- **Prepare a final copy.** Make a neat final copy of your cause-effect essay and check it for errors.

Struggling Learners

Help students avoid the *has-is-gets* trap in their future writing. Explain that like other essays, scientific essays benefit from well-chosen active verbs. To demonstrate, have students scan the sample essay on PE page 413 for active verbs (overcome, deal, climbed, cause, holds, suffer, risk, cough, break, punishes, endure).

Remind students that active verbs make writing more interesting and help readers understand and visualize the details.

* For more about active and passive verbs, see PE page 722.

Cause-Effect Essay

In this essay a student explains the effects of climbing above 25,000 feet.

Sample Essay

The **beginning** introduces the topic (cause) and leads to the thesis statement.

Into the Death Zone

Mountain climbers must overcome many dangers, and those who climb the world's highest peaks must deal with the greatest danger of all, the death zone. Hundreds of people have climbed above 25,000 feet and returned. They all know that a prolonged stay above that elevation will cause death because the air only holds a third as much oxygen as it does at sea level.

One effect of oxygen deprivation is pulmonary edema. Pulmonary edema is caused by the inability of the lungs to exchange gases and get rid of toxins. All climbers suffer from this condition to a degree, but some risk death if they do not immediately descend to much lower levels. A few mountain climbers cough so hard that they break ribs as their lungs battle for oxygen.

Each **middle** paragraph explains an effect of the lack of oxygen on mountain climbers.

The high altitude and lack of oxygen also affect the brain. The prolonged lack of oxygen causes the brain to swell, and in serious cases death follows quickly. Even breathing bottled oxygen cannot completely compensate for the oxygen-starved brain. Climbers are so impaired at times that they make foolish, often fatal mistakes. Climbers report hallucinations and headaches. One person who successfully climbed Everest found he could not even appreciate what he had done once he reached the peak.

The lack of oxygen also punishes the rest of the body. Hypothermia and frostbite are common because the body's metabolic functions need oxygen to operate efficiently. Climbers stumble, fatigue easily, endure frozen fingers and toes, and suffer nausea. A climber unable to walk is probably doomed because no one else will have the strength to help him or her.

The **ending** summarizes and emphasizes that the rewards of mountain climbing come with great risks.

Mountain climbing delivers spectacular rewards, and that is one reason why people risk so much. However, even the best-equipped climbers cannot endure the death zone for long. The lack of oxygen simply challenges climbers beyond their limits. Though climbers may reach their goals, they must quickly leave the place where no human was ever meant to live.

Cause-Effect Essay

Work as a class to analyze the sample essay to see how the writer has applied the traits of writing to produce an effective cause-effect essay.

Ideas

- The thesis statement tells the cause (a prolonged stay) and the effect (death) and focuses the essay.
- The writer explains three specific effects.

Organization

- Each effect is explained in a separate middle paragraph.
- The paragraphs are organized in logical order and connected by transitions to make the order clear (*one effect, also affect, also*).

Voice & Word Choice—The use of scientific terms, such as *hypothermia* and *metabolic function* helps to **create a knowledgeable voice** (*see below*).

Sentence Fluency—Sentences vary in pattern and length to create a smooth and interesting flow.

Conventions—The essay is free of careless mistakes.

Teaching Tip: Create a Knowledgeable Voice

Remind students that voice is the way a piece of writing sounds to readers. If a writer sounds knowledgeable, then readers will believe and accept what the writer has to say. To achieve a knowledgeable voice in a cause-effect science essay, students should do the following:

- Use scientific terms and language correctly.
- Define technical terms.
- Provide accurate details, statistics, and examples.
- Use active voice verbs (passive voice can weaken the sound of ideas).
- Choose specific nouns and verbs.

English Language Learners

Define the following words before reading the essay:

- overcome (survive)
- peaks (mountaintops)
- prolonged (for a long time)
- deprivation (lack of)
- toxin (poisonous thing)
- compensate (make up for)
- hallucinations (imaginary visions)
- hypothermia (dangerously low body temperature)

Writing Guidelines

Science-Article Summary

If there is time, have students practice **identifying the main idea** *(see below)* of short articles to prepare them for writing a summary.

- Divide students into groups of three.
- Assign each group three short articles from their science textbook or from magazines.
- Have students read each article silently and write its main idea.
- Have students compare main ideas.

414

Writing Guidelines Science-Article Summary

Scientists do a great deal of reading to keep up with new discoveries in their fields. The ability to read and summarize an article helps scientists and students alike. Use the guidelines below when you summarize a science article.

Prewriting

- **Find an article.** Browse periodicals like *National Geographic* or *Popular Science*, looking for articles that relate to your class work. Also check Internet sites like *www.nasa.gov* or *www.scitech.gov* and page through your science textbook.
- **Read the article.** Read the selection quickly to get its overall message. Then reread it more carefully for details.
- **Focus on the summary.** Write down the main idea of the article.
- **Gather details.** For your summary, select only the most important details that support the main point of the article. Your summary should be no more than one-third the length of the original.

Writing

- **Connect your ideas.** Write your topic sentence, stating the main point of the reading. Then follow with the key supporting details and an effective closing sentence.
- **Paraphrase information.** Use your own words for the summary. Avoid plagiarism by not copying phrases and sentences from the article itself.

Revising

- **Improve your writing.** Review your first draft for *ideas, organization,* and *voice.* Ask these questions: *Have I identified the main idea of the article? Have I included only the most important details? Have I used a topic sentence, body sentences, and a closing sentence? Have I put the ideas in my own words?*
- **Improve your style.** Check on your *word choice* and *sentence fluency,* asking these questions: *Have I used specific nouns and active verbs? Does my summary read smoothly?*

Editing

- **Check for conventions.** Proofread your summary for errors in punctuation, capitalization, spelling, and grammar.
- **Prepare a final copy.** Make a neat final copy of your summary.

Teaching Tip: Identifying the Main Idea

Most students can identify the main idea of a passage or selection when it is stated directly in a clear topic sentence that begins the passage. Point out, however, that a topic sentence may appear later, and that it sometimes is the concluding sentence. Students should also be aware that a main idea may be implied (the reader must infer it).

When the main idea is implied, readers have to identify the key points in the passage and then determine what all these points together have to say about the topic. Guide students to see that the main idea is implied in the sample article on SE page 415. Point out that the main idea includes two concepts, which the student writer combined in the topic sentence of the sample summary.

Provide small groups of students with at least one passage in which the main idea is implied. To help students write the main idea, have them complete this sentence: *The main point the writer wants me to understand is . . .*

Science-Article Summary

The following article, "The Debate on Cloning," is summarized in the student paragraph "Clones Aren't Just Copies."

Science

The Debate on Cloning

Cloning—the process of creating genetically identical organisms—has been a common science-fiction theme for more than 50 years. Today, cloning is making headlines around the world. The first cloned mammal was Dolly the sheep in 1997. Since then, scientists have cloned cats, deer, goats, horses, pigs, and endangered species like the banteng, gaur, and mouflon. Some commercial ventures even provide genetic clones of beloved pet dogs and cats.

In the science of reproductive cloning, the DNA of one animal is transplanted into the nucleus of an egg. The egg is then carried to term by a female of the same species or a similar one.

Advocates of reproductive cloning support the new science as a way to improve medical research. They claim that cloning can provide many medical advances: infertile couples can have children; genetically compatible organs or skin can be created for accident victims; and gene therapies may help doctors cure diseases like Alzheimer's or Parkinson's. However, the immediate use for reproductive cloning is to repopulate endangered animal species.

Opponents of cloning argue that the science faces great ethical problems. They consider it immoral to create life to use it selectively or destroy it in a lab. Indeed, the science-fiction stories that first explored the idea of human cloning depicted the horror of these kinds of abuses. Other opponents of human cloning point to legal issues. In the United States, for example, the constitutional guarantees of rights to individuals would cover any clone at birth. Opponents of cloning argue that the medical advances that cloning offer would come at an unthinkable ethical price.

The science of cloning continues to move forward. Like any science, it has potential to heal or harm. While scientists push the frontiers, opponents continue to protest. The debate is not likely to be resolved soon and may still be raging when the first human clone is old enough to speak for him- or herself.

Sample Summary

Topic Sentence

Body Sentences

Closing Sentence

Clones Aren't Just Copies

Despite deep concerns, cloning has moved from science fiction to science fact. Dolly the sheep was the first cloned mammal in 1997, and more animals have been cloned since then. Supporters say this technology can help infertile couples, provide organs for transplants, and cure diseases through gene therapies. Cloning also can help save endangered species. Opponents argue that cloning raises serious ethical concerns, especially in human cloning. They say that human clones should have rights and should not be test subjects. **Cloning isn't science fiction anymore, but science has not been able to dismiss long-standing ethical questions.**

Try It!

Write a summary of an assigned article or of one that interests you. Follow the writing guidelines on the previous page.

Science-Article Summary

Emphasize the importance of including only the most important details from the article in a summary. Then ask students to point out the following in the sample summary:

- important ideas from the original article that the writer paraphrased or combined
- less important details the writer omitted from the summary
- examples of specific nouns and verbs

Remind students that using specific nouns and verbs will not only make their ideas clearer, but it will also help them to convey their ideas concisely. Since a summary is much shorter than the original article, being able to write concisely is important.

✱ For more about using specific nouns and verbs, see SE pages 534 and 538.

Point out that although the sample summary is shorter than the article, it

- introduces the main idea,
- provides key arguments for and against the process, and
- restates the debate.

Emphasize that a summary does not include the writer's personal opinion.

English Language Learners

Define the following words before reading both samples:

- genetically identical (having exactly the same DNA)
- organisms (living things)
- endangered (close to extinct)
- advocates (people who support something)
- infertile (not able to have babies)

- compatible (able to work together)
- repopulate (make grow again)
- opponents (people who are against something)
- ethical (following standards of right and wrong)
- immoral (bad, wrong)
- potential (possibility, ability)
- frontiers (unknown areas of study)

Struggling Learners

Summarizing an entire article can feel daunting. To help students break down the assignment into manageable pieces, suggest that first they summarize each paragraph from the assigned article. Then they can use their paragraph summaries to better grasp the overall content of the article and craft a full summary.

Other Forms of Writing in Science

The first four forms of writing presented on this page (Process Essay, Classification Essay, Problem-Solution Essay, and Definition Essay) are examples of expository writing.

✽ If students choose one of these four ideas, refer them to the unit on expository writing on SE pages 144–199 for tips, guidelines, and models for these forms.

The last two forms of writing on this page (Opposing-Views Essay and Position Essay) are examples of persuasive writing.

✽ If students choose one of these two ideas, refer them to the unit on persuasive writing on SE pages 200–253 for tips, guidelines, and models for these forms.

416

Other Forms of Writing in Science

Process Essay

Biology—Write a process essay that describes a chronic illness or condition. Sample topics include arteriosclerosis, emphysema, cancer, or osteoporosis. Tell how the condition begins, how it progresses, and what it leads to.

Classification Essay

Climate Science—Write a classification essay about weather phenomena: types of cyclonic storms, types of fronts, types of clouds, or types of lightning.

Problem-Solution Essay

Life Science—Write a problem-solution essay about a current problem of conservation, such as disappearing wetlands, dying amphibians, or nonnative species. Suggest possible solutions to the problem.

Definition Essay

Geology—Write an essay that defines a major geological feature and explains how it came into being. Consider features like the Ring of Fire, the Great Barrier Reef, the forests of Petrified Forest National Park, the Great Lakes, or the Rocky Mountains.

Opposing-Views Essay

Earth-Space Science—Write an opposing-views essay about a controversial proposal in earth-space science: whether the moon should be mined, whether planets like Mars should be "terraformed" to make them earthlike, and so forth.

Position Essay

Any Science—Read about controversial new theories in biology, earth-space science, or any other area of science that interests you. Choose one theory and write a position essay that explains and defends it against opposing viewpoints.

417

Writing in Social Studies

In social studies, you are often asked to gather and interpret information from a variety of sources (texts, charts, graphs, maps, photos, and so on) and then respond to the information in writing. Learning to read and interpret data are important skills that will help you succeed when writing about key issues related to social studies.

This chapter models several types of writing you may be asked to do in your social studies classes. It addresses the descriptive report as well as responding to an editorial cartoon and responding to a series of documents.

- **Taking Notes**
- **Keeping a Learning Log**
- **Writing Guidelines: Descriptive Report**
- **Writing Guidelines: Editorial-Cartoon Response**
- **Writing Guidelines: Document-Based Essay**

"I was brought up to believe that the only thing worth doing was to add to the sum of accurate information in the world."

—Margaret Mead

Objectives

- practice taking notes for social studies
- keep a learning log for social studies
- apply the writing process and traits of writing to a descriptive report, an editorial-cartoon response, and a document-based essay

The lessons on the following pages provide samples of writing students might do in a social studies class. Assigning these forms of writing will depend on
- the skill level of your students,
- the subject matter they are studying, and
- the writing goals of your school, district, or state.

Taking Notes

Developing good listening skills will help students take better notes, and the ability to identify the most important ideas is key to taking the most useful notes. Explain that lecturers often provide visual and sound clues, such as the following, to help listeners identify key ideas.

- They pause and look up after making an important point.
- They change their intonation and adjust their rate. For example, they may suddenly speak louder and more slowly for emphasis.
- They repeat a phrase or an entire sentence.
- They write or draw on the board.

✱ For more tips on improving listening skills, have students see SE pages 464 and 466.

Taking Notes

Taking complete and accurate notes helps you understand new material. Effective notes are also one of your main resources when reviewing for tests and when completing writing assignments. Here are tips for taking notes.

Before you take notes . . .

- **Write the topic and date** at the top of each page.
- **Do your assigned reading** before you come to class. That will make it easier to follow what is being discussed. (See page **407**.)

As you take notes . . .

- **Listen to lectures carefully** and write down the main ideas.
- **Write down** what the teacher writes on the board or on an overhead.
- **Use your own words** for the most part.
- **Note new or unfamiliar terms** and add definitions later.
- **Condense information.** Write your notes in phrases and lists rather than in complete sentences.

After you've taken notes . . .

- **Review your notes** as soon as possible. Add information to clarify your notes.
- **Find answers** to any questions you still have.

The date and topic are noted.	September 5, 2011
	Themes for the Geographer
Main points are underlined.	Describing a place:
Dashes set off details.	– location (where it is)
	– features (what it's like)
	– region (how places are similar/different)
	– movement (how people move from place to place)
	– human-environment interaction (how people and animals relate to the physical world)

Geography is the study of the earth's surface features and how humans and animals interact with them.

 Try It!

Follow the tips and sample above the next time you take notes in class.

English Language Learners

Tell students they should listen for and write down words that they hear repeated often in a lecture. Suggest that students carry a pocket translation dictionary so that they can look up meanings of repeated words they do not understand.

Struggling Learners

Reviewing notes taken by their classmates will help students determine if their own note taking needs improvement. After a class activity that requires note taking, have students divide into groups of three to review one another's notes. Encourage them to consider the following points:

- Organization: Are the notes dated and titled?
- Thoroughness: Are the notes complete?
- Length: Are the notes in phrases and lists rather than full sentences?
- Neatness: Can the notes be read?

Social Studies

Keeping a Learning Log

A **learning log** is a specialized notebook in which you reflect on ideas and facts you are learning in class. Here are some tips on keeping a learning log.

Before you make an entry . . .

- **Write the date and topic** each time you make an entry.

As you make an entry . . .

- **Summarize key concepts** that you learned.
- **Connect to the material** by explaining what the ideas mean to you.
- **Write down questions** that you have.

After you've made an entry . . .

- **Review your entries** to see how well you understand the class material. Also research the questions you have.

The date and topic are given.	*September 5, 2011*
	Geography and Geographers
New information is reviewed.	Today we learned what geography is and how geographers do their work. I think it's fun to look at maps. Whenever my family goes on road trips, I am the map reader.
A personal connection is made.	I like visiting the forest, but I'm always happy to get home to the ocean shore where I can see for miles.
An assignment is discussed.	We learned about the five themes of geography. Each place is described by where it is, what it's like, how it's like other places, how people get around there, and how they interact with their surroundings. I need to write a descriptive report using these five themes.

What's the point of studying geography?

It helps you see connections between land and people.

Try It!

Freewrite for 5 minutes after your next class. Try to make a personal connection with what you learned.

Keeping a Learning Log

Remind students of the difference between taking class notes and writing learning-log entries.

- Notes summarize information and include specific facts and details presented in class.
- A learning-log entry personally connects what is learned in class or in a reading assignment to the writer's own experience.

To clarify the differences between the style and purpose of class notes and learning-log entries, have students compare the sample learning-log entry to the sample class notes on SE page 418. Guide students in a discussion of how the learning-log entry reflects on the information in those class notes.

Writing Guidelines

Descriptive Report

If you plan to have students write a descriptive report but do not want to assign a specific topic, consider providing a narrow list of suitable, course-related topics from which students can choose. This will eliminate an endless search by some students for the "perfect" topic. It also ensures that students write on topics that you can evaluate effectively without having to do extensive and time-consuming research of your own to verify information.

Whether you provide a specific topic, provide a list of topics, or allow students to choose their own topic, ask students to submit a **works-cited page** *(see below)* to support factual information that appears in their report.

Writing Guidelines Descriptive Report

Often in social studies, you will need to describe an event, a place, or a time in history. Use the following guidelines when you create a descriptive report.

Prewriting

- **Select a topic.** If your teacher does not assign a topic, you should choose a specific event, time, or place that relates to your course work and that you would like to know more about.
- **Gather details.** Learn all you can about your topic. Read books and Web-site articles. Study maps, graphs, and charts. All of this information will help you write a clear and interesting description.
- **Outline your report.** Organize your notes so that related details are together. If you are describing an event, consider organizing your details in chronological order. If you are describing a place, consider organizing your details by order of location or by some other logical order.

Writing

- **Connect your ideas.** Start by introducing your topic. Let the reader know the focus of your description. (Perhaps you will describe a place using the five themes of geography.) In the middle part, describe the topic using a clear and effective method of organization. Write an ending that sums up the topic.

Revising

- **Improve your writing.** Review your first draft for *ideas, organization,* and *voice.* Ask yourself if you have included details that help the reader clearly understand what you are describing.
- **Improve your style.** Check for *word choice* and *sentence fluency.* Ask these questions: *Have I correctly used and explained new terms? Do my sentences read smoothly?*

Editing

- **Check for conventions.** Proofread your report for errors in punctuation, capitalization, spelling, and grammar.
- **Prepare a final copy.** Make a neat final copy of your descriptive report. Proofread this copy before sharing it.

Teaching Tip: Works-Cited Page

By ninth grade, most students will have had opportunities to write a research report and create a works-cited page. Still, some students may benefit from a refresher on how to format reference sources for work cited.

✳ For specific details about how to format sources in a works-cited page, see SE pages 381–384.

Remind students that the purpose of a works-cited page is to allow readers to locate sources referenced in the report, in order to verify the information or to read more extensively about the topic. A works-cited page lists these sources in alphabetical order, making them easy for readers to find.

Descriptive Report

In this report, a student describes the city of Chicago, using the five themes of geography.

Sample Report

Writing in Social Studies **421**

Social Studies

Heart of the Midwest

Writers have called Chicago the "Windy City" to describe the wind off Lake Michigan. Carl Sandburg called it the "City of the Big Shoulders" when he wrote about Chicago's hardworking labor force. However, it's unlikely that anyone has ever described Chicago using the five themes of geography: location, features, region, movement, and human-environment interaction.

Location: Located in both the Northern and Western Hemispheres, Chicago is at about 42 degrees latitude and 87 degrees longitude in northeastern Illinois. Lake Michigan forms its eastern boundary.

Features: Chicago sits on a flat tract of land. The city's most unique geographical feature is its beautiful lake shore that borders the Loop, the city's downtown business district. The city's climate is one of extremes. Chicago experiences freezing winter temperatures and occasional heavy snowstorms. Then in summer, the temperature and humidity can almost reach tropical levels.

Region: Chicago is the most populous city in the Midwest region. Politically speaking, Chicago tends to be liberal, just like other large urban areas. A strong work ethic among the city's people means that many major industries and businesses have located in the region.

Movement: Many visitors arrive by air at O'Hare International Airport, one of the world's busiest airports, or at Midway Airport. Chicago provides public transportation for residents and tourists alike, including commuter trains and "el trains" (short for elevated trains). Cars, trucks, buses, and taxis crowd the city streets and expressways. Chicago is also a major Great Lakes port.

Human-Environment Interaction: As Chicago has grown, land has become more scarce. That is why developers have constructed skyscrapers in the Loop. The Sears Tower in Chicago is now the nation's tallest building. Businesses, such as those located on Navy Pier, have also expanded out into the lake on huge piers. Housing in the city and suburbs extends to the north, south, and west.

It's hard to describe a city as complex as Chicago. However, using the five themes of geography is a good starting point.

Descriptive Report

Point out that some topics have features that provide a built-in organizational plan for writers.

For example, as can be seen in the sample report, the five themes of geography provide an efficient and sensible organizational plan for a report about the city of Chicago. Explain that students can use this plan if they are writing a descriptive report about any specific geographical region.

If students are writing about the development of an idea over time, they will probably discover that a series of important dates in chronological order provides them with an efficient and sensible organizational plan.

Emphasize that whatever feature students use to organize their descriptive report, it should be logical and easy for readers to follow.

✱ For more about patterns of organization, see SE pages 571–574.

English Language Learners

Define the following words before reading the report:

- tract (area)
- populous (full of people)
- liberal (broad-minded, not conservative)
- work ethic (valuing hard work)
- elevated (raised off the ground, up high)
- scarce (difficult to find)
- developers (people who plan and build buildings)
- suburbs (towns close to a city)

Struggling Learners

Remind students to define new terms when writing a report. To help students focus on this task, point out two ways the writer defined new terms in the sample report.

- In the Features section, *the Loop* is followed by a comma and an appositive phrase.
- In the Movement section, *el trains* is explained parenthetically.

Writing Guidelines

Editorial-Cartoon Response

Explain to students that an editorial-cartoon response does not include a personal commentary, such as, "I thought this was a really funny cartoon." An editorial-cartoon response offers the writer's interpretation of the ideas represented in the cartoon. This means that the writer has to have a basic knowledge of the topic and be aware of controversies related to the topic. Otherwise, the writer will find it difficult to respond to the cartoon.

Provide students with practice **identifying and analyzing elements** (see below) in an editorial cartoon.

422

Writing Guidelines Editorial-Cartoon Response

Often in social studies, you will be asked to respond to an editorial cartoon, which uses words and images to comment on timely issues. Typically, editorial cartoons make their point through caricatures, symbols, labels, and brief captions. (A *caricature* is an exaggerated representation of a person, group, place, or thing.) Use the following guidelines to help you respond to an editorial cartoon.

Prewriting

- **Study the cartoon.** Carefully review the elements (*caricatures, symbols, text*) in the cartoon. If you're not sure about a particular element, ask someone for help.
- **Gather details.** List the different elements of the cartoon on a piece of paper. Write a brief description next to the element. (The two examples below relate to the cartoon on the next page.)

Caricature of NASA: NASA is represented by a young boy.

Slingshot: The slingshot may symbolize that the space program is "winging it."

- **Plan your response.** Identify the main point of the cartoon. Next, write a topic sentence for your response that focuses on the main point. Then determine which details from the cartoon you will include to support the topic sentence.

Writing

- **Connect your ideas.** Start with your topic sentence. In the body sentences of your response, include the key details. End with a closing sentence that reminds the reader of the main point of the cartoon.

Revising

- **Improve your writing.** Ask yourself if you have clearly and completely explained the editorial cartoon. Revise accordingly.
- **Improve your style.** Check for *word choice* and *sentence fluency.*

Editing

- **Check for conventions.** Proofread your response for errors in punctuation, capitalization, spelling, and grammar.
- **Prepare a final copy.** Make a neat final copy of your response.

Teaching Tip: Identifying and Analyzing Elements

Guide students to see how many elements are included in the editorial cartoon on SE page 423.

- Ask students to examine the cartoon before reading the sample response shown below it.
- Then ask them to identify additional elements in the cartoon besides the two examples shown on this page (Prewriting). List

these on the board. (the words *NASA* and *American taxpayer;* the image of the American taxpayer with stretched-out arms; the shuttle in the slingshot; the foolish, careless look on the boy's face; the crudeness of the slingshot.)

- Guide the class in a discussion of these elements and what they signify. Point out that there isn't

necessarily a right answer, that each reader will have his or her own interpretation. For example, do students agree with the description of the slingshot (under Prewriting)?

- Have students then read the sample response on SE page 423 to see which elements that they listed also appear in the response.

Writing in Social Studies **423**

Social Studies

Editorial Cartoon

Sample Response

Student writer Mai Yang wrote the following paragraph after taking some time to interpret the editorial cartoon shown above.

Slingshot Space Program

This editorial cartoon suggests two main problems with the United States space program. First, NASA is represented by a young boy pulling back a slingshot. This image suggests that NASA may be "winging" it with the space program, rather than spelling out a specific plan for the future. Just shooting rocket after rocket into space may not be serving the American public. Second, the space program is funded by the American taxpayers. And, as the cartoon suggests, taxpayers are being stretched to the limit to pay for NASA, not to mention all other government programs. The helpless taxpayer appears to have no control over what is happening. All in all, this cartoon raises some critical questions about NASA.

Try It!

Locate a political cartoon in an area newspaper or on the Internet. Respond to the cartoon using the information on page **422** and the sample above as a guide.

English Language Learners

Students may not be familiar with editorial cartoons, as they are not used in all cultures the way that they are here.

- Explain that political cartoons are created to call attention to something in the news.

- Show students examples from reliable news sources of cartoons about government, current events, and pop culture, and guide students in responding to editorial cartoons.

Editorial Cartoon

Consider having students all write a response for the same cartoon.

- Choose a cartoon with a topic that you are certain all or most students will know and understand.
- Display the cartoon in the classroom, or if you find the cartoon online, provide a link on the classroom Web site or give students the Web address.
- As part of prewriting, have students gather in small groups to discuss the various elements of the cartoon and share interpretations. This will help students who may not be familiar with the topic, as well as those who may be having doubts about their interpretations.

Writing Guidelines

Document-Based Essay

After students read the two opening paragraphs, have them skim SE pages 425–430 to see the examples of the different kinds of documents they may be asked to write about, and the kinds of questions they may be asked to answer about these documents.

Direct students' attention to the fourth bullet under Prewriting, and emphasize that students can use an outline to plan the flow of ideas in their essays. Tell them that when they write an outline, they should write a topic sentence for each middle paragraph. Then, when it is time to write, they can just add transitions to the topic sentences to create a smooth flow from one paragraph to the next.

✱ For more about creating outlines and for sample outlines, see SE pages 356, 372, and 528.

Focus on the first bullet under Writing. Provide students with examples of writing prompts and questions and have them practice **writing thesis statements** (see below) for an introductory paragraph.

424

Writing Guidelines Document-Based Essay

In social studies class, you may be asked to respond to a question or prompt based on a series of documents. The documents may include excerpts from books, magazines, letters, diaries, or other text sources. They may also include graphic documents, such as photos, maps, political cartoons, tables, or graphs.

In most cases, you will have several documents on the same subject to read and analyze. Along the way, you may be asked to answer a question about each document. Your main job, however, will be to write an extended essay using all the documents.

Prewriting

- **Read all the information thoroughly.** That includes your responses to questions for each document.
- **Look for clue words.** Make sure you understand your main task. Words such as *compare, explain, define,* and so on, indicate the type of thinking and writing you are to do. (See page **526**.)
- **Analyze each document.** Consider how the documents relate to each other and the main question or prompt you must answer.
- **Organize your facts.** Create an outline that pulls together information from all the documents and from your own previous knowledge.

Writing

- **Write your introductory paragraph.** Introduce the topic, give background information, and restate the question as a thesis statement.
- **Write the body of your essay.** Reword each main point in your outline as a topic sentence for a paragraph that explains part of your thesis. Include plenty of supporting detail in each paragraph.
- **Write a concluding paragraph** that briefly restates your position.

Revising

- **Improve your writing.** Review your essay for *ideas, organization,* and *voice*. Then check for *word choice* and *sentence fluency*.

Editing

- **Check for conventions.** Proofread your essay for errors in punctuation, capitalization, spelling, and grammar.
- **Prepare a final copy.** Make a neat final copy of your essay.

Teaching Tip: Writing Thesis Statements

Most students will benefit from a refresher on writing effective thesis statements. Remind students that a thesis statement sets forth the main idea that the writer plans to develop in an essay. An effective, well-written thesis statement

- lets readers know what they can expect to read about in the essay and

- guides the writer by controlling the details. Only details that support and help explain the thesis statement should be included in the essay.

✱ For more instruction and a formula for writing effective thesis statements, see SE page 594.

Struggling Learners

Students may find it difficult to keep track of the information needed for a document-based essay. To help them organize information for their outlines, encourage students to take notes while reading each document. If they are using photocopied documents, suggest they

- make margin notes and
- highlight, underline, and circle details on the page.

Sample Documents

Introduction: In many tropical areas around the world, rain forests are being cut down or burned in a process known as deforestation. At the current rate of deforestation, the rain forests will be gone within 100 years.

Document One

The Effects of Deforestation on Biodiversity

Leading biologists and ecologists estimate that as many as 30 million different plant and animal species may inhabit the earth. We have yet to identify and catalogue the vast majority of these species and are quickly losing our opportunity to do so. More than half can be found within an area that constitutes only 7% of the planet's total land mass, an area that is shrinking and could disappear altogether—the tropical rain forests.

Rain forests are being harvested at an alarming rate for their trees. Such deforestation could be causing an average of 100 living species to go extinct every day. Many plants and animals require the specialized habitats that only the rain forests can provide. Once those habitats are lost, so too are the species that populate them.

The world's biodiversity is a critical issue. What happens to the rain forests could have a significant impact on another species—the human species. The keys to curing such life-threatening diseases as cancer, AIDS, and heart disease could be lost along with the plants and animals that deforestation kills.

Source: Friends of the Rain Forests

> Only the most important information is included in the summary.

Task: Summarize the main concern of deforestation as presented in this document. Why is it important?

The majority of earth's 30 million species of plants and animals live in rain forests. Approximately 100 species are probably becoming extinct each day due to loss of habitat caused by deforestation. The effects of deforestation could mean losing the chance to cure life-threatening diseases.

Sample Documents

All the sample documents on the following pages include tasks and sample student responses. If you think it will benefit your students to practice reading and analyzing documents, have them create their own responses for each task before they read the sample response.

English Language Learners

Define the following words:

- deforestation (cutting down or clearing trees or forests)
- biodiversity (all of the different kinds of living things)
- species (kind or sort of living thing)
- habitat (the natural place where something lives)
- extinct (all of a kind of plant or animal have died)
- impact (effect, consequence)

Provide general information about deforestation so that students have some background knowledge in order to better understand each document in this section.

Discuss the benefits to a reader or writer using a graphic organizer to chart information from an article.

- The process forces students to identify key ideas and supporting details, which leads to a greater understanding of the selection.
- A graphic organizer makes it easy to see and recall the most important ideas, which will help when writing.

426

Document Two

Why Is Deforestation Happening?

Deforestation is the clearing of land by cutting or burning trees. It occurs for many reasons but can usually be traced to underlying economic issues. Most deforested land in tropical rain forests is cleared to make room for agriculture.

Individual farmers will clear a few acres of trees in order to have open land to plant crops. Many earn a living selling these crops and the wood from the trees. Subsistence farmers live off everything grown on the farm. For them, deforestation is necessary simply to eat and live.

Commercial loggers and big agri-businesses have the capacity to harvest many more square miles than small farmers. Logging companies cut down trees for timber and wood pulp, while corporate farmers clear whole tracts of land to accommodate large herds of livestock. The global demand for beef is a significant factor in deforestation.

Governments of economically deprived nations will sometimes sell logging rights that allow others to come deforest their land. These governments need the money to pay off debts, to fund agencies that provide services to their people, and to foster the growth of new industries. Some land is also cleared for new towns, to accommodate the expanding populations of developing nations.

Source: Friends of the Rain Forests

Task: Make a chart listing the groups who cause deforestation and the reasons they do it.

> A word or two is all that is needed to list the answers for this task.

Farmers	Businesses	Governments
– food	– make money	– pay off debts
– earn a living	– raise livestock	– fund government agencies
	– logging (timber, pulp)	– support new industries

English Language Learners

Define the following words:

- corporate (belonging to a large company)
- loggers (people who cut down and sell trees)
- pulp (crushed wood used for making paper)
- deprived (poor, limited)
- fund (provide money for)

Writing in Social Studies **427**

Social Studies

Document Three

Percentages of Species
Unique to Madagascar's
Rain Forests

Reptiles   Plants   Birds

Task: Explain the information in the bar graph. State at least two of the percentages in a different mathematical form (ratio, fraction, and so on).

> The bar graph shows species unique to Madagascar's rain forests. That means they are found nowhere else in the world. Nine out of ten of this island's reptiles, four-fifths of its plants, and 50 percent of its birds exist only in Madagascar.

Graph information is changed to text form.

Two percentages are stated in other ways.

Document Four

Rain Forests of the World

Equator

■ **Tropical** (thousands of species)
■ **Temperate** (dozens of species)

Task: Based on this map, tell why there are probably fewer species of plants and animals in temperate rain forests than there are in tropical rain forests.

> Temperate rain forests are farther from the equator. They are cooler and have a wider range of temperatures that many tropical rain-forest species cannot tolerate.

Previous knowledge is used to answer this question.

For additional practice, have volunteers suggest alternate ways the percentages could have been stated in the explanation for Document Three. For example, instead of saying "nine out of ten," the student could have said 90 percent or nine-tenths.

Document Five

We can't save all the forests. Let's say, hypothetically, that we can save 10 percent. We have to decide: What do we set aside? What do we let be destroyed?

—*Chris Raxworthy, Curator, Herpetology Department,
American Museum of Natural History, New York*

Task: What position does this quotation represent?

The main point is restated.

This quotation says that deforestation cannot just stop. A plan is needed to determine which rain forests to save.

Document Six

"Rain Forest" Coffee is the Bee's Knees

Your morning cup of joe might seem to taste better to you because of its certified eco-friendliness. Now comes word that coffee grown on farms that don't deforest might actually be better. A study recently published in the *Proceedings of the National Academy of Sciences* links the activity of rain-forest bees to bountiful coffee-bean yields and a tastier brew.

American researchers in Costa Rica found that where bees were in greater abundance—near their rain-forest habitat—coffee yields were 20% higher. What's more, coffee trees that bees had pollinated were far less likely to produce "peaberries," the small misshapen beans that produce poor-quality coffee.

The higher price tag of "Rain Forest" certified coffees, which must be grown according to strict forest-friendly specifications, already provides an economic incentive for local farmers to preserve trees. Thanks to the bees, you can be sure you're getting your money's worth.

—*Pacific Lifestyle Magazine*

Task: What's one way to save rain forests?

One way to save rain forests is to prove their value to local people who live near them.

English Language Learners

Define the following words before reading Document Six:

- bountiful (large amounts)
- researcher (someone who studies or investigates)
- incentive (motivation, reason)
- pollinated (fertilized)
- yields (amounts)
- misshapen (strange, wrong form)

Students may have an easier time summarizing this document by first paraphrasing each of the three paragraphs and then writing a one-sentence summary of the entire article, based on their three restatements.

Document-Based Essay

In this essay, a student writes an essay that pulls together the information presented in six original documents.

Social Studies

> **Task: Extended Essay**
> *Using all six documents provided and your own knowledge about this topic, write an essay in which you explain why deforestation occurs, what it leads to, and what can be done about it.*

Sample Essay

Documents 1, 2, and 4
The thesis is stated in the opening paragraph.

Is There Hope for the World's Rain Forests?

Deforestation of tropical rain forests occurs because economically challenged tropical nations find it difficult to compete in a world market. However, even though deforestation appears to make life better for people in the short term, it is impossible to replace the tropical rain forests. The world's temperate rain forests just don't offer the same variety of species. The nations of the world should try to reduce the loss of valuable plant and animal life since such loss is affecting the world in a devastating way in the long term.

Document 2
An overview of reasons for deforestation is presented.

In all cases, rain forests are destroyed for economic reasons. Farmers cut down trees on a few acres to grow crops or graze animals. A majority of people in these countries rely on the land to eat and to earn a living. In many areas, large logging businesses destroy huge areas of rain forest for lumber. On cleared land, corporate farms graze cattle for the world beef market. Governments also destroy rain forests by promoting industry to help pay debts. They also use some rain-forest land to construct new towns for growing populations.

Document 1
The importance of habitat is emphasized and previous knowledge is shared.

Losing rain forests means losing plants, reptiles, birds, and other wildlife. The majority of the world's species call rain forests home, so any loss of rain forest is a loss of vital habitat. Some species may live in more than one of the world's rain forests, but that isn't always true. Rain forests are very unique ecosystems. For example, in the rain forests of

Document-Based Essay

Before assigning an extended essay for students to write on their own, give them a chance to read and analyze the sample essay. Guide a class discussion of how the student writer pulled together information from the six documents on SE pages 425–428 to respond to the key ideas in the prompt.

This task may appear overwhelming for many students. If you intend to assign a document-based extended essay, assure students that you will supply the documents, and that you will provide time for students to discuss and respond to each document separately before they have to write the essay.

Remind students that they can apply all of the techniques that they have learned about the writing process and the traits of writing to any writing assignment.

✱ If students need a quick refresher on the steps of the writing process and the writing traits, refer them to SE pages 9–12 and 54.

430

Document 3
Specific facts from a graph emphasize the uniqueness of the rain-forest ecosystem.

Madagascar, 90 percent of the reptiles live nowhere else on earth. The same is true for 80 percent of Madagascar's plants and 50 percent of its birds. Many rain forest species are still unknown to humans, so the exact effect of their loss to the world is uncertain. However, any plant or animal that becomes extinct might have been the source of a cure for disease.

Documents 1, 2, and 4
The causes and effects of deforestation are revisited.

While the future of tropical rain forests is uncertain, two facts remain. As many as 100 species may be lost each day because rain-forest habitat is being destroyed. The world's few temperate rain forests don't support plants and animals being lost in the tropical rain forests. Populations of rain-forest countries keep growing, and so economic pressure keeps increasing for individuals, businesses, and governments who rely on rain forests for income.

Documents 5 and 6
The conclusion points to one way to slow or stop deforestation.

Scientists seem to agree that it may be impossible to stop deforestation. Instead, they call for a plan to slow the process. Questions remain about which rain forests will contribute most to the world and humankind. More research could find ways to prove the value of saving rain forests. For instance, in Costa Rica, researchers found that pollination by rain-forest bees increased nearby coffee crops 20 percent. More could be done to find out what people living in rain forests already know about the medical values of plants and animals so that people around the world would understand the value of saving irreplaceable rain forests.

Essay Checklist

_____ 1. Do all the ideas in my essay support and relate to my thesis statement?
_____ 2. Do I cover all the issues named in the task or prompt?
_____ 3. Do I summarize my main points in the conclusion?
_____ 4. Do I refer to information from all the documents?
_____ 5. Do I include some of my own knowledge about this topic?
_____ 6. Have I checked my punctuation, grammar, and spelling?

431

Writing in Math

Your understanding of mathematics rests upon a foundation laid down during your early years—from counting to adding to subtracting and on and on. Through the years, you have continued to build concept upon concept, much as construction workers frame in a building floor by floor.

When you attempt to explain a math concept in writing, you may discover you have gained a greater understanding of the idea. You may also find that striving to put math into words can actually improve your writing.

- **Taking Notes**
- **Keeping a Learning Log**
- **Writing Guidelines: Article Summary**
- **Writing Guidelines: Problem Analysis**
- **Writing Guidelines: Creation of a Chart or Graph**
- **Writing Guidelines: Response to a Math Prompt**
- **Other Forms of Writing in Math**

"The safest words are always those which bring us most directly to fact."
—Charles H. Parkhurst

Writing in Math

Objectives

- practice taking notes for math
- keep a learning log for math
- apply the writing process and traits of writing to a math article summary, a problem analysis, a graphic response, and a response to a math prompt

The lessons on the following pages provide samples of writing students might do in a math class. Assigning these forms of writing will depend on

- the skill level of your students,
- the subject matter they are studying, and
- the writing goals of your school, district, or state.

Taking Notes

As part of their regular note-taking habits, encourage students to create their own glossary of math terms.

- Suggest that students set aside a section of their binder for math terms and their definitions.
- If possible, students should try to keep these terms in alphabetical order to make the terms and their definitions easy to locate.

Taking Notes

Using your own words to write down mathematical steps and formulas can help you understand and remember them. Here are some note-taking tips.

Before you take notes . . .

- **Use a three-ring binder** to store your notes so that you can add handouts, worksheets, and so on.
- **Write the topic and date** at the beginning of each entry.

As you take notes . . .

- **Write down** what the teacher puts on the board or overhead. This information often contains main concepts, math terms, definitions, formulas, and important examples.
- **Put concepts in your own words.** Also write down questions you have about the material.
- **Draw pictures.** Use diagrams to help you visualize a process.

After you've taken notes . . .

- **Find answers** to your questions.
- **Study your notes** before the next class and again before exams.

Sample Notes

May 3, 2011
Two-Step Equations
- variable—represents the unknown
- inverse operation—doing the opposite (subtract, not add)
- solving for the variable—getting the variable alone on one side of the equation

Solving Two-Step Equations
1. Subtract (or add) the number without the variable to both sides.
2. Divide (or multiply) by the number attached to the variable on both sides of the equation.
3. Substitute the answer into the equation to check it.

Problem: Tulip bulbs cost $0.75 each plus $3.00 for shipping. With $14.00, how many bulbs can you order?

Form an equation: Let x represent the number of tulip bulbs. Then $0.75x + 3.00 = 14.00$

(1) Subtract 3.00 from both sides.
$0.75x + 3.00 - 3.00 = 14.00 - 3.00$
$0.75x = 11.00$

(2) Divide by 0.75 on both sides.
$\dfrac{0.75x}{0.75} = \dfrac{11.00}{0.75}$ $x = 14.67$
You can buy 14 bulbs.

(3) Check your solution.
$0.75 (14) + 3.00 = 13.50$.
You have $0.50 remaining.

Math

Keeping a Learning Log

In a learning log, you record new ideas and puzzle over questions related to what you are studying. Here are some tips for keeping a learning log.

Before you write . . .

- **Set up the log.** Use a notebook or a section of your binder.
- **Date each entry** so you can find it easily.
- **Leave wide margins** for writing questions and answers.

As you write . . .

- **Reflect on what you learn** by writing about what you understand and what you're still questioning.
- **Summarize key concepts** and think about how they connect to your own experience and to other ideas you have learned in math.

After you've written . . .

- **Review your log** before a test or when you study a new theorem.
- **Answer any questions** you may still have.

Sample Learning Log

May 3, 2011   Exponents

Exponents: n is the exponent in X^n (X to the nth power). An exponent tells how often the base is used as a factor.

$A^4 = A \times A \times A \times A$ (A to the 4th power)

1. When multiplying same-base variables with exponents, ADD exponents.

$A^x \times A^y = A^{x+y}$ $A^3 \times A^2 = A^5$

2. When raising a variable with an exponent to another power, MULTIPLY exponents.

$(A^x)^y = A^{xy}$ $(A^3)^2 = A^6$

3. When raising more than one variable to a power, raise BOTH by that exponent.

$(AB)^x = A^x B^x$ $(AB)^3 = A^3 B^3$

Base? Number raised to n^{th} power

Factor? Multiplying number

$3^4 = 3 \times 3 \times 3 \times 3 = 81$ (3=base)

1. product of powers

$2^3 \times 2^2 = 2^5 = 32$

2. power of a power

$(2^3)^2 = 2^6 = 64$

3. power of a product

$(2 \times 3)^3 = 2^3 \times 3^3 = 8 \times 27 = 216$

Try It!

Write a learning log entry about a topic you studied in math class.

Keeping a Learning Log

The need for accuracy is essential when taking math notes or keeping a math learning log. Remind students that while misspelling a word in their science or social studies notes will probably not interfere with comprehension in those subjects, copying a formula incorrectly or writing the wrong number in their math notes can lead to bigger mistakes.

One of the greatest benefits of keeping a learning log is that it gives students an opportunity to explore complex concepts.

- If, as they reflect on what they have learned, they find that they have questions about specific math concepts and procedures, tell them to circle those questions.
- Then they should review their class notes to find the answers or ask for help.

Writing Guidelines

Article Summary

Before asking students to write a summary of an article containing math data, make sure that
- students have reviewed the writing process steps shown here, and
- they have read and discussed the math article and sample summary on SE page 435 (see TE page 435).

Financial magazines and the business section of the newspaper often have articles that contain math data. Make available a variety of these print resources for students to look through to find articles to summarize.

Writing Guidelines Article Summary

You often encounter statistics or data analysis in the articles, books, or news stories you read. Use the following guidelines when you are asked to summarize a math-related article.

Prewriting

- **Find an article.** Choose a newspaper or magazine article that uses statistics and figures to support a story, a position, or an issue.
- **Read the article.** Read the selection first to get its overall message. Then reread it carefully, paying attention to details.
- **Find the focus.** Write down the main idea of the article.
- **Gather details.** Select only the most important details that support the main idea of the article. Arrange the details in the most logical order.

Writing

- **Write your first draft.** Write your topic sentence, stating the main point of the reading. Supply supporting details. Close with a sentence that summarizes your thoughts.

Revising

- **Improve your writing.** Review your first draft for *ideas, organization,* and *voice.* Ask these questions: *Have I identified the main idea of the article? Have I included only the most important details? Have I explained any math concepts in clear language?*
- **Improve your style.** Check on your *word choice* and *sentence fluency.* Ask these questions: *Have I used specific nouns and active verbs? Does my summary read smoothly?*

Editing

- **Check for conventions.** Proofread your summary for errors in punctuation, capitalization, spelling, and grammar.
- **Prepare a final copy.** Make a neat final copy of your summary.

Try It!

Find an article containing math data. Follow the tips above as you write your summary paragraph.

Math

Math Article and Summary

A student read the following article in the newspaper and wrote a brief summary, including a graph to illustrate the statistics in the article.

Teen Reading Habits Examined

Parents today are frequently reminded to monitor what their children are watching on television, downloading on the computer, or listening to on their MP3 players. Curiously, you seldom hear of parents being warned to monitor what books their children are checking out from the public library. Many libraries maintain a policy of no restrictions as to what young people may check out, and the Putnam City Library is no different. According to City Librarian Anna LaGrange, "If they have a card, they can check out anything."

While this might seem disconcerting to most parents, there is good news. According to Ms. LaGrange, the majority of books being read by young people in Putnam seem to be age appropriate. "While we don't censor reading materials, I keep records of what is checked out," she says. "Our teens make excellent choices of reading materials." She offers the following statistics from the past year to support her claim.

The books most often checked out in the past 12 months have been classified by the Young Adult Library Services Association (YALSA) as "Books that don't make you blush." These include teen romances, modern novels, and classics and contain no objectionable themes or language. Nearly 27% of books checked out by Putnam teens fall into this category. Mysteries are checked out by 21% of the city's teens and include adult mysteries as well as those for young adults. Science fiction runs a close third at 18%, and historical fiction is also popular, with a 16% readership. Health-related books capture 9% of our teens' interest. These can be either fiction, including medical thrillers, or nonfiction. The remaining 7% are books that contain inappropriate adult themes or language.

"While there is some wiggle room in the categories, on the whole, our children appear to be reading age-appropriate material," says Ms. LaGrange. She still encourages parents to talk with their children about their reading, and offers this advice to parents: "You judge what is appropriate. Read what your child is reading, and read good books on your own. Set an example, and then you can set your guidelines."

Sample Summary

Teen Reading: Right on Track

The article "Teen Reading Habits Examined" shows the types of books teenagers are checking out of the Putnam City Library. Statistics quoted by librarian Anna LaGrange indicate that student interests tend to be appropriate to their ages. Books most often checked out by local teens appear to be unobjectionable novels, classics, and mysteries. Science fiction and historical fiction also appear to be widely read, followed by health-related works. Only a few students check out books that might be unacceptable. The librarian suggests that parents should know what their children are reading.

Types of Literature Checked Out by Teens at Putnam City Library

science fiction 18% — good novels and classics 27% — mysteries 21% — inappropriate 7% — health related 9% — historical fiction 16%

Math Article and Summary

Explain that students will have an easier time deciding which details to include in a summary and which to leave out if they first identify the topic (what the article is generally about) and then the main idea (the important point the article is making about the topic). Then they can choose only those details that relate specifically to the main idea.

- Give students a few minutes to read the article "Teen Reading Habits Examined."
- Then have them identify its topic (teen reading habits) and its main idea (Most teens are making good choices when it comes to checking books out of the library.).
- Have students read the sample summary. Ask them to explain in their own words how the writer integrated relevant details from the article into the summary.
- Then have students point out details that the writer didn't include, and have them explain why. Students should recognize that while these details add interest to the article, they do not help explain the main idea.

English Language Learners

If students have difficulty comprehending the sample article, allow them to read it with the help of an English-proficient student who is able to clear up any confusion or misunderstanding that they may have.

Writing Guidelines

Problem Analysis

Help students recognize the benefits of writing a problem analysis.

- Point out that writing an analysis ensures that they do not skip any of the important steps in the problem-solving process.
- In addition, it can help them recognize specific weaknesses in their problem-solving methods. Once they have identified a weakness, they can decide how to address it. For example, they may need to reread their text, review their notes and learning-log entries, or ask for additional help.

Writing Guidelines Problem Analysis

In math class, you learn how to analyze problems by stating specific *assumptions, evaluations,* and *explanations* about them.

- **Assumptions** are statements that are believed to be true. These could be formulas or statements about variables. They provide the structure for solving the problem.

  Evaluate and solve $6x - (x + y)$, for $x = 4$ and $y = 5$ (assumptions).

- **Evaluations** are the calculations and manipulations needed to get to the answer. For this problem, show your work by replacing unknown variables (x or y) with their values.

  $6(4) - (4+5) = 6(4) - 9 = 24 - 9 = 15$ (evaluations)

- **Explanations** make any complex process clearer to the reader by explaining problem-solving steps.

  I solved this by replacing x and y with their assumed values; if $x = 4$ and $y = 5$, then the answer to $6x - (x + y)$ is 15 (explanation).

Prewriting

- **Select a topic.** If your teacher does not assign a specific math problem, review your learning log or textbook for ideas.
- **Study the problem.** Be sure you understand your assignment. Then write down assumptions you find in its instructions.
- **Plan the steps.** Write down each step in the correct order.

Writing

- **Write your first draft.** First, introduce the problem and explain it step-by-step, identifying any variables. Next, evaluate the problem by sharing all work. Finally, state your explanation.

Revising

- **Improve your writing.** Review your *ideas, organization,* and *voice. Do you identify the assumptions and explain the process clearly?*
- **Improve your style.** Check *word choice* and *sentence fluency. Have you correctly used and defined any math terms?*

Editing

- **Check for conventions.** Check punctuation, grammar, and spelling.
- **Prepare a final copy.** Make a neat final copy of your work.

Math

Analysis of a Problem

To analyze math problems, you need to show your work. Read the prompt and determine the assumptions (A). In the middle, show the calculations and manipulations (B–D). End with an explanation of the process (E).

Sample Analysis

For the past 50 years, kids have enjoyed coiled-spring toys. In those five decades of production, 3,030,000 miles of wire weighing 50,000 tons have been coiled, with each spring toy starting as 80 feet of wire.

(A) What assumptions can be made from the above information?
One toy uses 80 feet of wire. In 50 years, 3,030,000 miles and 50,000 tons of wire were used for the toys.

(B) Explain how to find out the number of toys made and then solve.
There are 5,280 feet in one mile. Divide 5,280 by 80 to find out how many toys are in one mile of wire (66). Multiply 66 times 3,030,000 to find out how many toys were produced in 50 years (199,980,000).

(C) Explain how to find out how much 1 mile of wire weighs and then solve.
A ton weighs 2,000 pounds. First multiply 2,000 times 50,000 to find out how many pounds all the wire weighs (100,000,000 pounds). Divide that by 3,030,000 miles to find the pounds per mile (33 pounds).

(D) The 3,030,000 miles of wire could go around the equator 126 times. What is the length of the equator? What is the diameter of Earth? Divide 3,030,000 by 126 to find the equator (24,048 miles). Find Earth's diameter by dividing 24,048 by 3.14 (7,659 miles).

(E) List known values and definitions you need to solve the questions.
I needed to know the number of feet in a mile, the number of pounds in a ton, that the length of the equator equals Earth's circumference, that circumference equals diameter times pi, and that pi is about 3.14.

Try It!

Eight public swimming pools hold a total volume of 17,500 cubic meters of water. Each pool is 1.75 meters deep and is half as wide as it is long. What assumptions can you make from this information? Explain how to find the dimensions of the pools. What do you need to know to find the dimensions? Use the example above as a model.

Analysis of a Problem

Discuss the sample analysis to make sure students understand how it works.

- Explain that the writer has broken down the original prompt into lettered sections and then responded to each section separately.
- Call attention to the **Try It!** prompt at the bottom of the page. Work with students to break the prompt into sections. Invite a volunteer to show the breakdown on the board.

Eight public swimming pools hold a total volume of 17,500 cubic meters of water. Each pool is 1.75 meters deep and is half as wide as it is long.
(A) What assumptions can you make from this information?
(B) Explain how to find the dimensions of the pools.
(C) What (values and definitions) do you need to know to find the dimensions?

Remind students to use complete sentences when they write their analysis.

Writing Guidelines
Creation of a Chart or Graph

Explain that graphics, such as charts, tables, and graphs, are often used to illustrate complex numerical concepts in math-based articles. The ability to read and to create such graphics greatly enhances students' ability to understand and communicate ideas in math.

Have students look back at the pie chart in the sample summary on SE page 435 for another example of how complex numbers can be incorporated into a graphic to create a visual reference.

✳ For more about using graphic elements to explain ideas, see SE pages 602–603.

438

Writing Guidelines Creation of a Chart or Graph

Sometimes figures, numbers, or statistics are best communicated in charts and graphs, which can express the relationship between facts at a glance.

- **Charts** often list the most important details from an article, such as the prices of certain grocery items. Tables are sometimes called charts.
- **Graphs** can plot the points of different variables to show how numbers change over time or in relation to other factors.

Prewriting

- **Select a topic.** If your teacher does not assign a specific topic, review your class notes, learning log, or textbook for ideas. Choose a topic from which you can develop a chart or graph.
- **Gather details.** Research your topic and write down the primary details. Use a chart if you are listing numbers. Develop a chart or a graph to show the relationship between variables.

Writing

- **Design your chart or graph.** Include the most important ideas and details on your chart or graph. Experiment to find the best way to display your information so that a reader understands it.

Revising

- **Improve your chart or graph.** Ask these questions: *Have I correctly used and defined any mathematical terms? Is the information clear, easy to follow, and labeled properly? Have I double-checked any calculations made to create this chart or graph?*

Editing

- **Check for conventions.** Check your work for errors in punctuation, capitalization, spelling, and grammar.
- **Prepare a final copy.** Make a neat final copy of your chart or graph and proofread it again.

Graphic Response

Yuri's teacher gave his class the following assignment about banking statistics.

Sample Assignment and Response

Many people borrow money to buy a car. The length of time they take to pay back the loan may range from two to six years. The chart below shows the monthly payments on a loan of $15,000 at 6 percent interest.

1. What can you tell, from the chart at the right, about the relationship between the length of the loan and the monthly payment?
2. Identify the independent and the dependent variables.
3. Graph the data.
4. Is the relationship between the variables clearer on the graph or in the chart? Explain your answer.

Length of Loan	Monthly Payment
Two years	$664.81
Three years	$456.33
Four years	$352.28
Five years	$289.99
Six years	$248.59

Yuri B.
Math 9, Period 7

> The student answers each question.

1. If you borrow money for a longer time, your monthly payment is lower.
2. The independent variable is the number of years; the dependent variable is the monthly payment. The monthly payment depends on the length of the loan.

> He makes a graph to show his answer.

3. See the graph.
4. The graph is clearer. You can spot the relationship of time against the payment.

Monthly Payments (in dollars)

Loan Years

Try It!

Figure out the total payment for each loan. Graph the data. The total payment is your dependent variable and time is the independent variable.

English Language Learners

Some students may have limited experience with graphing and charting information. Review parts of a graph and a chart, and tell students to write down the names of the parts in a notebook so that they can easily access the correct vocabulary.

Graphic Response

Help students understand that they will often have a choice of which graphic element to use to express the relationship between facts. When you assign the **Try It!** activity,

■ have one-third of the students graph the data in a line graph,
■ have one-third use a bar graph, and
■ have one-third use a table or a chart.

After they complete the assignment, have students compare their graphics and discuss the benefits and limitations of each.

Writing Guidelines

Response to a Math Prompt

Focus attention on the first bullet under Prewriting.

- Emphasize the importance of reading the prompt carefully and performing only the requested actions.
- Remind students that tests are usually timed. If students spend time performing actions that are not requested, it is likely that they will not have time to complete the actions that are requested. As a result, they may receive an unsatisfactory grade even if they know and understand the material.

Discuss the sample response to a math prompt on SE page 441 before assigning the **Try It!** activity.

Writing Guidelines Response to a Math Prompt

Math prompts are like word problems. To solve mathematical test prompts, you need good reading and thinking skills. By approaching the prompt one step at a time, you can solve the problem and explain your solution. Use the following guidelines when responding to a math test prompt.

Prewriting

- **Read the prompt.** Read the prompt carefully to understand it completely. Some problems have more than one part. Always pay attention to the directions in the prompt, performing the requested actions only.
- **Gather details and data.** Find the details given in the prompt as assumptions. Write down the data you will use to solve the prompt.

Writing

- **Build your solution.** Decide how to use the assumptions and data to solve the problem. Set up the mathematical formula or equation and show all your work.

Revising

- **Improve your response.** Reread the prompt after you do your calculations. If the problem has more than one part, be sure to answer every part. Always double-check your math to be sure your solution is correct.

Editing

- **Check for conventions.** Check your solution for errors in punctuation, capitalization, spelling, and grammar.
- **Prepare a final copy.** Make a neat final copy of your solution.

Try It!

Find a prompt and write a response. Choose a practice prompt from your math textbook or one recommended by your teacher. Follow the tips above to write your solution to the test prompt.

English Language Learners

If students have limited experience with state tests, show them examples of prompts from previous math tests, if available. Show students answers that received different scores, so that they can compare the writing of a well-written response to a poorly written one.

Response to a Math Prompt

Toni's algebra class was assigned the following math prompt. Toni's response below answers each question and shows all the work of her solution.

Sample Prompt and Response

Solving Systems of Equations

A. Solve one of the problems below using the appropriate method or methods—graphing, substitution, or elimination.

B. Justify your reason for choosing the method and explain how to solve the problem.

C. Solve the system of equations and show all your work.

1. $-5x + 2y = 14$
$-3x + y = -2$

2. $y = -2x + 7$
$y = 4x - 5$

3. $y = 4$
$3x - y = 5$

Toni Ortiz
Math 9, Period 4

A. I chose to solve problem #1 using both elimination and substitution.

B. The system of two equations is set up to use this method. I first have to multiply the bottom equation by −2 (because the top equation has a positive 2y I need to balance out). Then I can add the two equations together to "eliminate" the y variable (reduce it to 0). That shows the solution to the x variable. I then use substitution to solve for the y variable.

C. Steps of Solution

$-5x + 2y = 14$	$-5x + 2y = 14$	$-3(18) + y = -2$
$-2(-3x + y = -2)$	$+ 6x - 2y = 4$	$-54 + y = -2$
	$x \quad\quad = 18$	$+ \ 54 \quad\quad 54$
		$y = \ 52$

Solution of (x, y) is (18, 52)

This student breaks the answer into steps.

She shows all her work and gives the final answer.

Response to a Math Prompt

To reiterate the importance of reading the prompt carefully and completely, propose the following scenarios.

- What if a student read item A quickly and skipped over the words *one of*? (Thinking that all three problems had to be solved in the allotted time, the student would rush to complete them and possibly make mistakes.)
- What if a student read only the first part of item C? (The student might not show all the work and would lose points even if the answer were correct.)

Suggest that students check off each part of a prompt after they have answered it completely. This will ensure that they write a complete response.

Tell students to use *I* throughout the entire response, and to be careful not to slip into the second person, using the pronoun *you*. (For example, *First I have to multiply. Then you add the two equations.*)

English Language Learners

When students read answer B of the sample, point out that the writer used steps to explain the work clearly. Review time-order words, such as *first, second, next, then,* and *finally.* Explain that students can use these transition words to order their ideas clearly.

✱ For more time-order words, see SE page 592.

Struggling Learners

Sometimes students overlook a simple tool for responding to a math prompt. Remind them that one good way to be sure they have answered the prompt completely is to organize their answer using the same format as the prompt. Point out that the sample prompt is divided into steps *A, B,* and *C* and that the answer is also organized into steps *A, B,* and *C.*

Other Forms of Writing in Math

Encourage students to choose one of these other forms for writing in math. These assignments provide excellent opportunities for students to see the legitimate application of math to real-world situations.

✳ The Definition, Classification, and Process assignments are forms of expository writing. If students choose one of these ideas, suggest that they skim SE pages 144–199 for strategies that apply to expository writing.

✳ For help with the descriptive assignment, have students review SE pages 565 and 572.

✳ For help with narrative writing, have students see SE pages 88–143.

✳ A position essay is a form of persuasive writing. For help with persuasive writing techniques, have students see SE pages 200–253.

442

Other Forms of Writing in Math

Descriptive Writing

Geometry—Write a descriptive paragraph or essay using your knowledge of geometric shapes to describe your home.

Definition

Any Math—Write a detailed expository paragraph that defines a major mathematical concept, such as *coefficients, complementary angles, inductive reasoning, Pythagorean rule,* or *tessellation.*

Narrative

Personal Finance—Write a paragraph or an essay about converting currency while you are on a trip (real or imagined) to another country. Ask your teacher for help in finding the most up-to-date currency conversion rates.

Any Math—Write an anecdote or a longer narrative to tell about a time you used math skills in your daily life.

Classification

Geometry—Write a classification paragraph or essay about different types of polyhedrons: the five regular polyhedra, the different types of pyramids, and so on. Organize your writing to compare and contrast if you wish.

Position

Any Math—Read about controversial new theories in math or economics that interest you. Choose one theory and write a position essay that supports the theory and defends it against opposing viewpoints.

Process

Any Math—Write a process paragraph or essay about the history and development of calculators from the abacus to today's computers.

Writing in the Applied Sciences

443

Writing in the Applied Sciences

In some classes, you learn by reading a textbook, listening to lectures, and taking notes. In other classes, you learn by doing. Family and consumer science (FACS) and technical education (Tech Ed) are considered applied science classes because they give you hands-on experience.

Many teachers of applied sciences use writing assignments to complement the hands-on part of the class. After completing a project, students reflect on their experience, analyzing what went right as well as what went wrong.

In this section, you will learn about taking notes and keeping a learning log in a FACS or Tech Ed class. Then you will review forms of writing often assigned in these classes.

- **Taking Notes**
- **Keeping a Learning Log**
- **Writing Guidelines: Process Essay**
- **Writing Guidelines: Essay of Identification**
- **Writing Guidelines: Persuasive Poster**
- **Other Forms of Practical Writing**

"I hear and I forget; I see and I remember; I write and I understand."

—Chinese Proverb

Objectives

- practice taking notes for applied science classes
- keep a learning log for applied science classes
- apply the writing process and traits of writing to a process essay, essay of identification, and safety poster

The lessons on the following pages provide samples of writing students might do in a family and consumer science or technical education class. Assigning these forms of writing will depend on

- the skill level of your students,
- the subject matter they are studying, and
- the writing goals of your school, district, or state.

Copy Masters

Time Line (TE p. 447)

Taking Notes

The sample notes at the bottom of the page are written in sentence form. Point out that these notes could also be expressed in phrases and lists.

Taking Notes

Effective note taking is especially valuable in the applied sciences.

Before you take notes . . .

- **Keep your notes in a three-ring binder** so you can add work sheets and additional notes.
- **Write the date** at the beginning of each entry.
- **Divide your paper into two columns.** Write steps of a process on the left and comments, reasons, or other data on the right. Or put reading notes on the left and classroom notes on the right.

As you take notes . . .

- **Jot down important instructions** as they are given.
- **Don't write down every word.** Use phrases and lists.
- **Draw diagrams and graphic organizers** to help you remember.

After you've taken notes . . .

- **Review your notes** and highlight main ideas.
- **Study your notes** during a project or before a test.
- **Form study groups** for sharing notes and asking questions.

Oct. 12, 2011   Hybrid engines

A parallel hybrid engine has a fuel tank to run the gas engine and batteries to run the electric motor.

The gas and electric engines both connect to the transmission. Either one can turn the axle on its own, or they can turn it together.

A series hybrid engine is different. It uses a gas-driven generator to run the electric motor or recharge the batteries.

Parts of a parallel hybrid engine

electric motor   gas tank

gas engine

batteries

fuel line

transmission

Try It!

Prepare a binder for notes and take notes in your next class.

Keeping a Learning Log

A learning log is a journal with entries about the things you are learning in a specific class. In this type of journal, you can reflect on new ideas, puzzle over questions, and add drawings or comments on a project.

Writing in the Applied Sciences   **445**

Applied Sciences

Before you write . . .

- **Use a spiral notebook** or a section of your three-ring binder.
- **Date each entry.**
- **Leave wide margins** for writing questions and, later, for answers.

As you write . . .

- **Reflect on what you are learning.** Include what you experienced, what you wonder about, what worked and didn't work.
- **Predict what will come next.** Think about how the material connects to other classes or to what you already know.

After you've written . . .

- **Review your log** before a test and when you need an idea for a project.
- **Answer any questions** you may have written in the margins.

November 9, 2011—FACS

Sleeves are so complicated! I tried to save time by using only one row of basting stitches along the top edge of the sleeve, but I ended up with tucks when I tried to attach the sleeve to the bodice. I had to start over!

A sculptor must see a statue inside a block of marble, but a tailor must see a shirt inside out and right side out at the same time.

Of course, there are tricks, like pressing seams open before attaching pieces. That makes the seams lie flat so they are easier to match. I'll get the hang of this soon!

What's the point of two rows of basting stitches? They keep the shoulders from looking puffy.

▶ **Try It!**

Set up a learning log in a notebook or in a section of your three-ring binder. Be sure to date each entry.

Keeping a Learning Log

Focus attention on the first bullet under After you've written. The idea that a learning log is a good source for project ideas reinforces one of the main reasons students should be motivated to keep a learning log and a writer's notebook.

- Ask students how many times they have struggled to come up with interesting and challenging ideas for class projects.
- Explain that if they are keeping a learning log, they can use a colored pen to mark topics that truly interest them. Then when it is time to choose project ideas, they can flip through their learning log to easily identify topics that they already know intrigue them.

✱ For more about using a writer's notebook, see SE pages 4–5.

Writing Guidelines

Process Essay

Emphasize the importance of presenting the steps in the process in the proper sequence. Ask students to identify transitions in the sample process essay on SE page 447 that show the order in which steps are to be followed (before, to begin, next, meanwhile, when).

✽ For a list of transitions that show time, see SE page 592.

446

Writing Guidelines Process Essay

A process essay tells how to do something or how something works. You could write about how to make tortilla pinwheels, or you could describe how gas burns in an internal-combustion engine. Your goal in a process essay is to explain each step clearly and completely.

Prewriting

- **Select a topic.** If your teacher does not assign a specific topic, review your notes, manual, or textbook for ideas. Think of things you have made, skills you have mastered, or processes you have observed. Consider topics with steps or with a chain of causes and effects.
- **Gather details.** Freewrite about the topic, writing everything you know about it. Research the various steps in your notes, manual, or textbook. Then list needed materials or ingredients, equipment, and the steps in the process.
- **Plan and organize.** Outline your essay. First, list the materials and equipment. Then, in chronological order, list the steps of the process.

Writing

- **Connect your ideas.** Write a beginning paragraph, introducing the topic. Then discuss materials, ingredients, or equipment in the order used. Afterward, write about each step. The steps should logically follow each other, allowing the reader to understand the process. Use transition words and phrases to connect your ideas.

Revising

- **Improve your writing.** Review your first draft for *ideas, organization,* and *voice.* Ask these questions: *Is the process clear? Have I described all necessary materials or equipment? Do I have the steps in time order? Is my essay interesting to read?* Work with a partner to get suggestions for revision. Use the expository rubric (pages **180–181**) as a final check of your revising.
- **Improve your style.** Check your *word choice* and *sentence fluency.* Ask these questions: *Have I used correct terminology? Does each step lead naturally to the next step?* Revise to improve your essay.

Editing

- **Check for conventions.** Check punctuation, spelling, and grammar.
- **Prepare a final copy.** Make a neat final copy of your essay.

English Language Learners

When students write process essays, recommend that they ask classmates to read their essays and follow the instructions to make sure that the writing is clear and not missing any fundamental steps.

Writing in the Applied Sciences **447**

Recipe

Luz chose to explain the process of making tortilla pinwheels step by step.

The **beginning** introduces the topic.

Tasty Tortilla Pinwheels

Tortillas aren't just for tacos anymore. Try this tasty appetizer, which is easy to make and delicious.
- 2 8-oz. packages cream cheese
- 1 package dry ranch dressing mix
- 2 green onions
- 4 12-inch flour tortillas
- 1 small jar diced pimentos
- 3 jalapeño peppers, no seeds
- 3 green chili peppers
- 8 oz. black olives

The **middle** paragraphs list materials needed and explain the process.

Before you begin, be sure you have kitchen gloves handy to protect your hands from the juice of the jalapeño peppers. Also be careful not to rub your eyes when handling the peppers.

To begin, soften the cream cheese in a microwave. Set the microwave on medium power for 30 seconds at a time until the cheese is spreadable. Blend with the dry ranch dressing mix.

Next, finely chop the green onions and add to the cream-cheese mixture. Spread the mixture onto the four tortillas, covering all the way to the edges.

Drain the pimentos on paper towels. Meanwhile, wearing kitchen gloves, chop the jalapeños and discard the seeds. Dice the chiles and the olives. Sprinkle all ingredients evenly on the four tortillas.

The **ending** concludes with serving suggestions.

Starting on one side of the first tortilla, roll tightly. Do the same for each of the others. Wrap each in wax paper and chill at least two hours. When firm, unwrap from the wax paper, slice each tortilla into 1-inch-thick slices, and arrange on a plate.

Serve pinwheel tortillas as a colorful appetizer at your next family gathering or just as a tasty snack anytime.

Write a process essay. Select a process you know very well. Follow the guidelines on page 446 as you write your essay. Be sure to list any materials necessary and provide the steps in chronological order.

Recipe

Ask students if they think Luz explained the process of making tortilla pinwheels clearly enough for them to follow, and have them explain why.

Have students point out details that make the essay interesting, informative, and easy to read. For example, they may point out
- the bulleted list of ingredients,
- the caution to not rub your eyes after handling the peppers,
- and the specific directions to finely chop the green onions and to discard the seeds of the jalapeños.

Students may find it easier to organize the steps of the process using a time line or a process diagram as shown on SE pages 588 and 589. Distribute photocopies of the reproducible time line (TE page 816) for students who choose to use the time line.

English Language Learners

If students decide to use a recipe for their process essay assignment, suggest that they choose one for a typical food from their culture. If possible, invite students to read aloud their essay and share samples of their food with the class. Knowing that their culture is valued in class may motivate students.

Struggling Learners

Students may tend to phrase instructions in a process essay the same way they would give instructions in daily life. Point out, however, that using the standard conventions, such as *you should* or *please,* slow down how-to essays.

To help students avoid this pitfall, review how the sample essay uses command words and imperative phrasing to quickly relate a task. For example, *"next, finely chop"* and *"drain the pimentos"* are more concise than *"next, you should finely chop"* or *"please drain the pimentos."*

Writing Guidelines

Essay of Identification

Students often insist that they can't think of good topics. To prevent students from falling into this trap, help them

- brainstorm a list of tools and machines that they use and post the list in the classroom;
- eliminate those items on the list that, because of their complexity, would be impossible for the majority of students to explain; and
- group items that can be related, such as different types of saws.

448

Writing Guidelines Essay of Identification

An essay of identification names tools or the parts of a machine. It then explains what each of these items does and how they work together.

Prewriting

- **Select a topic.** If your teacher doesn't assign a specific topic, think of tools you use in class or machines that help you perform a task. Select a topic that has several elements to be identified.
- **Gather details.** Freewrite about your topic, describing it and telling what it is used for. Then think about how the different parts relate to each other.
- **Plan and organize.** Decide on the best order for arranging your information. If you are describing saws, for example, you could start with the most common (handsaw) and work up to the most unusual (radial-arm saw). If you are describing parts of a machine, you could organize them spatially (front to back, top to bottom, or left to right).

Writing

- **Connect your ideas.** Introduce the items or parts you will write about. Then devote a paragraph to each item, identifying it, describing it, and telling its uses. (Two closely related items can be covered in one paragraph.) Write an ending that explains how the items relate to each other, or sum up the essay in another way.

Revising

- **Improve your writing.** Review your writing for *ideas, organization,* and *voice.* Ask these questions: *Have I identified, described, and explained each item? Have I presented the items in the best order? Do I sound interested and knowledgeable?* Add, cut, or move details to improve your essay. Use the expository rubric on pages **180–181** as a final check of your revising.
- **Improve your style.** Check your *word choice* and *sentence fluency* to make sure that everything is stated clearly and effectively. Ask these questions: *Have I chosen specific words and explained technical terms? Do my sentences flow smoothly?*

Editing

- **Check for conventions.** Check punctuation, spelling, and grammar.
- **Prepare a final copy.** Make a neat final copy of your essay.

Essay of Identification

Ravi wrote the following essay of identification for his Drafting I class.

T-square

45° triangle

30°–60° triangle

Protractor

Applied Sciences

The beginning introduces the tools used.

It's hard to believe people could make complicated drawings using such simple tools. With a T-square, a couple of triangles, and a protractor, drafters can make surprisingly complex drawings.

The T-square is a straight plastic or metal measuring stick with a guide piece attached to one end at a right angle (90°). By placing the guide along the side of the drafting table, the T-square establishes the horizontal axis. The T-square is used to line up the paper and draw any horizontal line on it.

Each middle paragraph identifies a tool, describes it, and explains its uses.

The T-square works with two triangles to make vertical lines and various angles. The 45° triangle has one angle at 90° and two others at 45°. The 30°–60° triangle has one angle at 90°, one at 30°, and another at 60°. Each triangle is set on the T-square and used to draw lines. By using both triangles together, the following angles can be created: 75°, 105°, 120°, 135°, and 150°.

Another tool used with the T-square is the protractor. It is a semicircle with a straight side. The curved side is marked by degrees to help create any angles between 0° and 180°. The drafter aligns the protractor with one side of the angle. A mark is made through the hole in the center of the straight side for the vertex of the angle. Another dot is marked at the angle desired, and the two dots are connected to create the second side of the angle.

The ending reflects on the importance of all the tools.

With these simple tools, drafters have drawn entire cathedrals. At first, beginners may not be able to do more than draw a few lines, but with practice, they will be able to draw just about anything.

Write an essay of identification. Identify tools or parts of a machine. Define each item, show how it works, and tell how it relates to the others.

Essay of Identification

Focus attention on how the beginning paragraph introduces the tools in an interesting and personal way. Remind students that besides introducing the topic, the beginning of any piece of writing should grab the reader's attention and make the reader want to keep reading.

Ask students how Ravi accomplishes both these goals in his beginning paragraph.

- He introduces the topic, which is a group of drafting tools.
- He grabs the reader's attention in the second sentence when he says *I couldn't believe people could make such complicated drawings using such simple tools.*

Encourage students to write **a great beginning** *(see below)* for their essay of identification.

Teaching Tip: A Great Beginning

Getting started can be the hardest part of writing, yet developing a good beginning is essential to the success of any piece of writing. Discuss different methods that writers use to grab a reader's attention.

- Ask a "Do you know why" question that piques the reader's interest.
- Use a startling fact.
- Begin with a short quotation from a famous work.
- Tell a personal anecdote (a short amusing story).

* For more information and a step-by-step strategy for writing an opening paragraph, see SE page 595.

English Language Learners

Define the following words before reading the passage:

- drafting (drawing plans for buildings and machines)
- complicated (very detailed, having many parts)
- attached (connected)
- establishes (sets, places)
- vertex (center point of an angle)
- cathedrals (huge churches)

Writing Guidelines

Persuasive Poster

Display several examples of posters for students to evaluate. If possible, include handmade and professionally printed posters. Have students also evaluate the sample posters on SE page 451.

■ Give students time to study the design and message of all the posters.

■ Then have students discuss which posters they think are most effective and which they think are least effective. Have them give reasons to support their opinions.

Encourage students to incorporate elements from the effective posters in the persuasive poster they create themselves (**Try It!** SE page 451).

Writing Guidelines Persuasive Poster

A well-designed poster uses words and images to make a point quickly, clearly, and persuasively. In applied sciences, posters can convince the reader to attend important events, follow procedures, and avoid dangerous situations.

Prewriting

■ **Select a topic.** If your teacher doesn't assign a specific topic, think of things you'd personally like to promote—events, rules and safety procedures, or policies to keep the workplace running smoothly. Select a topic that you feel strongly about.

■ **Gather details.** Brainstorm a list of the points you wish to make. Think of as many as you can, and then select the most important ones. Write a slogan or catchphrase that sums up your points. Also think of a call to action: something you want the reader to do.

Writing

■ **Design your poster.** Sketch out your poster on a standard sheet of paper. Experiment with different elements—main headings, bullet points, and graphics. Also try various typestyles and colors. Your poster should be both eye catching and easy to read.

■ **Compare designs.** Review your designs, checking for *ideas, organization,* and *voice.* Ask these questions: *Which design effectively delivers my overall message, has the clearest organization, and is most convincing and eye catching?* Choose the best one and add, cut, or rearrange elements to improve your poster.

Revising

■ **Improve your poster's message.** Review your poster for *word choice* and *sentence fluency.* Ask these questions: *Do I use the best words to get my point across? Do I use command words to ask my reader to act? Do my ideas flow smoothly?* Make your revisions.

Editing

■ **Check for conventions.** Look for errors in punctuation, spelling, capitalization, and grammar. Use the persuasive rubric on pages 234–235 as a final check of your revising and editing.

■ **Prepare a final copy.** Transfer your corrected poster to a large piece of poster board. Proofread this final copy before posting it.

Struggling Learners

Coming up with a slogan or catch phrase for a poster takes creativity. This can be challenging. To help students with ideas and to provide good examples, ask the class to brainstorm slogans they know, such as ones the school sports teams use, as well as ones in ad campaigns they have seen on TV.

Write on the board slogans the students name. Which ones are most easily remembered? Why? Is it because they are short, funny, clearly understood, or intriguing? Is it because of how they sound? Do they roll easily off the tongue? Do they use alliteration (words that start with the same sound) or rhyme?

Encourage students to consider these questions when writing their slogans.

Applied Sciences

Safety Posters

The following posters for a shop class focus on safety and courtesy. You can try a variety of colors, type fonts, and images to present your message.

Command words get attention.

A graphic emphasizes the message.

Color highlights important words.

STAY SAFE IN SHOP!

Wear goggles **and hearing-protection equipment.**

Use tool guards!

Check tools **before using them.**

Walk, **don't run.**

Keep **your brain in gear!**

A question catches the reader's attention.

Short, parallel sentences get to the point.

Color highlights important words.

WHY SHOULD YOU KEEP THIS SHOP CLEAN?

Spills **can cause accidents.**

Dirty tools **can be dangerous.**

Messes **can waste time.**

Oily rags **can cause fires.**

Try It!

Create a persuasive poster promoting an event, highlighting classroom rules, or encouraging safety or courtesy.

English Language Learners

Ask students to look at the first poster on the page. Point out that all the sentences are simple commands. Remind students that in English the subject (you) of a command is implied but not written, and that commands start with the verb. If students write persuasive posters, check that they use the implied *you* in their command sentences.

Safety Posters

If students are interested in promoting an event but need an idea, have them look at the school calendar and the community events page of the school and local newspapers.

Display completed posters in appropriate places throughout the school. For example, if students make posters related to cafeteria rules, display the posters in the cafeteria.

Other Forms of Practical Writing

Point out that the lab report suggested here is for a foods class, not a science class. Have students turn to SE pages 410–411, and explain that although the writing guidelines and sample lab report shown there are for a science class, students can use them when they write a lab report in any class. Take this opportunity to emphasize how the writing process is applicable in all content areas.

If possible, provide real-world examples of press releases, work orders and estimates, observation/accident reports, letters of complaint, and résumés as models for students who choose one of these writing forms.

Other Forms of Practical Writing

Lab Report

Foods Class—Write a lab report based on an observation of yeast at various temperatures. Report your hypothesis about what will happen. Then note your observations and summarize the results.

Observation/Accident Report

Metal Shop—Observe students working on their projects and write a report on their use of equipment (tools and safety).

Letter and E-mail Message

Living-on-Your-Own Class—Write a letter of complaint about a product you recently bought that does not work properly. Include a detailed description of the problem and the action needed to remedy the situation. Keep your language neutral, cool, and professional.

Press Release

Any Class—Write a press release promoting a current class project. Focus on the positive aspects of the project as well as its importance to the general public.

Résumé

Career Explorations Class—Write your résumé for a career that interests you. Include your education and relevant talents and abilities. Add personal qualifications and name two references.

Work Order and Estimate

Auto Shop—Examine an engine that needs a tune-up. Write a description of the work that should be done along with a cost estimate for parts and labor charges. Explain the need for each item.

Writing in the Arts

Studying works of art or music can stimulate your mind and trigger many questions. Why did a painter use a particular medium? How did a composer develop his or her style? How has sculpting changed over time? How do different types of music affect people's feelings? Why do different countries have different styles of music?

As you study these creative fields, let writing deepen your understanding and enjoyment of the arts. This chapter will help you write learning-log entries, essays, and reports about the arts.

- ■ **Taking Classroom Notes**
- ■ **Keeping a Learning Log**
- ■ **Writing Guidelines: Response to an Art Prompt**
- ■ **Writing Guidelines: Research Report**
- ■ **Other Forms of Writing in the Arts**

"Art is a lie which
makes us realize
the truth."
—Picasso

Writing in the Arts

Objectives

- • practice taking notes for arts classes
- • keep a learning log for arts classes
- • apply the writing process and traits of writing to a response to an art prompt and a research report for art or music

The lessons on the following pages provide samples of writing students might do in an art or music class. Assigning these forms of writing will depend on

- ■ the skill level of your students,
- ■ the subject matter they are studying, and
- ■ the writing goals of your school, district, or state.

Taking Classroom Notes

Even though most of your work in art and music classes is applied (you paint, you sing, you play an instrument), there are times to take notes.

Take notes when . . .

- **your teacher writes information on the board or an overhead.**
  This information is obviously important. Copying it into your notes helps make the information part of your own thinking. Be sure to write down new vocabulary words, as well as names, dates, and key phrases.
- **you have a demonstration in class.**
  Your class may view slides of art pieces or listen to recordings of various musical styles. Taking notes will help you keep track of the individual works.
- **you have a guest speaker/performer.**
  Professional artists may demonstrate or discuss their work. Your notes can help you participate during a question-and-answer session after the presentation.

Tip

- Date each entry and give it a heading so you can quickly find the topic.
- Copy new vocabulary words and leave space so that you can fill in definitions or examples later.
- Write down hints or memory joggers to help you remember a name, term, or concept.
- Draw sketches to help you recall individual works.
- Mark the spot in your notes where you got lost so that you can come back and ask about it later.
- Divide your page into two columns (one side wider than the other). Write classroom notes in the wider column and questions in the other.
- Find a "study buddy" who will compare notes, go over questions, or review for tests with you.

Try It!

Set up a notebook for your art or music class with a wide right column and a narrower left column (see page **455**). Take notes during class.

Keeping a Learning Log

In any project-based class, such as art or music, a learning log can help you keep track of, and reflect on, your progress. Julia wrote the following entries in her learning log as she worked on a watercolor project. Notice that she divided her log, using the left side for the steps in the project and the right side for comments about her progress.

Arts

Sample Entry

Steps in watercolor painting	December 12
1. Tape the paper on the newspaper on the table.	Mr. Anderson told us to use scratch paper to practice on, but I won't need it.
2. Wet the paper and let it dry.	Last time I didn't do this, and the paper curled when I painted on it.
3. Make a light sketch.	Pressing too hard on the pencil made dents in the paper. Paint may pool in the dents.
4. Some ways to paint Wet on wet Wet on dry Dry on wet Dry on dry	Wet on wet made a nice background wash, but my sky and grass smeared together. Next time I'll use scratch paper for a new technique.
5. Fill large areas first.	Dry on wet worked better. The colors didn't bleed so much. I left space for my tree.
6. Use the smaller brush for details.	The paper was still too wet, and the details bled into the wash. Paint pooled in the pencil lines, but it looked kind of cool, so I used a dry brush to pull some of the paint out. It made nice shadows, blending out of the darker colors.
	I liked layering colors and got some nice effects. A light yellow wash over the dry, finished painting gave it a hazy look.

Try It!

Set up a learning log for your art or music class. Keep one side for class notes or instructions and the other side for your own comments.

Keeping a Learning Log

Analyzing the sample entries can help students recognize the benefit of keeping their own learning log in art or music.

- Give students time to read the sample entries.
- Then ask them how they think Julia could benefit from these entries. (The entries on the left remind her what steps to follow when doing watercolor painting. The entries on the right help her understand specifically what worked for her and what didn't work for her. She knows what not to do, to avoid particular problems, and what to try in order to achieve specific effects. The notes on the right also help her understand her own artistic preferences.)

Struggling Learners

Students may be more motivated to keep a learning log for an art or music class if you explain that they can express creative ideas in a learning log.

- Point out that at the end of the sample log, the writer notes that "*A light yellow wash over the dry, finished painting gave it a hazy look.*"
- The writer could also jot down an idea for another project, such as: "*I want to paint that dream I had about being on a boat lost at sea. Maybe using a yellow wash will give it a dream-like effect.*"

Explain that when students think of ideas for projects they want to do on their own, they should write them in their learning logs. These might include ideas for art projects they would do if they were professional artists, or lyrics for songs that come to mind while recalling topics covered in class.

Writing Guidelines

Response to an Art Prompt

Explain to students that one way to analyze a prompt is to use the STRAP questions. Display these questions on the board or on chart paper and have students refer to them whenever they are asked to respond to a prompt. Explain that the ideas given in parentheses for each of the STRAP questions are provided as examples of possible responses to that question. Each response, of course, depends on the specific prompt.

Subject: What topic (painting, musical piece, artist, art movement) should I write about?

Type: What form (evaluation, critique, review, essay, report) of writing should I create?

Role: What position (student, critic, reporter) should I assume as the writer?

Audience: Who (teacher, classmates) is the intended reader?

Purpose: What is the goal (persuade, respond, evaluate, explain, tell, describe) of my writing?

Writing Guidelines Response to an Art Prompt

Sometimes you will be asked to write a short essay in response to a prompt about art or music. This type of writing can be a regular class assignment or part of a test. In either case, responding to a prompt allows you to apply what you have learned about a specific work. Here are guidelines to follow as you write.

Prewriting

- **Understand the prompt.** Read through the prompt and focus on what it is asking you to do. Is the purpose of your response to explain, compare, describe, persuade?
- **Gather your details.** Go through your notes and any research materials you are allowed to use. Highlight or jot down the details that will help you respond to the prompt. Be sure to record the sources you use for quotations or facts.
- **Organize your details.** Decide on the best way to organize your information. Check the prompt for clues. For example, if the prompt is "compare and contrast the Roman Empire with the British Empire," you know you will be organizing details to show how the two topics are similar and different.

Writing

- **Write freely.** Use your notes as a guide, but don't worry too much about getting everything right. Just get all your ideas down on paper. Most short-response essays are one paragraph long. However, if a prompt calls for more than one main point, you should use a new paragraph for each main point.

Revising

- **Improve your writing.** Read your draft and cut any details that don't fit the prompt. Also add any information that will clarify your ideas or help answer the prompt. Be as complete as possible.
- **Improve your style.** Check your word choice and sentence fluency to make sure that your response reads smoothly.

Editing

- **Check for conventions.** Look for errors in spelling, punctuation, and grammar.
- **Prepare your final copy.** If necessary, and if time permits, copy your response onto a clean sheet of paper and proofread it a final time.

Struggling Learners

Art and music have their own vocabulary, and learning these words will help students better formulate their thoughts when responding to art prompts.

Ask students to skim the sample response on SE page 457 for words or phrases that helped the writer describe the painting. (Examples include *palette, composition, vertical lines, curves,* and *subjects.*)

- So that they, too, will have the words they need at their disposal, encourage students to build a word bank in their notes or learning logs that includes words or phrases that are specific to each subject.

- Each day, as they hear descriptive words and vocabulary, students should add them to the bank.
- When gathering details for a response to a prompt, students will have the vocabulary they need.

Writing in the Arts **457**

Arts

Response to an Art Prompt

In the following response, Roy Jones evaluates a painting.

Prompt

Evaluate Georges Seurat's Sunday Afternoon on the Island of La Grande Jatte. *Answer the questions in one or more paragraphs.*

1. *What are the important technical aspects of the painting? How did critics of the time react?* **2.** *What types of people are in the painting? Are any social comments being expressed?*

Sample Response

> **Response #1**
>
> The primary technical aspect of the painting is that it is composed entirely of dots of color. Seurat didn't mix colors on the palette. Instead, he let the colors be mixed naturally by the eye of the observer. Seurat's dots create a soft, hazy look.
>
> Another interesting technical aspect of the painting is the composition. Most of the people are in profile. Only one woman and her child are full face. The people create vertical lines in the painting. Curves in the umbrellas, boat sails, and the riverbank soften those vertical lines.
>
> When Seurat's work first came out, the technique of pointillism was new. The critics mostly hated it, even sneering at its first exhibition at the Independants (WebMuseum, Paris).
>
> **Response #2**
>
> Subjects in the painting appear to be middle-class people enjoying a holiday by the river. Some occupations are revealed by the way people are dressed. Two men in uniforms can be seen in the distance. There are two exceptions to the middle class. The couple on the far right appear to be wealthy. They stand extra straight, and the lady has a pet monkey on a leash. Interestingly, the only person dressed like a worker dominates the lower left-hand corner, and he is also the only person in the painting with a detailed face. Perhaps that was Seurat's way of snubbing the middle class.

The writer uses a separate paragraph to cover each main point of the answer.

The writer uses in-text citations to indicate sources of specific ideas.

The writer uses specific details and examples to show his understanding of the topic.

◀ Try It!

Respond to a short-essay prompt your teacher will supply about a topic you are studying. Write a one- or two-paragraph answer.

English Language Learners

Define the following words before reading the response:

- composed (made up of)
- palette (artist's paint-mixing board)
- hazy (unclear, fuzzy)
- composition (organization, structure)
- profile (side view of face)

- occupations (jobs, professions)
- dominates (stands out)
- snubbing (ignoring)

If possible, show students a print of the painting described in the writing so that they can more easily comprehend what is written about it.

Response to an Art Prompt

Tell students that one way to answer a question in a prompt is to reword the question as a statement, and then add details that help answer the question.

For example, Roy Jones rewords the first question of item 1 in the sample prompt *(What are important technical aspects of the painting?)* to create topic sentences for the first two paragraphs of Response #1. (First paragraph: *The primary technical aspect of the painting is that it is composed entirely of dots of color.* Second paragraph: *Another interesting technical aspect of the painting is the composition.*)

Ask students to point out details in the essay that specifically answer the other questions in the prompt.

Writing Guidelines

Research Report

Students may benefit from a refresher on writing effective thesis statements. Remind students that an effective thesis statement

- identifies a specific topic and
- tells a special feeling or feature about the topic.

✳ For more on writing thesis statements, see SE page 594.

Remind students that the best way to achieve a knowledgeable voice is to use facts, details, examples, quotations, and anecdotes that relate to their topic and that support the main idea expressed in their thesis statements. Caution students that listing facts just for the sake of filling space will result in a confusing report that lacks unity and focus.

458

Writing Guidelines Research Report

At some time, you may be asked to do a research report on an aspect of art or music. You may write a biographical piece about an artist or a musician, or an expository piece about a certain artistic style or time period. The following guidelines will help you write your report.

Prewriting

- **Gather what you know.** List what you already know about the subject and any questions you may have.
- **Begin your research.** Do an overview of your subject. Read articles and excerpts from books to find a specific area of the subject that interests you. Then choose a specific topic suitable for the length of your paper. The shorter your paper, the more focused your topic should be. Once you have narrowed your topic, write a thesis statement.
- **Plan and organize.** Decide on the type of organization you will use. For example, chronological order is effective when you are writing a biography. If you are explaining an art style, you may decide to put your main points in order of importance.

Writing

- **Connect your ideas.** Introduce your topic in the first paragraph and include the thesis statement for your report. As you begin writing, pretend you are explaining your topic out loud to a classmate.

Revising

- **Improve your writing.** Check your writing for *voice. Do you sound interested and knowledgeable? Do you include all the information you need to examine the topic?*
- **Improve your style.** Check your *word choice* and *sentence fluency* to make sure that everything is stated clearly and effectively. *Are your ideas easy to follow? Do your words effectively express your ideas? Do you connect your sentences and paragraphs with transitions? Does each sentence flow naturally into the next?*

Editing

- **Check for conventions.** Look for and correct any errors in punctuation, spelling, and grammar.
- **Prepare a final copy.** After you have made your changes, write a neat final copy and give it another proofreading.

Struggling Learners

Before students edit their work, explain that dates, years, and locations are common areas where all writers—not just students—make punctuation errors.

Point out in the sample essay on SE pages 459–460 examples of the following rules:

- **Dates** – A comma should follow both the day and the year (unless a period is required at sentence end.)
- **Decades** – The four-digit decade is followed *only* by an *s*. Do not insert an apostrophe. (*1950s,* not *1950's)* Remind students that an apostrophe indicates ownership.

- **Locations** – When writing only the name of a city, do not set it off with a comma. For example, *The jazz of Paris was different.* When both the city and the state or country are used, both are followed by commas. For example: *The jazz of Paris, France, was different.*

Research Report

You can learn about music by studying famous composers and their works. Tam wondered how modern classical music began and whether one composer played a key role in developing that style. After doing some research, he wrote the following essay on Aaron Copland.

Sample Report

The introduction presents the thesis statement for the report.

Aaron Copland: Our Nation's Musical Voice

Aaron Copland's life spanned nearly all of the twentieth century. Copland was an innovative composer who eventually became the musical voice of the United States.

Born in New York on November 14, 1900, Copland learned to play piano from his older sister. By the age of 15, he had already decided to be a composer and took a mail-order course on harmony. Later on he studied harmony and counterpoint with Rubin Goldmark. Goldmark had a classical background, but Copland was more modern.

The body of the report is organized in chronological order, beginning with the composer's early life and then moving decade by decade.

Even though Copland would develop a uniquely American sound, he actually left the United States in 1921 to study in Paris. Jazz was a strong influence there, just as it was in the United States. The jazz of Paris was different, though, and Copland returned home after three years with some new sounds and rhythms. Soon he completed his first large work, the ballet *Grohg.*

Copland's special style emerged in the second half of the 1920s. His jazz rhythms were important in his early work, including his *Piano Concerto* (1926). He produced new works that blended elegance with a concise, compact style (Washington State University).

In the 1930s, Copland developed a more popular sound. Trying to escape the economic troubles of the Depression, people were attracted to the upbeat sounds of the radio and theater. Copland understood this and created a series of ballets that boosted American pride. His ballet music for *Billy the Kid, Rodeo,* and *Appalachian Spring* (which earned him a Pulitzer Prize) celebrated the American spirit.

English Language Learners

Define the following words before reading the report:

- spanned (stretched over)
- innovative (taking a new and original approach)
- composer (someone who writes music)
- harmony (the combination of musical notes)

- counterpoint (two melodies in a piece of music)
- emerged (came out)
- concise (direct, to-the-point)
- boosted (lifted up, raised)
- dimension (aspect, part)
- pioneer (explorer)

Research Report

Use the side notes on SE pages 459 and 460, and the following questions, to help students recognize the elements that make this sample a well-written report.

- What special feature about Aaron Copland does Tam focus on in the essay? (how this innovative composer became the musical voice of the United States) Is this clearly stated in the thesis statement? (yes)
- How does each middle paragraph support the thesis statement? (with specific details that show how Copland was constantly developing new sounds and incorporating them into American music)
- What makes the ideas easy to follow? (the use of dates that move from decade to decade)

Point out the citations in parentheses here and on SE page 459. Explain that these citations refer to resources the writer used for specific facts. Tell students to show references this way in their report. If students are required to turn in a works-cited page with their report, take time to review the guidelines for formatting this page.

✱ See SE pages 381–384 for more about formatting works cited.

460

Citations are given for specific facts.

Copland visited Mexico often during this period and began using that country's folk sounds and rhythms in his music. He also visited Cuba and South America, seeking to create "American music for all Americans" (Aaron Copland Collection, Library of Congress). His music became the music of the masses: people felt his music, and they responded to it.

Movies were also very popular in the 1930s, and this was not lost on Copland. He saw a new way to introduce classical music to America. During the 1940s, he composed scores for many movies. These have been called "popular" works by some critics, but the music definitely added an important dimension to fine films such as *Of Mice and Men, Our Town, The Red Pony,* and *The Heiress,* for which Copland won an Academy Award for best score.

During the 1950s and 1960s, Copland began to do less composing. Instead, he traveled all over the world, conducting his work and the work of others. By the 1970s, Copland had pretty much stopped composing. He stopped conducting in 1983. He wrote more than 60 articles and essays and five books about music. Throughout his later career, he helped young American composers, encouraged school music programs, and lectured around the world, promoting music until he died at age 90 on December 2, 1990, in Tarrytown, New York.

The conclusion restates the thesis and offers a final wrap-up.

Copland had a passion for bringing music to the masses. His style influenced some of the best composers of modern music. Copland's music became a tribute to the pioneer spirit that formed our great nation. He remains to this day the ultimate American composer.

Try It!

Write a research report related to an area of art or music that interests you. Use the guidelines on page **458** and the model above as a guide.

Review a piece of writing. Read over something that you have recently written. Try to find two or three sets of sentences that you could combine. Write the combined sentences to see how they sound.

Writing in the Arts **461**

Other Forms of Writing in the Arts

Here are some more ways to explore the arts through writing.

Arts

Expository Writing

- Explain how basic sculpting tools are used.
- Examine the parts of a musical instrument and describe how each contributes to the final sound.
- Explain how to throw a pot.
- Review a book about a composer, musician, or band.
- Summarize a review of a concert or an art exhibit.

Descriptive Writing

- Describe the composition of a painting.
- Describe your feelings when listening to different types of music.
- Describe the use of color and texture in a painting.

Persuasive Writing

- Write a proposal for building a school sculpture garden.
- Write a letter to the school board requesting new jazz choir uniforms.
- Write an editorial addressing cuts in the school music program.

Narrative Writing

- Write about a time that music had a major impact in your life.
- Tell about the first time you worked on a group art project.
- Tell about a concert you attended.
- Write a journal entry as though you were Beethoven.

Creative Writing

- Create an imaginary encounter between Bach and John Lennon.
- Write a myth to fit an instrumental piece of music.
- Write about the music you would find on a distant, inhabited planet.
- Write a parody of a popular song, relating it to your school.
- Write a poem about a piece of art.

Other Forms of Writing in the Arts

Encourage students to choose one of the forms on this page to explore their interest in the arts.

You can also use this page as a resource for topic ideas throughout the year and to correspond with students' writing program. For example, when students are working on expository writing in writing class, they can choose one of the expository writing topics listed here.

The Tools of Learning Overview

Common Core Standards Focus

> **Writing 10:** Write routinely over extended time frames (time for research, reflection, and revision) and shorter time frames (a single sitting or a day or two) for a range of tasks, purposes, and audiences.

Skills

- listening and speaking in class
- taking class notes, notes from reading, minutes for a meeting
- reading critically to remember information
- summarizing and paraphrasing
- understanding word parts
- writing a business letter

Tools and Techniques

- note taking
- glossary of word parts

Test Taking

- test preparation
- four basic types of objective tests (true/false, matching, multiple choice, and fill-in-the-blanks)
- essay tests
- standardized tests

Technology Connections

 Write Source Online
www.hmheducation.com/writesource

- **Net-text**
- **Bookshelf**
- **GrammarSnap**
- **Portfolio**
- **Essay Scoring**
- **Writing Network features**
- **File Cabinet**

 Interactive Whiteboard Lessons

Teacher's Notes for The Tools of Learning

Each chapter description below will help you decide which parts of the unit to teach.

Listening and Speaking (pages 463–466)

In this section, students are reminded that education involves careful listening to the person speaking (for example, a teacher, a guest speaker, or a student answering a question) and clear speaking (loud voice, on topic, and facts).

Taking Notes (pages 467–472)

Taking careful notes is one of the best ways to keep track of what is said in class. Students are encouraged to review their notes as soon as possible after taking them, and add explanatory details as needed. They will also receive tips to help them take good reading notes.

Critical Reading (pages 473–482)

With each passing year, students encounter reading material that is more and more complex. To maintain a high level of reading comprehension, students must become more sophisticated readers. To help students read more effectively, the SQ3R system is explained. Then the reading steps (before, during, and after) are presented. The way to read fiction or poetry is also a part of this chapter.

Summarizing and Paraphrasing (pages 483–490)

Both summarizing and paraphrasing are modeled in this chapter. Students are given tips as well as opportunities to summarize and paraphrase.

Understanding Writing Assignments (pages 491–500)

One reason students fail to do well on assignments is that they may not understand the assignment. This chapter discusses various types of assignments and gives a detailed explanation of each level of thinking needed for different types of assignments.

Improving Your Vocabulary (pages 501–512)

Knowing many words makes communication easier and gets the attention of a reader or a listener. In this chapter, students are given some of the most common prefixes, roots, and suffixes to help them figure out the meaning of unfamiliar words, so that those words can become part of their vocabulary.

Writing Business Letters (pages 513–520)

A cover letter for a college application, a letter of complaint about a product, and a letter inquiring about a job opening are all examples of a business letter. Most students will one day write one of those letters. This chapter will give them the guidelines they need for the proper form and concise communication. Even though your students are very familiar with the Internet, e-mail messages, and so on, they may not use good etiquette or form in writing e-mail. Both are addressed near the end of the chapter. The last page in this section reviews the United States Postal Service guidelines for addressing an envelope.

Taking Tests (pages 521–531)

By ninth grade, students have taken many tests. However, the tests they will face now and in the future are likely to be more and more challenging. Concerns covered in this chapter include test preparation, tips for taking tests in general, as well as specific advice for objective tests, essay tests, and standardized tests.

Minilessons

In the News
Listening and Speaking

- Have a partner **READ** a short story from a newspaper. **LISTEN** carefully and **WRITE** down the *who, what, when, where, why,* and *how* of the story. If you don't get them all the first time, have your partner read the story again. **TRADE** roles; have your partner **LISTEN** as you read a different story.

Top 8
Taking Notes

- **LISTEN** as your teacher quickly reads the list of eight do's and don'ts of constructive criticism (SE page 57). **TAKE** notes. **TRY** to capture all eight ideas.

"Just the Facts, Please" vs. "Why did that happen?"
Summarizing and Paraphrasing

- **WATCH** a video clip of a minor car accident. Then **WRITE** a paraphrase of what happened, including why you think the accident happened.

Time, Time, Time
Understanding Writing Assignments

- **READ** the sample assignment schedule on SE page 500. **THINK** about your own reading, thinking, planning, and writing speeds. Then **REWORK** the sample schedule, using the same assignment, to fit your pace.

Understanding
Improving Your Vocabulary

- As a team, **SELECT** five prefixes and **WRITE** as many words with those prefixes as you can. After each word, **WRITE** the meaning of the word. Also, **WRITE** a sentence using the word. **CHECK** your words in a dictionary. **COMPARE** your number of correctly created words with those of another team. **GIVE** one point per correct word.

Determine My Purpose
Writing Business Letters

- **READ** the business-letter writing tips on SE page 515. **READ** the following and **DECIDE** why you would write a business letter about each item or issue. Also, **DETERMINE** to whom the letter should be addressed.

  a broken part on an old bicycle, a poorly lit street, a well-designed calculator, a missing part in a kit, polluted water, news coverage of a class trip

---

Academic Vocabulary

Read aloud the academic terms, as well as the descriptions and questions. Model for students how to read one question and answer it. Have partners monitor their understanding and seek clarification of the terms by working through the meanings and questions together.

462

The Tools of Learning

Academic Vocabulary
Work with a partner. Read the definitions below and share your answers to the questions that follow.

1. A summary of something is a shortened version that contains only the most important points.
   To whom might you give a summary of a movie you've seen? Why?

2. Context refers to the parts of a text that surround a particular word or idea.
   Can the meaning of a word change based on its context? Explain.

3. To evaluate is to judge the value of something.
   Why is it important to evaluate information you find on the Internet?

4. To eliminate is to get rid of something.
   When should you try to eliminate answer choices on a multiple-choice test?

463

Listening and Speaking

Effective listening and speaking are often called *people skills* or *group skills*. They help you succeed in the classroom, in extracurricular activities, and in the workplace. You've been using these skills for, well, for as long as you can remember. But you probably have not been using them as effectively as you could be.

Good listening requires practice. No one can listen with complete attention for very long unless they really concentrate and practice effective listening skills. Similarly, effective speaking takes effort. No one can speak convincingly without thinking first and being prepared. This chapter will help you improve your listening and speaking skills.

- **Listening in Class**
- **Speaking in Class**
- **A Closer Look at Listening and Speaking**

"Some people talk simply because they think sound is more manageable than silence."
—Margaret Halsey

Listening and Speaking

Objectives
- learn to become a good listener
- develop skills for participating in a group
- improve speaking skills

Note that because listening and speaking are such important parts of daily life, students will have ample opportunity to practice the skills presented in this section. From time to time as you go through the section, ask students to talk about ways they've been able to use speaking and listening skills in other classes and in their extracurricular life.

Listening in Class

Talk about the distinction between hearing and listening. Ask students to describe it.

- Hearing describes the act of passively perceiving sound.
- Listening is actively processing the sound that is heard.

Acknowledge that listening can be a challenge when students must pay attention for an extended period of time. Encourage them to practice using the tips, which will lead them to listen actively. Suggest more tips based on your experiences.

Listening in Class

When you really listen, you're doing more than simply hearing what is being said. Listening involves effort. The following tips will help you become a better listener.

- **Know why you're listening.** What is the speaker trying to tell you? Will there be a test? Are you being given an assignment?
- **Listen for the facts.** The 5 W's and H—*Who? What? When? Where? Why?* and *How?*—will help you identify the most important information.
- **Take notes.** When you hear important information, write it down in your notebook. Also write down questions and comments in the margins. Review and complete your notes as soon after class as possible.
- **Put the speaker's ideas into your own words.** Paraphrase the speaker's key points as you take notes. Add your own comments.

 Try It!

Take notes in your own words. In your notes, practice putting ideas in your own words and adding your own comments.

Magna Carta (1215)

means "great charter"
– King John's barons forced him to sign it
– signed at Runnymede near Windsor
basis for all modern laws
– set the stage for due process and
parliamentary rule
– forerunner of Declaration of Independence
and U.S. Constitution
revised throughout history—of more than 60
original clauses only 2 remain intact
– #39 (no judgment until proven guilty)
– #40 (equal justice in courts for all citizens)
Importance: Established equality among all—
        even rulers

Mostly the nobles wanted to set limits on the monarchy's control.

Gradually the Magna Carta extended to all English citizens.

English Language Learners

Students not yet proficient in English may find it difficult to take effective notes because they do not have the vocabulary necessary for identifying and recording important information in their own words. Supplement their note-taking efforts by arranging for English-proficient "note partners" to share and compare copies of their notes in all classes.

Speaking in Class

Speaking in class is a skill everyone needs to master. A good classroom discussion depends on cooperation. These basic strategies will help you and your classmates become better speakers.

Before you speak . . .

- **Listen** carefully and take notes.
- **Think** about what others are saying.
- **Wait** until it's your turn to speak.
- **Plan** how you can add something positive to the discussion.

As you speak . . .

- **Use a loud, clear voice.**
- **Stick to the topic.**
- **Avoid repeating what's already been said.**
- **Support your ideas with examples, facts, or anecdotes.**
- **Maintain eye contact with others in the group or class.**

Tip

- Focus your comments on ideas, not on personalities.
- Ask meaningful questions.
- Summarize what's been agreed upon in the discussion.
- Mention another person's comments and expand on them constructively.

Try It!

Play "Who, Where, and When." Exercise your speaking skills by completing the following game.

1. Form groups of five students. Have each group choose a speaker.
2. The speaker looks at the lists below and chooses one person, one place, and one time period. Then the speaker begins to speak like that person, in that place, at that time.
3. The one who guesses the person, place, and time becomes the speaker.

People	Places	Times
nanny	playground	Roman Empire
salesperson	restaurant	Colonial days
scientist	the opera	Civil War
cowhand	an art museum	1930s
computer technician	flea market	present day

Learning

Speaking in Class

Assure students that if they do not feel comfortable speaking in class, there are strategies that will help them feel more confident. Explain how these strategies can accomplish this.

- Along with regular class attendance, active listening and taking good notes keep students involved in the subject. Participating in discussions is easier when all students are up-to-date on the learning.
- Observing basic rules of group etiquette— such as waiting one's turn and speaking loudly enough to be heard—creates an encouraging, supportive environment.

Remind students that over time, as they participate in opportunities to speak in class, they will build communication skills and confidence.

English Language Learners

Students learning English go through a number of language acquisition stages before they are ready to speak in front of large groups. Modify speaking assignments to allow students to practice sharing in smaller groups until they develop the language proficiency to participate in whole-class discussions.

Watch for students who demonstrate difficulty initiating and maintaining eye contact while speaking. Some cultures avoid eye contact as a sign of respect. Meet individually with students and explain that eye contact is important and respectful in American culture. Have students practice with you.

A Closer Look at Listening and Speaking

Remind students to practice their listening and speaking skills as they go about their daily activities in school. To help them gauge their progress, have students work in small groups after they have taken notes during a presentation you make to the class.

- Have groups discuss the material you've covered, keeping in mind what they've learned about effective speaking and listening.
- Ask students to supplement the notes they took during the presentation as needed, based on their discussion.
- Circulate among groups as they talk, offering guidance and clarification.

Afterward, ask students to reflect in their journals by responding to these questions: Did you feel alert and focused or **distracted** (see below) during the presentation? How thorough and accurate were your notes? Did the group discussion cover material you missed or misunderstood? If so, what did you do about it?

Encourage students to refer to this reflection prior to the next presentation.

466

A Closer Look at Listening and Speaking

Improving your listening and speaking skills will help you increase your confidence and effectiveness. Follow these basic guidelines to carry on productive conversations and discussions.

Good Listeners . . .	Good Speakers . . .
- think about what the speaker is saying. - stay focused so that they are prepared to respond thoughtfully. - pay attention to the speaker's tone of voice, gestures, and facial expressions. - interrupt only when necessary to ask questions.	- speak loudly and clearly. - maintain eye contact with their listeners. - emphasize their main ideas by changing the tone and volume of their voice. - respect their audience by explaining and clarifying information that may be confusing. - use gestures and body language effectively to enhance their message.

Try It!

Focus on speaking and listening skills by doing the activity below.

1. Pick two classmates and number yourselves 1, 2, and 3.
2. Person 1 will take person 2 aside and read the paragraph below.
3. Person 2 will then take person 3 aside and try to repeat the paragraph from memory.
4. Person 3 will then try to repeat the paragraph from memory to the first two classmates.
5. Compare the original paragraph to what person 3 reports.

Gregor Mendel is credited with our modern-day theory of genetics. Interestingly, he was not a scientist, but an Augustinian monk who taught high school science in the nineteenth century. Thinking that the environment was the key to why plants developed as they did, he discovered heredity was far more important. He became more and more involved in his experiments and spent seven years crossing plants and recording the results. What he learned became the foundation of modern genetics.

Teaching Tip: Dealing with Distraction

Acknowledge that there will be times when, despite students' best efforts, they can become distracted. Suggest that they try the focusing series of actions.

- Check your focus regularly to maintain an optimum level of attention.
- Focus on active listening and note taking to prevent the mind from wandering.
- If important information is missed, consult with a classmate about what was said and supplement class notes with information from this conversation.

467

Taking Notes

Taking notes is an active approach to learning, one that gets you personally involved in the learning process. In your high school classes, notes help you learn as you read textbooks, listen to lectures in class, and complete homework assignments. You begin to understand even the most complex ideas as you put information into your own words. Note taking also helps you focus on and organize the information you need to study for tests.

This chapter presents strategies for taking notes while reading a text, listening to a lecture, or attending a meeting. As you master this useful skill, note taking will become one of your most important learning tools.

- **Taking Classroom Notes**
- **Taking Reading Notes**
- **Taking Minutes for a Meeting**

"Make your
 writing useful."
—William Zinsser

Taking Notes

Objectives
- use guidelines for taking classroom notes
- learn tips for taking reading notes
- use graphic organizers for taking notes
- practice taking minutes for a meeting

Encourage students to think about how they can make the information presented in this section work best for them. Explain that different people will prefer using different types of notes, and students should experiment until they find the approach that best suits their style of learning. Assure students that taking notes will not distract them from listening. For most students, taking notes—once the right method is learned—greatly improves both comprehension and retention of the material.

Taking Classroom Notes

Discuss the fact that good note taking during class presentations requires the ability to pick out essential information from less important details. Suggest strategies to help discern this difference.

- Be alert for lists. Often the cue is the mention of a number, as in the example, *here are the six essential steps in flying a hot-air balloon.*
- Instead of trying to write every detail, pause regularly to listen for the gist, or main point, of what's being said.
- Before the presentation begins, anticipate the kind of information that it will cover. While listening, try to guess what's coming up next. This can provide a sense of what direction to take in organizing the details.

Point out that reviewing their notes later (an important step discussed on SE page 470) can remind students of essential points they might not have written down. This is because even random, nonessential details can spark recollections of other things that were said—provided students review notes while the presentation is fresh in their memory.

468

Taking Classroom Notes

Your teacher may give a lecture to explain an important subject, introduce a new topic, or help the class review for a test. The following tips will help you take clear, organized lecture notes.

Guidelines for Class Notes

1. **Write the topic and date at the top of each page.** Number your pages so that you can sort them out if they get mixed up.
2. **Listen carefully.** This is the key to taking good notes. If you get busy writing, you may miss important clues. For example, if a teacher says, "There are six steps in flying a hot-air balloon," listen for the six steps. Also listen for key words such as *first, second, next,* or *most importantly.*
3. **Use your own words.** You can't write down everything your teacher says. Instead, try to put the main points into your own words. You can fill in the details later.
4. **Begin taking notes right away** or you may miss something important. It's hard to catch up while taking notes.
5. **Write quickly, but be neat.** Your notes won't be helpful if you can't read them.
6. **Condense information.**
   - Use lists, phrases, and abbreviations (*p = page, ex = for example*).
   - Skip the small, unnecessary words, such as articles (*a, an, the*).
   - Shorten some words (*intro* for *introduction, chap* for *chapter*).
   - Use numbers and symbols (*1st, 2nd, +, ↑, ↓,=*).
   - Develop a personal shorthand (*w = with, w/o = without*).
7. **Draw sketches and diagrams** to explain something more quickly than in words.
8. **Copy important information** your teacher writes on the board.
9. **Ask your teacher** to explain something you don't understand, to repeat something, or to please slow down.

Try It!

Review some of your recent class notes in light of the guidelines above. How could you improve your note-taking skills? Explain.

Setting Up Your Notes

Keep your notes in a notebook, preferably one for each subject. You can also take notes on loose-leaf paper kept in a three-ring binder, which lets you add or remove pages as needed. Write only on one side of the paper. This makes it easier to read and find portions of your notes.

Learning

Leave wide margins.

Skip a line between main ideas.

Make sketches.

Use bullets or numbers in lists.

page 14

How a Submarine Dives   Nov. 17

Theory
- Buoyancy keeps the sub floating above or at some point below the surface.
- Ballast causes the sub to dive beneath the surface.

Four parts of a submarine
1. double hull
2. ballast tanks
3. compressed-air tanks
4. crew quarters

conning tower
valves

Steps in submerging a submarine
1. Close all air valves and hatches.
2. Fill ballast tanks with water.
3. Angle bow planes to help the sub dive.
4. Level off for underwater travel.

Controlling the submarine
- Increase or decrease engine speed to drive the sub forward.
- Reverse engines to move sub backward.
- Adjust bow planes and rudders to control left/right and up/down motion.
- Bring the sub to surface by forcing compressed air into ballast tanks to push water out.

Setting Up Your Notes

Emphasize the importance of developing a personal shorthand and becoming familiar with useful abbreviations and symbols. Remind students, however, that they should spell out and underline specialized terms (such as *ballast, bow planes, rudders*) the first time they're mentioned. This way, students will be able later to locate the terms and learn their meaning.

English Language Learners

To provide additional support for note taking, introduce a three-column format.

- In the first column, have students take their notes using words from their first language as part of their personal shorthand if they do not yet take all notes in English.

- In the second column, students should add information their "note partners" (TE page 464) have that they are missing.
- In the third column, students should write questions they have as they review their notes (SE page 470).

Reviewing Your Notes

Students may feel that reviewing their notes is an extra, unnecessary step. Explain that reviewing notes as soon as possible can be just as important as taking the notes in the first place. Talk about the **benefits of reviewing** *(see below)*.

■ It reminds students of the details that were presented.

■ It presents the information as a visual (reading) experience, rather than an auditory (listening) one. Since the brain processes heard and read information differently, this allows students to make use of both processes.

■ It allows students to interact with the information on a deeper level, by analyzing the important points, asking questions, and researching those questions.

Remind students that they don't have to rewrite their notes in the same form that they took them. They can transfer the details into an appropriate graphic organizer, such as a process diagram or time line. This will help them to consider the information from a different angle.

✱ For more about graphic organizers, see SE pages 588–589.

470

Reviewing Your Notes

As you read over your notes, circle any words that may not be spelled correctly. Also underline any words or phrases that you don't understand. Look up these words in a dictionary or textbook glossary. Then write each word and its meaning in the margin of your notes.

1. **Write any questions you have in the margin.** Then look for the answers on your own. If you can't find an answer, ask a teacher or classmate. Write the answer near the question.

2. **Use a highlighter to mark the most important notes.** You can use a different colored pen to circle or underline key ideas instead.

3. **Rewrite your notes.** Making a neat, organized copy of your notes gives you another chance to learn the material.

4. **Review your notes.** Look over your notes before the next class, especially if you are having a test or class discussion.

---

page 14

How a Submarine Dives   Nov. 17

Theory

Buoyancy =
water
making
things float

• Buoyancy keeps the sub floating above or at some point below the surface.
• Ballast causes the sub to dive beneath the surface.

conning tower

Four parts of a submarine

valves

Ballast =
something
that adds
stability

1. double hull
2. ballast tanks
3. compressed-air tanks
4. crew quarters

1
2
3
4

Steps in submerging a submarine

1. Close all air valves and hatches.
2. Fill ballast tanks with water.
3. Angle bow planes to help the sub dive.
4. Level off for underwater travel.

Can it dive
if a valve is
stuck open?

Controlling the submarine

• Increase or decrease engine speed to drive . . .

Teaching Tip: The Benefits of Reviewing

To demonstrate how helpful reviewing notes can be, ask students to review their notes from a particular class as homework. The next day, discuss their experiences.

● Ask students to describe which reviewing strategies they used and how those worked for them.

● Do students understand the information better after their review?

● Are they more interested in the topic than before?

Many students, especially those who are new to the idea of reviewing notes, should report having a positive experience.

Taking Reading Notes

Taking notes while you read an assignment is easier than taking notes during a lecture. You can stop to write at any time, which means you can write more neatly and carefully. Here are some tips for taking reading notes.

Guidelines for Reading Notes

1. **Preview the assignment.** Look through your assignment to see what your reading is about. Look at the title, introduction, headings, and chapter summary. Also look at any pictures, maps, or graphics. (See pages **602–603**.)

2. **Quickly read the entire assignment** once before taking notes. This gives you an overview of the material and allows you to pick out the main ideas.

3. **Take notes while reading a second time.** Start taking notes as you read your assignment again. Read the material slowly and stop at new ideas or words.

   - **Write down the important information.**

   - **Put notes in your own words.** Don't just copy passages from the book. You learn more when you rewrite ideas in your words. (See pages **483–490** for more information on summaries and paraphrases.)

   - **Use headings or subtitles.** Headings and subtitles help to organize your notes. Write down the important information under each heading or subtitle.

   - **Include notes about pictures, charts, and illustrations.** You can also make quick sketches of these visual elements.

   - **Use graphic organizers.** (See pages **588–589**.)

   - **List and define any new words.** Look up each word in the glossary or in a dictionary. Write down the appropriate meaning in your notes. Also write down the number of the page where the word is located. This way you can easily find it again.

4. **Learn more.** See "Critical Reading" on pages **473–482** for more information on taking reading notes.

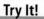

Try It!

For your next reading assignment, take notes using the tips above.

Learning

Taking Reading Notes

Students may be daunted by the prospect of going through the text three times in the process of taking reading notes. To reassure them that this is not as time consuming as it sounds, discuss how to preview a reading assignment.

- First, students should take just a few minutes to page through the selection, looking at the items specified. The idea is to get a broad idea of what will be covered.

- Next, students should **skim** *(see below)* the selection. This differs from a word-by-word close reading.

Explain that previewing will prepare students for reading the material closely. Acknowledge that this process will take more time than just reading the assignment through once. However, previewing the material at the start will be well worth it. Students will learn the information more thoroughly and remember it longer. This may even save them time in the end because they won't have to reread as much when preparing for a test.

Teaching Tip: Skimming

Discuss techniques students can use to skim a piece of writing.

- Take note of headings, subheadings, boldfaced vocabulary, graphics, and so on.
- Read the opening and closing paragraphs in each major section of the writing.

- Glance quickly through the body of each middle paragraph, looking for important details.

Distribute photocopies of a sample piece of writing for students to skim. Encourage them to continue practicing to improve their ability to skim effectively.

English Language Learners

A limited vocabulary and a slow reading rate may make skimming impractical. Demonstrate how, instead, students can write questions (SE page 476) on a graphic organizer while previewing a text and then take notes on the organizer the first time they read.

Taking Minutes for a Meeting

Discuss how minutes are taken at meetings and how they are used.

- One person, a secretary, is appointed to document what happens during the meeting.
- The secretary uses note-taking skills— including special shorthand and abbreviations—to record all the necessary information.
- Often, the secretary will transcribe (type up) the minutes and distribute copies to all members of the group.
- Usually the secretary will also read the minutes for the previous meeting at the start of a new meeting.

Taking Minutes for a Meeting

Recording the minutes of a meeting is another form of note taking. Minutes must be well organized and include everything from who is present to what is discussed and decided. Always report minutes in an objective (impersonal) voice. To record minutes during a meeting, you must listen carefully and write down information accurately. Below are some tips to follow.

Guidelines for Taking Minutes

- Begin with the organization's name, the date, location, and topic of the meeting.
- Record what time the meeting begins.
- List those present (or absent). Indicate who led the meeting and who recorded the minutes.
- Note "old business" (from a previous meeting) that is discussed or resolved.
- Note "new business" (plans or decisions to be handled in the current meeting).
- Record any votes taken and their result.
- Record when the meeting is adjourned.

McPherson High School Student Government Minutes
Date: October 13, 2011
Location: Room 115 (Mr. Troskas, Faculty Liaison)
Topic: Weekly Meeting

Attending
Madonna Armando, Maretta Cabaso, Ray Cadavico, James Conlan, Burt DiPerri (recording), Andreas Gallin, Rex Girtz, Tara Lehrer, Jonelle Levin, Sabrina Mocaryn, Wyatt Moody, Joey Righetti, Tamara Seung (chair), Lavinia Sidle, Carla Zacaggi

Old Business
Homecoming Committee: Supplies were purchased for gym decorations. Tara still needs volunteers to help with setup after school on October 27.

Fund-Raiser Committee: With last Friday's dance receipts, there is $460 in the fund. Another $40 is needed to pay for the homecoming band in two weeks.

New Business
Blood Drive: The local Blood Center, Principal Jackson, and Mr. Troskas all agreed to having the 14th Annual Blood Drive in February of 2008. Bring suggestions for a theme/title for the drive to next week's meeting.

School Spirit Committee: Fan attendance has been down at all nonvarsity sports events. Ideas for how to raise awareness included posters in halls and morning sports announcements. Joey will talk to Principal Jackson about adding announcements.
- Vote: 10 to 5 to paint posters for the halls next Monday evening (October 20) instead of tonight.

Meeting Time: 2:45 pm – 4:00 pm

Take minutes to tell what was discussed and decided upon by a group. When you take minutes, record only the main points, not all the details, of a discussion. Be sure to accurately record any votes or official action taken.

English Language Learners

Point out that the word *minutes* has multiple meanings. In this case, *minutes* not only refers to the notes taken during a meeting, but it also implies the passage of time. Explain that meeting *minutes* are a record of what people said and the actions they took during the time of a meeting.

Critical Reading

Does this ever happen to you? You read a paragraph, a page, or a chapter in a textbook—put the book down—and say, "I can't remember a thing!" Unfortunately, many students have that experience. However, the good news is that you *can* remember important information that you read. The way to do that is by reading critically.

Critical reading involves a number of important steps, including *surveying* a reading assignment, *questioning* what the text is about, *taking notes* as you read, and so on. If you have a tested reading plan in mind, and carry out that plan, you will be in control of your reading. This chapter gives you an effective critical-reading method to follow.

- Critical Reading: SQ3R
- Before You Read
- As You Read
- After You Read
- Reading Fiction
- Reading Poetry

"Meaning doesn't reside ready-made in the text or in the reader; it happens during the transaction between reader and text."

—Louise Rosenblatt

Critical Reading

Objectives
- use the five steps of the SQ3R method for reading nonfiction critically
- learn techniques for reading prose
- learn techniques for reading poetry

Tell students that the critical reading methods they will learn on the following pages are designed to help them as they read for classes. However, they may also find that some of the techniques will help them get more out of their extracurricular reading, too.

Discuss the quotation by Louise Rosenblatt. Ask students what they think she is saying about reading. Responses may include the following:
- Reading is an active process.
- Both the reader and the text (the writer's thoughts) contribute to the meaning.
- Reading is like an exchange between the reader and the text.

Critical Reading: SQ3R

To strengthen students' understanding of the term *critical reading,* talk about the meaning of the word *critical.*

- Do students tend to associate *critical* with having a negative opinion of something? (Some students will probably agree that they do.)
- Challenge students to give examples of other ways the word is used.
- Have a volunteer look up *critical* in the dictionary and read its many different definitions to classmates.
- Ask students which definition is more likely to apply to the term *critical reading* as it is described. (involving careful judgment or evaluation)

Critical Reading: SQ3R

An effective reading technique for all types of nonfiction is the SQ3R method. SQ3R stands for the five steps in this reading process: *survey, question, read, recite,* and *review.* The steps in this technique are explained below.

Before you read . . .

- **Survey** Preview the reading assignment for its general content. Read titles, subtitles, headings, and subheadings to see what is being covered. Take note of illustrations and terms in bold or italic type. Also read just the first and last paragraphs.
- **Question** Ask yourself what you already know about the topic of the reading. Write down questions you still want answered. To get started, you could turn the text's titles, subtitles, headings, and subheadings into questions. Asking questions keeps you actively involved while reading.

As you read . . .

- **Read** Read slowly and carefully. Look for the main idea in each paragraph, section, or chapter. Try to answer questions you have already identified. At different points, also ask these questions: *What does this mean? How does it connect with previous material? What will come next?* Take notes as you go along. Take the time to read difficult parts slowly. (Reread them if necessary.)
- **Recite** Test your comprehension of the material by summarizing the main points out loud. Reciting is one of the most valuable parts of SQ3R. After you read a page, section, or chapter, try to answer the 5 W's and H *(Who? What? Where? When? Why?* and *How?)* about that part. Reread any parts as needed.

After you read . . .

- **Review** Assess your knowledge by reviewing your notes. See how well you understand the entire reading assignment. Ask these questions: *Have all my questions been answered? Can I summarize each main section? Can I summarize or outline the whole assignment?* Consider outlining the material (or using another type of graphic organizer) to help you remember what you have read.

 Critical reading means looking beyond surface details and thinking carefully about the information that is presented.

Struggling Learners

To help students with the questioning part of the prereading process, model how to set up a KWL chart to set a purpose for reading and to guide their note taking as they read.

K (what I Know)	W (what I Want to know)	L (what I Learned)

Learning

Before You Read

Try to get the big picture with each assignment.

Surveying the Reading

To begin, **survey** or preview the text. This will give you a general understanding of the main points. Use the following guidelines:

- **Scan** chapter titles, subtitles, headings, and boldfaced type.
- **Identify the purpose of the material:** to inform, to persuade, to entertain.
- **Read** the first and last paragraphs.
- **List** the topic and the main points you identify.

Below, Marcus *surveys* the opening part of an article. He writes his notes on a copy of the article.

Sample Survey Notes

On Our Borders: Immigrants and Terrorists

Terrorism in the United States

Terrorism is a relatively new threat to the United States. Before the first attack on the World Trade Center in 1993, foreign terrorists had not successfully attacked a target on U.S. soil. Other countries—including Russia, Spain, and the United Kingdom—have dealt with terrorists for decades. Since 9/11, defending the security of our borders against terrorism has emerged as one of the key issues in this country.

Immigration Policies and a Protected Nation

All citizens want to feel protected against terrorism. However, tighter security may jeopardize civil liberties in this country. So a critical debate has developed between those individuals who want tighter immigration policies and people who are concerned that those policies will harm the American way of life. . . .

Purpose:
to inform

Topic:
connection
between
immigration
and terrorism

Key Points:
terrorism in
the U.S.

policies
protecting
immigrants/
the nation

Try It!

Survey a reading assignment. Choose a reading assignment from any of your classes. Identify its purpose, main topic, and the key points.

Before You Read

If students don't have a photocopy of the material they need to survey, suggest that they write their thoughts on sticky notes. They can then attach them to the first page of the selection.

Discuss the idea of surveying. Note that before building on a piece of land, a *surveyor* goes to the site to measure it and decide how the terrain, composition of the soil, size of the plot, and other factors will affect the proposed structure. Point out that this is similar to what students are doing when they survey an article. They are taking an overall look at what the reading covers—how the text is laid out—to decide how to proceed in order to construct their understanding of the content.

English Language Learners

Limited vocabulary makes it difficult for students to comprehend many books that are assigned for reading.

- Students should look up the unfamiliar words as they read.

- If students still have trouble understanding the general idea of the text after they look up the vocabulary, help them understand the meaning of the words in the context of the text.

Questioning the Material

Distribute copies of the reproducible 5 W's Chart (TE page 817) for students to use as they list their questions. Encourage them to think of at least one question for each *W* word and for *How*. This will help them cover the topic more thoroughly.

Draw students' attention to the *Already Know* column of the model notes. Point out that in this section the student writer doesn't just list factual details about the subject. He also

- tries to anticipate what he might learn when he reads the selection (*I think that "borders" might refer to . . .*) and
- records his feelings about the topic (*I want to be safe . . .*).

Explain that getting involved with topics in this way can really help students to understand the reading better.

Questioning the Material

After you have surveyed the entire text, ask **questions** about the reading. Use the following guidelines:

- **Ask what you already know** about the topic.
- **List questions** that you still want answered. Also ask the 5 W and H questions.
- **Turn headings and main points into questions.** For example, if the chapter title is "Scientific Discoveries of the Ancient World," your questions might be "What were those scientific discoveries? Who made them?"

Below, Marcus turned the main headings into questions and formed other questions that occurred to him. Next to his questions, he noted things he already knew about the topic.

Sample Question Notes

"On Our Borders: Immigrants and Terrorists"	Already Know:
1. How do terrorists get into this country?	Terrorists came to the
2. Does "borders" refer to national borders or other borders?	U.S. legally and attacked the World Trade Center
3. What are U.S. immigration policies?	more than once.
4. How do U.S. policies compare to policies in other countries?	I think that "borders" might refer to more than
5. What rights do immigrants have?	just national borders.
6. How would our country change if immigration policies changed?	I want to be safe from terrorists, but I also want immigrants to be able to come to the U.S.

Try It!

Ask questions. Write down questions you have about the reading assignment you surveyed. Also note what you already know about the topic.

As You Read

Once you have surveyed the assignment and formed questions about it, you are ready to read carefully. Try to turn your reading into a conversation with the text. Respect what the writer has to say even as you question certain parts. And stay open to the unexpected.

Reading (and Taking Notes)

Always have a goal in mind when you read. Use the following guidelines to read the material and answer the questions you listed.

- **Read slowly** so that you don't miss anything.
- **Reread parts** that seem challenging.
- **Write down boldfaced key concepts.**
- **Define key concepts** using context or a dictionary.
- **Record any additional questions** you may have.
- **Keep the following questions in mind** as you read:
  - What does this mean?
  - How does it connect with what I already know about the topic?
  - What will probably come next?

Try It!

Read your chosen assignment critically. Take careful notes as you go along, using the guidelines above.

Reciting Out Loud

After you complete the entire reading, it's time to reinforce what you have learned. Reciting or repeating the information out loud is an effective way to evaluate how well you understand information. Use the following guidelines:

- **Recite the key points** without looking at your notes.
- **Answer the 5 W's and H** (*Who? What? Where? When? Why?* and *How?*) about the material.
- **Discuss (and answer) your other questions** about the topic.
- **Identify any new questions** that occur to you.

Try It!

Recite what you have learned from your reading assignment. Use the guidelines above to help you complete this step.

Learning

As You Read

Suggest that one way of making the most of reciting out loud is for students to work with a study partner. They can

- take turns reciting the key points of sections of the reading to each other,
- identify the 5 W's and H for the piece,
- compare questions and discuss possible answers, and
- divide up the work of researching the still-unanswered questions.

To prepare students for working with study partners, have them choose partners and, during class time, go through the reciting stage together for a particular set of notes.

Then encourage students to continue meeting with their partners during their own study time.

Advanced Learners

Point out the last bulleted item in the Recite section. Encourage students to expand their learning by thinking of questions that require other sources, such as the library or the Internet, for finding answers to those questions. Have students use those sources to research the answers.

After You Read

Draw students' attention to the term *point/counterpoint* in the sample summary. Note that this is a writing form that describes a discussion that includes arguments for *and* against an issue. Often, the arguments are presented alternately—first the writer makes a *point,* then the writer mentions the *counterpoint,* or opposing point of view.

Note that distilling the information into concise summaries not only helps students understand the material better, but it also can serve as a **review resource** *(see below)* for them later.

After You Read

Having completed the first four steps in the SQ3R method, it's time to review the reading. Reviewing will help you see how well you understand the material.

Reviewing the Material

A final **review** of your reading assignment will make the information part of your own thinking. Use the following guidelines:

- **Go over your notes** one section at a time.
- **Keep searching for answers** if you have any unanswered questions.
- **Ask for help** if you cannot figure something out on your own.
- **Add illustrations or graphic organizers** to your notes to make complex ideas clearer.
- **Summarize the reading** at the end of your notes.

In the example below, Marcus summarized the entire article in a paragraph and added his own thoughts in the margin.

Sample Summary

> #### "On Our Borders"—Summary
>
> This point/counterpoint article argues both sides of immigration policies in the United States and discusses how to change these policies to deal with terrorism. Disagreements arise over limiting the freedoms of both U.S. citizens and immigrants. Tougher restrictions could lead to problems with global trade. Both sides agree something must be done to combat terrorism, but excluding immigrants goes against the ideals of this nation, which has always welcomed new citizens from around the globe.
>
> *The U.S. needs to track student and tourist visas more effectively. Don't those systems need fixing, too?*
>
> *Why do politicians make this an immigration issue? (I would like to do more research on this.)*

 Try It!

Review your reading assignment. Go over your notes and summarize the assignment. Be sure to include all the main ideas.

Teaching Tip: Review Resources

Suggest that students write their one-paragraph summaries of reading materials on note cards. Eventually, they will build up a useful collection of summaries for each reading assignment in every course. This way, they can remind themselves quickly of what is in a reading selection when they study for a test or write a paper.

Reading Fiction

Fiction uses made-up characters and events to reveal what is real or true about life. This makes fiction a great way to learn. Here are some tips for reading fiction.

Before you read . . .

- **Learn something about the author** and her or his other works.
- **React thoughtfully** to the title and opening pages.

As you read . . .

- **Identify** the following story elements: *setting, tone, main characters, central conflict,* and *theme.*
- **Predict** what will happen next.
- **Write** your reactions to the short story or novel in a reading journal as you go along.
- **Think** about the characters and what they do.
  - What motivates the characters?
  - Have you encountered people similar to these characters?
  - Have you faced situations similar to the ones faced by the main characters?
  - Would you have reacted in the same way?
- **Consider** how the author's life may have influenced the story.
- **Notice** the author's style and word choice. (See pages **298–299**.)
  - How effectively has the author used literary devices?
  - Why do you think the author used a particular word or phrase?
- **Discuss** the story with others who are reading it.

After you read . . .

- **Consider** how the main character changes during the course of the story. Often, this is the key to understanding a work of fiction.
- **Determine** the story's main message or theme; then decide how effectively this message is communicated.

Try It!

Use the information above as a guide to help you better understand and enjoy the next short story or novel you read.

Learning

Reading Fiction

Discuss the value of keeping a reading journal. Note that responses to reading can be included in a student's personal journal as well.

To encourage all students to try journaling, have them keep a reading journal for the **Try It!** activity. Assure students that they should not worry about whether their responses are right or wrong. Their goals are to be thoughtful in what they write and to cultivate the habits of active readers.

For their final journal entry, ask students to freewrite in response to the following prompts about keeping the journal:

- Did it help you to use the suggested tips for reading fiction?
- Did you enjoy the process of keeping a journal? Explain.
- Do you feel you understand the story better than you would have if you hadn't used the reading tips?
- Will you refer to your response notes later? Why?

Struggling Learners

Students may have difficulty making predictions and writing their reactions to a story (bullets 2 and 3 under As you read. . .) if they do not understand the basic elements of the plot or conflict. Have students create a story map as they read to track events of a narrative before they address the rest of the tips.

Reacting to Fiction

Note that, for shorter works, a student might prefer to read the story all the way through—perhaps jotting down questions and notable words or phrases only as they occur. Afterward, the student can go back and add to the notes.

Reacting to Fiction

The excerpt below is from the short story "Ghosts in the House" by Rob King. The margin notes reveal one student's reactions, which she wrote on a photocopy of the story. She makes observations, asks questions, and defines a term.

From "Ghosts in the House"

More than anything, I'll miss this.

Terrell sat on an old crate by the attic window and watched the sun set. It turned his neighborhood gold. From this window, even the worn-out rooftops shone like the streets of heaven.

> This simile helps me to "see" the setting.

"This is my house." The words sounded hollow. Somebody had bought the place to make it a parking lot. "This is *my* house."

Actually, it wasn't. The house had been abandoned for 10 years, and most of the neighborhood kids called it the "haunted house." Four years ago, Terrell explored it and liked it so well, he made it his own. He and his friends called themselves "the Ghosts," and they fixed up their Haunt and hung there every afternoon.

" 'Sup?" said Junior, coming up the stairs.

Terrell knocked knuckles with him. "Last day for the Ghosts."

> The dialogue sounds real.

Junior flopped down on the old beanbag. "Nah, we'll always be the Ghosts."

"What're Ghosts without a Haunt?"

Bill climbed in through the fire escape. " 'Sup?"

"I'm surprised you came," Terrell said.

Bill slouched against the wall. "It couldn't last forever, T. Two more years, and we'll graduate anyway."

> Why do the boys think the house is theirs?

Terrell said, "This is *our* house. We grew up here. Who can grow up in a parking lot?"

There was nothing more to say. Outside, the rooftops gave up their gold and became cracked black asphalt. Bill left, and then Junior. That left only Terrell and his window and the house that wasn't his.

> Violators means "people who break or disregard the law."

On the next day, the house was padlocked, and a sign was taped on the door: "PRIVATE PROPERTY. KEEP OUT. VIOLATORS WILL BE PROSECUTED."

The Ghosts weren't violators. They took care of this place, and it took care of them.

"The job of the poet is to render the world—
to see it and report it without loss. . . . "
—Mark Van Doren

Reading Poetry

You shouldn't expect to understand a poem completely in one reading, especially if it is lengthy or complex. In fact, each time you read a poem over again, you will probably discover something new about it. Reacting to poetry in a reading journal will also help you to appreciate it more. (See the next page.) Here are some strategies for reading poetry.

First Reading

- **Read the poem** at your normal reading speed to gain an overall first impression.
- **Jot down brief notes** about your immediate reaction to the poem.

Second Reading

- **Read the poem again**—out loud, if possible. Pay attention to the sound of the poem.
- **Note examples of sound devices** in the poem—alliteration, assonance, rhyme (see pages **340–341**). Finding a poem's phrasing and rhythm can help you discover its meaning.
- **Observe** the punctuation, spacing, and special treatment of words and lines.
- **Think** about what the poem is saying.

Third Reading

- **Identify** the type of poem you're reading. Does this poem follow the usual pattern of that particular type? If not, why not?
- **Determine** the literal sense or meaning of the poem. What is the poem about? What does it seem to say about its topic?
- **Look for** figurative language in the poem. How does this language—metaphors, similes, personification, symbols—support or add to the meaning of the poem? (See pages **340–341**.)

Try It!

Use the strategies above as a guide the next time you read a poem.

Reading Poetry

Extend the journaling exercise from TE page 479. Have students write journal entries about a poem of their choice.

- Provide a variety of poems for students to choose from. Have enough selections available so that each student can keep a chosen poem alongside his or her journal.
- Emphasize that students' main goal is to be active, thoughtful readers.

After students have completed their journal entries,

- have the class reflect on their journaling and
- invite interested students to meet as a group to share and discuss their poems and journal entries.

English Language Learners

Students who have difficulty reading fluently may not benefit from reading the poem aloud. Meet with these students to brainstorm ways to modify the second reading. For example, they could look for poems on tape or ask an English-proficient partner to read the poem aloud.

Struggling Learners

Provide guidance for students who may have difficulty writing a response to a poem as a journal entry.

- Assign a high-interest poem for students to read and respond to.

- Then, guide a group discussion about the poem, asking questions that help students respond to it thoughtfully.

After the group discussion, have students write their responses in their journals.

Reacting to Poetry

Draw students' attention to the techniques used to mark parts of the poem. Have them describe these techniques.

- Straight underlining identifies words that echo or comment on the previous stanza.
- Wavy underlining denotes single, contrasting words.
- Circled words indicate that the reader has questions about their meaning.
- A large, single bracket connected by a line to a margin note indicates the lines in the poem that apply to that note.

Help students to develop a similar note-taking system and to practice using it. (It doesn't have to be the same as these examples.) Using consistent marking techniques will help them analyze poems and other writings more efficiently.

482

Reacting to Poetry

The untitled poem below is by Stephen Crane. The notes on a copy of the poem show one student's reactions. He makes observations, asks questions, identifies figurative language, and so forth. Whenever you read a challenging poem, try to react to it in several different ways.

> **XXVII**
>
> The poet starts with a metaphor for truth.
>
> "Truth," said a traveler,
> "Is a rock, a mighty fortress;
> Often have I been to it,
> Even to its highest tower,
> From (whence) the world looks black."
>
> *What does "whence" mean?*
>
> "Truth," said a traveler,
> "Is a breath, a wind,
> A shadow, a phantom;
> Long have I pursued it,
> But never have I touched
> The hem of its garment."
>
> *The second stanza parallels the first.*
>
> *The poem uses repetition to make a point.*
>
> And I believed the second traveler;
> For truth was to me
> A breath, a wind,
> A shadow, a phantom,
> And never had I touched
> The hem of its garment.
>
> *The third stanza comments on the second.*
>
> *This poem does not rhyme or have a regular rhythm.*
>
> *The poem uses irony as each traveler describes truth in opposite terms. The same contrast is seen in the words often and never.*

Tip

Do a 5 to 10 minute freewriting when you finish reading a poem. Write down anything you can about the poem. Relate it to other poems you have read.

Advanced Learners

Students may enjoy keeping a poetry journal in which they can react to poetry on a regular basis. As they read poetry or listen to song lyrics, students should record lines or stanzas that have special meaning to them. Tell them to note the author and title of the poem or song before each entry. Then, they should

- write a journal entry reflecting on those lines, explaining what the words and images mean to them;
- make notes like the ones in the sample reaction; and
- follow the guidelines in the Tip.

Encourage students to add excerpts and reflections at least once a week.

Summarizing and Paraphrasing

Have you ever explained something to another person and found that, in making the explanation, you suddenly understood the topic better yourself? The same thing happens when you summarize or paraphrase a reading assignment. When you read a text and then put the main ideas into your own words, real understanding begins to take place.

When you summarize an article, you highlight its main points and arguments without writing down every single detail. Paraphrasing is similar to summarizing, except that paraphrasing requires you to interpret the main points and then put them in your own words. This chapter presents examples of both kinds of writing and shows you how to write concise summaries and accurate paraphrases.

- ■ **Sample Article and Summary**
- ■ **Guidelines for Summarizing**
- ■ **Summarizing an Article**
- ■ **Strategies for Paraphrasing**
- ■ **Sample Paragraphs and Paraphrases**
- ■ **Paraphrasing a Paragraph**

"It's good to rub and polish our brain against that of others."

—Montaigne

Copy Masters

5 W's Chart (TE p. 484)

Summarizing and Paraphrasing

Objectives
- learn techniques for summarizing a reading selection
- learn strategies for paraphrasing a passage

To help students better understand the distinction between summarizing and paraphrasing, talk more about the words themselves. For example:

- ■ *Summarize* comes from the Latin *summarium,* which means "a high point." It is related to the word *summit* ("peak") and *sum* ("total number"). Students can remember that a summary states the "high point" or the "sum total" of a piece.

- ■ *Paraphrase* comes from the Greek prefix *para-* ("by the side of") and the Greek root word *phrasis* ("speech"). Students can remember that a paraphrase interprets a text by putting it in the student writer's own words.

Sample Article

Suggest that students use the 5 W's and H strategy to identify the main points of a piece of writing. This can be done by underlining and making notations on the article or on sticky notes. Alternatively, students may prefer to use a graphic organizer, just as they would during the prewriting stage for any project. Then the ideas will be listed in a clear format that they can refer to as they write their summaries.

Distribute photocopies of the reproducible 5 W's Chart (TE page 817) for students to use when they read the sample article.

484

Sample Article

The following article is about a Native American tribe called the Mandan.

The Nearly Forgotten People

The Mandan tribe lived in what is now North Dakota, where they achieved a level of technology that was unique on the North American Great Plains. The Mandan lived in houses and tended gardens at the same time that neighboring nomadic tribes followed the buffalo. In the 1700s, the Mandan had twelve thriving villages along the Missouri River. Because smallpox ravaged the tribe in the early 1800s, the Mandan have been mostly forgotten in American popular culture. However, their living descendants and historians have passed on important information about them.

At one time, Mandan communities centered on a sacred cedar pole and a central plaza. The Mandan dwelled in sod-enclosed houses that were erected upon frames of wooden timbers. These structures were sturdy enough that people could sit on top of them. In fact, they used the buildings as makeshift grandstands to watch the elaborate ceremonies they held around their community's sacred pole.

Mandan tribal society had distinct male and female roles. Mandan women maintained elaborate and productive gardens, growing maize (corn), beans, pumpkins, sunflowers, and squash. They made baskets and were the only potters among all the Plains Indians. They used small, tub-shaped watercraft called "bull boats," made by stretching animal hide over a framework of sticks. The men served as hunters and warriors and were responsible for the tribe's spiritual life.

Although the Mandan were more agrarian than most of their neighboring cultures, they still relied upon the buffalo as a staple of survival just as other Plains tribes did. A Mandan buffalo hunt was generally preceded by an elaborate dance performed (sometimes for days) by hunters who had already slain buffalo. The hunters danced until a herd of buffalo was spotted. Then the hunt would commence.

By 1804, smallpox had reduced the Mandan to two large villages. In 1837, the Mandan were stricken for the last time, when smallpox swept through both of the remaining villages and reduced the tribal population from some sixteen hundred to only a few dozen. Yet, because of those survivors and others who have studied their culture, the Mandan are remembered to this day.

English Language Learners

The vocabulary in the sample article may make it difficult for students to complete the 5 W's chart. Have them use the modified SQ3R method (see TE pages 474–478) for each paragraph to reinforce how SQ3R develops vocabulary and improves understanding and note taking.

Summarizing and Paraphrasing **485**

Sample Summary

The following paragraph is a student summary of the preceding article. Pay special attention to the three main parts: the topic sentence, the body, and the closing sentence. (See the side notes.)

The **topic sentence** expresses the main idea.

Each sentence in the **body** summarizes one or even two paragraphs from the article.

The **closing sentence** adds the article's concluding thoughts.

The Mandan Tribe

The Mandan were a tribe of Native Americans living along the Missouri River in an area of the Great Plains that would become North Dakota. Unlike the nomadic tribes of the Great Plains, the Mandan were farmers who lived in permanent villages and sturdy houses. The women did most of the work and were skilled at gardening, making pots and baskets, and even building tub-like boats. The Mandan, like other Plains Indians, hunted buffalo. The men were the hunters, and they would do a dance that could last for days before they'd go hunting. **In the early 1800s, the tribe was nearly wiped out by smallpox, but the memory of the Mandan still lives on.**

Learning

 Respond to the reading. Answer the following questions.

Ideas (1) What main points from the article does the summary focus on? Name two. **(2)** What details are *not* included? Name two.

Organization (3) How is the summary paragraph organized?

Voice & Word Choice (4) How does the writer show that she or he has a clear understanding of the article? Identify two phrases or ideas from the summary in your explanation.

Tip

An effective summary includes only the necessary facts. Names, dates, times, places, and similar information are usually necessary, but examples and descriptive details are not. A summary should answer two questions: *What is the most important idea in the reading? What information supports this idea?*

English Language Learners

Help students recognize that all of the information in the sample summary comes from the sample article. To demonstrate that the information is the same,

- read aloud sentences from the sample summary and
- then guide students to identify the sentences in the sample article that contain the same information.

Sample Summary

After giving students time to read the article on their own, work through the **Respond to the reading** activity as a class.

 Respond to the reading.

Answers

Ideas 1. Possible responses:
- Tribe lived in what's now North Dakota.
- Women gardened, made baskets, pots, and boats.
- Men hunted buffalo.
- Smallpox killed all but a few in the early 1800s.

2. Possible responses:
- Villages had sacred cedar pole and plaza.
- Men were responsible for religion.
- Two villages were left in 1804.

Organization 3. roughly the same order as the original article

Voice & Word Choice 4. Possible response: The summary includes the main idea, conclusion, and main points from the middle paragraphs. The sentence beginning *Unlike the nomadic tribes* shows the writer understood that the Mandan were different. The sentence beginning *The women did most of the work* shows understanding of the meaning of paragraph 3, about gender roles.

Guidelines for Summarizing

Draw students' attention to the parenthetical instruction that says they should *not* include their personal opinions in a summary. Emphasize the importance of this rule. Summaries (and paraphrases) express the ideas of the original author only.

Point out to students that summarizing requires rewriting information from an original article. Encourage students to remain alert to the possibility of accidental plagiarism. Suggest that before editing, they check both the original article and their summary to make sure they've used only their own words.

✽ For more about avoiding plagiarism, see SE page 369.

Guidelines for Summarizing

Follow the guidelines below whenever you are asked to write a summary.

Prewriting

■ Select an article on a topic that interests you or relates to a subject you are currently studying. Make a photocopy of the article if possible.

■ Read the article once, quickly. Then read it again, underlining passages (if working from a photocopy) or taking notes on the key details.

■ Think about the article. Identify and write down the main idea. For example, here is the main idea of the sample article: **The Mandan were a tribe of Native Americans living along the Missouri River in an area of the Great Plains that would become North Dakota.**

Writing

Write a summary paragraph.

■ Write a topic sentence that states the main idea of the article.

■ Write body sentences that communicate the most important ideas of the article in your own words.

■ Conclude by reminding your reader of the main point of the article. (A summary should *not* contain your personal opinions.)

Revising **and** Editing

Read and revise your summary and make necessary changes. Also edit for conventions. Ask yourself the following questions:

Ideas Do I correctly identify the article's main idea in my topic sentence? Do my body sentences contain only the most important details from the article?

Organization Does my paragraph arrange ideas in the same order that the article does?

Voice Does my voice sound informed and interested?

Word Choice Have I used my own words for the most part? Are there terms that need to be defined?

Sentence Fluency Have I varied sentence structures and lengths?

Conventions Have I eliminated all errors in punctuation, spelling, and grammar?

Summarizing an Article

The following article is about the evolution and history of the horse.

Full Circle

The spread of horses around the world is well documented. Archaeologists report that horses first appeared on the plains of North America more than 55 million years ago. Then, about 8 to 10 thousand years ago, horses disappeared from the Western Hemisphere. It was not until the first Spanish expeditions to the New World that the horse returned to its original home.

By about 2.5 million years ago, ancestors of all modern breeds of horses had multiplied across the plains of the Americas and into the rest of the world, probably crossing to Asia on the Siberian land bridge that regularly rose above sea level during that time.

The horse disappeared from the Americas about 8000 B.C., but by then *Equus,* the scientific name for these animals, was already well established in Asia and Europe (as the horse and donkey) and in Africa (as the zebra). Several hypotheses seek to explain the horse's disappearance from the Western Hemisphere. Horses and other large animals all became extinct when humans migrated to the Americas. It is possible that these early humans killed off the horse through hunting. Alternately, a devastating disease might have destroyed them. In any event, there were no horses around as early human cultures developed in the Americas.

It was A.D. 1519 before the horse was finally returned to the continent of its origin. The Spanish conquistador Hernando Cortez took horses with him to Mexico. These animals quickly increased their numbers. In 1532, horses were taken to Peru. Within three years, wild horses were roaming the lush grass *pampas* of Argentina.

The horse moved north from Mexico, as well. By 1594, native tribes in northern Mexico were using horses, and in 1598 a band of Native Americans drove a herd all the way to what is now New Mexico. Less than 100 years later, Ute and Shoshone tribes brought the horse onto the Great Plains, and soon other tribes had horses, too.

Today, wild horses again range over the Western Hemisphere. No doubt, they will remain with humankind for many centuries to come.

Learning

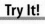

Try It!

Summarize the article above. Write a summary paragraph about this article, using the guidelines provided on page **486**.

English Language Learners

Students may resort to copying information verbatim when summarizing because of the time it takes them to read and restate the ideas. Break down the task. Instruct students to focus on one paragraph at a time and cover the rest of the text as they write the main idea of the paragraph in their own words.

Summarizing an Article

Before students write their summary, discuss the article. Have students describe the main idea, main points, and conclusion in their own words.

- **Main idea:** Horses first appeared in North America about 55 million of years ago, vanished around 8000 B.C., and returned with the Spanish in the 16th century.
- **Main point 1:** Ancestors of today's horse probably crossed from the Americas to Asia over the Siberian Land Bridge about 2.5 million years ago.
- **Main point 2:** Theories about what happened to the first horses in the Americas include the ideas that they were killed by newly arrived humans or by a disease.
- **Main point 3:** Hernando Cortez brought horses when he came to Mexico in 1519, and they quickly spread north and south.
- **Main point 4:** By the late 1600s, many Great Plains Indians rode horses.
- **Conclusion:** Wild horses are once more well established in the Western Hemisphere.

Strategies for Paraphrasing

Ask students to read the paraphrase examples at the bottom of the page. Why, exactly, does the first example lack voice?

- The language sounds more formal than the original.
- The words chosen (*commented, gathering*) are too general and don't convey the sense that the councilman is expressing disapproval.

488

Strategies for Paraphrasing

A paraphrase is a type of summary that is very effective for clarifying or explaining the meaning of an important passage that you would like to use in your research. A summary is shorter than the original text and attempts to state its meaning. A paraphrase, on the other hand, is sometimes longer than the original material and tries to *interpret* its meaning. Use the following strategies as a guide when you paraphrase.

Follow a plan: In order to complete an effective paraphrase, you must follow a series of important steps. There are no shortcuts.

- **Review the entire passage.** This will help you identify the main point and purpose of the material.
- **Carefully read the passage.** If necessary, reread parts that seem especially important or challenging.
- **Write your paraphrase.** Be sure your interpretation is clear and complete. For the most part, use your own words. (See below.)
- **Check your paraphrase.** Make sure that you have captured the tone and meaning of the passage.

Use your own words: Avoid the original writer's words as much as possible. Exceptions include key words (*tribe, repertory theater*) or proper nouns (*Iroquois, Lake Erie, New York*).

- **Consult a dictionary.** Refer to a dictionary to help you think of new ways to express certain terms or ideas.
- **Refer to a thesaurus.** Find synonyms to use in place of words in the original text. For example, if the writer is describing an empire, a thesaurus will suggest synonyms such as domain, realm, and kingdom. Pick the synonym that fits the context of the passage.

Capture the original voice: In a paraphrase, you should try to communicate the original writer's opinions and feelings. Read the examples that follow.

Original News Report

> Councilman Davis Miller declared that he is tired of kids with skateboards taking over the city parks and parking lots.

- **Paraphrase lacking voice:** Councilman Miller commented about the teenage skateboarders gathering in the city parks and parking lots.
- **Paraphrase with the proper voice:** Councilman Miller complained about the teenage skateboarders overwhelming the city parks and parking lots.

English Language Learners

Not all English or bilingual dictionaries and thesauruses provide enough context to be helpful resources for students learning the English language. Encourage students to ask English-proficient partners to help them decide which words they find in their resources are appropriate synonyms.

Sample Paragraphs and Paraphrases

The following expository paragraph from a longer article describes tribes of early American people.

> The League of the Iroquois was a confederacy of Native American tribes living in what is now the state of New York. From east to west, these tribes were the Mohawk, Oneida, Onondaga, Cayuga, and Seneca. Archaeological evidence suggests that the Iroquois lived along the lower Great Lakes for several centuries before the first European settlers arrived in North America. For all this time, the League stood united against hostile tribes to the north, west, and south.

A student wrote the following paraphrase to demonstrate her understanding of the above paragraph.

> Five tribes of Native Americans living in the area of New York State formed a confederacy, which is like a nation, called the League of the Iroquois. The tribes were the Seneca, Cayuga, Onondaga, Oneida, and Mohawk. They lived along Lake Erie and Lake Ontario for hundreds of years before Europeans arrived on the continent. They acted as allies of one another against neighboring tribes.

The following paragraph is a brief published review of a play performed at an area theater.

> The new comedy, *Who, Me?*, at the local repertory theater is a major disappointment, considering the talent of the cast and the excellent musical accompaniment. The actors do the best they can with material that is at best trite and at worst boring. The playwright's political ranting obscures the plot, and there is no significant plot development.

A student wrote this paraphrase of the review, taking care to reflect the writer's opinion in his paraphrase.

> You might be wasting your time if you go to the repertory theater's comedy <u>Who, Me?</u> The main problem seems to be a poor script, and good actors and musicians aren't enough to save it. The author of the play goes on and on about his political beliefs, and nothing happens with the plot.

Sample Paragraphs and Paraphrases

Ask students to examine the first sample paraphrase carefully and to describe exactly what the student writer did. For example, she

- states the number of tribes (five) that are in the League,
- defines *confederacy,*
- lists the tribes in the opposite order from the original,
- specifies *Lake Erie and Lake Ontario* instead of using the original phrase, *Lower Great Lakes,* and
- uses equivalent wording, such as *hundreds of years* instead of *several centuries* or *Europeans* instead of *European settlers.*

Point out that some information added by the writer is probably the result of research: To explain *confederacy* and specify which of the Great Lakes are the lower ones, she may have checked a dictionary, encyclopedia, or atlas. Remind students that, in order to paraphrase effectively, they must be sure to understand the original text. If they pause to define words or research details as they read, it might be helpful to include that clarification in the paraphrase.

Paraphrasing a Paragraph

Remind students to try to remain true to the voice of the author in their paraphrase for the **Try It!** activity. Ask students to discuss the author's voice for each passage. How would they describe it and why?

- Paragraph 1: The voice is fairly casual, as shown by the use of the wording *was inevitably bad news.*
- Paragraph 2: The voice is somewhat formal, as shown by the use of such words as *structures, predate,* and *annals of history.*
- Paragraph 3: The voice is enthusiastic and casual, as shown by the use of *rosy prediction,* and *blistered opposing defenses.* The use of the specialized language *both lines are also intact* and the mention of *receivers, linebackers,* and *defensive backs* suggests that the writing is geared toward a knowledgeable audience.

✳ For more about voice, see SE pages 46–47.

After students have completed their paraphrase, have volunteers read their work out loud to classmates. Ask that more than one version of each paraphrase be read so that students can compare the versions.

490

Paraphrasing a Paragraph

Here are three sample paragraphs. As you read them, you will see that each one has a specific main idea and a distinct author's voice.

> There exists a common misconception that the spread of European settlers across North America was inevitably bad news for the wild animals on the continent. Certainly the populations of large predators, such as wolves, cougars, and grizzly bears, suffered almost to the point of extinction. Other animals, however, thrived even as the population of humans increased. White-tailed deer, for example, maintain far higher populations amid the cornfields of farm country than they ever did in a pre-Columbian forest. Likewise, raccoons, coyotes, and squirrels are all thought to be more populous now than ever before.

> Near Mexico City rise two structures called the Pyramid of the Sun and the Pyramid of the Moon. Built long before the coming of the conquistadores, they even predate the Aztecs by many hundreds of years. The two pyramids are part of the complex known as Teotihuacán. The people who built it have been lost from the annals of history. Teotihuacán was certainly a center of religion and ritual, but it had been abandoned for centuries before the great clash of cultures that occurred in Mexico about 1520.

> Coach Renault has a rosy prediction for the Clinton Cougars' chances in the upcoming Division I football season. Star quarterback Derek "Duke" Wilson returns, having led the conference in passing and touchdowns last year. Also returning is running back Jeff Roberts, who blistered opposing defenses and school record books with his performance last year. Both lines are also intact, and a promising array of underclassmen forms a solid nucleus of receivers, linebackers, and defensive backs.

Try It!

Paraphrase a paragraph. Paraphrase one of the paragraphs above. Communicate all important details and the author's point of view, in your own words. Use the strategies on page **488** to guide you.

Understanding Writing Assignments

Writing is really thinking on paper. The type of thinking that you do depends on the writing assignment. In an English class, you may be asked to analyze a poem or evaluate a newspaper article. In a history class, you may be asked to explain a piece of legislation or to apply an event to your own experience. The key to doing well on these writing assignments is to understand the requirements of each.

This chapter explains the six basic levels of thinking as they relate to various writing assignments. The levels are *recalling, understanding, applying, analyzing, synthesizing,* and *evaluating.* It is important to know that as you work on an assignment, you will often use more than one type of thinking.

- **Types of Assignments**
- **Levels of Thinking**
- **Planning Your Writing Time**

"I learn by going
 where I have to go."
—Theodore Roethke

Understanding Writing Assignments

Objectives

- learn to recognize three types of writing assignments
- practice the six levels of thinking
- learn how to plan writing time for an assignment

Explain to students that many of the concepts they will learn on the following pages are undoubtedly things they already do to a great extent, maybe even without being aware of it. By becoming aware of what they are doing and by learning about the different stages of the thinking process, they will be able to exercise greater control over how they approach assignments. They may also identify new ways of thinking. Improving their abilities in those areas will greatly improve their ability to learn.

Types of Assignments

Discuss students' prior experiences with writing assignments.

- What type of writing assignments do they like best?
- Do they prefer to have lots of choices or fewer choices?
- What has been their favorite writing assignment so far? Was it specific, open-ended, or a combination?
- If students are working on a writing project now, is the assignment specific, open-ended, or a combination?

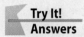
Try It!
Answers

1. combination
2. specific
3. open-ended

492

Types of Assignments

Throughout your school career, you will most often be assigned the following three basic types of writing.

Types	Examples
Specific You are given a specific topic.	Explain how an internal combustion engine works.
Open-ended You are given the chance to select your own topic.	Write a biographical essay about a person of significance who lived during the 1920s.
Combination You are given a subject area from which to choose a topic. This type of assignment is part specific and part open-ended.	Describe a key cultural event that occurred in the United States during the 1960s.

Try It!

Label each assignment below as open-ended, specific, or a combination.

1. Describe the features of a planet, a moon, or an asteroid in our solar system.
2. Explain the causes and effects of a tsunami.
3. Write a historical fiction story set in any time period.

Understanding Your Task

Different types of writing assignments require you to use different levels of thinking. These levels can range from simply recalling information to understanding, applying, analyzing, synthesizing, or evaluating it. (See the next page.) That is why it is so important that you clearly understand each assignment before you get started. Once you know exactly what you have to do, you can confidently plan, and carry out, your writing.

English Language Learners

Some students have trouble responding to writing prompts and directions for assignments because they fail to read them completely. Students may skip over small words, such as *or,* as they concentrate on the key words in the directions.

Explain that the word *or* in the first **Try It!** assignment example indicates that students have a choice of which item to describe. They are not being asked to describe all the items.

Understanding Writing Assignments **493**

Levels of Thinking

The chart on this page describes the levels of thinking inherent in different types of assignments; the next six pages give a closer look at each one.

Whenever you are asked to . . .		Be ready to . . .
RECALL		**Remember what you have learned.**
underline	circle	■ collect information
list	match	■ list details
name	label	■ identify or define key terms
cluster	define	■ remember main points
UNDERSTAND		**Explain what you have learned.**
explain	review	■ give examples
summarize	restate	■ restate important details
describe	cite	■ tell how something works
APPLY		**Use what you have learned.**
change	illustrate	■ select the most important details
do	model	■ organize information
demonstrate	show	■ explain a process
locate	organize	■ show how something works
ANALYZE		**Break down information.**
break down	rank	■ carefully examine a subject
examine	compare	■ identify important parts
contrast	classify	■ make connections and
tell why		comparisons
SYNTHESIZE		**Shape information into a new form.**
combine	connect	■ invent a better way of doing
speculate	design	something
compose	create	■ blend the old with the new
predict	develop	■ predict or hypothesize (make
invent	imagine	an educated guess)
EVALUATE		**Judge the worth of information.**
recommend	judge	■ point out a subject's strengths
criticize	argue	and weaknesses
persuade	rate	■ evaluate its clarity, accuracy,
convince	assess	value, and so on
weigh		■ convince others of its value/worth

Learning

Levels of Thinking

Ask students to examine the order in which the levels of thinking are presented. Does this order seem important? (They should agree that it does.) What do they notice about the sequence of the different skills? Guide them to the following realization:

- The skills are presented in an order that goes from basic to more complex.
- The first level, recall, requires simply that the thinker have memorized information.
- Progressively, at each level, the thinker engages more deeply with the information—understanding it, using it, examining its component parts, and combining it with other related ideas.
- At the highest level, the thinker is ready to evaluate the information—to express his or her opinion of it.

Struggling Learners

Help students realize that they probably have experience in thinking at all six levels. For example, they may have

- baked brownies (apply);
- compared two cell phones before deciding which one to buy (analyze);

- made a prediction about what would happen during a movie (synthesize); or
- recommended a CD to a friend (evaluate).

Ask students to give more examples for each level.

Advanced Learners

To extend students' understanding of all six levels of thinking, have small groups choose a nonfiction article from a magazine or newspaper. Then have them compose a writing assignment (such as the ones in Try It! on SE page 492) based on that article, to address as many of the levels of thinking as possible.

Recalling Information

Talk about ways to improve students' recall of information. Suggest techniques such as the following:

- Review class notes carefully and consistently. Remind students of the tips for reviewing on SE page 470.
- Make flash cards. This is common way to learn vocabulary words, but it also works well for other kinds of information. Students write a basic concept on one side of the card and put important facts about it on the other. To review the information, they look at the concept and try to recall all the facts listed on the other side of the card.
- Work with a study partner and quiz each other about important information.
- For a simple series of facts, try creating or finding a mnemonic device (memory aid) such as a rhyme. For example, many people remember the number of days in a month by reciting, *Thirty days hath September . . .*

494

Recalling Information

The most basic type of thinking you use in school is **recalling**. This type of thinking is needed when you are asked to remember and repeat what you have learned in class.

You recall when you . . .
- supply details such as dates or other facts.
- identify or define key terms.
- remember main points.

Recalling

Your teachers will give very few writing assignments that only require recalling information. However, you may encounter test questions that ask you simply to recall. Multiple-choice, fill-in-the-blank, and short-answer questions are examples of test questions asking students to recall information.

Directions: Underline the correct answer in each set of parentheses.

1. The civil rights leader who, in the spring of 1941, threatened to organize a march in Washington to protest racial segregation was *(Frederick Douglass, A. Philip Randolph)*.

2. On June 6, 1944, American, British, and Canadian armies invaded the mainland of Europe at *(Berlin, the Ardennes Forest, Normandy)*.

Directions: Define each term by completing the sentence.

1. The "dollar-a-year" men were _____

_____

2. Lobbyists are _____

_____

3. Rosie the Riveter was _____

_____

Try It!

Review your notes from a recent classroom lecture, underlining key ideas. Set the notes aside and write down all of the details you can recall. Check your notes again to see how much you were able to remember.

Understanding Information

Understanding is a level of thinking that is more advanced than simply recalling facts and information. You show that you understand something when you can write about it in your own words.

You understand when you . . .

- explain how something works.
- provide reasons for something.
- summarize or rewrite information in your own words.

Learning

Understanding

Often, you will be asked to show understanding by writing an essay or a paragraph. The following assignment asks the student to explain an executive order, which requires that the student understand it. (Graphic organizers, charts, or maps can also be used to show understanding.)

Directions: Explain some of the reasons for President Roosevelt's signing of Executive Order #8802, which prohibited racial discrimination in hiring, in March of 1941.

By 1941, the president could see that the United States would be drawn into World War II, which was already being waged in Europe and China. He felt that it was very important for American industries to be working at top speed. Still, many companies in the South were refusing to hire African American workers. An important civil rights leader named A. Philip Randolph was trying to organize a march in Washington, D.C., to protest this discrimination. Roosevelt was afraid this march would disrupt the country. He made a deal with Randolph and signed the executive order banning discrimination in exchange for the march being called off.

 Try It!

Write a paragraph that summarizes a detailed newspaper article. Be sure to use your own words.

Understanding Information

To make students aware of the vast difference between understanding and simply recalling, give the following examples of information students may recall but not understand:

- How many students recall the formula for Einstein's Theory of Relativity ($E=mc^2$)? How many of them can explain what it means?
- How many students recall the words to "The Star-Spangled Banner"? How many can explain what the song means?

Note also that people sometimes become familiar with words before understanding their meaning. For example, in "The Star-Spangled Banner," what do the words *spangled* and *ramparts* mean?

English Language Learners

Some students are able to demonstrate comprehension of content area information by filling in graphic organizers. Emphasize the importance of taking the time to use graphic organizers to plan their response to all assignments that call for more than recalling facts. Model using a graphic organizer to respond to the sample directions.

Have students turn in their graphic organizers along with their responses so that you have a more comprehensive view of their level of understanding.

Applying Information

Point out that there are two different ways of applying information presented here.

1. Applying information to a physical task. This is described in the example of using a manual to set up a computer. Other examples include using a recipe to bake a cake or reading a map to find a street. Applying information to a task is common in everyday life.
2. Applying information to a concept or an idea. This is illustrated in the sample paragraph and in the **Try It!** prompt. Students are often asked to apply information in order to demonstrate comprehension.

Note that both applications require advancing from simple recall to applying information.

Before students begin the **Try It!** activity, ask them to discuss how the question relates to the idea of applying information.

- It's important first to understand what gasoline is and how it is used globally.
- Then that knowledge is *applied* by imagining a world suddenly without gasoline.

496

Applying Information

When you are **applying** information, you must be able to use what you have learned to demonstrate, show, or model something. For example, using a manual to help you set up your computer requires you to apply the information from the manual to the job.

You apply when you . . .

- think about how you can use information.
- organize information so that it meets your specific needs.

Applying

Sometimes you will be asked to apply one type of information to another situation or idea. This assignment asks the writer to apply a specific concept to a foreign-policy decision made by Germany during World War II.

Assignment: Define the concept of *Lebensraum* and show how it applied to Nazi foreign policy during World War II.

The term *Lebensraum*, which means "living space" in German, was the idea that people should spread out from their homeland to occupy lands around them. The term became Hitler's main motive for World War II, and he saw Eastern Europe as a desirable "living space" for the German people. The first phase of Hitler's plan was to invade and take over countries such as Czechoslovakia and Poland. In these countries, he set up concentration camps meant to depopulate the countryside and make room for his people. At the same time, Hitler initiated so-called "eugenics" programs to produce more Germans to fill the emptied space. War and genocide were the natural results of applying the concept of *Lebensraum*. Whenever a country claims that it needs "living space," its neighbors should prepare for war.

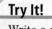

Try It!

Write a paragraph explaining what would happen if there were suddenly no gasoline in the world.

English Language Learners

Students may not recognize that the sample assignment asks students to recall (*define* the concept) as well as to apply (*show* how the concept is applied to a policy). Guide students to find *both* of the verbs in the assignment.

Explain to students that assignments frequently ask them to define a concept before explaining or using it in a new context. To help students make sure they know what they are being asked to do, tell them to circle or write down all the verbs in the directions when they read an assignment or test prompt.

Learning

Analyzing Information

You **analyze** information when you are able to break it down into parts that you can further explain.

You analyze when you . . .

- show how things are similar or different.
- identify which things are most important.
- arrange things in groups or categories.
- describe a process.
- discuss causes and/or effects.

Analyzing

Assignments that ask you to analyze information may require you to compare and contrast, discuss causes and effects, and so on. In this assignment, the writer discusses the causes of dramatic changes in the capital of the United States.

Assignment: In 1939, Washington, D.C., was a small city on the banks of the Potomac River. By 1945, it was one of the most important places in the world. Why did it change so much and so quickly?

During the 1930s, many citizens of the United States were "isolationists." They wanted this country to keep to itself. When World War II broke out in 1939, the U.S. had a small army. However, when the U.S. became involved in the war, isolationists could do nothing to stop it. The army expanded into one of the world's largest, and industries built more ships, tanks, and airplanes than anyone thought possible. This expansion was managed from Washington, D.C. Every bit of office space was used, and many temporary buildings were erected for government offices. More African Americans and women were hired than ever before, and the city more than doubled in population. Due to its distance from the fighting, Washington became the center for the Allied command.

Try It!

Think of a recent news event. Write a detailed paragraph describing the actions (causes) that led up to the event.

Analyzing Information

Point out that since analysis involves identifying different parts of information, a graphic organizer can be of great help in arranging all those parts in the right order. Review the use of graphic organizers that are especially suited to analysis.

- **Venn diagram:** Organizes details for a comparison-contrast essay by providing spaces for notes about how two items are different and how they are similar.
- **T-chart:** Organizes contrasting details in two columns so details can be viewed side-by-side.
- **Cluster chart:** Provides spaces for noting the component parts of an idea.
- **Cause-effect organizer:** Provides spaces for notes about causes and the effects that resulted from them.

✱ For more examples of graphic organizers, see SE pages 588–589.

English Language Learners

Some students have difficulty choosing the graphic organizer that is most appropriate to a specific assignment or test prompt. Provide an opportunity for them to see how their classmates make this choice.

- Have groups of students decide which graphic organizer they would use to plan a response to the sample assignment.

- Invite the groups to share their choices and their reasons with the class before they read the sample response.
- Did the groups all choose the same graphic organizer or different ones?
- Could different organizers work for this assignment or is there just one that is appropriate?

Synthesizing Information

Explain that synthesis combines complementary parts into a whole idea. At this level, thinkers contribute their own point of view, even imagination, to transform information. More than other levels of thinking, synthesis requires creativity.

Emphasize that the process of synthesis includes quite a bit of experimentation because ideas and details can be combined in so many different ways. When faced with a task that requires synthesis, students might try

- sharing their ideas with other people,
- writing more than one version of a project to see which works best, or
- keeping a journal to document their ideas for approaching a project.

498

Synthesizing Information

When you employ reasoning to combine parts into a whole, you are **synthesizing**.

You synthesize when you . . .

- add new ideas to existing information.
- use information to create a story, a poem, or other creative work.
- predict what will happen based on information that you have learned.

Synthesizing

The same thing that makes synthesizing a challenge also makes it fun: you get to use your imagination. This assignment asks the writer to use information to create imaginary diary entries about life in Washington, D.C., during World War II.

Assignment: Imagine that you are a "government girl" or a "dollar-a-year man" arriving in Washington, D.C., early in 1942. Write several diary entries about your life in this new city.

March 8, 1942—I arrived by bus after a long trip north from Montgomery, Alabama. There were lots of other young women on the bus, and the terminal in Washington was absolutely full of soldiers. In a very old building, I found a tiny apartment that I am sharing with five other girls.

March 12, 1942—Getting a job was easy because everyone needs workers who know how to type. I am working for the city draft board, helping young men (boys, really) fill out registration forms. We have a temporary office set up in a high school. Some of the boys act really tough, but I can tell that most of them are scared.

May 1, 1942—The cherry blossoms are blooming, and it is really beautiful. I got a letter from my brother Charlie, who is in the army in North Africa. I can't help but think of him every time I process new draftees.

▶ Try It!

Imagine living in the United States during World War II. Write several diary entries about what you might see and experience.

English Language Learners

Students who have not recently studied the conditions in the United States during World War II will have difficulty with the **Try It!** activity. If students have limited knowledge of the topic, have them write diary entries about living in their home country during a previous era.

Evaluating Information

When you are asked to express your opinion about an important issue, or to discuss the good and the bad points of a subject, you are **evaluating**. Evaluating is an advanced form of thinking that requires more thorough understanding and analysis of information.

You evaluate when you . . .

- give your opinion and support it.
- identify both the good and the bad points of a subject.

Evaluating

An effective evaluation is based on information. It often begins by identifying an overall opinion, or evaluation, and then adds supporting facts and details. This assignment asks the writer to evaluate the effects of a historical period.

Assignment: Can you think of two positive effects of the United States' involvement in World War II? If so, describe and discuss them.

The United States' involvement in World War II helped improve racial equality in the country. African Americans fought in the armed forces and performed very well. The Tuskegee Airmen, African American fighter pilots trained in Alabama, were one notable example. Besides that, minorities were hired for war jobs in areas that were closed to them previously.

Another positive effect was the end of the United States' isolationism. This country helped form the United Nations after the war and invited the organization to have its offices in New York. This showed that the U.S. was ready to play a positive role in world affairs.

Learning

Try It!

Write a paragraph discussing some of the positive or negative aspects of a topic you are studying in one of your classes.

Evaluating Information

Point out that evaluating—the most complex level of thinking—involves not only stating an opinion or preference but also giving reasons for it. This is something that people sometimes don't do in everyday conversation.

Encourage students to practice pausing to consider the reasons for their opinions. Emphasize that they use the skill of evaluating every day, both in and out of school.

Planning Your Writing Time

Students may have different needs as writers, and each project will have different requirements (a research report, for example, usually requires more prewriting time than a personal narrative). Encourage students to experiment with different schedules to see what suits them best.

When you give a writing assignment, consider providing a suggested writing schedule as well. Encourage students to meet with you to customize the schedule to suit their own writing habits and to meet the deadlines.

Also encourage students to use a daily planner to help them keep track of their school responsibilities. In it, they should write down
- their daily class schedule,
- homework and writing assignments,
- writing schedules,
- test dates and paper due dates, and
- school events.

500

Planning Your Writing Time

Be sure that you completely understand a writing assignment before you begin. Use the following guidelines.

1. **Read the directions** carefully.
2. **Focus on key words**—"describe," "evaluate," and so on—in order to understand the requirements of the assignment.
3. **Ask questions** if necessary.
4. **Plan your time** so that you can complete your work without rushing. (See the schedule below.)
5. **Review and revise** your writing.

The following schedule was created by a student who was asked to write a research report for a history class. The report was due in two weeks.

Sample Schedule

Week One	Week Two
Day 1 PREWRITING • Review the assignment. • Search for a topic.	**Day 1 REVISING** • Revise the draft for ideas, organization, and voice.
Day 2 PREWRITING • Choose a topic. • Start doing research.	**Day 2 REVISING** • Ask a peer to review the draft.
Day 3 PREWRITING • Gather and organize details. • Find a focus for the report.	**Day 3 REVISING** • Check word choice and sentence fluency.
Day 4 WRITING • Begin the first draft.	**Day 4 EDITING** • Check the report for convention errors. • Proofread the final copy.
Day 5 WRITING • Complete the first draft.	**Day 5 PUBLISHING** • Share the final copy.

Scheduling a Timed Writing

If you must complete your writing in one sitting, such as during a single class period, it is especially important to plan your work. For example, you might use 5 to 10 minutes at the beginning of the period to plan your writing, 30 to 40 minutes to write your draft, and 5 to 10 minutes at the end to make any necessary changes.

English Language Learners

During a timed writing, students may have difficulty conceptualizing the organization necessary to write effectively, because of the demands of writing in a second language. Remind students to use graphic organizers when they gather and organize details during the planning step of any timed writing task.

Improving Your Vocabulary

The words you know and use are important for three reasons: (1) They shape your thinking; (2) They influence how you communicate with your world; and (3) They affect how the world responds to you. You can improve your vocabulary by studying new subjects, having new experiences, increasing the amount of reading that you do, and listening carefully to other people. (Learning about any new subject requires learning the vocabulary that goes with it.)

This chapter contains a detailed glossary of prefixes, suffixes, and roots that will help you to learn many new words. By understanding these different word parts, you'll be able to figure out the meaning of even challenging words like *megalopolis* and *psychosomatic*. Consider this glossary as a special resource, much like a dictionary, that you can refer to again and again.

- **Understanding Word Parts**
- **Prefixes**
- **Suffixes**
- **Roots**

"We all come from the factory wired for language."
—Patricia T. O'Conner

Improving Your Vocabulary

Objectives

- use prefixes, suffixes, and roots to build vocabulary
- improve vocabulary skills

Explain to students that this section takes a different approach to building vocabulary than they may be used to. Students may be most familiar with learning words in context or by memorizing their meaning. In this section, they will learn instead how they can analyze an unfamiliar word by

- breaking it down into parts,
- learning the meaning of each part, and then
- making an informed guess about the word's meaning, based on the meaning of the parts.

Students will find that they can get a good idea of the meaning of many unfamiliar words by first learning the meaning of the parts that compose them.

Understanding Word Parts

Have students do the **Try It!** activity with a partner. Encourage partners to discuss possible definitions and to think of similar words they know.

Try It!
Answers

1. *geo = earth, centri = center, -ic = like*; *geocentric* = having the world at the center
2. *em = into, path = feeling, -ic = like*; *empathetic* = taking another's feelings in, as if they were your own
3. *syn = together, chron = time, -ize = to make*; *synchronize* = to make the timing the same
4. *volcan = fire, ology = the study or science of*; *volcanology* = the study of volcanoes
5. *bibl = book, phil = love*; *bibliophile* = book lover

Understanding Word Parts

Some English words such as *ground, age,* and *clock* are called base words. They cannot be broken down into word parts. However, many English words are made of prefixes, suffixes, and roots. Knowing the meanings of these parts can help you figure out the meanings of the words they form.

Unicyclist combines . . .

- the prefix *uni* (meaning *one*)
- the root *cycle* (meaning *wheel*)
- the suffix *ist* (meaning *a person who*)
  A *unicyclist* is a person who rides a one-wheeled vehicle.

Monochromatic combines . . .

- the prefix *mono* (meaning *one*)
- the root *chrom* (meaning *color*)
- the suffix *ate* (meaning *make*)
- the suffix *ic* (meaning *nature of*)
  A *monochromatic* painting is made of one color.

Try It!

Look through the following pages of prefixes, suffixes, and roots. Then write down the parts, their meanings, and a final definition for each of the following words.

1. geocentric
2. empathetic
3. synchronize
4. volcanology
5. bibliophile

Learning New Words

You already know and use many common prefixes, suffixes, and roots every day. To improve your speaking and writing vocabulary, study the meanings of prefixes, suffixes, and roots that are not familiar to you. The following pages contain nearly 500 word parts. Here is how to use these pages:

1. Scan the pages until you come to a word part that is new to you.
2. Learn its meaning and at least one of the sample words listed.
3. Apply your knowledge as you encounter new words in your course work.

Prefixes

Prefixes are those word parts that come *before* the root words (*pre* = before). Depending upon its meaning, a prefix changes the intent, or sense, of the base word. As a skilled reader, you will want to know the meanings of the most common prefixes in order to figure out the meanings of unfamiliar words.

a, an [not, without] amoral (without a sense of moral responsibility), atypical, atom (not cuttable), apathy (without feeling), anesthesia (without sensation)

ab, abs, a [from, away] abnormal, abduct, absent, avert (turn away)

acro [high] acropolis (high city), acrobat, acronym, acrophobia (fear of height)

ambi, amb [both, around] ambidextrous (skilled with both hands), ambiguous

amphi [both] amphibious (living on both land and water), amphitheater

ante [before] antedate, anteroom, antebellum, antecedent (happening before)

anti, ant [against] anticommunist, antidote, anticlimax, antacid

be [on, away] bedeck, belabor, bequest, bestow, beloved

bene, bon [well] benefit, benefactor, benevolent, benediction, bonanza, bonus

bi, bis, bin [both, double, twice] bicycle, biweekly, bilateral, biscuit, binoculars

by [side, close, near] bypass, bystander, by-product, bylaw, byline

cata [down, against] catalog, catapult, catastrophe, cataclysm

cerebro [brain] cerebral, cerebellum

circum, circ [around] circumference, circumnavigate, circumspect, circular

co, con, col, com [together, with] copilot, conspire, collect, compose

coni [dust] coniosis (disease that comes from inhaling dust)

contra, counter [against] controversy, contradict, counterpart

de [from, down] demote, depress, degrade, deject, deprive

deca [ten] decade, decathlon, decapod

di [two, twice] divide, dilemma, dilute, dioxide, dipole, ditto

dia [through, between] diameter, diagonal, diagram, dialogue (speech between people)

dis, dif [apart, away, reverse] dismiss, distort, distinguish, diffuse

dys [badly, ill] dyspepsia (digesting badly), dystrophy, dysentery

em, en [in, into] embrace, enslave

epi [upon] epidermis (upon the skin, outer layer of skin), epitaph, epithet

eu [well] eulogize (speak well of, praise), euphony, euphemism, euphoria

ex, e, ec, ef [out] expel (drive out), ex-mayor, exorcism, eject, eccentric (out of the center position), efflux, effluent

extra, extro [beyond, outside] extraordinary (beyond the ordinary), extrovert, extracurricular

for [away, off] forswear (to renounce an oath)

fore [before in time] forecast, foretell (to tell beforehand), foreshadow

hemi, demi, semi [half] hemisphere, demitasse, semicircle (half of a circle)

hex [six] hexameter, hexagon

homo [man] Homo sapiens, homicide (killing man)

hyper [over, above] hypersensitive (overly sensitive), hyperactive

hypo [under] hypodermic (under the skin), hypothesis

il, ir, in, im [not] illegal, irregular, incorrect, immoral

in, il, im [into] inject, inside, illuminate, illustrate, impose, implant, imprison

infra [beneath] infrared, infrasonic

inter [between] intercollegiate, interfere, intervene, interrupt (break between)

intra [within] intramural, intravenous (within the veins)

intro [into, inward] introduce, introvert (turn inward)

macro [large, excessive] macrodent (having large teeth), macrocosm

mal [badly, poorly] maladjusted, malady, malnutrition, malfunction

meta [beyond, after, with] metaphor, metamorphosis, metaphysical

mis [incorrect, bad] misuse, misprint

miso [hate] misanthrope, misogynist

mono [one] monoplane, monotone, monocle, monochrome

Learning

Prefixes

To demonstrate how prefixes change meaning, write on the board a list of words with the same root but different prefixes. Talk about the meaning of each prefix and each word. For example, using the base word: *cede (to move, yield, go)* and its variant form *ceed,* create this list:

- *antecedent*—something that goes before
- *concede*—to yield (literally, move together with)
- *exceed*—to go outside of, or beyond, what was expected
- *intercede*—to act as a go-between
- *precede*—to go first, be in front of
- *proceed*—to go forward (note variant spelling of root, *ceed*)
- *recede*—to go backward
- *secede*—to withdraw (literally, go to the side)
- *succeed*—to come next and, by extension, to turn out well (*suc-* being a form of the prefix *sub-,* which can mean *near* as well as *under*)

Advanced Learners

To extend students' practice using prefixes and suffixes, challenge them with the following game.

- Divide students into two teams. Name a prefix or suffix from the lists in their texts.
- Give each team two minutes to write down every word they can think of that contains that word part.

- Then have the teams compare lists. Any words that appear on both teams' lists should be crossed out.
- Then, read and count up the additional words. Each word is one point.

After a few rounds, tally up the points. The team with the most points wins.

Have the teams work together to compile their lists in a notebook for class reference. Tell them to write the word part and definition at the top and list all the words and their definitions.

Talk about common errors in identifying prefixes and give examples of tricky words.

- *anti-* and *ante-*: They sound the same but are not. *Antebellum* (note the root *belli*) means *before the war*, not *against war*.
- *inter-* and *intra-*: Suggest that students try remembering that the prefix with the letter *r within* it (*intra-*) means *within*. *Intrastate* means *within a state*. *Interstate* means *between states*—students can think of an *interstate highway,* which goes between states.
- *for-* and *fore-*: Again, these sound-alike prefixes mean different things, and they sometimes lead to sound-alike words. To *forgo* means to do without something (literally, *go away* from it). To *forego* means to *go before*.
- *il-, im-, in-* [not] and *il-, im-, in-* [into]: These **prefix groups** *(see below)* look the same but have different meanings. A good (but not foolproof) clue to their meaning is that *not* prefixes tend to form adjectives, while *into* prefixes tend to go with verbs.

multi [many] multiply, multiform
neo [new] neopaganism, neoclassic, neophyte, neonatal
non [not] nontaxable (not taxed), nontoxic, nonexistent, nonsense
ob, of, op, oc [toward, against] obstruct, offend, oppose, occur
oct [eight] octagon, octameter, octave, octopus
paleo [ancient] paleoanthropology (pertaining to ancient humans), paleontology (study of ancient life-forms)
para [beside, almost] parasite (one who eats beside or at the table of another), paraphrase, paramedic, parallel, paradox
penta [five] pentagon (figure or building having five angles or sides), pentameter, pentathlon
per [throughout, completely] pervert (completely turn wrong, corrupt), perfect, perceive, permanent, persuade
peri [around] perimeter (measurement around an area), periphery, periscope, pericardium, period
poly [many] polygon (figure having many angles or sides), polygamy, polyglot, polychrome
post [after] postpone, postwar, postscript, posterity
pre [before] prewar, preview, precede, prevent, premonition
pro [forward, in favor of] project (throw forward), progress, promote, prohibition
pseudo [false] pseudonym (false or assumed name), pseudopodia
quad [four] quadruple (four times as much), quadriplegic, quadratic, quadrant

quint [five] quintuplet, quintuple, quintet, quintile
re [back, again] reclaim, revive, revoke, rejuvenate, retard, reject, return
retro [backward] retrospective (looking backward), retroactive, retrorocket
se [aside] seduce (lead aside), secede, secrete, segregate
self [by oneself] self-determination, selfish, self-employed, self-service
sesqui [one and a half] sesquicentennial (one and one-half centuries)
sex, sest [six] sexagenarian (sixty years old), sexennial, sextant, sextuplet, sestet
sub [under] submerge (put under), submarine, substitute, subsoil
suf, sug, sup, sus [from under] sufficient, suffer, suggest, support, suspend
super, supr [above, over, more] supervise, superman, supernatural, supreme
syn, sym, sys, syl [with, together] system, synthesis, synchronize (time together), synonym, sympathy, symphony, syllable
trans, tra [across, beyond] transoceanic, transmit (send across), transfusion
tri [three] tricycle, triangle, tripod, tristate
ultra [beyond, exceedingly] ultramodern, ultraviolet, ultraconservative
un [not, release] unfair, unnatural, unknown
under [beneath] underground, underlying
uni [one] unicycle, uniform, unify, universe, unique (one of a kind)
vice [in place of] vice president, viceroy, vice admiral

Numerical Prefixes

Prefix	Symbol	Multiples and Submultiples	Equivalent	Prefix	Symbol	Multiples and Submultiples	Equivalent
tera	T	10^{12}	trillionfold	centi	c	10^{-2}	hundredth part
giga	G	10^{9}	billionfold	milli	m	10^{-3}	thousandth part
mega	M	10^{6}	millionfold	micro	u	10^{-6}	millionth part
kilo	k	10^{3}	thousandfold	nano	n	10^{-9}	billionth part
hecto	h	10^{2}	hundredfold	pico	p	10^{-12}	trillionth part
deka	da	10	tenfold	femto	f	10^{-15}	quadrillionth part
deci	d	10^{-1}	tenth part	atto	a	10^{-18}	quintillionth part

Teaching Tip: Prefix Groups

Explain to students that the variation in spelling within a group of prefixes is usually a result of the way the prefix combines with the word part adjacent to it. For example, here are guidelines for forming words with the prefix *in-* (and related forms) meaning *not:*

- Use *il-* if the next letter is *l* (*illegible*).
- Use *ir-* if the next letter is *r* (*irreversible*).
- Use *im-* if the next letter is *m* or *p* (*immobile* or *imperfect*).
- Use *in-* before other letters (*inadequate, incomplete, infelicitous . . .*).

- Sometimes the related prefix *un-* is used instead (*unbelievable, uncommon, ungrateful*).

Note that, while there are exceptions, students will see that these ideas are generally true and can be applied to other prefixes as well.

Suffixes

Suffixes come at the end of a word. Very often a suffix will tell you what kind of word it is part of (noun, adverb, adjective, and so on). For example, words ending in *-ly* are usually adverbs.

able, ible [able, can do] capable, agreeable, edible, visible (can be seen)

ade [result of action] blockade (the result of a blocking action), lemonade

age [act of, state of, collection of] salvage (act of saving), storage, forage

al [relating to] sensual, gradual, manual, natural (relating to nature)

algia [pain] neuralgia (nerve pain)

an, ian [native of, relating to] Canadian, African, Floridian

ance, ancy [action, process, state] assistance, allowance, defiance, truancy

ant [performing, agent] assistant, servant

ary, ery, ory [relating to, quality, place where] dictionary, bravery, dormitory

ate [cause, make] liquidate, segregate (cause a group to be set aside)

cian [having a certain skill or art] musician, beautician, magician, physician

cule, ling [very small] molecule, ridicule, duckling (very small duck), sapling

cy [action, function] hesitancy, prophecy, normalcy (function in a normal way)

dom [quality, realm, office] freedom, kingdom, wisdom (quality of being wise)

ee [one who receives the action] employee, nominee (one who is nominated), refugee

en [made of, make] silken, frozen, oaken (made of oak), wooden, lighten

ence, ency [action, state of, quality] urgency, difference, conference

er, or [one who, that which] baker, miller, teacher, racer, amplifier, doctor

escent [in the process of] adolescent (in the process of becoming an adult), obsolescent, convalescent

ese [a native of, the language of] Japanese, Vietnamese, Portuguese

esis, osis [action, process, condition] genesis, hypnosis, neurosis, osmosis

ess [female] actress, goddess, lioness

et, ette [a small one, group] midget, octet, baronet, majorette

fic [making, causing] scientific, specific

ful [full of] frightful, careful, helpful

fy [make] fortify (make strong), simplify, amplify

hood [order, condition, quality] manhood, womanhood, brotherhood

ic [nature of, like] metallic (of the nature of metal), heroic, poetic, acidic

ice [condition, state, quality] justice, malice

id, ide [a thing connected to or belonging to] fluid, fluoride

ile [relating to, suited for, capable of] missile, juvenile, senile (related to being old)

ine [nature of] feminine, genuine, medicine

ion, sion, tion [act of, state of, result of] contagion, aversion, infection (state of being infected)

ish [origin, nature, resembling] foolish, Irish, clownish (resembling a clown)

ism [system, manner, condition, characteristic] heroism, alcoholism, Communism

ist [one who, that which] artist, dentist

ite [nature of, quality of, mineral product] Israelite, dynamite, graphite, sulfite

ity, ty [state of, quality] captivity, clarity

ive [causing, making] abusive (causing abuse), exhaustive

ize [make] emphasize, publicize, idolize

less [without] baseless, careless (without care), artless, fearless, helpless

ly [like, manner of] carelessly, forcefully, quickly, lovingly

ment [act of, state of, result] contentment, amendment (state of amending)

ness [state of] carelessness, kindness

oid [resembling] asteroid, spheroid, tabloid, anthropoid

ology [study, science, theory] anthropology, biology, geology, neurology

ous [full of, having] gracious, nervous, spacious, vivacious (full of life)

ship [office, state, quality, skill] friendship, authorship, dictatorship

some [like, apt, tending to] lonesome, threesome, gruesome

tude [state of, condition of] gratitude, multitude (condition of being many), aptitude

ure [state of, act, process, rank] culture, literature, rupture (state of being broken)

ward [in the direction of] eastward, forward, backward

y [inclined to, tend to] cheery, crafty, faulty

Learning

Suffixes

Explain to students that suffixes can often be used to change one part of speech into another—few prefixes do this. Challenge students to identify such suffixes and use them to change one part of speech into another. For example:

- Verbs into nouns—*run, runner*; *believe, believer*; *argue, argument*; *escape, escapee*
- Nouns into verbs: *category, categorize*; *beauty, beautify*
- Nouns into adjectives: *wood, wooden*; *beauty, beautiful*; *hope, hopeless*; *peril, perilous*
- Adjectives into nouns: *happy, happiness*
- Verbs into adjectives: *inhabit, inhabitable*; *instruct, instructive*
- Adjectives into adverbs: *bad, badly*
- Adjectives into verbs: *active, activate*

Roots

Expand a little on what makes a word part a root rather than a prefix or suffix. (It expresses the word's basic idea, much as a topic sentence expresses a paragraph's basic idea.)

Note that while a word may or may not contain a prefix or suffix, it must contain at least one root. Students will have noticed as they did the **Try It!** activity on SE page 502 that words can have more than one root. Words with two or more roots are like compound words (two words joined into one, either with or without a hyphen). In compound words, the two parts have equal or nearly equal value. Give examples of words with two roots such as the following:

- *manufactured* (although it isn't used exactly the same way, the roots literally form the compound *handmade*),
- *geothermal* (having to do with the *heat* of the *earth*)
- *omnivore* (describing a creature that *eats everything*)

Challenge students to contribute other words that contain two roots and to talk about how each root participates equally in conveying the word's meaning.

506

Roots

A *root* is a base upon which other words are built. Knowing the root of a difficult word can take you a long way toward figuring out its meaning—even without a dictionary. For that reason, learning the following roots will be very valuable to you as you read.

acer, acid, acri [bitter, sour, sharp] acrid, acerbic, acidity (sourness), acrimony

acu [sharp] acute, acupuncture

ag, agi, ig, act [do, move, go] agent (doer), agenda (things to do), agitate, navigate (move by sea), ambiguous (going both ways), action

ali, allo, alter [other] alias (a person's other name), alibi, alien (from another place), alloy, alter (change to another form)

alt [high, deep] altimeter (a device for measuring heights), altitude

am, amor [love, liking] amiable, amorous, enamored

anni, annu, enni [year] anniversary, annually (yearly), centennial (occurring once in 100 years)

anthrop [man] anthropology (study of mankind), philanthropy (love of mankind), misanthrope (hater of mankind)

anti [old] antique, antiquated, antiquity

arch [chief, first, rule] archangel (chief angel), architect (chief worker), archaic (first, very early), monarchy (rule by one person), matriarchy (rule by the mother)

aster, astr [star] aster (star flower), asterisk, asteroid, astronomy (star law), astronaut (star traveler, space traveler)

aud, aus [hear, listen] audible (can be heard), auditorium, audio, audition, auditory, audience, ausculate

aug, auc [increase] augur, augment (add to; increase), auction

auto, aut [self] autograph (self-writing), automobile (self-moving vehicle), author, automatic (self-acting), autobiography

belli [war] rebellion, belligerent (warlike or hostile)

bibl [book] Bible, bibliography (list of books), bibliomania (craze for books), bibliophile (book lover)

bio [life] biology (study of life), biography, biopsy (cut living tissue for examination)

brev [short] abbreviate, brevity, brief

cad, cas [to fall] cadaver, cadence, caducous (falling off), cascade

calor [heat] calorie (a unit of heat), calorify (to make hot), caloric

cap, cip, cept [take] capable, capacity, capture, reciprocate, accept, except, concept

capit, capt [head] decapitate (to remove the head from), capital, captain, caption

carn [flesh] carnivorous (flesh eating), incarnate, reincarnation

caus, caut [burn, heat] caustic, cauterize (to make hot, to burn)

cause, cuse, cus [cause, motive] because, excuse (to attempt to remove the blame or cause), accusation

ced, ceed, cede, cess [move, yield, go, surrender] procedure, secede (move aside from), proceed (move forward), cede (yield), concede, intercede, precede, recede, success

centri [center] concentric, centrifugal, centripetal, eccentric (out of center)

chrom [color] chrome, chromosome (color body in genetics), chromosphere, monochrome (one color), polychrome

chron [time] chronological (in order of time), chronometer (time measured), chronicle (record of events in time), synchronize (make time with, set time together)

cide, cise [cut down, kill] suicide (killing of self), homicide (human killer), pesticide (pest killer), germicide (germ killer), precise (cut exactly right), incision, scissors

cit [to call, start] incite, citation, cite

civ [citizen] civic (relating to a citizen), civil, civilian, civilization

clam, claim [cry out] exclamation, clamor, proclamation, reclamation, acclaim

clud, clus, claus [shut] include (to take in), conclude, claustrophobia (abnormal fear of being shut up, confined), recluse (one who shuts himself away from others)

cognosc, gnosi [know] recognize (to know again), incognito (not known), prognosis (forward knowing), diagnosis

---

Advanced Learners

As an enrichment activity to the study of word parts, encourage interested students to research the Latin origin of many English words.

Point out that ancient Romans spoke Latin. As they conquered different regions in Europe, their language spread. Over time, the Latin language in each region developed into separate languages, such as Italian, Spanish, and French. Therefore, there are common word roots in all of these "sister languages."

Challenge students to list English words with Latin roots and then find Italian, Spanish, and French words that use the same root. For example:

English: *transcribe* means "to write down"

Latin root: *scrib* means "write"

All three of the following words mean "to write."

Italian: *scrivere*

Spanish: *escribir*

French: *écriver*

cord, cor, cardi [heart] cordial (hearty, heartfelt), concord, discord, courage, encourage (put heart into), discourage (take heart out of), core, coronary, cardiac

corp [body] corporation (a legal body), corpse, corpulent

cosm [universe, world] cosmic, cosmos (the universe), cosmopolitan (world citizen), cosmonaut, microcosm, macrocosm

crat, cracy [rule, strength] democratic, autocracy

crea [create] creature (anything created), recreation, creation, creator

cred [believe] creed (statement of beliefs), credo (a creed), credence (belief), credit (belief, trust), credulous (believing too readily, easily deceived), incredible

cresc, cret, crease, cru [rise, grow] accrue (to grow), crescendo (growing in loudness or intensity), concrete (grown together, solidified), increase, decrease

crit [separate, choose] critical, criterion (that which is used in choosing), hypocrite

cur, curs [run] concurrent, current (running or flowing), concur (run together, agree), incur (run into), recur, occur, precursor (forerunner), cursive

cura [care] curator, curative, manicure (caring for the hands)

cycl, cyclo [wheel, circular] Cyclops (a mythical giant with one eye in the middle of his forehead), unicycle, bicycle, cyclone (a wind blowing circularly, a tornado)

deca [ten] decade, decalogue, decathlon

dem [people] democracy (people-rule), demography (vital statistics of the people: deaths, births, and so on), epidemic (on or among the people)

dent, dont [tooth] dental (relating to teeth), denture, dentifrice, orthodontist

derm [skin] hypodermic (injected under the skin), dermatology (skin study), epidermis (outer layer of skin), taxidermy (arranging skin; mounting animals)

dict [say, speak] diction (how one speaks, what one says), dictionary, dictate, dictator, dictaphone, dictatorial, edict, predict, verdict, contradict, benediction

doc [teach] indoctrinate, document, doctrine

domin [master] dominate, predominant, dominion, domain

don [give] donate, condone

dorm [sleep] dormant, dormitory

dox [opinion, praise] doxy (belief, creed, or opinion), orthodox (having the correct, commonly accepted opinion), heterodox (differing opinion), paradox (contradictory)

drome [run, step] syndrome (run-together symptoms), hippodrome (a place where horses run)

duc, duct [lead] produce, induce (lead into, persuade), seduce (lead aside), reduce, aqueduct (water leader or channel), viaduct, conduct

dura [hard, lasting] durable, duration, endurance

dynam [power] dynamo (power producer), dynamic, dynamite, hydrodynamics

endo [within] endoral (within the mouth), endocardial (within the heart), endoskeletal

equi [equal] equinox, equilibrium

erg [work] energy, erg (unit of work), allergy, ergophobia (morbid fear of work), ergometer, ergonomic

fac, fact, fic, fect [do, make] factory (place where workers make goods of various kinds), fact (a thing done), manufacture, amplification, confection

fall, fals [deceive] fallacy, falsify

fer [bear, carry] ferry (carry by water), coniferous (bearing cones, as a pine tree), fertile (bearing richly), defer, infer, refer

fid, fide, feder [faith, trust] confidante, Fido, fidelity, confident, infidelity, infidel, federal, confederacy

fila, fili [thread] filament (a single thread or threadlike object), filibuster, filigree

fin [end, ended, finished] final, finite, finish, confine, fine, refine, define, finale

fix [attach] fix, fixation (the state of being attached), fixture, affix, prefix, suffix

flex, flect [bend] flex (bend), reflex (bending back), flexible, flexor (muscle for bending), inflexibility, reflect, deflect

flu, fluc, fluv [flowing] influence (to flow in), fluid, flue, flush, fluently, fluctuate (to wave in an unsteady motion)

form [form, shape] form, uniform, conform, deform, reform, perform, formative, formation, formal, formula

fort, forc [strong] fort, fortress (a strong place), fortify (make strong), forte (one's strong point), fortitude, enforce

fract, frag [break] fracture (a break), infraction, fragile (easy to break), fraction (result of breaking a whole into equal parts), refract (to break or bend)

Learning

Challenge students to choose 10 roots from the list and think of an example word for each that isn't already mentioned. Have them incorporate their example words into sentences, to demonstrate their use in context.

Invite volunteers to write one of their example sentences on the board. Discuss each sentence briefly.

- Can classmates pick out the word being demonstrated?
- What is that word's root?
- What prefixes and suffixes were used?
- Can students point out another word or two from the example sentence and identify roots, prefixes, and suffixes?

English Language Learners

Provide support by creating a web graphic organizer with a common root word and its meaning in the center. Help students think of words that contain the root word and write them around the center. Have students attach the meanings of the word parts and the definitions to the words. Encourage them to create webs for different root words to promote vocabulary development as they encounter new words in their reading.

Struggling Learners

The list of word roots in this section may be daunting to students, and they may have trouble with the activity. List a few of the more familiar roots on the board for students to use in this activity. For example:

auto	crit	cycle
form	fract	graph
mand	mego	micro
multi	prime	solv
spec	sphere	therm

Suggest that a good way to learn the prefixes, suffixes, and roots in this section would be to make flash cards. Encourage students to use three different colors of flash cards—one for each different kind of word part. Tell students to

- write the word part on one side of the card and
- write its meaning on the reverse side.

Students can use the flash cards to study independently or with a partner.

Students can also use the flash cards as puzzle pieces, arranging them next to one another to form words.

508

gam [marriage] bigamy (two marriages), monogamy, polygamy (many spouses or marriages)

gastr(o) [stomach] gastric, gastronomic, gastritis (inflammation of the stomach)

gen [birth, race, produce] genesis (birth, beginning), genetics (study of heredity), eugenics (well born), genealogy (lineage by race, stock), generate, genetic

geo [earth] geometry (earth measurement), geography (earth writing), geocentric (earth centered), geology

germ [vital part] germination (to grow), germ (seed; living substance, as the germ of an idea), germane

gest [carry, bear] congest (bear together, clog), congestive (causing clogging), gestation

gloss, glot [tongue] glossary, polyglot (many tongues), epiglottis

glu, glo [lump, bond, glue] glue, agglutinate (make to hold in a bond), conglomerate (bond together)

grad, gress [step, go] grade (step, degree), gradual (step-by-step), graduate (make all the steps, finish a course), graduated (in steps or degrees), progress

graph, gram [write, written] graph, graphic (written, vivid), autograph (self-writing, signature), graphite (carbon used for writing), photography (light writing), phonograph (sound writing), diagram, bibliography, telegram

grat [pleasing] gratuity (mark of favor, a tip), congratulate (express pleasure over success), grateful, ingrate (not thankful)

grav [heavy, weighty] grave, aggravate, gravity, gravitate

greg [herd, group, crowd] congregation (a group functioning together), gregarian (belonging to a herd), segregate (tending to group aside or apart)

helio [sun] heliograph (an instrument for using the sun's rays to send signals), heliotrope (a plant that turns to the sun)

hema, hemo [blood] hemorrhage (an outpouring or flowing of blood), hemoglobin, hemophilia

here, hes [stick] adhere, cohere, cohesion

hetero [different] heterogeneous (different in birth), heterosexual (with interest in the opposite sex)

homo [same] homogeneous (of same birth or kind), homonym (word with same pronunciation as another), homogenize

hum, human [earth, ground, man] humus, exhume (to take out of the ground), humane (compassion for other humans)

hydr, hydra, hydro [water] dehydrate, hydrant, hydraulic, hydraulics, hydrogen, hydrophobia (fear of water)

hypn [sleep] hypnosis, Hypnos (god of sleep), hypnotherapy (treatment of disease by hypnosis)

ignis [fire] ignite, igneous, ignition

ject [throw] deject, inject, project (throw forward), eject, object

join, junct [join] adjoining, enjoin (to lay an order upon, to command), juncture, conjunction, injunction

juven [young] juvenile, rejuvenate (to make young again)

lau, lav, lot, lut [wash] launder, lavatory, lotion, ablution (a washing away), dilute (to make a liquid thinner and weaker)

leg [law] legal (lawful; according to law), legislate (to enact a law), legislature, legitimize (make legal)

levi [light] alleviate (lighten a load), levitate, levity (light conversation; humor)

liber, liver [free] liberty (freedom), liberal, liberalize (to make more free), deliverance

liter [letters] literary (concerned with books and writing), literature, literal, alliteration, obliterate

loc, loco [place] locality, locale, location, allocate (to assign, to place), relocate (to put back into place), locomotion (act of moving from place to place)

log, logo, ogue, ology [word, study, speech] catalog, prologue, dialogue, logogram (a symbol representing a word), zoology (animal study), psychology (mind study)

loqu, locut [talk, speak] eloquent (speaking well and forcefully), soliloquy, locution, loquacious (talkative), colloquial (talking together; conversational or informal)

luc, lum, lus, lun [light] translucent (letting light come through), lumen (a unit of light), luminary (a heavenly body; someone who shines in his or her profession), luster (sparkle, shine), Luna (the moon goddess)

magn [great] magnify (make great, enlarge), magnificent, magnanimous (great of mind or spirit), magnate, magnitude, magnum

man [hand] manual, manage, manufacture, manacle, manicure, manifest, maneuver, emancipate

English Language Learners

Some students may realize that words created during the flash card activity appear similar to words in their first language. Point out that this can be a good way to determine meaning. However, caution students that the meanings aren't always the same, and they need to check a dictionary if they're not sure.

mand [command] mandatory (commanded), remand (order back), mandate

mania [madness] mania (insanity, craze), monomania (mania on one idea), kleptomania, pyromania (insane tendency to set fires), maniac

mar, mari, mer [sea, pool] marine (a soldier serving on shipboard), marsh (wetland, swamp), maritime (relating to the sea and navigation), mermaid (fabled sea creature, half fish, half woman)

matri [mother] maternal (relating to the mother), matrimony, matriarchate (rulership of women), matron

medi [half, middle, between, halfway] mediate (come between, intervene), medieval (pertaining to the Middle Ages), Mediterranean (lying between lands), mediocre, medium

mega [great, million] megaphone (great sound), megalopolis (great city; an extensive urban area including a number of cities), megacycle (a million cycles), megaton

mem [remember] memo (a reminder), commemoration (the act of remembering by a memorial or ceremony), memento, memoir, memorable

meter [measure] meter (a metric measure), voltameter (instrument to measure volts), barometer, thermometer

micro [small] microscope, microfilm, microcard, microwave, micrometer (device for measuring small distances), omicron, micron (a millionth of a meter), microbe (small living thing)

migra [wander] migrate (to wander), emigrate (one who leaves a country), immigrate (to come into the land)

mit, miss [send] emit (send out, give off), remit (send back, as money due), submit, admit, commit, permit, transmit (send across), omit, intermittent (sending between, at intervals), mission, missile

mob, mot, mov [move] mobile (capable of moving), motionless (without motion), motor, emotional (moved strongly by feelings), motivate, promotion, demote, movement

mon [warn, remind] monument (a reminder or memorial of a person or an event), admonish (warn), monitor, premonition (forewarning)

mor, mort [mortal, death] mortal (causing death or destined for death), immortal (not subject to death), mortality (rate of death), mortician (one who prepares the dead for burial), mortuary (place for the dead, a morgue)

morph [form] amorphous (with no form, shapeless), metamorphosis (a change of form, as a caterpillar into a butterfly), morphology

multi [many, much] multifold (folded many times), multilinguist (one who speaks many languages), multiped (an organism with many feet), multiply

nat, nasc [to be born, to spring forth] innate (inborn), natal, native, nativity, renascence (a rebirth, a revival)

neur [nerve] neuritis (inflammation of a nerve), neurology (study of nervous systems), neurologist (one who practices neurology), neural, neurosis, neurotic

nom [law, order] autonomy (self-law, self-government), astronomy, gastronomy (art or science of good eating), economy

nomen, nomin [name] nomenclature, nominate (name someone for an office)

nov [new] novel (new, strange, not formerly known), renovate (to make like new again), novice, nova, innovate

nox, noc [night] nocturnal, equinox (equal nights), noctilucent (shining by night)

numer [number] numeral (a figure expressing a number), numeration (act of counting), enumerate (count out, one by one), innumerable

omni [all, every] omnipotent (all-powerful), omniscient (all-knowing), omnipresent (present everywhere), omnivorous

onym [name] anonymous (without name), synonym, pseudonym (false name), antonym (name of opposite meaning)

oper [work] operate (to labor, function), cooperate (work together)

ortho [straight, correct] orthodox (of the correct or accepted opinion), orthodontist (tooth straightener), orthopedic (originally pertaining to straightening a child), unorthodox

pac [peace] pacifist (one for peace only; opposed to war), pacify (make peace, quiet), Pacific Ocean (peaceful ocean)

pan [all] panacea (cure-all), pandemonium (place of all the demons, wild disorder), pantheon (place of all the gods in mythology)

Learning

Point out that in addition to helping students decode words, learning prefixes, suffixes, and roots can help them decide how to **divide words into syllables** *(see below),* when for example, they need to

- properly break the word at the end of a line in a written piece,
- guess how to pronounce a long and complicated word, or
- determine the number of syllables for the purpose of analyzing meter in a work of poetry.

Have students look up words in the dictionary and examine the syllable divisions shown. Are they already familiar with the prefix, suffix, and root in each syllable? If not, remind them to check the etymology in the dictionary to learn about them.

✳ For more about etymology, see SE page 352.

Teaching Tip: Dividing Words into Syllables

Most students will benefit from a brief review of the guidelines of syllabication.

- There is one vowel sound per syllable.
- Divide between vowels, unless they combine to form a diphthong (single sound), such as the *oi* in *voice.*

- Divide between consonants, unless the consonants are a blend, such as the *st* in *lasting,* or a digraph, such as the *th* in *rather.*
- Divide words between prefixes, suffixes, and roots (though some word parts contain more than one syllable).

During the course of a week, have students keep a journal of words they encounter that they are able to decipher by using their knowledge of prefixes, suffixes, and roots. Request that students write down

- the word,
- its source, and
- the sentence in which it was used.

At the end of the week, invite volunteers to share a new word and tell where they discovered it.

510

pater, patr [father] paternity (fatherhood, responsibility), patriarch (head of the tribe, family), patriot, patron (a wealthy person who supports as would a father)

path, pathy [feeling, suffering] pathos (feeling of pity, sorrow), sympathy, antipathy (feeling against), apathy (without feeling), empathy (feeling or identifying with another), telepathy (far feeling; thought transference)

ped, pod [foot] pedal (lever for a foot), impede (get the feet in a trap, hinder), pedestal (foot or base of a statue), pedestrian (foot traveler), centipede, tripod (three-footed support), podiatry (care of the feet), antipodes (opposite feet)

pedo [child] orthopedic, pedagogue (child leader; teacher), pediatrics (medical care of children)

pel, puls [drive, urge] compel, dispel, expel, repel, propel, pulse, impulse, pulsate, compulsory, expulsion, repulsive

pend, pens, pond [hang, weigh] pendant pendulum, suspend, appendage, pensive (weighing thought), ponderous

phil [love] philosophy (love of wisdom), philanthropy, philharmonic, bibliophile, Philadelphia (city of brotherly love)

phobia [fear] claustrophobia (fear of closed spaces), acrophobia (fear of high places), hydrophobia (fear of water)

phon [sound] phonograph, phonetic (pertaining to sound), symphony (sounds with or together)

photo [light] photograph (light-writing), photoelectric, photogenic (artistically suitable for being photographed), photosynthesis (action of light on chlorophyll to make carbohydrates)

plac [please] placid (calm, peaceful), placebo, placate, complacent

plu, plur, plus [more] plural (more than one), pluralist (a person who holds more than one office), plus (indicating that something more is to be added)

pneuma, pneumon [breath] pneumatic (pertaining to air, wind, or other gases), pneumonia (disease of the lungs)

pod (see *ped*)

poli [city] metropolis (mother city), police, politics, Indianapolis, Acropolis (high city, upper part of Athens), megalopolis

pon, pos, pound [place, put] postpone (put afterward), component, opponent (one put against), proponent, expose, impose, deposit, posture (how one places oneself), position

pop [people] population, populous (full of people), popular

port [carry] porter (one who carries), portable, transport (carry across), report, export, import, support, transportation

portion [part, share] portion (a part; a share, as a portion of pie), proportion (the relation of one share to others)

prehend [seize] comprehend (seize with the mind), apprehend (seize a criminal), comprehensive (seizing much, extensive)

prim, prime [first] primacy (state of being first in rank), prima donna (the first lady of opera), primitive (from the earliest or first time), primary, primal, primeval

proto [first] prototype (the first model made), protocol, protagonist, protozoan

psych [mind, soul] psyche (soul, mind), psychiatry (healing of the mind), psychology, psychosis (serious mental disorder), psychotherapy (mind treatment), psychic

punct [point, dot] punctual (being exactly on time), punctuation, puncture, acupuncture

reg, recti [straighten] regiment, regular, regulate, rectify (make straight), correct, direction

ri, ridi, risi [laughter] deride (mock, jeer at), ridicule (laughter at the expense of another, mockery), ridiculous, derision

rog, roga [ask] prerogative (privilege; asking before), interrogation (questioning; the act of questioning), derogatory

rupt [break] rupture (break), interrupt (break into), abrupt (broken off), disrupt (break apart), erupt (break out), incorruptible (unable to be broken down)

sacr, sanc, secr [sacred] sacred, sanction, sacrosanct, consecrate, desecrate

salv, salu [safe, healthy] salvation (act of being saved), salvage, salutation

sat, satis [enough] satient (giving pleasure, satisfying), saturate, satisfy (to give pleasure to; to give as much as is needed)

sci [know] science (knowledge), conscious (knowing, aware), omniscient (knowing everything)

scope [see, watch] telescope, microscope, kaleidoscope (instrument for seeing beautiful forms), periscope, stethoscope

scrib, script [write] scribe (a writer), scribble, manuscript (written by hand), inscribe, describe, subscribe, prescribe

Improving Your Vocabulary **511**

Learning

sed, sess, sid [sit] sediment (that which sits or settles out of a liquid), session (a sitting), obsession (an idea that sits stubbornly in the mind), possess, preside (sit before), president, reside, subside

sen [old] senior, senator, senile (old; showing the weakness of old age)

sent, sens [feel] sentiment (feeling), consent, resent, dissent, sentimental (having strong feeling or emotion), sense, sensation, sensitive, sensory, dissension

sequ, secu, sue [follow] sequence (following of one thing after another), consequence, sequel, subsequent, prosecute, consecutive (following in order), second (following "first"), ensue, pursue

serv [save, serve] servant, service, preserve, subservient, servitude, conserve, deserve, reservation, conservation

sign, signi [sign, mark, seal] signal (a gesture or sign to call attention), signature (the mark of a person written in his or her own handwriting), design, insignia (distinguishing marks)

simil, simul [like, resembling] similar (resembling in many respects), assimilate (to make similar to), simile, simulate (pretend; put on an act to make a certain impression)

sist, sta, stit [stand] persist (stand firmly; unyielding; continue), assist (to stand by with help), circumstance, stamina (power to withstand, to endure), status (standing), state, static, stable, stationary, substitute (to stand in for another)

solus [alone] soliloquy, solitaire, solitude, solo

solv, solu [loosen] solvent (a loosener, a dissolver), solve, absolve (loosen from, free from), resolve, soluble, solution, resolution, resolute, dissolute (loosened morally)

somnus [sleep] insomnia (not being able to sleep), somnambulist (a sleepwalker)

soph [wise] sophomore (wise fool), philosophy (love of wisdom), sophisticated

spec, spect, spic [look] specimen (an example to look at, study), specific, aspect, spectator (one who looks), spectacle, speculate, inspect, respect, prospect, retrospective (looking backward), introspective, expect, conspicuous

sphere [ball, sphere] stratosphere (the upper portion of the atmosphere), hemisphere (half of the earth), spheroid

spir [breath] spirit (breath), conspire (breathe together; plot), inspire (breathe into), aspire (breathe toward), expire (breathe out; die), perspire, respiration

string, strict [draw tight] stringent (drawn tight; rigid), strict, restrict, constrict (draw tightly together), boa constrictor (snake that constricts its prey)

stru, struct [build] construe (build in the mind, interpret), structure, construct, instruct, obstruct, destruction, destroy

sume, sump [take, use, waste] consume (to use up), assume (to take; to use), sump pump (a pump that takes up water), presumption (to take or use before knowing all the facts)

tact, tang, tag, tig, ting [touch] contact, tactile, intangible (not able to be touched), intact (untouched, uninjured), tangible, contingency, contagious (able to transmit disease by touching), contiguous

tele [far] telephone (far sound), telegraph (far writing), television (far seeing), telephoto (far photography), telecast

tempo [time] tempo (rate of speed), temporary, extemporaneously, contemporary (those who live at the same time), pro tem (for the time being)

ten, tin, tain [hold] tenacious (holding fast), tenant, tenure, untenable, detention, content, pertinent, continent, obstinate, abstain, pertain, detain

tend, tent, tens [stretch, strain] tendency (a stretching; leaning), extend, intend, contend, pretend, superintend, tender, extent, tension (a stretching, strain), pretense

terra [earth] terrain, terrarium, territory, terrestrial

test [to bear witness] testament (a will; bearing witness to someone's wishes), detest, attest (bear witness to), testimony

the, theo [God, a god] monotheism (belief in one god), polytheism (belief in many gods), atheism, theology

therm [heat] thermometer, therm (heat unit), thermal, thermostat, thermos, hypothermia (subnormal temperature)

thesis, thet [place, put] antithesis (place against), hypothesis (place under), synthesis (put together), epithet

tom [cut] atom (not cuttable; smallest particle of matter), appendectomy (cutting out an appendix), tonsillectomy, dichotomy (cutting in two; a division), anatomy (cutting, dissecting to study structure)

Challenge students to use their knowledge of prefixes, suffixes, and roots to create—or *coin*—their own words. Suggest that they begin by browsing the lists of roots for inspiration. Or perhaps students have a concept for which they think a word should exist. Suggest an idea of your own to get them started, or provide examples of **clever new words** *(see below)*.

- Idea: writing a paper all in one night
  Word: *uninoctuscription*
  Word parts: *uni-* (one) + *nox-, noc-* (night) + *scrib, script* (write) + *-tion* (act of)

- Idea: to sleep until the last possible minute before having to get up
  Word: *ultimasecundusomniate*
  Word parts: *ultima-* (last, final) + *secu* (second) + *somnus* (sleep) + *-ate* (cause, make)

Invite volunteers to share their favorite word creation.

Teaching Tip: Clever New Words

Show students ways people play with words. The American Dialect Society holds an annual contest for "best new word of the year." Many of these new words make informed use of prefixes, suffixes, and roots. See www.americandialect.org for the current and past nominations and final choices for word of the year.

English Language Learners

The "clever new word" activity can reinforce the concept of using the meanings of roots and affixes to *figure out* the meaning of unfamiliar words. Have groups of students try to figure out the intended meanings before the volunteers share the definitions of their word creations.

To practice using prefixes, suffixes, and roots, have students play a dictionary game.

- Divide the class into small groups. Give each group a dictionary and note cards.
- Have one student in each group choose a word from the dictionary that the others are unlikely to know.
- Anyone who knows the word must admit it, so that another word can be chosen.
- The student writes the word on a note card and gives it to the other students to study.
- Using their knowledge of prefixes, roots, and suffixes, students work together to determine the meaning of the word.
- Encourage students to try to figure out the meaning on their own, but tell them that if they need help they can refer to SE pages 503–512.
- When they think they know the meaning, students should ask the dictionary holder for confirmation.

Continue playing until each student has had a turn to be the dictionary holder. Students could also choose new words in current reading assignments.

tort, tors [twist] torture (twisting to inflict pain), retort (twist back, reply sharply), extort (twist out), distort (twist out of shape), contort, torsion (act of twisting, as a torsion bar)

tox [poison] toxic (poisonous), intoxicate, antitoxin

tract, tra [draw, pull] tractor, attract, subtract, tractable (can be handled), abstract (to draw away), subtrahend (the number to be drawn away from another)

trib [pay, bestow] tribute (to pay honor to), contribute (to give money to a cause), attribute, retribution, tributary

turbo [disturb] turbulent, disturb, turbid, turmoil

typ [print] type, prototype (first print; model), typical, typography, typewriter, typology (study of types, symbols), typify

ultima [last] ultimate, ultimatum (the final or last offer that can be made)

uni [one] unicorn (a legendary creature with one horn), unify (make into one), university, unanimous, universal

vac [empty] vacate (to make empty), vacuum (a space entirely devoid of matter), evacuate (to remove troops or people), vacation, vacant

vale, vali, valu [strength, worth] valiant, equivalent (of equal worth), validity (truth; legal strength), evaluate (find out the value), value, valor (value; worth)

ven, vent [come] convene (come together, assemble), intervene (come between), venue, convenient, avenue, circumvent (come or go around), invent, prevent

ver, veri [true] very, aver (say to be true, affirm), verdict, verity (truth), verify (show to be true), verisimilitude

vert, vers [turn] avert (turn away), divert (turn aside, amuse), invert (turn over), introvert (turn inward), convertible, reverse (turn back), controversy (a turning against; a dispute), versatile (turning easily from one skill to another)

vic, vicis [change, substitute] vicarious, vicar, vicissitude

vict, vinc [conquer] victor (conqueror, winner), evict (conquer out, expel), convict (prove guilty), convince (conquer mentally, persuade), invincible (not conquerable)

vid, vis [see] video, television, evident, provide, providence, visible, revise, supervise (oversee), vista, visit, vision

viv, vita, vivi [alive, life] revive (make live again), survive (live beyond, outlive), vivid, vivacious (full of life), vitality

voc [call] vocation (a calling), avocation (occupation not one's calling), convocation (a calling together), invocation, vocal

vol [will] malevolent, benevolent (one of goodwill), volunteer, volition

volcan, vulcan [fire] volcano (a mountain erupting fiery lava), volcanize (to undergo volcanic heat), Vulcan (Roman god of fire)

volvo [turn about, roll] revolve, voluminous (winding), voluble (easily turned about or around), convolution (a twisting)

vor [eat greedily] voracious, carnivorous (flesh eating), herbivorous (plant eating), omnivorous (eating everything), devour

zo [animal] zoo (short for zoological garden), zoology (study of animal life), zodiac (circle of animal constellations), zoomorphism (being in the form of an animal), protozoa (one-celled animals)

The Human Body

capit	head	**gastro**	stomach	**osteo**	bone
cardi	heart	**gloss**	tongue	**ped**	foot
corp	body	**hema**	blood	**pneuma**	breathe
dent	tooth	**man**	hand	**psych**	mind
derm	skin	**neur**	nerve	**spir**	breath

Writing Business Letters

Well-written business letters are designed to get results. People in the workplace write business letters to apply for jobs, request information, promote products, make complaints, or answer questions. In addition, carefully written letters serve as accurate records, especially for businesses, organizations, and governing bodies. While telephone conversations and e-mails are frequently used to exchange information, letters are still regarded as the most reliable form of communication. In other words, if something is important, put it in writing.

As a student, you can also write business letters to get things done. You can request help, apply for jobs or admission to schools, or persuade others to support worthy causes. Developing good letter-writing skills will help you now and for years to come.

- **Writing a Business Letter**
- **Parts of a Business Letter**
- **Creating an E-Mail Message**
- **Sending a Letter**

"Make the most of yourself, for that is all there is of you."
—Ralph Waldo Emerson

Writing Business Letters

Objectives
- understand the purposes of business correspondence
- understand the content and form of a business letter
- learn tips for creating business-related e-mail messages
- learn how to address an envelope

Point out that the art of writing business letters is related to persuasive writing: the initial letter in a business interchange will have been written in order to persuade the recipient to do something for the sender.

✱ For more about persuasive writing, see SE pages 201–253.

Talk about your own letter-writing experiences and whether you were able to accomplish your goal (for example, a job-application letter or a letter of request for a refund for defective merchandise). Invite volunteers to describe business letters they have written.

Writing a Business Letter

Guide students in discussing the sample letter in terms of the traits of writing.

Ideas

- The writer clearly expresses his purpose (to request a recommendation).
- It would be good for Justin to ask Mr. Spencer to acknowledge receipt of the letter in some way so that Justin will know whether Mr. Spencer received the recommendation. Justin could, for example, ask if he may give Mr. Spencer's phone number to Mr. Perkins, instead of having Mr. Spencer call directly.

Organization

The letter is well organized. It (1) reminds the reader who Justin is and states his purpose, (2) tells the reader what he can do to help, and (3) thanks the reader for his time.

Voice & Word Choice

- The voice is polite and formal.
- The words are specific.

Sentence Fluency

The sentences vary in length and in the way they begin.

514

Writing a Business Letter

If you need information, resources, or a recommendation from an individual or group, a request letter is an effective way to accomplish this task. In the following letter, Justin Dobbs requests a job recommendation from a former employer. (See the writing tips on the next page.)

The letter follows the correct format. (See pages 516–517.)

717 Main Street
Sandusky, OH 44870
May 12, 2011

Mr. Sam Spencer
Sandusky Register
314 West Market Street
Sandusky, OH 44870

Dear Mr. Spencer:

The beginning introduces the request.

I delivered papers for you for two years when I was in seventh and eighth grade. Now I am at the end of my freshman year at Sandusky High School, and I am applying for a summer job at a Dollar General grocery store. Mr. Perkins, the store manager, asked me if I could get a reference from a previous employer. I immediately thought of you because you were my first employer.

The middle provides details of the request.

If you could give me a recommendation, please call Mr. Perkins at the store's office number, 555-1234, before May 18. You can reach me at 555-1086 if you have any questions.

The ending expresses thanks.

Thank you for considering my request. I would be very grateful for any help you could give me.

Sincerely,

Justin Dobbs

Justin Dobbs

"The best advice on writing I've ever received is: 'Write with authority.'"

—Cynthia Ozick

Writing Tips for Letters of Request

Use the following tips as a guide whenever you write a letter of request.

Before you write . . .

- **Determine your purpose.**
  Know exactly what you are requesting.
- **Gather information.**
  Collect information that supports your request, including specific dates, names, places, and so on. Also think about the best way to organize the information.
- **Consider your reader.**
  Decide what your reader must know to respond to your request.

As you write . . .

- **Keep it short.**
  Stay focused on the main idea and make your point quickly.
- **State your request.**
  Be specific about what you are asking the reader to do.
- **Be courteous.**
  Be polite.
- **Focus on the outcome.**
  What do you want the reader to do, and when, and how?

After you've written a first draft . . .

- **Check for completeness.**
  Be sure that your main point is clear and that you have included all important information.
- **Check for appropriate voice.**
  Did you use a respectful, sincere tone?
- **Check for correctness.**
  Double-check the address and spelling of all names. Correct errors in punctuation, capitalization, spelling, and grammar.

Try It!

Write a request letter to the appropriate person or organization, politely asking for help. (Send the letter or simply treat it as a school assignment.)

Writing Tips for Letters of Request

If your school holds a fund-raising event, such as an auction, try to coordinate the letter-writing practice with it. Have students use the **Try It!** activity to compose a letter to a local business owner, or other appropriate recipient, asking for a contribution.

Remind students that a letter of request should always be followed by a thank-you note after the recipient does what is requested. Challenge students to generate tips for writing this thank-you note, based on the tips for writing a request letter. For example:

- Before you write . . . Find out what the recipient did in response to the letter of request.
- As you write . . . Keep it short, acknowledge the recipient's actions, express thanks, focus on the positive results of the recipient's actions.
- Follow the same steps for checking the draft.

Encourage students to write thank-you notes as soon as possible after they learn the results of their request letter.

Parts of a Business Letter

Elaborate on the material presented in the text, using the following information:

- It's very important for students to include their address in the heading of the letter itself and not just as the return address on an envelope. Envelopes are often discarded immediately after a letter is opened.
- Students should always try to learn the exact name of the desired recipient. Addressing the letter to a specific person makes it less likely that the letter will get misdirected.
- Strongly encourage students to keyboard all business letters. A handwritten letter looks less professional and may be difficult for the recipient to decipher, thereby resulting in no reply.

Parts of a Business Letter

1. The **heading** includes the writer's complete address and the date. Write the heading at least one inch from the top of the page, at the left-hand margin.
2. The **inside address** includes the reader's name and address (including the company name).
   - If the person has a title, be sure to include it. (If the title is short, write it on the same line as the name. If the title is long, write it on the next line.)
   - If you are writing to an organization or a business—but not to a specific person—begin the inside address with the name of the organization or business.
3. The **salutation** is the greeting. Always put a colon after the salutation.
   - If you know the reader's name, use it in your greeting.
     Dear Mr. Perkins:
   - If you don't know the name of the person who will read your letter, use a salutation like one of these:
     Dear Store Manager:
     Dear Sir or Madam:
4. The **body** is the main part of the letter. Do not indent the paragraphs in your letter; instead, double-space between them. The body is organized into these parts: (1) the beginning states why you are writing, (2) the middle provides the needed details, and (3) the ending focuses on what should happen next.
5. The **complimentary closing** comes after the body. Use *Sincerely* or *Yours truly* to close a business letter. Capitalize only the first word of the closing and put a comma after the closing.
6. The **signature** ends the letter. If you are using a computer, leave four spaces under the closing; then type your name. Write your signature in the space between the closing and the typed name.

Tip

Check the help file in the word-processing program on your computer to see if it has templates (built-in patterns) that will help you set up your business letters. However, make sure that the templates closely follow the format of the letter on the next page before you use any of them.

Business-Letter Format

1
717 Main Street
Sandusky, OH 44870
May 6, 2011

Four to Seven Spaces

2
Mr. Anthony Perkins, Manager
Dollar General
1622 Cleveland Road
Sandusky, OH 44870

3
Dear Mr. Perkins:

Double Space

I noticed the sign in your store window about an opening for a
stocker/bagger. I asked my friend James Leonard, who works for you,
about it. He said the best way to apply for a job would be to send you
a letter of application.

Double Space

I am a freshman at Sandusky High School, and I would be able
to start work on June 4, the day after school gets out for summer
vacation. I have had one extended job before this as a paper carrier
for the *Sandusky Register*. I had that job for two years during seventh
4 and eighth grade. My boss, Mr. Spencer, said that I was the only
carrier who never had a customer complaint. If I work for you this
summer at Dollar General, I would also be interested in working
part-time during the school year, if there is an opening.

Double Space

If you would like more information, please call me at 555-1086. You
can also reach me at my dad's e-mail address <rdobbs@insight.com>.
Thanks for considering me. I look forward to hearing from you.

Double Space

5
Yours truly,

6
Justin Dobbs

Four Spaces

Justin Dobbs

Learning

Business-Letter Format

Focus students' attention on specific details in
the sample letter.

- The writer does not put his name over his
address in the heading. That is because his
name is typed in the signature.
- The writer mentions his friend James
Leonard by name and explains James's
relationship to Mr. Perkins. In doing so,
he shows that he has already done some
preliminary research and that he is
associated with someone whom the reader
already trusts enough to employ.
- The writer not only mentions that he was a
paper carrier but provides supporting details
(the paper's name, the name of his boss
there). This sets a knowledgeable tone.
- The writer encloses his e-mail address in
angle brackets. While this is not imperative,
it can help the address stand out.

Creating an E-Mail Message

Acknowledge that when students write e-mail messages to their friends, they might use abbreviations and unconventional spellings and ignore standard capitalization or punctuation rules. Remind students, however, that as with all writing, they must always consider their audience. While a very casual style is appropriate for family and close friends, it is not the right choice for more formal correspondence with an acquaintance, a coworker, a referral, or someone in a position of authority.

Encourage students to consider observing the usual conventions even when they write to friends. It always helps to get this practice.

518

Creating an E-Mail Message

E-mail has become an important, quick communication tool for teachers, students, and parents. However, in spite of e-mail's delivery speed, it still takes time to write a good message. In the following e-mail, a student asks a teacher for advice on a research project.

The **heading** includes the sending information.

New Message	
To:	jmueller@mountainairhigh.edu
Cc:	
Subject:	Research project on Robert Rauschenberg

Dear Ms. Mueller:

The **beginning** tells the reason for the e-mail message.

As you know, I chose Robert Rauschenberg as the subject of my research project for Art Foundations class. I have been finding a lot of information about him, but I'm having problems with the requirement that we include illustrations of some of the artist's work and point out its characteristics. Whenever I find a work that I want to use, the Web site either blocks me from downloading the picture or shows a word like "copy" across the artwork.

The **middle** asks for advice.

Do you know how I can get copies of pictures without having these problems? Should I make copies from art books at the library, or are there Web sites where I can get good downloads?

The **ending** politely thanks the reader for her help.

If you could answer these questions, I would really appreciate it. My project is working out well except for this one problem. Thanks for your help.

Sincerely,
Louvinia Moham
lmoham@mountainairhigh.edu

Tips for Writing E-Mail Messages

Show respect for the recipient of your e-mail messages. Check your spelling, punctuation, and grammar, just as you would in a more formal business letter.

Before you write . . .

- **Jot down the main points you want to make.**
  List other necessary details.
- **Complete the e-mail heading.**
  Fill in the address line by typing in each character of the address or by using your address book's automatic fill-in feature. Then write a subject line that briefly indicates the reason for the e-mail message.

As you write . . .

- **Greet the reader and give your reason for writing.**
  Start with a polite greeting. Then give the reason for your e-mail.
- **Use a conversational but proper tone.**
  Be sure your sentences are clear and complete. Even if you use an informal voice, your grammar should be correct.
- **Briefly state your main points.**
  Include only the most important information.
- **End politely.**
  Close with "Sincerely," or another appropriate closing. Type your name below it and add your e-mail address (if you wish).

After you have written a first draft . . .

- **Read over your e-mail.**
  Be sure your message is clear and complete.
- **Check attachments.** Don't forget to include any attachments you refer to in your message.
- **Check for correctness.**
  Check for errors in punctuation, capitalization, spelling, and grammar.
- **Finally, press "send."**

Try It!

Think of a school-related situation that may require an e-mail message. Write a message about the matter to a teacher or a fellow student. (You may send the e-mail or simply treat it as a class assignment.)

Tips for Writing E-Mail Messages

In addition to the strategies given in the pupil text, discuss the following:

- It's important to use a subject line for two reasons: First, some people automatically delete e-mail that arrives without a subject line, because this is one of the characteristics of unsolicited (and usually unwanted) commercial e-mails (also called spam). Second, having a subject line instantly alerts the reader to the purpose of the message and makes it easier to file for future reference if desired.
- It may be helpful to add the attachments before writing the message. It is very common to forget to include attachments after taking the time to write a note.
- Before pressing SEND, double-check the address to avoid the embarrassment of accidentally sending a message to the wrong person.

Learning

Sending a Letter

Challenge students to guess why the postal service form requires the use of capital letters without punctuation. (Envelopes are now sorted by machines that can recognize the form of letters if they're written legibly.)

If students will be using a computer to write their letters, show them how to set up the word-processing program and printer for printing envelopes as well. It may be most efficient to print all students' envelopes at once using a class computer. That way the envelope-feeding mechanism on the printer has to be adjusted only once.

Sending a Letter

Letters sent through the mail will get to their destinations faster if they are properly addressed and stamped. Always include a ZIP code.

Addressing the Envelope

Place the writer's name and address in the upper left corner of the envelope and the destination name and address in the center. Then put correct postage in the upper right corner of the envelope.

JUSTIN DOBBS
717 MAIN ST
SANDUSKY OH 44870

MR SAM SPENCER
SANDUSKY REGISTER
314 W MARKET ST
SANDUSKY OH 44870

There are two acceptable forms for addressing an envelope: the older, traditional form and the new form preferred by the postal service.

Traditional Form	**Postal Service Form**
Ms. Theresa Chang	MS THERESA CHANG
Goodwill Industries	GOODWILL INDUSTRIES
9200 Wisconsin Avenue	9200 WISCONSIN AVE
Bethesda, MD 20814-3896	BETHESDA MD 20814-3896

Following U.S. Postal Service Guidelines

1. Capitalize everything and leave out ALL punctuation.
2. Use the list of common address abbreviations located on page **660**. Use numerals rather than words for numbered streets and avenues (9TH AVE NE, 3RD ST SW).
3. If you know the ZIP + 4 code, use it.

521

Taking Tests

Teachers give tests to check how well you are learning. You may feel nervous while taking tests and have trouble remembering the important information, but this shouldn't happen if you are prepared. This is true of any test—objective, essay, or standardized. Plan properly, and you will perform at your best.

The preparation should start with your class work. Make sure that you understand the subjects you are studying. This means you must pay attention in every class, take good notes, and complete each assignment. You must also understand the test-taking process. This means you should know how to study for, and take, different types of tests.

This chapter will help you plan your test-taking strategies and make test taking less stressful for you. It includes tips for studying and for taking three types of tests.

- **Preparing for a Test**
- **Test-Taking Tips**
- **Taking Objective Tests**
- **Taking Essay Tests**
- **Taking Standardized Tests**
- **Tips for Standardized Tests**

"Man's mind,
stretched to a new
idea, never goes
back to its original
dimensions."
—Oliver Wendell Holmes

Taking Tests

Objectives

- learn ways to prepare for and approach tests
- learn about the different kinds of objective tests
- learn how to understand and respond to writing prompts
- learn techniques for taking standardized tests

Point out that many of the topics covered so far in this unit (note taking, summarizing and paraphrasing, understanding writing assignments) can help students when it is time to be tested. Encourage them to continue to practice those skills conscientiously.

Talk about students' experiences with test taking.

- Are there certain kinds of tests they prefer? Why?
- Have they ever been so well prepared for a test that they hardly felt nervous at all? How had they prepared?
- Does anyone have an effective technique to share?

Assure students that they can learn to ease test-related nervousness and to concentrate in spite of it. The following pages will help them.

Preparing for a Test

Encourage students to plan their study time for a test just as they plan their writing time for an assignment (SE page 500). Suggest that they try starting the review process two weeks before the test. This will allow them to meet several times with a study partner or a **study group** (*see below*) and to use the time in between meetings to prepare further. Remind students to use a daily planner to keep track of their study schedule.

Draw students' attention to the last step in the cycle, reviewing the completed test. Note that many people skip this stage, treating the test as if it is the end of the matter. Remind students, however, that their primary goal is to add to their personal knowledge for the long term. The best way to do this is to view the test itself as part of their learning process.

522

Preparing for a Test

In order to prepare for a test, you must know what to expect. Usually, you can expect a test to cover whatever you've learned in class. Every day in class, take good notes and review them often. Keep your graded assignments so you can look them over later. Follow the cycle below to do your best on every test.

Test-Prep Cycle

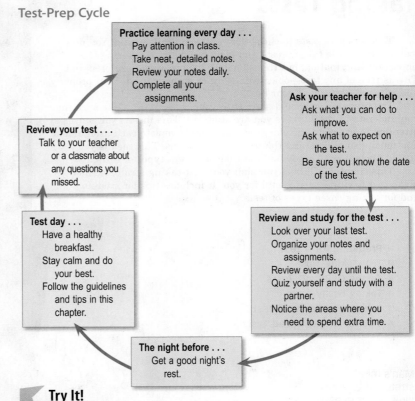

Practice learning every day . . .
Pay attention in class.
Take neat, detailed notes.
Review your notes daily.
Complete all your assignments.

Ask your teacher for help . . .
Ask what you can do to improve.
Ask what to expect on the test.
Be sure you know the date of the test.

Review and study for the test . . .
Look over your last test.
Organize your notes and assignments.
Review every day until the test.
Quiz yourself and study with a partner.
Notice the areas where you need to spend extra time.

The night before . . .
Get a good night's rest.

Test day . . .
Have a healthy breakfast.
Stay calm and do your best.
Follow the guidelines and tips in this chapter.

Review your test . . .
Talk to your teacher or a classmate about any questions you missed.

Try It!
Think of the ways you prepared for your last test. Did you leave out any of the above steps? See if you can improve your test scores by following this test-prep cycle.

Teaching Tip: Study Groups

Encourage students to get together with several classmates to form a regular study group and remind them that

- the more active a role they take in dealing with new information, the more thoroughly they will master it, and

- the conversations they have with members of their study group will not only help them to remember material better, but they will expose them to other points of view, which is an effective way to learn.

Struggling Learners

To help students remember to do each step in the process of preparing for a test, have them convert the Test-Prep Cycle (in writing or on the computer) to a checklist. Before each test, students can use this checklist to keep track of the steps, as well as to note important information such as the test date and subject.

Taking Tests **523**

Test-Taking Tips

- **Listen carefully** as your teacher gives directions, makes any corrections, or provides other information. And don't try to get a head start while your teacher is talking. You may miss important comments such as these:

"You have 30 minutes to finish the test."

"Make this change in number three."

"Write your answer to the final question on the back of the test sheet."

- **Put your name on the test right away.**
- **Take a quick look at the entire test.** This will help you decide how much time to spend on each section or question.
- **Begin the test.** Read the instructions before answering each set of questions. Do exactly what they tell you to do.
- **Read each question carefully.** Be sure you understand the question completely before answering it.
- **Answer all of the questions you are sure of first.** Then go back to the other questions and do your best to answer each one. Keep track of the time as you work on the more difficult questions.
- **Check over your answers when you finish the test.** If you skipped any really hard questions, try to answer them now.

Try It!

Review these tips right before your next test and then put them into practice. Upon completion of the test, determine how closely you followed this advice.

Test-Taking Tips

Focus attention on the third bullet: *Take a quick look at the entire test.* Discuss how students can preview a test before beginning it.

- Look at the total number of questions to get a general idea of the rate at which you'll have to work.
- Notice the objective types of questions (true/false, matching, multiple choice, and fill-in-the-blanks) and always allow more time for writing answers to essay questions.
- Check the point value of the questions and consider answering the more valuable ones first. (Note that some people might prefer to ease into a test by starting with the lower-value questions.)

English Language Learners

Help students analyze errors they've made in content-area tests to determine the specific types of questions and wording that pose the greatest problems. Have students recall strategies suggested earlier (TE pages 492–497) for understanding directions and organizing and responding to assignments. Discuss how those tips apply to test-taking.

Struggling Learners

Focus attention on the sixth bulleted item: *Answer all of the questions you are sure of first.* For many students, this strategy will help them take the test more calmly and will also help build their confidence.

Remind students that this strategy requires reviewing the whole test before starting. Emphasize that the extra time they spend reviewing will be worth it, as they will identify questions they are able to answer. This will build confidence to tackle the harder questions and complete the test.

Taking Objective Tests

Talk with students about the meaning of the term *objective tests*.

- Challenge students to define the word *objective* ("having to do with facts or conditions that are perceptible by all"). Ask students to look it up in a dictionary, if necessary.
- What does this imply about this type of test? (That it tests factual knowledge, rather than asking for students' thoughts and opinions.)

Point out that objective tests tend to focus more on the first level of thinking, recall (SE page 493). Encourage students always to ask whether a test will involve many objective questions, because then they can focus their study time on mastering names, dates, places, and other facts.

524

Taking Objective Tests

Tests often have four different types of objective questions: true/false, matching, multiple-choice, and fill-in-the-blanks.

True/False

In a true/false test, you decide if a statement is correct or incorrect. Most true/false questions focus on the details, so read each statement carefully.

- **Look for absolutes and qualifiers.** Statements with absolutes such as *always, never, all,* and *none* are often false. Statements that use qualifiers such as *often, rarely,* and *seldom* are more likely to be true.

    False 1. The Speaker of the House always presides over Senate sessions. *(When the Speaker is away, the president pro tem presides.)*

    True 2. Political parties sometimes make it difficult for Congress to pass a bill.

- **Test each part.** Even if only one word or phrase in a statement is false, then the entire statement is false.

    False 3. The legislative and the executive branch have the power to override the veto of a bill. *(Only the legislative branch has that power.)*

- **Watch for negatives.** Words such as *don't, can't, doesn't,* and *wasn't* can be confusing, so make sure you know what the statement means.

    False 4. The power to zone property doesn't belong to local governments.

Matching

In matching tests, you are asked to match items from one column to those in another column.

- **Read both columns before answering any questions.** This helps you find the best match for each item.
- **Match the items you know first.** If each answer is used only once, cross out the letter or number after you've used it.
- **Find grammar clues.** For example, plural subjects need plural verbs.

    _C_ 1. metabolism   A. Compounds that link with peptides to act as chemical messengers

    _A_ 2. amino acids   B. Fundamental components of all living cells that are made of substances like enzymes and hormones

    _B_ 3. proteins   C. The sum of all chemical reactions in an organism

Taking Tests 525

Multiple-Choice

In multiple-choice questions, you choose the right answer from several possibilities.

- **Read each question carefully.** Usually, you will be asked to choose the best answer. Sometimes your choices may include "all of the above" or "none of the above."

  1. All of the following are branches of government except
     A. Legislative   C. Executive
     B. Presidential   D. Judicial

- **Anticipate the answer.** Before reading the choices, try to answer the question or complete the sentence. That will help you recognize the right answer.

- **Read each choice.** It's tempting to choose the first answer that seems close, but there may be another choice that is better.

- **Consider the "all of the above" answer carefully.** If there is even one statement that you are sure is false, do not choose "all of the above." If there is one statement that you are sure is true, do not choose "none of the above."

- **Eliminate the wrong or unlikely choices first.**

  2. Washington was elected as the first president of the United States in
     A. 1620 *(too early)*   C. 1789
     B. 1776 *(too early)*   D. 1813 *(too late)*

Fill-in-the-Blanks

Fill-in-the-blank questions require you to complete a missing part of a statement.

- **Check the number of blanks.** Often, there is one for each word.

  1. Monosaccharides and disaccharides are ___simple___ ___carbohydrates___.

- **Check for grammar clues.** If there is an *a* before the blank, the answer should begin with a consonant. If there is an *an* before the blank, the answer should begin with a vowel.

  2. An educated guess or explanation based on current logic and data is called a ___hypothesis___.

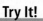

Try It!

Which types of objective questions are the most difficult for you? Which tips can you use to help you on your next test?

Learning

Ask students to note how many of the test-taking tips on SE pages 524–525 focus on the danger of misreading the question. Assure students that they have a great deal of control over this and can essentially eliminate this possibility if they

- pace themselves;
- focus on the test, ignoring outside distractions;
- use their critical-reading skills; and
- ask for clarification when they do not understand a question.

Encourage students working with study partners to make up objective tests for each other as part of their study process. Both creating and taking the test will increase their mastery of the material.

Struggling Learners

In addition to creating objective tests with a study partner, students can also study for objective tests by using flash cards.

- With their partner, have students create flash cards with important terms, dates, and definitions.

- Partners can use the cards to test each other. (Flash cards are a helpful tool for memorizing material.)

Students may also find it helpful to play memory games, such as Concentration.

- Students can use index cards to makes pairs of dates-events or terms-definitions.
- Students lay their cards face down.
- Partners take turns flipping over two cards. If the cards match, they keep the pair; if not, they turn the cards back over, and their partner takes a turn.

Taking Essay Tests

Refer students to the verbs in the levels of thinking chart on SE page 493 for more key words they might encounter in essay-test prompts.

Discuss students' feelings about whether essay questions are the hardest part of a test. Point out that

- unlike objective test questions, essay questions usually do not have a single correct answer;
- students will usually receive credit for strong writing and creative thinking, even if they make some editing mistakes.

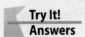
Try It!
Answers

Possible Answers

1. A space shuttle sends astronauts into space for short-term exploration, and a space station allow astronauts to spend extended time living in and exploring space.
2. Earth's water resources are threatened by sewage overflow, fertilizer run-off, and petroleum spills.

Taking Essay Tests

Many students feel that the essay questions are the hardest part of a test because, unlike other questions, possible answers are not given. Essay-test prompts require you to show how facts and supporting details are connected. The next few pages offer tips for taking an essay test.

Understanding and Restating the Prompt

- **Read the question carefully.**
- **Underline the key words** that explain what you are being asked to do. Here are some key words and their explanations.

Compare . . . . . tell how things are alike.
Contrast . . . . . tell how things are different.
Cause . . . . describe how one thing has affected another.
Define . . . . give a clear, specific meaning for a word or an idea.
Describe . . . . . use sensory details to explain how something looks, sounds, and so on.
Evaluate . . . . . . make a value judgment supported by facts or examples.
Explain . . . . use details and facts to tell what something means or how it works, or give reasons that tell why.
Identify . . . . . . answer the question using one or more of the 5 W's.
Illustrate . . . . . use examples to show how something works or why it's important.
Prove . . . . use facts and details to tell why something is true.
Review . . . . create an overall picture of the topic.
Summarize . . . tell the main idea and key points about the topic.

- **Rephrase the prompt into a thesis statement.** It often works well to drop the key word from your thesis statement.

  Prompt: Explain how a flat tax would affect people with low income levels.

  Thesis Statement: A flat tax would affect low-income people in a negative way because most of them would have to pay a higher percentage of their income in taxes.

Try It!

Turn each essay-test prompt below into a thesis statement. (Refer to your textbook or a Web site for information on these topics.)

1. Compare the effectiveness of a space shuttle and a space station.
2. Identify some of the major sources of water pollution.

Planning a One-Paragraph Response

Tests may include one or more prompts that call for a paragraph response rather than a full-length essay. The following guidelines will help you write an effective one-paragraph response to a prompt.

- **Read the prompt carefully.** Underline the key words or phrases.
- **Identify what the prompt is asking you to do** (explain, compare, prove, define).
- **Plan your response.**
  1. **Turn the prompt into a topic sentence.**
  2. **Include at least three supporting details.** Keep your topic sentence in mind when you select these details.

Learning

Prompt

Briefly explain the reason for the formation of the United Nations.

Planning Notes

Topic Sentence: The United Nations was formed after World War II to help countries work together.

Supporting details:
1. Prevent future wars
2. Help countries in conflict find peace
3. Defend human rights
4. Support nations in trouble
5. Promote social and economic progress

Response

Formation of the United Nations

The United Nations was formed after World War II to help countries work together. The founders of the United Nations wanted to protect future generations from the devastating effects of war. They believed the United Nations could help countries in conflict find peaceful solutions. They also wanted to defend human rights throughout the world, but especially in developing regions. Other priorities were to provide assistance for nations in crisis and promote social and economic progress in every country.

Planning a One-Paragraph Response

After students have read the sample response, ask them to respond to it. Do they think it answered the prompt adequately? (Most should agree that it does. If students disagree, have them explain their opinion.) Can students suggest any improvements? Possible responses:

- If the writer had included more specific details—such as the year the United Nations was founded, names of one or two people responsible, or the names of major countries involved—it would have demonstrated an even greater grasp of the information.
- The writer could have varied the sentence forms and used effective transitions.
- The writer could have ended with a sentence that emphasizes the importance of the topic.

✳ For more about writing effective paragraphs, see SE pages 561–579.

Planning an Essay Response

Explain that it is especially important for students to plan their time carefully when responding to essay questions. They must take care to

- allow time to complete any other questions on the test,
- decide what length of essay is realistic, given the requirements and the time frame, and
- rigorously stick to their writing schedule.

Acknowledge that this type of test will be a challenge for students who tend to write more slowly, but assure them that, with practice, they can master timed writing. Note also that often when a test includes an essay question, the teacher will inform students of this in advance. Even though they may not know what the exact question will be, students can still complete many prewriting tasks during their study process.

Planning an Essay Response

Some essay prompts require you to respond with a full-length essay. The following tips will help you write a clear, well-organized response essay.

- **Read the prompt** and restate it as a thesis statement.
- **Plan your response** by collecting and outlining details that support your thesis.
- **Write your essay answer.** Include your thesis statement in your opening paragraph. Each main point of your outline becomes the topic sentence for a body paragraph. In the final paragraph, write a meaningful conclusion that shows you truly understand the topic.

Prompt

> **Evaluate the effectiveness of the United Nations. Give at least three reasons to support your response.**

Planning Notes

Thesis Statement: Since its creation, the United Nations has helped those in need by improving health care, defending human rights, and assisting struggling countries.

Outline:
I. Improving health care
   A. Provides immunizations and safe water
   B. Fights against the spread of diseases
   C. Results in increased life expectancy
II. Defending human rights
   A. Offers assistance to women, children, and refugees
   B. Created Universal Declaration of Human Rights
III. Assisting struggling countries
   A. Provides about one-third of the world's food aid
   B. Has given more than $4.5 billion in aid

Try It!

Plan and respond to the following prompt: "Evaluate the effectiveness of _____ in your school." (Fill in the blank with a topic.)

Essay Response

The following essay response follows the outline on page **528**. The thesis statement appears at the end of the beginning paragraph. In the final paragraph, the writer restates the reasons she uses to defend her position on the prompt.

Sample Essay Response

Effectiveness of the United Nations

Clearly, the United Nations is more than a peacekeeping organization. In fact, billions of dollars raised by the United Nations have had a positive impact on people around the world. Since its creation, the United Nations has helped those in need by improving health care, defending human rights, and assisting struggling countries.

There are millions of people around the world whose health has improved because of the United Nations. With the help of other organizations, the United Nations provides immunizations and safe drinking water. This group has also led the fight against the spread of diseases such as malaria and AIDS. As a result, the life expectancy of people throughout the world has increased.

The United Nations has also worked very hard to defend human rights. The United Nations has created the Universal Declaration of Human Rights to describe the freedoms and rights of all people. This declaration has triggered programs to assist women and children. It has also prompted the United Nations to protect refugees when their freedoms are threatened and they are forced to leave their homes.

Countries facing all kinds of crises are a priority for the United Nations as well. More than one-third of the world's food aid comes from a United Nations' agency. Each year, more than $4.5 billion is raised to help countries affected by natural disasters or war and to help struggling countries develop.

Although the United Nations is known for supplying peacekeeping troops, and often faces criticism for its efforts to keep peace, it has other benefits for people around the world. Health care, human rights, and disaster aid are three of its most important roles in touching the lives of people.

Learning

Essay Response

Ask students to point out ways in which the writer demonstrates her command of the information and ways that show she worked efficiently within a limited amount of time.

- The writer's opening sentence reveals indirectly that she knows the UN is a peacekeeping organization. The thesis statement later in the paragraph lists three additional things the UN does.
- Each of the three things mentioned becomes the topic of one of the three middle paragraphs, which are presented in the same order. This reveals the information clearly and succinctly.
- The writer provides specific details that demonstrate her understanding—such as mentioning malaria and AIDS, naming the Universal Declaration of Human Rights, providing the dollar amounts ($4.5 billion) for aid given.
- The writer acknowledges in the closing paragraph that not everyone shares her positive opinion about the UN. This shows that she's aware there is another side to the story.

Taking Standardized Tests

Discuss the purpose of standardized tests. Note that they generally are created by organizations outside the school and are intended to be given to large numbers of students under set—standardized—conditions.

Most students will already have some experience with standardized testing. Talk about what tests they have taken and what they did to prepare for them.

530

Taking Standardized Tests

At certain times throughout your school life, you will be required to take standardized tests. The guidelines below will help you take these tests.

Before the test . . .

- **Know what to expect.** Ask your teacher what subjects will be covered on the standardized test, what format will be used, and what day the test will be given.
- **Get a good night's rest.** Also be sure to eat breakfast before any test.
- **Be prepared.** Bring extra pens, pencils, and erasers. Make sure to have enough blank paper for notes, outlines, or numerical calculations.

During the test . . .

- **Listen to the instructions and carefully follow directions.** Standardized tests follow strict guidelines. You will be given exact instructions on how to fill in information and supply answers.
- **Pace yourself.** In general, don't spend more than one minute on an objective question; move on and come back to it later.
- **Keep your eyes on your own work.** Don't worry if others finish before you.
- **Match question numbers to answer numbers.** If you skip a question in the question booklet, be sure to skip the corresponding number on your answer sheet. Every few questions, double-check the question number against your answer sheet.
- **Answer every question.** As long as there is no penalty for incorrect answers, you should always answer every question. First eliminate all the choices that are obviously incorrect, and then use logic to make your best educated guess.
- **Review your answers.** If you have time left, make sure that you've answered all the questions and haven't made any accidental mistakes. In general, don't change an answer unless you are sure that it's wrong. If you need to change an answer, erase the original answer completely.

After the test . . .

- **Make sure you have filled in all information correctly.**
- **Erase any unnecessary marks before turning in your test.**

English Language Learners

Some students may qualify for additional time or special accommodations when taking standardized tests. Check district and state requirements to determine which students qualify.

Tips for Standardized Tests

Standardized tests in language arts assess your skills in areas such as vocabulary, word analysis, conventions, and reading comprehension. Below are tips for responding to these kinds of questions.

Vocabulary and Word Analysis

Some questions on standardized tests assess your vocabulary knowledge. You are tested on your ability to identify a word's literal and figurative meanings, usage, concept, power, or origin.

1. Which underlined word has the most negative connotation?

   A. The man's testimony was unfounded.
   B. The man's testimony was malicious.
   C. The man's testimony was damaging.
   D. The man's testimony was hurtful.

Conventions

These questions assess your command of the conventions of grammar, sentence structure, spelling, and punctuation.

2. Read the following sentence.

   I realize that our school cannot afford brand-new uniforms every year, but absolutely we can surely replace uniforms that are faded and torn.

   Which is the BEST way to improve the underlined part of the sentence?
   A. but surely we can replace uniforms that are faded and torn.
   B. yet absolutely we can replace faded and torn uniforms.
   C. but we can replace uniforms that are faded and torn absolutely.
   D. yet uniforms that are faded and torn we can surely replace.

Reading Comprehension and Literary Responses

In this section of a test, you are given a text passage to read. Then you answer questions about it. These questions test your comprehension and ability to draw conclusions. Use the following guidelines to help you answer these kinds of questions efficiently.

■ **Skim the questions before you read the passage.**

■ **Read the passage quickly but carefully.**

■ **Read all the choices before deciding which answer is best.**

Learning

Tips for Standardized Tests

Note that standardized tests are largely objective tests, so students can refer to the test-taking tips on SE pages 524–525 for additional help.

Explain that standardized tests are intended to measure students' mastery of what they've learned in school, so if they have kept up with their studies, they should already be well prepared. However, there are also books and test-taking courses available to help with certain standardized tests, such as PSAT and ACT assessments.

Suggest that interested students start by finding resources in the library or online to see the sort of information covered. They'll find explanations of the types of questions asked, lists of vocabulary words that commonly appear, and practice tests. Familiarizing themselves with what to expect can help prepare students and build confidence. Point out that in some cases, students are even allowed to retake tests to achieve a better score.

Struggling Learners

Some students may have difficulty with comprehension questions on standardized tests. To provide support, focus attention on the first bulleted guideline: *Skim the questions before you read the passage.* Ask students why they think this is a vital step. Guide them to see that the questions will help set a purpose for their reading.

Suggest that whenever students are presented with a passage to read and comprehension questions to answer, they

● read the questions quickly but carefully to get a sense of what they need to understand and

● take notes based on the questions as they read the passage.

Writing Paragraphs Level 9 Write Source (One Week)

Day	Writing and Skills Instruction	Student Edition		SkillsBook
		Main Pages	Resource Units*	
1	**Writing Effective Paragraphs** (Models)	561–567		
	(Topic Sentences)	563		
2–4	(Guidelines and Details)	568–570		
	(Models and Order)			
	Revising Skills: • Word Choice		548	154
	Editing Skills: • Capitalization, Abbreviations, Numbers		614 (+), 650–651, 652 (+), 658–659, 660–663	38, 47, 48, 49, 50
	Using the Right Word	690–691, 692–693		61
5 opt.	**Paragraph to Essay**	577–578		

* These units are also located in the back of the *Teacher's Edition*. Resource Units include "Basic Grammar and Writing," "A Writer's Resource," and "Proofreader's Guide."

(+) This activity is located in a different section of the *Write Source Student Edition*. If students have already completed this activity, you may wish to review it at this time.

Academic Vocabulary

Read aloud the academic terms, as well as the descriptions and questions. Model for students how to read one question and answer it. Have partners monitor their understanding and seek clarification of the terms by working through the meanings and questions together.

WRITE SOURCE Online

www.hmheducation.com/writesource

Basic Grammar and Writing

Writing Focus

Academic Vocabulary

Work with a partner. Read the definitions below and share your answers to the questions that follow.

1. To indicate can mean to be a sign of something.
   What does a grade of A+ on a test indicate?

2. Something is versatile when it is able to do many different things.
   When does a writer need to be versatile? Explain.

3. Emphasis is special weight placed on something considered important.
   When speaking, how do you give emphasis to an important idea? How do you do so when writing?

4. Unnecessary words that repeat something already stated are redundant.
   Why should you avoid writing a redundant phrase or sentence?

Using Words Effectively

In the world of fashion, style comes and goes. One year, hip-hugger jeans with bell-bottoms are in style, and the next year, high-waisted, straight-legged jeans are all the rage. In her book, *Sisterhood of the Traveling Pants*, Ann Brashares claims that "you must never double-cuff the pants. It's tacky." But in the world of fashion, "never" is a very short time.

It's different in the world of writing; good style is always in fashion. If you place just the right word in just the right spot, your writing will be in style tomorrow and next month and next year. This chapter discusses the parts of speech, showing you how to improve your use of words.

■ **Nouns**
■ **Pronouns**
■ **Verbs**
■ **Adjectives**
■ **Adverbs**
■ **Prepositions**
■ **Conjunctions**
■ **Checking Your Word Choice**

"Remember that the basic rule of vocabulary is *use the first word that comes to your mind, if it is appropriate and colorful.*"
—Stephen King

Nouns Using Specific Nouns

Since a noun names something, the more specific your nouns are, the more colorful and more precise your writing will be. Specific nouns pin down exactly **whom** and **what** you are writing about. Proper nouns (names of actual people, places, and things) are the most specific nouns you can use. Always capitalize proper nouns.

Vague and Dull

The **guy** walked out of the **building** and handed me the **papers**.

Specific and Interesting

The **policeman** walked out of the **courthouse** and handed me the **subpoena**.

The **exterminator** walked out of the **basement** and handed me the **bill**.

Extremely Specific and Interesting

Albert Einstein walked out of the **Kaiser Wilhelm Institute for Physics** and handed me the **"General Theory of Relativity."**

Try It!

Rewrite each numbered sentence, replacing the general nouns with specific ones. Create three versions of each sentence. Include some proper nouns.

Example: The **person** was a **man**.

The superhero was Sarcasm Man.
The Viking was Eric the Red.
The pirate was Three-Toed Jack.

1. The **food** was good.
2. The **man** climbed out of the **car** and waved the **book**.
3. The **storm** battered the **house** and the **truck**.

FYI

Besides being **common** or **proper**, nouns can be **concrete** or **abstract**. A concrete noun names a thing that is tangible (*can* be seen, heard, smelled, tasted, or touched).

telephone   spaghetti   letters   Mia Hamm

An abstract noun names a thing that *cannot* be seen, heard, smelled, tasted, or touched.

loyalty   freedom   soccer   Coriolis effect

Creating Appositives

An **appositive** is an explanatory word or phrase that renames or adds more information about the noun or pronoun that comes before it.

Appositive Word

My oldest sister, Carla, **loves sports.** ("Carla" renames "sister.")

Appositive Phrase

Carla, my oldest sister, **loves sports.**

("My oldest sister" adds information about "Carla.")

Try It!

Rewrite each of the following sentences, using your imagination to create an appositive after each **boldfaced** noun. Your appositives should use other nouns to rename or add information to the preceding noun or pronoun.

1. Carla's favorite **sports** have no varsity teams at our school.
2. She created an after-school student **club** dedicated to her favorite sports.
3. The club will become citywide if Carla can convince nearby **schools** to start their own clubs.
4. **Carla** can be extremely convincing.
5. Carla and her **friends** have really changed sports in our **city**.

FYI

Some appositives are **restrictive**—which means that they *restrict* the meaning of the word they rename.

• Carla's friend **Judy** is a great tennis player.

The appositive "Judy" restricts the meaning of "friend" by identifying *which* friend. After all, Carla has other friends. A restrictive appositive is not set off with commas.

A **nonrestrictive** appositive doesn't restrict the meaning of the word it renames.

• Carla's best friend, **Frances**, is an athlete as well.

"Frances" does not restrict the meaning of "friend" because Carla can have only one best friend. The nonrestrictive appositive is set off by commas.

Word Style

Answers will vary. Possible answers:

1. The spaghetti was good. The French toast was good. The pizza was good.
2. The banker climbed out of the convertible and waved *The Sphere*. Mr. Jay climbed out of the SUV and waved his checkbook. The soldier climbed out of the jeep and waved *The Art of Roadblocking*.
3. The hurricane battered the mansion and the dump truck. Hurricane Alpha battered the Holiday Terrace Apartments and the semi. The tornado battered the split-level and the fire truck.

Answers will vary. Possible answers:

1. Carla's favorite sports, table tennis and volleyball, have no varsity teams at our school.
2. She created an after-school student club, Fans Without Teams, dedicated to her favorite sports.
3. The club will become citywide if Carla can convince nearby schools, Franklin High and Jones Central, to start their own clubs.
4. Carla, a brilliant debater, can be extremely convincing.
5. Carla and her friends, Emile and Lelah, have really changed sports in our city, Sailton.

Pronouns Establishing Voice with Pronouns

The form of a personal pronoun indicates its number (*singular* or *plural*), its person (*first, second,* or *third*), its case (*nominative, possessive,* or *objective*), and its gender (*masculine, feminine,* or *neuter*). You can use these versatile words to establish the voice of your writing.

- **Write in the first person** to focus on personal thoughts, feelings, and experiences. Use this voice in freewriting, journals, personal narratives, and so on.

  I really blew it at play practice last night. **I** was late making **my** entrance, *and* **I** forgot **my** line.

- **Write in the second person** to speak directly to your reader, as in letters and e-mail messages. Some fiction writers experiment with this voice, but it should be avoided in formal writing assignments.

  Before **you** log off, **you** will want to save **your** work to a backup file.

- **Write in the third person** to focus on the subject, not yourself. Use this voice in most formal writing and in stories that are not about you.

  Conflicts may be unavoidable, but **they** can provide an opportunity to improve friendships among students.

Try It!

Identify the *person* in which these sentences are written (first, second, or third). Then rewrite each sentence, changing the person of the pronouns. What effect does each change have on the voice of the writing?

1. When the team of horses hauled our wagon to the crest of the hill, we saw that the wildfire had destroyed our farm.
2. You looked in dread at your barn, gutted and blackened, and your house, still smoldering, and saw that everything you owned was in ruins.
3. She stepped down from their wagon and put her feet on the sooty stalks of corn she and her husband had planted.
4. I said, "We should be glad. We all survived, and our land has been fertilized by this fire."
5. You plowed the ash under and rebuilt your home and barn, and the next year, your crops were more bountiful than ever.

Creating Suspense with Indefinite Pronouns

Usually, writers use pronouns and antecedents that are specific and precise. Notice how each pronoun in the following story has a clear antecedent. (An *antecedent* is the noun that the pronoun refers to or replaces.)

David had nearly drifted off when he heard Joe outside. David sat up. Joe wasn't supposed to be awake. Still, he was walking outside the tent.

"Are you out there, Joe?" The footsteps stopped. David listened. "I can hear you, Joe. What do you want?"

He finally answered, "The flashlight."

You can create suspense by using indefinite pronouns such as *something, somebody, nobody, nothing,* and *anything.* This version of the story *withholds* information from the reader, creating suspense.

David had nearly drifted off when he heard something outside. He sat up. Nobody was supposed to be awake. Still, someone or something was walking outside the tent.

"Is somebody out there?" The footsteps stopped. David listened. "I can hear you. What do you want?"

Someone finally answered, "Everything."

Try It!

Write your own suspenseful scene, using indefinite pronouns to withhold information from the reader. You might set your scene in a subway at night, a classroom before a major test, or an abandoned mine. Below is a list of indefinite pronouns to choose from.

Singular				Plural	Singular/Plural
another	each	more	one	both	all
anybody	everybody	nobody	some	few	any
anyone	everyone	no one	somebody	many	most
anything	everything	nothing	someone	several	none

Note: For academic essays, use specific pronouns and antecedents because they make your writing clear and answer the reader's questions. But for personal narratives and fictional stories, use indefinite pronouns when you want to keep your reader guessing.

Word Style

Try It! **Answers**

Rewritten sentences and their effects will vary. Possible answers are shown.

1. first person; When the team of horses hauled their wagon . . . , they saw that the wildfire had destroyed their farm. (The change shifts from a personal feeling to being outside of the action.)
2. second person; I looked in dread at my barn, . . . , and my house, . . . everything I owned was in ruins. (The feeling becomes personal.)
3. third person; We stepped down from our wagon and put our feet on the . . . corn we had planted. (The feeling becomes personal.)
4. first person; He said, "You should be glad. You all survived, and your land . . . fertilized . . . ." (The reader is removed from what has happened.)
5. second person; They plowed the ash . . . rebuilt their home . . . next year, their crops were more bountiful than ever. (The voice establishes an objective observation.)

Try It! **Answers**

Answers will vary.

Verbs Using Verbs to *Show* Instead of *Tell*

Verbs can be described as *static* or *dynamic*. Static verbs are forms of the verb *to be* and often use the passive voice. Dynamic verbs convey action and often use the active voice. They add interest to your writing.

- **Static verbs** are *be* verbs that *tell* what happens.
  Jim was excited about the letter from Kurt Vonnegut.
- **Dynamic verbs** are *action* verbs that *show* what happens.
  Jim whooped and waved the letter from Kurt Vonnegut.

Try It!

Read the following sentences, each with a static verb. Then choose a dynamic verb or two and build a new sentence that shows instead of tells.

Example: Jim usually was glum when there was mail.

Jim usually moped when the mail slid through the slot.

1. On Tuesday, Jim was excited.
2. His brother was jealous about the letter.
3. Jim was tough to put up with.

Using Specific Verbs

Verbs can also be *general* or *specific*. Some writers prop up general verbs by adding modifiers, but a specific verb is always a better choice.

Instead of writing . . .	Write . . .
angrily looked	scowled
looked with amazement or shock	gaped
intently looked	stared

Try It!

Replace these general verbs and modifiers with specific verbs. Use a thesaurus if you get stuck.

1. quietly said
2. stepped on heavily
3. loudly spoke
4. eagerly took

 Use dynamic, specific verbs. Complete the following story starter, using as many dynamic and specific verbs as you can.

Just as our helicopter shot over the snowy peak, the blizzard began. . . .

Understanding Onomatopoeia

Some verbs simply tell the reader what is happening. Other verbs seem to let the reader actually *hear* the action. The English language has more verbs than any other language on the globe, and many of those verbs make the sounds they describe. (The term *onomatopoeia* is used to identify these types of words.) Here are some examples.

Plain Verbs	laugh	break	eat	yell
Onomatopoetic Verbs	chuckle giggle snicker guffaw cackle bray	crack smash shatter crunch rip split	gulp gobble chomp swallow nibble gnaw	holler bellow blare shriek roar blast

Poets regularly use onomatopoeia in their poems; careful prose writers do, too. Onomatopoetic verbs work well even in articles and reports.

Plain Verbs
The railroad crossing alarm sounded, Dad applied the brakes, the car rolled to a stop, and a freight train went past our bumper.

Onomatopoetic Verbs
The railroad crossing alarm clanged, Dad stomped on the brakes, the car screeched to a stop, and a freight train screamed past our bumper.

Try It!

Use a thesaurus, if necessary, to find two onomatopoetic synonyms for each of the following plain verbs:

shake   cut   speak   cry   fly

 Use onomatopoeia. Think of a noisy setting that you know well—perhaps the cafeteria, a busy intersection, or the garage where a friend's band is practicing. Write a one-paragraph description of the noisy setting and use at least two or three onomatopoetic verbs in your writing.

Word Style

Try It! Answers

Answers will vary. Possible answers:

1. On Tuesday, Jim jumped up and down.
2. His brother glared at him and his precious letter.
3. Jim kept shouting, leaping, and laughing.

Try It! Answers

1. whispered
2. stomped
3. hollered
4. snatched

Try It! Answers

Answers will vary. Possible answers:
shake: quiver, shiver
cut: slice, slit
speak: chatter, babble
cry: blubber, bawl
fly: flutter, flap

Adjectives Using Objective and Subjective Adjectives

In terms of style, adjectives can be objective or subjective, depending on what they describe.

- **Objective adjectives** focus on the noun itself, describing qualities that anyone can objectively see.

  The tall, thin **farmer ambled toward the** short, stout **dog.**

- **Subjective adjectives** focus on the writer's feelings about the noun.

  The gangly **farmer ambled toward the** pudgy **dog.**

Each type of adjective has its place. When you want to create a factual, knowledgeable voice (as in expository essays and research reports), consider using objective adjectives. When you want to create an emotional, personal voice (as in personal narratives and some persuasive essays), consider using subjective adjectives.

Try It!

In each word pair below, decide which adjective is objective and which is subjective.

1. empty—pointless
2. lush—fertile
3. old—haggard
4. warm—inviting
5. unique—peculiar
6. huge—staggering
7. baffling—complex
8. small—cozy
9. vibrant—colorful
10. amorphous—blobby

FYI

You can create a subtle effect by using objective and subjective adjectives together.

  Niagara Falls is a **huge, staggering** cascade.
  The Mesopotamian landscape once was a **lush, fertile** Eden.
  I sought out a **warm, inviting** corner of the library.

This technique should be used sparingly to provide special emphasis.

 Use objective and subjective adjectives. Create a T-graph, writing objective adjectives on one side and subjective adjectives on the other. Try to list four of each. Then spend 5 minutes freewriting a paragraph that uses as many of the adjectives as you can.

Emphasizing with Adjectives

When you want to focus on the specific qualities of a person, a place, a thing, or an idea, you can create emphasis by varying the placement of adjectives in the sentence. Here are some techniques to try.

- **Place the adjectives at the beginning of the sentence.**

  Cold, hungry, and weary, the prospector staggered into town with his last nugget of gold.

- **Place adjectives at the end of the sentence.**

  He looked dejected. He felt defeated. For this one man, prospecting had been many things, but most of all it had been hard.

- **Place adjectives after the noun.**

  In the town bank, the teller, shifty eyed and suspicious, stared at the prospector as he hiked up to the window.

- **Repeat an adjective to emphasize it.**

  The prospector released a gusty sigh and handed over the gold nugget. "It's been a bad day at the end of a bad month at the end of a bad year. Give me some good news."

- **Contrast adjectives within a sentence.**

  The teller lifted the nugget to his long face and took a short look. "The bad news is that this here's fool's gold." He grinned. "The good news is that there's a diamond stuck in it."

- **Create a series of adjectives.**

  The prospector felt confused, amazed, elated.

Try It!

 Write an ending to the story of the prospector and the teller. Experiment with different strategies for emphasizing adjectives.

FYI

As with nouns and verbs, adjectives can be general or specific; specific adjectives are usually better. Write about a *brisk* wind rather than a *cold* wind, or a *grating* sound instead of an *annoying* sound.

Word Style

Try It! Answers

	Objective	Subjective
1	empty	pointless
2	fertile	lush
3	old	haggard
4	warm	inviting
5	unique	peculiar
6	huge	staggering
7	complex	baffling
8	small	cozy
9	colorful	vibrant
10	amorphous	blobby

Try It! Answers

Answers will vary

Adverbs Answering Questions

An adverb (or a phrase or clause that functions as an adverb) answers questions such as *how? when? where? why? to what degree? how often?* The great advantage of the adverb is that it can be placed almost anywhere. Different adverb positions create different effects.

- **Begin with an adverb.** Start a sentence with an adverb to emphasize the quality of the action.

  Abruptly, **the party ended.**

    (adverb emphasizing *how*)

  When Mrs. Jones walked in, **the party ended.**

    (adverb clause emphasizing *when*)

- **Interrupt the flow of the sentence.** To give special emphasis to an adverb (word, phrase, or clause), place it in the middle of the sentence.

  Mrs. Jones deliberately **and** ferociously **met her son's gaze.**

  Mrs. Jones, with eyes like heat-seeking missiles, **met her son's gaze.**

- **End with an adverb.** Place the adverb (word, phrase, or clause) at the end of the sentence, set off by a comma or a dash, to create a strong sense of finality.

  Young Mr. Jones replied, "I'm sorry, Mom—very.**"**

  Young Mr. Jones replied, "I'm sorry, Mom, more than you know.**"**

FYI

Even though adverbs can be placed almost anywhere in a sentence, there are still a few places they should not appear. For example, adverbs should not appear between a verb and a direct or an indirect object.

Don't **write:**   Mrs. Jones scowled as her son opened **slowly** the door.
Do **write:**   Mrs. Jones scowled as her son **slowly** opened the door.

Also, an adverb that answers the question *when* should not appear between the subject and the verb.

Don't **write:**   The other party guests **at that moment** shouted, "Surprise!"
Do **write:**   **At that moment,** the other party guests shouted, "Surprise!"

 Experiment with adverb placement. Write an ending to the story about the surprise party for Mrs. Jones. Include adverbs, and experiment with placing them in different positions throughout the sentence.

Avoiding Unnecessary Adverbs

Adverb abuse is a sad fact of bad writing. Eliminate adverbs from your work when they contribute nothing to the meaning.

- **Eliminate redundant adverbs.** Adverbs are often not needed if you use strong verbs.

  Recently, the energy secretary growled angrily **at the press.**

  Recently, the energy secretary growled at the press.

- **Drop telling adverbs.** Don't try to persuade by overusing adverbs such as *absolutely, apparently, certainly, clearly, definitely,* and *undoubtedly.* These words are usually unnecessary to the real meaning. They only emphasize the writer's bias.

  Obviously, **politicians can't continue to let fuel prices rise.**

  Politicians can't continue to let fuel prices rise.

- **Avoid unnecessary amplifiers.** Speakers of British English commonly use *rather, really,* and *quite,* even though these words don't add any meaning to an idea. These words are not commonly used in American English, which is much more direct.

  Consumers are really quite **bothered by these** rather **high prices.**

  Consumers are bothered by these high prices.

Try It!

Read the following paragraph and identify unneeded adverbs.

1   When ancient plants and animals died completely, their bodies were
2 totally compacted to create coal, oil, and natural gas. These creatures certainly
3 transferred the carbon in their bodies to the fossil fuels we now obviously use.
4 When we burn up those fuels, we quite undoubtedly let out all that carbon into
5 the atmosphere again. This practice very definitely must stop before the world
6 turns back into a really hot planet.

FYI

Hopefully is a problem adverb: Hopefully, hybrid cars will help reduce pollution. What the writer means is "I hope hybrid cars will help reduce pollution," but the sentence actually means "Hybrid cars will help reduce pollution with hope." So avoid beginning sentences with *hopefully.*

Word Style

Try It!   **Answers**

Unneeded adverbs: completely, totally, certainly, obviously, up, quite, undoubtedly, out, again, very, definitely, back, really

Prepositions Accelerating Your Verbs

When a verb in a sentence shows movement, prepositions will direct the action. Consider the following simple sentence and notice how the prepositions extend and direct the motion of the verb *paddled*. This technique creates a strong sense of continuing action and is useful in writing about exciting events.

The kayaker paddled over a six-foot plunge, through a boiling cauldron, between towering rocks, down a channel of white water, and over a waterfall.

Creating an Appropriate Mood

In contrast to using multiple prepositional phrases to direct action, you can use a single prepositional phrase with multiple objects to create a dreamy, thoughtful feeling.

Marlene lingered beside the sun-dappled meadow, the corral where the foals trotted with their mothers, the barn her great-grandfather had built with his own hands, and the farmhouse that now bore the sign "For Sale."

Try It!

Complete each of the following sentence starters twice. First, complete the starter with a series of prepositional phrases to create strong, continuing action. Then try using a single preposition with multiple objects to create a thoughtful mood. (Some prepositions are listed below. See page **732** for more.)

1. A quarter horse galloped . . .
2. An old man sauntered . . .
3. The race car roared . . .
4. Some music blared . . .

above	behind	for	off	to
across	below	from	on	toward
after	beneath	in	onto	under
along	beside	inside	on top of	until
among	between	into	out	up
around	by	like	over	upon
at	down	near	past	within
away from	during	of	through	without

Experiment with prepositions. Freewrite for 5 minutes about a recent experience you have had. If the experience was fast paced and full of action, try using a series of prepositional phrases to extend the action of the verb. If the experience was quiet and reflective, try using a single preposition with many objects.

Creating Emphasis

Sometimes, prepositions work without calling attention to themselves. At other times, the preposition takes center stage, as in Abraham Lincoln's address at Gettysburg:

" . . . that government of the people, by the people, and for the people shall not perish from the earth."

You can use prepositional phrases to expand a sentence and create emphasis in a number of ways.

- **Begin a sentence with a series of prepositional phrases.** Use the phrases to build anticipation in the mind of the reader.

  On a dreamy evening, after a day of blazing sun, under the green arms of a chestnut tree, we met.

- **Use several prepositions with a single object.** In the style of Mr. Lincoln, create a string of prepositional phrases that have the same object but a different preposition.

  I'd rather have people laugh with me than at me, let alone without me.

- **Use a single preposition with several objects.** Create a strong rhythm by varying the objects but not the preposition.

  The army fought through the barricades, through the city streets, and through the enemy lines.

Try It!

Add prepositional phrases to the sentences below. Try a different strategy for each sentence.

1. The elk raised his antlered head.
2. Cyclists rode.
3. The reforms were denied.

FYI

Prepositions have a unique function: they turn nouns into modifiers. Take the noun *pajamas*. Add a preposition—*in pajamas*—and the combination becomes a modifier. Now you can add more modifiers—*in red-striped pajamas*, or *in the red-striped pajamas that Winston Churchill wore during the London air raids*. A single preposition can unlock a world of meaning.

Word Style

Try It! Answers

Answers will vary. Possible answers:

1. . . . galloped out of the gate, past the other horses, and across the finish line. . . . galloped away from the open gate, the sounding gun, and the noisy crowd.
2. . . . sauntered across the road, through the park, over the bridge, and down the bank of the river. . . . sauntered through the crowded streets, the city gardens, and the busy parking lot.
3. . . . roared down the straightaway, along cobblestone streets, and toward the final lap. . . . roared toward the dangerous curve, the city center, and the victor's circle.
4. . . . blared out the window, across the courtyard, and into the library reading room. . . . blared past the sleeping students, the sweating gardeners, and the focused readers.

Try It! Answers

Answers will vary. Possible answers:

1. The elk raised his antlered head above the small spruce tree beyond the stream in the evening twilight.
2. Cyclists in the off-road competition rode toward the storm, into the storm, and through the storm that decimated the course.
3. Before the school year, during the school committee meeting, for the sake of lower student fees, the reforms were denied.

Conjunctions Creating Rhythm with "And"

Instead of using commas to connect words, groups of words, and sentences, you can use the word *and*.

> lions, tigers, and bears

> lions and tigers and bears (oh my!)

This technique is called *polysyndeton*, which means "many conjunctions." Note how this gives every item special emphasis, doing as much to separate the items as to join them. This technique creates rhythm and emphasis.

> **The civil rights movement** and **the Watergate scandal** and **the equal rights movement** changed the United States profoundly during the '60s and '70s.

You may have used this same technique when you were trying to describe a hectic day.

> **After school, I ran laps** and **took a shower** and **worked in the deli** and **finished my homework** and **crawled into bed.**

Try It!

List the things you plan to do on Saturday. After you have four or five items, write a sentence with the list as a standard series, including commas and a single "and." Next, rewrite the sentence using polysyndeton. Then do the same for the main things that you would like to do next summer.

Tip

Limit your use of this technique to times when you want to create a special effect. In the following excerpt from *Dombey and Son*, Charles Dickens uses polysyndeton to create a sense of disorder as he describes the cluttered land near a new railroad. In the hands of a less skillful writer, this may have become simply a rambling sentence.

> "There were frowzy fields, and cow-houses, and dunghills, and dustheaps, and ditches, and gardens, and summer-houses, and carpet-beating grounds, at the very door of the Railway."

Using Subordinating Conjunctions

A subordinating conjunction shows the relationship between two clauses. Such conjunctions can show time, cause and effect, and logical connections.

Showing Time
After the mayor finished her speech, the press asked her questions.

> after, as, as long as, before, since, till, until, when, while

Showing Cause and Effect
She said the city budget was tight **because** spring floods required expensive cleanup.

> because, if/then, in order that, provided that, since, so that

Showing Logical Connections
"**Although** money is tight," the mayor said, "we have enough to keep the city running."

> although, as if, as though, that, though, unless, whereas, while

When two short sentences express ideas that are related by time, cause and effect, or a logical relationship, consider combining them with a subordinating conjunction.

Try It!

Combine the following pairs of sentences by selecting a subordinating conjunction showing the relationship between the ideas.

1. The spring rains raised the river to record heights.
   Public facilities along the river were flooded.
2. The cleanup effort after the flood helped the whole city.
   The whole city should be willing to pay for the cost.
3. Next year's budget will also be tight.
   The city will continue to look for sources of funds.
4. New funds will be found.
   Improvements will be made to the storm sewers.

Tip

If the clause with the subordinating conjunction comes first, place a comma after the clause. If the clause with the conjunction comes last, you usually do not need a comma. Use a comma, however, if the clause begins with a conjunction that expresses a contrast, such as *although, even though,* or *while*.

Word Style

Try It! **Answers**

Answers will vary.

Try It! **Answers**

Answers will vary. Possible answers:

1. When the spring rains raised the river to record heights, public facilities along the river were flooded.
2. Since the cleanup effort after the flood helped the whole city, the whole city should be willing to pay for the cost.
3. Because next year's budget will also be tight, the city will continue to look for sources of funds.
4. New funds will be found so that improvements will be made to the storm sewers.

Checking Your Word Choice

Writers often have difficulty evaluating and improving word choice. They see the essay, the paragraphs, the sentences, but somehow they gloss right over the individual words. Improving your word choice is just a matter of *looking*. The following scavenger hunt can help you evaluate the word choice in all your writing.

Word-Choice Scavenger Hunt

1. Find the three most specific nouns in your work. <u>Teddy Roosevelt, piranha, expedition</u>

2. Find the three most general nouns in your work and suggest specific nouns to replace them. <u>boat (dugout), river (Amazon), disease (malaria)</u>

3. Find three verbs with strong onomatopoeia. <u>pelted, trundled, slogged</u>

4. Find three verbs that could be stronger and suggest replacements. <u>wanted (longed for), tried (struggled), got (snatched)</u>

5. Find your most effective objective adjective. <u>detailed (plan)</u>

6. Find your most effective subjective adjective. <u>fanatical (vision)</u>

7. Find three adverbs that could be cut or replaced. <u>suddenly, very, extremely</u>

8. Find one sentence in which you have emphasized adjectives or prepositions. <u>Wounded, bleeding, and antagonized, Roosevelt pulled the speech from his breast pocket, showed the bullet hole in it, and declared, "It takes more than that to kill a bull moose!"</u>

9. Find three subordinating conjunctions you used. <u>when, although, despite</u>

 Try It!

Review your first draft of a current writing assignment. Evaluate your word choice by completing the scavenger hunt above.

Understanding Sentence Style

Writer Patricia T. O'Conner says that a well-written sentence really is "a triumph of engineering." On its own, an effective sentence states a complete thought, using just enough words and no more. As part of a longer piece of writing, it carries an important idea and connects the reader with the ideas that come before and after it.

To become sentence-smart, make reading and writing important in your life. Read anything and everything that you can get your hands on, and write regularly on your own. Your personal reading and writing will help you develop an ear for good sentences. In addition, follow the guidelines in this chapter for writing sentences.

- **Sentence Balance**
- **Sentence Length**
- **Sentence Variety**
- **Sentence Combining**
- **Sentence Problems**
- **Sentence Modeling**

"Don't be afraid to throw more than one verb in a sentence. I think She *twisted and fell* is more exciting than *She twisted. She fell to the ground.*"

—Martyn Godfrey

Try It! **Answers**

Answers will vary.

Sentence Balance Using Parallel Construction

You can create balance in sentences by using **parallel construction**. This means repeating similar grammatical elements (words or phrases) to give your writing rhythm. Here are some ways to make your sentences parallel.

Sentence Elements	Example	Technique Used
Words— All words in a series should be the same *parts of speech*.	**Not parallel:** Opera can amuse, sadden, or make you think. **Parallel:** Opera can **amuse**, **sadden**, or **inspire**.	All the words in the series are **verbs**.
	Parallel: Opera can be **amusing**, **depressing**, or **inspiring**.	All the words in the series are **adjectives**.
Phrases— All phrases in a series should be the same *type*.	**Not parallel:** The audience members reacted to the show by jumping to their feet, cheering for an encore, and with calls of "Bravo!" **Parallel:** The audience members reacted to the show by **jumping to their feet**, **cheering for an encore**, and **calling "Bravo!"**	All the phrases are **participial phrases** (they start with *-ing* words).
	Parallel: The audience began **to cheer**, **to jump to their feet**, and **to call "Bravo!"**	All the phrases are **infinitive phrases** (they start with *to*).

 Try It!

Rewrite each of the following sentences, using parallel construction.

1. I enjoy swimming, to play computer games, and when we go to the movies.
2. When I choose music, I listen to jazz, rock, and chilling out to Latin rhythms.
3. Our library contains study tables, computer stations, and it has a reading corner.
4. Korean summers are hot, it rains a lot, and humid.

Sentence Length Writing Short Sentences

The length of your sentences contributes to the effect you wish to establish in a piece of writing. Short sentences often make a strong point.

Creating Suspense

Short sentences add excitement to your writing by suggesting suspense. Compare the two paragraphs below.

> The room had always presented an uncomfortable feeling, but now, as the door slowly opened with a long, creaky sound, the inside seemed even less welcoming.

> With an eerie creak, the door slowly opened. The room had never before seemed so frightening.

Stepping Up the Pace

Short sentences help create a sense of speed and urgency by pulling the reader through a fast-moving situation. Again, compare the examples below.

> As the door opened with a weird creak, a spider ominously disappeared into the shadows. The dark room loomed, and I found that my feet were rooted to the ground, even as my mind was filled with thoughts of what awaited me.

> The door creaked. A spider disappeared into the shadows. Inside, the room was dark. My feet wouldn't move, but my imagination raced.

Emphasizing Key Points

Short sentences set among longer ones create emphasis.

> I called out into the darkness for the assurance that someone human would join me. There was no answer. Moving through the darkness, I tentatively eased my barefoot way across the cool wooden floor, hoping to find a light switch, a lamp, a candle. I found none. I tried to take a deep breath, to focus on adjusting my eyes to the blackness. The silence was thick as cotton, stuffing my ears and muffling even the sound of my heartbeat. Then I heard a crash.

Try It!

Write an ending to the story beginning above. Use some short sentences to create suspense, speed, or emphasis.

Sentence Style

Try It! **Answers**

1. I enjoy swimming, playing computer games, and going to the movies.
2. When I choose music, I listen to jazz, rock, and Latin rhythms.
3. Our library contains study tables, computer stations, and a reading corner.
4. Korean summers are hot, rainy, and humid.

Try It! **Answers**

Answers will vary.

Writing Long Sentences

Long sentences can effectively package important information. Here are three ways to build longer, more intricate sentences.

Type of Long Sentence	Uses	Example
Loose sentences express the main clause or idea near the beginning and follow with modifiers.	Add layers to the main idea, creating a more informative sentence.	**We ran drill after drill**, all the time with Coach Mayland encouraging us to pick up the pace.
Periodic sentences postpone the most important or most surprising idea until the end.	Add a sense of suspense as the reader works through to the main idea.	Following Coach's threats to make us run the "stops," **we almost immediately improved our footwork.**
Cumulative sentences place the main idea in the middle, with modifying phrases and clauses coming before and after.	Create a detailed, complex sentence.	Once we finished the passing drills, **Coach finally blew his whistle**, signaling a much-needed water break.

Try It!

Copy each of the following sentences on your own paper. Then underline the main clause or idea and identify the type of each sentence—either loose, periodic, or cumulative.

1. The tornado swept through the town, leaving a trail of destruction that shocked everyone.
2. Because the tornado was completely unexpected, it caused extensive damage, including uprooted trees, broken windows, and twisted road signs.
3. Within a matter of minutes during a warm summer evening, a small town changed forever.

Sentence Variety Varying Sentence Beginnings

In paragraphs and essays, varied sentence beginnings can make your writing interesting. Here are some different beginnings that will add variety to your sentences.

Beginning with a Subject

Chaya **spilled some of the chemicals used in the safety drill.**
The other students **followed safety procedures.**

Beginning with a Modifying Word or Phrase

Quickly, **they pulled on safety gloves and switched on the ventilation hoods.**

Standing quietly at the door, **the teacher made notes on a clipboard.**

As the seconds ticked by, **the class worked to clean up the chemicals.**

Because they had gone through the practice many times, **the students knew exactly what to do.**

Try It!

All of the sentences below begin with the subject. Create sentence variety by rewriting some of the sentences to begin with modifying words, phrases, or clauses.

1. Chelsey and her sister Kara both need rides from their after-school activities.
2. Chelsey volunteers at the city's homeless shelter two days a week.
3. Kara has soccer practice every day at the high school.
4. Their mother's office is not far from the shelter.
5. She picks Chelsey up after work.
6. Chelsey sometimes has to wait if her mother works late.
7. The girls' father picks up Kara at practice.
8. He often finishes work early, so he reads in the car until practice is over.
9. The girls would like to get their own car someday so their parents don't always have to pick them up.

Sentence Style

Try It! Answers

1. The tornado swept through the town; loose
2. it caused extensive damage; cumulative
3. a small town changed forever; periodic

Try It! Answers

Answers will vary. Possible answers:

1. unchanged
2. Two days a week, Chelsey volunteers at the city's homeless shelter.
3. unchanged
4. Because their mother's office is not far from the shelter, she picks Chelsey up after work.
5. combined with 4
6. Sometimes Chelsey has to wait if her mother works late.
7. unchanged
8. Since he often finishes work early, he reads in the car until practice is over.
9. Someday the girls would like to get their own car so that their parents don't always have to pick them up.

Expanding Sentences

You can use the 5 W's and H—*Who? What? Where? When? Why? How?*—to expand short sentences. For example, look at this basic sentence:

> Spices were important trade items.

Now see how using the 5 W's and H adds details and makes the sentence longer and more interesting.

Who?	Spices were important trade items **to European customers**.
What?	Spices **such as cinnamon and pepper** were important trade items to European customers.
Where?	Spices **from the East**, such as cinnamon and pepper, were important trade items to European customers.
When?	Spices from the East, such as cinnamon and pepper, were important trade items to European customers **in the thirteenth century**.
Why?	Spices from the East, such as cinnamon and pepper, were important trade items to European customers, **providing them a way to make plain food taste better**.
How?	Spices such as cinnamon and pepper, **brought with great difficulty in caravans from the East**, were important trade items to European customers in the thirteenth century.

Tip
How Usually, you will not use all of the 5 W's and H in one sentence. Be careful not to overload a sentence with details.

Try It!
Using the 5 W's and H to add details, rewrite one of the sentences below. Use as many details as you can without making the sentence cumbersome.

1. The employees loaded the trucks.
2. The mall bustled.
3. People hurried along.

Sentence Style Combining Short, Choppy Sentences

Sentence combining is the act of making one smoother, more detailed sentence from two or more short sentences.

Using a Series of Words
Ideas from short sentences can be combined into one sentence using a series of words.

- **Three Short Sentences:**
  Medications may cause insomnia.
  Caffeine may keep you from sleeping.
  Poor eating habits may also bring on sleep problems.
- **Combined Sentence:**
  Medications, caffeine, and poor eating habits may cause insomnia.

Using a Series of Phrases
These are all acceptable sentences, but see what happens when they are combined. The ideas flow more smoothly.

- **Three Short Sentences:**
  Carlos loves to play video games.
  He loves to watch movies.
  He loves to surf the Net.
- **Combined Sentence:**
  Carlos loves to play video games, watch movies, and surf the Net.

Try It!
Combine each group of short sentences into one smoother sentence.

1. Headaches can cause insomnia. Worry can cause a loss of sleep. Illness can cause insomnia.
2. Insomnia can be brought on by stress. Insomnia can be caused by excitement. Insomnia can be the result of outside noise.
3. Insomnia produces irritability. Sleeplessness causes nervousness. It also triggers memory problems.
4. Taking a warm bath can help you overcome insomnia. Drinking warm milk can help you sleep. Listening to soft music can help you sleep.

Try It! Answers

Answers will vary. Possible answers:

1. Yesterday in Atlanta, employees of Filmat's Industries, using heavy-duty forklifts, loaded relief supplies onto five semi trailers for Louisiana's hurricane victims.
2. As I was shopping for my mother's birthday present yesterday, the mall bustled with shoppers catching the end-of-year sales.
3. In the midst of the summer heat wave, people hurried along the subway platform, trying to seek relief in the fresh air.

Try It! Answers

Answers will vary. Possible answers:

1. Headaches, worry, and illness can cause insomnia.
2. Insomnia can be brought on by stress, excitement, and outside noise.
3. Insomnia produces irritability, causes nervousness, and triggers memory problems.
4. Taking a warm bath, drinking warm milk, or listening to soft music can help you overcome insomnia.

Using Other Types of Phrases

Ideas from shorter sentences can also be combined into one sentence by using phrases.

- **Short Sentences:**

  Most students need to be rested in order to do well.
  They need to do well in their classes.

- **Combined Using a Prepositional Phrase:**

  Most students need to be rested in order to do well in their classes.

- **Short Sentences:**

  Newborns are babies in their first few days of life.
  They need 17 hours of sleep per day.

- **Combined Using an Appositive Phrase:**

  Newborns, babies in their first few days of life, need 17 hours of sleep per day.

Try It!

Combine each set of short sentences into one sentence using a phrase.

1. Some adults are not getting enough sleep.
   These adults are in their working years.
2. Older adults need less sleep than young adults do.
   Older adults are people over 60.
3. Young adults really should sleep nine to ten hours per day.
   They should sleep this long during their formative years.
4. Dreams often last several hours.
   Dreams are an important part of sleep.
5. Thomas Edison took many short naps throughout the day.
   He was a very famous inventor.
6. Sleep is a time for the body to heal itself.
   Sleep is essential for good health.

 Review a piece of writing. Read over something that you have recently written. Try to find two or three sets of sentences that you could combine. Write them as combined sentences to see how they sound.

Sentence Problems Avoiding Sentence Errors

Avoid the following sentence problems when you write—or correct them as you revise.

Correcting Run-On Sentences

Run-on sentences occur when two sentences are joined without punctuation or without a connecting word (*and, but, or*).

- **Run-On Sentence:** Wing-walking was a popular stunt during the 1920s Ormer Locklear is credited with popularizing the activity among young daredevils.
- **Corrected as Two Sentences:** Wing-walking was a popular stunt during the 1920s. Ormer Locklear is credited with popularizing the activity among young daredevils.
- **Corrected as a Compound Sentence:** Wing-walking was a popular stunt during the 1920s, and Ormer Locklear is credited with popularizing the activity among young daredevils.

Eliminating Comma Splices

Comma splices occur when a comma is placed between two independent clauses without a conjunction.

- **Comma Splice:** Locklear liked to think he was providing a real service, he claimed he was showing people that anything was possible if they tried.
- **Corrected as Two Sentences:** Locklear liked to think he was providing a real service. He claimed he was showing people that anything was possible if they tried.
- **Corrected as a Compound Sentence:** Locklear liked to think he was providing a real service, and he claimed he was showing people that anything was possible if they tried.

Try It!

 Read the following paragraph. On your own paper, rewrite any run-on or comma splice, fixing the error.

(1) Wing-walking was not limited to men many women also tried the stunt high above the ground. (2) Gladys Ingle became famous for transferring from one plane's wing to another, she also practiced archery on the moving plane's wing. (3) Mabel Cody shared the adventurous spirit of her uncle "Buffalo Bill" Cody the daredevil became the first woman to successfully transfer from a boat to an airplane. (4) The first African American woman pilot was Bessie Coleman. She was best known as a parachute jumper.

Sentence Style

Try It!   Answers

1. Some adults in their working years are not getting enough sleep.
2. Older adults, people over 60, need less sleep than young adults do.
3. Young adults really should sleep nine to ten hours per day during their formative years.
4. Dreams, an important part of sleep, often last several hours.
5. Thomas Edison, a very famous inventor, took many short naps throughout the day.
6. Sleep, a time for the body to heal itself, is essential for good health.

Try It!   Answers

(1) Wing walking was not limited to men. Many women also tried the stunt high above the ground. (2) Gladys Ingle became famous for transferring from one plane's wing to another, and she also practiced archery on the moving plane's wing. (3) Mabel Cody shared the adventurous spirit of her uncle "Buffalo Bill" Cody. The daredevil became the first woman to successfully transfer from a boat to an airplane. (4) The first African American woman pilot was Bessie Coleman. She was best known as a parachute jumper.

Fixing Fragments

A fragment is not a sentence because it does not communicate a complete thought. In a sentence fragment, a subject, a predicate, or both are missing.

Fragment: Became a national park in 1919. (A subject is needed.)

The Grand Canyon **became a national park in 1919.**

Fragment: Sure-footed burros down paths in the canyon. (A predicate is needed.)

Sure-footed burros **walk** **down paths in the canyon.**

Fragment: Through the canyon. (A subject and a predicate are needed.)

People **raft** **through the canyon.**

Try It!

Rewrite each of the following fragments as a complete sentence. (Some of the examples are complete sentences.)

1. More than 270 miles long, 15 miles wide, and 5,000 feet deep.
2. The Colorado River carved out the Grand Canyon.
3. At the bottom of the canyon.
4. The river has been cutting the rock for six million years.
5. Filled with high ridges and deep valleys.
6. The rock formation known as "The Alligator" amazes people.
7. John Wesley Powell, the first geologist to explore the area.
8. Traveled through the canyon in a small boat.
9. The dangerous journey was completed in 1869.

Rewriting Rambling Sentences

Rambling sentences are those that seem to go on and on. Their parts are connected by coordinating conjunctions. While not grammatically incorrect, these sentences are hard to read. As a rule, if your sentence has more than two coordinating conjunctions, try to divide it into shorter sentences.

Rambling: The man in line in front of us had two little children, and he was having trouble keeping them quiet so Raul started doing some of his magic tricks and the children didn't make a sound until their dad got their tickets.

Better: The man in line in front of us had two little children. He was having trouble keeping them quiet, so Raul started doing some of his magic tricks. The children didn't make a sound until their dad got their tickets.

Moving Misplaced Modifiers

Misplaced modifiers are modifiers that have been placed incorrectly in a sentence. A modifier should be as close as possible to the word it modifies.

Misplaced: After finishing the last song, the press met with the singer.
(Did the press sing?)

Corrected: After finishing the last song, the singer met with the press.

Correcting Dangling Modifiers

A dangling modifier appears to modify a word that isn't in the sentence. It "dangles" because it's not attached to anything.

Dangling: Fighting for breath, the finish line seemed very far away.
(Who or what is fighting for breath?)

Corrected: Fighting for breath, Kali thought the finish line seemed very far away.

Try It!

Rewrite each of the sentences below so that it does not contain a misplaced modifier.

1. The boat puttered down the river loaded with excited tourists.
2. Hanging from the trees, we could see hundreds of monkeys.
3. Skewered by a spear, our guide removed the wriggling fish.

Changing Double Subjects

Do not use a pronoun immediately after the subject.

Double Subject: Felix's letter jacket **it** needs to be cleaned.

Corrected: Felix's letter jacket needs to be cleaned.

Correcting Double Negatives

Do not use two negative words together, like *never* and *no*, or *not* and *no*. Also, do not use *hardly, barely,* or *scarcely* with a negative word.

Double Negative: She **never** saw **no one** run so fast.

Corrected: She **never** saw **anyone** run so fast.

Try It!

Rewrite each of the sentences below so that it does not contain a double subject or a double negative.

1. Blue whales they are the largest mammals on earth.
2. The female blue whale she can be up to 110 feet long.
3. A baby blue whale doesn't eat no solid foods.

Sentence Style

Try It! Answers

Answers will vary. Possible answers:

1. The Grand Canyon is more than 270 miles long, 15 miles wide, and 5,000 feet deep.
2. complete
3. The Colorado River lies at the bottom of the canyon.
4. complete
5. The canyon is filled with high ridges and deep valleys.
6. complete
7. John Wesley Powell became the first geologist to explore the area.
8. He traveled through the canyon in a small boat.
9. complete

Sentence Modeling Writing Stylish Sentences

Many painters learn to paint by copying famous works of art. Writers, too, can learn to write better by modeling sentence patterns used by professional writers.

Model: I bought a jug of milk and fell off my bike, breaking the glass jug, cutting my leg.

—Thylias Moss, "Wings"

New Sentence: I found an album of family photographs and paged through it, enjoying each photo, losing track of time.

Try It!

Select two of the sentences below and write your own sentences, modeling the sentence structure as closely as possible.

1. The steam from the kettle had condensed on the cold window and was running down the glass in tear-like trickles.

—Jessamyn West, "Sixteen"

2. His hands were white and small, his frame was fragile, his voice was quiet, and his manners were refined.

—James Joyce, "A Little Cloud"

3. Jim dipped his hand into the trough and stirred the moon to broken, swirling streams of light.

—John Steinbeck, "The Murder"

4. In the darkness, Mr. Shiftlet's smile stretched like a weary snake waking up by a fire.

—Flannery O'Connor, "The Life You Save May Be Your Own"

5. In cotton-picking time the late afternoons revealed the harshness of Black Southern life, which in the early morning had been softened by nature's blessing of grogginess, forgetfulness, and the soft lamplight.

—Maya Angelou, *I Know Why the Caged Bird Sings*

Writing Effective Paragraphs

Writer Donald Hall calls a paragraph a "maxi-sentence" or a "mini-essay." What he means is this: A paragraph is a special unit of writing that does more than the typical sentence and less than the typical essay. If you can write strong paragraphs, you can develop effective essays, articles, and research papers.

A paragraph is made up of a group of sentences focused on one topic. A paragraph can tell a story, describe, share information, or express an opinion. Whatever form a paragraph takes, it must contain enough details to give the reader a complete picture of the topic. The first sentence usually identifies the topic, the middle sentences support it, and the last sentence wraps things up.

- The Parts of a Paragraph
- Types of Paragraphs
- Writing Guidelines
- Types of Details
- Patterns of Organization
- Modeling Paragraphs
- Connecting Paragraphs in Essays
- Paragraph Traits Checklist

"Writing is the solid construction of thoughts."

—Donald Murray

Try It! Answers

Answers will vary.

The Parts of a Paragraph

A typical paragraph consists of three main parts: a **topic sentence**, the **body sentences**, and a **closing sentence**. A paragraph can develop an explanation, an opinion, a description, or a narrative. Whatever form a paragraph takes, it must contain enough information to give readers a complete picture of the topic. The following expository paragraph provides information about a remarkable breed of dog. Notice that each detail in the body supports the topic sentence.

Topic Sentence

Body

Closing Sentence

Gentle Giants

Of all dogs, perhaps the greatest helper breed has been the Newfoundland. Because of their Canadian origin and English breeding, "Newfs" are ideally suited for life by the water. They boast great lung capacity, an oily outer fur, and webbed feet! This gentle animal is a natural retriever; at 150 pounds, it can easily bring a drowning human to safety. However, the dog's usefulness through the centuries has not been limited to lifesaving. These large canines can lug as much as 2,000 pounds, and in their native province, they were once used to haul fishing nets as well as carts of fish, milk, or mail. At one time, Newfs were part of a sailing ship's crew, sometimes used to swim a line to land in choppy waters. If a ship were sinking, the animals would be sent with lifelines to rescue drowning crew members. Newfs are as gentle as they are strong and can be loving, protective companions to children. Indeed, this huge, devoted dog is one of the greatest partners to bless humankind.

 Respond to the Reading. What main idea about the topic does this paragraph communicate? What specific details support this idea?

A Closer Look at the Parts

Whether a paragraph stands alone or is part of an extended piece of writing, it contains three elements.

The Topic Sentence

A **topic sentence** tells the reader what your paragraph is about. The topic sentence should do two things: (1) name the specific topic of the paragraph and (2) identify a particular feeling or feature about the topic. Here is a simple formula for writing a topic sentence.

a specific topic
+ a particular feeling or feature about the topic

= an effective topic sentence

Newfoundland dogs
+ perhaps the greatest helper breed

= Of all dogs, perhaps the greatest helper breed has been the Newfoundland.

Tip

How The topic sentence is *usually* the first sentence in a paragraph. However, it can also be located elsewhere. For example, you can present details that build up to an important summary topic sentence at the end of a paragraph.

The Body

The sentences in the **body** of the paragraph should all support the idea expressed in the topic sentence. Each sentence should add new details about the topic.

- Use specific details to make your paragraph interesting.

    These large canines can lug as much as 2,000 pounds, and in their native province, they were once used to haul fishing nets, as well as carts of fish, milk, or mail.

- Organize your sentences in the best possible order: time order, order of importance, classification, and so on. (See pages **571–574**.)

The Closing Sentence

The **closing sentence** comes after all the body details have been presented. This sentence can remind the reader of the topic, summarize the paragraph, or link the paragraph to the next one.

    Indeed, this huge, devoted dog is one of the greatest partners to bless humankind.

Paragraphs

Answers

Respond to the reading.

The paragraph emphasizes the ways in which Newfoundland dogs have served people.

The specific details include saving a drowning person; hauling fish, milk, and mail (up to 2,000 pounds); and rescuing people from sinking ships.

Types of Paragraphs

There are four basic types of paragraphs: *narrative, descriptive, expository,* and *persuasive.* Notice how the details support the topic sentence in each of the following paragraphs.

Narrative Paragraph

A **narrative paragraph** tells a story. It may draw from the writer's personal experience or from other sources of information. The details should answer the 5 W's *(who? what? when? where? and why?).* A narrative paragraph is almost always organized chronologically, or according to time.

Topic Sentence

Body

Closing Sentence

My Watch Dog

My morning routine is unusual because it has been established by my dog, Rolph. By nature, I'm not an early riser, but unfortunately for me, Rolph is always ready to go by 5:30 in the morning. He snorts and grunts for a while, but if I don't get out of bed, he'll start to bark. I can assure you that this works better than any alarm clock. Before I know it, I'm stumbling downstairs in my pajamas to let Rolph outside. By the time I get my face washed and teeth brushed, he's barking again, wanting to come in. Just after 6:00, he has to be fed; otherwise, he follows me around panting and drooling until I put his food out. Then he needs his exercise, so I take him for a walk through the park. Thanks to Rolph, I'm wide awake by 7:00 when I catch the bus for school. By then, Rolph is heading up to my room for his morning nap.

 Respond to the reading. What transitional words or phrases does the writer use to indicate the passage of time? Find three. What tone does the writer use—serious, entertaining, or surprising? Explain.

 Write a narrative paragraph. Write a narrative paragraph in which you share an experience dealing with a pet or some other animal. Make sure to answer the 5 W's. (Follow the guidelines on page 568.)

Descriptive Paragraph

A **descriptive paragraph** provides a detailed picture of a person, a place, an object, or an event. This type of paragraph should contain a variety of sensory details—specific sights, sounds, smells, tastes, and textures.

Topic Sentence

Body

Closing Sentence

A Champion Mix

Rolph has the look of a strange mix of breeds. His nose is pointed like a German shepherd, but his ears are long and floppy, suggesting some spaniel in his DNA. His eyes are as blue as arctic skies, hinting of a gene pool that includes a little husky or malamute somewhere in the history. His fur, gray streaked with black, has a large white patch on his chest, suggesting some schnauzer blood. His rough coat contains brushlike bristles along his back, yet the fluff around his head is curly and soft—almost poodlelike. His tail is soft, too, but bushy, perhaps conjuring up some collie heritage. (Rolph can dust a coffee table in nothing flat if he's in a good mood, and he's positioned just right.) Rolph's "woof" is deep enough to belong to a Saint Bernard, but when he gets excited he yips like a little Chihuahua! When he is running free in the park, someone may even mistake him for a nimble purebred retriever. From nose to tail Rolph appears as though he was assembled from a crazy collection of leftover pieces.

 Respond to the reading. What senses are covered in this paragraph? Which two or three details seem especially descriptive?

 Write a descriptive paragraph. Write a paragraph that describes something that is important to you. Use sensory details in your description. (Follow the guidelines on page 568.)

 Answers

Respond to the reading.

Transitional words and phrases include the following: before, by the time, just after 6:00, until, then, when, by then. The tone is entertaining because the focus is on how the dog gets the writer going in the morning, but then sleeps while his owner must go to school.

 Answers

Respond to the reading.

The senses covered are sight, touch, and sound. Descriptive details include the following: blue as arctic skies, gray streaked with black, brushlike bristles, the fluff around his head, yips like a Chihuahua.

Expository Paragraph

An **expository paragraph** shares information about a specific topic. Expository writing presents facts, gives directions, defines terms, explains a process, and so forth. It should clearly inform the reader.

Topic Sentence

Body

Closing Sentence

The Nose Knows

To a dog, the sense of smell is everything. The structure of a dog's nose accounts for its extraordinary sense of smell. Generally, the longer the dog's nose, the keener its sense of smell is. The wetness of the outer area of a dog's nose helps the animal detect and collect odors. Inside the nose, dogs have 25 times more smell receptors than humans. Sniffing activates these receptors, which send the odor "messages" to the olfactory lobe in the dog's brain. This lobe is four times larger than the corresponding area in the human brain and allows dogs to sort out and pinpoint many specific layers of smells. Dogs can pick up odors in concentrations 100 million times lower than humans can detect! A dog uses its sense of smell to evaluate its world, an ability that has proven to be of enormous help to humans. Some dogs can find people trapped in avalanches or collapsed buildings, while others are trained to hunt for those who have not survived. Patrol dogs prove invaluable for sniffing out drugs, smuggled goods, and bombs. Scientists are even exploring the medical "miracle" that dogs seem to be able to smell certain kinds of cancers before they are detected through lab tests. While people may not always agree with a dog about what does or does not smell delightful, they can surely appreciate the marvel that is a dog's nose.

 Respond to the reading. What is the specific topic of this paragraph? What supporting facts or examples does the writer include? Name three or four of them.

 Write an expository paragraph. Write a paragraph that shares information about a specific topic. Make sure to include plenty of details that support the topic. (Follow the guidelines on page 568.)

Persuasive Paragraph

A **persuasive paragraph** expresses an opinion and tries to convince the reader that the opinion is valid. To be persuasive, a writer must include effective supporting reasons and facts.

Topic Sentence

Body

Closing Sentence

Not So Fast . . . Or So Far

Sled dogs in the Iditarod race in Alaska should not be exposed to unnecessary health risks. The Iditarod race covers an incredible distance, approximately 1,150 miles, and takes a dog team from 9 to 14 days to complete. That amount of running in the course of that number of days puts an incredible strain on the dogs. In most of the Iditarod races, at least one dog has died. Causes of death include "strangulation in the towlines, internal bleeding from sled gouges, liver injuries, heart failure, and pneumonia" (Facts 2). Sled dogs are bred to obey commands under any circumstances, so they will continue to run even if they are injured or sick. Even if a dog wanted to stop, it couldn't because it is tied into the sled harness. A dog that happens to hesitate or fall could be trampled to death. Some health experts, including veterinarians, say that the number of deaths is not very surprising. With 800 dogs in the race, one or two deaths should be expected. That many deaths would just naturally occur over a two-week period. While that may be true, it must be remembered that the dogs have no choice but to run. As a result, race promoters must do everything possible to reduce health risks to these animals.

 Respond to the reading. What is the writer's opinion in the paragraph? What reasons does the writer include to support the opinion? Name two.

 Write a persuasive paragraph. Write a paragraph expressing your opinion about an event or an activity. Include at least two or three strong reasons that support your opinion. (Follow the guidelines on page 568.)

 ## Answers

Respond to the reading.

The specific topic of this paragraph is a dog's sense of smell.

Supporting information:

1. The longer the nose, the keener its sense of smell. **Fact**
2. Dogs have 25 times more smell receptors than humans have. **Fact**
3. Dogs can detect odors 100 million times less concentrated than humans can. **Fact**
4. Dogs can find people buried under avalanches or collapsed buildings. **Example**
5. Patrol dogs sniff out drugs or bombs. **Example**
6. Dogs can smell certain cancers. **Example**

 ## Answers

Respond to the reading.

The writer feels that health risks to sled dogs running in the Iditarod race should be reduced. Reasons that support this opinion include the following: The long race puts a strain on dogs. Usually at least one dog dies in each Iditarod. Dogs are trained to run even if they are hurt. Dogs have no choice but to run and couldn't stop if they wanted to since they are tied to the sled harness.

Writing Guidelines Developing a Paragraph

Before you begin your writing, make sure you understand the requirements of the assignment. Then follow the steps listed below.

Prewriting Selecting a Topic and Details

- Select a specific topic that meets the requirements of the assignment.
- Collect facts, examples, and other details about your topic.
- Write a topic sentence stating what your paragraph will be about. (See page 563.)
- Decide on the best way to organize the supporting details. (See pages 571–574.)

Writing Creating the First Draft

- Start your paragraph with the topic sentence.
- Follow with sentences that support your topic. Use your planning as a general guide.
- Connect your ideas and sentences with transitions.
- Close with a sentence that restates your topic, gives a final thought, or, in the case of an essay, leads into the next paragraph.

Revising Improving Your Writing

- Add information if you need to say more about your topic.
- Move sentences that aren't in the best order.
- Delete sentences that don't support the topic.
- Rewrite any sentences that are unclear.

Editing Checking for Conventions

- Check the revised draft for punctuation, capitalization, grammar, and spelling errors.
- Write a neat final copy and proofread it one last time.

Tip

When you write a paragraph, remember that the reader wants to . . .

- learn something. *(Offer new and interesting information.)*
- hear the writer's voice. *(Let your personality come through in the writing.)*

Types of Details

There are many types of details you can include in paragraphs (and in longer forms of writing). The purpose of your writing determines which details you should use. The key types are explained below and on the following page.

Facts are *details* that can be proven.

> Carnivores are animals that derive most of their sustenance from eating meat.

> In 2004, the Boston Red Sox won the World Series by sweeping the St. Louis Cardinals.

Statistics present *numerical information* (numbers) about a specific topic.

> A recent survey found that 16 percent of Whitewater High School students have family pets.

> Whole-grain bread contains up to six times more dietary fiber than regular white bread.

Examples are *statements that illustrate a main point.*

> Every region presents climate-related challenges *(main point)*. Southeastern coastal regions are subject to hurricanes. The Great Plains are vulnerable to tornadoes, while the northern regions experience howling blizzards and periods of dangerous subzero temperatures.

Anecdotes are *brief stories* that help to make a point about a topic. They can be much more effective than a matter-of-fact list of details.

> Abraham Lincoln had a dry wit and a sharp sense of humor. Two men once asked him to settle an argument they were having about the proper proportion of the length of a man's legs to his torso. After acknowledging the seriousness of the matter, Lincoln concluded:
> "After much thought and consideration, not to mention mental worry and anxiety, it is my opinion, all side issues being swept aside, that a man's lower limbs, in order to preserve harmony of proportion, should be at least long enough to reach from his body to the ground."

Quotations are *people's statements* repeated word for word. Quotations can provide powerful supporting evidence.

> Some people are concerned that bilingual education is a threat to English as our national language. This is obviously not the case, since the ultimate goal is to help all students become speakers of English. James Crawford, author of *Hold Your Tongue*, states, "Bilingualism is as American as apple pie—and has been ever since this nation's beginnings."

Definitions give the *meaning* of unfamiliar terms. Definitions of technical terms are especially important for the reader. Defining such terms makes your writing clear.

> That painting has a lot of texture because it is a fresco, a painting applied directly onto wet plaster.

> Manatees, large aquatic mammals sometimes called sea cows, can be found in the warm coastal waters of Florida.

Reasons answer *why* and can explain or justify ideas.

> High school athletes should avoid using creatine, a common training supplement. In the short term, creatine may cause diarrhea, nausea, dehydration, and cramping. While these side effects are rare, high school football players have been hospitalized for dehydration from using creatine. In the long term, taking creatine may lead to serious kidney problems and muscle tears. Some experts also believe that if athletes overload on creatine, their bodies may stop producing it naturally.

Comparisons address the *similarities or differences* between two things. It is especially helpful to compare something new or unknown to something your reader understands.

> Switzerland celebrates its founding on August 1st, much like the United States celebrates its independence on July 4th. Switzerland, however, is more than 700 years old, while the United States is little more than 200 years old.

Try It!

Find examples in this book's writing samples of any four types of details listed on the previous two pages. Write the examples and the pages where you found them on your own paper.

Patterns of Organization

On the following four pages, sample paragraphs show basic patterns of organization. Reviewing these samples can help you organize your own writing.

Chronological Order

Chronological (time) **order** is effective for explaining a process or sharing a story. Information is organized by what happens first, second, third, and so on. The paragraph below explains how to focus a microscope.

Time Line

"Focusing a Microscope" Time Line

| put lens in lowest position | turn on light, place slide on glass | open diaphragm | focus with coarse focusing knob | switch to higher power | focus using fine focus knob | move lens until specimen is in focus | check clarity of specimen |

Topic Sentence

Body

Closing Sentence

A Clear Specimen

Knowing how to focus a microscope properly can save time and frustration when viewing slides. Start with the lens on its lowest power—that's the shortest objective lens. Then turn on the viewing light and place your slide on the glass stage with the specimen centered. Open the diaphragm all the way to get the most light. Next, look through the eyepiece and begin focusing by slowly turning the coarse focus knob (the large outer knob) until the specimen is in focus. Reposition the slide as needed. At this point, switch to a higher power, but be careful not to touch the coarse focus knob again. Adjusting the coarse focus knob could scratch or crack the slide. Only use the smaller fine focus knob if needed to adjust the focus. Then slowly move the lens up until your specimen is in focus. Once the specimen is in focus, check to see if looks faint. If it does look faint, try closing the diaphragm a little. This will make the specimen brighter. A specimen will now be easy to identify and observe.

Paragraphs

Answers

Answers will vary. Possible answers:

1. Facts—*In 1841, Horace Greeley started another penny newspaper . . .* (page 361)
2. Statistics—*However, estimates indicate that up to 137 species disappear worldwide each day.* (page 425)
3. Examples—*An early example is a knight crashing through a stained-glass window in* Young Sherlock Holmes *(1985).* (page 29)
4. Anecdotes—*After paying 14 shillings to look around his dig site, she (Fossey) slipped down a rock slope, landed on his fossil find, sprained her ankle . . .* (page 149)
5. Quotations—*An article on WebMD reports, "The explosion of candy and soda machines in public schools is a relatively new phenomenon closely paralleling the rise in childhood obesity."* (page 203)
6. Definitions—*I'd never been in a mosque, but now I was going to a feast to celebrate the holiest month of the Islamic year: Ramadan.* (page 41)
7. Reasons—*First, keeping Hillhouse open is very important to the people who live and work there. If Hillhouse shuts down, twenty-six residents will need to find new homes, and seven staff members will lose their jobs.* (page 205)
8. Comparisons—*They tell us, sir, that we are weak; unable to cope with so formidable an adversary. But when shall we be stronger?* (page 308)

Order of Location

Order of location (spatial organization) is effective for organizing a description. It provides unity by arranging details in a logical way—left to right, top to bottom, and so on. A student who described Casa Loma, a castle located in Toronto, Canada, used the graphic organizer shown at the right to help him arrange his details.

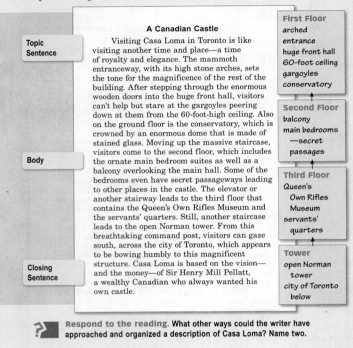

Topic Sentence

Body

Closing Sentence

A Canadian Castle

Visiting Casa Loma in Toronto is like visiting another time and place—a time of royalty and elegance. The mammoth entranceway, with its high stone arches, sets the tone for the magnificence of the rest of the building. After stepping through the enormous wooden doors into the huge front hall, visitors can't help but stare at the gargoyles peering down at them from the 60-foot-high ceiling. Also on the ground floor is the conservatory, which is crowned by an enormous dome that is made of stained glass. Moving up the massive staircase, visitors come to the second floor, which includes the ornate main bedroom suites as well as a balcony overlooking the main hall. Some of the bedrooms even have secret passageways leading to other places in the castle. The elevator or another stairway leads to the third floor that contains the Queen's Own Rifles Museum and the servants' quarters. Still, another staircase leads to the open Norman tower. From this breathtaking command post, visitors can gaze south, across the city of Toronto, which appears to be bowing humbly to this magnificent structure. Casa Loma is based on the vision—and the money—of Sir Henry Mill Pellatt, a wealthy Canadian who always wanted his own castle.

First Floor
arched entrance
huge front hall
60-foot ceiling
gargoyles
conservatory

Second Floor
balcony
main bedrooms
—secret passages

Third Floor
Queen's Own Rifles Museum
servants' quarters

Tower
open Norman tower
city of Toronto below

 Respond to the reading. What other ways could the writer have approached and organized a description of Casa Loma? Name two.

Classification

Classification is used when you need to break a topic down into categories and subcategories to help the reader better understand it. The following paragraph classifies the divisions of food according to kosher dietary laws. The writer used the following line diagram to help plan her writing.

Line Diagram

Topic Sentence

Body

Closing Sentence

Keeping Kosher

Silver's family keeps kosher, meaning they follow the Jewish dietary laws that divide food into three groups: dairy, meat, and pareve. Dairy foods include milk, cheese, and butter, as well as many prepared foods and mixes that contain milk products such as whey. Anything that contains dairy products must never be eaten with meat. The meat group includes beef, chicken, and lamb, but never ham or other pork products. Some dry mixes or powders may have meat flavorings or fat in them, and these, too, should never be served with dairy foods. Foods that are neither dairy nor meat are called pareve and include vegetables, fruits, and grains. Pareve foods may be eaten with either dairy or meat foods. Fish is also considered pareve, but it is not mixed with meat in a recipe and is usually served on a separate plate in a meat meal. (Shellfish such as lobster or shrimp are never kosher.) People who keep kosher often have two sets of dishes, utensils, and pots—one for dairy and one for meat—and some even go so far as to have separate dishwashers! According to Rachel, keeping kosher is easy once it becomes part of a family's daily routine.

 Respond to the reading. Answer this question: What facts or details did you learn about the topic? Name three.

Answers

Respond to the reading.

The writer could have written about the castle chronologically, explaining when each part was built. The writer could have talked about the purpose of each part of the castle, telling how each part was used. The writer could have started with the tower and worked down to the entrance.

Answers

Respond to the reading.

Answers will vary. Possible answers:

1. I learned that keeping kosher means eating dairy, meat, and pareve properly.
2. Foods that are called pareve include vegetables, fruits, and grains.
3. Lobster and shrimp are never kosher.

Comparison and Contrast

Organizing by **comparison** shows the similarities or differences between two subjects. To compare dairy farming of the past with that of today, one student used a Venn diagram. After organizing her details, she found that the two styles were more different than alike. Those differences are explained in her paragraph.

Venn Diagram

Then	Both	Now
family farms	sanitary conditions	owned by corporations
cows roamed free	affected by varying weather, prices	cows penned in "drylots"
all natural—no Rbgh	milk picked up by trucks	hormones used—Rbgh
milked twice a day		milked 3 times a day
milk cans		"bulk" tanks

Farming Then and Now

Topic Sentence

The family farm of the '50s had little in common with the modern dairy farm. Of course, dairy farms have always held sanitary conditions as a top priority, and farmers have always been at the mercy of both the weather and milk prices. The family farm gave way to farms owned by corporations and run by accountants. On the family farm, cows grazed rich pastures between milkings, while on modern farms, every inch of land is utilized for crops. That means many herds spend their lives in large barns or drylots (pens with no grass) with no room to roam. All feed and supplements were natural in the past, but today, hormones might be administered to promote milking three times a day rather than twice. Old-time farmers used individual milking machines: rubber cups suctioned the milk into a steel container. The machines were then emptied into a larger milk can, which was placed in a cooler until the milk truck came to pick it up. Today, the suction cups lead to sterile pipelines that run the milk directly into a large tank, which is then pumped into huge tanker trucks. Farming today is less of a personal relationship between farmer and animal and more of an efficient business.

Body

Closing Sentence

Modeling Paragraphs

When you come across paragraphs that you really like, practice writing examples of your own that follow the author's pattern of writing. This process is called **modeling**. Follow these guidelines:

Guidelines for Modeling

- **Find a paragraph** you would like to model.
- **Think of a topic** for your practice writing.
- **Follow the pattern** of the paragraph as you write about your own topic. (You do not have to follow the pattern exactly.)
- **Build your paragraph** one sentence or idea at a time.
- **Review your work** and change any parts that seem confusing.
- **Save your writing** and share it with your classmates.

Ending with the Topic Sentence

Sometimes a writer presents the topic sentence at the end of the paragraph. The details build suspense gradually until the final sentence, which serves as an effective summary (topic) sentence.

My toes curl in pain. Stepping forward only makes it worse because my ankles start to stiffen. Then the cramping begins in my calf as the pain moves up my body. My teeth also start to chatter uncontrollably. I wrap my arms around myself, hoping to gather a little warmth. Finally, I decide to take action because procrastinating only prolongs the agony. So I hold my breath and leap forward. My body momentarily goes into shock as I hit the cold water. I gasp and then relax. I have made my first dive into the lake.

 Respond to the reading. What is the topic of the paragraph? In which sentence is this topic identified? Which details build suspense into the paragraph? Name two or three of them.

 Try It!

Write your own narrative paragraph modeled after the sample above. Refer to the guidelines near the top of the page to help you complete your writing.

Paragraphs

 Answers

Respond to the reading.

The topic of the paragraph is the first dive into a lake. The topic is revealed in the last sentence. The details that build suspense include toes curling in pain, prolonged agony, momentary shock, calf muscles cramping, and teeth chattering uncontrollably.

Try It! **Answers**

Answers will vary.

*"Good writing has an aliveness that keeps the
reader reading from one paragraph to the next."*
—William Zinsser

Answering a Question

A topic sentence is usually a statement, but it doesn't have to be. A writer can ask a question in a topic sentence. The remaining sentences in the paragraph answer the question. In the expository paragraph that follows, the writer asks and answers a question about a common fastening device, the zipper.

What exactly makes a zipper work? A zipper works because the slide either joins or separates the two sides of the track. The key to understanding this is knowing that the two sides have perfectly matched teeth. Each tooth has a hook on the top and a hollow on the bottom. In order to join the sides, the moving slide wedges each hook into the hollow of the tooth directly across from it. When all of the hooks and hollows are joined, the zipper is closed. To open the zipper, the slide pops each hook out of its hollow. A zipper won't work if there is a piece of thread tangled in the works, a tooth is broken, or the hooks and hollows are not properly lined up. Of course, understanding this process will not make a person feel any less upset when a zipper gets stuck.

 Respond to the reading. What is the topic of this paragraph? In which sentence is the main idea about the topic identified? Does the writer supply enough supporting details? Explain.

Try It!

Write your own expository paragraph modeled after the sample above. Refer to the guidelines for modeling near the top of page **575** to help you complete your writing.

Connecting Paragraphs in Essays

To write strong essays, you must organize the ideas within each paragraph and then organize the paragraphs within the essay. The guidelines that follow will help you connect the paragraphs in your essay.

- **Be sure that your paragraphs are complete.** Each one should contain an effective topic sentence and supporting details.
- **Identify the topic and thesis (focus) of your essay** in the beginning paragraph. Start with some interesting details to get the reader's attention. Then share the focus of your writing.
- **Develop your ideas** in the middle paragraphs. Each middle paragraph should include information that explains and supports your focus. Often, the paragraph that contains the most important information comes right after the beginning paragraph or right before the final paragraph.
- **Review one or more of the main points in your essay** in the closing paragraph. The last sentence usually gives the reader a final interesting thought about the topic.
- **Use transition words or phrases** to connect the paragraphs. Transitions help the reader follow an essay from one paragraph to the next. In the sample below, the transitions are shown in red.

. . . Since that time, blue jeans have become much more than a symbol of the American West and are worn around the world.

In addition to jeans, other symbols of American culture include athletic shoes and sports jerseys. These two symbols have become especially important with the international popularity of basketball. . . .

For several reasons, many fashion trends have begun in the United States. Because of our wealth, free time, and technology, it's easy to understand why . . .

Try It!

Turn to pages **592–593** to see examples of transition words and phrases. On your own paper, list the transitions that you have used in your writing. *Special Challenge:* Find one or two writing samples that use some of the transitions from pages **592–593**.

Paragraphs

Answers

Respond to the reading.

The topic is how a zipper works, and the topic is revealed in the question in the first sentence.

Yes. The writer explains how a zipper is made and how the action of the slide closes or opens a zipper.

Try It! ## Answers

Answers will vary.

Try It! ## Answers

Answers will vary.

Sample Essay

Read this sample essay about leadership. Notice how the three parts—the beginning, the middle, and the ending—work together.

Becoming a Leader

Who is a leader? The simple answer is "someone who leads." But there isn't anything simple about leadership. As basketball coach Howard Brown states, "Leading a team, and getting the players to work toward a common goal, takes skill and a lot of effort." So how does someone take on this important role? To become a leader, a person must develop three main traits.

First of all, leaders must be confident. They must believe in their own abilities and know that these abilities will help the group reach its goals. This confidence comes mainly through training and experience. True leaders are willing to make decisions and stand behind them even when faced with detractors. Leaders know what needs to be done, and they act accordingly. They also make decisions based on good personal judgment, along with the wise input of others.

Second, leaders must display good work habits. Effective leaders lead by example, working longer and harder than the rest of the group. In many cases, a group's effort—or lack of it—will be a direct reflection of the leader's example. Leaders also keep up with the latest developments related to the group's work. In other words, true leaders change with the times and grow as individuals.

Third, and most important, leaders must earn the respect of the group. This respect is earned in a number of ways. Leaders must be organized, laying out an effective plan or schedule for the group to follow. They help the individuals in the group improve and grow. In addition, effective leaders treat everyone fairly and honestly. They offer praise when it is earned and criticism when it is necessary.

Becoming a good leader truly does take a lot of effort. A person earns that position by being confident, hardworking, and respected by others. There is an English proverb that says, "A smooth sea never made a skilled mariner." A leader, like a skilled mariner, has sailed and conquered rough seas and, from that experience, has learned how to lead.

 Respond to the reading. What transitions are used to connect the middle paragraphs in this essay? Does the writer present his most important supporting reason in the first middle paragraph or in the last middle paragraph? Why does he organize his reasons in this way?

Paragraph Traits Checklist

Use the checklist below as a basic guide when you review your paragraphs. If you answer "no" to any of the questions, continue to work with that part of your paragraph.

Revising Checklist

Ideas

_____ **1.** Have I selected a specific topic?
_____ **2.** Have I supported the topic with specific details?

Organization

_____ **3.** Is my topic sentence clear?
_____ **4.** Have I organized the details in an effective order?

Voice

_____ **5.** Do I sound interested in, and knowledgeable about, my topic?
_____ **6.** Does my voice fit the assignment and my audience?

Word Choice

_____ **7.** Do I use specific nouns, verbs, and modifiers?
_____ **8.** Do I define any unfamiliar terms?

Sentence Fluency

_____ **9.** Have I written clear and complete sentences?
_____ **10.** Do I vary my sentence beginnings and lengths?

Conventions

_____ **11.** Have I checked for punctuation, capitalization, and grammar errors?
_____ **12.** Have I checked for spelling errors?

Paragraphs

 Answers

Respond to the reading.

The transition words are the following: *first of all, second, third.* The most important supporting reason is in the third middle paragraph. I believe the writer organized his reasons to build up to the most important point.

580

A Writer's Resource

Writing Focus

Academic Vocabulary

Work with a partner. Read the definitions below and share your answers to the questions that follow.

1. To integrate something is to add it in, making it part of a larger whole.
   Why should you integrate information from sources into an expository essay?

2. Something that is visual relates to the sense of sight.
   How can visual elements make a text or presentation better?

3. A technique is a way of doing something that requires special knowledge or skill.
   What are some writing techniques that you use in creative writing?

4. Succinct writing uses few words to express ideas.
   Why would you prefer to read succinct writing?

581

A Writer's Resource

Writer Sholem Asch says, "Writing comes more easily if you have something to say." That is so true. If you know a lot about a topic, and have strong feelings about it, you're ready to write. But what about those times when you can't think of a writing topic, or you're not sure how to develop a writing idea? Then you should turn to this section for help.

This chapter contains tips and guidelines to help you complete any writing assignment. You'll find strategies for selecting topics, organizing details, writing thesis statements, and so on. Once you become familiar with this chapter, you'll always have something interesting to say in your writing.

- Finding a Topic
- Knowing the Different Forms
- Collecting and Organizing Details
- Creating an Outline
- Using Transitions
- Writing Thesis Statements
- Writing Great Beginnings and Endings
- Integrating Quotations
- Learning Key Writing Terms
- Using Writing Techniques
- Adding Graphics to Your Writing
- Using Editing and Proofreading Marks

"You can't wait for inspiration. You have to go after it with a club."
—Jack London

Academic Vocabulary

Read aloud the academic terms, as well as the descriptions and questions. Model for students how to read one question and answer it. Have partners monitor their understanding and seek clarification of the terms by working through the meanings and questions together.

Finding a Topic

In writing, everything starts with an idea. Sometimes your teacher will supply a general writing subject. Suppose your teacher assigns a paper on the Great Depression. It's a huge subject—you still need to find a specific writing topic. These two pages show different ways that students approached this task.

Using a Cluster Diagram

Cho used a cluster diagram to find her topic. She wrote the general subject in the center and then broke it down into three categories. Each category became another cluster. Cho could see which topic had the most information and looked most interesting to her. She decided to write about the New Deal.

Trying Freewriting

Jennifer tried freewriting. She wrote for 10 to 15 minutes about what she already knew about the subject as well as questions she had about it. Jennifer's freewriting led her to research and write about entertainment during the Great Depression.

> The movie we saw about the Depression was depressing! What did people do for fun during that time? I know they went to movies. How could they afford them? My grandma has some dishes her mother got when she went to the movies. That's weird. What was that all about? What kind of movies did people watch back then? Did they go to movies to take their minds off the Depression? What other types of entertainment did people find?

Reviewing a "Basics of Life" List

There are certain things people need to live a full life. Below is a list of these categories, called the "Basics of Life." By selecting one category and applying it to your subject, you can zero in on a topic. Randall selected the category "freedom/rights" and decided to explore civil rights during the Great Depression.

food	friends	land/property	heat/fuel
work/occupation	purpose/goals	community	natural resources
clothing	love	science	personality/identity
faith/religion	senses	plants/vegetation	recreation/hobbies
communication	machines	freedom/rights	trade/money
exercise	intelligence	energy	literature/books
education	history/records	rules/laws	health/medicine
family	agriculture	tools/utensils	art/music

Using Visual Images

Sometimes topic ideas are all around you. Juana used the Internet to help her find her topic. She was fascinated by the Depression-era images of dust storms and grasshopper damage, so she decided to research and write about the causes and effects of the Dust Bowl.

Resource

Using Writing Prompts

Every day is full of experiences that make you think. You do things that you feel good about. You hear things that make you angry. You wonder how different things work. You are reminded of a past experience. These everyday thoughts can make excellent starting points for writing. As you write about one of these prompts, a number of specific topics will come to mind.

Best and Worst

My most memorable day in school
My best hour
My encounter with a bully

It could only happen to me!

A narrow escape from trouble
I was so shocked when . . .
My life began in this way.
My strangest phone conversation
If only I had done that differently
Whatever happened to my . . .

Quotations

"Someone who makes no mistakes does not usually make anything."

"When people are free to do as they please, they usually imitate each other."

"More is not always better."

"It is easier to forgive an enemy than a friend."

"Never give advice unless asked."

"Honesty is the best policy."

"Know thyself."

"Like mother, like daughter."

"Like father, like son."

I was thinking.

Everyone should know . . .
Where do I draw the line?
Is it better to laugh or cry?
Why do people like to go fast?
I don't understand why . . .

First and Last

My first game or performance
My last day of _____
My last visit with _____

School, Then and Now

The pressure of tryouts
Grades—are they the most important part of school?
Finally, a good assembly
What my school really needs is . . .
A teacher I respect
I'm in favor of more . . .

People and Places

Who knows me best? What does he or she know?
Getting along with my brother, sister, or friend
A person I admire
My grandparents' house
The emergency room
A guided tour of my neighborhood

Using Sample Topics

People, places, experiences, and information you encounter all offer springboards for writing. Here are some topic ideas for descriptive, narrative, expository, and persuasive writing.

Descriptive

People: favorite relative, coach, friend, teacher, doctor or veterinarian, brother or sister, homeless person, local store worker

Places: band room, park, mall, art museum, wood shop, corner garage, observatory, science lab, laundromat, library, mountaintop, city street

Things: wedding cake, salt and pepper shakers, cell phone, locker, snowy road, bracelet, griffin, old car, photograph, potted plant, fish tank

Animals: buffalo, coyote, alley cat, goldfish, gorilla, mosquito, pigeon, opossum, whale, ostrich, wolverine, penguin, dove, porpoise

Narrative

Stories: trying out for a team, choosing a pet from a shelter, volunteering at a nursing home or day care, riding in an ambulance, acting in community theater, working on a farm, going fishing or hunting

Expository

Comparison-Contrast: football and rugby, baseball and cricket, the United States and Australia, squid and octopus, guitar and violin, U.S. Congress and British Parliament, tulip and Venus flytrap

Cause/Effect: shrinking polar ice caps, identity theft, deforestation, AIDS, drought, lab experiment, cosmetic surgery, rabies, rainbows

Classification: kinds of clouds, types of popular music, branches of the military, groups of vertebrates, kinds of cameras, types of waves

Persuasive

School: carrying backpacks to class, giving special privileges to students who earn them, offering weighted grades, opening a student lounge, adding a cafeteria vegetable bar

Home: getting a larger allowance, rotating chores, extending computer time, having parental blocks on TV channels, taking music/dance/karate lessons

Community: adding corner stoplights, building or repairing sidewalks, creating bicycle paths, extending weekend curfews, allowing skateboards on sidewalks, creating a teen center

Resource

Knowing the Different Forms

Finding the right form for your writing is just as important as finding the right topic. When you are selecting a form, be sure to ask yourself who you're writing for (your *audience*) and why you're writing (your *purpose*).

Anecdote	A brief story that helps to make a point
Autobiography	A writer's story of his or her own life
Biography	A writer's story of someone else's life
Book review	An essay offering an opinion about a book, not to be confused with *literary analysis*
Cause and effect	A paper examining an event, the forces leading up to that event, and the effects following the event
Character sketch	A brief description of a specific character showing some aspect of that character's personality
Descriptive writing	Writing that uses sensory details that allow the reader to clearly visualize a person, a place, a thing, or an idea
Editorial	A letter or an article offering an opinion, an idea, or a solution
Essay	A thoughtful piece of writing in which ideas are explained, analyzed, or evaluated
Expository writing	Writing that explains something by presenting its steps, causes, or kinds
Eyewitness account	A report giving specific details of an event or a person
Fable	A short story that teaches a lesson or moral, often using talking animals as the main characters
Fantasy	A story set in an imaginary world in which the characters usually have supernatural powers or abilities
Historical fiction	An invented story based on an actual historical event
Interview	Writing based on facts and details obtained through speaking with another person
Journal writing	Writing regularly to record personal observations, thoughts, and ideas

Literary analysis	A careful examination or interpretation of some aspect of a piece of literature
Myth	A traditional story intended to explain a mystery of nature, religion, or culture
Novel	A book-length story with several characters and a well-developed plot, usually with one or more subplots
Personal narrative	Writing that shares an event or experience from the writer's personal life
Persuasive writing	Writing intended to persuade the reader to follow the writer's way of thinking about something
Play	A form that uses dialogue to tell a story, usually meant to be performed in front of an audience
Poem	A creative expression that may use rhyme, rhythm, and imagery
Problem-solution	Writing that presents a problem followed by a proposed solution
Process paper	Writing that explains how a process works, or how to do or make something
Profile	An essay that reveals an individual or re-creates a time period
Proposal	Writing that includes specific information about an idea or a project that is being considered for approval
Research report	An essay that shares information about a topic that has been thoroughly researched
Response to literature	Writing that is a reaction to something the writer has read
Science fiction	Writing based on real or imaginary science and often set in the future
Short story	A short fictional piece with only a few characters and one conflict or problem
Summary	Writing that presents the most important ideas from a longer piece of writing
Tall tale	A humorous, exaggerated story about a character or an animal that does impossible things
Tragedy	Literature in which the hero fails or is destroyed because of a serious character flaw

Resource

Collecting and Organizing Details

Using Graphic Organizers

Graphic organizers can help you gather and organize your details for writing. Clustering is one method (see page 582). These two pages show other useful organizers.

Cause-Effect Organizer

Use to collect and organize details for cause-effect essays.

Problem-Solution Web

Use to map out problem-solution essays.

Time Line

Use for personal narratives to list actions or events in the order they occurred.

Evaluation Collection Grid

Use to collect supporting details for essays of evaluation.

Subject: _____

Points to Evaluate	Supporting Details
1.	
2.	
3.	
4.	

Venn Diagram

Use to collect details to compare and contrast two topics.

Line Diagram

Use to collect and organize details for academic essays.

Process (Cycle) Diagram

Use to collect details for science-related writing, such as how a process or cycle works.

5 W's Chart

Use to collect the *Who? What? When? Where?* and *Why?* details for personal narratives and news stories.

Subject: _____

Who?	What?	When?	Where?	Why?

Definition Diagram

Use to gather information for extended definition essays.

Sensory Chart

Use to collect details for descriptive essays and observation reports.

Subject: _____

Sights	Sounds	Smells	Tastes	Textures

Creating an Outline

An **outline** organizes a set of facts or ideas by listing main points and subpoints. An effective outline shows how topics or ideas fit together. A well-designed outline serves as a frame for an effective essay.

There are two types of outlines: *topic outlines* and *sentence outlines*. (See the samples below and on the next page.)

A Topic Outline

In a **topic outline**, main points and details appear as phrases rather than as complete sentences. Topic outlines are useful for short essays, including essay-test answers. The information after the Roman numerals (I., II., III., and so on) identifies the main points in the essay. The information after the capital letters (A., B., C., and so on) identifies the details that support the main points.

Sample Topic Outline

I. History of driver safety problems in Formula-One cars
  A. Bad accidents at the start
  B. Hazards due to the course
  C. Hazards due to the cars
II. Modifications to cars
  A. Single-shell construction and cockpit survival cells
  B. Fire extinguishers
  C. Escape systems
III. Modifications to driver equipment
  A. Helmet improvements
  B. Head-and-neck support systems
  C. Fireproof clothes
IV. Modifications to racetracks
  A. Track improvements
  B. Medical services upgraded

Note: Information for the opening and closing paragraphs is not included in this outline for an essay about safety in Formula-One cars.

Tip

In an outline, if you have a "I.," you must have at least a "II." If you have an "A.," you must have at least a "B.," and so on.

A Sentence Outline

A **sentence outline** is a detailed plan for writing. In this type of outline, the ideas are explained in complete sentences. This type of outline is useful for longer writing assignments like research reports and formal essays.

Sample Sentence Outline

I. Driver safety wasn't always a primary concern in Formula-One racing.
  A. Races have a history of bad accidents.
  B. The courses include hills and hairpin turns.
  C. The cars are the fastest in the world and jockey for position.
II. Many safety modifications have been made to cars.
  A. The body shell and cockpit survival cell are stronger now.
  B. Each car has several fire extinguishers.
  C. Escape systems allow drivers to escape after an accident.
III. Modifications have improved driver equipment.
  A. Helmets are stronger and lighter.
  B. The new head-and-neck support systems prevent spinal injuries.
  C. All clothing is fireproof.
IV. Modifications have made racetracks safer.
  A. Improvements in track layout help prevent crashes.
  B. Rescue and medical services are only seconds away.

A Quick List

Use a **quick list** when there is no time for an outline. A quick list organizes ideas in the most basic way, but it will still help you organize or structure your writing.

Sample Quick List

Formula-One Safety
  • history of automobile racing accidents
  • safety modifications in cars
  • modifications in race driver equipment
  • modifications in racetracks

Resource

Using Transitions

Transitions can be used to connect one sentence to another sentence within a paragraph, or to connect one paragraph to another within a longer essay or report. The lists below show a number of transitions and how they are used.

Each colored list below is a group of transitions that could work well together in a piece of writing.

Words used to show location

above	around	between	inside	outside
across	behind	by	into	over
against	below	down	near	throughout
along	beneath	in back of	next to	to the right
among	beside	in front of	on top of	under

Above	In front of	On top of
Below	Beside	Next to
To the left	In back of	Beneath
To the right		

Words used to show time

about	during	yesterday	until	finally
after	first	meanwhile	next	then
at	second	today	soon	as soon as
before	to begin	tomorrow	later	in the end

First	To begin	Now	First	Before
Second	To continue	Soon	Then	During
Third	To conclude	Eventually	Next	After
Finally			In the end	

Words used to compare things

likewise	as	in the same way	one way
like	also	similarly	both

In the same way	One way
Also	Another way
Similarly	Both

Words used to contrast (show differences)

but	still	although	on the other hand
however	yet	otherwise	even though

On the other hand	Although
Even though	Yet
Still	Nevertheless

Words used to emphasize a point

again	truly	especially	for this reason
to repeat	in fact	to emphasize	

For this reason	Truly	In fact
Especially	To emphasize	To repeat

Words used to conclude or summarize

finally	as a result	to sum it up	in conclusion
lastly	therefore	all in all	because

Because	As a result	To sum it up	Therefore
In conclusion	All in all	Because	Finally

Words used to add information

again	another	for instance	for example
also	and	moreover	additionally
as well	besides	along with	other
next	finally	in addition	

For example	For instance	Next	Another
Additionally	Besides	Moreover	Along with
Finally	Next	Also	As well

Words used to clarify

in other words	for instance	that is	for example

For instance	For example
In other words	Equally important

Resource

Writing Thesis Statements

An effective thesis statement tells the reader specifically what you plan to write about. In a longer essay or research report, your thesis statement generally comes at the end of the opening paragraph. It serves as a guide to keep you on track as you develop your writing.

The Process at Work

A thesis statement usually takes a stand or expresses a specific feeling about, or feature of, your topic. Write as many versions as it takes to hit upon the statement that sets the right tone for your writing. The following formula can be used to form your thesis statements.

> **A specific topic** (*Egypt's magnificent Sphinx*)
> + **a particular stand, feeling, or feature**
>   (*is being destroyed by pollution.*)
> = **an effective thesis statement.**

Sample Thesis Statements

Writing Assignment: Research report about a historical event
Specific Topic: The Monroe Doctrine
Thesis Statement: The Monroe Doctrine (**topic**) benefited England as much as it did the United States (**particular stand**).

Writing Assignment: Persuasive essay about a school problem
Specific Topic: Litter on the school grounds
Thesis Statement: The excessive litter on the school grounds (**topic**) reflects negatively on our school (**particular feeling**).

Writing Assignment: Analysis of a character in a story
Specific Topic: *"A Christmas Memory"* by Truman Capote
Thesis Statement: *"A Christmas Memory"* by Truman Capote (**topic**) examines the bond between a young boy and his special guardian (**particular feature**).

Thesis Checklist

Be sure that your thesis statement . . .

_____ identifies a limited, specific topic,
_____ focuses on a particular feature or feeling about the topic,
_____ is stated in one or more clear sentences,
_____ can be supported with convincing facts and details, and
_____ meets the requirements of the assignment.

Writing Great Beginnings

The opening paragraph of an essay should grab the reader's attention, introduce your topic, and present your thesis. To start your opening paragraph, try one of these approaches.

- **Start with an interesting fact.**
  King Kong by director Peter Jackson is a remake of the famous 1933 motion picture.
- **Ask an interesting question.**
  How many people know that the original King Kong was only eighteen inches tall?
- **Start with a quotation.**
  In the original *King Kong*, fictional showman Carl Denham said, "Why, the whole world will pay to see this"—and he was right.

Trying a Beginning Strategy

If you have trouble coming up with a good opening paragraph, follow the step-by-step example below.

First sentence—**Grab the reader's attention.**
Start with a sentence that catches your reader's attention (see above).

> How many people know that the original King Kong was only eighteen inches tall?

Second sentence—**Give some background information.**
Provide some background information about the topic.

> During most of the movie, Kong was actually a posable or movable model covered with rabbit fur.

Third sentence—**Introduce the specific topic of the essay.**
Introduce the topic in a way that builds up to the thesis statement.

> Stop-motion animation was just one of the techniques used to bring Kong to life.

Fourth sentence—**Give the thesis statement.**
Write the thesis statement of the paper (see page 594).

> Many special effects pioneered in the original *King Kong* appear in movies today.

Developing Great Endings

The closing paragraph of a paper should summarize your thesis and leave the reader with something to think about. When writing your closing paragraph, use two or more of the following ideas.

- Review your main points.
- Emphasize the special importance of one main point.
- Answer any questions the reader may still have.
- Draw a conclusion and put the information in perspective.
- Provide a final significant thought for the reader.

Trying an Ending Strategy

If you have trouble coming up with an effective closing paragraph, follow the step-by-step example below.

First sentence—**Reflect on the topic.**
Start by reflecting on the material presented previously about the topic.

Movie special effects have come a long way since 1933.

Second sentence—**Add another point.**
Include a final point of interest that you didn't mention before.

Computer-generated imagery (CGI) used today would astound early filmmakers.

Third sentence—**Emphasize the most important point.**
Stress the importance of one or more key points that support the thesis.

Despite the new technology, however, many basic techniques remain the same, including the use of miniatures, animation, and matte paintings.

Fourth sentence—**Wrap up the topic or draw a conclusion.**
Add one final thought about the topic or draw a conclusion from the points you've presented in the writing.

No matter how special effects are achieved, they continue to delight movie audiences everywhere.

Integrating Quotations

Always choose quotations that are clear and appropriate for your writing. Quotations should *support* your ideas, not replace them.

Trying Strategies for Using Quotations

Use the strategies below to get the most from quoted material in your writing.

- **Use quotations to support your own thoughts and ideas.**
  Effective quotations can back up your main points or support your arguments.

  Doing the right thing builds self-esteem. As Mark Twain noted, "A man cannot be comfortable without his own approval." That is why people must let their conscience be their guide.

- **Use quotations to lend authority to your writing.**
  Quoting an expert shows that you have researched your topic and understand its significance.

  Albert Einstein observed the growth of nuclear power with concern, stating, "I know not with what weapons World War III will be fought, but World War IV will be fought with sticks and stones." His disturbing comment reminds people that a nuclear war would result in unthinkable destruction.

- **Use quotations that are succinct and powerful.**
  Any quotation that you use must add value to your writing.

  Clearly, the education provided to today's students will determine the success of the country's future. As Benjamin Franklin put it, "An investment in knowledge always pays the best interest." A well-funded education system greatly benefits and enriches society.

Common Quotation Problems to Avoid

Keep these problems in mind when you consider using quotations.

- **Don't plagiarize.**
  Cite sources for all quotations (and paraphrases).
- **Don't use long quotations.**
  Keep quotations brief and to the point.
- **Don't overuse quotations.**
  Use a quotation only if you can't share the idea as powerfully or effectively in another way.

Resource

Learning Key Writing Terms

Here's a glossary of terms that describe aspects of the writing process.

Term	Definition
Balance	Arranging words or phrases in a way to give them equal importance
Body	The main part of a piece of writing, containing details that support or develop the thesis statement
Brainstorming	Collecting ideas by thinking freely about all the possibilities; used most often with groups
Central idea	The main point of a piece of writing, often stated in a thesis statement or a topic sentence
Closing sentence	The summary or final part in a piece of writing
Coherence	The logical arranging of ideas so they are clear and easy to follow
Dialogue	Written conversation between two or more people
Emphasis	Giving great importance to a specific idea in a piece of writing
Exposition	Writing that explains and informs
Figurative language	Language that goes beyond the normal meaning of the words used, often called "figures of speech"
Focus (thesis)	The specific part of a topic that is written about in an essay
Generalization	A general statement that gives an overall view, rather than focusing on specific details
Grammar	The rules that govern the standard structure and features of a language
Idiom	A phrase or an expression that means something different from what the words actually say **That answer was really** out in left field. (This means the answer was not even close to being correct.) **Next year you'll sing** a different tune. (This means you'll think differently.)
Jargon	The special language of a certain group or occupation **The weaver pointed out the fabric's unique** warp **and** woof. Computer jargon: byte icon server virus

Limiting the subject	Narrowing a general subject to a more specific one
Literal	The actual dictionary meaning of a word; a language that means exactly what it appears to mean
Loaded words	Words slanted for or against the subject **The new tax bill** helps the rich **and** hurts the poor.
Logic	Correctly using facts, examples, and reasons to support a point
Modifiers	Words, phrases, or clauses that limit or describe another word or group of words
Objective	Writing that gives factual information without adding feelings or opinions (See *subjective*.)
Poetic license	A writer's freedom to bend the rules of writing to achieve a certain effect
Point of view	The position or angle from which a story is told (See page 322.)
Prose	Writing in standard sentence form
Purpose	The specific goal of the writing
Style	The author's unique choice of words and sentences
Subjective	Writing that includes the writer's feelings, attitudes, and opinions (See *objective*.)
Supporting details	Facts or ideas used to sustain the main point
Syntax	The order and relationship of words in a sentence
Theme	The main point or unifying idea of a piece of writing
Thesis statement	A statement of the purpose, or main idea, of an essay
Tone	The writer's attitude toward the subject
Topic	The specific subject of a piece of writing
Topic sentence	The sentence that carries the main idea of a paragraph
Transitions	Words or phrases that connect or tie ideas together
Unity	A sense of oneness in writing in which each sentence helps to develop the main idea
Usage	The way in which people use language (*Standard* language follows the rules; *nonstandard* language does not.)
Voice	A writer's unique personal tone or feeling that comes across in a piece of writing

Resource

Using Writing Techniques

Experiment with some of these techniques in your own essays and stories.

Allusion A reference to a familiar person, place, thing, or event
Mario threw me my mitt. "Hey, Babe Ruth, you forgot this!"

Analogy A comparison of similar ideas or objects to help clarify one of them
There is no frigate like a book, to take us lands away.
—Emily Dickinson

Anecdote A brief story used to illustrate or make a point
It is said that the last words John Adams uttered were "Thomas Jefferson survives." Ironically, Jefferson had died just a few hours earlier. Both deaths occurred on July 4, 1826—the 50th anniversary of the Declaration of Independence shepherded by the two great men. (This ironic anecdote intensifies the importance of both men in our nation's history.)

Colloquialism A common word or phrase suitable for everyday conversation but not for formal speech or writing
"Cool" and "rad" are colloquialisms suggesting approval.

Exaggeration An overstatement or a stretching of the truth to emphasize a point (See *hyperbole* and *overstatement*.)
We opened up the boat's engine and sped along at a million miles an hour.

Flashback A technique in which a writer interrupts a story to go back and relive an earlier time or event
I stopped at the gate, panting. Suddenly I was seven years old again, and my brother was there, calling me "chicken" from the edge of the stone well. Then I opened my eyes and heard only the crickets chirping. The years, the well, and my brother were gone. I turned back to the road, determined to get home before nightfall.

Foreshadowing Hints about what will happen next in a story
As Mai explained why she had to break their date, she noticed Luke looking past her. Turning, she saw Meg smiling—at Luke.

Hyperbole (hi-púr-bə-lè) Exaggeration used to emphasize a point
The music was loud enough to make your ears bleed.

Irony An expression in which the author says one thing but means just the opposite
As we all know, there's nothing students love more than homework.

Juxtaposition Putting two words or ideas close together to create a contrasting of ideas or an ironic meaning
Ah, the sweet smell of fuel emissions!

Local color The use of details that are common in a certain place

Metaphor A figure of speech that compares two things without using the words *like* or *as*
The sheep were dense, dancing clouds scuttling across the road.

Overstatement An exaggeration or a stretching of the truth (See *exaggeration* and *hyperbole*.)
If I eat one more piece of turkey, I will burst!

Oxymoron Connecting two words with opposite meanings
small fortune, cruel kindness, original copy

Paradox A true statement that says two opposite things
As I crossed the finish line dead last, I felt a surge of triumph.

Parallelism Repeating similar grammatical structures (words, phrases, or sentences) to give writing rhythm
We cannot undo, we will not forget, and we should not ignore the pain of the past.

Personification A figure of speech in which a nonhuman thing is given human characteristics
The computer spit out my disk.

Pun A phrase that uses words that sound the same in a way that gives them a funny effect
I call my dog Trousers because he pants so much.

Simile A figure of speech that compares two things using *like* or *as*
Her silent anger was like a rock wall, hard and impenetrable.

Slang Informal words or phrases used by a particular group of people
cool it   hang out   shoot the curl

Symbol A concrete object used to represent an idea

Understatement The opposite of exaggeration; using very calm language to call attention to an object or an idea
". . . except for an interruption caused by my wife falling out of the car, the journey went very well."
—E. B. White

Resource

Adding Graphics to Your Writing

Graphics can enhance your writing by explaining your ideas in a visual manner. You can create graphics by hand or design them on a computer program and paste them into your document. Be sure to refer to the graphic in the text of your paper, either in the body of a paragraph or in a parenthetical reference. Here are some common types of graphics you can use.

Graphs

Graphs show information visually. Line graphs show change or trends across a period of time. Bar graphs compare data. Pie graphs show proportions and percentages of a whole. A graph should always include a clear title and labels for axes, sections, data points, and so forth.

Concentrations of CO2

Tables

Tables can organize information in a convenient manner. Most tables have rows (going across) and columns (going down). Rows contain one set of details, while columns contain another. At the left is a sample flight table, showing how far it is from one place to another. Check one place's column against the other's row.

Air Miles Between Major Cities

Diagrams

Diagrams are drawings that show how something is constructed, how it works, or how its parts relate to each other. A diagram may leave out parts to show you only what you need to learn.

Using Editing and Proofreading Marks

Use the symbols below to show where and how a composition should be changed. Your teacher may also use these symbols to mark errors in your writing. (This chart also appears on the inside back cover of your book.)

Symbols	Meaning	Example	Corrected Example
≡	Capitalize a letter.	Harper Lee wrote *To Kill a mockingbird*.	Harper Lee wrote *To Kill a Mockingbird*.
/	Make a capital letter lowercase.	Her novel tells the story of the Finch Family.	Her novel tells the story of the Finch family.
⊙	Insert (add) a period.	The book focuses on prejudice. It also . . .	The book focuses on prejudice. It also . . .
⬭ or sp.	Correct spelling.	Scout Finch is the narrater of the story.	Scout Finch is the narrator of the story.
ℒ	Delete (take out) or replace.	Scout and her brother Jem they make friends with Dill.	Scout and her brother Jem make friends with Dill.
∧	Insert here.	They plot to make a neighbor come out of his house.	They plot to make a reclusive neighbor come out of his house.
∧∧∧	Insert a comma, a colon, or a semicolon.	The three have many adventures some of the adventures are surprising.	The three have many adventures; some of the adventures are surprising.
∨∨∨	Insert an apostrophe or quotation marks.	Scouts father, Atticus Finch, is a dignified, respected attorney.	Scout's father, Atticus Finch, is a dignified, respected attorney.
? ! ∧∧	Insert a question mark or an exclamation point.	Atticus Finch also turned out to be an expert marksman!	Atticus Finch also turned out to be an expert marksman!
¶	Start a new paragraph.	The book takes on a more serious tone when Atticus defends Tom Robinson.	The book takes on a more serious tone when Atticus defends Tom Robinson.
∼	Switch words or letters.	Scout learns eventually not to prejudge people.	Scout eventually learns not to prejudge people.

Resource

Proofreader's Guide

Academic Vocabulary

Work with a partner. Read the definitions below and share your answers to the questions that follow.

1. When words, phrases, or clauses modify, they limit the meaning of other words, phrases, or clauses.
   What parts of speech do adverbs modify? (Consider these two examples of adverbs: *quickly* and *very*.)

2. Something that is compound is made up of two or more parts.
   What parts make up a compound sentence?

3. Something that is subordinate is secondary, less important, or dependent.
   What is a subordinate clause dependent upon in a sentence?

4. In grammar, the passive voice refers to clauses in which the subject receives the action. (In the active voice, the subject performs the action.)
   Why should you limit use of the passive voice in your writing?

Marking Punctuation

Period

605.1 At the End of a Sentence

Use a **period** at the end of a sentence that makes a statement, requests something, or gives a mild command.

(Statement) **The man who does not read good books has no advantage over the man who can't read them.**

—Mark Twain

(Request) **Please bring your folders and notebooks to class.**

(Mild command) **Listen carefully so that you understand these instructions.**

NOTE: It is not necessary to place a period after a statement that has parentheses around it and is part of another sentence.

My dog Bobot (I don't quite remember how he acquired this name) is a Chesapeake Bay retriever—a hunting dog—who is afraid of loud noises.

605.2 After an Initial or an Abbreviation

Place a period after an initial or an abbreviation (in American English).

Ms.   Sen.   D.D.S.   M.F.A.   M.D.   Jr.   U.S.   p.m.   a.m.
Edna St. Vincent Millay   Booker T. Washington   D. H. Lawrence

NOTE: When an abbreviation is the last word in a sentence, use only one period at the end of the sentence.

Jaleesa eyed each door until she found the name Fletcher B. Gale, M.D.

605.3 As a Decimal Point

A period is used as a decimal point.

New York City has a budget of $46.9 billion to serve its 8.1 million people.

Exclamation Point

605.4 To Express Strong Feeling

Use the **exclamation point** (sparingly) to express strong feeling. You may place it after a word, a phrase, or a sentence.

Imagine the sheer joy of shouting "Finished!" when you turn in your last assignment of the school year.

Academic Vocabulary

Read aloud the academic terms, as well as the descriptions and questions. Model for students how to read one question and answer it. Have partners monitor their understanding and seek clarification of the terms by working through the meanings and questions together.

Related Skills Activities

- **SkillsBook**
  End Punctuation 1 and 2, pp. 5–6
  Punctuation in Math, p. 38

Question Mark

606.1 Direct Question

Place a **question mark** at the end of a direct question.

> **Where should I go? I wondered. Do I climb the stairs or take the elevator? Why should I be discouraged by the sound of ringing in my ears?**

When a question ends with a quotation that is also a question, use only one question mark, and place it within the quotation marks.

> **On road trips, do you remember driving your parents crazy by asking, "Are we there yet?"**

NOTE: Do *not* use a question mark after an indirect question.

> **Out on the street, I picked out a friendly looking old man and asked him where the depot was.**

> —Wilson Rawls, *Where the Red Fern Grows*

606.2 To Show Uncertainty

Use a question mark within parentheses to show uncertainty.

> **This summer marks the 20th season (?) of the American Players Theatre.**

606.3 Short Question Within a Sentence

Use a question mark for a short question within parentheses.

> **We crept so quietly (had they heard us?) past the kitchen door and back to our room.**

Use a question mark for a short question within dashes.

> **Somewhere in all the confusion—how could it have happened?—the cat escaped through the front door.**

Grammar Practice

Periods and Question Marks

 Write the correct end punctuation for each of the following sentences. Also write the instances where a period is needed as a decimal point or after an initial or abbreviation (as shown in red).

Example: Bill Gates, worth an astounding $56 1 billion, became interested in writing software at age 13
> $56.1   13.

1. That was back in 1968—wasn't that before personal computers were even around

2. Gates went to Harvard, but he did not graduate

3. William H Gates III wanted to work at his own company instead

4. Few people question if that was a good decision

5. Gates had a hunch that personal computers would become common in homes and offices

6. The company he founded developed software for these personal computers

7. That company did $44 2 billion in business in 2006

8. Mr Gates and his wife, Melinda, are noted philanthropists

9. Only someone like John D Rockefeller knows how it feels to be as generous as the Gateses with a personal fortune

10. Can you imagine giving away billions of dollars

11. That is what the Gateses have given to the Gates Foundation since 2000

Model

Model the following sentences to practice using question marks.

> **Mara couldn't help but dream (did she really have a chance?) about her eligibility for the competition.**

> **Could it be possible that she was asking, "How can I be a member of this team? What must I do?"**

Related Skills Activities

- **SkillsBook**
  End Punctuation 1 and 2, pp. 5–6

Answers

1. around?
2. graduate.
3. H.
   instead.
4. decision.
5. offices.
6. computers.
7. $44.2
   2006.
8. Mr.
   philanthropists.
9. D.
   fortune.
10. dollars?
11. 2000.

Comma

608.1 Between Two Independent Clauses

Use a **comma** between two independent clauses that are joined by a coordinating conjunction *(and, but, or, nor, for, yet, so).*

> He stumbled in the dark, **but** he never fell off the narrow ledge.

NOTE: Do not confuse a sentence containing a compound verb for a compound sentence.

> I had to burn her trash **and** then sweep up her porches and halls.
> —Anne Moody, *Coming of Age in Mississippi*

608.2 To Separate Adjectives

Use commas to separate two or more adjectives that *equally* modify the same noun. (Note: Do not use a comma between the last adjective and the noun.)

> Bao's eyes met the **hard, bright** lights hanging directly above her.
> —Julie Ament, student writer

A Closer Look

To determine whether adjectives modify equally—and should, therefore, be separated by commas—use these two tests:

1. Shift the order of the adjectives; if the sentence is clear, the adjectives modify equally. (In the example below, *hot* and *smelly* can be shifted and the sentence is still clear; *usual* and *morning* cannot.)

2. Insert *and* between the adjectives; if the sentence reads well, use a comma when the *and* is omitted. (The word *and* can be inserted between *hot* and *smelly*, but *and* does not make sense between *usual* and *morning*.)

> Matty was tired of working in the **hot, smelly** kitchen and decided to take her *usual morning* walk.

608.3 To Separate Contrasted Elements

Use commas to separate contrasted elements within a sentence. Often the word or phrase that is set off is preceded by *not*.

> Working late hours in the hot sun, **not under cover of the trees,** she developed a deep tan.

Punctuation

Grammar Practice

Commas 1

- ■ Between Independent Clauses
- ■ To Separate Adjectives

Indicate where commas are needed in the following sentences by writing the commas along with the words that surround them (as shown in red).

Example: Walt and Wade are twins but they are not identical.
> . . . twins, but . . .

1. Walt is a tall dark-haired man.

2. Wade is the slightly shorter twin and he has long curly hair.

3. Wade enjoys long productive computer sessions or quick video games.

4. Walt enjoys those pursuits, too yet he is also a talented musician.

5. His blue bass guitar is his constant companion so he's always ready to jam.

6. Wade playfully calls his brother's wailing soulful rhythms "the bass-ment."

7. Despite their differences, the friendly intelligent brothers get along well.

8. They go to see the same movies or they hit the beach together.

9. They both plan to go to college but they'll attend different schools.

Model

Model the following sentences to practice using commas between independent clauses and to separate adjectives.

> I have caught rattlesnakes with a forked stick and my bare hands, but I'm not ashamed to say I jumped back from that cage.
> —Daniel P. Mannix, "A Running Brook of Horror"

> It was a small, black-covered book . . . with that ageless look that some books have.
> —Robert Sheckley, "Feeding Time"

Related Skills Activities

- ■ *GrammarSnap*
  Punctuating Compound and Complex Sentences

- ■ *SkillsBook*
  Commas Between Independent Clauses, p. 8
  Commas in a Series and Commas to Separate Adjectives
  1 and 2, pp. 9–10

Answers

1. tall, dark-haired
2. twin, and
   long, curly
3. long, productive
4. too, yet
5. companion, so
6. wailing, soulful
7. friendly, intelligent
8. movies, or
9. college, but

Comma *(continued)*

610.1 To Set Off Appositives

A specific kind of explanatory word or phrase called an **appositive** identifies or renames a preceding noun or pronoun.

Benson, *our uninhibited and enthusiastic Yorkshire terrier,* **joined our family on my sister's fifteenth birthday.**

—Chad Hockerman, student writer

NOTE: Do not use commas with *restrictive appositives*. A restrictive appositive is essential to the basic meaning of the sentence.

Sixteen-year-old student *Ray Perez* **was awarded an athletic scholarship.**

610.2 Between Items in a Series

Use commas to separate individual words, phrases, or clauses in a series. (A series contains at least three items.)

Dad likes *meat, vegetables, and a salad* **for dinner.** (words)

She went to the grocery store, set the table, and prepared the meal *before her guests arrived.* (phrases)

NOTE: Do not use commas when all the words in a series are connected with *or, nor,* or *and.*

The red leaves covered the ground *and* **the sidewalk** *and* **the driveway.**

610.3 After Introductory Phrases and Clauses

Use a comma after an introductory participial phrase.

Determined to finish the sweater by Friday, *my grandmother knit night and day.*

Use a comma after a long introductory prepositional phrase or after two or more short ones.

In the oddest places and at the strangest times, *my grandmother can be found knitting madly away.*

NOTE: You may omit the comma if the introductory phrase is short.

Before breakfast *my grandmother knits.*

Use a comma after an introductory adverb (subordinate) clause.

After the practice was over, *Tina walked home.*

NOTE: A comma is not used if an adverb clause *follows* the main clause and is needed to complete the meaning of the sentence.

Tina practiced hard *because she feared losing.*

However, a comma is used if the adverb clause following the main clause begins with *although, even though, while,* or another conjunction expressing a contrast.

Tina walked home, *even though it was raining very hard.*

Grammar Practice

Commas 2

■ To Set Off Appositives
■ Between Items in a Series

 Indicate where commas are needed in the following sentences by writing the commas along with the words that surround them (as shown in red). If no commas are needed, write "none needed."

Example: One of my cousins Pablo got the hiccups the other day and couldn't get rid of them.
One of my cousins, Pablo, . . .

1. The person who holds the world record for hiccups Charles Osborne had them for 68 years—from 1922 to 1990.

2. Hiccups are the result of an involuntary contraction of the diaphragm a large, convex muscle located underneath the lungs.

3. The diaphragm becomes irritated from eating or drinking too much swallowing too much air or feeling nervous.

4. The muscle contracts, causing a sudden gulp of air.

5. The glottis the opening of the air passage closes quickly, and this is what makes the "hic" sound.

6. Although scientists know *how* hiccups come about, they don't know why; hiccups serve no known function.

7. Hiccups can last a few minutes several hours or (as mentioned) many years.

Model

Model the following sentences to practice using commas between items in a series and to set off appositives.

More and more Americans are appalled by the ravages of industrial progress, by the defacement of nature, by man-made ugliness.

—John William Gardner, *No Easy Victories*

Months before he had lost his heart to young Elise, the blue-eyed, yellow-haired daughter of the lecturer.

—Arthur Conan Doyle, "The Great Keinplatz Experiment"

Related Skills Activities

■ **Basic Grammar and Writing**
Create Appositives, p. 535

■ *GrammarSnap*
Commas after Introductory Words, Phrases, and Clauses; Appositives and Appositive Phrases

■ *SkillsBook*
Commas to Set Off Explanatory Words and Appositives, p. 14
Commas After Introductory Phrases and Clauses 1 and 2, pp. 11–12

 ## Answers

1. hiccups, Charles Osborne,
2. diaphragm, a
3. much, swallowing too much air, or
4. none needed
5. glottis, the opening of the air passage,
6. none needed
7. minutes, several hours, or

Comma *(continued)*

612.1 To Enclose Parenthetical Elements

Use commas to separate parenthetical elements, such as an explanatory word or phrase, within a sentence.

> **Victor dived into the water,** toward the group of girls, **and emerged with a grin.**
>
> **Allison meandered into class,** late as usual, **and sat down.**

612.2 To Set Off Nonrestrictive Phrases and Clauses

Use commas to set off **nonrestrictive** (unnecessary) clauses and participial phrases. A nonrestrictive clause or participial phrase adds information that is not necessary to the basic meaning of the sentence. For example, if the clause or phrase (in red) were left out in the two examples below, the meaning of the sentences would remain clear. Therefore, commas are used to set them off.

> **The Altena Fitness Center and Visker Gymnasium,** which were built last year, **are busy every day.** (nonrestrictive clause)
>
> **Students and faculty,** improving their health through exercise, **use both facilities throughout the week.** (nonrestrictive phrase)

Do not use commas to set off a **restrictive** (necessary) clause or participial phrase, which helps to define a noun or pronoun. It adds information that the reader needs to know in order to understand the sentence. For example, if the clause and phrase (in red) were dropped from the examples below, the meaning wouldn't be the same. Therefore, commas are *not* used.

> **The handball court** that has a sign-up sheet by the door **must be reserved.** The clause identifies which handball court must be reserved. (restrictive clause)
>
> **Individuals** wanting to use this court **must sign up a day in advance.** (restrictive phrase)

A Closer Look: *That* and *Which*

Use *that* to introduce restrictive (necessary) clauses; use *which* to introduce nonrestrictive (unnecessary) clauses. When the two words are used in this way, the reader can quickly distinguish necessary and unnecessary information.

> The treadmill that monitors heart rate is the one you must use.
> (The reader needs the information to find the right treadmill.)
>
> This treadmill, which we got last year, is required for your program.
> (The main clause tells the reader which treadmill to use; the other clause gives additional, unnecessary information.)

Grammar Practice

Commas 3

- To Enclose Parenthetical Elements
- To Set Off Nonrestrictive Phrases and Clauses

Indicate where commas are needed in the following sentences by writing the commas along with the words that surround them (as shown in red).

Example: My mom who is really into her exercise program is always trying to get me off the couch.
> . . . mom, who is really into her exercise program, is . . .

1. She claims that aerobic exercise which gets oxygen to the brain would help me get better grades.

2. Mom feeling she is right about this usually manages to get me moving.

3. Yesterday I walked fast around our block the kind lined with nice shade trees exactly eight times.

4. That was a long hike which was just what I needed.

5. Back home I popped in a DVD one I'd seen already and made some microwave popcorn.

6. Mom having heard about a test I had the next day came in to talk.

7. Soon we were both eating popcorn while she quizzed me on my history notes which is probably why I got a B on the test today.

Model

Model the following sentences to practice using commas to enclose parenthetical elements and to set off nonrestrictive phrases.

> **It was growing dark before,** drunk with sun and air, **we all stumbled sleepily back to the houses.**
> —Frances Fowler, "The Day We Flew the Kites"
>
> **Farther down,** in the land of the Crows and Blackfeet, **the plain is yellow.**
> —M. Scott Momaday, "A Kiowa Grandmother"

Related Skills Activities

- **Basic Grammar and Writing**
  Sentence Combining, p. 555

- *GrammarSnap*
  Punctuating Parenthetical Elements with Commas, Dashes, or Parentheses; Restrictive/Nonrestrictive Relative Clauses and Relative Pronouns in Complex Sentences

- *SkillsBook*
  Commas with Nonrestrictive Phrases and Clauses 1, 2, and 3, pp. 15–18

Answers

1. . . . exercise, which gets oxygen to the brain, would . . .

2. Mom, feeling she is right about this, usually . . .

3. . . . block, the kind lined with nice shade trees, exactly . . .

4. . . . hike, which was just . . .

5. . . . DVD, one I'd seen already, and . . .

6. Mom, having heard about a test I had the next day, came . . .

7. . . . notes, which is probably . . .

Comma *(continued)*

614.1 To Set Off Dates

Use commas to set off items in a date.

> On September 30, 2002, my little sister entered our lives.
> He began working out on December 1, 2010, but quit by May 1, 2011.

However, when only the month and year are given, no commas are needed.

> He began working out in December 2010 but quit by May 2011.

When a full date appears in the middle of a sentence, a comma follows the year.

> On June 7, 1924, my great-grandfather met his future wife.

614.2 To Set Off Items in Addresses

Use commas to set off items in an address. (No comma is placed between the state and ZIP code.)

> Mail the box to Friends of Wildlife, Box 402, Spokane, Washington 20077.

When a city and state (or country) appear in the middle of a sentence, a comma follows the last item in the address.

> Several charitable organizations in Juneau, Alaska, pool their funds.

614.3 In Numbers

Use commas to separate numerals in large numbers in order to distinguish hundreds, thousands, millions, and so forth.

> 1,101   25,000   7,642,020

614.4 To Enclose Titles or Initials

Use commas to enclose a title or initials and names that follow a surname (a last name).

> Letitia O'Reilly, M.D., is our family physician.
> Hickok, J. B., and Cody, William F., are two popular Western heroes.

Grammar Practice

Commas 4

- To Set Off Dates
- To Set Off Items in Addresses
- In Numbers

 Indicate where commas are needed in the following sentences by writing the commas along with the words that surround them (as shown in red).

Example: Here are some facts about Washington D.C. the capital of the United States.
> . . . Washington, D.C., the . . .

1. On July 16 1790 Congress made it possible for George Washington to select our capital's present location.

2. It rests on the banks of the Potomac River, 35 miles southwest of Baltimore Maryland.

3. While the site was being prepared, Philadelphia Pennsylvania served as the temporary capital from 1790 to 1800.

4. Finally, Congress convened for the first time in the new capital on November 21 1800.

5. The transfer of the government from Philadelphia to Washington D.C. wasn't finished until June 1801.

6. Presently, the population of the capital city is 550521 (291226 female and 259295 male).

7. You can write to the City Museum of Washington D.C. 801 K Street Mount Vernon Square Washington D.C. 20001 for more information.

 Model

Model the following sentences to practice using commas in dates, addresses, and numbers.

> My best friend, who was born on August 31, 1993, lives at 2745 Market Place Drive, Phoenix, Arizona 85062.
>
> If I lived in Chicago, Illinois, and wanted to visit Seattle, Washington, I would have to travel 2,052 miles.

Related Skills Activities

- ***SkillsBook***
  Other Uses for Commas, p. 19
  Punctuation in Math, p. 38

Answers

1. . . . July 16, 1790, Congress . . .
2. . . . Baltimore, Maryland.
3. . . . Philadelphia, Pennsylvania, served . . .
4. . . . November 21, 1800.
5. . . . Washington, D.C., wasn't . . .
6. . . . is 550,521 (291,226 female and 259,295 male).
7. . . . Washington, D.C., 801 K Street, Mount Vernon Square, Washington, D.C. 20001, . . .

Comma (continued)

616.1 To Set Off Dialogue

Use commas to set off the speaker's exact words from the rest of the sentence. (It may be helpful to remember that the comma is always to the left of the quotation mark.)

"It's like we have our own government," adds Tanya, a 17-year-old squatter.
—Kyung Sun Yu and Nell Bernstein, "Street Teens Forge a Home"

616.2 To Set Off Interjections

Use a comma to separate an interjection or a weak exclamation from the rest of the sentence.

Wow, how will you reach such a high goal?

616.3 To Set Off Interruptions

Use commas to set off a word, a phrase, or a clause that interrupts the movement of a sentence. Such expressions usually can be identified through the following tests: (1) They may be omitted without changing the meaning of a sentence. (2) They may be placed nearly anywhere in the sentence without changing its meaning.

The laughter, thank goodness, broke out all around the stadium
The safest way to cross this street, as a general rule, is with the light.

616.4 In Direct Address

Use commas to separate a noun of direct address from the rest of the sentence. A *noun of direct address* is the noun that names the person(s) spoken to.

You can never know, James, how much your work meant to the people living on the streets.

616.5 For Clarity or Emphasis

You may use a comma for clarity or for emphasis. There will be times when none of the traditional rules call for a comma, but one will be needed to prevent confusion or to emphasize an important idea.

Those who can see tomorrow, can find the energy to continue. (emphasis)
What the crew does, does affect our voyage. (clarity)

Grammar Practice

Commas 5

■ To Set Off Dialogue
■ To Set Off Interruptions

 Indicate where commas are needed in the following sentences by writing the commas along with the words that surround them (as shown in red).

Example: Wolves as you may be aware completely disappeared from Yellowstone National Park by the 1970s.
Wolves, as you may be aware, completely . . .

1. These animals are very efficient predators, and this not surprisingly has given the wolf a bad name.

2. "As a child, I remember singing a song about the big bad wolf" says my grandpa.

3. Cruel eradication programs were in reality the cause of the wolf's decline.

4. During the past century as a matter of fact "humans . . . killed an estimated two million wolves" says CNN reporter Jack Hamann.

5. A 1995 wolf reintroduction program however has been successful in Yellowstone, even though it is controversial.

6. Ranchers for example worry about wolves wandering off parkland to prey on livestock.

7. I hope that, with education and cooperation, no one will again say "The only good wolf is a dead wolf."

Model

Model the following sentences to practice using commas to set off dialogue and interruptions.

"My son will go to school," he said, and the neighbors were hushed.
—John Steinbeck, *The Pearl*

The room, to tell the truth, was a barren, cold place with dirty walls.

Related Skills Activities

■ *SkillsBook*
Other Uses for Commas, p. 19

Answers

1. . . . this, not surprisingly, has . . .
2. . . . wolf," says . . .
3. . . . were, in reality, the . . .
4. . . . century, as a matter of fact, "humans . . .
   . . . wolves," says . . .
5. . . . program, however, has . . .
6. Ranchers, for example, worry . . .
7. . . . say, "The . . .

Semicolon

618.1 To Join Two Independent Clauses

Use a **semicolon** to join two or more closely related independent clauses that are not connected with a coordinating conjunction. (Independent clauses can stand alone as separate sentences.)

> Sylvia didn't call his name; she simply nodded her head in the poodle's direction.
>
> Regret froze him into indecision; he wanted so much to have that day to live over.

NOTE: When independent clauses are especially long or contain commas, a semicolon may punctuate the sentence, even though a coordinating conjunction connects the clauses.

> We waited all day in that wide line, tired travelers pressing in from all sides; and when we needed drinks or sandwiches, I would squeeze my way to the cafeteria and back.

618.2 With Conjunctive Adverbs

A semicolon is used *before* a conjunctive adverb (with a comma after it) when the word connects two independent clauses in a compound sentence. (Common conjunctive adverbs are *also, besides, finally, however, indeed, instead, meanwhile, moreover, nevertheless, next, still, then, therefore,* and *thus.*)

> "I am faced with my imminent demise; therefore, life becomes a very precious thing."
>
> — Amy Taylor, "AIDS Can Happen Here!"

618.3 To Separate Groups That Contain Commas

A semicolon is used to separate groups of words that already contain commas.

> Every Saturday night my little brother gathers up his things—goggles, shower cap, and snorkel; bubble bath, soap, and shampoo; tapes, stereo, and rubber duck—and heads for the tub.

Grammar Practice

Semicolons

■ To Join Two Independent Clauses

 Indicate where a semicolon is needed in the following sentences by writing the semicolon along with the words that surround it (as shown in red).

Example: Aliens from outer space are still a popular subject movies like *Independence Day, Signs,* and *Men in Black* attest to that.
. . . subject; movies . . .

1. Recently, the imagined aliens are unfriendly indeed, they are the "let's-take-over-the-earth" variety.

2. Long ago, people were crazy about the movie *Close Encounters of the Third Kind* however, this movie's aliens were a more friendly type.

3. You wanted to meet these guys you wanted to take a ride in their brightly lit, saucer-shaped spacecraft!

4. Their spaceship was gargantuan it dwarfed the Devils Tower National Monument in Wyoming!

5. Area 51, a military facility north of Las Vegas, is shrouded in secrecy at the center of this 60-square-mile plot of land, a site once used to test the U-2 spy plane, is an air base the government will not discuss.

6. Many unidentified flying object (UFO) stories are connected with this place Area 51 has become the symbol for the government's alleged UFO cover-up.

7. Whatever you choose to believe about aliens, they remain an interesting topic plenty of stories are yet to be told.

Model

Model the following sentences to practice using semicolons to join two independent clauses.

> No one dared touch the bowls of steaming food; instead, they sat quietly, waiting to be invited.
>
> —Lois Krenzke, "The Long Table"
>
> The small fox trembled a moment; it had heard something, a warning.

Related Skills Activities

■ *SkillsBook*
Semicolons to Join Independent Clauses, pp. 21–22

 ## Answers

1. . . . unfriendly; indeed, . . .
2. . . . Kind; however, . . .
3. . . . guys; you . . .
4. . . . gargantuan; it . . .
5. . . . secrecy; at . . .
6. . . . place; Area 51 . . .
7. . . . topic; plenty . . .

Colon

620.1 After a Salutation

Use a **colon** after the salutation of a business letter.
> Dear Judge Parker: Dear Governor Whitman:

620.2 Between Numerals Indicating Time

Use a colon between the hours, minutes, and seconds of a number indicating time.
> 8:30 p.m.   9:45 a.m.   10:24:55

620.3 For Emphasis

Use a colon to emphasize a word, a phrase, a clause, or a sentence that explains or adds impact to the main clause (also see **650.3**).
> The newest candidates announced their platforms today: Lower taxes and more efficient services are the consistent themes.

620.4 To Introduce a Quotation

Use a colon to formally introduce a quotation, a sentence, or a question.
> Directly a voice in the corner rang out wild and clear: "I've got him! I've got him!"
> —Mark Twain, *Roughing It*

620.5 To Introduce a List

A colon is used to introduce a list.
> I completed all the forms on my list: registration, health, logistics, and room reservation.

A Closer Look

Do not use a colon between a verb and its object or complement, or between a preposition and its object.

> **Incorrect:** Min has: a snowmobile, an ATV, and a canoe.
> **Correct:** Min has plenty of toys: a snowmobile, an ATV, and a canoe.
> **Incorrect:** I watch a TV show about: cooking wild game.
> **Correct:** I watch a TV show about a new subject: cooking wild game.

620.6 Between a Title and a Subtitle

Use a colon to distinguish between a title and a subtitle, volume and page, and chapter and verse in literature.
> *Encyclopedia Americana* IV: 211   Psalm 23:1–6

Grammar Practice

Colons

- For Emphasis
- To Introduce a List

Indicate where a colon is needed in the following sentences by writing the colon along with the words that surround it (as shown in red).

Example: Hawaii is a beautiful tropical paradise in my grandmother's mind a place she has only dreamed of visiting.
> . . . mind: a place . . .

1. Grandmother remembers the exact day that Hawaii became the 50th state in the Union August 21, 1959.

2. The Aloha State is composed of many islands, seven of which are inhabited Niihau, Kauai, Oahu, Molokai, Lanai, Maui, and Hawaii.

3. Niihau has been privately owned since 1864 and has an interesting nickname the Forbidden Island.

4. The owners are determined to preserve the traditional ways of life on Niihau, including their native language Hawaiian.

5. The 200 residents of the island still hunt and fish with traditional tools ropes, knives, spears, and nets.

6. Because this is an arid, flowerless island, residents make leis of another material tiny seashells.

7. Tourists can visit this paradise for half-day tours, reaching the island in a classy helicopter the Agusta 109A.

8. While there, they can spend a few hours at one of the pristine beaches, doing what Hawaiian vacations are famous for swimming, snorkeling, and just plain relaxing.

Model

Model the following sentences to practice using colons for emphasis and to introduce a list.

> Tilly received a surprise birthday gift: a round-trip ticket to Hawaii!
> She's busy packing the essentials: sunscreen, bathing suits, sandals, straw hats, a camera, film—and more sunscreen.

Related Skills Activities

- *GrammarSnap*
  Colon

- *SkillsBook*
  Colons, p. 23

Answers

1. . . . Union: August . . .
2. . . . inhabited: Niihau, . . .
3. . . . nickname: the . . .
4. . . . language: Hawaiian.
5. . . . tools: ropes, . . .
6. . . . material: tiny . . .
7. . . . helicopter: the . . .
8. . . . for: swimming, . . .

Test Prep!

Read the following paragraphs. From the choices given on the next page, write the letter of the correct way to punctuate each underlined part. If it is already correct, choose "D."

What does the future <u>hold</u>. If you were asked this question in the
(1)
mid-twentieth <u>century here's</u> what you may have <u>envisioned</u>, flying
(2)   (3)
automobiles, space travel to distant planets, and lifelike robots acting as
servants. Movies and books of that era are fascinating to look at now.

The 1930 movie *Just Imagine* depicted the future of 1980. People
had numbers rather than <u>names and</u> the government arranged all
(4)
marriages. Several movies from the 1970s and 1980s depicted a future
world run by computers. The *Mad Max* series of <u>movies on the other hand</u>
(5)
showed a <u>bleak orderless</u> future. Fortunately, none of these ideas has
(6)
come to pass . . . yet.

Unfortunately, some predictions have come true. Two of Aldous
Huxley's <u>books *Brave New World*</u> and <u>*Ape and Essence,* which</u> were
(7)   (8)
published in the 1930s and 1940s, described many of the social problems
we see <u>today; terrorism,</u> overpopulation, the loss of natural <u>resources and</u>
(9)   (10)
widespread drug use. In movies, destruction caused by huge bombs was
depicted before the nuclear age was a reality.

On the brighter side, movies and books that dreamed of "picture
phones" have of course, become a dream come true. (These dreams didn't
go far <u>enough, indeed,</u> no one saw the Internet coming!) And while human
(11)
travel to distant planets hasn't <u>evolved scientists</u> have been able to
(12)
explore beyond our galaxy with the help of a kind of robot.

No one knows what tomorrow has in store for <u>us, but</u> based on
(13)

technologies in development <u>today we</u> can make educated guesses.
(14)
Many predict a cashless <u>future, all</u> financial transactions will take place
(15)
electronically. Some see cures for <u>AIDS cancer,</u> and the common cold. And
(16)
a few envision molecular transport, as in *Star Trek*. Whatever we predict,
people of the future will either laugh—or be in awe of our insight.

1 Ⓐ hold!
　 Ⓑ hold?
　 Ⓒ hold,
　 Ⓓ correct as is

2 Ⓐ century, here's
　 Ⓑ century. Here's
　 Ⓒ century; here's
　 Ⓓ correct as is

3 Ⓐ envisioned.
　 Ⓑ envisioned;
　 Ⓒ envisioned:
　 Ⓓ correct as is

4 Ⓐ names and,
　 Ⓑ names: and
　 Ⓒ names, and
　 Ⓓ correct as is

5 Ⓐ movies, on the other hand,
　 Ⓑ movies, on the other hand
　 Ⓒ movies on the other hand,
　 Ⓓ correct as is

6 Ⓐ bleak orderless,
　 Ⓑ bleak, orderless
　 Ⓒ bleak; orderless
　 Ⓓ correct as is

7 Ⓐ books *Brave New World,*
　 Ⓑ books *Brave, New World*
　 Ⓒ books, *Brave New World*
　 Ⓓ correct as is

8 Ⓐ *Ape and Essence* which
　 Ⓑ *Ape and Essence* which,
　 Ⓒ *Ape, and Essence* which
　 Ⓓ correct as is

9 Ⓐ today: terrorism
　 Ⓑ today: terrorism,
　 Ⓒ today terrorism
　 Ⓓ correct as is

10 Ⓐ resources, and
　 Ⓑ resources and,
　 Ⓒ resources, and,
　 Ⓓ correct as is

11 Ⓐ enough indeed;
　 Ⓑ enough, indeed,
　 Ⓒ enough; indeed,
　 Ⓓ correct as is

12 Ⓐ evolved scientists,
　 Ⓑ evolved; scientists
　 Ⓒ evolved, scientists
　 Ⓓ correct as is

13 Ⓐ us but
　 Ⓑ us but,
　 Ⓒ us. but
　 Ⓓ correct as is

14 Ⓐ today, we
　 Ⓑ today; we
　 Ⓒ today we,
　 Ⓓ correct as is

15 Ⓐ future all
　 Ⓑ future; all
　 Ⓒ future all,
　 Ⓓ correct as is

16 Ⓐ AIDS cancer
　 Ⓑ AIDS, cancer
　 Ⓒ AIDS, cancer,
　 Ⓓ correct as is

Related Skills Activities

- **SkillsBook**
  End Punctuation Review, p. 7
  Review: Commas 1, p. 13
  Review: Commas 2, p. 20
  Review: Semicolons and Colons, p. 24
  Posttest: End Punctuation, p. 191
  Posttest: Commas, p. 192
  Posttest: Semicolons and Colons, p. 193

Answers

1. B
2. A
3. C
4. C
5. A
6. B
7. C
8. D

9. B
10. A
11. C
12. C
13. D
14. A
15. B
16. C

Hyphen

624.1 In Compound Words

Use the **hyphen** to make some compound words.

great-great-grandfather   maid-in-waiting   three-year-old

624.2 To Create New Words

Use a hyphen to form new words beginning with the prefixes *self-, ex-, all-,* and *half-*. Also use a hyphen to join any prefix to a proper noun, a proper adjective, or the official name of an office. Use a hyphen before the suffix *-elect*.

self-**contained**   ex-**governor**   all-**inclusive**   half-**painted**
pre-**Cambrian**   mid-**December**   president-**elect**

Use a hyphen to join the prefix *great-* only to the names of relatives.

great-**aunt**, great-**grandfather** (correct)   **great-hall** (incorrect)

624.3 To Form an Adjective

Use a hyphen to join two or more words that serve as a single adjective (a single-thought adjective) before a noun.

In real life I am a large, big-boned **woman with rough,** man-working **hands.**
—Alice Walker, "Everyday Use"

Use common sense to determine whether a compound adjective might be misread if it is not hyphenated. Generally, hyphenate a compound adjective that is composed of . . .

- a phrase   heat-and-serve **meal**   off-and-on **relationship**
- a noun + adjective   oven-safe **handles**   book-smart **student**
- a noun + participle (*ing* or *ed* form of a verb)   bone-chilling **story**

A Closer Look

When words forming the adjective come after the noun, do not hyphenate them.

In real life I am large and big boned.

When the first of these words is an adverb ending in *-ly*, do not use a hyphen.

delicately prepared **pastry**

Also, do not use a hyphen when a number or a letter is the final element in a single-thought adjective.

class B **movie**

624.4 To Join Letters and Words

Use a hyphen to join a capital letter or lowercase letter to a noun or participle. (Check your dictionary if you're not sure of the hyphenation.)

T-**shirt**   Y-**turn**   G-**rated**   x-**axis**

Grammar Practice

Hyphens 1

- To Create New Words
- To Form an Adjective

 For each sentence below, write the words that should be hyphenated (as shown in red). Some sentences contain two hyphenated words.

Example: Every spring, Nebraska's Platte River welcomes thousands upon thousands of long necked sandhill cranes to its banks.
long-necked

1. Many birders come to see the cranes and enjoy the three day Rivers and Wildlife Celebration held each March.

2. Long ago there were many wetlands along the Platte that offered nutrient rich worms, snails, and frogs to the migrating birds.

3. Because of water diversion projects, the Platte River is not the lush roosting place it once was.

4. In the 1970s, the National Audubon Society purchased a 1,248 acre sanctuary along an 80 mile stretch of the Platte to help the cranes and other wildlife.

5. Although dried up wetlands imposed food source changes on the cranes, they have proved to be adaptable creatures.

6. Cranes search cow pies for half digested corn or newly hatched grubs; they also feast on machine harvested corn left behind in the fields.

7. The sandhill cranes and other birds still look to the Platte as a fattening up stopover on their way to northern nesting grounds.

Model

Model the following sentences to practice using hyphens to create new words and to form adjectives.

By mid-June the self-assured little boy had earned fifty dollars doing errands for the neighbors.

That is what the two Helens and I were talking about the day we had lunch in a room up in a high-rise motel near the Kansas City airport. We had lunch there at the end of a two-day conference on families.
—Jane Howard, "All Happy Clans Are Alike"

Related Skills Activities

- *SkillsBook*
  Hyphens 1, p. 25

 ## Answers

1. three-day
2. nutrient-rich
3. water-diversion
4. 1,248-acre
   80-mile
5. dried-up
6. half-digested
   machine-harvested
7. fattening-up

Hyphen *(continued)*

626.1 Between Numbers and Fractions

Use a hyphen to join the words in compound numbers from *twenty-one* to *ninety-nine* when it is necessary to write them out (see 658.3).

Use a hyphen between the numerator and denominator of a fraction, but not when one or both of those elements are already hyphenated.

four-tenths   five-sixteenths   (7/32) seven thirty-seconds

626.2 In a Special Series

Use hyphens when two or more words have a common element that is omitted in all but the last term.

The ship has lovely two-, four-, or six-person cabins.

626.3 To Join Numbers

Use a hyphen to join numbers indicating the life span of a person or the score in a contest or a vote.

We can thank Louis Pasteur (1822–1895) for pasteurized milk.

In the 2000 Rose Bowl, Wisconsin defeated Stanford 17–9.

626.4 To Prevent Confusion

Use a hyphen with prefixes or suffixes to avoid confusion or awkward spelling.

re-create (not *recreate*) the image   re-cover (not *recover*) the sofa

626.5 To Divide a Word

Use a hyphen to divide a word, only between its syllables, at the end of a line of print. Always place the hyphen after the syllable at the end of the line—never before a syllable at the beginning of the following line.

Guidelines for Dividing with Hyphens

1. Always divide a compound word between its basic units: **sister-in-law**, not **sis-ter-in-law**.

2. Avoid dividing a word of five or fewer letters: **paper, study, July.**

3. Avoid dividing the last word in a paragraph.

4. Never divide a one-syllable word: **rained, skills, through.**

5. Never divide a one-letter syllable from the rest of the word: **omit-ted**, not **o-mitted.**

6. When a vowel is a syllable by itself, divide the word after the vowel: **epi-sode**, not **ep-isode.**

7. Never divide abbreviations or contractions: **shouldn't**, not **should-n't.**

8. Never divide the last word in more than two lines in a row.

Punctuation

Grammar Practice

Hyphens 2

- Between Numbers and Fractions
- To Join Numbers

For each sentence below, write the numerals or words that should be hyphenated (as shown in red). You may use more than one hyphen in some sentences.

Example: Wolfgang Amadeus Mozart (1756 1791) wrote his first compositions at age four.
(1756–1791)

1. Mozart's father took Wolfgang on an extended tour of Italy (1769 1773).

2. A mule is genetically one half horse and one half donkey.

3. Being sure-footed, a mule can serve as a good pack animal for 20 30 years of its life.

4. A four fifths majority vote in the Senate would settle the matter once and for all.

5. "Ninety nine out of a hundred people use this brand," bragged the salesperson.

6. A late fourth-quarter score of 112 110 kept the fans on their feet.

7. Forty eight of our classmates rode the school bus to the state championship game, and thirty two rode in private cars.

8. Fran Tarkenton completed 3,686 passes during his 1961 1978 professional football career.

9. Although he might have expected it, my uncle's college career (1968 1972) was not interrupted by a tour of duty in Vietnam.

Model

Model the following sentences to practice using hyphens between numbers and to join numbers.

Twenty-one other children went to school with him in first grade; in twelfth grade, ninety-five.
Yemen's coastal plain is 20-50 miles wide (32-80 kilometers).

Related Skills Activities

- **SkillsBook**
  Hyphens 2, p. 26
  Punctuation in Math, p. 38

Answers

1. (1769–1773)
2. one-half
   one-half
3. 20–30 years
4. four-fifths
5. Ninety-nine
6. 112–110
7. Forty-eight
   thirty-two
8. 1961–1978
9. (1968–1972)

Punctuation

Apostrophe

628.1 In Contractions

Use an **apostrophe** to show that one or more letters have been left out of a word group to form a contraction.

hadn't – **o** is left out   they'd – **woul** is left out   it's – **i** is left out

NOTE: Use an apostrophe to show that one or more numerals or letters have been left out of numbers or words in order to show special pronunciation.

class of '99 – **19** is left out   g'day – **ood** is left out

628.2 To Form Singular Possessives

Add an apostrophe and *s* to form the possessive of most singular nouns.

Spock's **ears**   Captain Kirk's **singing**   the ship's **escape plan**

NOTE: When a singular noun ends with an *s* or a *z* sound, you may form the possessive by adding just an apostrophe. When the singular noun is a one-syllable word, however, you usually add both an apostrophe and an *s* to form the possessive.

San Carlos' **government** (or) San Carlos's **government** (two-syllable word)
Ross's **essay** (one-syllable word)   The class's **field trip** (one-syllable word)

628.3 To Form Plural Possessives

The possessive form of plural nouns ending in *s* is usually made by adding just an apostrophe.

students' **homework**   bosses' **orders**

For plural nouns not ending in *s*, an apostrophe and *s* must be added.

children's **book**   men's **department**

A Closer Look

It will help you punctuate correctly if you remember that the word immediately before the apostrophe is the owner.

girl's **guitar** (*girl* is the owner)   boss's **order** (*boss* is the owner)
girls' **guitar** (*girls* are the owners)   bosses' **order** (*bosses* are the owners)

628.4 To Show Shared Possession

When possession is shared by more than one noun, use the possessive form for the last noun in the series.

Hoshi, Linda, and Nakiva's **water skis** (All three own the same skis.)
Hoshi's, Linda's, and Nakiva's **water skis** (Each owns her own skis.)

Grammar Practice

Apostrophes 1

- In Contractions
- To Form Singular Possessives

 Write the word or words from the following sentences that need apostrophes.

Example: Central Americas seven countries include Nicaragua, Guatemala, El Salvador, Panama, Honduras, Costa Rica, and Belize.
Central America's

1. Its basically an isthmus connecting North and South America.

2. Guatemalas Sierra Madre mountain range has more than 30 volcanoes.

3. Most of the regions volcanoes arent active, but some are.

4. Panamas canal provides ships a means to go quickly from the Atlantic to the Pacific Ocean.

5. Along with Belize and Costa Rica, Honduras popularity as a tourist destination is growing.

6. The countrys ancient ruins, beaches, rain forests, and mountains attract foreigners.

7. Native Hondurans dont mind the influx of tourist dollars.

8. Belize wasnt independent until 1993; before that, it was known as British Honduras.

9. Belizes coral reefs offer superior scuba diving.

Model

Model the following sentence to practice using an apostrophe in contractions and to show special pronunciation. Note that this use is often employed in dialogue.

"Why not 'fess up, Jimmy? Confession's good for the soul, they say."
—Stephen King, "The Little Sisters of Eluria"

Related Skills Activities

- ***SkillsBook***
  Apostrophes in Contractions and to Show Omitted
     Letters or Numbers, p. 29
  Apostrophes to Form Possessives 1 and 2, pp. 30–31

Answers

1. It's
2. Guatemala's
3. region's
   aren't
4. Panama's
5. Honduras's *or* Honduras'
6. country's
7. don't
8. wasn't
9. Belize's

Apostrophe *(continued)*

630.1 To Show Possession with Indefinite Pronouns

Form the possessive of an indefinite pronoun by placing an apostrophe and an *s* on the last word (see **704.1** and **706.3**).

everyone's   anyone's   somebody's

630.2 To Show Possession in Compound Nouns

Form the possessive of a compound noun by placing the possessive ending after the last word.

the secretary of the interior's (singular) **agenda**
her lady-in-waiting's (singular) **day off**

If forming a possessive of a plural compound noun creates an awkward construction, you may replace the possessive with an *of* phrase. (All four forms below are correct.)

their fathers-in-law's (plural) **birthdays**
or **the birthdays of their fathers-in-law** (plural)
the ambassadors-at-large's (plural) **plans**
or **the plans of the ambassadors-at-large** (plural)

630.3 To Express Time or Amount

Use an apostrophe and an *s* with an adjective that is part of an expression indicating time or amount.

a penny's worth   today's business   this morning's meeting
yesterday's news   a day's wage   a month's pay

630.4 To Form Certain Plurals

Use an apostrophe and *s* to form the plural of a letter, a number, a sign, or a word discussed as a word.

B – B's   C – C's   8 – 8's   + – +'s   *and* – *and*'s
Ms. D'Aquisto says our conversations contain too many *like's* and *no way's*.

NOTE: If two apostrophes are called for in the same word, omit the second one.

Follow closely the *do's* and *don'ts* (not *don't's*) on the checklist.

Punctuation

Grammar Practice

Apostrophes 2

■ To Show Possession with Indefinite Pronouns
■ To Show Possession with Compound Nouns

 Write the possessive form of the underlined words in the following sentences.

Example: The <u>middle class</u> aspirations are sometimes hindered by its members' collective debt.
middle class's

1. "I presume that this is <u>nobody</u> paper airplane," the teacher remarked.
2. The look on the <u>passerby</u> face was one of despair.
3. It is best that <u>one</u> thoughts converge prior to action.
4. Crystal borrowed her <u>brother-in-law</u> power drill.
5. Do not look at <u>one another</u> papers.
6. Not everyone accepts the <u>president-elect</u> agenda for the country.
7. <u>Everybody</u> opinion is valued in my ethics class.
8. The <u>post office</u> heavy glass doors are difficult to open.
9. My <u>half sister</u> mother lives in Ontario.
10. Is this <u>someone</u> towel?
11. The <u>nine-year-old</u> ability to play the piano was astounding.

Model

 Model the following sentence to practice using an apostrophe to show possession with indefinite pronouns.

There is no greater joy nor greater reward than to make a fundamental difference in someone's life.

—Sister Mary Rose McGeady

Related Skills Activities

■ **SkillsBook**
Apostrophes to Form Possessives 1, p. 30

Answers

1. nobody's
2. passerby's
3. one's
4. brother-in-law's
5. one another's
6. president-elect's
7. Everybody's
8. post office's
9. half sister's
10. someone's
11. nine-year-old's

Quotation Marks

632.1 To Set Off Direct Quotations

Place **quotation marks** before and after the words in direct quotations.

"Just come to a game," he pleads. "You'll change your mind."

—Sandra Lampe, "Batter UP!"

In a quoted passage, put brackets around any word or punctuation mark that is not part of the original quotation. (See **644.3**.)

If you quote only part of the original passage, be sure to construct a sentence that is both accurate and grammatically correct.

Much of the restructuring of the Postal Service has involved "turning over large parts of its work to the private sector."

632.2 Placement of Punctuation

Always place periods and commas inside quotation marks.

"Slow down, Olivia," Marcos shouted. "You will run out of energy long before the end of the race."

Place an exclamation point or a question mark *inside* quotation marks when it punctuates the quotation and *outside* when it punctuates the main sentence.

"Am I dreaming?"   Had she heard him say, "Here's the key to your new car"?

Always place semicolons or colons outside quotation marks.

I wrote about James Joyce's "The Dead"; I found it thought provoking.

632.3 For Long Quotations

If you quote more than one paragraph, place quotation marks before each paragraph and at the end of the last paragraph (Example A). If a quotation has more than four lines on a page, you may set it off from the text by indenting 10 spaces from the left margin (block form). Do not use quotation marks either before or after the quoted material, unless they appear in the original (Example B).

Example A

"
_____
_____.
  "
_____
_____.
  "
_____
_____."

Example B

_____.
_____
_____
_____
_____
_____
_____.

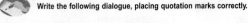

Grammar Practice

Quotation Marks 1

■ To Set Off Direct Quotations
■ Placement of Punctuation

 Write the following dialogue, placing quotation marks correctly.

Example: Hey, what's up? asked Raheema.
"Hey, what's up?" asked Raheema.

I'm trying to plan my class schedule for next year, Steve answered.

Are you going to take a foreign language? she asked.

I don't know, said Steve. There are a lot of other courses I want to take, like drama.

Yeah, me, too. Well, I'm going to take Chinese, Raheema said, rising from her seat.

Did Steve hear her right? Did he really hear her say, I'm going to take Chinese?

What did you say? he asked.

I said, Raheema answered, I'm going to get some take-out Chinese. Do you want any?

Model

Write a sentence that quotes part of this passage. Use quotation marks correctly.

When I first signed with the Chicago Bulls in 1984, the NBA's Uniform Player's Contract included a clause that prohibited players from certain activities during the off-season, including playing the game.

—Michael Jordan, *For the Love of the Game*

Related Skills Activities

■ *GrammarSnap*
Punctuating Dialogue

Answers

"I'm trying to plan my class schedule for next year," Steve answered.

"Are you going to take a foreign language?" she asked.

"I don't know," said Steve. "There are a lot of other courses I want to take, like drama."

"Yeah, me, too. Well, I'm going to take Chinese," Raheema said, rising from her seat.

Did Steve hear her right? Did he really hear her say, "I'm going to take Chinese"?

"What did you say?" he asked.

"I said," Raheema answered, "I'm going to get some take-out Chinese. Do you want any?"

Quotation Marks (continued)

634.1 Quotation Marks Within Quotations

Use single quotation marks to punctuate a quotation within a quotation. Use double quotation marks in order to distinguish a quotation within a quotation within a quotation.

> **"For tomorrow," said Mr. Botts, "read 'Unlighted Lamps.' "**
>
> **Sue asked, "Did you hear Mr. Botts say, 'Read "Unlighted Lamps" '?"**

634.2 For Special Words

You may use quotation marks (1) to distinguish a word that is being discussed, (2) to indicate that a word is unfamiliar slang, or (3) to point out that a word is being used in a special way (such as ironically).

> **(1) If I had to choose a word to describe his attitude, it would be "stoic."**
>
> **(2) Next time I hear a New Zealander say "ta," I will know that I'm being thanked.**
>
> **(3) Tom pushed the wheelchair across the street, showed the lady his "honest" smile . . . and stole her purse.**

NOTE: You may use italics (underlining) in place of quotation marks in each of these three situations. (See **636.3**.)

634.3 To Punctuate Titles

Use **quotation marks** to punctuate titles of songs, poems, short stories, one-act plays, lectures, episodes of radio or television programs, chapters of books, unpublished works, electronic files, and articles found in magazines, newspapers, encyclopedias, or online sources. (For punctuation of other titles, see **636.2**.)

> **"Santa Lucia"** (song)
>
> **"The Chameleon"** (short story)
>
> **"Twentieth-Century Memories"** (lecture)
>
> **"Affordable Adventures"** (magazine article)
>
> **"Dire Prophecy of the Howling Dog"** (chapter in a book)
>
> **"Dancing with Debra"** (television episode)
>
> **"Miss Julie"** (one-act play)

NOTE: Punctuate one title within another title as follows:

> **"Clarkson's 'Breakaway' Hits the Waves"**
> (title of a song in title of an article)

Grammar Practice

Quotation Marks 2

- Quotation Marks Within Quotations
- For Special Words
- To Punctuate Titles

 Write the word or words that should be enclosed in quotation marks in the following sentences.

Example: Marina and Dale moved to the dance floor when the deejay played Can't Get You Outta My Head as the last song.
"Can't Get You Outta My Head"

1. Dale shuffled his feet a bit and swung his arms slightly; he called this dancing.

2. "You should find the article Time Management for Students on the school Web site," the advisor said.

3. Ms. Poland got quite a variety of answers when she asked us to define the word morality.

4. Kenny explained, "When I asked him about my application, he said, Come on in, and we'll talk it over."

5. "I just finished reading a clever little story by Isaac Asimov, A Loint of Paw, and it really got me thinking," said Grant.

Model

Model the following sentence to practice using quotation marks within quotations.

> **"This song has invaded my brain, and I don't even know the name of it,"** Lee said. **"Maybe 'Bear It' or 'Dare It' or something like that—it's driving me nuts."**
>
> —Claire Ziffer, "Just Instinct"

Related Skills Activities

- **SkillsBook**
  Quotation Marks with Titles and Special Words, p. 33

Answers

1. "dancing."
2. 'Time Management for Students'
3. "morality."
4. 'Come on in, and we'll talk it over.'
5. 'A Loint of Paw'

Italics (Underlining)

636.1 Handwritten and Printed Material

Italics is a printer's term for a style of type that is slightly slanted. In this sentence, the word *happiness* is printed in italics. In material that is handwritten or typed on a machine that cannot print in italics, underline each word or letter that should be in italics.

> *My Ántonia* is the story of a strong and determined pioneer woman.
> (printed)
> Willa Cather's <u>My Ántonia</u> describes pioneer life in America.
> (typed or handwritten)

636.2 In Titles

Use italics to indicate the titles of magazines, newspapers, pamphlets, books, full-length plays, films, videos, radio and television programs, book-length poems, ballets, operas, paintings, lengthy musical compositions, sculptures, cassettes, CD's, legal cases, and the names of ships and aircraft. (For punctuation of other titles, see 634.3.)

> *Newsweek* (magazine) *Cold Sassy Tree* (book)
> *Shakespeare in Love* (film) *Law & Order* (television program)
> *Caring for Your Kitten* (pamphlet) *Hedda Gabler* (full-length play)
> *Chicago Tribune* (newspaper) *The Thinker* (sculpture)

636.3 For Special Uses

Use italics for a number, letter, or word that is being discussed or used in a special way. (Sometimes quotation marks are used for this reason. See 634.2.)

> I hope that this letter *I* on my report card stands for *incredible* and not *incomplete*.

636.4 For Foreign Words

Use italics for foreign words that have not been adopted into the English language; also use italics for scientific names.

> The voyageurs—tough men with natural *bonhomie*—discovered the shy *Castor canadensis*, or North American beaver.

Grammar Practice

Italics (Underlining)

- In Titles
- For Special Uses
- For Foreign Words

 Write and underline the word or words that should be italicized in the following sentences.

Example: There is a certain je ne sais quoi about the new restaurant; it's become quite popular.
<u>je ne sais quoi</u>

1. A large number 9 is the only image on the restaurant's sign.

2. A positive review appeared in the magazine Out and About.

3. Grandpa's directions read, "When you hit the fork in the road (where it splits like the letter Y), follow it left."

4. Chester's singing on Linkin Park's Collision Course CD is awesome.

5. Helenium autumnale, also known as the common sneezeweed, is a member of the aster family.

6. When did the word bad start to mean its opposite?

7. Reality shows such as American Idol cost television networks less than other types of shows.

8. In the United States, the highest-grossing film of 2008 was The Dark Knight.

9. The 1954 legal case Brown v. Board of Education, by a unanimous Supreme Court decision, mandated integration in all public schools.

Model

 Model the following sentence to practice using italics (underlining) for special uses.

> I do not evolve; I *am*.
>
> —Pablo Picasso, *The Art*

Related Skills Activities

- ***SkillsBook***
  Italics (Underlining) and Quotation Marks, p. 36

Answers

1. *9*
2. *Out and About*
3. *Y*
4. *Collision Course*
5. *Helenium autumnale*
6. *bad*
7. *American Idol*
8. *Pirates of the Caribbean: Deadman's Chest*
9. *Brown v. Board of Education*

638

Parentheses

638.1 To Set Off Explanatory Material

You may use **parentheses** to set off explanatory or added material that interrupts the normal sentence structure.

Benson (our dog) **sits in on our piano lessons** (on the piano bench), **much to the teacher's surprise and amusement.**

—Chad Hockerman, student writer

NOTE: Place question marks and exclamation points within the parentheses when they mark the added material.

Ivan at once concluded (the rascal!) **that I had a passion for dances, and . . . wanted to drag me off to a dancing class.**

—Fyodor Dostoyevsky, "A Novel in Nine Letters"

638.2 With Full Sentences

When using a full sentence within another sentence, do not capitalize it or use a period inside the parentheses.

With the judging already begun (the judges have narrowed their selections to the top six), **you will have to wait until next year to enter your onion pie.**

When the parenthetical sentence comes after the period of the main sentence, capitalize and punctuate it the same way you would any other complete sentence.

Register for the event by completing an application. (Use blue ink.)

NOTE: For unavoidable parentheses within parentheses (. . . [. . .] . . .), use brackets. Avoid overuse of parentheses by using commas instead.

Diagonal

638.3 To Show a Choice

Use a **diagonal** (also called a *slash* or *forward slash*) between two words, as in *and/or*, to indicate that either is acceptable.

Press the load/eject **button.**
Don't worry; this is indoor/outdoor **carpet.**

638.4 When Quoting Poetry

When quoting more than one line of poetry, use a diagonal to show where each line of poetry ends. (Insert a space on each side of the diagonal.)

Hear the mellow wedding Bells, / Golden bells! / What a world of happiness their harmony foretells!

—Edgar Allan Poe, "The Bells"

Grammar Practice

Parentheses and Diagonals

 Write the word or words that should be enclosed in parentheses or divided by a slash. (Use the correct punctuation.)

Example: Aunt Joanie my mom's sister is my favorite relative.
(my mom's sister)

1. When Octavio and Jude went snowboarding I was working and so couldn't go, they met Olympic medal winner Danny Kass.

2. Dad glared as he said, "This is not an either or decision, Son. Just do what I told you to do."

3. Travon lucky dog! already has a job lined up for the summer.

4. Lots of kids go to Skate U the local roller rink on Friday nights.

5. To adjust the dryer's alarm volume, turn the high low knob accordingly.

6. Now that Colleen has her room to herself her sister is away at college, she can play her music as loud as she likes it.

7. Rhea was walking her dog on the 16th? or 17th? when she witnessed a car crash into a stoplight.

Model

Model the following sentence to practice using parentheses with full sentences.

Donleavy looked at the audience once (on reflection, I'm sure that he wanted only to reassure himself that we were really there), adjusted his glasses, and began to read from a sheaf of papers.

—Maya Angelou, "Graduation"

Model

Write the lyrics to a favorite song to practice using diagonals when quoting poetry.

Tell them at home I long to be there, / While thro this wide world ever I roam; / Only to meet my darling so fair, / Only to see the dear folks at home.

Related Skills Activities

- **GrammarSnap**
  Punctuating Parenthetical Elements with Commas, Dashes, or Parentheses

- **SkillsBook**
  Punctuation in Math, p. 38

Answers

1. (I was working and so couldn't go),
2. either/or
3. (lucky dog!)
4. (the local roller rink)
5. high/low
6. (her sister is away at college)
7. (on the 16th? or 17th?)

Dash

640.1 To Indicate a Sudden Break

Use a **dash** to indicate a sudden break or change in the sentence.

> **Near the semester's end**—and this is not always due to poor planning—**some students may find themselves in a real crunch.**

NOTE: Dashes are often used in place of commas. Use dashes when you want to give special emphasis; use commas when there is no need for emphasis.

640.2 To Set Off an Introductory Series

Use a dash to set off an introductory series from the clause that explains the series.

> **A good book, a cup of tea, a comfortable chair**—these things always saved my mother's sanity.

640.3 To Set Off Parenthetical Material

You may use a dash to set off parenthetical material—material that explains or clarifies a word or a phrase.

> **A single incident**—a tornado that came without warning—**changed the face of the small town forever.**

640.4 To Indicate Interrupted Speech

Use a dash to show interrupted or faltering speech in dialogue.

> "Why—why are you doing this to me?"

640.5 For Emphasis

Use a dash to emphasize a word, a series, a phrase, or a clause.

> **After years of trial and error, Belther made history with his invention**—the unicycle.

> **After several hours of hearing the high-pitched yipping, Petra finally realized what it was**—coyote pups.

Grammar Practice

Dashes

- To Set Off An Introductory Series
- To Set Off Parenthetical Material
- For Emphasis

 A word, a phrase, or a clause follows each sentence below. Write the sentences to include those words, set off by one or two dashes.

Example: The book she left on the bed was probably some kind of hint. *(Cleaning in a Snap!)*
> The book she left on the bed—<u>Cleaning in a Snap!</u>—was probably some kind of hint.

1. The nine-day tournament over, a voice came over the loudspeaker announcing the winner. (my brother)

2. Many Native Americans are involved in the conservation movement today. (whose ancestors treated the land with respect)

3. No household will run smoothly without them. (scissors, tape, and string)

4. The museum would like to feature Mr. Saraee's car in an exhibit. (a 1954 Ferrari convertible)

5. It is strongly suggested that everyone make a $5 donation at the dance. (although not required)

Model

Model the following sentences to practice using dashes for emphasis and to set off an introductory series.

> There is but one success—to be able to spend your life in your own way.
>
> —Christopher Morley, *Where the Blue Begins*

> A tie, a little plastic comb, and a belt—those are three gifts that my grandparents thought I needed.

Related Skills Activities

- ***GrammarSnap***
  Punctuating Parenthetical Elements with Commas, Dashes, or Parentheses

- ***SkillsBook***
  Dashes, p. 27

 ## Answers

1. The nine-day tournament over, a voice came over the loudspeaker announcing the winner—my brother.

2. Many Native Americans—whose ancestors treated the land with respect—are involved in the conservation movement today.

3. Scissors, tape, and string—no household will run smoothly without them.

4. The museum would like to feature Mr. Saraee's car—a 1954 Ferrari convertible—in an exhibit.

5. It is strongly suggested—although not required—that everyone make a $5 donation at the dance.

Ellipsis

642.1 To Show Omitted Words

Use an **ellipsis** (three periods with one space before and after each period) to show that one or more words have been omitted in a quotation.

(Original)

We the people of the United States, in order to form a more perfect Union, establish justice, insure domestic tranquility, provide for the common defense, promote the general welfare, and secure the blessings of liberty to ourselves and our posterity, do ordain and establish this Constitution for the United States of America.

—Preamble, *U.S. Constitution*

(Quotation)

"We the people . . . in order to form a more perfect Union . . . establish this Constitution for the United States of America."

642.2 At the End of a Sentence

If words from a quotation are omitted at the end of a sentence, place the ellipsis after the period that marks the conclusion of the sentence.

"Standing at the entrance were small groups of students. . . . As Will walked by, he could not help but overhear the murmurs of discontent as they continued to wait for the signal to return to class."

—Pamela Brown, student writer

NOTE: If the quoted material is a complete sentence (even if it was not complete in the original), use a period, then an ellipsis.

(Original)

I am tired; my heart is sick and sad. From where the sun now stands I will fight no more forever.

—Chief Joseph of the Nez Percé

(Quotation)

"I am tired. . . . From where the sun now stands I will fight no more forever."

or

"I am tired. . . . I will fight no more. . . . "

642.3 To Show a Pause

Use an ellipsis to indicate a pause.

I brought my trembling hand to my focusing eyes. It was oozing, it was red, it was . . . it was . . . a tomato!

—Laura Baginski, student writer

Punctuation

Grammar Practice

Ellipses

- To Show Omitted Words
- To Show a Pause

 For each of the following paragraphs, select the least important information to replace with ellipses. Write the shortened paragraphs on your paper.

Example: Taneka Sills, a local girl who is a member of the high school forensics team, has been awarded a scholarship to the Young People's Peace Camp in Tillamook, Oregon.

Taneka Sills . . . has been awarded a scholarship to the Young People's Peace Camp in Tillamook, Oregon.

1. Simple braids are easy to make. First, divide the hair into three equal sections. You may fasten each with a small band at the bottom, if desired. Next, pull the section on the right into the middle of the two others; then do the same with the section on the left. Continue to alternate until the braid is the desired length (or you run out of hair!). Use a covered rubber band to tie the ends together, and finish with a hair decoration or barrette.

2. Polar bears live in a place where not many other animals live, on the coasts of the Arctic Ocean. They are powerful swimmers and can easily go 25 miles back and forth from the coast to drifting icebergs. Male polar bears can reach 10 feet tall and 1,700 pounds. The bears' heavy, white fur even covers the soles of their feet—a feature not seen in any other bear—to help them walk on the ice. The polar bear's only enemy is the human, and because of overhunting, the species is threatened.

Model

Model the following sentence to practice using an ellipsis to indicate a pause.

"Tell me something: those little plants there . . . " she said, nonchalantly, pointing to some rushes growing tall in the midst of the lagoon, "where do they put down their roots?"

—Italo Calvino, "The Aquatic Uncle"

Related Skills Activities

- **SkillsBook**
  Other Forms of Punctuation, p. 39

Answers

Answers will vary. Possible answers:

1. Simple braids are easy to make. First, divide the hair into three equal sections. . . . Next, pull the section on the right into the middle of the two others; then do the same with the section on the left. Continue to alternate . . . tie the ends together, and finish with a . . . barrette.

2. Polar bears live . . . on the coasts of the Arctic Ocean. They are powerful swimmers and can . . . reach 10 feet tall and 1,700 pounds. The bears' heavy, white fur even covers the soles of their feet . . . to help them walk on the ice. The polar bear's only enemy is the human, and . . . the species is threatened.

Brackets

644.1 To Set Off Clarifying Information

Use **brackets** before and after words that are added to clarify what another person has said or written.

> "They'd [the sweat bees] get into your mouth, ears, eyes, nose. You'd feel them all over you."
>
>   —Marilyn Johnson and Sasha Nyary, "Roosevelts in the Amazon"

NOTE: The brackets indicate that the words *the sweat bees* are not part of the quotation but were added for clarification.

644.2 Around an Editorial Correction

Place brackets around an editorial correction inserted within quoted material.

> "Brooklyn alone has 8 percent of lead poisoning [victims] nationwide," said Marjorie Moore.
>
>   —Donna Actie, student writer

NOTE: The brackets indicate that the word *victims* replaced the author's original word.

Place brackets around the letters *sic* (Latin for "as such"); the letters indicate that an error appearing in the material being quoted was made by the original speaker or writer.

> "When I'm queen," mused Lucy, "I'll show these blockheads whose [*sic*] got beauty and brains."

644.3 To Set Off Added Words

Place brackets around comments that have been added to a quotation.

> "Congratulations to the astronomy club's softball team, which put in, shall we say, a 'stellar' performance." [groans]

Punctuation Marks

´	Accent, acute	,	Comma	( )	Parentheses
`	Accent, grave	†	Dagger	.	Period
'	Apostrophe	—	Dash	?	Question mark
*	Asterisk	/	Diagonal/Slash	" "	Quotation marks
{ }	Brace	¨(ü)	Dieresis	§	Section
[ ]	Brackets	…	Ellipsis	;	Semicolon
^	Caret	!	Exclamation point	~	Tilde
(ç)	Cedilla	-	Hyphen	___	Underscore
^	Circumflex	…	Leaders		
:	Colon	¶	Paragraph		

Grammar Practice

Brackets

- ■ To Set Off Clarifying Information
- ■ Around an Editorial Correction

Follow the directions for each activity below.

Example: In the following quotation, the speaker is talking about influenza. Use words in brackets to clarify the quotation.

> "People hear about so many other diseases," said Dr. Pintar, "but we need to remember that this disease continues to exert a high toll on human life."
>
> *"People hear about so many other diseases," said Dr. Pintar, "but we need to remember that this disease [influenza] continues to exert a high toll on human life."*

1. In the following quotation, the speaker is talking about the earth. Use words in brackets to clarify the quotation.

   > "By measuring the level of decay of radioactive material in rocks, we can figure out how old it is," Jung noted.

2. In the following quotation, replace the speaker's use of the word *hypertrichosis* with *excessive hair*. Place brackets around your editorial correction.

   > "My father's hypertrichosis bothered him," she related.

3. Quote the following statement and show that the error was made by the original writer, Gary Sumter. (Use the word *sic* enclosed in brackets.)

   > The storm wreaked it's havoc for hundreds of miles along the coast.

Model

Model the following sentence to practice using brackets to set off clarifying information.

> There is no frigate [sailing vessel] like a book, to take us lands away.
>
>   —Emily Dickinson

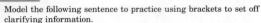

Answers

1. "By measuring the level of decay of radioactive material, we can figure out how old it [the earth] is," Jung noted.
2. "My father's [excessive hair] bothered him," she related.
3. Gary Sumter wrote, "The storm wreaked it's [*sic*] havoc for hundreds of miles along the coast."

Test Prep!

Read the following paragraphs. From the choices given below each paragraph, write the letter of the correct way to punctuate each underlined part. If it is already correct, choose "D."

The movie "You've Got Mail" is actually a remake of the 1940 film
(1)
"The Shop Around the Corner." While the previous film focused on a
(2)
romance conducted through the post office, the newer one (made in 1998)
(3)
had the romance happening through e mail.
(4)

1 Ⓐ "Youv'e Got Mail"
  Ⓑ *You've Got Mail*
  Ⓒ "You've Got Mail"
  Ⓓ correct as is

3 Ⓐ (made) in 1998
  Ⓑ (made in 1998
  Ⓒ made in 1998)
  Ⓓ correct as is

2 Ⓐ *The Shop Around the Corner.*
  Ⓑ "The Shop Around the Corner."
  Ⓒ "The Shop Around the Corner".
  Ⓓ correct as is

4 Ⓐ e'mail
  Ⓑ "e" mail
  Ⓒ e-mail
  Ⓓ correct as is

Sasha asked, "Do you know whose hat this is"? She held up a red
(5)   **(6)**
and white striped knit stocking cap.

Patrick said, "Its either Jacks' or Zack's hat, I'm pretty sure."
(7)   **(8)**

5 Ⓐ this is?
  Ⓑ this is?"
  Ⓒ this is"
  Ⓓ correct as is

7 Ⓐ "It's
  Ⓑ It's
  Ⓒ "Its'
  Ⓓ correct as is

6 Ⓐ a-red-and-white
  Ⓑ a red-and-white
  Ⓒ a red and-white
  Ⓓ correct as is

8 Ⓐ Jacks' or Zacks' hat
  Ⓑ Jack's or Zack's hat
  Ⓒ Jacks or Zack's hat
  Ⓓ correct as is

"The Black Eyed Peas released a new album, Kent said. Have
(9)
you heard any songs from it?"

"Iv'e heard "Union" a few times," said Fiona.
(10)
"Is this album as good as the one before it, *Elephunk?*" he asked.
(11)

"I think its the Pea's best one," she said.
(12)

9 Ⓐ album," Kent said. Have
  Ⓑ album, Kent said. "Have
  Ⓒ album," Kent said. "Have
  Ⓓ correct as is

11 Ⓐ *Elephunk*"?
  Ⓑ '*Elephunk*'?"
  Ⓒ '*Elephunk*?'"
  Ⓓ correct as is

10 Ⓐ "I've heard "Union"
  Ⓑ "Iv'e heard 'Union
  Ⓒ "I've heard 'Union'
  Ⓓ correct as is

12 Ⓐ it's the Peas'
  Ⓑ its' the Peas
  Ⓒ it's the Pea's
  Ⓓ correct as is

In general, dont make a U turn at an intersection with a
(13)
traffic light. Also, when someones' view of your car may be obstructed,
(14)
such as on a hill or a curve, do not do so. Always observe the right of
(15)
way rules. It's everyones' responsibility to prevent striking another
(16)
vehicle or pedestrian.

13 Ⓐ don't make a U turn
  Ⓑ do'nt make a U-turn
  Ⓒ don't make a U-turn
  Ⓓ correct as is

15 Ⓐ the-right-of-way rules
  Ⓑ the right of-way rules
  Ⓒ the right-of-way rules
  Ⓓ correct as is

14 Ⓐ someone's view
  Ⓑ someones view
  Ⓒ someones" view
  Ⓓ correct as is

16 Ⓐ Its everyone's responsibility
  Ⓑ It's everyones responsibility
  Ⓒ It's everyone's responsibility
  Ⓓ correct as is

Answers

1. B	5. B
2. A	6. B
3. D	7. A
4. C	8. B

Answers

9. C	13. C
10. C	14. A
11. D	15. C
12. A	16. C

Related Skills Activities

■ *SkillsBook*
Review: Hyphens and Dashes, p. 28
Review: Apostrophes, p. 32
Review: Quotation Marks and Italics (Underlining), p. 37
Posttest: Hyphens and Dashes, p. 194
Posttest: Apostrophes, p. 195
Posttest: Quotation Marks and Italics (Underlining),
  p. 196
Posttest: Punctuation, p. 197

Checking Mechanics

Capitalization

648.1 Proper Nouns and Adjectives

Capitalize proper nouns and proper adjectives (those derived from proper nouns). The chart below provides a quick overview of capitalization rules. The pages following explain some specific rules of capitalization.

Capitalization at a Glance

Names of people	Alice Walker, Matilda, Jim, Mr. Roker
Days of the week, months	Sunday, Tuesday, June, August
Holidays, holy days	Thanksgiving, Easter, Hanukkah
Periods, events in history	Middle Ages, the Battle of Bunker Hill
Official documents	Declaration of Independence
Special events	Elgin Community Spring Gala
Languages, nationalities, religions	French, Canadian, Islam
Political parties	Republican Party, Socialist Party
Trade names	Oscar Mayer hot dogs, Pontiac Sunbird
Official titles used with names	Mayor John Spitzer, Senator Feinstein
Formal epithets	Alexander the Great
Geographical names	
Planets, heavenly bodies	Earth, Jupiter, the Milky Way
Continents	Australia, South America
Countries	Ireland, Grenada, Sri Lanka
States, provinces	Ohio, Utah, Nova Scotia
Cities, towns, villages	El Paso, Burlington, Wonewoc
Streets, roads, highways	Park Avenue, Route 66, Interstate 90
Landforms	the Rocky Mountains, the Sahara Desert
Bodies of water	Yellowstone Lake, Pumpkin Creek
Buildings, monuments	Elkhorn High School, Gateway Arch
Public areas	Times Square, Sequoia National Park

Grammar Practice

Capitalization 1

■ Proper Nouns and Adjectives

 For each sentence below, write the words that should be capitalized (as shown).

Example: On the friday before the labor day weekend, mr. rayda invited us to his house in michigan.
Friday, Labor Day, Mr. Rayda, Michigan

1. Richard the lionhearted was the king of england for 10 years.

2. Of the five great lakes, only lake michigan is entirely within the united states.

3. Admission to the coronation ball required dressing in a renaissance-era costume.

4. When salvadore began going to hershey high school, he spoke fluent italian and a little english.

5. Although erica likes her car, she'd really like a mazda miata.

6. The december 2004 tsunami affected many countries surrounding the bay of bengal.

7. The only interstate highway that runs from canada to mexico is interstate 5 (from san diego to blaine, washington).

8. Is neptune or uranus the farthest planet from the sun?

9. A small part of russian land is lodged between lithuania and poland.

Model

Model the following sentences to practice capitalizing proper nouns and adjectives.

The train left the station promptly at 11 p.m. on July 1 to take us to Washington, D.C., for the Fourth of July extravaganza. The Atlantic coastline came into view at dawn. In only a few hours, the train would pull into Union Station and our sightseeing would officially begin.

Related Skills Activities

■ **Basic Grammar and Writing**
Nouns, p. 534

■ *GrammarSnap*
Common Uses of Capitalization

■ *SkillsBook*
Capitalization, pp. 41–42
Capitalization 1, 2, and 3, pp. 43–45

Answers

1. Lionhearted
England

2. Great Lakes
Lake Michigan
United States

3. Coronation Ball
Renaissance-era

4. Salvadore
Hershey High
School
Italian
English

5. Erica
Mazda Miata

6. December
Bay of Bengal

7. Canada
Mexico
Interstate 5
San Diego
Blaine, Washington

8. Neptune
Uranus

9. Russian
Lithuania
Poland

Capitalization (continued)

650.1 First Words

Capitalize the first word of every sentence, including the first word of a full-sentence direct quotation.

> **Ms. Andrews asked, "Who is your favorite poet?"**

650.2 Sentences in Parentheses

Capitalize the first word in a sentence enclosed in parentheses, but do not capitalize the first word if the parenthetical appears within another sentence.

> **In a bygone era, a fortunate paddleboat passenger could be entertained by a young Louis Armstrong playing the cornet. (A cornet is a kind of small trumpet with a mellower tone.)**
>
> **Damien's aunt (she's a wild woman) plays bingo every Saturday night.**

650.3 Sentences Following Colons

Capitalize the first word in a complete sentence that follows a colon when (1) you want to emphasize the sentence or (2) the sentence is a quotation.

> **When we quarreled and made horrible faces at one another, Mother knew what to say: "Your faces will stay that way, and no one will marry you."**

650.4 Sections of the Country

Capitalize words that indicate particular sections of the country; do not capitalize words that simply indicate direction.

> **Mr. Johnson is from the Southwest.** (section of the country)
>
> **After moving north to Montana, he had to buy winter clothes.** (direction)

650.5 Certain Religious Words

Capitalize nouns that refer to the Supreme Being, the word *Bible,* the books of the Bible, and the names for other holy books.

> **God   Jehovah   the Lord   the Savior   Allah   Bible   Genesis**

650.6 Titles

Capitalize the first word of a title, the last word, and every word in between except articles (*a, an, the*), short prepositions, and coordinating conjunctions. Follow this rule for titles of books, newspapers, magazines, poems, plays, songs, articles, films, works of art, photographs, and stories.

> ***Washington Post***   **"The Diary of a Madman"**   ***Nights of Rain and Stars***

Grammar Practice

Capitalization 2

■ Sentences in Parentheses
■ Sections of the Country
■ Titles

 For the paragraphs below, write the line number along with the words that should be capitalized (as shown in red below).

Example: 1. M**idwest**

1   When my grandfather was growing up in the midwest during the
2   1960s, he loved to listen to his little transistor radio. He could hear all
3   kinds of rock music, but his favorite bands were the "hot rod" groups.
4   (the genre was born in California but soon spread east.) Granddad
5   and his friends tuned in to that music as it became popular in their
6   area. They'd sing along to Jan and Dean's "Drag city" and "Dead man's
7   curve." They'd turn up the radio when the Beach Boys' "Little deuce
8   coupe" came on, and they'd dream about having their own hot rods
9   when they heard "Boss drag at Hot Rod beach."
10   By 1970, Granddad's family moved to the south, and the hot
11   rod craze had dried up. His next musical obsession was (naturally)
12   southern rock. He has some great stories about that time in his
13   life (this was in his late teens) and shares them with me often. It's
14   interesting to hear about someone's life through his love of music.

▶ Model

Model the following sentence to practice capitalizing sections of the country and titles.

> **We watched the University of Texas Longhorn Band (known as the Show Band of the Southwest) play "The Eyes of Texas."**

▶ Model

Model this sentence to practice *not* capitalizing a sentence in parentheses when it appears within another sentence.

> **They play cops and robbers (only they call it "Jail") and throw things at one another—snowballs in winter, rose hips in fall.**
>
> —E. B. White, "Education"

Related Skills Activities

■ **GrammarSnap**
Common Uses of Capitalization

■ **SkillsBook**
Capitalization 2 and 3, pp. 44–45

Answers

line 1: Midwest
line 4: (The
line 6: City
        Man's
line 7: Curve
        Deuce
line 8: Coupe
line 9: Drag
        Beach
line 10: South
line 12: Southern

Capitalization *(continued)*

652.1 Words Used as Names

Capitalize words like *father, mother, uncle,* and *senator* when they are used as titles with a personal name or when they are substituted for proper nouns (especially in direct address).

> **We've missed you, Aunt Lucinda!** (*Aunt* is part of the name.)
> **I hope Mayor Bates arrives soon.** (*Mayor* is part of the name.)

A Closer Look

To test whether a word is being substituted for a proper noun, simply read the sentence with a proper noun in place of the word. If the proper noun fits in the sentence, the word being tested should be capitalized; otherwise, the word should not be capitalized.

> **Did Mom (Sue) say we could go?** (*Sue* works in this sentence.)
> **Did your mom (Sue) say you could go?** (*Sue* does not work here.)

NOTE: Usually the word is not capitalized if it follows a possessive —*my, his, your*—as it does in the second sentence above.

652.2 Letters

Capitalize the letters used to indicate form or shape.

> **U-turn   I-beam   S-curve   T-shirt   V-shaped**

652.3 Organizations

Capitalize the name of an organization, an association, or a team.

> **Lake Ontario Sailors   American Indian Movement   Democratic Party**

652.4 Abbreviations

Capitalize abbreviations of titles and organizations. (Some other abbreviations are also capitalized. See pages 660–662.)

> **AAA   CEO   NAACP   M.D.   Ph.D.**

652.5 Titles of Courses

Capitalize words like *sociology* and *history* when they are used as titles of specific courses; do not capitalize these words when they name a field of study.

> **Who teaches History 202?** (title of a specific course)
> **It's the same professor who teaches my sociology course.** (a field of study)

NOTE: The words *freshman, sophomore, junior,* and *senior* are not capitalized unless they are part of an official title.

> **Rosa is a senior this year and is in charge of the Senior Class Banquet.**

Grammar Practice

Capitalization 3

- Organizations
- Abbreviations
- Titles of Courses

 For each of the following sentences, correctly capitalize or lowercase any word or word groups that are incorrect.

Example: The national audubon society is an Organization especially interested in birds.
> *National Audubon Society, organization*

1. Ms. Kincaid, who teaches biology II, is a member.

2. Other Conservation and Animal-Welfare organizations are the national wildlife federation (NWF) and the american society for the prevention of cruelty to animals (aspca).

3. The goal of the world wildlife fund (wwf) is "to build a future where people live in harmony with nature."

4. The Natural resources defense council (Nrdc) is an environmental group that takes action to protect wildlife and wild places.

5. We've learned about many of these groups in cultural geography, taught by Mr. Lee.

6. In addition, Luisa Rane, the president of the school's environmentalist club, made a presentation during earth science I.

7. I think I would like to get involved with greenpeace international.

Model

Model the following sentence to practice capitalizing abbreviations and the names of organizations.

> **Members of the International Ecology Society (IES) try to attain a better understanding of all life forms.**

Related Skills Activities

- ***GrammarSnap***
  Common Uses of Capitalization

- ***SkillsBook***
  Capitalization 2 and 3, pp. 44–45

Answers

1. Biology II
2. conservation
   animal-welfare
   National Wildlife Federation
   American Society for the Prevention Cruelty to Animals (ASPCA)
3. World Wildlife Fund (WWF)
4. Resources Defense Council (NRDC)
5. Cultural Geography
6. Environmentalist Club
   Earth Science I
7. Greenpeace International

Plurals

654.1 Most Nouns

Form the **plurals** of most nouns by adding *s* to the singular.

cheerleader – cheerleaders   wheel – wheels   crate – crates

654.2 Nouns Ending in *sh, ch, x, s,* and *z*

Form the plurals of nouns ending in *sh, ch, x, s,* and *z* by adding *es* to the singular.

lunch – lunches   dish – dishes   mess – messes   fox – foxes

EXCEPTION: When the final *ch* sounds like *k*, add an *s* (*monarchs*).

654.3 Nouns Ending in *y*

The plurals of common nouns that end in *y* (preceded by a consonant) are formed by changing the *y* to *i* and adding *es*.

fly – flies   jalopy – jalopies

Form the plurals of nouns that end in *y* (preceded by a vowel) by adding only an *s*.

donkey – donkeys   monkey – monkeys

NOTE: Form the plurals of all proper nouns ending in *y* by adding *s* (*Kathys*).

654.4 Nouns Ending in *o*

The plurals of nouns ending in *o* (preceded by a vowel) are formed by adding an *s*.

radio – radios   rodeo – rodeos   studio – studios   duo – duos

The plurals of most nouns ending in *o* (preceded by a consonant) are formed by adding *es*.

echo – echoes   hero – heroes   tomato – tomatoes

EXCEPTION: Musical terms always form plurals by adding *s*.

alto – altos   banjo – banjos   solo – solos   piano – pianos

654.5 Nouns Ending in *ful*

Form the plurals of nouns that end in *ful* by adding an *s* at the end of the word.

two tankfuls   three pailfuls   four mouthfuls

NOTE: Do not confuse these examples with *three pails full* (when you are referring to three separate pails full of something) or *two tanks full*.

654.6 Compound Nouns

Form the plurals of most compound nouns by adding *s* or *es* to the important word in the compound.

brothers-in-law   maids of honor   secretaries of state

Grammar Practice

Plurals 1

- Regular Nouns
- Nouns Ending in *sh, ch, x, s,* and *z*
- Nouns Ending in *y, o,* and *ful*

 Write the correct plurals of the underlined word or words in each sentence.

Example: Alahandra picked two <u>bunch</u> of <u>flower</u> for the kitchen table.
    bunches, flowers

1. The hidden <u>box</u> that Jake came upon intrigued him.
2. Some <u>job</u> offer several paid <u>holiday</u> per year.
3. The <u>piccolo</u> played the song over and over while the <u>dancer</u> gathered.
4. My aunts came from the <u>arbor</u> with <u>apronful</u> of <u>grape</u> for the special recipe.
5. We had a garden stew with lots of <u>potato</u>, onions, and <u>carrot</u> for supper, and cobbler made with <u>mango</u> for dessert.
6. The warm spell hatched many <u>insect</u> and brought new <u>buzz</u> to the evening air.
7. Soon the <u>boy</u> arrived at the campsite with <u>armful</u> of firewood.
8. The neighborhood looked interesting with its different-colored <u>chimney</u>.
9. Besides taking many biology <u>class</u>, Cecily toured the nation's major <u>zoo</u> and wrote a thesis to complete her major.
10. She plans to take several long <u>journey</u> to study exotic wildlife.
11. We wanted to get a picture, but the camera <u>battery</u> were dead.

Exercise

Write the plurals of the following words. Then use as many of the plurals as you can in one sentence.

handful, library, halo, wish, address, toy, sky

Related Skills Activities

- ### *SkillsBook*
  Pretest: Plurals and Spelling, pp. 51–52
  Plurals 1 and 2, pp. 52–53

 ## Answers

1. boxes
2. jobs
   holidays
3. piccolos
   dancers
4. arbors
   apronfuls
   grapes
5. potatoes
   carrots
   mangoes

6. insects
   buzzes
7. boys
   armfuls
8. chimneys
9. classes
   zoos
10. journeys
11. batteries

Exercise   ## Answers

handfuls, libraries, halos *or* haloes, wishes, addresses, toys, skies

Plurals (continued)

656.1 Nouns Ending in *f* or *fe*

Form the plurals of nouns that end in *f* or *fe* in one of two ways: if the final *f* sound is still heard in the plural form of the word, simply add *s;* but if the final *f* sound becomes a *v* sound, change the *f* to *ve* and add *s.*

Plural ends with *f* sound: roof – roofs; chief – chiefs
Plural ends with *v* sound: wife – wives; loaf – loaves

NOTE: Several words are correct with either ending.

Plural ends with either sound: hoof – hooves/hoofs

656.2 Irregular Spelling

A number of words form a plural by taking on an irregular spelling.

crisis – crises	child – children	radius – radii
criterion – criteria	goose – geese	die – dice

NOTE: Some of these words are acceptable with the commonly used *s* or *es* ending.

index – indices/indexes   cactus – cacti/cactuses

Some nouns remain unchanged when used as plurals.

deer   sheep   salmon   aircraft   series

656.3 Words Discussed as Words

The plurals of symbols, letters, numbers, and words being discussed as words are formed by adding an apostrophe and an *s.*

Dad yelled a lot of *wow's* and *yippee's* when he saw my A's and B's.

NOTE: You may omit the apostrophe if it does not cause any confusion.

the three R's or Rs   YMCA's or YMCAs

656.4 Collective Nouns

A collective noun may be singular or plural depending upon how it's used. A collective noun is singular when it refers to a group considered as one unit; it is plural when it refers to the individuals in the group.

The class was on its best behavior. (group as a unit)
The class are preparing for their final exams. (individuals in the group)

If it seems awkward to use a plural verb with a collective noun, add a clearly plural noun such as *members* to the sentence, or change the collective noun into a possessive followed by a plural noun that describes the individuals in the group.

The class members are preparing for their final exams.
The class's students are preparing for their final exams.

Grammar Practice

Plurals 2

- Nouns Ending in *f* or *fe*
- Irregular Spellings
- Words Discussed as Words

 For each sentence below, write the plural form of the word or words in parentheses.

Example: Not too long ago, when you saw (goose) in the sky, it meant winter was near.
geese

1. Now, however, it seems that a number of environmental (crisis) have changed weather patterns.

2. My grandparents say that they learned the 3 (R) in school—reading, 'riting, and 'rithmetic.

3. In the 1950s, it was usually the case that (man) went to work, (woman) stayed home, and (child) played outside—a lot.

4. Different religions naturally have different (belief).

5. The (leaf) on our maple tree are turning orange already.

6. The fisherman grinned as he showed us the nice-sized (salmon) and (trout) he had caught.

7. I've heard the (ABC) one too many times from my four-year-old sister.

8. Dad says we use too many (no way) and (whatever) in our conversations.

9. Board games usually involve throwing (die).

10. Our scrapping outdoor cat seems to have far more than the usual "nine (life)."

11. Long run-on sentences often have many (and) and (so) in them.

Exercise

Write sentences using plurals of these words:

cactus, mouse, ox, shrimp, moonfish

Related Skills Activities

- ***SkillsBook***
  Plurals 1 and 2, pp. 52–53

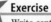 Answers

1. crises
2. R's *or* Rs
3. men
   women
   children
4. beliefs
5. leaves
6. salmon
   trout
7. ABC's *or* ABCs
8. no way's
   whatever's
9. dice
10. lives
11. and's   so's

Exercise **Answers**

cacti or cactuses, mice, oxen, shrimp *or* shrimps,
moonfish *or* moonfishes

Numbers

658.1 Numerals or Words

Numbers from one to nine are usually written as words; numbers 10 and over are usually written as numerals. However, numbers being compared or contrasted should be kept in the same style.

    8 to 11 years old   eight to eleven years old

You may use a combination of numerals and words for very large numbers.

    1.5 million   3 billion to 3.2 billion   6 trillion

If numbers are used infrequently in a piece of writing, you may spell out those that can be written in no more than two words.

    ten   twenty-five   two hundred   fifty thousand

658.2 Numerals Only

Use numerals for the following forms: decimals, percentages, chapters, pages, addresses, phone numbers, identification numbers, and statistics.

    26.2   8 percent   Highway 36   chapter 7
    pages 287–89 July 6, 1945   44 B.C.E.   a vote of 23 to 4

Always use numerals with abbreviations and symbols.

    8%   10 mm   3 cc   8 oz   90° C   24 mph   6' 3"

658.3 Words Only

Use words to express numbers that begin a sentence.

    Fourteen students "forgot" their assignments.

NOTE: Change the sentence structure if this rule creates a clumsy construction.

    Clumsy: *Six hundred thirty-nine* teachers were laid off this year.
    Better: This year, 639 teachers were laid off.

Use words for numbers that come before a compound modifier if that modifier includes a numeral.

    They made twelve 10-foot sub sandwiches for the picnic.

658.4 Time and Money

If time is expressed with an abbreviation, use numerals; if it is expressed in words, spell out the number.

    4:00 A.M. (or) four o'clock

If an amount of money is spelled out, so is the currency; use a numeral if a symbol is used.

    twenty dollars (or) $20

Grammar Practice

Numbers

- Numerals or Words
- Numerals Only
- Words Only

 For each sentence below, write the underlined numbers the correct way. If a number is already correctly presented, write "correct."

Example: The teacher assigned pages <u>two hundred thirty</u> to <u>two hundred forty-five</u>.
    230 to 245

1. A <u>nineteen forty-eight</u> flood in Woodland, Washington, caused $ <u>two hundred million</u> worth of damage.
2. The firebrick can withstand a temperature of at least <u>two thousand 760</u> degrees Fahrenheit.
3. The giant Ferris wheel at the 1893 World's Columbian Exposition in Chicago was <u>two hundred fifty</u> feet high; the next year, England built a Ferris wheel that was <u>three hundred twenty-eight</u> feet high.
4. The Chicago wheel had <u>thirty-six</u> cars, and each could hold <u>60</u> passengers; the London wheel had <u>40</u> cars, and each could hold <u>thirty</u> passengers.
5. When you think that these wheels were as high as <u>25-</u> or <u>32</u>-story buildings, it's amazing that they found people brave enough to ride them!
6. The museum offers art classes for children <u>six</u> to <u>13</u> years old.
7. <u>10</u> kids want cheese-and-sausage pizza; that's <u>fifty</u> percent of us.
8. The shop class ordered <u>14 12-foot</u> boards.
9. The Milky Way is <u>one hundred fifty thousand</u> light-years in diameter.

Exercise

Complete this sentence with your own numbers.

    The team has won _____ out of nine games, with their best game
    ending at ____–____.

Mechanics

Related Skills Activities

- **SkillsBook**
  Pretest: Numbers and Abbreviations, p. 47
  Numbers, p. 48

Answers

1. 1948
   $200 million
2. 2,760
3. 250
   328
4. 36
   correct
   correct
   30

5. correct
   correct
6. 6 correct *or*
   correct thirteen
7. Ten
   50
8. fourteen 12-foot
9. 150 thousand

Exercise | Answers

Answers will vary, but the first blank should have a spelled-out number and the score should use numerals.

Abbreviations

660.1 Formal and Informal Abbreviations

An **abbreviation** is the shortened form of a word or phrase. Some abbreviations are always acceptable in both formal and informal writing:

Mr.   Mrs.   Jr.   Ms.   Dr.   a.m. (A.M.)   p.m. (P.M.)

NOTE: In most of your writing, you do not abbreviate the names of states, countries, months, days, or units of measure. However, you may use the abbreviation *U.S.* after it has been spelled out once. Do not abbreviate the words *Street, Company,* and similar words, especially when they are part of a proper name. Also, do not use signs or symbols (%, &, #, @) in place of words. The dollar sign, however, is appropriate with numerals ($325).

660.2 Correspondence Abbreviations

United States

	Standard	Postal
Alabama	Ala.	AL
Alaska	Alaska	AK
Arizona	Ariz.	AZ
Arkansas	Ark.	AR
California	Calif.	CA
Colorado	Colo.	CO
Connecticut	Conn.	CT
Delaware	Del.	DE
District of Columbia	D.C.	DC
Florida	Fla.	FL
Georgia	Ga.	GA
Guam	Guam	GU
Hawaii	Hawaii	HI
Idaho	Idaho	ID
Illinois	Ill.	IL
Indiana	Ind.	IN
Iowa	Iowa	IA
Kansas	Kan.	KS
Kentucky	Ky.	KY
Louisiana	La.	LA
Maine	Maine	ME
Maryland	Md.	MD
Massachusetts	Mass.	MA
Michigan	Mich.	MI
Minnesota	Minn.	MN
Mississippi	Miss.	MS
Missouri	Mo.	MO
Montana	Mont.	MT
Nebraska	Neb.	NE
Nevada	Nev.	NV
New Hampshire	N.H.	NH
New Jersey	N.J.	NJ
New Mexico	N.M.	NM
New York	N.Y.	NY
North Carolina	N.C.	NC
North Dakota	N.D.	ND
Ohio	Ohio	OH
Oklahoma	Okla.	OK
Oregon	Ore.	OR
Pennsylvania	Pa.	PA
Puerto Rico	P.R.	PR
Rhode Island	R.I.	RI
South Carolina	S.C.	SC
South Dakota	S.D.	SD
Tennessee	Tenn.	TN
Texas	Texas	TX
Utah	Utah	UT
Vermont	Vt.	VT
Virginia	Va.	VA
Virgin Islands	V.I.	VI
Washington	Wash.	WA
West Virginia	W.Va.	WV
Wisconsin	Wis.	WI
Wyoming	Wyo.	WY

Canadian Provinces

	Standard	Postal
Alberta	Alta.	AB
British Columbia	B.C.	BC
Labrador	Lab.	NL
Manitoba	Man.	MB
New Brunswick	N.B.	NB
Newfoundland	N.F.	NL
Northwest Territories	N.W.T.	NT
Nova Scotia	N.S.	NS
Nunavut		NU
Ontario	Ont.	ON
Prince Edward Island	P.E.I.	PE
Quebec	Que.	QC
Saskatchewan	Sask.	SK
Yukon Territory	Y.T.	YT

Addresses

	Standard	Postal
Apartment	Apt.	APT
Avenue	Ave.	AVE
Boulevard	Blvd.	BLVD
Circle	Cir.	CIR
Court	Ct.	CT
Drive	Dr.	DR
East	E.	E
Expressway	Expy.	EXPY
Freeway	Fwy.	FWY
Heights	Hts.	HTS
Highway	Hwy.	HWY
Hospital	Hosp.	HOSP
Junction	Junc.	JCT
Lake	L.	LK
Lakes	Ls.	LKS
Lane	Ln.	LN
Meadows	Mdws.	MDWS
North	N.	N
Palms	Palms	PLMS
Park	Pk.	PK
Parkway	Pky.	PKY
Place	Pl.	PL
Plaza	Plaza	PLZ
Post Office Box	P.O. Box	PO BOX
Ridge	Rdg.	RDG
River	R.	RV
Road	Rd.	RD
Room	Rm.	RM
Rural	R.	R
Rural Route	R.R.	RR
Shore	Sh.	SH
South	S.	S
Square	Sq.	SQ
Station	Sta.	STA
Street	St.	ST
Suite	Ste.	STE
Terrace	Ter.	TER
Turnpike	Tpke.	TPKE
Union	Un.	UN
View	View	VW
Village	Vil.	VLG
West	W.	W

661.1 Other Common Abbreviations

abr. abridged; abridgment
AC, ac alternating current
ack. acknowledge; acknowledgment
acv actual cash value
A.D. in the year of the Lord (Latin *anno Domini*)
AM amplitude modulation
A.M., a.m. before noon (Latin *ante meridiem*)
ASAP as soon as possible
avg., av. average
BBB Better Business Bureau
B.C. before Christ
B.C.E. before the Common Era
bibliog. bibliographer; bibliography
biog. biographer; biographical; biography
C 1. Celsius 2. centigrade 3. coulomb
c. 1. circa (about) 2. cup
cc 1. cubic centimeter 2. carbon copy
CDT, C.D.T. central daylight time
C.E. of the Common Era
chap. chapter
cm centimeter
c.o., c/o care of
COD, C.O.D 1. cash on delivery 2. collect on delivery
co-op. cooperative
CST, C.S.T. central standard time
cu., c cubic
D.A. district attorney
d.b.a. doing business as
DC, dc direct current
dec. deceased
dept. department
DST, D.S.T. daylight saving time
dup. duplicate
DVD digital video disc
ea. each
ed. edition; editor
EDT, E.D.T. eastern daylight time
e.g. for example (Latin *exempli gratia*)
EST, E.S.T. eastern standard time
etc. and so forth (Latin *et cetera*)
ex. example
F Fahrenheit
FM frequency modulation
F.O.B., f.o.b. free on board
ft foot
g 1. gram 2. gravity
gal. gallon
gloss. glossary
GNP gross national product
hdqrs, HQ headquarters
HIV human immunodeficiency virus
Hon. Honorable (title)
hp horsepower
HTML hypertext markup language
Hz hertz
ibid. in the same place (Latin *ibidem*)
id. the same (Latin *idem*)
i.e. that is (Latin *id est*)
illus. illustration
inc. incorporated
IQ, I.Q. intelligence quotient
IRS Internal Revenue Service
ISBN International Standard Book Number
Jr., jr. junior
K 1. kelvin (temperature unit) 2. Kelvin (temperature scale)
kc kilocycle
kg kilogram
km kilometer
kn knot
kW kilowatt
l liter
lat. latitude
lb, lb. pound (Latin *libra*)
l.c. lowercase
lit. literary; literature
log logarithm
long. longitude
Ltd., ltd. limited
m meter
M.A. master of arts (Latin *Magister Artium*)
Mc, mc megacycle
M.C., m.c. master of ceremonies
M.D. doctor of medicine (Latin *medicinae doctor*)
mdse. merchandise
mfg. manufacturing
mg milligram
mi. 1. mile 2. mill (monetary unit)
misc. miscellaneous
ml milliliter
mm millimeter
mpg, m.p.g. miles per gallon
mph, m.p.h. miles per hour
MS 1. manuscript 2. Mississippi 3. multiple sclerosis
Ms., Ms title of courtesy for a woman
MST, M.S.T. mountain standard time
neg. negative
N.S.F., n.s.f. not sufficient funds
oz, oz. ounce
PA 1. public-address system 2. Pennsylvania
pct. percent
pd. paid
PDT, P.D.T. Pacific daylight time
Pfc, Pfc. private first class
pg., p. page
P.M., p.m. after noon (Latin *post meridiem*)
P.O. 1. personnel officer 2. purchase order 3. postal order; post office 4. (also **p.o.**) petty officer
pop. population
POW, P.O.W. prisoner of war
pp. pages
ppd. 1. postpaid 2. prepaid
PR, P.R. 1. public relations 2. Puerto Rico
P.S. post script
psi, p.s.i. pounds per square inch
PST, P.S.T. Pacific standard time
PTA, P.T.A. Parent-Teacher Association
qt. quart
RF radio frequency
RN registered nurse
R.P.M., rpm revolutions per minute
R.S.V.P., r.s.v.p. please reply (French *répondez s'il vous plaît*)
SASE self-addressed stamped envelope
SCSI small computer system interface
SOS 1. international distress signal 2. any call for help
Sr. 1. senior (after surname) 2. sister (religious)
ST standard time
St. 1. saint 2. strait 3. street
std. standard
syn. synonymous; synonym
TBA to be announced
tbs, tbsp tablespoon
TM trademark
tsp teaspoon
UHF, uhf ultra high frequency
UPC universal product code
UV ultraviolet
V 1. *Physics:* velocity 2. *Electricity:* volt 3. volume
V.A., VA Veterans Administration
VHF, vhf very high frequency
VIP *Informal:* very important person
vol. 1. volume 2. volunteer
vs. versus
W 1. *Electricity:* watt 2. *Physics:* (also **w**) work 3. west
whse., whs. warehouse
wkly. weekly
w/o without
wt. weight
yd yard (measurement)

Related Skills Activities

■ *SkillsBook*
Pretest: Numbers and Abbreviations, p. 47
Abbreviations, Acronyms, and Initialisms, p. 49

Acronyms and Initialisms

662.1 Acronyms

An **acronym** is a word formed from the first (or first few) letters of words in a phrase. Even though acronyms are abbreviations, they require no periods.

radar	radio detecting and ranging
CARE	Cooperative for American Relief Everywhere
NASA	National Aeronautics and Space Administration
VISTA	Volunteers in Service to America
LAN	local area network

662.2 Initialisms

An **initialism** is similar to an acronym except that the initials used to form this abbreviation are pronounced individually.

CIA	Central Intelligence Agency
FBI	Federal Bureau of Investigation
FHA	Federal Housing Administration

662.3 Common Acronyms and Initialisms

ADD	attention deficit disorder	MADD	Mothers Against Drunk Driving
AIDS	acquired immunodeficiency syndrome	MRI	magnetic resonance imaging
AKA	also known as	NASA	National Aeronautics and Space Administration
ATM	automatic teller machine	NATO	North Atlantic Treaty Organization
BMI	body mass index	OPEC	Organization of Petroleum-Exporting Countries
CD	compact disc	OSHA	Occupational Safety and Health Administration
DMV	Department of Motor Vehicles		
ETA	expected time of arrival	PAC	political action committee
FAA	Federal Aviation Administration	PDF	portable document format
FCC	Federal Communications Commission	PETA	People for the Ethical Treatment of Animals
FDA	Food and Drug Administration	PIN	personal identification number
FDIC	Federal Deposit Insurance Corporation	PSA	public service announcement
FEMA	Federal Emergency Management Agency	ROTC	Reserve Officers' Training Corps
FTC	Federal Trade Commission	SADD	Students Against Destructive Decisions
FYI	for your information		
GPS	global positioning system	SUV	sport utility vehicle
HDTV	high-definition television	SWAT	special weapons and tactics
IRS	Internal Revenue Service	TDD	telecommunications device for the deaf
IT	information technology		
JPEG	Joint Photographic Experts Group	VA	Veterans Administration
LCD	liquid crystal display		
LLC	limited liability company		

Grammar Practice

Abbreviations

In the following paragraph, some abbreviations are used incorrectly. If an underlined abbreviation is used incorrectly, write out what it stands for; if it is used correctly, write "correct."

Example: 1. *correct*

A survey of **(1)** Mrs. Reynolds' **(2)** apt. building at 1610 North Bunting **(3)** Rd., Sarton, **(4)** Ore., revealed that her property line is marked incorrectly. The neighboring **(5)** whse., owned by Roy Mitchel, **(6)** Jr., encroaches on the Reynolds property by 1 1/2 **(7)** ft. in the **(8)** NW corner of the lot. In a meeting on **(9)** Feb. 24 with **(10)** Mr. Mitchel and his wife, **(11)** Dr. Annemarie Tolbert, **(12)** Mrs. Reynolds agreed to a legal redefinition of the property line in exchange for a one-time cash payment of $32,500 to be made by 11:59 **(13)** p.m. **(14)** CST on **(15)** Mar. 15, 2006.

Model

Model the following acronyms and initialisms to come up with your own abbreviations. (Write at least one acronym and one initialism.)

scuba – self-contained underwater breathing apparatus
NOW – National Organization for Women
IQ – intelligence quotient
CPA – certified public accountant

Related Skills Activities

■ **SkillsBook**
Abbreviations, Acronyms, and Initialisms, p. 49

Answers

1. correct
2. apartment
3. correct
4. OR *or* Oregon
5. warehouse
6. correct
7. feet
8. northwest
9. February
10. correct
11. correct
12. correct
13. correct
14. correct
15. March

Spelling Rules

664.1 Write *i* before *e*

Write *i* before *e* except after *c*, or when sounded like *a* as in *neighbor* and *weigh*.

relief   receive   perceive   reign   freight   beige

EXCEPTIONS: There are a number of exceptions to this rule, including these:
neither, leisure, seize, weird, species, science.

664.2 Words with Consonant Endings

When a one-syllable word *(bat)* ends in a consonant *(t)* preceded by one vowel *(a)*, double the final consonant before adding a suffix that begins with a vowel *(batting)*.

sum—summary   god—goddess

NOTE: When a multisyllable word *(control)* ends in a consonant *(l)* preceded by one vowel *(o)*, the accent is on the last syllable *(con trol')*, and the suffix begins with a vowel *(ing)*—the same rule holds true: double the final consonant *(controlling)*.

prefer—preferred   begin—beginning
forget—forgettable   admit—admittance

664.3 Words with a Silent *e*

If a word ends with a silent *e*, drop the *e* before adding a suffix that begins with a vowel. Do not drop the *e* when the suffix begins with a consonant.

state—stating—statement   like—liking—likeness
use—using—useful   nine—ninety—nineteen

EXCEPTIONS: *judgment, truly, argument, ninth*

664.4 Words Ending in *y*

When *y* is the last letter in a word and the *y* is preceded by a consonant, change the *y* to *i* before adding any suffix except those beginning with *i*.

fry—fries—frying   hurry—hurried—hurrying   lady—ladies
ply—pliable   happy—happiness   beauty—beautiful

When *y* is the last letter in a word and the *y* is preceded by a vowel, do not change the *y* to *i* before adding a suffix.

play—plays—playful   stay—stays—staying   employ—employed

IMPORTANT REMINDER: Never trust your spelling even to the best spell-checker. Use a dictionary for words your spell-checker does not cover.

Mechanics

Grammar Practice

Spelling 1

Find the 10 words that are misspelled in the following paragraph and write them correctly. (Each misspelled word is in the "Commonly Misspelled Words" list on pages 666–667.)

Example: 1. abruptly

The music world changed abrubtly in August 1981: MTV broadcast its first music video. Twenty-five years later, record companies offen spend millions on a three-minute video—even more if the video is part of a movie campagne. Imagine what it must cost to design and build one of those elaberate sets! (Some videos, of course, have sevral sets.) Then figure in a variety of other costs, such as computer-generated animation, costumes and jewelery, and props. Sometimes an orchestra must be "rented." It adds up fast. The most ixpensive video, at an apsurd $7 million, was for Michael Jackson's song "Scream," feachering his sister, Janet. Since then, no one has come close to spending that much. Are we entertained yet?

Model

Model the following sentences to practice using the spelling rules that deal with adding a suffix.

Sometimes [the songs] are more than my real life and, conversely, my life is more than just my songs.
—Melissa Etheridge

To stop the flow of music would be like the stopping of time itself: incredible and inconceivable.
—Aaron Copland

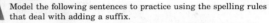

Related Skills Activities

■ *SkillsBook*
Spelling 1 and 2, pp. 54–55

Answers

1. abruptly
2. often
3. campaign
4. elaborate
5. several
6. variety
7. jewelry
8. expensive
9. absurd
10. featuring

Commonly Misspelled Words

A

abbreviate
abrupt
absence
absolute (ly)
absurd
abundance
academic
accelerate
accept (ance)
accessible
accessory
accidentally
accommodate
accompany
accomplish
accumulate
accurate
accustom (ed)
ache
achieve (ment)
acknowledge
acquaintance
acquired
across
address
adequate
adjustment
admissible
admittance
adolescent
advantageous
advertisement
advisable
aggravate
aggression
alcohol
alleviate
almost
alternative
although
aluminum
amateur
analysis
analyze
anarchy
ancient
anecdote
anesthetic

annihilate
announce
annual
anonymous
answer
anxious
apologize
apparatus
apparent (ly)
appearance
appetite
applies
appreciate
appropriate
approximately
architect
arctic
argument
arithmetic
arrangement
artificial
ascend
assistance
association
athlete
attendance
attire
attitude
audience
authority
available

B

balance
balloon
bargain
basically
beautiful
beginning
believe
benefit (ed)
biscuit
bought
boycott
brevity
brilliant
Britain
bureau
business

C

cafeteria
caffeine
calculator
calendar
campaign
canceled
candidate
catastrophe
category
caught
cavalry
celebration
cemetery
certificate
changeable
chief
chocolate
circuit
circumstance
civilization
colonel
colossal
column
commercial
commitment
committed
committee
comparative
comparison
competitively
conceivable
condemn
condescend
conference
conferred
confidential
congratulate
conscience
conscientious
conscious
consequence
consumer
contaminate
convenience
cooperate
correspondence
cough
coupon

courageous
courteous
creditor
criticism
criticize
curiosity
curious
cylinder

D

dealt
deceitful
deceive
decision
defense
deferred
definite (ly)
definition
delicious
descend
describe
description
despair
desperate
destruction
development
diameter
diaphragm
diarrhea
dictionary
dining
disagreeable
disappear
disappoint
disastrous
discipline
discrimination
discuss
dismissal
dissatisfied
dissect
distinctly
dormitory
doubt
drought
duplicate
dyeing
dying

E

earliest
efficiency
eighth
elaborate
eligible
eliminate
ellipse
embarrass
emphasize
employee
enclosure
encourage
endeavor
English
enormous
enough
enrichment
enthusiastic
entirely
entrance
environment
equipment
equipped
equivalent
especially
essential
eventually
exaggerate
examination
exceed
excellent
excessive
excite
executive
exercise
exhaust (ed)
exhibition
exhilaration
existence
expensive
experience
explanation
exquisite
extinguish
extraordinary
extremely

FG

facilities
familiar
fascinate
fashion
fatigue (d)
feature
February
fiery
financially
flourish
forcible
foreign
forfeit
fortunate
forty
fourth
freight
friend
fulfill
gauge
generally
generous
genuine
glimpse
gnarled
gnaw
government
gradual
grammar
gratitude
grievous
grocery
guard
guidance

H

happiness
harass
harmonize
height
hemorrhage
hereditary
hindrance
hoping
hopping
hospitable
humorous

hygiene
hymn
hypocrisy

IJ

ignorance
illiterate
illustrate
imaginary
immediately
immense
incidentally
inconvenience
incredible
indefinitely
independence
indispensable
industrial
industrious
inevitable
infinite
inflation
innocence
inoculation
inquiry
installation
instrumental
intelligence
interesting
interfere
interrupt
investigate
irregular
irresistible
issuing
itinerary
jealous (y)
jewelry
journal
judgment

KL

knowledge
laboratory
laugh
lawyer
league
legacy
legalize
legitimate
leisure

liaison
license
lightning
likable
liquid
literature
loneliness

MN

maintenance
maneuver
manufacture
marriage
mathematics
medieval
memento
menagerie
merchandise
merely
mileage
miniature
miscellaneous
mischievous
misspell
moat
mobile
mortgage
multiplied
muscle
musician
mustache
mutual
mysterious
naive
nauseous
necessary
neither
neurotic
nevertheless
ninety
nighttime
noticeable
nuclear
nuisance

OP

obstacle
obvious
occasion
occupant
occupation

occurred
occurrence
official
often
omitted
opinion
opponent
opportunity
opposite
optimism
ordinarily
organization
original
outrageous
pamphlet
parallel
paralyze
partial
particularly
pastime
patience
peculiar
pedestal
performance
permanent
permissible
perseverance
personal (ly)
personality
perspiration
persuade
petition
phenomenon
physical
physician
picnicking
planned
playwright
plead
pneumonia
politician
ponder
positively
possession
practically
precede
precious
preference
prejudice
preparation
presence
prevalent
primitive

privilege
probably
proceed
professional
professor
prominent
pronounce
pronunciation
protein
psychology
puny
purchase
pursuing

QR

qualified
quality
quantity
questionnaire
quiet
quite
quizzes
recede
receipt
receive
recipe
recognize
recommend
reference
referred
regard
regimen
religious
repel
repetition
residue
responsibility
restaurant
rheumatism
rhythm
ridiculous
robot
roommate

S

sacrifice
salary
sandwich
satisfactory
scarcely
scenic

schedule
scholar
science
secretary
seize
separate
sergeant
several
severely
sheriff
shrubbery
siege
signature
signify
silhouette
similar
simultaneous
sincerely
skiing
skunk
society
solar
sophomore
souvenir
spaghetti
specific
specimen
statue
stomach
stopped
strength
strictly
submission
substitute
subtle
succeed
success
sufficient
supersede
suppose
surprise
suspicious
symbolism
sympathy
synthetic

TU

tariff
technique
temperature
temporary
tendency

thermostat
thorough (ly)
though
throughout
tongue
tornado
tortoise
tragedy
transferred
tremendous
tried
trite
truly
unanimous
undoubtedly
unfortunately
unique
unnecessary
until
urgent
usable
usher
usually

V

vacuum
vague
valuable
variety
vengeance
versatile
vicinity
villain
visibility
visual

W

waif
Wednesday
weird
wholly
width
women
wrath
wreckage

Y

yesterday
yield
yolk

Related Skills Activities

■ *SkillsBook*
Spelling 1 and 2, pp. 54–55

Mechanics

Steps to Becoming a Better Speller

1. Be patient.
Becoming a good speller takes time.

2. Check the correct pronunciation of each word you are attempting to spell.
Knowing the correct pronunciation of a word can help you remember its spelling.

3. Note the meaning and history of each word as you are checking the dictionary for pronunciation.
Knowing the meaning and history of a word provides you with a better notion of how the word is properly used, and this can help you remember its spelling.

4. Before you close the dictionary, practice spelling the word.
Look away from the page and try to "see" the word in your mind. Then write it on a piece of paper. Check your spelling in the dictionary; repeat the process until you are able to spell the word correctly.

5. Learn some spelling rules.
For four of the most useful rules, see page **664**.

6. Make a list of the words that you often misspell.
Select the first 10 and practice spelling them.

STEP A: Read each word carefully; then write it on a piece of paper. Check to see that you've spelled it correctly. Repeat this step for the words that you misspelled.

STEP B: When you have finished your first 10 words, ask someone to read them to you as you write them again. Then check for misspellings. If you find none, congratulations! (Repeat both steps with your next 10 words, and so on.)

7. Write often.

Grammar Practice

Spelling 2

For each sentence below, fill in the blank with the correct word from the list of "Commonly Misspelled Words" (pages 666–667).

Example: A person who has p_____c__ can wait calmly.
  patience

1. You may not operate a car without a driver's l_____.

2. _____x_____ is an important part of physical fitness.

3. Zaida has not played in any professional tournaments yet; she still plays at the a_____ level.

4. Some sodas have as much _____f f_____ in them as coffee does.

5. Seth is always _____g his hair different colors.

6. Juries should assume a person's i___n_____ until guilt is proven.

7. Keep the dogs in s_____ kennels; they cannot be together.

8. Angel used a small v_____ to suck up the crumbs in the crevices of his car.

9. A cross is a r_____g_____ icon.

10. Angus kept asking Dom for the test answers, but Dom's _____s c_____ wouldn't let him do it.

11. These garlic potatoes are so d_____s, I'll have another serving!

Model

Model the following sentences to practice using the spelling rules for words ending in *y*.

She was overjoyed that the guests liked her curried lamb.

We were praying that the cub's pitiful whines would end soon.

Answers

1. license
2. Exercise
3. amateur
4. caffeine
5. dyeing
6. innocence
7. separate
8. vacuum
9. religious
10. conscience
11. delicious

Test Prep!

Read the following paragraphs. From the choices given on the next page, write the letter of the correct way to express each underlined part. If it is already correct, choose "D."

Although the United States was an ally of the Soviet Union during world war II, tensions afterward led to a period of time known as the Cold War. In particular, Western democracies disputed the Soviet Union's takeover of east european states. A vivid symbol of the Cold War was the Berlin Wall, separating west berlin from the territory of East Germany.

    (1)

    (2)

    (3)

The conflict never heated up into a full-scale war, but both the East and the West perceived each other as hostile, leading to the arms race. In nineteen forty-nine, the Soviets tested their first a-bomb. Of course, the u.s. had already used the bomb on Japan; nevertheless, president Truman's response was to further build up conventional and nuclear weapons. That the country took the Soviet "threat" very seriously was evident in its placement of Nike missiles around major U.S. cities. the hidden rockets, designed as antiaircraft weapons, were stored underground and could be raised into fireing position when needed. The first Nike missiles in 1954 carried conventional explosives and had a range of 25 miles; 4 years later the range was not only increased to seventy-five miles, but the missiles could carry nuclear warheads as well. The development of intercontinental ballistic missiles (IcbM's) in the late '50s made the Nike missile system obsolete. These self-propelled, unmanned missiles had a range of many thousand of miles and could be controlled remotely. They are still in use today.

    (4)

    (5)   (6)

    (7)

    (8)

    (9)

    (10)

    (11)

    (12)

    (13)

    (14)

Most analysts would agree that the Cold War fizzled as the Soviet Union broke up in the early '90s. The countries involved now cooperate on issues rather than focus on destroing each other. The current advances in international space exploration, for example, show that hostility between nations can be overcome—and that former allies can be allies again.

    (15)

    (16)

1 (A) World war II
(B) World War II
(C) world War II
(D) correct as is

2 (A) East European states
(B) East European States
(C) east European states
(D) correct as is

3 (A) West Berlin
(B) west Berlin
(C) West berlin
(D) correct as is

4 (A) east and the west
(B) east and the West
(C) East and the west
(D) correct as is

5 (A) 1949
(B) nineteen fourty-nine
(C) 19 forty-nine
(D) correct as is

6 (A) 1st a-bomb
(B) first A-bomb
(C) first A-Bomb
(D) correct as is

7 (A) The U.S.
(B) the U.S.
(C) the US
(D) correct as is

8 (A) president truman's
(B) President truman's
(C) President Truman's
(D) correct as is

9 (A) U.S. citys. The
(B) U.S. cities. The
(C) U.S. citys. the
(D) correct as is

10 (A) raised into firing
(B) raised into fiering
(C) raiseed into firing
(D) correct as is

11 (A) 25 miles; four years
(B) twenty-five miles; 4 years
(C) 25 mile; four years
(D) correct as is

12 (A) seventy-five mile
(B) 75 mile
(C) 75 miles
(D) correct as is

13 (A) IcBM's
(B) icbms
(C) ICBM's
(D) correct as is

14 (A) many thousands of mile
(B) many thousands of miles
(C) many thousand of mile
(D) correct as is

15 (A) distroing
(B) distroying
(C) destroying
(D) correct as is

16 (A) allys can be allys
(B) Allies can be Allies
(C) allys can be allies
(D) correct as is

Related Skills Activities

■ **SkillsBook**
Review: Capitalization, p. 46
Review: Numbers and Abbreviations, p. 50
Review: Plurals and Spelling, p. 56
Posttest: Capitalization, p. 198
Posttest: Numbers, Abbreviations, and Acronyms, p. 199
Posttest: Plurals and Spelling, p. 200

Answers

1. B		9. B	
2. A		10. A	
3. A		11. A	
4. D		12. C	
5. A		13. C	
6. B		14. B	
7. B		15. C	
8. C		16. D	

Understanding Idioms

Idioms are phrases that are used in a special way. You can't understand an idiom just by knowing the meaning of each word in the phrase. You must learn it as a whole. For example, the idiom *bury the hatchet* means "to settle an argument," even though the individual words in the phrase mean something much different. This section will help you learn some of the common idioms in American English.

apple of his eye	Eagle Lake is the apple of his eye. (something he likes very much)
as plain as day	The mistake in the ad was as plain as day. (very clear)
as the crow flies	New London is 200 miles from here as the crow flies. (in a straight line)
at a snail's pace	My last hour at work passes at a snail's pace. (very, very slowly)
axe to grind	The manager has an axe to grind with that umpire. (disagreement to settle)
bad apple	There are no bad apples in this class. (a bad influence)
beat around the bush	Don't beat around the bush; answer the question. (avoid getting to the point)
benefit of the doubt	Everyone has been given the benefit of the doubt at least once. (another chance)
beyond the shadow of a doubt	Beyond the shadow of a doubt, this is my best science project. (for certain)
blew my top	When I saw the broken statue, I blew my top. (showed great anger)
bone to pick	Alison had a bone to pick with the student who copied her paper. (problem to settle)
brain drain	Brain drain is a serious problem in some states. (the best students moving elsewhere)
break the ice	The nervous ninth graders were afraid to break the ice. (start a conversation)
burn the midnight oil	Devon had to burn the midnight oil to finish his report. (work late into the night)

bury the hatchet	My sisters were told to bury the hatchet immediately. (settle an argument)
by the skin of her teeth	Anna avoided an accident by the skin of her teeth. (just barely)
champing at the bit	The skiers were champing at the bit to get on the slopes. (eager, excited)
chicken feed	The prize was chicken feed to some people. (not worth much money)
chip off the old block	Frank's just like his father. He's a chip off the old block. (just like someone else)
clean as a whistle	My boss told me to make sure the place was as clean as a whistle before I left. (very clean)
cold shoulder	I wanted to fit in with that group, but they gave me the cold shoulder. (ignored me)
crack of dawn	Ali delivers his papers at the crack of dawn. (first light of day, early morning)
cry wolf	If you cry wolf too often, no one will believe you. (say you are in trouble when you aren't)
dead of night	Hearing a loud noise in the dead of night frightened Bill. (middle of the night)
dirt cheap	A lot of clothes at that store are dirt cheap. (inexpensive, costing very little money)
doesn't hold a candle to	That award doesn't hold a candle to a gold medal. (is not as good as)
drop in the bucket	The contributions were a drop in the bucket. (a small amount compared to what's needed)
everything from A to Z	That catalog lists everything from A to Z. (a lot of different things)
face the music	Todd had to face the music when he broke the window. (deal with the punishment)
fish out of water	He felt like a fish out of water in the new math class. (someone in an unfamiliar place)
fit for a king	The food at the athletic banquet was fit for a king. (very special)

Idioms

flew off the handle	Bill flew off the handle when he saw a reckless driver near the school. (became very angry)
floating on air	Celine was floating on air at the prom. (feeling very happy)
food for thought	The boys' foolish and dangerous prank gave us food for thought. (something to think about)
get down to business	After sharing several jokes, Mr. Sell said we should get down to business. (start working)
get the upper hand	The wrestler moved quickly on his opponent in order to get the upper hand. (gain the advantage)
give their all	Student volunteers give their all to help others. (work as hard as they can)
go fly a kite	Charlene stared at her nosy brother and said, "Go fly a kite." (go away)
has a green thumb	Talk to Mrs. Smith about your sick plant. She has a green thumb. (is good at growing plants)
has a heart of gold	Joe has a heart of gold. (is very kind and generous)
hit a home run	Rhonda hit a home run with her speech. (succeeded, or did well)
hit the ceiling	When my parents saw my grades, they hit the ceiling. (were very angry)
hit the hay	Exhausted from the hike, Jamal hit the hay without eating supper. (went to bed)
in a nutshell	Can you, in a nutshell, tell us your goals for this year? (in summary)
in one ear and out the other	Sharl, concerned about her pet, let the lecture go in one ear and out the other. (without really listening)
in the black	My aunt's gift shop is finally in the black. (making money)
in the nick of time	Janelle caught the falling vase in the nick of time. (just in time)
in the red	Many businesses start out in the red. (in debt)
in the same boat	The new tax bill meant everyone would be in the same boat. (in a similar situation)

iron out	Joe will meet with the work crew to iron out their complaints. (solve, work out)
it goes without saying	It goes without saying that saving money is a good idea. (it is clear)
it stands to reason	It stands to reason that your stamina will increase if you run every day. (it makes sense)
keep a stiff upper lip	Keep a stiff upper lip when you visit the doctor. (be brave)
keep it under your hat	Keep it under your hat about the pop quiz. (don't tell anyone)
knock on wood	My uncle knocked on wood after he said he had never had the flu. (did something for good luck)
knuckle down	After wasting half the day, we were told to knuckle down. (work hard)
learn the ropes	It takes every new employee a few months to learn the ropes. (get to know how things are done)
leave no stone unturned	The police plan to leave no stone unturned at the crime scene. (check everything)
lend someone a hand	You will feel good if you lend someone a hand. (help someone)
let the cat out of the bag	Tom let the cat out of the bag during lunch. (told a secret)
let's face it	Let's face it. You don't like rap. (let's admit it)
look high and low	We looked high and low for Jan's dog. (looked everywhere)
lose face	In some cultures, it is very bad to lose face. (be embarrassed)
needle in a haystack	Trying to find a person in New York is like trying to find a needle in a haystack. (something impossible to find)
nose to the grindstone	With all of these assignments, I have to keep my nose to the grindstone. (work hard)
on cloud nine	After talking to my girlfriend, I was on cloud nine. (feeling very happy)
on pins and needles	Nancy was on pins and needles during the championship game. (feeling nervous)

Idioms

out the window	Once the rain started, our plans were out the window. (ruined)
over and above	Over and above the required work, Will cleaned up the lab. (in addition to)
pain in the neck	Franklin knew the report would be a pain in the neck. (very annoying)
pull your leg	Cary was only pulling your leg. (telling you a little lie as a joke)
put his foot in his mouth	Lane put his foot in his mouth when he answered the question. (said something embarrassing)
put the cart before the horse	Tonya put the cart before the horse when she sealed the envelope before inserting the letter. (did something in the wrong order)
put your best foot forward	When applying for a job, you should put your best foot forward. (do the best that you can do)
red-letter day	Sheila had a red-letter day because she did so well on her math test. (very good day)
rock the boat	I was told not to rock the boat. (cause trouble)
rude awakening	Jake will have a rude awakening when he sees the bill for his computer. (sudden, unpleasant surprise)
save face	His gift was clearly an attempt to save face. (fix an embarrassing situation)
see eye to eye	We see eye to eye about the need for a new school. (are in agreement)
shake a leg	I told Mako to shake a leg so that we wouldn't be late. (hurry)
shift into high gear	Greg had to shift into high gear to finish the test in time. (speed up, hurry)
sight for sore eyes	My grandmother's smiling face was a sight for sore eyes. (good to see)
sight unseen	Liz bought the coat sight unseen. (without seeing it first)
sink or swim	Whether you sink or swim in school depends on your study habits. (fail or succeed)

spilled the beans	Suddenly, Jose realized that he had spilled the beans. (revealed a secret)
spring chicken	Although Mr. Gordon isn't a spring chicken, he sure knows how to talk to kids. (young person)
stick to your guns	Know what you believe, and stick to your guns. (don't change your mind)
sweet tooth	Chocolate is often the candy of choice for those with a sweet tooth. (a love for sweets, like candy and cake)
take a dim view	My sister will take a dim view of that movie. (disapprove)
take it with a grain of salt	When you read that advertisement, take it with a grain of salt. (don't believe everything)
take the bull by the horns	It's time to take the bull by the horns so the project gets done on time. (take control)
through thick and thin	Those two girls have remained friends through thick and thin. (in good times and in bad times)
time flies	Time flies as you grow older. (time passes quickly)
time to kill	Grace had time to kill, so she read a book. (extra time)
to go overboard	The class was told not to go overboard. A $50.00 donation was fine. (to do too much)
toe the line	The new teacher made everyone toe the line. (follow the rules)
tongue-tied	He can talk easily with friends, but in class he is usually tongue-tied. (not knowing what to say)
turn over a new leaf	He decided to turn over a new leaf in school. (make a new start)
two peas in a pod	Ever since kindergarten, Lil and Eve have been like two peas in a pod. (very much alike)
under the weather	Guy was feeling under the weather this morning. (sick)
wallflower	Joan knew the other girls thought she was a wallflower. (a shy person)
word of mouth	Joseph learns a lot about his favorite team by word of mouth. (talking with other people)

Idioms

Using the Right Word

a lot ▪ *A lot* (always two words) is a vague descriptive phrase that should be used sparingly.

> He reported to his teacher that he had a lot of unfinished assignments.

accept, except ▪ The verb *accept* means "to receive" or "to believe"; the preposition *except* means "other than."

> The principal accepted the boy's story about the broken window, but she asked why no one except him saw the ball accidentally slip from his hand.

adapt, adopt ▪ *Adapt* means "to adjust or change to fit"; *adopt* means "to choose and treat as your own" (a child, an idea).

> After a lengthy period of study, Malcolm X adopted the Islamic faith and adapted to its lifestyle.

affect, effect ▪ The verb *affect* means "to influence"; the verb *effect* means "to produce, accomplish, complete."

> Ming's hard work effected an A on the test, which positively affected her semester grade.

The noun *effect* means the "result."

> Good grades have a calming effect on parents.

aisle, isle ▪ An *aisle* is a passage between seats; an *isle* is a small island.

> Many airline passengers on their way to the Isle of Capri prefer an aisle seat.

all right ▪ *All right* is always two words (not *alright*).

allusion, illusion ▪ *Allusion* is an indirect reference to someone or something; *illusion* is a false picture or idea.

> My little sister, under the illusion that she's movie-star material, makes frequent allusions to her future fans.

already, all ready ▪ *Already* is an adverb meaning "before this time" or "by this time." *All ready* is an adjective meaning "fully prepared."

NOTE: Use *all ready* if you can substitute *ready* alone in the sentence.

> Although I've already had some dessert, I am all ready for some ice cream from the street vendor.

Grammar Practice

Using the Right Word 1

a lot; accept, except; **adapt, adopt**; affect, effect; **aisle, isle**; all right

 Read the following paragraphs. If an underlined word is used incorrectly, write the correct word. If it's correct as is, write "OK."

Example: 1. *OK*

Located in the middle of the Irish Sea between Liverpool and Belfast, the **(1)** <u>Isle</u> of Man is an independent country of approximately 75,831 people. **(2)** <u>Alot</u> of British people live there, but about half the population is native, known as Manx.

The island's status as an offshore financial center has had a positive **(3)** <u>affect</u> on the Manx economy. Current unemployment is only 1 percent, so a growing population of foreigners **(4)** <u>except</u> jobs on the Isle of Man to take advantage of the economic possibilities. Soon, they **(5)** <u>adopt</u> the island as their home—and **(6)** <u>adopt</u> to the damp climate. The island's weather is **(7)** <u>effected</u> by the Gulf Stream that runs through the Irish Sea, and there is not a wide fluctuation in temperatures: 68°F in summer and 48°F in winter. The precipitation is rain and fog **(8)** <u>accept</u> for snow that sometimes falls in late February or early March.

In the town of Douglas, young people visit shops and cafes, leisure centers, and bowling alleys. They descend the **(9)** <u>isles</u> at cinemas to see the latest movies. The area also boasts sports and facilities such as the skateboard, in-line skating, and BMX area. That sounds **(10)** <u>all right</u>!

Model

Model the following sentences to practice using the words *already* and *all ready* correctly.

> Advice is what we ask for when we already know the answer but wish we didn't.
>
> —Erica Jong

> I've prepared everything we need; I believe we're all ready to leave now.

Related Skills Activities

▪ **SkillsBook**
Using the Right Word 1, p. 58

Answers

1. OK
2. A lot
3. effect
4. accept
5. OK
6. adapt
7. affected
8. except
9. aisles
10. OK

Right Word

altogether, all together ■ *Altogether* means "entirely." The phrase *all together* means "in a group" or "all at once."

> "There is altogether too much gridlock," complained the Democrats. All together, the Republicans yelled, "No way!"

among, between ■ *Among* is typically used when speaking of more than two persons or things. *Between* is used when speaking of only two.

> The three of us talked among ourselves to decide between going out or eating in.

amount, number ■ *Amount* is used for bulk measurement. *Number* is used to count separate units. (See also *fewer, less*.)

> A substantial amount of honey spilled all over a number of my CD's.

annual, biannual, semiannual, biennial, perennial ■ An *annual* event happens once every year. A *biannual* or *semiannual* event happens twice a year. A *biennial* event happens every two years. A *perennial* event is one that is persistent or constant.

> Dad's annual family reunion gets bigger every year.
> We're going shopping at the department store's semiannual white sale.
> Due to dwindling attendance, the county fair is now a biennial celebration.
> A perennial plant persists for several years.

anyway ■ Do not add an *s* to *anyway*.

ascent, assent ■ *Ascent* is the act of rising or climbing; *assent* is "to agree to something after some consideration" (or such an agreement).

> We completed our ascent of the butte with the assent of the landowner.

bad, badly ■ *Bad* is an adjective. *Badly* is an adverb.

> This apple is bad, but one bad apple doesn't always ruin the whole bushel.
> In today's game, Ross passed badly.

base, bass ■ *Base* is the foundation or the lower part of something. *Bass* (pronounced like *base*) is a deep sound. *Bass* (pronounced like *class*) is a fish.

beside, besides ■ *Beside* means "by the side of." *Besides* means "in addition to."

> Mother always grew roses beside the trash bin. Besides looking nice, they also gave off a sweet smell that masked odors.

Grammar Practice

Using the Right Word 2

altogether, all together; among, between; **amount, number;** annual, biannual, biennial, perennial; **ascent, assent;** bad, badly

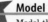 Write the correct choice from those given in parentheses.

Example: Shawn is such a cheerful guy—he seems to have *(an annual, a perennial)* smile on his face.
    a perennial

1. The *(amount, number)* of gray wolves in Minnesota increased dramatically from 1967 to 2007.

2. *(Altogether, All together)*, they numbered about 2,500 in 2007.

3. The consensus *(among, between)* experts is that the population will continue to grow.

4. The volunteer firefighters hold their *(biannual, biennial)* pancake breakfast every March and September.

5. Mom and Dad go to each one since their *(bad, badly)* accident a few years ago.

6. Everyone was surprised at Cruz's rapid *(ascent, assent)* to a leadership position in the student government.

7. He didn't do *(bad, badly)* in his first year's elections.

8. He is *(altogether, all together)* a great candidate for almost any office.

9. The *(amount, number)* of support he can count on is staggering.

10. People often *(ascent, assent)* to vote for him after meeting him just once.

11. Maybe he can fit in a political internship *(among, between)* high school and college.

◣ Model

Model the following sentence to practice using the word *anyway*.

> Courage is being scared to death—but saddling up anyway.
>   —John Wayne

Related Skills Activities

■ **SkillsBook**
Using the Right Word 1, p. 58

Answers

1. number
2. All together
3. among
4. biannual
5. bad
6. ascent
7. badly
8. altogether
9. amount
10. assent
11. between

board, bored ■ *Board* is a piece of wood. *Board* is also an administrative group or council.

The school board approved the purchase of fifty 1- by 6-inch pine boards.

Bored is the past tense of the verb "bore," which may mean "to make a hole by drilling" or "to become weary out of dullness."

Watching television bored Joe, so he took his drill and bored a hole in the wall where he could hang his new clock.

brake, break ■ *Brake* is a device used to stop a vehicle. *Break* means "to separate or to destroy."

I hope the brakes on my car never break.

bring, take ■ *Bring* suggests the action is directed toward the speaker; *take* suggests the action is directed away from the speaker.

Bring home some garbage bags so I can take the trash outside.

can, may ■ *Can* suggests ability while *may* suggests permission.

"Can I go to the mall?" means "Am I physically able to go to the mall?"
"May I go to the mall?" asks permission to go.

capital, capitol ■ The noun *capital* refers to a city or to money. The adjective *capital* means "major or important." *Capitol* refers to a building.

The state capital is home to the capitol building for a capital reason. The state government contributed capital for its construction.

cent, sent, scent ■ *Cent* is a coin; *sent* is the past tense of the verb "send"; *scent* is an odor or a smell.

For forty-one cents, I sent my girlfriend a mushy love poem in a perfumed envelope. She adored the scent but hated the poem.

cereal, serial ■ *Cereal* is a grain, often made into breakfast food. *Serial* relates to something in a series.

Mohammed enjoys reading serial novels while he eats a bowl of cereal.

chord, cord ■ *Chord* may mean "an emotion" or "a combination of musical tones sounded at the same time." A *cord* is a string or a rope.

The guitar player strummed the opening chord to the group's hit song, which struck a responsive chord with the audience.

chose, choose ■ *Chose* (chōz) is the past tense of the verb *choose* (chōōz).

Last quarter I chose to read Chitra Divakaruni's *The Unknown Errors of Our Lives*—a fascinating book about Indian immigrants.

Grammar Practice

Using the Right Word 3

board, bored; brake, break; can, may; capital, capitol; cent, sent, scent

 Select the correct word from the list above to complete each sentence. (One word is used twice.)

Example: I'll give you $12 for that CD, and not one _____ more.
    cent

1. My mechanic says my car needs _____ work.

2. A typical business start-up needs a _____ infusion of several thousand dollars.

3. Although most teens love summer, some are _____ by the lack of intellectual stimulation.

4. Most teachers require that you ask whether you _____ leave to use the washroom.

5. As Moira walked down the hall, the _____ of her perfume lingered after her.

6. Rap the egg sharply with a knife to _____ its shell.

7. We climbed up the grand staircase in the _____ to get to our senator's office.

8. My makeshift shelf consisted of a _____ laid across two milk crates.

9. _____ you help me move this sofa?

10. I _____ a job application to the zoo.

11. I hope I _____ get the job.

Model

Model the following sentences to practice using the words *can* and *may* correctly.

No one can make you feel inferior without your consent.
—Eleanor Roosevelt, *This Is My Story*

Conscience is the inner voice that warns us somebody may be looking.
—H. L. Mencken, *A Mencken Chrestomathy*

Right Word

Related Skills Activities

■ *SkillsBook*
Using the Right Word 2, p. 59

Answers

1. brake
2. capital
3. bored
4. may
5. scent
6. break
7. capitol
8. board
9. Can
10. sent
11. can

684

coarse, course ■ *Coarse* means "rough or crude"; *course* means "a path or direction taken." *Course* also means "a class or a series of studies."

> Fletcher, known for using coarse language, was barred from the golf course until he took an etiquette course.

complement, compliment ■ *Complement* refers to that which completes or fulfills. *Compliment* is an expression of admiration or praise.

> Kimberly smiled, thinking she had received a compliment when Carlos said that her new Chihuahua complemented her personality.

continual, continuous ■ *Continual* refers to something that happens again and again with some breaks or pauses; *continuous* refers to something that keeps happening, uninterrupted.

> Sunlight hits Iowa on a continual basis; sunlight hits Earth continuously.

counsel, council ■ When used as a noun, *counsel* means "advice"; when used as a verb, it means "to advise." *Council* refers to a group that advises.

> The student council counseled all freshmen to join a school club. That's good counsel.

desert, dessert ■ The noun *desert* (dĕz´ ərt) refers to barren wilderness. *Dessert* (dĭ zûrt´) is food served at the end of a meal.

> The scorpion tiptoed through the moonlit desert, searching for dessert.

The verb *desert* (dĭ zûrt´) means "to abandon"; the noun *desert* (dĭ zûrt´) means "deserved reward or punishment."

> The burglar's hiding place deserted him when the spotlight swung his way; his subsequent arrest was his just desert.

die, dye ■ *Die* (dying) means "to stop living." *Dye* (dyeing) is used to change the color of something.

different from, different than ■ Use *different from* in a comparison of two things. *Different than* should be used only when followed by a clause.

> Yassine is quite different from his brother.
> Life is different than it used to be.

farther, further ■ *Farther* refers to a physical distance; *further* refers to additional time, quantity, or degree.

> Alaska extends farther north than Iceland does. Further information can be obtained in an atlas.

fewer, less ■ *Fewer* refers to the number of separate units; *less* refers to bulk quantity.

> Because we have fewer orders for cakes, we'll buy less sugar and flour.

Grammar Practice

Using the Right Word 4

coarse, course; counsel, council; die, dye; farther, further; fewer, less

 Write the correct choice from those given in parentheses.

Example: Rae's *(coarse, course)* hair frizzed whenever it was humid.
> *coarse*

1. Last week, she sought the *(counsel, council)* of a trusted stylist.

2. The stylist encouraged Rae to *(die, dye)* her hair.

3. Quincy runs every other day; he enjoys trying to find a different *(coarse, course)* each week.

4. He is building his strength slowly, so he attempts to run a little *(farther, further)* each time he goes out.

5. He finds that he experiences *(fewer, less)* incidents of being totally out of breath now that he runs so often.

6. The Norwood city *(counsel, council)* meets once a month at city hall.

7. Tomorrow the members will *(farther, further)* discuss the drought's effect on local farmers.

8. Their crops will *(die, dye)* if we don't get rain soon.

9. The area has had *(fewer, less)* rain than it did during the drought of '86.

Model

Model the following sentences to practice using the words *farther* and *further* correctly.

> Gratitude is merely the secret hope of further favors.
> —Francois de La Rochefoucauld

> The farther behind I leave the past, the closer I am to forgiving my own character.
> —Isabelle Eberhardt

Right Word

Related Skills Activities

■ *SkillsBook*
Using the Right Word 2, p. 59

 ## Answers

1. counsel
2. dye
3. course
4. farther
5. fewer
6. council
7. further
8. die
9. less

flair, flare ■ *Flair* refers to style or natural talent; *flare* means "to light up quickly" or "burst out" (or an object that does so).

> Ronni was thrilled with Jorge's flair for decorating—until one of his strategically placed candles flared, marring the wall.

good, well ■ *Good* is an adjective; *well* is nearly always an adverb. (When *well* is used to describe a state of health, it is an adjective: He was happy to be *well* again.)

> The MP3 player works well.
> Our team looks good this season.

heal, heel ■ *Heal* means "to mend or restore to health." A *heel* is the back part of a foot.

> Achilles died because a poison arrow pierced his heel and caused a wound that would not heal.

healthful, healthy ■ *Healthful* means "causing or improving health"; *healthy* means "possessing health."

> Healthful foods build healthy bodies.

hear, here ■ You *hear* with your ears. *Here* means "the area close by."

heard, herd ■ *Heard* is the past tense of the verb "hear"; *herd* is a large group of animals.

hole, whole ■ A *hole* is a cavity or hollow place. *Whole* means "complete."

idle, idol ■ *Idle* means "not working." An *idol* is someone or something that is worshipped.

> The once-popular actress, who had been idle lately, wistfully recalled her days as an idol.

immigrate, emigrate ■ *Immigrate* means "to come into a new country or environment." *Emigrate* means "to go out of one country to live in another."

> Martin Ulferts immigrated to this country in 1882. He was only three years old when he emigrated from Germany.

imply, infer ■ *Imply* means "to suggest or express indirectly"; *infer* means "to draw a conclusion from facts." (A writer or speaker implies; a reader or listener infers.)

> Dad implied by his comment that I should drive more carefully, and I inferred that he was concerned for both me and his new car.

Grammar Practice

Using the Right Word 5

good, well; heal, heel; healthful, healthy; hear, here; hole, whole

 Write the correct choice from those given in each set of numbered parentheses.

Example: 1. healthful

There are questions about whether or not certain dietary supplements are, in fact, **(1)** *(healthful, healthy)*. People **(2)** *(hear, here)* all kinds of claims from the manufacturers. But do the supplements **(3)** *(heal, heel)* people of any medical conditions? Can they make weak, inactive people strong and **(4)** *(healthful, healthy)* again? Or is the supplement industry just a big **(5)** *(hole, whole)* where gullible people throw their money?

Since supplements are not regulated by the federal government, it is hard to find **(6)** *(good, well)*, solid evidence one way or the other. It's possible that supplements will work **(7)** *(good, well)* in some people and not in others. While only man-made pharmaceuticals might work **(8)** *(hear, here)*, herbal supplements might do fine there. But because supplements may actually be harmful to some individuals, the **(9)** *(hole, whole)* issue is an important one.

Some people rely solely on supplements, but many use a combination of therapies. For instance, I use a homeopathic ointment on my sore **(10)** *(heal, heel)*, but I also take ibuprofen for the pain. I take the most **(11)** *(healthful, healthy)* approach when it comes to taking care of myself.

▶ Model

Model the following sentences to practice using the words *good* and *well* correctly.

> In spite of everything I still believe that people are really good at heart.
> —Anne Frank

> People forget how fast you did a job—but they remember how well you did it.
> —Howard Newton

Related Skills Activities

■ *SkillsBook*
Using the Right Word 3, p. 60
Using *Good* and *Well*, p. 115

 ## Answers

1. healthful
2. hear
3. heal
4. healthy
5. hole
6. good
7. well
8. here
9. whole
10. heel
11. healthful

insure, ensure ■ *Insure* means "to secure from financial harm or loss." *Ensure* means "to make certain of something."

> To ensure that you can legally drive that new car, you'll have to insure it.

it's, its ■ *It's* is the contraction of "it is." *Its* is the possessive form of "it."

> It's hard to believe, but the movie *Shrek* still holds its appeal for many kids.

later, latter ■ *Later* means "after a period of time." *Latter* refers to the second of two things mentioned.

> Later that year we had our second baby and adopted a stray kitten. The latter was far more welcomed by our toddler.

lay, lie ■ *Lay* means "to place." *Lay* is a transitive verb. (See 716.1.)

> Lay your books on the big table.

Lie means "to recline," and *lay* is the past tense of *lie*. *Lie* is an intransitive verb. (See 716.1.)

> In this heat, the children must lie down for a nap. Yesterday they lay down without one complaint. Sometimes they have lain in the hammocks to rest.

lead, led ■ *Lead* (lēd) is the present tense of the verb meaning "to guide." The past tense of the verb is *led* (lĕd). The noun *lead* (lĕd) is a metal.

> We were led along the path that leads to an abandoned lead mine.

learn, teach ■ *Learn* means "to acquire information." *Teach* means "to give information."

> I learn better when people teach with real-world examples.

leave, let ■ *Leave* means "to allow something to remain behind." *Let* means "to permit."

> Would you let me leave my bike at your house?

lend, borrow ■ *Lend* means "to give for temporary use." *Borrow* means "to receive for temporary use."

> I told Mom I needed to borrow $18 for a CD, but she said she could only lend money for school supplies.

like, as ■ When *like* is used as a preposition meaning "similar to," it can be followed only by a noun, pronoun, or noun phrase; when *as* is used as a subordinating conjunction, it introduces a subordinate clause.

> You could become a gymnast like her, as you work and practice hard.

medal, meddle ■ *Medal* is an award. *Meddle* means "to interfere."

> Some parents meddle in the awards process to be sure that their kids get medals.

Grammar Practice

Using the Right Word 6

it's, its; later, latter; learn, teach; lend, borrow; medal, meddle

 For each paragraph below, choose the correct words from the list above to fill in the blanks.

Example: 1. it's

Clayton Dyer is a professional bass fisherman who was born without one arm and both of his legs. You can imagine that **(1)**_____ not easy to operate his boat and manipulate the rods, but Clayton has won more than one **(2)**_____ during his career. He has won 25 tournaments. When disabled children ask Clayton to **(3)**_____ them how to fish, he gladly does so. He says, "If I could **(4)**_____ how to fish, anyone can!"

My sister Mykaela loves to **(5)**_____ in my business. Once, I was trying to avoid facing my dad over a scratch on his car. I "repaired" the finish using some nail polish that matched **(6)**____color. She piped up, "You might think that's the right thing to do now, but you'll regret it **(7)**_____!" Recently she overheard me asking a friend to **(8)**_____ me some money. Mykaela said, "You shouldn't **(9)**_____ money from friends!" I don't know whether I should argue with her or ignore her. (Usually, I choose the **(10)**_____.)

 Model

Model the following sentences to practice using the words *learn* and *teach* correctly.

> A critic is a legless man who teaches running.
> —Channing Pollock

> We could never learn to be brave and patient if there were only joy in the world.
> —Helen Keller

Right Word

Related Skills Activities

■ *SkillsBook*
Using the Right Word 3, p. 60

Answers

1. it's
2. medal
3. teach
4. learn
5. meddle
6. its
7. later
8. lend
9. borrow
10. latter

metal, mettle ■ *Metal* is a chemical element like iron or gold. *Mettle* is "strength of spirit."

> Grandad's mettle during battle left him with some metal in his shoulder.

miner, minor ■ A *miner* digs for valuable ore. A *minor* is a person who is not legally an adult. A *minor* problem is one of no great importance.

moral, morale ■ A *moral* is a lesson drawn from a story; as an adjective, it relates to the principles of right and wrong. *Morale* refers to someone's attitude.

> Ms. Ladue considers it her moral obligation to go to church every day.
> The students' morale sank after their defeat in the forensics competition.

passed, past ■ *Passed* is a verb. *Past* can be used as a noun, an adjective, or a preposition.

> That old pickup truck passed my sports car! (verb)
> Many senior citizens hold dearly to the past. (noun)
> Tilly's past life as a circus worker must have been . . . interesting. (adjective)
> Who can walk past a bakery without looking in the window? (preposition)

peace, piece ■ *Peace* means "tranquility or freedom from war." *Piece* is a part or fragment.

> Grandma sits in the peace and quiet of the parlor, enjoying a piece of pie.

peak, peek, pique ■ A *peak* is a high point. *Peek* means "brief look" (or "look briefly"). *Pique*, as a verb, means "to excite by challenging"; as a noun, it is a feeling of resentment.

> The peak of Dr. Fedder's professional life was his ability to pique children's interest in his work. "Peek at this slide," he said to the eager students.

pedal, peddle, petal ■ A *pedal* is a foot lever; as a verb, it means "to ride a bike." *Peddle* means "to go from place to place selling something." A *petal* is part of a flower.

> Don Miller paints beautiful petals on his homemade birdhouses. Then he pedals through the flea market every weekend to peddle them.

personal, personnel ■ *Personal* means "private." *Personnel* are people working at a particular job.

plain, plane ■ *Plain* means "an area of land that is flat or level"; it also means "clearly seen or clearly understood."

> It's plain to see why settlers of the Great Plains had trouble moving west.

Plane means "flat, level"; it is also a tool used to smooth the surface of wood.

> I used a plane to make the board plane and smooth.

Grammar Practice

Using the Right Word 7

miner, minor; past, passed; peace, piece; pedal, peddle, petal; personal, personnel

 Write the correct choice from those given in parentheses.

Example: Would you care for a *(peace, piece)* of lasagna?
> piece

1. Soraya supervises all the maintenance *(personal, personnel)* at the hospital.

2. I haven't been feeling well for the *(past, passed)* few days, but I'm sure it's just a *(miner, minor)* bug.

3. We don't see many people who *(pedal, peddle, petal)* products door-to-door these days.

4. A *(miner, minor)* who does not take precautions is likely to get lung disease.

5. It's an uncomfortable situation when someone's *(personal, personnel)* hygiene leaves a little to be desired.

6. As Rohan *(past, passed)* his old girlfriend's house, he unconsciously hit the brake *(pedal, peddle, petal)*.

7. The *(peace, piece)* demonstrations of the 1960s affected public opinion about the Vietnam War.

8. This poor flower has just one *(pedal, peddle, petal)* left clinging to its stem.

Model

Model the following sentences to practice using the words *passed* and *past* correctly.

> Soon silence will have passed into legend.
> —Jean Arp, "Sacred Silence"

> The future, according to some scientists, will be exactly like the past, only far more expensive.
> —John Sladek

Related Skills Activities

■ ***SkillsBook***
Using the Right Word 4, p. 61

Answers

1. personnel
2. past
   minor
3. peddle
4. miner
5. personal
6. passed
   pedal
7. peace
8. petal

poor, pour, pore ■ *Poor* means "needy or pitiable." *Pour* means "to cause to flow in a stream." A *pore* is an opening in the skin.

Tough exams on late spring days make my poor pores pour sweat.

principal, principle ■ As an adjective, *principal* means "primary." As a noun, it can mean "a school administrator" or "a sum of money." *Principle* means "idea or doctrine."

His principal concern is fitness. (adjective) The principal retired. (noun)
During the first year of a loan, you pay more interest than principal. (noun)
The principle of *caveat emptor* is "Let the buyer beware."

quiet, quit, quite ■ *Quiet* is the opposite of "noisy." *Quit* means "to stop." *Quite* means "completely or entirely."

quote, quotation ■ *Quote* is a verb; *quotation* is a noun.

The quotation I used was from Woody Allen. You may quote me on that.

real, really, very ■ Do not use *real* in place of the adverbs *very* or *really*.

Mother's cake is usually very (not *real*) tasty, but this one is really stale!

right, write, wright, rite ■ *Right* means "correct or proper"; it also refers to that which a person has a legal claim to, as in copyright. *Write* means "to inscribe or record." A *wright* is a person who makes or builds something. *Rite* refers to a ritual or ceremonial act.

Write this down: It is the right of the shipwright to perform the rite of christening—breaking a bottle of champagne on the stern of the ship.

ring, wring ■ *Ring* means "encircle" or "to sound by striking." *Wring* means "to squeeze or twist."

At the beach, Grandma would ring her head with a large scarf. Once, it blew into the sea, so she had me wring it out.

scene, seen ■ *Scene* refers to the setting or location where something happens; it also may mean "sight or spectacle." *Seen* is a form of the verb "see."

Serena had seen her boyfriend making a scene; she cringed.

seam, seem ■ *Seam* (noun) is a line formed by connecting two pieces. *Seem* (verb) means "to appear to exist."

The ragged seams in his old coat seem to match the creases in his face.

set, sit ■ *Set* means "to place." *Sit* means "to put the body in a seated position." *Set* is transitive; *sit* is intransitive. (See **716.1**.)

How can you just sit there and watch as I set all these chairs in place?

Grammar Practice

Using the Right Word 8

poor, pour, pore; quiet, quit, quite; scene, seen; seam, seem

Select the correct word from the list above to complete each sentence.

Example: Yellow police tape often surrounds the _____ of a crime.
scene

1. Many teenagers know what happens when too much sebum clogs a _____.

2. Simon _____ his job last month.

3. He was _____ fortunate to find another one so soon.

4. Three more years until graduation might _____ like a long time—but to your parents, it's not.

5. Grandma says she is _____ in terms of cash but rich in many other ways.

6. Have you ever _____ a tornado?

7. Sometimes the bus is actually a _____ place to think.

8. The mistake most first-timers make when applying wallpaper is not matching a _____.

9. The pitcher doesn't have a spout, so it's difficult to _____ from it.

▶ Model

Model the following sentences to practice using the words *quiet* and *quite* correctly.

Full bottles are quiet; it's the empty ones that make all the noise.
—Chinese proverb

Nothing is quite as bad as being without privacy and lonely at the same time.
—Alexander Theroux

Right Word

Related Skills Activities

■ **SkillsBook**
Using the Right Word 4, p. 61

Answers

1. pore
2. quit
3. quite
4. seem
5. poor
6. seen
7. quiet
8. seam
9. pour

sight, cite, site ■ *Sight* means "the act of seeing"; a *sight* is what is seen. *Cite* means "to quote" or "to summon," as before a court. *Site* means "location."

> In her report, the general contractor cited several problems at the downtown job site. For one, the loading area was a chaotic sight.

sole, soul ■ *Sole* means "single, only one"; *sole* also refers to the bottom surface of the foot. *Soul* refers to the spiritual part of a person.

> As the sole inhabitant of the island, he put his heart and soul into his farming.

stationary, stationery ■ *Stationary* means "not movable"; *stationery* refers to the paper and envelopes used to write letters.

steal, steel ■ *Steal* means "to take something without permission"; *steel* is a type of metal.

than, then ■ *Than* is used in a comparison; *then* tells when.

> Abigail shouted that her big brother was bigger than my big brother. Then she ran away.

their, there, they're ■ *Their* is a possessive personal pronoun. *There* is an adverb used to point out location. *They're* is the contraction for "they are."

> They're a well-dressed couple. Do you see them there, with their matching jackets?

threw, through ■ *Threw* is the past tense of "throw." *Through* means "from beginning to end."

> Through seven innings, Egor threw just seven strikes.

to, too, two ■ *To* is a preposition that can mean "in the direction of." *To* is also used to form an infinitive. (See **726.2**) *Too* means "also" or "very." *Two* is a number.

vain, vane, vein ■ *Vain* means "valueless or fruitless"; it may also mean "holding a high regard for oneself." *Vane* is a flat piece of material set up to show which way the wind blows. *Vein* refers to a blood vessel or a mineral deposit.

> The vain prospector, boasting about the vein of silver he'd uncovered, paused to look up at the turning weather vane.

vary, very ■ *Vary* means "to change." *Very* means "to a high degree."

> Though the weather may vary from day to day, generally, it is very pleasant.

Grammar Practice

Using the Right Word 9

steal, steel; than, then; their, there, they're; threw, through; to, too, two

 Read the following paragraphs. If a numbered word is used incorrectly, write the correct word. If it's correct as is, write "OK."

Example: 1.Then

Sometimes it's not practical to build a bridge by sinking supports into the ground. **(1)** Than a suspension bridge is the answer. Early suspension bridges were made of rope and wood. Today, **(2)** their roadways supported by cables made of thousands of individual **(3)** steal wires bound tightly together. Huge main cables rest on top of high towers and extend from one end of the bridge **(4)** to the other. Anchorage systems at both ends are embedded in rock or concrete blocks. The cables are spread over a large area for **(5)** too reasons: to distribute **(6)** they're load, and to prevent them from breaking free.

Suspension bridges can span distances far longer **(7)** then any other kind of bridge. Currently, the longest bridge (at about 6,500 feet) is over the Akashi Strait in Japan. Since it is an earthquake-prone area **(8)** their, the bridge must withstand great forces of nature. As with most other suspension bridges, it must remain standing as 150-mph winds blast **(9)** threw its cables, **(10)** too. For these reasons, suspension bridges are built to be somewhat flexible. Fortunately, this type of bridge is usually quite pleasing to the eye, as well.

◀ Model

Model the following sentences to practice using the words *then* and *than* correctly.

> All you need in this life is ignorance and confidence; then success is sure.
> —Mark Twain

> You can no more win a war than you can win an earthquake.
> —Jeannette Rankin

Right Word

Related Skills Activities

■ **SkillsBook**
Using the Right Word 5, p. 62

 ## Answers

1. Then
2. they're
3. steel
4. OK
5. two
6. their
7. than
8. there
9. through
10. OK

696

vial, vile ■ *A vial* is a small container for liquid. *Vile* is an adjective meaning "foul, despicable."

It's a vile job, but someone has to clean these lab vials.

waist, waste ■ *Waist* is the part of the body just above the hips. The verb *waste* means "to spend or use carelessly" or "to wear away or decay"; the noun *waste* refers to material that is unused or useless.

Her waist is small because she wastes no opportunity to exercise.

wait, weight ■ *Wait* means "to stay somewhere expecting something." *Weight* refers to a degree or unit of heaviness.

ware, wear, where ■ *Ware* refers to a product that is sold; *wear* means "to have on or to carry on one's body"; *where* asks "in what place?" or "in what situation?"

The designer boasted, "Where can anybody wear my ware? Anywhere."

way, weigh ■ *Way* means "path or route." *Weigh* means "to measure weight" or "to have a certain heaviness."

My dogs weigh too much. The best way to reduce is a daily run in the park.

weather, whether ■ *Weather* refers to the condition of the atmosphere. *Whether* refers to a possibility.

Due to the weather, the coach wondered whether he should cancel the meet.

which, that ■ Use *which* to refer to objects or animals in a nonrestrictive clause (set off with commas). Use *that* to refer to objects or animals in a restrictive clause. (For more information about these types of clauses, see **612.2**.)

The birds, which stay in the area all winter, know where the feeders are located. The food that attracts the most birds is sunflower seed.

who, whom ■ Use *who* to refer to people. *Who* is used as the subject of a verb in an independent clause or in a relative clause. *Whom* is used as the object of a preposition or as a direct object.

To whom do we owe our thanks for these pizzas? And who ordered anchovies?

who's, whose ■ *Who's* is the contraction for "who is." *Whose* is a pronoun that can show possession or ownership.

Cody, whose car is new, will drive. Who's going to read the map?

your, you're ■ *Your* is a possessive pronoun. *You're* is the contraction for "you are."

Take your boots if you're going out in that snow.

Grammar Practice

Using the Right Word 10

waist, waste; wait, weight; way, weigh; who's, whose; your, you're

 Write the correct choice from those given in parentheses.

Example: Although Mariah and Sharlene have the same *(waist, waste)* measurement, they have very different body types.
  waist

1. Ms. Hull, *(who's, whose)* dog ran away last week, is offering a reward for its safe return.

2. I have a friend who refuses to *(wait, weight)* for me if I am late.

3. Can you bring *(your, you're)* CD's to my party?

4. Some people gain *(wait, weight)* over the winter holidays.

5. The grocery store cashier must *(way, weigh)* fresh fruits and vegetables to get a price.

6. "Gee, *(your, you're)* swell," said Biff to Bunny.

7. The lost tourists asked if we knew the *(way, weigh)* to the beach.

8. Kirk Swenson, *(who's, whose)* a volunteer firefighter, was able to help when Dillon fainted.

9. Is throwing a clock in a landfill a *(waist, waste)* of time?

▶ Model

Model the following sentences to practice using the words *your* and *you're* correctly.

Skiing combines outdoor fun with knocking down trees with your face.
—Dave Barry

The trouble with the rat race is that even if you win, you're still a rat.
—Lily Tomlin

Related Skills Activities

■ *SkillsBook*
Using the Right Word 5, p. 62

Answers

1. whose
2. wait
3. your
4. weight
5. weigh
6. you're
7. way
8. who's
9. waste

Test Prep!

Write the letter of the line in which an underlined word is used incorrectly. If all the words are correct, choose "D."

1
Ⓐ I don't really enjoy my <u>biannual</u> visits to the dental hygienist.
Ⓑ During my last visit, the dentist had <u>scene</u> a cavity.
Ⓒ She said, "<u>It's</u> best that we fill it right away."
Ⓓ All are used correctly.

2
Ⓐ Dale always <u>seams</u> surprised at the yield from his garden.
Ⓑ He harvests a huge <u>amount</u> of produce every year.
Ⓒ It never goes to <u>waste</u>, though; he donates it to the food pantry.
Ⓓ All are used correctly.

3
Ⓐ Try to eat foods made from <u>whole</u> grains.
Ⓑ They are better for you <u>than</u> processed foods are.
Ⓒ Some people find that <u>they're</u> also tastier.
Ⓓ All are used correctly.

4
Ⓐ "Is it difficult to <u>teach</u> young adults how to drive?" Shayla asked.
Ⓑ "It can be," the instructor said, "but I can <u>brake</u> if necessary."
Ⓒ He pointed to an extra <u>petal</u> on the floor by the passenger seat.
Ⓓ All are used correctly.

5
Ⓐ Keiko asked Deepak to <u>borrow</u> her some of his DVD's.
Ⓑ Deepak said he would give his <u>assent</u> on one condition.
Ⓒ "You must let me use some of <u>your</u> CD's," he said.
Ⓓ All are used correctly.

6
Ⓐ We went to the humane society to <u>adopt</u> a kitten.
Ⓑ It was hard to choose from <u>between</u> the nine or ten there.
Ⓒ We ended up taking <u>two</u> kittens home with us.
Ⓓ All are used correctly.

7
Ⓐ Monique could <u>hear</u> her brothers fighting.
Ⓑ "Please <u>quit</u> that!" she shouted.
Ⓒ "I need <u>piece</u> right now!"
Ⓓ All are used correctly.

8
Ⓐ No one likes to have to <u>wait</u> in line.
Ⓑ It's usually a <u>miner</u> inconvenience, but it still isn't fun.
Ⓒ In fact, it can be <u>quite</u> aggravating.
Ⓓ All are used correctly.

9
Ⓐ The music teacher <u>passed</u> out the lyric sheets.
Ⓑ He said, "Let's try an initial read-through <u>all together</u>."
Ⓒ A <u>number</u> of students did not participate.
Ⓓ All are used correctly.

10
Ⓐ Alyce took the team's loss <u>bad</u>.
Ⓑ She <u>threw</u> the volleyball up into the stands.
Ⓒ It hit some <u>poor</u> guy in the head.
Ⓓ All are used correctly.

11
Ⓐ The man in the desert thought he would <u>die</u> of thirst.
Ⓑ The <u>scene</u> before him was unbelievable: water in the distance.
Ⓒ Fortunately, it was not just an <u>allusion</u> of water.
Ⓓ All are used correctly.

12
Ⓐ When Francisco finished lunch, he asked, "<u>May</u> I be excused?"
Ⓑ "Wouldn't you like another <u>piece</u> of chicken?" Grandma asked.
Ⓒ "I couldn't <u>except</u> another bite," he said.
Ⓓ All are used correctly.

13
Ⓐ I am working <u>fewer</u> hours now than I did over the summer.
Ⓑ It has had a definite <u>affect</u> on my spending.
Ⓒ Sometimes I don't have a <u>cent</u> to my name!
Ⓓ All are used correctly.

14
Ⓐ Our neighbors often leave <u>their</u> dogs outside in a kennel.
Ⓑ They (the <u>latter</u>) will bark and bark and bark.
Ⓒ I think they must be <u>bored</u>.
Ⓓ All are used correctly.

15
Ⓐ Alejandra knows how to play the <u>steel</u> drums.
Ⓑ She plays them very <u>good</u>.
Ⓒ Last spring, her band played at the <u>capitol</u> building.
Ⓓ All are used correctly.

16
Ⓐ <u>Who's</u> supposed to take the garbage out?
Ⓑ We can't add anything <u>further</u> to this bag.
Ⓒ It must <u>way</u> a ton already.
Ⓓ All are used correctly.

Answers

1. B
2. A
3. D
4. C
5. A
6. B
7. C
8. B

9. D
10. A
11. C
12. C
13. B
14. D
15. B
16. C

Related Skills Activities

■ *SkillsBook*
  Review: Using the Right Word, pp. 63–64
  Posttest: Using the Right Word, p. 201
  Final Proofreading Posttest—Part 1 and 2, pp. 201–205

Parts of Speech

Words in the English language are used in eight different ways. For this reason, there are eight parts of speech.

700.1 Noun

A word that names a person, a place, a thing, or an idea
> Governor Smith-Jones   Oregon   hospital   religion

700.2 Pronoun

A word used in place of a noun
> I   you   she   him   who   everyone   these   neither
> theirs   themselves   which

700.3 Verb

A word that expresses action or state of being
> float   sniff   discover   seem   were   was

700.4 Adjective

A word that describes a noun or a pronoun
> young   big   grim   Canadian   longer

700.5 Adverb

A word that describes a verb, an adjective, or another adverb
> briefly   forward   regally   slowly   better

700.6 Preposition

The first word or words in a prepositional phrase (which functions as an adjective or an adverb)
> away from   under   before   with   for   out of

700.7 Conjunction

A word that connects other words or groups of words
> and   but   although   because   either, or   so

700.8 Interjection

A word that shows strong emotion or surprise
> Oh no!   Yipes!   Good grief!   Well, . . .

Noun

A **noun** is a word that names something: a person, a place, a thing, or an idea.
> governor   Oregon   hospital   Buddhism   love

Classes of Nouns

The five classes of nouns are *proper, common, concrete, abstract,* and *collective.*

701.1 Proper Noun

A **proper noun** names a particular person, place, thing, or idea. Proper nouns are always capitalized.
> Jackie Robinson   Brooklyn   World Series
> Christianity   Ebbets Field   Hinduism

701.2 Common Noun

A **common noun** does not name a particular person, place, thing, or idea. Common nouns are not capitalized.
> person   woman   president   park   baseball   government

701.3 Concrete Noun

A **concrete noun** names a thing that is tangible (can be seen, touched, heard, smelled, or tasted). Concrete nouns are either proper or common.
> child   Grand Canyon   music   aroma   fireworks   Becky

701.4 Abstract Noun

An **abstract noun** names an idea, a condition, or a feeling—in other words, something that cannot be touched, smelled, tasted, seen, or heard.
> New Deal   greed   poverty   progress   freedom   awe

701.5 Collective Noun

A **collective noun** names a group or a unit.
> United States   Portland Cementers   team   crowd   community

Parts of Speech

Related Skills Activities

- ***GrammarSnap***
  Nouns

- ***SkillsBook***
  Pretest: Nouns, p. 69
  Classes of Nouns 1 and 2, pp. 70–71

Forms of Nouns

Nouns are grouped according to their *number, gender,* and *case.*

702.1 Number of a Noun

Number indicates whether the noun is singular or plural.

A **singular noun** refers to one person, place, thing, or idea.

actor   stadium   Canadian   bully   truth   child   person

A **plural noun** refers to more than one person, place, thing, or idea.

actors   stadiums   Canadians   bullies   truths   children   people

702.2 Gender of a Noun

Gender indicates whether a noun is masculine, feminine, neuter, or indefinite.

Masculine: uncle   brother   men   bull   rooster   stallion

Feminine: aunt   sister   women   cow   hen   filly

Neuter (without gender): tree   cobweb   flying fish   closet

Indefinite (masculine or feminine): president   plumber   doctor   parent

702.3 Case of a Noun

Case tells how nouns are related to other words used with them. There are three cases: *nominative, possessive,* and *objective.*

■ A **nominative case** noun can be the subject of a clause.

> Patsy's heart was beating very wildly beneath his jacket. . . . That black horse there owed something to the orphan he had made.
> —Paul Dunbar, "The Finish of Patsy Barnes"

A nominative noun can also be a predicate noun (or predicate nominative), which follows a "be" verb *(am, is, are, was, were, be, being, been)* and renames the subject. In the sentence below, *type* renames *moth.*

> The brown moth was a different type than those we usually saw near our porch light.

■ A **possessive case** noun shows possession or ownership.

> The sweater's collar could be pulled up when the cold wind blew.

■ An **objective case** noun can be a direct object, an indirect object, or an object of the preposition.

> Marna always gives Mylo science-fiction books for his birthday.

(Mylo is the indirect object and *books* is the direct object of the verb "gives." *Birthday* is the object of the preposition "for.")

Grammar Practice

Nouns

- Classes of Nouns
- Gender of Nouns

 For each underlined noun, write its class (there are at least two classes for each) and gender, as shown.

Example: When I was a child, my family vacationed at <u>Parker Lake</u>.
    class: proper, concrete   gender: neuter

1. I was one of nine children in my <u>family</u>.

2. All 11 of us took the three-hour trip in our <u>Country Squire</u>—a station wagon with "wood" panels on the sides.

3. You can imagine that the <u>time</u> passed rather slowly on that drive.

4. My littlest <u>sister</u> would sit in my mom's lap.

5. The front bench seat would also accommodate <u>Dad</u> and another sibling.

6. The three oldest kids—two <u>boys</u> and a girl, all teenagers—got the middle seat.

7. The back of the station wagon had a couple of seats that folded up from the middle, and four <u>kids</u> sat there.

8. What a <u>relief</u> to finally get out of the car!

9. We spent a <u>week</u> at the cabin before piling in again for the long ride home.

Model

Model the following sentence to practice using proper, abstract nouns.

> Radical historians now tell the story of Thanksgiving from the point of view of the turkey.
> —Mason Cooley

Related Skills Activities

- **GrammarSnap**
  Nouns

- **SkillsBook**
  Nominative, Possessive, Objective Cases of Nouns, p. 73
  Subject-Verb Agreement 2, p. 146

Answers

1. class: common, concrete, collective   gender: indefinite
2. class: proper, concrete   gender: neuter
3. class: common, abstract   gender: neuter
4. class: common, concrete   gender: feminine
5. class: proper, concrete   gender: masculine
6. class: common, concrete   gender: masculine
7. class: common, concrete   gender: indefinite
8. class: common, abstract   gender: neuter
9. class: common, abstract   gender: neuter

Pronoun

A **pronoun** is a word used in place of a noun.

I, you, she, it, which, that, themselves, whoever, me, he, they, mine, ours

The three types of pronouns are *simple, compound,* and *phrasal.*

Simple: I, you, he, she, it, we, they, who, what

Compound: myself, someone, anybody, everything, itself, whoever

Phrasal: one another, each other

All pronouns have **antecedents.** An antecedent is the noun that the pronoun refers to or replaces.

Ambrosch was considered the important person in the family. Mrs. Shimerda and Ántonia always deferred to him, though he was often surly with them and contemptuous toward his father.   —Willa Cather, *My Ántonia*

(*Ambrosch* is the antecedent of *him, he,* and *his.*)

NOTE: Each pronoun must agree with its antecedent. (See page **756.**)

704.1 Classes of Pronouns

The six classes of pronouns are *personal, reflexive and intensive, reciprocal, relative, indefinite, interrogative,* and *demonstrative.*

Personal

I, me, my, mine / we, us, our, ours
you, your, yours / they, them, their, theirs
he, him, his, she, her, hers, it, its

Reflexive and Intensive

myself, yourself, himself, herself, itself, ourselves, yourselves, themselves

Reciprocal   Relative

each other, one another   what, who, whose, whom, which, that

Indefinite

all	both	everything	nobody	several
another	each	few	none	some
any	each one	many	no one	somebody
anybody	either	most	nothing	someone
anyone	everybody	much	one	something
anything	everyone	neither	other	such

Interrogative

who, whose, whom, which, what

Demonstrative

this, that, these, those

Grammar Practice

Pronouns 1

■ Antecedents

 For the following paragraphs, write the antecedent of each underlined pronoun.

Example: 1. Margaret Knight

In the 1850s, it was not uncommon for children to work in factories. One of these children, Margaret Knight, was only 12 years old when **(1)** she saw a coworker suffer a serious injury from a machine that wouldn't stop. She invented a stop-motion device to prevent **(2)** it from happening again.

Margaret went on to invent a lot of other things, but she is probably best known for her 1868 invention, **(3)** which she thought of while working in a paper-bag factory. **(4)** It was an addition to the machines that made the paper bags. This new part automatically folded and glued the bags so **(5)** they had square bottoms. Workmen who were installing the part didn't want to listen to a woman's advice, but **(6)** they had no choice. Of course, the part worked, and this type of paper bag is still in use today.

Margaret Knight patented **(7)** her invention and eventually received patents for 25 other inventions. Among **(8)** these were a numbering machine and a window frame and sash. Upon her death in 1914, Margaret was remembered as "the female Edison."

 Model

Model the following sentence to practice using a pronoun and an antecedent in the same sentence.

I never think of the future—it comes soon enough.

—Albert Einstein

Related Skills Activities

■ **Basic Grammar and Writing**
Pronouns, p. 536

■ *GrammarSnap*
Relative Pronouns; Reflexive and Reciprocal Pronouns

■ *SkillsBook*
Pretest: Pronouns, p. 75
Types of Pronouns, p. 76
Functions of Pronouns, p. 80

Answers

1. Margaret Knight
2. a serious injury
3. her 1868 invention
4. her 1868 invention
5. the bags
6. workmen
7. Margaret Knight
8. other inventions

706.1 Personal Pronoun

A **personal pronoun** can take the place of any noun.

Our coach made her **point loud and clear when** she **raised** her **voice.**

- A **reflexive pronoun** is formed by adding *-self* or *-selves* to a personal pronoun. A reflexive pronoun can be a direct object, an indirect object, an object of the preposition, or a predicate nominative.

   Miss Sally Sunshine loves herself. (direct object of *loves*)

   Tomisha does not seem herself **today.** (predicate nominative)

- An **intensive pronoun** is a reflexive pronoun that intensifies, or emphasizes, the noun or pronoun it refers to.

   Leo himself **taught his children to invest their lives in others.**

706.2 Relative Pronoun

A **relative pronoun** relates or connects an adjective clause to the noun or pronoun it modifies.

Students who study regularly get the best grades. **Surprise!**

The dance, which we had looked forward to for weeks, **was canceled.**

(The relative pronoun *who* relates the adjective clause to *students; which* relates the adjective clause to *dance.*)

706.3 Reciprocal Pronoun

An **reciprocal pronoun** refers to the individual members of a plural antecedent. It expresses mutual actions or relationships between those members.

The playgoers enjoyed talking with one another **about the amazing performance.**

706.4 Indefinite Pronoun

An **indefinite pronoun** refers to unnamed or unknown people or things.

I don't know anybody **who would come to my rescue on a cold, rainy night.**

706.5 Interrogative Pronoun

An **interrogative pronoun** asks a question.

Who **is the oldest among you?** What **does he know that you would like to learn?**

706.6 Demonstrative Pronoun

A **demonstrative pronoun** points out people, places, or things without naming them.

This **shouldn't be too hard.** That **looks about right.**

These **are the best ones.** Those **ought to be thrown out.**

NOTE: When one of these words precedes a noun, it functions as an adjective, not a pronoun. (See **728.1**.)

That **movie bothers me.** (*That* is an adjective.)

Grammar Practice

Pronouns 2

- Personal Pronouns (Reflexive and Intensive)
- Indefinite Pronouns
- Interrogative Pronouns

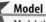 **Identify each underlined pronoun as *reflexive, intensive, indefinite,* or *interrogative.***

Example: Who **was the comic chosen to host** *Late Night* **in 1993?**
   interrogative

1. Many **applied for the position, but Conan O'Brien was the one selected for the comedy-variety show.**

2. **O'Brien got his comedy career going for** himself **at Harvard, where he was president of the** *Harvard Lampoon.*

3. **Did** anyone **there realize he was headed for fame?**

4. What **did Conan** himself **see in his future?**

5. **In the late '80s and early '90s,** everybody **loved his work as a writer for** *Saturday Night Live* **and** *The Simpsons.*

6. **Then, in 1993, he found** himself **hosting a new late-night talk show.**

7. Which **talk shows has he hosted since he left** *Late Night*?

8. **I** myself **see a long, successful future for Conan.**

 ### Model

Model the following sentences to practice using reflexive and intensive pronouns.

Never trust anything that can think for itself if you can't see where it keeps its brain.
   —J. K. Rowling, *Harry Potter and the Chamber of Secrets*

I was always looking outside myself for strength and confidence, but it comes from within.
   —Anna Freud

Related Skills Activities

- **Basic Grammar and Writing**
   Create Suspense with Indefinite Pronouns, p. 537

- *GrammarSnap*
   Relative Pronouns

- *SkillsBook*
   Personal Pronouns, p. 77
   Reciprocal Pronouns, p.85
   Relative Pronouns, p. 86
   Indefinite, Interrogative, and Demonstrative Pronouns, 87
   Subject-Verb Agreement 2, p. 150

Answers

1. indefinite
2. reflexive
3. indefinite
4. interrogative
   intensive
5. indefinite
6. reflexive
7. interrogative
8. intensive

Forms of Personal Pronouns

The form of a personal pronoun indicates its *number* (singular or plural), its *person* (first, second, third), its *case* (nominative, possessive, or objective), and its *gender* (masculine, feminine, or neuter).

708.1 Number of a Pronoun

Personal pronouns are singular or plural. The singular personal pronouns include *my, him, he, she, it.* The plural personal pronouns include *we, you, them, our.* (*You* can be singular or plural.) Notice in the caption below that the first *you* is singular and the second *you* is plural.

"Larry, you need to keep all four tires on the road when turning. Are you still with us back there?"

708.2 Person of a Pronoun

The **person** of a pronoun indicates whether the person, place, thing, or idea represented by the pronoun is speaking, is spoken to, or is spoken about.

- **First person** is used in place of the name of the speaker or speakers.

  "We don't do things like that," says Pa; "we're just and honest people. . . . I don't skip debts."

  —Jesse Stuart, "Split Cherry Tree"

- **Second-person** pronouns name the person or persons spoken to.

  "If you play through the rainstorm, will your uniform and instrument be ready for your next performance?" Arlene asked.

- **Third-person** pronouns name the person or thing spoken about.

  She had hardly realized the news, further than to understand that she had been brought . . . face to face with something unexpected and final. It did not even occur to her to ask for any explanation.

  —Joseph Conrad, "The Idiots"

Grammar Practice

Pronouns 3

- Number of a Pronoun
- Person of a Pronoun

 Identify the person and number of each underlined pronoun.

Example: "Rosa and Ruby, <u>your</u> bus is coming!" Mrs. Genara shouted.
second person plural

1. <u>They</u> missed the bus.

2. The bus driver said <u>he</u> couldn't wait for <u>them</u>.

3. Mrs. Genara was mad that they'd missed <u>it</u> and she would have to drive Rosa and Ruby to school.

4. As they rode in the car, Rosa said, "It's not <u>my</u> fault."

5. "Well, <u>I</u> wasn't ready yet!" Ruby pouted.

6. "Why does it take <u>you</u> so long to get ready, Ruby?" Mrs. Genara asked.

7. "<u>She</u> never gets up on time," Rosa said.

8. "Don't be mad at <u>us</u>, Mom," Ruby said.

9. "Do <u>me</u> a favor," Mrs. Genara said, "and try to be on time from now on."

10. "<u>We</u> will," the girls said.

11. They grabbed <u>their</u> books and ran into the school.

Model

Write a few sentences using the following forms of personal pronouns: *first person plural, second person singular,* and *third person singular.* Identify each one.

Parts of Speech

Related Skills Activities

- **SkillsBook**
  Number and Person of Personal Pronouns, p. 78

Answers

1. third person plural
2. third person singular
   third person plural
3. third person singular
4. first person singular
5. first person singular
6. second person singular
7. third person singular
8. first person plural
9. first person singular
10. first person plural
11. third person plural

710

710.1 Case of a Pronoun

The **case** of each pronoun tells how it is related to the other words used with it. There are three cases: *nominative, possessive,* and *objective.*

- A **nominative case** pronoun can be the subject of a clause. The following are nominative forms: *I, you, he, she, it, we, they.*

  I like life when things go well. You must live life in order to love life.

A nominative pronoun is a *predicate nominative* if it follows a "be" verb (*am, is, are, was, were, be, being, been*) or another linking verb (*appear, become, feel,* and so on) and renames the subject.

  "Oh, it's only she who scared me just now," said Mama to Papa, glancing over her shoulder.
  "Yes, it is I," said Mai in a superior tone.

- **Possessive case** pronouns show possession or ownership. Apostrophes, however, are not used with personal pronouns. (Pronouns in the possessive case can also be classified as adjectives.)

  But as I placed my hand upon his shoulder, there came a strong shudder over his whole person.
  —Edgar Allan Poe, "The Fall of the House of Usher"

- An **objective case** pronoun can be a direct object, an indirect object, or an object of the preposition.

  The kids loved it! We lit a campfire for them and told them old ghost stories. (*It* is the direct object of the verb *loved. Them* is the object of the preposition *for* and the indirect object of the verb *told.*)

Number, Person, and Case of Personal Pronouns

	Nominative	Possessive	Objective
First Person Singular	I	my, mine	me
Second Person Singular	you	your, yours	you
Third Person Singular	he	his	him
	she	her, hers	her
	it	its	it
	Nominative	Possessive	Objective
First Person Plural	we	our, ours	us
Second Person Plural	you	your, yours	you
Third Person Plural	they	their, theirs	them

710.2 Gender of a Pronoun

Gender indicates whether a pronoun is masculine, feminine, or neuter.

Masculine: he him his   Feminine: she her hers
Neuter (without gender): it its

Grammar Practice

Pronouns 4

■ Case of a Pronoun

 Identify each underlined pronoun as *nominative, possessive,* or *objective.*

Example: 1. possessive

Colton, my sister's boyfriend, was eating food from **(1)** <u>our</u> refrigerator, and it was also **(2)** <u>he</u> who just walked in our front door without knocking. Maybe **(3)** <u>we</u> ought to start charging **(4)** <u>him</u> an entry fee.

"Make **(5)** <u>yourself</u> comfortable," **(6)** <u>my</u> brother, Gavin, said.

"Are **(7)** <u>you</u> being sarcastic?" Colton asked dully. He pulled **(8)** <u>his</u> head out of the fridge and closed **(9)** <u>it</u>.

"I am merely making a suggestion," Gavin said. "In fact, is there anything **(10)** <u>I</u> can get for **(11)** <u>you</u>?"

"No," he said, "**(12)** <u>your</u> sister is already getting **(13)** <u>me</u> a drink from the basement."

"How kind of **(14)** <u>her</u>," Gavin snickered.

"Yeah, **(15)** <u>she</u>'s great," Colton said.

 Model

Use the following pronouns in a brief dialogue: *it, our, they,* and *you.* Identify the case of each one.

Related Skills Activities

■ **SkillsBook**
Number and Person of Personal Pronouns, p. 78
Nominative, Possessive, Objective Cases of Pronouns 1 and 2, pp. 80–82

Answers

1. possessive
2. nominative
3. nominative
4. objective
5. objective
6. possessive
7. nominative
8. possessive
9. objective
10. nominative
11. objective
12. possessive
13. objective
14. objective
15. nominative

Parts of Speech

Test Prep!

Read the following paragraphs. Write the letter of the part of speech of each underlined part from the choices given on the next page.

It took months to clear away the rubble remaining after the collapse of the <u>World Trade Center</u> in 2001. Once that was done, however, the rebuilding could begin. <u>What</u> could possibly replace <u>it</u>? An international contest to create a new design for the site resulted in the selection of architect Daniel Libeskind's ambitious plan. <u>His</u> design for the 16-acre site features a hanging garden and several new buildings.

The focal point of Libeskind's design is the <u>Freedom Tower</u>, topping out at a symbolic 1,776 feet. As it emits light skyward, it will remind people of the Statue of Liberty's torch—another beacon of freedom. With assistance from architect <u>David Childs</u>, the building was redesigned to use environmentally friendly <u>materials</u> and be a model of energy efficiency. By 2013, the Freedom Tower will open <u>its</u> doors to the world.

<u>People</u> will be able to view key 9/11 artifacts at the Memorial Museum. <u>It</u> will be adjacent to the World Trade Center Memorial. "Reflecting <u>Absence</u>," as the memorial is known, was the winning entry in the <u>World Trade Center Site Memorial Competition</u>. It consists of two pools recessed in the footprints of the twin towers. Visitors will descend from ground level into the memorial <u>itself</u> on ramps. <u>They</u> will enter a cool, dark space where a thin curtain of water falls from above into each pool. The names of the tragedy's <u>victims</u> will encircle the pools, and <u>everyone</u> will recall the enormity of the disaster.

(1) ... (16)

1.
(A) proper abstract noun
(B) proper concrete noun
(C) common abstract noun
(D) common concrete noun

2.
(A) intensive pronoun
(B) reflexive pronoun
(C) interrogative pronoun
(D) masculine pronoun

3.
(A) reflexive pronoun
(B) nominative pronoun
(C) possessive pronoun
(D) objective pronoun

4.
(A) intensive pronoun
(B) nominative pronoun
(C) possessive pronoun
(D) objective pronoun

5.
(A) antecedent of "it" (in the next sentence)
(B) objective pronoun
(C) indefinite pronoun
(D) common abstract noun

6.
(A) feminine noun
(B) masculine noun
(C) neuter noun
(D) indefinite noun

7.
(A) feminine noun
(B) masculine noun
(C) neuter noun
(D) indefinite noun

8.
(A) plural objective pronoun
(B) plural possessive pronoun
(C) singular objective pronoun
(D) singular possessive pronoun

9.
(A) proper abstract noun
(B) proper concrete noun
(C) common abstract noun
(D) common concrete noun

10.
(A) antecedent of "artifacts"
(B) nominative pronoun
(C) possessive pronoun
(D) objective pronoun

11.
(A) proper abstract noun
(B) proper concrete noun
(C) common abstract noun
(D) common concrete noun

12.
(A) proper abstract noun
(B) proper concrete noun
(C) common abstract noun
(D) common concrete noun

13.
(A) intensive pronoun
(B) reflexive pronoun
(C) interrogative pronoun
(D) feminine pronoun

14.
(A) first person plural pronoun
(B) third person plural pronoun
(C) third person singular pronoun
(D) second person plural pronoun

15.
(A) proper abstract noun
(B) proper concrete noun
(C) common abstract noun
(D) common concrete noun

16.
(A) intensive pronoun
(B) reflexive pronoun
(C) interrogative pronoun
(D) indefinite pronoun

Related Skills Activities

■ **SkillsBook**
Review: Nouns, p. 74
Review: Pronouns 1, p. 83
Review: Pronouns 2, p. 88
Posttest: Nouns, p. 206
Posttest: Pronouns, p. 207

Answers

1. B
2. C
3. D
4. C
5. A
6. B
7. C
8. D
9. D
10. B

11. C (The word *absence* by itself is a common, abstract noun. The full title of the memorial is a proper, abstract noun, so students may choose A for their answer.)
12. B
13. A
14. B
15. D
16. D

Verb

A **verb** is a word that expresses action (*run, carried, declared*) or state of being (*is, are, seemed*).

Classes of Verbs

714.1 Linking Verbs

A **linking verb** links the subject to a noun or an adjective in the predicate.

> In the outfield, the boy felt confident.
> He was the best fielder around.

Common Linking Verbs						
is	are	was	were	be	been	am

Additional Linking Verbs						
smell	seem	grow	become	appear	sound	
taste	feel	get	remain	stay	look	turn

714.2 Auxiliary Verbs

Auxiliary verbs, or helping verbs, are used to form some of the **tenses** (718.3), the **mood** (724.1), and the **voice** (722.2) of the main verb. (In the example below, the auxiliary verbs are in red; the main verbs are in blue.)

> The mud had flowed quickly down the mountain, covering everything in its path. By the time the rain had stopped, the rescue crews were faced with the daunting task of slogging through the mud to help those who had survived.

Common Auxiliary Verbs							
is	was	being	did	have	would	shall	might
am	were	been	does	had	could	can	must
are	be	do	has	should	will	may	

Grammar Practice

Verbs 1
- Linking Verbs
- Auxiliary Verbs

 Write whether each underlined word is a linking verb or an auxiliary verb.

Example: Yvette <u>is</u> a woman who loves to garden.
  linking verb

1. She <u>can</u> get just about anything to grow.

2. Several of her friends <u>are</u> helping her tend a vegetable garden this summer.

3. They <u>seem</u> happy to do it—especially since they <u>will</u> reap what they sow!

4. It <u>was</u> so exciting to see the seedlings pop up out of the rich soil.

5. Before long, the plants <u>were</u> reaching for the sky.

6. Because it had <u>been</u> so hot and dry, Yvette <u>would</u> water the garden often.

7. Her friends have <u>been</u> weeding all along.

8. Yvette and her helpers <u>might</u> begin harvesting soon.

9. They <u>are</u> sure that everything will <u>taste</u> great!

Model

Model the following sentence to practice using linking and auxiliary verbs.

> It is true that I was born in Iowa, but I can't speak for my twin sister.
> —Abigail Van Buren

Related Skills Activities

- **SkillsBook**
  Pretest: Verbs, p. 89
  Types of Verbs, p. 90
  Auxiliary (Helping) and Linking Verbs, 91

Answers

1. auxiliary
2. auxiliary
3. linking
   auxiliary
4. linking
5. auxiliary
6. linking
   auxiliary
7. auxiliary
8. auxiliary
9. linking
   linking

716.1 Action Verbs: Transitive and Intransitive

An **intransitive verb** communicates an action that is complete in itself. It does not need an object to receive the action.

> The boy flew on his skateboard. He jumped and flipped and twisted.

A **transitive verb** (red) is an action verb that needs an object (blue) to complete its meaning.

> The city council passed a strict noise ordinance.

While some action verbs are only transitive *or* intransitive, some can be either, depending on how they are used.

> He finally stopped to rest. (intransitive)
> He finally stopped the show. (transitive)

716.2 Objects with Transitive Verbs

■ A **direct object** receives the action of a transitive verb directly from the subject. Without it, the transitive verb's meaning is incomplete.

> The boy kicked his skateboard forward. (*Skateboard* is the direct object.)
> Then he put one foot on it and rode like a pro.

■ An **indirect object** also receives the action of a transitive verb, but indirectly. An indirect object names the person *to whom* or *for whom* something is done. (An indirect object can also name the thing *to what* or *for what* something is done.)

> Ms. Oakfield showed us pictures of the solar system.
> (*Us* is the indirect object.)
> She gave Tony an A on his project.

NOTE: When the word naming the indirect receiver of the action is in a prepositional phrase, it is no longer considered an indirect object.

> Ms. Oakfield showed pictures of the solar system to us.
> (*Us* is the object of the preposition *to*.)

Grammar Practice

Verbs 2

■ **Transitive and Intransitive Verbs**

 Write whether each underlined verb is transitive or intransitive. For a transitive verb, also write the direct object.

Example: Davonte <u>plays</u> the guitar as one of his hobbies.
transitive verb, guitar

1. Sometimes he <u>plays</u> with a bunch of friends in a band.
2. They really don't <u>sing</u> very well, if you ask me.
3. Despite that, they <u>auditioned</u> for the city talent show.
4. The judges <u>invited</u> the band back!
5. The band <u>bought</u> some funky clothes at a resale shop to wear at the show.
6. At the performance, they <u>sang</u> a song that one of them had written.
7. Simone <u>plucked</u> the strings of her bass.
8. The audience must have <u>liked</u> it, for they <u>called</u> for an encore.
9. Needless to say, that really <u>surprised</u> me.
10. Was I <u>missing</u> something that others <u>heard</u> in their music?
11. I had better <u>give</u> them another chance!

Model

 Model the following sentences to practice using transitive and intransitive verbs.

> He raised his head and gazed at me unblinking from beneath the rim of the dark hat.
> —Chaim Potok, *The Gift of Asher Lev*

> The hotel and its little outbuildings and the giraffe-like coconut palms hulked on shore, dark on darker.
> —Scott Turow, *Pleading Guilty*

Parts of Speech

Related Skills Activities

■ *GrammarSnap*
Transitive and Intransitive Verbs

■ *SkillsBook*
Types of Verbs, p. 90
Transitive and Intransitive Verbs, p. 98
Direct and Indirect Objects, p. 99

Answers

1. intransitive
2. intransitive
3. intransitive
4. transitive, band
5. transitive, clothes
6. transitive, song
7. transitive, strings
8. transitive, it
   intransitive
9. transitive, me
10. transitive, something
    intransitive
11. transitive, them

Forms of Verbs

A verb has different forms depending on its *number, person, tense, voice,* and *mood.*

718.1 Number of a Verb

Number indicates whether a verb is singular or plural. In a clause, the verb (in blue below) and its subject (in red) must both be singular or both be plural.

■ **Singular**

One large island floats off Italy's "toe."

Italy's northern countryside includes the spectacular Alps.

■ **Plural**

Five small islands float inside Michigan's "thumb."

The Porcupine Mountains rise above the shores of Lake Superior.

718.2 Person of a Verb

Person indicates whether the subject of the verb is first, second, or third person (is speaking, is spoken to, or is spoken about). The form of the verb usually changes only when a present-tense verb is used with a third-person singular pronoun.

	Singular	Plural
First Person	I sniff	we sniff
Second Person	you sniff	you sniff
Third Person	he/she/it sniffs	they sniff

718.3 Tense of a Verb

Tense indicates time. Each verb has three principal parts: the *present, past,* and *past participle.* All six tenses are formed from these principal parts. The past and past participle of regular verbs are formed by adding *ed* to the present form. For irregular verbs, the past and past participle are usually different words; however, a few have the same form in all three principal parts (see **720.2**).

718.4 Simple Tenses

■ **Present tense** expresses action that is happening at the present time, or action that happens continually, regularly.

In September, sophomores smirk and joke about the "little freshies."

■ **Past tense** expresses action that was completed at a particular time in the past.

They forgot that just ninety days separated them from freshman status.

■ **Future tense** expresses action that will take place in the future.

They will recall this in three years when they will be freshmen again.

Grammar Practice

Verbs 3

■ Number of a Verb

■ Simple Tenses

Write the verb or verbs in each sentence. Then identify each as *present, past,* or *future.* For present-tense verbs, write whether they are *singular* or *plural.*

Example: 1. is: present, singular

(1) The country of Taiwan, an island off the southeastern coast of China, is a bit smaller than the combined area of Maryland and Delaware. (2) Despite its size, its population is more than 23 million. (3) Its capitalist economy thrives as a result of its exports—especially electronics and textiles—to other countries. (4) The exports go mainly to China, the United States, and Japan.

(5) Taiwan was settled by people from China in the seventh century. (6) In 1895, Japan acquired the island and began to modernize it. (7) Following World War II, it was returned to China as a province. (8) Though it never seceded from China, Taiwan has a separate government. (9) Will the island reunite with China? (10) This continues to be a major political issue, so only time will tell.

Model

Model the following sentence twice; use past-tense verbs in one and future-tense verbs in the other.

We make a living by what we get; we make a life by what we give.

—Sir Winston Churchill

Related Skills Activities

■ **SkillsBook**

Present, Past, and Future Tense Verbs, p. 92

Subject-Verb Agreement 2, p. 150

Answers

1. is: present, singular
2. is: present, singular
3. thrives: present, singular
4. go: present, plural
5. was settled: past
6. acquired, began: past
   (to modernize: infinitive)
7. was returned: past
8. seceded: past
   has: present, singular
9. will reunite: future
10. continues: present, singular
    will tell: future

Forms of Verbs (continued)

720.1 Perfect Tenses

■ **Present perfect tense** expresses action that began in the past but continues in the present or is completed in the present.

Our boat has weathered **worse storms than this one.**

■ **Past perfect tense** expresses an action in the past that occurred before another past action.

They reported, wrongly, that the hurricane had missed **the island.**

■ **Future perfect tense** expresses action that will begin in the future and be completed by a specific time in the future.

By this time tomorrow, the hurricane will have smashed **into the coast.**

720.2 Irregular Verbs

Common Irregular Verbs and Their Principal Parts

Present Tense	Past Tense	Past Participle	Present Tense	Past Tense	Past Participle	Present Tense	Past Tense	Past Participle
am, be	was, were	been	go	went	gone	shrink	shrank	shrunk
begin	began	begun	grow	grew	grown	sing	sang, sung	sung
bite	bit	bitten	hang	hanged	hanged	sink	sank, sunk	sunk
blow	blew	blown	(execute)			sit	sat	sat
break	broke	broken	hang	hung	hung	slay	slew	slain
bring	brought	brought	(suspend)			speak	spoke	spoken
buy	bought	bought	hide	hid	hidden, hid	spring	sprang,	sprung
catch	caught	caught	know	knew	known		sprung	
choose	chose	chosen	lay	laid	laid	steal	stole	stolen
come	came	come	lead	led	led	strive	strove	striven
dive	dove	dived	leave	left	left	swear	swore	sworn
do	did	done	lie	lay	lain	swim	swam	swum
draw	drew	drawn	(recline)			swing	swung	swung
drink	drank	drunk	lie	lied	lied	take	took	taken
drive	drove	driven	(deceive)			teach	taught	taught
eat	ate	eaten	lose	lost	lost	tear	tore	torn
fall	fell	fallen	make	made	made	throw	threw	thrown
fight	fought	fought	ride	rode	ridden	wake	waked,	waked,
flee	fled	fled	ring	rang	rung		woke	woken
fly	flew	flown	rise	rose	risen	wear	wore	worn
forsake	forsook	forsaken	run	ran	run	weave	weaved,	weaved,
freeze	froze	frozen	see	saw	seen		wove	woven
get	got	gotten	shake	shook	shaken	wring	wrung	wrung
give	gave	given	show	showed	shown	write	wrote	written

These verbs are the same in all principal parts: *burst, cost, cut, hurt, let, put, set,* and *spread.*

Grammar Practice

Verbs 4

■ Irregular Verbs

 Write the correct form (past tense or past participle) of the verb shown in parentheses to complete each sentence.

Example: The bread dough had _____ enough, so it was ready to bake. *(rise)*
    risen

1. Sarika treasured the pendant her father had _____ her. *(give)*

2. Mustafa _____ me to the mall in his dad's new car. *(drive)*

3. When I was in grade school, Mr. McCall _____ music to the whole student body. *(teach)*

4. My oldest sister has _____ a lawyer for three years. *(be)*

5. When Alemba _____ home from school, he grabbed the mail. *(get)*

6. He looked at each piece as he _____ it into the house. *(bring)*

7. Then he _____ it on the kitchen table for his mom. *(leave)*

8. This is my good friend Beryl, whom I have _____ since I was four years old. *(know)*

9. Once, our dog _____ a dead mouse behind the sofa. *(hide)*

10. Wade said, "That's one too many tests I've _____ today." *(take)*

11. She looks like she has _____ her best friend. *(lose)*

 Model

Model the following sentences to practice using irregular verbs correctly.

We can't ask the middle class to pay more; their incomes went down and their taxes went up.
— Bill Clinton

Writers should be read, but neither seen nor heard.
— Daphne du Maurier

Related Skills Activities

■ *GrammarSnap*
Past Perfect and Past Continuous Verb Tenses; Shifting Verb Tenses in Analysis

■ *SkillsBook*
Perfect Tense Verbs, p. 93
Irregular Verbs 1, 2, and 3, pp. 101–104

Answers

1. given
2. drove
3. taught
4. been
5. got
6. brought
7. left
8. known
9. hid
10. taken
11. lost

722.1 Continuous Tenses

- A **present continuous tense** verb expresses action that is not completed at the time of stating it. The present continuous tense is formed by adding *am, is,* or *are* to the *-ing* form of the main verb.

  Scientists are learning **a great deal from their study of the sky.**

- A **past continuous tense** verb expresses action that was happening at a certain time in the past. This tense is formed by adding *was* or *were* to the *-ing* form of the main verb.

  Astronomers were beginning **their quest for knowledge hundreds of years ago.**

- A **future continuous tense** verb expresses action that will take place at a certain time in the future. This tense is formed by adding *will be* to the *-ing* form of the main verb.

  Someday astronauts will be going **to Mars.**

  This tense can also be formed by adding a phrase noting the future *(are going to)* plus *be* to the *-ing* form of the main verb.

  They are going to be performing **many experiments.**

722.2 Voice of a Verb

Voice indicates whether the subject is acting or being acted upon.

- **Active voice** indicates that the subject of the verb is, has been, or will be doing something.

  For many years Lou Brock held **the base-stealing record.**

Active voice makes your writing more direct and lively.

- **Passive voice** indicates that the subject of the verb is being, has been, or will be acted upon.

  For many years the base-stealing record was held **by Lou Brock.**

  NOTE: With a passive verb, the person or thing creating the action is not always stated.

  The ordinance was overturned. (Who did the overturning?)

Tense	Active Voice		Passive Voice	
	Singular	Plural	Singular	Plural
Present	I see you see he/she/it sees	we see you see they see	I am seen you are seen he/she/it is seen	we are seen you are seen they are seen
Past	I/he saw you saw	we/they saw you saw	I/it was seen you were seen	we/they were seen you were seen
Future	I/you/he will see	we/you/they will see	I/you/it will be seen	we/you/they will be seen

Grammar Practice

Verbs 5

- Active and Passive Verbs

 If any sentence or part of a sentence below is in the passive voice, rewrite it in the active voice. Write "active" if it's already in the active voice.

Example: 1. *active*

(1) In any election, young people have the most to gain by voting. **(2)** If the election isn't won by their favored candidate, these young people have to live with the consequences the longest. **(3)** Unfortunately, voting is done by only a low percentage of people from this age group (18 to 24).

(4) Although many young adults seem cynical about politics, some are taking action. **(5)** They are relying on more than just advertising to become informed. **(6)** Research is done to evaluate a candidate's record. **(7)** Personal connections are sought out. **(8)** A solid picture of each candidate—beyond sound bites and photo ops—is developed. **(9)** Then a decision on whom to vote for is made. **(10)** These young people are realizing the power they have to change things, and they are making a difference.

Model

Write the following sentences in the active voice.

The house was cleaned and dinner prepared by the young servant.
I like long walks, especially when they are taken by people who annoy me.

—Noel Coward

Related Skills Activities

- ***GrammarSnap***
  Past Perfect and Past Continuous Verb Tenses; Passive versus Active Voice; Past Perfect Passive & Past Continuous Passive

- ***SkillsBook***
  Active and Passive Voice, p. 93

Answers

1. active
2. If their favored candidates don't win the election . . .
3. Unfortunately, only a low percentage of people from this age group (18 to 24) vote.
4. active
5. active
6. They do research to evaluate a candidate's record.
7. They seek personal connections.
8. They develop a solid picture of each candidate—beyond sound bites and photo ops.
9. Then they decide whom to vote for.
10. active

724.1 Mood of a Verb

The **mood** of a verb indicates the tone or attitude with which a statement is made.

■ **Indicative mood** is used to state a fact or to ask a question.

Often I face the challenge of a test by making a study plan. I then work hard to stick to my plan so that I am ready for the test.

■ **Imperative mood** is used to give a command.

"Whatever you do, don't fly your kite during a storm."
—Mrs. Abiah Franklin

■ **Subjunctive mood** is not as commonly used in English as it once was; however, careful writers may choose to use it to express the exact manner in which their statements are meant.

Use the subjunctive *were* to express a condition that is contrary to fact.

If I were finished with my report, I could go to the movie.

Use the subjunctive *were* after *as though* or *as if* to express an unreal condition.

Mrs. Young acted as if she were sixteen again.

Use the subjunctive *be* in "that" clauses to express necessity, legal decisions, or parliamentary motions.

"It is moved and supported that no more than 6 million quad be used to explore the planet Earth."

"Ridiculous! Knowing earthlings is bound to help us understand ourselves! Therefore, I move that the sum be amended to 12 million quad."

"Stupidity! I move that all missions be postponed until we have living proof of life on Earth."

Grammar Practice

Verbs 6

■ Mood of a Verb

 Write whether each statement shows *indicative*, *imperative*, or *subjunctive* mood.

Example: Rhetta acts as though she were already selected prom queen.
subjunctive

1. Mr. Martinez asked, "When is the prom, anyway?"

2. Stand in that line over there to renew your driver's license.

3. Then sit in the waiting area until your name is called.

4. Malcolm would attend Carson's party if he were not grounded.

5. The gentle, all-day rain was a welcome respite from the summer's long streak of sunny, 90-degree days.

6. Where are the Pyrenees Mountains?

7. Find out—look in an atlas!

8. The doctor recommended that Leticia's broken ribs be wrapped for at least three weeks.

9. Her friends visit her after school.

Model

Model the following sentence to practice using the subjunctive mood.

The studio thought it best that the odd movie first be distributed in a limited area.

Related Skills Activities

■ **GrammarSnap**
Subjunctive Mood

■ **SkillsBook**
Indicative and Imperative Moods, p. 96
Subjunctive Mood, p.97

Answers

1. indicative
2. imperative
3. imperative
4. subjunctive
5. indicative
6. indicative
7. imperative
8. subjunctive
9. indicative

Verbals

A **verbal** is a word that is derived from a verb but acts as another part of speech. There are three types of verbals: *gerunds, infinitives,* and *participles.* Each is often part of a verbal phrase.

726.1 Gerunds

A **gerund** is a verb form that ends in *ing* and is used as a noun.

Swimming is my favorite pastime. (subject)

I began swimming at the age of six months. (direct object)

Swimming in chlorinated pools makes my eyes red. (gerund phrase used as a subject)

726.2 Infinitives

An **infinitive** is a verb form that is usually introduced by *to*; the infinitive may be used as a noun, an adjective, or an adverb.

Most people find it easy to swim. (adverb modifying an adjective)

To swim the English Channel must be a thrill. (infinitive phrase as noun)

The urge to swim in tropical waters is more common. (infinitive phrase as adjective)

726.3 Participles

A **participle** is a verb form ending in *ing* or *ed* that acts as an adjective.

The workers raking leaves are tired and hungry. (participial phrase modifies *workers*)

The bags full of raked leaves are evidence of their hard work. (participle modifies *leaves*)

Grammar Practice

Verbs 7

■ Verbals

 Write whether each underlined word or phrase is a *gerund*, a *participle*, or an *infinitive*.

Example: 1. gerund

(1) Eating gelatin dessert is a childhood memory for many. It may be one of Baby's first solid foods because it is so easy (2) to eat. Toddlers and older children like the (3) jiggling food.

(4) To make gelatin, protein called collagen is obtained from (5) cooked animal skin, bones, and tissues. It is filtered and double purified. When collagen is heated, its molecules trap tiny particles of water, resulting in the familiar jellylike substance. (At this point, the Food and Drug Administration no longer considers it a meat product.) Then sugar and other flavorings are mixed in (6) to create the fun dessert.

Peter Cooper invented gelatin in 1845, and fruit flavors were first added in 1897. It became such a staple in America's kitchens that immigrants (7) entering Ellis Island were served gelatin as a welcome to America. (8) Adding vegetables and fruit to gelatin was a way (9) to stretch the family budget in the 1940s. Today people appreciate this sweet, (10) satisfying snack for its low-calorie goodness.

◀ Model

Model the following sentences to practice using gerunds and participles.

Knowing that you know nothing makes you smartest of all.

—Aristotle

Failing to plan is planning to fail.

—Effie Jones

Related Skills Activities

■ **GrammarSnap**
Verbals: Gerund, Participle, & Infinitive
Dangling Participles

■ **SkillsBook**
Verbals: Gerunds, Infinitives, and Participles, p. 100

Answers

1. gerund
2. infinitive
3. participle
4. infinitive
5. participle
6. infinitive
7. participle
8. gerund
9. infinitive
10. participle

Adjective

An **adjective** describes or modifies a noun or a pronoun. The articles *a, an,* and *the* are also adjectives.

> The young **driver** peeked through the big **steering wheel**.
> (*The* and *young* modify *driver*; *the* and *big* modify *steering wheel*.)

728.1 Types of Adjectives

A **proper adjective** is created from a proper noun and is capitalized.

> In **Canada** (proper noun), you will find many cultures and climates.
> **Canadian** (proper adjective) winters can be harsh.

A **predicate adjective** follows a form of the "be" verb (or other linking verb) and describes the subject.

> Late autumn seems **grim** to those who love summer. (*Grim* modifies *autumn*.)

NOTE: Some words can be either adjectives or pronouns (*that, these, all, each, both, many, some,* and so on). These words are adjectives when they come before the nouns they modify; they are pronouns when they stand alone.

> Jiao made **both** goals. (*Both* modifies *goals;* it is an adjective.)
> **Both** were scored in the final period. (*Both* stands alone; it is a pronoun.)

728.2 Forms of Adjectives

Adjectives have three forms: *positive, comparative,* and *superlative.*

- The **positive form** describes a noun or a pronoun without comparing it to anyone or anything else.
   > The first game was **long** and **tiresome**.

- The **comparative form** (*-er, more,* or *less*) compares two persons, places, things, or ideas.
   > The second game was **longer** and **more tiresome** than the first.

- The **superlative form** (*-est, most,* or *least*) compares three or more persons, places, things, or ideas.
   > The third game was the **longest** and **most tiresome** of all.

NOTE: Use *more* and *most* (or *less* and *least*)—instead of adding a suffix— with many adjectives of two or more syllables.

Positive	Comparative	Superlative
big	bigger	biggest
helpful	more helpful	most helpful
painful	less painful	least painful

Grammar Practice

Adjectives

- Types of Adjectives

Write the adjectives (not including articles or possessive pronouns) in each of the following sentences. Label predicate adjectives with a "P" (as shown).

Example: Many Caribbean countries are troubled.
   many, Caribbean, troubled (P)

1. Pale North Americans and Europeans enjoy these warm havens during their hemisphere's long, cold winters.

2. All residents of the Caribbean, however, must deal with this natural hazard: hurricanes.

3. In addition, individual islands have their own dilemmas.

4. One Caribbean island, Anguilla, has no arable land (so crops do not grow).

5. Its economic health depends heavily on the tourist industry.

6. The small island of Montserrat is highly subject to volcanic explosions.

7. Two-thirds of its population of 12,000 fled following the frightening eruption of the Soufriere Hills Volcano in 1995.

8. Continued eruptions have left half of the island uninhabitable.

9. The poorest country in the Western Hemisphere is Haiti.

10. Although a mere 29 percent of the land is arable, 65 percent of its people farm for a meager income.

11. Puerto Rico, a U.S. territory, has problems, too, including a high unemployment rate.

Model

Model the following sentence to practice using adjectives well.

> He had broken thumbs and burnt fingers. He had thick, greasy fingernails he never cut and dusty hair.

—Sandra Cisneros, "One Holy Night"

Related Skills Activities

- ***GrammarSnap***
   Comparative and Superlative Adjectives

- ***SkillsBook***
   Pretest: Adjectives and Adverbs, p. 107
   Adjectives, p. 108
   Predicate Adjectives, p. 109
   Forms of Adjectives, p. 110
   Using *Good* and *Well,* p. 115

 ## Answers

1. pale, these, warm, hemisphere's, long, cold
2. all, this, natural
3. individual, own
4. one, Caribbean, no, arable
5. economic, tourist
6. small, subject (P), volcanic
7. frightening
8. continued, uninhabitable (P)
9. poorest
10. mere, arable (P), meager
11. U.S., high, unemployment

Adverb

An **adverb** describes or modifies a verb, an adjective, or another adverb.

She sneezed loudly. (*Loudly* modifies the verb *sneezed*.)
Her sneezes are really **dramatic.** (*Really* modifies the adjective *dramatic*.)
The sneeze exploded very **noisily.** (*Very* modifies the adverb *noisily*.)

An adverb usually tells *when, where, how,* or *how much.*

730.1 Types of Adverbs

Adverbs can be cataloged in four basic ways: *time, place, manner,* and *degree.*

TIME (These adverbs tell *when, how often,* and *how long.*)

today, yesterday   daily, weekly   briefly, eternally

PLACE (These adverbs tell *where, to where,* and *from where.*)

here, there   nearby, beyond   backward, forward

MANNER (These adverbs often end in *ly* and tell *how* something is done.)

precisely   effectively   regally   smoothly   well

DEGREE (These adverbs tell *how much* or *how little.*)

substantially   greatly   entirely   partly   too

NOTE: Some adverbs can be written with or without the *ly* ending. When in doubt, use the *ly* form.

slow, slowly   loud, loudly   fair, fairly   tight, tightly   quick, quickly

730.2 Forms of Adverbs

Adverbs of manner have three forms: *positive, comparative,* and *superlative.*

- The **positive form** describes a verb, an adjective, or another adverb without comparing it to anyone or anything else.

    Model X vacuum cleans well **and runs** quietly.

- The **comparative form** (*-er, more,* or *less*) compares how two things are done.

    Model Y vacuum cleans better **and runs** more quietly **than model X does.**

- The **superlative form** (*-est, most,* or *least*) compares how three or more things are done.

    Model Z vacuum cleans best **and runs** most quietly **of all.**

Positive	Comparative	Superlative
well	better	best
fast	faster	fastest
remorsefully	more remorsefully	most remorsefully

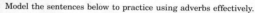

Grammar Practice

Adverbs

 Number your paper from 1 to 12 and write down each adverb you find in the following paragraphs.

Example: 1. *carefully*

Carefully reading old science fiction stories sometimes leads scientists to experiment with the theories presented within them. For instance, powering spacecraft with something other than bulky fuel has long been a popular idea in science fiction. In 2005, a partnership between private investors in the United States and Russia effectively produced the world's first solar sail spacecraft.

A solar sail is powered by light. Photons (light particles) bounce off the surface of the craft's broad sails, thereby pushing it forward. The sails slowly turn to catch the sun, changing the angle of reflection to move the craft diagonally.

Unfortunately, the attempt to launch *Cosmos 1*, the first such vehicle, was unsuccessful. Scientists launched it from a Russian nuclear submarine in the Barents Sea, but the engine of the booster rocket failed 83 seconds later. Future (successful) missions may go to other planets and eventually even to the stars.

 Model

Model the sentences below to practice using adverbs effectively.

The thing that is really hard, and really amazing, is giving up on being perfect and beginning the work of becoming yourself.
—Anna Quindlen

I've always thought that a big laugh is a really loud noise from the soul saying, "Ain't that the truth."
—Quincy Jones, *Victory of the Spirit*

Related Skills Activities

- **Basic Grammar and Writing**
  Adverbs: Answer Questions, p. 542

- *GrammarSnap*
  Adverbs

- *SkillsBook*
  Pretest: Adjectives and Adverbs, p. 107
  Adverbs, p. 112
  Types of Adverbs, p. 113
  Forms of Adverbs, p. 114
  Using *Good* and *Well,* p. 115

Answers

1. carefully
2. sometimes
3. long
4. effectively
5. thereby
6. forward
7. slowly
8. diagonally
9. unfortunately
10. later
11. eventually
12. even

Preposition

A **preposition** is the first word (or group of words) in a prepositional phrase. It shows the relationship between its object (a noun or a pronoun that follows the preposition) and another word in the sentence. The first noun or pronoun following a preposition is its object.

To make a mustache, Natasha placed the hairy caterpillar under **her** nose.
(*Under* shows the relationship between the verb, *placed*, and the object of the preposition, *nose.*)

The drowsy insect clung obediently to **the girl's upper** lip.
(The first noun following the preposition *to* is *lip; lip* is the object of the preposition.)

732.1 Prepositional Phrase

A **prepositional phrase** includes the preposition, the object of the preposition, and the modifiers of the object. A prepositional phrase functions as an adverb or as an adjective.

Some people run away from caterpillars.
(The phrase functions as an adverb and modifies the verb *run.*)

However, little kids with inquisitive minds **enjoy their company.**
(The phrase functions as an adjective and modifies the noun *kids.*)

NOTE: A preposition is always followed by an object; if there is no object, the word is an adverb, not a preposition.

Natasha never played **with caterpillars** before. (The word *before* is not followed by an object; therefore, it functions as an adverb that modifies *played*, a verb.)

Common Prepositions

aboard	before	from	of	save
about	behind	from among	off	since
above	below	from between	on	subsequent to
according to	beneath	from under	on account of	together with
across	beside	in	on behalf of	through
across from	besides	in addition to	onto	throughout
after	between	in back of	on top of	till
against	beyond	in behalf of	opposite	to
along	by	in front of	out	toward
alongside	by means of	in place of	out of	under
along with	concerning	in regard to	outside of	underneath
amid	considering	inside	over	until
among	despite	inside of	over to	unto
apart from	down	in spite of	owing to	up
around	down from	instead of	past	up to
aside from	during	into	prior to	upon
at	except	like	regarding	with
away from	except for	near	round	within
because of	for	near to	round about	without

Grammar Practice

Prepositions

 Write the prepositions you find in each sentence.

Example: The Sears Tower, in Chicago, Illinois, remains one of the world's tallest buildings since its completion on May 3, 1973.
in, of, since, on

1. At a height of 1,450 feet, it held the record as the tallest building for 25 years.

2. If spread across a single level, the building's 4.56 million square feet would cover 105 acres.

3. Miles of electrical wiring (1,500) and plumbing (25) run through the tower.

4. An elevator system with 104 cars services the 110 floors above three lower levels.

5. Each floor is divided into 75-square-foot column-free modules.

6. The building's base has nine modules, several of which terminate at different levels, leaving two at the top.

7. A restaurant on the 99th floor offers breathtaking views in all directions.

Model

As you scan the list of prepositions on the opposite page, you'll note that some of them can be used as other parts of speech as well. Model the following sentences, which use a word both as a preposition and as another part of speech.

Before our trip, we tied everything to the roof of the car, as we'd done many times before.
—Lisa Grossman

Time flies like an arrow. Fruit flies like a banana.
—Groucho Marx

Related Skills Activities

■ **Basic Grammar and Writing**
Prepositions, pp. 544–545
Using Other Types of Phrases, p. 556

■ *GrammarSnap*
Prepositions

■ *SkillsBook*
Pretest: Prepositions, Conjunctions, and Interjections, p. 117
Prepositions and Interjections, p. 118
Prepositional Phrases, p. 133

Answers

1. at, of, as, for
2. across
3. of, through
4. with, above
5. into
6. of, at, at
7. on, in

Conjunction

A **conjunction** connects individual words or groups of words. There are three kinds of conjunctions: *coordinating, correlative,* and *subordinating.*

734.1 Coordinating Conjunctions

Coordinating conjunctions usually connect a word to a word, a phrase to a phrase, or a clause to a clause. The words, phrases, or clauses joined by a coordinating conjunction are equal in importance or are of the same type.

I could tell by my old man's eyes that he *was nervous* and *wanted to smooth things over,* but Syl didn't give him a chance.
—Albert Halper, "Prelude"

(*And* connects the two parts of a compound predicate; *but* connects two independent clauses that could stand on their own.)

734.2 Correlative Conjunctions

Correlative conjunctions are conjunctions used in pairs.

They were not only *exhausted by the day's journey* but also *sunburned.*

734.3 Subordinating Conjunctions

Subordinating conjunctions connect two clauses that are *not* equally important, thereby showing the relationship between them. A subordinating conjunction connects a dependent clause to an independent clause in order to complete the meaning of the dependent clause.

A brown trout will study the bait *before he eats it.* (The clause *before he eats it* is dependent. It depends on the rest of the sentence to complete its meaning.)

> ### Kinds of Conjunctions
>
> Coordinating: **and, but, or, nor, for, yet, so**
> Correlative: **either, or; neither, nor; not only, but also; both, and; whether, or**
> Subordinating: **after, although, as, as if, as long as, as though, because, before, if, in order that, provided that, since, so that, that, though, till, unless, until, when, where, whereas, while**

NOTE: Relative pronouns (see **706.2**) and conjunctive adverbs (see **618.2**) can also connect clauses.

Interjection

An **interjection** communicates strong emotion or surprise. Punctuation—a comma or an exclamation point—sets off an interjection from the rest of the sentence.

Oh no! The TV broke. Good grief! I have nothing to do! Yipes, I'll go mad!

Grammar Practice

Conjunctions

Number your paper from 1 to 12. Write the conjunctions you find in the following paragraphs and label them *coordinating, subordinating,* or *correlative.* (Write both correlative conjunctions as one answer.)

Example: 1. *yet – coordinating*

Stem cells are cells whose functions are not specific, yet they have the potential to become any kind of body cell. They can be "trained" to become part of the surrounding tissue when they are injected into the body. Scientists hold great hope that stem cells will help cure not only organ diseases and various cancers but also neurological diseases such as Parkinson's, Alzheimer's, and multiple sclerosis. Provided that research continues, stem cells might also be coaxed to help repair damage from heart disease, strokes, and spinal cord injuries.

Stem cells from human embryos have generated controversy, but these amazing cells have also been found in liposuctioned fat. The fat stem cells have been programmed to work as muscle, bone, and cartilage cells. Since this source has been discovered only recently, it remains to be seen whether they will work or not in other areas of the body, too.

◄ Model

Model the following sentences to practice using interjections effectively.

"Eureka!" shouted Gran. "This is what my recipe has been missing!"
Ahhh, a man with a sharp wit. Someone ought to take it away from him before he cuts himself.
—Peter da Silva

Parts of Speech

Related Skills Activities

- **Basic Grammar and Writing**

- *GrammarSnap*
  Commas Splices and Run-On Sentences

- *SkillsBook*

Answers

1. yet – coordinating
2. when – subordinating
3. that – subordinating
4. not only . . . but also – correlative
5. and – coordinating
6. and – coordinating
7. provided that – subordinating
8. and – coordinating
9. but – coordinating
10. and – coordinating
11. since – subordinating
12. whether , or – correlative

Test Prep!

Read the following paragraphs. Write the letter of the answer that best describes each underlined part from the choices given on the next page.

Everyone thinks of Thomas Jefferson as a statesman—a <u>founding</u> **(1)** father who served as secretary of state, vice president, and president. In addition, he <u>is remembered</u> **(2)** as a writer, author of the Declaration of Independence. But not everyone knows about the other sides of Thomas Jefferson. He was a scientist, an architect, and a musician, as well.

Jefferson enjoyed all aspects of science, including astronomy, anatomy, mathematics, physics, meteorology, and anthropology. As an inventor, he <u>devised</u> **(3)** machines such as the dumbwaiter, a machine for <u>copying</u> **(4)** handwriting, and the swivel chair. Jefferson <u>was</u> **(5)** president of the American Philosophical Society, the main scientific organization of the time, and he wrote <u>scholarly</u> **(6)** papers on paleontology. In botany, Jefferson experimented with new varieties of vegetable seeds <u>from</u> **(7)** Europe.

<u>Another</u> **(8)** interest Jefferson explored was architecture. He designed his own home, the magnificent Monticello, as well as the Virginia State Capitol. <u>Although</u> **(9)** his work <u>was influenced</u> **(10)** by European design, he helped develop the unique Federalist style of architecture that became popular in America.

<u>Along with</u> **(11)** his <u>more</u> **(12)** technical interests, Thomas Jefferson was an accomplished musician. He played the violin, practicing three hours a day as a young man. His wife, Martha, played piano and guitar, and he encouraged their children and grandchildren <u>to study</u> **(13)** music as well. His

vast collection of music shows an eclectic taste that <u>included</u> **(14)** chamber pieces, historical works, orchestral music, song collections, and operas.

Scientist, architect, musician, <u>and</u> **(15)** so much more: <u>truly</u>, **(16)** Thomas Jefferson was the most versatile of American presidents.

1
- Ⓐ verb
- Ⓑ verbal – gerund
- Ⓒ verbal – infinitive
- Ⓓ verbal – participle

2
- Ⓐ verb – active voice
- Ⓑ verb – passive voice
- Ⓒ verbal – participle
- Ⓓ preposition

3
- Ⓐ action verb
- Ⓑ linking verb
- Ⓒ auxiliary verb
- Ⓓ verbal – participle

4
- Ⓐ verb
- Ⓑ verbal – gerund
- Ⓒ verbal – infinitive
- Ⓓ verbal – participle

5
- Ⓐ action verb
- Ⓑ linking verb
- Ⓒ auxiliary verb
- Ⓓ verbal – gerund

6
- Ⓐ adverb
- Ⓑ adjective
- Ⓒ preposition
- Ⓓ conjunction

7
- Ⓐ adverb
- Ⓑ adjective
- Ⓒ preposition
- Ⓓ conjunction

8
- Ⓐ adverb
- Ⓑ adjective
- Ⓒ preposition
- Ⓓ conjunction

9
- Ⓐ coordinating conjunction
- Ⓑ subordinating conjunction
- Ⓒ correlative conjunction
- Ⓓ adverb

10
- Ⓐ verb – active voice
- Ⓑ verb – passive voice
- Ⓒ verbal – infinitive
- Ⓓ verbal – gerund

11
- Ⓐ adverb
- Ⓑ adjective
- Ⓒ preposition
- Ⓓ conjunction

12
- Ⓐ adverb
- Ⓑ adjective
- Ⓒ preposition
- Ⓓ conjunction

13
- Ⓐ verb
- Ⓑ verbal – gerund
- Ⓒ verbal – infinitive
- Ⓓ verbal – participle

14
- Ⓐ action verb
- Ⓑ linking verb
- Ⓒ auxiliary verb
- Ⓓ verbal – participle

15
- Ⓐ coordinating conjunction
- Ⓑ subordinating conjunction
- Ⓒ correlative conjunction
- Ⓓ preposition

16
- Ⓐ adverb
- Ⓑ adjective
- Ⓒ preposition
- Ⓓ conjunction

Related Skills Activities

■ **SkillsBook**
Review: Verbs 1, p. 94
Review: Verbs 2, pp. 105–106
Review: Adjectives, p. 111
Review: Adverbs, p. 116
Review: Prepositions, Conjunctions, and Interjections,
   p. 122
Review: Parts of Speech, pp. 123–124
Posttest: Verbs, p. 208
Posttest: Adjectives and Adverbs, p. 209
Posttest: Prepositions, Conjunctions, and Interjections,
   p. 210
Final Parts of Speech Posttest—Parts 1 and 2,
   pp. 211–214

Answers

1. D		9. B	
2. B		10. B	
3. A		11. C	
4. B		12. A	
5. B		13. C	
6. B		14. A	
7. C		15. A	
8. B		16. A	

Understanding Sentences

Constructing Sentences

A **sentence** is made up of one or more words that express a complete thought. Sentences begin with a capital letter; they end with a period, a question mark, or an exclamation point.

> What should we do this afternoon? We could have a picnic. No, I hate the ants!

Using Subjects and Predicates

A sentence usually has a *subject* and a *predicate*. The subject is the part of the sentence about which something is said. The predicate, which contains the verb, is the part of the sentence that says something about the subject.

> We write from aspiration and antagonism, as well as from experience.
> —Ralph Waldo Emerson

738.1 The Subject

The **subject** is the part of the sentence about which something is said. The subject is always a noun; a pronoun; or a word, clause, or phrase that functions as a noun (such as a gerund or a gerund phrase or an infinitive).

> Wolves **howl.** (noun)
> They **howl for a variety of reasons.** (pronoun)
> To establish their turf **may be one reason.** (infinitive phrase)
> Searching for "lost" pack members **may be another.** (gerund phrase)
> That wolves and dogs are similar animals **seems obvious.** (noun clause)

- A **simple subject** is the subject without its modifiers.
  > Most wildlife biologists **disapprove of crossbreeding wolves and dogs.**

- A **complete subject** is the subject with all of its modifiers.
  > Most wildlife biologists **disapprove of crossbreeding wolves and dogs.**

- A **compound subject** is composed of two or more simple subjects.
  > Wise breeders and owners **know that wolf-dog puppies can display unexpected, destructive behaviors.**

738.2 Delayed Subject

In sentences that begin with *There* or *It* followed by a form of the "be" verb, the subject comes after the verb. The subject is also delayed in questions.

> There was nothing in the refrigerator. (The subject is *nothing*; the verb is *was*.)
> Where is my sandwich? (The subject is *sandwich*; the verb is *is*.)

Grammar Practice

Constructing Sentences 1

- Simple, Complete, and Compound Subjects
- Delayed Subjects

 Write the complete subject of each sentence. Circle the simple subject or subjects.

Example: There is always talk about alternative sources of energy.
 (talk) about alternative sources of energy

1. Off the coast of Portugal, a truly unique power plant is starting to generate electricity.

2. Ocean waves are the source of the energy.

3. Giant sausage-shaped generators float on the water, using its wave motion to create electricity.

4. A Norwegian energy company and a Scottish manufacturer combined resources to build the generators.

5. The wave farm, consisting of about 30 generators, produces clean, renewable energy.

6. How much energy can the system generate?

7. Three generators can produce enough electricity to supply 1,500 homes.

8. For countries on oceans, renewable wave energy seems like the "wave" of the future.

Model

Model the following sentences to practice using a delayed subject.

> Why are our days numbered and not, say, lettered?
> —Woody Allen

> There is no cure for curiosity.
> —Dorothy Parker

Related Skills Activities

- ***SkillsBook***
  Pretest: Subjects and Predicates, p. 127
  Simple Subjects and Predicates, p. 128
  Simple, Complete, and Compound Subjects and
      Predicates, p. 129
  Subject-Verb Agreement 3, p. 151

Answers

1. a truly unique power (plant)
2. Ocean (waves)
3. Giant sausage-shaped (generators)
4. A Norwegian energy (company) and a Scottish (manufacturer)
5. The wave (farm), consisting of about 30 generators,
6. the (system)
7. Three (generators)
8. renewable wave (energy)

740

740.1 The Predicate

The **predicate** is the part of the sentence that shows action or says something about the subject.

> **Giant squid** do exist.

■ A **simple predicate** is the verb without its modifiers.

> **One giant squid** measured **nearly 60 feet long.**

■ A **complete predicate** is the simple predicate with all its modifiers.

> **One giant squid** measured nearly 60 feet long.
> (*Measured* is the simple predicate; *nearly 60 feet long* modifies *measured*.)

■ A **compound predicate** is composed of two or more simple predicates.

> **A squid** grasps **its prey with tentacles and** bites **it with its beak.**

> **NOTE:** A sentence can have a **compound subject** and a **compound predicate.**
> Both **sperm whales and** giant squid **live and occasionally** clash **in the deep waters off New Zealand's South Island.**

■ A **direct object** is part of the predicate and receives the action of the verb. (See **716.2**.)

> **Sperm whales sometimes eat** giant squid.
> (The direct object *giant squid* receives the action of the verb *eat* by answering the question *whales eat what*?)

> **NOTE:** The **direct object** may be compound.
> In the past, **whalers harvested** oil, spermaceti, **and** ambergris **from slain sperm whales.**

740.2 Understood Subject and Predicate

Either the subject or the predicate may be "missing" from a sentence, but both must be clearly **understood.**

> Who is in the hot-air balloon?
> (*Who* is the subject; *is in the hot-air balloon* is the predicate.)
> No one.
> (*No one* is the subject; the predicate *is in the hot-air balloon* is understood.)
> Get out of the way!
> (The subject *you* is understood; *get out of the way* is the predicate.)

Grammar Practice

Constructing Sentences 2

■ Simple, Complete, and Compound Predicates

 Write the complete predicate of each sentence. Circle the simple predicate or compound predicate.

Example: North America's greatest earthquake did not happen in California, Alaska, or Mexico.
(did)not(happen) in California, Alaska, or Mexico

1. A series of terrible earthquakes rattled the ground in the Mississippi River valley in the winter of 1811–1812.

2. The series of quakes are named after the town most affected by them, New Madrid, Missouri.

3. New Madrid lies on the Mississippi River at the confluence of southeastern Missouri, southern Illinois, western Kentucky, and northwest Tennessee.

4. Few structures within 250 miles of the town escaped damage that winter.

5. People as far away as Charleston, South Carolina, and Washington, D.C., felt the tremors.

6. The quakes disrupted the bed of the Mississippi and changed its course in two places.

7. The strongest three quakes of the series are estimated to have measured at least 8.0 on the Richter scale.

8. The area was sparsely settled and so suffered few fatalities.

9. Scientists warn, however, of another quake happening on the New Madrid fault within 35 years.

◀ Model

Model the following sentence to practice using a compound predicate.

> They come in once a week and weave up and down every aisle and arrive at the cash register, exhausted, with a tipsy heap of groceries.
> —Susan Orlean, "All Mixed Up"

Sentences

Related Skills Activities

■ **SkillsBook**
Pretest: Subjects and Predicates, p. 127
Simple Subjects and Predicates, p. 128
Simple, Complete, and Compound Subjects and
  Predicates, p. 129

Answers

1. (rattled) the ground in the Mississippi River valley in the winter of 1811–1812

2. (are named) after the town most affected by them, New Madrid, Missouri

3. (lies) on the Mississippi River at the confluence of southeastern Missouri, southern Illinois, western Kentucky, and northwest Tennessee

4. (escaped) damage that winter

5. (felt) the tremors

6. (disrupted) the bed of the Mississippi and (changed) its course in two places

7. (are estimated) to have measured at least 8.0 on the Richter scale

8. (was) sparsely (settled) and so (suffered) few fatalities

9. (warn), however, of another quake happening on the New Madrid fault within 35 years

Using Phrases

A **phrase** is a group of related words that function as a single part of speech. The sentence below contains a number of phrases.

Finishing the race will require running up some steep slopes.

finishing the race (This gerund phrase functions as a subject noun.)
will require (This phrase functions as a verb.)
running up some steep slopes (This gerund phrase acts as an object noun.)

742.1 Types of Phrases

■ An **appositive phrase,** which follows a noun or a pronoun and renames it, consists of a noun and its modifiers. An appositive adds new information about the noun or pronoun it follows.

> The Trans-Siberian Railroad, the world's longest railway, stretches from Moscow to Vladivostok. (The appositive phrase renames *Trans-Siberian Railroad* and provides new information.)

■ A **verbal phrase** is a phrase based on one of the three types of verbals: *gerund, infinitive,* or *participle.* (See 726.1, 726.2, and 726.3.)

> ■ A **gerund phrase** consists of a gerund and its modifiers. The whole phrase functions as a noun.
>
> > Spotting the tiny mouse was easy for the hawk.
> > (The gerund phrase is used as the subject of the sentence.)
> > Dinner escaped by ducking under a rock.
> > (The gerund phrase is the object of the preposition *by.*)
>
> ■ An **infinitive phrase** consists of an infinitive and its modifiers. The whole phrase functions either as a noun, an adjective, or an adverb.
>
> > To shake every voter's hand was the candidate's goal.
> > (The infinitive phrase functions as a noun used as the subject.)
> > Your efforts to clean the chalkboard are appreciated.
> > (The infinitive phrase is used as an adjective modifying *efforts.*)
> > Please watch carefully to see the difference.
> > (The infinitive phrase is used as an adverb modifying *watch.*)
>
> ■ A **participial phrase** consists of a past or present participle and its modifiers. The whole phrase functions as an adjective.
>
> > Following his nose, the beagle took off like a jackrabbit.
> > (The participial phrase modifies the noun *beagle.*)
> > The raccoons, warned by the rustling, took cover.
> > (The participial phrase modifies the noun *raccoons.*)

Sentences

Grammar Practice

Constructing Sentences 3

■ Appositive Phrases
■ Verbal Phrases

 Identify each underlined phrase as an *appositive,* a *gerund,* an *infinitive,* or a *participial* phrase.

Example: More than 3,000 years ago, <u>making glass</u> out of sand became a reality.
gerund phrase

1. In Iraq and Syria, archaeologists have found pieces of glass <u>made in the third millennium B.C.E.</u>

2. The land was then known as Mesopotamia, <u>the land between the Tigris and Euphrates rivers.</u>

3. Glass was considered precious because it was difficult <u>to make</u> and, therefore, uncommon.

4. First silica, <u>the base material of glass,</u> had to be reduced to powder.

5. Then it was melted in a furnace, wrapped around a core <u>shaped from clay and dung,</u> and rolled on a smooth surface.

6. About 2,000 years ago, someone figured out how <u>to blow glass.</u>

7. At the same time, glassmakers started <u>adding lime and soda to the silica</u> prior to heating, making it softer and easier to mold.

8. Oddly enough, the addition of lead to the mixture, first <u>done in 1676,</u> makes the glass sparkle and shine even more.

9. Lead crystal, as it's called, is softer and easier <u>to cut</u> than other kinds of glass.

 Model

Model the following sentence to practice using an appositive phrase.

My very existence, my life in the world, seemed like a hallucination.
—Haruki Murakami, "Sleep"

Related Skills Activities

■ **Basic Grammar and Writing**
Sentence Combining, pp. 555–556

■ *GrammarSnap*
Appositives and Appositive Phrases; Commas after Introductory Words, Phrases, and Clauses

■ *SkillsBook*
Pretest: Phrases, p. 131
Verbal Phrases, p. 132
Appositive Phrases, p. 134

 Answers

1. participial phrase
2. appositive phrase
3. infinitive phrase
4. appositive phrase
5. participial phrase
6. infinitive phrase
7. gerund phrase
8. participial phrase
9. infinitive phrase

Using Phrases (continued)

■ A **verb phrase** consists of a main verb preceded by one or more helping verbs.

Snow has been falling **for days.** (*Has been falling* is a verb phrase.)

■ A **prepositional phrase** is a group of words beginning with a preposition and ending with a noun or a pronoun. Prepositional phrases function mainly as adjectives and adverbs.

Reach for that catnip ball behind the couch. (The prepositional phrase *behind the couch* is used as an adjective modifying *catnip ball.*)

Zach won the wheelchair race in record time. (*In record time* is used as an adverb modifying the verb *won.*)

■ An **absolute phrase** consists of a noun and a participle (plus the participle's object, if there is one, and any modifiers). An absolute phrase functions as an adjective that adds information to the entire sentence. Absolute phrases are always set off with commas.

Its wheels clattering rhythmically over the rails, **the train rolled into town.** (The noun *wheels* is modified by the present participle *clattering.* The entire phrase modifies the rest of the sentence.)

Using Clauses

A **clause** is a group of related words that has both a subject and a predicate.

744.1 Independent and Dependent Clauses

An **independent clause** presents a complete thought and can stand alone as a sentence; a **dependent clause** (also called a *subordinate* clause) does not present a complete thought and cannot stand alone as a sentence.

Sparrows make nests in cattle barns (independent clause) so that they can stay warm during the winter (dependent clause).

744.2 Types of Dependent Clauses

There are three basic types of dependent clauses: *adverb, noun,* and *adjective.*

■ An **adverb clause** is used like an adverb to modify a verb, an adjective, or an adverb. Adverb clauses begin with a subordinating conjunction. (See 734.3.)

If I study hard, **I will pass this test.** (The adverb clause modifies the verb *will pass.*)

■ A **noun clause** is used in place of a noun.

However, the teacher said that the essay questions are based only on the last two chapters. (The noun clause functions as a direct object.)

■ An **adjective clause** modifies a noun or a pronoun.

Tomorrow's test, which covers the entire book, **is half essay and half short answers.** (The adjective clause modifies the noun *test.*)

Grammar Practice

Constructing Sentences 4

■ Dependent Clauses

 Write the first word of each dependent clause found in each sentence below, and then write its type: *adverb, adjective,* or *noun clause.* Note that some sentences have more than one dependent clause.

Example: Our language technically began when the Germanic tribes of Angles, Saxons, and Jutes began populating England around 400–500 C.E.

when—adverb clause

1. Their West Germanic dialects developed into a language that they could all understand.

2. When the Vikings invaded around 850 C.E., they added their North Germanic dialects to the mix that became known as Old English.

3. Middle English is generally dated back to the 1066 Norman invasion of England, which ended Anglo-Saxon rule there.

4. The Normans spoke a Germanic language that had been influenced by the Roman occupation and included Latin roots.

5. That modern English began around the time of Shakespeare shows his strong influence on the language; he added some 2,000 words to it.

6. As technology has grown, so has our language.

7. Most changes that have occurred since Shakespeare's time consist of the addition of names for things that did not exist when the language was new.

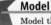
Model

Model the following sentences to practice using noun clauses effectively.

I've found students shocked to learn that it can take me three years to finish a poem.

—Carolyn Forche

Suburbia is where the developer bulldozes out the trees and then names the streets after them.

—Bill Vaughan

Sentences

Related Skills Activities

■ **Basic Grammar and Writing**
Using Other Types of Phrases, p. 556

■ *GrammarSnap*
Restrictive/Nonrestrictive Relative Clauses and Relative Pronouns in Complex Sentences

■ *SkillsBook*
Prepositional Phrases, p. 133
Pretest: Clauses, p. 136
Independent and Dependent Clauses, p. 137
Adverb, Adjective, and Noun Clauses, p. 138

Answers

1. that—adjective clause
2. when—adverb clause
   that—adjective clause
3. which—adjective clause
4. that—adjective clause
5. that—noun clause
6. as—adverb clause
7. that—adjective clause
   that—adjective clause
   when—adverb clause

Using Sentence Variety

A **sentence** may be classified according to the type of statement it makes, the way it is constructed, and its arrangement of words.

746.1 Kinds of Sentences

Sentences can make five basic kinds of statements: *declarative, interrogative, imperative, exclamatory,* or *conditional.*

- **Declarative sentences** make statements. They tell us something about a person, a place, a thing, or an idea.
    > The Statue of Liberty stands in New York Harbor.
    > For over a century, it has greeted immigrants and visitors to America.

- **Interrogative sentences** ask questions.
    > Did you know that the Statue of Liberty is made of copper and stands over 150 feet tall?
    > Are we allowed to climb all the way to the top?

- **Imperative sentences** make commands. They often contain an understood subject *(you)* as in the examples below.
    > Go see the Statue of Liberty.
    > After a few weeks of physical conditioning, climb its 168 stairs.

- **Exclamatory sentences** communicate strong emotion or surprise.
    > Climbing 168 stairs is not a dumb idea!
    > Just muster some of that old pioneering spirit, that desire to try something new, that never-say-die attitude that made America great!

- **Conditional sentences** express wishes ("if . . . then" statements) or conditions contrary to fact.
    > If I could design a country's flag, then I would use six colors behind a sun, a star, and a moon.
    > I would feel as if I were representing many cultures in my design.

Grammar Practice

Kinds of Sentences

- Sentence Variety

 Write the kind of statement each sentence makes: declarative, interrogative, imperative, exclamatory, or conditional.

Example: Take a good look at your body.
imperative

1. Did you know that you had 350 bones in your body when you were born?

2. Now 144 of them have fused together.

3. Your hands and feet contain more than half the bones in your body.

4. If your stomach did not produce a new lining every three days, it would digest itself in its own acid.

5. Over your lifetime, you will drink more than 16,000 gallons of water!

6. Has your brain stopped growing yet?

7. Most people's brains stop growing after the age of 15.

8. Move your little finger.

9. Your nervous system transmitted the messages enabling you to do that—at 180 miles per hour!

10. If your small intestine were not looped and folded inside you, it wouldn't fit in the abdomen.

11. It averages about 20 feet long.

Model

Model the following exclamatory sentences.

> What a blessing it would be if we could open and shut our ears as easily as we open and shut our eyes!
>
> —Georg Christoph Lichtenberg

> When I'm asked how to write, I answer—"Tell me a story!"
>
> —Anne McCaffrey

Sentences

Related Skills Activities

- **Basic Grammar and Writing**
  Sentence Variety, p. 553

- *GrammarSnap*
  Kinds of Sentences: Declarative, Interrogative, Imperative

- *SkillsBook*
  Pretest: Sentences, p. 141
  Basic Sentence Patterns, p. 142
  Kinds of Sentences, p. 143

Answers

1. interrogative
2. declarative
3. declarative
4. conditional
5. exclamatory
6. interrogative
7. declarative
8. imperative
9. exclamatory
10. conditional
11. declarative

748.1 Types of Sentence Constructions

A sentence may be *simple, compound, complex,* or *compound-complex.* It all depends on the relationship between independent and dependent clauses.

- A **simple sentence** can have a single subject or a compound subject. It can have a single predicate or a compound predicate. However, a simple sentence has only one independent clause, and it has no dependent clauses.

  My back aches.
  (single subject; single predicate)

  My teeth **and my** eyes hurt.
  (compound subject; single predicate)

  My throat **and** nose feel **sore and** look red.
  (compound subject; compound predicate)

  I must have caught the flu **from the sick kids in class.**
  (independent clause with two phrases: *from the sick kids* and *in class*)

- A **compound sentence** consists of two independent clauses. The clauses must be joined by a comma and a coordinating conjunction or by a semicolon.

  I usually don't mind missing school, but **this is not fun.**

  I feel too sick to watch TV; I feel too sick to eat.

  NOTE: The comma can be omitted when the clauses are very short.

  I wept and **I wept.**

- A **complex sentence** contains one independent clause (in black) and one or more dependent clauses (in red).

  When I get back to school, **I'm actually going to appreciate it.**
  (dependent clause; independent clause)

  I won't even complain about math class, although I might be talking out of my head because I'm feverish.
  (independent clause; two dependent clauses)

- A **compound-complex sentence** contains two or more independent clauses (in black) and one or more dependent clauses (in red).

  Yes, I have a bad flu, and because I need to get well soon, **I won't think about school just yet.**
  (two independent clauses; one dependent clause)

Grammar Practice

Types of Sentence Constructions

- Types of Sentences

 Identify each of the following sentences as a *simple, compound, complex,* or *compound-complex* sentence.

Example: How often do you grab a clear plastic bottle of water when you need a drink?
complex

1. If you are like the average U.S. citizen, you drink 61 liters of bottled water each year—and you pay more than 200 times the amount that you pay for a gallon of tap water.

2. You're paying for the convenience, not the safety.

3. Although there are federal standards for the safety of bottled water, rules for city tap water are stricter.

4. In addition, the standards do not even apply to bottled water that is not distributed across state lines.

5. State laws require little or no testing for impurities in bottled water.

6. Most city water is chlorinated to kill organisms, but bottlers seldom add it due to its taste.

7. Labels often do not indicate the source of the water; sometimes it is actually just bottled tap water.

8. Perhaps the bottler has added vitamins, herbs, flavoring, or sweeteners to the water to make it more appealing.

9. To be careful with your health, you may want to choose tap water over bottled, which would also save you money; and that's always a good thing.

◀ Model

Model the following sentences to practice forming compound and complex sentences.

I slept, and dreamed that life was Beauty; I woke, and found that life was Duty.
—Ellen Sturgis Hooper

If fifty million people say a foolish thing, it is still a foolish thing.
—Anatole France

Sentences

Related Skills Activities

- *GrammarSnap*
  Sentence Types: Simple, Compound, Complex, and Compound-Complex

- *SkillsBook*
  Types of Sentences, p. 144

Answers

1. compound-complex
2. simple
3. complex
4. complex
5. simple
6. compound
7. compound
8. simple
9. compound-complex

750

750.1 Arrangements of Sentences

Depending on the arrangement of the words and the placement of emphasis, a sentence may also be classified as *loose, balanced, periodic,* or *cumulative.*

■ A **loose sentence** expresses the main thought near the beginning and adds explanatory material as needed.

> We hauled out the boxes of food and set up the camp stove, all the time battling the hot wind that would not stop, even when we screamed into the sky.

> Memory performs the impossible for man—holds together past and present, gives continuity and dignity to human life.
>
> —Mark Van Doren, *Liberal Education*

■ A **balanced sentence** is constructed so that it emphasizes a similarity or a contrast between two or more of its parts (words, phrases, or clauses).

> The wind in our ears drove us crazy and pushed us on.
> (The similar wording emphasizes the main idea in this sentence.)

> Sarcasm makes us either laugh aloud or weep silently.

■ A **periodic sentence** is one that postpones the crucial or most surprising idea until the end.

> Following my mother's repeated threats to ground me for life, I decided it was time to propose a compromise.

> Our finest hour lies just ahead; we will either triumph or be spared the knowledge of what we have done.

■ A **cumulative sentence** places the general idea in the middle of the sentence with modifying clauses and phrases coming before and after.

> With careful thought and extra attention to detail, I wrote out my plan for being a model teenager, a teen who cared about neatness and reliability.

> Surrounded by friends and family, I stepped onto the stage and stood tall at the podium, no longer fearing the task that had earlier seemed almost impossible.

Grammar Practice

Arrangements of Sentences

■ Sentence Arrangements

 Classify each of the following sentences as *loose, balanced, periodic,* or *cumulative.*

Example: Arturo is a good singer but not an exceptional one.
balanced

1. Going through the motions of an audition for each school play, he usually got a starring role.

2. Until last spring, anyway, that was the case.

3. A new student auditioned—one who could sing quite well.

4. With unusual modesty, Victor belted out his own rendition of "If I Were a Rich Man," the same song that Arturo was going to use.

5. The drama teacher was impressed; Arturo was upset.

6. At that point, Arturo decided to sing a different song for his audition.

7. He remembered well a particular song from a play the school had presented two years ago.

8. Despite the blow to his self-esteem, Arturo did a credible job.

9. As it turned out, neither Arturo nor Victor got the lead role because it required someone who could dance like Fred Astaire.

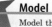 **Model**

Model the following balanced sentences.

> Be sincere; be brief; be seated.
>
> —Franklin D. Roosevelt

> Men are mortal, but ideas are immortal.
>
> —William Lippmann

Sentences

 ## Answers

1. periodic
2. periodic
3. balanced
4. cumulative
5. balanced
6. periodic
7. loose
8. periodic
9. cumulative

Getting Sentence Parts to Agree

Agreement of Subject and Verb

A verb must agree in number (singular or plural) with its subject.

The student was **proud of her quarter grades.**

NOTE: Do not be confused by words that come between the subject and verb.

The manager, as well as the players, is required to display good
sportsmanship. (*Manager*, not *players*, is the subject.)

752.1 Compound Subjects

Compound subjects joined by *or* or *nor* take a singular verb.

Neither Bev **nor** Kendra is **going to the street dance.**

NOTE: When one of the subjects joined by *or* or *nor* is singular and one is plural,
the verb must agree with the subject nearer the verb.

Neither Yoshi **nor his** friends are **singing in the band anymore.** (The plural subject
friends is nearer the verb, so the plural verb *are* is correct.)

Compound subjects connected with *and* require a plural verb.

Strength **and** balance are **necessary for gymnastics.**

752.2 Delayed Subjects

Delayed subjects occur when the verb comes before the subject in a sentence.
In these inverted sentences, the delayed subject must agree with the verb.

There are **many hardworking** students **in our schools.**
There is **present among many young people today a** will **to succeed.**
(*Students* and *will* are the true subjects of these sentences, not *there*.)

752.3 "Be" Verbs

When a sentence contains a form of the "be" verb—and a noun comes before and
after that verb—the verb must agree with the subject, not the *complement* (the
noun coming after the verb).

The cause **of his problem was the bad** brakes.
The bad brakes were **the** cause **of his problem.**

752.4 Special Cases

Some nouns that are **plural in form but singular in meaning** take a singular
verb: *mumps, measles, news, mathematics, economics, gallows, shambles.*

Measles **is still considered a serious disease in many parts of the world.**

Some nouns that are plural in form but singular in meaning take a plural verb:
scissors, trousers, tidings.

The scissors are **missing again.**

Grammar Practice

Agreement of Subject and Verb 1

■ Subject-Verb Agreement

For each sentence, write the correct verb from the choice given in
parentheses.

Example: Marlon and his brothers (*plays, play*) instruments in the
marching band.
play

1. The name of their school's team (*is, are*) the Bulldogs.

2. Tia or Eve (*works, work*) in the office a few hours a week.

3. Every morning in the school parking lot, there (*is, are*) seagulls
looking for food.

4. Mahender thinks that most news (*is, are*) biased.

5. Neither the nectarines nor the watermelon (*is, are*) on sale this week.

6. All of the monkeys, in addition to the puma, (*was, were*) unusually
noisy at the zoo today.

7. My pants (*has, have*) a big hole in the knee.

8. The ankle weights (*was, were*) the perfect gift for Marc.

9. Dad or my little sisters (*chooses, choose*) the bedtime book each night.

Model

Model the following sentences to practice subject-verb agreement.

**Canada is a country whose main exports are hockey and cold fronts.
Our main imports are baseball players and acid rain.**

—Pierre Trudeau

The future belongs to those who believe in the beauty of their dreams.

—Eleanor Roosevelt

Sentences

Related Skills Activities

■ *GrammarSnap*
Subject-Verb Agreement

■ *SkillsBook*
Pretest: Subject-Verb Agreement, p. 148
Subject-Verb Agreement 1, p. 149

Answers

1. is
2. works
3. are
4. is
5. is
6. were
7. have
8. were
9. choose

Agreement of Subject and Verb *(continued)*

754.1 Collective Nouns

Collective nouns *(faculty, committee, team, congress, species, crowd, army, pair, squad)* take a singular verb when they refer to a group as a unit; collective nouns take a plural verb when they refer to the individuals within the group.

> **The favored** team **is losing, and the** crowd **is getting ugly.** (Both *team* and *crowd* are considered units in this sentence, requiring the singular verb *is*.)
> **The** pair **were finally reunited after 20 years apart.**
> (Here, *pair* refers to two individuals, so the plural verb *were* is required.)

754.2 Indefinite Pronouns

Some **indefinite pronouns** are singular: *each, either, neither, one, everybody, another, anybody, everyone, nobody, everything, somebody,* and *someone.* They require a singular verb.

> **Everybody is invited to the cafeteria for refreshments.**

Some **indefinite pronouns** are plural: *both, few, many,* and *several.*

> **Several like chocolate cake. Many ask for ice cream, too.**

NOTE: Do not be confused by words or phrases that come between the indefinite pronoun and the verb.

> **One of the participants is** (not *are*) **going to have to stay late to clean up.**

A Closer Look

Some **indefinite pronouns** can be either singular or plural: *all, any, most, none,* and *some.* These pronouns are singular if the number of the noun in the prepositional phrase is singular; they are plural if the noun is plural.

> **Most of the food complaints are coming from the seniors.**
> (*Complaints* is plural, so *most* is plural.)

> **Most of the tabletop is sticky with melted ice cream.**
> (*Tabletop* is singular, so *most* is singular.)

754.3 Relative Pronouns

When a **relative pronoun** *(who, which, that)* is used as the subject of a clause, the number of the verb is determined by the antecedent of the pronoun. (The antecedent is the word to which the pronoun refers.)

> **This is one of the books that are required for geography class.**
> (The relative pronoun *that* requires the plural verb *are* because its antecedent, *books,* is plural.)

NOTE: To test this type of sentence for agreement, read the "of" phrase first.

> **Of the books that are required for geography class, this is one.**

Grammar Practice

Agreement of Subject and Verb 2

■ Subject-Verb Agreement

 For each underlined verb, state the reason it does not agree with its subject.

Example: 1. *Are* is plural, and its subject, *one,* is singular.

One of the themes Shakespeare presents in the play Romeo and Juliet **(1)** <u>are</u> that the stars (representing fate) determine a person's life. During Shakespeare's time, people commonly believed that all of life **(2)** <u>were</u> governed by the stars. The play carries this theme throughout, with frequent references to heavenly bodies.

In the play's prologue, the couple **(3)** <u>is</u> referred to as "star-crossed lovers" whose lives are set by the fates. When Romeo thinks that Juliet is dead, he cries out, "I defy you, stars!" He is indicating that anyone who **(4)** <u>use</u> free will can determine his own fate. Just before he kills himself, he comments that by dying he will "shake the yoke of inauspicious stars." He is suggesting that nobody **(5)** <u>lose</u> the hold fate has on him or her until death.

Fate controlling us, represented by the skies, is one of the ideas that **(6)** <u>is</u> present throughout Romeo and Juliet. From beginning to end, the lovers are doomed, yet everyone **(7)** <u>continue</u> to love the story because it is as beautiful as the stars.

Model

Model the following sentences to practice subject-verb agreement with indefinite pronouns.

> **Everybody likes a kidder, but nobody lends him money.**
> —Arthur Miller

> **To create one's own world in any of the arts takes courage.**
> —Georgia O'Keeffe

Sentences

Related Skills Activities

- ■ *GrammarSnap*
  Subject-Verb Agreement

- ■ *SkillsBook*
  Subject-Verb Agreement 1, 2, and 3, p. 146

Answers

1. *Are* is plural, and its subject, *one,* is singular.
2. *Were* is plural, and its subject, *all,* is singular in this sentence.
3. *Is* is singular, and its subject, *couple,* is plural because it refers to two individuals.
4. *Use* is plural, and its subject, *who,* is singular because its antecedent is *anyone,* which is singular.
5. *Lose* is plural, and its subject, *nobody,* is singular.
6. *Is* is singular, and its subject, *that,* is plural because its antecedent is *ideas,* which is plural.
7. *Continue* is plural, and its subject, *everyone,* is singular.

Agreement of Pronoun and Antecedent

A pronoun must agree in number, person, and gender with its *antecedent*. (The *antecedent* is the word to which the pronoun refers.)

> Cal **brought** his **gerbil to school.** (The antecedent of *his* is *Cal*. Both the pronoun and its antecedent are singular, third person, and masculine; therefore, the pronoun is said to "agree" with its antecedent.)

756.1 Agreement in Number

Use a **singular pronoun** to refer to such antecedents as *each, either, neither, one, anyone, anybody, everyone, everybody, somebody, another, nobody,* and *a person.*

> **Neither of the brothers likes** his **(not their) room.**

Two or more singular antecedents joined by *or* or *nor* are also referred to by a **singular pronoun.**

> **Either** Connie **or** Sue **left** her **headset in the library.**

If one of the antecedents joined by *or* or *nor* is singular and one is plural, the pronoun should agree with the nearer antecedent.

> **Neither the** manager **nor the** players **were crazy about** their **new uniforms.**

Use a **plural pronoun** to refer to plural antecedents as well as compound subjects joined by *and.*

> Jared **and** Carlos **are finishing** their **assignments.**

756.2 Agreement in Gender

Use a **masculine** or **feminine pronoun** depending upon the gender of the antecedent.

> **Is either** Connor **or** Grace **bringing** his **or** her **baseball glove?**

When *a person* or *everyone* is used to refer to both sexes or either sex, you will have to choose whether to offer optional pronouns or rewrite the sentence.

> **A person** should be allowed to choose her **or** his **own footwear.**
> (optional pronouns)
> People **should be allowed to choose** their **own footwear.**
> (rewritten in plural form)

Grammar Practice

Agreement of Pronoun and Antecedent

■ Pronoun-Antecedent Agreement

 For each sentence below, first write the antecedent of the pronoun that appears later in the sentence. Then replace the incorrect pronoun with one that agrees with the antecedent. If the pronoun is correct as is, write "C."

Example: Should a driver always know the basic things about maintaining her car?
driver, his or her

1. Everyone should at least know how to take a flat tire off and put their spare tire on.
2. Neither of my two best friends, Lasandra and Renee, knows how to change the oil in their car.
3. Phillip and Benito, on the other hand, know a lot about his cars.
4. Both of them work at tricking out their rides.
5. Benito or Phillip works at their brother's garage.
6. The mechanic or the lube techs were eating his lunch in the break room.
7. One of the lube techs was trying to clean their fingernails.
8. Lasandra's brakes were squealing, so a mechanic checked it for excessive wear.
9. The mechanic said that Lasandra was probably riding her brakes too much.

Model

Model the following sentences to practice making a pronoun and its antecedent agree.

> Some people have so much respect for their superiors that they have none left for themselves.
> —Peter McArthur

> Never judge a book by its movie.
> —J. W. Eagan

Related Skills Activities

■ *GrammarSnap*
Pronoun-Antecedent Agreement

■ *SkillsBook*
Pretest: Pronoun-Antecedent Agreement, p. 153
Pronoun-Antecedent Agreement 1 and 2, pp. 154–155

Answers

1. everyone, his or her
2. Lasandra nor Renee, her
3. Phillip and Benito, his
4. both, C
5. Benito or Phillip, his
6. mechanic or lube techs, their
7. one, his or her
8. brakes, them
9. Lasandra, C

Test Prep!

Read the following paragraphs. Write the letter of the best answer or answers for each underlined part from the choices given on the next page.

Strong women have always helped make the United States great. Three <u>who made life better for women</u> were Elizabeth Cady Stanton,
(1)
Susan B. Anthony, and Jane Addams.

<u>The American Revolution began with the Boston Tea Party, and the</u>
(2)
<u>women's rights movement began with a tea party of its own.</u> Elizabeth
<u>Cady Stanton and four women friends</u> met for tea one day in 1848. They
(3)
discussed the importance of women gaining rights equal to men. This
innocent tea party <u>led</u> to the formation of the Seneca Falls Convention.
(4)
<u>Its members drew up a declaration of women's rights that would serve as</u>
(5)
<u>the foundation for the women's rights movement.</u>

Susan B. Anthony's "radical" ideas included <u>paying women and men</u>
<u>equally.</u> She also campaigned for women <u>to receive the same civil and</u>
(6)
<u>political rights</u> that African American males had. The <u>adoption</u> of the
(7)   (8)
nineteenth amendment, which gave women the right to vote, came about
largely due to her efforts.

<u>Jane Addams</u>, a tireless reformer, left a trail of accomplishments
(9)
<u>matched by few.</u> She founded Hull-House in Chicago, <u>a "settlement" house</u>
(10)   (11)
<u>that attracted well-educated people to poor areas.</u> Hull-House <u>provided</u>
(11)
<u>services such as day care, libraries, an employment office, music and art</u>
(12)
<u>classes, and a little theater for the immigrants pouring into the country.</u>
Addams pushed legislators for child labor laws and laws on education. <u>For</u>
<u>these and other efforts, she was awarded the Nobel Peace Prize in 1931.</u>
(13)

The efforts of these three strong women—and many others like them—have advanced equal rights. <u>Although there is still much to do,</u>
(14)
American women <u>have made</u> great strides toward equality in the eyes of
(15)
men, the law, and the world.

1
- (A) independent clause
- (B) dependent clause
- (C) verbal phrase
- (D) appositive phrase

2
- (A) simple sentence
- (B) compound sentence
- (C) complex sentence
- (D) dependent clause

3
- (A) complete predicate
- (B) simple predicate
- (C) simple subject
- (D) complete subject

4
- (A) complete predicate
- (B) simple predicate
- (C) simple subject
- (D) complete subject

5
- (A) simple sentence
- (B) compound sentence
- (C) complex sentence
- (D) dependent clause

6
- (A) gerund phrase
- (B) infinitive phrase
- (C) participial phrase
- (D) appositive phrase

7
- (A) gerund phrase
- (B) infinitive phrase
- (C) participial phrase
- (D) appositive phrase

8
- (A) complete predicate
- (B) simple predicate
- (C) simple subject
- (D) complete subject

9
- (A) complete predicate
- (B) simple predicate
- (C) simple subject
- (D) complete subject

10
- (A) gerund phrase
- (B) infinitive phrase
- (C) participial phrase
- (D) appositive phrase

11
- (A) gerund phrase
- (B) infinitive phrase
- (C) participial phrase
- (D) appositive phrase

12
- (A) complete predicate
- (B) simple predicate
- (C) simple subject
- (D) complete subject

13
- (A) simple sentence
- (B) compound sentence
- (C) complex sentence
- (D) dependent clause

14
- (A) independent clause
- (B) dependent clause
- (C) verbal phrase
- (D) appositive phrase

15
- (A) complete predicate
- (B) simple predicate
- (C) simple subject
- (D) complete subject

Sentences

Related Skills Activities

- **SkillsBook**
  Review: Phrases, p. 135
  Review: Clauses, p. 139
  Review: Phrase or Clauses?, p. 140
  Review: Sentences, p. 147
  Review: Subject-Verb Agreement, p. 152
  Review: Pronoun-Antecedent Agreement, p. 156
  Posttest: Subjects and Predicates, p. 215
  Posttest: Phrases, p. 216
  Posttest: Clauses, p. 217
  Posttest: Kinds and Types of Sentences, p. 218
  Posttest: Subject and Verb Agreement, p. 219
  Posttest: Pronoun-Antecedent Agreement, p. 220

Answers

1. B		9. C	
2. B		10. C	
3. D		11. D	
4. B		12. A	
5. C		13. A	
6. A		14. B	
7. B		15. B	
8. C			

Diagramming Sentences

A **graphic diagram** of a sentence is a picture of how the words in that sentence are related and how they fit together to form a complete thought.

760.1 Simple Sentence with One Subject and One Verb

Chris fishes.

760.2 Simple Sentence with a Predicate Adjective

Fish are delicious.

760.3 Simple Sentence with a Predicate Noun and Adjectives

Fishing is my favorite hobby.

NOTE: When possessive pronouns (*my, his, their,* and so on) are used as adjectives, they are placed on a diagonal line under the word they modify.

760.4 Simple Sentence with an Indirect and Direct Object

My grandpa gave us a trout.

NOTE: Articles (*a, an, the*) are adjectives and are placed on a diagonal line under the word they modify.

Grammar Practice

Sentence Diagramming 1

■ Diagramming Sentences

 Diagram the following sentences.

Example: Jogging is a healthy activity.

1. Jogging is fun.
2. Amanda jogs.
3. Thad's mom offered me a ride.
4. I gave her my new address.
5. Woodworking combines two different talents.
6. One is carpentry.
7. Jorge built a beautiful cabinet.
8. Ronald lent me his blue jacket.
9. His other jacket was dirty.

Model

Model the following sentences to practice writing simple sentences with either a predicate noun or a predicate adjective.

The great omission in American life is solitude.
—Marya Mannes

People with courage and character always seem sinister to the rest.
—Hermann Hesse

Sentences

Answers

1. Jogging | is \ fun

2. Amanda | jogs

3. mom | offered | ride
   Thad's / me / a

4. I | gave | address
   her / my / new

5. Woodworking | combines | talents
   two / different

6. One | is \ carpentry

7. Jorge | built | cabinet
   a / beautiful

8. Ronald | lent | jacket
   me / his / blue

9. jacket | was \ dirty
   His / other

Diagramming Sentences *(continued)*

762.1 Simple Sentence with a Prepositional Phrase

I like fishing by myself.

762.2 Simple Sentence with a Compound Subject and Verb

The team and fans clapped and cheered.

762.3 Compound Sentence

The team scored, and the crowd cheered wildly.

762.4 Complex Sentence with a Subordinate Clause

Before Erin scored, the crowd sat quietly.

Grammar Practice

Sentence Diagramming 2

 ■ Diagramming Sentences

Diagram the following sentences.

Example: The Rands enjoy rides in a hot-air balloon.

1. Kelli and Maria giggled and whispered.
2. The music started, but we could not stay for the dance.
3. As the ship pulled away, the passengers waved.
4. The cat disappeared into the night.
5. Grandpa shouted, and my brother stopped immediately.
6. I prefer bicycling on forest trails.
7. Although we rushed, we missed the bus.

Model

Model the following sentences to practice writing compound and complex sentences.

> Don't become a mere recorder of facts, but try to penetrate the mystery of their origin.
> —Isabel Allende

> I used to think the phrase "burst into the room" was only for detective fiction until my son got his growth.
> —Garrison Keillor, "Something from the Sixties"

Sentences

Answers

1.

2.

3.

4.

Answers

5.

6.

7.

Credits

Text:

p. 353: Copyright © 2010 by Houghton Mifflin Harcourt Publishing Company. Adapted and reproduced by permission from *The American Heritage College Dictionary,* Fourth Edition.

Photos:

pp. 81, 340 (b) ©Photodisc/Getty Images; **334, 339** (c), **340** (t), **341** (b) ©Photos.com/Jupiter Images; **338** ©Thinkstock/Getty Images; **339** (t) ©Purestock/Getty Images; **339** (b), **endsheet** ©Ablestock.com/Jupiter Images; **340** (c) ©Corbis; **341** (c) ©Digital Vision/Getty Images; **341** (t) Harcourt School Publishers; **583** (tl, tr, b) Courtesy of The Library of Congress.

ASSESSMENT SHEET AND RUBRICS

BENCHMARK PAPERS

GRAPHIC ORGANIZERS

GETTING STARTED

Assessment Sheet

 Directions Use one of the rubrics listed below to rate a piece of writing. Circle the rubric your teacher tells you to use. If you need information about assessing with a rubric, see pages 68–72 in your Write Source book.

- ■ Narrative Rubric (pages 124–125)
- ■ Expository Rubric (pages 180–181)
- ■ Persuasive Rubric (pages 234–235)
- ■ Response to Literature (pages 290–291)

Title _____

____ **Ideas**

____ **Organization**

____ **Voice**

____ **Word Choice**

____ **Sentence Fluency**

____ **Conventions**

Evaluator_____

© Houghton Mifflin Harcourt Publishing Company

6-Point

Rubric for Narrative Writing

Ideas

6 The narrative shares a memorable event. Details bring the essay to life.
5 The writer shares an interesting experience. Specific details help maintain interest.
4 The writer tells about an interesting experience. Details need to show, not tell.
3 The writer should focus on one event. Some details do not relate to the essay.
2 The writer should focus on one experience. More details are needed.
1 The writer should select an experience and provide details.

Organization

6 The structure of the narrative makes it enjoyable and easy to read.
5 The narrative has a clear beginning, middle, and ending. Transitions are helpful.
4 For the most part, the narrative is organized. Most of the transitions are helpful.
3 The order of events must be corrected. More transitions are needed.
2 The beginning, middle, and ending all run together. The order is unclear.
1 The narrative must be organized.

Voice

6 The writer's voice captures the experience for the reader.
5 The writer's voice sounds natural. Dialogue helps hold the reader's interest.
4 The writer's voice creates interest in the essay, but dialogue needs to sound more natural.
3 The writer's voice can usually be heard. More dialogue is needed.
2 The voice is weak. Dialogue is needed.
1 The writer sounds uninvolved or disinterested in the essay.

Word Choice

6 The writer's excellent word choice creates a vivid picture of the event.
5 Specific nouns, verbs, and modifiers create clear images and feelings.
4 Some stronger nouns, verbs, and/or modifiers would create a clearer picture.
3 More specific nouns, verbs, and modifiers would paint a clearer picture of the event.
2 Better words are needed. Words are overused or too general to paint a clear picture.
1 The writer has not considered word choice or has used words incorrectly.

Sentence Fluency

6 The sentences are skillfully written to hold the reader's interest.
5 The sentences are skillfully written, show variety, and are easy to understand.
4 The sentences are varied, but some should flow more smoothly.
3 A better variety of sentences is needed. Sentences do not flow smoothly.
2 Many incomplete or short sentences make the writing choppy.
1 Few sentences are written well. Help is needed.

Conventions

6 The narrative has no errors in spelling, grammar, or punctuation.
5 The narrative has one or two errors in spelling, grammar, or punctuation.
4 The narrative has a few minor errors in punctuation, grammar, or spelling.
3 The narrative has several errors.
2 Numerous errors make the narrative hard to read and confusing.
1 Help is needed to find errors and make corrections.

© Houghton Mifflin Harcourt Publishing Company

6-Point

Rubric for Expository Writing

Ideas
6 The ideas in the essay are compelling from start to finish.
5 The essay is informative with a clear thesis and specific details.
4 The essay is informative with a clear thesis. More specific details are needed.
3 The thesis of the essay should be clearer, and more specific details are needed.
2 The topic should be narrowed or expanded. Many more specific details are needed.
1 The writer should select a new topic.

Organization
6 The essay shows thoughtful use of an organizational pattern. Transitions are strong.
5 The beginning interests the reader. The middle supports the focus. The ending works well. Transitions are used.
4 The essay is divided into a beginning, a middle, and an ending. Some transitions are used.
3 The beginning or ending is weak. The middle needs a paragraph for each main point. More transitions are needed.
2 The beginning, middle, and ending all run together. Paragraph breaks and transitions are needed.
1 The essay should be reorganized.

Voice
6 The writing voice is lively, engaging, and memorable.
5 The writer's voice sounds knowledgeable and confident. It fits the audience.
4 The writer's voice sounds knowledgeable most of the time and fits the audience.
3 The writer sometimes sounds unsure, and the voice needs to better fit the audience.
2 The writer sounds unsure. The voice needs to fit the audience.
1 The writer needs to learn about voice.

Word Choice
6 Word choice is vivid and precise. Special terms are defined or explained.
5 Specific nouns and action verbs make the essay clear and informative.
4 Some nouns and verbs could be more specific.
3 Too many general words are used. Specific nouns and verbs are needed.
2 General or missing words make this essay difficult to understand.
1 The writer needs help finding specific words.

Sentence Fluency
6 Sentences are carefully crafted. Sentences flow naturally and vary in type and length.
5 The sentences have flair and flavor, and the reader will enjoy them.
4 Most of the sentences read smoothly, but some are short and choppy.
3 Short, choppy sentences need to be rewritten to make the essay read smoothly.
2 Many sentences are choppy or incomplete and need to be rewritten.
1 Most sentences need to be rewritten.

Conventions
6 Editing shows mastery of conventions. The essay is error free.
5 The essay has one or two errors.
4 The essay has some errors in punctuation, spelling, or grammar.
3 Several errors confuse the reader.
2 Many errors make the essay difficult to read.
1 Help is needed to make corrections.

© Houghton Mifflin Harcourt Publishing Company

6-Point

Rubric for Persuasive Writing

Ideas

6 The position is convincingly presented and supported; it compels the reader to act.
5 The position is convincingly supported and defended.
4 Most reasons support the writer's position. An important objection is addressed.
3 More supporting reasons and a more convincing response to an objection are needed.
2 A clearer position statement is needed. Better support for the position must be provided.
1 A new position statement and reasons are needed.

Organization

6 All parts of the essay work together to build a very thoughtful, convincing position.
5 The opening states the position, the middle provides clear support, and the ending reinforces the position.
4 Most parts of the essay are organized adequately except for one part.
3 Some parts of the essay need to be reorganized.
2 The beginning, middle, and ending run together.
1 The organization is unclear and incomplete.

Voice

6 The writer's voice is completely confident, knowledgeable, and convincing.
5 The writer's voice is confident, knowledgeable, and convincing in the main.
4 The writer's voice is respectful, but needs to sound more persuasive or knowledgeable.
3 The writer's voice needs to be more persuasive and respectful.
2 The writer's voice sounds too emotional and unconvincing.
1 The writer needs to learn about voice in persuasive writing.

Word Choice

6 The writer's choice of words makes a powerful case and helps persuade the reader.
5 The writer's choice of words makes a powerful case.
4 The writer avoids inflammatory (unfair) words but needs to remove some qualifiers.
3 The writer needs to change some inflammatory words and remove some qualifiers.
2 The words do not create a clear message. Some inflammatory words are used.
1 Word choice for persuasive writing has not been considered.

Sentence Fluency

6 The sentences flow smoothly throughout the strong essay.
5 The sentences spark the reader's interest in the essay.
4 Variety is seen in both the types of sentences and their beginnings.
3 Variety is seen in most of the sentences.
2 More variety is needed in the beginnings or kinds of sentences used.
1 Sentence fluency has not been considered.

Conventions

6 The writing is error free.
5 The writing has one or two errors.
4 Grammar and punctuation errors are few. The reader is not distracted by the errors.
3 Several distracting grammar and punctuation errors confuse the reader.
2 Frequent errors make the essay difficult to read.
1 Nearly every sentence contains errors.

© Houghton Mifflin Harcourt Publishing Company

Rubric for Response to Literature

Ideas

6 The ideas show a complete understanding of the reading and form a compelling analysis.

5 The ideas show a complete understanding of the reading.

4 The essay has a clear focus statement. Unnecessary details need to be cut.

3 The focus statement is too broad. A variety of details is needed.

2 The focus statement is unclear. More details are needed.

1 The essay needs a focus statement and details.

Organization

6 All the parts work together to create an insightful essay.

5 The organization pattern fits the topic and purpose. All parts of the essay are well developed.

4 The organization pattern fits the topic and purpose. A part of the essay needs better development.

3 The organization fits the essay's purpose. Some parts need more development.

2 The organization doesn't fit the purpose.

1 A plan needs to be followed.

Voice

6 The voice expresses interest and complete understanding. It engages the reader.

5 The voice expresses interest and complete understanding.

4 The voice expresses interest but needs to show more understanding.

3 The voice needs to be more interesting and express more understanding.

2 The voice does not show interest in or an understanding of the topic.

1 The writer needs to understand how to create voice.

Word Choice

6 The word choice is precise and colorful and reflects a thorough understanding of the reading.

5 The word choice, including the use of figures of speech, creates a clear message.

4 The word choice is clear, but more figures of speech would improve the essay.

3 The word choice is too general, and more figures of speech are needed.

2 Little attention was given to word choice.

1 The writer needs help with word choice.

Sentence Fluency

6 The sentences in the essay are skillfully written and create a clear flow of ideas.

5 The sentences flow well and make the ideas plain.

4 No sentence problems exist. More sentence variety is needed.

3 A few sentence problems need to be corrected.

2 The essay has many sentence problems.

1 The writer needs to learn how to construct sentences.

Conventions

6 Grammar and punctuation are correct, and the copy is free of errors.

5 Grammar and punctuation are correct in the main, with one or two errors.

4 The essay has a few careless errors in punctuation and grammar that do not interfere with the reader's understanding.

3 The errors in the essay confuse the reader.

2 The number of errors make the essay hard to read.

1 Help is needed to make corrections.

© Houghton Mifflin Harcourt Publishing Company

5-Point

Rubric for Narrative Writing

Use this rubric for guiding and assessing your narrative writing. Refer to it whenever you want to improve your writing using the six traits.

Ideas

5 The writer shares an interesting experience. Specific details help maintain interest.

4 The writer tells about an interesting experience. Details need to show, not tell.

3 The writer should focus on one event. Some details do not relate to the essay.

2 The writer should focus on one experience. More details are needed.

1 The writer should select an experience and provide details.

Organization

5 The narrative has a clear beginning, middle, and ending. Transitions are helpful.

4 For the most part, the narrative is organized. Most of the transitions are helpful.

3 The order of events must be corrected. More transitions are needed.

2 The beginning, middle, and ending all run together. The order is unclear.

1 The narrative must be organized.

Voice

5 The writer's voice sounds natural. Dialogue helps hold the reader's interest.

4 The writer's voice creates interest in the essay, but dialogue needs to sound more natural.

3 The writer's voice can usually be heard. More dialogue is needed.

2 The voice is weak. Dialogue is needed.

1 The writer sounds uninvolved or disinterested in the essay.

Word Choice

5 Specific nouns, verbs, and modifiers create clear images and feelings.

4 Some stronger nouns, verbs, and/or modifiers would create a clearer picture.

3 More specific nouns, verbs, and modifiers would paint a clearer picture of the event.

2 Better words are needed. Words are overused or too general to paint a clear picture.

1 The writer has not considered word choice or has used words incorrectly.

Sentence Fluency

5 The sentences are skillfully written, show variety, and are easy to understand.

4 The sentences are varied, but some should flow more smoothly.

3 A better variety of sentences is needed. Sentences do not flow smoothly.

2 Many incomplete or short sentences make the writing choppy.

1 Few sentences are written well. Help is needed.

Conventions

5 The narrative has no errors in spelling, grammar, or punctuation.

4 The narrative has a few minor errors in punctuation, grammar, or spelling.

3 The narrative has several errors.

2 Numerous errors make the narrative hard to read and confusing.

1 Help is needed to find errors and make corrections.

© Houghton Mifflin Harcourt Publishing Company

© Houghton Mifflin Harcourt Publishing Company

5-Point

Rubric for Expository Writing

Use this rubric for guiding and assessing your expository writing. Refer to it to help you improve your writing using the six traits.

Ideas

5 The essay is informative with a clear thesis and specific details.
4 The essay is informative with a clear thesis. More specific details are needed.
3 The thesis of the essay should be clearer, and more specific details are needed.
2 The topic should be narrowed or expanded. Many more specific details are needed.
1 The writer should select a new topic.

Organization

5 The beginning interests the reader. The middle supports the focus. The ending works well. Transitions are used.
4 The essay is divided into a beginning, a middle, and an ending. Some transitions are used.
3 The beginning or ending is weak. The middle needs a paragraph for each main point. More transitions are needed.
2 The beginning, middle, and ending all run together. Paragraph breaks and transitions are needed.
1 The essay should be reorganized.

Voice

5 The writer's voice sounds knowledgeable and confident. It fits the audience.
4 The writer's voice sounds knowledgeable most of the time and fits the audience.
3 The writer sometimes sounds unsure, and the voice needs to better fit the audience.
2 The writer sounds unsure. The voice needs to fit the audience.
1 The writer needs to learn about voice.

Word Choice

5 Specific nouns and action verbs make the essay clear and informative.
4 Some nouns and verbs could be more specific.
3 Too many general words are used. Specific nouns and verbs are needed.
2 General or missing words make this essay difficult to understand.
1 The writer needs help finding specific words.

Sentence Fluency

5 The sentences have flair and flavor, and the reader will enjoy them.
4 Most of the sentences read smoothly, but some are short and choppy.
3 Short, choppy sentences need to be rewritten to make the essay read smoothly.
2 Many sentences are choppy or incomplete and need to be rewritten.
1 Most sentences need to be rewritten.

Conventions

5 The essay is error free.
4 The essay has some errors in punctuation, spelling, or grammar.
3 Several errors confuse the reader.
2 Many errors make the essay difficult to read.
1 Help is needed to make corrections.

© Houghton Mifflin Harcourt Publishing Company

5-Point

Rubric for Persuasive Writing

Use the following rubric for guiding and assessing your persuasive writing. Refer to it whenever you want to improve your writing using the six traits.

Ideas

5 The position is convincingly supported and defended; it compels the reader to act.

4 Most reasons support the writer's position. An important objection is addressed.

3 More supporting reasons and a more convincing response to an objection are needed.

2 A clearer position statement is needed. Better support for the position must be provided.

1 A new position statement and reasons are needed.

Organization

5 The opening states the position, the middle provides clear support, and the ending reinforces the position.

4 Most parts of the essay are organized adequately except for one part.

3 Some parts of the essay need to be reorganized.

2 The beginning, middle, and ending run together.

1 The organization is unclear and incomplete.

Voice

5 The writer's voice is extremely confident, knowledgeable, and convincing.

4 The writer's voice is respectful, but needs to sound more persuasive or knowledgeable.

3 The writer's voice needs to be more persuasive and respectful.

2 The writer's voice sounds too emotional and unconvincing.

1 The writer needs to learn about voice in persuasive writing.

Word Choice

5 The writer's choice of words makes a powerful case and helps persuade the reader.

4 The writer avoids inflammatory (unfair) words but needs to remove some qualifiers.

3 The writer needs to change some inflammatory words and remove some qualifiers.

2 The words do not create a clear message. Some inflammatory words are used.

1 Word choice for persuasive writing has not been considered.

Sentence Fluency

5 The sentences spark the reader's interest in the essay.

4 Variety is seen in both the types of sentences and their beginnings.

3 Variety is seen in most of the sentences.

2 More variety is needed in the beginnings or kinds of sentences used.

1 Sentence fluency has not been considered.

Conventions

5 The writing is error free.

4 Grammar and punctuation errors are few. The reader is not distracted by the errors.

3 Several distracting grammar and punctuation errors confuse the reader.

2 Frequent errors make the essay difficult to read.

1 Nearly every sentence contains errors.

© Houghton Mifflin Harcourt Publishing Company

5-Point

Rubric for Response to Literature

Use this rubric for guiding and assessing your writing. Refer to it whenever you want to improve your writing using the six traits.

Ideas

5 The ideas show a complete understanding of the reading.
4 The essay has a clear focus statement. Unnecessary details need to be cut.
3 The focus statement is too broad. A variety of details is needed.
2 The focus statement is unclear. More details are needed.
1 The essay needs a focus statement and details.

Organization

5 The organization pattern fits the topic and purpose. All parts of the essay are well developed.
4 The organization pattern fits the topic and purpose. A part of the essay needs better development.
3 The organization fits the essay's purpose. Some parts need more development.
2 The organization doesn't fit the purpose.
1 A plan needs to be followed.

Voice

5 The voice expresses interest and complete understanding. It engages the reader.
4 The voice expresses interest but needs to show more understanding.
3 The voice needs to be more interesting and express more understanding.
2 The voice does not show interest in or an understanding of the topic.
1 The writer needs to understand how to create voice.

Word Choice

5 The word choice, including the use of figures of speech, creates a clear message.
4 The word choice is clear, but more figures of speech would improve the essay.
3 The word choice is too general, and more figures of speech are needed.
2 Little attention was given to word choice.
1 The writer needs help with word choice.

Sentence Fluency

5 The sentences are skillfully written and make the ideas really stand out.
4 No sentence problems exist. More sentence variety is needed.
3 A few sentence problems need to be corrected.
2 The essay has many sentence problems.
1 The writer needs to learn how to construct sentences.

Conventions

5 Grammar and punctuation are correct, and the copy is free of all errors.
4 The essay has a few careless errors in punctuation and grammar that do not interfere with the reader's understanding.
3 The errors in the essay confuse the reader.
2 The number of errors make the essay hard to read.
1 Help is needed to make corrections.

4-Point

Rubric for Narrative Writing

Use this rubric for guiding and assessing your narrative writing. Refer to it whenever you want to improve your writing using the six traits.

Ideas
4 The writer shares an interesting experience. Specific details help maintain interest.
3 The writer tells about an interesting experience. Details need to show, not tell.
2 The writer should focus on one event. More details are needed.
1 The writer should select an experience and provide details.

Organization
4 The narrative has a clear beginning, middle, and ending. Transitions are helpful.
3 For the most part, the narrative is organized. Most of the transitions are helpful.
2 The order of events must be corrected. More transitions are needed.
1 The beginning, middle, and ending all run together. The narrative must be organized.

Voice
4 The writer's voice sounds natural. Dialogue helps hold the reader's interest.
3 The writer's voice creates interest in the essay, but dialogue needs to sound more natural.
2 The writer's voice is weak. More dialogue is needed.
1 The writer sounds uninvolved or disinterested in the essay.

Word Choice
4 Specific nouns, verbs, and modifiers create clear images and feelings.
3 More specific nouns, verbs, and modifiers would paint a clearer picture of the event.
2 Better words are needed. Words are overused or too general to paint a clear picture.
1 The writer has not considered word choice or has used words incorrectly.

Sentence Fluency
4 The sentences are skillfully written, show variety, and are easy to understand.
3 The sentences are varied, but some should flow more smoothly.
2 A better variety of sentences is needed. Sentences do not flow smoothly.
1 Few sentences are written well. Help is needed.

Conventions
4 The narrative has no errors in spelling, grammar, or punctuation.
3 The narrative has several errors.
2 Numerous errors make the narrative hard to read and confusing.
1 Help is needed to find errors and make corrections.

© Houghton Mifflin Harcourt Publishing Company

4-Point

Rubric for Expository Writing

Use this rubric for guiding and assessing your expository writing. Refer to it to help you improve your writing using the six traits.

Ideas

4 The essay is informative with a clear thesis and specific details.

3 The thesis of the essay should be clearer, and more specific details are needed.

2 The topic should be narrowed or expanded. Many more specific details are needed.

1 The writer should select a new topic.

Organization

4 The beginning interests the reader. The middle supports the focus. The ending works well. Transitions are used.

3 The essay is divided into a beginning, a middle, and an ending. Some transitions are used.

2 The beginning or ending is weak. The middle needs a paragraph for each main point. More transitions are needed.

1 The beginning, middle, and ending all run together. Paragraph breaks and transitions are needed. The essay should be reorganized.

Voice

4 The writer's voice sounds knowledgeable and confident. It fits the audience.

3 The writer's voice sounds knowledgeable most of the time and fits the audience.

2 The writer sounds unsure. The voice needs to fit the audience.

1 The writer needs to learn about voice.

Word Choice

4 Specific nouns and action verbs make the essay clear and informative.

3 Some nouns and verbs could be more specific.

2 Specific nouns and verbs are needed. General or missing words make this essay difficult to understand.

1 The writer needs help finding specific words.

Sentence Fluency

4 The sentences have flair and flavor, and the reader will enjoy them.

3 Most of the sentences read smoothly, but some are short and choppy.

2 Many sentences are choppy or incomplete and need to be rewritten.

1 Most sentences need to be rewritten.

Conventions

4 The essay is error free.

3 The essay has some errors in punctuation, spelling, or grammar.

2 Many errors make the essay difficult to read.

1 Help is needed to make corrections.

© Houghton Mifflin Harcourt Publishing Company

© Houghton Mifflin Harcourt Publishing Company

4-Point

Rubric for Persuasive Writing

Use the following rubric for guiding and assessing your persuasive writing.
Refer to it whenever you want to improve your writing using the six traits.

Ideas

4 The position is convincingly supported and defended; it compels the reader to act.

3 Most of the reasons support the writer's position. An important objection is addressed.

2 More supporting reasons and a more convincing response to an objection are needed.

1 A clearer position statement is needed. Better support for the position must be provided.

Organization

4 The opening states the position, the middle provides clear support, and the ending reinforces the position.

3 Most parts of the essay are organized adequately except for one part.

2 Some parts of the essay need to be reorganized.

1 The beginning, middle, and ending run together.

Voice

4 The writer's voice is extremely confident, knowledgeable, and convincing.

3 The writer's voice is respectful, but needs to sound more persuasive or knowledgeable.

2 The writer's voice sounds too emotional and unconvincing.

1 The writer needs to learn about voice in persuasive writing.

Word Choice

4 The writer's choice of words makes a powerful case and helps persuade the reader.

3 The writer avoids inflammatory (unfair) words but needs to remove some qualifiers.

2 The writer needs to change some inflammatory words and remove some qualifiers.

1 The words do not create a clear message. Some inflammatory words are used.

Sentence Fluency

4 The sentences spark the reader's interest in the essay.

3 Variety is seen in both the types of sentences and their beginnings.

2 More variety is needed in the beginnings or kinds of sentences used.

1 Sentence fluency has not been considered.

Conventions

4 The writing is error free.

3 Grammar and punctuation errors are few. The reader is not distracted by the errors.

2 There are a number of distracting grammar and punctuation errors that may confuse the reader.

1 Nearly every sentence contains errors.

Rubric for Response to Literature

Use this rubric for guiding and assessing your writing. Refer to it whenever you want to improve your writing using the six traits.

Ideas

4 The ideas show a complete understanding of the reading.

3 The essay has a clear focus statement. Unnecessary details need to be cut.

2 The focus statement is unclear. More details are needed.

1 The essay needs a focus statement and details.

Organization

4 The organization pattern fits the topic and purpose. All parts of the essay are well developed.

3 The organization pattern fits the topic and purpose. A part of the essay needs better development.

2 The organization fits the essay's purpose. Some parts need more development.

1 The organization doesn't fit the purpose. A plan needs to be followed.

Voice

4 The voice expresses interest and complete understanding. It engages the reader.

3 The voice expresses interest but needs to show more understanding.

2 The voice does not show interest in or an understanding of the topic.

1 The writer needs to understand how to create voice.

Word Choice

4 The word choice, including the use of figures of speech, creates a clear message.

3 The word choice is clear, but more figures of speech would improve the essay.

2 The word choice is too general, and more figures of speech are needed.

1 The writer needs help with word choice.

Sentence Fluency

4 The sentences are skillfully written and make the ideas really stand out.

3 No sentence problems exist. More sentence variety is needed.

2 A few sentence problems need to be corrected.

1 The essay has many sentence problems.

Conventions

4 Grammar and punctuation are correct, and the copy is free of all errors.

3 The essay has a few careless errors in punctuation and grammar that do not interfere with the reader's understanding.

2 The errors in the essay confuse the reader.

1 The number of errors make the essay hard to read.

© Houghton Mifflin Harcourt Publishing Company

Narrative Rubric Checklist

Title _____

____ # Ideas
- Is the essay about an important accomplishment?
- Does it have enough specific details about the event?
- Does it <u>show</u> the event rather than <u>tell</u> about it?

____ # Organization
- Does the beginning grab the reader?
- Does the middle part follow chronological order and increase the narrative tension?
- Does the ending work well?

____ # Voice
- Is the dialogue realistic?
- Is the narrative voice natural and consistent?

____ # Word Choice
- Do the words have the right connotation?
- Are the nouns and verbs specific?

____ # Sentence Fluency
- Is there a good variety of sentences?
- Do the sentences flow smoothly?

____ # Conventions
- Does the essay avoid errors in punctuation, spelling, and grammar?
- Is the dialogue punctuated correctly?

© Houghton Mifflin Harcourt Publishing Company

Expository Rubric Checklist

Title _____

____ Ideas
- Is the essay informative?
- Does it have a clear thesis?
- Are the details specific?

____ Organization
- Is the beginning interesting?
- Does the middle support the focus?
- Does the ending work well?

____ Voice
- Is the voice knowledgeable?
- Does it sound confident?
- Does the voice fit the audience?

____ Word Choice
- Are the verbs active?

____ Sentence Fluency
- Are the sentences varied?
- Do the sentences read smoothly?

____ Conventions
- Does this essay avoid most errors in punctuation, spelling, or grammar?
- Are sources correctly cited?

© Houghton Mifflin Harcourt Publishing Company

Persuasive Rubric Checklist

Title _____

____ Ideas
- Does my essay have a clear position statement?
- Is my position backed with solid reasons?
- Does my essay have any logic errors?

____ Organization
- Does the beginning introduce the issue and state my opinion?
- Are my reasons arranged by order of importance?
- Does my ending sum up my reasons and opinion and leave the reader with something to think about?

____ Voice
- Is the tone of my writing appropriate?
- Did I connect with my audience?

____ Word Choice
- Did I use too many qualifying words?
- Does my essay have any inflammatory words?

____ Sentence Fluency
- Did I use different kinds of sentences?
- Did I vary my sentence beginnings?

____ Conventions
- Does my essay avoid most errors in punctuation, spelling, and grammar?

© Houghton Mifflin Harcourt Publishing Company

Response-to-Literature Rubric Checklist

Title _____

____ Ideas
- Does my analysis focus on an interesting story?
- Do I have a clear thesis statement?
- Do I include effective supporting details?

____ Organization
- Does the beginning identify the story and the thesis statement?
- Does the middle show how the theme develops?
- Does the ending share a meaningful analysis?

____ Voice
- Does my voice sound natural?
- Do I sound engaging?

____ Word Choice
- Did I use specific nouns and active verbs?
- Have I included one of the author's significant figures of speech?

____ Sentence Fluency
- Do I use tense shifts correctly?
- Do my sentences read smoothly?

____ Conventions
- Do I correctly cite sources?
- Are my punctuation, capitalization, spelling, and grammar correct?

© Houghton Mifflin Harcourt Publishing Company

Narrative Writing

It's a Boy!

1   "Congradulations, you have a new baby boy!" my Child

2 Development teacher said as she handed over the ten-pound bundle.

3 It had come at last: my turn to take the Think-It-Over baby home for

4 a night to get a taste of parenthood. This baby had a computer inside

5 its body that was programmed to make crying sounds at any given

6 moment. I was the only person who could stop the crying because I

7 had the key. The key was tied to my wrist and could be inserted in

8 the doll's back to stop the crying.

9   It was a Friday night when my turn came to take the ten pound

10 plastic doll home. The doll really did look like a live baby from a

11 distance. It even had a pleasent baby powder smell. After I took

12 the baby home in the car seat, I changed him into some really cute

13 clothes because my friends and I were going out that night. I then

14 decided to name him Tyler. So far, so good. The doll had not cried yet.

15   My friends came over, and we all piled into the car. It was kind

16 of squished because we had the baby's seat, too. I had to treat the

17 doll like a real baby because the computer inside measured any types

18 of abuse to the doll such as shaking or neglect. The hour-long drive

19 to our destination was uneventful until we got to the restaurant. Of

20 course, it was Friday night, so there were a lot of people waiting in

21 line to get a table. It was rather chilly, so I decided to wrap Tyler up

© Houghton Mifflin Harcourt Publishing Company

22 in a blanket and carry him in that way. I also had a diaper bag with

23 diapers, a bottle, and an extra set of clothes hanging on my arm.

24 When I walked into the crowded entryway, I got some very wierd

25 looks. I could also see quite a few raised eyebrows in my direction.

26 My friends also noticed the glares and stares. I overheard one couple

27 say, "Why would she bring a baby here?" These people were giving me

28 rude looks and forming judgments about me. Others just smiled at

29 me sympathetically.

30 We finally got a table and the waiter, asked me if I needed a

31 highchair or something. I told him it was just a doll, but a highchair

32 would be good. He thought it was funny and brought a highchair and

33 even a red balloon for the "little one".

34 Again during our meal my friends and I received strange looks

35 from the others in the restaurant. One couple kept walking by our

36 table just to get a look at my baby. As the couple walked by, my

37 friends and I started discussing how people were being towards us

38 because they thought I was the mother. We decided that we probably

39 would do the same if we saw a teenage girl coming in with a baby

40 and a group of friends. Teenage pregnancy is not accepted where I

41 live and is definitely not the norm, so many girls would hide their

42 pregnancy if they decided to keep the baby.

43 We went to the mall after we were finished eating and I had to

44 take Tyler with me. My friends were looking at clothes but I couldn't

© Houghton Mifflin Harcourt Publishing Company

45 because I was carrying this baby (which was becoming quite heavy).

46 So I just roamed around wishing I could try on clothes too. Then

47 the baby started to cry this horrible imitation of a real baby's cry. It

48 was so loud and terrible. I quickly put the key into the doll's back

49 so it would quit crying. I had to explain to the sales clerk why I was

50 carrying around a plastic doll. I was so glad to finally go home.

51   I learned a lot with the Think-It-Over baby. The doll definitely

52 told me that I was not ready to be a parent, but it also made me

53 understand the big picture. This experience opened my eyes to what

54 other people think about others. People do not realize that some

55 things are not the way they seem. The doll seemed like it was my

56 baby, but that was not the case. I was only carrying it around for a

57 class project.

58   I sometimes catch myself judging people I do not know, just

59 because of the first impression they give. In reality, I do not have a

60 clue about their real story. I especially think people judge teenage

61 girls with babies too quickly. Sure, they may have made a mistake,

62 but the girl usually knows that and is the one has to pay the price.

63 I only experienced the glares and rude comments one night, but I

64 thought of all the girls who have to deal with these looks wherever

65 they go. We should all be slow to judge these girls as well as everyone

66 else and realize that some things do not seem as they appear.

© Houghton Mifflin Harcourt Publishing Company

Narrative Rubric Checklist

Title _It's a Boy!_

__4__ Ideas
- Is the essay about an important accomplishment?
- Does it have enough specific details about the event?
- Does it show the event rather than tell about it?

__4__ Organization
- Does the beginning grab the reader?
- Does the middle part follow chronological order and increase the narrative tension?
- Does the ending work well?

__4__ Voice
- Is the dialogue realistic?
- Is the narrative voice natural and consistent?

__4__ Word Choice
- Do the words have the right connotation?
- Are the nouns and verbs specific?

__5__ Sentence Fluency
- Is there a good variety of sentences?
- Do the sentences flow smoothly?

__4__ Conventions
- Does the essay avoid errors in punctuation, spelling, and grammar?
- Is the dialogue punctuated correctly?

© Houghton Mifflin Harcourt Publishing Company

OVERALL COMMENTS

It's a Boy!

- This experience was a *good* choice for a personal essay. Your narrative *tells* about your night with Tyler. Adding sensory details, dialogue, and more of your personal thoughts and feelings would *show* readers what it was like to be Tyler's parent for a night.

- Your beginning grabs the reader's attention. You do, however, get off the topic a bit in your discussion of teenage pregnancy.

- Your ending could have been stronger. What exactly *do* you want to say? Do you want to make a statement about quickly judging others or about the difficulties of teenage motherhood?

- Your voice shows that you found the experience interesting and quite memorable. Including more dialogue would have made your writing sound more natural.

- Revising your writing to include stronger nouns, verbs, and specific modifiers would create a clearer picture for your readers.

- Your narrative contains a variety of sentences that flow smoothly.

- Your narrative has a few errors in spelling (see <u>congratulations</u>, <u>pleasant</u>, and <u>weird</u>) and punctuation.

© Houghton Mifflin Harcourt Publishing Company

Narrative Writing

My Cousin's Wedding

1   One day this past summer I was in my cousins wedding. It was

2   a small wedding because it was in a small church in our town, so

3   they couldn't invite many people. Still it was a neat day. On Saturday

4   morning, I woke up early and ate breakfast as usual. My mom was

5   all nervus. I was pretty calm. I got dressed. I showered. My mom

6   didn't like they way i comed my hair over, and she kept trying to

7   change it. I had to get dressed in my tux after we got to the church.

8   My dad was just relaxing in the family room and wasn't too excited.

9   Listening to the music in the church made me start to get a little

10   nervus. I'll bet the groom was even worse. The bride looked pretty.

11   Soon it was time for us to go out and watch her come down the isle.

12   My cousin Jon looked pretty nervus too. She came down the isle he

13   was looking at the minister and then at the bride the whole time. My

14   aunt cried the most. He is her youngest she's going to miss him when

15   he moves out.

16   While I was standing up their. I really wanted to turn around

17   and see who all was in the church, but I kept my back to them,

18   because I didn't want my mom to get mad. I could hear my little

19   brother once during the quiet parts. The woman who sang two songs

20   was all right, but the song she sang while they lit the candle was way

21   too sad it sounded more like a funeral song!

© Houghton Mifflin Harcourt Publishing Company

22   Finally we were at the reception. My favorit part of a wedding.

23   Because I like to eat. I also like dancing. There wasn't many girls

24   their around my age, so I ended up dancing just one slow dance with

25   my cousin, the bride. I payed a buck just to dance with her too. Which

26   was ok except she's so short. I got tired stooping over that long. I

27   danced all the fast songs. The DJ was great. Before I knew it, they

28   were getting ready to throw the garter and take off. I tried to catch

29   it, but this other grooms men got in front of me and won. Then they

30   left on their honeymoon. I think they went to a resort in Florida

31   somewhere. I'd probably go farther away, like to an island. The

32   wedding cake ran out so my mom and Aunt Sue weren't too happy

33   with that otherwise the day was great. I'll always remember being in

34   the wedding.

© Houghton Mifflin Harcourt Publishing Company

Narrative Rubric Checklist

Title <u>My Cousin's Wedding</u>

__2__ Ideas

- Is the essay about an important accomplishment?
- Does it have enough specific details about the event?
- Does it <u>show</u> the event rather than <u>tell</u> about it?

__1__ Organization

- Does the beginning grab the reader?
- Does the middle part follow chronological order and increase the narrative tension?
- Does the ending work well?

__4__ Voice

- Is the dialogue realistic?
- Is the narrative voice natural and consistent?

__2__ Word Choice

- Do the words have the right connotation?
- Are the nouns and verbs specific?

__1__ Sentence Fluency

- Is there a good variety of sentences?
- Do the sentences flow smoothly?

__1__ Conventions

- Does the essay avoid errors in punctuation, spelling, and grammar?
- Is the dialogue punctuated correctly?

© Houghton Mifflin Harcourt Publishing Company

OVERALL COMMENTS

My Cousin's Wedding

- This experience was a good choice for a personal essay. However, you skim through the whole day. It would have been more effective to focus on one part of the day, such as the reception, and develop it in detail. You could *show* readers what the reception was like by including sensory details, dialogue, and your personal thoughts.

- Your beginning does not grab the readers' attention. You do attempt to describe the events in some order. However, more transitions are needed to create a clear beginning, middle, and ending. Also, you do not explain why this event is memorable.

- Your voice shows that you found the experience interesting and enjoyable. Including dialogue would make your writing more interesting to readers.

- Your writing contains words that are overused or too general to paint a clear picture of what happened that day. You should include stronger nouns, verbs, and specific modifiers.

- Your narrative contains many incomplete or short sentences that make the writing choppy. A better variety of sentences is needed.

- Your narrative contains numerous errors in spelling, grammar, and punctuation that make the narrative hard to read and confusing.

© Houghton Mifflin Harcourt Publishing Company

Expository Writing

Pull the Plug and Play Corks

1   Lately I can't even suggest a simple board game without getting

2 weird looks. The basic pleasure of dice and checkers have been long

3 replaced by electronic games. Is there no end to the latest electronic

4 gadgets with cartridges and cords? But I have hope . . . hope that

5 there is a game out there that can surpass our 10-second attention

6 spans. I am confident that games which cost under ten dollars can

7 still be entertaining. And I am convinced that the game of Corks is

8 our relief from electronic race cars and karate kicks.

9   The game of Corks doesn't require a six-way plug or a spare

10 generator to play. It doesn't come with a 300-page instruction booklet

11 and 20 little buttons to memorize and tap simultaneously. Corks are

12 much simpler. The game board is a wooden slab with a circle drawn

13 in the middle. Doesn't sound too complicated, does it? There should

14 also be something else at stake. It works best when each player has

15 some hard-earned pennies they don't mind getting rid of.

16   This game isn't one to be played alone in the dark in your

17 bedroom on a Saturday night. This game requires several players

18 and a limited amount of conversation the game pieces are corks with

19 string tied through them, a large funnel and two dice. Start by the

20 first player holding the funnel and rolling the dice. (Those dice have

21 a mind of their own so be gentle when you throw them.) The tension

© Houghton Mifflin Harcourt Publishing Company

22 is always thick as the dice roll onto the table and come to a rest.

23 Suddenly all chaos breaks as everyone catches a glimpse of the dice.

24 The player who rolled the dice hurls the funnel towards the circle

25 faking out the others as they whip their corks from the circle and

26 retracts it successfully. Those players now have to pay one penny to

27 the roller.

28   The same player rolls the dice again, the tension increasing with

29 each roll. Finally a seven or eleven is rolled. Corks fly, strings tangle.

30 The funnels slam onto the board. The person holding the funnel

31 must pay each player who escaped from their delayed reflexes. The

32 payment is one penny. Now that a seven or eleven has been rolled,

33 the funnel is passed around the circle to the next player.

34   Other solitary electronic games determine a winner by how

35 many times they can punch the enemy or by the number of

36 mushrooms or some other object they have accumulated. Gaining the

37 high score is the ultimate triumph. But in corks accomplishment isn't

38 only measure by how many pennies you end up with. Concentration

39 and quick reflexes (and a little pride) help gain self-satisfaction.

40   So if you are sick of spending hundreds of dollars on manipulated

41 plastic, molded into gray boxes and shipped out by the truckload, I

42 suggest the game of Corks. Corks is entertaining, social, and won't

43 corrupt your mind with road rage and senseless killing.

© Houghton Mifflin Harcourt Publishing Company

Expository Rubric Checklist

Title   *Pull the Plug and Play Corks*

__3__ Ideas

- Is the essay informative?
- Does it have a clear thesis?
- Are the details specific?

__3__ Organization

- Is the beginning interesting?
- Does the middle support the focus?
- Does the ending work well?

__4__ Voice

- Is the voice knowledgeable?
- Does it sound confident?
- Does the voice fit the audience?

__4__ Word Choice

- Are the verbs active?

__4__ Sentence Fluency

- Are the sentences varied?
- Do the sentences read smoothly?

__5__ Conventions

- Does this essay avoid most errors in punctuation, spelling, or grammar?
- Are sources correctly cited?

© Houghton Mifflin Harcourt Publishing Company

OVERALL COMMENTS

Pull the Plug and Play Corks

- Your essay has a clear thesis. However, the reader may not be able to play corks just by reading your essay. The object of the game and some of the steps are unclear.

- The title and beginning of your essay are clever. You do attempt to carefully explain the steps of this game in the middle sections, but the process is unclear. Using subheadings and lists could help the reader understand your explanation.

- Your voice shows that you are knowledgeable and enthusiastic about playing Corks.

- Your writing contains specific nouns and action verbs that are informative.

- Your writing contains some sentences with different lengths and structures. This helps the essay flow.

- Your essay contains a few errors in punctuation and grammar.

© Houghton Mifflin Harcourt Publishing Company

Expository Writing

Changing Students

1 Students have changed a lot in the last twenty-five years.

2 Twenty-five years ago the chance that both parents were working

3 was really rare. Back then teachers had more say or disciplin over

4 students. There was very little TV back then. TV's were rare. Drugs

5 weren't really a big thing back then. Hardly anyone knew about

6 drugs. Technogy has sort of changed a lot. These changes have really

7 had serious affects on the schools today.

8 There are lots of changes in students today. Todays student's

9 are kind of presured lots more than twenty-five years ago by drugs,

10 alcohol, and other influnces. And there are lots of distractions. Such

11 as TV, and more after school activities and friends. Jobs are also

12 really distracting students from there school work.

13 When your in school it's kind of hard to do good in your classes.

14 You have lots of distractions from your friends. After school activities

15 are a big distraction. There is really no time to get your studies done.

16 Jobs are also kind of a problem; if you work week nights there is no

17 time to get school work done.

18 Students seen on TV shows are not real life teens. They seem

19 to do well in school. Even though they are dating and holding down

20 jobs and all that. Most of there parents work. They sort of seem to be

21 around a lot to help the kids with there problems. And there teachers

© Houghton Mifflin Harcourt Publishing Company

22 are a lot nicer than real life teachers. Most teachers today have to

23 many students in their classrooms. To get to know anyone really

24 well to be able to help them with their problems. One last thing. The

25 teens on television are sort of better looking than the students in my

26 school. So that's another way they are not like real life kids.

27   So with all of the changes, like drugs, parents are not being

28 around, TV, and technogy. It's no wonder that today's student isn't at

29 all like the students of twenty-five years ago. How could they be with

30 the world the way it is?

© Houghton Mifflin Harcourt Publishing Company

Expository Rubric Checklist

Title *Changing Students*

___2___ **Ideas**
- Is the essay informative?
- Does it have a clear thesis?
- Are the details specific?

___1___ **Organization**
- Is the beginning interesting?
- Does the middle support the focus?
- Does the ending work well?

___4___ **Voice**
- Is the voice knowledgeable?
- Does it sound confident?
- Does the voice fit the audience?

___2___ **Word Choice**
- Are the verbs active?

___1___ **Sentence Fluency**
- Are the sentences varied?
- Do the sentences read smoothly?

___1___ **Conventions**
- Does this essay avoid most errors in punctuation, spelling, or grammar?
- Are sources correctly cited?

© Houghton Mifflin Harcourt Publishing Company

OVERALL COMMENTS

Changing Students

- Your essay lacks a clear thesis. Are you comparing students of today with those of twenty-five years ago? Or are you comparing real-life students with characters in television programs?

- Your essay lacks logical organization and effective development. You should have focused on three or four ways that students of today differ from those of the past and examined each way in great detail.

- Your voice sounds knowledgeable, but it could be more engaging.

- Your writing contains too many empty modifiers (<u>kind of</u>, <u>sort of</u>, <u>really</u>) that that make your essay difficult to follow.

- Your sentences do not flow smoothly. Using a variety of compound and complex sentences would create variety and make your writing more interesting.

- Your writing contains many errors in punctuation, spelling, and grammar that make the essay confusing and hard to read.

© Houghton Mifflin Harcourt Publishing Company

Persuasive Writing

Athlete of the Century

1   How could one athlete be chosen as "Athlete of the Year"? Such

2 a choice would be very difficult. Now consider this. How could one

3 athlete be chosen as "Athlete of the Century"? Imagine only one great

4 athlete out of thousands to hold this title? I feel that this athlete

5 would have to be like no one else. Some might foolishly think that

6 superstars like Michael Jordan or Wayne Gretzky could claim this

7 prize. However, it seems to me that the only athlete who deserves

8 this title is the baseball player George Herman "Babe" Ruth. In my

9 opinion he is positively, definitely the greatest performer in America's

10 greatest game.

11   First of all, Babe Ruth was a really amazing player. In 1936,

12 Ruth became one of the first players elected to the Baseball Hall of

13 Fame. In a typical year, he hit more home runs that most teams did.

14 In addition, he hit more home runs in one season than many of his

15 contemporaries did in their entire careers. He was the first man in

16 history to hit 60 home runs in one season, and he did so when the ball

17 did not travel as far as the juiced-up balls of today. Also, the number

18 of games played was different. In Ruth's time, he played about 10–15

19 fewer games per season than ballplayers do now. Think of how many

20 home runs he would have hit if he played today. In a single season, he

21 might have been able to hit more than 70 home runs.

© Houghton Mifflin Harcourt Publishing Company

22   Another good reason for choosing Babe Ruth is he set the

23   standard for power hitting. Ruth was the first man to become what we

24   know today as a power hitter. When he was traded to the New York

25   Yankees, Ruth attracted so many fans that Yankee Stadium became

26   known as the "the house that Ruth built." He hit 714 home runs and

27   had a .342 lifetime batting average. No one could live up to what he

28   did at the time. Pitchers seemed afraid of him. They would throw four

29   balls to him on purpose. He was walked 2,056 times during his career.

30   Outfielders would fall back to the fence, and the crowd would be on

31   their feet, waiting for the Babe to hit another home run.

32   Ruth was not only a great hitter, but also a great pitcher. He won

33   96 games as a pitcher. In one World Series, he pitched $29\frac{2}{3}$

34   consecutive scoreless innings. How many so-called "great"

35   pitchers could hit as Babe Ruth did? None. Babe Ruth was, and is,

36   the only player that could do it all. However, because his talents as a

37   hitter were so great, he gave up pitching early in his career.

38   Babe Ruth changed the game. Before, the game was about boring

39   strategy and keeping the ball in the park. When Ruth came on the

40   scene, everything changed. He made the home run an establishment

41   part of baseball. When I think of baseball, I think of Babe Ruth because

42   he had such an influence on the game. Yes, he had personal difficulties,

43   but his love of the game and his dedication to his sport changed the

44   game of baseball forever. He is truly our "Athlete of the Century."

© Houghton Mifflin Harcourt Publishing Company

Persuasive Rubric Checklist

Title <u>**Athlete of the Century**</u>

___3___ ## Ideas

- Does my essay have a clear position statement?
- Is my position backed with solid reasons?
- Does my essay have any logic errors?

___3___ ## Organization

- Does the beginning introduce the issue and state my opinion?
- Are my reasons arranged by order of importance?
- Does my ending sum up my reasons and opinion and leave the reader with something to think about?

___5___ ## Voice

- Is the tone of my writing appropriate?
- Did I connect with my audience?

___3___ ## Word Choice

- Did I use too many qualifying words?
- Does my essay have any inflammatory words?

___3___ ## Sentence Fluency

- Did I use different kinds of sentences?
- Did I vary my sentence beginnings?

___6___ ## Conventions

- Does my essay avoid most errors in punctuation, spelling, and grammar?

© Houghton Mifflin Harcourt Publishing Company

OVERALL COMMENTS

Athlete of the Century

- Your essay has a clear position statement, which is backed with solid reasons. However, few people would dispute that Babe Ruth was a great baseball player. This is not a compelling topic.

- The beginning of your essay grabs the reader's attention, introduces your topic, and states your position. However, your reasons are not presented in order of importance. You mention an objection for naming Ruth "Athlete of the Century" in your conclusion. This point should be made and addressed in the last middle paragraph.

- Your voice is persuasive and respects your audience. Your essay includes a balance of facts and feelings.

- Your writing contains some inflammatory words and qualifiers. These weaken your argument. Also, defining terms such as <u>power hitter</u> and <u>outfielder</u> would help readers unfamiliar with the game of baseball better understand your essay.

- Many of your sentences begin with a prepositional phrase starting with <u>In</u>. Your writing should contain a variety of sentence beginnings. This will make the essay flow smoothly.

- Your essay lacks errors in punctuation, spelling, and grammar. Good work!

© Houghton Mifflin Harcourt Publishing Company

Persuasive Writing

ATVs vs. Snowmobiles

1   My favorit season is winter. It is a good time to have a little

2 fun on your recretional vehical, and most people appear to be in the

3 snowmobile crowd now. It seems as if everyone have forgotten about

4 the other great winter vehical; the ATV. My favorit winter toy is the

5 ATV, because it's safer and more fun than a snowmobile.

6   My favorit form of fun is the ATV, or four-wheeler. They are

7 much cheaper than a snowmobile. A new ATV costs around $4,500,

8 while a new snowmobile can cost up to $7,000–$8,000. This is a

9 large difference of money. It seems most people will really apreciate

10 saving a couple thousand dollars. If you went to buy a used ATV, you

11 might pay about the same for a 5-year-old ATV as for a 10-year-old

12 snowmobile.

13   A snowmobile is driven by a single track. The power is

14 distributed to one part of the snowmobile, and it doesn't have an

15 off-road capability. The four-wheel drive ATV delivers power to all

16 four wheels and is high off the ground. These factor into its great

17 off-road capability. Snowmobiles might be driven in snow or on ice.

18 The ATV can tackle mud, rocks, gravle, and just about anything. This

19 allows owners to drive their ATV in all seasons and weather. The

20 snowmobile is strictly for winter.

© Houghton Mifflin Harcourt Publishing Company

21   The most important thing that separates the ATV is that riders

22   can have more fun. It is more fun to take your vehical out whenever

23   you want, instead of waiting for snow. Snowmobiles appear to be

24   faster. But how many people need to go 110 mph anyways? The

25   60–70 mph range of an ATV is sure fast enough and with their great

26   off-road capability, you'll never run out of fun challenges.

© Houghton Mifflin Harcourt Publishing Company

Persuasive Rubric Checklist

Title _ATVs vs. Snowmobiles_

__3__ Ideas

- Does my essay have a clear position statement?
- Is my position backed with solid reasons?
- Does my essay have any logic errors?

__3__ Organization

- Does the beginning introduce the issue and state my opinion?
- Are my reasons arranged by order of importance?
- Does my ending sum up my reasons and opinion and leave the reader with something to think about?

__3__ Voice

- Is the tone of my writing appropriate?
- Did I connect with my audience?

__2__ Word Choice

- Did I use too many qualifying words?
- Does my essay have any inflammatory words?

__2__ Sentence Fluency

- Did I use different kinds of sentences?
- Did I vary my sentence beginnings?

__2__ Conventions

- Does my essay avoid most errors in punctuation, spelling, and grammar?

© Houghton Mifflin Harcourt Publishing Company

OVERALL COMMENTS

ATVs vs. Snowmobiles

- You identified two strong examples to support your opinion: An ATV is more economical and more versatile than a snowmobile. At least one more argument should have been included to solidify your position.

- Parts of your essay are organized well. You mention in your opinion statement that ATVs are safer than snowmobiles. Yet, there is no mention of this point in the rest of your essay.

- Your voice respects your audience. Including additional facts would make you sound more knowledgeable about your topic.

- Your writing contains many overused qualifiers, such as <u>seems,</u> <u>appears,</u> and <u>might.</u> These words make you seem unsure of your topic.

- Many of your sentences begin the same way. Varying your sentence beginnings and sentence types will make your essay flow smoothly.

- Your essay contains errors in punctuation, spelling, and grammar that make your writing difficult to understand.

© Houghton Mifflin Harcourt Publishing Company

Response to Literature

The Color Purple

1   Confidence is an extraordinary quality that most people aren't
2 just born with. It is something you have to continually strive to
3 develop through experences. I think that this lesson is exquistely
4 portrayed in the character of Celie in the novel *The Color Purple.*
5 Celie was a woman who never went through many confidence-
6 building experiences as she was growing up. Most of the time she
7 is put down. Her own father would say severly destructive things
8 to her like, "She ugly, but she ain't no stranger to hard work." Celie
9 needed confidence in her hard life; confidence is one of the essential
10 ingredients to happiness. The more confidence you gain, the more
11 risks and chances you take. You build opportunities in your life and
12 make something of it.

13   In this book, Celie really didn't learn how to build her confidence
14 up until she meets Shug Avery. Shug influences Celie just by the way
15 she dressed. The first time she met Shug, she expressed her feelings
16 of this. She describes her as "dressed to kill". She goes on to say, "She
17 got a red wool dress and a chestful of black braids. A shiny black hat
18 with what look like chickenhawk feathers curve down side one cheek,
19 and she carrying a little snakeskin bag, match her shoes." Deep
20 down, I think that Celie wishes she could be that daring and dress
21 like Shug.

© Houghton Mifflin Harcourt Publishing Company

© Houghton Mifflin Harcourt Publishing Company

22 Shug influenced Celie by the way she was so blunt about

23 everything. She tells people exactly what she is thinking and she

24 doesn't care if it hurts them. She does not like to be treated badly

25 by men, either. Celie watches and she sees Mr. trying to hold Shug's

26 hand. Shug says, "turn loose my hand. What's the matter with you . . .

27 I don't need no weak little boy can't say no to his daddy hanging on

28 me." Celie watched Shug so much that she learned how to stand up

29 to Mr. on her own.

30 Celie became friends with Shug. When Celie told Shug some of

31 the horrors of her past, Shug loved her anyway. That definitly made

32 Celie feel better about herself, knowing that someone loved her

33 despite her past. Someone loving her gave her confidence a boost.

34 Celie gained enough confidence to tell Mr. that he had made her

35 life miserable and that she was leaving. I thought that was great. She

36 had the power to defend herself and she knew she was too good to

37 live with an abusive man any more. Celie had gained the confidence

38 to stand up for herself and move out on her own.

39 Confidence is really the key to growing up and becoming

40 yourself. If you must take chances that you may never usually take,

41 then that is what has to be done. Gaining confidence takes work and

42 time. Some gain it faster than others, but it is necessary to make life

43 happy. As Celie found out in *The Color Purple*, gaining confidence

44 allows you to do what is right and what makes you happy.

Response-to-Literature Rubric Checklist

Title _The Color Purple_

__5__ Ideas

- Does my analysis focus on an interesting story?
- Do I have a clear thesis statement?
- Do I include effective supporting details?

__4__ Organization

- Does the beginning identify the story and the thesis statement?
- Does the middle show how the theme develops?
- Does the ending share a meaningful analysis?

__3__ Voice

- Does my voice sound natural?
- Do I sound engaging?

__2__ Word Choice

- Did I use specific nouns and active verbs?
- Have I included one of the author's significant figures of speech?

__4__ Sentence Fluency

- Do I use tense shifts correctly?
- Do my sentences read smoothly?

__5__ Conventions

- Do I correctly cite sources?
- Are my punctuation, capitalization, spelling, and grammar correct?

© Houghton Mifflin Harcourt Publishing Company

OVERALL COMMENTS

The Color Purple

- Your essay has a clear thesis statement (the importance of confidence) and necessary supporting details. In addition, you use quotations and paraphrasing to support your main points.

- You connect your thesis statement and final analysis in your closing sentences. You should include more transitions in your middle paragraphs to make your ideas flow more smoothly.

- In the first paragraph of your essay, your voice is overly formal. You should revise this paragraph to match the interesting and natural voice used in the other parts of your writing.

- The second-person pronoun (you) references in the opening and closing paragraphs are distracting and confusing. You should have used the third person (he, she, or it). Also, the comment "I thought that was great" in the fifth paragraph disrupts the flow of your writing.

- Most of your sentences read smoothly. However, your writing contains some errors in tense shifts.

- Your narrative has a few minor errors in spelling. (See <u>experiences</u> and <u>definitely</u>.)

© Houghton Mifflin Harcourt Publishing Company

Response to Literature

The Call of the Wild

1   When gold was discovered in the Yukon in 1869, Jack London

2   catches the get rich quick fever and rushes to the northlands. When

3   he returned home, he had not mined a single ounce of gold but brings

4   back a greater treasure, he brings back vivid recolections of the

5   rugged life in the frozen wastes. He converted his experiences into

6   exciting adventure tails which continue to thrill readers. The Call

7   of the Wild has been called his masterpiece, as well as the best dog

8   story ever told. As mentioned the above story was about a dog, named

9   Buck. This story contained naturalism because Jack London doesn't

10 place humans above animals, but sometimes the other way around.

11   Anyway, the story starts out with Buck at his master's house in

12 the Santa Clara Valley. He was the master of all the animals there

13 and he likes his life of leisure. Unfotrunately for him he is kidnapped

14 from his nice house and was used as a sled dog in the north.

15   As a sled dog he learned many lessons of survival. He also learns

16 to not try to raise against humans in charge of the dogs or he will

17 serve the consequences.

18   I would encourage anybody who can read to read this book. I

19 would highly recommend it not only to the outdoorsman/woman, but

20 to everyone because it was not just about the wilderness but a good

21 plot line as well.

© Houghton Mifflin Harcourt Publishing Company

Response-to-Literature Rubric Checklist

Title _The Call of the Wild_

__1__ Ideas

- Does my analysis focus on an interesting story?
- Do I have a clear thesis statement?
- Do I include effective supporting details?

__2__ Organization

- Does the beginning identify the story and the thesis statement?
- Does the middle show how the theme develops?
- Does the ending share a meaningful analysis?

__5__ Voice

- Does my voice sound natural?
- Do I sound engaging?

__2__ Word Choice

- Did I use specific nouns and active verbs?
- Have I included one of the author's significant figures of speech?

__1__ Sentence Fluency

- Do I use tense shifts correctly?
- Do my sentences read smoothly?

__4__ Conventions

- Do I correctly cite sources?
- Are my punctuation, capitalization, spelling, and grammar correct?

© Houghton Mifflin Harcourt Publishing Company

OVERALL COMMENTS

The Call of the Wild

- Your essay lacks a clear thesis statement. You provide a brief summary of the story rather than identify a specific point you want to make about the novel.

- You attempt to arrange your ideas in a logical order. However, the middle section of your essay is brief and needs more development.

- Your voice shows that you are interested in the story and understand the plot.

- Your word choice is too general. Your writing lacks figures of speech that London used in the story.

- Your writing contains many errors in tense shifts that make the essay difficult to read.

- Your narrative has a few minor errors in spelling. (See <u>recollections,</u> <u>tales,</u> and <u>unfortunately.</u>)

© Houghton Mifflin Harcourt Publishing Company

Editing and Proofreading Marks

Use the symbols and letters below to show where and how your writing needs to be changed. Your teachers may also use these symbols to point out errors in your writing.

Symbols	Meaning	Example	Corrected Example
≡	Capitalize a letter.	Harper Lee wrote *To Kill a mockingbird*.	Harper Lee wrote *To Kill a Mockingbird*.
/	Make a capital letter lowercase.	Her novel tells the story of the Finch Family.	Her novel tells the story of the Finch family.
⊙	Insert (add) a period.	The book focuses on prejudice It also . . .	The book focuses on prejudice. It also . . .
⬯ or sp.	Correct spelling.	Scout Finch is the narrater of the story.	Scout Finch is the narrator of the story.
⌿	Delete (take out) or replace.	Scout and her brother Jem they make friends with Dill.	Scout and her brother Jem make friends with Dill.
∧	Insert here.	They plot to make a reclusive neighbor come out of his house.	They plot to make a reclusive neighbor come out of his house.
∧ ∧ ⌄	Insert a comma, a colon, or a semicolon.	The three have many adventures some of the adventures are surprising.	The three have many adventures; some of the adventures are surprising.
⌄ ⌄ ⌄	Insert an apostrophe or quotation marks.	Scouts father, Atticus Finch, is a dignified, respected attorney.	Scout's father, Atticus Finch, is a dignified, respected attorney.
? ! ∧ ∧	Insert a question mark or an exclamation point.	Atticus Finch also turned out to be an expert marksman	Atticus Finch also turned out to be an expert marksman!
¶	Start a new paragraph.	¶ The book takes on a more serious tone when Atticus defends Tom Robinson.	The book takes on a more serious tone when Atticus defends Tom Robinson.
∼	Switch words or letters.	Scout learns eventually not to prejudge people.	Scout eventually learns not to prejudge people.

© Houghton Mifflin Harcourt Publishing Company

Time Line

Topic: _____

© Houghton Mifflin Harcourt Publishing Company

5 W's Chart

Topic: _____

Who?	
What?	
When?	
Where?	
Why?	
How?	

© Houghton Mifflin Harcourt Publishing Company

T-Chart

Topic:

© Houghton Mifflin Harcourt Publishing Company

Venn Diagram

Subject A

Differences

Similarities

Subject B

© Houghton Mifflin Harcourt Publishing Company

Sensory Chart

Subject: _____

Sights	Sounds	Smells	Tastes	Textures

© Houghton Mifflin Harcourt Publishing Company

Details Chart

© Houghton Mifflin Harcourt Publishing Company

Quick List

1. First Point:

    ■

    ■

2. Second Point:

    ■

    ■

3. Third Point:

    ■

    ■

© Houghton Mifflin Harcourt Publishing Company

Scavenger Hunt 1: Find It!

© Houghton Mifflin Harcourt Publishing Company

> **Directions** — Find the following information in your book by turning to the pages listed in parentheses.

1. Which traits to focus on during each step of the writing process (page 12)

_____

_____

_____

2. Places to which you can send your writing for publication (page 75)

_____

_____

3. What STRAP stands for (pages 138, 142, 194, 248, 252)

_____

4. How to tell if you have repeated a word too often in your writing (page 171)

_____

5. A reference book you could use to find quotations from famous people (page 351)

_____

6. A form of writing to use when writing in life science (page 416)

_____

7. What to do after you make an entry in a social studies learning log (page 419)

_____

_____

8. How to correct run-on sentences and comma splices (page 557)

_____

9. When to use a semicolon (page 618)

_____

_____

10. What the idiom *as the crow flies* means (page 672)

_____

Scavenger Hunt 2: What Is It?

> **Directions**   Find the answers to the following questions using the index in the back of the book.

1. What are imperative sentences?

   _____

2. What can you do to connect with your audience when writing?

   _____

3. What are inflammatory words?

   _____

4. What is the definition of a thesis statement?

   _____

5. What are the three moods of a verb?

   _____

6. What is the new form preferred by the U.S. Postal Service for addressing envelopes?

   _____

7. What should you concentrate on when delivering an oral presentation?

   _____

8. What is the difference between restrictive and nonrestrictive clauses?

   _____

   _____

   _____

9. What are the three principal parts of the irregular verb *wake*?

   _____

10. What can you do to avoid plagiarism?

   _____

11. What are two things to check for when revising for word choice in narrative writing?

   _____

12. What should you include to make sure your sentences *show, don't tell*?

   _____

© Houghton Mifflin Harcourt Publishing Company

Getting to Know *Write Source*

Directions Locate the pages in *Write Source* where answers to the following learning tasks can be found. Both the index and the table of contents can help you.

_____ 1. You want to write a business letter to a store owner to ask her to support your school's fund-raising event. You need to know the parts of a business letter.

_____ 2. When you tell your mother that you did bad on your English test, she says she can see why. You need to know the difference between *bad* and *badly*.

_____ 3. You and a classmate have been asked to model peer responding to a seventh-grade class. You need to review peer-responding guidelines.

_____ 4. A local bookstore is holding a poetry contest that you would like to enter. You need help writing a free-verse poem.

_____ 5. Your science teacher has assigned an experiment that requires you to write a lab report. You need guidelines for writing a lab report.

_____ 6. Your teacher reminds you to use the SQ3R critical reading strategy as you read the article she handed out. You need to remind yourself what SQ3R stands for.

_____ 7. Your teacher asks you to write a summary of the article she handed out. You need to know how to write a summary.

_____ 8. Your personal narrative essay is excellent, but your teacher wants you to correct the pronoun-antecedent agreement problems. You need help making the pronouns agree with their antecedents.

_____ 9. You are supposed to use both primary and secondary sources for your research report. You need to understand what each one is.

_____ 10. Your teacher tells you that you can use a rubric to guide your writing as well as to assess it. You need to understand more about using a rubric.

© Houghton Mifflin Harcourt Publishing Company

Getting-Started Activity Answers

Scavenger Hunt 1: Find It!

1. During prewriting, focus on ideas, organization, and voice. Writing incorporates ideas, organization, and voice. Revising uses ideas, organization, voice, word choice, and sentence fluency. Editing focuses on conventions, and publishing uses all of these traits.

2. Some places to send your writing are a local newspaper, magazines, Web sites or E-zines, writing contests, and young writers' conferences.

3. STRAP stands for Subject, Type, Role, Audience, and Purpose.

4. The best way to know if you have repeated a word too often is to read your work aloud.

5. Bartlett's Familiar Quotations lists thousands of quotations from famous people.

6. A problem-solution essay is a form of writing in which you state a problem and convince the reader of your solution.

7. After you make an entry in a social studies learning log, you should review your entries to see how well you understand the class material.

8. Correct run-on sentences and comma splices by either using two sentences or combining the two sentences into a compound sentence.

9. Use a semicolon with conjunctive adverbs, to join two independent clauses, or to separate groups that contain commas.

10. The idiom as the crow flies means "in a straight line."

© Houghton Mifflin Harcourt Publishing Company

Getting-Started Activity Answers

Scavenger Hunt 2: What Is It?

1. Imperative sentences make commands or requests (p. 226).
2. Writing with an appealing voice will help you connect with your reader (p. 46).
3. An inflammatory word is a word using strong language aimed at someone or something (p. 225).
4. A thesis statement is defined as a statement of the purpose, or main idea, of an essay (p. 599).
5. The three moods of a verb are indicative, imperative, and subjunctive (p. 724.1).
6. The new form preferred by the U.S. Postal Service for addressing envelopes has several guidelines. First, capitalize everything and leave out all punctuation. Next, use the list of common address abbreviations from page 660. Also, use numerals rather than words for numbered streets and avenues. Finally, if you know the ZIP + 4 code, use it (p. 520).
7. When you deliver an oral presentation, concentrate on your voice and body language (p. 400).
8. A restrictive clause adds information that the reader needs to know in order to understand the sentence, whereas a nonrestrictive clause adds information that is not necessary to the basic meaning of the sentence (p. 612.2).
9. The three principal parts of the irregular verb wake are wake, waked (or woke), and waked (or woken) (p. 720.2).
10. You can avoid plagiarism by always giving the author credit when using a quotation (p. 274).
11. When you revise for word choice in narrative writing, be sure to use specific verbs and words with the right connotation, or feeling (p. 114).
12. Make sure your sentences show and not just tell by containing action, sensory details, dialogue, and your personal thoughts and feelings (p. 108).

Getting to Know *Write Source*

1. 516–517
2. 730.1
3. 56–57
4. 334
5. 410–411
6. 474–478
7. 484–487
8. 121, 756
9. 344
10. 61–72

© Houghton Mifflin Harcourt Publishing Company

Index